This page has been designed to fold out for easy reference, particularly when using

How to use this book

Explore Australia begins with an introduction giving information on planning a trip, accommodation, driving in outback conditions, breakdowns and travelling with children. From page 37 both text and maps are colour coded on a state-by-state basis.

The text

Each state section has a general introduction, a detailed description of the capital city and suggested tours, followed by an A–Z listing of towns. Each town description includes:

- a population figure (taken from the most recent Census statistics available and intended to provide only an approximate idea of the size of the town)
- a listing of what is of interest in the town and in the area
- an address for the local tourist information centre
- a guide to the minimum family accommodation available
- a reference to the map/s on which the town appears

The maps

Every part of Australia is mapped in *Explore Australia*. Heavily-populated areas are mapped in greater detail. Distance is shown by black and red markers on the maps and a scale bar at the top of each map. A ❶ symbol alongside a town name indicates there is a description of the town in the A–Z listing for that state.

Continuation of another there is same scale. The sy the next map page that should be turned to. **283**

Feature maps of holiday regions: Holiday regions are mapped to show tourist highlights in detail.

Intercity route maps: These maps have been designed to help you plan your route between major cities. Information is given on distances between the towns along each route, roadside rest areas and road conditions where relevant.

Cross-references

Text to maps: Each town described in the A–Z listings includes a reference to the map/s on which the town appears.

Maps to text: The ❶ symbol alongside a town name on the maps indicates there is a description of that town in the text.

The index

To find out about a particular place mentioned in the text or shown on a map, it is essential to use the index. For example:

Sale	**Vic.**	25 M6,		179, 190,	**194**
Town	State	Sale appears on this map page	Grid reference	Sale is mentioned on these pages	Main text entry about Sale

Symbols used on the maps

Freeway with Freeway Route Number	**F3**	State capital city	**DARWIN**
Freeway under construction		Town, over 50 000 inhabitants	**GEELONG** ○
Highway, sealed, with National Route Number	**31**	Town, 10 000–50 000 inhabitants	**Bairnsdale** ○
Highway, sealed, with Sydney Metroad Number	**5**	Town, 5 000–10 000 inhabitants	Hamilton ○
Highway, unsealed, with Tasmania Route Number	**A10**	Town, 1 000–5 000 inhabitants	Maffra ○
Highway under construction		Town, 200–1 000 inhabitants	Omeo ○
Major road, sealed, with State Route Number	**156**	Town, under 200 inhabitants	Eskdale ○
Major road, unsealed		Locality	BUNGALLA
Major road under construction		Suburb	GLENORCHY
Distributor road, with Tourist Route		Pastoral station homestead	Alroy Downs ■
Distributor road unsealed		Closed Aboriginal town	Murgenella ○
Minor road, with traffic direction arrow	→	Roadhouse	Fortesque
Minor road, unsealed		Commercial airport	✈
Vehicle track		Place of interest	• ■
Walking track		Landmark feature	•
Railway with station	Paratoo	General interest feature	■
Underground railway with station	Flagstaff	Accommodation	■
Total kilometres between two points	114	Hill, mountain	+
Intermediate kilometres	77	Lighthouse	★
State border		Route destination	*GOULBURN*
Major fence line	Vermin Proof Fence	Adjoining page number	**125**
Lake		National parks	
Intermittent lake		Prohibited areas	
Aboriginal land		Other named areas	

Road Distances Between Main Cities

This distance chart shows distances by road between cities. The distances shown are in kilometres and are based on the most direct route, not necessarily the most practical.

	Adelaide	Brisbane	Canberra	Darwin	Melbourne	Perth	Sydney
Adelaide		2062	1204	3024	725	2707	1424
Albury	913	1545	343	3937	310	3620	563
Alice Springs	1534	2946	2680	1490	2259	3933	2958
Ballarat	616	1765	762	3640	109	3323	982
Bendigo	641	1632	642	3665	149	3348	862
Birdsville	1202	1619	2153	2246	2470	3293	2129
Brisbane	2062		1268	3399	1686	4363	982
Broken Hill	509	1553	1073	3127	820	2810	1174
Broome	4271	4646	4975	1875	4996	2258	5112
Cairns	3384	1697	2922	2885	3008	6050	2679
Canberra	1204	1268		3917	653	3911	286
Darwin	3024	3399	4170		3749	4163	3994
Geelong	862	1760	727	3852	74	3410	947
Geraldton	3131	4787	4335	3739	3856	424	4555
Kalgoorlie	2188	3634	3392	4760	2913	597	3465
Katherine	2710	3085	3856	314	3435	3718	3588
Mackay	2666	979	2204	2913	2290	5275	1941
Melbourne	725	1686	653	3749		3432	873
Mildura	397	1671	807	3421	554	3104	1027
Mount Gambier	454	2071	1068	3478	482	3161	1288
Newcastle	1599	807	461	3819	1048	4159	175
Perth	2707	4363	3911	4163	3432		3984
Port Augusta	308	1754	1512	2716	1037	2399	1585
Port Hedland	4831	5178	5536	2482	5057	1625	5609
Rockhampton	2329	642	1867	2954	1953	5199	1624
Sydney	1424	982	286	3994	873	4131	
Tennant Creek	2040	2440	3186	984	2765	4622	3010
Townsville	3038	1351	2576	2541	2662	5911	2313
Wagga Wagga	959	1285	245	3672	438	3666	465

Hobart to Launceston **200 kilometres**

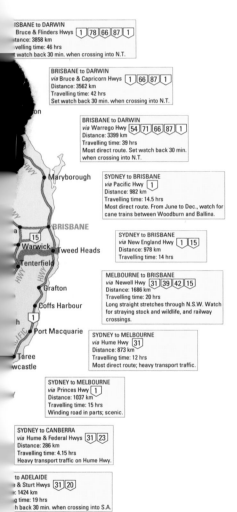

Warning

Driving in northern and outback Australia can be extremely hazardous. During the wet season from October to March torrential rains frequently flood large areas, making roads impassable for weeks on end. When planning journeys into these areas read carefully the section on Outback Motoring in this book. Always:

- Check the road conditions before departure.
- Notify a responsible person of your planned route.
- Check that your car is in good mechanical order.
- Carry plenty of water and supplies of food.
- Stay with the car in case of breakdown.

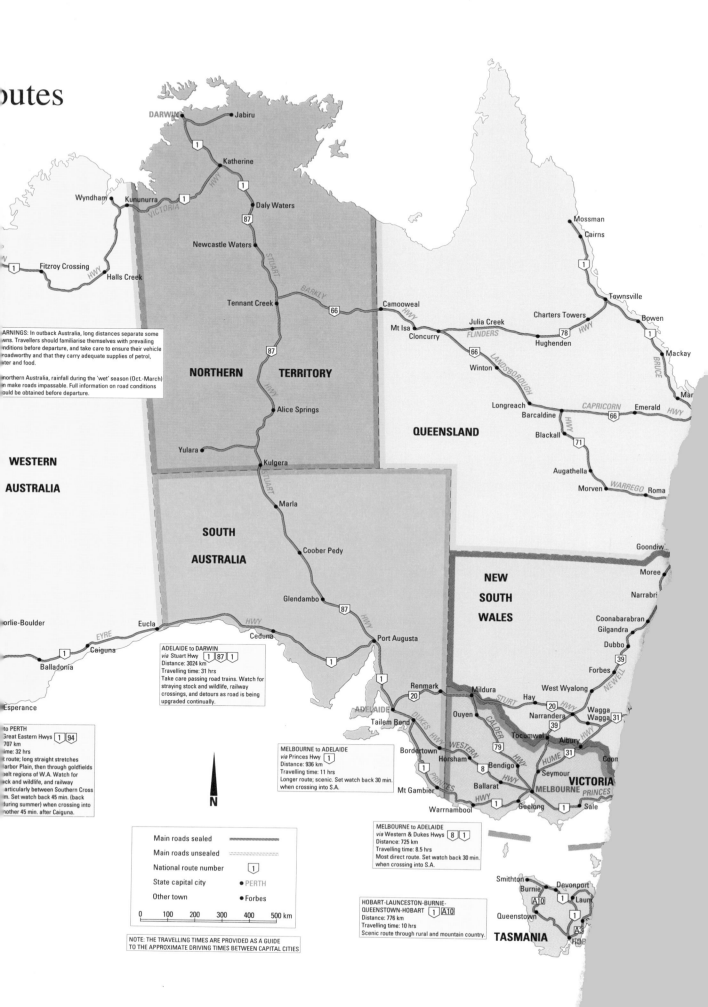

outes

DARWIN • Jabiru

Katherine

Wyndham Kununurra

Daly Waters

Newcastle Waters

Fitzroy Crossing

Halls Creek

Tennant Creek

Camooweal

Mossman

Cairns

Townsville

Charters Towers

Bowen

Mt Isa
Cloncurry

Julia Creek

Hughenden

Mackay

NORTHERN   TERRITORY

Winton

QUEENSLAND

Alice Springs

Longreach

Barcaldine

Emerald

Mar

Blackall

Yulara

Kulgera

Augathella

WESTERN

Morven   Roma

AUSTRALIA

Marla

SOUTH

AUSTRALIA

Coober Pedy

Goondiw...

Moree

NEW

SOUTH

Narrabri

WALES

Glendambo

Coonabarabran

Gilgandra

Dubbo

...orlie-Boulder   Eucla

Ceduna

Forbes

Caiguna

Port Augusta

Balladonia

Renmark

Mildura

West Wyalong

Hay

Wagga
Wagga

...Esperance

20

ADELAIDE

Ouyen

Narrandera

Tailem Bend

Bordertown

Tocumwal

Albury

VICTORIA

Horsham

Bendigo

Seymour

Coon

Ballarat

MELBOURNE

Mt Gambier

PRINCES

Warrnambool

Geelong

Sale

Smithton

Devonport

Burnie

Laun...

N

Main roads sealed
Main roads unsealed
National route number   1
State capital city   PERTH
Other town   Forbes

Queenstown

1

0 100 200 300 400 500 km

TASMANIA

NOTE: THE TRAVELLING TIMES ARE PROVIDED AS A GUIDE
TO THE APPROXIMATE DRIVING TIMES BETWEEN CAPITAL CITIES

EXPLORE AUSTRALIA

Robert Hale Ltd
Clerkenwell House
Clerkenwell Green
London EC1R OHT

This thirteenth edition published in Great Britain by Robert Hale Ltd, 1994
First published by George Philip & O'Neil Pty Ltd, 1980
Second edition 1981
Third edition 1983
Reprinted 1984
Fourth edition 1985
Fifth edition 1986
Sixth edition published by Penguin Books Australia, 1987
Seventh edition 1988
Eighth edition 1989
Ninth edition 1990
Tenth edition 1991
Eleventh edition 1992
Twelfth edition 1993
Copyright © Penguin Books Australia Ltd, 1994

ISBN 0 7090 5453 X

Map digital prepress by Tennyson Graphics, Melbourne
Text digital prepress by Eastern Studios, Melbourne
Printed and bound in Australia by McPherson's Printing Group, Melbourne

Disclaimers: The publisher cannot accept responsibility for any
errors or omissions. The representation on the maps of any road
or track is not necessarily evidence of public right of way.

The population figures given in Explore Australia have been taken
from the most recent Census results available (1991). They are
intended to provide only an approximate idea of the size of the
various cities and towns.

Accommodation listed is a guide to the minimum available family
accommodation in each town.

HALF-TITLE PAGE: Black Spur, Maroondah Highway, Victoria (Richard I'Anson)
TITLE PAGE: Uluru (Ayers Rock) Northern Territory (Richard I'Anson)

EXPLORE AUSTRALIA

The Complete Touring Companion

ROBERT HALE • LONDON

Acknowledgements

Editor
Fran Church

Chief cartographer
Colin Critchell

Design
Guy Mirabella

Cover design
Smartworks, Melbourne

Copy editor
Jenny Lang

Editorial assistance
Astrid Browne

Indexing assistance
Graham Lang

Research
Claire Kirkwood, Elizabeth O'Brien, Margaret Slessar, Jim Murcott, Michael Vella

Motoring consultant
Royal Automobile Club of Victoria (RACV)

Desktop publishing
Claire Kirkwood, Debra Wager

Cartographers
David Golding, Mark Griffiths, Ann-Marie McCarthy, Bruce McGurty, Charles Moscato, Julie Sheridan

State Cartographic Consultants
Australian Capital Territory: Paul Sjoberg
New South Wales: Bruce Vaughan
Northern Territory: Len Carter, AMAIC
Queensland: Bruno Scaggiante, MID (Aust.), MAIC
South Australia: George Ricketts, MAIC
Tasmania: Phil Broughton, FAIC
Victoria: Tim Corr, B.App.Sc. (Cartog.)
Western Australia: Peter Tarwin, AMAIC

Photographers
George Bareth, Andrew Chapman, G.A. & V. M Crimp, Stuart Grant, Richard I'Anson, Gary Lewis, PD Munchenberg, Nick Rains, Don Skirrow, Robin Smith, Ken Stepnell, Bruce Stewart, Stock Photos: David Austen, Bill Bachman, Benaji, Roger Du Buisson, Excitations, Ron Gale, Noeline Kelly, James Lauritz, David Marshall, Natfoto, Lance Nelson, Otto Rogge, Paul Steel, Ken Stepnell, Stocktake, Ken Straiton.

Text
For the preparation of this edition, each tourist information centre for the 800 towns described was contacted and the information for each town checked. The revision of this edition could not have occurred without their assistance, many of whom also supplied photographs. As well, assistance was received from the following organisations:

NSW Travel Centre
Sydney Visitors & Convention Centre
ACT Tourism Commission
Tourism Victoria
Melbourne Tourism Authority
South Australian Tourism Commission
WA Tourist Centre
Darwin Region Tourism Association
Queensland Government Travel Centre
Tasmanian Visitor Information Centre
National Parks and Wildlife Service
Department of Conservation and Natural Resources
South Australian Natural Resources Information Centre
Department of Conservation and Land Management
Conservation Commission of the Northern Territory
Department of Environment & Heritage
Parks and Wildlife Service

Maps
The publisher acknowledges the assistance to revise and check the maps from the various regional tourism authorities and state cartographic consultants.

Contents

Mount Sonder, Northern Territory

Australian Capital Territory

Victoria

Aboriginal rock art

South Australia

Western Australia

Opera House and Harbour Bridge, Sydney

Calendar of Events

Note: The information given here was accurate at the time of printing. However, as the timing of events held annually is subject to change and some events may extend into the following month, it is best to check with the local tourism authority or event organisers to confirm the details. The calendar is not exhaustive. Most towns and regions throughout Australia hold sporting competitions, regattas and rodeos, arts and craft, and trade exhibitions, agricultural and flower shows, music festivals and other such events annually. Details of these events are available from tourism outlets in each state.

JANUARY

ALL STATES Public holidays: New Year's Day; Australia Day.
NSW Sydney: Sydney Festival and Carnivalé. **Manly:** Iron Man Gold. **Bowral:** Horse Show. **Brunswick Heads:** Fish and Chips (wood chop) Festival. **Corowa:** Federation Festival. **Culburra–Orient Point:** Open Fishing Carnival. **Deniliquin:** Sun Festival. **Forbes:** Australian Flatlands Hang Gliding Titles. **Guyra:** Lamb and Potato Festival. **Hay:** Australia Day 'Surf' Carnival. **Kiama:** Agricultural Show. **Tamworth:** Australian Country Music Festival; Akubra National Finals Rodeo. **The Entrance:** Australia Day family concert and fireworks. **Wentworth Falls:** Australia Day Regatta.
ACT Canberra: Australia Day in the National Capital; Australia Day Cup; Embassies Open Day; Multicultural Festival.
VIC. Melbourne: Australian Open (grand slam tennis championships); Summer in the City. **Eltham:** Montsalvat Jazz Festival. **Cobram:** 'Peaches and Cream' Festival (biennial). **Hanging Rock:** New Year's Day Picnic Race Meeting. **Heyfield:** Timber Festival. **Inverloch:** Fun Festival. **Mount Beauty:** Conquestathon (race to summit of Mt Bogong). **Natimuk:** Tractor Pull. **Orbost:** Snowy Mountain Country Music Festival. **Port Fairy:** Moyneyana Festival. **Portland:** Country and Western Music Festival; Fishing Carnival. **Terang:** Horse Carnival.
SA Adelaide: Sheffield Shield Cricket. **Glenelg:** Greek Blessing of the Waters. **Hahndorf:** Founders Day; Schutzenfest German Festival. **Kingston:** Yachting Regatta. **Loxton:** Apex Fisherama. **Murray Bridge:** State Championship Swimming. **Port Germein:** Festival of the Crab. **Port Lincoln:** Port Lincoln Rodeo; Lincoln Week Regatta; Tunarama Festival. **Port Vincent:** Gala Day; Birdman Event; Classic Yacht Race. **Robe** Beer Can Regatta. **Streaky Bay:** Aquatic Sports Day and Mardi Gras; Family Fish Day Contest and Sailboat Regatta; Perlubie Beach Sports and Race Day. **Tanunda:** Oom Pah Festival.
WA Perth: Hopman Cup (tennis); Matilda Festival; Perth Cup (horse racing); Vines Golf Classic. **Albany:** Wittenoom Cup (golf). **Busselton:** Festival of Busselton. **Denmark:** Rainbow Festival. **Esperance:** Oz Rock Festival. **Mandurah:** Kanyana Carnival. **Narrogin:** State Gliding Championships. **Rockingham:** Cockburn Yachting Regatta.
QLD Clermont: Beef 'N Beer Festival. **Gold Coast:** Carrara: Albert Aussie Weekend. **Hervey Bay:** Hervey Bay Rodeo. **Redcliffe:** Blessing of the Waters Theophania. **Stanthorpe:** Agricultural Show. **Warwick:** Antique and Collectables Fair.
TAS. Hobart: Summer Festival. **Burnie:** New Year's Day Athletic Carnival. **Cygnet:** Huon Folk Festival. **Triabunna:** Spring Bay Crayfish Derby.

FEBRUARY

NSW Sydney: Gay and Lesbian Mardi Gras. **Blue Mountains:** Blue Mountains Summer Classic held at Blackheath, Leura and Katoomba golf courses. **Bungendore:** Country Music Muster. **Cessnock:** Hunter Vintage Walkabout. **Gosford:** Agricultural Show. **Kiama:** Jazz Festival. **Mittagong:** Dahlia Festival. **Nelson Bay:** Festival of Port Stephens. **Orange:** Banjo Paterson Festival. **Temora:** Golden Gift Foot Race. **Tenterfield:** Highland Gathering. **Ulladulla:** Open Game Fishing Tournament. **Wagga Wagga:** Gumi Festival.
ACT Canberra: Royal Canberra Show; St Valentine's Day Jazz Festival, Australian National University; Canberra Symphony Orchestra at Government House, Annual Prom Concert.
VIC. Melbourne: Australian Masters Golf Tournament; Formula 5000 (motor racing). **Chinatown:** Chinese New Year Festival. **St Kilda:** St Kilda Festival. **Bacchus Marsh:** Apple Valley Festival (biennial). **Bendigo:** Go-Cart Grand Prix. **Buninyong:** Gold King Festival. **Camperdown:** Leura Festival. **Clunes:**

Horseracing in outback WA

Clown at Melbourne's Moomba Festival

Golden Pyramid Festival. **Coal Creek:** Twilight Music and Theatre Festival. **Edenhope:** Henley-on-Lake Wallace. **Geelong:** National Aquatic Festival; Pako Festa. **Hanging Rock:** Harvest Picnic. **Maldon:** Camp Draft. **Maryborough:** Country Music Festival. **Torrumbarry:** Southern 80 (ski-race to Echuca). **Warrnambool:** Wunta Fiesta.
SA Adelaide: Adelaide Festival Fringe (biennial). **Berri:** Speedboat Spectacular. **Goolwa:** Wooden Boat Festival (odd numbered years). **Kadina:** Miners Ball. **Kingscote:** Kangaroo Island Racing Carnival. **Loxton:** Mardi Gras. **Millicent:** Radiata Festival. **Mount Compass:** Compass Cup Cow Race. **Port Lincoln:** Adelaide to Lincoln Yacht Race. **Tailem Bend:** Gumi Racing Festival. **Waikerie:** Rotary International Food Fair.
WA Perth: Chinese New Year Festival; Festival of Perth; Kyana Aboriginal Festival; Moon Chow Festival. **Boyup Brook:** Country Music Awards. **Katanning:** Katanning Triathlon. **Margaret River:** Leeuwin Estate Concert.
QLD Yeppoon: Surf Life Saving Championships.
TAS. Public holidays: Hobart Cup Day and Hobart Regatta Day (southern Tas. only); Launceston Cup Day (northern Tas. only). **Hobart:** Hobart Cup; Royal Hobart Regatta. **Devonport:** Food and Wine Fun Festival. **Evandale:** Village Fair, incorporating Penny Farthing Championships. **Fingal:** Fingal Valley Festival, incorporating Coal Shovelling Championships and Roof Bolting Championships. **Golconda:** Tasmanian Circus Festival. **Launceston:** Great Tasmanian Bike Ride (biennial). **New Norfolk:** Soroptimists Duck Race. **Oatlands:** Rodeo. **Richmond:** Country Music Festival.

MARCH

NSW Albury: World Cup Festival of Sport. **Alstonville:** Tibouchina Festival. **Blayney:** Agricultural Show. **Coonabarabran:** Warrumbungle Arts and Crafts Exhibition. **Dubbo:** Orana Country Music Festival. **Jamberoo:** Illawarra Folk Festival. **Lismore:** Kidsfest. **Molong:** Sheepdog Trials. **Moree:** NSW Mud Trials Championship. **Moss Vale:** Agricultural Show. **Myall Lakes:** Prawn Festival. **Parkes:** Marbles Tournament. **Robertson:** Agricultural Show. **Wellington:** Wellington Boot. **Wyong:** Festival of Arts.
ACT Public holiday: Canberra Day. **Canberra:** Black Opal Stakes; Canberra Festival;, Autumn Flower Show; Jewish Food Fair; Antique Fair.
VIC. Public holiday: Labour Day. **Melbourne:** Autumn Racing Carnival; International Dragon Boat Festival; Moomba Festival. **Bairnsdale:** Riviera Festival. **Ballan:** Arcadian Festival. **Ballarat:** Antique Fair; Begonia Festival; Super Southern Swap Meet. **Bendigo:** Eaglehawk Dahlia and Arts Festival. **Branxholm:** Bushwackers Carnival. **Cavendish:** Wannon River Regatta. **Chiltern:** Street Bazaar and Market. **Colac:** Kana Festival. **Corryong:** High Country Festival. **Daylesford:** Highland Gathering. **Dooen:** Wimmera Machinery Field Days. **Geelong:** Highland Gathering. **Hamilton:** Pastoral Museum Pioneer Day. **Horsham:** Apex Fishing Contest. **Koo-wee-rup:** Potato Festival. **Korumburra:** Karmai (Giant Worm) Festival. **Kyabram:** Rodeo. **Latrobe Valley:** Latrobe Valley Festival. **Maffra:** Mardi Gras. **Moe:** Jazz Festival. **Mount Beauty:** The Conquestathon, footrace. **Myrtleford:** Tobacco, Hops and Timber Festival. **Port Albert:** Seabank Fishing

Competition. **Port Fairy:** Folk Festival. **Portland:** Dahlia Festival. **Rutherglen:** Tastes of Rutherglen. **Seymour**: Rafting Festival. **Warragul:** Gippsland Field Days. **Yackandandah:** Country Music Festival. **Yarram:** Seabank Fishing Contest. **Yarra Valley:** Grape Grazing Festival.
SA Adelaide: Adelaide Festival of Arts (biennial, even years). **Thebarton:** Glendi Greek Festival. **Coonawarra:** Centenary Festival. **Lucindale:** Field Days and Tractor Pull. **Streaky Bay:** Streaky Bay Cup Race Meeting. **Tanunda:** Essenfest. **Wudinna:** Street Party and Annual Keg Roll.
WA Bridgetown: Carnival. **Brookton:** Old Time Motor Show. **Geraldton:** Kite Festival and Wind on Water. **Greenough:** Wind on Water Day (canboat regatta/kite flying). **Kalbarri:** Sports Fishing Classic. **Kambalda:** Rock Drilling Competition. **Kun-nurra:** Dam to Dam Regatta. **Margaret River:** Drug Offensive Masters (surfing). **Mount Barker:** The Field Day. **Pemberton:** King Karri Karnival. **Wagin:** Woolorama.
QLD Burketown: Barramundi Competition. **Einasleigh:** Races and Rodeo. **Emerald:** Sunflower Festival. **Gold Coast (Surfers Paradise):** Grand Prix. **Gympie:** Spring Valley Fair. **Kingaroy:** Peanut Festival (biennial). **Logan City:** Command Performance. **Stanthorpe:** Apple and Grape Harvest Festival (biennial). **Warwick:** Agricultural Show.
TAS. Public holiday: Eight Hours Day. **Hobart:** Garden Week. **Cygnet:** Port Cygnet Fishing Carnival. **Kingsborough:** Kingsborough Festival. **Longford:** Targa Tasmania. **New Norfolk:** Hop Festival. **St Helens/Port Arthur:** Tasmanian Sport and Game Fishing Festival.

EASTER

ALL STATES Public holidays: Good Friday; Easter Monday; Easter Tuesday (Tas. and Vic. only).
NSW Sydney: Royal Easter Show. **Bathurst:** James Hardie 12 hour car race. **Bingara:** Easterfish. **Bourke:** Festival of Sport. **Brunswick Heads:** Blessing of the Fleet and Fishing Festival. **Cowra:** Easter Golf Classic; Festival of Lachlan Valley. **Deniliquin:** Jazz Festival. **Grenfell:** Guinea Pig Races. **Griffith:** Wine and Food Festival (biennial). **Kempsey:** Cavalcade of Sport. **Leeton:** Sunwhite

Rice Festival (even years). **Maclean:** Highland Gathering. **Oxley:** Gymkhana. **Ulladulla:** Blessing of the Fleet. **Wentworth:** Henley on the Darling Rowing Regatta.
VIC. Easterbike (various locations). **Alexandra:** Easter Art Show. **Ballarat:** Eureka Jazz Festival; Opera Festival. **Beechworth:** Golden Horseshoes Festival. **Bendigo:** Easter Fair and Chinese Dragon Procession. **Dargo:** Walnut Festival. **Echuca:** Tisdalls Winery Vintage Festival and Grape Stomp. **Kyabram:** Antique Aeroplane Fly-in. **Kyneton:** Antique Fair; Autumn Flower Show. **Lake Bolac:** Easter Yachting Regatta. **Maldon:** Easter Fair. **Mallacoota:** Carnival in 'Coota. **Mildura:** Great Mildura Paddleboat Race. **Numurkah:** Rose Festival. **Quambatook:** Australian Tractor Pull Championships. **Stawell:** Easter Gift (professional footrace). **Torquay:** Bells Beach Easter Surfing Classic. **Warracknabeal:** Wheatlands Easter Carnival. **Wonthaggi:** Easter Carnival. **Yarram:** Tarra Valley Festival.
SA Andamooka: Annual Family Fun Day and White Dam Walk. **Berri:** Easter Carnival and Rodeo. **Clare:** Clare Valley Easter Festival; Racing Carnival. **Coober Pedy:** Opal Festival; Outback Festival. **Kadina:** Bowling Carnival. **Kapunda:** Celtic Festival (weekend before Easter). **Loxton:** Historical Village Fair (odd-numbered years). **Oakbank:** Easter Racing Carnival (picnic race meeting). **Port Victoria:** Annual Fishing Competition. **Waikerie:** Horse and Pony Club.
WA Perth: BMX National Championships. **Donnybrook:** Apple Festival (odd-numbered years). **Guilderton:** King of the River. **Lancelin:** National Beach Buggy Championships. **Nannup:** Folk Festival. **Northcliffe:** Forest Festival.
NT Borroloola: Fishing Classic.
QLD Brisbane: Brisbane–Gladstone Yacht Race. **Boulia:** Rodeo/gymkhana. **Bundaberg:** Easter Roundup. **Burketown:** World Barramundi Handline—Rod Fishing Championships. **Gladstone:** Harbour Festival. **Hamilton Island:** Race Week. **Roma:** Easter in the Country. **Scarness (Hervey Bay):** Yachting Regatta. **Tin Can Bay:** Easter Parade. **Townsville:** Gamefishing Club Easter Classic. **Warwick:** Easter Rock Swap.
TAS. Hobart/Devonport/Pipers River: Tazz Jazz.

APRIL

ALL STATES Heritage Week. Public holiday: Anzac Day.
NSW Sydney: AJC Racing Carnival; Australian International Dragon Boat Festival; finish of Great NSW Bike Ride; Sydney Cup Week. **Armidale:** New England Wool Expo. **Broken Hill:** St Patricks Races. **Bowral:** Southern Highlands Antique Fair. **Bundanoon**: Brigadoon at Bundanoon (Highland Gathering). **Cooma:** Man From Snowy River Marathon. **Leeton:** Sunwhite Rice Festival (biennial, even years). **Lightning Ridge:** Great Goat Race. **Narrabri:** Agricultural Show. **Tumut:** Tumut Valley Festival of the Falling Leaf. **Wee Waa:** Agricultural Show.
ACT Canberra: Marathon; Anzac Day Service, Australian War Memorial.
VIC: Melbourne: Comedy Festival. **Barmah:** Barmah Muster. **Bright**: Autumn Festival; Heritage Festival. **Lake Goldsmith (Beaufort):** Steam Rally.
SA Aldgate: Autumn Leaves Festival. **Barossa Valley:** Vintage Festival (biennial, odd years). **Burra:** Three Days Orienteering. **Goolwa:** Boat Rally and Picnic Races. **Kimba:** Yeltana Horse Spectacular. **Laura:** Folk Fair. **Stansbury:** Oyster Festival.
WA Perth: National Trust Heritage Week. **Albany:** Yachting Masters Australia. **Balingup:** Small Farm Field Day. **Northam:** Blue Gum Camel Farm Races.
NT Darwin: Barra Classic. **Alice Springs:** Country Music Festival.
QLD Comet: Rodeo. **Kingaroy:** Peanut Festival (biennial). **Manly:** XXXX Gold Cup Regatta. **Mount Isa:** Country Music Festival. **Rockhampton:** Beef Exposition. **Surfers Paradise**: Gold Coast Cup.
TAS. Hobart: Three Peaks Race (Mts Strzelecki/Freycinet/Wellington). **Launceston:** Targa Tasmania (car rally).

MAY

NSW Boggabri: Wean Picnic Races. **Casino:** Beef Reach Festival. **Dangar Island:** Bridge to Bridge Power Boat Race. **Dubbo:** Agricultural Show. **Lismore:** Gemfest. **Liverpool:** Sydney–Melbourne Marathon. **Scone:** Horse Week. **Tweed Heads:** Wintersun Carnival. **Ulladulla:** Fishing Carnival. **Wagga Wagga:** Winfield Gold Cup; Golden Gown Fashion Awards. **Wee Waa:** Cotton Festival (biennial).
ACT Canberra: Rock Eisteddfod.
VIC. Melbourne: Next Wave Festival. State-wide: Victoria's Garden Scheme closes. **Bendigo:** Gold Rush Fun Day. **Kalorama:** Chestnut Festival. **Warrnambool:** Southern right whales due at Logans Beach; Three-day May Racing Carnival.
SA Public holiday: Adelaide Cup Day. **Adelaide:** Adelaide Cup Carnival; Come Out Youth Festival (biennial, odd numbered years). **Ceduna:** Regional 'Come Out' Week. **Clare Valley:** Clare Valley Gourmet Weekend. **Hawker:** Horseracing Carnival. **Mannum:** Houseboat Hirers Open Days. **Nuriootpa:** Hot Air Balloon Regatta. **Yorke Peninsula: (Kadina/Moonta/Wallaroo):** Kernewek Lowender (Cornish Festival, biennial, odd years). **Yunta:** Races.
WA Boyup Brook: Autumn Art Affair. **Broome:** Kimberley Tourism and Trade Expo. **Carnarvon:** Mirari Festival. **Fremantle:** Fremantle–Exmouth Yachting Classic. **Toodyay:** Moondyne (Colonial and Convict) Festival. **York:** Theatre Festival (biennial); Winter Music Festival (biennial).
NT Darwin: Bougainvillea Festival; Expo NT; On the Beach Day. **Alice Springs:** Bangtail Muster; Camel Cup; Food and Wine Festival. **Katherine:** Rel Week (parachuting). **Tennant Creek:** Goldrush Festival; Tennant Creek Cup Day.
QLD Public holiday: Labour Day. **Charters Towers:** Country Music Festival. **Chinchilla:** May Day Spectacular. **Dimbulah:** Tobacco Festival. **Dysart:** Coal and Country Festival. **Fraser Island:** Orchid Beach Fishing Expo. **Hervey Bay:** Bay Carna. **Julia Creek:** Rodeo. **Kuranda:** Folk Festival. **Laidley:** Clydesdale Society Show and Field Day. **Mingeba:** Rodeo and Picnic Race Meeting. **Normanton:** Show, Rodeo and Gymkhana. **Noosa:** Festival of the Arts. **Port Douglas:** Reef and Rainforest Festival. **Richmond:** Rodeo. **Taroom:** Agricultural Show. **Thursday Island:** Cultural Festival. **Warwick:** Bush Week.
TAS. Carrick: Agfest. **Glenorchy:** City to Casino Fun Run. **Stanley:** Literature Fair.

JUNE

ALL STATES Public holiday: Queen's Birthday (except WA).
NSW Sydney: Sydney Film Festival.

Manly: Food and Wine Festival. **Albury:** Woolcraft and Sheep Show. **Blue Mountains:** Yulefest. **Bourke:** Bourke to B—Bash (charity car rally). **Dubbo:** Stampede. **Gloucester:** Billykart Derby. **Grenfell:** Henry Lawson Festival of Arts. **Gulgong:** Henry Lawson Birthday Celebrations. **Lake Keepit:** Keepit Kool Regatta. **Merimbula:** Jazz Festival. **Narrabri:** Cotton Fibre Exhibition. **Parkes:** Picnic Races and Jazz Convention. **Snowy Mtns:** Opening of Ski Season (long weekend). **Southern Highlands:** Christmas in June.

ACT Canberra: Embassies Open Day; National Eisteddford. **Duntroon:** Trooping the Colour.

VIC. Melbourne: Melbourne International Film Festival. **Echuca–Moama:** Steam, Horse and Vintage Car Rally. **Hamilton:** Eisteddfod. **Rutherglen:** Winery Walkabout Weekend. **Sea Lake:** Mallee Desert Car Rally.

SA Barmera: SA Country Music Festival. **Gawler:** Gawler 3 Day Event (dressage, cross-country riding and show-jumping). **Kingscote:** Half Marathon. **Renmark:** Riverland Citrus Week.

WA Public holiday: Foundation Day. West Week (week-long celebration of foundation of state). **Broome:** Fringe Arts Festival. **Cossack:** Cossack Fair and Yachting Regatta. **Kambalda:** Sky Diving Gathering. **Manjimup:** 15 000 Motocross. **Northam:** Soiree Avon Valley Arts Society. **Pannawonica:** Panna Regatta. **Wyndham:** Parrys Creek Picnic (Foundation Day bush carnival). **York:** Theatre Festival.

NT Darwin: Bougainvillea Festival; Darwin Cup Carnival; City to Surf Fun Run. **Adelaide River:** Bush Race Meeting. **Alice Springs:** Finke Desert Race; Gemtree World Paddymelon Bowls Championship. **Katherine:** Barunga Sport and Cultural Festival; Katherine Cup; Canoe Marathon. **Lake Bennett:** Birdman Rally. **Tennant Creek:** Brunette Downs Races.

QLD Brisbane: Eagle Farm: QTC Sires Produce Stakes. **Birdsville:** Gymkhana. **Blackall:** Race Meeting. **Cardwell:** Coral Sea Crab Racing Championships. **Cloncurry:** Agricultural Show. **Cooktown:** Discovery Festival. **Croydon:** Rodeo. **Gayndah:** Orange Festival (biennial). **Georgetown:** Rodeo. **Laura:** Aboriginal Dance Festival (odd-numbered years). **Longreach:** Hall of Fame Race Meeting. **Magnetic Island:** Rediscovery Weekend. **Monto:** Dairy Festival (biennial). **Mossman:** Bavarian Festival. **Mount Surprise:** Rodeo. **Rockhampton:** Agricultural Show. **Taldora Station:** Saxby Roundup. **Whitsunday:** Festival of Sail.

TAS. St Helens: Suncoast Jazz Festival.

JULY

NSW Barraba: Frost Over Barraba Art Show. **Blue Mountains:** Yulefest. **Cowra:** Wine Show. **Grafton:** Racing Carnival. **Gunnedah:** Dorothea Mac-Kellar Anniversary Day. **Iluka:** Amateur Fishing Classic. **Port Macquarie:** Life Style Expo. **Singleton:** Art Show. **Stroud:** International Brick and Rollingpin Throwing Contest. **Sussex Inlet:** Fishing Carnival. **Toukley:** Azalea Festival.

VIC. Bendigo: Wine Festival. **Daylesford:** Mid-Winter Festival. **Hamilton:** Wool Heritage Week. **Swan Hill:** Italian Festa.

SA Cowell: Jade Marathon. **Morgan:** Fun Run, Walk, Cyclathon. **Willunga:** Almond Blossom Festival.

WA Perth: Perth Marathon. **Broome:** Broome Cup. **Carnarvon:** Tropical Festival and Rodeo. **Denmark:** Winter Festival. **Derby:** Boab Festival; Country and Western Music Festival. **Exmouth:** Gala Week; Independence Day Celebrations. **Kalgoorlie:** Great Gold Festival. **Marble Bar:** Marble Bar Cup Race Weekend. **Roebourne:** Royal Show, Roebourne Cup. **Wickham:** Cossack–Wickham Fun Run.

NT Darwin: Agricultural Show (regional public holiday). **Alice Springs:** Agricultural Show (regional public holiday). **Katherine:** Agricultural Show (regional public holiday). **Tennant Creek:** Agricultural Show (regional public holiday). **Wauchope:** Wauchope v. the World Cricket Match.

QLD Brisbane: Jumbo Tennis Day. **Atherton:** Agricultural Show. **Broadbeach:** Gold Coast International Marathon. **Burketown:** Rodeo and Races. **Cairns:** Agricultural Show. **Chinchilla:** Polocrosse Carnival. **Cleveland:** Flinders Day (enactment of landing on Coochiemudlo Island). **Ipswich:** Limelight Festival. **Laura:** Cape York Aboriginal Dance Festival. **Mackay:** Festival of the Arts. **Mareeba:** Rodeo. **Mission Beach:** Banana Festival. **Pomona:** King of the Mountain Festival. **Stanthorpe:** Brass Monkey Month. **Texas:** Agricultural Show. **Townsville:** Turf Club Winter Carnival.

TAS. Hobart: Brighton Craft Fair.

AUGUST

NSW Sydney: Sun City to Surf (fun run to Bondi Beach). **Bellingen:** Jazz Festival. **Blue Mountains:** Yulefest. **Bourke:** Picnic Races. **Brewarrina:** Rodeo. **Cootamundra:** Wattle Time. **Euston:** Polocross Carnival. **Inverell:** Grafton to Inverell International Cycle Classic. **Junee:** Art & Crafts Festival. **Leeton:** Edisteddfod. **Murwillumbah:** Tweed Banana Festival. **Narrandera:** Camellia Show. **Quirindi:** Polo Carnival. **Thredbo:** FIS Australian Championships and Continental Cup (snow skiing).

VIC. State-wide: Victoria's Garden Scheme opens. **Falls Creek:** International Ski Marathon Kangaroo Hoppet. **Mt Buller/Mt Hotham:** FIS Australian Championships and Continental Cup (snow skiing).

Face painter at the Warana Festival, Brisbane

SA Adelaide: Festival City Marathon. Barossa Valley: Classic Gourmet Weekend. Cleve: Eyre Peninsula Field Days (biennial). Crystal Brook: Agricultural Show. Kadina: Agricultural Show. Mt Gambier: Eisteddfod. Paringa: Billy Boiling Championships and Bush Picnic. Strathalbyn: Collectors, Hobbies and Antique Fair. Whyalla: Harrier's Show; King and Queen of the Mountain.

WA Perth: City to Surf Fun Run. Badgingarra: Shearing Competition. Broome: Shinju Matsuri (Festival of the Pearl). Carnarvon: Dry River Regatta. Dampier/Karratha: FeNaCLNG Festival, incorporating Dampier Game Fishing Classic. Dowerin: Machinery Field Days. Fitzroy Crossing: Fun Run; Race Meeting and Rodeo. Kununurra: Ord River Festival. Newman: Fortescue Festival. Northam: Avon Descent (whitewater raft race) and Festival. Onslow: Bougainvillea Festival. Tom Price: Nameless Festival. Pingelly: Tulip and Art Festival. Port Hedland: Spinifex Spree. Wyndham: Top of the West Festival and Race Meeting.

NT Public holiday: Picnic Day. Darwin: Australian Safari; Darwin Cup; Darwin Rodeo; Mud Crab Tying Competition. Alice Springs: Harts Range Races; Old Timers Fete; Rodeo; Yuendumu Aboriginal Sports Carnival. Tennant Creek: Goldrush Folk Festival; Tennant Creek Rodeo.

QLD Public holiday: Brisbane Show Day. Brisbane: Brisbane International Film Festival; Royal Brisbane National Show (Ekka). Anakie: Gemfest Festival of Gems. Bowen: Art, Craft and Orchid Expo. Cloncurry: Merry Muster Rodeo. Cunnamulla/Eulo: Opal Festival. Eulo: World Lizard Racing Championships. Gympie: Country Music Muster. Hervey Bay: Whale Festival. Ingham: Herbert River Rodeo. Innisfail: Sugar Festival. Jondaryan: Australian Heritage Festival. Malanda: Dairy Festival. Mount Isa: Rotary Rodeo. Moura: Coal and Country Festival. Tin Can Bay: Country Music Muster. Tully: Rain Festival.

SEPTEMBER

NSW Sydney: Carnivale; Rugby League Grand Final. Bondi: Festival of the Winds (kite flying). Bellingen: Azalea Festival. Boggabri: Gum Tree Clay Pigeon Shoot. Bourke: Engonnia Picnic Races; Mateship Festival and Outback Trek. Bowral: Tulip Time Festival. Brewarrina: Festival of Fisheries. Canowindra: Ballooning Festival. Cessnock: Wine and Food Affair. Coffs Harbour: Buttercup Buskers Festival. Glen Innes: Minerama Gem Festival. Gloucester: MMI Mountain Man Triathlon. Hay: Festival of the Plains (biennial). Henty: Machinery Field Days. Kiama: Art Show. Maclean: Cane Harvest Festival. Mudgee: Wine Festival. Mullumbimby: Chincogan Fiesta. Oberon: Daffodil Festival. Taroom: Leichhardt Festival. Tibooburra: Gymkhana and Rodeo. Wauchope: Colonial Week. Wollongong: Festival of Wollongong. Yamba: Leisure Spectacular.

ACT Canberra: Floriade Spring Festival; Spring Bulb and Camelia Show; Red Cross Embassy Open Days.

VIC. Public holiday: Show Day. Springbike (various locations). Melbourne: Antiquarian Book Fair; Australian Football League and Association Finals; Fringe Arts Festival; Royal Melbourne Show. Anglesea–Aireys Inlet: Angair Festival. Bendigo: Monster Antique Fair; Red Ribbon Rebellion Re-enactment at Sandhurst Town. Halls Gap: Wildflower Exhibition, Grampians National Park. Kyneton: Daffodil and Arts Festival. Leongatha: Daffodil and Floral Festival. Little Desert: Wildflower Exhibition, Little Desert Lodge. Maryborough: Golden Wattle Festival. Olinda: Rhododendron Festival (3 months). Rutherglen: Spring Wine and Art Show. Shepparton: Sheptember Festival. Silvan: Tulip Festival. Yarrawonga: Ice Breaker Yacht Regatta.

SA Adelaide: Royal Adelaide Show. Adelaide Hills: Spring Festival; Handmade in the Hills. Beltana: Picnic Races and Gymkhana. Glenelg: Bay to Birdwood Run (vintage car rally; biennial). Hawker: Art Show; Photographic Show. Mannum: River Festival (Spring). Paskeville: Yorke Peninsula Field Days. Port Pirie: Blessing of the Fleet. Robe: Blessing of the Fleet. Stirling: Food and Wine Affair.

WA Perth: Football League Finals; Kings Park Wildflower Festival; Perth Royal Show; Rally Australia. Bencubbin: WA State Marbles Championships. Coolgardie: Camel Races; Coolgardie Day. Cranbrook: Wildflower Show. Kalgoorlie: Kalgoorlie Cup; Spring Festival. Katanning: Art Exhibition. Mount Magnet: Fun Day. Narrogin: Three-day Horse Competition. Port Hedland: All Can Regatta. Stirling Range National Park: Awareness Week. Three Springs: White Rock Stakes Wheelbarrow Relay. Toodyay: Folk Festival. York: Jazz Festival.

NT National Aboriginal Week (statewide). Darwin: Beer Can Regatta. Alice Springs: Alice Springs Rodeo; Henley-on-Todd. Bathurst Island: NT Barra Classic. Katherine: Caulfield Cup. Tennant Creek: Mary Ann Dam Yacht Regatta.

QLD Brisbane: City of Brisbane Chelsea Flower Show; Spring Hill Festival; Warana Festival. Airlie Beach: Fun Race. Atherton: Maize Festival. Biggenden: Rose Festival (biennial). Birdsville: Birdsville Races. Caboolture: Historical Village Open Day. Charleville: Booga Woongaroo Festival. Dunk Island: Billfish Classic. Herberton: Tin Festival. Hervey Bay: Pier Festival. Kalbar: Fassifern German Festival. Kynuna: Surf Carnival. Laidley: Tourist Festival. Logan City: Spring Fair. Mackay: Sugartime Festival. Maryborough: Heritage Festival. Miles: Wildflower Festival. Redland Bay: Strawberry Festival. Rockhampton: Capricana (Springtime Festival). Sunshine Coast: Festival of the Gardens. Toowoomba: Carnival of Flowers. Townsville: Pacific Festival. Winton: Outback Festival (biennial). Yeppoon: Pineapple Festival.

TAS. Hobart: Film Festival; TFL Grand Final; Tasmanian Tulip Festival. Burnie: Burnie Festival. Sheffield: Daffodil Festival. Stanley: Circular Head Arts Festival.

OCTOBER

NSW Albury: Agricultural Spring Show. Armidale: Spring Floral Festival. Balranald: Flower Show. Bathurst: Mt Panorama Tooheys 1000 car races. Berry: Antique Fair. Boggabri: Gum Tree Clay Pigeon Shoot. Bourke: Outback Surf Classic. Casino: Agricultural Show. Cessnock: Jazz in the Vines. Cowra: Sakura Bonsai and Japanese Cultural Exhibition. Forster–Tuncurry: Oyster Festival. Gilgandra: Cooee Festival. Glen Innes: Australian Bush Music Festival. Gosford: Mangrove Mountain District Country Fair. Goulburn: Lilac City Festival. Grafton: Jacaranda Festival; Bridge to Bridge Ski Race. Griffith: Festival of Gardens.

Gundagai: Spring Flower Show. **Inverell:** Sapphire City Floral Festival; Art Exhibition, and Collectables and Bottle Show. **Kempsey:** Country Truck Show. **Kiama:** Seaside Festival. **Leura:** Gardens Festival. **Lord Howe Island:** Lion IslandLord Howe Island Yacht Race. **Murrurundi:** Bushman's Carnival. **Narrabri:** Spring Festival. **Newcastle:** Folk Festival. **Parkes:** Country Music Spectacular; Antique Motorbike Rally. **Port Kembla:** Put Into Port Festival. **Port Macquarie:** Carnival of the Pines. **Raymond Terrace:** Twin Rivers Festival. **Singleton:** Agricultural Show; Romance of the Rose Festival. **Tenterfield:** Federation Festival; Spring Wine Festival. **Tibooburra:** Gymkhana and Rodeo. **Walcha:** Timber Expo (biennial). **Wentworth:** Country and Western Festival. **West Wyalong:** Highway Festival. **Windsor/Richmond:** Macquarie Towns Festival. **Wyong:** Historical Bush Picnic. **Young:** Cherry Festival.

ACT Canberra: Canberra Cup; Canberra Quilters Exhibition of Work; Embassies Open Day; Floriade Spring Festival; Oktoberfest; Winery Walkabout.

VIC. Melbourne: Fantastic Entertainment in Public Places (FEIPP) summer program begins; Oktoberfest; Spring Racing Carnival, including Caulfield Cup; Sun Tour of Victoria; International Festival of the Arts. **Chinatown:** Autumn Moon Lantern Festival. **Ararat:** Golden Gateway Festival. **Avoca:** Wool and Wine Festival. **Ballarat:** Kite Festival. **Bendigo:** Mandurang Arts and Orchid Festival. **Bright:** Springtime in Bright. **Chiltern:** Art Show. **Dunolly:**

Gold Rush Festival. **Echuca–Moama:** Rich River Festival, including Tisdall Winery Fine Food and Wine Day and Jazz Night. **Eildon:** Water Festival. **Euroa:** Wool Week. **Geelong:** Spring Festival. **Hamilton:** Spring Flower Show. **Marysville:** Wirreanda Festival. **Melton:** Djerriwarrh Festival. **Mildura:** Bottlebrush Festival. **Port Fairy:** Spring Classical Music Festival. **Tallangatta:** Arts Festival. **Wangaratta:** Wangaratta Festival. **Warrnambool:** Melbourne–Warrnambool Cycling Classic.

SA Adelaide: League Football Finals. **Andamooka:** Opal Festival. **Balaklava:** Festival of Wineries and Galleries. **Barmera:** Show. **Barossa Valley:** Music Festival. **Berri:** Multicultural Festival (even numbered years). **Bordertown:** Clayton Farm Vintage Field Day. **Coober Pedy:** Races. **Goolwa:** Folk and Steam Festival. **Hawker:** Henley-on-Arkaba fun day. **Kingscote:** Blessing of the Fleet. **Koppio:** Smithy Museum Open Day. **Loxton:** Show. **Marrabel:** Rodeo. **McLaren Vale:** Bushing Festival. **Naracoorte:** Show. **Penola:** Petticoat Lane Street Party. **Port Pirie:** Festival of Country Music. **Renmark:** Show. **Strathalbyn:** Glenbarr Scottish Festival. **Wellington:** Strawberry Fair. **Yorke Peninsula:** (**Ardrossan, Maitland, Port Victoria**) Barley Festival. **Yorketown:** Picnic races and Gymkhana.

WA Perth: Spring in the (Swan) Valley Festival. **Bridgetown:** Blackwood Classic (powerboat race); Blackwood Marathon Relay. **Bunbury:** Octoberfest. **Dunsborough:** Naturaliste Triangle Funfest. **Eucla:** Eucla Shoot. **Exmouth:** Game Fishing Competitions.

Geraldton: Blessing of the Fleet; Geraldton–Batavia Coast Sunshine Festival. **Harvey:** Harvey Show. **Kukerin:** Trach Mach Vintage Fair. **Manjimup:** Timber Festival. **Margaret River:** Margaret River Masters (windsurfing/surfing competitions); Spring Festival. **Morawa:** Music Spectacular. **Mount Barker:** Wine Show. **Nannup:** Jarrah Jerker's Jog (railway-sleeper teams race). **Narrogin:** Spring Festival. **York:** Flying 50 (vintage car rally; biennial, even years).

NT Darwin: Octoberfest. **Alice Springs:** Beerfest; Central Australian Masters Olympic Games (biennial); Henley-on-Todd Regatta.

QLD Brisbane: Colonial George Street Festival. **Ayr:** Water Festival. **Bowen:** Coral Coast Festival. **Cairns:** Fun in the Sun Festival. **Dalby:** Harvest Festival. **Gatton:** Potato Carnival. **Gold Coast:** Tropicarnival. **Goondiwindi:** Spring Festival. **Gympie:** Gold Rush Festival. **Hervey Bay:** Hervey Bay–Fraser Island Sailboard Marathon. **Ingham:** Maraka Festival. **Ipswich:** Goodna and District Jacaranda Festival. **Lake Tinnaburra:** Tablelands Water Sports Festival. **Mapleton:** Yarn Festival. **Mount Isa:** Oktoberfest. **Mount Tamborine:** Avocado and Rhubarb Festival. **Nanango:** Mardi Gras. **Noosa:** Festival of the Waters. **Normanton:** Races and B & S Ball. **Ravenshoe:** Torimba Forest Festival. **Stanthorpe:** Granite Belt Spring Wine Festival. **Thangool:** Arts Festival. **Townsville:** Aquatic Festival. **Warwick:** Rose and Rodeo Festival. **Yandina:** Spring Flower and Ginger Festival.

TAS. Public holidays: Hobart Show Day (S. Tas. only); Launceston Show Day (N. Tas. only). **Hobart:** Royal Hobart Agricultural Show. **Burnie:** Rhododendron Festival. **Deloraine:** Tasmanian Cottage Industry Exhibition and Craft Fair. **Derby:** Derby Day. **Great Lake:** Tasmanian Trout Fishing Championships. **Kingston:** Oliebollen Festival. **Launceston:** Garden Festival; Royal National Show; Tasmanian Poetry Festival. **Richmond:** Village Fair. **Wynyard:** Tulip Festival.

NOVEMBER

NSW Bellingen: Agricultural Show. **Brunswick Heads:** River Festival. **Campbelltown:** Fishers Ghost Festival. **Carcoar:** Ben Hall Festival. **Glen Innes:** Land of the Beardies Bush Festival.

Camel Cup, Alice Springs

Kyogle: Fairmont Festival. **Lithgow:** Festival of the Valley. **Moree:** Carnival of the Golden Grain. **Narrandera:** Country Music Festival. **Newcastle:** Surfest. **Nowra:** Shoalhaven Fun Festival Triathalon. **Penrith:** City Jazz Festival. **Rylstone:** Village Festival. **Shoalhaven:** Fun Festival. **Tenterfield:** Gem Festival. **Warren:** Cotton Cup Carnival. **Windsor:** Bridge to Bridge Water Ski Classic. **Young:** Cherry Festival.

ACT Canberra: Horticultural Society, Annual Spring Show; Wine Show; Australian Craft Show.

VIC. Public holiday: Melbourne Cup Day. **Melbourne:** Spring Racing Carnival, including Melbourne Cup and Oaks Day. **Carlton:** Melbourne Lygon Arts Festival. **Ballarat:** Rowing Regatta. **Benalla:** Rose Festival. **Bendigo:** National Swap Meet (vintage cars/bikes). **Casterton:** Agricultural Show. **Castlemaine:** State Festival (biennial, even years); Spring Garden Festival (odd years). **Harrow:** National Bush Billycart Championships. **Lake Goldsmith:** Steam Rally. **Macedon:** Mt Macedon Festival. **Maldon:** Folk Festival. **Mansfield:** Mountain Country Festival. **Maryborough:** Energy Breakthrough Festival. **Ouyen:** Farmers Festival. **Port Fairy:** Heritage Discovery Weekend. **Portland:** Pioneer Week. **Wandin:** Victorian Cherry Festival. **Wangaratta:** Festival of Jazz.

SA Adelaide: Australian Formula One Grand Prix; Christmas Pageant. **Ardrossan:** Wine and Cheese Tasting. **Bordertown:** Camel Race Festival. **Ceduna:** Grand Prix Sailing Carnival. **Hahndorf:** Blumenfest (Festival of Flowers). **Kapunda:** Antique and Craft Fair. **Mount Gambier:** Blue Lake Festival. **Murray Bridge:** Big River Challenge Festival. **Riverland:** Multicultural Festival (biennial, even years); Wine Festival (biennial, odd years). **Streaky Bay:** Snapper Fishing Contest.

WA Albany: Perth–Albany Ocean Yacht Race. **Bridgetown:** Agricultural Show and Blues Music Festival. **Broome:** Mango Festival. **Bunbury:** Pram Race. **Denison:** Blessing of the Fleet. **Exmouth:** Gamex, world class game fishing. **Fremantle:** Fremantle Festival. **Kambalda:** Raft Regatta. **Manjimup:** Timber Festival. **Mount Barker:** Agricultural Show. **Northam:** Avon Valley Country Music Festival.

NT Alice Springs: Corkwood Festival.

QLD Atherton: Tablelands Band Festival. **Bribie Island:** Bribie Cup Yacht Race. **Heron Island:** Dive Festival. **Home Hill:** Harvest Festival. **Logan City:** River Festival and Raft Race. **Whitsunday Passage and Outer Reef:** Game Fishing Championships.

Tas. Public holiday: Recreation Day (N. Tas. only). **Hobart:** North Hobart Fiesta. **Battery Point:** Salamanca's Writers Weekend. **Campbell Town:** Country Music Festival. **Penguin:** Town Fiesta. **Ross:** Rodeo. **Westbury:** Maypole Festival. **Zeehan:** King of the Mountain Fun Run.

DECEMBER

ALL STATES Public holidays: Christmas Day; Boxing Day.
Carols by Candlelight (various locations).

NSW Sydney: Hot Summer Festival; Scottish Week; Sydney–Hobart Yacht Race. **Manly:** Summer Festival. **Abaercrombie Caves:** Underground music in caves. **Coffs Harbour:** South Pittwater–Coffs Harbour Race Series. **Cowra:** International Motor Boat and Ski Challenge. **Mulwala:** Red Cross Murray River Canoe Marathon. **The Entrance:** Tuggerah Lakes Mardi Gras Festival. **Yass:** Warrambalulah Festival.

ACT Canberra: Street Machine Summernats (national hot-rod exhibition and races); Fiesta Capitale.

VIC. Melbourne: Finish of Great Victorian Bike Ride. **Bendigo:** Tram Spectacular (procession). **Corryong:** Nariel Creek Folk Music Festival. **Daylesford:** Highland Gathering; New Year's Eve Festival. **Gisborne:** Gisborne Festival. **Horsham:** Kannamaroo Festival. **Moyston:** World Rabbit Skinning Championships. **Nagambie:** Rowing Regatta.

SA Public holiday: Proclamation Day. **Adelaide:** Christmas Pageant. **Barmera:** Christmas Pageant. **Berri:** Rowing Regatta. **Glenelg:** Proclamation Day Celebrations. **Jamestown:** Christmas Pageant. **Naracoorte:** Street Traders Party; Carols by Candlelight. **Renmark:** Christmas Pageant; Rowing Regatta. **Streaky Bay:** Carols by the Sea.

WA Perth: Australian Derby; Christmas Pageant; Tennis, Hopman Cup; City Beach Fun Run. **Derby:** Kimberley Boxing Day Sports (cockroach and frog races, egg and nose race, seed spit competition, etc.). **Jurien:** Slalom Carnival. **Katanning:** Katanning Caboodle. **Lancelin:** Ledge Point Ocean Race.

NT Darwin: Darwin–Adelaide World Solar Challenge Race for Solar-powered Vehicles (biennial).

QLD Beaudesert: Lions Christmas Carnival. **Innisfail:** Opera Festival. **Karumba:** Fisherman's Ball. **Logan City:** Christmas Spectacular. **Maleny:** Folk Festival. **Whitsunday:** Festival of Sail.

TAS. Hobart: Brighton Craft Fair; Christmas Pageant; Summer Festival; Sydney–Hobart/Melbourne–Hobart Yacht Races. **Battery Point:** Salamanca's All Ears World Music Festival. **Burnie:** Christmas Festival. **Latrobe:** Latrobe Wheel Race and Latrobe Gift. **Port Arthur:** Chopping Carnival. **Triabunna:** Tandara Woodchoppers Classic. **Ulverstone:** Ulverstone Fiesta.

Hobart end of the Sydney-Hobart yacht race

Introduction

Exploring Australia by motor vehicle provides the traveller with the opportunity to venture into remote areas, tropical rainforests and inland deserts; to visit large cosmopolitan cities and tiny outback settlements.

Australia's deserts are as vast as the Sahara; its snowfields rival those of Switzerland; its surfing beaches are among the best in the world. The entire continent is criss-crossed by a combination of bitumen highways and rough bush tracks, almost all navigable in the modern motor car, although some demand 4WD vehicles.

Australia comprises an area of some 8.5 million square kilometres; it covers a distance of 3700 kilometres from north to south, and 4000 kilometres east to west. Within these boundaries there is an extraordinary range of flora and fauna, a variety of climatic extremes and a host of geological wonders.

Australia's temperatures vary from an average 30°C in the midsummer of the Centre to an average of 6°C in the highlands in winter.

It is a land of extremes. The parched deserts of central Australia may be totally dry for years until flooding rains produce a short-term sea. Sydney has a population of around 4 million, whereas Innamincka in South Australia, near the New South Wales and Queensland borders, has only 14 permanent residents.

The predominant colours of Australia are red, blue and green. Inland, the stark red of the Simpson Desert sand dunes contrasts dramatically with the deep azure blue of the noonday sky. Dotted here and there are clumps of velvet-green scrub and, after recent rains, Sturt's desert pea blooms scarlet.

Australia has been the home of Aboriginal tribes for a period in excess of 40 000 years and evidence of their occupation abounds. Many cave paintings and rock carvings made thousands of years ago are found at Ayers Rock, that superb monolith sited almost in the centre of this island continent.

Despite its name, the so-called 'Dead Centre' is far from dead, even in times of drought, and the moonscapes of sand and rocky tors and hardy bush scrub have a forbidding beauty all their own.

Across the Far North, from the Cape York Peninsula in the east to the Kimberleys in the west, tropical rainforests are so lush in parts as to be impenetrable and of a green so green as to rival the colour from an artist's paintbox.

Almost all of Australia is accessible to the explorer. It is possible to drive from Melbourne at the base of the mainland to Cairns in the Far North.

The intrepid explorer can plan a trip from the Pacific to the Indian Ocean; from the rainforest in the north, to the temperate, breeze-washed beaches of the southern coast. And for the traveller seeking peace and tranquillity, there is the further, ever-beckoning green pasturelands and rugged mountainous interior of Tasmania, the Island State.

Simply put, all Australia is a wonderland. And in order to discover what it has to offer, either for a one-day tour or as a full-year once-in-a-lifetime adventure, *Explore Australia* is an invaluable travelling companion. It is designed to be of assistance with every facet of your travel itinerary. It is an encouragement and an almanac; a manual and a tour guide. It is recommended that you read it as part of your travel planning, particularly for long-distance journeys. For experienced road travellers, it will reinforce knowledge acquired in the past; for 'new chums', it can ensure the utmost pleasure from the holiday you have planned and help to make it trouble-free.

Have a good trip—and drive carefully!

Shark Bay, near Monkey Mia

Planning Ahead

There is so much of Australia to see and so many ways to see it. Today, even the most remote sections of this vast continent are accessible, particularly to 4WD vehicles designed for use on bush tracks and unmade roads.

For some, exploring Australia will mean touring the made highways and staying in motels and hotels. Others will tow their accommodation behind them in the form of a caravan or camper and probably, as a result, stay mainly on made roads. Still others will fit out a commercial van with sleeping and cooking facilities and produce a mobile home, and yet another group, perhaps the true adventurers, will load a tent, a mobile fridge and a barbecue unit into the back of a 4WD station wagon and go bush. The country is there to be seen and enjoyed, whatever the style and method of travel, but in all cases, careful planning will enhance the journey immeasurably.

Obviously, a one-, two- or three-day tour will not require the time and effort necessary for a round-Australia jaunt, but in any case, advance planning of the route, an estimate of travel time and, where appropriate, use of overnight accommodation will need to be considered. So, indeed, will the roadworthiness of the vehicle. While it is reasonable to expect that all vehicles are properly maintained and in reliable condition, some extra attention will not go astray, and more particularly for long journeys. More of that later.

Advance Information

Any journey will benefit from careful **advance planning**. The idea of throwing a bag in the back and taking off is attractive in theory but creates complications in practice.

Try to gather as much information as possible as far ahead of your planned departure as you can. Remember, the planning is half the fun. Research will confirm, or perhaps deny, your original choice of destination; it also will reveal ways and means, and problems involved, where they exist. And bear in mind that although information sources are extensive, there is nothing like local knowledge. So remember to re-check everything you have learned as you go.

The first places to obtain information are the relevant **State tourist bureaus** and **motoring organisations (see:** Useful Information). They are excellent sources for travel brochures, regional maps and accommodation guides, and they usually have up-to-date knowledge of local conditions. For details of specific areas, they can put you in touch with the appropriate tourist authority.

If you are planning a fly/drive holiday, or intend to combine rail and motor travel, the various **travel agencies**, **airline travel centres** and the **main railway booking offices** in each State can provide advice and information.

Also, read this book. The introductions to each State provide basic information on main tourist areas. Once you have decided on your destination, check it out by consulting the gazetteer entries for specific towns and other points of interest. Do note that while the capital cities and towns have been covered quite comprehensively, the fine detail will be available locally.

On arrival, visit a local newsagent or bookshop and see what is available; for example a place will mean more to you if you can read a history of the area. All cities and most major towns will have a pocket-sized guide detailing points of interest, and listing sporting events and local entertainment venues.

How Far Ahead to Start

It can be a major disappointment to decide on a certain destination and then discover that motels, caravan parks and camping grounds in the area are booked out. In some regions at certain times of the year—Christmas, Easter, school holiday periods—accommodation can be booked out a year in advance. Explore all possibilities and, on long journeys, remember the travel-time factor. When booking accommodation in advance, allow enough time to travel comfortably to your destination. Your trip will lose a great deal of its charm if you have to rush from one point to the next (**see:** Itineraries).

While all popular destinations are likely to be busy at holiday peak times, some will be booked out around the time of special events: Melbourne at Melbourne Cup time; Adelaide at the time of the Australian Formula One Grand Prix, for example (**see:** Calendar of Events). Check ahead for the timing of local special events.

If you wish to return to a favourite hotel or try a special type of accommodation—a farm homestead, a houseboat or charter boat—book well ahead. Other holiday makers will have the same interests.

And remember, most national parks require advance notice to give permission for camping within their boundaries.

When to Go

With a few exceptions, you can travel Australia at any time of the year. The exceptions include the Far North, between October and May, in the 'wet' or tropical monsoon season (this applies particularly if you plan to use bush tracks and unmade roads, many of which are

Useful Information

Motoring Organisations

There are motoring organisations in all Australian States and territories. All are affiliated under the Australian Automobile Association and reciprocal rights are available to their members. Membership can consist of service and social membership or service membership only.

When planning a trip it would be advisable for you to take out **service membership** of the motoring organisation in your home State. Not only will this ensure that you receive service in that State, but by producing your membership card you can request assistance from the equivalent organisation in other States.

The advantages of service membership of a motoring organisation are wide-ranging. They include emergency breakdown and towing services, vehicle inspection and 'approved repairer' services; tuition in safe and defensive driving for licensed drivers; legal advice on matters like the procedure to be followed after motor vehicle accidents or traffic charges, and the possible penalties; and motor vehicle insurance cover.

Service membership also makes available touring information and advice for motoring holidays, including guides, maps and reports on road conditions, accommodation and travel bookings; and special tours, package holidays and accommodation at concessional rates, as well as car accessories.

Social or 'club' membership entitles members to the use of club facilities and accommodation, including reciprocal use in some 50 clubs throughout Australia.

New South Wales
National Roads & Motorists'
Association (NRMA)
151 Clarence St, Sydney 2000
(02) 260 9222. Fax: (02) 260 8472

Australian Capital Territory
National Roads & Motorists'
Association (NRMA)
92 Northbourne Ave, Braddon 2601
(06) 243 8805. Fax: (06) 243 8892

Victoria
Royal Automobile Club of Victoria Ltd
(RACV)
422 Little Collins St, Melbourne 3000
(03) 790 3333. Fax: (03) 607 2325

South Australia
Royal Automobile Association of
South Australia Inc. (RAA)
41 Hindmarsh Sq, Adelaide 5000
(08) 223 4555. Fax: (08) 202 4520

Western Australia
Royal Automobile Club of Western
Australia Inc. (RAC)
228 Adelaide Tce, Perth 6000
(09) 421 4444. Fax: (09) 221 2708

Northern Territory
Automobile Association of the
Northern Territory Inc. (AANT)
7– 81 Smith St, Darwin 0800
(089) 81 3837. Fax: (089) 41 2965

Queensland
Royal Automobile Club of Queensland
(RACQ)
300 St Pauls Tce, Brisbane 4000
(07) 361 2444. Fax: (07) 257 1863

Tasmania
Royal Automobile Club of Tasmania
(RACT)
Cnr Patrick and Murray Sts, Hobart 7000
(002) 32 6300. Fax: (002) 34 8784

Tourist Bureaus

New South Wales
NSW Travel Centre
19 Castlereagh St, Sydney 2000
(02) 231 4444. Fax: (02) 232 6080

Australian Capital Territory
ACT Tourism Commission
Visitor Information Centre
Northbourne Ave, Dickson 2602
(06) 205 0044. Fax: (06) 205 0776

Victoria
RACV Travel Centre
230 Collins St, Melbourne 3000
(03) 790 3333. Fax: (03) 790 2844

South Australia
South Australian Tourism Commission
1 King William St, Adelaide 5000
(08) 212 1505. Fax: (08) 303 2249

Western Australia
WA Tourist Centre, Albert Facey House
Cnr Forrest Place and Wellington St,
Perth 6000
(09) 483 1111. Fax: (09) 481 0190

Northern Territory
Darwin Region Tourism Association
33 Smith St Mall
Darwin 0800
(089) 81 4300. Fax: (089) 81 7346

Queensland
Queensland Government Travel Centre
Cnr Adelaide and Edward Sts,
Brisbane 4000
(07) 221 6111. Fax: (07) 221 5320

Tasmania
Tasmanian Visitor Information Centre
20 Davey St, Hobart 7000
(002) 30 8233. Fax: (002) 24 0289

Other Accommodation

Backpackers Resorts (head office)
PO Box 1000, Byron Bay NSW 2481
(018) 66 6888 (9–5, Mon.–Fri.)

Bed and Breakfast (head office)
PO Box 408, Gordon NSW 2072
(02) 498 5344, (02) 498 1539 (AH)

Farm holidays
The following is a list of contact addresses in each State if you wish to arrange a farm holiday.

New South Wales
Australian Farm Host Holidays Pty Ltd
PO Box 65, Culcairn 2660
(060) 29 8621. Fax: (060) 29 8770
(Properties available Australia-wide)

Victoria
Host Farms Association Inc.
332 Banyule Rd, View Bank 3084
(03) 457 5413. Fax: (03) 457 6725

South Australia
SA Host Farms Association Inc.
'Glenbower'
PO Box 14, Morgan 5320
(085) 81 0586

Western Australia
WA Farm and Country Holidays
Association
Munaleeun Farm
Jackson Road
Albany via Narrikup 6326
(098) 53 2091. Fax: (098) 53 2090

Northern Territory
Northern Territory Government Tourist
Bureau in any State

Queensland
Queensland Host Farm Association
c/o RACQ Travel Service
GPO Box 1403
Brisbane 4001
(07) 361 2390. Fax: (07) 257 1504

Tasmania
Homehost Tasmania Pty Ltd
PO Box 780, Sandy Bay 7005
(002) 24 1612. Fax: (002) 24 0472

Youth Hostels (head office)
10 Mallett St, Camperdown NSW 2050
(02) 565 1699. Fax (02) 565 1325

Emergency (for all States)

For police, ambulance and fire-brigade services, dial 000.

impassable for months). Tropical cyclones are random summer hazards between November and March. In the NSW and Victorian high country, from about May to August, many roads will be snowbound. The Centre is not especially inviting in midsummer, when daytime temperatures can reach 45°C plus, while it can be bitterly cold at night.

Otherwise, remember the **holiday peaks.** If you can avoid the dense traffic during the major vacation periods, do so.

Which Way to Go

If you quail at the thought of driving seemingly endless kilometres, you should consider an alternative: both fly/drive packages and MotoRail facilities eliminate time-consuming travel and allow for concentration on areas of interest. Given fuel costs, both these are not necessarily extravagances. Cost them out against the expenses involved in using your own car for the entire trip.

MotoRail: For information on this easy way of covering long distances, contact the State tourist bureaus or the main State railway offices. Enquire about **CAPER fares:** a reduction in rail fare is available on some interstate services if travel is booked and paid for in advance. For rail enquiries in each State, contact:

New South Wales
Country Link Travel Centre,
Wynyard Station
11–31 York St, Sydney 2000
(02) 224 4744, (008) 043 126
Victoria
V/Line Reservations and Information
Level 2, Transport House
589 Collins St, Melbourne 3000
(03) 619 5000, (008) 136 109
South Australia
Australian National Passenger
Reservations and Enquiries
1 Richmond Rd, Keswick 5035
(08) 231 7699, (008) 888 417
Western Australia
Westrail Centre
West Pde, East Perth 6000
(09) 326 2222
Queensland
Queensland Railways
305 Edward St, Brisbane 4000
(07) 235 2222

MotoRail services available are: **Perth–Sydney–Perth**
Indian–Pacific
Two services a week each way;
66 hours.

Perth–Adelaide–Perth
Indian–Pacific
Two services a week each way; 38 hours. This service connects with *The Overland* to Melbourne.
Melbourne–Adelaide–Melbourne
The Overland
Daily, each way (overnight); 12 hours.
Adelaide–Alice Springs–Adelaide
The Ghan
May–October, 2 services a week each way; November– April, 1 service a week each way; 23 hours.
Brisbane–Townsville–Cairns–Townsville–Brisbane
The Queenslander
One service a week each way; 33 hours. An extra service each way a week including Proserpine stop; check frequency.
Note: No MotoRail services between Melbourne–Sydney and Sydney–Brisbane.

Other Touring Possibilities

The **Spirit of Tasmania** car and passenger ferry makes three return voyages weekly between Melbourne and Devonport in northern Tasmania. Bookings can be made through the TT-Line Tasmania at Port Melbourne and Dockside, Devonport, or through your local Tasmanian Travel Centre. One warning: if you are prone to sea sickness, Bass Strait is often a rough crossing and you may not enjoy the voyage. An option to explore Tasmania is a **fly/drive holiday**, with a rental car awaiting your aircraft.

Houseboat, Richmond River, NSW

Campervan rental is available in all States and most cities and major towns. Campervans are fully equipped and vary in size and level of luxury. Costs vary accordingly and also with the season. There are often restrictions on where you can take a campervan. Check first.

If you are interested in a 'full-on' **adventure tour**, but are intimidated by the thought of doing it alone, there are motoring organisations and many private tour operators that provide escorted group trips into more remote areas, Cape York for example. These tag-along tours save you the worry of navigation and planning (except for your vehicle) and also provide expert help and back-up in case of a mechanical breakdown.

You also could leave your vehicle behind and tour in a 4WD coach, or take a **camel trek** or try a **canoe adventure**— or almost any way you want. Check with your travel agent or Government tourist bureau (**see:** Useful Information).

For the young at heart, there are over 100 **youth hostels** throughout Australia. For information, contact the main headquarters of the Australian Youth Hostels Association, 10 Mallett St, Camperdown, NSW 2050; (02) 565 1699.

If you are planning a stay in a city or at a resort area for any length of time, a sensible family alternative to motel or hotel accommodation is a **serviced** or **self-service flat.** The relevant tourist bureau (**see:** Useful Information) will provide details.

House swapping is yet another possibility for a lengthy stay. Advertisements for those seeking a house-swapping holiday often appear in the classified sections of the newspapers. Make sure you are totally satisfied with the arrangements made concerning your commitments and with the people with whom you are dealing. Also check that your householder's insurance covers you in such circumstances (**see:** Insurance).

A **host farm** can make a refreshing change from the norm. Such accommodation varies from spartan to luxurious and, in some cases, guests are invited to take part in farm life. Associations in each State (**see:** Farm Holidays) or tourist authorities will provide details.

If you would prefer **bed and breakfast** accommodation only in a 'homestay' or 'farmstay' environment throughout Australia, contact: Bed & Breakfast, PO Box 408, Gordon NSW 2072; (02) 498 5344, 498 1539 (AH).

Not to be confused with bushwalking, **backpacking** is a mode of travel using accommodation provided at budget rates in a communal environment. Note, however, the accommodation offered is not always suitable for children. During the high season, resort hostels may not accept telephone reservations without payment and it is advisable to book well in advance. For information on the range of accommodation available, contact: The Secretary, Backpackers Resorts of Australia Pty Ltd, PO Box 1000, Byron Bay NSW 2481; (018) 66 6888 (9–5, Mon.–Fri.). Backpackers VIP Discount Kit $15; accommodation guide to 93 hostels Australia-wide free; both plus $2 postage and handling.

If you are into **staying afloat**, consider hiring a paddle-wheeler on the Murray or a houseboat on the Hawkesbury or Eildon Weir, or even chartering a yacht to cruise in the Whitsundays. Check with your travel agent or Government tourist bureau (**see:** Useful Information).

Dividing Up the Dollars

Very few people can afford the 'money-no-object' approach to holidays, no matter what the length of stay. Your planning should include budgeting. You will need principally to consider accommodation, food, fuel and entertainment, although emergency funds should not be forgotten. **Travel insurance** is a wise precaution (**see:** Insurance). Accommodation costs can be estimated when you book, but you might simply average the figure. If you do, estimate high rather than low. **Food** is a matter of personal choice: you may eat out every night or prepare all or some of your meals yourself. Be realistic when budgeting the cost of eating out or preparing meals: allow for the unexpected, and for the higher cost of food and meals in popular holiday destinations or in remote areas. If you are travelling with children, budget for snacks and recreational treats.

Once you know your vehicle's fuel consumption you can work out your **fuel** costs in advance. The usual method is based on litres per 100 kilometres. If your vehicle uses 16 litres per 100 km and your journey distance works out at 5000 km, you will use 50 times 16 litres of fuel, or 800 litres. Allow for rises in petrol and charges and also for the fact that fuel is more expensive in remote areas.

When **budgeting**, allow for such 'budget biters' as admission charges, postcards, camera film, chemist's items, tips, bridge tolls and car repairs. Remember also that accommodation, travel and rental charges rise during peak periods.

Carrying large amounts of **cash** with you is not a good idea, which is why travellers cheques were invented. Use them, but also make arrangements with your bank to enable you to draw from the bank's branches on your route.

Car Maintenance Courses

If you plan to tour in the remoter areas, you should acquire basic mechanical knowledge and skills. In general, you should have a broad understanding of the technology of your vehicle and know how much roadside repair is possible in the event of a breakdown (**see also:** Breakdowns). You should also have some specific knowledge; for example how to change a tyre on the vehicle you will be using; and whether you can use jumper leads to start your car, and if so, how it is done. Car care and basic car-maintenance courses are run by Adult Education centres, TAFE Colleges and automobile clubs in all States. The courses vary widely in content and length. A call to these organisations will ascertain what course is available and appropriate. Test your knowledge by reading through the flow-charts and the list of tools and spare parts (**see:** Breakdowns).

Insurance

The benefits of a comprehensive insurance policy on your vehicle, caravan or trailer are obvious. Apart from cover against loss or damage due to accident, theft or vandalism, your personal effects are covered against loss or damage when they are in the insured vehicle. Additional policies will cover such eventualities as the cost of temporary accommodation should your caravan become uninhabitable, for example. Some companies provide short-term (maximum 6 weeks) travel insurance, for example to cover loss of luggage or the cancellation of accommodation bookings. Information and advice can be obtained from the various motoring organisations and insurance companies.

Itineraries

Some people make itineraries and stick to them. Others do not. At the very least, a rough schedule to ensure a mixture of travel and sightseeing time is essential.

Allow some flexibility. You never know what might detain you: the weather, for example (rest breaks are necessary in extreme heat), or children, who have a low tolerance for long stretches of driving without a break (**see:** Child's Play).

Clothing

Be strict with yourself and the family when you are packing and travel as lightly as you can. It is better to spend an hour at a laundromat than overburden your vehicle with clothing you probably will not wear.

Essentials are a warm **sweater** or **jacket**, even in summer, sensible **comfortable shoes** and a **wide-brimmed hat** to protect yourself from the sun at all times. Non-irons are practical. Carry items like swimwear, towels, spare socks and sweaters in a loose bag, which can be kept within easy reach. **Gumboots** are a handy item also.

First-aid Kit

A first-aid kit is essential. Include bandaids, antiseptic, bandages, headache tablets, extra blockout, sunburn cream, insect repellent and a soothing lotion for bites. Eye drops are a good idea, as is a thermometer and a tourniquet. A range of such kits is available from the St John Ambulance Service, which also conducts basic courses in first aid. As **car sickness** is often a problem on long journeys, particularly with young children, include medication to counter this. Your local chemist or a doctor will advise you on what is available.

Useful Extras

Depending on the length and nature of your tour, some items are valuable, some essential (**see:** Tools and Spare Parts). Carry picnic and barbecue equipment, tissues, toilet paper and a container or plastic bag for rubbish—and take it with you rather than leaving it behind, at least until you can find a legitimate rubbish tip. Rugs or blankets are a necessary extra (**see:** Natural Hazards: Bushfire), as is a large sheet of plastic, which can be used as an emergency windscreen (**see also:** How to Obtain Water). Having a mobile phone may be useful if you are travelling within signal range; check the coverage before you buy. If you are going outback, some type of shade cover, such as a tarpaulin, as sun protection is a necessary item in case of an emergency stop (**see:** Surviving in the Outback).

6

Other Information

Pets

Don't forget: whether you are leaving your pets behind or taking them with you, you will need to make a booking for them also.

Leaving them behind:
- Pet care services (*Yellow Pages*). These provide care of pets in their own environment. They also will care for plants and property, etc.
- Dog boarding kennels and catteries (*Yellow Pages*): provide care and accommodation. Some have pickup and delivery services.
- Animal welfare organisations/veterinary surgeons (*Yellow Pages*): For advice and information.

Taking them with you:
- Make sure, in advance, that the accommodation or mode of travel booked permits animals. Many caravan parks and most national parks do not admit animals.
- During the trip, carry additional water and stop at regular intervals to provide an opportunity for toileting and exercise.
- Do not leave an animal unattended in a vehicle for any length of time; always provide a source of fresh air.
- Allow sufficient room in the vehicle to comfortably accommodate the animal.
- Do not transport an animal in a moving caravan.

Before Departure

- Cancel newspapers, mail deliveries.
- Make arrangements for the garden to be watered and the lawns mowed. Board out your indoor plants, or if this is not possible, place the pots in the sink, surround them with damp peat and water thoroughly. Encasing each in a sealed polythene bag also helps during summer months.
- If you have a pet, arrange for its safekeeping well in advance (**see:** Pets).
- Arrange for a neighbour to keep an eye on the house. Your local police will cooperate. Alternatively, consult a professional home security service (*Yellow Pages*).
- Valuable items, such as jewellery, are best left for safekeeping at your bank.
- Before leaving, turn the electricity off at the mains, but leave the fridge door open. Make sure that everything else that should be turned off is off.
- Check that all windows and doors are locked; then check again.
- Make sure you leave a contact address with a friend or neighbour.

Carrying a Camera

You probably will want to preserve the highlights of you trip on film. Check the following points.
- If you have recently purchased or hired a camera, take at least one test film so that you know how the equipment reacts to different light conditions.
- As weather conditions may vary on your trip, it is a good idea to carry film with a range of speeds. If you are not an expert, talk to your local dealer about the varieties of film available.
- Before you leave, ensure that you have a good supply of film, batteries and a lens brush. Other useful accessories are a close-up lens, exposure meter, lens hood, filters and a tripod.
- To safeguard your equipment from damage by water, heat, sand and dust, protect it in a plastic bag inside a camera bag. It can get very hot in a closed car, so always keep the camera in the shade. The best place is on the floor, on the opposite side to the exhaust pipe. Make sure, however, that the bag can't rattle around.
- High temperatures and humidity can damage colour film. Store your film in the coolest spot available and do not break the watertight vapour seal until just before use. Once the film is used, remove it from the camera, mark it with an E for 'exposed' and send it for processing as soon as possible.
- Even with automatic exposure, when filming in hot conditions it may be necessary to allow one stop or half of a stop down to compensate for the brilliance of the light. If in doubt, consult the instruction sheet included with the film.
- Check that your personal property insurance covers the loss of cameras and photographic equipment while travelling (**see:** Insurance).

Time Zones

Australia has 3 time zones:
- **Eastern Standard Time** (EST), in Queensland, New South Wales, Victoria and Tasmania.
- **Central Standard Time** (CST is half an hour behind EST), in South Australia and Northern Territory.
- **Western Standard Time** (WST is 2 hours behind EST), in Western Australia.

Daylight saving is adopted by some States in the summer months. In New South Wales, Victoria, Tasmania, Australian Capital Territory, Western Australia and South Australia, clocks are put forward 1 hour at the beginning of summer. Northern Territory and Queensland do not have daylight saving.

Quarantine Regulations

Throughout Australia, State quarantine regulations prohibit the transport by travellers of certain plants and foods, and even soil, across State borders. Further information is available from offices of agricultural departments in all States.

Yampire Gorge, Hamersley Range National Park, WA

Intercity Route Maps

The following intercity route maps will help you to plan your route between major cities. As well, you can use the individual maps while undertaking your journey, since they provide information on distances between all towns along the route, roadside rest areas and road conditions, where relevant.

The map below provides an overview of the routes mapped together with a listing of the maps and the pages on which they appear.

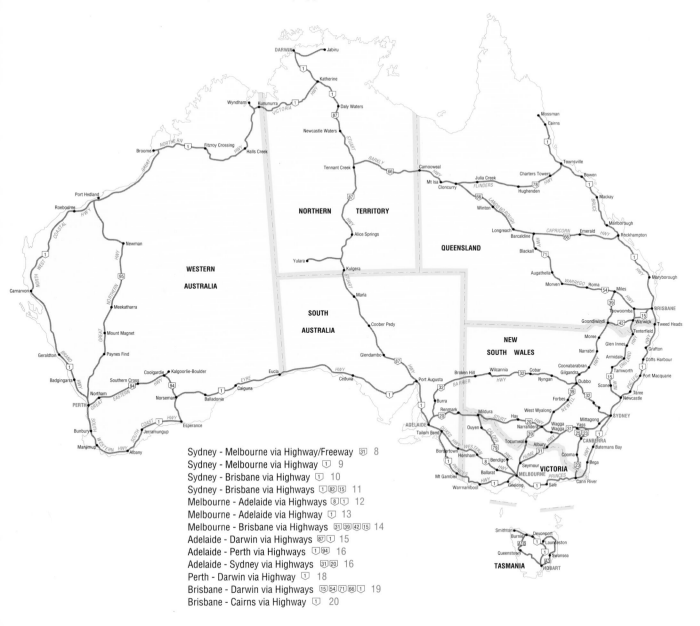

Sydney-Melbourne
via Hume Highway/Freeway ③①

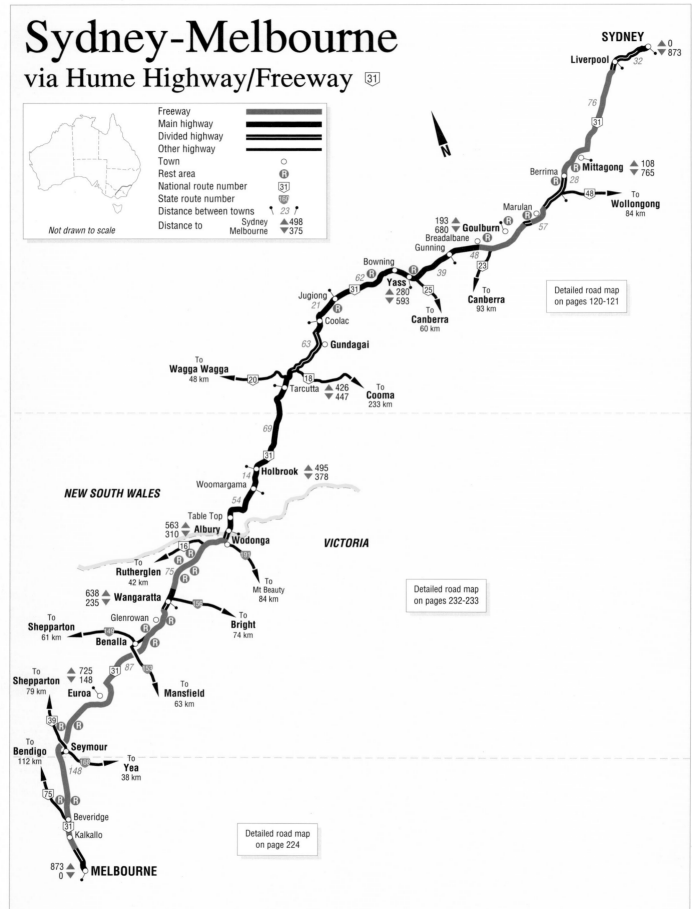

Freeway	
Main highway	
Divided highway	
Other highway	
Town	○
Rest area	Ⓡ
National route number	③①
State route number	⑯⓪
Distance between towns	23
Distance to	Sydney ▲498
	Melbourne ▼375

Not drawn to scale

SYDNEY ▲0 ▼873
Liverpool 32
76
③①
Mittagong ▲108 ▼765
Berrima Ⓡ 28
Marulan 48 To Wollongong 84 km
193 ▲ Goulburn
680 ▼ 57
Breadalbane
Gunning 48
②③
Bowning Ⓡ 39 To Canberra 93 km
62 Yass ②⑤
Jugiong ③① ▲280 ▼593 To Canberra 60 km
21 Ⓡ
Coolac
63 Gundagai
To Wagga Wagga 48 km ②⓪ ⑱ ▲426 ▼447 To Cooma 233 km
Tarcutta

Detailed road map on pages 120-121

69
③①
Holbrook ▲495 ▼378
14
Woomargama
NEW SOUTH WALES 54
Table Top
563 ▲ Albury
310 ▼ Wodonga
⑯ Ⓡ ⑲① **VICTORIA**
To Rutherglen 42 km Ⓡ 75 Ⓡ
638 ▲ Wangaratta To Mt Beauty 84 km
235 ▼ ⑮⑥
Glenrowan To Bright 74 km
To Shepparton 61 km ⑭⑨ Ⓡ
Benalla Ⓡ
725 ▲ ③① 87 ⑮③
148 ▼ To Mansfield 63 km
To Shepparton 79 km Euroa
③⑨ Ⓡ Ⓡ
To Bendigo 112 km Seymour
⑯⑧ To Yea 38 km
148
⑦⑤ Ⓡ Ⓡ
Beveridge
③① Kalkallo
873 ▲ **MELBOURNE**
0 ▼

Detailed road map on pages 232-233

Detailed road map on page 224

Sydney-Melbourne
via Princes Highway ⬡1

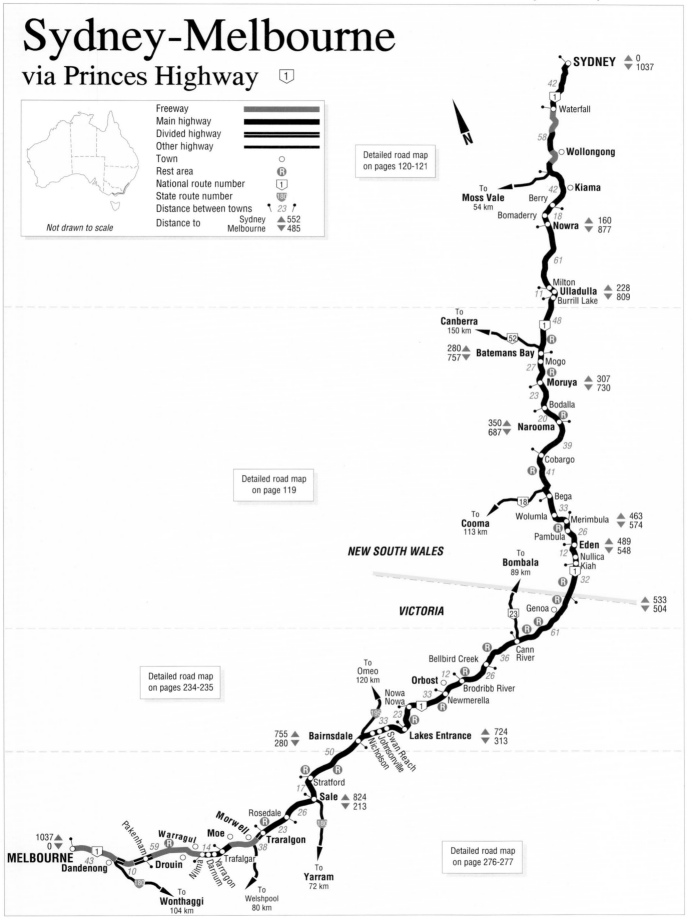

Freeway		
Main highway		
Divided highway		
Other highway		
Town	○	
Rest area	Ⓡ	
National route number	⬡1	
State route number	180	
Distance between towns	23	
Distance to	Sydney	▲552
	Melbourne	▼485

Not drawn to scale

Detailed road map on pages 120-121

SYDNEY ▲0 ▼1037

42
⬡1 Waterfall

58

Wollongong

○Kiama

To **Moss Vale** 54 km *42* Berry

Bomaderry *18* **Nowra** ▲160 ▼877

61

Milton ▲228 ▼809
Ulladulla *11* Burrill Lake

To **Canberra** 150 km ⬡1 *48*
52 Ⓡ
280▲ 757▼ **Batemans Bay** Mogo
27 Ⓡ
Moruya ▲307 ▼730
23 Bodalla
20 Ⓡ
350▲ 687▼ **Narooma**
39
Cobargo
Ⓡ *41*

Detailed road map on page 119

18 Bega
To **Cooma** 113 km Wolumla *33* Merimbula ▲463 ▼574
26 Ⓡ
Pambula **Eden** ▲489 ▼548
To **Bombala** 89 km *12* Nullica Ⓡ Kiah
⬡1 *32*

NEW SOUTH WALES

▲533 ▼504

VICTORIA

23 Genoa ○
Ⓡ
61

Ⓡ Cann River
Bellbird Creek *36*
Ⓡ *26*
Orbost ○ *12* Ⓡ
33 Brodribb River
Nowa Nowa Newmerella
⬡1
23
195 Ⓡ
33 Swan Reach **Lakes Entrance** ▲724 ▼313
755▲ 280▼ **Bairnsdale** Johnsonville
Nicholson
50

Detailed road map on pages 234-235

Ⓡ Ⓡ
Stratford
17
Sale ▲824 ▼213
Rosedale *26*
Morwell Ⓡ *23* 180
1037▲ 0▼ Pakenham Warragul **Moe** **Traralgon**
MELBOURNE ⬡1 *59* Ⓡ *14* Trafalgar *38* To **Yarram** 72 km
43 Drouin Nilma Yarragon
Dandenong *10* Darnum
180 To **Wonthaggi** 104 km To **Welshpool** 80 km

Detailed road map on page 276-277

Sydney-Brisbane
via Pacific Highway ①

QUEENSLAND

Detailed road map on page 475

NEW SOUTH WALES

BRISBANE ▲ 0 ▼ 982

Loganholme
Beenleigh Ⓡ
Yatala
Ormeau
67
Oxenford
Nerang **Southport**
Surfers Paradise
Mudgeeraba *32* **Coolangatta** ▲ 99 ▼ 883
Tweed Heads
31
Murwillumbah
15 Burringbar
17 Ocean Shores
Brunswick Heads ▲ 162 ▼ 820
21
Bangalow
To **Lismore** 35 km *26* Newrybar
④④ **Ballina** ▲ 209 ▼ 773
9
18 Wardell
12 Broadwater
Ⓡ Woodburn
43 ①
Chatsworth
To **Glen Innes** 159 km
③⑧ Ⓡ Tyndale Maclean
13 *40*
344 ▲ 638 ▼ **Grafton** Ulmarra
58
Detailed road map on page 123
Woolgoolga ▲ 402 ▼ 580
25 Emerald Beach
Moonee Beach
29 **Coffs Harbour** ▲ 427 ▼ 555
Ⓡ Sawtell
Urunga
30 Valla Beach
486 ▲ 496 ▼ **Macksville** **Nambucca Heads**
Ⓡ
46
Frederickton
7 ①
To **Walcha** 172 km **Kempsey** ▲ 539 ▼ 443
31 Ⓡ Kundabung
③④ *42* Telegraph Point
○ **Port Macquarie**
Kew Ⓡ
49
661 ▲ 321 ▼ **Taree**
Coopernook
Ⓡ *28*
48 Nabiac
To **Maitland** 18 km *43* **Bulahdelah** ▲ 737 ▼ 245
Ⓡ
① Karuah *37* Ⓡ
Kurri Kurri ○ **Raymond Terrace** ▲ 807 ▼ 175
To **Newcastle** 49 km
① *165*
Ⓡ
○ **Gosford**
Detailed road map on page 121
SYDNEY ▲ 982 ▼ 0

N

Freeway	
Main highway	
Divided highway	
Other highway	
Town	○
Rest area	Ⓡ
National route number	①
State route number	⑯⓪
Distance between towns	*23*
Distance to	Brisbane ▲ 539 Sydney ▼ 443

Not drawn to scale

Sydney-Brisbane
via New England Highway ① ⑧² ⑮

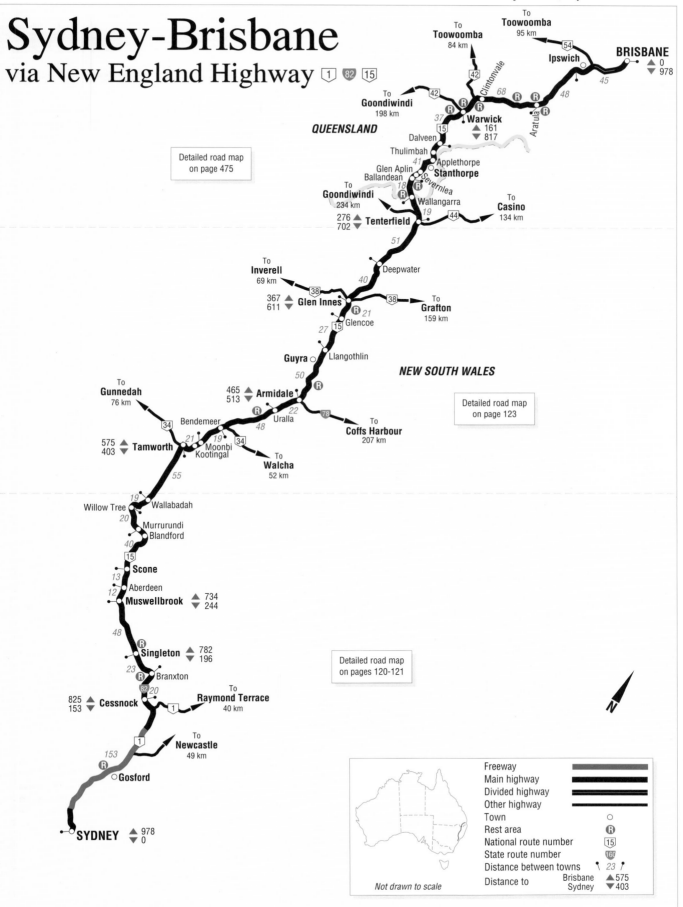

To Toowoomba 84 km
To Toowoomba 95 km
54
Ipswich
BRISBANE ▲ 0 ▼ 978
42
Clintonvale
68
45
42
To Goondiwindi 198 km
R R
R R
48
Aratula
QUEENSLAND
37
15
Warwick ▲ 161 ▼ 817
Dalveen
Thulimbah
41
Applethorpe
Glen Aplin
Stanthorpe
Ballandean
Severnlea
18
To Goondiwindi 234 km
R
R
Wallangarra
276 ▲ 702 ▼ **Tenterfield**
19
44
To Casino 134 km
51
To Inverell 69 km
Deepwater
40
38
367 ▲ 611 ▼ **Glen Innes**
38
To Grafton 159 km
R 21
Glencoe
27
15
Guyra ○ Llangothlin
50
NEW SOUTH WALES
465 ▲ 513 ▼ **Armidale**
R
22
To Gunnedah 76 km
R
Uralla
78
To Coffs Harbour 207 km
34
Bendemeer
48
21
19
575 ▲ 403 ▼ **Tamworth**
Moonbi
34
Kootingal
To Walcha 52 km
55
19
Willow Tree
Wallabadah
20
Murrurundi
Blandford
40
15
Scone
13
Aberdeen
12
Muswellbrook ▲ 734 ▼ 244
48
R
Singleton ▲ 782 ▼ 196
23
R
Branxton
82 20
To Raymond Terrace 40 km
825 ▲ 153 ▼ **Cessnock**
1
1
To Newcastle 49 km
153
R
○ Gosford
SYDNEY ▲ 978 ▼ 0

Detailed road map on page 475

Detailed road map on page 123

Detailed road map on pages 120-121

Freeway	
Main highway	
Divided highway	
Other highway	
Town	○
Rest area	®
National route number	⑮
State route number	⑯⁰
Distance between towns	23
Distance to	Brisbane ▲575 Sydney ▼403

Not drawn to scale

Melbourne-Adelaide
via Western & Dukes Highways ⑧ ①

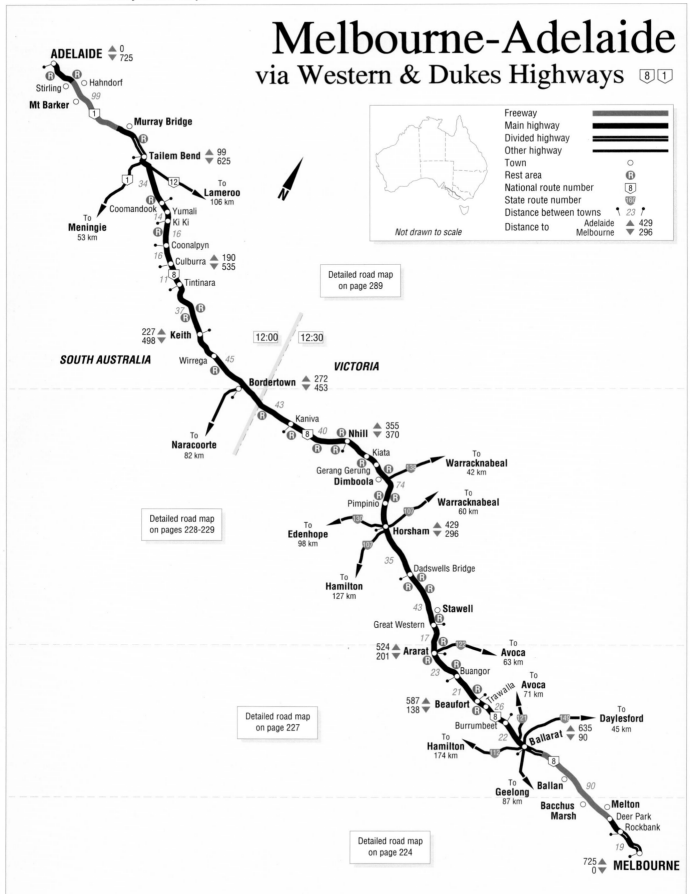

ADELAIDE ▲ 0 ▼ 725

Stirling ○
Hahndorf ○
Mt Barker
99
①
Murray Bridge

Tailem Bend ▲ 99 ▼ 625

① 34
⑫
To Lameroo 106 km

Coomandook
Yumali
To Meningie 53 km
14
Ki Ki
16
Coonalpyn
16
Culburra ▲ 190 ▼ 535
⑧
11
Tintinara

37

227 ▲ 498 Keith

SOUTH AUSTRALIA
Wirrega 45
12:00   12:30
VICTORIA
Bordertown ▲ 272 ▼ 453

43
Kaniva
To Naracoorte 82 km
⑧ 40
Nhill ▲ 355 ▼ 370

Kiata
Gerang Gerung   138   To Warracknabeal 42 km
Dimboola
74
Pimpinio   107   To Warracknabeal 60 km
130
To Edenhope 98 km
Horsham ▲ 429 ▼ 296
107

35
Dadswells Bridge
To Hamilton 127 km

43   Stawell
Great Western
17   122   To Avoca 63 km
524 ▲ 201 Ararat
23   Buangor
21   Trawalla   To Avoca 71 km
587 ▲ 138 Beaufort
26
⑧   121   149   To Daylesford 45 km
Burrumbeet   Ballarat ▲ 635 ▼ 90
22
To Hamilton 174 km   112
⑧
To Geelong 87 km   Ballan   90
Bacchus Marsh   Melton
Deer Park
Rockbank
19
725 ▲ 0 ▼ **MELBOURNE**

Legend

Freeway	
Main highway	
Divided highway	
Other highway	
Town	○
Rest area	Ⓡ
National route number	⑧
State route number	160
Distance between towns	23
Distance to	Adelaide ▲ 429
	Melbourne ▼ 296

Not drawn to scale

N

Detailed road map on page 289

Detailed road map on pages 228-229

Detailed road map on page 227

Detailed road map on page 224

Melbourne-Adelaide
via Princes Highway [1]

Legend	
Freeway	
Main highway	
Divided highway	
Other highway	
Town	○
Rest area	R
National route number	[1]
State route number	[160]
Distance between towns	23
Distance to	Adelaide ▲454
	Melbourne ▼482

Not drawn to scale

0 / 936 ▲▼ ADELAIDE
R — Stirling ○ — ○ Hahndorf — R
Mt Barker ○ — *99*
[1] — **Murray Bridge**
Tailem Bend — ▲ 99 / ▼ 837
32
[12] — To **Lameroo** 106 km
[8]
Ashville — *21*
152 / 784 ▲▼ **Meningie** — R — *22* — To **Coomandook** 34 km
Magrath Flat
30 — Woods Well
Policemans Point — *10*
Salt Creek — R
R — [1]
R — *84*
R

SOUTH AUSTRALIA

Detailed road map on page 287

Kingston S.E. — R
298 / 638 ▲▼
R — R — *91*
Clay Wells — 12:00 | 12:30
R
Hatherleigh — *15* — To **Penola** 53 km
R — **VICTORIA**
Millicent — R — To **Penola** 52 km
Snuggery — *10*
R — *40*
[1]
454 / 482 ▲▼ **Mt Gambier** — R — [12] — To **Casterton** 61 km
Dartmoor — To **Hamilton** 58 km
108
R — [107]
Narrawong
543 / 393 ▲▼ **Heywood** — R
19
Portland ○ — Codrington — Rosebrook
Yambuk — *27* — To **Mortlake** 50 km
Port Fairy — R — [104] — Panmure — Garvoc — **716 / 220** ▲▼ — **741 / 195** ▲▼
28 — Boorcan
661 / 275 ▲▼ **Warrnambool** — R — *34* — **Terang** — *21* — *72* — **Camperdown** — Pomborneit
[100] — Pirron Yallock — To **Mortlake** 147 km
Stoneyford — R — To **Ballarat** 87 km
788 / 148 ▲▼ **Colac** — R — [1] — *37* — [149] — Werribee ○
To **Port Campbell** 66 km — **Winchelsea** — *19* — Mt Moriac — [106] — *74*
[100] — **Geelong** — **MELBOURNE**
825 / 111 ▲▼ — To **Lorne** 69 km — ▲ 936 / ▼ 0

Detailed road map on page 224

Detailed road map on pages 226-227

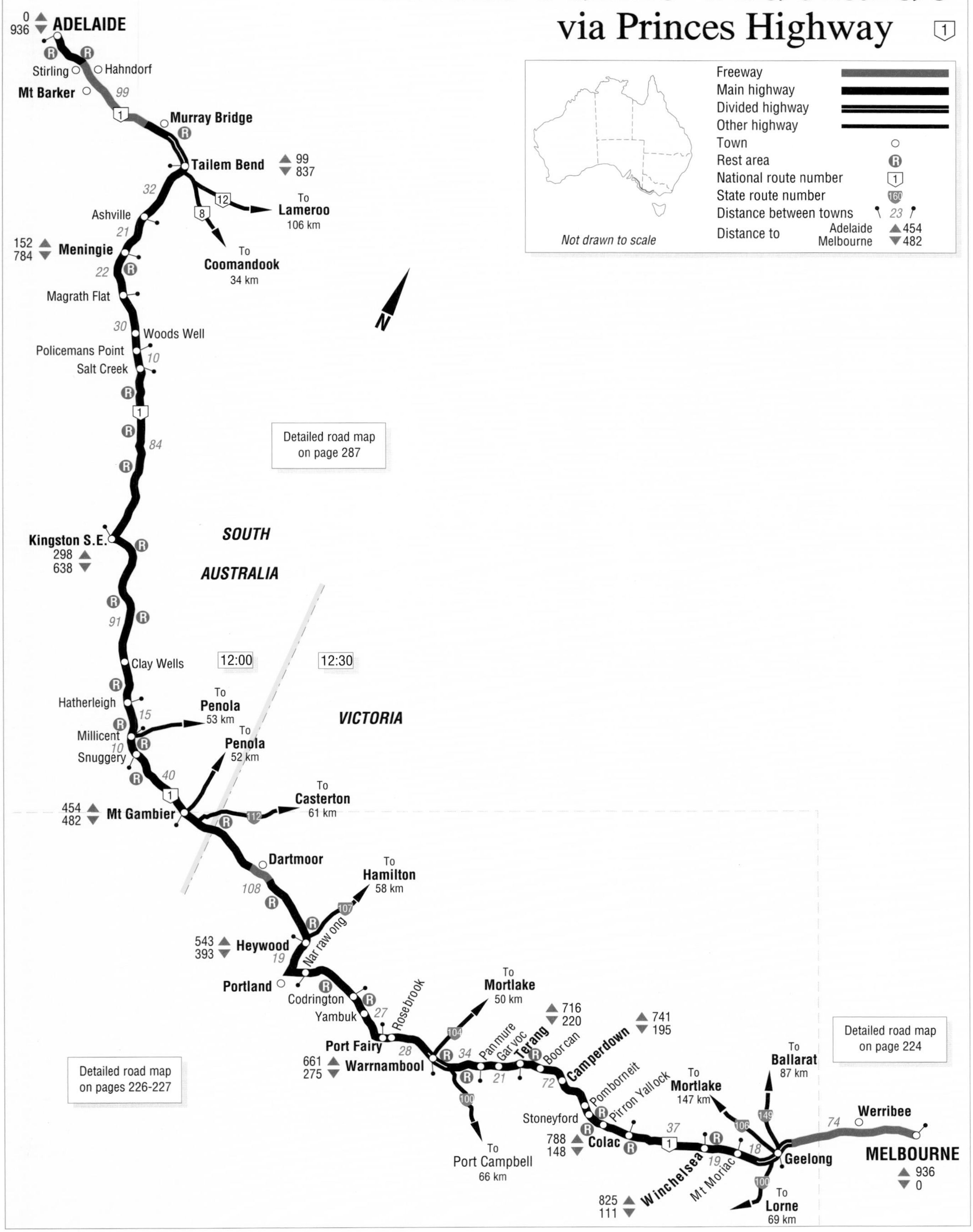

Melbourne-Brisbane
via Newell Highway 31 39 42 15

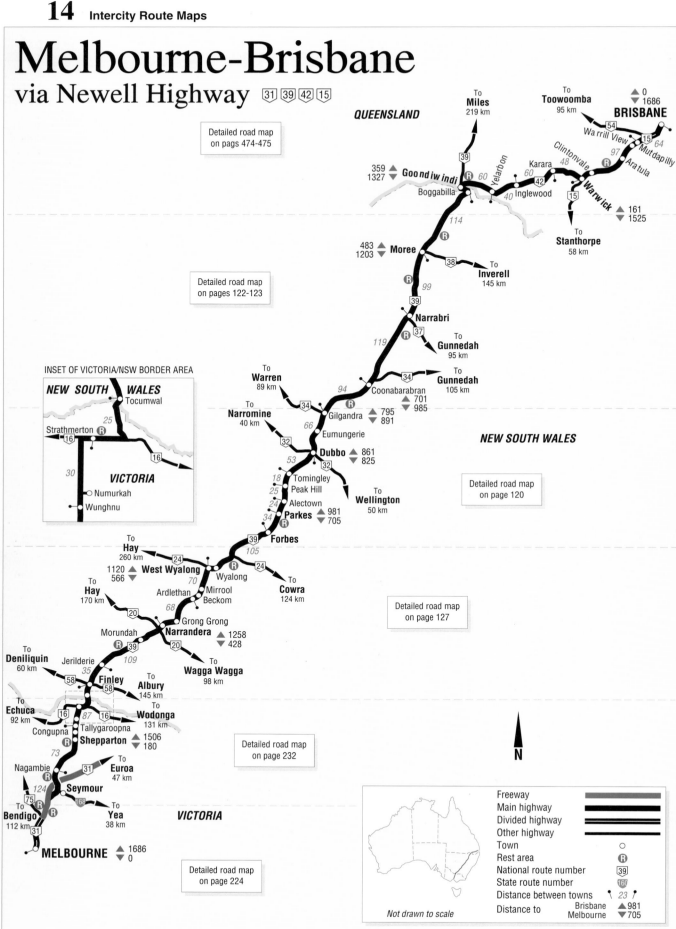

Detailed road map
on pags 474-475

QUEENSLAND

To
Miles
219 km

To
Toowoomba
95 km

▲ 0
▼ 1686
BRISBANE

54
Warrill View
15
64
Mutdapilly
97
Clintonvale
48
Aratula
Warwick

39
Yelarbon
60
Karara
60
42
Inglewood
15

359 ▲
1327 ▼ **Goondiwindi**
Boggabilla

40

161 ▲
1525 ▼

To
Stanthorpe
58 km

114

483 ▲
1203 ▼ **Moree**

38
To
Inverell
145 km

Detailed road map
on pages 122-123

99

39
Narrabri

37
To
Gunnedah
95 km

NEW SOUTH WALES

119

To
Warren
89 km

34
Coonabarabran
▲ 701
▼ 985

34
To
Gunnedah
105 km

94

To
Narromine
40 km
Gilgandra
795 ▲
891 ▼

66
Eumungerie

32
Dubbo ▲ 861
▼ 825

Detailed road map
on page 120

53
32

18
Tomingley
Peak Hill
To
Wellington
50 km

INSET OF VICTORIA/NSW BORDER AREA

NEW SOUTH WALES
Tocumwal
25
Strathmerton R
16
16

30

VICTORIA
Numurkah
Wunghnu

25
Alectown
Parkes ▲ 981
▼ 705

34

39
Forbes

To
Hay
260 km
24
105

24

1120 ▲
566 ▼ **West Wyalong**
Wyalong
To
Cowra
124 km

To
Hay
170 km
70
Ardlethan
Mirrool
Beckom

Detailed road map
on page 127

20
68

Morundah
Grong Grong
Narrandera ▲ 1258
▼ 428

To
Deniliquin
60 km
R 39
Jerilderie
109
20
To
Wagga Wagga
98 km

35
58
Finley
58
To
Albury
145 km

To
Echuca
92 km
16
87
16
To
Wodonga
131 km

Congupna
Tallygaroopna

R
Shepparton ▲ 1506
▼ 180

Detailed road map
on page 232

73

Nagambie
R
31
To
Euroa
47 km

124
Seymour

75
168
To
Yea
38 km

VICTORIA

R
To
Bendigo
112 km
31

MELBOURNE ▲ 1686
▼ 0

Detailed road map
on page 224

N

	Freeway
	Main highway
	Divided highway
	Other highway
Town	○
Rest area	R
National route number	39
State route number	160
Distance between towns	*23*
Distance to	Brisbane ▲ 981
	Melbourne ▼ 705

Not drawn to scale

Adelaide-Darwin
via Stuart Highway 87 1

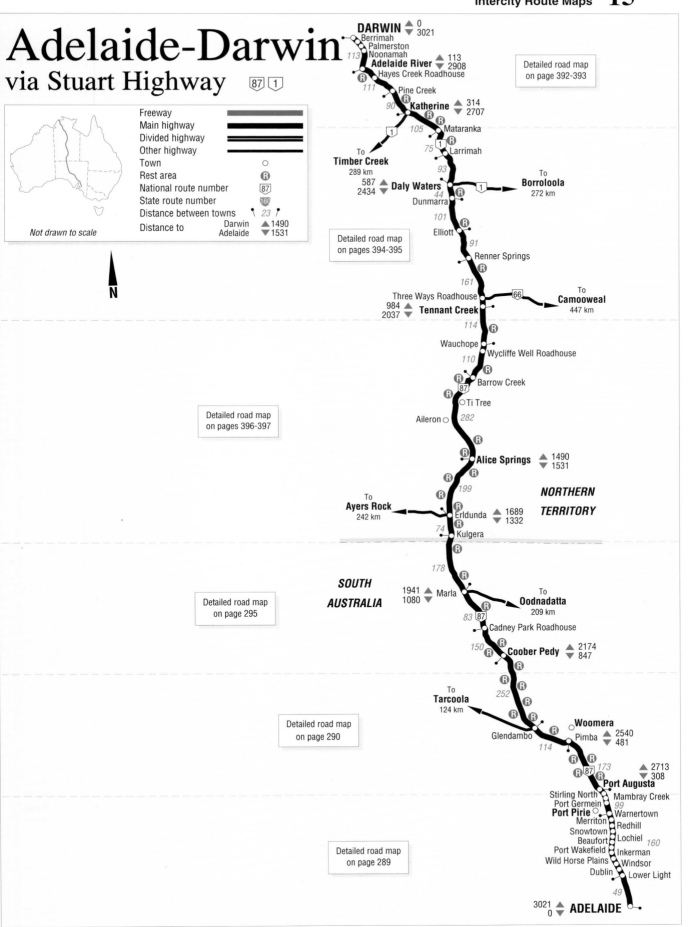

Freeway	
Main highway	
Divided highway	
Other highway	
Town	○
Rest area	®
National route number	87
State route number	160
Distance between towns	23
Distance to	Darwin ▲1490
	Adelaide ▼1531

Not drawn to scale

N

DARWIN ▲ 0 ▼ 3021
Berrimah
Palmerston
113 Noonamah
Adelaide River ▲ 113 ▼ 2908
Hayes Creek Roadhouse
111 Pine Creek
90 **Katherine** ▲ 314 ▼ 2707
105 Mataranka
To
Timber Creek
289 km
75 Larrimah
93
587 **Daly Waters** ▲
2434 ▼ 44
Dunmarra
101 To **Borroloola** 272 km
Elliott
91
Renner Springs
161
Three Ways Roadhouse 66 To **Camooweal** 447 km
984 **Tennant Creek** ▲
2037 ▼
114
Wauchope
Wycliffe Well Roadhouse
110
Barrow Creek 87
○Ti Tree
Aileron ○ 282
Alice Springs ▲ 1490 ▼ 1531

NORTHERN TERRITORY

To **Ayers Rock** 242 km
199
Erldunda ▲ 1689 ▼ 1332
74 Kulgera

SOUTH AUSTRALIA
178
1941 ▲ Marla To **Oodnadatta** 209 km
1080 ▼
83 87
Cadney Park Roadhouse
150 **Coober Pedy** ▲ 2174 ▼ 847
To **Tarcoola** 124 km
252
Woomera
Glendambo Pimba ▲ 2540 ▼ 481
114
87 173 ▲ 2713 ▼ 308
Port Augusta
Stirling North Mambray Creek
Port Germein 99
Port Pirie ○ Warnertown
Merriton Redhill
Snowtown Lochiel 160
Beaufort
Port Wakefield Inkerman
Wild Horse Plains Windsor
Dublin Lower Light
49
3021 ▲ **ADELAIDE** 0

Detailed road map on page 392-393

Detailed road map on pages 394-395

Detailed road map on pages 396-397

Detailed road map on page 295

Detailed road map on page 290

Detailed road map on page 289

Adelaide-Perth
via Eyre & Great Eastern Highways ⬡1 ⬡94

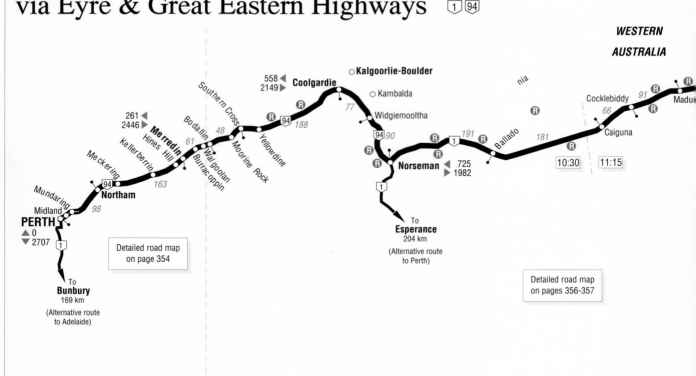

WESTERN AUSTRALIA

Kalgoorlie-Boulder

558 ◀
2149 ▶ Coolgardie

Kambalda

Cocklebiddy   91   Madu

261 ◀
2446 ▶ Merredin

Widgiemooltha

nia

Southern Cross

Bodallin   48

Hines Hill   61

Yellowdine   188

94   90

77

191   Ballado   181   Caiguna

66

Kellerberrin   Walgoolan

Meckering   Burracoppin   Moorine Rock   163   Norseman   725 ◀
1982 ▶   10:30   11:15

Mundaring   Northam   98

Midland
PERTH
▲ 0
▼ 2707   1

To Esperance
204 km
(Alternative route to Perth)

Detailed road map on page 354

Detailed road map on pages 356-357

To Bunbury
169 km
(Alternative route to Adelaide)

Adelaide-Sydney
via Hume & Sturt Highways ⬡31 ⬡20

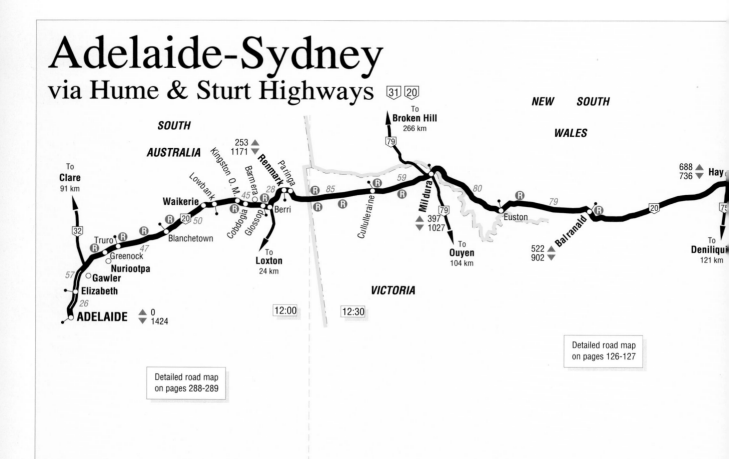

NEW SOUTH WALES

To Broken Hill
266 km

SOUTH AUSTRALIA

253 ▲
1171 ▼ Renmark

Paringa   79

688 ▲
736 ▼ Hay

To Clare
91 km

Kingston O. M.

Lowbank   Barmera   28

Waikerie   45   Berri   59   Mildura   80   Euston   79

20   50   Cobdogla   Glossop   85   Cullulleraine   397 ▲
1027 ▼   79   Balranald   75

Truro   47   Blanchetown

Greenock

Nuriootpa
Gawler   57

Elizabeth

ADELAIDE   ▲ 0
▼ 1424   26   32

To Loxton
24 km   12:00   12:30

VICTORIA   To Ouyen
104 km   522 ▲
902 ▼

To Deniliqu
121 km

Detailed road map on pages 126-127

Detailed road map on pages 288-289

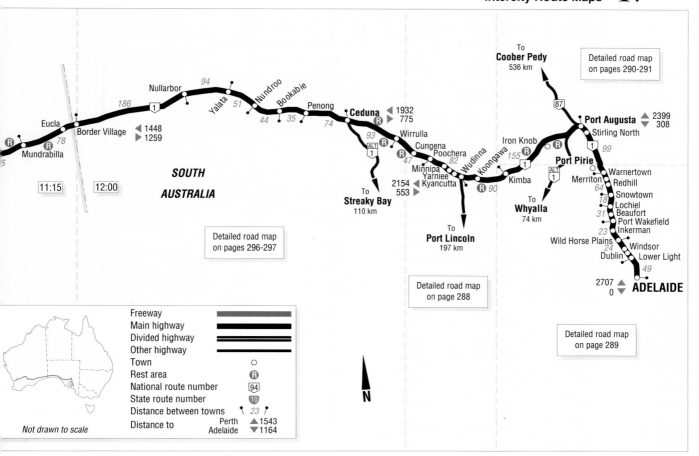

SOUTH
AUSTRALIA

11:15   12:00

Detailed road map
on pages 296-297

Detailed road map
on page 288

Detailed road map
on pages 290-291

Detailed road map
on page 289

To
Coober Pedy
536 km

Port Augusta ▲ 2399
308

Stirling North

Port Pirie

Iron Knob

To
Whyalla
74 km

Warnertown
Redhill
Snowtown
Lochiel
Beaufort
Port Wakefield
Inkerman
Windsor
Lower Light

Merriton

Wild Horse Plains
Dublin

2707 ▲
0 ▼ **ADELAIDE**

Freeway
Main highway
Divided highway
Other highway
Town ○
Rest area Ⓡ
National route number 94
State route number 10
Distance between towns 23
Distance to   Perth ▲ 1543
Adelaide ▼ 1164

Not drawn to scale

N

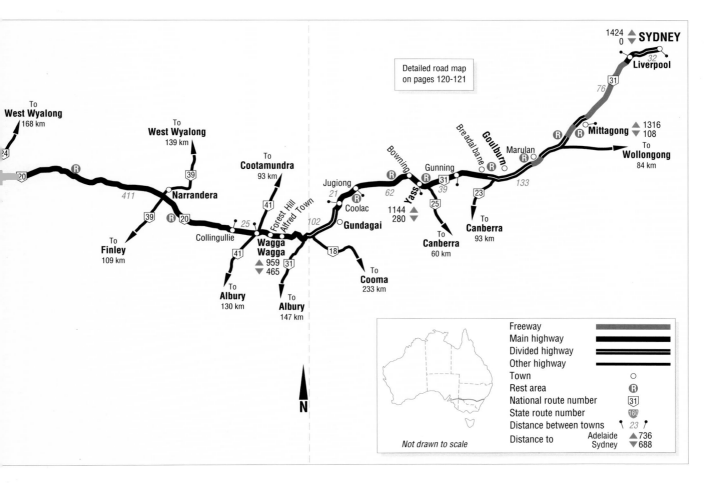

To
West Wyalong
168 km

To
West Wyalong
139 km

To
Cootamundra
93 km

Narrandera

Collingullie

To
Finley
109 km

Wagga Wagga ▲ 959
▼ 465

To
Albury
130 km

To
Albury
147 km

Forest Hill
Alfred Town

To
Cooma
233 km

Jugiong
Coolac
Gundagai

Yass
1144 ▲
280 ▼

To
Canberra
60 km

Bowning

Gunning

To
Canberra
93 km

Breadalbane

Goulburn

Marulan

Detailed road map
on pages 120-121

1424 ▲ **SYDNEY**
0 ▼

Liverpool

Mittagong ▲ 1316
▼ 108

To
Wollongong
84 km

Freeway
Main highway
Divided highway
Other highway
Town ○
Rest area Ⓡ
National route number 31
State route number 160
Distance between towns 23
Distance to   Adelaide ▲ 736
Sydney ▼ 688

Not drawn to scale

N

Perth-Darwin
via Brand, Northwest Coastal, Great Northern, Victoria & Stuart Highways ①

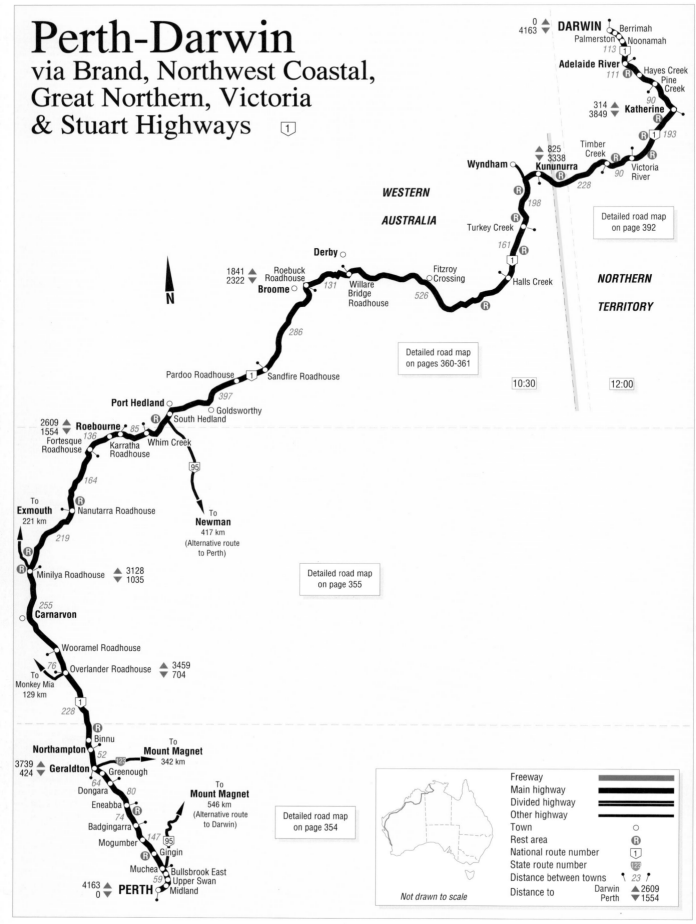

DARWIN
0 ▲ 4163

Berrimah
Palmerston
Noonamah
113

Adelaide River
111

Hayes Creek
Pine Creek
90

314
3849
Katherine
193

825 ▲
3338 ▼

Timber Creek

Victoria River
90

Wyndham
Kununurra
228

198

Turkey Creek
161

WESTERN
AUSTRALIA

Detailed road map
on page 392

NORTHERN
TERRITORY

Halls Creek
526

Derby
Roebuck Roadhouse
1841 ▲
2322 ▼
Broome
131
Willare Bridge Roadhouse

Fitzroy Crossing

Detailed road map
on pages 360-361

10:30   12:00

286

Pardoo Roadhouse   Sandfire Roadhouse
397

Port Hedland
Goldsworthy
South Hedland

2609 ▲
1554 ▼
Roebourne
85
136
Karratha
Whim Creek
Fortesque Roadhouse
Roadhouse
95

164

To Exmouth
221 km
Nanutarra Roadhouse

To Newman
417 km
(Alternative route to Perth)

219

Detailed road map
on page 355

3128 ▲
1035 ▼
Minilya Roadhouse

255

Carnarvon

Wooramel Roadhouse

To Monkey Mia
129 km
76
Overlander Roadhouse
3459 ▲
704 ▼

228
①

Binnu
To Mount Magnet
342 km

Northampton
52
123
3739 ▲
424 ▼
Geraldton
Greenough
64

Dongara
80

Eneabba
74

Badgingarra
Mogumber
147
95
Gingin

To Mount Magnet
546 km
(Alternative route to Darwin)

Detailed road map
on page 354

Muchea   Bullsbrook East
59   Upper Swan
4163 ▲
0 ▼
PERTH   Midland

Freeway
Main highway
Divided highway
Other highway
Town ○
Rest area ®
National route number ①
State route number 123
Distance between towns ▸ 23 ◂
Distance to   Darwin ▲2609
Perth ▼1554

Not drawn to scale

Brisbane-Darwin
via Warrego, Landsborough, Barkly & Stuart Highways ⑮ �54 �71 �66 ①

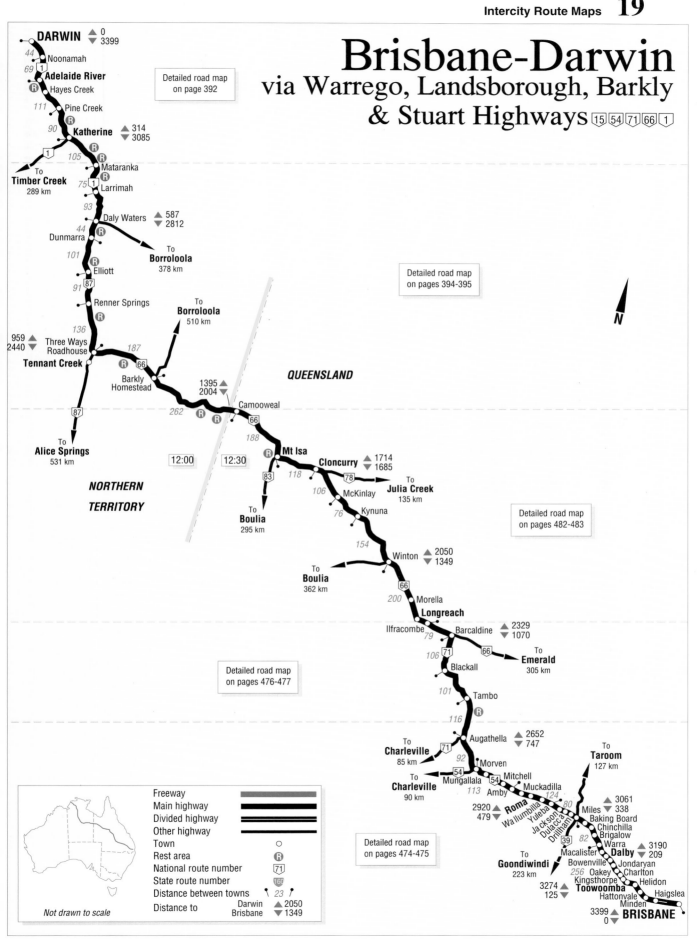

DARWIN ▲ 0 ▼ 3399

44 Noonamah
69 Adelaide River
Ⓡ Hayes Creek
111 Pine Creek
90 Ⓡ Katherine ▲ 314 ▼ 3085
Ⓡ *105* Ⓡ Mataranka
To Timber Creek 289 km
75 Larrimah
93 Daly Waters ▲ 587 ▼ 2812
44 Ⓡ Dunmarra
To Borroloola 378 km
101 Ⓡ Elliott ⑧7
91 Renner Springs Ⓡ
To Borroloola 510 km
136 Three Ways Roadhouse
959 ▲ 2440 ▼
Tennant Creek *187*
Ⓡ �66 Barkly Homestead
262 Ⓡ Ⓡ 1395 ▲ 2004 ▼
⑧7 Camooweal
To Alice Springs 531 km
188 �66
Ⓡ Mt Isa Cloncurry ▲ 1714 ▼ 1685
⑧3 *118* ㊁8 To Julia Creek 135 km
To Boulia 295 km
106 McKinlay
76 Kynuna
154
Winton ▲ 2050 ▼ 1349
To Boulia 362 km
�66 *200* Morella
Longreach
Ilfracombe *79* Barcaldine ▲ 2329 ▼ 1070
106 �71 �66 To Emerald 305 km
Blackall
101 Tambo Ⓡ
116
To Charleville 85 km �71 Augathella ▲ 2652 ▼ 747
92 Morven To Taroom 127 km
㊄4 Mitchell
To Charleville 90 km ㊄4 Muckadilla
Mungallala *113* Amby *124*
Roma *80*
2920 ▲ 479 ▼ Wallumbilla Yuleba Miles ▲ 3061 ▼ 338
Jackson Baking Board
Dulacca Chinchilla
Drillham Brigalow
39 Warra ▲ 3190 ▼ 209
Macalister *82* Dalby
To Goondiwindi 223 km Bowenville Jondaryan
256 Oakey Charlton
Kingsthorpe Helidon
3274 ▲ 125 ▼ Toowoomba Hattonvale
3399 ▲ 0 ▼ Minden Haigslea
BRISBANE

QUEENSLAND
12:00 12:30
NORTHERN TERRITORY

Detailed road map on page 392
Detailed road map on pages 394-395
Detailed road map on pages 482-483
Detailed road map on pages 476-477
Detailed road map on pages 474-475

N

Legend:
Freeway
Main highway
Divided highway
Other highway
Town ○
Rest area Ⓡ
National route number �71
State route number ㊉0
Distance between towns *23*
Distance to Darwin ▲ 2050 Brisbane ▼ 1349
Not drawn to scale

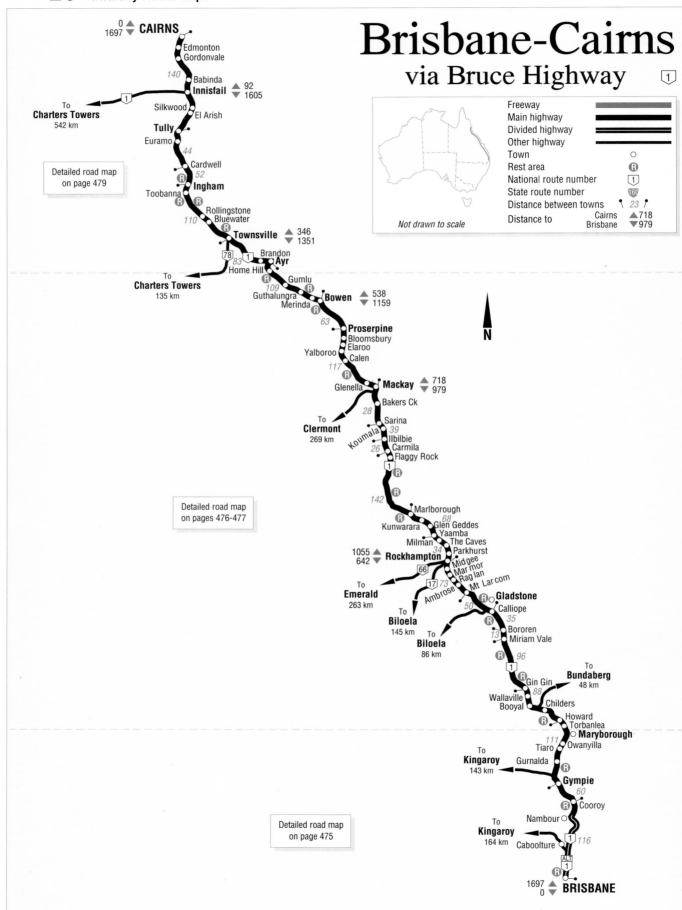

Brisbane-Cairns
via Bruce Highway [1]

CAIRNS
0
1697

Edmonton
Gordonvale

140

Babinda
Silkwood
Innisfail ▲ 92 ▼ 1605

To
Charters Towers
542 km

El Arish

Tully
Euramo *44*

Cardwell
52
Ingham

Toobanna

Rollingstone
Bluewater
110

Townsville ▲ 346 ▼ 1351

Brandon
[78] *83* [1]
Ayr
Home Hill

To
Charters Towers
135 km

109 Gumlu
Guthalungra
Merinda
Bowen ▲ 538 ▼ 1159

63

Proserpine
Bloomsbury
Elaroo
Yalboroo Calen
117

Glenella
Mackay ▲ 718 ▼ 979

Bakers Ck
28

To
Clermont
269 km

Sarina
Koumala *39*
Ilbilbie
26 Carmila
Flaggy Rock
[1]

142

Marlborough
68
Kunwarara
Glen Geddes
Yaamba
Milman The Caves
34 Parkhurst
Rockhampton 1055 ▲ 642 ▼
Midgee
Mar mor
Rag lan
[66]
[17] *73* Mt Lar com
Ambrose

To
Emerald
263 km

Gladstone ℝ ○
Calliope
50 *35*
To Bororen
Biloela Miriam Vale
145 km *13*

To
Biloela
86 km

96
To
[1] **Bundaberg**
Gin Gin 48 km
Wallaville *88*
Booyal Childers
Howard
Torbanlea
111 **Maryborough**
Tiaro Owanyilla

To
Kingaroy
143 km
Gurnalda
ℝ
Gympie
60

To ℝ Cooroy
Kingaroy Nambour ○
164 km [1] *116*
Caboolture
[ALT 1]

1697 ▲ **BRISBANE**
0 ▼

Detailed road map on page 479

Detailed road map on pages 476-477

Detailed road map on page 475

N

Freeway	
Main highway	
Divided highway	
Other highway	
Town	○
Rest area	ℝ
National route number	[1]
State route number	[160]
Distance between towns	*23*
Distance to	Cairns ▲718
	Brisbane ▼979

Not drawn to scale

Have A Good Trip

Checking the Car

All the care that you devote to your own comfort can be for nothing if you do not make sure that the car checks out too.

For a one-, two- or three-day tour, you could simply fuel up, check the tyre pressures, clean all the windows and head off, and if you maintain your vehicle at all times in reasonable condition—as indeed you should—probably little further preparation is required. However, a vacation of a week or more, or any time long-distance driving is involved, will require more thorough preparation. If you intend travelling through remote areas, for example, you first should check that your vehicle is able to handle off-road conditions. The service department of your State motoring organisations (**see:** Motoring Organisations) will give advice and carry out a preliminary inspection of your vehicle.

Regardless of the length of your tour, you should check the wheelbrace, jack and under-vehicle jacking points, in case you have to change a tyre.

Unless you are able to undertake the necessary servicing of your vehicle yourself, this preparation should be left in the hands of your mechanic. You will be particularly concerned to avoid breakdowns and to confirm the reliability of safety-related items; therefore your instructions will include a check of the fuel supply, electrics, brakes, tyres and certain ancillary equipment, as follows.

- **Fuel supply** Check fuel pump for flow. Check carburettor for wear and potential blockages *or* check condition of electronic or mechanical fuel injection. When the tank is almost empty, remove the drain plug and drain the tank, to check that the remaining fuel is perfectly clean. Check fuel-supply lines for cracks and poor connections, and make sure no fuel line is exposed to damage by rocks or low-clearance projections.
- **Electrics** Check battery output and condition (including terminals), alternator/generator output and condition, spark plugs, condenser, coil, distributor and all terminals and cables. If the vehicle is fitted with electronic ignition, it should be checked in the prescribed manner.
  Check all lights, not just to see that they work, but to make sure that they are aligned correctly and are likely to continue to work. It is very, very dark at night in outback Australia.
- **Brakes** Check wear of pads and/or linings and check discs for runout and drums for scoring. Brake dust should be cleaned off. Check brake lines and hoses for cracks and wear. Make sure brake lines are not liable to be damaged by rocks or low projections. Check parking brake for adjustment and cable stretch.
- **Tyres** Check for uneven or excessive wear. Check walls for cracks and stone or kerb fractures. Check pressures. Include spare (or spares) in all checks. Make sure that the spare wheel matches those on the car, and uses the same kind of wheel nuts.
- **Other items** Check windscreen-wiper blades for wear and proper contact and washers for direction and effectiveness. Include rear wiper and washer, where fitted.
- Check **windscreen glass** for cracks and replace if necessary.
- Check **seat mountings and adjustments.**
- Check **levels** of all **lubricants** (including brake and clutch fluid) and either top up or drain and refill.
- Check **wheel bearings** for play and adjust or replace.
- Check **universal and constant velocity joints,** where appropriate, and replace if necessary.
- Check **dust and water sealing.** (A pre-run test in appropriate conditions will reveal any problems. What you do not need is dust, exhaust fumes or water inside the vehicle.)
- If you carry a **roof rack**, check mounts and welds for weaknesses and cracks.
- Check all **seat belts** for tears or sun-hardening. Replace if necessary. Also check inertia reels.
- Check **radiator water level and condition**. Drain and flush, if necessary. Check radiator for leaks and radiator pressure cap for pressure release accuracy. Check water-pump operation. Check radiator and heater hoses for cracks and general condition, and replace if necessary. Check hose clamps.
- Check **fan belt** for tension and fraying.
- Check anything else you might think is worthwhile.
- This should be done as near as practicable to your departure date. Allow time for unexpected work or part replacement, and for a return to the garage if a particular problem persists. *Nothing should be overlooked*—lives may be at stake.

Packing the Car

First and most important, you should carry only those items that are absolutely necessary with you in the passenger compartment. In a sedan, this is not difficult. You have a boot, and that is where most items should be carried; but in a station sedan or wagon, it is much more difficult to isolate everything. This is important, because loose items in the passenger compartment get under your feet (fatal

Hazards

Flood

In some remote areas, floods can occur without warning. Do not camp in dry river beds or close to the edges of creeks or streams. Always exercise extreme caution when approaching flooded roads or bridges. Floodwaters are deceptive; always check the depth before attempting to cross. If you do find yourself stranded in deep water:

- Do not panic.
- Wind up all the windows, to slow down or prevent water entering. (You should have closed all the windows before you tried to cross.)
- When the car has stabilised, undo the seatbelts.
- Turn the headlights on to help rescuers locate the car.
- If the car does not sink, but drifts (which is often the case with a well-sealed car), wait until it reaches shallow water or is close to the bank, then open the door or windows and climb out.
- Form a human chain and help children to keep their heads above water.
- If the car is sinking, it will be necessary to wait for the water pressure to equalise before you can open the doors or windows. As a last resort, kick out the windscreen or rear window.

Bushfire

If you have to travel on days of critical fire danger (i.e. total fire ban days), make sure you carry some woollen blankets and a filled water container. If you are trapped as a bushfire approaches:

- Do not panic.

- Stop the car in the nearest cleared area.
- Wind up all the windows.
- Turn on the hazard lights to warn any other traffic.
- DO NOT GET OUT OF YOUR CAR. The temperature may become unbearably hot, but it is still safer to stay in the car.
- Lie on the car floor, below window level, to avoid radiant heat.
- Cover yourself and your passengers with blankets.
- The car will not explode, or catch on fire, and a fast-moving wildfire will pass quickly overhead.

Animals

Although some species of Australia's unique wildlife are immensely appealing, some species are extremely dangerous.

Marine life

Box jellyfish (or sea wasps) are found in the coastal waters of Queensland and northern Australia in the summer months (end November–end April). A sting from their many long tentacles can be lethal, and for that reason swimming on coastal beaches north of Rockhampton is prohibited at this time. Also, walking barefoot at the water's edge in this region in summer is not advisable.

Among Australia's several species of poisonous stinging fish, the **stonefish**, found all around the northern coastline, is best avoided.

The small **blue-ringed octopus** is common in Australian coastal waters. Its bite can paralyse in 15 minutes. Do not handle in any circumstances.

Sharks are common in Australian waters. Avoid swimming in deep water and do not swim where sharks have been seen.

Freshwater and saltwater crocodiles are found in north and northwestern Australia. The saltwater crocodile is particularly dangerous and may be found in both salt water and fresh water. The freshwater crocodile will bite if disturbed. Neither species is easy to see in the water. Heed local warning signs and do not swim or paddle in natural waterways or allow children or animals near the water's edge.

Snakes

Snakes are timid and generally do not attack unless threatened. However, several species are highly venomous.

Spiders

The bite from both the funnel-web and red-back spider can be deadly. The funnel-web is found in and around Sydney. The red-back is widespread.

Insects

Wasps, bees, ticks, ants (particularly the bull-ant), scorpions and centipedes are found throughout Australia. Their sting or bite normally is not harmful, except to those people who are allergy-prone, but it may cause pain and discomfort. Ticks should be removed promptly.

Study Australia's wildlife and learn to identify dangerous species. Remember also that some plant species are poisonous. When visiting a new area, check with local authorities to ascertain which dangerous species, if any, are found there.

Check depth of floodwaters before crossing

for the driver), interfere with your comfort and will become potentially dangerous projectiles in the event of a collision. So for your station-wagon, buy or rig up a safety net, which can be fitted at the back of the rear seat to separate you from the objects that otherwise could harm you.

This rule applies also to food and drink. Empty bottles and cartons should be stowed out of the way in a small carry-bag for rubbish, until you are able to dispose of them.

And if you are short of space, cull some non-essential items.

In order to provide extra space, many drivers fix a **roof rack** to their vehicle. This is not recommended. Laden roof racks upset the balance of the vehicle by changing its centre of gravity, making it top-heavy. They disturb the air flow, which can destabilise the vehicle, and they certainly increase fuel consumption by interfering with the aerodynamics. In some circumstances, they can snag on overhanging limbs of trees.

If you must use a roof rack, carry as little on it as possible and keep the maximum loading height as low as you can. Protect the load by wrapping it in a tarpaulin or groundsheet and, if possible, create a sharp (aerofoil) leading edge on the load to improve air flow.

A better alternative to a roof rack is a small, strong, lightweight **trailer,** but

there are times when this will be a disadvantage also.

If you are towing a **caravan,** some items can be carried inside the van, on the floor, preferably strapped down (anything loose will be flung about) and located over the axle/s. In some States, caravans must be fitted with a fire extinguisher. (And remember, no people or animals are to be transported in a towed caravan.)

Once your vehicle is loaded, and preferably with the passengers aboard (yes, even as you leave home on day one), check the **tyre pressures**. The additional load will mean higher pressures are needed. The tyre placard or owner's handbook can be used as a guideline, but modern steel radials, fully laden, are best inflated to around 250 kilopascals (36 psi). This is not too high. For a country trip with a heavy load on a hot day 280 kPa (40 psi) is about right. Light vans and 4WD vehicles should have higher pressure: at least 315 kPa (45 psi) for the highway, and as high as 350 kPa (50 psi) for highway travel on a hot day with a heavy load. The tyre will bag if it is under-inflated and destabilise the car. It also will offer a baggy sidewall to rocks and stones, and encourage wall fractures and potential blowouts. Laden tyre pressure requirements vary with tyre size and design, but the pressure is important. If

you are in any doubt, contact the tyre manufacturer. (**See also:** Outback Motoring).

When to Set Off

There is evidence to suggest that people drive best during the hours in which they are accustomed to being awake, and probably at work. As drowsiness is deadly in drivers, this is worth noting. Leaving home, for example, at 1 a.m. might avoid the heat of the day and beat the traffic to a large extent, but somewhere between 3 and 5 a.m. you may find yourself wanting to doze off again.

Plan to share long-distance driving as much as possible and depart around or just before sunrise and stop no later than sun-down. Allow regular stops, not just to stretch your legs but to take nourishment as well. Food helps keep the energy levels up. You might care to leave later, if you are travelling east, to avoid the rising sun, and finish earlier if you are travelling west, for the converse reason.

Leaving Home

Everyone knows the feeling that usually comes when you are a good distance from home: did I lock all the windows, turn off the electricity at the meter...? Usually all is well, but it is reassuring to double-check everything before you leave (**see**: Before Departure).

An early start, Mt Rowland, Tas.

Better Driving

The two most important ingredients in skilful driving are **concentration** and **smoothness.**

To facilitate the first, get comfortable and stay comfortable. Discomfort destroys concentration. Lack of concentration is the biggest single cause of road accidents.

Wear the right clothes: loose-fitting, cool or warm as appropriate, but capable of being changed (not while you are driving!) as temperatures change. Lightweight shoes are better than boots. (There are such things as driving shoes, which are excellent.) Wear good quality antiglare sunglasses. Sit comfortably: neither too close to the steering wheel and cramped, nor too far back and stretching; and be sure you can reach the foot controls through the entire length of their movement. Drive with both hands all the time. No one can control a car properly with one hand. Driving gloves are recommended. Make all seat, belt and rear-view mirror adjustments before you drive off. (This is especially relevant if you share the driving with someone not your size.)

Concentration means *no distractions.* It is probably unrealistic to suggest that no conversation takes place while you are driving, but do not allow conversations to interfere with your concentration. Aim to keep the children quiet and amused (**see:** Child's Play)**. If an important issue needs to be resolved, first stop the car and then sort it out.**

Smoothness is vital for the vehicle's safe, effective operation, but unfortunately many people are not smooth drivers. A vehicle in motion is a tonne or so of iron, steel and plastic sitting atop a set of springs. It is inherently unstable and prone to influences such as pitch and roll. This is difficult enough to control in normal motion, but worse when the driver exaggerates these instabilities by stabbing at the brakes, jerking the steering wheel and crashing the gears. Two things derive from being a smooth driver: the first is passenger comfort. On a long trip, everyone will arrive much fresher and more relaxed if the driver has provided a smooth and therefore pleasant journey. The second is increased safety. The vehicle will react better to smooth, controlled input than it will to hamfisted driving. Smooth driving could bring even further benefits: less wear and tear and lower fuel consumption.

However, to define better driving as a combination of concentration and smoothness only would not be wholly accurate. There are other factors:

- **Know your vehicle.** Understand its breaking capacities, especially in emergencies—some cars move around a lot; or become directionally unstable under harsh braking. Be aware of its usable power and its limitations. And drive well within the cornering and road-holding limits of the vehicle's suspension and tyre combination.
- **Drive defensively.** Assume all other drivers are asleep, inattentive or devoid of skill. It is remarkable how such an attitude will increase driving awareness.
- **Do not be impatient.** Advance planning should have provided you with ample time for the day's journey.
- **Do not drive with an incapacitating illness or injury.** Something as simple as a bruised elbow might restrict rapid arm movement when you most need it.

Emergencies

Of course, the best way to handle emergencies is to avoid them. However, to suggest one problem or another will never occur is unrealistic. (A course in defensive driving is an advantage. **See:** Motoring Organisations.)

The possibility of **skidding** worries most drivers, as well it should. There are a number of causes of a skid, some of them composite. Essentially, skidding occurs when the tyres lose their grip on the road. The most common form is a front-wheel (or sometimes all-wheel) skid caused by over-braking. When the wheels stop rolling, the vehicle will no longer react to steering input. If you avoid jumping on the brake pedal, (i.e. drive smoothly), you will avoid this type of skid. However, if you do skid, quickly try to ease just sufficient pressure off the brake pedal to allow the wheels to roll again. The steering will come back, which at least will allow you to take avoiding action, as well as slow down. A rear-wheel skid also may occur as a result of harsh braking, usually while turning at the same time (e.g. corner entry speed too high, braking too harsh). In slippery conditions, the tail of the car also may fishtail because of excessive speed of entry into a corner or, in rear-wheel drive vehicles, because too much power has been applied too soon, causing the rear tyres to break traction. A rear-wheel skid of any kind requires some reverse steering, often only briefly. It is not enough to advise turning the steering in the direction of the skid: the question is, by how much? Turn the steering wheels to point them in the direction you wish to travel and, at the same time, try to recognise what you did to cause the skid in the first place. If it was because of excessive acceleration, back off a little and re-apply the accelerator more gently. If it was because of excessive speed of entry into the corner and/or braking at the same time, ease the brakes and let your corrective steering realign the car and then,

Safe Driving

Basic Traffic Laws

There are variations in road traffic laws from State to State throughout Australia. Some affect the traveller, some do not. Drivers are expected to know and observe those rules that apply to a vehicle's operation; however, specific State laws that affect the registration of vehicles, trailers or caravans, for example, are not enforced between States.

The city of Melbourne, which is the last stronghold of the tram, has its unique hook turn, where at some inner-city intersections a vehicle making a righthand turn must move to the far left of the intersection and wait until the traffic clears and the traffic lights change before completing the turn. Overtaking on the right of a tram is forbidden and no vehicle may pass a stationary tram at a recognised tram stop.

Drink driving laws are extremely strict in all States and drivers can be pulled up at random and be required to take a blood alcohol test.

Speed regulations vary in each state. In some States, the use of cameras to catch speeding drivers, both in the city and country, is widespread; as well, cameras are positioned at traffic lights on many intersections to record drivers who do not stop at the red light.

In most other respects, the road traffic laws are essentially the same from State to State. However, legislation is subject to change and the cautious driver will check first with the relevant State motoring organisation (**see**: Motoring Organisations) for answers to any questions raised on specific regulations.

Positioning

Positioning is vital on any road.
*   Try to stagger the position of your car in the line of traffic so that you can see well ahead.

Incorrect

Out of vision

Out of vision

Correct

*   When turning right on a two-lane highway, do not angle the car; keep it square to the other traffic so cars can pass on the left.

Incorrect

Correct

In Case of Accident

In all States of Australia, any accident in which someone is injured or killed *must* be reported to police at once, or within 24 hours. In Western Australia, any accident involving a car must be reported.

It is highly advisable to report to police any accident that involves substantial property damage. Police may or may not decide to attend the scene, but they at least will have your report on record, which may well be useful should there be legal proceedings or insurance claims.

When involved in an accident and if required by police, you *must* give your name and address and produce your driver's licence. If you do not have it with you, you may be liable for an on-the-spot fine. It is advisable to obtain the insurance details of the other parties involved.

All parties involved in the accident should exchange names and addresses and insurance details. **Do not volunteer any other information**. In particular, do not discuss the accident. Should court action result, you may find something said in the stress of the aftermath of the accident used against you. Above all, **do not admit you are at fault in any way**, even if you think you may be.

You are not obliged to make a statement to police. If you are disturbed and upset, wait until you can think clearly.

An accident that involves damage to persons or property should be reported to your insurance company as soon as possible.**See also:** Accident Action.

---

smoothly, increase the power again.

Skids can be complex and difficult to control. Over-correction is common, with the result that the vehicle swings into another skid in the opposite direction. Do not panic and be smooth in your reaction. Easy to say—not so easy to do.

Aquaplaning is a form of skidding where the tyres roll a layer of water up in front of the vehicle and then ride on to it, breaking contact with the adhesive road surface. What you sense is a sudden loss of driving 'feel'. Slow down, very smoothly, until the tyres come off the layer of water and then proceed more carefully. Watch out for deep puddles: they are the danger.

Driving in snow, ice and mud also produces adhesion problems. Once again, smooth, steady progress, while 'feeling' the vehicle and staying on top of its movements, is the only answer.

For a visit to the **snow,** your vehicle should be fitted with chains. If it is not and the car's back wheels begin to spin wildly on packed and rutted snow or ice:
*   Stop the car.
*   Look for and remove any obstructions under the car.
*   Pack loose gravel, sticks or vegetation under the driving wheels.
*   Remember that on a level surface, a gentle push sometimes will get the car going.

*   Because it cannot be seen, ice can be more dangerous than snow.
    When driving in **fog:**
*   Switch on dipped headlights, or foglights if your car is fitted with them.
*   Use front and back demisters.
*   If visibility is reduced to such an extent that driving becomes an ordeal, pull as far off the road as you can and wait until you feel able to continue.

The advice in this section applies equally to driving in the cities and in the outback. The techniques are the same; only the conditions vary. (**see**: Outback Motoring for more detail on bush driving.)

Towing

Towing your accommodation behind you will provide the advantage of low-budget touring and flexibility with stop-overs. It can be a disadvantage also, in that it may restrict access to some areas and locations. You can, however, use the caravan for most sections of your journey and park it somewhere while you go off and explore the more difficult tracks.

If you are new to towing, the first thing you must do is to get expert advice on your **towing hitch** (**see:** Motoring Organisations). It is very important that **the rig** (i.e. car and caravan, boat or trailer) is balanced and the weight over the tow ball is not excessive. An adjustable height hitch with spring bars is best.

Once you have decided on the hitch, and you have learned how to hook up and unhook, you must learn to **reverse** the rig. Find a wide open area, an empty car park for example, and practise. Get the feel of the rig and aim to be proficient before you depart.

On the road, remember to make allowances for the added overall length and give yourself extra space for turning and extra distance for overtaking. The added weight will obviously affect the towing vehicle's performance in acceleration and braking.

In most States there are **speed limits** on articulated vehicles and you should know what they are and abide by them (**see:** Basic Traffic Laws). High-speed towing of vans and trailers can cause major difficulties, magnifying driving problems substantially.

Cross-winds can be a problem when towing a caravan, the van's slab sides acting like sails. The combination of high speed and cross-winds can cause **'trailer sway'**, a dangerous characteristic that dramatically destabilises both towing vehicle and caravan. You probably will feel it happening before you see it, but checking in the rear-view mirrors will confirm it. Should the trailer begin to move about, ease back on your speed, braking if necessary, but very gently. Harsh or sudden braking will compound the problem. When the caravan stabilises, resume speed, perhaps very gradually if you are continuing in a cross-wind area.

Fit good-quality towing mirrors on your vehicle. It is very important that your rear view down both sides of the trailer or caravan is not obscured.

If, because of the relative slowness of your progress, you find a line of vehicles banking up behind you, be courteous and pull over when and where you can, to allow vehicles to overtake.

The carrying of goods and equipment in a caravan has been mentioned, but it is worth repeating that such items should be located as much as possible over and just to the front of the caravan axle/s; never behind, which will lift the front of the caravan and the tow ball.

Before setting off and every day of the trip, whatever the vehicle, always **check and double-check that the hitch is secure**, that the **safety chains are correctly fitted** and that the **electrical connections are working,** so that indicator lights function at the rear of the towed vehicle.

Finally, when towing, remember to allow extra time for each day's travel, and remain alert.

Checklist

When towing anything:
- Check the hitch for security. The law in most States demands that tow bars are fitted with safety chains.
- Check that the tail and stop lights, marker lights and signal lights are working.
- Remember to check the air in the caravan or trailer tyres.
- If towing a boat, check the lashings.
- Check that caravan doors, windows and roof vents are closed before departure.
- If the caravan or trailer is fitted with separate brakes, check these as soon as you start to move.

Towing your accommodation requires extra care

Outback Motoring

Australia's size and remoteness deter many people from exploring it. However, properly set up and equipped, and armed with common sense and a little background knowledge, every intending traveller can explore the country's huge open spaces.

If you intend travelling in the outback, planning ahead is vital for it is possible to travel in some sections of the Australian outback and not see another vehicle or person for several days. (The Canning Stock Route is a good example.)

It is possible to travel in some areas of the outback in a 2WD vehicle, but it is safer and much more practical to do so in a 4WD vehicle suited to off-road conditions (**see:** Checking the Car).

Remember that if you rent a vehicle, there may be restrictions on insurance if you drive on unclassified roads; seek advice before you make plans.

Your vehicle should be fitted with **air conditioning** to counteract high inland daytime temperatures and make it possible to drive with all the windows closed through dusty areas. You should be able to carry out **small running repairs** and must carry a workshop manual for the vehicle, tools and spare parts (**see:** Tools and Spare Parts).

Outback **driving conditions** vary greatly. The deserts are usually dry; conditions change after rain. Much of the tropics is accessible only in the 'dry' season, and even then there are streams to ford and, washaways to contend with.

Pre-reading **road conditions** is vital. Recognising that a patch of different colour may represent a change in surface is an example. Sand can give way to rock; rock may lead to mud; hard surfaces become bulldust with little warning.

Soft sand, bulldust and mud are best negotiated at the highest reasonable speed and in the highest possible gear *and* in 4WD. However, examine the road surface first. Do not enter deep mud or mud covered with water without first establishing the depth of either or both.

Deep **sand** requires low tyre pressures. Carry a tyre pressure gauge and drop pressures to about 10 psi. Reinflate once on gravel or bitumen roads again, because the soft tyres will perform very badly and may blow out as a result of stone fractures on hard surfaces.

When **crossing a creek or stream,** stop to check the track across for clear passage and water depth. If the water is deep but fordable, cover the front of the vehicle with a tarpaulin and remove the fan belt to stop water being sprayed over the engine electrics. Drive through in low range second gear or high range first gear, and clear the opposite embankment before stopping again. If it has rained, beware of flash flooding.

Dips are common on outback roads and can break suspension components if you enter too fast. To cross a dip, brake on entry to drop the vehicle's nose, and hold the brake on until just before the bottom of the depression. Then accelerate again to lift the nose and therefore the suspension, as you exit. This will prevent the springs from bottoming out and will give maximum clearance.

Cattle grids are also a potential hazard. They are often neglected, with broken approaches and exits. If a grid appears to be in disrepair, stop and check first, before attempting to cross.

Road trains operate in many parts of outback Australia. These long, multi-trailered trucks are difficult and often dangerous to overtake particularly on dusty roads. Wait for a chance to get the front of your vehicle out to a position where the road train driver can see you in the rear-view mirror, but even then do not try to overtake until he has signalled that he knows you are there. Sometimes it is prudent to stop and take a break, rather than try to overtake a road train. If you meet an oncoming road train, pull over and stop until it has passed.

Animals present hazards on outback roads. There are vast areas of unfenced property where stock roam free. A bullock or a large kangaroo can seriously damage your vehicle. Be especially wary around sunrise and sunset when animals are more active. A bull-bar or roo-bar gives limited protection at low speeds only, especially against larger animals.

Despite the loneliness of the outback, driver concentration should be at as high a level as in city peak hours.

Surviving in the Outback

You might be stranded in a remote area with a major mechanical breakdown or if your vehicle becomes bogged. Should either occur, you should be equipped to wait until found. Always carry a week's supply of spare water, minimum 20 litres per head. **Keep it for an emergency.**

Iron rations of dry biscuits and some canned food will keep hunger at bay, but body evaporation and thirst is the vital factor. Do not drink radiator coolant. Often it is not water but a chemical compound, and even if it is water, usually it has been treated with chemicals.

Do not try to walk out of a remote area. You are going to survive only if you wait by the car. Before entering a remote area, check with police or a local authority, and tell them where and when you are going, and when you expect to arrive. When you reach your destination, telephone and advise of your arrival.

If stranded, set up some type of shelter and, in the heat of the day, remain in its shade as motionless as possible. Movement accelerates fluid loss. (**See also:** How to Obtain Water.)

Outback Advice

Critical Rules for Outback Motoring

- Check intended routes carefully.
- Check the optimum time of year to travel.
- Check that your vehicle is suited to the conditions.
- Check your load; keep it to a minimum.
- Check ahead for local road conditions, weather forecasts and fuel availability.
- Check that you have advised someone of your route, destination and arrival time.
- Check that you have essential supplies: water, food, fuel, spare parts.
- Carry detailed maps.
- Carry one week's extra supply of food and water in case of emergency.
- **Always remain with your vehicle if it breaks down.**

Warning: When Driving on Desert Roads

Remember:

- There is no water, except after rains.
- Unmade roads can be extremely hazardous, especially when wet.
- Traffic is almost non-existent, except on main roads.

Outback Advice Service

The Royal Flying Doctor Service of Australia offers a service to tourists who plan to tour the outback. RFDS bases and Visitors Centres provide advice on outback touring and on proper emergency procedures. Bases at Broken Hill (NSW), Charleville (Qld) and Jandakot (WA) also hire out transceiver sets with a fixed emergency call button in case of accident or sickness, at a very reasonable cost. Those bases that do not hire out sets, can suggest local outlets for them.

New South Wales
*Broken Hill: Broken Hill Airport 2880; (080) 88 0777
South Australia
*Port Augusta: 4 Vincent St 5700; (086) 42 2044
Western Australia
Carnarvon: 29 Douglas St 6701; (099) 41 1758
*Derby: Clarendon St 6728; (091) 91 1211
*Jandakot: 3 Eagle Dr, Jandakot Airport 6164; (09) 332 7733
*Kalgoorlie: 46 Picadilly St 6430; (090) 21 2899
Meekatharra: Main St 6642; (099) 81 1107
Port Hedland: The Esplanade 6721; (091) 73 1386
Northern Territory
*Alice Springs: Stuart Tce 0870; (089) 52 1033
Queensland
*Cairns: 1 Junction St 4870; (070) 53 1952
*Charleville: Old Cunnamulla Rd 4470; (076) 54 1233
*Mount Isa: Barkly Highway 4825; (077) 43 2800
Tasmania
Launceston: 17 Adelaide St 7250; (003) 31 6039
*These bases have Visitors Centres; check opening times.

For general information relating to the services offered by the RFDS, contact: The Australian Council of the Royal Flying Doctor Service of Australia, Level 5, 15–17 Young St, Sydney 2000; (02) 241 2411, fax (02) 247 3351.

Sharing the Outback

As you travel through the outback, remember: You are sharing the land with its traditional Aboriginal owners, pastoralists, other tourists—and even nature itself. In order to protect and preserve the outback for future visitors:

- Respect Aboriginal sacred and cultural sites, and heritage buildings and pioneer relics.
- Protect native flora and fauna: take photographs not specimens.
- Follow restrictions on the use of firearms and shooting. These restrictions protect wildlife and stock.
- Carry your own fuel source (e.g. portable gas stove), to avoid lighting fires in fire-sensitive areas.
- When lighting a campfire (if you must), keep it small and use any fallen wood sparingly. Never leave a fire unattended and extinguish completely, covering the remains.
- Do not drive off-road.
- Do not camp immediately adjacent to water sources (e.g. on riverbanks or by dams). Allow access for stock and native animals.
- Do not bury your rubbish: carry out everything you take in.
- Dispose of faecal waste by burial.
- Leave gates as you find them: open or shut.
- Do not ignore signs warning of dangers or entry restrictions. These have been erected for your protection.

Road sign beside Eyre Highway, SA

Direction Finding

Clever electronic hand-held navigation devices, using the Global Positioning System (GPS), are now available from walking shops and outdoor centres. These can be used with or without a map and are much more sophisticated and accurate than a magnetic compass.

If you cannot read a map or use a compass—or if you do not have any navigational device with you—it is vital to have some means of orientating yourself if you are lost.

A simple method of finding north is to use a conventional wristwatch.

Place the 12 on the watch in line with the sun and bisect the angle between it and the hour hand. This will give a fairly accurate indication of north.

At night, the Southern Cross can be used to determine south.

When exploring a side track off the main road, make a rough sketch of the route you are following, noting all turn-offs, and distances between them, using the speedometer, together with any prominent landmarks. When you return reconcile your return route with the sketch, point by point.

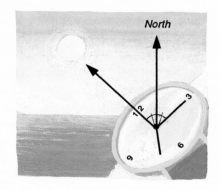

How to Obtain Water

Less than 24 hours without water can be fatal in outback heat.

It is essential to conserve body moisture. Take advantage of any shade that can be found.

Do not leave your vehicle. It may be the only effective shade available.

Ration your drinking water. **Do not drink radiator coolant**.

Although a river or creek bed may be dry, there is often an underground source of water. A hole dug about a metre deep may produce a useful soak.

Where there is vegetation, it is possible to extract water from it using an '**Arizona still**'.

- Dig a hole about one metre across and a little more than half as deep. Put a vessel of some kind in the hole's centre to collect the water.
- Surround the vessel with cut vegetation. (Fleshy plants, such as succulents, will hold more moisture than drier saltbush.)
- Cover the hole with a plastic sheet held down by closely packed rocks, so that the hole is sealed off. Put a small stone in the centre of the sheet, directly above the collection vessel.

The sun's heat will evaporate moisture from the plants. This moisture will condense on the inside of the plastic, run down the cone formed by the weight of the stone and drip off into the vessel.

In uninterrupted sunlight, with suitable plants, about one litre of water should be collected about every six hours.

The still takes about three hours to start producing and it will become less efficient as the ground moisture dries out. A new hole will need to be dug at intervals.

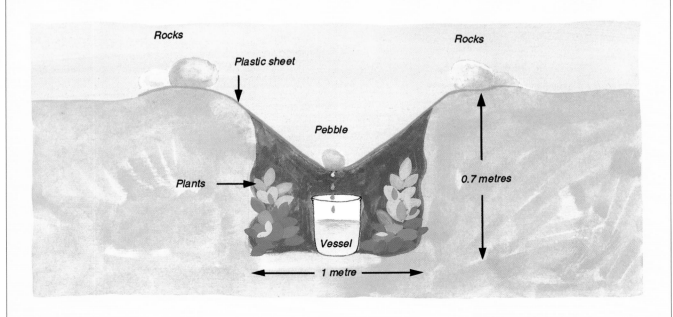

30

Breakdowns

There are many causes of motor vehicle breakdown, but fortunately modern vehicle technology has vastly reduced the possibility of being stuck by the roadside. Breakdowns that do occur can sometimes be cured with a roadside 'fix'; but this is less often possible with today's computer-driven vehicles. Inexpert or makeshift repairs may lead to further complications and a bigger repair bill.

Proper **vehicle preparation and maintenance** should reduce the possibility of roadside breakdowns and, on long journeys, the regular vehicle service schedule should be maintained.

In areas where you have access to service through a motoring organisation, it is better to leave even slightly complicated repairs to the specialist. (Remember to carry your membership card, which entitles you to assistance in other States. **See:** Motoring Organisations.)

If you are driving a **rental car**, most rental companies list their recognised repair organisations in the manual supplied. (Before you drive the car you should check that these details are provided.) If your rental vehicle cannot be repaired immediately, you should request an exchange vehicle.

If you plan to journey into remote areas, it is a good idea to first take a basic course in vehicle maintenance (**see:** Car Maintenance Courses). As well, you should carry a range of tools and spare parts (**see:** Tools and Spare Parts).

Most **modern vehicles** are fitted with electronic engine management systems, or with electronic ignition and fuel injection. Generally, these are more reliable than older systems and usually, in case of partial failure of the system, they have a 'limp home' mode, which enables travelling a limited distance at limited speed. However, total failure of such a system is difficult or impossible to remedy at the roadside without expert knowledge and equipment. This means that travel into remote areas is rendered much safer by travelling with at least one other vehicle, and by installing or hiring an appropriate long-range radio

transmitter, receiver and aerial. (**See:** Outback Advice Service.)

For those who drive **earlier-model vehicles** with less complex electrics and fuel systems, the trouble-shooting flow-charts are designed to be of assistance. But first, always remember to:

- **Watch warning gauges:** These have been installed to warn that things *may* be going wrong. A flickering battery warning light will suggest all is not well with the generator/alternator charge rate and should be attended to. A fluctuating temperature gauge *may* suggest the onset of a problem with the cooling system. Act on the warning at the earliest opportunity.
- **Make a daily check** of levels of fuel, water and oil (including spare supplies). Also check tyre pressures and fan belt tension and condition.
- **Make a regular check** of brake-fluid and battery-acid levels, and pressure of spare tyre.
- **Strange sounds:** If the vehicle develops an unexplained sound, move to the side of the road as soon as possible. Park on flat ground, if you can; you may have to spend some time under the bonnet, so look for shade or shelter. A loud, 'serious' sound usually indicates a major problem. Try to locate the source of the sound. If it is coming from the engine, do nothing and seek help.

When the Engine Stops

When the engine either splutters to a stop, constantly misfires or stops suddenly but was otherwise running smoothly, the problem is probably in one of two areas: fuel supply or electrics. Use the flow-charts to establish where the problem lies. If the problem is within the drive-train—gearbox, drive-shaft or differential—once again, seek help.

Roadside repairs, north Qld

Tools and Spare Parts

Remote-area travelling requires that someone in the vehicle knows, at least, the basics of breakdown repairs (**see**: Breakdowns). This means carrying emergency tools, spare parts and spare fuel. The following is a guide to what may be appropriate to your vehicle:

Tools

- Set of screwdrivers
- Small set of socket spanners
- Set of open-end/ring combination spanners
- Small ball pein (engineer's) hammer
- Pliers and wire-cutters
- Small and medium adjustable wrenches
- Hand drill and bits
- Workshop scissors
- Tyre-pressure gauge
- Wheel brace

- Jack with supplementary wide base for sand or mud (block of wood, slightly bigger than a brick but not as thick)
- Battery-operated soldering-iron
- Jumper leads
- Hydrometer
- Small backpackers shovel
- Pair of vice grips
- Small bolt-cutters
- Good quality tow-rope
- Heavy duty torch, spare batteries

Spare Parts

- Epoxy resin bonding 'goo'
- Plastic insulating tape
- Roll of cloth adhesive tape
- 1 metre fuel line (reinforced plastic)
- Spare electrical connections (range)
- Spare hose-clips (range)
- Distributor cap
- Set of high tension leads

- Condenser (where appropriate)
- Rotor
- Set of spark plugs
- Set of points
- Coil
- Spare fuel filters (replace daily in areas of constant dust)
- Fuel pump kit, water pump kit
- Small-diameter plastic tubing
- Nuts, bolts, washers, split pins
- At least one spare tyre, mounted, in good condition and over-inflated (to allow for some air loss)
- Tube of hand cleaner, clean rags

Fuel

- Spare fuel (40 litres minimum) in steel jerry cans. (Do *not* use plastic containers; some plastics react with fuel.) Check fuel range and distance between refuelling points.

Be prepared when travelling in remote areas

Trouble Shooting (for earlier-model vehicles)

Engine will not turn over

Check battery for charge.

If flat...
recharge or replace, or tow-start (if manual transmission vehicle) until next service opportunity. (If automatic, check handbook. Most autos cannot be tow- or clutch-started.)

If battery OK...
check if battery terminals and straps are loose, broken or dirty. If so, clean, repair or replace.

If terminals OK...
check for jammed starter motor. For manual vehicle, put in top gear and rock back and forth to try to free pinion. An indication that starter may be jammed is an audible click when you try to start the engine and it will not turn over. With an automatic vehicle, try to turn engine back and forth with a spanner on crankshaft pulley to free pinion. Put gearbox into 'N' first.

If the starter motor is free...
it is possible a solenoid has failed. Unless you are an auto electrician and carry a spare, seek help.

Starter motor whirrs but will not turn engine

Very likely, you have stripped a starter ring-gear, which means major repair work. But check to see that the starter motor is fully bolted to its mounting bracket, and tighten if not.

Engine turns over but will not fire, or fires but will not run cleanly, or misfires regularly, or runs and stops

Problem may be electrics or fuel supply. If unsure, begin with electrics.

Electrics

1 Check that spark is getting to spark plugs. Remove high tension (HT) lead from No. 1 plug and remove No. 1 plug. Reattach HT lead to plug and hold plug body with pliers 1 mm from cylinder-head bolt or similar and turn engine over. Plug should produce strong blue spark at regular intervals.

2 If not...
the simplest and fastest way to deal with an electrical problem is to replace parts, either at once or progressively, with spares (see: Tools and Spare Parts). Replace coil and all HT leads and try engine. If problem persists, remove distributor cap and replace condenser and points. Re-set points and fit new rotor and distributor cap. Engine should start and run cleanly.

3 If you carry no spare parts, you can still confirm electrics as the problem by a process of elimination. If there is no spark at the spark plugs, the problem has to be between battery and plug. Check that low tension lead at side of distributor is connected properly and tightly mounted. If so, remove distributor cap and check for cracks. If there is a crack, repair with an epoxy glue/filler until it can be replaced. Check that condenser is tightly mounted and its LT wire is connected. Check that points open and close properly by turning engine over by hand slowly and watching for a spark between points. Points may be burned or deeply pitted. If so, remove points and use nail-file to clean up faces, then replace and re-set. If, however, you have established an electrical problem and you have no spares, seek assistance.

4 If you have a spark at the plugs, most likely you have a fuel-supply problem.

Fuel supply

Check fuel tank for fuel, despite gauge reading. (It may be faulty.)

1 If fuel OK...
Check accelerator cable connection and for free operation and check choke cable and operation. For vehicle with automatic choke, remove air-cleaner carrier and element and look down choke tube. If choke butterfly is not fully open, open it and check to see if it stays open. If it closes again, engine is flooding, and may not run for that reason. A faulty auto choke cannot be repaired at the roadside.

2 If accelerator and choke cables are operating correctly...
do not replace air cleaner; remove fuel line to carburettor and turn engine over. Fuel should flow freely. If so, check it is not contaminated by pumping small amount into clear glass or plastic container and examine for water and/or dirt.

3 If water or dirt are apparent...
check and replace fuel filter and remove and check fuel pump. Examine glass for contamination. If none or very little, replace fuel line to carburettor and try engine again.

4 If there is substantial contamination...
it may be coming from fuel tank. Tank will need to be drained and perhaps flushed. Drained fuel should be saved and strained back. If you are travelling a long way before next fuel stop, be careful not to waste fuel.

5 If no fuel at fuel line and no apparent blockage...
fuel pump has failed for some reason. If you are carrying a spare, replace pump. If not, seek assistance.

6 If fuel is clean and running freely...
blockage may be inside carburettor. Carefully remove top and then main jet and float. Clear main jet and clean out float bowl. Be careful not to interfere with float level. Replace parts and try engine again.

Overheating in a water-cooled engine

(Occurs when coolant level falls or circulation is interrupted. Dash gauge gives warning, but vehicle also will lose power.)

1 Stop vehicle. Do not remove radiator cap. Check hoses and hose connections for signs of leakage—steam if system is boiling. Any identified leak can be cured temporarily with spare hoses or binding with cloth tape.

2 If no sign of leakage...
After about 10 minutes and holding radiator cap with a thick cloth, slowly remove cap, letting out steam under pressure at same time. Top up radiator and fill with engine running and car's heater on hot setting. Do not add cold water until engine is running and then mix cold with hot water.

3 Check again for leaks.

4 If there is a slow drip from radiator core itself...
fix with an internal chemical sealant or externally with an epoxy filler or adhesive.

5 If no leak is apparent...
check fanbelt for tension. It may be slipping and not driving water pump. If so, tighten by releasing bolts on generator/alternator and increasing tension and re-tightening.

6 If you cannot account for overheating by any of the preceding, you may have a failed water-pump, a blocked system, a failed pressure cap or a combination of all three. Seek help as soon as possible, but you may drive on if you can continue topping up.

top: Great Ocean Road, Vic.
bottom: Touring near the Hamersley Range, WA

Child's Play

Everyone in the family looks forward to a holiday, but most parents dread a long car trip, when children travelling in the back seat can become bored and irritable passengers.

Most children are good travellers, but there are some car journeys that are inappropriate for small children (say, under the age of 10). Usually, however, children will consider every trip an adventure, looking forward to it for weeks ahead. A little thought and planning by parents will avoid the boredom of a long drive and ease the strain on all concerned, and particularly the driver, who needs to be able to apply total concentration.

Dos and Donts

Several days before setting out, make a list of 'dos' and 'donts' for the children and explain, seriously, why their cooperation is necessary. Make it quite clear that you expect them to observe the rules because they are safety measures, and reinforce this message at the time of departure. For example:

- DO NOT fight or yell while the car is in motion. This distracts the driver and can cause a collision or a serious mishap, which might bring the holiday to an abrupt end.
- DO NOT play with door handles or locks. (Set the child-proof locks on rear doors before departure.)
- DO keep head, arms and hands inside the car. DO NOT lean out of the windows, ever.
- DO NOT unbuckle seat belts or restraints while the car is in motion.

Handy Hints

- Any long car trip, even with frequent stops, can be tiring. Make sure the children are as cool and comfortable as possible. Curtains (or substitutes, e.g. a towel) or sun screens on rear windows are advisable. Babies and pre-school children may need their security blankets or favourite soft toy. These items can save the day if the children are upset or sleepy.
- Pack a small bag—a cosmetic bag is ideal—with packets of moist towelettes or a damp face cloth.
- Make sure your first-aid kit contains some junior aspirin and supplies of any other medication taken by the children. It is important to carry some insect repellent and sunblock, since children tend to get bitten easily, and their skin must be protected from the sun. Also bring a mosquito net to cover your baby's bassinette when you are outdoors.
- Make up a 'busy box' for the children to take on the trip. Use a small box—a shoe box is best—and keep it on the back seat where the children can reach it easily. Fill the box with small note-pads, crayons or felt-tipped pens (pencils break and need to be sharpened) and activity books. Choose activity books for each child's age group. Do not forget to include your children's favourite storybooks.
- If your car has a radio and cassette player, include some tapes of stories and children's songs for 'quiet times'. Music soothes and lulls children to sleep.
- Although your main concern will be to keep the children happy and occupied during the car trip, it is also important to take along some games, such as snakes and ladders or Monopoly, or a pack of cards, to keep them amused in the evenings and on rainy days. Encourage older children to keep a diary. A rubber ball and skipping rope will be welcomed by young children who like to play outdoors.
- If you have room, breakfast trays can be used as book supports for colouring-in or drawing. If not, a clipboard will serve as well.
- When travelling with young children, make sure that you stop the car every hour or so, so that they can stretch their legs and let off steam. Try to stop at a park or an area with some play equipment. If it is raining, stop at a newsagent or bookshop where the children can browse and perhaps buy something to read.
- If children complain of feeling sick, stop the car as soon as possible and let them out for some fresh air. Sit with them for a while and persuade them to take a sip of water before continuing the trip.
- When approaching a rest area or a small town, offer the children a toilet stop. Do not delay until they get desperate and cannot wait.
- Even though you plan to stop for meals and snacks on your journey, you should still pack some food and drink. Children become very hungry and thirsty when travelling and it is important that they eat little but often. Pack small snacks in their own lunch boxes. Avoid chocolate, which is messy and can make children feel sick, and potato chips which are almost as messy and encourage thirst. Avoid greasy foods. Good for snacks are sultanas, nuts (for older children only), bananas, grapes, cheese cubes, celery and carrot sticks, boiled sweets. For lunches, pack easy-to-eat meals like chicken drumsticks or bite-size rolled-up pieces of cold meat with ready-spread bread on the side. Children can find large sandwiches difficult to handle, so remember to cut their sandwiches small. Sandwich fillings require some thought: avoid anything moist or runny.

Safety

Note the following safety hints:

Safe Swimming & Surfing

- Swim or surf only at those beaches patrolled by lifesavers.
- Swim or surf within the safe swimming area indicated by the red and yellow flags.
- An amber flag indicates the surf is dangerous.
- A red flag and sign 'Danger—closed to bathing' indicates the beach is unsafe. Do not swim or surf in this area.
- Do not enter the water directly after a meal or under the influence of alcohol.
- If you are caught in a rip or strong current, swim diagonally across it. If you tire or cannot avoid the current, do not panic. Straighten and raise one arm as a distress signal and float until help arrives.
- If seized with a cramp, keep the affected part perfectly still, raise one arm as before and float until help arrives.

Safe Skiing

Skiing is fun, but like any other sport, there is the risk of injury. It is also a strenuous sport. Avoid overdoing it when you go on the slopes. All ski resorts have instructors if you need to take lessons. Choose slopes that suit your ability. Wear clothing suited to the conditions. Check equipment before setting out. Avoid skiing alone. If you must, then tell someone where you are going. If lost, stay where you are, or retrace your tracks if they are very clear. **Cross-country skiing** requires careful planning. Tell someone in authority of your intended route; travel in a group; take plenty of food and adequate equipment for your survival; protect yourself against sunburn; and watch the weather. Be alert for signs of exposure (hypothermia)—tiredness, reluctance to carry on, clumsiness, loss of judgement, collapse.

Safe Boating

- Tell someone where you are going.
- Carry adequate equipment.
- Carry effective life jackets.
- Carry enough fuel and water.
- Ensure engine reliability.
- Guard against fire.
- Do not overload the craft.
- Know the boating rules and local regulations; also distress signals.
- Watch the weather.

- Avoid spills and breakages by buying milk or fruit juice in small cartons and making sure you have a good supply of drinking straws. If you carry drinks in a flask, take training cups for younger children. For older children use paper or styrofoam cups with tight-fitting lids and straws, and recycle as much as possible.
- Have plastic bags for waste paper and empty drink cartons in the cars.
- When eating out, choose places that have fast service—or have meals sent to your room.

Games

To while away the long hours you will spend in the car with your children, here are some games for them to play.

For younger children

Colour contest: Each child selects one colour, then tries to spot cars of that colour. The first with ten cars wins.

Spot the mistake in the story: Either you or an older child tells a story with obvious mistakes. For example, 'Once upon a time, there was a boy called Goldilocks, and he visited the house of the seven dwarfs.'

Scavenger: Make a list of 10 things you are likely to come across during your trip, e.g. farmhouse, bus stop, cow, lamb, chemist shop, woman with a hat. Ask the children to spot them, one at a time. Older children cross the objects off the list as they are seen.

Alphabet game: Select a letter and ask the children to spot as many things as possible beginning with that particular initial.

For older children

Rhyme stories: One child starts a story, and the next has to take up the story with a line that rhymes. The second child also continues the story with a line of new rhyme. For example:
1st child: 'I know a man called Sam.'
2nd child: 'He loves to eat ham.
   The more he eats the more he wants.'
Cliff-hangers: One child begins a story and stops at the most exciting part, leaving the next child to continue.
I packed my bag . . .(a good memory game): Each player has to name one object she or he puts into a bag. As each child takes a turn, she or he lists all the objects in order and adds a new item to the list. For example:
1st child: 'I packed my bag and put an apple in it.'
2nd child: 'I packed my bag and put an apple and a comb in it.'
3rd child: 'I packed my bag and put an apple, a comb and a key in it.'
4th child: 'I packed my bag and put an apple, a comb, a key and a ball in it.'
What am I? This is an old favourite. One player thinks of an object or an animal and keeps it secret. The others take turns to ask questions, which must be answered only by 'Yes' or 'No', for clues to the player's identity.
Number-plate messages: Take the letters of a number plate on a nearby car and ask the children to make up a message or conversation from them. For example:
WFL: 'What's for lunch?'
EYH: 'Eat your hat.'
Navigation: Older children enjoy this game very much. All you need is a spare road-map covering the route you are taking. The children can follow your progress with a coloured marker.

The following games take only a few minutes to prepare:
Word scramble: Prepare a list of words with jumbled letters and get the children to unscramble them.
Crossword: Draw crossword squares on several notepads. During the trip, play the crossword game by calling out letters at random. The children write the letters in any square they wish and try to make up words.

New South Wales

Founding State

In 1770 Captain Cook took possession for the British of all Australian territories east of the 135th meridian of east longitude and named them New South Wales. Today the founding state has shrunk somewhat and occupies just ten per cent of the continent. It is a state of contrasts, covering an area of 801 428 square kilometres, with extremes of country ranging from subtropical to alpine.

The state's capital, Sydney, is Australia's largest city. Established as the site of a penal colony in 1788, the settlement at Sydney Cove was developed under the guiding hand of Governor Arthur Phillip. Following his departure in 1792, however, much of Arthur's initial planning was negated owing to the influence of the infamous NSW Corps, until 1810 heralded the arrival of the redoubtable Governor Macquarie.

In 1813 Blaxland, Lawson and Wentworth discovered the lands to the west of the Blue Mountains. Further exploration quickly followed and settlement fanned out from Sydney. Sydney itself thrived and its citizens agitated against the stigma of the penal presence, with the result that transportation of convicts ended in 1840. The gold-rushes of the 1850s swelled the population and led to much development throughout the state. With the granting of responsible government in 1856, the founding state was well on its way.

Today New South Wales is the most populous state and its central region, around Sydney, Newcastle and Wollongong-Port Kembla, has been described as 'the heart of industrial Australia'. New South Wales produces two-thirds of the nation's black coal from huge deposits in the Hunter Valley, the Blue Mountains and the Illawarra Region. Its other main source of mineral wealth is the silver-lead-zinc mines of Broken Hill. Primary production is diversified and thriving—New South Wales is the nation's main wheat producer and has more than one-third of the nation's sheep population.

The state is divided naturally into four regions—the sparsely populated western plains, which take up two-thirds of the state; the high tablelands and peaks of the Great Dividing Range; the pastoral and farming country of the Range's western slopes; and the fertile coastal region.

The climate varies with the landscape: subtropical along the north coast; temperate all year round on the south coast. The north-west has fearsome dry summers; and the high country has brisk winters with extremes of cold in the highest alpine areas. Sydney has a midsummer average of 25.7°C, a midwinter average of 15.8°C and boasts sunshine for 342 days a year.

Lively and sophisticated, Sydney offers the shopping, restaurants and nightlife expected of a great cosmopolitan city, yet within a 200 kilometre radius is much of the best country in New South Wales: superb beaches, the myriad of intricate bays and inlets of Pittwater, the Hawkesbury and Tuggerah Lakes and the breathtaking Illawarra coastline. The scenic Blue Mountains and the Jenolan Caves can be reached in a day trip. Most of the state's highways lead out from the capital. The Pacific Highway runs north to Port Macquarie and the industrial city of Newcastle. Inland, you can sample the products of the rich Hunter Valley vineyards. Further north, the country becomes hilly and subtropical, with irresistible golden beaches, and the New England tablelands inland—high mountain and grazing country, at its best in autumn.

The state's extreme north and west is still frontier territory, with limited tourist facilities. If you enjoy getting off the beaten track, and if you and your car are well-prepared, the region can be very rewarding. Highlights include the spectacular Nandewar and Warrumbungle Ranges, Lightning Ridge and the green oasis of Broken Hill, the state's storehouse of mineral wealth.

Many relics of the early gold mining and agricultural history of the rich central tablelands and plains region can be seen in and around such towns as Bathurst, Dubbo, Wellington, Griffith and Wagga Wagga. Towards the Victorian border, where the Murray River forms a natural state boundary, irrigation greens the countryside and supports many vineyards and citrus groves. The Murray River towns retain much of the history of the riverboat era when the Murray was a major transport route.

The Princes Highway leads south from Sydney down the Illawarra Coast, famous for its panoramic views, excellent beaches and numerous national parks. Good fishing of all kinds can be enjoyed and there is splendid bushwalking and climbing in the nearby foothills of the southern highlands.

The Snowy Mountains area includes the natural grandeur of the Kosciusko National Park and the man-assisted grandeur of the Snowy Mountains hydro-electric scheme.

Linked by a network of freeways, highways and roads, New South Wales offers a wide variety of regions to explore.

During January 1994 the east coast of the State was savaged by devastating bushfires. Large tracts of bushland and national parks, on the central and south coast in particular, suffered enormous damage.

Bondi, one of Sydney's famous beaches

Sydney

Australia's First City

Sydney, a thriving harbourside metropolis populated by almost 4 million people, is Australia's largest and probably best-known city. It was the first site of European settlement on the Australian continent, a settlement vastly different from today's cosmopolitan showcase.

As Captain Cook sailed up the east coast of Australia in 1770, he noted the entrance to what is now Sydney Harbour and named the craggy headland Port Jackson, in honour of the then Secretary of the British Admiralty, Sir George Jackson.

'New Holland', as the continent was known, was deemed a perfect spot for a penal colony, providing also a reason for a British presence in the South Pacific. Command of the first colonial expedition was entrusted to Captain Arthur Phillip. On his arrival at Botany Bay in 1788, Phillip was not impressed with this proposed settlement site. Looking further afield, on January 26 he sailed into a beautiful natural harbour, where he dropped anchor, named the area Sydney Cove, hoisted the flag and proclaimed the colony of New South Wales.

Sydney Cove, now Circular Quay, saw those first fleet convicts toiling to clear a site for the settlement that was to become the city of Sydney. Testament to their endeavours is **The Rocks**, an area of winding lanes and sandstone buildings situated near the **Harbour Bridge**. An integral part of Sydney's history, providing rich memories of how the city was forged, today The Rocks features outdoor cafes, art and craft centres, museums, curio shops, and a retinue of rollicking pubs. The **Sydney Observatory**, a group of colonial buildings, houses a museum of astronomy with some hands-on displays. Another attraction with interactive exhibits at The Rocks is the **Earth Exchange** (formerly the Geological and Mining Museum), 18 Hickson Road, where visitors can journey across millions of years from the creation of our earth to the present.

In the sandstone building alongside the Sydney Cove Passenger Terminal is the **Museum of Contemporary Art**, which houses the J.W. Power Collection of some 4500 works of art, including Australian and Aboriginal art. It is Australia's first major museum dedicated to the contemporary visual arts.

Sydney Cove has remained the gateway to Australia, situated in calm waters some eleven kilometres from the towering bluffs that flank the harbour mouth: **North Head** and **South Head**. Both headlands command a breathtaking view back along the harbour to the city, automatically drawing the focus to the shimmering city skyline which highlights the **Harbour Bridge**, the **Opera House** and **Sydney Tower**.

While these three structures may be the city's best known landmarks, it is the harbour itself that is Sydney's pride and joy. Its innumerable waterways extend in

The Rocks from Observatory Hill

Harbour Bridge and city

all directions, the product of a drowned valley system that finds bottom in the depths of the Pacific. Its surface, however, is a glistening blue aquatic playground for Sydneysiders.

With the harbour as its heart, the city proper is bounded by water to the north and west and fringed to the east by the extensive green parklands of the Botanic Gardens and the Domain. **Hyde Park**, sitting in the middle of the city, provides areas of tranquil, verdant delight in a bustling central business district.

Within these boundaries, Sydney is an exciting and rewarding city to explore — elegant, lively, relaxed, solemn, Georgian, Edwardian, Victorian and dazzlingly contemporary; a perfect blend of historic bedrock and futuristic planning.

In line with Sydney's boundaries, the city's bus services terminate at three main points: **Circular Quay** in the north, **Wynyard Square** in the west and, in the south, **Central Railway Station**, the grand, domed building that is the outlet for all country and interstate train services. An underground train service goes aboveground outside the central business area and connects the city with outlying suburbs. The **Sydney Explorer** tourist bus loops around 28 km of the city daily, stopping at 27 leading attractions and allowing passengers to alight and rejoin following buses at will.

Where Phillip's First Fleet dropped anchor, the shoreline has become a neat U-shaped area, with major wharves on either arm and harbour ferry terminals at its base. **Circular Quay** is the hub of Sydney's water traffic and a bright, colourful part of town where buskers play amid strolling lunchtime shoppers.

The Quay was built in the nineteenth century to handle overseas shipping and, in the final great era of sail, the days of the superb clipper ships, Sydney Cove was a forest of majestic masts. Today it boasts a huge international shipping terminal with anchorage for ships of 40 000 tonnes. Nearby are several five-star restaurants where patrons dine while overlooking the harbour lights and the luxurious **Park Hyatt** hotel.

Across the water from the Quay, the Harbour Bridge disgorges its congested traffic into Sydney's mini-twin — **North Sydney**, a high-rise, high-density satellite of the 1960s. The **Harbour Tunnel** which runs beneath the harbour, links both business districts.

Under the shadow of the Bridge to the

Hotels
Hotel Intercontinental
117 Macquarie St, Sydney
(02) 230 0200
Observatory
89-113 Kent St, The Rocks
(02) 256 2222
Park Hyatt
7 Hickson Rd, The Rocks
(02) 241 1234
Park Lane
161 Elizabeth St, Sydney
(02) 286 6000
Sydney Renaissance
30 Pitt St, Sydney
(02) 259 7000
Sebel Town House
23 Elizabeth Bay Rd, Elizabeth Bay
(02) 358 3244
Ritz Carlton
93 Macquarie St, Sydney
(02) 252 4600
Sydney Hilton
259 Pitt St, Sydney
(02) 266 0610

Regent, Sydney
199 George St, Sydney
(02) 238 0000

Family and Budget
Russell
143a George St, Sydney
(02) 241 3543
Jackson
94 Victoria St, Potts Point
(02) 358 5144
YWCA
5–11 Wentworth Ave, Darlinghurst
(02) 264 2451
The York
5 York St, Sydney
(02) 210 5000

Motel Groups: Bookings
Flag 13 2400
Best Western (008) 22 2166
Travelodge (008) 22 2446
Golden Chain (008) 02 3966

This list is for information only; inclusion is not necessarily a recommendation.

west of the harbour is **Pier One**, a complex of shops, restaurants (specialising in seafood) and a tavern decorated in Old Sydney style. Once a disembarkation point for immigrants, Pier One has been remodelled to reflect its original purpose.

In keeping with the maritime atmosphere is nearby **Pier Four**, which has been converted into a permanent home for the Sydney Theatre Company. The Wharf Theatre is a modern, yet moody, venue for the Sydney Theatre Company's year-round calendar, while the Wharf Restaurant, with award-winning cuisine, commands one of Sydney's best views.

Standing sentinel at the eastern end of Sydney Cove is the **Sydney Opera House**, a building whose aspect is breathtaking against the blue of the harbour. Its white arches seem to flow out of the water, just as designer Joern Utzon intended, like sails scudding up from the waves. At weekends, the Opera House promenade is alive with audiences listening to free outdoor concerts.

The Quay is typically waterfront. **Circular Quay Plaza** and the Rocks area are the home of some of the city's oldest pubs, many of which are 'early openers' catering for night-shift workers from 6 a.m.

Detached from these, and from its high-rise neighbours, in the centre of the Plaza the old **Customs House** continues to preside over the scene, a monument in

sandstone to nineteenth-century Sydney. Its time-honoured clock is surrounded by tridents and dolphins, and the coat of arms above the entrance is one of the best stone carvings in Australia.

Immediately behind Circular Quay Plaza, a series of maritime-flavoured lane-ways and narrow streets culminates in **Macquarie Place** and its sheltering canopies of giant Moreton Bay fig trees. An anchor and a cannon from Phillip's flagship HMS *Sirius* are preserved in the park, which they share with gas lamps, an 1857 drinking fountain, an ornate Victorian 'gents' (classified by the National Trust) and a weathered obelisk from which distances to all points in the colony used to be measured.

In the surrounding laneways look for one of the world's smallest churches, the tiny **Marist Chapel** at 5 Young Street, run by the Marist Fathers.

Government House is an imposing neo-Gothic sandstone mansion of the 1840s, not open to the public but easily admired from the adjacent Botanic Gardens. Between the entrances to both, the fortress-like lines of the **NSW Conservatorium of Music** successfully conceal the building's origin as stables, designed in 1816 by the renowned convict architect Francis Greenway, and completed in 1821 as part of an earlier Government House on the site.

The Royal Botanic Gardens, more than twenty-four hectares of formal

landscaping, were originally dedicated in 1816. Today they are a perennial landscape of colour where more than 17 000 native and exotic plants bloom throughout the year. In one small corner there is a stone wall, over 200 years old, marking the original plot of the colony's first vegetable garden, planted at the direction of Governor Phillip. The Pyramid greenhouse contains Australian tropical plants, and nearby is the elegant glass Ark, a major tropical plant centre housing some of the world's rarest plants.

An imposing sandstone building on the western side of **Macquarie Street**, the **State Library of New South Wales**, overlooks the Botanic Gardens. In the library's Mitchell and Dixson wings is one of the world's great repositories of national archives and memorabilia, a priceless collection of Australiana and historical records. The new wing of the State Library is sited between the old building and Parliament House. This high-tech building features the latest technology, including study aids for the disabled. A brochure for a self-guide tour of the library is available.

Adjacent to the Library are two of Sydney's oldest buildings, the **New South Wales Parliament** and the **Colonial Mint** (now a museum). Between them, in all its dour Victorian splendour, is **Sydney Hospital**, a city institution, which opened in 1879.

Parliament House and the former

Circular Quay and city buildings

City on the Water

In the arid continent of Australia, Sydney is a cosmopolitan subtropical oasis, set around the bays and inlets of Port Jackson, where some 250 kilometres of unspoiled foreshore is scalloped with white sandy beaches. The southern Pacific Ocean caresses the shores in sheltered coves and thunders in on some of the best surf beaches in the country. The climate is mild, the water warm enough for swimming nine months of the year.

Australia's best-known city sits majestically on the shores of its beautiful natural harbour — a harbour bustling with commuter ferries and jetcats, small tugs and massive container ships, and visiting luxury liners. Sydneysiders are rightly proud of their city. It is the cradle of Australian history and, industrially and commercially, the focal-point of the South Pacific. The people are relaxed yet sophisticated. The water that surrounds them has a major impact on their lifestyle; many office workers commute by ferry and spend their lunch hours by the foreshore, enjoying the cool sea breeze in hot summer months. At weekends Sydneysiders collectively stretch out on the beaches, set sail, swim or surf. Year-round, Sydneysiders ensure their harbour is a hub of activity.

Sydney owes a lot to its harbour, first discovered in 1770 by Captain James Cook, who named it Port Jackson. In 1788, Captain Arthur Phillip declared it 'the finest harbour in the world'. Today, due to its vast size, its protection from storms, its uniform depth, small tides, freedom from silting, and lack of navigational hazards, together with its wharves, conveniently situated close to the city's business centre, it is arguably the world's best natural harbour. It embraces more than fifty-five square kilometres of water and caters for more than 6000 vessels each year.

Sydneysiders take delight in the water and at weekends sailboats, speedboats, yachts and launches join the busy harbour traffic. Sydney Harbour is also the venue of many boating classics, including the Festival of Sydney's Ferry Boat Race in January and the classic Sydney to Hobart yachting classic, which sets out from Sydney on Boxing Day each year, escorted to the Heads by a colourful fleet of pleasure boats.

Between Sydney's two most famous landmarks, the Opera House and the Harbour Bridge, is Sydney Cove — the birthplace of city, state and nation. In 1788, Captain Arthur Phillip chose this inlet to establish the first colony because of its

Yachts on Sydney Harbour

deep bay and running stream of fresh water. Its foreshore, now Circular Quay, in the heart of the city, is dwarfed by skyscrapers, with the City Circle Railway passing immediately overhead and the Cahill Expressway forming a canopy over the railway.

Circular Quay is the nucleus of a network of ferry services that links the city to its suburbs (Manly, Mosman, Neutral Bay, Balmain), popular beaches, Darling Harbour and Taronga Zoo. Most ferry routes pass close to Fort Denison, also known as 'Pinchgut', where convicts were once imprisoned on a diet of bread and water. Today this fortress island can be hired as a perfect festive location for special functions. It is possible also to hire an aqua cab (water taxi) to take you to any point around the harbour, while special cruises go to Middle Harbour, the Lane Cove and Parramatta Rivers, and up the coast to Broken Bay and the Hawkesbury River.

The ferry service to Manly dates back to 1854. This resort suburb took as its slogan around the turn of the century: 'seven miles from Sydney and a thousand miles from care' and it stands as true today. Named by Captain Phillip after the 'manly' behaviour of the Aborigines, this suburb can be reached by a 35-minute ferry ride, a 15-minute journey in a jetcat or an even quicker trip in a UTA catamaran. Manly stands at the gateway to Sydney Harbour, and each summer its population doubles due to the mild climate and the popularity of the eighteen harbour and ocean beaches nearby. Manly Oceanarium enables visitors to 'walk under the ocean' to view the amazing marine life.

Between Grotto Point and Middle Head is the fishing and boating haven of Middle

Harbour. Here the Spit Bridge opens for vessels visiting the area's many channels and bays, which are rich in small coves and beaches.

Along the northern shore of Port Jackson are several well-known beaches: Chowder Bay, where American whalers concocted their famous dish using Sydney rock oysters; Neutral Bay, where ships from foreign countries once anchored; and the picturesque Mosman Bay and Chinamans Beach, a favourite haunt of artists.

On the southern foreshore, almost 100 hectares of parkland in the Domain and Royal Botanic Gardens beckons office workers, who flock to the gardens for a quiet lunch break, a stroll or a jog along the foreshore or a quick game of cricket.

Sydney is also renowned for its fine surf beaches. The scenic northern beaches stretch from Manly to Palm Beach. To the south, Bondi, just seven kilometres from the General Post Office, is the most popular and most famous metropolitan beach. Coogee and Cronulla are also popular. The smaller beaches at Clovelly, Tamarama and Bronte offer quiet seclusion from crowds. Sydney's thirty-four surfing beaches are patrolled by volunteer life-savers, who stage colourful large-scale carnivals throughout the summer months to test their mettle against other clubs. Lady Jane and Reef beaches on the harbour cater to nude sunbathers.

Surfers should take heed of warning flags placed on the sand, which mark the areas safe for surfing on that day. Rock pools are abundant and are ideal for children. It is not advisable to swim in the harbour.

Monorail and city buildings

Mint were once a part of the original colonial hospital, which was known as the Rum Hospital. When there was a shortage of coinage in the colony and rum was the currency, the builders were paid in casks of the spirit. Behind the buildings, the **Domain** — a Sunday afternoon forum for 'soap-box' orators — separates the rear of Macquarie Street from the **Art Gallery of New South Wales**.

During January, when the annual **Sydney Festival and Carnivalé** is in full swing, the Domain becomes a giant outdoor concert hall where hundreds of thousands of Sydneysiders flock to hear jazz, opera and symphonies in the park.

Macquarie Street finally leads into **Queens Square**, arguably one of Sydney's most elegant precincts. The square is encircled by Hyde Park, the towering **Law Courts** building and Francis Greenway's pre-1820 masterpieces, **St James's Church** and **Hyde Park Barracks** (now a social history

museum with unique relics from Sydney's convict origins). Flowing harmoniously on from the old barracks are two great neo-Gothic triumphs of the nineteenth century: the **Registrar-General's Building** and **St Mary's Roman Catholic Cathedral**.

Hyde Park is divided into two sections by **Park Street**. One half is dominated by the **Archibald Fountain** — a legacy to the city from the first publisher of the *Bulletin* — and the other by a **Pool of Remembrance** and the **Anzac War Memorial**. At night, Hyde Park's avenues of trees are lit with thousands of fairy-lights. On the eastern boundary of the park, in College Street, stand the **Australian Museum**; one of Sydney's oldest colleges, **Sydney Grammar School**; and two high-rise neighbours, the **Returned Servicemen's League** headquarters and the **NSW Police Department** administration building.

On the city side of Hyde Park runs **Elizabeth Street.** No longer the major

city artery it once was, now it serves as a vital, almost continuous, bus feeder route, particularly where two underground railway stations, **St James** and **Museum**, disgorge. It is still, however, noteworthy for one of Sydney's historic buildings, the **Great Synagogue**, and for the headquarters of one of Australia's great retailing empires, **David Jones**.

David Jones, with its marble floors, liveried doormen and title of 'the most beautiful store in the world', stands on the corner of Elizabeth Street and Market Street and is a Sydney landmark. 'I'll see you on DJ's corner' was, and still is, a regular Sydney rendezvous. From here, Elizabeth Street continues north to the spacious semicircle of Chifley Square, named in honour of former Prime Minister J.B. Chifley.

In a wedge-shaped sector of blocks made by Bent, Bridge, Young, Phillip and Loftus Streets stand the office buildings of colonial New South Wales, elaborately constructed from Sydney's superb Hawkesbury sandstone, on which the city is built. Mostly late Victorian, the buildings still serve their original purpose as housing for state departments, such as Education and Agriculture.

All are massively solid and ornamented with either statues, gargoyles, handsomely worked-stone, or all three. Within them, cedar-lined offices open on to marbled corridors with staircases with wrought-iron balustrades and ceilings so high and arched as to be almost vault-like. The ministerial offices still within are treasure-troves of priceless colonial artefacts, from grandfather clocks to richly panelled fireplaces.

The disordered pattern of the surrounding streets is a product of the complete lack of planning that occurred once Governor Phillip was recalled from Sydney. Bullock-tracks and wandering cow-paths determined the town plan until Governor Macquarie attempted to impose order some twenty years later. Today the result contributes to Sydney's charm.

Castlereagh Street, parallel to Elizabeth Street, also loses itself in the tangle of colonial office blocks above the Quay. In **Martin Place**, a traffic-free plaza running from Elizabeth Street through Castlereagh and Pitt Streets and finishing at George Street, lunchtime office-workers attend outdoor concerts in the amphitheatre, flower-sellers hawk their wares from colourful barrows and cut-price theatre and concert tickets are on sale at a Halftix booth. The **GPO** sits in Martin Place, between Pitt and George Streets. South of Martin Place the character of the area changes from a merchant belt to a shopping mecca. The **MLC Centre** dominates almost a whole block and contains suites of luxurious offices above and, at ground level, some exclusive shops, mostly jewellers and fashionable boutiques. The complex also houses a convenient fast-food area, the Australia Tavern, a cinema (the Dendy) and, for the theatre-goer, Sydney's prestigious **Theatre Royal**. The King and Castlereagh Streets crossroads, with its collection of elite retail traders such as Chanel and Gucci, has been compared to New York's Fifth Avenue and London's Bond Street.

There are more cinemas nearby and a less expensive shopping complex: **Centrepoint.** Here you can visit the 270-metre-high golden **Sydney Tower**, with its two revolving restaurants. From the observation decks at the summit, high-powered binoculars and a video television camera offer spectacular views of Sydney landmarks.

Only two of Sydney's north–south arteries actually make a complete journey from Circular Quay to Central Railway Station: Pitt Street and George Street. As Pitt Street between King and Market Streets is a pedestrian mall, traffic must make this journey using George Street only.

Sydney has several shopping arcades that run off Pitt and George Streets. One of these, **the Strand**, is particularly noteworthy, having been restored to its 1892 splendour, and housing some of Australia's leading fashion designers, jewellers and crafts people.

In both Pitt and George Streets there is little trace of colonial Sydney, although handsome turn-of-the-century commercial buildings are carefully watched over by devoted citizens and the National Trust, lest developers' ambitions exceed their sense of history and good taste.

Of the two streets, Pitt Street is probably the more exciting in terms of shops, cafes and street hawkers.

The monorail beside Pitt Street worms through the city above street level, linking it to the **Darling Harbour Complex**.

Between King and Park Streets, Pitt Street comes into its own: department stores, including Grace Bros and Centre-

Darling Harbour Complex

point; another popular sporting club, **City Tattersalls**; the Pitt Street side of the Methodist Church's Wesley headquarters; cinemas, one a complex of several choices; and, dominating the two blocks, the sumptuous **Sydney Hilton Hotel**, now out-stripped by its soaring neighbour, Sydney Tower, Sydney's tallest building.

Pitt Street becomes rather nondescript as it heads south towards Central Railway Station, with some secondhand stores, places offering cheap accommodation, and a laneway that leads to a nineteenth-century police headquarters building, now more a city watch-house and serving as cells for the grim **Central Criminal Court** building on one of the cross streets, Liverpool Street.

On carnival-thronged evenings along George Street's entertainment section, cinema complexes, fast-food houses and pin-ball alleys, all-night bookshops and erotic movie houses all compete for the jostling crowd's attention.

Apart from its entertainment area that makes its nights so boisterous, by day George Street boasts a number of Sydney's most important and interesting buildings, both old and new. Until a few years ago, Sydney's and Australia's tallest building was the **Australia Square Tower**. Tall and circular in shape, it has an observation platform on the forty-eighth floor and a revolving restaurant,

the 'Summit'. These days, the tower is dwarfed by the AMP and MLC buildings on Sydney's rocketing skyline, and now more recently by the **Sheraton Wentworth Hotel**, situated opposite on Phillip Street.

South from here are Wynyard underground railway station, the GPO, Sydney's Victorian massif, and the remarkable **Queen Victoria Building** (QVB), which monopolises an entire block. The QVB has been restored by the Sydney City Council, in conjunction with an Asian consortium, including the reburnishing of its enormous copper dome, which once loomed over the older city skyline. The building now houses many restaurants and over 160 shops. A landmark of the city's earlier days is to be found opposite the Queen Victoria building, through the George Street entrance to the Hilton Hotel. In the hotel's basement, restored to its original ornate detail, is the superb **Marble Bar** of the old Adams Hotel, which once stood on the site of the Hilton. On the next corner stands the spiralling blue **Coopers and Lybrand tower**. With its art deco design, it has been dubbed the 'Superman' building because of its similarity to the fictitious *Daily Planet* building of comic-strip fame.

The **Town Hall**, now dwarfed but not overshadowed by a modern council administration block, is Italian Renaissance

A Colonial Past

At the first settlement at Sydney Cove, Captain Watkin Tench of the Marines wrote that 'to proceed on a narrow, confined scale in a country of the extensive limits we possess, would be unpardonable . . . extent of Empire demands grandeur of design'.

Such 'grand design' began in 1810, when the vision of the new Governor, Lachlan Macquarie, was put into practice by the convict architect Francis Greenway, giving us a heritage of splendid buildings, many of which are landmarks today. It continued through nearly a century of growth and lofty ideals to create a prosperous and busy metropolis—a great symbol of colonial aspirations.

As it developed, **Sydney** was both 'mean and princely', a mixture of broad, tree-lined avenues and narrow streets and alleys, grand buildings and crowded cottages and terraces. Its switchback, craggy hills around the indented harbour made orderly Georgian-style planning impossible, and the grand outlines of earlier days soon became blurred by the city's growth from first settlement to colonial seat, to state capital, to modern city.

In modern Sydney, however, with its gleaming towers, its crowds and its traffic, substantial remnants of old Sydney can still be seen. Some parts of the city, like the Rocks area, adjacent to Circular Quay, are almost pure history. The old pubs and bandstands, sandstone cottages and terrace houses, the Argyle Cut and Agar Steps, the Garrison Church and the village green are an oasis separated from the bustling city by Flagstaff Hill, where the old Observatory stands, and the approaches to the Harbour Bridge are seen.

There are many other inner suburban areas that are reminiscent of the feeling of old Sydney. Paddington is the showplace historic suburb, with its picturesque terraces and cottages, many superbly restored by proud owners. The narrow streets of this once working-class suburb provide an intimate, neighbourly feeling. Balmain, Leichhardt and Redfern are becoming popular as the advantages of inner-suburban living attract owners who are conscious of the aesthetic quality of the old sandstone cottages.

In the city itself, the street that best reflects the past is probably Macquarie

Street, which overlooks both the Botanic Gardens and the Domain, where Government House, the Conservatorium of Music, the State Library and Art Gallery of NSW are situated. Governor Macquarie planned for the east side of the street to be occupied by official buildings and for the west to contain the town houses of wealthy citizens, now occupied mainly by members of the medical profession.

Other interesting buildings in Macquarie Street are: Parliament House (1816), a verandahed sandstone building, originally one wing of the Rum Hospital; the adjoining Mint Building, restored from the other wing of the original Rum Hospital; Sydney Hospital: these buildings replaced the central block of the Rum Hospital; the Royal College of Physicians; and the Hyde Park Barracks (1819), now a museum. In nearby Queens Square is the classical St James's Church.

At the harbour end of Mrs Macquarie's Road is a reminder of the Macquarie era—a sandstone shell known as Mrs Macquarie's Chair. The Governor's wife is said to have sat here and gazed out upon the great harbour, now one of the world's busiest and most picturesque waterways.

There are a number of other major buildings in or near the city: such buildings as Elizabeth Bay House, in Regency style, now restored and a showplace for the rich furnishings of the time when it looked out over a harbour verged by cliff and woodland; the General Post Office in Martin Place, completed in 1887 in classic Renaissance style; the Great Hall of Sydney University, and St Andrew's Cathedral, both designed by Edmund Blacket; St Mary's Cathedral, designed by William Wardell; the Greek Revival courthouse in Taylor Square, designed by Mortimer Lewis; and Vaucluse House, the former home of William Charles Wentworth, father of the NSW Constitution. Perhaps the most striking example of colonial architecture in Sydney is Victoria Barracks in Darlinghurst. This two-storeyed building of severe Georgian style, 74 metres long, with white-painted upper and lower verandahs, is a model of elegance. (Visit on Thursday at 10 a.m., watch the changing of the guard and entertainment provided by the Australian Army Band, Sydney, followed by guided tours of this historic group of buildings.)

As settlement extended from the harbourside colony, villages were established, first in the upper **Hawkesbury region** to the north-west, then to the south and, finally, as the Blue Mountains were

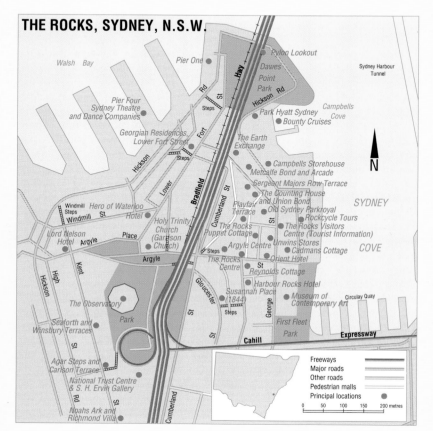

THE ROCKS, SYDNEY, N.S.W.

breached, out to the western plains and throughout New South Wales.

In the upper Hawkesbury valley are the sister towns of Windsor and Richmond, two of the Macquarie Towns, beautifully sited on the river and retaining the peaceful charm and many of the buildings of earlier days. Windsor has a number of fine buildings: Claremont Cottage, St Matthew's Anglican Church, the Macquarie Arms, Tebbutt's Observatory, the Doctor's House and the Toll House, to name but a few. At Richmond are Belmont, Hobartville, Toxana House, the School of Arts and St Peter's Anglican Church.

In the **Southern Highlands**, the settlements of Mittagong, Moss Vale, Berrima and Bowral are full of historic interest. The Berrima Village Trust is responsible for its preservation as it was in the 19th century. Sited in a valley, Berrima contains a number of fine sandstone buildings grouped around a central common, among them the gaol and courthouse, the Surveyor-General Inn, the Church of the Holy Trinity, Harper's Mansion and Allington. Throughout New South Wales, there are many other historic towns and properties bearing the hallmarks of the nation's foundation.

For further information on colonial towns and buildings, contact the National Trust of Australia office in your state. **See also:** Individual A–Z town listings.

The Rocks

Moss Vale, Southern Highlands

in style. Built of mellow brown sandstone, it was completed in 1874. A graceful, shaded pedestrian plaza, **Sydney Square,** is located around the Town Hall and separates it from Sydney's Anglican Cathedral, **St Andrew's**. Erected in stages from 1839 onwards, it was not until the final additions and alterations were completed that the present main entrance on to George Street finally was opened in 1919.

Further west is **Darling Harbour**, an ambitious public centre, opened on Australia Day 1988, which has become an entertainment centre for Sydneysiders. This impressive complex features the **Chinese 'Garden of Friendship'**, an exhibition and convention centre, waterside walks, a variety of eating places, seven-day-a-week shopping, and splendid parklands around a busy harbour inlet that was once a dull industrial port. At the western end of the National Trust classified Pyrmont Bridge is the National **Maritime Museum** and near the eastern end of this one-time traffic carrier, now used as a walkway, is the **Sydney Aquarium**.

The Powerhouse Museum on the southern edge of the Darling Harbour Complex is also well worth a visit. Its size is such that it can exhibit aeroplanes, trams, boats and steam-engines, as well as many equally fascinating smaller exhibits. Opposite is the **Sydney Entertainment Centre,** a major venue for concerts and conventions. Nearby lies **Dixon Street**, the pedestrianised heart of **Sydney's China Town**, a traditional area of restaurants, warehouses, specialty stores and Chinese grocers, where even the banks and service stations are labelled in Chinese script.

Not far from Darling Harbour is Australia's largest fish market, the **Sydney Fish Market** at **Pyrmont;** it has retail stores, coffee shops, souvenir outlets and Australia's first seafood school.

Of the city's cross-streets, two handsome boulevards are noteworthy: Park Street and Martin Place. The authentic heart of the city, **Martin Place**, with its memorial **Cenotaph** to Australia's war dead, is the annual stage for the city's Anzac Day March on April 25. It is also a stage for a variety of lunch-time entertainment.

Park Street ambles east, its footpaths splitting Hyde Park in two and providing a pleasant walk before turning into William Street, which inevitably leads to

Kings Cross, Sydney's version of Soho and Greenwich Village. The Cross, though, has its own unique flavour: the breath of a Sydney Harbour breeze and a glimpse of blue water are a delight. Whatever the Cross has borrowed from other cities in its strip joints, gaudy nightspots and colourful characters, it has its own bohemian traditions to draw on. In its backyard are **Garden Island** dockyard, where the Fleet is nearly always in, and the encircling apartment houses of select **Elizabeth Bay**. On its boundaries are the lively suburbs of Darlinghurst and Woolloomooloo.

The once notorious **Darlinghurst,** a long-time haunt of pimps, prostitutes and gangsters, boasts the historic Darlinghurst Gaol (where bushrangers were hanged) as one of its attractions. Today, however, the face of Darlinghurst has changed dramatically and it is now the home of artists, musicians and poets. Its main artery, **Oxford Street**, with its 'adult' bookshops, pubs, clothing stores and restaurants is the 'gay' capital of Australia.

Woolloomooloo (the famous Loo) has seen its cramped houses and narrow streets predictably skyrocket in price as the desire for trendy inner-city living escalates. Individual restaurants and bars are many and various — too numerous to list. Trendy brasseries compete amid the leftovers of 'sleaze' on Bayswater Road and Kellett Street, where the gentrification of the Cross is most apparent. But, even so, there are a great number of erotic movie-houses and specialty bookshops — with the red-light-district flavour that seems to go with them — still left in the Cross. A less controversial landmark is the dandelion-shaped **El Alamein Fountain** commemorating the World War II battle.

In the other direction, Darlinghurst Road and Bayswater Road lead to Sydney's 'trendiest' area, **Paddington**, a suburb of steep hills, unplanned streets and picturesque terrace houses, hardly one without ornate Victorian wrought-iron railings and fences and lots of trees. The old-fashioned pubs are now terribly chic; well-spoken children and large dogs exercise on streets once the domain of street-urchins before Paddington underwent its fashionable revival back in the late fifties. Next door to 'Paddo' is **Centennial Park**, Sydney's equivalent to New York's Central and London's Regent Park, where horseriding, cycling

and picnicking are weekend activities.

Paddington's counterpart on the other side of Sydney, **Glebe** (bordering historic **Sydney University**) is not quite so leafy or picturesque, and certainly not as expensive but is seeing a revival. Nearby **Balmain** with its harbour frontage also has undergone a fashionable revival.

At every turn of a corner these three suburbs reveal something old and handsome in weathered sandstone: a church, a cottage, a school from Sydney's past. They also have given rise to a Sydney phenomenon: the advent of the 'Church Bazaar'. These village markets, usually held on Saturdays, feature colourful identities plying their wares at open-air stalls in the grounds of schools or churches. For this reason alone, the suburbs are worth a visit.

So is the rest of Australia's first city: from Paddington's neighbours, **Woollahra** and **Rushcutters Bay** through the harbourside suburbs of exclusive **Double Bay**, **Rose Bay** and **Vaucluse** to **The Gap** and **South Head**; or across the harbour by the ferry, jetcat or Harbour Bridge to **Manly** and the long line of beaches stretching north to **Palm Beach**, competing in terms of wealth and privilege with the precipitous bush gorges and superior heights of the elegant **North Shore** suburbs. Beyond all that again lies the metropolitan heartland of Sydney's great urban sprawl — 75 km from the harbour across the vast, flat western suburbs to the foothills of the **Blue Mountains**.

A floatplane service at **Rose Bay** has flights between Sydney and Palm Beach, Gosford and Newcastle; and the Manly Ferry *Collaroy* offers cruises from Circular Quay up the coast into Broken Bay and the Hawkesbury River. Near the Hawkesbury at **Berowra** is the famous Berowra Waters Inn, ranked as one of the best restaurants in Australia.

It is not possible to list all of Sydney's restaurants. In Sydney one can dine out on the cuisines of virtually every nation in the world. However, it should be mentioned that Sydney is famous for its rock oyster and the Balmain Bug—an odd-looking but tasty crustacean. The choice of cinema, live theatre and live theatre-restaurants is just as comprehensive.

For further information, contact the NSW Travel Centre, 19 Castlereagh St, Sydney 2000; (02) 231 4444.

Tours from Sydney

Sydney's range of available day tours out and about is almost unrivalled for the variety of scenic and recreational attractions on offer.

In the frantic rush to get out of the city, however, it is easy to overlook two of Sydney's greatest assets: **Royal National Park**, little more than an hour's drive south from the GPO, and **Ku-ring-gai Chase National Park**, 40 km N.

Harbour Cruises from Circular Quay

An ideal way to view Sydney and its harbour is by boat. Several cruises are available. State Transit run three daily: a two-and-a-half hour harbour sights or harbour history cruise, and a one-and-a-half hour harbour lights cruise. Harbour lights does not run on Sun. evening. Bookings not necessary; for further information: (02) 956 4790.

'Coffee cruises' operated by Captain Cook Cruises run twice daily through Main and Middle Harbours and the same company's luncheon cruises travel up the Parramatta and Lane Cove Rivers daily. The *John Cadman* makes a 'dinner cruise' daily. The 38-m cruise ship *Proud Sydney* offers overnight harbour cruises. Experience the thrill of sailing on a harbour luncheon cruise aboard the *Solway Lass,* a restored sailing-ship.

Captain Cook Cruises also conducts tours to Fort Denison, one of the most historic relics in Australia, Tues.– Sun.

Taronga Zoo, 12 minutes by ferry from Circular Quay, Wharf 5

Taronga is set in 30 ha of harbourside bushland, giving it a magnificent and unique setting: the views back to the city are splendid. Of particular interest are the displays of Australian native animals and the nocturnal house. Children will enjoy meeting the tame animals at the Friendship Farm (open daily).

Palm Beach, 48 km from Sydney via Pittwater Rd

This beautiful beach in bush surroundings offers swimming and boating facilities and a choice of ocean or Pittwater beaches. The drive from Sydney reveals many of Sydney's lovely northern beaches and it is tempting to stop at every one. The Mona Vale road provides a shorter route if you are based in the northern suburbs; allow time for a visit to the fauna reserve Waratah Park at Terrey Hills.

Captain Cook's Landing Place, Kurnell, 35 km from Sydney via Princes Hwy and Captain Cook Bridge

The site of the first recorded landing by Europeans on the east coast of Australia in 1770 is set aside as a historic site on a pleasantly laid-out reserve. An excellent museum displays items related to Captain James Cook's life and

Cruise boat at Circular Quay

The Blue Mountains

The Blue Mountains have been a favourite holiday resort for Sydneysiders for more than a century. Rising from the coastal plain 65 kilometres west of Sydney, they combine a unique blend of superb mountain scenery and outstanding geographical features with a plethora of highly developed tourist attractions. In January 1994 devastating bushfires destroyed large areas of bushland and some property.

The towering cliffs of the Blue Mountains presented a seemingly impassable barrier to the early settlers until Blaxland, Lawson and Wentworth made their historic crossing in 1813—thus opening up much-needed pasture-land beyond.

In the late 1870s, the well-to-do of Sydney discovered the area's charms as a resort, and started to build elaborate holiday houses to escape the summer heat of the coast. At first they travelled by Cobb & Co. coach, later by train. Now the mountains are less than two hours from Sydney by road or rail. One-day round-trip coach tours run daily between Sydney and Katoomba.

The Blue Mountains are justly famous for their spectacular scenery of high precipices rising from densely wooded valleys. Their highest point is about 1100 metres above sea-level. Although the area has been developed for tourism, deep gorges and high rocks make much of the terrain inaccessible, except to skilled bushwalkers and mountaineers. Climbing schools offer rock-climbing weekends for beginners, and there are day courses in beginners' abseiling.

The panoramic **Blue Mountains National Park**, which covers an area of 216 000 hectares, is the 4th largest national park in the state.

The City of Blue Mountains incorporates over 20 towns and villages, including the main towns of **Katoomba**, **Blackheath**, **Wentworth Falls**, **Springwood** and **Glenbrook**. All these towns depend on tourism and are geared for the holiday trade. They offer a wide range of accommodation, from bed and breakfast at old-style guest houses to luxury living at modern resorts.

The Blue Mountains' reputation for natural wonders is rapidly being rivalled by its popularity as a gastronomic centre. Wining and dining to suit all tastes and budgets, combined with an overnight or weekend stay, is attracting further visitors to the area.

For further information, contact the Blue Mountains Tourism Authority, PO Box 8, Gembrook 2773; (047) 39 6266, or visit the Information Centres at Echo Point, Katoomba or Glenbrook on the Great Western Hwy. The BMTA produces a *Holiday Book*, detailing activities and accommodation in the area. **See also:** Katoomba–Wentworth Falls in A–Z listing. **Note** detailed map of Blue Mountains on page 106.

Why are the Blue Mountains so blue?
The whole area is heavily timbered with eucalypts, which constantly disperse fine droplets of oil into the atmosphere. These droplets cause the blue light-rays of the sun to be scattered more effectively, thus intensifying the usual light refraction phenomenon (known as Rayleigh Scattering), which causes distant objects to appear blue.

The Three Sisters

discoveries. A short 'historical walk' takes visitors past several points of interest. There are picnic/barbecue facilities in the grounds.

Parramatta, 22 km from Sydney via Great Western Hwy

Although it has now become a city within Sydney, Parramatta retains its individuality and has some interesting buildings. Pick up a Historic Houses self-guide leaflet from the tourist centre in Prince Alfred Park ((02) 630 3703). Elizabeth Farm (1793), in Alice St, contains part of the oldest surviving building in Australia and, as the home of Elizabeth and John Macarthur, was for the first 40 years of the colony the social, political and agricultural centre. Don't miss the audio-visual and period (1830s) gardens. Experiment Farm Cottage in Ruse St was the site of James Ruse's 'experiment' to support himself from the land in the early years of the colony. Closer to the centre of the city are two historic sites: Old Government House in attractive Parramatta Park has been beautifully restored from its 1799 (enlarged 1815) beginnings and is maintained by the National Trust. Take the guided tour to learn more. The guide will explain the significance of St John's Church (1850s), in the heart of the shopping district too. St John's cemetery is now a block away from the church itself and contains the oldest headstone in the colony, dated January 1791.

Windsor and Richmond, 60 km from Sydney via Great Western Hwy and Windsor Rd

These two towns on the Hawkesbury River are reminders of the earliest days of settlement in New South Wales. In Windsor, there are many historic buildings in George Street and Thompson Square. The Doctor's House, Thompson Square, built in 1844, is one of the most impressive, but the courthouse and the many churches and hotels in both towns are all of interest. The Hawkesbury Museum at 7 Thompson Square, Windsor, is housed in an old colonial building. It contains various items of historic interest relating to pioneer days. **See also:** Entries in the A–Z listing.

Historic Camden and Campbelltown, 60 km from Sydney via Liverpool, on Hume Hwy

Liverpool, situated 32 km from Sydney and a major retail and commercial centre, has many historic buildings of interest: St Luke's Church (1818), Liverpool Hospital (1825–30), designed by Francis Greenway and now the Liverpool College of TAFE, and Glenfield Farm (1817). The ultra-modern Liverpool Museum, built as a bicentennial project, fronts Collingwood Cottage, built in 1810 for a whaling captain. A good stopping-point is Chipping Norton Lakes, a reclaimed area with picnic and barbecue facilities, and walking tracks. Further down the highway, lovers of history can enjoy a relaxed stroll around the streets of two early towns of New South Wales, Camden and Campbelltown. (**See:** Entries in A–Z listing.) Although most of the historic buildings are not open for inspection, a pleasant day can be spent just taking in the atmosphere. A self-guide walking-tour booklet is available from the Macarthur Country Tourist Association, Liverpool. Between Camden and Campbelltown, off Narellan Road, is the 400-hectare Mt Annan Botanic Garden, the native plant garden of the Royal Botanic Gardens, Sydney, opened in 1988.

Katoomba and the Blue Mountains via Penrith, 104 km from Sydney via the Great Western Highway (or by minifare excursion, State Rail)

The historic town of Penrith, 57 km from Sydney, dates back to the opening of the Blue Mountains road in 1815 when a courthouse and a small gaol were built there. Today it makes a pleasant stopover en route to the Blue Mountains. Penrith's attractions include the Museum of Fire in Castlereagh St, the *Nepean Belle* paddleboat, which cruises the Nepean Gorge, Vicary's Winery south of town and the Lewers Regional Art Gallery at Emu Plains. **See also:** The Blue Mountains; and Katoomba entry in A–Z listing.

The Hunter Valley Vineyards, 160 km from Sydney via Pacific Hwy

Although it is possible to do this trip in a day, this certainly would not do the area justice — and it is definitely not a good idea if you plan to do any wine tasting!

The best time to visit the Hunter Valley is at vintage time, when you can see the grapes being fermented in great open vats. Picking starts any time from the end of January, but this can vary considerably, and sometimes does not start until well into February.

Most of the wineries welcome visitors. It is well worth while visiting a few of the smaller wineries. Tyrrell's and Drayton's wineries were established within a few years of each other in the 1850s and at Tyrrell's you can still see the classic hand presses being used during vintage and fermentation.

Most of the wineries are open every day. Inspections can be arranged with the wineries direct or by calling at the Tourist Information Centre, cnr Mt View and Wollombi Rds, Cessnock; (049) 90 4477. **See also:** Vineyards and Wineries.

Rhododendron Gardens, Blackheath, Blue Mountains

New South Wales from A to Z

Adaminaby
Pop. 375

This small town on the Snowy Mountains Hwy is renowned as a base for cross-country skiers, and the ski area of Mt Selwyn is nearby. It is the stepping-off point for Lake Eucumbene, where many holiday resorts around the lakeshore offer varied accommodation. Excellent fishing and boats for hire. At Providence Portal water can be seen gushing from one of the giant Snowy Mountains tunnels into the lake. **In the area:** Cruisers for hire at Buckenderra, 44 km S. Yarrangobilly Caves and thermal pool, off Snowy Mountains Hwy, 53 km N. Horseriding and alpine horseback safaris. Farm holidays. **Tourist information:** Snowy River Shire Council, 2 Myack St, Berridale Sth; (064) 56 3251. **Accommodation:** 1 hotel/motel, 3 motels, 1 caravan/camping park.
MAP REF. 118 H5, 119 D8, 140 E9, 235 K1

Adelong
Pop. 795

Both fossickers and goldfields historians are attracted to this picturesque tablelands town on the Snowy Mountains Hwy. In the mid-1850s it produced 200 tonnes of gold and drew many thousands of hopeful miners. **Of interest:** Tumut St, from Campbell to Neil Sts, classified by National Trust; some buildings, such as Bank of NSW, rated as being of great historic interest. Also in Tumut St: Gold Fields Galleries art and craft centre; restored Old Pharmacy with Old Prison Clock (over 125 years old) originally from Kiandra courthouse, and accommodation and restaurant. **In the area:** Adelong Falls, 2 km N, on Tumblong–Gundagai Rd; scenic picnic area; also gold fossicking. Oasis coloured-sheep farm, 8 km along same road; spinning, shearing and sales of wool and garments.

Tourist information: York's Newsagency, Tumut St; (069) 46 2051. **Accommodation:** 2 hotels, 1 camping/caravan park.
MAP REF. 119 B6, 120 C13

Albury
Pop. 39 975

Albury–Wodonga is situated on the Murray River, 572 km SW from Sydney. Once the meeting-place for local Aboriginal tribes, today the Albury region makes a convenient stopover point for motorists driving via the Hume Hwy between Sydney and Melbourne. The building of the Hume Weir in 1936 created Lake Hume, one of the most extensive and beautiful man-made lakes in Australia. This huge expanse of water is a paradise for swimmers, sailors, canoeists, water-skiers, speedboat enthusiasts, windsurfers and anglers. **Of interest:** Albury Regional Museum, in former Turk's Head Hotel, Wodonga Pl. Botanical Gardens (1871), cnr Wogonga Pl. and Dean St. The Parklands, comprising Noreuil and Australia Parks and Hovell Tree

Reserve, on western side of Wodonga Pl at entrance to town. Riverside walks, river swimming, kiosk and picnic areas. PS *Cumberoona* offers Murray River cruises; embarkation points within parks. Albury Regional Art Centre, Dean St. Performing Arts Centre, Civic Centre, Swift St. 360° views of surrounding area from Albury Monument Hill at end of Dean St. Frog Hollow Leisure Park, Olive St; maze, theatre, mini-golf. Haberfield's Milk Dairy Shop, Hovell St; sales of local dairy products, tours during business hours. **In the area:** Ettamogah Wildlife Sanctuary, 12 km NE on Hume Hwy. Cartoonist Ken Maynard's Ettamogah Pub; worth photographing. Cooper's Ettamogah Winery, 3 km further along hwy. Jindera Pioneer Museum, 14 km NW; former general store. Australian Newsprint Mill, 15 km N; tours by appt. Hume Weir Trout Farm, 14 km E; trout feeding, fishing and tastings. Bogong Mountains, gateway to Victorian snowfields and high country, 130 km S. Day trips to wineries of Rutherglen, 47 km W,

Lake Eucumbene, near Adaminaby

and into Mad Dan Morgan country, 200 km round trip N. Hume and Hovell Walking Track from Albury to Gunning, over 300 km NE. Farm holidays. **Tourist information:** Crossing Place Visitors Centre, Hume Hwy; (060) 21 2655; accommodation booking line (008) 80 6939. **Accommodation:** Albury–Wodonga, 2 hotels, 55 motels, 13 caravan/camping parks.
MAP REF. 126 P13, 208 B2, 233 P4

Alstonville   Pop. 3678
The village of Alstonville nestles in lush surroundings at the top of the Ballina Cutting between Ballina and Lismore. Famous for the beautiful purple Tibouchina tree, the town holds a Tibouchina Festival during blossom time in March. Surrounding properties produce potatoes, sugarcane, tropical fruits, macadamia nuts and avocados. **Of interest:** Prize-winning town in 'Tidy Towns' competition since 1986. Lumley Park, Bruxner Hwy; open-air pioneer transport museum. Kolinda Gallery, Budgen Ave; local art and crafts. **In the area:** House With No Steps, 10 km S; nursery, crafts, fruit sales and tearooms run by disabled. Victoria Park, 10 km S; boardwalks and picnic area. **Tourist information:** Ballina Tourist Information Centre, Las Balsa Plaza, Ballina; (066) 86 3484. **Accommodation:** 1 hotel, 1 motel.
MAP REF. 123 P3, 475 O9

Armidale   Pop. 21 605
Situated midway between Sydney and Brisbane in the New England Ranges (altitude 900 m), this city is the centre of the New England district and an attractive tourist centre, with over 30 National Trust buildings and a blaze of garden colour in spring and autumn. **Of interest:** New England Regional Art Museum, Kentucky St; contains Hinton Collection, most valuable provincial art collection in Australia. Also in Kentucky St, Aboriginal Centre and Keeping Place; museum and education centre. Folk Museum with display of pioneer relics, in classified National Trust building, cnr Faulkner and Rusden Sts. In Dangar St, St Mary's Roman Catholic Cathedral (1912), magnificent Gothic revival structure, and St Peter's Anglican Cathedral (1875), built of 'Armidale blues' bricks. The Stables (1872), Moore St; now craft shop. Courthouse (1860) and Imperial Hotel (1889), both in Beardy St. Central Park, Dangar St; pleasant city park with

useful relief map of area. Market in Mall, last Sun. of month; Spring Floral Festival in Oct. **In the area:** University of New England, 5 km NW, with historic Booloominbah homestead now administration building, Antiquities Museum, Zoology Museum, and kangaroo and deer park. National Trust-owned Saumarez Homestead (1888), 6 km S. Rural Life and Industry Museum at ghost town of Hillgrove, 27 km E; exhibits of goldmining equipment. Oxley Wild Rivers National Park, 39 km E, includes Wollomombi Falls, highest falls in Australia, plunging 457 m. Fine views from Point Lookout (1500 m) in New England National Park, 80 km E. Self-guide leaflets available for National Parks. Mt Yarrowyck Aboriginal rock-art site and cultural walk, 23 km NW off Bundarra Rd. **Tourist information:** Visitors Centre & Coach Station, cnr Marsh & Dumaresq Sts; (067) 73 8527. **Accommodation:** 5 hotels, 22 motels, 2 caravan/camping parks. **See also:** New England.
MAP REF. 123 L8, 475 K12

Ashford   Pop. 567
This small New England town is the centre of a tobacco-growing district. **In the area:** Network of limestone caves and spectacular Macintyre Falls, 36 km NW. Pindari Dam, 20 km S; bushwalking, swimming, fishing, camping, picnic/barbecue facilities. **Tourist information:** Shire Tourism Committee, Water Towers Complex, Campbell St, Inverell; (067) 22 1693. **Accommodation:** 1 hotel, 1 caravan/camping park. **See also:** New England.
MAP REF. 123 J4, 475 J10

Ballina   Pop. 14 554
A fishing town at the mouth of the Richmond River in northern NSW, Ballina's ideal year-round temperatures, picturesque farmlands, golden beaches and friendly rural atmosphere make the area a popular family holiday destination. Cedar cutters were among the first settlers, attracted by the red cedar trees along the shores of the river. Farmers followed and by 1900 the dairy-farming industry was established alongside sugarcane plantations. **Of interest:** Ballina Maritime Museum, in Tourist Information Centre; steam riverboat exhibit and restored Las Balsas Expedition rafts that sailed from South America in 1973. Framed Gallery, River St. Opal and Gem

Museum, Pine St. Quilts and Collectables, Martin St. Balina Outdoor Entertainment Reserve, Canal Rd. The Big Prawn, Pacific Hwy; fresh seafood, antiques, arts and crafts. *Richmond Princess* river cruises. **In the area:** MacKay Harrison Galleries, 2 km N on Lennox Head Rd. Freshwater Lake Ainsworth, 12 km N, at Lennox Head. Macadamia Land, 17 km N, at Knockrow; entertainment park. Broadwater Sugar Mill, on Pacific Hwy at Broadwater, 19 km S; inspection tours during sugar season; covered shoes must be worn. Thursday Plantation Tea Tree Oil, 3 km W; guided tours. Macadamia Magic at Alphadale, 25 km W; processing and packaging of nuts. **Tourist information:** Las Balsa Plaza; (066) 86 3484. **Accommodation:** 14 motels, 8 caravan/camping parks.
MAP REF. 123 P3, 475 O9

Balranald   Pop. 1327
On the Murrumbidgee River, 438 km NW of Melbourne, in a wool, cattle, wheat, fruit and timber area. **Of interest:** Historical Museum and Heritage Park, Market St. Old Police Station, River St; open to public. Lions Park picnic/barbecue facilities and children's playground. **In the area:** Balranald (low-level) Weir for picnics, barbecues and fishing. Yanga Lake, 7 km SE; good fishing and water sports. Historic Homebush Hotel (1878), 25 km N. Mungo National Park, 150 km NW; Walls of China; Willandra Lakes preserve record of 40 000 years of Aboriginal life. **Tourist information:** Market St; (050) 20 1599. **Accommodation:** 1 hotel/motel, 4 motels, 1 caravan/camping park.
MAP REF. 126 H9, 231 N7

Bangalow   Pop. 819
Discover the rustic charm of this delightful village, set amid magnificent scenery. **Of interest:** Art, craft and antique shops. Colourful market, held every 4th Sun. **In the area:** Byron Creek walking track, through splendid rainforest to picnic area. Beaches at Byron Bay, 12 km E. **Tourist information:** Byron Tourist Information Office, 80 Jonson St, Byron Bay; (066) 85 8050. **Accommodation:** 1 hotel, 1 motel.
MAP REF. 123 P2, 475 J10

Barham–Koondrook
Pop. 1217
These twin towns, situated on either side of the Murray River, are centres for the

The Hawkesbury

The Hawkesbury River, one of the most attractive rivers in Australia, is located north of Sydney. The river and its surrounds played an important role in Sydney's early colonial history. The first settlers arrived in the area in 1794 to establish farming settlements to help feed the starving colony. In 1810, Governor Macquarie founded the towns of **Windsor**, **Richmond**, **Castlereagh**, **Wilberforce** and **Pitt Town** in the upper Hawkesbury valley. Today much of this land is still used for agriculture and there are many oyster leases on the lower river.

Although farming has been pursued since the late 18th century, the charm of the Hawkesbury lies mainly in the fact that the river is still surrounded by large areas of untouched bushland. Large tracts of bushland were destroyed in the terrible bushfires that swept through the area in January 1994. Two major national parks front the river: upstream the Dharug National Park, noted for its Aboriginal rock carvings, and downstream the Ku-ring-gai Chase National Park.

The Hawkesbury River is a popular recreational waterway, particularly at its lower and wider reaches between Brooklyn and Pittwater.

One of the best ways of exploring the Hawkesbury is by boat. Craft of all types from small rowing dinghies to cruisers and houseboats are available for hire at **Brooklyn**, a small town near the Hawkesbury River Bridge, and also at **Bobbin Head**, **Berowra Waters** and **Wisemans Ferry**. A delightful way to see the river is to join the river mailboat run, which leaves Brooklyn on weekdays and takes 3 hours. Cruises on the river are also available, from 2 hours to 2 days, on the luxury catamaran *Windsor Princess*.

If you are travelling north from Sydney by road, the Newcastle–Sydney Freeway crosses the Hawkesbury and its tributary, Mooney Mooney Creek. This section of the freeway cuts through magnificent sandstone cliffs and offers spectacular views.

For further information, contact the Hawkesbury Regional Tourist Centre, Ham Common Bicentennial Park, Richmond Rd, Clarendon; (045) 88 5895. **See also:** Individual town entries in A–Z listing. **Note** detailed map of Hawkesbury and Central Coast on page 108.

Berowra Waters

Near Wisemans Ferry

timber, fat-lamb, cattle, dairying and tourism industries. **Of interest:** Barham Lakes Complex, Murray St; man-made lakes, 4-km walking track, picnic/barbecue facilities, swimming, paddle-boats and canoes for hire. Bonum Red Gum Saw Mill, Moulamein Rd. **In the area:** Gannawarra Wetlander Cruises, 15 km s via Koondrook. Kerang Ibis Rookery, 28 km sw from Koondrook on Murray Valley Hwy. Shannkirst Cashmere Stud, Koondrook. Koondrook State Forest, East Barham Rd. Brady's Burls, 2½ km N of Koondrook on Murrabit Rd; local red-gum woodcraft. **Tourist information:** 25 Murray St, Barham; (054) 53 3100. **Accommodation:** 3 hotels, 6 motels, 3 caravan/camping parks.
MAP REF. 126 I12, 229 Q3, 231 Q13, 232 B1

Clyde River Bridge, Batemans Bay

Barooga   Pop. 843
A small, but rapidly growing town near the Victorian town of Cobram. Barooga's beautiful setting and abundant wildlife make it a popular holiday resort. **Of interest:** Sandy beaches along Murray River. Barooga Sportsmen's Club, with poker machines, and Cobram–Barooga Golf Club; both offer entertainment and restaurants. Binghi Boomerang Factory, Tocumwal Rd. **In the area:** Kramner Cellars (Seppelts Vineyards), Mulwala Rd, 2 km E. Brentwood Fruit Juices, 6 km E. Drop-irrigation junction at bridge on Berrigan Rd, 20 km N. Citrus and grape growing. **Tourist information:** The Old Grain Shed, cnr Station St and Punt Rd, Cobram; (058) 72 2132. **Accommodation:** 1 hotel, 6 motels, 3 caravan/camping parks.
MAP REF. 127 M13, 233 J3

Barraba   Pop. 1427
Surrounded by magnificent mountain scenery on the Manilla River in the Nandewar Ranges, Barraba is an agricultural and pastoral centre and an ideal base for exploring the eastern part of the Nandewar Mountains. **Of interest:** Nandewar Historical Museum, Queen St; open by appt. Clay Pan Fuller Gallery, Queen St. St Laurence's Anglican Church, Fitzroy St; beautiful old organ recently restored. **In the area:** Adam's Lookout, 4 km N. Breathtaking views from Mt Kaputar's summit, via road from Narrabri. Horton River Falls and Horton Valley, 38 km NW towards Mt Kaputar

National Park; picnic/barbecue facilities. **Tourist information:** 116 Queen St; (067) 82 1255. **Accommodation:** 3 hotels, 1 motel, 2 caravan/camping parks. **See also:** New England.
MAP REF. 122 I7, 474 I12

Batemans Bay   Pop. 8320
Crayfish and oysters are the specialty of this attractive resort town on the Princes Hwy. The charming site, at the estuary of the Clyde River, 294 km s of Sydney, makes it an ideal picnic and bushwalking spot. **Of interest:** Birdland Animal Park, Beach Rd; native and exotic birds, wildlife, rainforest trail. Excellent swimming, diving, surfing, fishing; and bowling club. **In the area:** Shell Museum, Batehaven, 1 km E; shells from all over world. Mogo Goldfields Park, Mogo, 8 km s; features working goldmine. Old Mogo Town; 19th century goldmining town recreated. Mogo Zoo; native and exotic animals. Surfing at Malua Bay, 10 km SE. Durras Lake, 10 km N, for fishing, swimming and varied wildlife; houseboats for hire. Murramarang National Park, 10 km N; rainforest and popular swimming beaches. Nelligen, 10 km NW, on Clyde River, for picnics, water-skiing and cruises. Araluen, old goldmining town, 82 km NW. **Tourist information:** Eurobodalla Coast Visitors Centre, cnr Princes Hwy and Beach Rd; (044) 72 6900. **Accommodation:** 16 motels, 4 caravan/camping parks. **See also:** The South Coast.
MAP REF. 119 G7, 141 N7

Bathurst   Pop. 24 682
This sedate city, 209 km w of Sydney on the Macquarie River, and the centre of a pastoral and fruit- and grain-growing district, has many historic connections. The birthplace of former Prime Minister, J.B. Chifley, it is possibly better known today for its famous motor racing circuit, Mount Panorama. **Of interest:** Self-guide Historic Walking Tour. Ben Chifley's Cottage, Busby St. Historical Society Museum in East Wing of courthouse, Russell St. Miss Traill's house (c. 1845), 321 Russell St; contents, collected by one family over 100 years, record history of town and reflect family's passion for horse breeding and racing. Bathurst Regional Art Gallery, Keppel St. **In the area:** Fossicker's Self-drive Tour of Bathurst (60–90 min.). South of town, on Panorama Ave, Mt Panorama: Bathurst Gold Diggings, Karingal Village; reconstruction of goldmining era. Motor races held at Mt Panorama Circuit in Oct. Bathurst Motor Racing Museum nearby. Magnificent views from lookout at summit of Mt Panorama; picnic area in McPhillamy Park. Sir Joseph Banks Nature Reserve in park. Bathurst Sheep and Cattle Drome at Rossmore Park, 6 km NE on Limekilns Rd, Kelso; performing sheep and cattle; milking, shearing, sheepdog demonstrations. Abercrombie Caves, 72 km s, via Trunkey, on Bathurst–Goulburn Rd; limestone cave system containing spectacular Arch Cave, considered one of finest natural arches in world and larger than Grand Arch at

Port Stephens

The white volcanic sand and aquamarine waters of the beaches of Port Stephens have a distinctly tropical look, and the annual average temperature is within about 2°C of that of the Gold Coast. This large deep-water port, less than an hour's drive from Newcastle, is one of the most unspoiled and attractive seaside holiday areas on the New South Wales coast. Two-and-a-half times the size of Sydney Harbour, and almost enclosed by two volcanic headlands, the large harbour is fringed by sheltered white sandy beaches backed by stretches of natural bushland. In spring, wildflowers grow in profusion.

The deep, calm waters of the harbour are ideal for boating and offer excellent fishing. A wide range of boats, from aquascooters and catamarans to sailing and power boats, can be hired. Various cruises that explore the harbour and Myall River are available. Big-game fishing waters are within reach outside the harbour, but local fishing clubs warn against leaving the heads unless you are an experienced sailor with a two-motor boat.

The best way to reach these waters is aboard one of the many charter boats licensed to take fishermen and sightseers outside the heads. Early in the afternoon you can watch the local fishing fleet coming into **Nelson Bay**, the main anchorage of the port.

Restaurants in the area—not surprisingly—offer fresh seafood as a specialty. You can sample a superb lobster supreme, washed down by a fine Hunter Valley wine. What more could you ask? For dedicated oyster lovers, a trip to Moffat's Oyster Barn, Swan Bay, is a must. As well as seeing oysters under cultivation and learning about their four-year life cycle, you can enjoy a delicious meal of oysters. Bookings are essential. If you go by boat, make sure you do not run aground on an oyster lease!

You can hire almost anything in the area: bicycles (how about a tandem?), beach umbrellas, fishing tackle; there are also golf courses, bowling greens and all the other usual sporting facilities.

For surfing, you can visit the spectacular ocean beaches that stretch in both directions outside the harbour. Within about 6 kilometres of Nelson Bay are Zenith, Wreck and Box Beaches, Fingal Bay and One Mile Beach.

Other local attractions include art galleries; craft markets on the first and third Sunday of the month; Aussie Ewe and Lamb Centre, Anna Bay; the toboggan run at Toboggan Hill Park, Salamander Bay; Oakvale Farm and Fauna World; and Fighter World, RAAF Base Williamtown. Accommodation, including hotels, motels and modern holiday flats, is available throughout the area and there are caravan and camping parks. The main resorts, apart from Nelson Bay, are **Shoal Bay**, **Fingal Bay**, **Anna Bay**, **Tanilba Bay**, **Salamander Bay**, **Soldiers Point**, **Corlette** and **Lemon Tree Passage** on the south shore, and **Tea Gardens** and **Hawks Nest** on the north.

For further information about the area, including such nearby attractions as the Myall Lakes National Park, contact the Port Stephens Visitors Centre, Victoria Pde, Nelson Bay; (049) 81 1579. **See also:** Individual town entries in A–Z listing. **Note** detailed map of Newcastle Region on page 112.

The Illawarra Coast

The magnificent panoramic views along the rugged Illawarra coast more than compensate for the sometimes winding route of the Princes Highway, which runs the length of it. 'Illawarra' is a corruption of an Aboriginal word appropriately meaning 'high and pleasant place by the sea'. Stretching from Sydney south to Batemans Bay, the Illawarra coast is bounded on the west by the Southern Highlands.

Fine surf beaches stretch along Illawarra's craggy coast, which is liberally dotted with mountain streams, waterfalls, inlets and lakes—ideal for prawning and water sports. Wildflowers and fauna abound in the many reserves along the coast, and the distinctive vegetation includes cabbage palms, tree ferns and giant fig trees. Some of these reserves were burnt out

Lookout near Wollongong

during the devastating bushfires in January 1994. This is the setting for the State's third largest city—**Wollongong**, which has many tourist attractions, scenic lookouts and beautiful beaches.

The other main towns on the coast are **Shellharbour**, a popular holiday resort and residential town south of Lake Illawarra; **Kiama**, the centre of a prosperous dairying and mixed-farming district;

Nowra, the main town of the fascinating Shoalhaven River district; and **Ulladulla**, a picturesque little fishing town and popular summer holiday resort.

For further information, contact Tourism Wollongong, 93 Crown St, Wollongong; (042) 28 0300. **See also:** Individual town entries in A–Z listing. **Note** detailed map of Southern Highlands on page 116.

The South Coast

The southern coast of New South Wales — from Batemans Bay down to the Victorian border — is a fisherman's paradise. Hemmed in by the Great Dividing Range, it is one of the finest areas for fishing in southern Australia. It is also a haven for anyone who enjoys swimming, surfing or bushwalking in an unspoiled setting.

One of the attractions of this stretch of coast is the variety of country to be seen: superb white surf beaches, and crystal-clear blue sea against a backdrop of craggy mountains, gentle hills, lakes, inlets and forests. The coast is dotted with quaint little fishing and holiday resorts, which have a wide range of hotel, motel and holiday-flat accommodation, as well as many caravan parks. These towns are not highly commercialised, although many of them triple their population in the peak summer months. Boats of all kinds can be hired at the major resorts.

Peaceful **Batemans Bay**, at the estuary of the Clyde River, has become very popular with Canberra people since the road linking the Monaro and Princes Highways was updated. **Narooma**, **Montague Island** and **Bermagui** are famous for their big-game fishing. Black marlin, blue fin and hammerhead sharks are the main catch. Narooma also boasts an 18-hole cliff-side golf course where you tee off from the third hole across a narrow canyon.

Bega, to the south, is the unofficial capital of the area and is an important dairying and cheese-making centre. As Bega is about 10 minutes inland from the coast and 2 hours from the snow fields, the town's proud boast is that you can ski in the Snowies and surf in the Pacific on the same day. Further south is the popular holiday resort of **Merimbula** and its sister village of **Pambula**.

The southernmost town of the region is the quaint old fishing village of **Eden**, and its former rival settlement, **Boydtown**, both reminders of the colourful whaling days of the last century.

Fishing is excellent all along the coast. You can catch a wide variety of fish, including rock cod, bream and jew-fish, from the beach or net crayfish off the rockier parts of the coast. Prawning is good in the scattered inlets; and trout and perch can be caught in the many rivers draining from the mountains.

Because of its position, the South Coast attracts tourists from Victoria and Canberra, as well as from other parts of New South Wales. The region's all-year-round mild climate has made it a favourite with visitors, but you must book well ahead in the peak holiday period.

For further information, contact the Sapphire Coast Tourist Association, Zingle Pl, Pacific Hwy (PO Box 424), Bega; (064) 92 3313. **See also:** Individual town entries in A–Z listing. **Note** detailed map of South Coast on page 117.

Coast near Merimbula

Jenolan Caves. Kanangra–Boyd National Park; major access off Oberon–Jenolan Caves Rd, 5 km s of caves. Abercrombie House (1870s), 6 km w, on Ophir Rd; baronial-style Gothic mansion. Hill End Historic Site, 86 km nw; former goldfield, many original buildings, some restored. Visitor Centre in old Hill End Hospital. Equipment for panning and fossicking for hire in village. Other old gold towns nearby include Rockley, O'Connell, Trunkey Creek and Sofala. Farm holidays available; check with tourist information centre. **Tourist information:** William St; (063) 33 6288. **Accommodation:** 7 hotels, 12 motels, 3 caravan/camping parks.
MAP REF. 104 A3, 120 F7

Batlow   Pop. 1143

This timber-milling and former gold-mining town in the Great Dividing Range 33 km s of Tumut is situated in a district renowned for its apples, pears and berry fruits. **Of interest:** Granny Smith's Country Cottage, Pioneer St; arts, crafts, teas and tourist information. Historical Society Museum, Mayday Rd. Mountain Maid Cannery, off Kurrajong Ave, and Batlow Fruit Packing Complex, Forest Rd. Superb town views from Weemala Lookout Flora and Fauna Reserve, H.V. Smith Dr. **In the area:** Hume and Hovell's Lookout, 6 km e; views over Lake Blowering and picnic area at site where explorers paused in 1824. Lake Blowering, 20 km e; picnic/barbecue facilities. Spectacular Buddong Falls, 25 km s; picnic/barbecue facilities, fine-weather road only. Bushwalks and drives through scenic areas on south-west slopes of Bago State Forest. Access points to 370 km Hume and Hovell Walking Trail, which runs from Yass to Albury. Several farms on Tumut Rd offer pick-your-own berry fruits and cherries. **Tourist information:** Pioneer St; (069) 49 1447. **Accommodation:** 1 hotel, 1 motel, 1 camping/caravan park.
MAP REF. 119 B6, 120 C13, 140 A4

Bega   Pop. 4202

It is possible to surf and ski on the same day when staying at Bega, set as it is between the beach and the Kosciusko snow resorts. The town is sited at the junction of the Princes and Snowy Mountains Hwys, which link Sydney, Melbourne and Canberra. **Of interest:** Bega Family Historical Museum, cnr Bega and Auckland Sts. Grevillea Estate Winery, Buckajo Rd; tastings and sales. Inspection of Bega Cheese Factory, North Bega (well signposted). **In the area:** Bega Valley Lookout (2 km n) and Dr George Lookout (8 km ne) for fine views. Brogo Valley Rotolactor, 18 km n; see cows being milked. Tathna, 18 km e; beautiful beaches and historic wharf. Mimosa Rocks National Park, 17 km n of Tathra, offers swimming, fishing and bushwalking. Water sports on Wallagoot Lake, 10 km s of Tathra. Bushwalking, fishing and canoeing at Bournda National Park, 20 km se of Bega. Historic village of Candelo, 23 km sw, untouched by time; art gallery and monthly market. **Tourist information:** Gipps St; (064) 92 2045. **Accommodation:** 5 hotels, 5 motels, 2 caravan/camping parks. **See also:** The South Coast.
MAP REF. 117 F7, 119 F10, 235 P6

Bellingen   Pop. 2298

Attractive tree-lined town on the banks of the Bellinger River in the rich dairylands of the Bellinger Valley. In pioneer days it was a timber-getting and ship-building centre. **Of interest:** Much of town classified by Heritage Commission. Restored Hammond and Wheatley Emporium. Jazz Festival held Aug. Azalea Fair Sept. Agricultural Show in Nov. **In the area:** River walks. Scenic island in river, with flying fox colony. Picnicking at Thora, 14 km w, at foot of Mt Dorrigo. State forests for bushwalking and horseriding. Trout fishing in streams on Dorrigo Plateau. **Tourist information:** Yellow Shed, cnr High and Prince Sts; (066) 55 1189. **Accommodation:** 1 hotel, 1 motel, 1 caravan/camping park.
MAP REF. 123 O8, 475 M12

Bermagui   Pop. 1166

Fishing in all forms—lake, estuary, deep-sea and big-game—is excellent in this delightful small port, 13 km from the Princes Hwy. It was much publicised for its fishing by American novelist-sportsman Zane Grey in the 1930s. **Of interest:** Beautiful rock pools, rugged coastline and unspoiled countryside. **In the area:** Mimosa Rocks National Park, 20 km s; spectacular coast and mountain scenery, and Mumbula Mountain. Wallaga Lake National Park, 8 km n; boating, fishing, swimming, bushwalking and picnicking. Montague Island, 23 km n; mecca for big-game fishermen. Cobargo, on Princes Hwy, 19 km w; unspoiled old working village with several art galleries, wood and leather crafts, pottery and tea-rooms. **Tourist information:** 8 Coluga St; (064) 93 4174. **Accommodation:** Bermagui: 1 hotel, 4 motels, 5 caravan/camping parks. Cobargo: 1 motel. **See also:** The South Coast.
MAP REF. 117 H4, 119 G9, 141 M13, 235 Q4

Berridale   Pop. 949

A rural town near Lake Eucumbene, Lake Jindabyne and the southern ski fields. **Of interest:** St Marys Church (1860), off Kosciusko Rd. Berridale School (1883), Oliver St. In Exchange Sq., Berridale Inn (1863). Snowy River Ag Barn and Fibre Centre, and Snowy River Winery, on road south to Dalgety. **In the area:** Eucumbene Trout Farm, 30 km n; fishing sales, horseriding, animals and farm tours. Llama farm, on Snowy Mountains Hwy, 43 km ne. **Tourist information:** Snowy River Shire Council, 2 Myack St; (064) 56 3251. **Accommodation:** 1 hotel, 5 motels, 1 caravan/camping park.
MAP REF. 118 I10, 119 D9, 140 E12, 235 K4

Berrigan   Pop. 949

A traditional country town with many old buildings reflecting a bygone era, Berrigan is the headquarters of the Berrigan Shire Council and is best known for its connections with horseracing. **Of interest:** Historic buildings. Berrigan Racecourse and Kilfenora Racing Stables. Sojourn Station Art Studio. Golf course and other sports amenities. **Tourist information:** River Foreshore, Tocumwal; (058) 74 2131. **Accommodation:** 3 hotels, 1 hotel/motel, 1 motel, 1 caravan/camping park.
MAP REF. 127 M12, 233 J1

Berrima   Pop. 723

A superbly preserved 1830s Australian town. **Of interest:** Many old buildings restored as craft and antique shops, restaurants and galleries. White Horse Inn (1832). Australia's oldest licensed hotel, the Surveyor General (1834), still operating. Harper's Mansion (1834). Historical Museum. Gaol (1839), still in use. Courthouse; display and excellent video of early Berrima. Australian Alpaca Centre, Market Pl; knitwear, chat to alpacas at weekends. **Tourist information:** Winifred West Park, Old Hume

Hwy, Mittagong; (048) 71 2888. **Accommodation:** 2 motels.
MAP REF. 116 B7, 119 H3, 120 H10

Berry   Pop. 1570
Old English trees add to the charm of this picturesque township on the Princes Hwy, 18 km N of Nowra. In rich dairying country, it was founded by David Berry, whose brother Alexander was the first European settler in the Shoalhaven area. **Of interest:** Several buildings with National Trust classifications, including Historical Museum, Queen St. Antique shops; art and craft centres. Antique Fair Oct. Market at Showgrounds, first Sun. in month. **In the area:** Cambewarra Lookout, 14 km W. Coolangatta, 11 km SE, on site of first white settlement in area in 1822; group of convict-built cottages, restored and converted into historic village and resort. **Tourist information:** Princes Hwy, Bomaderry; (044) 21 0778. **Accommodation:** 1 hotel, 2 motels.
MAP REF. 116 F11, 119 H4, 120 I11

Bingara   Pop. 1231
Diamonds, sapphires, tourmalines and gold may be found in the creeks and rivers of this fascinating town. **Of interest:** All Nations Gold Mine, top of Hill St. Historical Society Museum (1860), in slab building thought to be town's first hotel and classified by National Trust; houses collection of old furniture and photographs depicting early days of district. Murray Cod Hatchery, Bandalong St; inspection by appt. Good fishing in town's rivers and creeks. **In the area:** Upper Bingara goldfields, 24 km S; remains of old gold and copper mines, also Chinese cemetery. Glacial area at Rocky Creek, 37 km SW; scenic, good spot for gold panning. Copeton Dam, 42 km E; fishing and boating, excellent camping and holiday accommodation. **Tourist information:** Bingara Advocate, 34 Maitland St; (067) 24 1127. **Accommodation:** 2 hotels, 1 motel, 1 caravan/camping park. **See also:** New England.
MAP REF. 122 I6, 474 I11

Blayney   Pop. 2652
A rural town close to the historic villages of Carcoar and Millthorpe, on the Mid Western Hwy between Cowra and Bathurst. **Of interest:** Forever Country, Adelaide St; local crafts. Agricultural Show held March. **In the area:** Taroona

Wool Pack, 8 km E, on Bathurst Rd. Cottesbrook Galleries, on Mid Western Hwy, 15 km E. Carcoar, 14 km SW, reminiscent of English village and scene of NSW's first bank hold-up in 1863; many delightful buildings and shops, pleasant picnic areas and Stokes Stable Museum. Carcoar Dam, 15 km S; picnic areas, fishing, water sports and overnight camping. Golden Memories Museum and Millthorpe Crafts and Book Store at Millthorpe, 13 km N. **Tourist information:** Blayney City Council, 91 Adelaide St; (063) 68 2104. **Accommodation:** 4 hotels, 1 motel, 1 caravan/camping park.
MAP REF. 120 F7

Boggabri   Pop. 751
Situated 115 km NW of Tamworth, this town is the centre of a wool, wheat and cotton area. **Of interest:** Historical Museum, Brent St. Honey factory, Lynn St; inspection by appt. Wean Picnic Races held in May. Gum Tree Clay Pigeon Shoot, Oct. Labour Day weekend. **In the area:** Gemstone fossicking. Fishing. Gin's Leap, rock formation, 4 km N. Dripping Rock waterfall, on Manilla Rd, 35 km E. Farm visits and accommodation. **Tourist information:** Newell Hwy, Narrabri; (067) 92 3583. **Accommodation:** 3 hotels, 1 motel, 1 caravan/camping park.
MAP REF. 122 G8, 474 H13

Bombala   Pop. 1404
This small town on the Monaro Hwy, 89 km S of Cooma, supports wool, beef cattle, sheep, vegetables and timber-milling and is a rich trout-fishing area. **Of interest:** Self-guide Historical Walk (1 hr) around town includes Old Mechanics Institute and courthouse. White House Gallery (c.1835), Caveat St. Folk Museum, Mahratta St; local artefacts, farm implements. **In the area:** Historic homestead, Burnima, 6 km N on Monaro Hwy; open by arrangement. Coolumbooka Nature Reserve, 15 km NE. Goldmines at Craigie, 33 km SW. Scenic drive to Bendoc Mines, 57 km SW into Vic.; gold fossicking along route, with landowners' permission. **Tourist information:** The White House, 34 Caveat St; (064) 58 3751. **Accommodation:** 3 hotels, 1 motel, 1 caravan/camping park.
MAP REF. 117 A9, 119 E11, 235 M7

Bourke   Pop. 2976
Anything 'Back o' Bourke is the real outback. Bourke itself is the service centre of a vast area of sheep country that produces up to 55 000 bales of wool a year. It is claimed to be the largest centre for wool shipment in the world. **Of interest:** Tourist Centre in Old Railway Station, Anson St; Aboriginal artefacts, products of local industries, historic displays. Fred Hollows' grave and Memorial in cemetery, Cobar Rd. Cotton Gin,

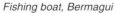
Fishing boat, Bermagui

National Parks

The national parks of New South Wales encompass areas ranging from World Heritage-listed rainforests to unspoiled beaches. Tourists return time and time again to these popular scenic retreats, which offer a wide range of activities for holiday-makers. Many of the parks, particularly those on the eastern edge of the State, suffered damage during the devastating bushfires in January 1994. At the time of going to press, the extent of damage to those parks affected and to their visitor facilities was unavailable. Visitors planning to visit national parks along the central and south coasts should check first with the National Parks and Wildlife Service; (02) 585 6333.

Many of the State's parks are found along the coast, their rugged headlands, quiet inlets and sweeping beaches pounded by the crashing surf. The easy accessibility of these coastal parks accounts for their popularity. **Sydney Harbour National Park** is made up of pockets of bushland encircling Sydney Harbour and is the closest National Park to the city.

Among the 76 parks proclaimed in New South Wales is Australia's first, the Royal National Park, just 32 kilometres south of Sydney. Established in 1879, **Royal National Park** has over 16 000 hectares of sandstone plateau country, broken here and there by fine surf beaches, including Wattamolla and Garie. Over 90 per cent

of the Park was destroyed in the bushfires. The Hacking River runs almost the entire length of the park. Boats may be hired at Audley and visitors can row in leisurely fashion up the river, following its twisting course.

Also south of Sydney is **Botany Bay National Park** in two sections: the northern section contains the sandy beaches of La Perouse and features a maritime museum (guided tours available) while the southern section at Kurnell protects the site of Captain Cook's first Australian landing in 1770. Here a staffed Discovery Centre has exhibitions of the history of the area.

Just north of Sydney are two prominent national parks, on the southern and northern shores of the Hawkesbury River: **Ku-ring-gai Chase** and **Brisbane Water National Parks,** which are renowned for their sheltered creeks and inlets, ideal for boating, and bushland walking tracks adorned with wildflowers. Both suffered bushfire damage.

Ku-ring-gai Chase, established in 1894 and only 24 kilometres from Sydney, hugs the shores of Cowan Creek, Broken Bay and Pitt Water. Comprising 15 000 hectares of open rainforest, eucalypt forests, scrub and heath, it is the home of a wide range of animal life, including the shy swamp wallaby, the elusive lyrebird, honeyeaters, waterbirds, colourful parrots and lorikeets. A small colony of koalas

dwells in the eucalypt forest. Aboriginal hand stencils and rock engravings are accessed by a network of walking tracks.

Brisbane Water also has sandstone landscapes rich in Aboriginal art. There are scenic views from Warrah Trig and Staples Lookout, while Somersby Falls and Girakool picnic areas mark the beginning of rainforest walks.

Nearby is **Dharug National Park,** its sandstone cliffs rising high above the meandering Hawkesbury River; it too suffered bushfire damage. A network of walking tracks includes a section of the convict-built Old Great North Road.

Further inland, to the west of Sydney, are splendid parks nestling in the mountains that overawed the early explorers. Year after year, innumerable visitors return to the **Blue Mountains National Park**, where mysterious blue mists shroud the immense valleys of the Grose and Coxs Rivers, creating ever-changing patterns of colours: green, blue and purple. Large sections were burnt out during the January fires.

At Katoomba, pillars of weathered sandstone rise abruptly like isolated church spires: these are the Three Sisters, the most popular tourist attraction in the Blue Mountains.

The World Heritage **New England National Park**, which preserves one of the largest remaining areas of rainforest in New South Wales, is 576 kilometres

Kinchega National Park

north-east of Sydney. Its 29 985 hectares cover three distinct zones: subalpine with tall snow gums; temperate forests of ancient moss-covered Antarctic beeches; and true subtropical rainforests, rich in ferns, vines and orchids. The park has a diverse range of flora and fauna including the rare rufous scrub-bird. Some 20 kilometres of walking tracks reveal to visitors the silent charm of the rainforest, while the trackless wilderness attracts more experienced bushwalkers. The World Heritage **Dorrigo National Park** protects the rainforests of northern NSW. At the Rainforest Centre, visitors can experience the sights, sounds and smells of rainforests. The Skywalk provides magnificent panoramas over the rainforest canopy to the Bellinger Valley and Pacific Ocean beyond. **Yuraygir** and **Bundjalung National Parks** to the north and south respectively of the mighty Clarence River on the far north coast, are a water wonderland with isolated beaches, quiet lakes and striking scenery. The parks deserve their reputation as prime areas for fishing. Surfing is also popular; their waterways invite exploration by canoe; and the estuaries offer safe swimming. Heathwalking offers opportunities for birdwatching and nature photography, particularly in spring when both parks explode in a spectacle of colour.

In the far north of the State, **Border Ranges**, **Mount Warning** and **Nightcap National Parks** offer the visitor vistas of World Heritage-listed rainforest. The 31 508 hectare Border Ranges includes the rim of the ancient volcano once centred on Mt Warning to the east. This is best accessed via the spectacular Tweed Scenic Drive. Stunning escarpments, waterfalls, and walking tracks from picnic areas abound in the eastern part.

Known to the Aborigines as 'Wollumbin', the cloud-catcher, Mt Warning (1157 metres) dominates the landscape and catches the first rays of the rising sun on the continent. A walk through Breakfast Creek rainforest leads to a steep climb and the summit viewing platform. Nightcap National Park is also part of the volcanic remnants of Mt Warning and contains the famous summit viewing platform and Protector Falls, a popular destination.

One park popular throughout the year is **Warrumbungle National Park**, located on the western slopes of the Great Divide, 491 kilometres north-west of Sydney. Here is some of the most spectacular scenery in the nation: sheltered gorges, rocky spires, permanent freshwater springs.

At Warrumbungle, east meets west: the dry western plains and moist eastern coast combine to give high peaks covered with gums and lower forests filled with fragrant native trees and shrubs. Walking trails lead to lookout points where hikers are rewarded with the fascinating colours of sunrise and sunset. In the spring and summer months, the colourful displays of wildflowers and the calls of brightly plumaged birds lure many visitors. Easy access tracks for families and the disabled are also available.

Mount Kaputar National Park, near Narrabri, is one of Australia's most accessible wilderness areas. Its vegetation ranges from rainforest to subalpine, and the park is rich in flora and fauna. One of the highlights in the park is Sawn Rocks, a 40-metre-high rock formation resembling a series of organ pipes. This is some of the finest columnar jointing in the country and represents one of the various volcanic formations found in the park.

The largest coastal lake system in New South Wales is protected by the **Myall Lakes National Park**, an important waterbird habitat. Water is the focus of tourist activities: sailing and canoeing on the quiet lake waters; surfing and beach fishing off the shores of the Pacific Ocean.

The largest national park in New South Wales is **Kosciusko**. Its 690 000 hectares include mainland Australia's only glacial lakes, as well as limestone caves, grasslands, heaths and woodlands. Situated 450 kilometres south-west of Sydney, this park is of particular significance because it embraces a large area of the continent's largest alpine region and contains Australia's highest mountains as well as the sources of the important Murray, Snowy and Murrumbidgee Rivers. Here are the most extensive snowfields of the nation, ski resorts including Thredbo, Perisher, Smiggin Holes, Blue Cow mountain, Mt Selwyn and Charlotte Pass. There are easy grades for beginners and slopes for expert skiers. Although Kosciusko is associated with winter sports, it is also a superb summer retreat with its crisp, clean air, crystal-clear lakes and a wonderful display of alpine wildflowers. This is a popular venue for those who enjoy camping, fishing, boating and bushwalking. Yarrangobilly Caves, perhaps the first site within the park to be developed for tourism, is open all-year round subject to winter road conditions. Yarrangobilly boasts 4 tourist caves—one with wheelchair access—a naturally heated thermal pool, nature trails, facilities for BYO picnics and historic grounds.

There are a number of national parks in the southern part of the State, some of which suffered bushfire damage, including **Morton National Park**, particularly renowned for the Fitzroy, Belmore and Carrington Falls, and **Budderoo National Park** which boasts the award-winning Minnamurra Rainforest Centre.

Over 9000 hectares of rocky but beautiful coastline flanking Twofold Bay make up **Ben Boyd National Park**. Flowering heaths and colourful banksias add to the area's attraction. Boyd's Tower, constructed in the 1840s, is a prominent feature of the park.

In the far west of New South Wales are four outstanding national parks. **Kinchega**, 110 kilometres south-east of Broken Hill, contains the beautiful saucer-shaped overflow lakes of the Darling River. The lakes provide a most important breeding ground for a wide variety of waterbirds, including herons, ibises, spoonbills and black swans. Walking tracks through forests of river red gums and scenic drives follow the course of the river and the lake shores.

North-east of Wentworth is the World Heritage-listed **Mungo National Park**, part of the Willandra Lakes World Heritage Area. The shores of the now dry lake hold a continuous record of Aboriginal life dating back more than 40 000 years. The remarkable 'Walls of China', a great crescent-shaped dune, stretches along the eastern shore of the lake bed. Visitors can enjoy the park on a day trip or take advantage of the shearers' quarters accommodation or camping facilities available. A 60-km, self-guide drive tour and self-guide walking tracks provide visitors with the opportunity to see and learn about the many attractions of the parks.

Mootwingee National Park, covering an area of 68 912 hectares and 130 kilometres north-east of Broken Hill, offers breathtaking scenery and a rich heritage of Aboriginal art.

The most remote national park in the State is **Sturt**, 1400 kilometres from Sydney and 330 kilometres north of Broken Hill. This is an ideal place for those who want to get away from it all and experience the real Australian outback. The park's 310 634 hectares comprise scenic red sand dunes, rocky ridges, ephemeral lakes and billabongs and Mitchell grass plains. Visitors must come well prepared but may camp within the park and enjoy bushwalking over the sandplains. Wildflowers, which include the scarlet and black blooms of Sturt's desert pea, are abundant in good seasons. Fort Grey, where Sturt and his party built a stockade to protect their supplies, will repay a visit, even though there is little evidence of his occupation today.

For further information about the national parks of New South Wales, contact the National Parks and Wildlife Service, 43 Bridge St (PO Box 1967), Hurstville, NSW 2220; (02) 585 6333.

Lighthouse at Cape Byron, Byron Bay

Cobar Rd; open for tours. Fishing for cod in Darling River. Annual events include: Festival of Sport at Easter, Breakaway to Bourke and Bourke to B— (a different destination each year, but always a name starting with 'B') Bash in June, picnic races in Aug. and Sept., Mateship Festival and Outback Trek in Sept. and Outback Surf Classic in Oct. Annual Explorers Trial car rally leaves Bourke for Warrumbungle National Park each Easter. **In the area:** Mt Gunderbooka, 74 km S; caves with Aboriginal art. Fort Bourke Stockade, 20 km SW; testament to early explorer Major Thomas Mitchell. Mt Oxley, 40 km E; superb views of plains. **Tourist information:** Old Railway Station, 45 Anson Street; (068) 72 2280. **Accommodation:** 4 hotels, 4 motels, 2 caravan/camping parks.
MAP REF. 125 N6, 474 A12, 485 P12

Bowral   Pop. 7929

The friendly township of Bowral nestles below Mount Gibraltar, 114 km S of Sydney. Originally a popular summer retreat for wealthy Sydney residents, who left a legacy of stately mansions and beautiful gardens, Bowral today is a thriving town with a harmonious blending of modern and colonial architecture. **Of interest:** Corbett Gardens, Merigang St, showpiece of Tulip Time Festival held in Sept., as are Milton Park Gardens, Horderns Rd. Bradman Oval, near house where cricketer Sir Donald Bradman spent his youth, and the Bradman Museum, St Jude St. Specialty shopping in

antiques, especially Bong Bong St. Alpaca Haven, Bong Bong St; knitwear and fleeces, pat alpacas at weekends. Many restaurants, and a variety of accommodation from country resorts to guest houses and bed-and-breakfast cottages. **In the area:** Lookout on Mt Gibraltar, 2 km N. **Tourist information:** Winifred West Park, Old Hume Hwy, Mittagong; (048) 71 2888. **Accommodation:** 2 hotels, 6 motels.
MAP REF. 116 C7, 119 H3, 120 I10

Braidwood   Pop. 976

This old town, 84 km S of Goulburn, has been declared an historic village by the National Trust. Gold was discovered in the area in 1852 and Braidwood developed as the principal town of the southern goldfields. Much of the architecture from this period has survived. **Of interest:** Museum, churches, old hotels, restaurants, galleries, craft and antique shops. Self-guide tour of town's historic buildings. Scenic drive of area; leaflet at Museum. **Tourist information:** Museum, Wallace St; (048) 42 2310. **Accommodation:** 1 hotel, 3 motels.
MAP REF. 119 F6, 120 G13, 141 L4

Brewarrina   Pop. 1168

Located 95 km E of Bourke, this town takes its name from an Aboriginal word meaning 'good fishing', which is still appropriate. Pastoral activities include grazing and wheat production. **Of interest:** Aboriginal fisheries in bed of Darling River. Aboriginal Cultural Museum,

Bathurst St, presents aspects of Aboriginal life from Dreamtime to present. Festival of Fisheries held in early Sept. Wildlife park in Doyle St. **In the area:** Narran Lake, 40 km E, for native birdlife and other fauna. **Tourist information:** Shire Offices, Bathurst St; (068) 39 2308. **Accommodation:** 2 hotels, 1 motel, 1 caravan/camping park.
MAP REF. 125 P5, 474 C11, 485 R12

Broken Hill   Pop. 23 263

This artificial oasis in the vast arid lands of far western NSW was created to serve the miners working in the rich silver-lead-zinc mines of the Barrier Range. The green parks and colourful gardens, 1170 km W of Sydney, seem unreal in the semi-desert setting. The city's water supply comes from local storage schemes and from the Menindee Lakes on the Darling River. The mines produce 2 million tonnes of ore annually. Note that Broken Hill operates on Central Standard Time, that is, half an hour behind the rest of NSW. **Of interest:** Self-guide Heritage Trails. Historic streetscape (Argent St) classified by National Trust. Railway, Mineral and Train Museum, cnr Blende and Bromide Sts. Geo Centre Museum, cnr Crystal and Bromide Sts. White's Mineral Art and Mining Museum, Allendale St. Many art galleries, including Entertainment Centre, cnr Blende and Chloride Sts, featuring Silver Tree, commissioned by Charles Rasp, discoverer of Broken Hill ore-body in 1883. Broken Hill is home of legendary Brushmen of the Bush, group of artists that includes Pro Hart and Jack Absalom. Inspection of School of the Air, cnr McCulloch and Lane Sts. Mine tours to Delprat's Mine, off Crystal St. Moslem Mosque (1891), Buck St; built by Afghan community then living in town. **In the area:** Inspection of Royal Flying Doctor Service, 10 km E, at airport. Zinc Twin Lakes, off Wentworth Rd, South Broken Hill. Water sports, fishing and camping at Menindee Lakes, 110 km SE. Fred Hollows Sculpture Symposium, 6 km N on Nine Mile Rd; leaflet at tourist office. Sundown Nature Trail, 9 km N on Tibooburra Rd. Silverton, 24 km NW, where silver chlorides were discovered in 1883; used as location for *Wake in Fright*, *Mad Max 2* and *A Town Like Alice*. At Silverton: tours of Day Dream Mine; Heritage Walking Trail; Peter Browne's Art Gallery; Horizon Gallery; Silverton Hotel; Silverton Gaol Museum; camel rides. Mundi Mundi Plains Lookout, 4 km further N, and Umberumberka Reservoir Lookout, 39 km NW. Mootwingee National Park, 130 km NE of Broken Hill; magnificent scenery and rich in Aboriginal rock art and stencils. Visitors are advised to be fully self-sufficient in food, water and fuel. **Tourist information:** Cnr Blende and Bromide Sts; (080) 87 6077. **Accommodation:** 12 hotels, 13 motels, 3 caravan/camping parks. MAP REF. 124 C12

Brunswick Heads   Pop. 1662

This town at the mouth of the Brunswick River is renowned for its outstanding fishing, and a large commercial fishing fleet is based here. **Of interest:** Canoes for hire; good surfing, swimming. Annual events: Fish and Chips (wood chop) Festival in Jan.; Blessing of the Fleet and Fishing Festival at Easter; River Festival in Nov. Popular Brunswick Heads Markets held first Sat. of month. **In the area:** New Brighton Hotel, old pub with character, at Billinudgel, 7 km N. Pioneer Plantation at Mooball, 14 km N, offers guided tours of banana farm and walk-through wildlife habitat. Crystal Castle, outside Mullumbimby, 10 km W; collection of crystal. Cape Byron lighthouse at Byron Bay, 19 km S. Minyon Falls, 50 km SW; picnic area in Rummery Park, with walking tracks. **Tourist information:** 69 Jonson St, Byron Bay; (066) 85 8050. **Accommodation:** 1 hotel, 4 motels, 3 caravan/camping parks. MAP REF. 123 P2, 475 O8

Bulahdelah   Pop. 1097

Situated on the Pacific Hwy at the foot of Alum Mountain, Bulahdelah is a good base for a bushwalking or houseboating holiday. **Of interest:** Mountain, which has huge alonite rock deposits, also well known for its rare varieties of rock orchids. **In the area:** Bulahdelah Logging Railway, 19 km N; full-size steam tourist train, runs Fri., Sat. and school holidays. Myall Lakes National Park, 12 km E, one of State's largest networks (10 000 ha) of coastal lakes; water activities, and bushwalking and camping in rainforest. **Tourist information:** Little St, Forster; (065) 54 8799. **Accommodation:** 4 motels, 2 caravan/camping parks. MAP REF. 121 M3

Bundanoon   Pop. 1513

This charming township is 32 km S of Mittagong. The area is renowned for its deep gullies and magnificent views over the rugged mountains and gorges of the Morton National Park. Lookouts can be reached by car or on foot. In April, when the mists roll in, Bundanoon becomes Brigadoon for a day and celebrates with highland games. Bundanoon was once well known as a honeymoon resort: today it boasts an English-style pub, delightful guest houses and a health resort. The train stops in the heart of the town. **Tourist information:** Winifred West Park, Old Hume Hwy, Mittagong; (048) 71 2888. **Accommodation:** 1 hotel, 2 motels, 2 caravan/camping parks. MAP REF. 116 A9, 119 H3, 120 H11

Byron Bay   Pop. 5001

Surfers from near and far gravitate to Wategos Beach, on Cape Byron. Its northerly aspect makes it one of the best beaches for surfboard riding on the east coast. Dairy products, bacon, beef and tropical fruits are produced locally. Visitors can go bushwalking, horseriding, fishing, swimming, scuba diving or paragliding, or just enjoy the delightful climate and relaxing lifestyle of this idyllic spot. **In the area:** Australia's most powerful lighthouse, 3 km SE at Cape Byron, most easterly point on Australian mainland; walking trail and lookout. Award-winning Wheel Resort, 3 km S; caters especially for disabled visitors. Ocean Shores Golf Course; 1½ km N, considered best in State. **Tourist information:** 80 Jonson St; (066) 85 8050.

Accommodation: 1 hotel, 22 motels, 6 caravan/camping parks. MAP REF. 123 Q2, 475 O8

Camden   Pop. 8440

In 1805, John Macarthur was granted 5000 acres at what was known as the Cowpastures, where he began his famous sheep-breeding experiments. The township of Camden dates from 1840, and is 60 km SW of Sydney on Camden Valley Way. **Of interest:** Many historic buildings, including Belgenny Farm (1819) and Camden Park House (1834), both part of Macarthur's Camden Estate, Elizabeth Macarthur Dr; Church of St John the Evangelist (1840–49), John St; Camelot, designed by J. Horbury Hunt, and Kirkham Stables (1816), both in Kirkham Lane. Camden History Museum, John St. **In the area:** Struggletown Fine Arts Complex, 3 km N. El Caballo Blanco, featuring famous dancing Andalusian horses; also horse-drawn carriage museum, large wildlife reserve and fun park. Historic Gledswood Homestead and winery, next door to El Caballo Blanco; both at Catherine Field, 10 km N. Museum of Aviation at Narellan, 3 km NE. Mt Annan Botanic Garden on Narellan Rd. Camden Aerodrome, 3 km NW; ballooning, gliding, vintage aircraft. Oran Park Raceway, 4 km W; bike, car and truck racing. **Tourist information:** Macarthur Country Tourist Assocn, cnr Hume Hwy and Congressional Dr, Liverpool; (02) 821 2311. **Accommodation:** 4 motels, 1 hotel, 1 caravan/camping park. **See also:** Vineyards and Wineries. MAP REF. 104 I11, 116 F1, 119 I2, 120 I9

Camden Haven   Pop. 4384

A fisherman's dream, consisting of the villages Laurieton, North Haven and Dunbogan, less than 3 km apart, 44 km S of Port Macquarie; Camden Haven has a tidal inlet for estuary fishing. **Of interest:** Oysters, lobsters, crabs, bream and flathead, in local rivers and lakes. Seafront well-known fishing spot. Delightful bushwalks along seafront and around lakes. River cruises. Panoramic views from North Brother Mountain. **In the area:** Rainforest with waterfalls, 60 km W at Comboyne Plateau. Timbertown, 34 km NW at Wauchope; re-creation of 1880s town, open daily. **Tourist information:** Pacific Hwy, Kew; (065) 59 4400. **Accommodation:** Laurieton: 1 hotel, 3 motels, 2 caravan/camping

The Snowy Mountains

The Snowy Mountains are a magnet to tourists all year round. The combination of easily accessible mountains, alpine heathlands, forests, lakes, streams and dams is hard to beat. In winter, skiers flock to the snug, well-equipped snow resorts in the area. As the snow melts, anglers, bushwalkers, water-skiers and boating enthusiasts move in. The ski resorts are popular in both summer and winter.

The creation of the Snowy Mountains Hydro-electric Scheme was indirectly responsible for boosting tourism. The roads built for the Scheme through the previously inaccessible mountain country helped to open up the area, which is now used for winter sports.

All the snow resorts of the Snowy Mountains are within Kosciusko National Park, which is the largest national park in the State and includes the highest plateau in the Australian continent. Mount Kosciusko (2228 m) is its highest peak.

The major ski areas are: Thredbo, Perisher, Smiggin Holes, Mt Blue Cow–Guthega, and Charlotte Pass in the southern part of the Kosciusko National Park; and Mt Selwyn in the north.

The resorts are easily accessible and the major centres have first-class amenities such as chairlifts, ski-tows, motels, hotels, restaurants, lodges, apres-ski entertainment, and expert instruction. The snow sports season officially begins on the long weekend in June and continues until mid- or late-October.

Thredbo Village, 96 kilometres from Cooma at the foot of the Crackenback Range. This world-class resort has the only giant slalom course in Australia approved by the world skiing control board. It is the site for international skiing events. There is a wide range of facilities for skiers at all levels. The chairlift to the summit of Mt Crackenback operates through the summer. Thredbo has a wide range of amenities, restaurants and entertainment, including year-round paragliding. Ski hire and instruction.

Charlotte Pass, 98 kilometres from Cooma and 8 kilometres from the summit of Mt Kosciusko. A convenient base for ski tours to some of Australia's highest peaks and most spectacular ski runs.

Perisher, 90 kilometres from Cooma. One of the highest and most popular ski resorts in the area; caters for both downhill and cross-country skiers. Ski hire and instruction.

Smiggin Holes, 89 kilometres from Cooma. Linked to Perisher by ski-lifts and a free shuttle bus service. Ski hire and instruction.

Mt Selwyn, at the northern end of Kosciusko National Park, has been designed for beginners, families and school groups. Mt Selwyn is one of the main centres for cross-country skiing. No overnight accommodation. Ski hire and instruction.

Mt Blue Cow–Guthega can be reached only by the Skitube underground railway, which runs from Bullocks Flat terminal near Jindabyne up to Perisher Valley and on to Mt Blue Cow. No overnight accommodation. Ski hire and instruction.

For further information on the Snowy Mountains, contact the Visitors Centre at Sawpit Creek; (064) 56 2102. **See also:** Safe Skiing. **Note** detailed map of Snowy Mountains on page 118.

Guthega Dam

parks; North Haven: 2 motels, 3 caravan/camping parks; Dunbogan: 2 caravan/camping parks.
MAP REF. 109 G10

Campbelltown   Pop. 10 004

Named by Governor Macquarie in 1820 after his wife's maiden name, Campbelltown is now a rapidly growing city. It is also the location for the legend of Fisher's ghost: the ghost of a murdered convict is alleged to have pointed to the place where his body was subsequently found and as a result the murderer was brought to justice. **Of interest:** Campbelltown City Bicentennial Art Gallery and Japanese Gardens, Art Gallery Rd, cnr Camden and Appin Rds. Historic buildings include Glenalvon (1840) and Richmond Villa (1830–40) in Lithgow St; Colonial Houses at 284–298 Queen St; St Peter's Church (1823), Cordeaux St; Old St John's Church, cnr Broughton and George Sts, with grave of James Ruse; Emily Cottage (1840), cnr Menangle and Camden Rds; and Campbelltown Art and Craft Society (licensed as Farrier's Arms Inn in 1843) and Fisher's Ghost Restaurant, formerly Kendall's Millhouse (1844), both in Queen St. Annual Festival of Fisher's Ghost held in Nov. **In the area:** Eschol Park House (1820), 15 km N. Mount Annan Botanic Garden, 10 km W, on Narellan Rd. Steam and Machinery Museum, 5 km S on Menangle Rd. Menangle House (1839) and St James's Church at Menangle, 9 km SW. Horseriding available. **Tourist information:** Macarthur Country Tourist Assocn, cnr Hume Hwy and Congressional Dr, Liverpool; (02) 821 2311. **Accommodation:** 4 motels.
MAP REF. 105 J11,   116 G1,   119 I2, 121 J9

Canowindra   Pop. 1721

Bushranger Ben Hall and his gang commandeered this township in 1863. Canowindra today is known as the 'Balloon Capital of Australia'; hot-air balloons fly every weekend, March–Nov. Situated on the Belubula River, Canowindra is noted for its curving main street and notable buildings; the entire commercial section has been classified by the National Trust as a Heritage Conservation Area. **Of interest:** Fish fossils of world significance, 360 million years old; discovered 1956. Museum, antique shops and display gallery for Knitters Guild of NSW. **Tourist information:** Canowindra

Bakery, Gaskill St; (063) 44 1399. **Accommodation:** 3 hotels, 1 motel, 1 caravan/camping park.
MAP REF. 120 D7

Casino   Pop. 10 850

This important commercial centre on the Richmond River could be dubbed the city of parks. There are about 20 in all, most with picnic/barbecue facilities. **Of interest:** Casino Folk Museum, Walker St. Freshwater fishing on Cooke's Weir and Richmond River. Beef Reach 12-day festival in May; street parades, tours of meat works. **In the area:** Aboriginal rock carvings, 20 km W on Tenterfield Rd; take Dyrabba turnoff. **Tourist information:** Memorial Baths Centre, Centre St; (066) 62 3566. **Accommodation:** 3 hotels, 5 motels, 2 caravan/camping parks.
MAP REF. 123 O3, 475 N9

Cessnock   Pop. 17 506

Many excellent Hunter River table wines are produced in the Cessnock district. The economy of the city, formerly based on coal mining, is now centred on wine and tourism. **Of interest:** Galleries, antique and craft shops. Hunter Vintage Walkabout held Feb.–March. Wine and Food Affair Sept. Jazz in the Vines held Oct. **In the area:** Hot-air ballooning at Rothbury, 11 km N. Rusa Zoo, exotic wildlife park, at Nulkaba, 7 km NW. Peppers, guest house resort at Pokolbin, 14 km NW. Over 50 quality wineries open for tastings and sales in Pokolbin area. At Pelaw Main, 17 km E, Richmond Main Mining Museum; steam train rides. Picturesque village of Wollombi, 29 km SW, with wealth of historic buildings, including beautiful St John's Anglican Church, courthouse (now Endeavour Museum) and old-style general store-post office. Aboriginal cave paintings; tours. Horseriding. Watagan Mountains and State Forest, 33 km SE; picnic/barbecue facilities at Heaton, Hunter's and McLean's Lookouts. **Tourist information:** Turner Park, Aberdare; (049) 90 4477. **Accommodation:** 11 hotels, 28 motels, 3 caravan/camping parks.
MAP REF. 112 B10, 113 E11, 121 K5

Cobar   Pop. 4138

A progressive copper, gold, silver, lead and zinc mining town with wide tree-lined streets, Cobar is 723 km NW of Sydney. The town is on the Barrier Hwy, used by travellers to visit outback areas

of NSW, Qld and NT. Since the opening of the CSA Copper Mine in the mid-1960s, and the introduction of a channel water supply, the town has been transformed from an arid landscape to a green oasis. The CSA Mine, the most highly mechanised mine in Australia, has an annual output of 600 000 tonnes of copper and copper-zinc ores. The Elura silver-lead-zinc mine opened in 1983 and the Peak goldmine in 1992. Wool is the main local primary industry. **Of interest:** Regional Museum, Barrier Hwy; pastoral, mining and technological displays. Fine early architecture, including courthouse and police station, Barton St; St Laurence O'Toole Catholic Church, Prince St; and Great Western Hotel, Marshall St, with longest iron-lace verandah in State. **In the area:** Commonwealth Meteorological Station, 4 km NW; inspection by appointment. Mt Grenfell Aboriginal cave paintings, turn-off 40 km W on Barrier Hwy, near Mt Grenfell homestead; human and animal figures densely cover walls of rock shelters; picnic area nearby. **Tourist information:** Cobar Regional Museum, Barrier Hwy; (068) 36 2448. **Accommodation:** 2 hotels, 1 hotel/motel, 6 motels, 1 caravan/camping park.
MAP REF. 125 N10

Coffs Harbour   Pop. 20 326

One of the larger centres on the Holiday Coast, this subtropical resort town is 580 km N of Sydney on the Pacific Hwy. The surrounding districts produce timber, bananas, vegetables, dairy products and fish. Coffs Harbour is really two towns—one on the highway and the other near the artificial harbour and railway station. **Of interest:** Historic buildings include Pier Hotel (rebuilt 1920s) and jetty (1892). Coffs Harbour Museum, High St. Pet Porpoise Pool, Orlando St; sea circus with performing porpoises and seals, also research and nursery facilities. Aquajet Waterslide, Park Beach Rd. Mutton Bird Island National Park, 1 km walk on sea wall. North Coast Regional Botanical Gardens complex, Hardacre St. **In the area:** Clog-making and Dutch village at Clog Barn on Pacific Hwy, 2 km N. The Big Banana, 4 km N along Pacific Hwy; unusual concrete landmark in form of huge banana has displays inside illustrating banana industry; Big Banana Theme Park includes Aboriginal Dreamtime Cave experience and 'realistic' bunyip; World of Horticulture, with monorail, is nearby. Coastline views from surrounding area. Nude bathing at Little Digger Beach, 4 km N. Coffs Harbour Zoo, 14 km N; koalas, kangaroos, deer and wombats; also Devonshire teas. Bruxner Park Flora Reserve, Korora, 9 km NW; dense tropical jungle area of vines, ferns and orchids; bushwalking tracks and picnic area at Park Creek. Georges Gold Mine tours, 38 km W. Hot-air ballooning, white-water rafting, canoeing, game-fishing, scuba diving, horseriding, golf and 4WD tours. Self-guide tours through Wedding Bells State Forest and the Dorrego Region; 4WD only. **Tourist information:** Orara Pk, Pacific Hwy; (066) 52 1522. **Accommodation:** 9 hotels, 35 motels, 6 caravan/camping parks. MAP REF. 123 O7, 475 N12

Coleambally   Pop. 580

This, the State's newest town, officially opened in June 1968 and the centre of the Coleambally Irrigation Area, is south of the Murrumbidgee River. Rice is the main crop of the 87 600 ha under irrigation; vegetables, grain, sorghum, safflower and soya beans also are grown. The town has a modern shopping centre and a rice mill. **Of interest:** Wineglass Water Tower. **Tourist information:** Cnr Banna and Jondaryan Aves, Griffith; (069) 62 4145. **Accommodation:** 1 hotel, 1 motel. MAP REF. 127 N9

Condobolin   Pop. 3163

On the Lachlan River, 475 km W of Sydney, Condobolin is the centre of a red-soil plains district producing wool, fat lambs, fruit and mixed farm products. **Of interest:** Community Centre, in old hotel, cnr Bathurst and Dennison Sts. Gum Bend Lake and olympic swimming pool. **In the area:** Aboriginal relics, 40 km W, including monument marking burial place of one of last Lachlan tribal elders. Agricultural research station, 10 km E. Mt Tilga, 8 km N, said to be geographic centre of NSW; stiff climb to summit but view is worth it. **Accommodation:** 3 hotels, 1 hotel/motel, 2 motels, 1 caravan/camping park. MAP REF. 127 Q4

Cooma   Pop. 7385

This lively, modern tourist centre at the junction of the Monaro and Snowy Mountains Hwys, on the Southern Tablelands of NSW, was once dubbed Austra-

lia's most cosmopolitan town. Thousands of migrants from many different countries worked here on the Snowy Mountains Scheme. Today it is a busy tourist centre year-round, and the jumping-off point for the Snowies. (Motorists are advised to check their tyres and stock up on petrol and provisions before setting off for the snow country.) **Of interest:** Self-guide Lambie St Walk; historic buildings classified by National Trust. Old Gaol Museum, Vale St. Clog Maker, Sharp St; clog-making demonstration by Dutch craftsman. International Avenue of Flags, Centennial Park, Sharp St; flags of 27 countries, unfurled 1959 to commemorate 10th anniversary of Snowy Mountains Hydro-electric Authority and in recognition of nationalities of people who worked on project. The Time Walk, also in park; Bicentennial project presenting district history in 40 ceramic mosaics. Snowy Mountains Authority Information Centre, Monaro Hwy; displays, tours. Dodgem City Entertainment, Commissioner St. **In the area:** Southern Cloud Park, on Snowy Mountains Hwy, 1 km W; display (with audiotape) of remains of *Southern Cloud* aircraft, which crashed here in 1931, found 1958. Llama Farm, 13 km W on Snowy Mountains Hwy. Cloyne Rose Gardens, 4 km N. **Tourist information:** 119 Sharp St; (064) 50 1742. **Accommodation:** 7 hotels, 19 motels, 3 caravan/camping parks. MAP REF. 117 A2, 119 E9, 140 G11, 235 L3

Coonabarabran   Pop. 2959

A tourist-conscious town in the Warrumbungle Mountains on the Castlereagh River, 465 km NW of Sydney, near Warrumbungle National Park. **Of interest:** Woollen Yarn and Exhibition, Dalgarno St; shearing demonstrations during school holidays. Crystal Kingdom, Oxley Hwy, with unique collection of minerals from Warrumbungle Range. **In the area:** At Miniland, 8 km W, life-size models of prehistoric animals displayed in bushland setting; also children's fun park, kiosk, picnic/barbecue facilities and historical museum. Siding Spring Observatory set atop an extinct volcano, 24 km W, has largest optical telescope (150 in) in southern hemisphere, and permanent hands-on exhibition, Exploring the Universe. Warrumbungle National Park, 35 km W; bushwalking, rock climbing, nature study, photography. Pilliga

Scrub at Baradine, 44 km NW; 450 000 ha forest (biggest in NSW) consisting mainly of white cypress pine and broom plains of dense heath and scrub; location of picnic areas and walking tracks from Baradine Forestry Office. **Tourist information:** Bicentennial Centre, Newell Hwy; (068) 42 1441. **Accommodation:** 3 hotels, 12 motels, 2 caravan/camping parks. **See also:** The Newell. MAP REF. 122 F10

Coonamble   Pop. 2886

This town on the Castlereagh Hwy is situated on the Western Plains, 518 km NW of Sydney. It serves a district that produces wheat, wool, lamb, beef, cypress pine and hardwood timber. **Of interest:** Historical Museum, former police station and stables, Aberford St. Warrana Creek Weir; boating and swimming. **In the area:** Youie Bore, 20 km N on Castlereagh Hwy; water from bore is hot and supplies 5 properties with stock water. Macquarie Marshes, 80 km NW; breeding-ground for waterbirds. Warrumbungle National Park and Siding Springs Observatory, 80 km SE. Farm holidays. **Tourist information:** Coonamble Motel, Castlereagh St; (068) 22 1400. **Accommodation:** 5 hotels, 3 motels, 1 caravan/camping park. MAP REF. 122 C9

Cootamundra   Pop. 6386

This town on the Olympic Way, 427 km SW of Sydney, is less than 2 hours' drive from Canberra, and is well known for the Cootamundra wattle (*Acacia baileyana*). It has a strong retail sector and is a large stock-selling centre for the surrounding pastoral and agricultural rural holdings. **Of interest:** Self-guide 'Two Foot Tour' leads visitors on walk around town, taking in historic buildings, many restored. Birthplace of Sir Donald Bradman, town's most famous son, at 89 Adams St; open weekends. Cootamundra Public School Museum, Cooper St. **In the area:** Yandilla Mustard Seed Oil, 26 km N; tours by appt. Inglenook Deer Farm at Wallendbeen, 19 km NE; bus tours by appt. Wineries in the Harden area, 78 km E; tastings, sales, picnic/barbecue facilities. Merriwonga sheep and grain property, Old Nubba Schoolhouse, Appletrees Cottage and Winona Homestead, all offer farm holidays. **Tourist information:** Business Enterprise Centre, Hovell St (at railway station);

Japanese Garden, Cowra

(069) 42 1400. **Accommodation:** 7 hotels, 4 motels, 1 caravan/camping park. MAP REF. 119 B3, 120 C11

Corowa
Pop. 5064

Birthplace of Australia's Federation, Corowa took its name from *Currawa*, an Aboriginal word describing pine trees that once grew there in profusion. A typical Australian country town, Corowa's wide main street, Sanger St, lined with turn-of-the-century verandahed buildings, runs down to the banks of the Murray River. The town offers visitors opportunities for tennis, swimming, water-skiing, birdwatching and bushwalking. Tom Roberts' painting *Shearing of the Rams*, in the National Gallery of Victoria, was completed nearby in 1889. **Of interest:** Federation Museum, Queen St. National Federation Festival held in Jan. **In the area:** Rutherglen wineries, only a short drive or bicycle ride away. Scenic drives from the town. **Tourist information:** Railway Station Building, John St; (060) 33 3221. **Accommodation:** 4 hotels, 20 motels, 4 caravan/camping parks. MAP REF. 127 O13, 233 M4

Cowra
Pop. 8422

The peaceful air of this busy country town on the Lachlan River belies its dramatic recent history. On 5 August 1944, over 1000 Japanese prisoners attempted to escape from a nearby POW camp. Four Australian soldiers and 231 Japanese prisoners were killed in the ensuing struggle. **Of interest:** Australia's World Peace Bell, Darling St. Army Vehicle Museum, River Park Rd. Cowra Rose Garden, adjacent to Tourist Information Centre. **In the area:** Australian and Japanese War Cemeteries, 5 km N, beside Cowra–Canowindra Rd. Australian soldiers who died are buried in Australian War Cemetery. Japanese soldiers who died during escape, and Japanese internees who died elsewhere in Australia, are buried in Japanese War Cemetery. Sakura Ave, 5 km of flowering cherry trees, links site with that of POW camp, with Breakout Walking Track, and Japanese Garden and Cultural Centre. Gardens cover 5 ha; Cultural Centre includes traditional teahouse, bonsai house, pottery and display of Japanese artefacts. Quarry Cellars, 4 km S, on Boorowa Rd; tastings and sales. Conimbla National Park, 27 km W. Wyangala State Recreation Area, 40 km SE, mecca for water sports and fishing enthusiasts. Historic Croote Cottage, Gooloogong, 25 km NW; built by convicts and raided by bushrangers; visits by appt. **Tourist information:** Mid Western Hwy, near Boorowa turnoff; (063) 42 4333. **Accommodation:** 4 hotels, 2 hotel/motels, 8 motels, 3 caravan/camping parks. MAP REF. 119 C1, 120 D8

Crookwell
Pop. 1966

Located 45 km NW of Goulburn, Crookwell is the centre of a rich agricultural and pastoral district, producing apples, pears and cherries, and is the State's major supplier of certified seed potatoes. **Of interest:** Stevensons Mill, Spring St; flour mill restored by local historians; open Wed. or by appt. Crookwell Memorial Park, Spring St. **In the area:** Redground Lookout, 8 km NE. Many quaint historic villages associated with gold and copper mining and bushranging: Tuena, Peelwood, Laggan, Bigga, Binda (all north of town) and Roslyn (south, and birthplace of poet Dame Mary Gilmore). Willow Vale Mill at Laggan, 9 km N; restored flour mill with restaurant and accommodation. Upper reaches of Lake Wyangala and Grabine State Recreation Area, 65 km NW; water-skiing, picnicking, fishing, sailing, bushwalking and camping. Abercrombie Caves, 64 km further N along Bathurst Rd; guided tours. Farm holidays. **Tourist information:** 44 Goulburn St; (048) 32 1988. **Accommodation:** 2 hotels, 2 motels, 1 caravan/camping park. MAP REF. 119 E3, 120 F10

Culburra–Orient Point
Pop. 3145

Famous for its prawning and fishing, this unspoiled resort is situated 23 km E of

Nowra on an ocean beach near Wollumboola Lake. **Of interest:** Surfing, swimming, lake, shore and rock fishing. Beach is patrolled in summer holidays. **Tourist information:** Shoalhaven Tourist Centre, 254 Princes Hwy, Bomaderry; (044) 21 0778. **Accommodation:** 1 motel, 2 caravan/camping parks.
MAP REF. 116 G13, 119 I4, 120 I11

Culcairn   Pop. 1175

Dating back to 1880 and planned to service the railway between Sydney and Melbourne, the township today reflects the district's rural prosperity. Bushranger Dan Morgan began his life of crime at Round Hill Station, with a hold-up on 19 June 1864. Once known as the oasis of the Riverina because of its unlimited underground water supply (discovered in 1926), the town owes its picturesque tree-lined streets and parks to this artesian water. **Of interest:** Historic Culcairn Hotel (1891), Railway Pde. Many buildings in Railway Pde and on Olympic Way classified by National Trust. Centenary Mural, Main St. Artesian pumping station, Gordon St. **In the area:** John McLean's Grave, 3 km E; a price was put on Morgan's head after he shot McLean. Round Hill Station, on Holbrook Rd. At Walla Walla, 18 km W, Old Schoolhouse (1875) Museum and largest Lutheran church in NSW (1924); and 4 km N, Morgan's Lookout. Premier Yabbies, 7 km S of Culcairn; farm and catch-out. Pioneer Museum at Jindera, 42 km S. **Tourist information:** Billabong Craft Shop, Railway Pde. **Accommodation:** 1 hotel, 1 motel, 1 caravan/camping park.
MAP REF. 127 P12, 233 P2

Deniliquin   Pop. 7895

At the centre of the largest irrigation complex in Australia, on the Edward River, 750 km SW of Sydney, Deniliquin has the largest rice mill in the southern hemisphere. The northern part of the district is famed for merino sheep studs, such as Wanganella and Boonoke. **Of interest:** Sunrice Visitors Centre, Saleyard Rd. Peppin Heritage Centre (1879), former school, George St. Waring Gardens, in town centre. Island Sanctuary, off Cressy St footbridge; free-ranging animals and birds. River beaches, including McLean and Willoughby's Beaches. 18-hole competition golf course. Sun Festival held in Jan. Jazz Festival at Easter. **In the area:** Pioneer Tourist Park and Garden Centre, 6 km N; antique steam

and pump display. Bird Observatory Tower at Mathoura, 34 km S. Irrigation works include Lawsons Syphon, 6 km E, and Stevens Weir, 26 km W. **Tourist information:** Cressy St; (058) 81 2878. **Accommodation:** 4 hotels, 3 hotel/motels, 8 motels, 5 caravan/camping parks.
MAP REF. 127 K11, 232 F1

Dorrigo   Pop. 1135

Magnificent river, mountain and forest scenery is a feature of this important timber town. **Of interest:** Calico Cottage, Hickory St; crafts and Devonshire teas. Dorrigo Pottery, Tyringham Rd. **In the area:** Dangar Falls, 2 km N. Dorrigo National Park, 5 km E; birds' eye views over canopy of World Heritage-listed rainforest from Skywalk, beginning at Rainforest Centre. Excellent trout fishing in district. Dutton Trout Hatchery at Ebor, 49 km W. **Tourist information:** Dorrigo Hotel, Hickory St; (066) 57 2016. **Accommodation:** 2 hotels, 3 motels, 1 caravan/camping park.
MAP REF. 123 N7, 475 M12

Dubbo   Pop. 28 064

This pleasant city lies on the banks of the Macquarie River, 420 km NW of Sydney, is recognised as the regional capital of western NSW, and supports many agricultural and secondary industries. **Of interest:** Old Dubbo Gaol, Macquarie St, with original gallows and solitary confinement cells; animatronic robots tell story of convicts. Dubbo Museum, Macquarie St. Dubbo Regional Art Gallery, Darling St. Indoor Kart Centre, Mountbatten Dr. Agricultural Show in May. **In the area:** Western Plains Zoo, 5 km S, Australia's first open-range zoo with over 300 ha of landscaped park; animals from 6 continents, some roaming in natural surroundings. Military Museum, 8 km S; open-air exhibits. Yarrabar Pottery, 4 km further S. Restored Dundullimal Homestead (1840s), 7 km SE, on Obley Rd. Golfworld, Fitzroy St, 3 km N; driving range and mini-golf course. Jinchilla Gardens and Gallery, 12 km N, off Gilgandra Rd. **Tourist information:** cnr Erskine and Macquarie Sts; (068) 84 1422. **Accommodation:** 6 hotels, 32 motels, 5 caravan/camping parks. **See also:** The Newell.
MAP REF. 120 D3, 122 D13

Dungog   Pop. 2187

These days an ideal base for bushwalking enthusiasts, Dungog was established in

1838 as a military post to prevent bushranging in the area. Situated on the upper reach of the Williams River, it is on one of the main access routes to Barrington Tops National Park. **In the area:** Chichester Dam, 23 km N, in picturesque mountain setting; Duncan Park within is ideal spot for picnic/barbecue. Telegherry Forest Park, 30 km N; walking trails to waterfalls along Telegherry River; picnic, swimming and camping spots. Barrington Tops National Park, 40 km N; Barrington Brush noted for its unusual native flora and rich variety of wildlife. Superb views from Mt Allyn (1100 m), 40 km NW. Clarence Town historic village, 25 km S. **Tourist information:** Shire Offices; (049) 92 1224. **Accommodation:** 3 hotels, 1 motel.
MAP REF. 121 L3

Eden   Pop. 3277

Quiet former whaling town on Twofold Bay, 512 km S of Sydney, with an outstanding natural harbour. Fishing and timber-getting are the main industries. **Of interest:** Eden Killer Whale Museum, Imlay St; exhibits include skeleton of notorious 'Tom the killer whale' and 70-million-year-old snail fossils. Whale-watching Oct.–Nov. Bay cruises. **In the area:** Ben Boyd National Park, extending 8 km N and 19 km S of Eden; outstanding scenery and ideal for fishing, swimming, camping and bushwalking. Prominent park feature, Boyd's Tower (1840s), at Red Point. On perimeter of park, at Nullica Bay, 9 km S, former rival settlement of Boydtown, including convict-built Sea Horse Inn, still licensed; safe beach and excellent fishing. Davidson Whaling Station Historic Site on Kiah Inlet. Good fishing at Wonboyn Lake Resort, 40 km S, surrounded by Ben Boyd National Park and Nadgee Nature Reserve. Harris Daishowa Chipmill Visitors Centre at Jews Head, 26 km S; video and static display on logging and milling operations. **Tourist information:** Princes Hwy; (064) 96 1953. **Accommodation:** 2 hotels, 10 motels, 6 caravan/camping parks. **See also:** The South Coast.
MAP REF. 117 F11, 119 F11, 235 P8

Eugowra   Pop. 572

'The great gold-escort robbery' occurred near this small town on the Orange–Forbes road in 1862. **Of interest:** Eugowra Museum; Aboriginal skeleton and artefacts, gemstones, early farm equipment and wagons. Nangar Gems, Norton St; sapphires, opals, emeralds, garnets. **In the area:** Escort Rock, 3 km E, where bushranger Frank Gardiner and gang hid before ambush of Forbes gold escort. Rock is on private property, but plaque on road gives details and unlocked gate allows entry. Picnic area. **Tourist information:** Visitors Centre, Civic Gardens, Byng St, Orange; (063) 61 5226, or Molong Railway Station Complex, Mitchell Hwy, Molong; (063) 66 8404. **Accommodation:** 2 hotels. MAP REF. 120 C7

Evans Head   Pop. 2375

This holiday and fishing resort, and centre of the NSW prawning industry, is situated off the Pacific Hwy via Woodburn. It has safe surf beaches and sandy river flats. **Of interest:** Rock, beach and ocean fishing, boating, windsurfing. **In the area:** Broadwater National Park, 5 km N, between Evans Head and Broadwater; bushwalking, birdwatching, fishing and swimming. Bundjalung National Park, on southern edge of Evans Head; Aboriginal relics, varied wildlife. **Tourist information:** McCormack's Real Estate, 9 Oak St; (066) 82 4611. **Accommodation:** 1 hotel, 1 motel, 1 caravan/camping park. MAP REF. 123 P4, 475 N9

Finley   Pop. 2220

This town on the Newell Hwy, 20 km from the Victorian border, is the centre of the Berriquin irrigation scheme. **Of interest:** Log Cabin (replica) and Museum, Mary Lawson Wayside Rest, Newell Hwy; display of rural heritage, open daily. Finley Lake, Newell Hwy; boating and sailing, picnic areas on lake banks. **Tourist information:** River Foreshore, Tocumwal; (058) 74 2131. **Accommodation:** 3 hotels, 5 motels, 1 caravan/camping park. MAP REF. 127 M12, 232 I1

Forbes   Pop. 7552

Noted bushranger Ben Hall is buried in this former goldmining town, 386 km W of Sydney on the Lachlan River. He was shot by police just outside the town in 1865. Today the town's industries include an abattoir, feed lots, and export of beef and hay. **Of interest:** Many historic buildings, especially in Camp and Lachlan Sts. Historical museum, Cross St; relics associated with Ben Hall. Forbes Cemetery, Bogan Gate Rd; contains graves of Ben Hall, Ned Kelly's sister, Kate Foster, and Captain Cook's niece, Rebecca Shields. Historical sites include memorial in King George V Park, where 'German Harry' discovered gold in 1861. Another memorial marks the spot where

explorer John Oxley first passed through Forbes; in small park in Dowling St. **In the area:** Lachlan Vintage Village, recreation of gold-rush era, 1 km S; 73-ha site with restaurant and picnic areas. Sandhills Vineyard, 6 km E on Eugowra Rd; tastings, sales and picnic/barbecue facilities. **Tourist information:** Old Railway Station, Union St; (068) 52 4155. **Accommodation:** 9 hotels, 6 motels, 4 caravan/camping parks. **See also:** The Newell. MAP REF. 120 C7

Forster–Tuncurry
Pop. 14 578

Twin towns on opposite sides of Wallis Lake, a holiday area in the Great Lakes district, Forster and Tuncurry are connected by a bridge. Launches and boats may be hired for lake and deep-sea fishing, and tours are available. The area is renowned for its fishing, including flathead, bream and whiting, as well as oysters and prawns. **Of interest:** Forster Art and Craft Centre. Oyster Festival held in Oct. **In the area:** Curtis Collection, 3 km S; vintage cars. The Green Cathedral, at Tiona on shores of Wallis Lake, 13 km S; unusual 'open-air cathedral'. Booti Booti State Recreation Area, 17 km S. Sugar Creek Toymakers at Bungwahl, 22 km S. Wallingat State Forest, 25 km S. Myall

Ben Boyd National Park, near Eden

New England

If you pull over for a rest in the New England area, it is worth keeping your eyes on the ground, despite the scenery. Some of the best fossicking specimens in the district have been found by the roadside. Jaspers, serpentine, all kinds of quartz, crystal and chalcedony are found right throughout this area—not to mention sapphires, diamonds and gold, though these require a little more effort to find.

The round trip from Nundle, through Tamworth, Manilla, Barraba, Bingara, Warialda, then on to the New England towns of **Inverell** and **Glen Innes** and back, is known as 'The Fossickers' Way' and tourist signs have been placed at intervals to guide the motorist. Nearby is the Copeton Dam, which holds two-and-a-half times as much water as Sydney Harbour, with part of its foreshores forming Copeton State Recreational Area.

Glen Innes and Inverell have nearby sapphire reserves where fossickers may hire tools and try their luck. Anything you find is yours; but remember, you must have a fossicker's licence, available from all New South Wales courthouses, tourist centres, and some sporting stores. The largest find in the Nullamanna Fossicking Reserve, near Inverell, to date is a 70-carat blue, valued at $3000.

The New England district is the largest area of highlands in Australia, and has plenty to offer besides gemstones. The countryside is varied and lovely, with magnificent mountains, and streams cascading into spectacular gorges, contrasting with the rich blacksoil plains of wheat and cotton to the west. Some of the State's most outstanding national parks and World Heritage features are found in New England, and the southern hemisphere's largest granite monolith, Bald Rock, is near **Tenterfield**.

Fishing is excellent, with trout in the streams of the tablelands, and cod and yellow-belly in the lower New England rivers to the west. You can also fish, picnic, swim, sail or water-ski at Pindari and Copeton Dam.

Other towns in New England, **Ashford**, **Delungra**, **Guyra**, **Tingha**, **Walcha**, **Uralla**, and **Deepwater**, and the city of **Armidale**, have much to offer.

For further information, contact the Visitors Centre and Coach Station, cnr Marsh and Dumaresq Sts, Armidale; (067) 73 8527. **See also:** Individual town entries in A–Z listing.

The Newell

With its excellent bitumen surface and long, straight stretches, the Newell provides fast and easy driving right across New South Wales. Driving time between Melbourne and Brisbane is up to 6 hours quicker by this route. The time you save could be put to good use enjoying the many interesting towns and attractions along the way.

From the Murray River town of **Tocumwal** to the Queensland border town of **Goondiwindi**, the highway runs through a wide range of scenery and is well served with motels, roadside cafes and service stations.

Tocumwal, with sandy beaches on the Murray, offers swimming and fishing as well as boating. At **Jerilderie**, 57 kilometres further north, visit the tiny restored post office held up by the Kelly gang in 1879. At **Narrandera** there is an excellent caravan park on the shore of Lake Talbot, a popular water sports centre. Beyond **West Wyalong** to the north is Lake Cowal, the largest natural lake in New South Wales and an important bird sanctuary; further north out of **Forbes** is a major tourist attraction—the Lachlan Vintage Village, a re-creation of a 19th-century goldmining town.

There is plenty to see in **Parkes**, including a vintage car museum and the Henry Parkes Museum. The famous radio telescope is on the highway, north of the town. **Dubbo** boasts what is probably the most popular tourist attraction on the Newell—the Western Plains Zoo, claimed to be the best open-range wildlife park in Australia.

From Dubbo, the highway passes through the spectacular volcanic Warrumbungle National Park, which is ideal for bushwalking. If you have children aboard, do not miss the award-winning fantasy park, Miniland, with its life-size prehistoric animals, just west of **Coonabarabran**. Once you get beyond the Warrumbungle Ranges, the scenery changes dramatically to the vast Pilliga scrub country. **Narrabri**, in the heart of 'Cotton Country', offers a diversity of attractions, including Mt Kaputar National Park, Sawn Rocks, the CSIRO Telescope and gemstone fossicking. The northern town of **Moree**, not far from the Queensland border, is famed for its artesian spa baths and pecan nut farm.

Western Plains Zoo, Dubbo

For further information, contact the Tourist Information Office, Kelly Reserve, Newell Highway, Parkes 2870; (068) 62 4365. A booklet on the Newell is available at tourist information centres. **See also:** Individual town entries in A–Z listing.

Lakes National Park, 35 km S; house-boats for hire. Camping and beaches at Seal Rocks, 40 km S. The Grandis, accessed from The Lakes Way, 48 km S in Bulahdelah State Forest, tallest tree in NSW. **Tourist information:** Great Lakes Tourist Board, Little St; (065) 54 8799. **Accommodation:** 2 hotels, 19 motels, 12 caravan/camping parks.
MAP REF. 121 N3, 123 N13

Gerringong Pop. 2478

Spectacular views of white sand and rolling breakers can be seen from this resort, 11 km S of Kiama on the Illawarra coast. **Of interest:** Surfing, fishing and swimming at local beaches. Gerroa and Seven Mile are world-famous as windsurfing locations. Memorial to pioneer aviator Sir Charles Kingsford Smith at northern end of Seven Mile Beach, site of his takeoff to New Zealand in the Southern Cross in 1933. Wild Country Park at Fox Ground, 6 km S. Bushwalks through Seven Mile Beach National Park, 13 km S; camping and picnic areas. **Tourist information:** Visitors Centre, Blowhole Pt, Kiama; (042) 32 3322. **Accommodation:** 1 hotel, 3 motels, 3 caravan/camping parks.
MAP REF. 116 G10, 119 I4, 121 J11

Gilgandra Pop. 2890

An historic town at the junction of three highways, in timber, wool and farming country. Home of the famous Coo-ee March, which left from Gilgandra for Sydney in 1915 in a drive to recruit more soldiers for World War I. Also known for its windmills, which once provided residents with sub-artesian water. **Of interest:** Australian Collection, Miller St; Aboriginal artefacts, display of minerals, fossils and marine specimens, Gwen Collison watercolours. The Observatory and Display Centre, cnr Wamboin and Willie Sts, with 31 cm telescope. Museum, Newell Hwy; displays of memorabilia from Coo-ee March. Film *The Chant of Jimmy Blacksmith* was based on Breelong Massacre, which took place near Gilgandra; related items in museum. Orana Cactus World, Newell Hwy. **In the area:** Gilgandra Flora Reserve, 14½ km N; wild-flowers in spring. Warrumbungle National Park, 82 km NE. **Tourist information:** Coo-ee March Memorial Park, Newell Hwy; (068) 47 2045. **Accommodation:** 3 hotels, 8 motels, 3 caravan/camping parks.
MAP REF. 120 D1, 122 D12

Celtic monument, Glen Innes

Glen Innes Pop. 6140

Gazetted in 1852, this mountain town was the scene of many bushranging exploits. In a beautiful setting, at an altitude of 1073 m, it is now the centre of a lush farming district where sapphire mining is an important industry. **Of interest:** Many original public buildings, particularly in Grey St; self-guide walks. Centennial Parklands with Martin's Lookout, now site of Australian Standing Stones, Celtic monument. Land of the Beardies History House, cnr Ferguson St and West Ave, folk museum housed in town's first hospital and set in extensive grounds; reconstructed slab hut, period room settings and pioneer relics. Local art and craft. Minerama Gem Festival held Sept.; Australian Bush Music Festival on Oct. long weekend; Land of the Beardies Bush Festival in Nov. **In the area:** Gibraltar Range National Park, 70 km NE; impressive Dandahra Falls, and The Needles and Anvil Rock, famous granite formations. World Heritage-listed Washpool National Park 75 km NE; rainforest wilderness area. Guy Fawkes River National Park, 77 km SE; wild river area for bushwalking, canoeing and fishing. Convict-carved tunnel, halfway between Glen Innes and Grafton, on road east, passing through scenic mountain and riverside country. Fishing; trout, perch

and cod. Fossicking for sapphire, topaz and quartz, within 45-km radius of town. Horse treks, with accommodation at historic bush pubs. **Tourist information:** Church St (New England Hwy); (067) 32 2397. **Accommodation:** 4 hotels, 10 motels, 5 caravan/camping parks. **See also:** New England.
MAP REF. 123 L5, 475 K11

Gloucester Pop. 2465

This quiet town lies at the foot of a range of monolithic hills called 'the Bucketts'. It is at the junction of three tributaries of the Manning River, the upper reaches of which are excellent for trout and perch fishing. **Of interest:** Folk Museum in Church St. The Bucketts Walk, immediately west of town. Gloucester Park, outstanding sporting complex. Billykart Derby, June. MMI Mountain Man Triathlon, Sept.; mountain-biking, kayaking and running. **In the area:** Scenic views from Mograni Lookout (5 km E), Kia-ora Lookout (4 km N) and Berrico Trig Station (14 km W). Mountain Maid Gold Mine at Copeland, 16 km W. Altamira Holiday Ranch, 18 km E. **Tourist information:** Great Lakes Tourist Board, Little St, Forster; (065) 54 8799. **Accommodation:** 1 hotel, 1 hotel/motel, 2 motels, 1 caravan/camping park.
MAP REF. 121 L2, 123 L13

Gosford Pop. 38 205

Gosford is 85 km N of Sydney on beautiful Brisbane Water. **Of interest:** Henry Kendall Cottage, built 1838 as inn, where poet lived 1874–5; picnic/barbecue facilities in pleasant grounds. **In the area:** Australian Reptile Park and Wildlife Sanctuary, Pacific Hwy north; taipans, pythons, goannas and a platypus. Old Sydney Town, 9 km W; reconstruction of early pioneer settlement, re-created from carefully researched pre-1810 material. Somersby Falls, near Old Sydney Town; ideal picnic spot. Central Park Family Fun Centre at Forresters Beach, 31 km E. The Ferneries, Oak Rd, Matcham, 11 km NE; rainforest area with picnic/barbecue facilities, paddle-boats, children's playground, and Devonshire teas. Bouddi National Park, 17 km SE; bushwalking, camping, fishing and swimming. Brisbane Water National Park, 10 km SW; spectacular waratahs in spring. **Tourist information:** 200 Mann St; (043) 25 2835. **Accommodation:** 3 hotels, 10 motels, 1 caravan/camping parks.
MAP REF. 105 O5, 108 F6, 121 K7

Goulburn   Pop. 21 451

This provincial city, steeped in history (it was proclaimed a town in 1833), is on the Hume Hwy 209 km sw of Sydney. It is the centre of a wealthy farming district (including wool, wheat, stud cattle and horses) at the junction of the Wollondilly and Mulwarry Rivers beyond the Southern Highlands. **Of interest:** Riversdale (1840), Maud St; National Trust classified coaching-house. St Clair History House (c.1843), Sloane St; 20-room mansion, restored by local historical society. Regional Art Gallery, Bourke St. Garroorigang and Hume Dairy, South Goulburn (1857), in almost original condition; private home, open by appt. Old Goulburn Brewery Hotel, Bungonia Rd. Goulburn Courthouse, Montague St. Cathedral of St Saviour, Bourke St. Cathedral of St Peter and St Paul, cnr Bourke and Verner Sts. Sun. aftn concerts at The Towers (c.1842) guest house, Braidwood Rd. Farm holidays at a wide variety of nearby properties. Gulfon's Craft Village, Common St, housed in old brickworks (1884); working displays and sales. Goulburn Yurt Works, Copford Rd; inspection tours (by appt) of factory making prefabricated round houses. The Big Merino, a 15-m-high sculptured relief, Hume Hwy; displays of wool products and Australiana. Goulburn Steam Museum, Fitzroy St; rides on Leisureland Express. Black Stag Deer Park, Gorman Rd. South Hill, Garooigang Rd; woollen art, accommodation. Barbecue facilities on Wollondilly River at nearby Marsden Weir. Rocky Hill War Memorial, Memorial Dr; city's best-known landmark, built in memory of local World War I soldiers. **In the area:** Bungonia State Recreation Area, 35 km E; range of walks, incl. through Bungonia Canyon. Pelican Sheep Station, 10 km s; shearing and sheepdog demonstrations by appt. **Tourist information:** 6 Montague St; (048) 21 5343. **Accommodation:** 7 hotels, 1 hotel/ motel, 13 motels, 3 caravan/camping parks.
MAP REF. 119 F4, 120 G11

Grafton   Pop. 16 642

A garden city, famous for its riverbank parks and the jacaranda, wheel and flame trees lining its wide streets, Grafton is situated at the junction of Pacific Hwy and Gwydir Hwy, 665 km N of Sydney. A colourful Jacaranda Festival is held in the last week of Oct. and first week of Nov. **Of interest:** Numerous National Trust buildings. Schaeffer House (1900), Fitzroy St; now district historical museum. Stately Prentice House, Fitzroy St; one of Australia's finest regional art galleries. Susan Island in Clarence River; recreation reserve covered with rainforest and home to large fruit bat colony. Water sports on river include annual bridge to bridge ski race in Oct. Passenger ferry services and river cruises; houseboats for hire. **In the area:** Weekend gliding at Eatonsville, 18 km NW. Canoeing and rafting on wild-river systems in surrounding shires such as Nymboida; also many scenic drives. Ulmarra village, 12 km N, classified by National Trust and a fine example of turn-of-the-century river port; art, craft and antique shops. Riverboats for hire at Brushgrove, 20 km NE. Four major national parks within hour's drive: Yuraygir (50 km E) and Bundjalung (70 km N) coastal parks, and Washpool (88 km) and Gibraltar Range (92 km) W. World Heritage-listed rainforest in Washpool National Park and at Iluka offers walking tracks and wildlife. **Tourist information:** Cnr Spring St and Pacific Hwy, South Grafton; (066) 42 4677. **Accommodation:** 17 hotels, 14 motels, 3 caravan/camping parks.
MAP REF. 123 O5, 475 N11

Grenfell   Pop. 2037

The birthplace of poet and short-story writer Henry Lawson, and the background for many of his verses and stories, this small town on the Mid Western Hwy, 377 km w of Sydney, is also noted for the Guinea Pig Races held on Easter Sunday and during the Henry Lawson Festival of Arts in June. **Of interest:** Grenfell Museum, Camp St. O'Brien's Lookout, where gold was discovered; walkway and picnic facilities. Henry Lawson Obelisk, next to Lawson Park, on site of house where poet is believed to have been born. **In the area:** Weddin Mountains National Park, 18 km SW; bushwalking, camping and picnicking. Area was used as hideout by bushrangers Ben Hall, Frank Gardiner, Johnnie Gilbert and others. Easy walk to Ben Hall's Cave. **Tourist information:** CWA Craft Centre, 68 Main St; (063) 43 1612. **Accommodation:** 5 hotels, 1 motel, 1 caravan/camping park.
MAP REF. 119 B1, 120 C8

Griffith   Pop. 13 296

A thriving city that developed as a result of the introduction of irrigation, Griffith was designed by Walter Burley Griffin, architect of Canberra, and named after Sir Arthur Griffith, the first Minister for Public Works in the NSW government. Of a diversity of industries, rice is the most profitable, followed by citrus fruits, grapes, vegetables, eggs and poultry. Griffith is well known as a wine-producing area; there are over a dozen wineries in the district. The Murrumbidgee Irrigation Area produces 80 per cent of the State's wines. The Griffith Wine and Food Festival is held over Easter. Griffith Festival of Gardens held every October. **Of interest:** Tours of Viticultural Research Station, agricultural, horticultural and viticultural farms, and various food-processing factories such as Koala Gourmet Foods. Regional Theatre, Banna Ave; stage curtain designed and created by combined efforts of 300 residents of Griffith to reflect city, surrounding villages and industries. Regional Art Gallery, Banna Ave; monthly exhibitions. Griffith Cottage Gallery, Bridge Rd; and Crafty Spot, Benerembah St. **In the area:** Many wineries open for sales, tastings and guided tours. Pioneer Park Museum, set in 18 ha of bushland, 2 km N; drop-log buildings and collection of memorabilia from early 20th century. Bagtown village recreated here to give insight into development of area. Bagtown Cemetery, 5 km s; reminder of pioneering days. Lake Wyangan, 10 km NW; water sports and picnic areas. Cocoparra National Park, 25 km NE. **Tourist information:** Cnr Banna and Jondaryan Aves; (069) 62 4145. **Accommodation:** 2 hotels, 1 hotel/motel, 8 motels, 2 caravan/camping parks. **See also:** Vineyards and Wineries.
MAP REF. 127 N7

Gulgong   Pop. 2042

This fascinating old goldmining town, 29 km NW of Mudgee, is known as 'the town on the (original) $10 note'. In its heyday in the 1870s it was packed with fortune hunters from all over the world. Some of its glory remains in the form of many restored buildings. The town's narrow streets are lined with clapboard and iron buildings decorated in their original iron lace. **Of interest:** Henry Lawson Centre, Mayne St; largest collection of Lawson memorabilia outside Sydney's Mitchell Library. Historic buildings to note on self-guide Town Trail include Prince of Wales Opera House, Mayne St; Ten Dollar Town Motel (formerly Royal Hotel), cnr Mayne and Medley Sts; American Tobacco Warehouse and Fancy Goods Emporium, Mayne St; and Gulgong Pioneers Museum, cnr Herbert and Bayly Sts. **Tourist information:** 84 Market St, Mudgee; (063) 72 5874. **Accommodation:** 4 hotels, 3 motels. MAP REF. 120 F3

Gundagai   Pop. 2069

Much celebrated in song and verse, this town on the Murrumbidgee River at the foot of Mt Parnassus, 398 km sw of Sydney, has become part of Australian folklore. Its history includes Australia's worst flood disaster in 1852 when 89 people drowned, nearby gold rushes, and many bushranging attacks. Today it is the centre of a rich pastoral and agricultural district that produces wool, wheat, fruit and vegetables, and is a convenient overnight stopping-place for motorists using the Hume Hwy. **Of interest:** Marble carving of cathedral, comprising over 20 000 pieces, by Frank Rusconi, sculptor of tuckerbox dog, on display in Tourist Information Centre, Sheridan St. Outstanding collection of early photographs with letters and possessions of poet Henry Lawson at Gabriel Gallery, Sheridan St. Historical museum, Homer St. Courthouse (built 1859 and still in use), classified by National Trust as building of great architectural merit; scene of many historic trials, including that of notorious bushranger Captain Moonlite. St John's Anglican Church (1861), cnr Otway and Punch Sts, and Prince Alfred Bridge (1866), longest timber viaduct in Australia, classified by National Trust. Views from Mt Parnassus Lookout, Hanley St, and Rotary Lookout, South Gundagai. Spring Flower Show held in Oct. **In the area:** Dog on the Tuckerbox at Caltex service station, 'five miles from' or 8 km N; monument to pioneer teamsters and their dogs, celebrated in song by Jack O'Hagan, and larger-than-life copper statues of Dad and Dave characters. Nearby kiosk, fern-house and ruins of Five Mile Pub, where teamsters and goldminers once broke their journeys. **Tourist information:** Sheridan St; (069) 44 1341. **Accommodation:** 5 hotels, 5 motels, 2 caravan/camping parks. MAP REF. 119 B5, 120 C12

Gunnedah   Pop. 8874

A prosperous town on the banks of the Namoi River, Gunnedah is recognised as the centre of rich pastoral and agricultural country, and is one of the largest stock-marketing and killing centres in NSW. Other industries include a brickworks, a tannery, flour mills and open-cut and underground coal mining. **Of interest:** Water Tower Museum, Anzac Park. Dorothea MacKellar Memorial statue in park. Rural Museum, Mullaley Rd. Red Chief Memorial, State Office building, Abbott St. Old Bank Gallery, Conadilly St. Creative Arts Centre, Chandos St. 8th Division Memorial Avenue of flowering gums. Self-drive town tour and self-guide Bindea Town Walk. **In the area:** Porcupine Lookout, 3 km SE; picnic spot. 150° East Time Meridian, 28 km w. Lake Keepit Dam and State Recreation Centre, 34 km NE, for water sports, bushwalking, picnicking and camping; caravan park and gliding club. **Tourist information:** Anzac Park; (067) 42 1564. **Accommodation:** 6 hotels, 7 motels, 1 caravan/camping park. MAP REF. 122 H9

Courthouse, Grafton

Gunning   Pop. 497

In the centre of lush pastoral country on the Hume Hwy between Goulburn and Yass. **Of interest:** Pye Cottage, a slab-style pioneer cottage, post office, Royal Hotel, old courthouse (now church), Do Duck Inn, Caxton House and Cottage—all in Hume Hwy. **In the area:** Greendale Pioneer Cemetery, Gunning–Boorowa Rd. Hume and Hovell Walking Track extends from Gunning to Albury. **Tourist information:** Yass Information Centre, Coronation Park, Cooma St, Yass; (06) 226 2557. **Accommodation:** 1 hotel, 1 motel. MAP REF. 119 E4, 120 F11

Guyra   Pop. 1942

Guyra is Aboriginal for 'fish may be caught', and the local streams are excellent for fishing, including trout and eels. At 1300 m, this small town in the Great Dividing Range is one of the highest in NSW, with occasional snowfalls in

Witcombe Memorial Fountain, Lachlan St, Hay

winter. Guyra is the centre of a highly productive rural area known for fat lambs, wool and potatoes. **Of interest:** Historical Society Museum, Bradley St; open Sun. or by appt. Waterbirds at Mother of Ducks Lagoon. Lamb and Potato Festival held in Jan. **In the area:** Chandler's Peak for spectacular views. Thunderbolt's Cave, 10 km S. Llangothlin Handcraft Hall on hwy, 13 km N. Unusual balancing rock formation and gem fossicking at Backwater, 34 km NE. Ebor Falls and picnic reserve, 75 km E. Copeton Dam, 90 km W; fishing, boating and camping. Farm holidays at Wattleridge, Mosgiel, Milani Trout Cottage and Cabar Feidh. **Tourist information:** Guyra Nursery, Nincoola St; (067) 79 1420. **Accommodation:** 2 hotels, 2 motels, 1 caravan park. **See also:** New England.
MAP REF. 123 L7, 475 K12

Harden–Murrumburrah
Pop. 2016
Twin towns, 357 km SW of Sydney. Settled in 1830, the area is rich grain- and stock-producing country. **Of interest:** Harden–Murrumburrah Historical Museum and Witch Craft and Coffee Cottage, both in Albury St. Newson Park, in Harden, with picnic/barbecue facilities. **In the area:** Barwang Vineyard, 20 km N. Asparagus plantation at Jugiong, 30 km S. **Tourist information:** Shire

Offices; (063) 86 2305. **Accommodation:** 4 hotels, 1 motel, 1 caravan/camping park.
MAP REF. 119 C3, 120 D10

Hartley   Pop. 5
This historic village just off the Great Western Hwy, 134 km W of Sydney, used to be an important stopover for travellers in the early colonial days. Situated in the Hartley Valley, it is now administered by the National Parks and Wildlife Service. **Of interest:** Self-guide leaflet introduces historic buildings, including: convict-built courthouse (1837), designed by colonial architect Mortimer Lewis, Royal Hotel (early 1840s), Old Trahlee Cottage, post office (1846), St Bernard's Church and Presbytery (1842), Farmer's Inn, Ivy Cottage and Shamrock Inn. **Tourist information:** 285 Main St, Lithgow; (063) 51 2307. **Accommodation:** 1 caravan/camping park.
MAP REF. 104 F5

Hay   Pop. 2817
Hay serves as the commercial centre for the huge area of semi-arid grazing country on the Murrumbidgee River at the junction of the Cobb, Mid Western and Sturt Hwys. Increasing irrigation from the Murrumbidgee has led to an expansion in vegetable- and fruit-growing. Many world-famous sheep studs are in the area. **Of interest:** Historic

buildings in Lachlan St. Witcombe Memorial Fountain (1883) and plaque in Lachlan St to commemorate journey of explorer Charles Sturt along Murrumbidgee and Murray rivers in 1829–30. Hay Gaol Museum, Church St; pioneer relics. Restored courthouse, Moppett St. Coachhouse in main shopping area; original Cobb & Co. coach that plied Deniliquin–Hay–Wilcannia run until 1901. Hay Park, with picnic/barbecue facilities and children's playgrounds. Signposted scenic drive around town. Sandy river beaches along Murrumbidgee for swimming, boating and fishing; Sandy Point Beach venue for Australia Day 'Surf' Carnival. Birdwatching area close to town; breeding ground for inland species. Bishop's Lodge, South Hay (1888); restored as museum, exhibition gallery and conference centre. **In the area:** Ruberto's Winery, Sturt Hwy, South Hay. Weir on Murrumbidgee River, 12 km W. Sunset viewing area, 16 km N on Booligal Rd. Famous sheep studs of Mungadal, Uardry and Cedar Grove. **Tourist information:** 407 Moppett St; (069) 93 1003. **Accommodation:** 7 hotels, 6 motels, 2 caravan/ camping parks.
MAP REF. 127 K8

Henty   Pop. 840
The historic pastoral township of Henty, the 'home of the header', is in the heart of 'Morgan Country', so called because of the famous but ill-fated bushranger Dan Morgan. Almost midway between Albury–Wodonga and Wagga Wagga, Henty can be reached by the Olympic Way or by the Hume Hwy and Boomerang Way. **Of interest:** Headlie Taylor Header Memorial, Henty Park, off Allen St; tribute to machine (invented 1914) that revolutionised grain industry. Annual Henty Field Days held in Sept. **In the area:** Sergeant Smith Memorial Stone, 2 km W on Pleasant Hills Rd, marks site where Dan Morgan fatally wounded a policeman. Doodle Cooma Swamp (2000 ha), breeding area for waterbirds, visible from memorial stone. Built of chocks and logs (no nails), Buckarginga Woolshed, on Cookardinia Rd, 11 km E. Squatters Arms Inn (1848) at Cookardinia, 24 km E. **Tourist information:** Billabong Craft Shop, Railway Pde, Culcairn. **Accommodation:** 1 hotel, 1 motel, 1 caravan/camping park.
MAP REF. 127 P11, 233 P1

Vineyards and Wineries

A vineyard holiday takes you through peaceful, ordered countryside and gives you the chance to learn more about wine and its making at first hand. It also gives you a perfect excuse for wine tasting and, later, sampling the local wines with a meal in a first-class restaurant in the area. The obvious place to head for in New South Wales is the famous **Hunter Valley**. It is not far from Sydney (2 hours' drive each way) and, with some 70 wineries, must rate as one of the most important wine-growing districts in Australia. Although it can be a pleasant day trip from Sydney to the Hunter, it is well worth booking into a motel in the area for at least one night, to do it justice. Mid-week is the best time to visit, with lower tariffs and fewer crowds.

The Hunter is Australia's oldest commercial wine-producing area, wine having first been made there in the 1830s. The Hunter's table wines, both red and white, still rank as among the best in Australia.

Most of the early colonial vineyards have vanished and some family concerns have been taken over by the larger companies with such well-known names as Lindemans and McWilliams.

The high reputation of the district is maintained by such well-known properties as Mount Pleasant, Oakvale, Drayton's Bellevue, Tyrrell's and Tulloch's Glen Elgin.

Most wineries welcome visitors and are open for inspection and wine tastings daily. Several have picnic grounds, barbecue facilities and excellent restaurants.

Restaurants in the area include the Pokolbin Cellars at Hungerford Hill, Blaxland's at Pokolbin and the Casuarina at North Pokolbin.

The Hungerford Hill Wine Village at Pokolbin has wine tastings, wine sales, a gallery, accommodation at the Quality Pokolbin Resort, specialty shops, a restaurant, kiosk and picnic facilities, an adventure playground for children, plus an aquagolf driving range and clay pigeon shooting with laser beams.

It is best to go at vintage time—usually around February in the Hunter—if you want to see a vineyard in full swing. However, this is the most hectic time of year for vignerons, so do not expect their undivided attention. For an idea of the range of wineries in the district, try Tyrrell's and Drayton's wineries for a glimpse of the more traditional family approach, and Lindeman or Hunter Estate for the modern 'big company' style.

South of Sydney at **Camden** is Gledswood, birthplace of Australia's wine

Lindemans Winery, Pokolbin

Vineyard, Mudgee

industry. The first vines were planted in 1827 and the winery was re-established as Gledswood Cellars in 1970. The winery offers wine tastings and sales, an art gallery, shearing demonstrations and picnic facilities. Hay-rides and candle-lit dinners for parties can be arranged.

You could have an equally enjoyable wine tasting holiday in the Riverina towns of **Griffith** and **Leeton**, in the other main winegrowing area of the State. Griffith, Leeton and **Narrandera** are the main towns in the **Murrumbidgee Irrigation Area**, which grows 80 per cent of the State's wine-producing grapes. Well known wineries such as McWilliam's, de Bortoli and Rosetto & Sons are open to

visitors who wish to taste the wines of the Riverina. In Leeton, visitors are welcome to sample the vintages at Toorak Winery and Lillypilly Estate. **Mudgee**, 261 kilometres north-west of Sydney, is also in an area where fine wines are produced from around a dozen wineries. Other smaller vineyards are scattered throughout the State—some of them quite close to Sydney.

For further information, contact Lower Hunter Tourism Authority. **See also:** Individual town entries in A–Z listing. **Note** detailed map of Lower Hunter Vineyards on page 113.

Holbrook   Pop. 1369

This small town, 521 km SW of Sydney on the Hume Hwy, is a noted stock-breeding centre. **Of interest:** Commander Holbrook submarine in Holbrook Park, Hume Hwy; replica of submarine in which Commander N. D. Holbrook won VC in World War I. Town (formerly Germanton) was renamed in his honour. Woolpack Inn Museum, located in former hotel built in 1860, open daily; exhibits include complete plant of old cordial factory, bakery, horse-drawn vehicles and farm equipment. **In the area:** Ultralight Centre at Holbrook airport. Glenfalloch for farm holidays. **Tourist information:** Woolpack Inn Museum, 83 Albury St (Hume Hwy); (060) 36 2131. **Accommodation:** 2 hotels, 6 motels, 1 caravan/camping park.
MAP REF. 127 Q12, 233 Q2

Iluka   Pop. 1795

A coastal resort on the Clarence River, known for its fishing. A deep-sea fishing fleet operates from the harbour. **Of interest:** Daily passenger ferry services to Yamba. River cruises. Iluka Amateur Fishing Classic held in July. **In the area:** Woombah Coffee Plantation, 14 km W; tours of world's southernmost coffee plantation. Bundjalung National Park and World Heritage-listed Iluka Rainforest, northern edge of town. Riverboats for hire at Brushgrove, 33 km W. **Tourist information:** Cnr Spring St and Pacific Hwy, South Grafton; (066) 42 4677. **Accommodation:** 1 motel, 3 caravan parks.
MAP REF. 123 P4, 475 N10

Inverell   Pop. 9736

Known as 'Sapphire City', this town, 69 km W of Glen Innes, is in fertile farming land also rich in minerals. Industrial diamonds, zircons, tin and 75% of the world's sapphires are mined in the area. **Of interest:** Courthouse, Otho St, classified by National Trust. Pioneer Village, Tingha Rd; buildings dating from 1840, moved from their original sites, include Grove Homestead, Paddy's Pub and Mt Drummond Woolshed. Tour Centre–Mining Museum in Water Towers Complex, Campbell St. Art Society Gallery, Evans St. Gem Centre, Byron St. Sapphire City Floral Festival, Art Exhibition, and Collectables and Bottle Show, all held in Oct. **In the area:** Lake Inverell Reserve, 3 km E. Draught Horse Centre, Fishers Rd, 4 km E; 6 breeds, display of harness and memorabilia. DeJon

Sapphire Centre, 19 km E on Glen Innis Rd; inspection of working sapphire mine. Honey Farm and Bottle Museum, 8 km W. Gwydir Ranch 4WD Park, 28 km W. Goonoowigall Bushland Reserve, 5 km S. Gilgai Winery, 12 km S; tastings and sales. Conrad and Kin Conrad Silver Mine, 29 km S; inspection tours. Green Valley Farm, 35 km S, with museum. Copeton Dam State Recreation Area, 40 kmSW; boating, water-skiing, swimming and fishing, bushwalking, rock climbing, children's adventure playgrounds, picnic/barbecue facilities. Whole area renowned for fossicking. **Tourist information:** Water Towers Complex, Campbell St; (067) 22 1693. **Accommodation:** 4 hotels, 6 motels, 3 caravan/camping parks. **See also:** New England.
MAP REF. 123 J6, 475 J11

Jamberoo   Pop. 704

Jamberoo, 13 km W of Kiama, is one of the most picturesque areas of the NSW coast with lush pastures surrounded by towering escarpments. The district has been famous for the quality of its dairy products since the early settlement days. **Of interest:** Jamberoo Hotel, Allowrie St; bush bands Sun. aftn. Illawarra Folk Festival held March. **In the area:** Jamberoo Recreation Park, 3 km N. Breathtaking, State award-winning Minnamurra Rainforest, 4 km W. **Tourist information:** Kiama Visitors Centre, Blowhole Point, Kiama; (042) 32 3322. **Accommodation:** 1 hotel, 1 motel/lodge, 1 guest house.
MAP REF. 116 F9, 119 I3, 120 I11

Jerilderie   Pop. 898

This town on the Newell Hwy was held by the Kelly gang for two days in 1879 when they captured the police station, cut the telegraph wires and robbed the bank. Today it is the centre of the largest merino stud area in NSW and also supports an expanding vegetable industry. **Of interest:** Telegraph Office Museum, Powell St; next door The Willows historic home offers crafts, Devonshire teas and tourist information. Courthouse, Newell Hwy. Lake Jerilderie for water sports; adjacent Luke Park features 'Steel Wings', one of largest windmills in southern hemisphere, also shady picnic areas. **Tourist information:** The Willows, Powell St; (058) 86 1666. **Accommodation:** 1 hotel/motel, 3 motels, 1 caravan/camping park. **See also:** The Newell.
MAP REF. 127 M11

Jindabyne   Pop. 4601

Now situated on the shores of Lake Jindabyne at the foothills of the Snowy Mountains, the original township was located on the banks of the Snowy River. From 1962, residents of the old town moved up to the new site chosen by the Snowy Mountains Hydro-electric Authority. This made way for the damming of the Snowy River to form a water storage as part of the Snowy Mountains Scheme. At an altitude of 930 m and situated in the heart of the Snowy Mountains, Jindabyne attracts skiers in winter and anglers, water-sports enthusiasts and bushwalkers in summer. **Of interest:** Lake Jindabyne is well stocked with trout and is ideal for boating, water-skiing, and other water sports. **In the area:** Kosciusko National Park Headquarters and Information Centre, Sawpit Creek, 20 km W, on Mt Kosciusko Rd. Winter shuttle-bus service to Perisher, Smiggin Holes and Thredbo. After snow has melted, 50-min. drive W from Jindabyne leads to Charlotte Pass, where there is choice of 300-m boardwalk to view main range or 16-km round trip to summit of Mt Kosciusko. At Thredbo, 37 km W, chairlift operates all year and in summer provides easy access over steel-mesh track to summit of Mt Kosciusko, 13-km round trip. Eagles Range for farm holidays. **Tourist information:** Snowy River Information Centre, Petamin Plaza; (064) 56 2444. **Accommodation:** 1 hotel/motel, 5 motels, 2 caravan/camping parks.
MAP REF. 118 G11, 119 C9, 140 C12, 235 J4

Junee   Pop. 3673

An important railhead town and commercial centre 482 km SW of Sydney on the Olympic Way. **Of interest:** 'Monte Cristo' homestead overlooking township; the (47 bay) Rail Round House; the famous wine family's (McWilliam's) vineyard and winery; Endeavour Park, Memorial Park & Hobbin Pond. **In the area:** The Bethungra Rail Spiral, a unique engineering feat. **Tourist information:** Tarcutta St, Wagga Wagga; (069) 23 5402 or Junee Council, Belmore St; (069) 24 1277. **Accommodation:** 4 hotels, 1 motel, 1 caravan/camping park.
MAP REF. 119 A4, 120 B11, 127 R9

Katoomba–Wentworth Falls   Pop. 16 927

Visitors are big business in Katoomba, the highly developed tourism centre of the Blue Mountains. At least 3 million people visit the area each year. Katoomba and the smaller towns of Leura and Wentworth Falls have many interesting features as well as superb mountain scenery. Originally developed as a coal mine last century, it was not long before Katoomba was attracting wealthy Sydney holiday-makers. Word of the area's attractions spread and guest and holiday houses sprang up almost overnight. The coal mine foundered, but Katoomba continued to develop as a tourist resort. The Blue Mountains region abounds in natural and man-made attractions: the Blue Mountains National Park (parts of which were destroyed in the January bushfires), historic sites, art galleries, gift, craft and antique shops, as well as cosy tearooms and fine restaurants. **Of interest:** Scenic Skyway and Railway Complex, Violet St/Cliff Dr; first horizontal passenger-carrying ropeway in Australia, the Scenic Skyway travels about 350 m across mountain gorge above Cooks Crossing, giving magnificent views of Katoomba Falls, Orphan Rock and Jamison Valley. Built in late 1800s by founder of Katoomba coal mine to bring out coal and transport miners, and reputed to be world's steepest railway, the Scenic Railway descends into Jamison Valley at an average incline of 45°, through a sunlit, tree-clad gorge approximately 445 m in length. Famous rock formations (The Three Sisters and Orphan Rock) and Katoomba Falls are floodlit at night. At Wentworth Falls, Yester Grange (1870s), colonial homestead-museum on 4.7 ha site; restored and furnished to late-Victorian splendour. Horse-drawn carriage rides through Leura's tree-lined streets. Everglades Garden, Everglades Ave in Leura, one of Australia's great gardens. Leuralla, Olympian Pde in Leura; historic art deco mansion, houses major collection of 19th-century Australian art, Australia's biggest collection of toys, dolls, trains and railway memorabilia, and memorial museum to Dr H. V. Evatt. Cliff Drive follows cliff tops around Katoomba–Leura, offering spectacular views at many lookouts and picnic spots. Walking tracks along cliff tops and descending into Jamison Valley offer chance to experience delights of heathland and rainforest. Wide selection of accommodation available at such superb resorts as Fairmont at Leura with its indoor pool and spa, Carrington Hotel at Katoomba, luxurious guest houses,

South West Rocks, near Kempsey

modern motels, holiday cottages and cabins. Visitors can enjoy horseriding, four wheel driving, cycling and scenic flights. **In the area:** Dramatic views from Sublime Point (on Blue Mountains Scenic Drive from Leura) and Hanging Rock (NE of Blackheath on 4WD track). Jemby-Rinjah Lodge at Blackheath, 12 km N, has environmental studies centre set on edge of Blue Mountains National Park. Govett's Leap and Evans Point Lookouts in park. Hydro Majestic Hotel at Medlow Bath, 5 km NW; once a health resort, dates from around turn of century. Norman Lindsay Gallery and Museum at Faulconbridge, 32 km E; picnic area in grounds. Mount Victoria, 16 km N, National Trust classified village with craft shops and museum; nearby waterfalls, Pulpit Rock reserve and Mount York Historic Site. Yerranderie, abandoned old silver-mining town, 70 km S of Blackheath, surrounded by 2430 ha wildlife reserve. Jenolan Caves, containing some of most splendid underground caves and above-ground arches in Australia, in recreation reserve 80 km S of Katoomba. Australia Day Regatta at Wentworth Falls Lake in Jan. Blue Mountains

Summer Classic held in Feb. at Blackheath, Leura and Katoomba golf courses. Yulefest, traditional snow-clad Christmas in July. Leura Gardens Festival in Oct. **Tourist information:** Echo Point, Katoomba; or the Blue Mountains Information Centre, Gt Western Hwy, Glenbrook; (047) 39 6266. **Accommodation:** In Katoomba: 2 hotels, 7 motels, 1 caravan/camping park. **See also:** The Blue Mountains.
MAP REF. 104 G7, 106 E9, 106 G8, 120 H8

Kempsey

Pop. 9049

Kempsey is situated in the Macleay River Valley, 480 km N of Sydney, and is the commercial centre of a growing district of dairying, tourism and light industry, including the Akubra hat factory. The town celebrated its sesquicentenary in 1986. **Of interest:** Macleay River Historical Society Museum, Pacific Hwy, South Kempsey. Number of 19th-century buildings in Kemp, Elbow, Sea and Belgrave Sts, West Kempsey. **In the area:** Trial Bay Gaol, 40 km NE; built by prisoners in 1880s. South West Rocks, 35 km NE, beach resort; river

cruises. Bellbrook, 47 km W; village classified by National Trust. Crescent Head, 20 km SE. Limeburners Creek Nature Reserve, further 10 km S of village. Hat Head National Park, 32 km E. Fish Rock Cave, noted for scuba diving, 5 km off Smoky Cape. **Tourist information:** Pacific Hwy, South Kempsey; (065) 63 1555. **Accommodation:** 6 hotels, 10 motels, 5 caravan/camping parks.
MAP REF. 109 G3, 123 O10

Khancoban   Pop. 416

Situated in the lush green Murray Valley at the western end of the Alpine Way, 109 km NW of Jindabyne, this small modern town was built by the Snowy Mountains Authority and is now an administrative centre. Khancoban offers a variety of accommodation from a luxurious alpine retreat to a caravan park. National Parks and Wildlife Service have videos of Snowy Mountains Scheme and Kosciusko National Park. **In the area:** Inspections of Murray 1 Power Station; trout fishing, water sports, whitewater rafting. Fishing tours. Excellent picnic and rest areas along Alpine Way and spectacular mountain views from Scammel's Spur Lookout. Brilliant roadside displays of wildflowers in spring and autumn. **Tourist information:** National Parks and Wildlife Service, Scott St; (060) 76 9373. **Accommodation:** 1 hotel/motel, 1 caravan/camping park.
MAP REF. 118 A9, 119 B8, 234 H3

Kiama   Pop. 10 631

The spectacular Blowhole is the best-known attraction of this resort town. Discovered by explorer George Bass in 1797, it sprays water up to heights of 60 m and is floodlit each evening. Kiama is the centre of a prosperous dairying and mixed farming district. **Of interest:** Kiama Beach for surfing, swimming and fishing. Pilots Cottage Historical Museum, beside Kiama Visitors Centre and restaurant at Blowhole Point. Terrace houses, specialty and craft shops in Collins St. Family History Centre, Railway Pde; world-wide collection of records for tracing family history. Agricultural Show held Jan. Jazz Festival in Feb. Art Show Sept. Seaside Festival Oct. **In the area:** Little Blowhole, 2 km S, off Tingira Cres; although smaller, sometimes outblows its famous brother. Cathedral Rocks, 3 km N, at Jones Beach; scenic rocky outcrop, best viewed at dawn. **Tourist information:** Blowhole Point; (042) 32 3322.

Accommodation: 2 hotels, 6 motels, 4 caravan/camping parks. **See also:** The Illawarra Coast.
MAP REF. 116 G9, 119 I4, 121 J11

Kyogle   Pop. 2912

Kyogle makes a good base for exploring the mountains nearby. It is also the centre of a lush dairy and mixed-farming area on the upper reaches of the Richmond River near the Qld border. **In the area:** World Heritage-listed Border Ranges National Park, 27 km NE; walking tracks and forestry road access. Views of Mt Warning and Tweed Valley from park lookouts. Tweed Range Scenic Drive (64 km), through eastern section; pristine rainforest and deep gorges with waterfalls plunging into crystal-clear creeks. Magnificent views from Mt Lindesay, 45 km NW, on NSW-Qld border. Wiangaree State Forest, 30 km N; rainforest with elevated coastal views. Toonumbar Dam, 31 km W, offers conference centre, bushwalking and picnic/barbecue facilities; freshwater fishing and camping at Bell's Bay. Picnic spots include Roseberry Nursery and Moore Park (23 km and 27 km N), Tooloom Falls (95 km NW) and scenic area at Nimbin Rocks (32 km E). **Tourist information:** 29 Summerland Way; (066) 32 1044. **Accommodation:** 2 hotels, 1 motel, 1 caravan/camping park.
MAP REF. 123 O2, 475 N8

Lake Cargelligo   Pop. 1256

A small township, 586 km W of Sydney, of the same name as the lake, which serves the surrounding agricultural and pastoral district. **Of interest:** Fishing, boating, water-skiing and swimming on lake; picnic/barbecue facilities. Lake is home to many species of bird, including pelicans, wild ducks, geese and black swans, galahs, cockatoos and, at times, the rare black cockatoo. **Tourist information:** Kelly Reserve, Newell Hwy, Parkes; (068) 62 4365. **Accommodation:** 3 hotels, 2 motels, 1 caravan/camping park.
MAP REF. 127 O4

Lake Macquarie

Pop. 158 300
Lake Macquarie is a city without a town centre, but boasts the largest saltwater coastal lake in Australia as its hub. The northern shore townships of Lake Macquarie such as Toronto, Speers Point, Belmont and Boolaroo contain many

restaurants and sailing clubs. The lake is excellent for swimming, sailing, fishing and associated water sports. **Of interest:** Lake cruises on *Nambucca Princess* and MV *Macquarie Lady*, both leaving from Toronto Wharf and Belmont Public Wharf. Dobell House, 47 Dobell Dr., Wangi Wangi; home of Australian artist Sir William Dobell, with collection of his work and memorabilia. Eraring Power Station; guided tours. **In the area:** Bahtabah Land Council Visitors Centre, Lakeview Pde, Blacksmiths; Aboriginal art and crafts, open daily. **Tourist information:** 72 Pacific Hwy, Blacksmiths; (049) 72 1172. **Accommodation:** Belmont, 2 hotels, 10 motels, 9 caravan/camping parks. Charlestown: 2 hotels, 5 motels. Toronto: 1 hotel/motel, 1 caravan/camping park.
MAP REF. 105 Q2, 112 G11

Leeton   Pop. 6245

Located 560 km SW of Sydney, Leeton is the first of the planned towns in the Murrumbidgee Irrigation Area and was designed by American architect Walter Burley Griffin. The town is an important administrative and processing centre for this intensive fruit-, rice- and wine-grape-growing area. **Of interest:** Historic Hydro Hotel (1919), Chelmsford Pl. Letona Fruit Cannery, Wamoon Ave; Sunrice Country Visitors Centre at rice mill, Calrose St; Quelch Juice Factory, Brady Way; guided tours weekdays. Leeton Sunwhite Rice Festival every even year, 11 days including Easter. **In the area:** Toorak and Lillypilly Estate Wineries, both close to town. Fivebough Swamp, 2 km N; famous waterbird sanctuary. Yanco Agricultural High School, 10 km S. Murrumbidgee State Forests, 12 km S. Gogeldrie Weir, 23 km SW. Yanco Weir, 25 km SE. Aquatic Park near Yanco. Whitton Court House Museum, 23 km W. Gliding and hot-air ballooning. **Tourist information:** Chelmsford Pl.; (069) 53 2832. **Accommodation:** 3 hotels, 4 motels, 2 caravan parks. **See also:** Vineyards and Wineries.
MAP REF. 127 O8

Lennox Head   Pop. 3036

Just north of Ballina, Lennox Head has retained its charming seaside village atmosphere. The area is famous for its surfing beaches. **Of interest:** Freshwater Lake Ainsworth, 50 m from surfing beach; popular with windsurfers. **In the area:** Swimming, surfing, snorkelling.

Many scenic walks and rainforests a short drive away. **Tourist information:** Ballina Tourist Information Centre, Las Balsas Plaza, Ballina; (066) 86 3484. **Accommodation:** 3 motels, 1 caravan/camping park.
MAP REF. 123 Q3, 475 O9

Lightning Ridge
Pop. 1522

Small opal-mining township in the famous Lightning Ridge opal fields, 74 km N of Walgett, via the Castlereagh Hwy. The valuable black opal found in the area attracts gem enthusiasts world-wide. **Of interest:** Bowling Club and Diggers Rest Hotel, Morilla St, share township's social life. Underground mine tours, opal-cutting demonstrations; museums, potteries, and displays of local art and craft, including opal jewellery and gem opals. **In the area:** Cactus Nursery, 2 km N, off Bald Hill Rd. Fauna Orphanage, Opal St, 3 km S. Hot Artesian Bore Baths (free), 2 km NE. Nature reserves and fossicking. **Tourist information:** 77 Fox St, Walgett; (068) 28 1399. **Accommodation:** 3 motels, 5 caravan/camping parks.
MAP REF. 122 B5, 474 E10

Lismore
Pop. 27 246

Regional centre of the Northern Rivers district of NSW, a closely settled and intensively cultivated rural area producing dairy products, tropical fruits, beef, timber and fodder crops, Lismore is situated on Wilsons River (formerly the north arm of the Richmond River), 821 km N of Sydney. It is best known for its rainforest heritage, including the Rotary Rainforest Reserve, situated within the residential area of the city, Wilsons Park and the Boatharbour Reserve. **Of interest:** Lismore Tourist Information Centre; Rainforest Exhibition, Cultural Gallery and other displays. Surrounding Heritage Park (picnic areas), cnr Ballina and Molesworth Sts. Cedar Log Memorial, Ballina St. Richmond River Historical Museum and Lismore Regional Art Gallery, both in Molesworth St. Robinson's Lookout, Robinson Ave. Claude Riley Memorial Lookout, New Ballina Rd. River cruises on MV *Bennelong*, The Wharf, Magellan St. Kidsfest held March. Gemfest in May. **In the area:** Macadamia Magic at Alphadale, 11 km E; macadamia processing plant and tourist complex. Rocky Creek Dam, 25 km N. Minyon Falls and Peates Mountain Lookout, in Whian Whian State Forest, 25 km N. Spectacular volcanic Nimbin Rocks, 3 km S of Nimbin (29 km N). World Heritage-listed Border Ranges National Park, 25 km N of Nimbin, and Nightcap National Park, 25 km N of Lismore. Lismore Lake, 3 km S; picnic/barbecue facilities, pleasant lagoon for swimming, children's adventure park. Tucki Tucki Koala Reserve, 15 km S, adjacent to Lismore–Woodburn Rd;

Aboriginal ceremonial ground nearby. **Tourist information:** Cnr Ballina and Molesworth Sts; (066) 22 0122. **Accommodation:** 10 hotels, 4 motels, 5 caravan/camping parks.
MAP REF. 123 P3, 475 N9

Lithgow
Pop. 11 968

This important coal-mining city on the north-west fringes of the Blue Mountains is a must for railway enthusiasts. The city itself is highly industrialised with two power stations and several large factories, but the surrounding countryside is beautiful. **Of interest:** Eskbank House, Bennett St, built in 1841 by Thomas Brown, who discovered Lithgow coal seam; now museum with fine collection of 19th-century furniture and vehicles, and displays depicting industrial history of area. Blast Furnace Park, off Inch St; ruins of Australia's first blast furnace complex. Festival of the Valley held in Nov. **In the area:** Zig Zag Steam Railway, 10 km E, via Bells Line of Road; breathtaking stretch of railway, regarded as engineering masterpiece when built in 1869, and restored by enthusiasts; train trips and picnic/barbecue facilities. Sweeping views from Hassan Walls Lookout, 5 km S, via Hassans Wall Rd. Historic village of Hartley, 12 km SE, off Great Western Hwy, has convict-built courthouse (1837) of outstanding architectural and historic interest. Jenolan

View from Mt Pleasant, south of Kiama

Caves, 60 km SE. Lake Lyall, 6 km E; power boating, water-skiing, trout fishing. Mt Piper Power Station, 21 km NW; Lake Wallace, at Wallerawang, 11 km W; sailing and trout fishing. **Tourist information:** 285 Main Street; (063) 51 2307. **Accommodation:** 8 hotels, 5 motels, 1 caravan/camping park.
MAP REF. 104 F4, 120 H7

Lockhart
Pop. 887
This pleasant historic town, situated 65 km SW of Wagga, was originally known as Green's Gunyah and was renamed Lockhart in 1897. A distinctive feature of the commercial centre is the wide, shady shopfront verandahs, a fine example of a turn-of-the-century streetscape, for which it received a classified listing by the National Trust. **Tourist information:** Tarcutta St, Wagga Wagga; (069)23 5402. **Accommodation:** 1 hotel, 1 motel, 1 caravan park.
MAP REF. 127 P10

Macksville
Pop. 2869
An attractive town on the Nambucca River, south of Nambucca Heads. **Of interest:** Mary Boulton Pioneer Cottage, River St; replica of pioneer home, includes furniture, costumes and museum of horse-drawn vehicles in its collection. **In the area:** Cosmopolitan Hotel (1903), the 'pub with no beer', made famous by song, at Taylors Arm, 26 km W; surrounded by lawns and trees, with picnic/barbecue area. Joseph and Eliza Newman Folk Museum at unspoiled Bowraville (the 'verandah post town'), 16 km NW. **Tourist information:** Ridge St, Nambucca Heads; (065) 68 6954. **Accommodation:** 2 hotels, 3 motels, 2 caravan parks.
MAP REF. 123 O9, 475 M13

Maclean
Pop. 2890
Fishing and river prawning fleets are based at Maclean, known as 'the Scottish town in Australia', on the Clarence River, about 740 km N of Sydney. Fishermen from here and from the nearby towns of Yamba and Iluka catch about 20% of the State's seafood. Sugarcane, maize and mixed farm crops are grown in the area. **Of interest:** Scottish Corner, River St; shop with tourist information. Bicentennial Museum and adjoining Stone Cottage (1879), Wharf St. Maclean Lookout and Pinnacle Rocks. Rainforest walking track from High School. Maclean Highland Gathering held Easter. Cane Harvest

Festival in Sept. **In the area:** Houseboats for hire at Brushgrove, 21 km SW. Yuraygir National Park, 24 km SE. **Tourist information:** Shire Offices; (066) 45 2266. **Accommodation:** 3 hotels, 2 motels, 3 caravan/camping parks.
MAP REF. 123 P5, 475 N10

Maitland
Pop. 45 209
On the Hunter River, 28 km NW of Newcastle, Maitland dates back to the early days of the colony. The flourishing city's winding High St has been recorded by the National Trust as a Conservation Area and over 90% of the buildings date back to the 1800s. First settled in 1818, when convicts were put to work as cedarcutters, it was a flourishing township by the 1840s. **Of interest:** National Trust properties Grossmann House, Georgian-style folk museum, and Brough House (1870), containing city's art collection, in Church St, are mirror images of each other. Cintra, Regent St; Victorian mansion offering b & b accommodation. Self-guide Heritage Walk of East Maitland and Morpeth. **In the area:** Walka Waterworks, 3 km N; former pumping station, excellent bushwalking and picnic site. At Morpeth, 5 km NE: historic buildings with superb iron lace and specialty craft shops. At Lochinvar, 13 km W: Windermere Colonial Museum, built of sandstone brick by convict labour in 1820s, later occupied by William Charles Wentworth; also NSW Equestrian Centre. **Tourist information:** Hew Cottage, cnr Banks St and New England Hwy; (049) 33 2611. **Accommodation:** 4 hotels, 6 motels, 1 caravan/camping park.
MAP REF. 112 C7, 121 K4

Manilla
Pop. 2110
This small town, set in beautiful countryside, boasts Dutton's Meadery, one of only two meaderys in the State. Visitors can sample and buy fresh honey and mead. **Of interest:** Picturesque street setting with antique stores and coffee shops. Royce Cottage Historical Museum, Manilla St. **In the area:** Manilla Ski Gardens on Lake Keepit, 20 km SW. Muluerindie Country Holidays, 22 km E. Split Rock Dam Recreation Area, 28 km NE. Warrabah National Park, 40 km N, peaceful riverside retreat; fishing, swimming and canoeing on Namoi and Manilla Rivers. **Tourist information:** Cnr New England Hwy and Kable Ave, Tamworth; (067) 68 4462. **Accommodation:**

1 motel, 1 caravan/ camping park. **See also:** New England.
MAP REF. 122 I9

Menindee
Pop. 467
It was at this small township, 110 km SE of Broken Hill, that the ill-fated Burke and Wills stayed in 1860 on their journey north. **Of interest:** Maiden's Hotel (where they lodged). Ah Chung's Bakehouse Gallery, Menindee St. Menindee Lakes Lookout. **In the area:** Menindee Lakes, upstream from township; water-storage scheme that guarantees an unfailing water supply to Broken Hill. Yachting, fishing and swimming on lakes; nearby Copi Hollow attracts water-skiers and power boat enthusiasts. Kinchega National Park, 1 km W; emus, red kangaroos and waterbirds; shearers' quarters accommodation. **Tourist information:** Broken Hill Tourist Information Centre, cnr Blende and Bromide Sts, Broken Hill; (080) 87 6077. **Accommodation:** 2 hotels, 1 motel, 2 caravan/ camping parks.
MAP REF. 124 E13, 126 E1

Merimbula
Pop. 4259
Excellent surfing, fishing and prawning make this small sea and lake town a popular holiday resort. Its sister village of Pambula also offers fine fishing and surfing. **Of interest:** Aquarium at Merimbula Wharf, Lake St. Old School Museum, Main St. Magic Mountain Family Recreation Park, Sapphire Coast Dr. Jazz Festival held June. **In the area:** Cruises on lakes. Boats for hire. Tura Beach, 5 km N. Pambula Beach, 10 km S, with walking track and lookout. Ben Boyd National Park, 13 km S. **Tourist information:** Beach St; (064) 95 1129. **Accommodation:** 16 motels, 4 caravan/ camping parks. **See also:** The South Coast.
MAP REF. 117 F9, 119 F11, 235 P7

Merriwa
Pop. 962
This small township in the western Hunter region is noted for its many historic buildings. **Of interest:** Self-guide Historic Walks; buildings of note in Vennacher, Bay and McCartney Sts. Historical Museum housed in stone cottage (1857), Bettington St. Bottle Museum in Tourist Information Centre, Vennacher St. **In the area:** Convict-built Flags Rd, runs from town to Gungal, 25 km SE. The Drip picnic area, at Goulburn River National Park, 35 km S. Official

gem-fossicking area 27 km sw. Cassilis, 45 km NW; historic sandstone buildings. Aboriginal paintings of hands, on rocks in caves just off Mudgee Rd, 32 km sw of Cassilis. Ulan coal mine, further 8 km sw; largest open-cut mine in southern hemisphere; viewing area. **Tourist information:** Vennacher St; (065) 48 2505. **Accommodation:** 2 hotels, 1 motel, 1 caravan/camping park.
MAP REF. 120 H3, 122 H13

Mittagong — Pop. 5666

The gateway to the Southern Highlands, Mittagong is 110 km s of Sydney. **Of interest:** Historic cemeteries and many gracious old buildings. Butterfly House and The Maze, Bessemer St. Natural wonders of Lake Alexandra, Queen St; walking tracks, Old Anthracite Mines, falls; mecca for children. Mt Gibraltar, once volcanic, access from Oxley Dr; picnic facilities, walking tracks, spectacular views. **In the area:** Well-planned walks through nearby hills include Box Vale and Natural Arch Walks; follow Hume Fwy from Mittagong to Berrima turnoff, 15 km sw. Laopline Scenic Drive includes Thirlmere Lakes National Park, Thirlmere Railway Museum, potteries and orchards. **Tourist information:** Winifred West Park, Old Hume Hwy; (048) 71 2888. **Accommodation:** 2 hotels, 6 motels, 1 caravan/camping park.
MAP REF. 116 C6, 119 H3, 120 I10

Menindee Lakes

Moama–Echuca — Pop. 9438

Moama and its twin city Echuca, on the Victorian side of the Murray River, embody the age of the paddle-steamer, when the port of Echuca was a major outlet for agricultural products. **Of interest:** Restored port at Echuca; Coach House Carriage Museum, Historical Museum, Njernda Aboriginal Museum, National Holden Museum, Gem Club, Gumnutland Model Village, Port Antique Photographics and Penny Arcade. **In the area:** Murray River tours aboard cruise boats or paddle-steamers. Moira and Barmah red gum forests, 35 km SE. Joy flights, go-karts and poker-machine clubs. Houseboats. **Tourist information:** 2 Leslie St, Echuca; (054) 80 7555. **Accommodation:** 4 hotels, 1 hotel/ motel, 28 motels, 11 caravan/camping parks.
MAP REF. 127 K13, 232 E4

Molong — Pop. 1563

The grave of Yaranigh, the Aboriginal guide of explorer Sir Thomas Mitchell, is 2 km E of this Mitchell Hwy town. Yaranigh was buried there in 1850, according to the rites of his tribe. The grave is marked by a headstone that pays tribute to his courage and fidelity. Four trees, one dead but preserved for its Aboriginal carvings, mark the four corners of the burial ground. **Of interest:** Yarn Market, Craft Cottage and Coach House Gallery, Bank St. Annual sheepdog trials held in March. **In the area:** Mitchell's Monument, 21 km s, marks site of explorer's base camp. **Tourist information:** Civic Gardens, Byng St, Orange; (063) 61 5226. **Accommodation:** 2 hotels, 1 motel, 1 caravan/camping park.
MAP REF. 120 E6

Moree — Pop. 10 062

Situated on the Mehi River, 640 km NW of Sydney, this town is the nucleus of a large beef-, wool-, cotton- and wheat-producing region. It is best known for its artesian spa baths, said to relieve arthritis and rheumatism. **Of interest:** Spa complex, Anne St; with olympic swimming pool. Mary Brand Park, Gwydir St. Meteorological station, Jones Ave. Moree Lands Office (1894), National-Trust-classified, cnr Frome and Heber Sts; self-guide Mehi River Walking Track. Moree Plains Regional Gallery, Heber St. Yurundiali Aboriginal Corporation, Endeavour Lane; screen printing clothing factory. **In the area:** Pecan Nut Farm, 35 km E; tours in season. Inspection of cotton gins during harvesting season. **Tourist information:** Lyle Houlihan Park, Alice St; (067) 52 9559. **Accommodation:** 6 hotels, 1 hotel/ motel, 18 motels, 3 caravan/camping parks. **See also:** The Newell.
MAP REF. 122 G5, 474 H10

Moruya — Pop. 2520

Many well known old dairying estates were founded near this town, which was once a gateway to the Araluen and Braidwood goldfields. Situated on the Moruya River, 322 km s of Sydney, it is now a dairying, timber and oyster-farming centre. Granite used in the pylons of the Sydney Harbour Bridge was quarried in the district. **Of interest:** Eurobodalla Historic Museum, in town centre, depicts discovery of gold at Mogo and general history of district. Courthouse (1880), on Princes Hwy. Catholic Church (1889), Queen St; built in blue granite, by local builder Joseph Ziegler. Moruya River; black swan and sea eagle colonies up-river at Yarragee. **In the area:** Mort Memorial Church and historic cemetery at Moruya Heads, 7 km E. Coomerang House at Bodalla, 24 km S; home of 19th-century industrialist and dairy farmer Thomas Sutcliffe Mort. Nerrigundah, 44 km SW; former gold-mining town. Deua National Park, 20 km W; Hanging Mountain and Mt Wanderer lookouts. Fishing, surfing and water sports. **Tourist information:** Cnr Princes Hwy and Beach Rd, Batemans Bay; (044) 72 6900, and Narooma; (044) 76 2881. **Accommodation:** 1 hotel, 2 motels, 2 caravan/camping parks. MAP REF. 119 G8, 141 M18, 235 Q1

Moss Vale   Pop. 5690
The industrial and agricultural centre of the Southern Highlands, this town stands on part of the 1000-acre parcel of land granted to Charles Throsby in 1819. **Of interest:** Leighton Park, running almost half length of main street. Cecil Hoskins Reserve with abundance of birdlife. Historic Throsby Park, on northern edge of town; open to public on special occasions. **In the area:** At township of Sutton Forest, 6 km S on Illawarra Hwy, Old Butcher Shop Gallery has items ranging from shortbread to antiques. Exeter, 4 km further S. Fitzroy Falls in Morton National Park, 20 km SE. **Tourist information:** Winifred West Park, Old Hume Hwy, Mittagong; (048) 71 2888. **Accommodation:** 2 hotels, 2 motels, 1 caravan/camping park. MAP REF. 116 B8, 119 H3, 120 H10

Moulamein   Pop. 459
This is the oldest town in the Riverina, already well established in the 1870s as a prosperous inland port on the Edward River. Today the town is noted for its fishing. **Of interest:** Old wharf, Main St. Restored courthouse. Riverside picnic areas. Lake Moulamein and nearby State forests. **Tourist information:** Golden Rivers Tourism, 25 Murray St,

Barham; (054) 53 3100. **Accommodation:** 1 hotel, 1 caravan/camping park. MAP REF. 126 I10, 231 P10

Mudgee   Pop. 7447
This attractively designed town is the centre of a productive agricultural area on the Cudgegong River, 264 km NW of Sydney. Wine grapes, fine wool, sheep, cattle and honey are among the local produce. There are horse studs in the area. **Of interest:** Many fine buildings in town centre, including St John's Church of England (1860), St Mary's Roman Catholic Church, railway station, town hall and Colonial Inn Museum, all in Market St. Mt Vincent Meadery, Common Rd. Honey Haven, cnr Hill End and Gulgong Rds, and Mudgee Honey, Robertson St. Mudgee Creative Yarns, Sydney Rd; tours of working mill, sales. **In the area:** Henry Lawson's boyhood home memorial; plaque on remains of demolished cottage, 6 km N. Cudgegong River Park, 14 km W, on eastern foreshores of Burrendong Dam; water sports and excellent fishing. Windamere Dam, 24 km E, with camping facilities. Langton's Roses, 5 km S; tours and sales. Pick-Your-Own Farm, 12 km S; variety of fruit and vegetables, Oct.–May. Eighteen local wineries, including Craigmoor, Montrose, Huntington Estate, Botobolar; tasting and sales. **Tourist information:** 84 Market St; (063) 72 5874. **Accommodation:** 5 hotels, 9 motels, 3 caravan/camping parks. **See also:** Vineyards and Wineries. MAP REF. 120 F4

Mullumbimby   Pop. 2612
Situated in lush subtropical country, Mullumbimby is some 850 km NE of Sydney. **Of interest:** Art Gallery, cnr Burringbar and Stuart Sts. Restored Cedar House, Dalley St; classified by National Trust, with antiques gallery. Brunswick Valley Historical Museum, in old post office (1907), Stuart St. Brunswick Valley Heritage Park, Tyagarah St. **In the area:** Nightcap National Park to north, and Tuntable Falls to south. Sakura Farm, 15 km W, in hills at Mullum; run by Buddhist monk, it offers unique retreat-style holidays. Crystal Castle, 7 km N; large display of natural quartz. Wanganui Gorge and rainforest walking track, 20 km W. Skydiving and paragliding at airstrip at Tyagarah, on Pacific Hwy, 13 km SE. **Tourist information:** 80 Jonson St, Byron Bay; (066) 85 8050.

Accommodation: 2 hotels, 2 motels, 1 camping park. MAP REF. 123 P2, 475 N8

Mulwala   Pop. 1330
On the foreshores of Lake Mulwala, the town is a major aquatic centre. Lake Mulwala is a man-made lake of over 6000 ha, formed by the damming of the Murray River at Yarrawonga Weir in 1939 to provide water for irrigation. **Of interest:** Yachting, water-skiing, sailboarding, swimming, canoeing and fishing. Linley Animal Park, Corowa Rd; native and exotic animals, horse and pony rides. Tunzafun Amusement Park offers entertainment for young. Bowlers and golfers are well catered for in area with excellent facilities and licensed clubs. Cruise boats operate scenic tours on Lake Mulwala. **Tourist information:** Irvine Pde, Yarrawonga; (057) 44 1989. **Accommodation:** 2 hotels, 10 motels, 6 caravan/camping parks. MAP REF. 127 N13, 233 K3

Murrurundi   Pop. 983
This picturesque town on the New England Hwy, set in a lush valley on the Pages River, is overshadowed by the Liverpool Ranges. **Of interest:** St Joseph's Catholic Church, Polding St; contains 1000 pieces of Italian marble. Murrurundi Museum, Main St. Paradise Park, Paradise Rd; horseshoe-shaped, surrounded by mountains; visits by wildlife in evening. Bushman's Carnival held Oct. **In the area:** Chilcott's Creek, 15 km N, where huge diprotodon remains, now in Sydney Museum, were found. Burning Mountain at Wingen, 20 km S. Timor Limestone Caves, 43 km E. **Tourist information:** Council Offices, 47 Mayne St; (065) 46 6205. **Accommodation:** 3 hotels, 2 motels, 1 caravan/camping park. MAP REF. 120 I1, 122 I12

Murwillumbah   Pop. 8003
Situated on the banks of the Tweed River, 31 km S of the Qld border in the beautiful Tweed Valley, Murwillumbah's local industries include cattle-raising and the growing of sugarcane, tropical fruits, tea and coffee. **Of interest:** Tweed River Regional Art Gallery, Tumbulgum Rd. **In the area:** Tweed River Houseboats for hire, on Pacific Hwy, 1 km N of Visitors Centre. Condong sugar mill, 5 km N; inspections July–Dec. Avocado Adventureland, 15 km N. Griffith Furniture

Mt Warning, near Murwillumbah

Park, 8 km NE. World Heritage-listed areas within radius of 50 km include Mt Warning, Nightcap and Border Ranges National Parks. Madura Tea Estates, 12 km NE. Pioneer Plantation, 25 km SE; banana plantation, farm animals, native gardens, tours; open daily. Hare Krishna Community Farm, Eungella, 10 km W; visitors welcome. Farm holidays specialty of area; at Uki Village Guesthouse, Crystal Creek Rainforest Retreat, Midginbil Hill, Bushranger Hideaway, Mt Warning Forest Hideaway, Wollumbin Caravan Park and Tyalgum Tops. **Tourist information:** Cnr Pacific Hwy and Alma St; (066) 72 1340. **Accommodation:** 6 hotels, 4 motels, 3 caravan/camping parks.
MAP REF. 123 P1, 475 N8

Muswellbrook   Pop. 10 140

In the Upper Hunter Valley, Muswellbrook is the centre of pastoral enterprises, including fodder crops, stud cattle and horses, wineries and dairy products. There is also a large open-cut coal-mining industry. **Of interest:** Muswellbrook Art Gallery in old town hall. **In the area:** Matt Peel's Quarter Horse Stud and Rural Museum, 12 km W. Denman, unspoilt 1930s town, 25 km W; horsedrawn tours of area. Bayswater Power Station, 16 km S; inspection tours. Wollemi National Park, 30 km SW. Ten local wineries open daily for tastings and sales. **Tourist**

information: Old Teahouse and Gift Shoppe, 208 Bridge St; (065) 43 3599. **Accommodation:** 1 hotel, 8 motels, 1 caravan/camping park.
MAP REF. 121 J3, 122 I13

Nambucca Heads   Pop. 5683

At the mouth of the Nambucca River, 552 km N of Sydney, this beautifully sited town is ideal for boating, fishing and swimming. **Of interest:** Nambucca Historical Museum, Headland Reserve; many old photographs. Model Train Museum, Pelican Cres. **In the area:** Breathtaking views from several local lookouts. Bakers Creek Station, 40 km SW; horseriding, fishing, canoes, rainforest walks, picnic/barbecue facilities, cabins. **Tourist information:** Ridge St; (065) 68 6954. **Accommodation:** 1 hotel, 9 motels, 6 caravan/camping parks.
MAP REF. 123 O8, 475 N13

Narooma   Pop. 3443

This popular fishing resort at the mouth of the Wagonga River on the Princes Hwy, 360 km S of Sydney, is well known for its rock oysters. **Of interest:** Excellent golf course on scenic cliff top. Mystery Bay near Lake Corunna, famous for coloured sands and strange rock formations, and other inlets and lakes north and south of town. Cruises on *Wagonga Princess*. **In the area:** Tuross and other nearby lakes and inlets. Montague

Island, wildlife sanctuary 5.7 nautical miles offshore; large colony of Little Penguins and Australian Fur Seals, year-round tours, prebooking necessary. Historic villages; Central Tilba is Heritage Area, 17 km S of Narooma, just off Princes Hwy, classified as 'unusual mountain village' by National Trust; founded in 1894, old buildings in original 19th-century condition, new buildings to NT specifications. **Tourist information:** Princes Hwy; (044) 76 2881. **Accommodation:** 1 hotel, 13 motels, 4 caravan/camping parks. **See also:** The South Coast.
MAP REF. 117 I2, 119 G8, 141 N11, 235 Q3

Narrabri   Pop. 6694

Situated between the Nandewar Range, including Mt Kaputar National Park and the extensive Pilliga scrub country, this town has become a phenomenally successful cotton-producing centre. **Of interest:** Historic buildings include courthouse (1886), Maitland St. Self-guide town tour. Riverside picnic area, Tibbereena St. Agricultural show held in April and Spring Festival Oct. long weekend. **In the area:** Guided tours of cotton fields and gins, April–June. Plant Breeding Institute, 9 km N, on Newell Hwy. CSIRO Telescope Complex, 25 km W; 6 giant radio telescopes, Visitors Centre, open daily. Yarrie Lake, 32 km W.

Pilliga State Forest, 23 km SW. Sawn Rocks, 35 km NE, on Bingara Rd within park; spectacular basaltic formation. Mt Kaputar National Park, 53 km E; 360° views from peak take in one-tenth of NSW: spectacular volcanic blue mountain country. **Tourist information:** Newell Hwy; (067) 92 3583. **Accommodation:** 6 hotels, 2 hotel/motels, 8 motels, 3 caravan/ camping parks. **See also:** National Parks; The Newell.
MAP REF. 122 G7, 474 H12

Narrandera   Pop. 4649

This historic town on the Murrumbidgee River, at the junction of the Newell and Sturt Hwys, has been declared an urban conservation area with buildings classified/listed by the National Trust. Located 580 km SW of Sydney, it is the gateway to the Murrumbidgee Irrigation Area. **Of interest:** Lake Talbot Aquatic Playground and caravan/camping complex; 100 m water-slide, 3 pools, ski area, fishing, bushwalking tracks and koala reserve. Antique Corner, Larmer St. NSW Forestry Tree Nursery, Branch St. Tiger Moth Memorial, Narrandera Park, Newell Hwy. Parkside Cottage Museum and Narrandera Park and Miniature Zoo, Newell Hwy. **In the area:** Inland Fisheries Research Station (with star, Percy the Murray Cod) and John Lake Centre, 6 km SE. Berembed Weir, 40 km SE. Pine Hill Nursery, 5 km NE. Robertson Gladioli Farm, 8 km W; group tours by arrangement. Sheep dairy, 5 km NW; milking-time tours, tastings and sales. Deer Farm, 6 km NW; tours daily. Alabama Ostrich Farm, 30 km N; group tours by arrangement. **Tourist information:** Narrandera Park, Newell Hwy; (069) 59 1766. **Accommodation:** 5 hotels, 10 motels, 2 caravan/camping parks. **See also:** The Newell; Vineyards and Wineries.
MAP REF. 127 O9

Narromine   Pop. 3378

On the Macquarie River, 457 km NW of Sydney, renowned for quality agricultural products, including citrus fruit, tomatoes, corn, sheep, cattle and cotton. **In the area:** Water-slide and Rural Museum, Mitchell Hwy. Gin Gin Weir. Gliding and ultralight flying at airport. Trangie Agricultural and Yates Research Stations. Swane's Rose Production Nursery, 5 km W. Narromine Transplants, 2 km N, seedlings grown; open for inspection by appt. **Tourist information:** 84/86 Dandaloo

St. **Accommodation:** 4 hotels, 3 motels, 3 caravan/camping parks.
MAP REF. 120 C3, 122 C13

Nelson Bay   Pop. 6766

The beautiful bay on which this town is sited is the main anchorage of Port Stephens, about 60 km N of Newcastle. **Of interest:** Restored Inner Lighthouse, Nelson Head. Self-guide Heritage Walk, from Dutchmans Bay to Little Beach. Native Flora Reserve at Little Beach. Cruises on harbour and Myall River; also boats for hire. **In the area:** Gan Gan Lookout, 2 km SW on Nelson Bay Rd. Toboggan Hill Park at Salamander Bay, 5 km SW; toboggan runs, mini-golf course, fun shed. Gemstone House, on Shoal Bay Rd, 8 km SW. Oakvale Farm and Fauna World, 16 km SW on Nelson Bay Rd at Salt Ash. Fighter World, displays of modern and historic aircraft, at RAAF base, Williamtown, 35 km W. Convict-built Tanilba House (1831), 37 km W. Tomaree National Park, 50 km W; nude bathing at Samurai Beach, within park. Festival of Port Stephens held Feb.–March. **Tourist information:** Victoria Pde, Nelson Bay; (049) 81 1579. **Accommodation:** 11 motels, 1 caravan/camping park. **See also:** Port Stephens.
MAP REF. 112 H2, 121 M4

Newcastle   Pop. 262 331

Australia's largest industrial city is encircled by some of the finest surfing beaches in the world. Overlooking a huge, spectacular harbour, Newcastle, just 158 km N of Sydney, was always uniquely positioned to claim the image of an aquatic playground. While modern technology successfully tackled pollution, the City Fathers of Australia's sixth largest city called for a plan to ensure that residents and visitors could take full advantage of its superb location. The $13-million answer was a brilliant foreshore redevelopment scheme. Rebuilding in some areas has followed an earthquake that struck the city in December 1989. Named in a recent survey as the 'best city in Australia', Newcastle is experiencing a boom in tourism as visitors are attracted to the wineries and vineyards and picturesque villages of the surrounding Hunter Valley region. **Of interest:** Queens Wharf, colourful and cosmopolitan centrepoint of foreshore redevelopment, with everything from an ice-cream parlour to indoor and outdoor restaurants, 'boutique' brewery, brewing range

of specialty beers, and observation tower; linked by walkway to City Mall, part of Hunter St. Scenic walks along foreshore with its sweeping lawns and swaying palms, and along nearby city streets lined with Sydney-style terrace houses. City parks and gardens. Art gallery, Laman St. Maritime and military museums, Fort Scratchley, Nobbys Rd. City Hall, Laman St. Many fine surf beaches. River and harbour cruises. **In the area:** Shortland Wetlands, 15 km W; bird habitat with other wildlife and canoe trail. Fighter Aviation Museum and high-tech exhibition at Williamtown RAAF base, 20 km N. Lake Macquarie, 27 km S, huge aquatic playground with well-maintained parks lining foreshore; picnic/barbecue facilities. About 50 km NW is Australia's famous wine region, the Hunter Valley. Yuelarbah Track, part of Great North Walk from Sydney to Newcastle, covers 25 km from Lake Macquarie to Newcastle harbour. **Tourist information:** 150 Wharf Rd; (049) 29 9299. **Accommodation:** 27 hotels, 30 motels, 13 caravan/camping parks.
MAP REF. 110, 112 G8, 121 L5

Nimbin   Pop. 274

The Festival of Aquarius in 1973 established Nimbin as the alternative culture capital of Australia. Today, it is a thriving, colourful, environmentally aware town. Its peaceful, friendly atmosphere, and the buildings designed and decorated to reflect the community's ideas and beliefs, attract visitors wishing to experience an alternative lifestyle. **Of interest:** Shops in Cullen St, painted in psychedelic colours, feature home-made products and local art and crafts. Jem's Restaurant with 'food from the fourth dimension'; original Rainbow Cafe, serving fresh local organic produce; Nimbin Museum, dedicated to hippy culture and history of St Aquarius; Town Hall, with mural featuring Aboriginal art; all in Cullen St. Rainbow Power Company, Alternative Way; alternative power supplier, inspection tours. Nimbin Country Market, held in Showgrounds 4th Sun. of month; outlet for local craftspeople. **In the area:** Spectacular volcanic Nimbin Rocks, 3 km S, on Lismore Rd. Nimbin Rocks Gallery nearby; high-quality art in all mediums. Channon Craft Market, 15 km SE, held 2nd Sun. of month at Coronation Park; items on sale must be 'made, baked, sewn or grown'. Calurla Tea Gardens, 10 km N, on Lillian

Rock Rd; spectacular views, farmhouse cooking, live music. World-Heritage-listed Nightcap National Park, 10 km NE; walking track (1.4 km through rainforest) to Protestors Falls. **Tourist information:** Cullen St; (066) 89 1577. **Accommodation:** Limited.
MAP REF. 123 P2, 475 N8

Nowra–Bomaderry
Pop. 21 942
Rapidly becoming a popular tourist centre, Nowra is the principal town of the Shoalhaven district. Bomaderry is directly opposite on the northern side of the river. **Of interest:** Meroogal (1885), cnr Worrigee and West Sts; Historic House Trust property open to public. Shoalhaven Historical Museum, cnr Plunkett and Kinghorn Sts, in old police station. Fishing, water-skiing, canoeing and sailing on Shoalhaven River. Hanging Rock, via Junction St, for fine views. Nowra Animal Park, Rockhill Rd; native fauna and peacocks in rainforest setting. **In the area:** HMAS *Albatross* Naval Air Station, South Nowra; two hangars converted to navy museum. Kangaroo Valley, 23 km NW; many old buildings, including Friendly Inn (classified by National Trust) and Pioneer Farm Museum, reconstruction of typical dairy farm of 1880s. Fitzroy Falls in Morton National Park, 38 km NW. Many beautiful beaches within 30 km radius of town. Camping and cabin/bunkhouse accommodation at Coolendel, 30 km W of Nowra, near Albatross; picnic/barbecue facilities, free-ranging wildlife, canoeing and bushwalks. **Tourist information:** Shoalhaven Tourist Centre, 254 Princes Hwy, Bomaderry; (044) 21 0778. **Accommodation:** Nowra: 11 motels, 5 caravan/camping parks. Bomaderry: 1 hotel, 4 motels, 1 caravan/camping park. **See also:** The Illawarra Coast.
MAP REF. 116 E12, 119 H4, 120 I11

Nundle
Pop. 261
The history of this small town began in the early gold-rush era during the 1850s. Renowned for its fishing, Nundle is situated 60 km SE of Tamworth, at the foot of the Great Dividing Range, in a district that produces sheep, cattle, wheat and timber. **Of interest:** Courthouse and antique shop, old bakery store and historic Peel Inn (1860s), all in Jenkins St. Gold-mining display in restored coffin factory, Gill St. **In the area:** Hanging Rock and Sheba Dams, picnic and camping area,

11 km E. Chaffey Dam, 11 km N. Fossicking at Hanging Rock and gold panning on Peel River. **Tourist information:** Cnr New England Hwy and Kable Ave, Tamworth; (067) 68 4462. **Accommodation:** 1 hotel, 1 motel, 1 caravan/camping park.
MAP REF. 123 J11

Nyngan
Pop. 2311
The centre of a wool-growing district on the Bogan River, 603 km NW of Sydney. **Of interest:** Historic buildings, especially in Cobar and Bogar Sts. **In the area:** Cairn marking geographic centre of NSW, 65 km S. Grave of Richard Cunningham, botanist with Major Mitchell's party, speared by Aborigines in 1835, on private property, 70 km S. Bird sanctuary in Macquarie Marshes, 64 km N. **Tourist information:** Burns Video, Pangee St; (068) 32 1155. **Accommodation:** 3 hotels, 2 hotel/motels, 3 motels, 2 caravan/camping parks.
MAP REF. 125 Q11

Orange
Pop. 29 635
A prosperous city set in rich red volcanic soil and famous for its apples, parks and gardens, Orange is situated 264 km NW of Sydney on the slopes of Mt Canobolas. An obelisk marks the birthplace of the

city's most famous citizen, poet A. B. (Banjo) Paterson; his birthday is celebrated with the Banjo Paterson Festival, mid-Feb. to mid-March. **Of interest:** Historic Cook Park, Summer St; begonia conservatory (flowers Feb.–May), duck ponds, fernery and picnic area. Museum, McNamara St. Orange Civic Centre, Byng St; $5-million complex comprising a theatre, Regional Art Gallery, City Library, Visitors Centre and exhibition rooms. **In the area:** Campbell's Corner, 8 km S on Pinnacle Rd, attractive roadside picnic/barbecue spot. Agriculture Research Centre, 5 km N; field days held Nov. Ophir goldfields, 27 km N, site of first discovery of payable gold in Australia in 1851; still fossicking centre with picnic area and walking trails to historic gold tunnels. Gallery of Minerals, 1 km E; mineral and fossil collection. Apple Stop Antiques at Lucknow Village, 10 km E. Golden Memories Museum at Millthorpe, 22 km SE; over 5000 exhibits, including grandma's kitchen, blacksmith's shop and art and craft centre. Lake Canobolas Park, 8 km SW via Cargo Rd; recreation and camping area with deer park, children's playground, picnic/barbecue facilities; also trout-fishing. Mt Canobolas Park, 1500-ha bird and animal sanctuary, 14 km SW. **Tourist**

Queens Wharf, Newcastle

Caves and Caverns

Magical underground limestone caves are one of the wonders of New South Wales. Glittering limestone stalactites and stalagmites, caused by the ceaseless dripping of limestone-impregnated water over tens of thousands of years, glow eerily in cathedral-like caves. These delicate formations of ribbed columns, frozen cascades, 'tapestries' and 'shawls' look like part of a subterranean fairyland.

The **Jenolan Caves** are the most famous. Since they were opened in 1866, several million people have visited them. Situated on a spur of the Great Dividing Range, a few kilometres to the south-west of the Blue Mountains, they are open daily for guided tours. The caves are surrounded by a 2430 hectare flora and fauna reserve with walking trails, kiosk, licensed cafe and picnic/barbecue facilities. The charming tudor-style guest house, Jenolan Caves House, provides accommodation, as do Binda Bush Cabins.

The **Wombeyan Caves** are set in a pleasant valley in the Southern Highlands, 193 kilometres south-west of Sydney. They can be reached from the Wombeyan turn-off, 60 kilometres northwest of Mittagong. From here a well-surfaced but narrow road winds through spectacular mountain scenery. The alternative route (recommended for caravanners) is via Goulburn, Taralga and Richlands. Five of the caves are easily accessible by graded paths. They are fully developed for visitors, with steps and handrails, and are open daily or on demand for self-guide, historical and adventure caving tours. There is a Visitors Centre and facilities exist for camping and family/group accommodation. Three walking tracks lead from the reserve to attractions in the area.

The **Yarrangobilly Caves**, 6.5 kilometres off the Snowy Mountains Highway, 109 kilometres north of Cooma, are open daily (subject to winter road conditions) for self-guide or guided tours. On weekends, school and public holidays, additional tours are available, subject to demand. Among some 250 caves in the area only 5 have been developed and are open for inspection (one with wheelchair access). An added attraction here is a thermal pool. Originally a mineral spring, the pool is heated to a constant temperature of 27°C all the year round, and the water is slightly mineralised. Tours include the Adventure Cave Walk during school holidays. The reserve surrounding the caves contains some of the most beautiful unspoiled country in the State. But bring your own food and drink; there is no kiosk in the area.

For further information, contact Jenolan Caves Reserve Trust; (063) 59 3311; Wombeyan Caves; (048) 43 5976; and Yarrangobilly Caves; (064) 54 9597. **See also**: Individual town entries in A–Z listing.

Jenolan Caves House

information: Civic Gardens, Byng St; (063) 61 5226. **Accommodation:** 7 hotels, 9 motels, 2 caravan/camping parks. MAP REF. 120 E6

Parkes Pop. 8784

Situated 364 km W of Sydney on the Newell Hwy, and often referred to as the 'gateway to the stars', Parkes is the commercial and industrial centre of an important agricultural area. **Of interest:** Motor Museum, cnr Bogan and Dalton Sts; vintage and veteran vehicles, and local art and craft. Henry Parkes Museum, Clarinda St; memorabilia and library of 1000 volumes. Pioneer Park Museum, Pioneer St, in historic school and church; displays of early farm machinery and transport. Kelly Reserve, on northern outskirts of town; picnics and barbecues in bush setting. Imposing views from Shrine of Remembrance at eastern end of Bushman St. Annual marbles tournament held March at Parkes Golf Club. Picnic races and Jazz Convention in June. Country Music Spectacular and Antique Motorbike Rally in Oct. **In the area:** Mugincoble Wheat Sub-terminal, 8 km SE. CSIRO Radio Telescope Visitors Centre, 23 km N; many educational aids explain use of giant saucer-shaped telescope. Peak Hill, 48 km N; open-cut goldmine, camel park, and accommodation. **Tourist information:** Kelly Reserve, Newell Hwy; (068) 62 4365. **Accommodation:** 8 hotels, 11 motels, 4 caravan/camping parks. **See also:** The Newell. MAP REF. 120 C6

Picton Pop. 2116

Picton, named after Sir Thomas Picton, hero of Waterloo, is 80 km SW of Sydney on Remembrance Drive (former Hume Hwy). The old buildings and quiet hills of this small town seem to echo the past. **Of interest:** Historic buildings include: old railway viaduct (1862) over Stonequarry Creek, seen from Showgrounds, off Menangle St; St Mark's Church (1848), Menangle St; George IV Inn, which incorporates Scharer's Little Brewery, Argyle St. **In the area:** Sydney Skydiving Centre, 5 km E. Jarvisfield (1865), family home of pioneer landholders, now clubhouse of Antill Park Golf Club, 2 km N, on Remembrance Dr. Woolaway Woolshed, 3 km N on Remembrance Dr; bush dances nightly, special fixtures. Wollondilly Heritage Centre and slab-built St Matthew's

Church (1838) at The Oaks, 21 km N. Burragorang Lookout, 15 km W of The Oaks. Railway Museum at Thirlmere, 5 km S. Thirlmere Lakes National Park, 8 km S. Wirrimbirra Sanctuary, 13 km S; National Trust sanctuary; native flora and fauna, overnight cabins. Mowbray Park, 8 km NW; farm holidays. **Tourist information:** Macarthur Country Tourist Assocn, cnr Hume Hwy and Congressional Dr., Liverpool; (02) 821 2311. **Accommodation:** 2 hotels, 1 motel, 1 caravan park. MAP REF. 104 I12, 116 E3, 119 H2, 120 I9

Pitt Town Pop. 632

One of the 5 Macquarie Towns, Pitt Town was named after William Pitt the elder, and marked out on a site to the east of the present village in January 1811. The surrounding rich alluvial river flats provided early Sydney with almost 50% of its food supply, which was transported by boat down the Hawkesbury River and around to Sydney Town. Pitt Town did not develop a 20th-century town centre and thus remains more modest in architectural style than Windsor. Location for *A Country Practice*. **Of interest:** Curious reminder of importance of river, at end of Bathurst St, overlooking Pitt Town Bottoms. Old Manse, belonging to oldest Presbyterian (now Uniting) Church in Australia, 8 km N at Ebenezer. **Tourist information:** Ham Common Bicentennial Park, Richmond Rd, Clarendon; (045) 88 5895. **See also:** The Hawkesbury. MAP REF. 105 K6

Port Macquarie Pop. 26 798

Founded as a convict settlement in 1821, and one of the oldest towns in the State, Port Macquarie (known locally as 'Port') is now a major holiday resort, situated at the mouth of the Hastings River, 423 km N of Sydney. **Of interest:** Award-winning Hastings Historical Museum, Clarence St, housed in 15 rooms of commercial building, built 1835–40; convict and pioneer relics. St Thomas's (1824), Church St; convict-built church designed by convict architect Thomas Owen. Historic cemetery, Horton St; graves dating from 1842. Roto House and Macquarie Nature Reserve, Lord St; koala hospital and study centre. Port Macquarie Observatory, William St. Fantasy Glades, Pacific Dr; re-creation of story of Snow White and other fairytale characters, with

birds, animals, bushwalks, children's playground and kiosk. Billabong and Kingfisher Parks; close-up look at Australian animals. Town Beach; surf at one end and sheltered coves at other. Kooloonbung Creek Nature Reserve; 50 ha of natural bushland, with walking trails. Peppermint Park; slides and roller-skating. River cruises daily. Orchid World, Ocean Dr.; Australian and exotic plants, camel rides and safaris. Old World Timber Art on Hastings River Dr. **In the area:** Exceptionally good fishing and all water sports. Charter fishing, including reef fishing. Shelly Beach Resort, 3 km SE on Pacific Dr. The Big Bull at Redbank Farm, working dairy farm, 20 km W, via Wauchope. Sea Acres Rainforest Centre, Pacific Drive, 5 km S; some 30 ha of rainforest, multi-level boardwalk allows viewing of flora and fauna. Cassegrain Winery, 12 km W; tastings and sales. Harley Davidson motorbike tours, horseriding and abseiling. **Tourist information:** Cnr Clarence and Hay Sts; (065) 83 1293. **Accommodation:** 1 hotel/motel, 47 motels, 17 caravan/camping parks. MAP REF. 109 G7, 123 O11

Queanbeyan Pop. 19 383

Adjoining Canberra, Queanbeyan has a special relationship with the Australian capital. The town, proclaimed in 1838, is named from a squattage held by an ex-convict innkeeper, Timothy Beard, on the Molonglo River called 'Quinbean' ('clear waters'). **Of interest:** Queanbeyan History Museum, Farrer Pl. Rehwinkel's Animal Farm. Byrne's Mill. Mill House Gallery. Design Plus Gallery, Monaro St; pottery, silk and leatherwork. Michelago Steam Train rides; first Sun. in month and special trips. **In the area:** At Bungendore, 26 km NE, historic village square and exhibition depicting story of Jacky Jacky, Aboriginal bushranger; also wood-turning, antiques and herbal farm. Bywong Mining Town, 31 km NE. **Tourist information:** Cnr Farrer Place and Lowe St; (06) 298 0241. **Accommodation:** 4 hotels, 18 motels, 2 caravan/camping parks. MAP REF. 119 E6, 120 F13, 137 G4, 140 H3

Quirindi Pop. 2830

Appropriately named after an Aboriginal word meaning 'nest in the hills', this town in the Liverpool Ranges was proclaimed in 1856. **Of interest:** Historical

Cottage and Museum, Station St; Fri. p.m., Sat. a.m. One of the first towns in Australia to organise the game of polo, it still holds an annual polo carnival in first week of Aug. **In the area:** Who'd-A-Thought-It Lookout, 2 km NE. Many properties offer farm holidays. **Tourist information:** Sports Centre, 248 George St; (067) 46 2128. **Accommodation:** 5 hotels, 2 motels, 1 caravan/camping park.
MAP REF. 120 I1, 122 I11

Raymond Terrace   Pop. 11 159
Several historic buildings remain in this town, which was an important wool-shipping centre in the 1840s. **Of interest:** Self-guide Heritage Town Walk takes in significant buildings, including court-house (1838), still in use; Irrawang (1830), homestead of pioneer James King; Church of England and rectory, built of hand-hewn sandstone in 1830s; and Sketchley Cottage, once sited at Sea-ham, 8 km N. Twin Rivers Festival held Oct.; water-skiing and motorboat racing. **In the area:** Hunter Region Botanic Gardens, on Pacific Hwy at Motto Farm, 2 km S. Fighter World, RAAF Base Wil-liamtown, 16 km E. **Tourist information:** Neighbourhood Centre, 14 King St; (049) 87 1331. **Accommodation:** 4 motels, 2 caravan/camping parks.
MAP REF. 112 E6, 121 L4

Richmond   Pop. 18 766
One of the 5 Macquarie towns and sister town to Windsor, 5 km E, Richmond was proclaimed a town in 1810. **Of interest:** Hobartville, Castlereagh Rd. Toxana (1841), Windsor St. St Peter's Church (1841), Windsor St; graveyard where notable pioneers, including William Cox and Australia's convict chronicler Margaret Catchpole, are buried. **In the area:** RAAF base, 3 km E on Windsor–Richmond Rd; oldest Air Force establishment in Australia, used for civilian flying from 1915. University of Western Sydney, 3 km S; foundation-stone laid in 1895. **Tourist information:** Ham Common Bicentennial Park, Richmond Rd, Clarendon; (045) 88 5895. **Accommodation:** 1 hotel, 1 hotel/motel, 2 motels. **See also:** The Hawkesbury.
MAP REF. 105 J6, 120 I7

Robertson   Pop. 252
The link between the Southern High-lands and the coast, Robertson sits at the top of the Macquarie Pass and vantage points offer spectacular views of the coast. It is the centre of the largest potato-growing district in NSW. **In the area:** Fitzroy, Belmore and Carrington Falls, all in Morton National Park, 10 km S. **Tourist information:** Winifred West Park, Old Hume Hwy, Mittagong; (048) 71 2888. **Accommodation:** 1 hotel, 1 motel.
MAP REF. 116 D8, 119 H3, 120 I10

Rylstone–Kandos   Pop. 721
Aboriginal hand-paintings on a sand-stone rock overhang are a feature of the region, which is west of the Great Divi-ding Range on the Cudgegong River, north-east of Bathurst. **Of interest:** Industrial Museum at Kandos. **In the area:** Fern Tree Gully, 16 km N; magnificent tree ferns in subtropical forest. Glen Davis, 56 km SE on Capertee River, sur-rounded by sheer cliff faces. Many camp-ing spots and fishing areas on Capertee, Cudgegong and Turon rivers. **Tourist information:** Shire Council, Liuee St, Rylstone; (063) 79 1205. **Accommodation:** 4 hotels, 1 motel, 1 caravan/camp-ing park.
MAP REF. 120 G5

Sawtell   Pop. 10 809
This peaceful family holiday resort, 8 km S of Coffs Harbour, has safe beaches and tidal creeks for fishing, swimming and surfing. Playground and picnic/barbecue facilities at Boambee Creek Reserve, Sawtell Rd. Enchanting walks and drives in the surrounding bush and mountains, including Sawtell Reserve. **In the area:** White-water rafting on Nymboida, Gwydir and Murray rivers. **Tourist information:** Orara Park, Pacific Hwy, Coffs Harbour; (066) 52 1522. **Accommodation:** 2 hotels, 3 motels, 1 caravan/camping park.
MAP REF. 123 O7, 475 N12

Scone   Pop. 3329
This pleasant town set in beautiful country on the New England Hwy, 280 km N of Sydney, is the second largest thoroughbred and horse-breeding centre in the world. **Of interest:** Scone Histori-cal Society Museum, Kingdon St. Grass-root Art Gallery and Restaurant, part of well-equipped tourist information centre opp. Elizabeth Park, near mare and foal sculpture. **In the area:** Glenbawn Dam, 15 km E; water sports and picnic/bar-becue facilities. Hunter Valley Museum of Rural Life, 2 km W of dam. Burning Mountain at Wingen, 20 km N; deep coal seam that has been smouldering for at least 1000 years. Barrington Tops Nat-ional Park, 80 km NE; scenic drives and walks. **Tourist information:** Cnr Susan and Kelly Sts; (065) 45 1526. **Accommo-dation:** 1 hotel, 5 motels, 1 caravan/camping park.
MAP REF. 121 J2, 122 I13

Shellharbour   Pop. 1754
This attractive holiday resort 7 km S of Lake Illawarra is one of the oldest settle-ments on the south coast. A thriving port in the 1830s, its importance declined once the south coast railway opened. **In the area:** Blackbutt Forest Reserve and Killalea Recreation Park. Bass Point Headland and Marine Reserve, 3 km S; picnic area with views. Scuba diving and snorkelling at Bass Point. Lake Illawarra, 7 km N; boats for hire. Fine beaches for fishing, surfing and boating on Windang Peninsula, 10 km N. Jamberoo Valley and Minnamurra Rainforest Centre, 20 km SW. Bike paths and bike hire. BMX circuit at Croome Rd Sporting Complex. **Tourist information:** 93 Crown St, Wollongong; (042) 28 0300. **Accommo-dation:** 1 hotel, 1 motel, 1 caravan/camping park. **See also:** The Illawarra Coast.
MAP REF. 116 G8, 120 I3, 121 J10

Singleton   Pop. 11 861
Located beside the Hunter River in rich grazing land, Singleton is the geographi-cal heart of the Hunter Valley. New wealth in the form of huge open-cut coal mines has joined the traditional rural in-dustry and transformed Singleton into one of the most progressive country centres in the State. **Of interest:** Built as Bicentennial project, monolithic sundial, largest in southern hemisphere; on river-bank, in James Cook Park. Gardens of historic home, Townhead; sales of herbs. Art Show held July. Agricultural Show and Romance of the Rose Festival in Oct. **In the area:** Nearby Lake St Clair, with magnificent views of Mt Royal Range; extensive recreational and waterway fa-cilities, including camping. Township is home of Singleton Army Camp, whose Royal Australian Infantry Corps Mu-seum of Small Arms, 5 km S, traces de-velopment of firearms from 15th century. On New England Hwy between Single-ton and Muswellbrook, 26 km NW, Bays-water Power Station, biggest thermal power station in southern hemisphere.

The Big Oyster, Taree

Singleton is central location for visits to wineries of upper and lower Hunter Valley. **Tourist information:** Shire Offices; (065) 72 1866. **Accommodation:** 6 hotels, 2 hotel/motels, 5 motels, 2 caravan/camping parks.
MAP REF. 121 J4, 346 C7

Stroud   Pop. 556
There are many historic buildings in this small country town, 75 km N of Newcastle. One of the finest is the convict-built Anglican Church of St John, built in 1833 of local clay bricks, with its beautiful stained glass windows and cedar furnishings. **Of interest:** Rectory of St John's (1836), Stroud House (1832), Parish House (1837), courthouse, post office and Quambi House. Underground silo (one of 8 built in 1841) at Silo Hill Reserve. Self-guide Heritage Tour. **Tourist information:** Great Lakes Tourist Board, Little St, Forster; (065) 54 8799. **Accommodation:** 1 hotel.
MAP REF. 121 L3

Tamworth   Pop. 31 716
This prosperous city at the junction of the New England and Oxley Hwys is the country music capital of Australia, as well as being the heart of many other cultural and musical activities. Thousands of fans flock here for the 10-day Australian Country Music Festival, held each Jan. since 1973. Tamworth, with its attractive public buildings and parks and gardens, is also the commercial capital of northern NSW. **Of interest:** Country Music Hands of Fame cornerstone at CWA park, Kable Ave (outside Tamworth Tourism), has hand imprints of country music stars, including Tex Morton, Slim Dusty and Smoky Dawson. Country music Roll of Renown at Radio Centre, Calala, dedicated to country music artists who have contributed to Australia's heritage. Calala Cottage, Denison St, home of Tamworth's first mayor, classified by National Trust and restored by Tamworth Historical Society. Tamworth City Gallery, Marius St; works by Turner, Hans Heysen and Will Ashton, and home of National Fibre Collection. Oxley Gallery, Peel St (specialising in gemstones), Weswal Gallery, Brisbane St, and Tininburra Gallery, Moore Creek Rd. Country Collection on New England Hwy features fascinating gemstone collection, Gallery of Stars Wax Museum, Great Australian Icecreamery and famous Longyard Hotel. Oxley Park Wildlife Sanctuary north off Brisbane St; bushwalks, picnic/barbecue facilities and friendly kangaroos. Oxley Lookout; panoramic views of city and rich Peel Valley. Powerstation Museum traces Tamworth's history as first city in southern hemisphere to have electric street lighting. Fred Hilliers 'Backtracks'; humorous and informative commentaries for self-guide tours through countryside. **In the area:** Lake Keepit State Recreation Area, 57 km NW; ideal for water sports and visitor facilities. Warrabah National Park, 75 km NE. Historic goldmining township of Nundle nestled in 'Hills of Gold', a 63-km scenic drive SE. Chaffey Dam, 45 km SE, for sailing; Dulegal Arboretum on foreshore. **Tourist information:** Cnr New England Hwy and Kable Ave; (067) 68 4462. **Accommodation:** 7 hotels, 2 hotel/motels, 28 motels, 4 caravan/camping parks.
MAP REF. 123 J10

Taree   Pop. 16 303
Attractively laid out, Taree serves as the manufacturing and commercial centre of the Manning River district, on the Pacific Hwy, 320 km N of Sydney. **Of interest:** Manning River cruises. The Big Oyster. **In the area:** Easy access by car to top of Ellenborough Falls, on Bulga Plateau, 50 km NW. Crowdy Bay National Park, 40 km NE; wildflowers in spring, fishing, swimming, bushwalking. Railway Crossing Family Fun Park at Harrington, 30 km N. The Bird Tree, 50 km N. Forest drives and walking trails in Manning Valley. Taree–Forster Grass Ski Park. Farm holidays at many properties. Fine surfing beaches on coast 16 km E. **Tourist information:** Manning Valley Tourist Information Centre, Pacific Hwy, Taree North; (065) 52 1900 or (008) 80 1522. **Accommodation:** 5 hotels, 27 motels, 3 caravan/camping parks.
MAP REF. 109 C13, 121 N2, 123 N12

Bald Rock National Park, near Tenterfield

Tathra   Pop. 1571

Tathra is a relaxed seaside township, centrally located on the south coast of NSW, 18 km E of Bega and midway between Merimbula and Bermagui. Tathra is an ideal place for a family holiday, with its patrolled 3-km long surf beach, safe swimming for small children at Mogareka Inlet (the sandy mouth of the Bega River), and good fishing spots. **Of interest:** Sea Wharf, classified by National Trust. Above wharf; Maritime Museum; memorabilia of visiting ships. **In the area:** Bournda State Recreation Area, immediately south of town; camping and bushwalking. Fishing and water sports on Lake Wallagoot. Mimosa Rocks National Park, 17 km N. Diving and deep-sea fishing charters at Kianniny Bay. **Tourist information:** Tathra Wharf; (064) 94 4062. **Accommodation:** 1 motel, 1 hotel/motel, 4 caravan/camping parks.
MAP REF. 117 G7, 119 G10, 235 P6

Temora   Pop. 4279

Commercial centre for the rich wheat district of the northern and western Riverina, which also produces oats, barley, fat lambs, pigs and cattle. **Of interest:** Temora Rural Museum with large number of working displays; also rock and mineral collection. Scenic walk around town. Golden Gift foot race in Feb. **In the area:** Lake Centenary, 3 km N. Paragon Gold Mine at Gidginbung, 15 km N. **Tourist information:** White Rose Cafe, 186 Hoskins St; (069) 77 2131. **Accommodation:** 2 hotels, 3 motels, 1 caravan/camping park.
MAP REF. 120 A10, 127 R8

Tenterfield   Pop. 3310

Tenterfield sits astride the Great Dividing Range at the northern end of the New England Highlands in northern NSW, and offers a contrast of rugged mountains and serene rural landscapes. Autumn in Tenterfield (April) is particularly spectacular. Primarily a sheep- and cattle-grazing area, the district has a variety of other industries, including orchards, logging and sawmilling, a silica mine, a goldmine, various farm crops and the growing industry of tourism. **Of interest:** Centenary Cottage (1871), Logan St; local history collection. Self-guide Logan St Historic Walk. Sir Henry Parkes Library and Museum in School of Arts (1876), Rouse St; relics relating to Sir Henry Parkes, who made his famous Federation speech in this building in 1889. Tenterfield Saddler (1860s), High St. Federation Festival and Spring Wine Festival held Oct. Gem Festival in Nov. **In the area:** Mt McKenzie Granite Drive, 30-km circular route west of town, includes Ghost Gully. Bluff Rock, 10 km S on New England Hwy; unusual granite outcrop. Thunderbolt's Hideout, 11 km NE. Bald Rock National Park, 35 km NE; panoramic views from summit of Bald Rock, largest granite monolith in Australia. Spectacular Boonoo Boonoo Falls (210-m drop), within Boonoo Boonoo National Park, 32 km N. **Tourist information:** 157 Rouse St; (067) 36 1082. **Accommodation:** 3 hotels, 2 hotel/motels, 6 motels, 3 caravan parks. **See also:** New England.
MAP REF. 123 L3, 475 L9

Terrigal–Wamberal

Pop. 7453

Excellent surfing is one of the main attractions of this popular holiday resort on the Central Coast. **In the area:** Bouddi National Park, 17 km S; bushwalking, camping, fishing and swimming. **Tourist information:** Rotary Park, Terrigal Dr, Terrigal; (043) 85 4430. **Accommodation:** 1 hotel, 5 motels, 2 caravan/camping parks.
MAP REF. 105 P5, 108 H5, 121 K7

The Entrance   Pop. 37 831

Blessed with clear, clean beaches, this beautiful lakeside and ocean resort located between Sydney and Newcastle is the family holiday playground of these two cities. **Of interest:** Daily pelican feeding in Memorial Park, 3.30 p.m. 'Concerts by the Sea', bi-monthly events, but weekly in Jan. Annual Tuggerah Lakes Mardi Gras Festival held first weekend in Dec. Australia Day family concert and fireworks. **In the area:** Fishing on lakes—Tuggerah, Budgewoi and Munmorah—and ocean beach. During summer months, prawning on lakes. Water sports on Lake Tuggerah. Lake cruises depart from The Entrance public wharf. **Tourist information:** Tuggerah Lakes Tourist Assocn, Memorial Pk, Marine Pde; (043) 32 9282. **Accommodation:** 3 hotels, 10 motels, 12 caravan parks.
MAP REF. 105 P4, 108 H2, 121 K6

The Rock   Pop. 809

This small township, 32 km SW of Wagga Wagga, is noted for its unusual scenery. Walking trails through a flora and fauna reserve lead to the summit of The Rock (about 365 m). One species, the groundsel plant, is believed to be unique to the area. **Of interest:** Fantasia Dolls,

Olympic Way; hand-made porcelain dolls. **Accommodation:** 1 hotel/motel. MAP REF. 127 Q11

Tibooburra   Pop. 150

The name of this former gold town, 337 km N of Broken Hill, comes from an Aboriginal word meaning 'heaps of boulders'. The town is surrounded by granite outcrops and was known as The Granites. **Of interest:** Buildings of local stone, including courthouse (1888), Family Hotel (1888) and Tibooburra Hotel (1890). School of the Air buildings, Briscow St; tours during term time. Gymkhana and rodeo held in Oct. on NSW Labour Day weekend. **In the area:** Self-guide Golden Gully Scenic Walk, 3 km N. Nearby goldfields. Sturt National Park, 20 km N; semi-desert area, noted for its wildlife and geological features. Pastoralists display at Mt Wood, 27 km E, within park. Former gold township of Milparinka, 42 km S; restored courthouse, together with remains of old police station, bank, general store and post office, but Albert Hotel is town's only active concern. Further 11 km NW of Milparinka are Mt Poole Homestead and Mt Poole, where cairn commemorates Charles Sturt's expedition. Cameron's Corner, 150 km NW, where 3 States meet. **Tourist information:** National Parks and Wildlife Service, Tibooburra; (080) 91 3308. **Accommodation:** 2 hotels, 1 motel, 1 caravan/camping park. MAP REF. 124 D4, 484 I10

Tingha   Pop. 831

This small tin-mining town is 28 km SE of Inverell. **Of interest:** Campbells Honey Farm, Swimming Pool Rd. Nucoorilma Aboriginal Arts and Crafts. **In the area:** Smith's Mining and Natural History Museum at Green Valley Farm, 10 km S; Aboriginal artefacts, antiques, mineral and gemstone collection; also cabin accommodation. Fossicking for gems. Water sports on Copeton Dam, 15 km W. **Tourist information:** New England Hwy, Guyra; (067) 79 1420. **Accommodation:** 1 hotel, 1 caravan park. **See also:** New England. MAP REF. 123 J6, 475 J11

Tocumwal   Pop. 1587

This peaceful Murray River town on the Newell Hwy is ideal for swimming, fishing and boating. **Of interest:** Huge fibreglass codfish in town square represents

Pelicans, Terrigal

Aboriginal legend about giant Murray cod that lived in nearby blowhole. Old Railway Store, Deniliquin St; scale models of Australian trains. Picnic area with lawns and sandy river beach, 200 m from town square. **In the area:** River Murray Heritage Centre, 3 km N. Aerodrome, 5 km NE, largest RAAF base in Australia during World War II, now houses world-renowned Sportavia Soaring Centre; gliding joy flights and tuition packages. Flights and tuition at Ultralight Aviation, Tocumwal Aerodrome. The Rocks and Blowhole, 11 km NE on Rocks Rd; once stone quarry, now popular picnic spot. Binghi Boomerang Factory at Barooga, 19 km E. Several golf courses. Ulupna Island flora and fauna reserve. Nallama, 14 km W on Tuppal Rd; historic farm settlement with grave site and giant gum. **Tourist information:** Tocumwal River Foreshore; (058) 74 2131. **Accommodation:** 3 hotels, 1 hotel/motel, 10 motels, 6 caravan/camping parks. **See also:** The Newell. MAP REF. 127 M12, 206 I2

Tooleybuc   Pop. 300

A quiet, tranquil, riverside town with a village atmosphere, Tooleybuc's social centre is its Sporting Club. The town boasts a range of recreational facilities, including fishing, bowls, picnicking and riverside walks. **Of interest:** The Opal Shack; demonstrations of opal cutting. **Tourist information:** 25 Murray St, Barham; (054) 53 3100.

Accommodation: 1 hotel, 3 motels, 1 caravan/camping park. MAP REF. 126 H10, 231 M9

Toukley   Pop. 6520

Situated on the peninsula between Tuggerah and Budgewoi Lakes, this delightful coastal hamlet offers a holiday experience with pollution-free beaches and breathtaking scenery. **Of interest:** Toukley open-air markets, every Sun. at shopping centre carpark. Shark-free lakes provide venue for all forms of water sports. During summer months prawning from lake foreshores. Azalea Festival held in July. **In the area:** Rock pool at Cabbage Tree Bay, 5 km E. Norah Head Lighthouse, 5 km E; inspections by appt. Many bushwalking trails in magnificent Munmorah State Recreation Area, 10 km N, or Red Gum Forest in Wyrrabalong National Park, 4 km S. **Tourist information:** Memorial Park, Marine Pde, The Entrance; (043) 32 9282. **Accommodation:** 1 hotel/resort, 6 motels, 4 caravan/camping parks. MAP REF. 105 P3, 121 K6

Tumbarumba   Pop. 1548

A former goldmining town situated in the western foothills of the Snowy Mountains, 504 km SW of Sydney, Tumbarumba has much to offer the visitor who prefers to get off the beaten track. It is an ideal base for day trips to the Snowy Mountains. **Of interest:** Historical Society Museum, Bridge St; working model of water-powered timber mill. Castanea Orchards, Adelong Rd; hazelnuts, chestnuts, cherries; open daily. **In the area:** Henry Angel Trackhead on Hume and Hovell Walking Track; facilities for campers and picnickers, starting point for bushwalks. Site of old Union Jack Mine, 3 km N. Pioneer Women's Museum, 5 km W. William's mini hydro-electric scheme and Lake Mannus, 7 km S. Paddy's River Falls, 16 km S; spectacular cascades drop 60 m; walking track and picnic area. Tooma, 34 km S; historic hotel and store. Mt Selwyn Ski Resort, 70 km SE. Murray 1 Power Station, SW of Khancoban on Alpine Way; guided tours daily. Whitewater rafting, fly fishing, paragliding, trail rides. Pioneer Women's Hut, 8 km NW on Wagga Rd; domestic rural history museum, check times. **Tourist information:** Tumbarumba Wool and Craft Centre, 10 Bridge St; (069) 48 2805. **Accommodation:** 2

hotels, 1 motel, 2 caravan/camping parks.
MAP REF. 119 B7

Tumut — Pop. 5955

Situated on the Snowy Mountains Hwy, 424 km sw of Sydney, Tumut attracts visitors all year round. Close to ski resorts and the great dams of the Snowy Mountains Hydro-electric Scheme, it is also renowned for spectacular mountain scenery. **Of interest:** Inspections of local power station, marble and millet broom factories. Festival of the Falling Leaf held April–May. **In the area:** Two access points for Hume and Hovell Walking Track. Orchard tours and pick-your-own farms at Batlow, 33 km sw. Largest African violet farm in Australia, 7 km s on Tumut Plains Rd. Blowering Lake, 10 km s, major centre for water sports; fishing for rainbow trout, brown trout and perch. Talbingo Dam and Reservoir, 40 km s; second tallest rock-filled dam in Australia, set in steep wooded country and renowned for large trout. Excellent fishing on Tumut and Goobraganda Rivers. Whitewater rafting, canoeing, horseriding, abseiling, powered hang-gliding, scenic flights. Local art, craft and pottery. **Tourist information:** Fitzroy St (Snowy Mountains Hwy); (069) 47 1849. **Accommodation:** 2 hotels, 6 motels, 2 caravan/camping parks.
MAP REF. 119 B6, 120 C13, 140 A2

Tweed Heads — Pop. 5360

This exciting town on the NSW–Qld border combines the attraction of being a comprehensive shopping venue with the pleasurable entertainment provided by its licensed clubs. **Of interest:** World's first laser-beam lighthouse sits atop Point Danger, one half in NSW and the other in Qld. **In the area:** Tweed Endeavour cruise boats, operating from River Tce, visit locations along Tweed River. Minjungbal Museum and Resource Centre, just over Boyds Bay Bridge; Aboriginal ceremonial bora ring, museum and nature walk through sections of mangroves and rainforest. Avocado Adventureland, 15 km s on Pacific Hwy. Cabarita Gardens Lake Resort, 20 km s on Tweed Coast Rd. **Tourist information:** Cnr Pacific Hwy and Alma St, Murwillumbah; (066) 72 1340. **Accommodation:** 2 hotels, 22 motels, 9 caravan/camping parks.
MAP REF. 123 P1, 475 O7

Ulladulla — Pop. 7381

Ulladulla, a fishing town, and nearby Milton are at the northern end of a stretch of beautiful coastal lakes and lagoons with white sandy beaches. **Of interest:** Town's oldest building (c.1868) houses Millard's Cottage Restaurant, Princes Hwy, with harbour views. Finland, Princes Hwy; large indoor family fun park. Lighthouse at Wardens Head; views and walking tracks. South Pacific Heathland Reserve, Dowling St; native plants and birdlife, walks. Ulladulla Wildflower Reserve, cnr Green and Warden Sts. Colourful Blessing of the Fleet ceremony held each Easter. **In the area:** Mollymook, 2 km N, for surfing, excellent fishing and golf. Narrawallee Beach, 4 km N, for surfing; but nearby Narrawallee Inlet has calm shallow water ideal for children. Bendalong, 36 km N, for surfing and swimming. Sussex Inlet, 47 km N; fishing carnival in May. Lakes Conjola (23 km N) and Burrill (5 km sw); swimming, fishing and water-skiing. Views from summit of Pigeon House Mountain in Morton National Park, 25 km w. **Tourist information:** Princes Hwy; (044) 55 1269. **Accommodation:** 1 hotel, 7 motels, 4 caravan/camping parks. **See also:** The Illawarra Coast.
MAP REF. 119 H6, 120 I3, 141 Q3

Uralla — Pop. 2324

'Gentleman' bushranger Captain Thunderbolt was shot dead by a local policeman in 1870, in the swampy country south-east of this New England town. Rich gold discoveries were made in the vicinity in the 1850s. **Of interest:** Self-guide Heritage Walking Tour introduces town's historic buildings. Hassett's Military Museum, Bridge St; local and national military history, memorabilia. McCrossin's Mill (1870), Salisbury St; museum includes goldfields history, joss house, local Aboriginal tribe and Thunderbolt exhibits. Statue of Thunderbolt in Bridge St and grave in Uralla Cemetery. **In the area:** Mt Yarrowyck Aboriginal rock-art site, 23 km NW off Bundarra Rd. Fossicking at Old Rocky River diggings, 5 km w; pleasant picnic spot. Gostwyck, 11 km SE; one of oldest properties in area; inspection of private chapel by appointment. **Tourist information:** Bridge St; (067) 78 4496. **Accommodation:** 2 hotels, 2 motels, 2 caravan/camping parks. **See also:** New England.
MAP REF. 123 K8

Urunga — Pop. 2666

One of the best fishing spots on the north coast, 32 km s of Coffs Harbour at the mouth of the Bellinger River, the town is separated from the ocean by a broad lagoon. **Of interest:** Safe river swimming pool for children, with picnic reserve. **Tourist information:** The Honey Place, Pacific Hwy; (066) 55 6160. **Accommodation:** 1 hotel, 4 motels, 5 caravan/camping parks.
MAP REF. 123 O8, 475 N12

Wagga Wagga — Pop. 40 875

This prosperous city—the largest inland city in NSW—is located 478 km sw of Sydney just off the Hume Hwy and a major centre for industry, commerce, education, agriculture and the home of two important military bases. It is renowned for its cultural pursuits and performing arts. **Of interest:** Botanic Gardens and Zoo on Willans Hill; miniature railway runs through gardens. Historical Museum, adjacent to gardens; indoor and outdoor exhibits, City Art Gallery, Gurwood St, with National Art Glass collection and Riverina Galleries on The Esplanade. **In the area:** Lake Albert, 7 km s, for water sports. Murray Cod Hatcheries and Fauna Park, 5 km E. Wagga Wagga Winery, 15 km NE, has early Australiana theme and restaurant and Eunonyhareenyha Cottage. Charles Sturt University-Riverina, 6 km NW, includes Charles Sturt Winery on campus; tastings and sales. Aurora Clydesdale Stud and Pioneer Farm, 9 km w of Collingullie on Sturt Hwy towards Narrandera. Tours of military base at Kapooka, 9 km sw. **Tourist information:** Tarcutta Street; (069) 23 5402. **Accommodation:** 12 hotels, 24 motels, 6 caravan/camping parks.
MAP REF. 120 A12, 127 Q10

Walcha — Pop. 1782

This small town on the eastern slopes of the Great Dividing Range was first settled in 1832. **Of interest:** Pioneer Cottage and Museum, Derby St; includes Tiger Moth plane, first to be used for crop-dusting in Australia, and replica of blacksmith's shop. Fenwicke House, 19th-century terrace in Fitzroy St; art gallery and b & b accommodation. **In the area:** Ohio homestead (1842), 4 km E; inspection by appt. Oxley Wild Rivers National Park, 20 km E; areas around Oxley, Tia and Wollomombi Falls developed for picnicking and camping.

Tumut River valley, near Tumut

Several properties offer farm holidays. Trout fishing in many streams (with access to private property by request). **Tourist information:** Craft Centre, Fitzroy St (Oxley Hwy); (067) 77 2802 or (067) 77 1075. **Accommodation:** 2 hotels, 2 motels, 1 caravan/camping park. **See also:** New England.
MAP REF. 123 K9

Walgett   Pop. 2091
A small rural community situated at the junction of the Barwon and Namoi Rivers, 300 km N of Dubbo. **Of interest:** Barwon Aboriginal Community, Fox St. First European settler's grave. Good fishing all year. **In the area:** Grawin, Glengarry and Sheepyard opal fields, 70 km W. (Motorists are warned water is scarce; adequate supply should be carried.) Narran Lake, 96 km W, via Cumborah Rd, one of largest inland lakes in Australia; wildlife sanctuary, no facilities for private visits, but light aircraft tours can be arranged through Walgett Aero Club; (068) 28 1344. **Tourist information:** 77 Fox St; (068) 28 1399. **Accommodation:** 2 hotel/motels, 3 motels, 1 caravan/camping park.
MAP REF. 122 C6, 474 E11

Warialda   Pop. 1285
The first administrative centre in the north-west of the State, this small town on Gwydir Hwy, 63 km W of Inverell, is in a stud farm district. **Of interest:** Historical buildings, especially along Stephen and Hope Sts. Carinda House, Stephen St; historic house, local crafts. Pioneer Cemetery, Queen and Stephen Sts; graves date from 1850s. Well's Family Gem and Mineral Collection in the Heritage Centre, Hope St; also Aboriginal artefacts and bottle display. Self-guide walk around town. **In the area:** Fossicking, bushwalking, wildflowers. Picnic spots and free-ranging native animals at Cranky Rock Nature Reserve, 8 km E. **Tourist information:** Shire Offices, Hope St; (067) 29 1016. **Accommodation:** 1 hotel, 1 motel, 1 caravan/camping park.
MAP REF. 122 I5, 474 I10

Warren   Pop. 2036
In a wool and cotton-growing district on the Macquarie River, this Oxley Hwy town, 134 km NW of Dubbo, offers excellent fishing. **Of interest:** Macquarie Park, on banks of river, and Tiger Bay Wildlife Park. **In the area:** Excellent racecourse, 3 km W; Cotton Cup carnival in Nov. Austcott Cotton Farm, 10 km SW; inspection tours late April–June. Warren Weir, 5 km SE. Visits to merino studs. **Tourist information:** Shire Offices, Dubbo St; (068) 47 4606; Craft Shop, Burton St; (068) 47 3181.

Accommodation: 2 hotels, 2 motels, 1 caravan/camping park.
MAP REF. 120 B1, 122 B12

Wauchope   Pop. 4297
Nearby Timbertown, a major re-creation of a typical timber town of the 1880s, has put Wauchope on the tourist map. The town itself is the centre of a timber-getting, dairying, beef-cattle and mixed-farming area on the Oxley Hwy, 19 km W of Port Macquarie. **Of interest:** Hastings Dairy Co-operative, Randall St; demonstrations of cheese production. Train Meadows, King Creek Rd; model train display. **In the area:** Timbertown, re-created village with shops and school, on edge of Broken Bago State Forest, 3 km W; working bullock team, horse-drawn wagons, smithy, steam-powered train and sleeper-cutting demonstrations. Small weatherboard church adjacent houses Historical Society Museum. The Big Bull, 2 km E off Oxley Hwy; dairy farming display, hay rides, animal nursery. **Tourist information:** Cnr Hay and Clarence Sts, Port Macquarie; (065) 83 1293. **Accommodation:** 2 hotels, 2 motels, 1 caravan/camping park.
MAP REF. 109 E8, 123 N11

Wee Waa   Pop. 2030
This small town near the Namoi River is the centre of a cotton-growing district

producing the highest cotton yield in Australia. **Of interest:** Guided tours from Namoi Cotton Co-op, Short St, to Merah North Cotton Gin (9 km), April–Aug. Agricultural Show held in April. Cotton Festival held biennially in May. **In the area:** Yarrie Lake, 24 km S, for boating and birdwatching. Cuttabri Wine Shanty, 25 km SW; original Cobb & Co. coaching stop between Wee Waa and Pilliga. Cubbaroo Winery, 45 km W; tastings and sales, tour groups welcome. **Tourist information:** Newell Hwy, Narrabri; (067) 92 3583. **Accommodation:** 1 hotel, 2 motels, 2 caravan parks. MAP REF. 122 F7, 474 G12

Wellington   Pop. 5433

Limestone caves are one of the interesting features of this town at the junction of the Macquarie and Bell Rivers, 362 km NW of Sydney. **Of interest:** Historical Museum in old bank (1883), cnr Percy and Warne Sts. From Mt Arthur Reserve, 3 km W of town, walking trails to Mt Binjang with lookout at summit. Maps available from Visitors Centre in Cameron Park, attractive area on western side of main street (Mitchell Hwy). **In the area:** Wellington Caves, 9 km S; guided tours of Cathedral Cave, and smaller Gaden Cave with its rare cave coral; picnic/barbecue facilities, kiosk, aviary and animal enclosure, fossil and clock museum. Wellington Golf Club (18 hole) next to caves open to public. Glenfinlass Wines, 8 km SW on Parkes Rd. Nangara Gallery, 26 km SW; Australia-wide collection of Aboriginal artefacts. Markeita Cellars, 16 km S in village of Neurea. Rabbit Farm 20 km S; alpacas and shearing of angora rabbits; coach and group tours by appt. Burrendong Dam, 32 km E; panoramic views from spillway; also Arboretum, native flora reserve open daily. Areas for water-skiing, sailing, power boating and fishing nearby; camping facilities and cabin accommodation. **Tourist information:** Cameron Park, Nanima Cr.; (068) 45 2001. **Accommodation:** 7 hotels, 4 motels, 4 caravan/camping parks. MAP REF. 120 E4

Wentworth   Pop. 1447

Wentworth is a historic town at the junction of the Murray and Darling Rivers. At one time a busy riverboat and customs port, today it is a quiet holiday town. **Of interest:** Rotary Folk Museum and Old Wentworth Gaol (1881), both in Beverly

St. Courthouse (1870s), Darling St. Apphara Art Gallery, Adams St. Historic PS *Ruby*, Fotherby Park, Wentworth St. Riverboat cruises on MV *Loyalty*. Lock 10, weir and park, for picnics. Poker machines in town service clubs. Horseracing on Melbourne Cup Day. **In the area:** Houseboats for hire. Championship golf courses. Model aircraft display at Yelta, 12 km E. Orange World and Stanley Wine Co. on Silver City Hwy, 26 km E, at Buronga. Mungo National Park, 157 km NE, via Pooncarie. **Tourist information:** Shop 4, Wentworth Pl, Adams St; (050) 27 3624. **Accommodation:** 3 hotels, 6 motels, 2 caravan parks. MAP REF. 126 D7, 230 F3

West Wyalong   Pop. 3458

This former goldmining town, at the junction of the Mid Western and Newell Hwys, celebrated its centenary in 1994. It is now the business centre of a prosperous wheat, wool and mixed-farming area. **Of interest:** Aboriginal Artefacts Gallery, Newell Hwy. Bland District Historical Museum, Newell Hwy; scale model of goldmine, historical displays and archives. Highways Festival held long weekend in Oct. **In the area:** Lake

Bottle House, White Cliffs

Cowal, 48 km NE, via Clear Ridge, largest natural lake in NSW; also important bird sanctuary and popular fishing spot. Weethalle Whistlestop, 65 km W, on Hay Rd; Devonshire teas, art and crafts. At Barmedman, 32 km SE, Mineral Water Pool, believed to provide relief from arthritis and rheumatism. **Tourist information:** McCann Park, Newell Hwy; (069) 72 3645. **Accommodation:** 7 hotels, 11 motels, 2 caravan/camping parks. **See also:** The Newell. MAP REF. 120 A8, 127 Q6

White Cliffs   Pop. 219

White Cliffs Pioneer Opal Fields, 97 km NW of Wilcannia, is a town where pioneering is a way of life. The opal fields were the first commercial fields in NSW; the first lease was granted in 1890, and in the boom years at the turn of the century the fields were supporting 4500 people. Precious opal is still mined today. Jewelled opal 'pineapples' are found only in this area. **Of interest:** Underground Art Gallery; Eagles Gallery Pottery; Rosavilla with antiques and rock and mineral collections; Jock's Dugout Museum. Historic buildings include the now restored police station (1897), post

office (1900) and public school (1900). Pioneer children's cemetery. Unique underground motel and dugout homes; underground guest house in Turley's Hill. Many opal showrooms where opal cutting and polishing can be seen; Stubby Bottle Showroom, built from glass stubbies. Fossicking for opal in old field. Experimental solar power station. Camping, picnic/barbecue facilities and swimming-pool in Town Reserve. **In the area:** Mootwingee National Park, 90 km SW; guided tours of Aboriginal rock-art sites in cooler months (extremely hot in summer). **Tourist information:** Association Secretary; (080) 91 6611. **Accommodation:** 1 hotel, 1 motel, 1 caravan/ camping reserve.
MAP REF. 124 G8, 485 K13

Whitton   Pop. 340

Whitton, 24 km W of Leeton, is the oldest town in the Murrumbidgee Irrigation Area and has large rice and grain storage facilities. **Of interest:** Whitton Courthouse and Gaol Museum. **In the area:** Gogeldrie Weir, 14 km SE. **Tourist information:** Chelmsford Pl, Leeton; (069) 53 2832. **Accommodation:** 1 hotel.
MAP REF. 127 N8

Wilcannia   Pop. 942

Once the 'queen city of the west', this quaint township still has many impressive sandstone buildings. It was proclaimed a town in 1864 and was once a key inland port in the days of paddle-steamers. Gradually declining in the early 1920s with the advent of the car, today it is the service centre for a far-flung rural population. **Of interest:** Self-guide Historic Town Tour introduces several fine stone buildings, including post office, prison and courthouse (1880) and Athenaeum Chambers (1890), which houses Tourist Information Centre; also opening bridge (1895) across Darling River and paddle-steamer wharf upstream. **In the area:** Opal fields at White Cliffs, 97 km NW. **Tourist information:** Central Darling Shire, Athenaeum Chambers, Reid St; (080) 91 5909. **Accommodation:** 2 hotels, 2 motels, 1 caravan/camping park.
MAP REF. 124 G11

Windsor   Pop. 1869

An exciting town for lovers of history and early architecture, Windsor is one of the oldest towns in Australia, situated 56 km NW of Sydney. **Of interest:** St Matthew's Church, Moses St, oldest Anglican Church in Australia, designed by Francis Greenway and convict-built in 1817. Nearby graveyard is even older. Courthouse, Court St, is another Greenway building. The Doctor's House (1844), Thompson Sq.; privately owned. Many other fine buildings in historic George St and Thompson Sq. Hawkesbury Museum, Thompson Sq.; formerly Daniel O'Connell Inn, built in 1843. **In the area:** Australiana Pioneer Village, 6 km N; Rose Cottage, oldest timber dwelling in Australia, wagon and buggy collection, picnic/barbecue facilities and lake with paddle-boats. Tizzana Winery, 14 km N at Ebenezer; tastings and sales of fortified wines and picnic/barbecue facilities. Ebenezer Uniting Church (1809), claimed to be oldest church in Australia still holding regular services. Nearby, old cemetery and schoolhouse (1817). Cattai Park State Recreation Area, 14 km NE; historic homestead, friendship farm, horse and pony rides, canoe hire, picnic/barbecue facilities and camping area. **Tourist information:** Ham Common Bicentennial Park, Clarendon; (045) 88 5895. **Accommodation:** 2 hotels, 3 motels. **See also:** The Hawkesbury.
MAP REF. 105 K6, 121 J7

Wingham   Pop. 4407

The oldest town on the Manning River, 13 km NW of Taree, Wingham was established in 1836. **Of interest:** Wingham Museum, part of attractive village square with several prominent historic buildings, bounded by Isabella, Bent, Farquhar and Wynter Sts. The Wingham Brush, close to town centre, is one of the few remaining subtropical flood-plain rainforests in NSW, with orchids, ferns, Moreton Bay fig trees, subtropical flowers, and flying foxes year-round. Agricultural Show and Rodeo held Nov. **Tourist information:** Pacific Hwy, Taree North; (065) 52 1900 or (008) 80 1522. **Accommodation:** 2 hotels, 1 motel.
MAP REF. 109 B13, 121 M2, 123 M12

Wisemans Ferry   Pop. 400

Situated on the southern side of the Hawkesbury River, 66 km NW of Sydney, Wisemans Ferry is an important recreational area for those interested in water sports. Two vehicular ferries provide transport across the river. **Of interest:** Wisemans Ferry Inn, named after founder of original ferry service and innkeeper; said to be haunted by his wife, whom he allegedly pushed down front steps of inn to her death. Dharug National Park, on northern side of river, named after local Aboriginal tribe, is important for its wealth of Aboriginal rock engravings. Convict-built Old Great North Road in park, one of great engineering feats of early colony; walk or cycle along lower section (closed to vehicles) from ferry. **Tourist information:** Ham Common Bicentennial Park, Richmond Rd, Clarendon; (045) 88 5895. **Accommodation:** 1 hotel, 1 motel, 4 caravan/camping parks. **See also:** The Hawkesbury.
MAP REF. 105 L4, 121 J6

Wollongong   Pop. 211 417

The third largest city in NSW. Clustered around Port Kembla Harbour is the highly automated steel mill operated by BHP, an export coal loader and the largest grain-handling facility in NSW. The area surrounding the city contains some of the South Coast's most spectacular scenery. **Of interest:** Illawarra Historical Society Museum, Market St; includes handicraft room and furnished Victorian parlour. Wollongong City Gallery, cnr Burrelli and Kembla Sts. Spectacular mall shopping area with soaring steel arches and water displays. Botanic Gardens and Rhododendron Park. Surfing beaches and rock pools, to north and south. Foreshore parks for picnicking. Wollongong Harbour, fishing fleet and fish market. Historic lighthouse (1872). **In the area:** Lake Illawarra, 5 km S, stretching from South Pacific Ocean to foothills of Illawarra Range, for prawning, fishing and sailing; boats for hire. Seaside village of Shellharbour, 22 km S; walking trails in nearby Blackbutt Reserve. Many lookouts with superb views of coast, including Bald Hill Lookout, 36 km N; site of aviator Lawrence Hargrave's first attempt at flight in early 1900s, now favourite spot for hang-gliding. Symbio Animal Gardens, 44 km N at Helensburgh; free-roaming wombats, kangaroos, donkeys and other animals. Mt Kembla Village, 15 km W, scene of tragic mining disaster in 1902; features monument in church; original miners' huts; and several historic buildings, including Historical Museum housed in former post office, with pioneer kitchen, blacksmith's shop and

reconstruction of Mt Kembla disaster. **Tourist information:** 93 Crown St; (042) 28 0300. **Accommodation:** 4 hotels, 8 motels. **See also:** The Illawarra Coast.
MAP REF. 114, 116 H6, 119 I3, 121 J10

Woodburn
Pop. 592

Woodburn is a pleasant town on the Pacific Hwy, astride the Richmond River. **Of interest:** Riverside Park. Monument and remains of settlement at New Italy, result of ill-fated Marquis de Rays' expedition in 1880. Houseboats for hire. **Tourist information:** Cnr Ballina and Molesworth Sts, Lismore; (066) 22 0122. **Accommodation:** 1 motel.
MAP REF. 123 P3, 475 N9

Woolgoolga
Pop. 3660

This charming seaside town on the Pacific Hwy, 26 km N of Coffs Harbour, is excellent for crabbing, prawning and whiting fishing. Good surf beaches. **Of interest:** Guru Nanak Sikh Temple, River St; place of worship for town's Indian population. Raj Mahal Indian Cultural Centre. Woolgoolga Art Gallery on Turon Parade; paintings, pottery, workshops. **In the area:** Yuraygir National Park, 10 km N; bushwalking, canoeing, fishing, surfing, swimming, and picnic and camping areas on beautiful stretch of unspoiled coastline. Wedding Bells State Forest. **Tourist information:** Mobil Service Station, Pacific Hwy; (066) 54 1603. **Accommodation:** 7 motels, 3 caravan/camping parks.
MAP REF. 123 O7, 475 N12

Woy Woy
Pop. 12 206

Situated 90 km N of Sydney and 6 km S of Gosford. **Of interest:** Boating, fishing and swimming on Brisbane Water, Broken Bay and Hawkesbury River. Centre for Brisbane Water National Park, 3 km SW, noted for spring wildflowers, bushwalking, birdwatching and Aboriginal rock-art sites. **Tourist information:** Umina Visitors Centre and Tea Rooms, cnr Bullion and West Sts, Umina; (043) 43 2200. **Accommodation:** On peninsula: 3 hotels, 2 motels, 3 caravan/camping parks.
MAP REF. 105 O6, 108 F8, 121 K7

Wyong
Pop. 3902

Wyong is pleasantly situated on the Pacific Hwy between the Tuggerah Lakes and the State Forests of Watagan, Olney and Ourimbah. **Of interest:** Wyong District Museum, Cape Rd; recalls early ferry services across lakes, and forest logging. Many sports catered for, including golf, swimming, most water sports, horse and dog racing. Festival of Arts held in March. Historical Bush Picnic in Oct. **In the area:** Hinterland popular for bushwalking and camping. Burbank Nursery, at Tuggerah; 20 ha of azaleas, open daily, flowering time July–Sept. Award-winning Forest of Tranquillity at Ourimbah, 12 km S. **Tourist information:** Tuggerah Lakes Tourist Assocn, Memorial Park, Marine Pde, The Entrance; (043) 32 9282. **Accommodation:** 2 hotels, 1 motel, 2 caravan/camping parks.
MAP REF. 105 P4, 108 F1, 121 K6

Yamba
Pop. 3707

This prawning and fishing town at the mouth of the Clarence River offers sea, lake and river fishing. It is the largest coastal resort in the Clarence Valley. **Of interest:** Story House Museum, River St; historical records of early Yamba. Views from base of lighthouse, reached via steep Pilot St. **In the area:** Daily passenger ferry services to Iluka. River cruises. Lake Wooloweyah, 4 km S, for fishing and prawning. Yuraygir National Park, 5 km S; swimming, fishing and bushwalking in area dominated by sand ridges and banksia heath. The Blue Pool at Angourie, 5 km S; only 50 m from ocean, freshwater pool of unknown depth and origin; popular swimming and picnic spot. Houseboats for hire at Brushgrove, 35 km SW. **Tourist information:** Pacific Hwy, South Grafton; (066) 42 4677. **Accommodation:** 1 hotel, 8 motels, 3 caravan parks.
MAP REF. 123 P5, 475 N10

Yanco
Pop. 651

Located 8 km S of Leeton, this is where Sir Samuel McCaughey developed his own irrigation scheme, which led to the establishment of the Murrumbidgee Irrigation Area. His mansion is now an agricultural high school and with the nearby Yanco Agricultural Institute is open to the public. Yanco Powerhouse Museum has interesting displays and the Yanco Aquatic Park is nearby. There are extensive red gum forests along the Murrumbidgee River and well-marked forest drives lead to sandy beaches and fishing spots. **Tourist information:** Chelmsford Pl, Leeton; (069) 53 2832. **Accommodation:** 1 hotel.
MAP REF. 127 O8

Yass
Pop. 4828

Close to the junction of two major highways (the Hume and the Barton), this interesting old town is on the Yass River, surrounded by beautiful, rich, rolling country, 280 km SW of Sydney and 55 km from Canberra. **Of interest:** Grave of Hamilton Hume, who discovered Yass Plains in 1824, in Yass Cemetery; signposted from Ross St. He lived at Cooma Cottage (1830), 3 km E, for 40 years; cottage classified by National Trust, closed Tues. Hamilton Hume Museum, Comur St. Self-guide walk introduces many old buildings in town that relate to Australia's heritage. **In the area:** Burrinjuck State Recreation Area, 54 km SW off Hume Hwy; bushwalking, water sports and fishing. At Wee Jasper, 53 km SW; Goodradigbee River for trout fishing, Micalong Creek, Carey's Cave, with superb limestone formations, and Hume and Hovell Walking Track. **Tourist information:** Coronation Park, Cooma St; (06) 226 2557. **Accommodation:** 4 hotels, 6 motels, 1 caravan/ camping park.
MAP REF. 119 D4, 120 E11

Young
Pop. 6666

Attractive former goldmining town in the western foothills of the Great Dividing Range, 395 km SW of Sydney. Today cherries and prunes are the area's best-known exports, as well as flour, steel, tiles and magnesium oxide. **Of interest:** Lambing Flat Historic Museum, Campbell St; fascinating reminders of town's colourful history, including 'roll-up' flag carried by miners during infamous anti-Chinese Lambing Flat riots of 1861. Art Gallery, Olympic Way. Backguard Gully with historic Pug-mill, on Boorowa Rd; reconstruction showing early goldmining methods. **In the area:** Chinaman's Dam, 4 km SE, recreation area with picnic/barbecue facilities, children's playground and scenic walks. At Murringo Village, 24 km E; several historic buildings and home of crystal designer and engraver Helmut Heibel. Five wineries in area, all open for tastings and sales. **Tourist information:** Olympic Way; (063) 82 3394. **Accommodation:** 6 hotels, 6 motels, 1 hotel/ motel, 1 caravan/ camping park.
MAP REF. 119 B2, 120 C10

New South Wales

Location Map

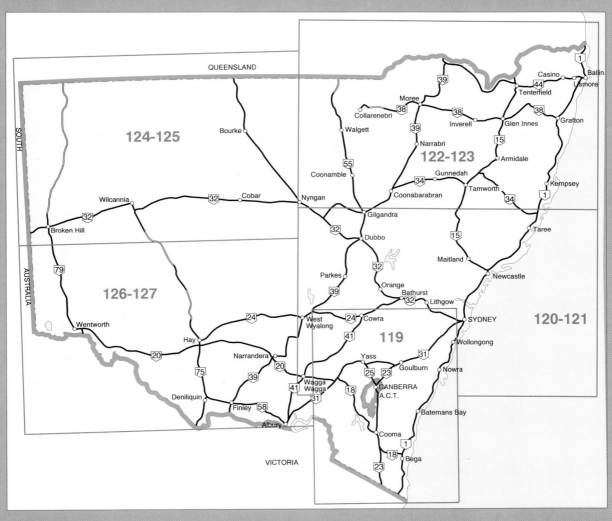

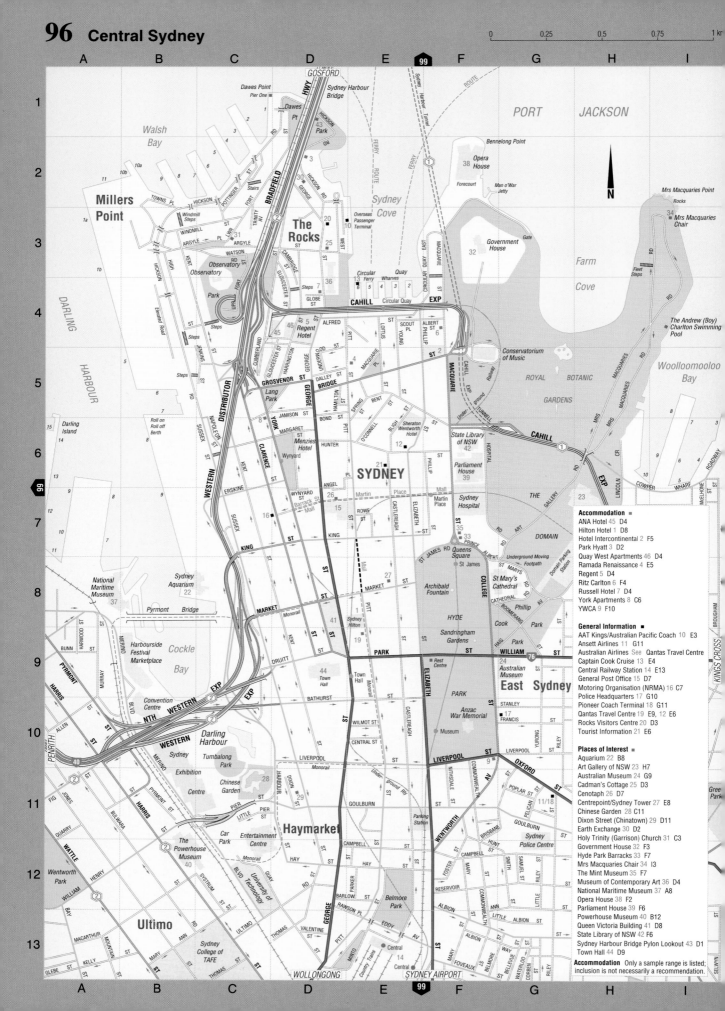

0   0.25   0.5   0.75   1 kr

PORT   JACKSON

N

Walsh
Bay

**Millers
Point**

Dawes Point
Pier One

Dawes
Pt

43
Park

Sydney Harbour
Bridge

**The
Rocks**

Bennelong Point

38
Opera
House

Forecourt   Man o' War
Jetty

Mrs Macquaries Point
Rocks

34   Mrs Macquaries
Chair

Observatory

Observatory
Park

Overseas
Passenger
Terminal

Sydney
Cove

32   Government
House

Gate

Farm

Fleet
Steps

Cove

Circular
Ferry   Quay
Wharves

CAHILL   Circular Quay

Conservatorium
of Music

The Andrew (Boy)
Charlton Swimming
Pool

DARLING

Regent
Hotel

45   46

Sheraton
Wentworth
Hotel

ROYAL   BOTANIC

**Woolloomooloo
Bay**

HARBOUR

Lang
Park

Menzies
Hotel

Wynyard

Martin   Place

SYDNEY

21

Martin
Place

Sydney
Hospital

Parliament
House
39

State Library
of NSW
42

GARDENS

Roll on
Roll off
Berth

Queens
Square

St James

Sydney
Hilton

Archibald
Fountain

St Mary's
Cathedral

HYDE

23

THE

DOMAIN

Darling
Island

Wynyard

**National Maritime
Museum**
37

**Sydney
Aquarium**
22

Pyrmont   Bridge

27

Sandringham
Gardens

PARK

Town
Hall

Town Hall

44

East   Sydney

24
Australian
Museum

**Cockle
Bay**

**Harbourside
Festival
Marketplace**

**Convention
Centre**

Sydney
Exhibition

**Darling
Harbour**

Tumbalong
Park

Chinese
Garden

28

WILLIAM

76

STANLEY

17
FRANCIS

Anzac
War Memorial

Museum

Liverpool

**Wentworth
Park**

Ultimo

**The
Powerhouse
Museum**
40

Car
Park

**Entertainment
Centre**

Chinese
Garden

Haymarket

Belmore
Park

**University
of
Technology**

**Sydney
College of
TAFE**

Sydney
Police Centre

Central Trains

Central   14

Central

WOLLONGONG   **SYDNEY AIRPORT**

Accommodation ▪
ANA Hotel 45 D4
Hilton Hotel 1 D8
Hotel Intercontinental 2 F5
Park Hyatt 3 D2
Quay West Apartments 46 D4
Ramada Renaissance 4 E5
Regent 5 D4
Ritz Carlton 6 F4
Russell Hotel 7 D4
York Apartments 8 C6
YWCA 9 F10

General Information ▪
AAT Kings/Australian Pacific Coach 10 E3
Ansett Airlines 11 G11
Australian Airlines See Qantas Travel Centre
Captain Cook Cruise 13 E4
Central Railway Station 14 E13
General Post Office 15 D7
Motoring Organisation (NRMA) 16 C7
Police Headquarters 17 G10
Pioneer Coach Terminal 18 G11
Qantas Travel Centre 19 E9, 12 E6
Rocks Visitors Centre 20 D3
Tourist Information 21 E6

Places of Interest ▪
Aquarium 22 B8
Art Gallery of NSW 23 H7
Australian Museum 24 G9
Cadman's Cottage 25 D3
Cenotaph 26 D7
Centrepoint/Sydney Tower 27 E8
Chinese Garden 28 C11
Dixon Street (Chinatown) 29 D11
Earth Exchange 30 D2
Holy Trinity (Garrison) Church 31 C3
Government House 32 F3
Hyde Park Barracks 33 F7
Mrs Macquaries Chair 34 I3
The Mint Museum 35 F7
Museum of Contemporary Art 36 D4
National Maritime Museum 37 A8
Opera House 38 F2
Parliament House 39 F6
Powerhouse Museum 40 B12
Queen Victoria Building 41 D8
State Library of NSW 42 F6
Sydney Harbour Bridge Pylon Lookout 43 D1
Town Hall 44 D9

Accommodation Only a sample range is listed;
inclusion is not necessarily a recommendation.

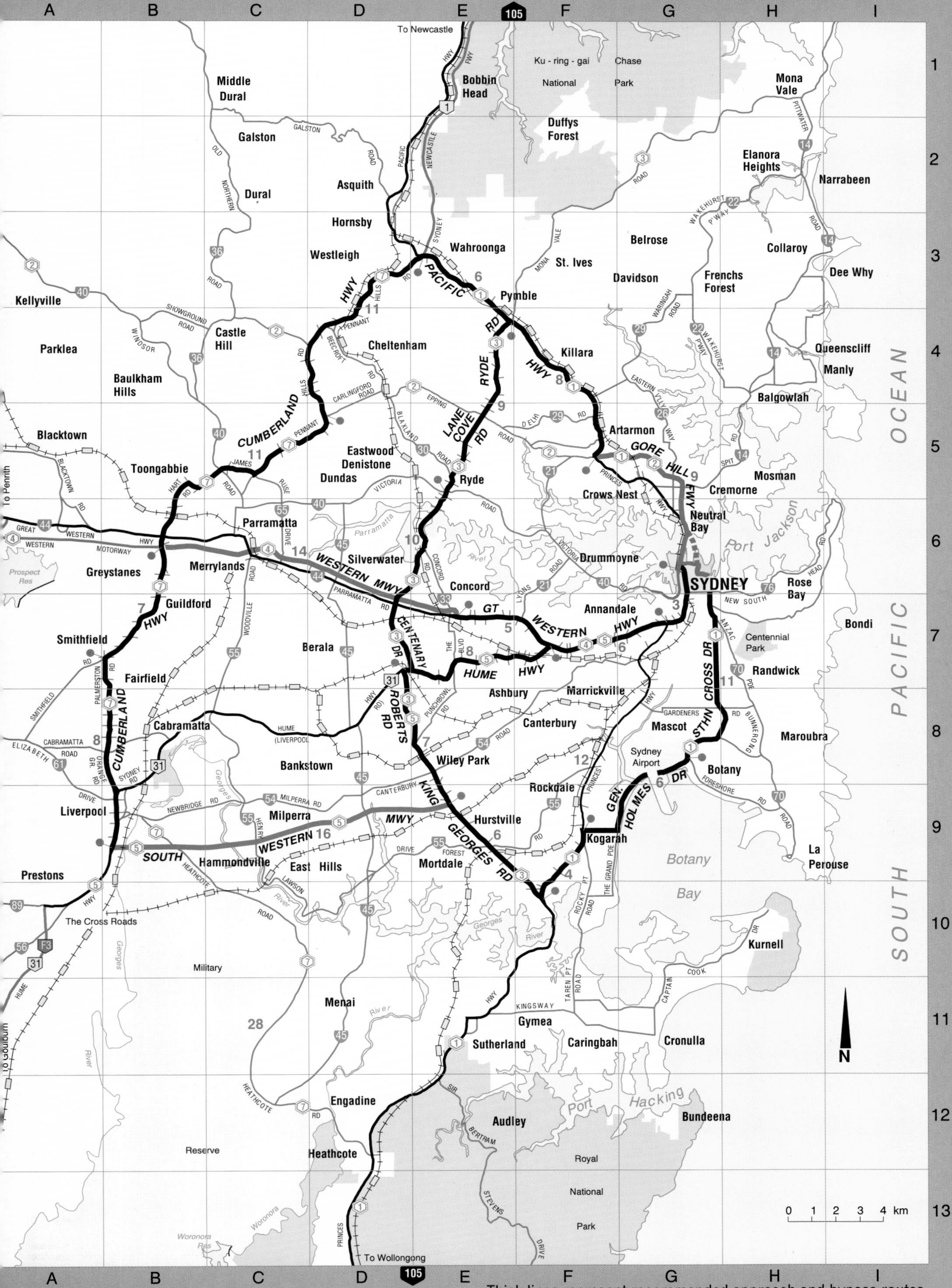

A B C D E F G H I

1 2 3 4 5 6 7 8 9 10 11 12 13

To Newcastle

Ku - ring - gai Chase
National Park

Bobbin Head

Middle Dural

Galston

Dural

Asquith

Hornsby

Westleigh

Wahroonga

Pymble

St. Ives

Duffys Forest

Belrose

Davidson

Frenchs Forest

Mona Vale

Elanora Heights

Narrabeen

Collaroy

Dee Why

Queenscliff

Manly

Kellyville

Parklea

Castle Hill

Cheltenham

Killara

Balgowlah

OCEAN

Baulkham Hills

Eastwood
Denistone
Dundas

Artarmon

Crows Nest

Mosman

Cremorne

Neutral Bay

Blacktown

Toongabbie

Parramatta

Ryde

Concord

Drummoyne

SYDNEY

Rose Bay

Port Jackson

Greystanes

Merrylands

Silverwater

Concord

Annandale

Bondi

Guildford

Smithfield

Fairfield

Berala

Ashbury

Marrickville

Mascot

Centennial Park

Randwick

Maroubra

PACIFIC

Cabramatta

Bankstown

Canterbury

Wiley Park

Rockdale

Sydney Airport

Botany

La Perouse

Liverpool

Milperra

Hurstville

Mortdale

Kogarah

Botany Bay

Kurnell

Prestons

The Cross Roads

Hammondville

East Hills

Menai

Gymea

Caringbah

Cronulla

SOUTH

Sutherland

Bundeena

Engadine

Audley

Royal

Heathcote

National Park

Reserve

Port Hacking

To Wollongong

N

0 1 2 3 4 km

Thick lines represent recommended approach and bypass routes.

100

102

105

A B C D E F G H I

1 2 3 4 5 6 7 8 9 10 11 12 13

Rogans Hill
Castle Hill
Thornleigh
Pennant Hills
Normanhurst
Fox Valley
Cumberland State Forest
Koala Park
Beecroft
Cheltenham
West Pymble
Lane Cove National Park
Macquarie University
Epping
Baulkham Hills
Excelsior Park
Darling Mills State Forest
Muirfield Golf Course
North Rocks
Carlingford
Eastwood
North Ryde
Winston Hills
Dundas Valley
Denistone
North Ryde Golf Course
Lake Parramatta Reserve
Pennant
Telopea
West Ryde
Old Toongabbie
Northmead
Oatlands Golf Course
Dundas
Ryde
Pendle Hill
Wentworthville
Rydalmere
Ryde-Parramatta Golf Course
Meadowbank
Melrose Park
Westmead
Parramatta
Ermington
Rhodes
Putney
Mays Hill
Camellia
Rosehill Racecourse
Silverwater Corrective Services Complex
Harris Park
Rosehill Showground
Silverwater
Concord Repatriation General Hospital
Granville
Parramatta River
Concord
Mortlake
Cabarita
Merrylands
Auburn
Homebush Bay
Homebush
Guildford
Bi-Centennial Park
Main Venue for Olympic Games
Concord Golf Course
Canada Bay
Fairfield
Auburn Golf Course
Lidcombe
Flemington
Strathfield
Burwood
Yennora
Berala
Rookwood Cemetery
Hudson Park Golf Course
Chester Hill
Rookwood
Strathfield Golf Course
Enfield
Croydon
Carramar
Villawood
Leightonfield
Regents Park
Chullora
Ashfield
Lansvale
Sefton
Birrong
Croydon Park
Bass Hill
Mirambeena Regional Park
Lansdowne Park
Lansdowne
Yagoona
Greenacre
Belfield
Ashbury
Motor Racing Circuit
Liverpool Golf Course
Georges Hall
Crest Of Bankstown
Hume Hwy
Mt Lewis
Punchbowl
Belmore
Warwick Farm Racecourse
Chipping Norton
Riverwood Golf Course
Condell Park
Bankstown Airport
Bankstown
Punchbowl
Lakemba
Clemton Park
Campsie

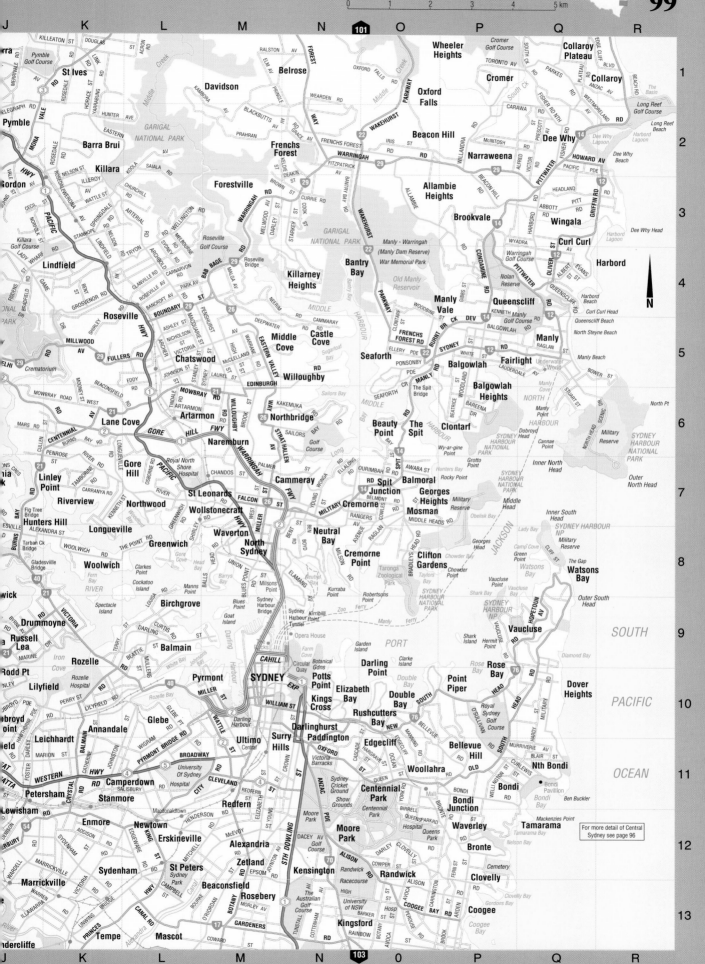

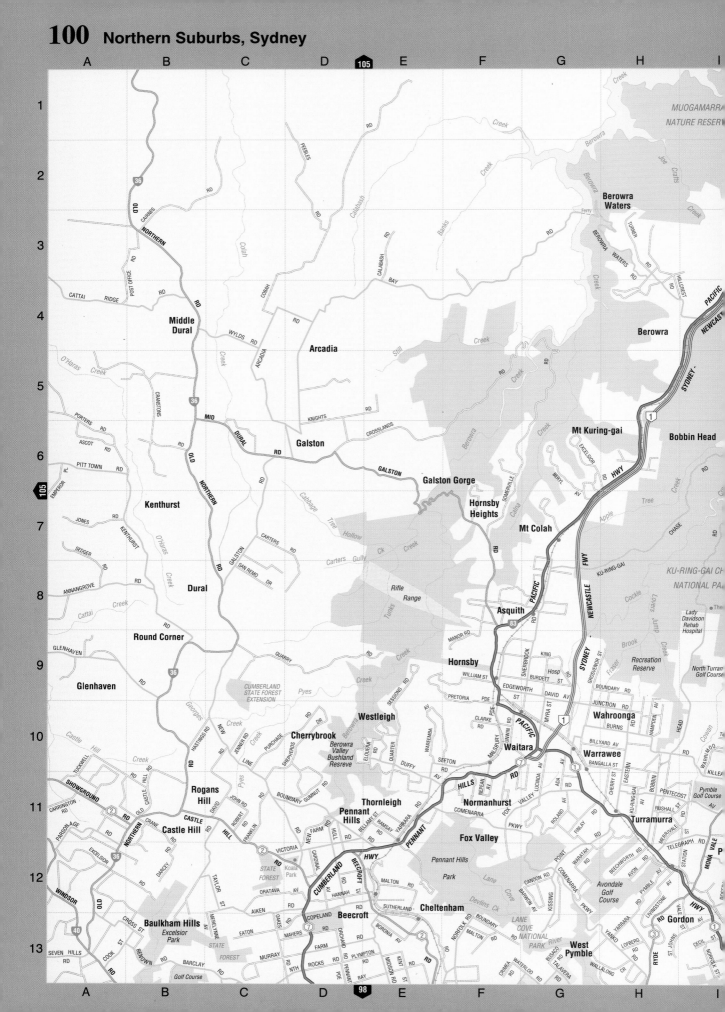

Berowra Waters

MUOGAMARRA NATURE RESERV

Middle Dural

Arcadia

Berowra

Galston

Galston Gorge

Mt Kuring-gai

Bobbin Head

Kenthurst

Hornsby Heights

Mt Colah

Dural

KU-RING-GAI CH NATIONAL PA

Round Corner

Asquith

Lady Davidson Rehab Hospital

Glenhaven

CUMBERLAND STATE FOREST EXTENSION

Hornsby

North Turra Golf Course

Westleigh

Wahroonga

Cherrybrook

Berowra Valley Bushland Resreve

Waitara

Warrawee

Rogans Hill

Thornleigh

Normanhurst

Pennant Hills

Turramurra

Castle Hill

Fox Valley

Pennant Hills Park

Avondale Golf Course

Baulkham Hills
Excelsior Park

Beecroft

Cheltenham

West Pymble

Gordon

WINDSOR

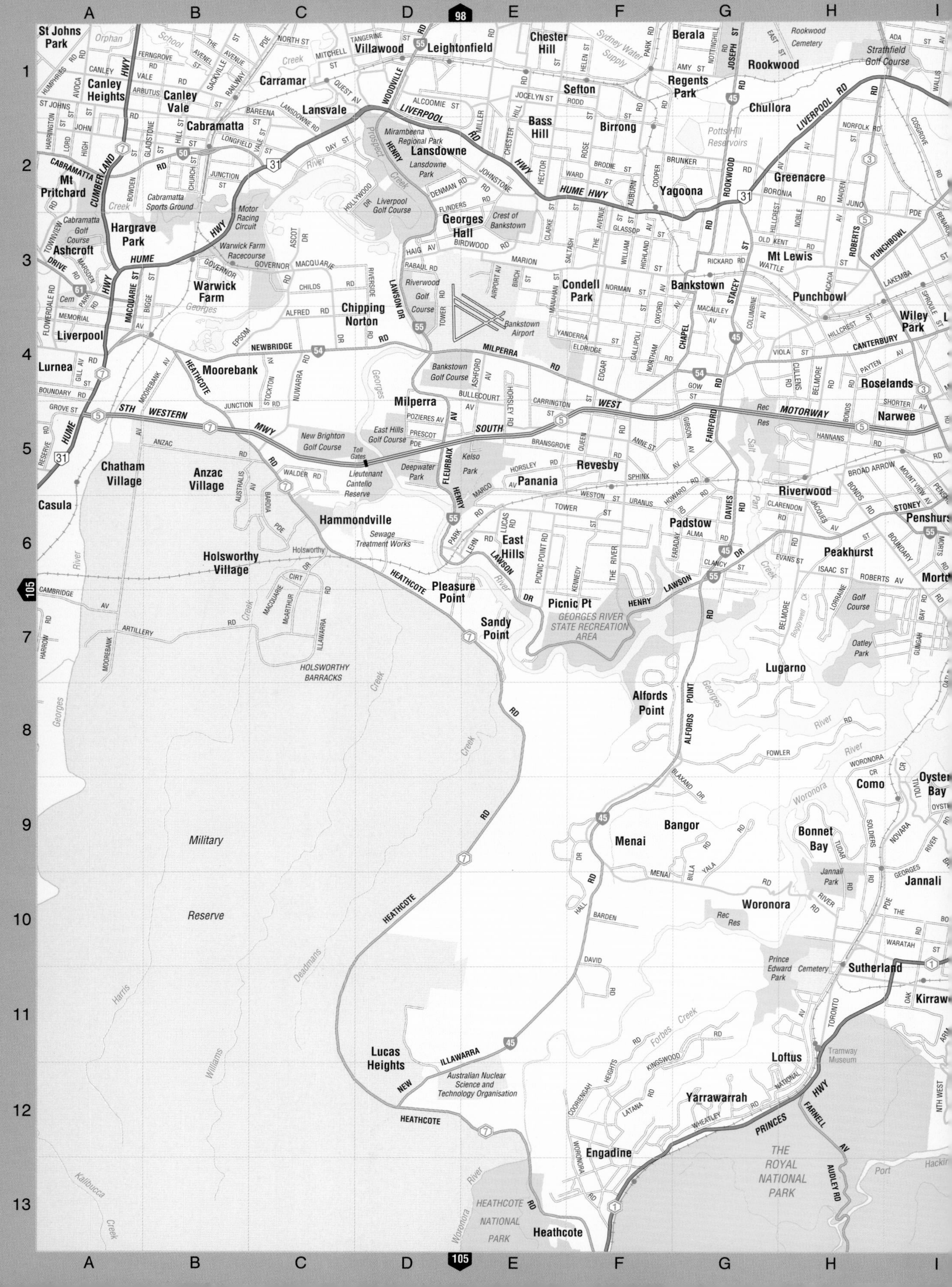

St Johns Park
Canley Heights
Canley Vale
Carramar
Cabramatta
Lansvale
Villawood
Leightonfield
Chester Hill
Berala
Rookwood
Sefton
Regents Park
Chullora
Mt Pritchard
Hargrave Park
Ashcroft
Lansdowne
Lansdowne Park
Georges Hall
Bass Hill
Birrong
Yagoona
Greenacre
Liverpool
Warwick Farm
Chipping Norton
Condell Park
Bankstown
Mt Lewis
Punchbowl
Lurnea
Moorebank
Milperra
Bankstown Airport
Chapel
Wiley Park
Roselands
Chatham Village
Anzac Village
Holsworthy Village
East Hills Golf Course
Deepwater Park
Revesby
Panania
Padstow
Narwee
Riverwood
Peakhurst
Penshurst
Casula
Hammondville
Pleasure Point
Sandy Point
East Hills
Picnic Pt
Georges River State Recreation Area
Alfords Point
Lugarno
Como
Oyster Bay
Military Reserve
Holsworthy Barracks
Menai
Bangor
Woronora
Bonnet Bay
Jannali
Sutherland
Kirraw
Lucas Heights
Australian Nuclear Science and Technology Organisation
Loftus
Yarrawarrah
Engadine
Heathcote National Park
Heathcote
THE ROYAL NATIONAL PARK
Prince Edward Park Cemetery

A B C D E 120 F G H I

1 Capertee · Newnes · RANGE

Palmers Oakey · PANTONEYS CROWN NATURE RESERVE · Colo River · DIVIDING · River · CULOUL

2 LIMEKILNS · WINBURNDALE NATURE RESERVE · Peel · TURON STATE FOREST · DARK CORNER STATE FOREST · SUNNY CORNER STATE FOREST · Ben Bullen · 34 · Wolgan · Glow Worm Tunnel · WOLLEMI · River · River

Winburndale · 21 · Cullen Bullen · Angus Place · NATIONAL

3 TO ORANGE · DUNKELD · Bathurst T · Walang · Glanmire · WINBURNDALE NATURE RESERVE · Portland · Pipers Flat · 86 · Lidsdale · 14 · GREAT · Mt Tootie 795m · Mount Irvine

Evans Plains · Mt Panorama Motor Racing Circuit · ORTON PARK · Meadow Flat · Yetholme · GREAT · Wallerawang · 2 · Marrangaroo · Zig Zag Railway · Clarence · Newnes Junction · DIVIDING · NATIONAL

4 TO COWRA · Perthville · WHITE ROCK · 31 · 37 · 5 · 11 · 13 · 32 · 19 · 8 · 11 · Mt Walker 1189m · 3 · 40 · 16 · Bell · Mount Wilson · PARK · Bilpin · 18

Georges Plains · 21 · Brewongle · SUNNY CORNER STATE FOREST · Sodwalls · Rydal · Lithgow T · WESTERN · 11 · Hartley Vale · 5 · 8 · 17 · Berambing · Kurrajong Hei · Panorama Po

5 COW FLAT · The Lagoon · 12 · O'Connell · LOCKSLEY · Tarana · EVANS CROWN NAT RES · Lake Lyell · GLENROY · Hartley T · Little Hartley · Mt York Explorers Monument · Mt Tomah Botanic Gardens · BLUE MOUNTAINS · Bow Moun · Vale Lo

19 · Ben Chifley Dam · Carlwood · 36 · Cox · River · 22 · 20 · Mount Victoria · Perrys Lookdown · Pulpit Rock · NATIONAL PARK

6 Rockley Historic Town · 18 · ESSINGTON · Wisemans Creek · 47 · LOWES MOUNT STATE FOREST · Lowes Mount · 25 · Hazelgrove · Bonfire Hill 1286m · Hampton · Lowther · 14 · Mt Piddington 1078m · Blackheath · Govetts Leap · The Bridal Veil · Evans Lookout · Mt Blackheath Lookout SHIPLEY · Beauchamp Falls

7 Mount David · 16 · Oberon · 26 · Duckmaloi · 29 · 32 · JENOLAN STATE FOREST · Gibraltar Rocks 1057m · Medlow Bath · Hargraves Lookout · Megalong · Explorers Tree · Katoomba T · Leura · Wentworth Falls · Faulconbridge · Winmalee · Springwo · Lawson · WESTERN · Valley

24 · 5 · 24 · Edith · BLACK RANGE · Scenic Skyway & Railway · Echo Point · The Three Sisters · Bullaburra · Hazelbrook · 32 · Woodford · Linden · Warrimoo · Bl

8 Burraga · Black Springs · 19 · 23 · 5 · Jenolan Caves · For more detail of the Blue Mountains see page 106 · Queen Victoria Hospital · JAMISON · Mt Bedford 639m · VALLEY · The Oaks Picnic Ground · Glenbrook · 21

9 CAMPBELLS RIVER · Shooters Hill · Mt Guouogang 1290m · KANANGRA · BOYD · River · RANGE · BLUE MOUNTAINS · McMahons Lookout · NATIONAL PARK · Mulgoa · Wallacia · Warragamba

Campbells · Tuglow Caves · 27 · GANGERANG RANGE · SCOTTS MAIN RANGE · Lake · Burragorang · Silverdale · Werombi · 29

10 Porters Retreat · Kanangra Walls · Mt Pallin 1210m · NATIONAL PARK · Green · Wattle · River · Creek · Burragorang Lookout · Orangeville · Glenmore · Nattai River · 14 · There · Cobbi · Brownlow Hill · Cam · 13

11 37 · 68 · Mt Werong 1214m · RANGE · GINGRA RANGE · Butchers · Mt Colong 1047m · Yerranderie Historic Town · Oakdale · The Oaks · Mount · Cawdor · 11 · 8 · 14

Mt Armstrong 1091m · DIVIDING · River · Mowbray Park · 6

12 Vaughan · Creek · GREAT · GOLSPIE · 22 · GOODMANS FORD · Lords Mountain 845m · NATTAI · River · Lake · NATIONAL · Lakesland · THIRLMERE LAKES NP · Thirlmere · Maldon · Picton T · 13 · 5 · 10 · 15

13 Richlands · 29 · Wollondilly · Bullio · Burragorang Lookout · Tunnel · Mt Wanganderry 835m · PARK · THE WATTLE RIDGE · Buxton · Balmoral · Bargo · Couridjah · Tahmoor · 89 · Yanderra · Wilton · 88 · SOUTH · TO MITTAGONG

A B C D E 120 F G H I

BUSHWALKS:
There are a number of scenic walks throughout the Blue ▨
These include:

1. The Fairfax Heritage Track (2km, approx. 1 hour) : ▨
starts at Heritage Centre, finishes at Govetts Leap; several
wheelchair access.

2. Popes Glen Nature Track (2km, approx. 3 hours) : Mode▨
at Dell St, finishes at Govetts Leap; meanders through woo▨

3. Pulpit Rock Nature Track (5km, approx. 4 hours) : Modera▨
Govetts Leap, finishes at Pulpit Rock; splendid views of Horse▨

4. Lyre Bird Dell / Pool of Siloam Track (2km, approx. 2 hours)▨
starts at Gordon Falls Picnic Area, finishes at Lyre Bird Dell; varie▨

5. Cascades / Fernbower Track (3km, approx. 2 hours) : Mode▨
and finishes at Leura Falls Picnic Area; magnificent▨
the Jamison Valley.

MOUNT VICTORIA: A blend of weatherboard and sandstone
colonial buildings, Mount Victoria is a National Trust classified
village with craft shops, a historical museum and a quaint
cinema, Mt Vic Flicks.

GARDENS: The Blue Mountains region is justly famous for
its beautiful gardens. One of the most famous is the Everglades
Gardens, created by the Danish landscaper Paul Sorenson; open
daily. The Rhododendron Gardens, at Blackheath, lovely all-year
round, are at their peak in late Spring; open daily.

LEURA: Home to some of Australia's most beautiful gardens.
The village with its unhurried atmosphere also offers
beautifully restored historic buildings, charming tea houses,
craft shops and galleries displaying the work of local artists.

KATOOMBA: The tourism centre of the Blue Mountains. A
wealth of natural and man-made attractions abound in the
area. Echo Point lookout provides magnificent views of the
Jamison Valley and the famous rocky pinnacles - the Three
Sisters.

SCENIC SKYWAY AND SCENIC RAILWAY: The Scenic Skyway,
Violet St / Cliff Dr., Katoomba is the first horizontal passenger-
carrying ropeway in Australia. It travels about 350m across the
mountain gorge above Cooks Crossing and provides stunning
views of Katoomba Falls, Orphan Rock and Jamison Valley.
The Scenic Railway was built in the 1880s by the founder of the
Katoomba coalmine to bring out the coal and transport the
miners. Reputed to be the steepest railway in the world, it
descends into the Jamison Valley at an average incline of 45
degrees through a sunlit, tree-clad gorge approximately 445m
in length.

THE THREE SISTERS: The foremost attraction of the Blue
Mountains and one of Australia's best known rock formations.
This trio of rocky pinnacles is floodlit at night.

Map labels:

TO LITHGOW · DARLING CAUSEWAY · Mt Victoria 1044m · Sunset Rock · Mount Victoria · Toll House Gallery · Mt Piddington 1078m · Coxs Cave · Killibinbin Arabian Stud · Colliers Lookout · Rhododendron Gardens · GREAT 32 · BLACKHEATH PLATEAU · HAT HILL · Mount Blackheath Lookout · Mt Blackheath · Mermaids Cave · Govetts Leap Statue · Blackheath · NP & W Heritage Centre · GOVETTS LEAP RD · Bridal Veil Falls · Trinity Falls · Cripps Lookout · Pulpit Rock Lookout · Hat Hill 1033m · Luchetti Lookout · Perry's Lookdown · Anvil Rock · Bennett Lookout · Baltzer Lookout · Walls Lookout · Rigby Hill 924m · Victoria Falls · Victoria Falls Lookout · Mt Banks 1058m · Edgeworth David Hill 864m · Lockley Pylon · Fortress Hill 954m · The Pinnacles · Mt Hay 944m · BLUE MOUNTAINS RANGE · HAY · MOUNT · LYCON PLATEAU · NATIONAL PARK · 4WD · Flat Top 928m · Arethusa Falls · Beauchamp Falls · Evans Lookout · THE GRAND CANYON · Walls Cave · Lake Medlow · EVANS LOOKOUT RD · WESTERN · Shipley Tea Rooms · Tuckers Lookout · SHIPLEY · Medlow Bath · Hydro Majestic · Cascade Creek Dams · Sugarloaf Peak · Hargreaves Lookout · KANIMBLA VALLEY · MEGALONG VALLEY · Megalong · Werribee Trail Rides · Megalong Valley Farm · Megalong Head · Katoomba · Explorers Tree · Scenic Skyway · Scenic Railway · Echo Point · Giant Stairway · The Three Sisters · CLIFF DR · FIRE TRAIL · Billy Healy Hill 637m · Pinnacle Hill · Euroka · Mountain River Riders · Packsaddlers Safaris · NARROW NECK · Castle Head 986m · Ruined Castle · MITCHELLS CREEK · JAMISON VALLEY · BLUE MOUNTAINS · Greenfields Lookover · Mt Solitary 965m · Melvilles Lookdown · CEDAR VALLEY · NATIONAL PARK · KEDUMBA VALLEY · Leura · HIGHWAY · BARTON ST · KATOOMBA ST · MEGALONG ST · Gordon Falls · Leura Falls · Everglades Gardens · Pool of Siloam · Conservation Hut · Natural History Museum · Wentworth Falls · Wentworth Falls Lake · Pointon Galleries · BLAXLAND · FALLS RD · Strathmore Historic Home · Yester Grange · Kings Table 883m · Lawson · Bullaburra · RAILWAY · GENEVIEVE RD · Queen Victoria Hospital · Hobbys Reach Museum · QUEEN · KINGS · KEDUMBA · ELIZABETH · TABLELAND · ERSKINE · KANGAROO VALLEY · EXPLORERS · Grose River

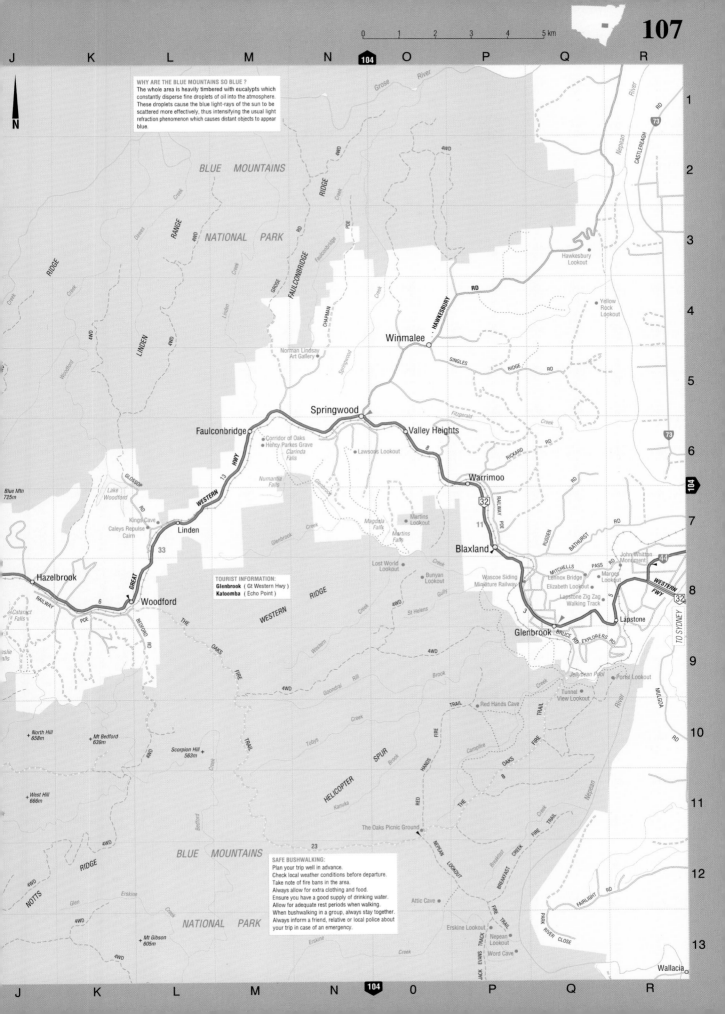

WHY ARE THE BLUE MOUNTAINS SO BLUE ?
The whole area is heavily timbered with eucalypts which constantly disperse fine droplets of oil into the atmosphere. These droplets cause the blue light-rays of the sun to be scattered more effectively, thus intensifying the usual light refraction phenomenon which causes distant objects to appear blue.

TOURIST INFORMATION:
Glenbrook (Gt Western Hwy)
Katoomba (Echo Point)

SAFE BUSHWALKING:
Plan your trip well in advance.
Check local weather conditions before departure.
Take note of fire bans in the area.
Always allow for extra clothing and food.
Ensure you have a good supply of drinking water.
Allow for adequate rest periods when walking.
When bushwalking in a group, always stay together.
Always inform a friend, relative or local police about your trip in case of an emergency.

0 2 4 6 8 km

A   B   C   D   E   F   G   H   I

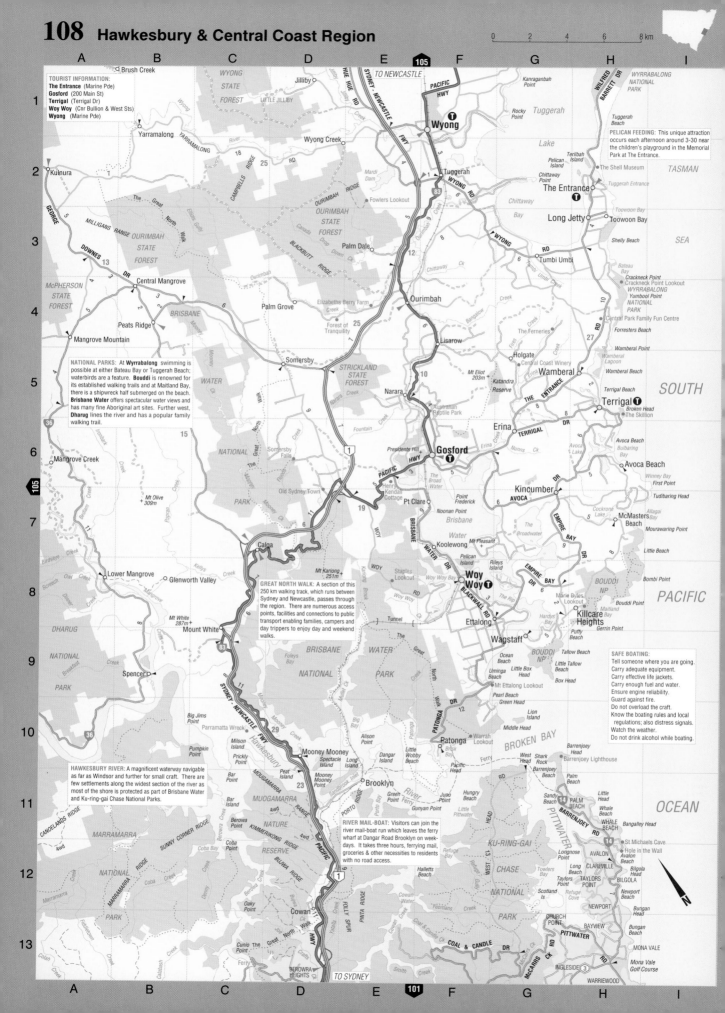

TOURIST INFORMATION:
The Entrance (Marine Pde)
Gosford (200 Main St)
Terrigal (Terrigal Dr)
Woy Woy (Cnr Bullion & West Sts)
Wyong (Marine Pde)

PELICAN FEEDING: This unique attraction occurs each afternoon around 3-30 near the children's playground in the Memorial Park at The Entrance.

NATIONAL PARKS: At **Wyrrabalong** swimming is possible at either Bateau Bay or Tuggerah Beach; waterbirds are a feature. **Bouddi** is renowned for its established walking trails and at Maitland Bay, there is a shipwreck half submerged on the beach. **Brisbane Water** offers spectacular water views and has many fine Aboriginal art sites. Further west, **Dharug** lines the river and has a popular family walking trail.

GREAT NORTH WALK: A section of this 250 km walking track, which runs between Sydney and Newcastle, passes through the region. There are numerous access points, facilities and connections to public transport enabling families, campers and day trippers to enjoy day and weekend walks.

SAFE BOATING:
Tell someone where you are going.
Carry adequate equipment.
Carry effective life jackets.
Carry enough fuel and water.
Ensure engine reliability.
Guard against fire.
Do not overload the craft.
Know the boating rules and local regulations; also distress signals.
Watch the weather.
Do not drink alcohol while boating.

HAWKESBURY RIVER: A magnificent waterway navigable as far as Windsor and further for small craft. There are few settlements along the widest section of the river as most of the shore is protected as part of Brisbane Water and Ku-ring-gai Chase National Parks.

RIVER MAIL-BOAT: Visitors can join the river mail-boat run which leaves the ferry wharf at Dangar Road Brooklyn on weekdays. It takes three hours, ferrying mail, groceries & other necessities to residents with no road access.

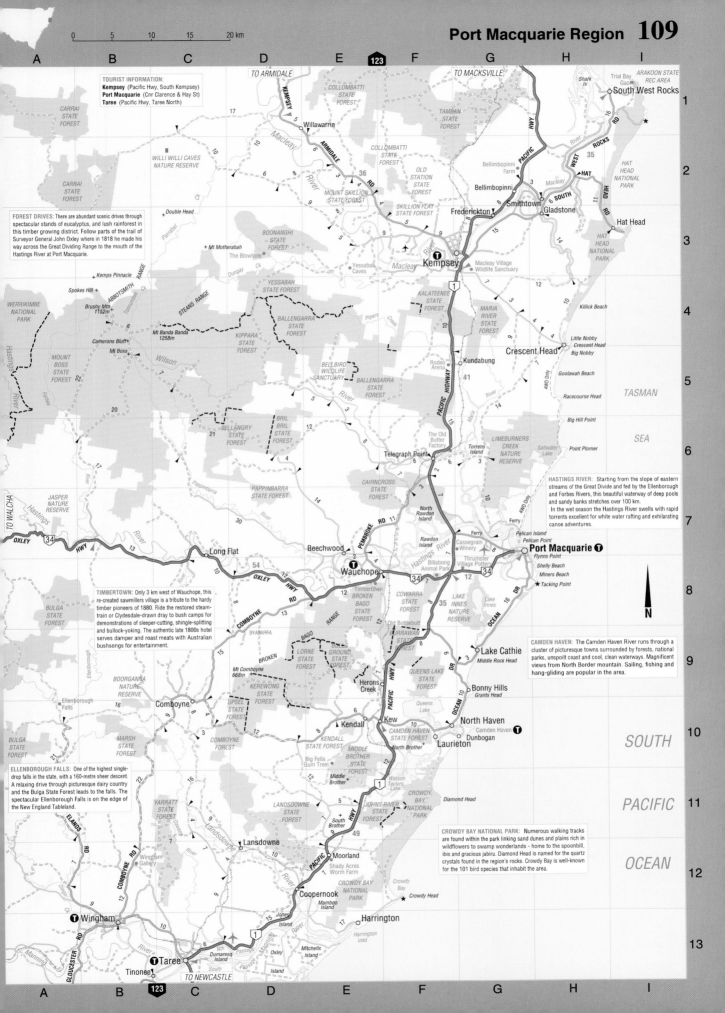

0 0,5 1 1,5 2 km
A B C D E F G H I
112
1 2 3 4 5 6 7 8 9 10 11 12 13
BHP Steel International
Iron and Steel Works
Mayfield East
Port Waratah Coal Loader
KOORAGANG ISLAND
Industrial Area
Walsh Point
North Harbour
Stockton
NEWCASTLE BIGHT
Maryville
Carrington
Islington
Wickham
Hamilton
PORT
HUNTER RIVER
The Basin
State Dockyard
Newcastle Harbour
Queens Wharf
Fort Scratchley
Harbourside Park (The Foreshore)
Horseshoe Beach
Nobbys
NEWCASTLE
Cooks Hill
National Park
Broadmeadow Racecourse
Hamilton South
Bar Beach
Merewether
TASMAN SEA
Sewage Treatment Works
Accommodation
Aloha Motor Inn 1 B10
Lucky Lil's 2 E7
Newcastle Backpackers 3 C7
Newcastle Star Hotel 4 E7
Noahs on the Beach 5 I7
Novocastrian Motor Inn 6 I7
Radisson Hotel 7 D7
The Esplanade Motel 8 I7
General Information
Ansett Airlines 9 F7
Australian Airlines see Qantas Travel Centre
City Hall 10 F7
Motoring Organisation (NRMA) 11 F7
Police 12 H7
Post Office 13 H7
Qantas Travel Centre 14 F7
Newcastle Railway Station 15 H6
Royal Newcastle Hospital 16 H7
Tourist Information 17 G6
Places of Interest
Bogey Hole 18 H8
Christ Church Cathedral 19 G7
Convict Stockade 20 H7
Fort Scratchley 21 I6
Hunter Street Mall 22 G7
King Edward Park 23 G8
Maritime & Military Museum 24 I6
Newcastle Workers Club 25 E7
Queens Wharf 26 G6
Regional Art Gallery 27 F7
Regional Museum 28 C7
Supernova 29 C7
Sydney Harbour Seaplanes 30 G6
War Memorial Cultural Centre 31 F7
William IV Steamship 32 G6
Accommodation Only a sample range is listed; inclusion is not necessarily a recommendation.

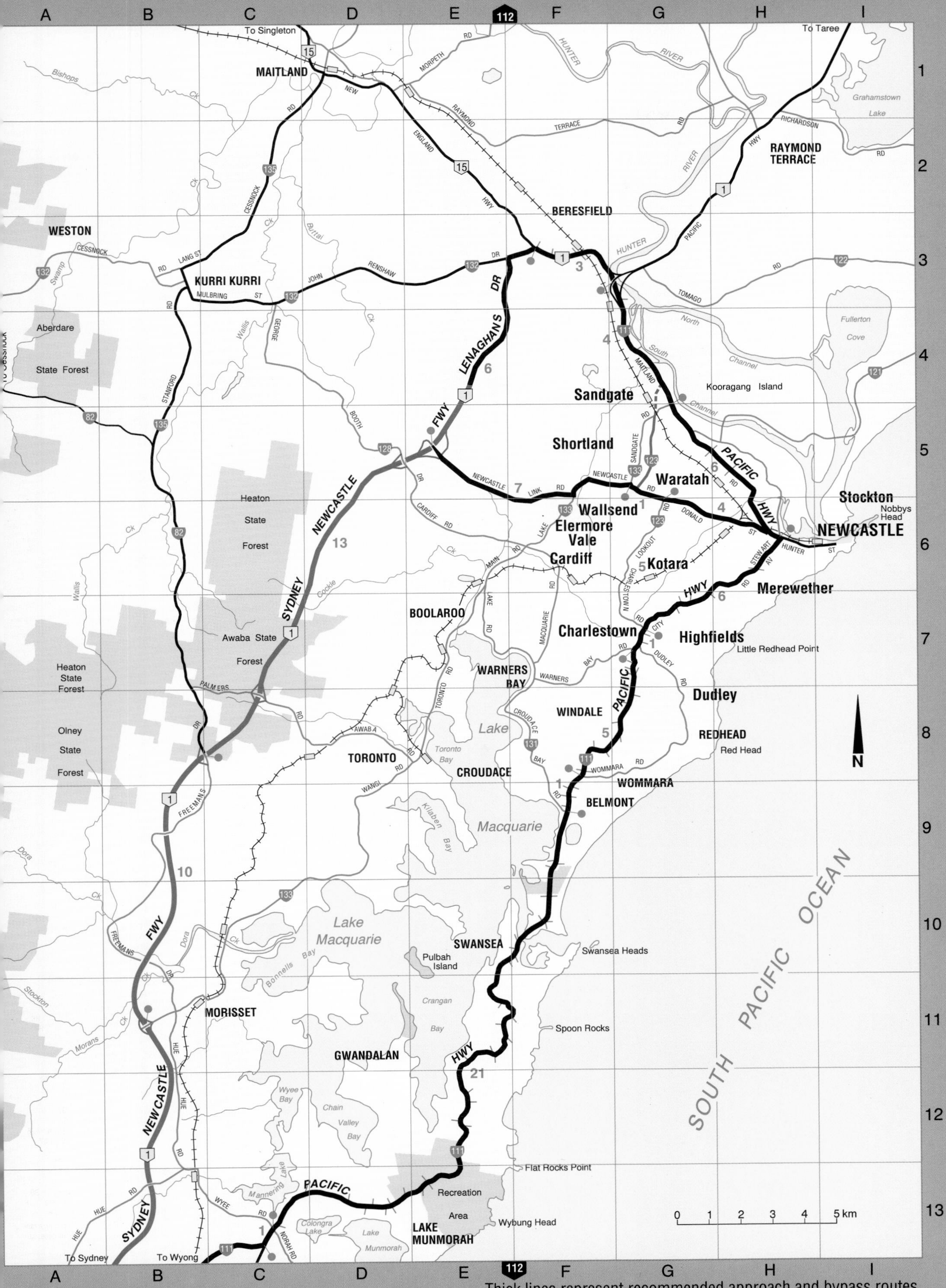

A B C D E F G H I

112

1

MAITLAND
To Singleton
15

To Taree

**RAYMOND
TERRACE**

2
15
135

BERESFIELD

WESTON

KURRI KURRI
132
132
1
3

132

Sandgate
4

LENAGHANS DR
6

Shortland

FWY
1

PACIFIC HWY

Waratah

NEWCASTLE
Stockton
Nobbys Head

5
128

Wallsend
133

7

Elermore Vale
Cardiff

133

4

4

NEWCASTLE FWY
13

SYDNEY

Kotara
Merewether
6

Highfields
Little Redhead Point
Charlestown
7

BOOLAROO

WARNERS BAY

Windale
Dudley

REDHEAD
Red Head
5

8

TORONTO
CROUDACE
131

WOMMARA
BELMONT

9
Macquarie

10

FWY
10

Lake Macquarie

133

SWANSEA
Swansea Heads

10

Pulbah Island

MORISSET
Spoon Rocks
11

NEWCASTLE
1

GWANDALAN

HWY
21

12

HUE
1

PACIFIC
111

Flat Rocks Point

Recreation Area

13
0 1 2 3 4 5 km
To Sydney
To Wyong
111

SYDNEY
1

LAKE MUNMORAH
Wybung Head

SOUTH PACIFIC OCEAN

A B C D E F G H I

112

Thick lines represent recommended approach and bypass routes.

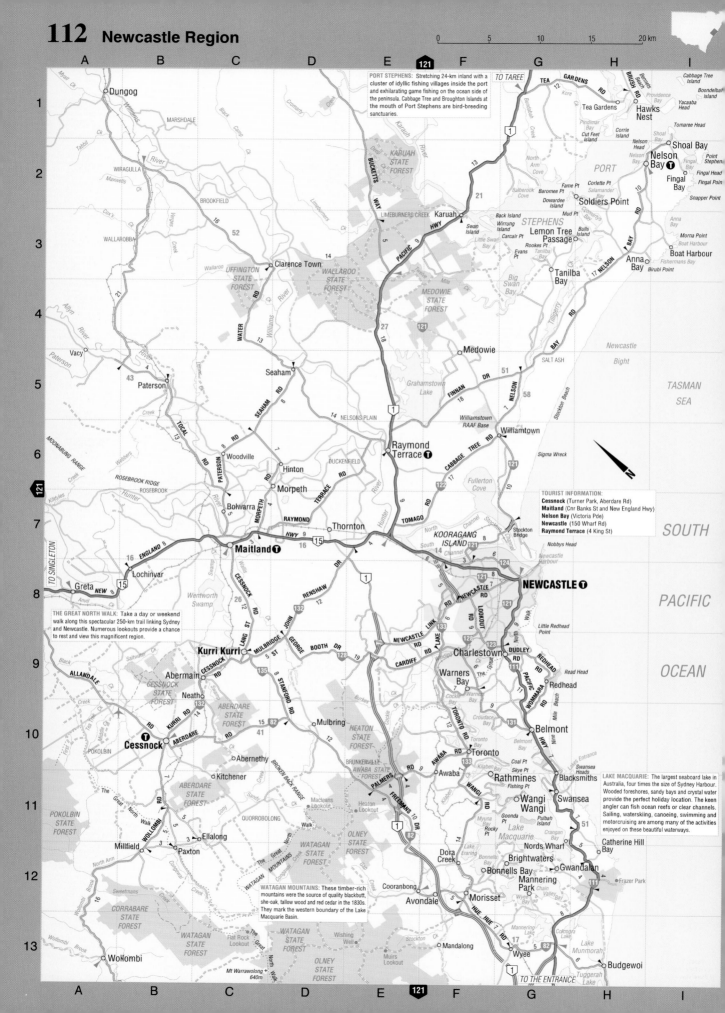

PORT STEPHENS: Stretching 24-km inland with a cluster of idyllic fishing villages inside the port and exhilarating game fishing on the ocean side of the peninsula. Cabbage Tree and Broughton Islands at the mouth of Port Stephens are bird-breeding sanctuaries.

THE GREAT NORTH WALK: Take a day or weekend walk along this spectacular 250-km trail linking Sydney and Newcastle. Numerous lookouts provide a chance to rest and view this magnificent region.

TOURIST INFORMATION:
Cessnock (Turner Park, Aberdare Rd)
Maitland (Cnr Banks St and New England Hwy)
Nelson Bay (Victoria Pde)
Newcastle (150 Wharf Rd)
Raymond Terrace (4 King St)

LAKE MACQUARIE: The largest seaboard lake in Australia, four times the size of Sydney Harbour. Wooded foreshores, sandy bays and crystal water provide the perfect holiday location. The keen angler can fish ocean reefs or clear channels. Sailing, waterskiing, canoeing, swimming and motorcruising are among many of the activities enjoyed on these beautiful waterways.

WATAGAN MOUNTAINS: These timber-rich mountains were the source of quality blackbutt, she-oak, tallow wood and red cedar in the 1830s. They mark the western boundary of the Lake Macquarie Basin.

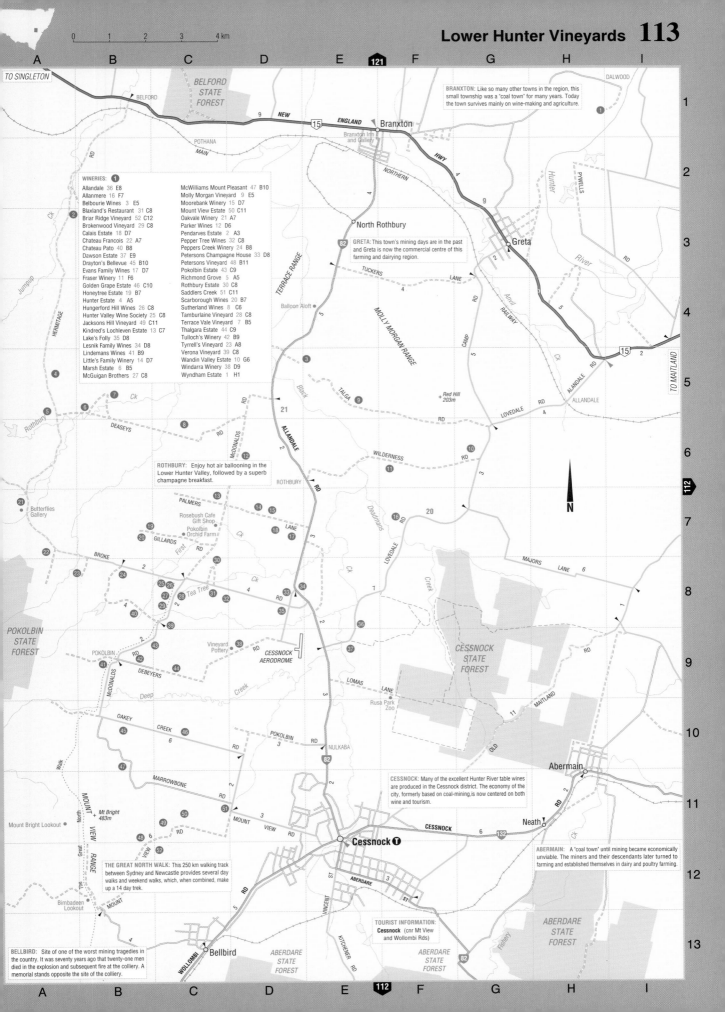

0   1   2   3   4 km

TO SINGLETON

WINERIES: ⓵

Allandale 36 E8
Allanmere 16 F7
Belbourie Wines 3 E5
Blaxland's Restaurant 31 C8
Briar Ridge Vineyard 52 C12
Brokenwood Vineyard 29 C8
Calais Estate 18 D7
Chateau Francois 22 A7
Chateau Pato 40 B8
Dawson Estate 37 E9
Drayton's Bellevue 45 B10
Evans Family Wines 17 D7
Fraser Winery 11 F6
Golden Grape Estate 46 C10
Honeytree Estate 19 B7
Hunter Estate 4 A5
Hungerford Hill Wines 26 C8
Hunter Valley Wine Society 25 C8
Jacksons Hill Vineyard 49 C11
Kindred's Lochleven Estate 13 C7
Lake's Folly 35 D8
Lesnik Family Wines 34 D8
Lindemans Wines 41 B9
Little's Family Winery 14 D7
Marsh Estate 6 B5
McGuigan Brothers 27 C8

McWilliams Mount Pleasant 47 B10
Molly Morgan Vineyard 9 E5
Moorebank Winery 15 D7
Mount View Estate 50 C11
Oakvale Winery 21 A7
Parker Wines 12 D6
Pendarves Estate 2 A3
Pepper Tree Wines 32 C8
Peppers Creek Winery 24 B8
Petersons Champagne House 33 D8
Petersons Vineyard 48 B11
Pokolbin Estate 43 C9
Richmond Grove 5 A5
Rothbury Estate 30 C8
Saddlers Creek 51 C11
Scarborough Wines 20 B7
Sutherland Wines 8 C6
Tamburlaine Vineyard 28 C8
Terrace Vale 7 B5
Thalgara Estate 44 C9
Tulloch's Winery 42 B9
Tyrrell's Vineyard 23 A8
Verona Vineyard 39 C8
Wandin Valley Estate 10 G6
Windarra Winery 38 D9
Wyndham Estate 1 H1

BRANXTON: Like so many other towns in the region, this small township was a "coal town" for many years. Today the town survives mainly on wine-making and agriculture.

GRETA: This town's mining days are in the past and Greta is now the commercial centre of this farming and dairying region.

ROTHBURY: Enjoy hot air ballooning in the Lower Hunter Valley, followed by a superb champagne breakfast.

CESSNOCK: Many of the excellent Hunter River table wines are produced in the Cessnock district. The economy of the city, formerly based on coal-mining, is now centered on both wine and tourism.

ABERMAIN: A "coal town" until mining became economically unviable. The miners and their descendants later turned to farming and established themselves in dairy and poultry farming.

THE GREAT NORTH WALK: This 250 km walking track between Sydney and Newcastle provides several day walks and weekend walks, which, when combined, make up a 14 day trek.

TOURIST INFORMATION:
Cessnock (cnr Mt View and Wollombi Rds)

BELLBIRD: Site of one of the worst mining tragedies in the country. It was seventy years ago that twenty-one men died in the explosion and subsequent fire at the colliery. A memorial stands opposite the site of the colliery.

Branxton

North Rothbury

Greta

Balloon Aloft

Red Hill 203m

Butterflies Gallery

Rosebush Cafe Gift Shop

Pokolbin Orchid Farm

Tea Tree

Vineyard Pottery

POKOLBIN STATE FOREST

CESSNOCK AERODROME

Pokolbin

Rusa Park Zoo

CESSNOCK STATE FOREST

Abermain

Neath

Cessnock

Mt Bright 483m

Mount Bright Lookout

MOUNT VIEW RANGE

Bimbadeen Lookout

Bellbird

ABERDARE STATE FOREST

ABERDARE STATE FOREST

ABERDARE STATE FOREST

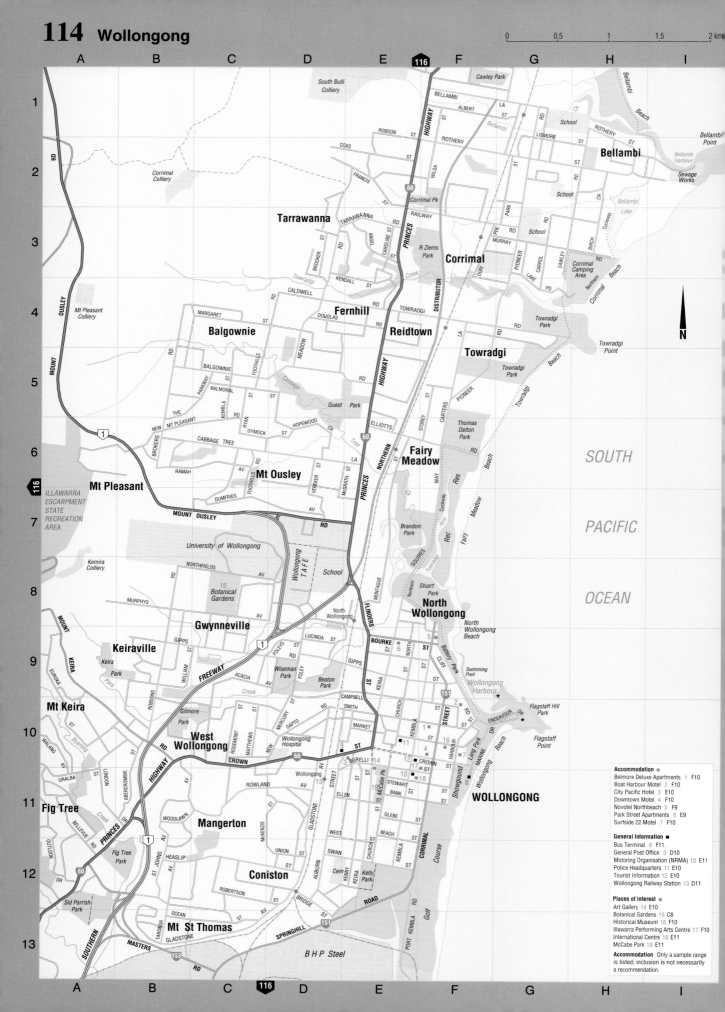

114 Wollongong

Accommodation ■
Belmore Deluxe Apartments 1 F10
Boat Harbour Motel 2 F10
City Pacific Hotel 3 E10
Downtown Motel 4 F10
Novotel Northbeach 5 F9
Park Street Apartments 6 E9
Surfside 22 Motel 7 F10

General Information ■
Bus Terminal 8 F11
General Post Office 9 D10
Motoring Organisation (NRMA) 10 E11
Police Headquarters 11 E10
Tourist Information 12 E10
Wollongong Railway Station 13 D11

Places of Interest ■
Art Gallery 14 E10
Botanical Gardens 15 C8
Historical Museum 16 F10
Illawarra Performing Arts Centre 17 F10
International Centre 18 E11
McCabe Park 19 E11

Accommodation Only a sample range
is listed; inclusion is not necessarily
a recommendation.

A B C D E 116 F G H I

0 1 2 3 km

1

To Sydney

Thirroul

MOUNT OUSLEY ROAD

BULLI PASS

4

The Elbow

Hewitt

Woodland

Hargrave Dr

Lawrence Ck

2

POINT ST

Bulli Point

PARK RD

Bulli

BLACKALL ST

TRINITY ROW

CARRINGTON

3

Woonona Heights

HIGHWAY

FARRELL

Waniora Point

Bulli Beach

VOGTOK

9.7

Ck

GRAY ST

PARK RD

Woonona

THOMPSON ST

MITCHELL RD

Woonona Beach

4

Collins

Russell Vale

Farrahars Ck

YORK ST

Bellambi

Bellambi Beach

5

MOUNT OUSLEY RD

PRINCES

BELLAMBI LA

ROTHERY

Bellambi Point

DISTRIBUTOR

60

RAILWAY

Bellambi Lake

6

TARRAWANNA RD

Tarrawanna

PIONEER

MURRAY RD

Corrimal

ST

Corrimal Beach

LAKE PDE

7

Towradgi

Fernhill

MEADOW

2

TOWRADGI

Towradgi

Balgownie

BALGOWNIE

Reidtown

CARTERS

Fairy Meadow Beach

8

1

4

KEMBLA ST

RYAN ST

NEW MT PLEASANT

CABBAGE TREE LA

ELLIOTTS

2

Fairy Meadow

WAY

NORTHERN

SQUIRES

Mt Ousley

MT OUSLEY RD

9

Mt Pleasant

North Wollongong

HANLEY DR

University of Wollongong

NORTHFIELDS AV

FREEWAY

4

FLINDERS ST

Virginia

CRWE ST

Wollongong Harbour

10

Gwynneville

3.5

BOURKE ST

Keiraville

GIPPS

VICKERY ST

FOLEYS

2

KEIRA

RD

Mt Keira

MT KEIRA

ROBSONS RD

GILMORE

ACACIA AV

NEW DAPTO RD

MERCURY ST

ROW LAND AV

Mall

CROWN ST

WOLLONGONG

11

2.7

60

West Wollongong

CROWN

SOUTHERN

McArthur

GLADSTONE AV

CORRIMAL

Mangerton

HEASLIP ST

12

Figtree

THE AVENUE

ST JOHNS AV

Coniston

BRIDGE ST

Golf Course

SPRINGHILL

Mt St Thomas

GLADSTONE

MT KEMBLA

CORDEAUX

Byarong Ck

American Ck

MASTERS RD

13

60

PRINCES HWY

To Dapto

To Kiama

BHP Steel Works

A B C D E 116 F G H I

SOUTH PACIFIC OCEAN

N

88

PICTON RD

MT KEIRA RD

MT KEIRA RD

Thick lines represent recommended approach and bypass routes

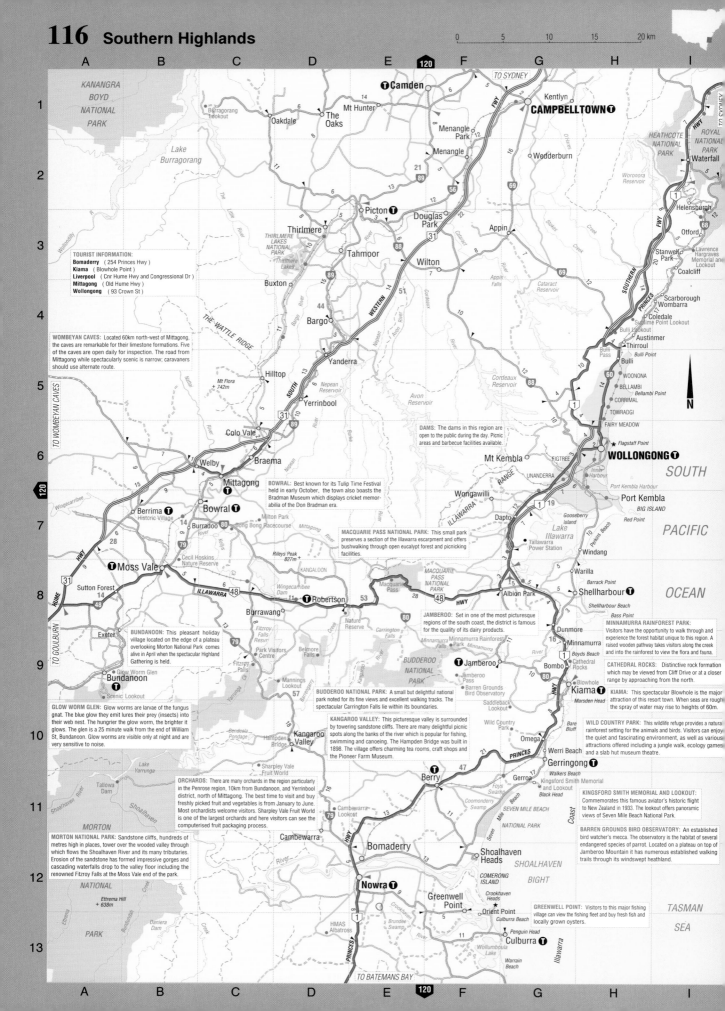

TOURIST INFORMATION:
Bomaderry (254 Princes Hwy)
Kiama (Blowhole Point)
Liverpool (Cnr Hume Hwy and Congressional Dr)
Mittagong (Old Hume Hwy)
Wollongong (93 Crown St)

WOMBEYAN CAVES: Located 60km north-west of Mittagong, the caves are remarkable for their limestone formations. Five of the caves are open daily for inspection. The road from Mittagong while spectacularly scenic is narrow; caravaners should use alternate route.

BOWRAL: Best known for its Tulip Time Festival held in early October, the town also boasts the Bradman Museum which displays cricket memorabilia of the Don Bradman era.

DAMS: The dams in this region are open to the public during the day. Picnic areas and barbecue facilities available.

MACQUARIE PASS NATIONAL PARK: This small park preserves a section of the Illawarra escarpment and offers bushwalking through open eucalypt forest and picnicking facilities.

BUNDANOON: This pleasant holiday village located on the edge of a plateau overlooking Morton National Park comes alive in April when the spectacular Highland Gathering is held.

GLOW WORM GLEN: Glow worms are larvae of the fungus gnat. The blue glow they emit lures their prey (insects) into their web nest. The hungrier the glow worm, the brighter it glows. The glen is a 25 minute walk from the end of William St, Bundanoon. Glow worms are visible only at night and are very sensitive to noise.

MORTON NATIONAL PARK: Sandstone cliffs, hundreds of metres high in places, tower over the wooded valley through which flows the Shoalhaven River and its many tributaries. Erosion of the sandstone has formed impressive gorges and cascading waterfalls drop to the valley floor including the renowned Fitzroy Falls at the Moss Vale end of the park.

ORCHARDS: There are many orchards in the region particularly in the Penrose region, 10km from Bundanoon, and Yerrinbool district, north of Mittagong. The best time to visit and buy freshly picked fruit and vegetables is from January to June. Most orchardists welcome visitors. Sharpley Vale Fruit World is one of the largest orchards and here visitors can see the computerised fruit packaging process.

BUDDEROO NATIONAL PARK: A small but delightful national park noted for its fine views and excellent walking tracks. The spectacular Carrington Falls lie within its boundaries.

KANGAROO VALLEY: This picturesque valley is surrounded by towering sandstone cliffs. There are many delightful picnic spots along the banks of the river which is popular for fishing, swimming and canoeing. The Hampden Bridge was built in 1898. The village offers charming tea rooms, craft shops and the Pioneer Farm Museum.

JAMBEROO: Set in one of the most picturesque regions of the south coast, the district is famous for the quality of its dairy products.

MINNAMURRA RAINFOREST PARK: Visitors have the opportunity to walk through and experience the forest habitat unique to this region. A raised wooden pathway takes visitors along the creek and into the rainforest to view the flora and fauna.

CATHEDRAL ROCKS: Distinctive rock formation which may be viewed from Cliff Drive or at a closer range by approaching from the north.

KIAMA: This spectacular Blowhole is the major attraction of this resort town. When seas are rough the spray of water may rise to heights of 60m.

WILD COUNTRY PARK: This wildlife refuge provides a natural rainforest setting for the animals and birds. Visitors can enjoy the quiet and fascinating environment, as well as various attractions offered including a jungle walk, ecology games and a slab hut museum theatre.

KINGSFORD SMITH MEMORIAL AND LOOKOUT: Commemorates this famous aviator's historic flight to New Zealand in 1933. The lookout offers panoramic views of Seven Mile Beach National Park.

BARREN GROUNDS BIRD OBSERVATORY: An established bird watcher's mecca. The observatory is the habitat of several endangered species of parrot. Located on a plateau on top of Jamberoo Mountain it has numerous established walking trails through its windswept heathland.

GREENWELL POINT: Visitors to this major fishing village can view the fishing fleet and buy fresh fish and locally grown oysters.

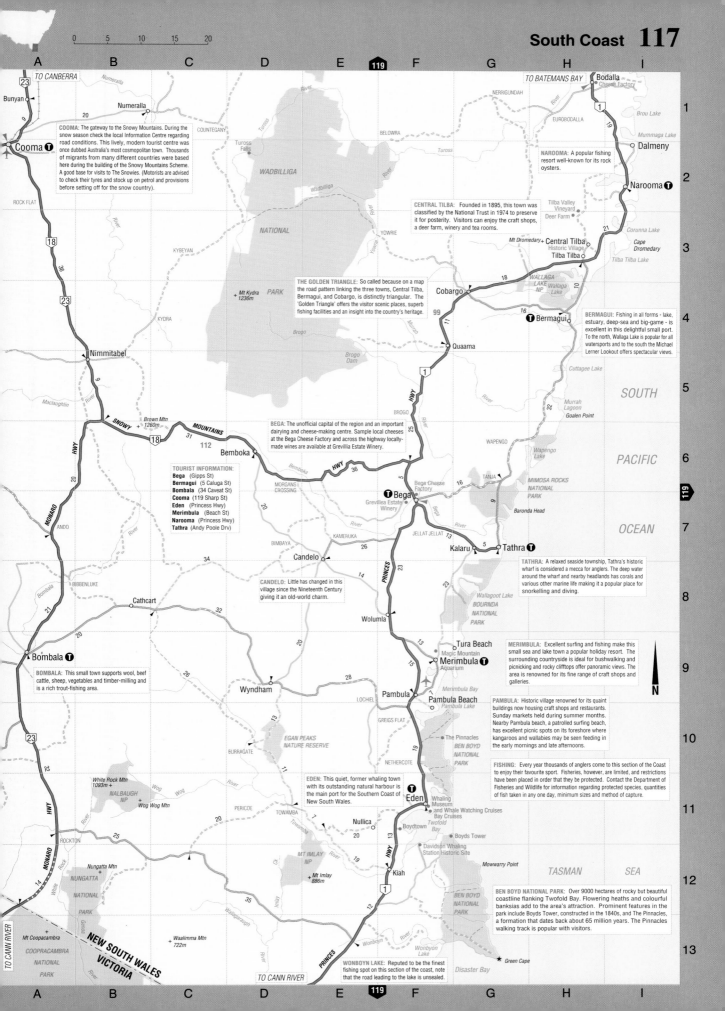

TO CANBERRA

0 5 10 15 20

A B C D E [119] F G H I

TO BATEMANS BAY

Bunyan

Numeralla

Numeralla

Cooma

NERRIGUNDAH

Bodalla
Cheese Factory

EUROBODALLA

Brou Lake

Dalmeny

Mummaga Lake

COOMA: The gateway to the Snowy Mountains. During the snow season check the local Information Centre regarding road conditions. This lively, modern tourist centre was once dubbed Australia's most cosmopolitan town. Thousands of migrants from many different countries were based here during the building of the Snowy Mountains Scheme. A good base for visits to The Snowies. (Motorists are advised to check their tyres and stock up on petrol and provisions before setting off for the snow country).

COUNTEGANY

Tuross Falls

Tuross

BELOWRA

Tuross

NAROOMA: A popular fishing resort well-known for its rock oysters.

Narooma

ROCK FLAT

WADBILLIGA

YOWRIE

Tilba Valley Vineyard
Deer Farm

CENTRAL TILBA: Founded in 1895, this town was classified by the National Trust in 1974 to preserve it for posterity. Visitors can enjoy the craft shops, a deer farm, winery and tea rooms.

Mt Dromedary

Central Tilba
Historic Village

Tilba Tilba

Cape Dromedary

Corunna Lake

Tilba Tilba Lake

NATIONAL

Nimmitabel

KYBEYAN

KYDRA

Mt Kydra
1236m

THE GOLDEN TRIANGLE: So called because on a map the road pattern linking the three towns, Central Tilba, Bermagui, and Cobargo, is distinctly triangular. The 'Golden Triangle' offers the visitor scenic places, superb fishing facilities and an insight into the country's heritage.

Brogo

Cobargo

WALLAGA
LAKE NP

Wallaga Lake

Bermagui

BERMAGUI: Fishing in all forms - lake, estuary, deep-sea and big-game - is excellent in this delightful small port. To the north, Wallaga Lake is popular for all watersports and to the south the Michael Lerner Lookout offers spectacular views.

PARK

Brogo Dam

Quaama

Cuttagee Lake

SOUTH

Maclaughlin

Brown Mtn
1260m

SNOWY MOUNTAINS

Murrah Lagoon

Goalen Point

PACIFIC

Bemboka

BEGA: The unofficial capital of the region and an important dairying and cheese-making centre. Sample local cheeses at the Bega Cheese Factory and across the highway locally-made wines are available at Grevillia Estate Winery.

WAPENGO

Wapengo Lake

TANJA

MIMOSA ROCKS
NATIONAL
PARK

TOURIST INFORMATION:
Bega (Gipps St)
Bermagui (5 Caluga St)
Bombala (34 Caveat St)
Cooma (119 Sharp St)
Eden (Princess Hwy)
Merimbula (Beach St)
Narooma (Princess Hwy)
Tathra (Andy Poole Drv)

MORGANS CROSSING

Bega Cheese Factory

Bega

Grevillea Estate Winery

Baronda Head

OCEAN

ANDO

MONARO

BIMBAYA

KAMERUKA

JELLAT JELLAT

Kalaru

Tathra

TATHRA: A relaxed seaside township, Tathra's historic wharf is considered a mecca for anglers. The deep water around the wharf and nearby headlands has corals and various other marine life making it a popular place for snorkelling and diving.

BIBBENLUKE

Candelo

Wallagoot Lake

BOURNDA
NATIONAL
PARK

CANDELO: Little has changed in this village since the Nineteenth Century giving it an old-world charm.

PRINCES

Cathcart

Wolumla

Bombala

Tura Beach

Magic Mountain

Merimbula
Aquarium

MERIMBULA: Excellent surfing and fishing make this small sea and lake town a popular holiday resort. The surrounding countryside is ideal for bushwalking and picnicking and rocky clifftops offer panoramic views. The area is renowned for its fine range of craft shops and galleries.

N

BOMBALA: This small town supports wool, beef cattle, sheep, vegetables and timber-milling and is a rich trout-fishing area.

Wyndham

LOCHIEL

Pambula

Pambula Beach
Pambula Lake

Merimbula Bay

PAMBULA: Historic village renowned for its quaint buildings now housing craft shops and restaurants. Sunday markets held during summer months. Nearby Pambula beach, a patrolled surfing beach, has excellent picnic spots on its foreshore where kangaroos and wallabies may be seen feeding in the early mornings and late afternoons.

GREIGS FLAT

EGAN PEAKS
NATURE RESERVE

BURRAGATE

NETHERCOTE

The Pinnacles

BEN BOYD
NATIONAL
PARK

FISHING: Every year thousands of anglers come to this section of the Coast to enjoy their favourite sport. Fisheries, however, are limited, and restrictions have been placed in order that they be protected. Contact the Department of Fisheries and Wildlife for information regarding protected species, quantities of fish taken in any one day, minimum sizes and method of capture.

White Rock Mtn
1093m

NALBAUGH
NP

Wog Wog Mtn

Wog

EDEN: This quiet, former whaling town with its outstanding natural harbour is the main port for the Southern Coast of New South Wales.

Eden

Whaling Museum and Whale Watching Cruises
Bay Cruises

Twofold Bay

PERICOE

Nullica

Boydtown

Boyds Tower

ROCKTON

TOWAMBA

Davidson Whaling Station Historic Site

Mowarry Point

TASMAN   SEA

Nungatta Mtn

MONARO

NUNGATTA

NATIONAL

MT IMLAY
NP

Mt Imlay
886m

Kiah

BEN BOYD
NATIONAL
PARK

BEN BOYD NATIONAL PARK: Over 9000 hectares of rocky but beautiful coastline flanking Twofold Bay. Flowering heaths and colourful banksias add to the area's attraction. Prominent features in the park include Boyds Tower, constructed in the 1840s, and The Pinnacles, a formation that dates back about 65 million years. The Pinnacles walking track is popular with visitors.

Mt Coopacambra

COOPRACAMBRA

NATIONAL

PARK

NEW SOUTH WALES
VICTORIA

Waalimma Mtn
722m

WONBOYN LAKE: Reputed to be the finest fishing spot on this section of the coast, note that the road leading to the lake is unsealed.

Green Cape

Wonboyn Lake

Disaster Bay

PRINCES

TO CANN RIVER

TO CANN RIVER

TO CANBERRA

A B C D E [119] F G H I

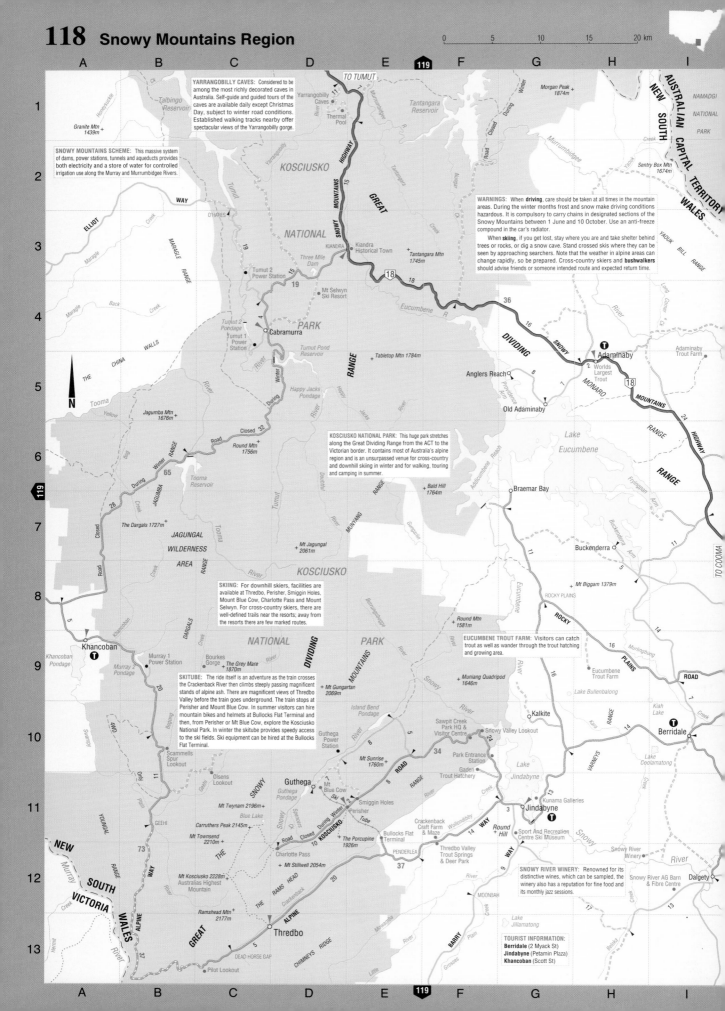

YARRANGOBILLY CAVES: Considered to be among the most richly decorated caves in Australia. Self-guide and guided tours of the caves are available daily except Christmas Day, subject to winter road conditions. Established walking tracks nearby offer spectacular views of the Yarrangobilly gorge.

SNOWY MOUNTAINS SCHEME: This massive system of dams, power stations, tunnels and aqueducts provides both electricity and a store of water for controlled irrigation use along the Murray and Murrumbidgee Rivers.

WARNINGS: When **driving**, care should be taken at all times in the mountain areas. During the winter months frost and snow make driving conditions hazardous. It is compulsory to carry chains in designated sections of the Snowy Mountains between 1 June and 10 October. Use an anti-freeze compound on the car's radiator.

When **skiing**, if you get lost, stay where you are and take shelter behind trees or rocks, or dig a snow cave. Stand crossed skis where they can be seen by approaching searchers. Note that the weather in alpine areas can change rapidly, so be prepared. Cross-country skiers and **bushwalkers** should advise friends or someone intended route and expected return time.

KOSCIUSKO NATIONAL PARK: This huge park stretches along the Great Dividing Range from the ACT to the Victorian border. It contains most of Australia's alpine region and is an unsurpassed venue for cross-country and downhill skiing in winter and for walking, touring and camping in summer.

SKIING: For downhill skiers, facilities are available at Thredbo, Perisher, Smiggin Holes, Mount Blue Cow, Charlotte Pass and Mount Selwyn. For cross-country skiers, there are well-defined trails near the resorts; away from the resorts there are few marked routes.

SKITUBE: The ride itself is an adventure as the train crosses the Crackenback River then climbs steeply passing magnificent stands of alpine ash. There are magnificent views of Thredbo Valley before the train goes underground. The train stops at Perisher and Mount Blue Cow. In summer visitors can hire mountain bikes and helmets at Bullocks Flat Terminal and then, from Perisher or Mt Blue Cow, explore the Kosciusko National Park. In winter the skitube provides speedy access to the ski fields. Ski equipment can be hired at the Bullocks Flat Terminal.

EUCUMBENE TROUT FARM: Visitors can catch trout as well as wander through the trout hatching and growing area.

SNOWY RIVER WINERY: Renowned for its distinctive wines, which can be sampled, the winery also has a reputation for fine food and its monthly jazz sessions.

TOURIST INFORMATION:
Berridale (2 Myack St)
Jindabyne (Petamin Plaza)
Khancoban (Scott St)

A
B
C
D
E
F
G
H
I
1
2
3
4
5
6
7
8
9
10
11
12
13
122
127
119
MITCHELL HIGHWAY
OXLEY HWY
NEWELL HWY
MITCHELL
WESTERN
HUME
BARTON HWY
FEDERAL HWY
KINGS HWY
Binnaway
Warren
Collie
Gilgandra
Nevertire
Mendooran
Merrygoen
Coolah
Blackville
Quirindi
Willow Tree
Eumungerie
Trangie
Dunedoo
Leadville
Merriwa
Tottenham
Narromine
Dubbo
Ballimore
Wongarbon
Geurie
Goolma
Gulgong
Ulan
Albert
Munghorn Gap
Sandy Hollow
Denman
GREAT DIVIDING RANGE
Wellington
Wellington Caves
Tomingley
Mudgee
Lue
Tullamore
Peak Hill
Yeoval
Mumbil
Stuart Town
Rylstone
Kandos
Fifield
Trundle
Alectown
Cumnock
Ilford
Hill End Historic Site
Sofala Historic Town
Bogan Gate
Parkes
Molong
Capertee
Manildra
Orange
Cullen Bullen
Portland
Lidsdale
Cudal
Lucknow
Wallerawang
Forbes
Eugowra
Cargo
Spring Hill
Forest Reefs
Millthorpe
Bathurst
Peel
Yetholme
Rydal
Lithgow
Bilpin
Burcher
Blayney
Perthville
O'Connell
Hartley
Mount Victoria
Blackheath
Richmond
Canowindra
Gooloogong
Mandurama
Carcoar
Lyndhurst
Newbridge
Rockley Historic Town
Oberon
Springwood
Katoomba
Lawson
Hampton
Edith
Woodstock
Marsden
Cowra
Grenfell
Caragabal
West Wyalong
Wyalong
Warragamba
Abercrombie Caves
Wyangala Dam
Tuena
Bigga
Quandialla
Greenethorpe
Koorawatha
The Oaks
Oakdale
Camden
Barmedman
Bribbaree
Bendick Murrell
Young
Thirlmere
Buxton
Bargo
Ariah Park
Binda
Hilltop
Colo Vale
Wombat
Boorowa
Rugby
Laggan
Crookwell
Taralga
Berrima
Mittagong
Temora
Stockinbingal
Wallendbeen
Murrumburrah
Harden
Rye Park
Grabben Gullen
Moss Vale
Bowral
Burrawang
Bundanoon
Cootamundra
Binalong
Gurrundah
Penrose
Goulburn
Marulan
Marulan South
Bowning
Gunning
Breadalbane
Kangaroo Valley
Marrar
Coolamon
Junee
Illabo
Bethungra
Jugiong
Bookham
Yass
Bungonia
Bomaderry
Nowra
Greenwell Point
Coolac
Murrumbateman
Collector
Gundaroo
Tarago
Nangus
Gundagai
Wee Jasper
Huskisson
St Georges Basin
Wagga Wagga
Alfred Town
Brungle
Sutton
Sussex Inlet
Forest Hill
Uranquinty
CANBERRA
Bungendore
Berrara
Lake Conjola
Tarcutta
Adelong
Tumut
Milton
Ulladulla
Mangoplah
ACT
Tidbinbilla Tracking Station
Queanbeyan
Braidwood
Burrill Lake
Batlow
KOSCIUSKO NATIONAL PARK
NAMADGI NP
Bawley Point
WOLLEMI NATIONAL PARK
GOULBURN RIVER NATIONAL PARK
BLUE MOUNTAINS NATIONAL PARK
MORTON NATIONAL PARK
BUDAWANG NATIONAL PARK
WEDDIN MTNS NP
CONIMBLA NATIONAL PARK
CURUMBENYA NATURE RESERVE
For more detail of Canberra Region see page 140

0 20 40 60 80 100 km

Nowendoc

Comboyne
Ellenborough
Falls
Kendall
Watson Taylor Lake
Lake Cathie
Bonny Hills
North Haven
Kew
Laurieton

WOKO NP

BARRINGTON TOPS
NATIONAL PARK

GREAT
DIVIDING
RANGE

Lansdowne
Coopernook
CROWDY BAY NP

Wingham
Tinonee
Harrington

Gundy
Lake Glenbawn

Barrington
Gloucester
Mt McKenzie

Taree
Old Bar

deen

Stratford
Nabiac
Diamond Beach
Hallidays Point

swellbrook

Wards River
Tuncurry
Forster

Dungog
Lake
Liddell

Gresford
Booral
Stroud
Bulahdelah
Seal Rocks

Singleton
Branxton
Paterson
Clarence
Town
Karuah
BOOTI BOOTI NP
Elizabeth Bay
Wallis Lake
164
MYALL LAKES
NATIONAL PARK
Tamboy

Maitland
Morpeth
Raymond
Terrace
Tea Gardens
Hawks Nest
Port Stephens
Nelson Bay
Anna Bay
TOMAREE NP

Cessnock
Millfield
Paxton
Abernethy
Williamtown

Ellalong
NEWCASTLE

Vollombi
Rathmines
Avondale
Wangi Wangi
Belmont

Kulnura
St Albans
Peats Ridge
Mannering Park
Catherine Hill Bay
Budgewoi
Toukley
Lake
Munmorah

Wyong
The Entrance

Gosford
Terrigal
Kincumber

Woy
Woy
Killcare

KURING-GAI
CHASE NP

SYDNEY
Cape Banks

SOUTH

PACIFIC

OCEAN

PBELLTOWN
Waterfall
ROYAL
NATIONAL
PARK

For more detail of Newcastle
Region see page 112

For more detail of Sydney
Suburbs see pages 98 - 103

LLONGONG
llongong Harbour

lharbour

gong

N

1
2
3
4
5
6
7
8
9
10
11
12
13

A B 474 C D E F G 475 H I

CARNARVON

1
Waltom River
River
Creek
Nindigully
BARWON
65
16 HWY
Commoron
Toobeah
18
BENDIDEE NATIONAL PARK
CUNNINGHAM
50
HY

2
Culgoa
River
25 Dirranbandi T
20
44
Thallon
32
Daymar
76
Bungunya
22
62
Goondiwindi T
Yelarb
12
Boggabilla
49
37
153
40
River
62
BRUXNER

3
63
Hebel
19
QUEENSLAND
NEW SOUTH WALES
99
49
Mungindi
26
18
30
18
41
42
50
NEWELL
90
18
103
MASTERMANS
RANGE
39
Yetn
Coola

474
38
Birrie
River
4
Goodooga
27
47
20
31
Angledool Lake
107
50
Gundabloui
OTC Satellite Tracking Station
50
95

21
Narran
Opal Mines
57
142
74
38
Moree T
29
Pallamallawa
50 HWY
Warial
5
Lightning Ridge T
55
CASTLEREAGH
Collarenebri
74
75
89
GWYDIR
68
39
53
64
41
De
106
Gravesend

6
Cumborah
Narran Lake
Barwon River
Rowena
97
44
36
Bingar
62

70
Castlereagh River
92
Walgett T
Burren Junction
50
Wee Waa T
32
Grattai Mtn 1310m
Upper Horton
7
69
Namoi River
Come-by-chance
Pilliga
57
River
Mt Kaputar 1508m
MOUNT KAPUTAR NP
Narrabri T
Deriah Mtn 855m
NANDEWAR
Barra

363
99
CSIRO Observatory
8
Carinda
115
Wingadee
85
Gwabegar
68
53
96
28
Up Ma
56
58
HWY

9
Macquarie Marshes
42
Quambone
Coonamble T
71
56
Baradine
118
39
Boggabri T
42
OXLEY
Gunnedah T
HWY
Some A
27
17
55
PILLIGA SCRUB
44
NEWELL
43
30
76

10
43
24
21
Beladerie Dam
28
WARRUMBUNGLE
Bullaway Mtn 1003m
Siding Spring Observatory
Bulleamble Mtn 1014m
Coonabarabran T
39
Black Mt 502m
108
Mullaley
Curlewis
84
37
Werr
Currabubula

125
31
16
Gulargambone
42
WARRUMBUNGLE NATIONAL PARK
The Breadknife
Mt Cenn Cruaich
Mt Spire 1071m
Mt Exmouth 1205m
Tooraweenah
34
RANGE
Tambar Springs
Premer
94
Caroona
Spring Ridge
Quirindi T
Wallab

11
77
Reedy Corner
47
48
Dragon Cowal
46
94
Binnaway
85
43
46
Blackville
44
Willow Tree
19
Murru

12
MITCHELL
20
Warren T
164
49 OXLEY
Collie
36
Gilgandra T
55
52
Mendooran
Merrygoen
Coolah
37
LIVERPOOL
RANGE
55
Nevertire
73
65
Old Harbor Lagoon
52
86
48
Belaringar
Euloon Cowal
Dunedoo
84

13
33
HWY
Trangie
33
Buddah Lake
39
Eumungerie
74
Leadville
21
69
44
Merriwa T
Ab
Narromine T
32
40
Minore Falls
Dubbo 84
Ballimore
38
33
GOULBURN RIVER NP
Muswell

A B C D 120 E F G H I

Scale: 0 20 40 60 80 100 km

Grid columns: J K L M N O P Q R
Grid rows: 1 2 3 4 5 6 7 8 9 10 11 12 13

QUEENSLAND

NEW SOUTH WALES

SOUTH

PACIFIC

OCEAN

GREAT DIVIDING RANGE

Karara
Warwick
Mt Burrabaranga 794m
Rathdowney
Hillview
Springbrook
Tweed Heads
Bogangar
Killarney
Tannymorel
Main Range NP
Mt Barney NP
Mt Warning NP
Murwillumbah
Tyalgum
Pottsville Beach
Legume
Woodenbong
Urbenville
Uki
Burringbar
Ocean Shores
Brunswick Heads
Dalveen
Pozieres
Thulimbah
Applethorpe
Haystack Mtn 878m
Border Ranges NP
Nightcap NP
Mullumbimby
Nimbin
Cape Byron
Byron Bay
Amiens
Stanthorpe
Severnlea
Kyogle
Bangalow
Clunes
Newrybar
Lennox Head
Ballandean
Glen Aplin
Bonalbo
Boonoo Boonoo Falls
Boonoo Boonoo NP
Richmond Range
Mummulgum
Lismore
Alstonville
Ballina
Texas
Bald Rock NP
Tabulam
Mallanganee
Casino
Coraki
Wardell
Wallangarra
Drake
Woodburn
Broadwater
Broadwater NP
Evans Head
Tenterfield
Mt Belmore 650m
Baryulgil
Mt Bajimba 1446m
Washpool NP
Mt Marsh 501m
Laurence Road
Chatsworth
The Broadwater
Iluka
Torrington
England Hwy
Deepwater
Gibraltar Range National Park
Copmanhurst
Maclean
Yamba
Emmaville
Carrs Creek Junction
Lawrence
Brooms Head
Inverell
Glen Innes
Red Range
Grafton
Tyndale
Ulmarra
Yuraygir NP
Minnie Water
Gilgai
Balancing Rock
Glencoe
Coutts Crossing
Power Station
Wooli
Tingha
Ben Lomond
The Black Mtn 591m
Guy Fawkes National Park
Red Rock
North West Solitary Island
Bundarra
Llangothlin
Mt Hyland 1439m
Glenreagh
Arrawarra
Woolgoolga
North Solitary Island
Guyra
Thunderbolts Cave
Dorrigo
Dorrigo NP
Coramba
Emerald Beach
Moonee Beach
Coffs Harbour
Muttonbird Island
Armidale
Hillgrove
Wollomombi Falls
Cathedral Rock NP
Ebor
Bellingen
Sawtell
Mylestom
Urunga
Uralla
Dangars Falls
Mihi Falls
New England National Park
Valla Beach
Nambucca Heads
Bowraville
Macksville
Scotts Head
Stuarts Point
Walcha Road
Walcha
Apsley Falls
Stoney Ck Falls
Oxley Wild Rivers National Park
Bellbrook
Trial Bay Gaol
South West Rocks
Hat Head NP
Dungowan
Werrikimbe National Park
Tia Falls
Willawarrin
Frederickton
Smithtown
Gladstone
Hat Head
Niangala
Yarrowitch Falls
Kempsey
Crescent Head
Nundle
Tuggolo Falls
Mt Seaview
Point Plomer
Telegraph Point
Limeburners Creek Nature Reserve
Nowendoc
Long Flat
Beechwood
Wauchope
Port Macquarie
Ellenborough
Combyne
Kew
Lake Cathie
Bonny Hills
North Haven
Laurieton
Kendall
Crowdy Bay NP
Woko National Park
Lansdowne
Wingham
Coopernook
Harrington
Crowdy Head
Barrington Tops National Park
Mt Mckenzie
Tinonee
Taree
Old Bar
Gloucester
Diamond Beach
Hallidays Point
Stratford
Nabiac
Tuncurry
Forster
Wards River

For more detail of the Port Macquarie Region see page 109

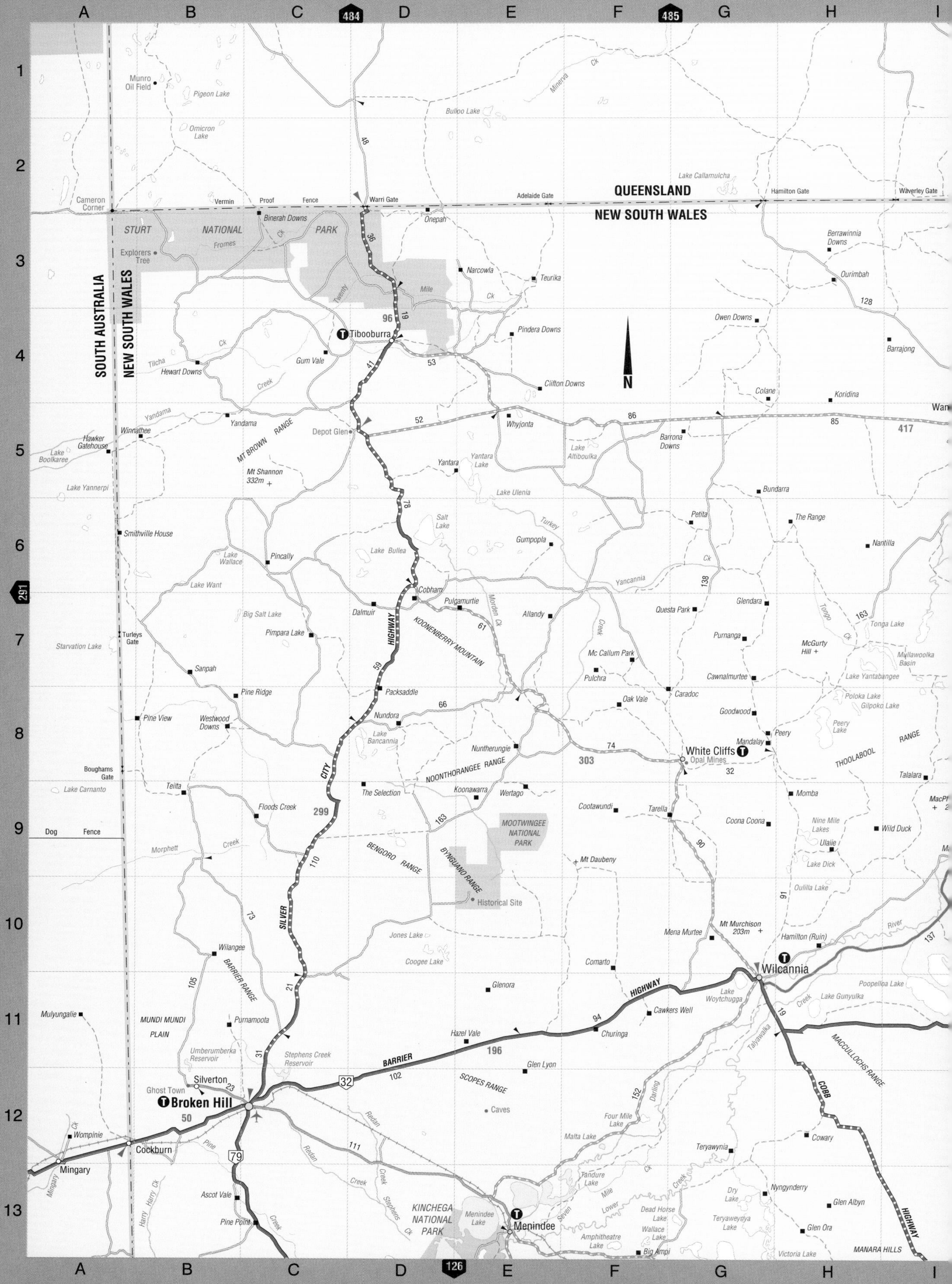

A B C 484 D E F 485 G H I

1 2 3 4 5 6 291 7 8 9 10 11 12 13

QUEENSLAND
NEW SOUTH WALES

SOUTH AUSTRALIA
NEW SOUTH WALES

STURT NATIONAL PARK
Fromes

Munro Oil Field
Pigeon Lake
Omicron Lake

Cameron Corner

Vermin Proof Fence
Binerah Downs
Warri Gate
Onepah
Adelaide Gate
Lake Callamulcha
Hamilton Gate
Waverley Gate
Berrawinnia Downs

Explorers Tree
Narcowla
Teurika
Ourimbah
128

Twenty
Mile
96 19
Tibooburra
Pindera Downs
Owen Downs
Barrajong

Gum Vale
41
53
Clifton Downs
Colane
Koridina
War

Tilcha
Hewart Downs
MT BROWN RANGE
Yandama
Yandama
52
Whyjonta
86
Barrona Downs
85
417

Hawker Gatehouse
Lake Boolkaree
Winnathee
Depot Glen
Yantara
Yantara Lake
Lake Altiboulka
Bundarra

Lake Yannerpi
Mt Shannon 332m
78
Salt Lake
Lake Ulenia
Turkey
Petita
The Range

Smithville House
Lake Wallace
Pincally
Lake Bullea
Gumpopla
Yancannia
138
Glendara
163
Tonga Lake
Nantilla

Lake Want
Cobham
Pulcamurtie
Morden Ck
Questa Park
Purnanga
McGurty Hill
Mullawoolka Basin

Starvation Lake
Turleys Gate
Big Salt Lake
Dalmuir
61
HIGHWAY
KOONENBERRY MOUNTAIN
Allandy
Creek
Cawnalmurtee
Lake Yantabangee
Poloka Lake
Gilpoko Lake

Sanpah
Pimpara Lake
Packsaddle
59
Mc Callum Park
Pulchra
Caradoc
Goodwood
Peery
Peery Lake
RANGE

Pine Ridge
Pine View
Westwood Downs
Nundora
66
Oak Vale
74
White Cliffs Opal Mines
Mandalay
Peery
THOOLABOOL
Talalara

Boughams Gate
Lake Carnanto
Teilta
CITY
Lake Bancannia
Nunthorangee
NOONTHORANGEE RANGE
303
32
Momba
MacP
Wild Duck

Dog Fence
Morphett
Floods Creek
299
The Selection
Koonawarra
Wertago
163
BYNGUANO RANGE
Cootawundi
Tarella
Coona Coona
Nine Mile Lakes
Ulaie

MOOTWINGEE NATIONAL PARK
Historical Site
BENGORO RANGE
Jones Lake
Mt Daubeny
90
Lake Dick

110
73
SILVER
Coogee Lake
Comarto
91
Oulilla Lake
Mt Murchison 203m
Mena Murtee
Hamilton (Ruin)
River
137

Wilangee
21
BARRIER RANGE
105
Glenora
HIGHWAY
Wilcannia
19
Poopelloa Lake
Lake Gunyulka

Mulyungalie
MUNDI MUNDI PLAIN
Purnamoota
Hazel Vale
94
Churinga
Cawkers Well
Lake Woytchugga
Taljinaalka
MACCULLOCHS RANGE

Umberumberka Reservoir
Stephens Creek Reservoir
31
BARRIER
196
Glen Lyon
152
Darling
COBB

Ghost Town
Silverton 23
32
102
SCOPES RANGE
Caves
Four Mile Lake
Teryawynia
Cowary

Broken Hill
50
Redan
111
Malta Lake
Dead Horse Lake
Dry Lake
Nyngynderry
Glen Albyn

Wompinie
Cockburn
79
Ascot Vale
Tandure Lake
Wallace
Teryaweynia Lake
Glen Ora

Mingary
Pine Point
KINCHEGA NATIONAL PARK
Menindee Lake
Menindee
Amphitheatre Lake
Big Ampi
Victoria Lake
MANARA HILLS
HIGHWAY

126

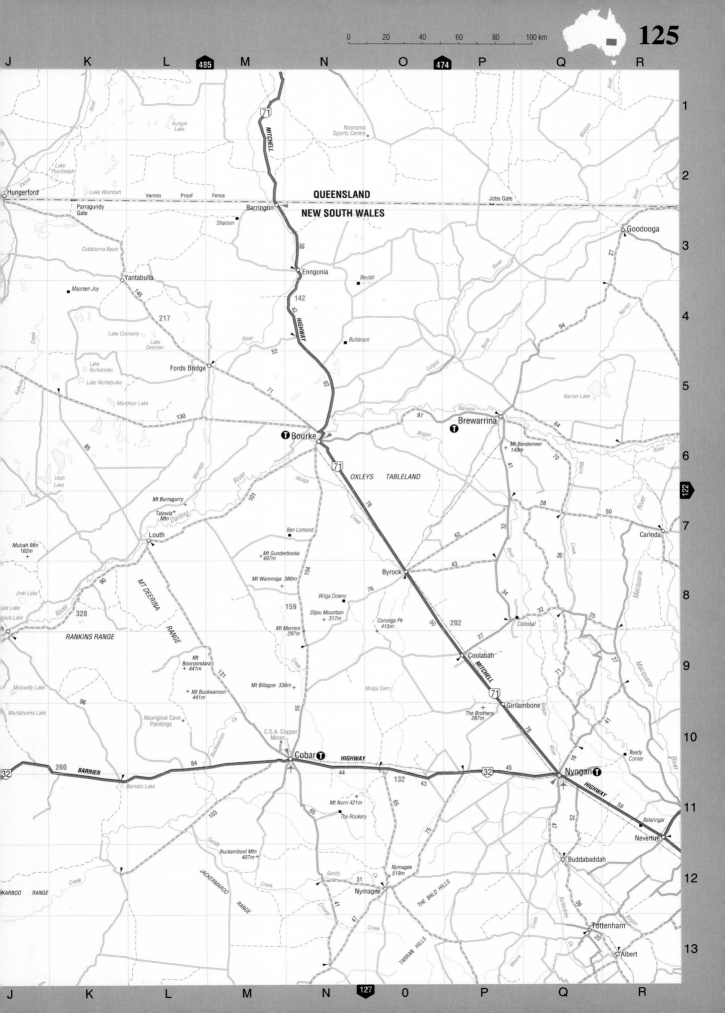

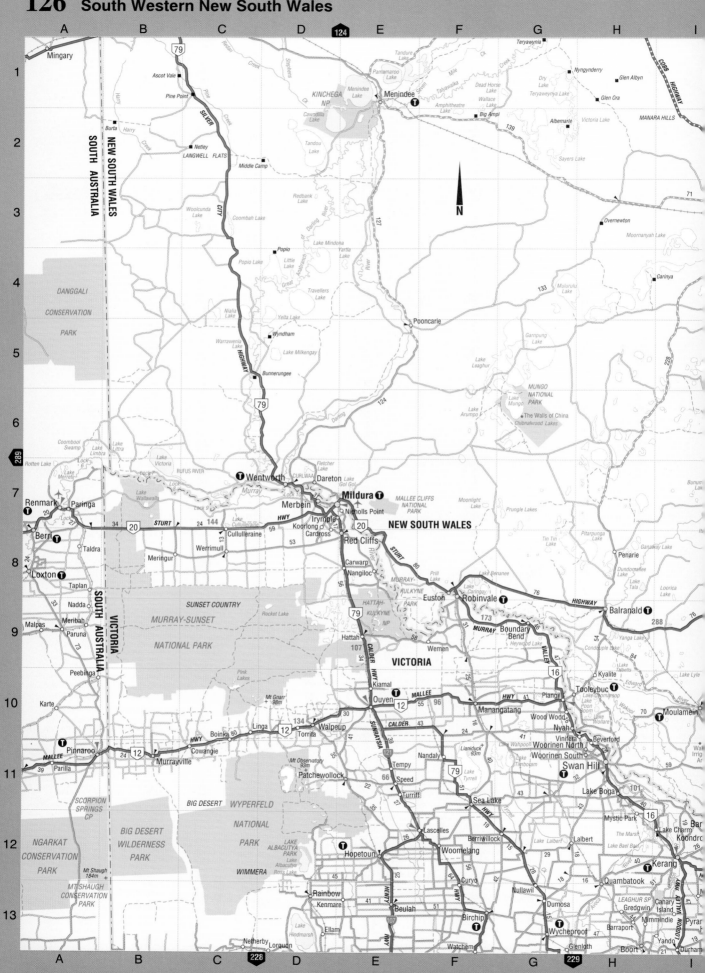

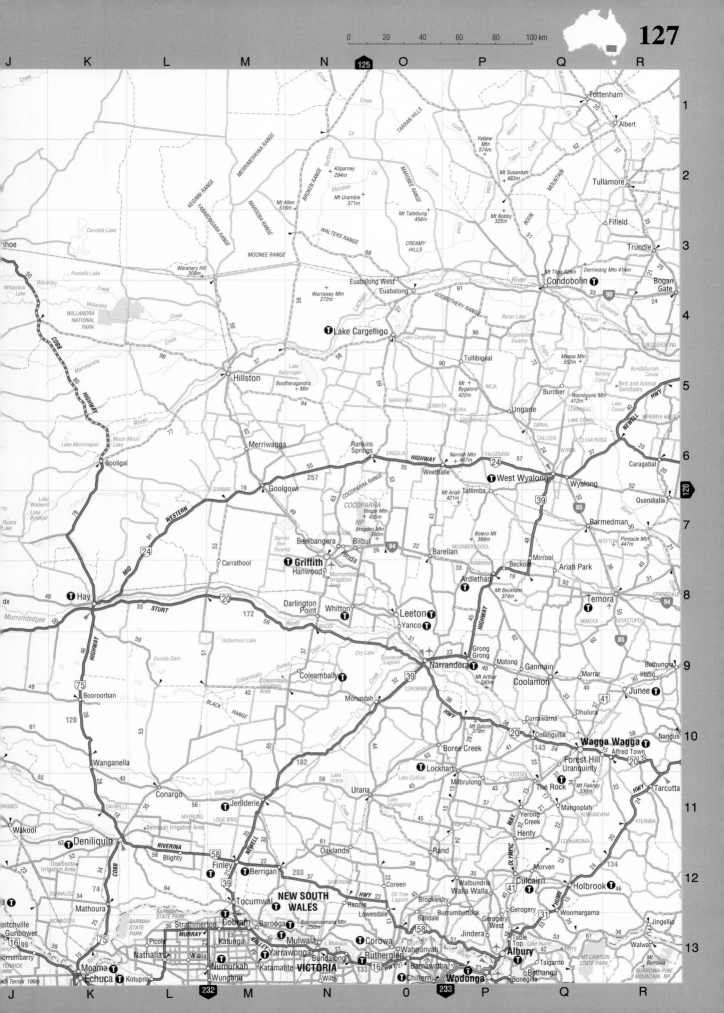

Australian Capital Territory

The Capital State

The ACT is a 250 000-hectare area which has an air of spaciousness and grace enhanced by the beautiful valley of the Molonglo River and the surrounding hills, mountains and pastureland, typical of eastern rural Australia. The capital State is surrounded by New South Wales and lies roughly halfway between Sydney and Melbourne. The ACT was created by the Commonwealth Constitution Act of 1901 when the Commonwealth of Australia was inaugurated: a nation was formed from the six colonies. One of the provisions of the Act was that the seat of government should be on land vested in the Commonwealth. Nine years of prolonged wrangling followed, as two Royal Commissions and parliamentary committees considered the various claims of established towns and cities to be the federal capital, before the location of the new territory and the site for the new city was decided. In addition the area of Jervis Bay was ceded to the Commonwealth to provide a seaport for the nation's capital. Melbourne was the provisional seat of government until 1927 when a temporary building was erected in Canberra. This building was used until 1988 when the new House of Parliament was completed.

Canberra, Australia's modern capital city, was built on an undulating plain in an amphitheatre of the Australian Alps. The Molonglo River, a tributary of the Murrumbidgee, runs through the city and was dammed in 1964 to create Lake Burley Griffin, around which Canberra has been developed.

It is one of the world's best-known fully-planned cities and over the last 60 years has become an increasing source of pride and interest for Australians and for overseas visitors. Its impressive public buildings, its areas of parkland and bush reserves, its leafy suburbs and broad tree-lined streets have resulted from brilliant planning by its architect, Walter Burley Griffin, and from care and pride taken in its development over the years. Its architecture and its atmosphere are unique and stimulating in that there is so little that is more than 50 years old. Because of this the city exudes an air of being contrived and self conscious, but it contains so much that will educate, absorb and stimulate the visitor that this somewhat sterile quality is soon forgotten.

The land on which the city is sited was discovered in 1820 by Charles Throsby Smith and his party of explorers. The area became known as Limestone Plains and was destined for settlement as grazing property. The first white settler, Joshua Moore, took up a thousand acres of land on the Murrumbidgee River in 1824 and named his property Canberry, an Aboriginal word meaning 'meeting place'. A year later Robert Campbell, a wealthy Sydney merchant, took up 4000 acres of land, which formed the first part of the Duntroon estate.

When the land on which the city is now built was acquired by the Commonwealth Government in 1911, it contained only two small villages.

Construction of the first public buildings started in 1913, and in 1914 a rail service was opened between Sydney and the new capital. The Depression and World War II slowed building construction, but the rate of development has been spectacular since the mid-1950s and the population is now over 285 000.

There are four distinct seasons: a warm spring, a hot dry summer, a brilliant cool autumn, and a cold winter with occasional snow. Perhaps the best time to visit the ACT is in the autumn, when there is a magnificent display of golden foliage. Over two million Australian and overseas visitors come to the ACT each year.

Spring in Canberra

Australia's Coat of Arms, Parliament House

Canberra   The Nation's Capital

As well as being Australia's capital, Canberra is a model city. Its unique concentric circular streets, planted with more than 10 million trees and shrubs, are set graciously on the shores of the manmade Lake Burley Griffin. Driving in Canberra can be confusing; it is wise to study a map before beginning to tour.

The old Parliament House, completed in 1927, a number of government department buildings and hostels for public servants were among the first buildings in the national capital. They are now dwarfed by the grand buildings of later development, which have turned Canberra into a showplace.

A number of lookouts on the surrounding hills give superb views of the city. The 195-metre **Telecom Tower** on Black Mountain is the highest. **Mount Ainslie** offers fine views of central Canberra and Lake Burley Griffin. **Red Hill** overlooks Parliament House, South Canberra and the Woden Valley. **Mount Pleasant** has memorials to the Royal Regiment of Australian Artillery and the

Royal Australian Armoured Corps at its summit.

The city took on a new character in 1964 when Lake Burley Griffin was created. The shoreline totals 35 kilometres and the lake has become popular for swimming, sailboarding, rowing, sailing and fishing, while ferries operating from Acton Jetty offer day and dinner cruises.

In recent years Canberra has spread outwards into the plains, with satellite towns at Belconnen, Woden, Tuggeranong, Weston Creek and Gungahlin, but the focus is still the city centre and the modern architectural development around Lake Burley Griffin.

Black Mountain, close to the city centre and the lakeshore, is topped by a telecommunications tower with public-viewing galleries and a revolving restaurant. On the lower slopes of Black Mountain are Canberra's **Botanic Gardens**. They follow Walter Burley Griffin's original plan for an Australian native garden. The superbly laid-out gardens have arrowed walks, which allow

for varying degrees of stamina, and take visitors through areas of foliage indigenous to various Australian regions. In the rainforest area a misting system simulates rainforest conditions. The **Australian Institute of Sport** is on the edge of Black Mountain Reserve in **Bruce**. Tours of training facilities and stadiums are conducted daily.

Most of Canberra's major buildings lie within a triangle formed by **Constitution**, **Commonwealth** and **Kings Avenues**, with Capital Hill at the apex and the central business district on the northern corner. On Capital Hill is the new **Parliament House**, topped by its massive flagpole. A grassed walkway forms the roof of Parliament House and provides visitors with splendid views of Canberra. In front is the **old Parliament House**, open to the public.

A new attraction in Constitution Avenue is the **Canberra Casino** at the National Convention Centre, which opened in late 1992.

On the southern foreshore of **Lake**

Parliament House

The imposing Anzac Parade

Burley Griffin is the **Australian National Gallery**, which houses an outstanding collection of modern and post-modern art, including a wide representation of Australian painters. In the grounds, works by Australian and international sculptors are placed in a landscape setting. The gallery has a restaurant overlooking the lake. A footbridge connects the National Gallery and the **High Court of Australia**, the nation's final court of appeal. The court's lofty public gallery is encircled by open ramps that lead off to the courts, and it features Jan Senbergs' murals reflecting the history, functions and operations of the High Court.

Further along the foreshore is the **National Library**, which contains over 5 million books, as well as newspapers, periodicals, films, documents and photographs. The foyer features three magnificent tapestries woven from Australian wool in Aubusson, France, and superb stained glass windows, the work of the Australian artist Leonard French.

Also on the foreshore of the lake between the National Library and the High Court is **Questacon**, the **National Science and Technology Centre** in King Edward Terrace. The Centre features hands-on science displays where simple do-it-yourself experiments and explanations make the understanding of everyday scientific principles easy. Adults and children alike are enthralled for hours by the hundreds of exhibits in the five galleries (Waves, Microcosm, Forces,

Visions, and 0011–OTC). Further south of the lake is the **Canberra Railway Museum**, which has Australia's oldest working steam locomotive (built in 1878), as well as four other engines and 40 carriages.

Lake Burley Griffin is the centrepiece of Canberra. On the lake are three places of interest: the **Carillon**, a three-column belltower that was a gift from the British Government to mark Canberra's Jubilee; the **Captain Cook Memorial**, a 150-metre water jet and terrestrial globe on the foreshore; and the **Canberra Planning Exhibition** at Regatta Point, which has a pavilion with exhibits showing Canberra's development. Overlooking the lake is the Australian–American Memorial, which celebrates America's contribution to Australia's defence during World War II.

The lake is surrounded by parklands, most with picnic facilities. One of the largest is **Commonwealth Park** on the northern foreshore, with its wading pools and cherry-tree grove. Another lakeside park is **Weston Park**, which features superb conifer trees, a miniature train, a maze and a playground for able and disabled children. Cycling is popular in Canberra; there are more than 200 km of cycle paths. It is possible to cycle right round the lake. Bikes can be hired near the ferry terminal. Sightseeing cruises of the lake are available, and also occasional inspections of the Murray paddle-steamer *Enterprise*. Paddle-boats, windsurfers and sailing boats also can be hired. Hot-air ballooning is popular throughout the year, and during the **Canberra Festival** in March and the **Floriade**, Canberra's Spring Festival, a fleet of balloons take flight each morning. Although the **National Museum of Australia** is still in the planning stage, its Yarramundi Visitor Centre off Lady Denman Drive on the shores of the lake features a model and plans of the project, objects from the museum's extensive collections, a viewing platform and a theatrette. The **National Aquarium**, further along Lady Denman Drive near Scrivener Dam, has over 60 display tanks containing marine life from giant sharks to tiny reef fish.

Imposing **Anzac Parade** stretches from the northern side of the lake to the **Australian War Memorial,** one of Australia's most frequently visited attractions. The War Memorial houses a huge collection of relics, models and paintings

Hotels

Capital Parkroyal
1 Binara St, Canberra City
(06) 247 8999
The Hyatt
Commonwealth Ave, Yarralumla
(06) 270 1234
Lakeside Hotel
London Circuit, Acton
(06) 247 6244
The Pavilion
Cnr Canberra Ave and National Circuit, Forrest
(06) 295 3144

Family and Budget

Canberra City Motor Inn
74 Northbourne Ave, Braddon
(06) 249 6911

Eagle Hawk Hill Resort
Federal Hwy, Sutton
(06) 241 6033
Heritage Motor Inn
203 Goyder St, Narrabundah
(06) 295 2944
Macquarie Private Hotel
18 National Circuit, Barton
(06) 273 2325

Motel Groups: Bookings

Flag (008) 01 1177
Best Western (008) 22 2166
Travelodge (008) 22 2446

This list is for information only; inclusion is not necessarily a recommendation.

from all theatres of war. Its cloisters, pool of reflection, hall of memory and many galleries of war relics provide an unforgettable experience. An interesting walk to the summit of **Mount Ainslie** starts from the picnic grounds behind the War Memorial.

Another distinctive landmark in Canberra is the **Academy of Science**, situated in Gordon Street, **Acton**. Its copper-covered dome rests on arches set in a circular pool. Nearby, the **National Film and Sound Archive** in McCoy Circuit displays movie memorabilia and has public screenings from its collection of historic films, radio and television programs. Also at Acton is the **Australian National University**, set in 145 hectares of landscaped gardens.

Diplomatic missions bring an international flavour to the city's architecture. It is well worth driving around the suburb of Yarralumla to see the many embassy buildings. The official residence of Australia's Governor-General is on Dunrossil Drive at Yarralumla. In **Deakin**, on the corner of Adelaide Avenue and National Circuit, is the **Prime Minister's Lodge**, the official residence of the Australian Prime Minister. The **Royal Australian Mint** in Denison Street, Deakin, has plate-glass windows in its visitors' gallery, allowing excellent views of the money-making process.

Despite the gleaming modern style of the city of Canberra, there are still interesting vestiges of the old Limestone Plains settlement. In Campbell the sandstone homestead of the **Duntroon estate**, now the Officer's Mess at Duntroon Royal Military College, is the finest old house in the ACT. The single-storey part of the house was built in 1833 and the two-storey extension was completed in 1856. Tours of the **Australian Defence Force Academy** and the **Royal Military College** are available.

The **Church of St John the Baptist** off Anzac Park dates back to 1841 and its tombstones and other memorials provide a record of much of the area's early history. The adjacent schoolhouse containing relics of this history is regularly open to visitors. Many of the stained-glass windows of St John's Church commemorate members of the pioneer families, including Robert Campbell, the founder of Duntroon estate. **Blundell's farmhouse** on the northern shore of the lake was built in 1858 by Campbell for his ploughman

and has been furnished by the Canberra and District Historical Society with pieces contemporary to the district's early history.

The **Central Business District** for Canberra surrounds London Circuit at the end of Commonwealth Avenue. **Civic Centre** is the major retail area. At the head of the **Civic Square** is the **Canberra Theatre Centre** and nearby in **Petrie Plaza** is the old St Kilda merry-go-round, a favourite with children. The **General Post Office** in Alinga Street displays Australia's largest and most valuable collection of stamps. For touring the city's attractions, the **Canberra Explorer** bus service runs every hour, 7 days a week, around a 25-km route with 19 stops. Leave the bus any time and reboard, or take the full hour tour.

Around Canberra too there are many attractions. **Cockington Green** on the Barton Highway, 9 km north of the city, is a miniature English village (named after Cockington in Devon, UK). Adjacent is the historic village of **Ginninderra**, featuring craft studios, an art gallery, shops and a restaurant. Adjacent is a new shopping area, Federation Square, with a number of craft and specialty shops, and children's play areas. Directly opposite Ginninderra is the 300-exhibit **National Dinosaur Museum**, on the Barton Highway between Gold Creek Road and Northbourne Avenue.

Telecom Tower

The **Australian Heritage Village**, on the corner of Federal Highway and Antill Street, features shops, eating houses and amusements in a parkland setting, and is open daily, admission free. Further north off the Federal Highway is **Rehwinkel's Animal Park**, popular for its Australian fauna collection displayed in a natural bushland setting. The **Bywong Mining Town** at Geary's Gap NSW (off the Bugendore Road), is a recreation of the mining settlement that prospered in the late 1800s. Tourists can see working machinery and enjoy panning for gold. Bywong is open daily. Guided tours and special programs are available.

At the **Tidbinbilla Nature Reserve**, 40 km south-west of the city, an area of more than 5000 hectares has been developed to enable visitors to see Australian flora and fauna in natural surroundings. Nearby is the **Corin Forest Recreation Area**, with a 1-km alpine slide, bushwalking, and skiing in winter. Another favourite spot is the **Cotter Dam** and Reserve, 22 km west of the city, where there are pleasant picnic and camping areas, a restaurant, river swimming and a children's playground. Nearby is the **Mount Stromlo Observatory**, its large silver domes and buildings housing the huge telescope of the Department of Astronomy of the Australian National University. Further south at Tidbinbilla, the **Canberra Space Centre**, a deep-space tracking station, features spacecraft models and audio-visual presentations. It is operated by the Department of Science for the US National Aeronautics and Space Administration.

The historic homestead **Lanyon**, 30 km south of the city, enjoys the National Trust's highest classification. Set in landscaped gardens and parklands on the banks of the Murrumbidgee River, Lanyon serves as a reminder of nineteenth-century rural living. As well there is a gallery housing a collection of Sidney Nolan paintings. Further south and also on the Murrumbidgee River is the historic **Cuppacumbalong** homestead with its cottages, outbuildings and private cemetery. A craft centre, restaurant, picnic areas and river swimming are features.

For further information on Canberra and the ACT, contact the ACT Tourism Commission, Visitors Information Centre, Northbourne Ave, Dickson; (06) 205 0044.

Early morning, Lake Burley Griffin

The Carillon

Cockington Green

Tours from Canberra

Although Canberra is primarily urban, the Australian bush is only minutes away from the city centre. A leisurely drive takes the visitor to the heart of the Snowy Mountains in the south or to the picturesque coastal resorts in the east.

Bungendore and Braidwood, 35 km and 90 km from Canberra via the Kings Highway

This is a popular drive with the locals, particularly on Sundays. The route passes Lake George, which mysteriously empties periodically. At Bungendore, the Village Square features a historic re-creation from the 1850s telling the story of a local bushranger. The entire town of Braidwood is classified by the National Trust. Antique and art and craft shops, museums and restaurants are found in many of the town's lovely old sandstone buildings.

Batemans Bay, 150 km from Canberra via the Kings Highway

This popular resort is at the mouth of the Clyde River. Of particular interest are the penguins and other birds at Tollgate Island Wildlife Reserve. In the area are many picturesque coastal resorts and the old gold-mining towns of Mogo and Araluen.

The Snowy Mountains, 228 km from Canberra via the Monaro and Snowy Mountains Highways

The Snowy Mountains, centre of the world-famous hydro-electric scheme, is an all-year-round resort and tourist area. Thredbo is the centre of activity during the ski season. Lake Eucumbene is popular for water sports and trout fishing.

Jervis Bay, 285 km from Canberra via the Kings and Princes Highways

This fine natural port has never been developed commercially. It was the site of the Royal Australian Navy Training College, established in 1915. In that year its jurisdiction was transferred from New South Wales to the ACT, to give the federal capital sea access. Fifteen years later the Naval College was transferred to Flinders in Victoria; in 1958 the Navy returned to Jervis Bay. Of particular interest in the area are several pleasant holiday resorts, ideal for swimming, fishing, boating and bushwalking.

Namadgi National Park, 30 km from Canberra via the Tuggeranong Parkway and Tharwa Drive to Tharwa

This park, the most northerly alpine environment in Australia, covers some 40 per cent of the ACT. The special qualities of remoteness and rugged beauty that make up a wilderness are evident in the area surrounding the park's highest point, Bimberi Peak (1911 m).

Public access roads within the park pass through majestic mountain scenery. Picnic areas, some with barbecues and toilets, are located along most roads. The pleasant bushland settings at Mt Clear and Orroral are ideal for low-key camping. Much of Namadgi's attractions lie beyond its main roads and picnic areas. Over 150 km of marked walking tracks allow further exploration. Bushwalkers who venture into Namadgi's more remote parts reap some of the park's greatest rewards. Namadgi streams attract trout fishermen, horseriding is permitted in certain areas and cross-country skiing is possible when snow conditions permit.

Batemans Bay, south-east of Canberra

Australian Capital Territory

Location Map

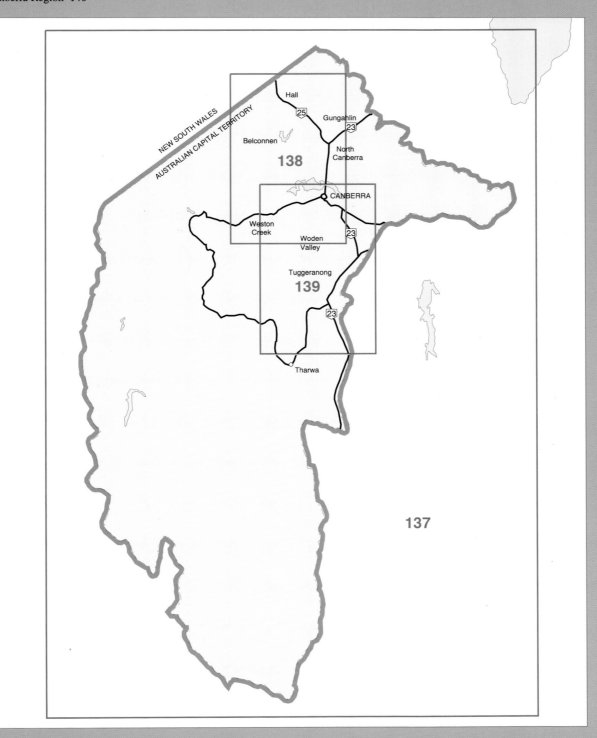

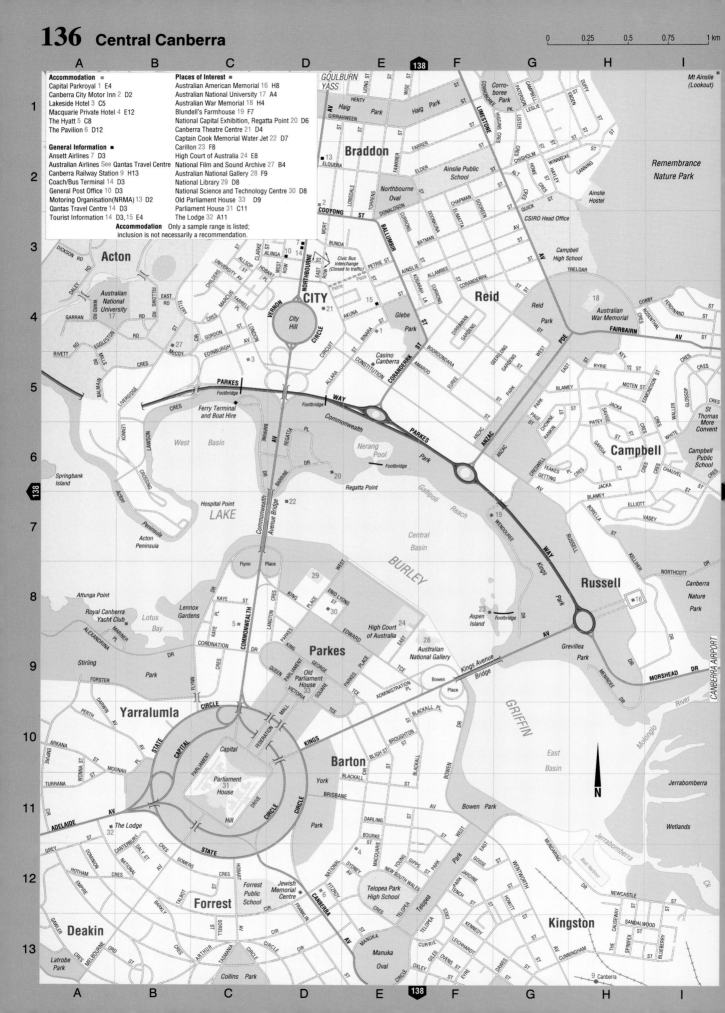

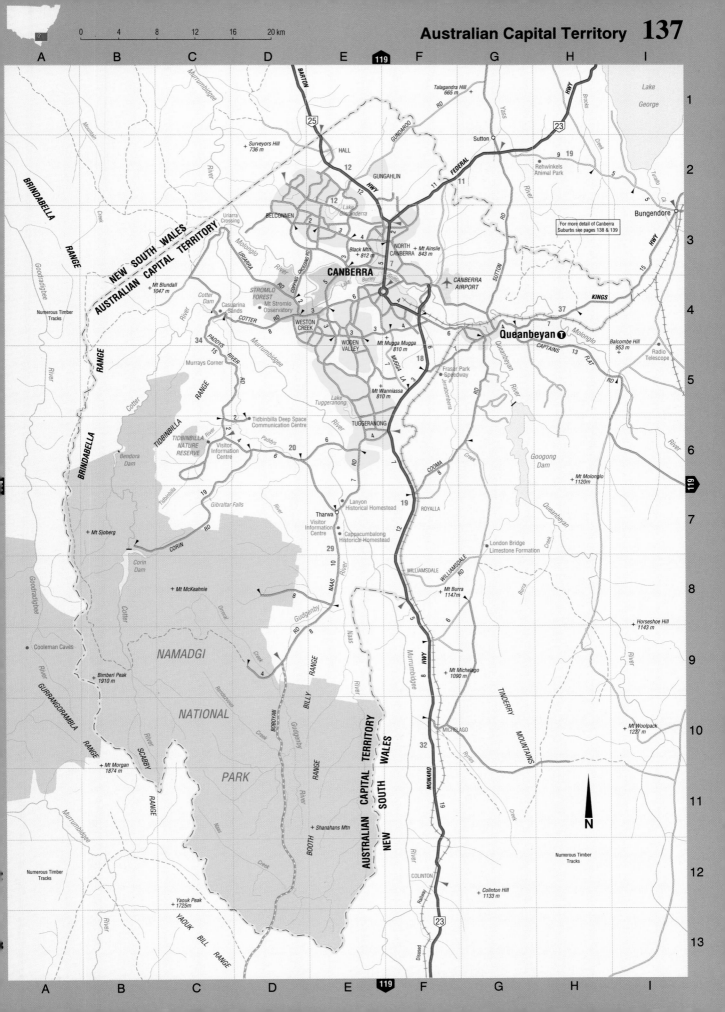

0 4 8 12 16 20 km

A B C D E **119** F G H I

BRINDABELLA
RANGE

NEW SOUTH WALES
AUSTRALIAN CAPITAL TERRITORY

Numerous Timber
Tracks

Goodradigbee River

BRINDABELLA RANGE

+ Mt Sjoberg

GURRANGORAMBLA RANGE

+ Bimberi Peak
1910 m

+ Mt Morgan
1874 m

NAMADGI

NATIONAL

PARK

Cooleman Caves

SCABBY RANGE

Numerous Timber
Tracks

Yaouk Peak
+ 1725 m

YAOUK BILL RANGE

Murrumbidgee River

Cotter River

Murrumbidgee River

BARTON
119

25

Surveyors Hill
+ 736 m

+ Mt Blundall
1047 m

Uriarra
Crossing

Cotter
Dam

Casuarina
Sands

COTTER

Molonglo River

URIARRA RD

COPPINS CROSSING RD

STROMLO
FOREST

Mt Stromlo
Observatory

34 PADDYS RIVER

Murrays Corner

TIDBINBILLA
RANGE

Tidbinbilla River

TIDBINBILLA
NATURE
RESERVE

Bendora
Dam

Cotter River

19

Gibraltar Falls

CORIN RD

Corin
Dam

+ Mt McKeahnie

Tidbinbilla River

Paddys River

Gudgenby River

Orroral River

Rendezvous Creek

BOBOYAN RD

Naas River

Gudgenby River

BILLY RANGE

GUDGENBY RANGE

BOOTH RANGE

Gudgenby River

+ Shanahans Mtn

AUSTRALIAN CAPITAL TERRITORY
NEW SOUTH WALES

HALL

12

12

12

GUNGAHLIN

BELCONNEN

Lake Ginninderra

2

3

4

Black Mtn
+ 812 m

WESTON
CREEK

3

3

3

WODEN
VALLEY

5

2

CANBERRA

Lake Burley Griffin

6

4

4

3

3

+ Mt Mugga Mugga
810 m

MUGGA LA

Mt Wanniassa
810 m

18

3

Lake
Tuggeranong

TUGGERANONG

A

Paddys River

Murrumbidgee River

2

Tidbinbilla Deep Space
Communication Centre

Visitor
Information
Centre

2

2

4

6

20

6

6

Tharwa

Lanyon
Historical Homestead

Visitor
Information
Centre

Cappacumbalong
Historical Homestead

29

10

12

MAAS RD

Naas River

8

8

4

5

GUNDAROO RD

NORTH
CANBERRA

+ Mt Ainslie
843 m

7

CANBERRA
AIRPORT

4

4

6

6

7

7

Jerrabomberra

Frasar Park Speedway

COOMA RD

ROYALLA

19

12

WILLIAMSDALE

WILLIAMSDALE RD

+ Mt Burra
1147m

6

MONARO HWY

5

+ Mt Michelago
1090 m

MICHELAGO

32

19

COLINTON

+ Colinton Hill
1133 m

23

Railway

Disused

Talagandra Hill
665 m +

9 19

5

RD

FEDERAL HWY
11

Sutton

11

SUTTON RD

For more detail of Canberra
Suburbs see pages 138 & 139

37

KINGS HWY

Queanbeyan T

13

CAPTAINS FLAT RD

Molonglo River

Queanbeyan River

Googong
Dam

Queanbeyan River

Burra Creek

London Bridge
Limestone Formation

+ Mt Molonglo
1120 m

TINDERRY
MOUNTAINS

Ryries Creek

Numerous Timber
Tracks

YASS RD

Yass River

23

Brooks Creek

Rehwinkels
Animal Park

5

Bungendore

15

Balcombe Hill
953 m +

Radio
Telescope

Lake
George

Turallo Ck

+ Horseshoe Hill
1143 m

Molonglo River

+ Mt Woolpack
1227 m

N

119

1
2
3
4
5
6
7
8
9
10
11
12
13

For more detail of Australian Capital Territory see page 137

TO ALBURY
TO YASS
TO GOULBURN
TO BEGA

NEW SOUTH WALES
AUSTRALIAN CAPITAL TERRITORY

CANBERRA

Queanbeyan

Tumut

Batlow

Talbingo

Cabramurra

Adaminaby

Old Adaminaby

Anglers Reach

Buckenderra

Middlingbank

Berridale

Jindabyne

Cooma

Bunyan

Bredbo

Michelago

Colinton

Numeralla

Sutton

Hall
Gungahlin
Belconnen
North Canberra
Woden Valley
Weston Creek
Tuggeranong
Tharwa

Cockington Green Model Village
Rehwinkel's Animal Park
Casuarina Sands
Mt Stromlo Observatory
Cotter Dam
Tidbinbilla Deep Space Communication Complex
Tidbinbilla Peak 1562m
TIDBINBILLA NATURE RESERVE
Visitors Information Centre
Bendora Dam
Corin Reservoir
Lanyon Historical Homestead
Cuppacumbalong Craft Centre
Visitors Information Centre
Fraser Park Speedway
Canberra Airport

Lake Burley Griffin
Lake Ginninderra
Lake Tuggeranong

Googong Dam
Mt Molonglo 1120m
London Bridge Limestone Formation
Mt Burra 1147m
Williamsdale
Royalla
TINDERRY MOUNTAINS
Tinderry Peak 1618m
Mt Holland 1392m
Mt Dowling 1198m
McInally Mtn 1085m
Jerangle
Peakview
Chakola
Billilingra Siding
Captain

KOSCIUSKO NATIONAL PARK
NAMADGI NATIONAL PARK
BRINDABELLA
Brindabella
Bimberi Peak 1910m
Mt Morgan 1874m
Yaouk
Mt Nungar 1710m
Yaouk Peak 1725m
Shannons Flat

BOGONG MOUNTAINS
THE FIERY RANGE
Bogong Peaks 1717m
Yarrangobilly
Yarrangobilly Caves
Tantangara Reservoir
Talbingo Reservoir
Kiandra
Sue City
Tumut 2 PS
Tumut 1 PS
Tumut Pond Reservoir
Tooma Reservoir
The Big Dargal 1713m

GREAT DIVIDING RANGE
SNOWY MOUNTAINS
MONARO HIGHWAY
SNOWY MOUNTAINS HIGHWAY

Mt Jagungal 2060m
Mt Gungartan 2069m
Kalkite Mtn
Muniang Quadripod 1646m
Island Bend Pondage
Snowy Valley Lookout
Lake Eucumbene
Rocky Plains
Mt Biggam 1379m
Kalkite
Kiah Lake
Lake Jindabyne
Lake Coolamatong
Gaden Trout Hatchery
Sawpit Creek Visitor Centre Tourist Information
Guthega PS
Mt Sunrise 1760m
Island Bend
Mt Blue Cow
Guthega
Smiggin Holes
Perisher
Charlotte Pass
Thredbo
Mt Twynam 2196m
Mt Townsend 2210m
Mt Kosciusko 2228m Australia's Highest Mountain
Ramshead Mtn 2177m
Olsens Lookout
Bourkes Gorge
Geehi Reservoir
Blue Lake
DEAD HORSE GAP
Thredbo Trout Springs & Deer Park
Bullocks Flat Terminal

KOSCIUSKO NATIONAL PARK
GREAT DIVIDING RANGE
THE ALPINE WAY
MARAGLE RANGE
BAGO RANGE
Murray 1 PS
Gocup
Gadara
Gilmore
Windowie
Wereboldera
Blowering Dam Lookout
Blowering Reservoir
Pilot Hill
Tumut 3 PS
Jounama Pondage

Tumorrama
Argalong
Lacmalac
Goobarragandra

MONARO RANGE
Cootralantra Lake
Killmacoola Lake
Arable Lake
Long Lake
O'Neill Lagoon
Muddah Lake
Cooma Llama Farm
Lookout & Fairytale Park
Worlds Largest Trout
Thurbergal Lake
Rock Flat
Dalgety
Buckleys Lake
Cooneran Siding

Mt Flinders 1484m

WARNING: During the winter months (June to October), travellers should check prevailing conditions before departure.

J K L M N O P Q R

0 5 10 15 20 km

119

TO NOWRA

Tomerong
Huskisson
Vincentia
Wandandian
St Georges Basin
13
Hyams Beach
Sanctuary Point
Jervis Bay
HWY
St Georges Basin
10
Sussex Inlet
Green Patch
Swan Lake
Swanhaven
PRINCES
9
Berrara
Lake Conjola
Bendalong
Manyana
Cunjurong Point
Lake Conjola
Narrawallee
Milton
Mollymook
Ulladulla
Burrill Lake
Burrill Lake
16
TERMEIL
Bawley Point
1
East Lynne
15
PRINCES
HWY
Cullendulla
Long Beach
Durras
Batemans Bay
Batehaven
Shell Museum
Surf Beach
Mogo
Malua Bay
27
BIMBIMBIE
Tomakin
Mossy Point
Broulee
MOGENDOORA
GUNDARY
Moruya
Moruya Heads
THE ANCHORAGE
KIORA
Congo
BERGALIA
MERINGO
Coila Lake
TURLINJAH
Tuross Lake
43
Tuross Head
Bodalla
The Big Cheese
Eurobodalla
Brou Lake
Mummunga Lake
Dalmeny
Kianga
Narooma
Little Lake
Corunna Lake
MONTAGUE IS NATURE RESERVE
Corunna
Tilba Tilba
Central Tilba
Historic Town Deer Park
Tilba Tilba Lake
HWY
PRINCES
Cobargo
WALLAGA LAKE NP
Wallaga Lake
Bermagui

TO BEGA
119

SOUTH

PACIFIC

OCEAN

MT FAIRY
BORO
LOWER BORO
Mt Coghill 806m
BUTMAROO
RANGE
NERRIGA
CORANG
MORTON NATIONAL PARK
Mt Sassafras 823m
Mt Tianjara 768m
HWY
KINGS
BUDAWANG
RANGE
Mt Corang 863m
BUDAWANG
NATIONAL
PARK
Pigeon House Mtn 719m
Lookout
DIVIDING
Braidwood
Historic Town
MONGARLOWE
52
Mt Mogood 391m
Burrill Lake
Majors Creek
REIDSDALE
MONGA
HWY
CURROWAN CREEK
Round Mtn 1224m
ARALUEN NORTH
Nelligen
BENANDARAH
Durras Lake
PEBBLY BEACH
GUNDILLION
Wyanbene Caves
RUNNYFORD
MURRAMARANG NATIONAL PARK
Wandera Mtn 580m
DEUA
NATIONAL
Mt Donovan 784m
MULLENDEREE
Bendethera Caves
Bendethera Mtn 997m
PARK
Jinden
Peak Alone 954m
WADBILLIGA
NATIONAL
PARK
BODALLA
STATE
FOREST
WANDELLA
Digmans
YOWRIE
Baragoot Lake
N

Victoria

Garden State

Victoria is an ideal state for the motoring tourist. In one day's drive, explore mountain country, pastoral landscape and spectacular coastline, yet still arrive at your destination in time to watch the sunset.

Victoria's earliest explorers, of course, were from a pre-motor age. What they saw did little to arouse their enthusiasm. After an unsuccessful attempt at settlement in the Port Phillip area in 1803, it was not until 1834 that parties from Van Diemen's Land, searching for more arable land, settled along the south-west coast of Victoria. Their glowing reports prompted John Batman and John Fawkner to investigate the Port Phillip area and then purchase land on opposite sides of the Yarra from Aboriginal tribes. The Colonial Office in London expressed disapproval of these transactions, but in those times possession was nine points of the law. A squatting colony grew up rapidly in the district and the new town was named Melbourne after the British prime minister of the day.

Nervous of inheriting the penal system of settlement, Victoria sought separation from New South Wales; it was granted in 1851. At about that time, gold was discovered near Ballarat and the state's population more than doubled within a year. Apart from a serious, but short-lived, setback caused by land speculation in the early 1890s, Victoria has gone from strength to strength ever since.

Today Victoria is the most closely settled and industrialised part of the nation, responsible for about one-third of the gross national product. Melbourne has been traditionally regarded as the 'financial capital' of the country.

Melbourne's inner areas are graced by spacious parks and street upon street of elegant and well-preserved Victorian and Edwardian architecture, contrasting strongly with modern tower blocks. Other attractions include the city's parks and gardens and its renowned retail shopping, theatres, restaurants and unusual theatre restaurants.

Beyond the city, the Dandenong Ranges, fifty kilometres to the east, are noted for their forests of eucalypts and graceful tree ferns, their many established European-style gardens and an increasing number of good restaurants and galleries. Phillip Island, less than two hours' drive away, is famed for its unique fairy penguin parade as well as for its good surfing. To the south-east and south-west, the Mornington and Bellarine Peninsulas provide Melbourne with its seaside playgrounds, extremely popular during the summer months.

The weather can be unpredictable in Victoria, particularly along the coastal regions. Despite its rather volatile weather, however, the state enjoys a generally temperate climate. Spring, late summer and autumn provide the most settled and pleasant touring weather. The state's road system is good and penetrates most areas; much of the state can be reached easily in a day's driving.

Each of Victoria's five main geographical regions has its own special attraction. The central and western districts, due north and west of Melbourne, offer touring highlights such as the historic gold-rush areas, with well-preserved, attractive towns such as Bendigo, Castlemaine and Ballarat—which is always popular during its March Begonia Festival—and the Grampians, Victoria's most beautiful national park, particularly with its spring wildflowers. Travelling south from these impressive ranges brings you into the Western District, where rich grazing land is dotted with splendid old properties. No exploration of this region would be complete without a drive along the Great Ocean Road, which runs for 320 kilometres along the dramatic south-west coast. The spectacular rock formations in the Port Campbell National Park are without doubt its most imposing sights, but along its length there are excellent beaches and pleasant small resort towns.

The north-east high-country region has equally magnificent scenery and is dotted with well-patronised winter ski resorts. Popular in spring and summer, this region would hardly ever be described as crowded and the wildflowers, sweeping views and clear air can be enjoyed with a fair degree of solitude. Fishing, bushwalking and climbing are well provided for and, down in the foothills, the Eildon Reservoir and Fraser National Park area are good for water sports.

Gippsland stretches to the south-east; it contains some of the state's most beautiful and varied country. Rolling pastures lead to densely wooded hill country, still relatively unpopulated and peaceful. National parks such as the Tarra-Bulga and Wilsons Promontory Park are all well worth visiting. The coastal region of Gippsland includes the Ninety Mile Beach bordering the Gippsland Lakes system, Australia's largest inland waterway network, and Croajingolong National Park, a wilderness area.

Following the Murray can be an interesting way of exploring Victoria's north. The river begins as a narrow, rapidly flowing alpine stream near Mt Kosciusko, and changes to a broad expanse near the aquatic playgrounds of Lakes Hume and Mulwala; it has water-bird and wildlife reserves and sandy river beaches and offers fascinating glimpses of life in the riverboat era at cities such as Echuca, Swan Hill and Mildura. Perhaps the Murray best sums up the contrasting landscape which is Victoria, the Garden State.

The Otways, south-western Victoria

Melbourne The Shopping City

At first glance Melbourne may look like any other modern city with its skyline chock-a-block with concrete and glass. However, if you look a little closer you'll find the real Melbourne: clanging trams, swanky boutiques, friendly taxi drivers, Australian football, fickle weather, and 'BYOs' (restaurants to which you bring your own liquor) by the hundred. Add to this Melbourne's traditional virtues of tree-lined boulevards, glorious parks, elegant buildings and imposing Victorian churches and banks—and the Melbourne Cricket Ground and you'll have some idea of the city.

In recent years it has become a polyglot society with its huge influx of migrants from many countries, particularly Greece. The city has one of the largest Greek-speaking populations in the world. This cosmopolitan influence is reflected in Melbourne's bustling markets, delicatessens and restaurants. Eating out has become one of the great Melbourne pastimes and the city and suburban restaurants give an opportunity to literally eat your way around the world; the food of almost every nation imaginable is available.

At the head of Port Phillip Bay and centred on the north bank of the Yarra River, Melbourne's population of over three million lives in the flat surrounding suburbs which stretch in all directions, particularly round the east coast of the bay right out to the Dandenongs, an impressive range of mountains to the east of the city.

Both John Batman and John Pascoe Fawkner were associated in the founding of Melbourne in 1835, and Melbourne soon entered a boom period with the discovery of gold in the state in 1851. The goldfields of Bendigo, Ballarat and Castlemaine attracted fortune-hunters from all over the world, and by 1861 Melbourne had become Australia's largest city. By the end of the century it was firmly established as the business and cultural centre of the colony.

Today Melbourne's traditional position as the financial and cultural centre of the nation has been challenged by Sydney, but it still has an unruffled elegance and style all its own. Melbourne was the only Australian capital to retain its network of pollution-free electric trams, and the clang of the old green thunderers adds a special flavour to the city. Many of these have been given a new lease of life after being decorated by leading artists, while others have been replaced by new trams and the light rail. The World

The Southgate riverside development

Building facades in Collins St

Health Organisation has rated Melbourne as one of the least polluted cities of its size; Melbourne has also been acclaimed the world's most livable city by the internationally renowned Population Crises Centre, based in Washington D.C., USA.

Melbourne has a huge range of retail stores, and shopping in the city and in suburbs such as fashionable **South Yarra** is one of the joys of the city. Several other suburbs such as **Carlton**, **Prahran**, **Armadale**, **Toorak** and **Camberwell** rival the city centre with their retail stores and restaurants.

Melburnians are also great sports lovers and this is reflected in the huge crowds that attend cricket and Australian football matches. A peculiarly Melbourne phenomenon is the 'football fever' which grips the city each year, with enthusiasm building up to mass hysteria on Grand Final day in September.

The **Melbourne Cricket Ground** is the venue for many sporting and entertainment fixtures. Just outside the Members' entrance, the **Australian Gallery of Sport** celebrates Australian sporting history. The **Olympic Museum**, located in the Gallery of Sport, houses memorabilia dating back to the first modern Olympics, held in Olympia in 1896.

Horseracing is another popular Melbourne spectator sport and the **Melbourne Cup** at Flemington Racecourse brings Australia to a halt for three minutes each first Tuesday in November. Melbourne's other main racecourses are at Caulfield, Moonee Valley and Sandown Park; the **Victorian Racing Museum** is at Caulfield Racecourse. The city's 3½- week spring racing carnival runs from mid-October to early November. **Moomba** in March, **Comedy Festival** in April and **Melbourne International Festival of the Arts** in October are other outstanding events on the Melbourne calendar.

The **National Tennis Centre** at Flinders Park hosts the first leg of the international grand slam in January each year. The Centre Court with its unique retractable roof seats 16 000 people and is used also as a venue for entertainment extravaganzas. Tours of the city's top sporting venues are available through the Melbourne Sports Network.

For cyclists, there is a comprehensive network of trails throughout the city and suburbs. Skiers can practise all year round on a dry ski slope conveniently

Hotels
The Hotel Como
630 Chapel St, South Yarra
(03) 824 0400
Grand Hyatt Melbourne
123 Collins St, Melbourne
(03) 657 1234
Le Meridien Melbourne
495 Collins St, Melbourne
(03) 620 9111
The Regent Melbourne
25 Collins St, Melbourne
(03) 653 0000
Rockmans Regency
Cnr Exhibition and Lonsdale Sts, Melbourne
(03) 662 3900
The Windsor
103 Spring St, Melbourne
(03) 653 0653

Family and Budget
Lygon Carlton
220 Lygon St, Carlton
(03) 663 6633

City Limits
20 Little Bourke St, Melbourne
(03) 662 2544
The Victoria
215 Little Collins St, Melbourne
(03) 653 0441
YWCA Family Accommodation
489 Elizabeth St, Melbourne
(03) 329 5188

Motel Groups: Bookings
Flag 13 2400
Best Western (008) 22 2166
Travelodge (008) 22 2446

This list is for information only; inclusion is not necessarily a recommendation.

Yarra River and city skyline

located at Ski Haus in the north-eastern suburb of **Ivanhoe**.

The **World Congress Centre** is on the corner of Flinders and Spencer Streets. Next door are the **Centra Melbourne on the Yarra** hotel and the **World Trade Centre** which hosts international trade displays. Further along Flinders Street past the Banana Alley Vaults is the **Flinders Street Station** complex with its restaurants and shops. It is the main terminus for the suburban rail system. Melbourne's **Underground Rail Loop** has three stations located on the edge of the central business district. Above ground, the **City Explorer** tourist bus departs Flinders Street Station hourly between 10 a.m. and 4 p.m., stopping at some major attractions. To get a different view of Melbourne, take a river cruise on the Yarra, departing from the **Princes Walk Terminal**.

On the opposite banks of the river is the new and exciting **Southgate** development. Restaurants, wine bars, a licenced food court, shops and the **Sheraton Towers Southgate** are part of this popular riverside development. As well, **Experience Australia**, a sensor vision theatre, provides a thrilling means to experience Australia—its historical, natural and cultural aspects.

The city centre is compact, its wide streets laid out in a grid system. Take a tram to the top of **Collins Street** and wander down—the street somehow epitomises Melbourne. At night, hundreds

of small bud lights in the trees lining the street create a spectacular effect.

Looking down on Collins street, in Spring Street, is the elegant **Old Treasury Building**, which was built in 1853, and just down from Spring Street is the august **Melbourne Club**, mecca of Melbourne's Establishment. On the opposite side of the street on the Exhibition Street corner is **Collins Place**, a multi-storey complex which houses **The Regent Melbourne** in one of its high towers. Called 'the City within a City', many of the shops and boutiques in this complex are open all weekend. Another tall building, **Nauru House**, is diagonally opposite.

Continuing down the hill you will see fashionable boutiques and two old churches, the **Uniting Church** and **Scots Church**. Across the road the **Grand Hyatt** hotel complex has an interesting food hall and shopping plaza. Between Russell and Swanston Streets there are pavement tables shaded by colourful sunshades. Opposite these is a unique Melbourne institution—**Georges**, Australia's most elegant department store. Just down the hill is the graceful porticoed **Baptist Church**, built in 1845. Melbourne's imposing **Town Hall** and soaring **St Paul's Cathedral** in Swanston Walk provide an attractive contrast to the modern **City Square** on the corner of Collins Street and Swanston Walk with its huge glass canopy, shady trees and fountains; this is an ideal place for relaxing or meeting a friend. Other

popular meeting places are the Sportsgirl complex in Collins Street and the stylish Australia-on-Collins complex and the Centreway Arcade nearby.

Further down Collins Street is the elegant old **Block Arcade** with its mosaic floor, glass and iron-lace roof and stylish shops. The small lane at the back of this arcade (Block Place) leads through to Little Collins Street and to another gracious old arcade. This is the **Royal Arcade** where, every hour, the huge statues of mythical figures, Gog and Magog, strike the hour. This arcade leads through to the **Bourke Street Mall**, between Elizabeth and Swanston Streets. Several department stores and fashion chains including **Myer**, Australia's largest department store, and **David Jones** front on to the mall. David Jones has another store on the opposite side and its food hall is worth a visit to see the beautifully presented displays. Nearby the shopping complex **Centre Point** is a handy place to browse under shelter, or to stop for a snack in one of its many coffee bars. You can sit and watch city buskers from the seats provided in the mall, but beware of the trams—the only traffic, apart from delivery and emergency vehicles, allowed in this block. The **Half-Tix** booth in the mall offers the opportunity to purchase theatre tickets for the day's performances at reduced prices.

Swanston Street Walk, a recently developed and innovative pedestrian mall, encourages a stroll between Flinders and Latrobe Streets. Window-shop at your leisure or take time for coffee at one of the many sidewalk cafes. An appealing combination of bookshops and bistros has sprung up in the uppermost block of **Bourke Street**. The front coffee bar at Pellegrini's, a bustling Italian restaurant, is a great favourite, and the BYO restaurant at the rear is an Italian-style cafeteria where you make your selection from mouth-watering hot and cold dishes. On the Spring Street corner is one of the last of Melbourne' grand old hotels, the elegant twin-towered **Windsor** (1883), which looks over the peaceful **Treasury Gardens**. Proudly surveying the city from Spring Street is the impressive classical-style **State Parliament House**. The plush Corinthian style of the Legislative Council Chamber is legacy of Melbourne's golden era. The spires of massive bluestone **St Patrick's Cathedral** can be seen beyond. Melbourne's elegant and beautifully restored

Princess Theatre, is also in Spring Street.

At the top of Little Bourke Street is **Gordon Place**, a unique old building designed by the colonial architect William Pitt in 1883. The building is now an attractive tourist apartment complex.

If you like Chinese food don't miss Melbourne's **Chinatown** in Little Bourke Street, between Exhibition and Swanston Streets. Dozens of fascinating oriental restaurants, quaint grocery shops and mixed stores dates back to Melbourne's post-gold-rush days, when it became the city's Chinese quarter. The standard of the restaurants is good and prices vary from fairly cheap to very expensive. Among the outstanding restaurants are the Bamboo House, the Flower Drum and the Mask of China. Located in the heart of Chinatown at Cohen Place, the **Museum of Chinese Australian History** is worth a visit.

Further down Little Bourke Street is the **Information Victoria Centre**, which provides the public with access to Victorian Government information resources, including public record research facilities.

Just half a block away in Lonsdale Street, is the huge retail complex **Melbourne Central** and department store **Daimaru**, which together occupy most of the block bounded by Lonsdale, Swanston, Latrobe and Elizabeth Streets. There is a direct walk-through access between Melbourne Central and the Myer department store. Further east along Lonsdale Street, Greek music cafes, and flaky pastry shops make Melbourne a mini-Athens for a couple of blocks.

The **Science Museum** in Swanston Street has many interesting exhibits, including Australia's first plane and car. This imposing old building also houses the **Planetarium** (where slides are projected on the ceiling of the dome); the magnificent domed **State Library**; the **La Trobe Library**; and the **National Museum**, which includes a large collection of Australiana, natural history exhibits—including the legendary racehorse Phar Lap—and the **Children's Museum**, a first in Australia.

A block away, opposite the Russell Street Police Station, is the grim **Old Melbourne Gaol** and **Penal Museum** with its chillingly macabre exhibits, including the gallows where folk-hero and bushranger Ned Kelly swung.

Shot tower and dome at Melbourne Central

More cheerful sights such as cheeses, sausages and decoratively arrayed vegetables can be seen at Melbourne's bustling **Queen Victoria Market**, at the corner of Peel and Victoria Streets, held on Tuesdays, Thursdays, Fridays, Saturdays and Sundays. Opposite the market on the corner of Queen and Franklin Streets is the fascinating **Queen Victoria Arts and Craft Centre**, open daily. From here it's only a short stroll to the beautiful **Flagstaff Gardens**, once used as a pioneer graveyard and later a signalling station. Today this is a pleasant place to relax, with shady old trees and a children's playground. Facing the park in King Street you can see **St James' Old Cathedral**, which was built in 1839.

The lower part of the city is the sedate legal and financial sector. Back towards the city centre along William Street are the former **Royal Mint** and the **Supreme Court** and **Law Courts**, which were built between 1877 and 1884. At the bottom end of Collins Street is the luxury hotel **Le Meridien Melbourne**. The elaborate Rialto building and its neighbours, erected between 1889 and 1893, have been retained as a facade to this towering hotel and office complex, the tallest building in the southern hemisphere. An observation deck is planned for the top of the south tower.

In complete contrast, two of Melbourne's finest city parks, the quiet old **Treasury Gardens** and the beautiful **Fitzroy Gardens**, lie to the eastern boundary of the central city 'grid'. The John F. Kennedy Memorial is located beside the lake in the Treasury Gardens. The Fitzroy Gardens have superb avenues of huge English elms planted along gently contoured lawns, giving them a serene beauty all year round. Attractions within the gardens include **Cook's Cottage**, the 'Fairy Tree', a model Tudor village, a restaurant and kiosk, and a children's playground. In summer the Fitzroy Gardens and other city parks have a programme of entertainment called Fantastic Entertainment in Public Places (FEIPP), including the Melbourne Symphony Orchestra's Prom Concerts, art shows, children's plays, jazz and ballet.

The **Carlton Gardens**, north-east of the city, flank the **Exhibition Buildings**—a grandiose domed hall originally built for the Great Exhibition in 1880 and still used for trade fairs. The southern side of the gardens has an ornamental pond and ornate fountain and the northern section an adventure playground and mini-traffic circuit popular with junior cyclists.

The **Victorian Arts Centre** is just over Princes Bridge on St Kilda Road, south of the central business area, and comprises the **National Gallery of Victoria**, the **Melbourne Concert Hall**, the **Theatres**, a variety of restaurants and bars, and the imposing Spire. The National Gallery features a fine collection of

Australian and overseas masterpieces. The intricate stained-glass ceiling of the Great Hall was designed by Australian artist Leonard French. The Concert Hall is used for symphony music and concerts. It also contains the **Performing Arts Museum**, which offers a programme of regularly changing exhibitions covering the whole spectrum of the performing arts. The theatres include the State Theatre for opera, ballet and large musicals, the Playhouse for drama and the Studio for experimental theatre; not far away at the Malthouse, 117 Sturt Street, South Melbourne, the Playbox Theatre Company has two theatres.

The **Kings Domain**, across St Kilda Road, is a huge stretch of shady parkland where you will see the **Myer Music Bowl**, used in the summer months as the venue for outdoor concerts and in the winter months as an ice-skating rink; the tower of **Government House** (tours operate at set times); the majestic, pyramid-style **Shrine of Remembrance,** which dominates St Kilda Road and is open to the public; the **Old Observatory** in Birdwood Avenue and, just past this, **La Trobe's Cottage**, Victoria's first Government House. This quaint cottage with many original furnishings—a reminder of Melbourne's humble beginnings—was brought out from England by the first Governor (La Trobe) in prefabricated sections. It is now a National Trust property, furnished in the original style with many of La Trobe's personal belongings and open daily. The main entrance to the **Royal Botanic Gardens** is nearby. These lush, beautifully landscaped gardens with gently sloping lawns, attractively grouped trees and shrubs, shady ferneries and ornamental lakes, are a peaceful retreat for city-dwellers. Many of the majestic old oaks in the western end of the garden are more than 100 years old. The kiosk, open daily, serves morning and afternoon teas and lunch. Guided walks operate at 10 a.m. and 11 a.m. daily (not Mondays, Saturdays and public holidays) departing from the Visitor Centre; there is no charge.

If you walk through the gardens you will come to shady **Alexandra Avenue**, which runs beside the Yarra River. Barbecues are dotted along the Yarra's grassy banks. At weekends, hire bicycles and ride the scenic **Yarra River Cycle Path,** or take a ferry trip from Princes Bridge downriver to Morrell Bridge, or past historic **Como House**.

Nearby **Albert Park**, just south of St Kilda Road, is another good place for families—and sports enthusiasts. There are barbecues on the edge of the huge Albert Park Lake and boats are available for hire. You can jog or cycle around the lake, or play golf on the adjoining public golf course.

Albert Park and its neighbouring suburbs, **South Melbourne** and **Port Melbourne**, are popular places with their trendy restaurants, bookshops, pubs and markets leading down to Melbourne's bayside beaches. **Albert Park Beach** has a brightly equipped playground with a tunnel slide on to the sand. In summer you can hire windsurfers on the beach near Fraser Street, West St Kilda.

Cosmopolitan **St Kilda** is a combination of London's 'Soho' and an old-fashioned fun resort. **Luna Park** and the enormous **Palais Theatre** are relics of the days when St Kilda was Melbourne's leading seaside playground. St Kilda is worth a visit, particularly on Sundays, when a collection of art and craft stalls appears on the **Esplanade** and **Acland Street** offers bookshops, restaurants and luscious continental cakes. For a delightful fish meal, visit Jean Jacques restaurant or take-away on the Lower Esplanade.

Just outside St Kilda at 192 Hotham Street, Elsternwick, is **Rippon Lea**, a National Trust property open daily. This huge Romanesque mansion is famed for its beautiful English-style landscaped gardens, which contain ornamental ponds and bridges, sweeping lawns, herbaceous borders, a superb fernery and strutting peacocks.

Two of Melbourne's wealthiest suburbs are **South Yarra** and **Toorak**. **Como**, another magnificent National Trust mansion, is in Como Avenue, off Toorak Road. Set in pleasant gardens, which once spread right down to the river, charmingly balconied Como is a perfectly preserved example of nineteenth-century colonial grandeur.

Although many of Toorak's and South Yarra's grand old estates have been subdivided, there is no shortage of imposing gates and high walls screening huge mansions. You could easily spend the best part of a day strolling down **Toorak Road**. This is a place to see and be seen—where there are probably more boutiques, expensive restaurants and gourmet food shops per metre than in any other part of Melbourne. The **Jewish**

Museum is on the corner of Toorak Road and Arnold Street in South Yarra.

Another of Melbourne's great shopping streets, **Chapel Street**, crosses Toorak Road in South Yarra. Here yet more fashion boutiques and antique and jewellery shops abound, but the air is not quite so rarefied, nor are the price tags quite as high. The **Jam Factory** is a huge redbrick building, which still looks like a factory from the outside but inside there is an arcade of shops, an attractive glass-topped courtyard and a restaurant. Further on towards Malvern Road, Chapel Street becomes more cosmopolitan and the emphasis shifts from fashion to food. The **Prahran Market** is just around the corner in Commercial Road. This market springs to life on Tuesdays, Thursdays, Fridays and Saturdays. Catch a tram down nearby **High Street** to Armadale and you will come upon Melbourne's antique area. Art and craft galleries, antique shops and designer-clothes shops stretch along High Street for several blocks.

Melbourne's city centre has been revitalised by Sunday trading, Swanston Walk, and the popularity of the various shopping complexes. Her once-depressed inner suburbs north of the Yarra have also been recharged with life. Theatres, theatre restaurants, antique shops, fashion boutiques and dozens of BYOs have bloomed in the suburbs of **Carlton**, **North Fitzroy** and **Richmond**. Most of the elegant iron-lace terrace houses in the more fashionable inner suburbs have been lovingly restored, but these areas still have a lively mixture of migrants and Australian old-timers. **Carlton**, the site of **Melbourne University**, also has one of the largest concentrations of beautiful Victorian houses in Melbourne. Its shady wide streets and squares of restored terraces can make you forget you are within walking distance of a modern city.

Lygon Street, known locally as 'little Italy', has three blocks of Italian restaurants, delicatessens, bookshops, boutiques and 'arty' shops. Have lunch and take in the Carlton scene at Jimmy Watson's, Melbourne's oldest wine bar, at 333 Lygon Street. The wine is good but cheap, the food self-service and the atmosphere frenetic, with everyone talking at once. If the weather is good the clientele spills out into the rear courtyard.

Walk through the Melbourne University grounds—a mixture of original ivy-clad buildings and modern blocks — and you come to **Parkville**, another little pocket of gracious Victorian terraces and shady streets. And at the **Melbourne Zoo**, just across nearby **Royal Park**, you can see a magnificent collection of butterflies in the unique walk-through Butterfly House, and families of lions at play from the safety of a 'people cage', an enclosed bridge which takes you right through the lions' large, natural-looking enclosure. This innovation is typical of the zoo's policy of providing enclosures for animals which are as large and as natural as possible, with a minimum of bars. There is also an amusement park and kiosk.

Melbourne's old metropolitan meat market at 42 Courtney Street, North Melbourne has been converted to a large craft gallery and workshop complex. The **Meat Market Craft Centre** features changing exhibitions, demonstrations and sales of high-quality crafts. For more information on craft shops and galleries, contact Craft Victoria on (03) 417 3111.

Another old inner suburb worth exploring is **Fitzroy**, which is similar in character to Carlton. Raffish Brunswick Street, Fitzroy, has an interesting mixture of antique shops, bookshops, clothes boutiques, pubs and first-class BYOs. In the suburb of **Fairfield**, a few kilometres east of Fitzroy, are the Fairfield Park Boathouse and Tea Gardens, with rowing skiffs and canoes for hire.

East Melbourne, another extremely well-preserved area of beautiful terrace houses, has such 'grand old ladies' as **Clarendon Terrace** (in Clarendon Street) with its graceful, colonnaded central portico and **Tasma Terrace** in Parliament Place, which now houses the National Trust Preservation Bookshop. The **Fire Services Museum of Victoria** is at 48 Gisborne Street, East Melbourne.

Swan Street, **Richmond** has one of the best selections of Greek restaurants in Melbourne. There is no need to book: if one is full, you try the next. Most are cheap and unpretentious with excellent food enhanced by a lively atmosphere. **Victoria Street** is the Vietnamese heartland of the city. Restored Victorian shops in **Bridge Road** house both boutiques and bargain 'seconds' outlets. As well as Bridge Road, factory outlets and seconds shops can be found in Swan Street and Chuch Street making Richmond the bargain shopping district of Melbourne.

St Kilda pier

It is possible in Melbourne to dine and see the sights at the same time. The Colonial Tramcar Company runs a restaurant aboard a 1927 tram, thus allowing patrons to enjoy a meal in elegant style while travelling through Melbourne and some of its suburbs. This has proved so popular that two old-style trams are now in use with a third planned. Another novel way to dine is aboard Lighters on the Yarra, where you can wine and dine while anchored on the Yarra River, opposite the World Trade Centre. A water taxi from Princes Bridge will take passengers to Cafe Alma in **Abbotsford**. Or try a Bar-B-Boat, a novel way to enjoy a barbecue while cruising on the Yarra past parks, gardens and the busy port area.

South-west of the city is Melbourne's oldest suburb, **Williamstown**, founded in the 1830s. This fascinating former maritime village has many quaint old seafront pubs, historic churches, fishermen's cottages and relics of its days as an important seaport. Because it was shielded from modern development until the completion of the **West Gate Bridge** to the city centre, much of Williamstown has changed little and retains a strong seafaring character. At weekends you can see over HMAS *Castlemaine*—a World War II minesweeper restored by the Maritime Trust—and picnic along the grassy foreshore. You can also see model ships, early costumes and relics at the Williamstown **Historical Museum** in Electra Street and look over a superb exhibition of old steam locomotives at the **Railway Museum** in Champion Road, North Williamstown. Williamstown Bay and river cruises are available.

The science and technology museum, **Scienceworks**, is located in a former pumping station in the suburb of **Spotswood**, close to Williamstown and only a ten-minute drive from the city. Scienceworks won the prestigious Australian Tourism Industry Association Award.

Closer to the city is the **Living Museum of the West** at Pipemakers Park, Van Ness Avenue, in the suburb of **Maribyrnong**; Australia's first ecomuseum, it presents the environment and heritage of the total community, the focus being upon the people of the region. Cruises on the Maribyrnong River visit some of the attractions to the west and north-west of Melbourne. At the **Craigieburn** note-printing branch of the Reserve Bank of Australia, visitors can observe the printing of Australian currency notes; appointment required (03) 303 0444.

The *Polly Woodside*, a square-rigged commercial sailing ship built in 1885, is moored at the old Duke and Orr's Dry Dock at the corner of Phayer Street and Normanby Road (near Spencer Street Bridge), **South Melbourne**, and is the focal point of the **Melbourne Maritime Museum**. In Coventry Street, South Melbourne are three portable houses, assembled in the 1850s, of the kind popular in Victoria during the gold-rush era.

For detailed information on Melbourne there are a number of guidebooks available. **Victorian Information Centre**, 230 Collins Street; (03) 790 3333, and the **Royal Automobile Club of Victoria (RACV)**, 422 Little Collins Street; (03) 790 3333, provide maps, brochures and other information. **The Met**, Melbourne's public transport system, offers a tourism package, the Met Pass, which includes an all-day ticket for all Met services, a map and a 92-page booklet of tourist attractions in and around Melbourne and suggested day-trips on public transport. Contact (03) 617 0900 or visit the Met shop at 103 Elizabeth Street.

Parks and Gardens

Rhododendron Gardens at Olinda, the Dandenongs

Melbourne is a city which has grown to become a place of dignity and beauty, designed as it was with wide, tree-shaded streets and magnificent public gardens. The feeling for greenery and open space has been maintained by individual residents, many of whom take great pride in their gardens, whether they be planted with European species or with the increasingly popular native trees and shrubs.

The jewel of Victoria is the **Royal Botanic Gardens**, situated beside the Yarra River, only two kilometres from the city. Here there are thirty-six hectares of plantations, flower-beds, lawns and ornamental lakes, so superbly laid out and cared for that they are considered to be among the best in the world.

The site for the gardens was selected in 1845 but the main work of their development was carried out by Baron Sir Ferdinand von Mueller, who was appointed Government Botanist in 1852. He was succeeded by W. R. Guilfoyle, a landscape artist, who further remodelled and expanded the gardens. The gardens and the riverside are now a favourite place for Melburnians on Sundays. Families flock to picnic, feed the swans and waterbirds on the lakes or simply take a pleasant stroll.

Adjoining the gardens and flanking St Kilda Road is another large area of parkland, the **Kings Domain**, which comprises forty-three hectares of tree-shaded lawns and contains the Shrine of Remembrance, La Trobe's Cottage, which was the first Government House, and the Sidney Myer Music Bowl, an unconventional aluminium and steel structure which creates a perfect amphitheatre for outdoor concerts in the summer months. During winter, the Bowl is converted into an ice-skating rink. This vast garden area is completed by the adjoining **Alexandra and Queen Victoria Gardens**, a further 52 hectares of parkland.

The city's first public gardens were the **Flagstaff Gardens** at William Street, West Melbourne. A monument in the gardens bears a plaque describing how the site was used as a signalling station to inform settlers of the arrival and departure of ships at Williamstown. On the other side of the city, not far from the centre, in East Melbourne are the **Treasury and Fitzroy Gardens** close by the State Government offices. In the Fitzroy Gardens is Captain Cook's cottage, which was transported in 1934 from the village of Great Ayton, Yorkshire, where Cook was born, and which was re-erected to commemorate Melbourne's centenary. Also in these gardens is a model Tudor village, laid out near an ancient tree trunk, a fairy tree carved with tiny figures by the late Ola Cohn. Another garden close to the city is the **Carlton Gardens**, in which the domed Exhibition Buildings are situated. They were erected for the Great Exhibition of 1880. The building was for twenty-seven years the meeting-place of the Victorian Parliament, while Federal Parliament met in the State Parliament buildings awaiting the building of Canberra.

Apart from these formal gardens—Melbourne's suburbs are endowed with large municipal garden areas Melbourne also has large recreational areas around the city and throughout the urban regions, and these are always expanding to meet the demands of a sport-loving populace. The most notable is Albert Park, where there are golf courses, indoor sports centres, two major cricket and football grounds and many other ovals, and a lake for sailing and rowing. Another large sporting area in East Melbourne contains the famous **Melbourne Cricket Ground**, which has been established for more than 100 years as a venue for test cricket and football and which now has stands that can accommodate 110 000 people. Nearby is the architecturally award-winning **National Tennis Centre**, the venue for international tennis tournaments. Courts are available for public hire. The Melbourne metropolitan area has eighty golf courses, many of which are accessible to the public. The **Royal Melbourne Golf Club** ranks sixth in world ratings, and hosts many world-class tournaments.

The man-made beauty of Melbourne is surpassed by nature in the Dandenong Ranges, about forty-nine kilometres from the city. The heavily forested ranges have trees such as mountain ash, grey gums, messmate, peppermint and box eucalypts interrupted by spectacular fern gullies. A network of good roads connects the many small towns in the Dandenongs, most of which blend into their bushland surroundings. The private gardens in the district are beautifully maintained and a drive through the hills is delightful at any time of the year, but particularly so in spring when fruit trees and ornamentals are in blossom, or in autumn when the European trees are at their most colourful.

There are a number of natural forests in the Dandenongs with tracks for bushwalkers. The best known is **Sherbrooke Forest**, which seems beautifully unspoiled despite the fact that it is visited by tens of thousands of people every year. It is a bird sanctuary and a home of the famous, but shy, lyrebird. A rare delight is to see the elaborate mating dance and display of these birds and to hear their brilliant mimicking calls.

A fascinating way to see the Dandenongs is to take a trip on the Puffing Billy, a delightful narrow-gauge steam railway maintained by a preservation society. It runs from Belgrave to Emerald Lake through bushland and flower farms. Visits to art galleries, antique shops, restaurants, sanctuaries or plant nurseries can add to the pleasure of a visit to the Dandenongs.

There are many other spectacular natural areas throughout Victoria and over the years the Government has been active in preserving many of these for the people—places such as the **Wilsons Promontory National Park** with its secluded beaches and superb coastal scenery; the **Tarra-Bulga National Park** in the Strzelecki Ranges, with its mountain ash trees and rainforest vegetation; the **Wyperfeld National Park** in the northwest, with its spring wildflowers and dry-country birdlife; the **Alpine National Park** which stretches across 6460 square kilometres of the state's high country; and many others.

The quality of Victoria's public and private gardens is exceptional wherever you go. Each year, Australia's Open Garden Scheme, publishes a guidebook to numerous private gardens open throughout spring, summer and autumn, right across Victoria as well as the other states. Most major towns have large, meticulously maintained garden areas, each with its own special quality. The **Ararat** Botanical Gardens are noted for their orchid glasshouse displays. The gardens at **Ballarat** are the centre of the famous annual Begonia Festival held in March. **Benalla** conducts a rose festival every year. In autumn, visitors are attracted to the colours of autumn foliage on the trees in and around the small town of Bright.

For further information on various garden festivals and displays contact the Victorian Information Centre, 230 Collins St, Melbourne; (03) 790 3333. **See also:** National Parks.

Sherbrooke Forest

Tours from Melbourne

Some of Australia's most beautiful and interesting tours emanate from Melbourne and include historic towns and stunning scenery. Many require an overnight stop to do them justice and in such cases booking ahead is recommended.

Ballarat and Sovereign Hill, 110 km from Melbourne via the Western Freeway

A must for the tourist if only to visit Sovereign Hill, arguably the most authentic reconstruction of a nineteenth-century goldmining township in the world. Ballarat is one of Victoria's most attractive old cities with many splendid colonial buildings, parks and gardens. Other attractions in Ballarat include the Eureka Stockade and the Begonia Festival held in March. Allow plenty of time for your Sovereign Hill visit. At Sovereign Hill you can stay overnight in the re-creation of Government Camp. **See also:** The Golden Age and Ballarat entry in A–Z listing.

Geelong, Queenscliff and Point Lonsdale, 107 km from Melbourne via the Princes Highway and Bellarine Highway

Allow two days for this tour. Spend some time in Geelong, especially around the historic waterfront and at the National Wool Museum, before continuing to Queenscliff, Melbourne's favourite summer resort of the late nineteenth century and still a popular weekend spot. Look for the lost treasure of Pirate Benito reputedly buried here and visit Fort Queenscliff, Melbourne's first defence establishment, before continuing on to William Buckley's cave at Point Lonsdale. Stay overnight at a classic nineteenth-century hotel; try the Vue Grand, Ozone or the Queenscliff, each located in Queenscliff. **See also:** Individual entries in A–Z listing.

Werribee Park, 35 km from Melbourne via the Princes Highway

Just outside the township of Werribee, now almost a suburb of Melbourne, Werribee Park is a large estate with a magnificent Italianate mansion of some sixty rooms, built in the 1870s for the Chirnside brothers, who had established a pastoral 'empire' in the Western District. Now owned by the Victorian Government, Werribee Park is open daily. There are extensive formal gardens, including the Victorian State Rose Garden, a wildlife reserve, a friendship farm, restaurant, kiosk, picnic facilities, electric barbecues, a golf course and tennis courts. Nearby Point Cook RAAF Museum (open Sun.–Fri.) has adjacent picnic and barbecue facilities. There is nude bathing at Campbell's Cove.

The Great Ocean Road and the Otway Range, 200 km from Melbourne along the south-west coast
See: The Great Ocean Road.

Port Phillip Bay Cruises from 11 North Wharf

The steam tug *Wattle*, a beautifully restored 1933 tugboat, makes daytrips to Portarlington on the Bellarine Peninsula on Saturdays, and fascinating two-hour trips around the Port of Melbourne on Sundays and public holidays. In January the *Wattle* runs daily seal-colony cruises

Fort Queenscliff

View from Bass Hwy, South Gippsland

from Rye. The *Wattle* does not operate during July and August. Bookings are essential; contact (03) 328 2739.

Healesville Sanctuary, 60 km from Melbourne via the Maroondah Highway

To see all of Australia's distinctive fauna in one huge natural enclosure, take a one-day tour to Healesville Sanctuary. Many of the animals roam freely; there are 'walk-through' aviaries, excellent nocturnal displays and viewing of the extraordinary platypus. However, the highlight is the new 'Where Eagles Fly' exhibit, where rangers and birds of prey combine in an awe-inspiring display. Open daily, with kiosk, picnic and barbecue facilities. Mt Saint Leonard north of Healesville offers a fine 360 degree view, but requires a one-kilometre uphill walk. **See also:** Healesville entry in A–Z listing.

The Dandenong Ranges, 49 km from Melbourne via the Burwood Highway

See: The Dandenongs.

Phillip Island, 140 km from Melbourne via the Mulgrave Freeway and the South Gippsland and Bass Highways

Famous for the nightly parade at dusk of little fairy penguins up to their burrows at Summerland Beach, Phillip Island attracts thousands of visitors annually. Other wildlife attractions include fur seals all year, but especially in November–December and mutton birds in spring and summer. The island is situated in Western Port and also offers excellent surfing and fishing. There is usually some activity at the Phillip Island Motor Racing Circuit, venue for the first 500 cc motorcycle Australian Grand Prix. **See also:** Phillip Island; and Cowes entry in A–Z listing.

South Gippsland and Wilsons Promontory, 180 km from Melbourne via the South Gippsland Highway

Leaving Melbourne behind, this tour takes you through the townships of Cranbourne, Korumburra and Leongatha and through the lush, rolling hills and the spectacular countryside of South Gippsland to Foster, where you turn right for the southern most point on the Australian mainland at Wilsons Promontory National Park. See kangaroos and koalas and take some short (or long) bushwalks to tiny coves and sandy beaches. This tour deserves at least two days. Return along the coast road through Inverloch and Wonthaggi. **See also:** Individual entries in A–Z listing.

Warburton and the Upper Yarra Dam, 120 km via the Maroondah and Warburton Highways

On the way to some of Victoria's high country, visit wineries in the Yarra Valley region and sample some superb vintage reds and whites. Some of this region is snow-covered in mid-winter. If you visit during the warmer months, picnic by the Upper Yarra Dam and go trout fishing at Tommy Finn's Trout Farm. Hot-air balloon flights are available at Yarra Glen. Warburton has giant waterslides and an art gallery; the La La Falls are just outside of town. You can cross the range to Noojee (but take care as the road is unsealed), and return via Warragul and the Princes Highway. The Gippsland region produces some of the world's great cheeses. **See also:** Warburton entry in A–Z listing.

Mornington Peninsula, 100 km from Melbourne via the Nepean Highway

See: The Mornington Peninsula.

Yarra Valley wineries, 40–60 km from Melbourne via the Maroondah and Melba Highways, or via Heidelberg, Greensborough and the Diamond Valley

Throughout the Yarra Valley, centred on Coldstream/Yarra Glen, 37 wineries and 82 vineyards produce premium and quality wines that are acclaimed worldwide. Of these, 20 have cellar-door facilities, mostly open on weekends and public holidays; several—such as Fergusson's, De Bortoli, Kellybrook and Yarra Burn—include restaurants on the premises. Further information and a listing of cellar-door details from the Yarra Valley Wine Growers Association, (059) 64 2016.

The Mornington Peninsula

This boot-shaped promontory separates Port Phillip Bay and Western Port and provides Melburnians with a beachside playground. It is a mixture of resort towns, varying in size and tourist development, and inland rural countryside. As well as safe bayside beaches, there are excellent surf beaches, particularly along the stretch of rugged coast between Portsea and Cape Schanck at the end of the Peninsula. The Point Nepean National Park includes the key beaches in this area—**Portsea**, **Sorrento**, **Diamond Bay**, **Koonya** and **Gunnamatta**. A number of walking tracks have been established. Swimming is considered safe only in those areas controlled by the Surf Lifesaving Association.

The Western Port side of the Peninsula is less developed, much of its foreshore having remained relatively unspoiled and being still devoted to farming and grazing land. **French Island**, which is set in the centre of this bay, was a Victorian penal settlement for forty years and is now administered by the Victorian government as a state park. The island is notable for its fauna.

Port Phillip Bay is linked for vehicle access by the Peninsula Searoad Transport ferry which operates between Sorrento and Queenscliff. Quaint passenger ferries link Sorrento, Portsea and Queenscliff in the summer season as well.

Frankston, now mainly a residential area for Melbourne commuters, could also be considered the gateway to the Peninsula. It is a thriving town within easy reach of good beaches on Port Phillip Bay at Daveys Bay, Canadian Bay and Mount Eliza. McClelland Art Gallery is open daily. Sage's Cottage (1850), at nearby Baxter, is now a colonial-style restaurant.

The Peninsula itself is well developed for tourists, with good sporting facilities and many art galleries, craft shops, restaurants and take-away food shops. Because of its popularity, it is advisable to book accommodation, whatever your choice, well ahead during the summer and Easter seasons. The Port Phillip Bay foreshore from **Dromana** to **Blairgowrie** is almost entirely devoted to campers and caravans during these peak seasons.

Mornington was established in 1864. The deep safe harbour at Point Schnapper first attracted settlers to this area and it has been a popular resort town ever since. Today it is a pleasant commercial, farming and recreational centre. Street

Point Nepean National Park, near Portsea

Market operates on Wednesday mornings and the second Sunday in each month. Between the town and nearby Mount Martha stretches a fine coastline with sheltered sandy bays separated by rocky bluffs and backed by steep wooded slopes. A self-guided walk introduces the town's historic buildings, including the gaol and courthouse on the Esplanade, and the old post office on the Esplanade corner, which is now a historic museum. The Australian Museum of Modern Media, 1140 Nepean Highway, has film, television, radio and pop music memorabilia. The new Mornington Peninsula Arts Centre is in the Civic Reserve, Duns Road. Fossil Beach, between Mount Martha and Mornington, is one of only two exposed fossil plains in the world. Parasailing is available at Mount Martha Beach. Located at Mount Martha, 'The Briars', an old homestead (1866) and property, incorporates wetland areas, bird hides, a Woodland Walk and the Briars Peninsula Wine Centre.

Dromana rests at the foot of Arthurs Seat, the 305-metre-high mountain that provides the Peninsula with panoramic views over both bays. Safety Beach has boat-launching ramps and trailer facilities. A good road leads to the summit and a chair-lift operates at weekends and school and public holidays May to mid September, but daily from then until to the end of April. At the summit there are a lookout tower, picnic reserve and licensed restaurant. Also nearby is Seawinds, a section of the Arthurs Seat State Park, which has beautiful gardens complete with sculptures, picnic facilities and great views.

Main Ridge and **Red Hill**, in the hinterland behind Arthurs Seat, are known for wineries. At Main Ridge attractions include Kings Waterfall, also in Arthurs Seat State Park, the Drum Drum wildflower farm, Seaview Nursery and tearooms, Sunny Ridge Strawberry Farm, a riding school and the Pine Ridge Car Museum. Red Hill is particularly well known for its Community Market, held on the first Saturday of the months September to May.

McCrae is a small resort centre, noted for the McCrae Homestead, built in 1844, now a National Trust property, open daily. It was the first homestead on the Peninsula.

Rosebud is a busy commercial centre with wide foreshore camping areas. Just outside the town is the Peninsula Gardens Sanctuary, set back from the Nepean Highway.

Rye has extensive camping, picnicking and recreational foreshore areas, and boat-launching facilities.

Sorrento was the site of Victoria's first settlement in 1803, when Colonel Collins landed in this area. The early settlers' graves and a memorial to Collins can be found in the cliff-top cemetery overlooking Sullivans Bay. Sorrento was energetically developed as a 'watering place' by George Coppin in the 1870s; the Sorrento, Koonya and Continental Hotels have been restored as fine examples of early Victorian architecture. At nearby Point King, the Union Jack was raised for the first time in Australia. South Channel Fort, a man-made island that is now a bird habitat, lies 6 kilometres off Sorrento and is open to visitors.

Portsea, situated at the end of the Nepean Highway, is an attractive resort with excellent deepwater bayside beaches and first-class surfing at its Back Beach. Victoria's first Quarantine Station (now an Army training camp) was built here in 1856 after 82 deaths from smallpox on the vessel *Ticonderoga* anchored in Weeroona Bay. Off-limits to the public until recently, this area is now incorporated into the Point Nepean National Park; open daily. Panoramic views of the impressive rocky coastline abound and near Back Beach is London Bridge, a spectacular rock formation created by sea erosion.

Flinders is the most southerly Peninsula township, on Western Port. It is a fishing and holiday resort, with good surfing, swimming and fishing. Cape Schanck lighthouse (1859) with its museum, the Blowhole and Elephant Rock are worth visiting.

Hastings, also fronting Western Port, is an attractive fishing port and holiday centre with a sea-water swimming pool, yacht-club, marina and boat-launching ramps south of the pier. There is a fauna park next to the high school in High St, and over 50 000 hectares of designated wetlands north of town.

Ashcombe Maze, near Shoreham

Other towns in Western Port include **Shoreham**, a sprawling holiday settlement on Stony Creek, close to the sea. On Red Hill Road is Ashcombe Maze, which features hedge mazes surrounded by gardens. Five kilometres from Shoreham is **Point Leo**, which has one of the safest surf beaches on the Peninsula. Between Point Leo and **Balnarring**, short access roads from the main Flinders–Frankston road lead to very pleasant beaches at Merricks, Coles, Point Sumner and Balnarring.

Somers, a quiet village with many holiday homes, has good beaches, excellent fishing, tennis and yacht-clubs. Coolart mansion, a National-Trust-classified homestead dating from the 1890s, is set on 87 hectares, with landscaped gardens, a lagoon and walking trails. Between Somers and Crib Point is HMAS *Cerberus*, a Royal Australian Navy training establishment.

The Mornington Peninsula is a rapidly growing wine-producing area. From the hinterland of Mount Martha to the shores of Western Port, 17 vineyards open regularly for cellar-door tastings and sales; 13 more open by appointment. For further detailed information, contact the Mornington Peninsula Vignerons Association; PO Box 400, Mornington 3931; (059) 74 4200.

For further information on the area contact the Dromana Information Centre, Nepean Hwy, Dromana; (059) 87 3078; the Frankston Information Centre, 54 Playne St, Frankston; (03) 781 5244; or the Mornington Information Centre, cnr Main and Elizabeth Sts, Mornington; (059) 75 1644. **Note** detailed map of Mornington Peninsula on page 212.

The Dandenongs

These ranges, 50 kilometres from the centre of Melbourne, are a renowned beauty area and tourist attraction. Heavy rainfall and rich volcanic soil have created a lush vegetation with spectacular hills and gullies crowded with creepers, tree ferns and soaring mountain ash. The area is fairly closely settled and there are a number of pretty townships dotted about the hills.

It has long been a traditional summer retreat for people from Melbourne and many of the gracious old homes have now been converted into guest houses and restaurants.

The entire area is famous for its beautiful gardens and for its great variety of European trees, particularly attractive in spring and autumn. Many excellent restaurants, art and craft galleries, antique shops and well-stocked plant nurseries add to the charm of these hills, ideally placed for a relaxed day's outing from Melbourne. At 633 metres, Mount Dandenong is the highest point of the ranges, and at its summit there are excellent views, picnic facilities and the Skyhigh Restaurant from which a magnificent night-time view of Melbourne can be seen.

Ferntree Gully National Park, Doongalla and Sherbrooke Forest are now the 1900-hectare Dandenong Ranges National Park, where you can see lush trees and ferns and a wide variety of flora and fauna. The lyrebird and eastern whipbird can be heard here. Sherbrooke Forest, on the road from **Belgrave** to **Kallista**, is unspoiled bushland with many lyrebirds. A tourist road runs through the park area from **Ferntree Gully** to **Montrose**. At Montrose, visit Gumnut Village in the Austraflora plant nursery, Belfast Road (open daily). William Ricketts Sanctuary (open daily), on Mount Dandenong Tourist Road, is a natural forest area in which Ricketts, a musician and naturalist, who died in 1993, sculpted in clay a number of Aboriginal figures and symbolic scenes. Near **Sherbrooke**, the Nicholas Memorial Gardens, 13 hectares of a formerly private garden, are open daily.

'Puffing Billy', one of the Dandenongs' most famous attractions, leaves from **Belgrave** and travels 13.5 kilometres to **Emerald Lake**. The Puffing Billy Steam Museum at **Menzies Creek**, open Saturday, Sunday and public holidays, displays some restored locomotives and rollingstock. Puffing Billy runs daily throughout the year, except on Christmas Day and fire-ban days. A timetable is available from the Victorian Information Centre, 230 Collins St, Melbourne, (03) 790 3333; or telephone (03) 870 8411 for recorded information. Each April, the Great Train Race is held: runners attempt to race Puffing Billy from Belgrave to Emerald Lake Park.

Emerald was the first settlement in the area and is situated on a high ridge. It has a number of interesting galleries and in the surrounding countryside there are lavender farms and attractive picnic spots. **Olinda** is a pretty township with some good restaurants. The home of one of Victoria's first settlers, Edward Henty, is now sited here on Ridge Road. Constructed from prefabricated sections brought from England, the house has a number of historic domestic items and original furnishings; open daily except Friday. Also of interest is the National Rhododendron Garden, especially in spring, when the annual show is held. Another spring flower festival is held at **Silvan**, where tulip bulbs are cultivated. **Ferntree Gully**, at the foot of the ranges, is now virtually an outer suburb of Melbourne.

For further information on the Dandenongs, contact the Victorian Information Centre, 230 Collins St, Melbourne; (03) 790 3333. **See also:** Individual town entries in A–Z listings. **Note** detailed map of Yarra Valley Region on page 214.

Nicholas Memorial Gardens, near Sherbrooke

Victoria from A to Z

Alexandra   Pop. 1965

Alexandra is a farming and holiday centre, 24 km W of Lake Eildon. **Of interest:** Timber and Tramway Museum housed in former railway station, Station St. Historic buildings include National-Trust-classified Post Office and adjacent Law Courts, Downey St (Goulburn Valley Hwy). Community Market, usually held last Sat. of month. Easter Art Show. **In the area:** Fraser National Park, 12 km E; excellent walks. Southern edge of town, McKenzie Nature Reserve; virgin bushland with an abundance of orchids in winter and spring. Stonelea Country Retreat at Acheron, 8 km S. Taggerty, 18 km S in the Acheron Valley; good trout fishing. Taggerty Pioneer Settlement. Cathedral Range State Park, 3 km further S from Taggerty, for camping, bushwalking, rock climbing and fishing. Bonnie Doon, 37 km NE, on Lake Eildon; base for trail riding, bushwalking, water sports and scenic drives. Starglen Lodge, Bonnie Doon, offers comfortable accommodation with horseriding, 4WD tours or relaxing. **Tourist information:** Redgate Nursery and Craft Cottage, 73 Downey St; (057) 72 2169. **Accommodation:** 4 hotels, 2 motels, 2 caravan/camping parks.
MAP REF. 211 O2, 233 J11

Anglesea   Pop. 1965

This attractive seaside town on the Great Ocean Road has excellent swimming and surfing. The golf course, has tame kangaroos, and Taberet facilities at the clubhouse. Behind the town, in Coalmine Rd, there is an open-cut brown-coal mine and power station with a viewing platform and information. **Of interest:** Melaleuca Gallery, Gt Ocean Rd. Coogoorah Park; bushland reserve, picnics and bushwalking. Annual Angair Festival in Sept. **In**

the area: J.E. Loveridge Lookout, 1 km W. Point Roadknight beach, 2 km W. Angahook–Lorne State Park, an attractive reserve with many walking tracks; access from either behind Anglesea or from Aireys Inlet, 10 km SW, on Gt Ocean Rd; features include Ironbark Basin, Currawong Falls, Treefern Grove and Melaleuca Swamp. **Tourist information:** Christmas–Easter from caravan, Anglesea Riverbank; other months from Shire Offices, Grossmans Rd, Torquay; (052) 61 4202. **Accommodation:** 3 motels, 4 caravan/camping parks. **See also:** The Great Ocean Road; The Western District.
MAP REF. 210 E11, 217 C11, 227 Q9

Apollo Bay   Pop. 894

The Great Ocean Road leads to this attractive coastal town, the centre of a rich dairying and fishing area and the base for a huge fish-freezing plant. The wooded mountainous hinterland offers memorable scenery and there is excellent sea and river fishing in the area. The rugged and beautiful coastline has been the scene of many shipwrecks in the past. **Of interest:** Bass Strait Shell Museum, Noel St. Old Cable Station Museum, Gt Ocean Rd. **In the area:** Self-guide walks available from Tourist Information Centre. Grey River Scenic Reserve, 24 km NE. Elliot River, 6 km SW, and adjacent Shelly Beach Viewpoint. Otway National Park, 13 km SW; excellent for bushwalking through park to sea or through forest to waterfalls. Turton's Track, 25 km N and Wild Dog Road, 3 km E, are scenic touring roads. Follow signs to Barham Paradise Scenic Reserve, 10 km NW, in beautiful Barham River Valley. Lavers Hill, 53 km W; tiny now in comparison with the booming timber centre of its heyday. Enchanting Melba Gully State Park, 3 km W of Lavers Hill; covers

49 ha, self-guide rainforest walk; a glow-worm habitat. Hang-gliding and horse-riding. **Tourist information:** 5 Moore St; (052) 37 6263. **Accommodation:** 2 hotels, 20 motels, 6 caravan/camping parks. **See also:** The Great Ocean Road. MAP REF. 215 G12, 227 N11

Ararat   Pop. 7633

The Ararat area gold boom came in 1857. It was short-lived, however, and sheep farming became the basis of the town's economy. Today the town is the commercial centre of a prosperous farming and winegrowing region. The area also produces fine merino wool. The first vines in the district were planted by Frenchmen in 1863 and the little town of Great Western, 16 km NW of Ararat, gave its name to some of Australia's most famous champagnes and wines. **Of interest:** Beautiful bluestone buildings in Barkly St: Post Office, the splendid Town Hall, Civic Square and War Memorial. Chinese Gold Discovery Memorial, Lambert St. Langi Morgala Folk Museum, Queen St; includes collection of Aboriginal weapons and artefacts. Ararat Art Gallery; regional gallery specialising in wool and fibre pieces by leading artists. Alexandra Park and Botanical Gardens, noted for their orchid glasshouse display, walk-in fernery and herb garden. Water sports at Green Hill Lake, a man-made lake, close to Western Hwy. Golden Gateway 10-day festival held Oct. J-Ward, Old Ararat Gaol, off Lowe St; open Sun. guided tours, groups by appt. **In the area:** Langi Ghiran State Park, 13½ km E off Western Hwy; scenic walks to nearby reservoir, picnic/barbecue facilities, children's playground. Buangor, 5 km E; century-old Buangor Hotel, Buangor Store, and opposite, old Cobb & Co. changing station (c. 1860).

Mt Buangor State Park and Fern Tree Waterfalls, with picnic facilities, 18 km further on. Several wineries in the area: Seppelt's Great Western Vineyards, 17 km NW, specialises in dry red wines and champagnes. Vineyard established in 1865; underground cellars classified by National Trust. Best's Wines, 2 km on through Great Western; open for inspection, tastings and sales. Mt Langi Ghiran Wines, 20 km E on Western Hwy. Montara Winery, 3 km S of Ararat, on Chalambar Rd. Cathcart Ridge Winery at Cathcart, 6 km W. Cathcart and, 20 km further west, Mafeking, are historic gold areas. Mafeking, once a bustling settlement with 10 000 people, has picnic facilities. Care must be taken when walking in these areas: many deep mine shafts. **Tourist information:** Barkly St; (053) 52 2096. **Accommodation:** 5 hotels, 6 motels, 2 caravan/camping parks. MAP REF. 220 D8, 227 K2, 229 K13

Avoca   Pop. 1004

In the Central Highlands region, Avoca was established with the discovery of gold in the area in 1852. Located at the junction of the Sunraysia and Pyrenees Hwys, the surrounding Pyrenees Range foothills offer attractive bushwalking and are the home of numbers of kangaroos, wallabies and koalas. **Of interest:** Early bluestone buildings classified by National Trust include the old gaol and powder magazine in Camp St, the courthouse and one of the State's earliest pharmacies, Lalor's, in High St. Rock and Gem Museum in High St. Wool and Wine Festival in Oct. **In the area:** Avoca and Wimmera Rivers, through town and 42

Bacchus Marsh

km W respectively, and Bet Bet Creek, 11 km E, are popular for fishing. Several wineries within easy driving distance of town include: Mt Avoca vineyard, 7 km W; Chateau Remy Vineyards, 8 km W on Vinoca Rd; Redbank Winery at Redbank, 20 km NW; Summerfield Winery in Moonambel Village, 20 km N; Warrenmang Vineyard, 1 km E; Taltarni and Dalwhinnie wines, each another 2 km further east. **Tourist information:** High St; (054) 65 3767. **Accommodation:** 2 hotels, 2 motels, 1 caravan/camping park. **See also:** Wine Regions. MAP REF. 210 A1, 220 I5, 227 M1, 229 M12

Bacchus Marsh   Pop. 13 000

The trees of the Avenue of Honour provide an impressive entrance to Bacchus Marsh, 49 km from Melbourne on the Western Hwy. This long-established town is situated in a fertile valley, once marshland, between the Werribee and Lerderderg Rivers. **Of interest:** Manor House, home of town's founder, Captain Bacchus, in Manor St; privately owned. In Main St, original blacksmith's shop and cottage, courthouse, lockup and National Bank, all classified by National Trust. Border Inn, opened in 1850, also in Main St; thought to have been first coaching service stop in Victoria; Bacchus Marsh was staging post for Cobb & Co. coaches travelling to goldfields. Holy Trinity Anglican Church (1877), Gisborne Rd. Gallery 22, Maddingley Blvd. Express Building Art Gallery, Gisborne Rd. Ra Ceramics and Crafts, Station St. Big Apple Tourist Orchard, Avenue of Honour. **In the area:**

Werribee and Lerderderg Gorges, 10 km W and 10 km N respectively; picnics, bushwalking and swimming. All popular with anglers and bushwalkers: Merrimu Reservoir and Wombat State Forest, both about 10 km N; Brisbane Ranges National Park, 16 km SW, and Anakie Gorge, 26 km SW; Long Forest Fauna Reserve, 2 km NE, with its bull mallee, some specimens centuries old. On the Western Fwy, 6 km W: St Anne's Vineyard; old bluestone cellar, built from remains of old Ballarat gaol; open daily. Willows Historical Homestead at Melton, 14 km E. Craiglee Winery and Goonawarra Vineyard at Sunbury, 47 km NE and Wildwood Vineyard, 9 km SE at Bulla. Mineral Springs Reserve and Garden of St Erth at Blackwood, 26 km NW. Maddingley open-cut coal mine, 3 km S. **Tourist information:** Shire Offices, Main Street; (053) 67 2111. **Accommodation:** 4 hotels, 2 motels, 1 caravan/camping park. **See also:** The Golden Age. MAP REF. 210 G5, 221 R13, 224 A3, 227 R5

Bairnsdale   Pop. 10 770

This Gippsland trade centre and holiday town is at the junction of the Princes Hwy, the Omeo Hwy and the road east to Lakes Entrance, which makes it an excellent touring base. It is a pleasant town with good sporting facilities and attractive gardens. **Of interest:** Historical Museum, Macarthur St; building (1891) houses furnishing and memorabilia, grounds display photographs, family histories, publications. St Mary's Church, Main St; wall and ceiling murals by an Italian artist. Bairnsdale Recreation Centre, McKeen St; includes sports hall. Port of Bairnsdale site and river walk, below post office; picnic facilities. **In the area:** Lindenow, 19 km W, close to Mitchell River National Park. Park has good bushwalking tracks and, in a gorge on the Mitchell River, the Den of Nargun, an Aboriginal cultural site. River empties into Lake King at Eagle Point Bluff, where world's second longest silt jetties can be seen. Jolly Jumbuk Country Craft Centre; 3 km E on Princes Hwy; woollen products for sale, workshops. Adjacent, Archery and Mini Golf Park; family fun centre. Metung, 30 km E; picturesque fishing village on shores of Lake King; some solid pioneer holiday homes still standing. About 2 km S, a boardwalk (closed during duck season) leads across part of McLeod's Morass, a bird wetland

habitat; main access about 10 km S. Scenic drive north along Omeo Hwy through Tambo River valley; stunning in spring when wattles are in bloom. Nicholson River Winery, 10 km E, and Golvinda winery, 5 km N. **Tourist information:** 240 Main Street; (051) 52 3444. **Accommodation:** 3 hotels, 8 motels, 3 caravan/camping parks. **See also:** Gippsland Lakes.
MAP REF. 225 P4, 234 E13

Ballan
Pop. 1053

A small township on the Werribee River, noted for its mineral springs. **Of interest:** Caledonian Park, eastern edge of town; picnic areas and swimming. **In the area:** Pikes Creek Reservoir, 12 km E, with good trout fishing. **Tourist information:** Shire Offices, cnr Stead and Steiglitz Sts; (053) 68 1001. **Accommodation:** 3 hotels, 2 caravan parks.
MAP REF. 210 F4, 221 P12, 227 Q4

Ballarat
Pop. 64 980

Ballarat is Victoria's largest inland city, situated in the Central Highlands. Its inner areas retain much of the charm of its gold-boom era, with many splendid original buildings still standing and parks and gardens adding to its attractive appearance. The begonia is the city's floral emblem and the Begonia Festival in March attracts many enthusiasts. Ballarat was just a small rural township in 1851, when its enormously rich alluvial goldfields were discovered. Within two years it had a population of nearly 40 000. Australia's only civil battle occurred here in 1854, when miners refused to pay Government licence fees and fought with police and troops at the Eureka Stockade. Today Ballarat is a bustling city with the added attraction of many galleries, museums, antique and craft shops. It has excellent recreational facilities and beautiful garden areas, making it most attractive to visitors. The Royal South Street Eisteddfod, which focuses on music and the dramatic arts, is held each Sept.–Oct. Bridge Street Mall in the centre of the city has many shops in a relaxed atmosphere. **Of interest:** Man-made Lake Wendouree, accessed from Hamilton Ave; water sports. Paddle-steamer tours; commentary on history of city. Adjoining the lake area: Botanic Gardens (40 ha); splendid begonia conservatories, Prime Ministers' Avenue, displaying busts of Australian prime ministers. Elegant statuary pavilion nearby. Vintage Tramway, access in

Main street, Ballarat

Wendouree Pde; rides weekends, public and school holidays. Fine Art Gallery in Lydiard St Nth; comprehensive collection of Australian art, including works by the Lindsay family. Montrose Cottage (1856), Eureka St; the first masonry cottage built on the goldfields; winner of Tourism Award of Social History. Adjacent, Eureka Museum; large collection of gold-era relics. Golda's World of Dolls, Eureka St; antique and modern dolls. Eureka Exhibition and Orpheus Radio Museum, cnr Stawell and Eureka Sts; historical information on Eureka Rebellion as well as comprehensive range of radios from past times. The Old Curiosity Shop, Queen St; collection of pioneer relics. In Stawell St Sth: Eureka Stockade Park, with life-size replica of the famous battle. Self-guide Eureka Trail for visitors. Ballarat Wildlife and Reptile Park, cnr of York and Fussell Sts. Craig's Royal Hotel, George Hotel, and Ballarat Terrace (1889) all in Lydiard St; dining and accommodation in old-world surroundings. Antique Fair, and Super Southern Swap Meet at Ballarat Airport, in Feb. Music Festival and Jazz Festival at Easter. **In the area:** Sovereign Hill, major tourist attraction 2 km S; is a reconstruction of a goldmining settlement with orientation centre and working displays. Blood on the Southern Cross; night sight-and-sound exhibition. During Begonia Festival in March; guided lamplight tours of Sovereign Hill. Excellent barbecue facilities, kiosk, restaurant and licensed hotel offer refreshments. Government Camp provides comfortable family-type accommodation. Adjoining Sovereign Hill, Gold Museum; exhibits of gold history, large collection of gold coins and display of the uses of

gold 'today and tomorrow'. Kryal Castle, 8 km E on Western Hwy; reconstruction of a medieval castle, offers entertainment for all the family. On western edge of the city: Avenue of Honour (22 km) and Arch of Victory, honouring those who fought in World War I. Lake Burrumbeet, 22 km NW; water sports, picnic spots and excellent trout fishing. Lal Lal Falls (30 m) on Moorabool River, 25 km SE of city. Lal Lal Blast Furnace; beautiful archaeological remains from 19th century. White Swan Reservoir, 8 km N off Daylesford Rd; attractive picnic spot with lawns, water views, picnic/barbecue facilities. Mooramong Homestead, National Trust property at Skipton, 53 km W; open by appt. Mt Widderin Caves, 6 km S of Skipton. Yellowglen Winery, 24 km SW, at Smythesdale. Berringa Mines Historic Reserve, 8 km from Smythesdale. Wallace Cheesery, 8 km E of Ballarat. Ballarat Aviation Museum, 4 km NW on Learmonth Rd. Enfield State Park, near Enfield, 16 km S of Ballarat. Pyrenees Vignerons, 8 wineries located at Avoca and district; open for tastings and cellar-door sales. **Tourist information:** Cnr Sturt and Albert Sts; (053) 32 2694. **Accommodation:** 15 hotels, 21 motels, 5 caravan/camping parks. **See also:** The Golden Age.
MAP REF. 210 C4, 219, 221 M12, 227 O4

Beaufort
Pop. 1171

This small town on the Western Hwy, midway between Ballarat and Ararat, has a gold-rush history, like so many of the other towns in this area. The discovery of gold at Fiery Creek swelled its population in the late 1850s to nearly 100 000. Today Beaufort is primarily a centre for

The Golden Age

The cities and towns of the goldfields region of Victoria came to a peak of style and affluence in the 1880s, an affluence built on the first gold discoveries in the 1850s. The towns display all the frivolity and grandeur of Victorian architecture, having grown up in an age when it was believed that gold and wealth would be a permanent benefit in Victoria.

The two major cities of the region are Ballarat and Bendigo, but there are many other towns, large and small, in the area. They all have beautiful old houses and public buildings, and many have other trappings of the past—statues, public gardens (sometimes with lakes), ornamental bandstands and grand avenues of English trees. Spring and autumn are the best seasons to visit this region, because then there are not the extremes of summer and winter temperatures and the flowers and foliage are at their best.

It is a quiet region now. The remaining small towns serve the rich pastoral district, and secondary industries and services centre on the two cities.

It was once, however, an area of frantic activity. Gold was found at Clunes in 1851 and within three months 8000 people were on the diggings in the area between Buninyong and Ballarat. Nine months later 30 000 men were on the goldfields and four years later 100 000. The population of the city of Melbourne dwindled alarmingly and immigrants rushed to the diggings from Great Britain, America and many other countries. Ships' crews, and sometimes even their captains, abandoned their vessels and trekked to the diggings to try their luck. Tent cities sprang up on the plains as men dug and panned for gold. There were remarkable finds of huge nuggets in the early days but, finally, the amount of gold obtained by panning in the rivers and by digging grew less and less. The communities were remarkable: there were shanty towns, the streets crowded day and night with hawkers and traders; there were pubs and dancing-rooms and continuous sounds of music and revelry.

As time went on, the surface gold was worked out and expensive company-backed operations followed, mining in deep shafts, stamping and crushing the ore in steam-powered plants on the surface.

The success of these methods heralded a new era, that of the company mines, outside investors and stock

Botanic Gardens, Ballarat

exchange speculation. It led to a more stable workforce and to the well-established communities that slowly evolved into towns of the region today. As the pastoral potential began to be fully exploited, it was the perfect scene for expansion and optimism.

The years between 1870 and 1890 saw the towns embellished with fine civic buildings, mansions, solid town houses, churches, hotels and all the trappings of affluence. Thus Ballarat, Bendigo, Castlemaine and, to a lesser extent, Clunes, Creswick, Daylesford and Maldon became extraordinary *nouveau riche* visions of the current British taste.

The Western Highway between Melbourne and Ballarat is at its most scenic as it rises into the Pentland Hills. Rounded volcanic hills encircle **Bacchus Marsh**, which is approached by a magnificent avenue of North American elms commemorating soldiers who died in the Great War. Bacchus Marsh is adjacent to the Lerderderg and Werribee Rivers, which enter dramatic gorges close to the town. Just off the highway are the small rural towns of Myrniong and Ballan, Gordon and Bungaree. South of the highway near Bungaree is Dunnstown, dominated by its bluestone distillery and the bulk of Mount Warrenheip, where an excellent view of the district can be had from the summit.

A turnoff to the south near Ballarat leads to **Buninyong**, the scene of one of the first gold strikes in Victoria. This impressive township with a grand tree-lined main street has a number of striking buildings—the Crown Hotel and white-walled Uniting Church are of the 1860s, while the combined council chambers and courthouse of 1886 are in rich Italianate design, unified by a central clock tower.

The city of **Ballarat** was laid out to the

west of the diggings within twelve months of the first discovery of gold. The design included a magnificent chief thoroughfare, Sturt Street, wide enough for future plantations and monuments. The primitive buildings of early settlement were gradually replaced by boom-style architecture in the 1880s. Italianate, Romanesque, Gothic and French Renaissance styles mingle together; porticoes, colonnades and ornamental stone facades vie with verandahs of lavish cast-iron decoration. There are many superb buildings, the most notable being the post office, the railway station, the town hall, the stock exchange, the former Ballarat gaol, the Wesley Church, the George Hotel, Reids Coffee Palace, the Bailey Mansion, the Roman Catholic bishop's residence, Loreto Abbey and the art gallery. It is a city of many beautiful gardens, particularly the Botanical Gardens adjacent to Lake Wendouree, famous for the annual begonia display in March.

Without doubt Ballarat's major attraction is **Sovereign Hill**. This re-created goldmining township is a fascinating place for a day's outing to interest all the family. Begin your outing by visiting the excellent Voyage to Discovery orientation centre, near the main entrance.

Gold was discovered in Ballarat in 1851, and a visit to the Red Hill Gully Diggings at Sovereign Hill will show you something of the life of those early days. Your visit will not be complete without the chance to pan for 'colour'. A friendly digger will give you a lesson, but you must be sure to purchase your licence first or you may find yourself being arrested by the watchful trooper!

Main Street is lined with faithfully re-created shops and businesses of the 1851–1861 period. These are based on actual shops and businesses that were

Panning for gold at Sovereign Hill, Ballarat

operating in Ballarat at that time. Perhaps you will be tempted by the aroma of freshly-baked bread from the wood-fire brick oven of the Hope Bakery. Next door you may dress in topcoat or crinoline and be photographed in true Victorian pose. Across the road, mid-nineteenth-century printing-presses in the Ballarat *Times* office can be used to print your name on a WANTED poster, similar to that issued for Lalor and Black after the uprising at the Eureka Stockade in 1854.

Few can even pass the well-stocked grocery without a surge of nostalgia for days gone by. The tiny sweet shop nearby sells all manner of sweets made to Victorian recipes at Brown's confectionery factory, further up the street.

Those with larger appetites may wine and dine at the United States Hotel or enjoy a digger's lunch of soup, roast meat and apple pie at the New York Bakery. For some energetic relaxation, try your hand at ninepin bowling on the 40-metre-long alley in the Empire Bowling Saloon. The accommodation complex, Government Camp, provides comfortable and inexpensive lodging ranging from tents to self-contained units.

During school terms you will be enchanted to watch a 'class of 1856' at the Red Hill National School. Here children dress in period costume, learn from actual 1850s texts, and are totally involved in living the life of a mid-nineteenth-century goldfields child.

The towering poppet-head, the hiss of steam and the thunder of the stamper battery will draw you to the Sovereign Quartz Mine. Take a guided tour of the underground area; here you will see examples of early mining techniques and even some original workings of the 1880s.

As you wander through the streets you will meet costumed diggers and business-folk, and ladies in bell-shaped crinolines and bonnets. Stop and talk to them and you will learn more about life in the days of the 'rush'.

Sovereign Hill is open daily, except on Christmas Day. There are admission charges, and ample parking is available. Enquiries to the Marketing Department, Sovereign Hill Post Office, Ballarat 3350.

The Gold Museum, opposite Sovereign Hill, has a collection of nuggets, alluvial gold and coins, as well as a Eureka Exhibition outlining the Eureka rebellion.

Beyond Ballarat, on the Midland Highway is **Creswick**, a picturesque valley town with a wonderfully ornate town hall. The bluestone tower of St John's Church dominates the town's western hill and on the hilltop across the valley is a Tudor-style hospital building which is now a school of forestry.

To make a turn off the highway to **Clunes** is well worth while. Gold was first discovered here in July 1851, but it proved difficult to get supplies to this remote township, so the rush was limited and the later discoveries at Buninyong and Ballarat quickly diverted attention from the area. Of particular interest in Clunes are the rich verandahed facades in the shopping area of Fraser Street and the elegant architectural style of the banks, hotels, post office and town hall.

On the Western Highway, 133 kilometres north-west of Ballarat, past **Ararat** (where a gold rush began in 1857), is **Stawell**. Gold was discovered at the present site of Stawell in 1853; by 1857 there was a population of 30 000, and the township was proclaimed the following year. Goldmining continued in the area until 1920. Today visitors can recapture some of the atmosphere of the gold-rush era at the Mount Pleasant Diggings and Alluvial Gold Memorial.

North-east of Ballarat up the Midland Highway is **Daylesford**, another former goldmining town set in picturesque wooded hills around Wombat Hill Gardens and Lake Daylesford. The town has a number of churches in the Gothic Revival style and an imposing town hall, post office and school. On the hill are groves of rhododendrons, exotic trees and a lookout tower that provides a view of Mount Franklin (a perfectly preserved volcanic crater) and Mount Tarrengower. Several kilometres north of Daylesford are natural springs containing lime, iron, magnesia and other minerals. This is the famed Hepburn Spa, which attracted visitors in the nineteenth century for its medicinal properties. Bottling mineral water is still the town's main industry.

Further north on the road to Bendigo is **Castlemaine**, a larger town and one of the most picturesque in the region. The streetscape in the centre of the town has remained virtually unaltered since the early days, for the prosperity of the 1860s diminished and the town settled down to a quieter rural life. One of the most notable buildings is the Castlemaine Market, an unusual Palladian-inspired building which was restored in 1974 and which now contains a museum portraying the history of the town and the Mount Alexander goldfields. The town boasts some other fine buildings, including the great post office in Italianate style with a central clock tower, the former telegraph office, the mechanics' institute, the Imperial Hotel and the Commercial Banking Company building. High on a hill above the town are the stone and redbrick gaol and the obelisk built in 1862 to commemorate the ill-fated Burke and Wills expedition.

Nearby **Maldon** was declared a notable town by the National Trust in 1962. The winding streets are flanked by low buildings, with deep verandahs shading the bluestone pavements laid in 1866.

The city of **Bendigo** is the jewel of the region and is Victoria's most outstanding example of a boom town. Gothic- and classical-style buildings have been designed in vast proportions, richly ornamented and combined with the materials of the age, cast iron and cast cement.

The post office and law courts are among the most impressive high-Victorian public buildings in Australia. Opposite the post office is the Shamrock Hotel—a massive, verandahed structure that once boasted an electric bell to ring for service in each of its 100 rooms. Many of Bendigo's important buildings were designed by the German architect William Charles Vahland. His work included the Benevolent Asylum and Hospital, the school of mines, the mechanics' institute,

the town hall, the Masonic hall, the Capital Theatre, four banks and the handsome Alexandra fountain at Charing Cross, the centre of Bendigo.

Bendigo Art Gallery houses a large collection of 19th-century British and European artworks and decorative arts, which complements its outstanding collection of Australian paintings.

Central Deborah Goldmine was the last deep-reef goldmine in Bendigo. Sunk in 1909 and closed in 1954, it has been restored and is open for inspection. The mine is 411 metres deep with seventeen levels, and the visitor level at 61 metres has a 350-metre circuit illustrating the geological features of the Bendigo region and the machinery used in the gold-retrieval process. At ground level are the 21-metre poppet head, the engine room, installations and other exhibits, all of which can be inspected. The mine is also the point of departure for the 8-kilometre (1-hour) tour through Bendigo by the city's famous vintage talking trams, with their taped commentary on attractions and historic points of interest.

Sandhurst Town, off the Loddon Valley Highway, 12 kilometres from Bendigo, represents a typical country town of 1929 with all the glamour of the gold-rush days. Its attractions include the Fair Dinkum Eucalyptus Distillery, the Honey Pavilion and various fascinating shops. The Red Rattler train leaves the town regularly to travel through the Whipstick Forest to the Goldrush Gully diggings with its

entertaining street theatre involving colourful characters. In the third week in September every year, Sandhurst Town stages a re-enactment of Bendigo's gold-digger uprising of 1854, in which more than 80 actors replay the struggle against the injustice of the Gold Licence.

Australian Designer Travel, Bendigo, organise personal itineraries to include accommodation in homes, farms, retreats and cottages throughout the goldfields area. Bendigo Goldseeker Tours organise gold fossicking excursions and include instruction in the use of metal detectors.

The goldfields region can be enjoyed in three days or three weeks according to time and taste. Reasonably priced accommodation is available throughout the region. An excellent way to see the region is via the **Goldfields Tourist Route**, a 450-kilometre triangle road route linking Ballarat, Ararat, Stawell, Bendigo and Castlemaine. Free maps marking the route are available at the Victorian Information Centre, RACV offices and various tourist information centres throughout the goldfields.

More detailed information can be obtained also from the Bendigo Tourist Information Centre, 26 High St, Kangaroo Flat; (054) 47 7788 and Charing Cross, Bendigo; (054) 41 5244. **See also:** Individual town entries in A–Z listing. **Note** detailed map of Goldfields Region on page 220.

Conservatory Gardens, Bendigo

the surrounding pastoral and agricultural district. **Of interest:** Historic courthouse. Turn-of-century band rotunda. **In the area:** Mt Cole State Forest, part of Great Dividing Range, 16 km NW, via Raglan; peaceful natural area with camping grounds, ideal for bushwalks, picnics and observation of native flora and fauna. Lake Goldsmith, 14 km S of Beaufort. Steam Rally held 2 km E of lake in May and Nov. Hang-gliding and paragliding. **Tourist information:** Shire Offices, cnr Lawrence St and Main Rd; (053) 492 000. **Accommodation:** 3 hotels, 1 motel, 2 caravan/camping parks.
MAP REF. 220 H10, 227 M3

Beechworth   Pop. 3136
Once the centre of the great Ovens gold-mining region, Beechworth lies 24 km off the Ovens Hwy, between Wangaratta and Wodonga on 'The Kelly Way' (Old Sydney Rd). This is one of Victoria's best-preserved and most beautiful gold towns, magnificently sited in the foot-hills of the Alps. Its public buildings are of architectural merit and the whole town has been classified as historically import-ant by the National Trust. The rich allu-vial goldfield at Woolshed Creek was discovered by a local shepherd during the 1850s. A total of 1 121 918 ounces of gold was mined in 14 years. A story is told of Daniel Cameron, campaigning to represent the Ovens Valley community: he rode through the town at the head of a procession of miners from Woolshed, on a horse shod with golden shoes. Sceptics claim they were merely gilded, but the tale is an indication of what Beechworth was like during the boom, when its popu-lation was 42 000 and it boasted 61 hotels and a theatre at which international cele-brities performed. **Of interest:** Fine gov-ernment buildings built of local honey-coloured granite in the 1850s, all still in use; especially in Camp and Ford Sts. Daily historic town tour from Tourist Information Centre; bookings essential. In Albert Rd: Harness and Carriage Mu-seum, run by National Trust; Tanswell's Hotel, privately restored lacework build-ing; under Shire Offices, Ned Kelly's cell; and Beechworth Gaol (1859), still used as a prison. Bank of Victoria build-ing, cnr Camp and Ford Sts; Rock Ca-vern, gemstone collection. Historic former Bank of Australasia, Ford St; fine dining in elegant surroundings. Country Rustica and Buckland Gallery, Ford St. Beechworth Galleries in Camp St. Ro-

bert O'Hara Burke Memorial Museum, Loch St; relics of gold rush and group of 16 mini-shops depicting town's main street as it was more than 100 years ago. **In the area:** Golden Hills Trout Farm, 2 km S. Fletcher Dam, on Beechworth Forest Drive, 2½ km S towards Stanley; picnic facilities. Historic village of Stan-ley, 4 km S; in hills above Beechworth, among apple orchards, berry farms, nut plantations and tall forests. Kelly's lookout, at Woolshed Creek, about 4 km N. Waterfalls at Reids Creek, Woolshed and Clear Creek. Black Springs Bakery, National Trust property 5 km W; early goldfields bakery (no interior inspec-tion). On road north to Chiltern, at Beechworth Cemetery, Chinese burning towers and Chinese cemetery. At Chil-tern, 26 km N, 'Lake View', home of Henry Handel Richardson; restored and landscaped by National Trust, open daily. Beechworth Historic Park with Wool-shed Falls historic walk, Gorge Scenic Drive (5 km), and gold fossicking in limited areas. Lake Sambell; fishing, swimming, sailing, boating, canoeing. **Tourist information:** The Rock Cavern, cnr Ford and Camp Sts; (057) 28 1374. **Accommodation:** 2 hotels, 5 motels, 2 caravan/camping parks.
MAP REF. 233 N6, 234 A4

Benalla   Pop. 8334
This small city on the Hume Hwy is 40 km S of Wangaratta. Lake Benalla was created in the Broken River, which runs through the city, and there are recreation and picnic facilities there, with a pro-tected sanctuary area for birdlife. During the late 1870s Benalla was a focal point of the activities of the notorious Kelly Gang, who were eventually captured at nearby Glenrowan in 1880. **Of interest:** Botanical Gardens, Bridge St, includes splendid rose gardens. Benalla Art Gal-lery, Bridge St, on shores of lake; import-ant Ledger Collection of Australian paintings. Pots 'n' More in Mair St; paint-ings, pottery and craftwork. Costume and Pioneer Museum, also in Mair St; Ned Kelly's cummerbund on display. Three-dimensional ceramic mural, Mair St. Gliding Club of Victoria, on outskirts of town, at aerodrome. Also at aerodrome, hot-air ballooning. Rose Festival held Nov. **In the area:** Lake Mokoan, 11 km NE; offers swimming, boating, picnic and camping facilities. West of Midland Hwy about 4 km, Reef Hills State Park, 2030 ha of forest and wide variety of native

flora and fauna. Pleasant day trips to King Valley and spectacular Paradise Falls. Winton Motor Raceway, 10 km NE. **Tourist information:** Pots 'n' More, 14 Mair St; (057) 62 1749. **Accommoda-tion:** 3 hotels, 8 motels, 1 caravan/camp-ing park.
MAP REF. 222 A2, 235 K7

Bendigo   Pop. 57 427
This is one of Victoria's most famous goldmining towns. Sited at the junction of 5 highways, it is centrally located for trips to many of the other gold towns in the surrounding areas. Bendigo's history is indeed golden: the rush began here in 1851 and gold production continued for 100 years. The affluence of the period can still be seen today in many splendid public and commercial buildings. Built in 1897, the Shamrock Hotel has been restored to its original charm. **Of inter-est:** Many attractive lacework-veran-dahed buildings: Sacred Heart Cathedral, Wattle St, largest outside Melbourne, with a 92-m spire; Alexandra Fountain at Charing Cross; Renaissance-style Post Office (1887) and Law Courts (1896) in Pall Mall. Self-guide Heritage Walk. Bendigo Art Gallery (1890), View St. Central Deborah Mine, Violet St in work-ing order; vivid reminder of Bendigo's history; open daily. Vintage Talking Trams run daily from mine on 8-km city trip, including stop at Tram Depot Mu-seum; 30 vintage trams on display. Taped commentary gives information about points of interest. Golden Dragon Mu-seum, Bridge St; Chinese history of the goldfields, largest display of Chinese processional regalia in the world, includ-ing world's oldest imperial dragon 'Loong' and largest imperial dragon, 'Sun Loong', more than 300 m long. Bendigo's Easter Fair (first held 1871) features the Chinese dragon. Dudley House (1859), View St, classified by Nat-ional Trust; gracious old home in lovely gardens, now houses historical display. Lookout tower in Rosalind Park. Aus-tralia's largest National Swap Meet for vintage car and bike enthusiasts held Nov. **In the area:** Fortuna Villa mansion (1871), Chum St, 2 km S; open Sunday. Chinese Joss House at Emu Point, 1 km N; built by Chinese miners who worked diggings here; classified by Nat-ional Trust, open daily. At Myers Flat, 12 km NW: Sandhurst Town, re-creation of a colonial town; gold diggings, euca-lyptus distillery, antique vehicles and

working 2-ft-gauge railway. At Epsom, 6 km NE, Epsom Market held Sun. Hartland's Eucalyptus Factory and Historic Farm, Whipstick Forest, off Neilborough Rd, 12 km N; built in 1890 to process eucalyptus oil obtained from surrounding scrub. Bendigo Mohair Farm at Lockwood, 15 km SW of town; open daily with guided tours. All in Mandurang Valley, 8 km S: Adventure Park and Water Playland; pick-your-own berries, water sports, trout fishing, Thunder Cave rapid-river ride and picnicking; historic Chateau Dore winery; Orchid Nursery; Tannery Lane Pottery. Vineyards and wineries, many open for sales and tastings, include Chateau Le Amon winery, 10 km S; Balgownie Vineyard, 10 km W at Maiden Gully. Pratts Park Pottery, 29 km S, in Harcourt Valley, surrounded by apple and pear orchards. Lake Eppalock, 26 km SE of town; camping, fishing, water sports, picnics and barbecues. Horsedrawn caravans can be hired at Bridgewater on Loddon, 37 km NW. **Tourist information:** Charing Cross; (054) 41 5244; 26 High St, Kangaroo Flat; (054) 47 7788. **Accommodation:** 10 hotels, 25 motels, 9 caravan/camping parks. **See also:** The Golden Age; Wine Regions. MAP REF. 218, 221 Q2, 229 Q10, 232 C8

Birchip
Pop. 827

On the main rail link between Melbourne and Mildura, Birchip gets its water supply from the Wimmera–Mallee stock and domestic channel system. **Of interest:** In Cumming Ave: Big Mallee Bull; in old courthouse, Historical Society Museum, open on request. **In the area:** Junction of two major irrigation channels constructed in early 1900s, 1 km N of town. Sections of original Dog Fence, 20 km N, vermin-proof barrier constructed in 1883 between Murray River near Swan Hill and South Australian border. Tchum Lake, 8 km E, with facilities for motor boats; caravan park at lake has excellent facilities. Sites of historic interest within Shire are indicated by markers; descriptive brochure from Shire Offices, Main St. **Tourist information:** Birchip Motel, Sunraysia Hwy; (054) 92 2566. **Accommodation:** 2 hotels, 1 motel, 1 caravan/camping park. MAP REF. 126 F13, 229 K5

Boort
Pop. 801

A pleasant rural and holiday town on the shores of Lake Boort, with excellent sporting facilities. The lake is popular for water sports, has good picnic facilities and beaches, and offers trout and redfin fishing. There is prolific native birdlife in the area. **Tourist information:** Lake Boort Motel, opposite lake; (054) 55 2106. **Accommodation:** 1 motel, 1 caravan/camping park. MAP REF. 126 H13, 229 O6

Bright
Pop. 1881

In the heart of the beautiful Ovens Valley and at the foothills of the Victorian Alps, Bright is an attractive tourist centre and a base for winter sports enthusiasts. The town offers easy access to the resorts at Mt Hotham, Mt Buffalo and Falls Creek, and a number of ski-hire shops in the town stay open late during the winter season. The area is excellent for bushwalking and trout fishing, and is very photogenic, particularly in autumn. The discovery of gold was responsible for the town's beginnings. Tensions between white and Chinese miners led to the notorious Buckland Valley riots of 1857 in which the Chinese were driven from their claims with some brutality. The remains of the alluvial goldfields can still be seen about the area. There is a good variety of restaurants, counter meals, cafes and take-away food shops. **Of interest:** European trees in Bright display spectacular autumnal colours. Bright holds Spring and Autumn Festivals in Oct. and May respectively. In Main St: Gallery 90 and Country Collectables. Bright Art Gallery and Cultural Centre, Mountbatten Ave. Historical Museum, in old railway station, Station Ave. Lotsafun Amusement Park adjacent, entrance in Mill Rd. Ovens River runs through town; riverbank has picnic and camping spots; walk to Riverside Canyon. Excellent summer swimming in deep weir next to Memorial Park in Main St; coin-operated barbecues, children's playground and shallow pool. **In the area:** Pleasant walking tracks lead to Clearspot Lookout, from Bakers Gully Rd, and Huggins Lookout, from Deacon Ave. The Alpine Road south-east to Mt Hotham gives superb views of Mt Feathertop, the Razor Back and Mt Bogong. Wandiligong, a National-Trust-classified hamlet in a scenic valley, 6 km S, is linked to Bright by a walking and cycle track. At Harrietville, a tiny and tranquil township 25 km S of Bright, Pioneer Park open-air museum; 4 km N of town, two trout farms. Porepunkah, 6 km NW of Bright, at junction of Ovens and Buckland Rivers with convenient access to Mt Buffalo, has Boyntons of Bright Winery and Restaurant; open daily. Horseriding available. **Tourist information:** Delany Ave, opposite Centennial Park; (057) 55 2275, Sports Centre, Gavan St; (057) 55 1339. **Accommodation:** 2 hotel/motels, 9 motels, 7 caravan/camping parks. MAP REF. 223 L5, 233 P8, 234 B6

Broadford
Pop. 2215

A small town off the Hume Hwy near Mt Disappointment, the State Forest and Murchison Falls. Picnic facilities at Anderson's Gardens, at the entrance to the State Forest. **Of interest:** Display of old printing equipment in *Broadford Courier* building, High St. Barbecues and picnic facilities in park in town centre; also replica of drop-slab pioneer cottage. **In the area:** Turn-off 20 km E to Strath Creek for scenic drive through Valley of a Thousand Hills. At Kilmore, 14 km SW: fine old buildings, including Whitburgh Cottage (1857); cable tram rides in Hudson Park. **Tourist information:** Shire Offices, 113 High St; (057) 84 1204. **Accommodation:** 2 hotels, 1 motel. MAP REF. 211 K2, 232 F11

Buchan
Pop. 220

This small township, set in the heart of Gippsland mountain country north-east of Bairnsdale, is famous for its remarkable series of limestone caves. Tours of two main caves, Royal and Fairy are conducted daily. A park and a spring-fed swimming pool are located in the hills behind the caves. **Of interest:** Conorville Heritage Model Village, Main St; display of Australian building to 1900. **In the area:** Spectacular views from lookout over Little River Gorge, 70 km N on road to McKillops Bridge. Litte River Falls near Gorge. Suggan Buggan schoolhouse (1865), 64 km N. Cobberas–Tingaringy National Park, 10 km NW of Suggan Buggan; spectacular mountain scenery. Stonehenge Rockhounds Museum at Buchan South, 7 km SW. **Tourist information:** General Store, Main St; (051) 55 9202. **Accommodation:** 1 motel, 1 hotel, 2 caravan/camping parks. MAP REF. 119 B13, 225 R2, 234 H11

Camperdown
Pop. 3315

This south-western town on the Princes Hwy has the English-style charm of gracious buildings and avenues of elms. Over 50 buildings are of historical

Phillip Island

Situated at the entrance to Western Port, 120 kilometres south-east of Melbourne, Phillip Island (10 300 hectares) is a year-round destination for those who want to get away from it all.

Once over the bridge between **San Remo** and **Newhaven**, the visitor is greeted by wide open spaces of farming land with panoramic views of ocean and bay. Most of the native bush has been cleared, although there are remnant pockets of native vegetation.

The greatest attraction for visitors is the fascinating fairy penguins on Summerland Beach. The penguins spend the day out at sea, catching whitebait for their young. Each evening at sunset they return in small groups and waddle up the beach to their sand dune burrows. Visitors watch the parade under subdued floodlights from elevated stands and walkways. No flashlight photography is permitted. The Phillip Island Penguin Reserve is open daily. Enquiries (059) 56 8300; bookings for parade (059) 56 8691.

Seal Rocks at the south-west tip of the island is the home of colonies of fur seals. A ferry service from Cowes allows close-up views of the seals sunbathing on the rocks. Coin-operated telescopes give landlubbers a view of the seals from The Nobbies kiosk.

Take the road down to the surf beach at Cape Woolamai, a rugged granite headland. A 2-hour walk leads to the highest point on the island, from where there are breathtaking views of the coastline. The sand dunes all along the Cape are the home of many short-tailed shearwaters. Arriving from Siberia on their annual migration, the birds nest in the rookeries here in spring and summer. Koalas also make their home on this island and can be viewed at the Koala Conservation Centre.

Visit nearby historic Churchill Island, reached by bridge near Newhaven. A pamphlet available at the island shop outlines the Homestead Walk and there are several walking trails.

Everyone will enjoy hand-feeding the tame emus, kangaroos and wallabies at the Phillip Island Wildlife Park, which is set in 32 hectares of bushland. Other fauna to be seen there include wombats, venomous and non-venomous snakes, eagles and pelicans. Nearly 7 hectares is wetlands: ponds and waterways that are breeding grounds for rare and endangered birds.

Some unusual bird species make their homes in The Nits at **Rhyll**, a fishing resort on the northern side of the island. Pelicans, ibis, royal spoonbills, swans and gulls inhabit the swamplands there.

Also on the north coast is **Cowes**, the most popular summer resort on Phillip Island. Its unspoilt beaches are sheltered for safe swimming, yachting and other water sports.

For further information, ticket sales for penguins and other attractions, free map and visitors guide as well as interesting displays, contact the Phillip Island Information Centre, Phillip Island Rd, Newhaven; (059) 56 7447. **See also:** Individual town entries in A–Z listing. **Note** detailed map of Mornington Peninsula on page 212.

Fairy penguins

significance and can be viewed by following the Heritage Trail; brochure from Tourist Information Centre. The centre for a rich pastoral district, Camperdown is also noted for the fishing in the volcanic crater lakes in the area. **Of interest:** Clock Tower (1896), cnr Manifold and Pike Sts. Historical Society Museum in Manifold St. Buggy Museum, Ower St. Courthouse and Post Office, both in Manifold St. Elm Avenue Tearooms. **In the area:** Lookout at Mt Leura, 1 km W, extinct volcano next to the perfect cone shape of Mt Sugarloaf; views over numerous crater lakes and volcanoes north across plains to the Grampians. Lake Corangamite, salt lake 13 km E, is Victoria's largest. Excellent fishing lakes include Bullen Merri, 3 km E, and Purrumbete, 4 km SE; latter well stocked with Quinnat salmon amd has excellent water sports facilities, picnic spots and a caravan park. Cobden, 13 km S; peaceful dairying town. Timboon, 27 km further S; pretty timbered township also centred on dairying. Timboon Farmhouse Cheese, just south of the township; tastings and door sales. Old Timboon Railway Line Walk (10 km); 3–4 hours and requires 14-km car shuttle. Picturesque road leads 18 km S from Timboon to tiny seaside village of Port Campbell; good rock fishing and close to a spectacular stretch of scenery along Great Ocean Road. Adjacent, Port Campbell National Park; camping and caravan facilities. Otway Ranges Deer and Wildlife Park, 20 km E of Port Campbell. At Mt Noorat: Alan Marshall Memorial Walking Track off Glenormiston Rd, Noorat, 20 km NW; 3-km summit and return (1 hr) or crater-rim 1.5-km circuit (30 mins); perfect volcanic cone provides excellent views over Western District. **Tourist information:** Fragrant Cottage in Old Courthouse building, Manifold St; (055) 93 2288. **Accommodation:** 3 hotels, 3 motels, 1 caravan/ camping park. **See also:** The Western District.
MAP REF. 215 C5, 227 L8

Cann River   Pop. 336
A popular stop for Sydney–Melbourne motorists using the Princes Hwy. Excellent fishing and bushwalking in the rugged hinterland. **Of interest:** Croajingolong National Park, main access 50 km S; stretches from Sydenham Inlet to the NSW border, incorporating the Captain James Cook Lighthouse Reserve at Point Hicks, Wingan, Timboon and

Mallacoota Inlets. **Tourist information:** Conservation and Environment Information Centre, Princes Hwy; (051) 58 6351. **Accommodation:** 1 hotel, 3 motels, 1 caravan/camping park.
MAP REF. 119 E13, 235 M11

Casterton   Pop. 1808
Given the Roman name meaning 'walled city' because of lush hills surrounding the valley, Casterton is on the Glenelg Hwy, 42 km E of the South Australian border. The Glenelg River runs through the town and provides excellent fishing and mineral and gem fossicking along its banks near the town as well as water-skiing at Nelson, some 70 km S. Launch trips can be taken at Nelson to the river's mouth, on the coast at Discovery Bay. **Of interest:** Casterton Historical Museum in old Railway Buildings, cnr Jackson and Clarke Sts; open by appt. Bryan Park, Henty St; children's playground. David Geschke Fine Porcelain Gallery, Casterton Racecourse Rd. Alma and Judith Zaadstra Fine Art Gallery, Henty St. Excellent sporting facilities, swimming pool and trail-bike riding facilities at Long Lead Swamp, Penola Rd. Tourist Information Centre has displays of local art and craft, and picnic/barbecue facilities. Motorcycle Hill climb held March. Agricultural Show in Nov. **In the area:** Angling Club Reserve at Roseneath, 24 km NW; picnic and camping facilities. Warrock Homestead (1843), classified by National Trust, 26 km NE; unique collection of buildings, open for inspection. Area around Casterton is mainly grazing land with rolling hills and areas of natural forest with excellent bushwalks and a variety of fauna and flora. Baileys Rocks, 50 km N; giant granite boulders of a unique green colour. Other interesting geological formations at the Hummocks, 12 km NE, and Bahgalah Bluff, 20 km SW. Camel treks. **Tourist information:** Shiels Tce; (055) 81 2070. **Accommodation:** 2 hotel/motels, 1 motel, 1 caravan/camping park. **See also:** The Western District.
MAP REF. 226 D4

Castlemaine   Pop. 6812
Along with Kyneton and Maldon, Castlemaine epitomises the goldmining towns of north-western Victoria. A very attractive and interesting town, it is built on low hills at the foot of Mt Alexander, on the Calder Hwy, 119 km from Melbourne. During the 1850s and 1860s

enormous quantities of gold were found in its surface fields. This gold boom saw Castlemaine grow rapidly and many of the fine old buildings that remain today were built during this period. **Of interest:** Town Market (1862), Mostyn St, classical-Roman style building; National-Trust-operated and open weekends, houses audiovisual displays, photographic collection, relics of district. Other splendid buildings: Midland and Imperial hotels, Templeton and Lyttleton Sts respectively; iron lacework verandahs. Courthouse, town hall and library, art gallery and museum; all in Lyttleton St. Buda, Urquhart St, home from late 1850s of silversmith and jeweller Ernest Leviny and his family; beautifully preserved gardens of the era, delightful house. Botanic Gardens, Parker St. Castlemaine State Festival incorporates theatre, opera, children's shows, art, craft and music for all, early Nov. (Melbourne Cup week), even-numbered years; in odd-numbered years Spring Garden Festival is held. **In the area:** Excellent restaurants, antique shops, b & b accommodation. Pottery at Newstead, 16 km NW. Burnett Gallery and Garden on Burnett Road in North Castlemaine; open weekends. At Harcourt, 10 km N: Skydances, walk-through butterfly house; good fishing and picnic spots; Harcourt Valley Estate and Mt Alexander wineries. Nearby on Mt Alexander, koala reserve. Wattle Gully goldmine at Chewton, 4 km SE. Duke of Cornwall mine buildings at Fryerstown, 10 km SE. Chinese cemetery and mineral springs at Vaughan, 12 km SE. Big Tree at Guildford, 11 km SW. **Tourist information:** Duke St; (054) 72 2480. **Accommodation:** 5 hotels, 3 motels, 2 caravan/camping parks. **See also:** The Golden Age.
MAP REF. 210 F1, 221 P5, 227 Q1, 229 Q12, 232 C10

Charlton   Pop. 1182
A supply centre for a rich wheat district, Charlton is set on the banks of the Avoca River, at the intersection of the Calder and Borung Hwys in north-central Victoria. **Of interest:** Fishing in Avoca River. Walking track along river, about 2 km one way, from town to weir. **In the area:** Wooroonook Lake, 12 km W, for swimming and boating. Bish Deer Farm, further 18 km W. Wychitella State Forest, 27 km E, for interesting native flora and fauna, including the lowan (mallee fowl). **Tourist information:** Shire Offices,

High St; (054) 91 1755. **Accommodation:** 2 hotels, 2 motels, 1 caravan/camping park.
MAP REF. 229 M7

Chiltern
Pop. 1157

Halfway between Wangaratta and Wodonga, Chiltern is 1 km off the Hume Hwy. It was once a goldmining boom town with 14 suburbs. Many of its attractive buildings have been classified by the National Trust; Historic Walk leaflet available. **Of interest:** Athenaeum Museum, Conness St (1866); contains Goldfields Library collection. The Pharmacy, Conness St, (1868); chemist shop with all original features. Stephen's Motor Museum, Conness St; collection of motoring memorabilia. *Federal Standard* newspaper office, Main St; dating from gold-mining era (1860-61) and classified by National Trust; open by appt for groups. Grape Vine Gallery, formerly Grape Vine Hotel, cnr Conness and Main Sts; boasts a vast grape vine. Picnic spots with barbecues at Lake Anderson, access Main St. Walking track from lakeshore over bridge to 'Lake View', Victoria St, home of well-known author Henry Handel Richardson, classified by National Trust; open weekends, public and school holidays. Street bazaar and market in March. Annual Art Show held Oct. **In the area:** Chiltern State Park surrounds town; historic drive, bushwalking, nature observation and picnicking. Magenta open-cut mine, 2 km E. Black Dog Creek Pottery, 3 km NW on Chiltern Valley Rd. Pioneer Cemetery, 2 km SW. **Tourist information:** Shire Offices, Main St; (057) 26 1206. **Accommodation:** 1 hotel, 1 motel, 1 caravan/camping park. **See also:** Wine Regions.
MAP REF. 127 O13, 233 N5

Clunes
Pop. 846

The first reported gold find in the State was made at Clunes on 7 July 1851 when James Esmond announced his discovery of 'pay dirt'. The town, some 40 km N of Ballarat, has several sandstone buildings classified by the National Trust and the verandahed elegance of Fraser St is worth noting. Surrounding the town are a number of rounded hills (extinct volcanoes) and a good view of them can be obtained about 3 km S, on the road to Ballarat. **Of interest:** Old Post Office (1873), cnr Bailey and Service Sts; houses second-hand book store. Town hall and courthouse (1870), Baily St. Clunes, Fraser St. Bottle Museum, Baily St; in former Clunes State School. Keebles of Clunes guest house, Baily St. Queens Park, maintained as garden, established over 100 years ago on banks of Creswick Creek; picnic/barbecue facilities, playground. Butter Factory Gallery, Cameron St; sculpture and art gallery. Jindalee Arts and Crafts Centre, Talbot Rd; handmade pottery. The Weavery, Fraser St; handwoven fabrics. **In the area:** Mt Beckworth, 8 km W; scenic reserve, variety of birds and native flora and fauna, picnic/barbecue facilities. Clunes Homestead Furniture, 1 km N on Talbot Rd. Possum Road Gallery, 20 km N; sculpture and paintings, major and local artists. Talbot, 18 km NW; historic town featuring many 1860–1870 buildings, particularly in Camp St and Scandinavian Cres. Talbot Arts and Historical Museum, Camp St; in former Primitive Methodist Church (1870). Bull and Mouth restaurant; bluestone building (1860s) housed former hotel of same name. **Tourist information:** (053) 45 3020, or Clunes Museum, Fraser St; (053) 45 3592. **Accommodation:** 1 hotel, 1 motel, 1 caravan/camping park.

See also: The Golden Age.
MAP REF. 210 C2, 221 L8, 227 O2, 229 O13, 232 A12

Cobram
Pop. 3797

Magnificent wide sandy beaches are a feature of the stretch of the Murray River at Cobram, so picnicking and water sports can be enjoyed. This is fruit-growing country and Cobram is well known for its 'Peaches and Cream' Festival held Australia Day weekend every odd-numbered year. **Of interest:** Rotary dairy, 200 cows, on outskirts of town; open at milking time, 3–4 daily. Houseboats for hire. **In the area:** Tyrrell's Heritage Farm Winery, on Murray Valley Hwy, 5 km W; 116-m woodcarving depicting scenes of early River Murray life. Binghi Boomerang Factory and Kramner Cellars at Barooga, 4 km NE. Spikes and Blooms cactus farm and Coonanga Homestead at Strathmerton, 16 km W. Monichino Wineries, 15 km S towards Numurkah. Matata Deer Farm on Tocumwal road, 5 km NW of Cobram. Sportavia Soaring Centre, at Tocumwal airport, 20 km NW. **Tourist information:** The Old Grain Shed, cnr Station St and Punt Rd; (058) 72 2132. **Accommodation:** 2 hotels, 5 motels, 4 caravan/camping parks. **See also:** The Mighty Murray.
MAP REF. 127 M13, 232 I3

Cohuna
Pop. 2071

Between Kerang and Echuca on the Murray Valley Hwy, Cohuna is beside Gunbower Island, formed by the Murray on the far side and Gunbower Creek just across the highway from the town. This island is covered in red gum and box forest, which provides a home for abundant waterfowl and other birdlife, as well as kangaroos and emus. The central zone of the forest is a sanctuary. The forest is

Cattle on the move, Cobram

National Parks

Coastal scene, Otway National Park

Although it is Australia's smallest mainland State, Victoria houses over 100 national, state, wilderness and regional parks; among them there will be something for everyone in every season.

Victoria's parks protect the wide range of the State's land and vegetation types: from alps, open grasslands and desert mallee, to rainforests, tall forests, coasts, volcanic plains and heathlands. Spring and summer are the best seasons to visit, when wildflowers bloom in natural surroundings and sun lovers can head for parks along the coast to swim, surf, canoe, boat or fish. Autumn, with its mild weather, beckons the bushwalker, and winter means skiing at alpine parks.

The 646 000 hectare **Alpine National Park**, created in December 1989, is the State's largest national park. Stretching along the Great Dividing Range, the park links with the Kosciusko National Park in New South Wales and its neighbour Namadgi National Park in the Australian Capital Territory. The park protects the habitats of a variety of flora and fauna, including the rare mountain pygmy possum (the world's only exclusively alpine marsupial). The Alps are renowned for their sublime landscapes, features characterised by Mount Bogong and Mount Feathertop (Victoria's highest mountains) and the unique Bogong High Plains. During spring and summer the high plains are carpeted with wildflowers; more than 1100 native plant species are found in the park, including 12 found nowhere else in the world. The park is ideal for bushwalking, horseriding and cross-country skiing. In the summer months most roads provide easy access for conventional vehicles, allowing a range of scenic drives with short walks to lookouts and other points of interest. Some huts in the park are being restored for the use of walkers.

Yanga-nyawi (Murray Sunset) National Park in the north-west, is the State's most recent, and, at 633 000 hectares, the second largest national park. It contains a diversity of semi-arid environments from riverine floodplains to heathlands, salt lakes and woodlands, which support a tremendous variety of wildlife, particularly birdlife. This park is best avoided in the heat of summer. **Wyperfeld National Park** nearby, also contains hundreds of species of plants and birdlife and is also best avoided in the high heat of summer. It's a great park to visit in the winter and spring in good rainfall years for wildflower displays, and also in autumn for crisp, clear days—perfect for bushwalking and birdwatching.

Another park in the north west of the State is the smaller **Hattah-Kulkyne National Park**. Typically, summers here are long, hot and dry: rainfall is usually under 300 mm per year. Both plants and animals of this area have evolved strategies for avoiding or tolerating heat and dryness. Some animals burrow and others just rest during the heat of the day and feed and drink early and late; while some birds catch thermals to cooler air. After rainfall and flooding from the Murray River, the serenely beautiful Hattah Lakes sytem transforms the park into a bird haven and a wonderful wildflower landscape.

The **Grampians National Park** is the State's third largest. Its 167 000 hectares comprise marvellous scenery, wildlife and tourist facilities. The park is famous for its rugged sandstone ranges, waterfalls, wildflowers, wide variety of birds and mammals, as well as its Aboriginal rock art sites. The peaks rise to heights of over 1000 metres and form the western edge of the Great Dividing Range. The Grampians is no doubt best seen by foot and there are many interesting walking tracks, such as the easy graded, well marked Wonderland Track, through to the more challenging walks across the Major Mitchell Plateau. Those with limited time or who don't want to walk are not left out of the feeling of spaciousness and grandeur, since many scenic drives are available on good roads.

The main thing most visitors to the **Little Desert National Park** discover is that it is neither little nor a desert. It is best known for its amazing displays of wildflowers in spring; more than 600 species of flowering plants are found here, including more than 40 ground orchids. Another special thing about the Little Desert is that it is the home of the mallee fowl. These birds build mounds for eggs that can be as much as 5 metres in diameter and 1.5 metres high.

Several parks contain rock formations of great geological interest. At **Mount Eccles**, an extinct volcano in south-west Victoria, a lava canal, lava cave and the formation called the Stony Rises are exceptional features, while the crater contains the tranquil Lake Surprise.

More well-known and unusual rock structures are found at **Port Campbell National Park**: The Twelve Apostles, The Arch and Loch Ard Gorge are majestic formations sculpted out of soft limestone cliffs by the restless sea.

Obviously it is the spectacular coastal scenery that makes this park so popular. However, this is an interesting linear park for birds, with around 100 species being recorded. It was a popular place with Aboriginal people too if the number of shell middens along the coast is an indication. And it is especially notorious for being part of the shipwreck coast.

Closer to Melbourne are the beautiful lush tree fern gullies and towering mountain ash forests of the **Otway National Park** and the special **Melba Gully State Park** to the north-west of the national park near Lavers Hill. Because of the treacherous nature of the waters, a lighthouse was the first piece of 'civilisation', opened in 1848 after two years in the building. Activities to be enjoyed include sightseeing all year (even in winter storms), while camping, surfing, fishing and walking are most enjoyed in spring and summer. There are guided walks in summer to see the glow-worms at Melba Gully.

Eastern Victoria's mild and fairly wet climate, combined with rich soils, has produced vast areas of dense forest, particularly in the uplands. These are especially attractive to bushwalkers and campers, who will find here a wide range of trees—mainly eucalypts, but also native pines, banksias and paperbarks. In summer, many bushwalkers prefer to explore a coastal park; **Wilsons Promontory National Park** is the best known and one of the most popular in Gippsland. The Prom, as it is known, really does have something for everyone. There is the concentration of amenities and accommodation, including camping and caravan sites, at Tidal River, as well as the visitor information centre and park office. Leaflets for 80 km of walking tracks are available here, and visitors should enquire about the lighthouse walk. Other natural attractions include secluded bays and magnificent stretches of beaches, granite outcrops, and wildflowers that begin blooming in late winter and keep spring colourful. In summer there is the highest usage of everything, with campsites available only by ballot!

At **Organ Pipes National Park**, only 20 km north-west of Melbourne, there are more interesting rock formations: a series of hexagonal basalt columns rising more than 20 metres above Jacksons Creek.

These 'organ pipes' were formed when lava cooled in an ancient river bed. While this is the best known feature of the small, 85-hectare park, it is also excellent for picnics, walks and bird-observing. Another favourite haunt of bushwalkers 50 km north-east of Melbourne is **Kinglake National Park**, where wooded valleys, fern gullies and timbered ridges provide a perfect setting for two breathtakingly beautiful waterfalls, Masons and Wombelano Falls. From a lookout, visitors can take in a panoramic view of the Yarra Valley, Port Phillip Bay and the You Yangs Range.

Just 35 kilometres east of Melbourne is the green wonderland of the 1900-hectare **Dandenong Ranges National Park**. This park includes pockets of rainforest in which huge fronds of ferns form a canopy overhead, screening the sun and creating a cool, moist environment in which mosses, delicate ferns and flowers, including over thirty species of orchids, all thrive. There are more than 20 species of native animals, including echidnas, platypuses, ringtail possums and sugar gliders, in the park; kookaburras, rosellas and cockatoos often visit picnic areas. The spectacular rufous fantail can be seen in the summer months. There are over 100 species of birds, but make sure you identify them by sight and not only by sound, because the lyrebird can mimic their calls.

Point Nepean National Park is probably the most interesting park close to Melbourne, mainly because for more than 100 years it has been out of bounds to most people. It has associations with early settlement, shipping, quarantine and defence. As one of Victoria's major bicentennial projects, an information centre, walking tracks, displays and other facilities were provided during 1988–9. Today the total area of the park, including former Cape Schanck Coastal Park, is 2200 hectares.

To prevent overcrowding and damage

to the environment, no more than 600 people are permitted in the Point Nepean area at one time; so bookings for day visits (with a park-use fee) are required, especially during summer. Vehicles are not permitted beyond the orientation centre, so walking or taking the transporter are the ways to get around. Highlights of the park are Fort Nepean itself, the cemetery with burials dating from the 1850s, and the Cheviot Hill walk.

Canoeists will find excitement shooting the rapids or exploring the gorge of **Snowy River National Park** or **Mitchell River National Park**, while bushwalkers can hike through forests of native pine, alpine ash, messmate and shining gum.

Some of the most attractive coastal scenery close to any major regional centre can be found in and around **The Lakes National Park**. The park is surrounded by the waters of the Gippsland Lakes, ideal for sailing and boating. The 2390 hectares is based on Sperm Whale Head and harbours a large population of kangaroos and more than 140 bird species. Camping, picnicking and an excellent network of walking tracks provide distractions for those who are land-based.

Croajingolong National Park has 87 500 hectares of coastline and hinterland stretching from Sydenham Inlet to the New South Wales border. The area contains remote rainforest, woodland, ocean beaches, rocky promontories, inlets and coves. Several rare species of wildlife can be found here, such as the smoky mouse and the ground parrot, and an array of spring wildflowers. There is a wide range of activities for visitors at Croajingolong, with a resort centre at Mallacoota and other towns along the Princes Highway offering accommodation and fine food.

For more information, contact the Department of Conservation and Natural Resources at 240 Victoria Pde, East Melbourne; (03) 412 4011.

Tidal River, Wilsons Promontory National Park

subject to flooding and a large part of the island has breeding rookeries during the flood periods. Picnic/barbecue facilities can be found on the island, and forest tracks give access for driving and riding. Maps are available from the Forests Officer or from stores in Cohuna. **Of interest:** Two-hr cruises in the *Wetlander*, along Gunbower Creek. Cohuna swimming pool with 45-m waterslide; open daily from November to Easter. **In the area:** Box Bridge, at Kow Swamp, 23 km S; in sanctuary, picnic spots and good fishing. Mount Hope (110 m), about 28 km S; easy rock climbing, good views from summit, beautiful wildflowers in spring, picnic facilities. Craft Cottage, 4 km SE; antiques, nursery, gifts, tearoom. Torrumbarry Lock, 40 km SE; during winter, entire weir structure is removed from the river; in summer, water-skiing above the weir. Two potteries open to the public. **Tourist information:** Rotunda, Main St. **Accommodation:** 1 hotel/motel, 1 caravan/camping park.
MAP REF. 127 J12, 229 Q4, 232 B2

Colac   Pop. 10 241
Colac is situated on the eastern edge of the volcanic plain that covers much of the Western District of Victoria. It is the centre of a prosperous, closely settled agricultural area and is sited on the shores of Lake Colac, which has good fishing and a variety of water sports. **Of interest:** Historical Centre, Gellibrand St; open Thurs., Fri., Sun. 2–4. Sculpture Park on Princes Hwy; permanent and special exhibitions. Historic homes, not open to the public: Balnagowan in Balnagowan Ave; The Parsonage, 81 Wallace St; The Elms, 16 Gellibrand St. Self-guide town walk and full-day mountain car-tour available. Botanic Gardens (18 ha), Queen St; picnic/barbecue facilities. Barongarook Creek; walking track to sculpture park, also birdwatcher's haven. Annual Kana Festival in March. **In the area:** Alvie Red Rock Lookout, 22 km N, from which 30 of the surrounding volcanic lakes can be seen, including Lake Corangamite, Victoria's largest saltwater lake. Gellibrand Pottery, 10 km S; open daily for sales; cottage accommodation. Barongavale Winery, 15 km S; cellar-door sales and berry fruits; (052) 33 8324 for opening times. The beautiful Otway Ranges lie about 30 km S. Winding roads pass through them, revealing lush mountain scenery, and lead down to the coast. Floating Island Reserve, 17 km W;

lagoon with islands that change position. Birregurra, about 20 km E, has interesting old buildings. **Tourist information:** Cnr Murray and Queen Sts; (052) 31 3730. **Accommodation:** 1 hotel, 5 motels, 3 caravan/camping parks.
MAP REF. 210 A10, 215 F7, 227 N9

Coleraine   Pop. 1089
Situated in the attractive Wannon River valley, 35 km W of Hamilton, the Coleraine area was first settled by the Henty and Whyte brothers in 1838 for pastoral grazing. The primary products are fine-wool sheep and beef cattle. **In the area:** The Wannon Falls, 14 km SE, and Nigretta Falls, 24 km SE. Point's Reserve, lookout on western edge of town; unique planting of over 700 species of native trees and shrubs. Historic homesteads include Warrock Homestead (1843), classified by National Trust, with some 30 buildings to explore, 20 km NW towards Casterton; and Glendinning Homestead, near Balmoral, 50 km N, with a wildlife sanctuary and farm holiday accommodation. Rocklands Reservoir, 12 km E of Balmoral; excellent fishing and boating, caravan park nearby. Black Range State Park, northern shores of reservoir, has walking tracks and picnic areas. Gardens of 'Nareen', property of Malcolm and Tamie Fraser, 31 km NW, are open weekdays by appt, (055) 79 0244, and through Victoria's Open Garden Scheme (closed Christmas, Easter and May–Aug). **Tourist information:** Cobb & Co. Cafe, 75 Whyte St; (055) 75 2386. **Accommodation:** 2 hotels, 1 caravan/camping park. **See also:** The Western District.
MAP REF. 226 E4

Corryong   Pop. 1226
Situated in alpine country, Corryong is at the gateway to the Snowy Mountains. The district offers superb mountain scenery and excellent trout fishing. The Murray near Corryong is a brisk and gurgling stream running through forested hills. **Of interest:** Jack Riley, reputedly 'The Man from Snowy River', came from these parts and his grave is in Corryong cemetery. The Man from Snowy River Folk Museum, Hanson St; antique ski collection, replica of Riley's original shack. High Country Festival in March. Nariel Creek Folk Music Festival in late Dec. **In the area:** Playles Hill Lookout, 1 km SE of town. Cudgewa Bluff Falls area, 27 km NW of Corryong in Burrowa–

Pine Mountain National Park; excellent scenery and bushwalking tracks. At Upper Nariel, 43 km S; Upper Murray Fish Farm and Upper Murray Historical Society. Trout fishing at Tintaldra, 23 km N. Canoeing and mountain-bike excursions from Walwa, 47 km NW. Khancoban, 27 km E; horse-trekking and whitewater rafting. Scenic drive west from Corryong. Towong, 12 km NE; lookout with views over Kosciusko National Park. Mt Mittamite and Emberys Lookout, 10 km N, and Sassafras Gap, 66 km S; scenic views. **Tourist information:** Corryong Newsagency, 43–49 Hanson St; (060) 76 1381; or Mt Mittamite Caravan Park, Tallangatta Rd; (060) 76 1152. **Accommodation:** 2 hotel/motels, 2 motels, 2 caravan/camping parks.
MAP REF. 119 A8, 234 F3

Cowes   Pop. 2658
This is the main town on Phillip Island, a popular resort area in Western Port linked to the mainland by a bridge at San Remo. Cowes is on the northern side of the island and is the centre for hotel and motel accommodation. It has pleasant beaches, safe for children, and the jetty is popular for fishing and swimming. The town has a number of art and craft shops, an amusement centre and a variety of restaurants. **Of interest:** Down Under Clock Display, Findlay St. **In the area:** Summerland Beach, on southern shore, about 13 km SW; famous for its nightly penguin parade. Colonies of fur seals can be seen year-round on Seal Rocks, off southern shores, and short-tailed shearwaters Oct.–April. Mini Europe, Ventnor Rd; display of 200 miniature European buildings. Australian Dairy Centre at Newhaven, 16 km SE; museum and cheese factory. Phillip Island Wildlife Park, Main Tourist Rd; koalas, wombats, kangaroos in a natural environment. Churchill Island, 2 km from Newhaven; historic homestead and walking tracks. **Tourist information:** Phillip Island Rd, Newhaven; (059) 56 7447 (includes tickets for Phillip Island attractions). **Accommodation:** 17 motels, 11 caravan/camping parks. **See also:** Phillip Island.
MAP REF. 211 L12, 213 O11, 224 D8

Creswick   Pop. 2387
This picturesque township, 18 km N of Ballarat, nestles at the foot of the State Forest. One of the richest alluvial goldfields in the world was discovered here.

Convent Gallery, Daylesford

Of interest: Mullock heaps on Lawrence Rd. Gold panning. Surrounding volcanic bushland and forest areas attract field naturalists and bushwalking enthusiasts. Creswick Historical Museum, Albert St; collection of early history of area. Gold Battery, Battery Cres. Local cemetery, Clunes Rd; early miners' graves and a Chinese section. Koala Park and St Georges Lake, both in Melbourne Rd; picnic facilities. Olympic pool at Calambeen Park, Cushing St. **In the area:** World of Dinosaurs, 1.5 km E off Midland Hwy; life-size models in bushland setting. Creswick Forest Nursery, 1 km E. Tumblers Green Nursery, 1 km W. At Smeaton, 16 km N: Smeaton House (1850s); Anderson's Mill (1860s); and Tuki Trout Farm. **Tourist information:** Shire Office, cnr Raglan and Cambridge Sts; (053) 45 2000. **Accommodation:** 1 motel, 1 caravan/camping park. **See also:** The Golden Age.
MAP REF. 210 C3, 221 M10, 227 O3, 232 A13

Daylesford   Pop. 3347

Daylesford and Hepburn Springs, 5 km N, are popular holiday centres, set in attractive hill country. They are both spa towns, with 65 documented mineral springs, many with hand pumps. Hepburn Springs Spa Complex within the Mineral Springs Reserve, Main Rd, offers public and private baths, floatation tanks, massage and a sauna; open daily. Daylesford rambles up the side of Wombat Hill, at the top of which are the Botanical Gardens in Central Springs Rd, with a lookout tower from which there are commanding views in all directions.

Convent Gallery, in former girls' school, Daly St; seven galleries, meals; open daily. Alpha Hall Galleria, in former movie house, Vincent St; closed Tues.– Wed. **Of interest:** Jubilee Lake, Lake Rd; Daylesford Lake, Leggatt St; and Central Springs Spa Reserve, Central Springs Rd, for picnicking. Historical museum in former School of Mines, Vincent St. Market near railway station, Sun. During market, Central Highlands Tourist Railway runs rail-motor services between Daylesford and Musk on 1st and 3rd Sundays and ganger's trolleys operate to Wombat Forest on alternate Sundays. **In the area:** Breakneck Gorge, 5 km N. Sailors Falls, 10 km S. Mt Franklin, an extinct volcano, 13 km N. Trentham Falls, 15 km N. Bin Billa Winery, 6 km S; open daily. Farm holidays available at Truro Dairy Farm, Franklinford, 15 km N, Oldeborg Family Farm and Holcombe Homestead near Glenlyon, 12 km NE. Yandoit, a town of Swiss–Italian heritage, 18 km NW of Daylesford: Jajarawong Holiday Park offers bushwalking, water sports and wildlife. Horseriding at Boomerang Holiday Ranch, 2 km SW. **Tourist information:** Spa Centre Variety Store, 49 Vincent St; (053) 48 3707. **Accommodation:** 8 hotels, 3 motels, 3 caravan/camping parks. **See also:** The Golden Age.
MAP REF. 210 E2, 221 P9, 227 Q2, 229 Q13, 232 B12

Derrinallum   Pop. 280

Small rural town servicing the local pastoral farming community and surrounded by volcanic plains typical of the Western District of Victoria. **In the area:** Mt Elephant, 2 km SW; scoria cone of volcanic origin rising high above surrounding plains. Deep Lake, 5 km NW; fishing and water sports. Significant dry-stone walls, immediately west of town. Elephant Bridge Hotel, at Darlington, 15 km W; 2-storey bluestone building classified by National Trust. Lake Tooliorook, 6 km SE; fishing and swimming. Rockbank Farmstay; (055) 97 6626, 5 km SW; splendid views of Mt Elephant. **Accommodation:** 1 hotel/motel.
MAP REF. 215 C2, 227 L6

Dimboola   Pop. 1581

This is a peaceful town on the tree-lined Wimmera River, 35 km NW of Horsham. **Of interest:** Rowing regatta in Nov. **In the area:** Little Desert National Park, 6 km N; self-guide walks include Pomponderoo Hill Nature Walk (1 km) from Horseshoe Bend picnic and camping area at river's edge. Ebenezer Mission Station (founded 1858), on Jeparit Rd, 15 km N; restored by National Trust. At Kiata, 26 km W, mallee fowl can be seen in Lowan Sanctuary all year. Pink Lake, a coloured salt lake, 9 km NW. Wail, 11 km S, has well-stocked forest nursery run by Department of Conservation and Natural Resources. **Tourist information:** Horsham Information Centre, 20 O'Callaghan's Pde, Horsham; (053) 82 1832. **Accommodation:** 2 hotels, 1 motel, 1 caravan/camping park. **See also:** The Wimmera.
MAP REF. 228 G8

Donald   Pop. 1505

At the junction of the Sunraysia and Borung Hwys, Donald is situated on the

Richardson River and in a Wimmera district renowned for its fine wheat, sheep and fat lambs. **Of interest:** Historic police station (1874), Wood St. Railway steam engine in Steam Loco Park, cnr Hammill and Walker Sts. Agricultural museum in Hammill St. Historic water pump by lake in caravan park. Bullocks Head Lookout, Byrne St; large, unusual growth on box tree beside Richardson River. **In the area:** Quail-shooting in season. Lake Buloke, 10 km N; wetlands area, duck-shooting in season. Mt Jeffcott, 20 km N; flora and fauna, views of Lake Buloke. Watchem Lake, 30 km N; fishing, water sports, picnic/barbecue facilities. **Tourist information:** Shire Offices, McCulloch St; (054) 97 1300. **Accommodation:** 2 hotels, 2 motels, 1 caravan/camping park.
MAP REF. 229 K7

Drouin   Pop. 4455
Drouin is on the Princes Hwy not far from Warragul and the Latrobe Valley. A large milk products factory is a major industry. **In the area:** Camping and picnic spots on Tarago River at Glen Cromie, 8 km N, and Picnic Point on the Princes Hwy, 10 km W. At Nayook, 38 km N: Nayook Fruit and Berry Farm, and Country Farm Perennials Nursery and Gardens. At Drouin West, 3 km W: Fruit and Berry Farm and Hilston Lodge Deer Farm. At Neerim South, 31 km N: Gippsland Blue Cheese farm factory, and picnic/barbecue area at Tarago Reservoir; Woodlyn Park offers horseriding into adjacent State forest. Alpine Trout Farm at Noojee, 40 km N. Jindivick Smokehouse (handmade smallgoods) and Hirschberg Deer Farm at Jindivick, 19 km N. Gumbaya Park, 25 km W on Princes Hwy; wildlife and family fun park. The Farm Shed, Princes Hwy, Tynong, 22 km W; farm animal and agricultural displays, including shearing, sheepdog workouts and milking; open daily. Many of the food attractions are featured on the Gourmet Deli Trail; brochure available locally and at the Victorian Information Centre, 230 Collins St, Melbourne; (03) 790 3333. **Tourist information:** Hilston Lodge Deer Farm, Jackson's Track; (056) 28 7526. **Accommodation:** 2 hotels, 2 motels, 3 caravan/camping parks.
MAP REF. 211 P9, 224 G6

Drysdale   Pop. 1166
This is primarily a service centre for the local farming community on the Bellarine Peninsula. **Of interest:** Old Courthouse Museum and Drysdale Community Crafts, both in High St. Community Market, Recreation Reserve, Duke St; every 3rd Sunday, Sept.–April. **In the area:** Lake Lorne picnic area, 1 km SW; nearby Bellarine Peninsula Railway offers steam-train rides between Drysdale and Queenscliff; locomotives and carriages dating back to the 1870s on display. Adjoining township of Clifton Springs had a brief burst of fame in the 1870s when the therapeutic value of its mineral-spring water was discovered; today it offers sporting facilities and a restaurant. **Tourist information:** A Maze'N Things, cnr Bellarine Hwy and Grubb Rd, Wallington; (052) 50 2669. **Accommodation:** 1 hotel.
MAP REF. 210 H9, 217 H7, 224 A6

Dunkeld   Pop. 440
On the Glenelg Hwy, 31 km from Hamilton, Dunkeld is the southern gateway to the Grampians and is conveniently located for trips to the Victoria Valley (world-famous fine-wool district), the Chimney Pots and Billywing Plantation within Grampians National Park, 25 km N. **Of interest:** Historical museum, Templeton St; history of area's Aboriginal tribes and explorer Major Mitchell's journeys. Detailed map available of historic sites and buildings. Skin Inn (sheepskin products and crafts) and The Chimney Pot (handcrafts and light refreshments), both in Parker St. **In the area:** Walking tracks to top of Mt Sturgeon and Mt Abrupt; both climbs steep, but fine views rewarding. Picnic spots at Freshwater Lake Reserve, 8 km N. **Tourist information:** Dunkeld Cafe, Parker St; (055) 77 2256. **Accommodation:** 1 hotel/motel, 2 caravan/camping parks. **See also:** The Western District.
MAP REF. 226 H4

Dunolly   Pop. 686
A small township in north-central Victoria, in the heart of the gold country and on the Goldfields Tourist Route. 'Welcome Stranger', claimed to be the largest nugget ever discovered, was found 15 km NW at Moliagul. The district has produced more nuggets than any other goldfield in Australia; 126 were unearthed in the town itself. **Of interest:** Handsome original buildings in Broadway, the main street. Goldfields Historical and Arts Museum, Broadway; replicas of some of town's most spectacular nuggets; open weekends or by arrangement. Bonsai shop, Broadway. Restored Dunolly Courthouse, Market St; information centre and display relating to historic gold discoveries in area. Goldrush Festival held Oct. **In the area:** Melville Caves, 30 km N; haunt of bushranger Captain Melville. Laanecoorie Reservoir, 16 km E; picnic spot. Countryside around Dunolly abounds with wildflowers in spring; many native birds and animals. Gold panning in local creeks. Monuments at Moliagul; mark spot where Welcome Stranger nugget was found 1869, and birthplace of Rev. John Flynn, founder of Royal Flying Doctor Service. **Tourist information:** Market St; (054) 68 1205. **Accommodation:** 2 hotels, 1 motel, 1 caravan/camping park.
MAP REF. 221 L3, 229 O10

Echuca–Moama   Pop. 9438
These twin towns are at the junction of the Murray, Campaspe and Goulburn Rivers. Echuca, once Australia's largest inland port, took its name from an Aboriginal word meaning 'meeting of the waters', while Moama means 'place of the dead'. An iron bridge joins the city of Echuca to the NSW town of Moama, on the other side of the Murray River. **Of interest:** Along the Murray Esplanade, Port of Echuca, massive red gum wharf restored to the period of its heyday: includes paddle-steamer *Pevensey* (renamed *Philadelphia* for TV mini-series *All the Rivers Run*, filmed here), which cruises during peak periods, D26 logging barge, PS *Alexander Arbuthnot* (being restored) and PS *Adelaide*; Star Hotel, with underground bar and escape tunnel; and Bridge Hotel, built by Henry Hopwood, founder of Echuca, who ran original punt service across river. Also part of the Port's attractions: the Red Gum Works; Sharp's Magic Movie House and Penny Arcade (winner of State and National Tourism Awards); Echuca Wharf Pottery; Tisdall Wines and Cellar Door Restaurant; Wistaria Tearooms; and the Coach House Carriage Collection: all in Murray Esplanade. In High St: Echuca Historical Society Museum (1867) in former police station, classified by National Trust; Gumnutland; and World in Wax Museum. Njernda Aboriginal Cultural Centre in former Law Courts, and National Holden Museum in Warren St. One-hr cruises on paddlewheelers *Canberra* and *Pride of the Murray*. Accommodation and 1-hr cruises on

Alpine Country

To the east and north-east of Melbourne, the gently rounded peaks of the Victorian Alps stretch, seemingly endlessly, under clear skies. They are much lower than alpine ranges in other parts of the world, lacking sheer escarpments and jagged peaks, but they still stand majestic, especially when covered in snow. These blue ranges are not high enough to have a permanent cover of snow, but the expanses of the rolling mountains are ideal for cross-country skiing as well as for the downhill variety.

The skiing season officially opens on the Queen's Birthday long weekend each June and closes in October, but it often actually extends beyond these dates. Each year, thousands of people flock to the snow: for the enjoyment of downhill skiing, for leisurely cross-country skiing, for snowboarding or just to enjoy the beauty of nature. Children can have a great time throwing snowballs and building snowmen.

There is bountiful fishing in the lakes and trout streams. Tennis, rock-climbing, sailing, swimming, canoeing and water-skiing are popular sports in the summer. Many riding schools in the valleys provide a leisurely pastime for those who want to explore the countryside on horseback. For the more energetic, bushwalking in this beautiful rugged country is a must. Despite their summer beauty, however, the Alps can still claim the life of an ill-prepared bushwalker. Make sure you have the necessary equipment and knowledge to tackle this recreational activity, and always tell someone where you are going and when you expect to be back.

Victoria has nine ski resorts, all within easy reach of Melbourne.

Falls Creek, 356 km from Melbourne, via the Snow Road through Oxley. Protected ski runs for novices, intermediate and advanced skiers; good cross-country skiing. Ski hire and instruction.

Lake Mountain, 120 km from Melbourne, via Healesville. Sightseeing and cross-country skiing.

Mount Baw Baw, 177 km from Melbourne, via Drouin. Beginners, novices and cross-country skiing.

Mount Buffalo, 331 km from Melbourne, via Myrtleford. Includes Dingo Dell and Cresta. Beginners, families and cross-country skiing. Ski hire and instruction.

Mount Buller, 221 km from Melbourne, via Mansfield. For beginners to advanced skiers. Ski hire and instruction.

Mount Stirling, 250 km from Melbourne, near Mount Buller. Cross-country skiing. Most trails start at Telephone Box Junction, which has a visitor centre with public shelter, ski hire and trail maps.

Mount Donna Buang, 95 km from Melbourne, via Warburton. Sightseeing and novice skiing.

Mount Hotham, 367 km from Melbourne, via Wangaratta. The 'powder snow capital' of Australia. For experienced downhill skiers; unlimited cross-country skiing. Ski hire and instruction.

Dinner Plain, is a 10-minute ski-shuttle ride from Mount Hotham and offers cross-country skiing and horseriding.

For further information on all resorts, contact the Alpine Resorts Commission, Amev House, Whitehorse Road, Box Hill; (03) 895 6900; or the Falls Creek Information Centre, Bogong High Plains Tourist Rd, Falls Creek; (057) 58 3224. **See also:** Safe Skiing. **Note** detailed map of Alpine Region on page 222.

Snow gums, Mount Baw Baw

Puffing Billy

paddle-steamer *Emmylou*. MV *Mary Ann* and PB *Captain Proud* are cruising restaurants. Gem Club, in old pump station near bridge to Moama; also Oz Maze. Houseboat hire. Southern 80 Ski Race from Torrumbarry Weir to Echuca, held Feb. Rich River Festival in Oct. Steam, Horse and Vintage Car Rally in June. Barmah Muster in April. **In the area:** Camping, fishing, kayaking, canoeing, swimming, bushwalking and water-skiing. Excellent sporting facilities including golf, tennis, bowls, croquet. Harness and horse races 18–20 times annually. Joalah Fauna Park, Rich River Yabbie Farm and Raverty's Auto Museum, all on Cornelia Creek Rd, 4 km s. In Moama: Silverstone Go Kart Track, Aqua Farms Yabbie Farm and 4 clubs with poker machines. Barmah Red Gum Forest and Moira Forest, 41 km NE, cover some 100 000 ha. At Barmah Lakes; wetlands cruise in the *Kingfisher*. Dharnya Centre, 36 km N within Barmah Forest; illustrates traditions and lifestyle of area's Aboriginal inhabitants. Golden Cow Educational Centre at Tongala, 27 km SE. Upside Down Pub, 15 km E on Murray Valley Hwy. Kyabram Fauna Park, 35 km SE; one of Victoria's best. **Tourist information:** 2 Leslie St, Echuca; (054) 80 7555; or Cobb Hwy, Moama; (054) 80 9555. **Accommodation:** 42 motels, hotels, homesteads and holiday units, 11 caravan parks. **See also:** The Mighty Murray; Wine Regions. MAP REF. 127 K13, 232 E4

Edenhope   Pop. 821

On the Wimmera Hwy, just 30 km from the border, Edenhope is situated on the shores of Lake Wallace, a haven for waterbirds. When full, the lake is popular for water sports and has a boat ramp; golf course and tennis courts nearby, and sports centre with squash courts and pool off Lake St. **Of interest:** Cairn beside the lake in Lake St, commemorating visit of first all-Aboriginal cricket team to England. Team was coached by T.W. Willis, who was also the founder of Australian Rules football. Henley-on-Lake Wallace; show day with floats, Feb. **In the area:** Harrow, 32 km SE; one of Victoria's oldest inland towns, with many interesting buildings, including Hermitage Hotel (1851) and log gaol (1862). About 50 km w, over SA border, Naracoorte Caves Conservation Park. Rocklands Reservoir, 65 km E of Edenhope, part of Wimmera–Mallee irrigation system; popular for fishing and boating. **Tourist information:** Shire Offices, Elizabeth St; (055) 85 1011. **Accommodation:** 1 hotel, 1 motel, 1 caravan/camping park. MAP REF. 228 C11

Eildon   Pop. 740

Built to irrigate a vast stretch of northern Victoria and to provide hydro-electric power, Lake Eildon is the State's largest man-made lake and is a very popular resort area, surrounded by the beautiful foothills of the Alps within Eildon State Park. There are excellent recreational facilities around the foreshores, two major boat harbours, launching ramps, picnic grounds and many lookout points. The towns of Eildon and Bonnie Doon, 42 km N, are popular holiday centres. Power boats and houseboats can be hired at the boat harbours. **In the area:** Signposted Lake Eildon Wall lookout. Lake cruises depart from Eildon Boat Harbour. Mt Pinninger (503 m), 3 km E; panoramic views of Mt Buller, the Alps and lake. Snobs Creek Fish Hatchery, 6 km SW; millions of trout bred and used to stock lakes and rivers; visitors welcome. Eildon Deer Park nearby, on Goulburn Valley Hwy; open weekends and public holidays. Just past the hatchery, Snobs Creek Falls, Rubicon Falls, 18 km SW, via Thornton. Jamieson, 57 km SE; old mining town at junction of Goulburn and Jamieson Rivers, surrounded by dense, bush-clad mountain countryside. Mt Skene, 48 km SE of Jamieson; usually covered with wildflowers Dec.–Feb. (road closed in winter). Eildon Pondage and Goulburn River offer excellent fishing. There is no closed season for trout in Eildon Lake, which is also stocked with Murray cod; redfin abound naturally. Inland fishing licence required for anglers over 16. Sailing, water-skiing. Fraser National Park, 13 km NW, and Eildon State Park surrounding town; bushwalking, camping, boating and fishing. Candlebark Gully Nature Walk, popular walk within Fraser National Park. **Tourist information:** Redgate Nursery and Craft Cottage, 73 Downey St, Alexandra; (057) 72 2169. **Accommodation:** 4 motels, 6 caravan/camping parks. MAP REF. 211 Q2, 222 A12, 233 K11

Emerald   Pop. 4693

The Puffing Billy steam railway runs between this pretty township, which was the first European settlement in the Dandenong Ranges and Belgrave. **Of interest:** Number of galleries and craft shops; restaurants include Choo Choos, Monbulk Rd, a restored Victorian 'red rattler' train with gallery and model railway. Emerald Lake Park, Emerald Lake Rd, once part of famous Nobelius Nursery; walking tracks and free barbecues. Emerald Lake, one of hills' most attractive and best-equipped picnic and swimming sites; water-slides, paddle-boats, model railway and tearooms. Lake sited on Dandenongs Walk Track, 40-km trail stretching from Cockatoo and Gembrook

The Great Ocean Road

Very few roads in Australia can offer a continuous stretch of more than 300 kilometres of breathtaking scenery, but the Great Ocean Road, along Victoria's south-west coast, does exactly that. This area suffered devastation on Ash Wednesday 1983 as bushfires burned from Lorne through to Aireys Inlet and Anglesea.

Built to honour the servicemen of World War I and completed in 1932, the road has dramatic stretches of precipitous cliffs, idyllic coves, and wide beaches.

The Great Ocean Road begins at **Torquay**, not far from Geelong. This is a popular surfing spot and the Road leads past a collection of famous surfing and safe swimming beaches and resorts. **Lorne** is one of the most charming of these. Despite offering modern holiday amenities and plenty of seaside entertainment for families, its gracious old hotels and guest houses remain as a reminder of days gone by. Behind the town, the **Otway Ranges**, which stretch from **Anglesea** to **Cape Otway**, offer beautiful hills, waterfalls, excellent walking tracks and lovely picnic spots. At **Apollo Bay**, the Road leaves the coast and winds through the ferny slopes of Cape Otway. This is rainforest country, silent and untouched, and well worth exploring. Many of the roads are unsealed but quite adequate for standard cars. Do try to visit the Melba Gully State Park to the west of the tiny township of **Lavers Hill**. Shipwreck trail signs begin on the eastern side of Lavers Hill. This point marks the beginning of the 'Shipwreck Coast', which stretches through **Port Campbell** and **Warrnambool** to **Port Fairy**. Photographers can be seen risking life and limb to take advantage of the dramatic coastal scenery. It is advisable, however, for drivers to keep their eyes firmly on the road. The coastline takes on tortured, twisted shapes, with amazing rock formations like The Twelve Apostles—huge stone pillars looming out of the surf, carved over time by the incessantly boiling sea. A one-and-a-half-hour nature trail runs between Port Campbell and Two Mile Bay to the west; self-guide leaflets are available from the Port Campbell and Warrnambool information centres.

At **Princetown**, the Great Ocean Road returns to hug the coastline along the entire length of the **Port Campbell National Park** and follows the coast to the Bay of Islands, 8 kilometres east of the small seaside township of **Peterborough**, where four shipwrecks are located. Here the Curdies River enters the sea in a wide, sandy inlet beloved of fishermen.

For further information, contact the Great Ocean Road Tourism Association, 5 Moore St, Apollo Bay; (052) 37 6263. **See also:** Individual town entries in A–Z listing.

The Prom

Wilsons Promontory, at the southernmost tip of the Australian mainland, is one of Victoria's largest and most spectacular national parks. 'The Prom', as it is affectionately known to Victorians, has an impressive range of landscapes, including tall forested ranges, luxuriant tree fern valleys, open heaths, salt marshes and long drifts of sand dunes. Its wide, white sandy beaches are magnificent, some dominated by spectacular granite tors and washed by spectacular rolling surf. There are also very safe swimming beaches, particularly at Norman Bay near the main camping area at Tidal River and also the aptly named Squeaky Beach, where the sands squeak underfoot.

Birds and other wildlife abound on the Prom; flocks of lorikeets, rosellas and flame robins, kookaburras and blue wrens are in evidence, even in the main general store area at Tidal River village, and for the more dedicated and patient birdwatcher, sightings of treecreepers, herons and lyrebirds can be the reward.

Refuge Cove

Emus feed unperturbed on the open heath by the side of the main road at the park entry area at Yanakie Isthmus, and kangaroos and wallabies seem unimpressed by their human observers. At night wombat-spotting by torchlight is a favourite pastime with children staying in the Tidal River area.

There are more than 80 kilometres of walking tracks in the Wilsons Promontory National Park. Some cover short walks, such as the nature trail in Lilly Pilly Gully, where the vegetation varies from bushland, inhabited by many koalas, to rainforest, with ancient tree ferns and trickling streams; other longer walks can be taken to such places as Sealers Cove or to the tip of the Prom, where there is a lighthouse dating from 1859. Hikers should consider tide times to make creek crossing easier.

At the visitor information centre and park office at **Tidal River**, leaflets are available detailing walking tracks and the flora and fauna of the park. During summer and Easter, information officers give talks and spotlight tours as well as leading children's nature activities. Permits are required for all overnight hikes.

For further information telephone (056) 80 9555, or for bookings (056) 80 9500.

to Sassafras. **In the area:** At Menzies Creek, 5 km W: Cotswold House, fine food and views; Lake Aura Vale for sailing and picnics. Monbulk Animal Kingdom in Swales Rd, Monbulk, 11 km N. Tulip farms at Silvan, 14 km N. Bimbimbie Wildlife Park in Paternoster Rd, Mount Burnett, 12 km SE. Sherbrooke Art Gallery, 8 Monbulk Rd, Belgrave, 11 km W. Olinda, 18 km N, a picturesque town: antique gallery; National Rhododendron Garden and nursery; good restaurants; home of settler Edward Henty on Ridge Rd. Australian Rainbow Trout Farm at Macclesfield, 8 km N of Emerald. **Tourist information:** Emerald Lake Kiosk; (059) 68 4109. **Accommodation:** 1 resort. **See also:** The Dandenongs.
MAP REF. 211 M8, 224 E5

Euroa   Pop. 2772
A small town 151 km NE of Melbourne, recently bypassed by the Hume Hwy, Euroa is a good base from which to explore the Strathbogie Ranges and tablelands. It was at Euroa that the Kelly gang pulled off a daring robbery, rounding up some 50 hostages at the nearby Faithfull Creek station and then making off with £2200. **Of interest:** Farmers Arms historical museum, Kirkland Ave. **In the area:** Seven Creeks Run Woolshed complex, 1 km N; sheepdog and shearing demonstrations, also bush market, pottery and souvenirs. Faithfull Creek homestead, 9 km NE near Balmattum; burnt out in 1939 bushfires, but ruins remain. Nearby, Faithfull Creek Waterfall, with picnic facilities. Euroa Soaring Club offers glider flights; also Balloon Flights Victoria, 10 km S. At Violet Town, 20 km NE: parachuting centre; Dorset Hill Wildlife Park. Forlonge Memorial, off Euroa–Strathbogie road, 10 km SE, commemorates Eliza Forlonge, who with her sister imported first merino sheep into Victoria. Scenic drive to Gooram Falls and around Strathbogie Ranges to SE. **Tourist information:** Goulburn Tourism, 320 High St, Nagambie; (057) 94 2647. **Accommodation:** 3 motels, 1 caravan/camping park.
MAP REF. 232 I8

Foster   Pop. 1078
A picturesque small township within easy reach of Corner Inlet, Waratah Bay and Wilsons Promontory on the southeast coast of Victoria, about 170 km from Melbourne. **Of interest:** In Main St: His-torical Museum, housed in old post office; Stockyard Gallery. **In the area:** Scenic drive to Fish Creek, 11 km SW; Fish Creek Potters. Waratah Bay, 34 km SW, Walkerville, 36 km SW and Port Franklin, 12 km SE, all pleasant beach resorts. Cape Liptrap, 46 km SW; excellent views of rugged coastline and Bass Strait. Toora, 12 km E; new SECV windfarm, and home of Bonlac milk products. Good surf beach at Sandy Point, 22 km S; surrounding protected waters of Shallow Inlet popular for fishing and swimming. Foster North Lookout, 6 km NW. Turtons Creek, 18 km N; old gold-rich village where lyrebirds can sometimes be seen in tree fern gullies nearby. Horse-drawn wagons and trail riding near Turtons Creek. **Tourist information:** Stockyard Gallery/Dept. of Conservation and Natural Resources, Main St; (056) 82 2133/82 2466. **Accommodation:** 2 motels, 1 caravan/camping park.
MAP REF. 224 I9

Geelong   Pop. 126 306
Geelong, on Corio Bay, is the largest provincial city in Victoria. A major manufacturing and processing centre, Geelong also has a large petroleum refinery. It is also a traditional wool-selling centre. The Corio Bay area was first settled in the 1830s and, apart from a rush to the diggings during the gold boom, Geelong has grown and prospered steadily. It is a pleasant and well-laid-out city with more than 14% of its area reserved for parks and sports grounds. **Of interest:** National Wool Centre and Museum, cnr Moorabool and Brougham Sts; museum has 3 galleries. Geelong Otway Convention and Visitors Bureau in foyer. Swimming at Eastern Beach and Park. Geelong Beachfront Scenic Drive. Botanic Gardens in Eastern Park, Garden St, overlooking Corio Bay. Johnstone Park, cnr Mercer and Gheringhap Sts; art gallery, war memorial, library and city hall, and Geelong Historical Records Centre. Queens Park, Queens Park Rd, Newtown; golf course, sports oval, and walks to Buckley's Falls. Geelong boasts many interesting buildings, more than 100 with National Trust classifications. They include: Merchiston Hall, Garden St, East Geelong, 8-roomed stone house built 1856 for early settler, James Cowie. In North Geelong, Osborne House in Swinburne St, bluestone mansion built 1858. At Eastern Beach, beautiful Corio Villa, prefabricated cast-iron house built 1856.

The Heights, Aphrasia St, Newtown, 14-roomed prefabricated timber mansion built 1855 for Charles Ibbotson; open to public. Also open: Barwon Grange (1855), Fernleigh St, Newtown. Oldest Anglican church in Victoria still in continuous use, Christ Church in Moorabool St. Also of interest, Customs House and Maritime Museum in Brougham St. Performing Arts Centre in Little Malop St. Pegasus Antiques, 560a Latrobe Tce. Wintergarden Gallery, 51 McKillop St. Pottage Crafts, 189 Moorabool St. Deb's Cottage Collections Crafts, 178 Swanston St, South Geelong. Great Galah Australiana and Gifts, 91 Little Malop St. Balyang Bird Sanctuary in Shannon Ave, Newtown. Boat ramps on the Corio Bay beaches. Area offers good river and bay fishing. Annual Show, Geelong Cup Carnival and Spring Festival in Oct.–Nov. **In the area:** Norlane Water World, 7 km N. Deakin University's Institute of the Arts, 13 km SW at Waurn Ponds. Fyansford, 5 km W, on outskirts of city, one of oldest settlements in region; Monash Bridge across Moorabool River thought to be one of first reinforced-concrete bridges in Victoria. Also at Fyansford, historic buildings include: Swan Inn; Balmoral Hotel (1854), now an art gallery; and Fyansford Hotel. Brownhill Observation Tower at Ceres, 10 km SW, for excellent view of surrounding areas. Batesford, 10 km NW of Geelong; now a picturesque market-garden township, with a history of wine-making. Idyll Vineyard, 11 km NW on Ballan road; open Tues.–Sun. for tastings and sales. The sandstone Travellers Rest Inn was built in 1849 and is across the Moorabool River from the present hotel. Lara (pop. 6318), 19 km N of Geelong; swept by bushfires in 1969, but some historic buildings remaining; located at foot of the You Yangs, a range of granite hills, which feature the You Yangs Forest Park. Between Lara and You Yangs is the Serendip Sanctuary, once purely a wildlife research station but now open to the public, with visitors centre, walking tracks, bird hides and picnic area. Some 46 km NW, along the Midland Hwy; Happy Hens Egg World at Meredith, one of the oldest towns in Victoria, and once an important stopping-place for diggers on their way to the goldfields. Shire hall, railway station and bluestone State school are of interest. Anakie, 31 km N, and the Anakie Gorge, 36 km N (picnic area). Accessed via Batesford, township is at the foot of the

Grampians National Park, near Halls Gap

Brisbane Ranges, a national park area. Many species of ferns and flowering plants in the park; walking tracks lead to the gorge and adjoining wildlife sanctuary. Nearby Fairy Park displays quaint miniature houses and scenes from fairytales. Mt Anakie Winemakers, 4 km N of Anakie on Staughton Vale Rd, produces local wines; open Sat. Steiglitz, 10 km NW of Anakie; popular camping ground, courthouse dating back to 1875. The Bellarine Peninsula begins about 16 km E and includes Queenscliff, Portarlington, Ocean Grove and Barwon Heads (see separate town entries). Horseriding at Koombahla Park in Wallington, 16 km E of Geelong. Also at Wallington, A Maze'N Things. Lake Connewarre Wildlife Reserve, 2 km S of Leopold. Bellarine Peninsula Railway; steam and diesel trains on 16-km track between Drysdale (see separate town entry) and Queenscliff. Venturing further afield, Great Ocean Rd to Torquay and Lorne provides spectacular coastal scenery. At Moriac, 20 km SW, horse-drawn caravans for hire. Vineyards in area include Rebenberg and Tarcoola. Alden Lodge Museum and Coral Gardens at Grovedale, 6 km S of Geelong; shell and coral displays, and flower gardens. **Tourist information:** National Wool Centre, Bay end of Moorabool St; (052) 22 2900. **Accommodation:** 2 hotels, 24 motels, 9 caravan/camping parks. **See also:** The Great Ocean Road; Wine Regions.
MAP REF. 210 F9, 216, 217 E6, 227 Q7

Gisborne   Pop. 2819
Once a stopping-place for coaches and foot travellers on their way to the Castlemaine and Bendigo goldfields, Gisborne is an attractive township (now bypassed by the Calder Hwy) on the way to Woodend and Kyneton. **In the area:** Mount Macedon, 20 km N; memorial cross at summit. Mt Aitken Estates Winery, 6 km S of Gisborne. **Tourist information:** Ampol Road Pantry; (054) 282 541. **Accommodation:** 1 motel, 1 caravan/camping park (at Macedon). **See also:** Wine Regions.
MAP REF. 210 H4, 224 A2, 232 D13

Glenrowan   Pop. 345
Glenrowan is the famous site of the defeat of Ned Kelly and his gang by the police in 1880. Today the village, set in picturesque country, has craft and souvenir shops, nurseries and tea and coffee shops. **Of interest:** All along Old Hume Hwy: Ned Kelly Memorial Museum and Homestead; Kate's Cottage Gifts in front and huge statue of Ned Kelly; Tourist Centre, with engrossing computer-animated show of capture of Ned Kelly. **In the area:** Warby Ranges and State Park, 12 km N; historic villages, scenic drives, walking tracks and picnic spots. Lake Mokoan, 5 km W; boating, fishing and water-skiing. Glenrowan wineries include Booth's Winery, Auldstones Cellars, H.J.T. Vineyards and Bailey's Bundarra Vineyards. Milawa–

Oxley wineries, 16 km E. **Tourist information:** Wangaratta and Region Visitors Information Centre, Hume Hwy, Wangaratta; (057) 21 5711. **Accommodation:** 1 motel, 1 caravan park. **See also:** Wine Regions.
MAP REF. 222 D1, 233 L6

Halls Gap   Pop. 334
Beautifully sited in the heart of the Grampians, this little town is adjacent to Lake Bellfield and surrounded by the Grampians National Park and a network of scenic roads. **Of interest:** Tearooms, restaurants, an art gallery and potteries; also good sporting facilities. The area is famous for its wildflowers, and Halls Gap holds an annual spring wildflower exhibition in Sept.–Oct. **In the area:** Bushwalking, camping, rock climbing and abseiling in national park, one of the largest in the State; Visitors Centre 2 km from town; open daily for films and park information. Brambuk Aboriginal Living Cultural Centre, 2 km S. Reids Lookout and The Balconies, 12 km NW. McKenzie Falls, 17 km NW. Lake Fyans, 17 km E, for swimming, fishing, yachting and water-skiing. Wallaroo Wildlife Park, 5 km SE, open daily. Roses Gap Recreation Centre, 21 km N. Boroka Vineyards, 2 km E; open daily. Wartook Pottery and Restaurant, 20 km NW. **Tourist information:** Halls Gap Newsagency, Grampians Rd; (053) 56 4247. **Accommodation:** 8 motels, 4 caravan/camping parks. **See also:** The Grampians; National Parks.
MAP REF. 226 I1, 228 I12

Hamilton   Pop. 10 200
Known as the 'Wool Capital of the World', Hamilton is a prosperous and pleasant city less than an hour's drive from the coastal centres of Portland, Port Fairy and Warrnambool on the south coast and the Grampian Ranges to the north. **Of interest:** Big Woolbales Complex, Henty Hwy, recreates the story of wool production and processing; shearing demonstrations, woolshed memorabilia, craft centre and cafeteria. HIRL (Hamilton Institute of Rural Learning), North Boundary Rd; community, craft and educational centre surrounded by gardens, nature trail and breeding area for eastern barred bandicoots. HEAL (Hamilton Environmental Awareness and Learning) conducts tours in area to discover how to care for the land; bookings essential; (055) 78 6223. Hamilton

Art Gallery, Brown St; varied collections, including decorative arts. Trout fishing in Lake Hamilton, Ballarat Rd; sandy beach, water sports and picnic facilities. On banks of lake, Sir Reginald Ansett Transport Museum; history and memorabilia of Sir Reginald's life and transport industry begun in Hamilton in 1931. Small zoo at Botanical Gardens, French St (established 1870); free-flight aviary, duck pond and children's playground. Hamilton Pastoral Museum, Glenelg Hwy, housed in former St Luke's Lutheran Church; open by appt. Hamilton History Centre and Aboriginal Keeping Place, Gray St; aspects of local Aboriginal culture. **In the area:** Summit Park, Nigretta Rd, 15 km NW; specialises in raising Saxon-Merino sheep for superfine wool production; open daily. Wannon and Nigretta Falls, 15 km NW. Mt Eccles National Park, near Macarthur, 35 km S. Mt Eccles, with its crater Lake Surprise, one of 3 extinct volcanoes nearby. For a pleasant day trip from Hamilton, the Grampians Tour (about 250 km N), to Dunkeld, Halls Gap, Ararat and back via Glenthompson. Several historic homes and gardens of note; also b & b accommodation. **Tourist information:** Lonsdale St; (055) 72 3746 and (008) 807 056. **Accommodation:** 6 hotels, 7 motels, 2 caravan/camping parks. **See also:** The Western District.
MAP REF. 226 G5

Harrietville   Pop. 250

Tucked into the foothills of Mt Hotham and Mt Feathertop, Harrietville is a convenient accommodation centre for those who want to ski at Mt Hotham or sightsee in north-east Victoria. Gold was discovered here in 1862, and the gold-rush village was proclaimed a township in 1879. **Of interest:** Bicycles, fishing rods and gold panning dishes for hire. Horse-riding and golfing. Pioneer Park, open-air museum and picnic area, Alpine Rd. Audrey's Dolls and Crafts, Cobungra Court; hand-made porcelain dolls. **In the area:** Walking tracks to Mt Feathertop (1922 m), 20 km return, and Mt Hotham (1859 m), about 32 km one way. Bushwalking in high mountain country of Bogong National Park, which surrounds town (weather conditions can vary and must be considered). Crystal Waters Trout Farm and adjacent Mountain Fresh Trout Farm, 4 km N; fishing and educational facilities. **Tourist information:** Old General Store, Alpine Rd; (057) 59 2553. **Accommodation:** 1 hotel/motel, 1 resort, 1 lodge, 1 caravan/camping park.
MAP REF. 223 M7, 233 P9, 234 C7

Healesville   Pop. 6264

Surrounded by mountain forest country, Healesville is about an hour's drive from Melbourne along the Maroondah Hwy. It has been a popular resort town since the turn of the century, as the climate is cool and pleasant in summer and the area offers excellent bushwalks and scenic drives. **Of interest:** Trolley rides from Healesville railway station to Yarra Glen, Sun. Bicentennial National Trail, Healesville–Cooktown, 5000 km, for horseriders and walkers. Yarra Valley Winery Tours, Birdwood Ave. **In the area:** Famous Healesville Sanctuary, 4 km S, on Badger Creek Rd; open daily. This 32-ha reserve houses a variety of native animals and birds in a largely natural bushland setting. Key attractions are the close-up displays: see animals in close proximity; check times. Picnic/ barbecue facilities and restaurant. Corranderrk Aboriginal Cemetery, 5 km S. Pottery, lapidary and art gallery at Nigel Court, off Badger Creek Rd, 2 km S; open daily. Drives from Healesville: Toolangi State Forest, criss-crossed with logging roads, 14 km N; Donnelly's Weir Reserve, 4 km NE; Marysville, 37 km NE, via the Black Spur, passing Maroondah Reservoir (picnic/barbecue facilities) and towering stands of mountain ash and lush tree fern glades. Steavensons Falls is an attraction, 4 km SE of Marysville. Nearly 40 wineries in the Yarra Valley; many open for sales and tastings, including Warramate Winery at Gruyere, 8 km SW of Healesville, and others in surrounding areas, such as Bianchet, Yering Station, Coldstream Hills, Domaine Chandon, De Bortoli, Fergusson's, Kellybrook, Lillydale, Long Gully, Shantell, St Hubert's, Yarra Burn, Lovey's Estate, Silvan Winery, Stringybark Winery and Lovegrove of Cottles Bridge. Gulf Station Homestead (1854), 2 km N of Yarra Glen, itself 14 km W of Healesville. **Tourist information:** Piquant Palate, 278 Maroondah Hwy; (059) 62 3625. **Accommodation:** 2 hotels, 5 motels, 3 caravan/camping parks.
MAP REF. 211 N5, 214 E7, 224 F3

Heathcote   Pop. 1507

In attractive countryside on the McIvor Hwy, Heathcote is set along the McIvor Creek, 47 km S of Bendigo. **Of interest:** McIvor Cottage Industry Coop, High St, in old courthouse; historical display, craft marketing, tourist information. **In the area:** Lake Eppalock, 10 km W, one of the State's largest lakes; popular for motorboat racing. Excellent views from Mount Ida Lookout, 4 km N. Scenic attraction: the Pink Cliffs, created by eroded spoil from gold sluices, with their brilliant mineral staining. McIvor Range Reserve; historic powder magazine. Old Heathcote Hospital (1859), listed for preservation by National Trust. Wineries include Wild Duck Creek Estate, Heathcote Winery and Zuber Estate, within town; Jasper Hill and Huntleigh Vineyards, 6 km N, McIvor Creek Wines and Eppalock Ridge vineyards, 10 km and 22 km SW respectively. Central Victorian Yabbie Farm, on Northern Hwy at South Heathcote. **Tourist information:** Shire Offices, 125 High St; (054) 33 3211. **Accommodation:** 1 hotel, 1 hotel/motel, 1 motel, 1 caravan/camping park.
MAP REF. 232 E9

Koala, Healesville Sanctuary

Gippsland Lakes

Many people regard the area of the Gippsland Lakes as Victoria's most outstanding holiday area. Dominated as it is by Australia's largest system of inland waterways, it certainly does live up to all the superlatives accorded it. With the foothills of the high country just to the north and the amazing stretch of the Ninety Mile Beach separating the lakes from the ocean, the region offers an incredible variety of natural beauty and recreation activities. Here the choice really is yours—lake, river or ocean fishing, boating, cruising, surfing, birdwatching or just sitting by the water.

Within easy reach of the Lakes area the high country begins, so it is possible to vary a waterside trip with days exploring the alpine reaches and some of the fascinating little old townships such as **Walhalla**, **Omeo**, **Briagolong** and **Dargo**. The road across the Dargo High Plains and the Omeo Highway leading to Hotham Heights pass through some stunning country. Check your car thoroughly before you set off—service stations are scarce along the way.

Wellington, King, Victoria, Tyers, Reeve and Coleman—these 6 lakes cover more than 400 square kilometres and stretch parallel to the Ninety Mile Beach for almost its entire length. **Sale**, at the western edge of the region, is the local base for the development of the Bass Strait oil and gas fields. Both Sale and **Bairnsdale**, further east on the banks of the Mitchell River, make excellent bases for holidays on the Lakes or alpine trips. The main resort towns are **Lakes Entrance**, at the mouth of the Lakes, **Paynesville**, a mecca for boating and fishing enthusiasts, and **Metung**, where a cruising holiday on the Lakes can be commenced, and **Loch Sport**, nestled between Ninety Mile Beach, Lake Victoria and the national park.

The **Lakes National Park**, the **Mitchell River National Park** and the hills and valleys of the alpine foothills to the north all provide plenty of opportunities for bushwalking or for simply enjoying the peace.

For further information on the Gippsland Lakes, contact the local tourist information centres: cnr Esplanade and Marine Pde, Lakes Entrance; (051) 55 1966, 240 Main St, Bairnsdale; (051) 52 3444; and Princes Hwy, Sale; (051) 44 1108. **See also:** Individual town entries in A–Z listing.

Lakes Entrance

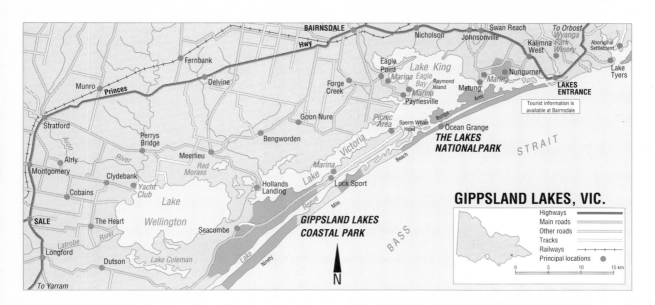

Hopetoun   Pop. 704

This small Mallee town, just south of Wyperfeld National Park, was named after the seventh Earl of Hopetoun, first Governor-General of Australia. Hopetoun was a frequent visitor to the home of Edward Lascelles, who was largely responsible for opening up the Mallee area. **Of interest:** Hopetoun House, built for Lascelles; classified by National Trust. Mallee Mural, and leadlight window in Shire Office, Lascelles St; depict history of the Mallee. Coorong Homestead (1846), Evelyn St; National-Trust-classified, home of first European settler in area, Peter McGinnis. Lake Lascelles for boating, swimming and picnics. **In the area:** Wyperfeld National Park, 50 km W; information centre within park. Swamp Tank Museum at Turriff, 45 km NE of Hopetoun. **Accommodation:** 1 hotel, 1 motel, 1 caravan/camping park. MAP REF. 126 E12, 228 H3

Horsham   Pop. 12 552

At the junction of the Western, Wimmera and Henty Hwys, Horsham is generally regarded as the capital of the Wimmera region. Its location makes it a good base for tours of the region, particularly to the Little Desert National Park, 40 km W, and to the Grampians, some 50 km SE. **Of interest:** Botanic Gardens, cnr Baker and Firebrace Sts. Wool Factory, Golf Course Rd, 3 km SW, produces top-quality, extra-fine wool from Saxon-Merino sheep; tours daily. Horsham Art Gallery, Wilson St; collection of photography and Mack Jost collection of Australian art. Slip-rail Art Gallery, Dimboola Rd. Olde Horsham Village, 3 km SE; collection of historic buildings, art, craft and antique market, also fauna park; open daily. Wimmera River; runs through town, attractive picnic spots, good fishing for trout, redfin and Murray cod. Apex Fishing Contest held March, Labour Day weekend. Victorian Institute of Dry Land Agriculture, Natimuk Rd, and Victorian College of Agriculture and Horticulture cereal research centre, 13 km NE at Longerenong; inspections by arrangement. Cottage Delights, Dooen Rd; plants and crafts. **In the area:** Black Range Cashmere and Thryptomene Farm, 40 km S, 4WD tours and inspection; bookings essential through Tourist Information Centre. Rocklands Reservoir, 90 km S on Glenelg River, built to supplement Wimmera–Mallee irrigation scheme; popular for water sports. Picnics, caravan and camping at lake's western edge, 14 km from Balmoral. Green Lake, 13 km SE of city, and Lake Natimuk, 24 km NW; picnic/barbecue facilities. Toolondo Reservoir, 44 km S, home of the fighting brown trout; excellent fishing, caravan park. **Tourist information:** 20 O'Callaghan's Pde; (053) 82 1832. **Accommodation:** 6 hotels, 15 motels, 2 caravan/camping parks. **See also:** The Wimmera. MAP REF. 228 G9

Inglewood   Pop. 740

North along the Calder Hwy from Bendigo are the 'Golden Triangle' towns of Inglewood and Bridgewater on Loddon. Sizeable gold nuggets have been found in this area, the largest being the 'Welcome Stranger', which weighed 65 kg. **Of interest:** Old eucalyptus oil distillery. Inglewood Gipsy Tours, Grant St; wagons drawn by Clydesdales. **In the area:** Kooyoora State Park, 16 km W of Inglewood; within park the Melville Caves, once haunt of notorious bushranger Captain Melville. Loddon River, at Bridgewater, 8 km SE, popular spot for fishing and water-skiing, picnic/barbecue facilities. Parachute jumping at Bridgewater. Horsedrawn caravans for hire at Inglewood and Bridgewater. **Tourist information:** 74 Brook St; (054) 38 3175. **Accommodation:** 1 motel, 1 camping/caravan park. MAP REF. 229 O9, 232 A7

Inverleigh   Pop. 282

On the Leigh River, this little town 29 km W of Geelong has a number of historic buildings. **Of interest:** Former Horseshoe Inn and 2-storey hotel opposite; Church of England, Presbyterian Church, State School and Whistler's Cottage Art Gallery, all on Hamilton Hwy. **In the area:** Fishing in Leigh and Barwon Rivers. Inverleigh Common, 2 km N; bushland with fauna reserve. Barunah Plains homestead, 17 km W; open by appt. **Tourist information:** National Wool Centre, Moorabool St (Bay end), Geelong; (052) 22 2900. **Accommodation:** Limited. MAP REF. 210 D9, 217 B6, 227 P7

Inverloch   Pop. 2195

This is a small seaside resort on Anderson Inlet, east of Wonthaggi. It has good surf and long stretches of excellent beach, and is very popular in summer. **Of interest:** South Gippsland Conservation Society, Environment Centre and Shell Museum, in Information Centre building, The Esplanade. Fun Festival held Oct. **In the area:** Inverloch–Cape Paterson Scenic Road, through Bunurong Cliff Coastal Reserve, 15 km SW; views equal those on Great Ocean Rd. Spear fishing and surfing at Cape Paterson. Adjacent to the town, Anderson's Inlet, the most southerly habitat of mangroves. Townsend Bluff and Maher's Landing for birdwatching. Tarwin River, 20 km SE; good fishing. Nearby, Venus Bay; beaches, natural bushland, wildlife, sporting facilities. **Tourist information:** Cnr Ramsay Blvd and The Esplanade; (056) 74 2706. **Accommodation:** 1 motel, 4 caravan/camping parks. MAP REF. 224 G9

Jeparit   Pop. 440

This little town in the Wimmera, 37 km N of Dimboola, is on the shores of Lake Hindmarsh, which is the largest natural freshwater lake in Victoria with many km of safe, sandy beaches, good fishing and a variety of birdlife. **Of interest:** Spire, illuminated at night, commemorates the fact that the town is the birthplace of Sir Robert Menzies. Wimmera–Mallee Pioneer Museum, 4-ha complex of colonial buildings at southern entrance to town; furnished in period, with displays of restored farm machinery. Beach Carnival held Jan. Agricultural Show in Oct. **In the area:** Near Antwerp, 20 km S, Ebenezer Mission, founded in 1859 by Moravian missionaries and restored by National Trust. Wyperfeld National Park, 44 km N and Little Desert National Park, 40 km NW; wildflowers, native animals and birds, walking. **Tourist information:** Shire Offices, Roy St; (053) 97 2070. **Accommodation:** 2 hotels, 1 caravan/camping park. MAP REF. 228 G6

Kaniva   Pop. 762

Kaniva in the west Wimmera, 43 km from Bordertown, SA, is just north of the Little Desert, which is famous for its wildflowers in spring. **Of interest:** Historical museum, Commercial St; large collection of items of local history. Old Kaniva railway station houses Luigi's Restaurant. **In the area:** Billy-Ho Bush Walk begins some 10 km S of town; 3-km self-guide walk in Little Desert National Park, numbered pegs allow identification of various species of desert flora. Big Desert, just north of town; walking trails, wildflowers and wildlife. Waterbird farm

20 km NW; breeding of black swans and many other varieties; open by appt, (053) 93 1347. Mooree Reserve, 20 km SW of town, a pleasant picnic spot. Farm holidays at Parlawidgee cropping and grazing farm, 10 km S. Railway station (1889) at Serviceton, 23 km W, classified by National Trust. **Tourist information:** 41 Commercial St; (053) 92 2418. **Accommodation:** 1 hotel, 2 motels, 1 caravan/camping park.
MAP REF. 228 C7

Kerang
Pop. 4024
Some 30 km from the Murray and 60 km from Swan Hill, Kerang is the centre of a productive rural area and lies at the southern end of a chain of lakes and marshes. Some of the largest breeding-grounds in the world for ibis and other waterfowl are found in these marshes. The ibis is closely protected because of its value in controlling locusts and other pests. **Of interest:** Old water tower, cnr of Murray Valley Hwy and Shadforth St; Gem Club and tourist information. Museum, Riverwood Drive; cars and farm machinery. Apex Park recreation area is sited by the first of the three Reedy Lakes; the second has a large ibis rookery and Lake Charm is popular for water sports. All the lakes in the Kerang area are popular for sailing and boating and have picnic facilities. Excellent year-round bowling, tennis and fishing. **In the area:** Lake Boga, 44 km NW; good sandy beaches. Murrabit, 29 km N, on the Murray and surrounded by picturesque river forests; country market on first Sat. of month. Australian Tractor Pull Championships at Quambatook, 42 km SW, on Easter Sunday. Sharnnkirst Cashmere Stud Farm and Riverside Crafts at Barham, 24 km NE. **Tourist information:** 25 Murray St, Barham; (054) 53 3100. **Accommodation:** 4 hotels, 3 motels, 2 caravan/camping parks. **See also:** The Mighty Murray.
MAP REF. 126 I12, 229 P3, 232 A2

Koo-wee-rup
Pop. 1106
Well known for its annual Potato Festival every March, this town is in the middle of a rich market-garden area near Western Port, and is the biggest asparagus-growing area in the Southern Hemisphere. **Of interest:** Historical Society Museum, Rossiter Rd; open Sun. **In the area:** Bayles Flora and Fauna Park, 8 km NE. Royal Botanic Gardens Cranbourne Garden, 28 km NW. Berwick–

Pakenham Historical Society Museum in John St, Pakenham, 21 km N. Military Vehicle Museum in Army Rd, Pakenham. Tooradin, 10 km W, situated on Sawtell's Inlet; popular with fishing and boating enthusiasts. Between Tooradin and Koo-wee-rup, on Sth Gippsland Hwy: Harewood House (1860s); original furnishings, open weekends. At Cardinia: Australian Pioneer Farm; re-created farm buildings, opportunities to shear sheep and milk cows. Victoria's Farm Shed displays at Tynong, 20 km NE. Also at Tynong, Gumbaya Fun Park, set in landscaped native bushland. **Accommodation:** 1 motel.
MAP REF. 211 N10, 224 F7

Koroit
Pop. 968
Koroit is 18 km W of the coastal resort of Warrnambool in the south-west of Victoria. It is an agricultural town with historic botanic gardens. The commercial and church precincts of the town, both containing historic buildings, have been classified by the National Trust. **In the area:** Tower Hill State Game Reserve, a volcanic area 3 km S; walking tracks, Natural History Centre, bird hides. The coast between Port Fairy and

Lake Boga, near Kerang

Warrnambool offers some delightful scenery. Mahogany Walking Track; 22-km of walking track between Port Fairy and Warrnambool. **Tourist information:** Warrnambool Tourist Information Centre, 600 Raglan St, Warrnambool; (055) 64 7837. **Accommodation:** 1 hotel, 1 caravan/camping park.
MAP REF. 226 H8

Korumburra
Pop. 2906
The giant Gippsland earthworm, sought by fishermen and geologists alike, is found in the area. Situated on the South Gippsland Hwy, 116 km SE of Melbourne, the area surrounding the town is given to dairying and agriculture, and the countryside is hilly. **Of interest:** Coal Creek Historical Village, cnr Sth Gippsland Hwy and Silkstone Rd, re-creation of 19th-century coal-mining village; located on original site of Coal Creek mine, begun in 1890s; orientation centre in Mechanics' Institute, inside village near entrance, open daily. Ten-day Karmai (giant worm) Festival held March. **In the area:** Gooseneck Pottery at Ruby, 4 km S. Leongatha, 14 km SE, for Southern Hemisphere's largest dairy factory. Beaches and excellent fishing at Waratah

Bay (66 km) and Corner Inlet (58 km). Top Paddock Cheeses at Bena, 4 km SW; tastings and sales of their traditional, curd and soft cheeses. Loch, 16 km W; antiques and arts and crafts. At Poowong, 18 km NW: Poowong Pioneer Chapel, fine example of German architecture, and Mudlark Pottery. **Tourist information**: Coal Creek Historical Village, Sth Gippsland Hwy; (056) 55 2233. **Accommodation:** 2 hotels, 1 motel, 1 caravan/camping park.
MAP REF. 211 P12, 224 G8

Kyabram   Pop. 5540
A prosperous town in the Murray–Goulburn area, just 40 km NW of Shepparton, Kyabram is in a rich dairying and fruit-growing district. **Of interest:** Community-owned waterfowl and fauna park on Lake Rd has 5 lakes with duck, ibis, swans and pelicans, a 16-ha enclosure for emus and kangaroos, a huge flight aviary and a reptile house; open daily. The Stables, adjacent to fauna park, for pottery and crafts. Mr Ilzyn's Cottages, Breen Ave; mansions, pubs, farmhouses from around the world, all in miniature. Antique Aeroplane Fly-in at Easter. Rodeo on March Labour Day holiday. **Tourist information:** Fauna park, 75 Lake Rd; (058) 52 2883. **Accommodation:** 3 hotels, 2 motels, 2 caravan/camping parks. **See also:** The Mighty Murray.
MAP REF. 232 F6

Kyneton   Pop. 3940
Little more than an hour's drive from Melbourne, along the Calder Hwy, Kyneton is an attractive and well-preserved town with several interesting bluestone buildings. Farms around the town prospered during the gold rushes, supplying large quantities of fresh food to the diggings at Ballarat and Bendigo. **Of interest:** Kyneton Museum, Piper St, housed in what was a two-storey bank (c.1865); drop-log cottage in grounds. Botanic Gardens, Clowes St; area of 8 ha above the river, contains 500 specimen trees. Historic buildings: town's churches, mechanics' institute and old police depot. Willis Flour Mill in Piper St; restored to operational condition, open weekends. Also in Piper St, Meskills Woolstore; wool spinning mill, yarn and garments for sale. Magnolia Cottage Nursery in Fiddlers Green Rd. Antique fair at Easter and Daffodil Festival in Sept. **In the area:** Two-storey bluestone mills on either side of town. Upper

Coliban, Lauriston and Malmsbury Reservoirs, all 8 km W. At Malmsbury, 10 km NW: historic bluestone railway viaduct, Bleak House (1850s) with rose garden, and Etherlings of Malmsbury for crafts. Carlsruhe Gallery and Campaspe Art Gallery at Carlsruhe, 5 km SE. At Trentham: 22 km SW: historic foundry; Jargon crafts; and Minifie's Berry Farm, pick-your-own in season. At Blackwood, further 14 km S, the Garden of St Erth. Turpins Falls at Metcalfe, 22 km N. **Tourist information:** Dapples and Darrell Lea, 6 High St; (054) 22 6075. **Accommodation:** 1 hotels, 2 motels, 1 caravan/camping park.
MAP REF. 210 G2, 224 A1, 227 R2, 229 R13, 232 D12

Lake Bolac   Pop. 266
In the Western District plains area, this small town on the Glenelg Hwy is by a 1460-ha freshwater lake that has good sandy beaches around a 20-km shoreline and is very popular for fishing (eels, trout, perch and yellow-belly), boating and swimming. There are several boat-launching ramps and an aquatic club. A sporting complex is located between town and lake. A 4-day yachting regatta is held at Easter. **Tourist information:** Lake Bolac Motel, Glenelg Hwy; (053) 50 2218. **Accommodation:** 1 motel, 1 caravan/camping park.
MAP REF. 220 C13, 227 J5

Lakes Entrance   Pop. 4622
This extremely popular holiday town is at the eastern end of the Gippsland Lakes, which form the largest inland network of waterways in Australia. They cover an area of more than 400 sq km and are separated from the ocean by a thin sliver of sand dunes forming a large part of the Ninety Mile Beach, which stretches south to Seaspray. A bridge across the Cunningham Arm gives access to the surf beach from Lakes Entrance. The town is well developed for the holidaymaker, catering for both seaside recreation and exploration of the mountain country to the north. It is the home port for a large fishing fleet and also for many pleasure craft. Large cruise vessels conduct regular sightseeing tours of the lakes throughout the year. Boats can also be hired. Fishing, both ocean and beach, is popular, as are swimming and surfing on a variety of good beaches. **Of interest:** Fisherman's Co-operative, Bullock Island; viewing platform and fish for sale. Shell Museum, the Esplanade. Potteries and galleries. **In the area:** Kinkuna Country fauna park and family entertainment centre, Princes Hwy, 3.5 km E. Good views from Jemmy's Point, 1 km W, and Nyerimilang Park, 10 km NW. Within the park is the original homestead, the north wing built in 1892; open for inspection. The sheltered waters of Lake Tyers (6–23 km E, depending on access point) are popular for fishing, swimming and boating; cruises depart from Fishermans Landing. Braeburne Park Orchards and tearooms; 6 km N. Woodsedge, 8 km N on Baades Rd; gallery, furniture workshop, glass-blowing demonstrations, refreshments. Buchan Caves, 55 km N, are well worth a visit. Day trips can be made to the old mining

Buchan Caves, near Lakes Entrance

Wine Regions

Viticulture developed in Victoria following the 1850s gold rush. Unsuccessful diggers began planting vines as a source of income. Later, Edward Henty and William Rye brought cuttings to the new colony and by 1868 more than 1200 hectares of vines had been established.

The light, dry wines produced in these vineyards won wide acclaim, but the event of phylloxera saw a promising industry decline until the early 1960s, when it started to re-emerge and develop into what it is today. One of the oldest regions is in the north-east of the State, 270 kilometres from Melbourne. **Rutherglen** and the other nearby wine-making towns of **Wahgunyah**, **Glenrowan** and **Milawa** produce distinct wine unique to each of the region's environmental subcultures. Many of the wineries are still managed by the descendants of the founders. The wines of the region are famed for their rich flavoursome red, and the exotic range of fortified wines such as Rutherglen Muscat, Rutherglen Tokay and their famous Port-style wine. On the June long weekend, a winery walkabout is organised so that wine lovers can visit the vineyards and sample some of the fine wines of the north-east. It is advisable to book your accommodation in advance if you plan to visit the area at this time.

West along the Murray, the towns of **Echuca**, **Swan Hill** and **Mildura** are part of the Murray Valley and north-west region known for the production of every-day-drinking wines.

About 200 kilometres west of Melbourne, between Stawell and Ararat, is the little town of **Great Western**, where the Seppelt and Best wineries developed in the 1860s. Since then they have consistently produced fine wines, including the renowned champagne-style Great Western Special Reserve from the Seppelt winery. The vineyards of Great Western are also noted for their rich red and full-flavoured white table wines.

At **Ararat**, Trevor Mast's Mt Langi Ghiran vineyard and the Montara vineyard both produce excellent wine with their own individual character.

To the north-east of Great Western is the region of the Pyrenees with the townships of **Avoca**, **Redbank** and **Moonambel**. Here are the Taltarni, Mt Avoca, Redbank, Chateau Remy, Summerfield, Dalwhinnie and Warrenmang wineries.

Stretching from **Shepparton** along to **Nagambie**, **Seymour** and **Mansfield** is the picturesque region of the Goulburn Valley with a contrast in wineries from the

Yarra Valley vineyard

historic, classified buildings of Chateau Tahbilk to the modern wineries of Delatite and Mitchelton. One grape variety from the region that has won acclaim is the Marsanne, a white wine that is distinct and rather unusual.

One of the two oldest regions near Melbourne is the Yarra Valley region, which is centred round **Cottles Bridge**, and the towns of **Yarra Glen**, **Lillydale**, **Coldstream** and **Seville**. This region's premium wine has had a rebirth after starting in the early 1850s and petering out as late as the 1920s. There is a wide range of wines produced in the area, from sparkling wine to quality reds and white table wines. In the Yarra Valley, wineries of particular interest include Domaine Chandon for its sparkling wines, and, as each has a restaurant, Fergusson's, Kellybrook, Yarra Burn and De Bortoli for an enjoyable lunch in the Valley, especially near to vintage. There are many other wineries worth visiting, including Bianchet for the merlot and verduzzo wines, and St Huberts, for it was one of the first wineries in the re-birth of the district.

Another wine-producing area close to Melbourne is the burgeoning Mornington Peninsula area. A cool-climate winegrowing district, its 83 vineyards nestle in between farming and coastal hamlets. The main spread covers the area from **Dromana**, through **Red Hill** and across the Peninsula to **Merricks** and **Balnarring**, with **Mornington**, **Main Ridge** and **Mt Martha** offering isolated vineyards. Of these, 17 vineyards are open, usually on weekends and public holidays, for cellar-door tastings and sales. Another 13 cellar doors are open for sales and visits by appointment.

North of Melbourne's Tullamarine Airport, wineries dot the landscape with pockets of vines stretching into the Macedon Ranges; some were established in the 1860s, others more recently. They include Knight's Granite Hills, Wildwood, Hanging Rock, Virgin Hills, Craiglee, Goonawarra, Cleveland, Cope-Williams, Flynn and Williams—each with its own distinct quality and character.

The Heathcote–Bendigo region is, like so many of Victoria's wine regions, gold-mining country that gave up much of its hidden wealth in the period 1850–1900. Today there are many wineries scattered throughout the region, around the townships of **Heathcote**, **Kingower**, **Bendigo** and **Bridgewater on Loddon**. Wineries include Passing Clouds, Jasper Hill, Osicka's, Zuber Estate, Water Wheel, Le Amon and Mildara's Balgownie.

In the last 20 years Victoria's wine industry has changed from an industry in decline, with about 25 commercial vineyards, to a flourishing concern with about 300 commercial vineyards and 100 smaller ones.

Most larger wineries are open daily for tastings and sales; some of the small wineries have restricted opening times, so it is worth checking before visiting.

For more information contact: the Victorian Wine Centre; (03) 699 6082; Mornington Peninsula Vignerons Association; (059) 74 4200; or Yarra Valley Wine Growers Association; (059) 64 2016. For tourist information, contact the Victorian Information Centre; (03) 790 3333. See also: Individual town entries in A–Z listing. **Note** detailed map of Yarra Valley Region on page 214.

areas around Omeo, 126 km N. Boats for hire at Metung, 15 km W by road. Lake Bunga, 3 km E; nature trail. Wyanga Park Vineyard and Winery, 10 km N; reached by boat trips from town. Nicholson River, 24 km W, and Golvinda wineries, 50 km NW, via Bairnsdale. Blue Gum Ostriches, 6 km NW on Hoggs Lane; tours, display of painted eggs; closed Tues. **Tourist information:** Cnr Esplanade and Marine Pde; (051) 55 1966. **Accommodation:** 2 hotels, 17 motels, 22 caravan/camping parks. **See also:** Gippsland Lakes; Wine Regions.
MAP REF. 225 Q4, 234 G13

Lancefield
Pop. 1063

This historic township with its wide streets and Victorian buildings is located 67 km NW of Melbourne. **Of interest:** Mechanics Hall (1868), old Macedonia House, now Antique Centre of Victoria (1889) and Cleveland, an historic home. In High St; paintings, ceramics and glass at The Gallery, and local crafts at Crafts Cottage. **In the area:** A number of wineries and nurseries. Burke and Wills Camel Farm, 12 km N, on Burke & Wills Track; 'hands on' workshops and education days; camel safaris and 1-day camel trek (12 km) to Knight's Winery. **Tourist information:** Centre Vic Motor Inn, Main Rd; (054) 29 1777. **Accommodation:** 1 motel.
MAP REF. 210 I2, 224 B1, 232 E12

Leongatha
Pop. 3968

Near the foothills of the Strzelecki Ranges, Leongatha, the centre of a dairying area, is a good base from which to make trips to Wilsons Promontory National Park and the seaside and fishing resorts on the coast. **Of interest:** Murray Goulburn Co-operative, one of Australia's largest dairy factories. Historic Society Museum, McCartin St. Magic Mushroom Pottery, Roughend St. Cycling Carnival held Feb. Daffodil and Floral Festival Aug.–Sept. **In the area:** Along the coast road there are impressive plantations of English trees, areas of natural bushland, picnic and camping facilities. About 21 km N, the Grand Ridge Rd offers excellent scenic driving and can be followed into the Tarra–Bulga National Park. Firelight Museum, 9 km N, displays antique lamps and firearms. Mossvale Park, 16 km NE, has picnic/barbecue facilities. At Mirboo North, 23 km NE: Grand Ridge Brewing Company for inspection of beer-brewing process; also Erimae Lavender Farm and Colonial Bank Antiques. Korumburra, with its Coal Creek Historical Park, 14 km W along South Gippsland Hwy. Brackenhurst Rotary Dairy on Christoffersens Rd, Nerrena; 350 cows, museum and bottle collection; open from 3.30 daily. **Tourist information:** Shire Offices, Woorayl; (056) 62 2111. **Accommodation:** 2 motels, 1 caravan/camping park.
MAP REF. 211 P12, 224 H8

Lorne
Pop. 1143

The approaches to Lorne along the Great Ocean Road, whether from east or west, are quite spectacular. The town is one of Victoria's most attractive coastal resorts, with the superb mountain scenery of the Otways behind, and a year-round mild climate. Captain Loutit gave the district the name of Loutit Bay. The village of Lorne was established in 1871, became popular with pastoralists from inland areas, and developed rather in the style of an English seaside resort. When the Great Ocean Road opened in 1932 Lorne grew more popular; however, the town itself has remained relatively unspoiled, with good beaches, surfing, and excellent bushwalking in the hills. **Of interest:** Teddy's Lookout, at the edge of George St behind town; good bay views. Foreshore reserve; children's playground, pool, trampolines, tennis courts and picnic ground. Shipwreck Walk along beach. Pedal boats for hire. Qdos Contemporary Art Gallery, Mountjoy Pde. Lorne Fisheries on pier; daily supplies from local fleet. Shell Shop and Museum, William St. Cumberland Resort, Mountjoy Pde. **In the area:** Angahook–Lorne State Park, surrounding town; many walking tracks, including one to Kalimna and Phantom waterfalls from Sheoak Picnic area; about 4 km from town. Erskine falls and rapids, 8 km N. Gentle Annie Berry Gardens, 26 km NW, via Deans Marsh. Mt Defiance, 10 km SW. Cumberland River Valley, 4 km S; walking tracks, camping ground. Allenvale, 2 km W; walking. Wye River, 17 km SW; fishing and surfing, limited accommodation. Scenic drives to west in the Otway Ranges and to south-west along Great Ocean Rd. **Tourist information:** 144 Mountjoy Pde; (052) 89 1036. **Accommodation:** 2 hotels, 5 motels, 5 caravan/camping parks. **See also:** The Great Ocean Road.
MAP REF. 210 D12, 217 A13, 227 P10

Macedon
Pop. 1137

Macedon is situated off the Calder Hwy, an hour from Melbourne. Large sections of the area were destroyed by bushfires in 1983. Today it is difficult to imagine this devastation, as the residents have rebuilt homes and re-established the beautiful gardens for which the area is renowned. Mount Macedon, formed by volcanic activity, is 1011 m high. At its summit is the memorial cross, erected in honour of those who died in World War I. **Of interest:** Coventry Antiques and Giftware and Lavender Place at Mount Macedon township; art and craft. **In the area:** Wineries include Hanging Rock near Hanging Rock, 8 km NW, Cope–Williams Vineyards at Romsey, 21 km E,

Erskine Falls, near Lorne

The Grampians

The massive sandstone ranges of the Grampians in Western Victoria provide some of the State's most spectacular scenery. Rising in peaks to heights of over 1000 metres, they form the western extremity of the Great Dividing Range. Major Mitchell climbed and named the highest peak, Mt William, in July 1836 and gave the name 'The Grampians' to the ranges because they reminded him of the Grampians in his native Scotland.

On 1 July 1984 these rugged mountain ranges became a national park. It is a superb area for scenic drives on good roads; bushwalking and rock climbing are also popular. Lake Bellfield provides for sailing and rowing, and there is trout fishing in the lake and in Fyans Creek. The Western and Northern Grampians have Aboriginal rock-art sites.

There is plenty of wildlife to be seen; koalas and kangaroos are numerous, and echidnas, possums and platypuses can be found, while more than 100 species of birds have been identified.

Apart from their scenic grandeur, the Grampians are best known for the beauty and variety of their wildflowers. There are more than 1000 species of ferns and flowering plants native to the region and they are at their most colourful from August to November. The Halls Gap Wildflower Exhibition is held annually in the Grampians National Park in September–October.

Halls Gap, which takes its name from a pioneer pastoralist who settled in the eastern Grampians in the early 1840s, is the focal point of the area; its wide variety of accommodation includes motels, guest houses, bed-and-breakfast options, holiday flats, cottages and cabins, a youth hostel and caravan and camping parks.

For further information, contact the Halls Gap Newsagency, Grampians Rd, Halls Gap; (053) 56 4247; the Stawell and Grampians Information Centre, 54 Western Hwy, West Stawell; (053) 58 2314; or the Grampians National Park Visitors Centre, Grampians Rd, Halls Gap; (053) 56 4381. **See also:** Entry for Halls Gap in A–Z listing.

and Lancefield, and Cleveland Winery, 30 km NE. Woodend, 10 km N, is an attractive old township at the safe 'wood's end' of the dangerous 'Black Forest' where more than a century ago, brigands lurked! Hanging Rock, made famous by Joan Lindsay's story, and the subsequent film, 7 km NE of Woodend; massive rock formation, ideal for climbing, viewing koalas; picnic reserve at base. Harvest Picnic, last Sun. in Feb.; Picnic races at Hanging Rock on New Year's Day and Australia Day. Trentham, potato-growing area and former gold-mining town, 25 km W of Woodend; historic foundry; crafts at 'Jargon'; Minifie's Berry Farm, pick your own in season. **Tourist information:** Woodend Information Centre; (054) 27 2033. **Accommodation:** 1 hotel, 1 motel, 1 caravan park.
MAP REF. 210 H3, 224 A2, 232 D13

Maffra–Heyfield
Pop. 3879, 1614
The Shire of Maffra includes both these towns and extends from the farming lands of the Macalister Irrigation Area north to the mountain scenery of the Great Dividing Range. **Of interest:** Maffra Sugar Beet Museum, River St. All Seasons Herb Gardens, Foster St. **In the area:** Lake Glenmaggie, 11 km N of Heyfield; popular water sports venue; camping facilities. The forest road north (closed in winter) that follows the Macalister Valley to Licola (49 km from Heyfield), or to Jamieson, (147 km), passes through spectacular scenery, leads to Mt Tamboritha (20 km N of Licola) and Mt Howitt (50 km); access to alpine country and the snowfields. The road north from Maffra, via Briagalong (14 km), leads over the Dargo High Plains and follows Freestone Creek; the Blue Pool and Quarries for swimming. Lake Tarli Karng, within the Alpine National Park, 60 km NE of Licola, is a major focus for bushwalking in the park. Trail-riding and horseback tours of area start from Valencia Creek, 17 km N of Maffra, and from Licola. Historic hotel, art and craft shops and Avonlea Gardens at Briagalong. **Tourist information:** Princes Hwy, Sale; (051) 44 1108. **Accommodation:** Maffra: 3 hotels, 1 motel, 1 caravan/camping park. Heyfield: 2 hotels, 1 motel.
MAP REF. 225 L5, 225 M5

Maldon
Pop. 1174
The National Trust has declared Maldon the 'First Notable Town' in Victoria, on the basis that no other town has such an interesting collection of 19th-century buildings, nor such a collection of European trees. Situated 20 km NW of Castlemaine in central Victoria, Maldon is very popular with tourists, especially during the Maldon Easter Fair, and in spring when the wildflowers are in bloom. The deep reef goldmines were among Victoria's richest, and at one stage 20 000 men worked on the nearby Tarrangower diggings. Enthusiasts still search for gold in the area. **Of interest:** Anzac Hill, at southern end of High St, affords a good view of the town. Many of the town's buildings, mostly constructed of local stone, are notable: in particular, Maldon Hospital (1860), cnr Adair and Chapel Sts; Post Office (1870), High St; old council offices, High St (now a folk museum); and Dabb's General Store in Main St, where the old storefront has been faithfully restored. Former Denominational (Penny) School and Welsh Congregational Church, cnr Camp and Church Sts; National Trust properties. In High St, Cumquat Tea Rooms. The Beehive Chimney (1862); south end of Church St. Castlemaine and Maldon Preservation Society runs steam trains from railway station, Hornsby St, Sun. Town walking tour brochure available. Derby Hill Accommodation Complex for school and family groups, Phoenix St. **In the area:** Delightful bushwalks and intriguing rock formations. Panoramic views from Mt Tarrangower Lookout Tower, 2 km W. Cairn Curran Reservoir, 10 km NW; water sports, fishing and picnics; sailing club near spillway. Nuggetty Ranges and Mt Marvel, 2 km N. Carmen's Tunnel, 2 km SW, vivid reminder of hardships of goldmining days; open

for inspection. Goldmining dredge beside road to Bendigo. To the northwest, Tarnagulla (38 km), Dunolly (37 km) and Bealiba (58 km), all former gold settlements. **Tourist information:** High St; (054) 75 2569. **Accommodation:** 1 motel, 2 caravan/camping parks. **See also:** The Golden Age.
MAP REF. 221 O4, 229 P11, 232 B10

Mallacoota   Pop. 961
On the Gippsland coast, at the mouth of a deep inlet of the same name, Mallacoota is a seaside and fishing township and a popular holiday centre. It offers the Croajingolong National Park, which surrounds the town, as well as beaches and fishing (Mallacoota's specialties are oysters and abalone). Bushwalking and birdwatching are also popular. **In the area:** Scenic lake and river cruises. Gipsy Point, 16 km N, is set in attractive countryside. Genoa, 24 km N, on Princes Hwy, is the last township before entering NSW, and nearby Genoa Peak has magnificent views. Karbeethong Lodge, on inlet 4 km from Mallacoota. Bastion Point and Betka surfing beaches. **Tourist information:** 57 Maurice Ave; (051) 58 0788. **Accommodation:** Mallacoota: 3 motels, 5 caravan/camping parks. Genoa: 1 motel, 4 caravan/camping parks. **See also:** National Parks.
MAP REF. 119 F13, 235 O11

Mansfield   Pop. 2178
A popular inland resort at the junction of the Midland and Maroondah Hwys, Mansfield is 3 km E of the northern arm of Eildon Weir. It is the nearest sizeable town to the Mt Buller Alpine Village. **Of interest:** In High St, marble obelisk erected to the memory of three police officers shot by Ned Kelly at Stringybark Creek, near Tolmie, in 1878. Their graves are in the Mansfield cemetery. Highton Manor (1896), Highton Lane. Annual Mountain Country Festival held Nov. **In the area:** Horse and trail-bike riding. The road north-east over the mountains to Whitfield in the King River Valley (62 km) passes through spectacular scenery. To the south are the Goulburn and Jamieson Rivers; trout fishing and gold fossicking. Delatite Winery on Pollards Rd, 7 km S. Mt Samaria State Park, 14 km N; scenic drives, picnics, camping and bushwalking. Nearby Lake Nillahcootie; boating, fishing, canoeing and sailing. Children's Adventure Camps; Nillahcootie camps. Howqua Dale Gourmet

Retreat, at Howqua, 29 km S; food weekends and sporting facilities. Historic buildings at old goldmining town of Jamieson, 37 km S, on Jamieson River. Lake William Hovell, 85 km NE; picnic/barbecue facilities, children's playground, boating, canoeing and fishing. Merrijig, 18 km SE, and Craig's Hut, at Clear Hills, 50 km E; used for filming *The Man from Snowy River*. Hot-air balloon flights available. Alpine National Park, 60 km E, is less accessible than other Victorian national parks but offers bushwalks through remote terrain. Kratlund Park, Mansfield; farm holidays. Houseboats for hire on Lake Eildon. **Tourist information:** Visitors Centre, 11 High St; (057) 75 1464. **Accommodation:** 3 hotels, 3 motels, 2 caravan/camping parks. **See also:** Wine Regions.
MAP REF. 211 R1, 222 C10, 233 K10

Maryborough   Pop. 7623
First sheep farming, then the gold rush, contributed to the development of this small city on the northern slopes of the Great Dividing Range, 70 km N of Ballarat. Modern Maryborough is in the centre of an agricultural and forest area and is highly industrialised. **Of interest:** Pioneer Memorial Tower, Bristol Hill. Worsley Cottage (1894), Palmerston St; historical museum. Maryborough railway station, Victoria St. Imposing Civic Square buildings, Clarendon St. Princes Park, Park Rd; good sports facilities. Maryborough Highland Gathering on New Year's Day. Country Music Festival held Feb. Race meetings April and Oct. Trotting meeting July. Golden Wattle Festival Sept.–Oct. Three-day Energy Breakthrough, Nov., energy expo, machine races, team competitions, music, food and entertainment. **In the area:** Aboriginal wells, 4 km S. To the north, the once thriving gold towns of Bowenvale–Timor (6 km), Dunolly (23 km) and Tarnagulla (37 km). **Tourist information:** Cnr Tuaggra and Alma Sts; (054) 60 4509. **Accommodation:** 1 hotel/motel, 6 motels, 2 caravan/camping parks.
MAP REF. 221 L5, 229 O12

Marysville   Pop. 662
The peaceful and attractive sub-alpine town of Marysville, which owes its existence first to gold, as it was on the route to the Woods Point goldfields, and later to timber milling, is 37 km N of Healesville, off the Maroondah Hwy. The town is surrounded by attractive forest-clad

mountain country and is a popular resort all year. **Of interest:** Hidden Talents, Murchison St. Arbour Green Gallery, Falls Rd. Goulds Sawmill, Racecourse Rd; open for inspection. Nicholl's Lookout, Cumberland Rd; excellent views. Burrengeen Park, Murchison St; historic display within park. **In the area:** Numerous bushwalking tracks lead to beauty spots in the area, including 4-km loop walk in Cumberland Memorial Scenic Reserve, 16 km E, 2-hr walk to Keppel's Lookout, 90-min. walk to Mt Gordon and 2-hr walk to Steavenson Falls (illuminated at night). Lake Eildon, 46 km NE, and Fraser National Park, 59 km NE, are within easy driving distance. Lake Mountain, 19 km E; accessible walking and cross-country skiing trails, tobogganing. Buxton Camel Farm, Buxton Trout Farm and Australian Bush Pioneer's Farm, at foot of Mt Cathedral, 10 km N. Marysville Trout Farm, Marysville Rd, 2 km SW. Big River State Forest, 30 km E, for camping, fishing, hunting, trail-bike riding and gold fossicking. **Tourist information:** The Old Yarra Track Shoppe, 18 Murchison St; (059) 63 3453. **Accommodation:** 1 hotel, 4 motels, 1 caravan/camping park.
MAP REF. 211 P4, 214 I4, 224 G2, 233 J13

Milawa–Oxley   Pop. 120
On what is known as the Snow Road, Milawa, 16 km SE of Wangaratta, is the home of Brown Brothers Vineyard. John Gehrig's and Read's wineries are to be found at Oxley, 4 km W, and the Markwood Estate Vineyard is 6 km E. Bogong Jack Adventures runs a range of bicycle tours from Oxley. The Snow Road links Oxley, Milawa and Markwood with Wangaratta to the west and the Ovens Hwy to the east. **Of interest:** In Snow Rd: Milawa Royal general store for light meals, and Old Emu Restaurant. Milawa Mustards, off Snow Rd; specialist mustards in cottage-garden setting. Milawa Cheese Company in Factory Rd; specialist cheeses and ploughman's lunches. **Tourist information:** Wangaratta and Region Visitors Information Centre, Hume Hwy; (057) 21 5711. **Accommodation:** 1 motel, 1 caravan/camping park. **See also:** Wine Regions.
MAP REF. 222 F1, 233 M6

Mildura   Pop. 23 176
Sunny mild winters and picturesque locations on the banks of the Murray make

Mildura and neighbouring towns popular tourist areas. Mildura, on the Sunraysia Hwy, 557 km N of Melbourne, is a small and pleasant city that developed along with the irrigation of the area. Alfred Deakin, statesman and advocate of irrigation, persuaded the Chaffey brothers, Canadian-born irrigation experts, to visit this region. They recognised its potential and selected Mildura as the first site for development. The early days of the project were fraught with setbacks, but by the turn of the century the citrus-growing industry was well established and with the locking of the Murray completed in 1928, Mildura soon afterwards became a city. **Of interest:** W.B. Chaffey became Mildura's first mayor; statue in Deakin Ave. Mildura Arts Centre, Chaffey Ave; includes first irrigation pump and Rio Vista, original Chaffey home, now a museum with a collection of colonial household items. Paddle-steamers leave from Mildura Wharf, end of Madden Ave, for trips on the Murray and Darling Rivers. PS *Melbourne* does 2-hr round trips. PS *Avoca* has luncheon and dinner cruises. PS *Coonawarra* offers 5- and 6-day cruises. Humpty Dumpty Tourist Farm, Cureton Ave, and Sultana Sam Vineyard, Benetook Ave, are popular with children. Mildura Lock Island and Weir can be inspected. Other attractions include: Aquacoaster waterslide, cnr Seventh St and Orange Ave; Dolls on the Avenue, Benetook Ave; Pioneer Cottage, Hunter St. The Citrus Shop, Pine Ave; educational aids and sales. Great Mildura Paddleboat Race held Easter Mon. **In the area:** River Road Pottery, 10 km W.

Woodsie's Gem Shop, 6 km SW. Many vineyards, including Lindemans (largest winery in southern hemisphere), Mildura Vineyards, Stanley, Trentham Estate and Mildara Blass; open weekdays, tastings and sales. Capogreco Wines, Riverside Ave; open Mon.–Sat. Orange World, 6 km N in NSW, offers tours of citrus-growing areas. Golden River Zoo, 3 km NW; large collection of native and exotic species in natural surroundings. PS *Rothbury* offers day cruises. Yabbies at Gol Gol Fisheries, 2 km N in NSW; open daily. Hattah–Kulkyne National Park, 70 km S, for bushwalking. At Irymple, 6 km S, Sunbeam Dried Fruits; tours. Red Cliffs, 15 km S; important area for citrus and dried fruit industries. 'Big Lizzie' steam traction engine at Red Cliffs. **Tourist information:** 41 Deakin Ave; (050) 21 4424. **Accommodation:** 3 hotels, 45 motels, 25 caravan/camping parks. **See also:** The Mighty Murray; Wine Regions.
MAP REF. 126 E7, 230 G4

Moe
Pop. 17 000

Situated on the Princes Hwy, 134 km SE of Melbourne, Moe is a rapidly growing residential city in the Latrobe Valley and gateway to the alpine region. **Of interest:** Old Gippstown Pioneer Township, Lloyd St; re-creation of 19th-century community, with over 30 restored buildings brought from surrounding areas; fine collection of fully restored horse-drawn vehicles; picnic/barbecue facilities, adventure playground; open daily. Jazz Festival in March. Trout fishing in Narracan Creek. **In the area:**

Mair's Coalville Vineyard at Moe South. A scenic road leads north-east 46 km to the picturesque old mining township of Walhalla, Thomson Dam nearby, and through the mountains to Jamieson, 147 km further north. The Baw Baw plateau and Mt Baw Baw and Mt Saint Gwinear, cross country and downhill skiing are accessed 47 km N via Willow Grove. The plateau is the highest alpine point in central Gippsland; and has abundant wildflowers in summer, excellent for bushwalking. Blue Rock Dam, 20 km N of Moe; fishing, swimming, sailing, picnic facilities. **Tourist information:** Old Gippstown Pioneer Township, Lloyd St; (051) 27 6928. **Accommodation:** 3 motels, 1 caravan/camping park.
MAP REF. 211 R10, 224 I6

Morwell
Pop. 15 423

Morwell, 150 km SE of Melbourne, is situated in the heart of the Latrobe Valley. This valley contains one of the world's largest deposits of brown coal. Morwell is an industrial town with a number of secondary industries. **Of interest:** State Electricity Commission's Visitors Centre; open daily for free guided tours. La Trobe Regional Gallery, Commercial Rd. **In the area:** Scenic day tours can be made from the three main cities in the Latrobe Valley: Morwell; Moe, 20 km W; and Traralgon, 12 km E. Lake Narracan and the Hazelwood pondage, 5 km S of Morwell; water sports and picnics. Morwell National Park, walking tracks, picnic facilities, 12 km S. Views of Moe, Yallourn North and the valley between Strzelecki Ranges and Baw Baw

PS Melbourne, *Murray River, Mildura*

mountains at Narracan Falls, about 27 km w. Tarra–Bulga National Park, 47 km SE, renowned for its fern glades, waterfalls, rosellas, lyrebirds and koalas. To the north, 66 km through dense mountain country, old mining township of Walhalla, and further on, Moondarra Reservoir and the beautiful Tanjil and Thomson River valleys. **Tourist information:** SEC Visitors Centre, off Commercial Rd; (051) 35 3170. **Accommodation:** 2 hotels, 9 motels, 2 caravan/camping parks.
MAP REF. 225 J7

Mount Beauty   Pop. 1837

Situated in the Upper Kiewa Valley, 344 km NE of Melbourne, Mount Beauty was originally an accommodation township for workers on the Kiewa Hydro-electric Scheme in the 1940s. An ideal holiday centre, the town lies at the foot of Mount Bogong, Victoria's highest mountain (1986 m). **Of interest:** Leaflets outlining walks, excursions and other activities; from tourist information centres and National Parks Office. The Conquestathon, family day and climb to the summit of Mt Bogong; held March, Labour Day weekend. The Kangaroo Hoppet; cross-country ski event in Aug. **In the area:** Scenic road, 32 km SE to Falls Creek and the Bogong High Plains. Mountain-bike hire, horseriding and 4WD tours. Excellent hang-gliding. Mount Beauty Pondage; water sports and fishing. Bogong Village, 16 km SE; walks around Lake Guy. Tours of the Kiewa and other power stations; advance bookings through SEC recommended. Skiing holidays to suit both cross-country and downhill skiers available at Mount Beauty and Falls Creek. **Tourist information:** Pyles Coach Service; (057) 57 3172, or SEC Information Centre, Kiewa Valley Hwy; (057) 57 2307. **Accommodation:** 6 motels, 2 caravan/camping parks.
MAP REF. 223 N5, 233 Q8, 234 C6

Murtoa   Pop. 878

Murtoa is situated on the edge of picturesque Lake Marma, 30 km NE of Horsham on the Wimmera Hwy. It is in the centre of Victoria's wheat belt and with two other old wheat towns, Minyip and Rupanyup, makes up the Shire of Dunmunkle. **Of interest:** Huge wheat-storage silo. Four-storey railway watertower (1886); now a museum, includes James Hill's taxidermy collection of some 500 birds, prepared between 1885

Snow slopes, Falls Creek

and 1930; open Sun. p.m. Lake Marma; trout and redfin fishing, caravan park on eastern side. Lake also offers birdwatching and spectacular sunsets. Major race meeting New Years Day; 6 other meetings annually. **In the area:** Rupanyup, 16 km E; attractive old township, and administrative centre of Shire. Barrabool Forest Reserve, 7 km S; attractive spring display of wildflowers. **Tourist information:** Marma Gully Antiques, 50 Marma St; (053) 85 2422. **Accommodation:** 2 hotels, 1 caravan/camping park.
MAP REF. 228 I9

Myrtleford   Pop. 2862

On the Ovens Hwy, 45 km SE of Wangaratta, the town of Myrtleford is surrounded by a rich hops- and tobacco-growing area. It also has some of the largest walnut groves in the southern hemisphere. The Ovens Valley was opened up by miners flocking to the area and creeks there are still popular for gold panning and gem fossicking. **Of interest:** The Phoenix Tree, sculptured butt of a red gum crafted by Hans Knorr; on highway at town entrance. Reform Hill Lookout, end of Halls Rd. Jaycees Historic Park and Swing Bridge, Standish St. Many other delightful picnic spots and rest areas. Tobacco, Hops and Timber Festival held March, Labour Day weekend. **In the area:** Lake Buffalo, 25 km S, Ovens River and Buffalo River, 31 km S; good fishing. Mt Buffalo National Park and historic towns of Beechworth, Yackandandah and Bright are within easy

driving distance (4WD vehicles for hire in Myrtleford). Swinburne Reserve, 5 km S of Myrtleford on road to Bright, is starting point for self-guide forest walks and a fitness track; picnic facilities. Historic Merriang Homestead, 6 km SW. Guided tours to hop and tobacco farms. **Tourist information:** Ponderosa Cabin, 29–31 Clyde St; (057) 52 1727. **Accommodation:** 1 hotel, 1 hotel/motel, 2 motels, 2 caravan/camping parks.
MAP REF. 223 J2, 233 N7, 234 A5

Nagambie   Pop. 1215

Between Seymour and Shepparton on the Goulburn Valley Hwy, Nagambie is on the shores of Lake Nagambie, which was created by the construction of the Goulburn Weir in 1891. Rowing and yachting regattas, speedboat and water-ski tournaments are held here throughout the year. There is a 65-m water-slide at one of the swimming areas. **Of interest:** Several buildings classified by National Trust. Historical Society display of colonial Victoriana and early horsedrawn vehicles. Annual Boxing Day rowing regatta. Pottery, art and craft shops. **In the area:** Two of Victoria's best-known wineries, Chateau Tahbilk and Mitchelton. Buildings at Chateau Tahbilk, 6 km SW, have been classified by the National Trust and cellars are open for tastings, inspections and sales. Mitchelton Winery, 10 km SW, off Goulburn Valley Hwy, has cellar-door sales and tastings, tours available; open daily. Mitchelton's features a 60-m observation tower; licensed restaurant—open daily. Scenic river cruises on the Goulburn River from Mitchelton's; frequently in the summer, and weekends and public holidays throughout the year. At Graytown, 24 km W; Osicka's Vineyard. David Traeger Wines; on Goulburn Valley Hwy at northern end of town. Italian War Memorial and chapel at Murchison, 23 km N. Meteorite Park, Murchison; site of 1969 meteorite fall. Longleat Winery, 2 km S of Murchison. Days Mill, flour mill with buildings dating from 1865, 5 km S of Murchison. **Tourist information:** 320 High St; (057) 94 2647. **Accommodation:** 5 motels, 2 caravan/camping parks. **See also:** Wine Regions.
MAP REF. 232 G9

Natimuk   Pop. 464

This Wimmera town, 27 km W of Horsham, is close to the striking Mt Arapiles, a 356-m sandstone monolith that has

been described as 'Victoria's Ayers Rock'. This monolith is in the Mount Arapiles–Tooan State Park. A drive to the summit reveals a scenic lookout and a telecommunications relay station. The mountain was first climbed by Major Mitchell in 1836 and is popular with rock-climbing enthusiasts. **Of interest:** Arapiles Historical Society museum in old courthouse, Main St. **In the area:** Lake Natimuk, 2 km N; water sports. Mount Arapiles–Tooan State Park, 12 km SW. Duffholme Cabins and Museum, 21 km W. **Tourist information:** Natimuk Hotel, Main St; (053) 87 1300. **Accommodation:** 1 hotel, 1 caravan/camping park.
MAP REF. 228 F10

Nhill   Pop. 1891
The name of this town is possibly derived from the Aboriginal word *nyell*, meaning 'white mist on water'. A small wheat town on the Western Hwy, exactly halfway between Melbourne and Adelaide, it claims to have the largest single-bin silo in the southern hemisphere. **Of interest:** Historical Society Museum, McPherson St; open weekends. Cottage of John Shaw Neilson, lyric poet, in Shaw Neilson Park, Western Hwy. Draught Horse Memorial in Goldsworthy Park, built to the memory of the famous Clydesdales, which were indispensable in opening up the Wimmera region. Nhill's Post Office, built in 1888, classified by National Trust. The Wagan Inn; information display with farming relics. Lowana Craft Shop; handcrafted local goods, refreshments. **In the area:** Self-guide car-tour leaflets available. Access to Little Desert National Park and Little Desert Lodge via Kiata, 23 km E. Little Desert Wildflower Exhibition each spring. Lake Hindmarsh, largest freshwater lake in Victoria, 45 km N. Access to the Big Desert Wilderness via Yanac, 32 km NW, on track north to Murrayville; exploration of this remote area by walking tracks only. **Tourist information:** Victoria St; (053) 91 3086 or (053) 91 1811. **Accommodation:** 3 hotels, 5 motels, 1 caravan/camping park.
MAP REF. 228 E7

Numurkah   Pop. 3128
Numurkah, 35 km N of Shepparton on the Goulburn Valley Hwy, is only a half-hour drive from some excellent beaches and fishing spots on the Murray River. The town is in an irrigation area concentrating on fruit-growing and dairying, and was originally developed through the Murray Valley Soldier Settlement Scheme. **Of interest:** Steam and Vintage Machinery Display. Rose Festival each Easter. **In the area:** Barmah Red Gum Forest, 40 km NW. Morgan's Beach Caravan Park, at edge of forest on bank of Murray, offers bushwalking, horseriding and resident koalas and kangaroos. Glen Arran, 4 km N; tourist farm and dairy. Monichino's Winery at Katunga, 11 km N. Ulupna Island flora and fauna reserve, near Strathmerton, 21 km N. Kraft cheese factory, and Spikes and Blooms cactus garden (1 ha), both at Strathmerton. Brookfield Historic Holiday Farm and Museum, 6 km SE. Historic buildings set on banks of Broken Creek, at Nathalia, 12 km W. **Tourist information:** Chicken Ranch, 1 Melville St; (058) 62 2020. **Accommodation:** 2 hotels, 2 motels, 1 caravan/camping park.
MAP REF. 127 M13, 232 H4

Ocean Grove–Barwon Heads   Pop. 10 069
At the mouth of the Barwon River, the resort of Ocean Grove offers fishing and surfing, while nearby Barwon Heads offers safe family relaxation along the shores of its protected river. Both resorts are popular in the summer months as they are the closest ocean beaches to Geelong, 22 km to the NW. **Of interest:** Ocean Grove Nature Reserve, Grubb Rd. **In the area:** Jirrahlinga Koala and Wildlife Sanctuary, Taits Rd, Barwon Heads; open daily. At Wallington, 8 km N: A Maze'N Things, Moorfield Wildlife Park, Koombahla Park Equestrian Centre and Country Connection Trout Farm. At Lake Connewarre, 7 km N; mangrove swamps and Lake Connewarre State Game Reserve. **Tourist information:** A Maze'N Things, cnr Bellarine Hwy and Grubb Rd, Wallington; (052) 50 2669. **Accommodation:** Ocean Grove: 2 motels, 5 caravan/camping parks. Barwon Heads: 1 hotel, 1 motel, 2 caravan/camping parks.
MAP REF. 210 G10, 217 G8, 217 G9, 224 A7, 227 R8, 227 R9

Omeo   Pop. 274
The high plains around Omeo were opened up in 1835 when overlanders from the Monaro region moved their stock south to these lush summer pastures. Its name is an Aboriginal word meaning mountains, and the township is set in the heart of the Victorian Alps at an altitude of 643 m. It is used as a base for winter traffic approaching Mt Hotham from Bairnsdale, 120 km S, and for bushwalking and fishing expeditions to the Bogong High Plains in summer and autumn. **Of interest:** Omeo has suffered several natural disasters: it was devastated by earthquakes in 1885 and 1892 and was destroyed by the Black Friday bushfires of 1939. Nevertheless, several old buildings remaining in the area are of historic interest, some seen in the A.M. Pearson Historical Park, Main St; including old courthouse (1892), at rear of present courthouse. Also in park: log gaol (1858); stables; blacksmith's shop. **In the area:** Scenic road leads to Corryong, 148 km NE, past the Dartmouth Reservoir; difficult to negotiate in bad weather; motorists should be alert for timber trucks and wandering cattle. Tambo River valley to the south; especially

Big Desert Wilderness, near Nhill

beautiful in autumn. Omeo has a gold-rush history; high cliffs left after sluicing for gold can be seen at the Oriental Diggings. Gold panning is still popular along Livingstone Creek; pans for hire from Shire Offices. Blue Duck Inn (1890s) is a base for fishing at Anglers Rest, 29 km NW. High-country horseback and 4WD tours, walking, skiing, rafting and abseiling. **Tourist information:** Octagon Bookshop, Day Ave; (051) 59 1411. **Accommodation:** 2 hotels, 1 motel, 1 caravan/camping park.
MAP REF. 119 A11, 234 E8

Orbost   Pop. 2515
Situated on the banks of the Snowy River, this Gippsland timber town is on the Princes Hwy, surrounded by spectacular coastal and mountain territory. **Of interest:** Historical Museum, Nicholson St. Old Pump House, behind Slab Hut Information Centre (1872); hut relocated from its original site 40 km from Orbost. Rainforest Interpretation Centre, Lockiel St; audiovisual display explaining complex nature of rainforest ecology. Croajingolong Mohair, Nicholson St; garments, yarns, fleeces, fabrics and leathergoods. Gemstone and Art Gallery, cnr Browning and Carlyle Sts. **In the area:** Beautiful Bonang Hwy, unsealed in parts, leads north through mountains to Delegate in NSW. Spectacular road to Buchan leads to Little River Falls and McKillop's Bridge on the Snowy River. At Bonang, 97 km NE; Aurora Mine, working goldmine, open daily; fishing; walking in nearby national parks, including rainforest boardwalk at Errinundra, 30 km SE. Tranquil Valley Tavern, on the banks of the Delegate River near the NSW border; log cabin accommodation and licensed restaurant. For a coastal drive, Cape Conran Rd, just west of Orbost, to Marlo. Marlo–Cape Conran road (18 km); coastal views. Cape Conran Reserve; accommodation in holiday cabins. Bemm River, on Sydenham Inlet, 57 km from Orbost; popular centre for bream fishermen. Baldwin Spencer Trail, 262-km driving circuit. Cabbage Tree Palms Flora Reserve, 27 km E of Orbost. Coopracambra National Park, 136 km NE, near NSW border. Errinundra National Park, 83 km NW. Croajingolong National Park, west along coast, from Sydenham Inlet to border. **Tourist information:** The Slab Hut, cnr Nicholson and Clarke Sts; (051) 54 2424.

Accommodation: 2 hotels, 3 motels, 2 caravan/camping parks.
MAP REF. 119 C13, 234 I12

Ouyen   Pop. 1337
On the Sunraysia Hwy, Ouyen is about 100 km S of Mildura, north-east of the Big Desert area. **Of interest:** Farmers Festival in Nov. **In the area:** Hattah–Kulkyne National Park, 34 km N; habitats for abundant wildlife; birdwatching, bushwalking, canoeing, wildflowers in spring. Pink Lakes State Park, 60 km W; lakes are outstanding subjects for photography. Tag-along and 4WD tours. **Tourist information:** Resource Centre, Oke St; (050) 92 1763. **Accommodation:** 1 hotel, 2 motels, 1 caravan/camping park. **See also:** The Mallee.
MAP REF. 126 E10, 230 H9

Paynesville   Pop. 2444
A popular tourist resort 18 km from Bairnsdale on the McMillan Straits, Paynesville is a mecca for the boating enthusiast, and is famous for yachting and speedboat racing as well as water-skiing. It is the headquarters of the Gippsland Lakes Yacht Club, and speedboat championships are held each Christmas and Easter. **Of interest:** St Peter-by-the-Lake (1961); incorporates seafaring symbols. Community Craft Centre. Captain Petries; mini-golf and bike hire. Market 2nd Sun. in month. **In the area:** Ninety Mile Beach, 10 km S by boat; punt crosses Straits to Raymond Island. Koala Reserve on Raymond Island. The Lakes National Park, 5 km by boat to Sperm Whale Head; otherwise accessed via Loch Sport. Rotomah Island Bird Observatory, 8 km S by boat. Cruises on MV *Lakes Odyssey*. Boat charter and hire. Organised scenic tours of lakes. Dolphins in bay. **Tourist information:** Mobil Service Centre, Esplanade; (051) 566 5504. **Accommodation:** 1 motel, 5 caravan/camping parks. **See also:** Gippsland Lakes.
MAP REF. 225 P5, 234 F13

Port Albert   Pop. 307
This tiny and historic township on the south-east coast, 120 km from Morwell, was the first established port in Victoria. Sailing boats from Europe and America once docked at the large timber jetty here. Boats from China brought thousands of Chinese to the Gippsland goldfields. Originally established for trade with Tasmania, Port Albert was the supply port

for Gippsland pioneers for many years until the railway line from Melbourne to Sale was completed in 1878. The timber jetty is still crowded with boats as it is a commercial fishing port and its sheltered waters are popular with fishermen and boat owners. Some of the original stone buildings are still in use and are classified by the National Trust. **Of interest:** Historic buildings in Tarraville Rd include: original government offices and stores; Bank of Victoria (1861), housing the Maritime Museum, with photographs and relics of the area. Port Albert Hotel, Wharf St, first licensed in 1842, possibly the oldest hotel still operating in state. Warren Curry Art Gallery, Tarraville Rd; Australian country-town streetscapes. Seabank fishing competition on Sun. of March Labour Day weekend. **In the area:** Christ Church at Tarraville (1856), 5 km NE; first church in Gippsland. Also to north-east (8 km), Alberton, once the administrative capital of Yarram (14 km) and Gippsland. Swimming at Mann's Beach, 10 km E. Wildlife sanctuary on St Margaret Island, 12 km E. Tarra–Bulga National Park, 41 km NW. Surfing at Woodside on Ninety Mile Beach, 34 km NE. **Accommodation:** 1 hotel/motel, 2 caravan/camping parks.
MAP REF. 225 K10

Port Campbell   Pop. 234
This small crayfishing village and seaside resort is situated in the centre of the Port Campbell National Park and on a spectacular stretch of the Great Ocean Road. **Of interest:** Historical Museum, Lord St; open school holidays. Loch Ard Shipwreck Museum, Lord St. Self-guide Discovery Walk. Good fishing from rocks and pier. **In the area:** Otway Deer and Wildlife Park, 20 km E. Port Campbell National Park, surrounding town; includes world-famous Twelve Apostles and Loch Ard Gorge, 5–10 km E, and London Bridge (now fallen down), 5 km W. Walking tracks and historic shipwreck sites; Historic Shipwreck Trail links sites along 'Shipwreck Coast', from Princetown to Port Fairy. **Tourist information:** National Parks Office, Tregea St; (055) 98 6382. **Accommodation:** 1 hotel, 4 motels, 1 caravan/camping park. **See also:** The Great Ocean Road.
MAP REF. 215 A10, 227 K10

Port Fairy   Pop. 2467
The home port for a large fishing fleet and an attractive, rambling holiday

resort, Port Fairy is 29 km w of Warrnambool with both ocean and river as its borders. The town's history goes back to whaling days. At one time it was one of the largest ports in Australia. Many of its small cottages and bluestone buildings have been classified by the National Trust—over 50 in all. This charming old-world fishing village is popular with heritage lovers and holidaymakers. **Of interest:** History Centre, Gipps St; in old courthouse, several display rooms. Booklet and map for Town Walk and Port Fairy Shipwreck Walk available. Battery Hill, end Griffith St; old fort and signal station at mouth of river. National Trust classifications: splendid timber home of Captain Mills, Gipps St; Mott's Cottage, 5 Sackville St; and 48 other houses in the area. Other attractive buildings include: Old Caledonian Inn, Bank St; Seacombe House and ANZ Bank building, Cox St; St John's Church of England (1856), Regent St; *Gazette* Office (1849), Sackville St. Main annual events include New Year's Eve procession, Moyneyana Festival in Jan., award-winning Port Fairy Folk Festival in March (Labour Day weekend), Spring Classical Music Festival in Oct., Heritage Discovery Weekend in Nov. **In the area:** Griffiths Island, connected to east of town by causeway; lighthouse and muttonbird rookeries; spectacular nightly return of the mutton-birds to island during Sept.–April. Other rookeries at Pea Soup Beach and South Beach, on southern edge of town; Australia's only mainland colony of mutton-birds. Lady Julia Percy Island, 10 km off coast, home for fur seals; only accessible by experienced boat operators in calm weather; tours available in summer, weather permitting. Waters off coast also attract big-game fishing for the white pointer shark. Tower Hill, a fascinating area with an extinct volcano, crater lake and islands, 14 km E. Mt Eccles National Park, 56 km NW. Yambuk and Lake Yambuk, 17 km w. **Tourist information:** 22 Bank St; (055) 68 2682. **Accommodation:** 6 motels, 6 caravan/camping parks. **See also:** The Great Ocean Road. MAP REF. 226 H9

Portarlington
Pop. 2553

Named after an Irish village and with a history of Irish settlement in the area, Portarlington is a popular seaside resort on the Bellarine Peninsula, 31 km E of Geelong. It has a safe bay for children to swim, good fishing and a variety of water

Pyramid Hill

sports. **Of interest:** Historic flour mill (1857), Turner Crt; restored by National Trust, houses historical and educational display. Isadora's Coffee and Collectables, Geelong Rd. Lavender Cottage Gallery, Fenwick St. Public Reserve, Sprout St; picnic facilities. **Tourist information:** A Maze'N Things, cnr Bellarine Hwy and Grubb Rd, Wallington; (052) 50 2669. **Accommodation:** 1 motel, 3 caravan/camping parks. MAP REF. 210 H9, 217 I6, 224 B6

Portland
Pop. 10 115

Portland, situated about 75 km E of the South Australian border, is the most western of Victoria's major coastal towns and is the only deep-water port between Melbourne and Adelaide. It was the first permanent settlement in Victoria, founded by the Henty brothers in 1834. Today it is an important industrial and commercial centre and a popular summer resort with beaches, surfing, fishing and outstanding coastal and forest scenery. There are a number of short walks in and around Portland; self-guide brochures are available at the Tourist Information Centre. For the more energetic, the 250-km Great South West Walk, a circular track that begins and ends at the Centre and travels through national parks and State forests to Discovery Bay and Cape Nelson, can be covered in easy stages. **Of interest:** Botanical Gardens,

Cliff St, established 1857. Many early buildings, some National-Trust-classified; among them customs house and court-house in Cliff St, and several old inns, including Steam Packet Hotel (1842) and Mac's Hotel in Bentinck St. History House; historical museum in old town hall (1864). Fawthrop Lagoon, Glenelg St; 140 bird species. Nearby, Powerhouse Museum in Percy St. Good views and picnic facilities at Portland Battery on Battery Hill. Guided tours of Portland Aluminium Smelter Tues. p.m.; bookings (008) 035567 and (055) 23 2671. Award-winning wineries: Kingsley Winery, Bancroft St; and Barrett's Gorae West Wines, Gorae Rd. **In the area:** Historic homesteads, including Maretimo, 3 km N, and Burswood, Cape Nelson Rd. Cape Nelson State Park, 11 km SW; spectacular coastal scenery and lighthouse classified by National Trust. At Cape Bridgewater, 16 km SW; petrified forest, blowholes, freshwater springs and the Watering Place, as well as walks to Discovery Bay and Cape Duquesne, both further west. Good swimming and surfing. Mt Richmond National Park, 45 km NW; displays of spring wildflowers. Narrawong State Forest, 18 km NE. Cave Hill Gardens at Heywood, 27 km N; picnic facilities. Bower Birds Nest Museum at Heywood. Caledonian Inn Museum, 8 km N. The Princes Hwy swings inland at Portland, but 70 km w along coastal road is the tiny, charming hamlet of Nelson, favoured by holidaymakers from Mt Gambier. Nearby Princess Margaret Rose Caves; worth a visit. Pleasant tours up the Glenelg River. Lower Glenelg National Park, 44 km NW via Kentbruck and 73 km via Nelson; spectacular gorges, colourful wildflowers, native birds, excellent fishing, limited accommodation. Farm holidays available at Quamby Park near Tyrendarra, 25 km NE, Nioka, near Mt Richmond National Park, and Bonnie View at Heathmere. **Tourist information:** Cliff St; (055) 23 2671 or (008) 03 5567. **Accommodation:** 10 motels, 7 caravan/camping parks. MAP REF. 226 E9

Pyramid Hill
Pop. 546

A small country town some 40 km SW of Cohuna and 100 km N of Bendigo, Pyramid Hill was named for its unusually shaped hill, 187 m high. **Of interest:** Historical museum, McKay St. A climb to the top of Pyramid Hill itself (also Braille walking trail) allows scenic views

of the surrounding irrigation and wheat district. **In the area:** Mt Hope, 10 km NE, named by Major Mitchell. To south, 2833-ha Murray Pine forest reserve with numerous granite outcrops. Terrick Terrick State Forest, with southernmost outcrop, Mitiamo Rock; picnic ground, walks, variety of birdlife and other fauna. **Tourist information:** Newsagency; (054) 55 7036. **Accommodation:** 1 hotel, 1 caravan/camping park.
MAP REF. 126 I13, 229 P5, 232 B4

Queenscliff–Point Lonsdale
Pop. 3681

Queenscliff, 31 km E of Geelong on the Bellarine Peninsula, was established as a commercial fishing centre in the 1850s and still has a large fishing fleet based in its harbour. The town looks out across the famous and treacherous Rip at the entrance to Port Phillip Bay. **Of interest:** Queenscliff Maritime Centre, Weeroona Pde; explores town's long association with the sea and the days of sailing ships. Adjacent Marine Studies Centre; summer holiday programme for visitors. Queenscliff Fine Arts Gallery in old Wesleyan Church, Hesse St. Hobson's Choice Gallery, Hobson St. Seaview Gallery in Seaview House, Hesse St. Many old buildings, including Fort Queenscliff (1882), built during the Crimean War, and the Black Lighthouse (1861), King St; some grand old hotels including the Vue Grand in Hesse St, the Ozone and the Queenscliff in Gellibrand St. Queenscliff Historical Tours leave from Queenscliff Pier. Steam train operates between Queenscliff (station in Symonds St) and Drysdale; weekends, daily in summer holidays. Regular passenger ferry service operates between Queenscliff and Portsea across the bay; summer and school holidays. Car and passenger ferry service between Queenscliff and Sorrento (about 35 min.); daily all year. 'Snorkelling with the seals' can be arranged through tourist information centre. Point Lonsdale has been extensively developed as a holiday and tourist resort; good swimming and surfing. Queenscliff Market, Symonds St; last Sun. of months Aug.–April. Pt Lonsdale Sunday Market, Bowen Rd; 2nd Sun. in month. **In the area:** Marine life viewing at Harold Holt Marine Reserve, which includes Mud Island and coastal reserves. Lake Victoria, 1 km W of Point Lonsdale. **Tourist information:** A Maze'N Things, cnr Bellarine Hwy and Grubb Rd, Wallington; (052) 50 2669. **Accommodation:** Queenscliff: 3 hotels, 4 caravan/camping parks. Point Lonsdale: 2 motels, 2 caravan/camping parks. MAP REF. 210 H10, 212 A5, 217 I9, 224 B7

Rainbow
Pop. 587

This Wimmera township, 70 km N of Dimboola, is near Lake Hindmarsh, popular for fishing, boating and water-skiing. **Of interest:** Pascoes Cash Store, Federal St; original country general store. Yurunga homestead, on northern edge of town, classified by National Trust; large selection of antiques, and retaining original fittings. **In the area:** Old Lutheran church (1901) at Pella, 10 km W. Lake Albacutya Park, 12 km N; camping facilities. Wyperfeld National Park, 40 km N; access via sealed road north from Yaapeet. **Tourist information:** Mid Lakes Mixed Business, 12 Federal St; (053) 95 1002. **Accommodation:** 2 hotels, 1 motel, 1 caravan/camping park.
MAP REF. 126 D13, 228 F4

Robinvale
Pop. 1795

This small, well-laid-out town on the NSW border, 80 km from Mildura, is almost entirely surrounded by bends in the Murray River, and the surrounding area is ideal for the production of citrus, dried fruit and wine grapes. It is a picturesque town, and water sports and fishing are popular along the river. **Of interest:** McWilliams Wines and the Lexia Room, with historical exhibits, in Moore St. **In the area:** Euston weir and lock on Murray, 2.5 km downstream. Robinvale Wines, Greek-style winery, 5 km S on Sea Lake road. Kyndalyn Park almond farm, 23 km SE of Robinvale. Hattah–Kulkyne National Park, 66 km SW. **Tourist information:** Swan Hill Regional Information Centre, 306 Campbell St, Swan Hill; (050) 32 3033. **Accommodation:** 1 hotel, 3 motels, 2 caravan/camping parks. **See also:** Wine Regions.
MAP REF. 126 F8, 231 J6

Rochester
Pop. 2527

On the Campaspe River, 28 km S of Echuca, Rochester is the centre for a rich dairying and tomato-growing area. A small, busy town, it has some attractive older buildings and boasts the largest dairy factory in Australia. **Of interest:** Historical Plaque Trail. **In the area:** An engineering achievement, the Campaspe Siphon, 3 km N, where the Waranga–Mallee irrigation channel runs under the Campaspe River. District channels are popular with anglers; cod and bream are plentiful. Random House homestead, amid 4 ha of gardens beside river in Bridge Rd, on eastern edge of town. Pleasant lakes in the district, popular for fishing and water sports, include Greens Lake and the Corop Lakes, 14 km SE. Scenic Mt Camel Range attracts gem fossickers. Field's Cactus Farm and Lochlomand Gardens and Tearooms near Tennyson, 18 km NW. **Tourist information:** Railway Station, Moore St; (054) 84 1860. **Accommodation:** 3 hotels, 1 motel, 1 caravan/camping park.
MAP REF. 232 E6

Romsey
Pop. 2033

Romsey, 7 km S of Lancefield, was settled in the mid 1850s and possesses some excellent Victorian architecture. **Of interest:** Historic Glenfern Horse Stud, Glenfern Rd. **In the area:** Cope Williams Romsey Vineyard. Mintaro, at nearby Monegeetta, built by Captain Gardiner in 1882; smaller replica of Melbourne's Government House. Huntingdon, just north of Romsey township. The Chase at Monegeetta North. **Accommodation:** 1 hotel.
MAP REF. 210 I3, 224 B1, 232 E12

Rushworth
Pop. 1012

Rushworth, 20 km from Murchison, off the Goulburn Valley Hwy, still shows traces of its gold-rush days. **Of interest:** Many of the town's attractive original buildings still stand, witnesses to the days when Rushworth was the commercial centre for the surrounding mining district. Nearly all the buildings in High St are classified by the National Trust: St Pauls Church of England, the band rotunda, the former Imperial Hotel (now a private residence), the Glasgow Buildings and the Whistle Stop. History Museum in Mechanics Institute (1913), High St; open p.m. weekends. **In the area:** Rushworth State Forest, 3 km S; 24 300 ha of ironbark forest, only natural ironbark forest remaining in the world. Whroo Historic Area, 7 km S; Balaclava Hill Open Cut, Whroo Cemetery and Aboriginal Waterhole, all with visitor access; sites of 20,000 mines, walking tracks. Further south, remnants of deserted goldmining towns Bailieston, Angustown and Graytown. Waranga

The Mighty Murray

As a present-day explorer, a trip following the course of the Murray gives you a chance to discover a rich cross-section of Australian country and history, as well as the infinite variety of natural beauty and wildlife the river itself supports.

The Source
The Murray has its source on the slopes of Mount Pilot, high in the Alps. Here it is just a gurgling mountain stream, rushing through some breathtaking mountain scenery. This is the area of the Snowy Mountains Scheme and the great Australian snowfields.

The Upper Murray
The river flows through the scenic area around **Jingellic** and **Walwa** and on to the beautiful Lake Hume near **Albury** and **Wodonga** before continuing past **Corowa**, the birthplace of Federation, and into Lake Mulwala.

Lakes, Beaches and Red Gums
As it flows from the aquatic play-grounds of Lakes Hume and Mulwala, the Murray becomes a wide and splendid river. Lined with magnificent red gums, in the region around **Cobram**, the riverbanks are transformed into wide sandy beaches. This is ideal holiday country, with pleasant resort towns to be found at **Yarrawonga–Mulwala**, **Barooga** and **Tocumwal**.

Wine Country
Victoria's main winegrowing area is centred around **Rutherglen** and extends to the wineries of Cobram and the Ovens and Goulburn Valleys. The wineries welcome visitors and many offer conducted tours.

The Heyday of the Riverboats
Famous river towns like **Echuca**, **Swan Hill** and **Wentworth** have carefully preserved much of the history of this colourful era. The Port of Echuca, the Swan Hill Pioneer Settlement and the historic Murray Downs homestead are a must if you are in the area. Children especially will delight in the 'living museum', where original buildings, paddlesteamers and old wharves have been restored.

Wildlife
The Murray's abundant bird and animal life is protected in a number of sanctuaries and reserves surrounding the banks of the river. Spoonbills, herons, eagles, harriers and kites are plentiful. Near Picnic Point in the Moira State Forest, which is near **Mathoura**, waterbirds and wildlife abound and can be seen from the observatory in this beautiful red gum forest. At **Kerang**, which lies at the beginning of a chain of lakes and marshes, you can see huge breeding grounds for the splendid ibis. **Kyabram** has a famous community-owned fauna and waterfowl park which is open daily, and almost all of Gunbower Island is a protected sanctuary for wildlife.

Sunraysia
The beautiful climate of **Mildura** supports flourishing citrus and winegrowing industries as well as attracting countless holidaymakers to the Mildura area during both the summer and winter seasons. Upstream is **Red Cliffs**, a town founded after World War I by returned soldiers, who turned it into a model irrigation town, and the surrounding areas into prosperous winelands. At the junction of the Murray and the Darling lies **Wentworth**, one of the oldest of the river towns, with an historic gaol and the beautifully preserved paddle-steamer *Ruby*. From Wentworth, holidaymakers can cruise along the Darling River in MV *Loyalty*.

Riverland
The Murray crosses into South Australia and at **Renmark** begins its splendid flow down to its mouth at Lake Alexandrina. The banks are lined with such historic river towns as **Renmark**, **Morgan** and **Murray Bridge**. **Goolwa** at its mouth has a strong tradition of shipbuilding, originating from the busy riverboat days. Renmark, like Mildura, is famous for its year-round sunshine. All these towns make attractive and interesting places for a holiday. This South Australian stretch of the Murray offers splendid river scenery and birdlife, excellent fishing and water sports and the chance to enjoy the many wineries in the area.

Further information is available from the tourist information centres in the various towns along the river, including Swan Hill; (050) 32 3033; Mildura; (050) 21 4424; Cobram; (058) 72 2132; Echuca–Moama; (054) 80 7555 and Yarrawonga–Mulwala; (057) 44 1989. **See also**: Individual town entries in A–Z listing.

Red gums, Murray River

Basin, 6 km N; water sports, fishing and camping; excellent picnic facilities. Longleat Winery and Campbell's Bend picnic reserve, 20 km E. At Murchison, 20 km E; Meteorite Park, site of meteorite fall in 1969. **Tourist information:** Guided Tours of Victoria, 31 High St; (058) 56 1612. **Accommodation:** 1 hotel, 1 hotel/motel, 2 caravan/camping parks.
MAP REF. 232 F7

Rutherglen   Pop. 1876
Rutherglen is the centre of the most important winegrowing area in Victoria. There is a cluster of vineyards surrounding the town, with winegrowing country stretching south to the Milawa area. Most wineries reflect their history; of particular interest is the winery building at All Saints, 10 km NW, which has a National Trust classification. Other wineries include Anderson's, Bullers, Campbells, Chambers, Cofield, Fairfield, Gehrig Brothers, Jones, Morris's, Mount Prior, Pfeiffers, Stanton and Killeen, and St Leonards. Rutherglen sponsors 3 major events: Tastes of Rutherglen, March Labour Day weekend; Winery Walkabout Weekend June long weekend; and Rutherglen Wine Show in Sept. Most wineries are open daily for tastings and sales. **Of interest:** The House (1882) at Mount Prior Vineyard, 14 km NE, now a guest house. **In the area:** Lake Moodemere, 8 km W; water sports, fauna sanctuary nearby. Old Customs House at Wahgunyah, 10 km NW relic of days when duty was payable on goods coming from NSW. History walk at Wahgunyah traces the area's beginnings. Rutherglen is well situated for day trips to Albury–Wodonga, Yarrawonga, Lake Mulwala, Corowa, Beechworth, Bright and Mt Buffalo. **Tourist information**: Walkabout Cellar, 84 Main St; (060) 32 9784. **Accommodation:** 2 hotels, 4 motels, 1 caravan/camping park. **See also:** The Mighty Murray; Wine Regions.
MAP REF. 127 O13, 233 M4

St Arnaud   Pop. 2741
This old goldmining town is on the Sunraysia Hwy between Donald and Avoca and is surrounded by forest and hill country. Many of the town's historic iron-lacework-decorated buildings have been classified by the National Trust. **Of interest:** Josephine Coppens Gallery, Napier St. Squash, basketball, badminton, table tennis and indoor tennis facilities at local sports stadium. Queen Mary Gardens, pleasant site for picnics. **In the area:** Good fishing in Avoca River and at Teddington Reservoir, 28 km S. At Lake Batyo Catyo, 35 km NW; fishing, water sports and camping. Melville Caves, 38 km E, between St Arnaud and Inglewood; famous as haunt of bushranger Captain Melville, picnic facilities nearby. St Peter's Church (1869) at Carapooee, 11 km SE; made of pebbles. **Tourist information:** Josephine Coppens Gallery, 2 Napier St; (054) 95 2313. **Accommodation:** 2 hotels, 2 motels, 1 caravan/camping park.
MAP REF. 229 L9

St Leonards   Pop. 1206
A small beach resort, 11 km SE of Portarlington on the Bellarine Peninsula, St Leonards has excellent coastal fishing, calm waters for boating and yachting, and is popular for family summer holidays. **Of interest:** Edwards Point Wildlife Reserve, Beach Rd; varied birdlife, picnic facilities. Memorial on The Esplanade commemorating landing by Matthew Flinders in 1802 and John Batman and his party in 1835. **Tourist information:** A Maze'N Things, cnr Bellarine Hwy and Grubb Rd, Wallington; (052) 50 2669. **Accommodation:** 1 hotel, 2 caravan/camping parks.
MAP REF. 210 I9, 212 B2, 217 I7, 224 B6

Sale   Pop. 13 858
Sale is the main administrative city in Gippsland. In nearby Bass Strait, there is a concentration of offshore oil development. Just over 200 km E of Melbourne on the Princes Hwy, it is conveniently located for exploration of the whole Gippsland Lakes area, which extends from Wilsons Promontory to Lakes Entrance, and is bordered to the north by the foothills and mountains of the Great Divide and most of the way along the coast by the famous Ninety Mile Beach. **Of interest:** Unique art of Annemieke Mein, wildlife-in-textiles artists, at Central Gippsland Tourism Assocn Inc., on Princes Hwy at western approach to city. Port of Sale, thriving during the days of the paddle-steamers; picnic facilities and boat-launching ramps. Cruises from here through 400-sq-km lakes system. Lake Guthridge, on Foster St in city centre; popular picnic spot, also fauna park and adventure playground. Historical Museum, located in Foster St nearby. City has many attractive buildings, including Our Lady of Sion Convent, the clock tower, Victoria Hall, and the Criterion Hotel with beautiful lacework verandahs. RAAF base, home of the famous Roulettes aerobatic team. Sale Regional Arts Centre, Macalister St. Pedestrian Mall, cnr Cunningham and Raymond Sts; local art. Sale Common and State Game Refuge, on southern edge of town; protected wetlands area, boardwalk. **In the area:** To the north, towns of Maffra and Heyfield (18 km), in intensively cultivated country, and Lake Glenmaggie, 6 km N of Heyfield. Road from Stratford, 18 km N, leads across the Dargo High Plains to Mt Hotham; scenic drive through the high country. Australian Wildlife Gallery, 15 km W of Stratford; stone sculptures of wildlife. Further on is Black Cockatoo Pottery. To the south, Seaspray, on Ninety Mile Beach, 32 km from Sale; excellent surfing and fishing; also Golden and Paradise Beaches, 35 km from Sale, and Loch Sport, another 30 km. Nearby are The Lakes National Park and Rotamah Island Bird Observatory, 15 km from Loch Sport. Marlay Point, on shores of Lake Wellington, 25 km from Sale; extensive launching facilities. Yacht club here sponsors overnight yacht race to Paynesville each March. Popular fishing rivers include the Avon, close to Marlay Point, and the Macalister, Thomson and Latrobe, especially at Swing Bridge (1883), 5 km S of Sale. Holey Plains State Park, 14 km SW, for wildlife and wildflowers. **Tourist information:** Central Gippsland Tourism, Princes Hwy; (051) 44 1108. **Accommodation:** 9 motels, 2 caravan/camping parks. **See also:** Gippsland Lakes.
MAP REF. 225 M6

Seymour   Pop. 6558
On the Goulburn River, at the junction of the Goulburn Valley Hwy and Hume Fwy, Seymour is a busy commercial, industrial and agricultural town, serving the local rural community. The area was recommended by Lord Kitchener during his visit in 1909 as being particularly suitable for a military base. Nearby Puckapunyal, 18 km W, was an important training base for troops during World War II and is still operating as a major army base. **Of interest:** In Emily St: Royal Hotel, featured in Russell Drysdale's famous 1941 painting, Moody's Pub; Studio Roest, fine art and restaurant; Somerset Crossing Vineyard and

restaurant. Goulburn Park, cnr Progress and Guild Sts; picnic and swimming areas, caravan park adjoining. Old Goulburn Bridge (1891), at end of Emily St; preserved as historic relic. Steam Train Preservation Society; rides Sun. by appt. **In the area:** Mitchelton and Chateau Tahbilk Vineyards, near Nagambie, 23 km N. Other wineries include Somerset Crossing Vineyards, 2 km S, Hankin's Wines, 5 km NW on Northwood Rd, and Hayward's Winery, 12 km SE near Trawool. Army Tank and Transport Museum at Puckapunyal, 10 km W. Trawool Valley Angora Stud and Tearooms, 11 km SE. Spotted Jumbuk, Highland Rd, 5 km E; spotted sheep. Capalba Park Alpacas, on Kobyboyne Rd, 11 km E. **Tourist information:** Old Court House Craft Shop, Emily St; or 320 High St, Nagambie; (057) 94 2647. **Accommodation:** 5 motels, 3 caravan/camping parks. **See also:** Wine Regions.
MAP REF. 211 L1, 232 G10

Shepparton–Mooroopna
Pop. 30 511

The 'capital' of the rich Goulburn Valley, this thriving, well-developed city, now known as The Solar City, 175 km N of Melbourne, has 4000 ha of orchards within a 10-km radius and 4000 ha of market gardens along the river valley nearby. The area is irrigated by the Goulburn Irrigation Scheme and is on the junction of the Goulburn and Broken Rivers. The central shopping area of Shepparton is surrounded by 68 ha of parkland, including an open-air music bowl and a Civic Centre housing an art gallery, town hall, theatre and municipal centre. **Of interest:** Solar display at Tourist Information Centre, Wyndham St. Art gallery at Civic Centre, Wellford St; traditional Australian paintings and collection of Australian ceramics. On Parkside Dr, the International Village and Aboriginal Keeping Place; tourist, educational and cultural centre. Historical Museum, within the Historical Precinct, High St; open Sun. afternoons. Redbyrne Pottery, on Old Dookie Rd; wide variety of locally made pottery and ceramics. Victoria Park Lake, Tom Collins Dr; yachting, water sports and a caravan park. Shepparton Preserving Company, Andrew Fairley Ave, largest cannery in southern hemisphere; guided inspections during canning period Jan.–April. Lemnos–Campbells soup cannery and Ardmona fruit cannery at Mooroopna;

Museum, Shepparton

direct sales. Driver Education Centre of Australia, on Wanganui Rd. Reedy Swamp Walk, at end of Wanganui Rd; wetland area abundant with birdlife. Fruit Connection, at rest stop on causeway between towns; crafts, wine tasting and sales, walks. **In the area:** Mud Factory Pottery, 6 km S on Goulburn Valley Hwy. Boxwood Pottery, Elm Vale Nursery and Le-Bella Ostrich Farm at Kialla, 5 km SE. Vineyards, including Gravina Winery, Old Dookie Rd, and Broken River Wines at Lemnos, 10 km E. Chateau Tahbilk (1860), 36 km S on Goulburn Valley Hwy, near Nagambie; recorded by National Trust. Historic Brookfield Homestead, 20 km N on Goulburn Valley Hwy; old farm machinery and shearing sheds; open by appt. Victoria's Irrigation Research Institute, east of Tatura, 16 km W of Shepparton. **Tourist information:** Wyndham St, Shepparton; (058) 32 9870. **Accommodation:** Shepparton: 3 hotels, 19 motels, 6 caravan/camping parks. Mooroopna: 4 motels, 5 caravan/camping parks. **See also:** Wine Regions.
MAP REF. 232 H6

Skipton
Pop. 462

This township on the Glenelg Hwy, south-west of Ballarat, lies in an important pastoral and agricultural district. The town was an important centre for merino sheep sales in the 1850s. **Of interest:** Eel factory; eels netted in region, snap-frozen and exported mainly to Germany. Adjacent to eel factory, Gibson's Doll Display. Bluestone Presbyterian Church, classified by National Trust. **In the area:** Mooromong, 11 km NW, notable historic

homestead; property donated to National Trust by D.J.S. and C. Mackinnon (formerly Claire Adams, silent movie star); open by appt and on National Trust open days; accommodation available in converted shearers' quarters. Mt Widderin Cave, 6 km S; volcanic cave with large underground chamber; tours by appt. Kaolin Mine, 10 km E. **Accommodation:** 1 hotel.
MAP REF. 220 H13, 227 M4

Stawell
Pop. 6339

North-east of Halls Gap and 123 km NW of Ballarat on the Western Hwy, Stawell is well sited for tours to the northern Grampians. It is the home of the Stawell Easter Gift, Australia's most famous professional foot race, held annually. **Of interest:** Stawell Gift Hall of Fame Museum, within Athletic Club, Central Park, cnr Seaby and Napier Sts; history of the footrace. Big Hill, local landmark and goldmining site; Pioneers Lookout at summit with indication of locations of famous mines. Casper's World in Miniature Tourist Park, London Rd; re-creation in miniature of scenes of life in Australia and Pacific countries, using indoor and outdoor scale working models with dioramas and commentaries; open daily. Doll and Toy Museum, Main St; private collection, Mon.–Fri. p.m. Pleasant Creek Courthouse Museum, Western Hwy. **In the area:** Goldmining at Stawell Joint Venture; public viewing areas off Reefs Rd. Bunjil's Cave; Aboriginal rock paintings in ochre, off Pomonal Rd, 11 km S. The Sisters Rocks, collection of huge granite tors beside Western Hwy, 3 km SE; saved from destruction in 1867 by

a local resident, who bought and fenced off the land on which they rest. Grampians scenic flights available. Bellellen Rise, merino sheep station, for farm holidays. Deep Lead Flora and Fauna Reserve, 6 km W, off Western Hwy. Tottington Woolshed, National Trust property and rare example of 19th-century woolshed, 55 km NE on road to St Arnaud. Boating on Lake Fyans, 15 km SW, near Halls Gap; picnic and camping facilities. Wineries include Stawell, Great Western, Garden Gully, Saint Gregory's, Ararat and Halls Gap. Great Western, 14 km SE, picturesque wine village; hotel, tearooms, craft and antique shops. Overdale Station, Landsborough Rd, 10 km E; guided tours during school holidays; farm holidays available. Old Coongee, host farm. Roses Gap Recreation Centre, holiday centre within Grampians National Park, 34 km W, off Western Hwy. **Tourist information:** 54 Western Hwy; (053) 58 2314. **Accommodation:** 8 motels, 2 caravan/camping parks, holiday cottages. **See also:** The Grampians; The Golden Age; Wine Regions.
MAP REF. 220 C5, 229 J12

Swan Hill   Pop. 9357

When the explorer Thomas Mitchell camped on the banks of the Murray, he named the spot Swan Hill because the local black swans had kept him awake all night. The township became a busy 19th-century river port and today it is a pleasant city and major holiday centre on the Murray Valley Hwy, 338 km NW of Melbourne. The climate is mild and sunny and the river offers good fishing, boating and water-sports relaxation. Swan Hill is a well-laid-out city with a unique garden-like main street. The street design is similar to that of Grand Junction, Colorado. **Of interest:** Swan Hill won recognition by establishing Australia's first Folk Museum, the Pioneer Settlement, at end of Gray St on Little Murray River, which depicts, in a natural environment, life in the last century and local Aboriginal culture; staff wear period costume and old-fashioned forms of transport are used. The Settlement features Sound and Light tour, nightly theatrical performance of music, lighting and dialogue—an exciting journey back into the pioneering past (bookings essential). Swan Hill Regional Gallery of Contemporary Art and Dowling House Art and Craft Centre; both in Gray St. Llanvair Gallery, Beveridge St.

Military Museum, Campbell St. Riverboats: PS *Pyap* offers Murray cruises; stationary PS *Gem* has restaurant. Annual Italian Festa held mid-July. Heritage Walk; brochure available from tourist information centre. **In the area:** Daily river cruises, including lunch cruise, on MV *Kookaburra*. Historic Tyntyndyer Homestead (c. 1846), classified by National Trust, 17 km N on Murray Valley Hwy. Murray Downs Homestead, 2 km NW over bridge into NSW on Moulamein Rd; historic sheep, cattle and irrigation property, with animal park and children's playground. Murray Downs Golf and Country Club, 5 km NW over bridge into NSW. Pheasant farm and aviaries at Nowie North, 32 km NW. Buller's winery at Beverford, 11 km N, Horseriding at Mulberry Farm, Vinifera, 20 km N. Lake Boga, 16 km S; for water sports and picnicking. Best's St Andrew's Vineyard near Lake Boga, 16 km S. Amboc Mohair Farm at Mystic Park, 29 km S. Tooleybuc, 45 km N, pleasant spot for fishing, birdwatching and picnics. Piambie State Forest, 70 km N. **Tourist information:** 306 Campbell St; (050) 32 3033. **Accommodation:** 4 hotels, 16 motels, 5 caravan/camping parks. **See also:** The Mighty Murray; Wine Regions.
MAP REF. 126 H11, 229 N1, 231 N11

Tallangatta   Pop. 1021

When the old town of Tallangatta was submerged for the construction of the Hume Weir, many of its buildings were moved to a new location above the shoreline. Today, situated 42 km from Wodonga on the Murray Valley Hwy, the town has the benefit of this large lake and boasts an attractive inland beach. It is the easternmost main Murray River town and is directly north of the beautiful alpine region of Victoria. The centre of a productive dairying area since early settlement, Tallangatta is the home of the Australian Red Breed Society, established to recognise red dairy cattle breeds throughout the world as a single breeding population. **Of interest:** The Hub, Tallangatta's Community Centre, in Towong St; art and craft. Arts Festival held Oct. **In the area:** Traron Alpacas at Bullioh, 15 km E; alpacas and other animals, yarns and garments, *Paulownia* trees. Laurel Hill Trout Farm at Eskdale, 33 km S; buy or catch-your-own, picnic/barbecue facilities. Forest drives recommended by the Forests Commission extends from Mitta Mitta down the

Omeo Hwy, and include trips to Cravensville, Mt Benambra, Tawonga and Omeo via Snowy Creek Rd. Alpine Walking Track passes over Mt Wills, 48 km S of Mitta Mitta. Lake Dartmouth, 58 km SE of Tallangatta, has good trout fishing, boating, picnic/barbecue facilities. Self-guide walks in the area. **Tourist information:** The Hub, Towong St; (060) 71 2695. **Accommodation:** 2 hotels, 1 motel, 1 caravan/camping park. **See also:** The Mighty Murray.
MAP REF. 233 Q5, 234 C3

Terang   Pop. 1937

Terang, located on the Princes Hwy in a predominantly dairy farming area, is a well-laid-out town with grand avenues of deciduous trees: recognised by the National Trust. The town has excellent sporting facilities with a particular emphasis on horse sports and a good polo field. **Of interest:** Early 20th-century commercial architecture and a classic Gothic sandstone Presbyterian church. Cottage crafts shop in century-old cottage, originally the police station. Self-guide Historic Town Walk. Horse carnival held Jan. **In the area:** Noorat, 6 km N, birthplace of Alan Marshall, author of *I Can Jump Puddles* and many other stories. Here, Alan Marshall Walking Track makes a gentle climb to summit of an extinct volcano; excellent views of crater, surrounding district and across to the Grampians. Farm accommodation available. Glenormiston Agricultural College, 4 km further N, tastefully developed around an historic homestead mansion. **Tourist information:** Clarke Saddlery, High St; (055) 92 1164. **Accommodation:** 4 hotels, 2 motels, 1 caravan/camping park.
MAP REF. 215 A6, 227 K8

Torquay   Pop. 4887

The popularity of this resort, 22 km S of Geelong, is well known. Close to the town, the excellent surfing beaches, Bells and Jan Juc, attract surfers from all over the world. Bells Beach Surfing Championships are held at Easter. The Torquay Surf Lifesaving Club is the largest in the State. Torquay also marks the eastern end of the Great Ocean Road, offering spectacular drives west to Anglesea and beyond. **Of interest:** Surfing products at Surf Coast Plaza, Geelong Rd. Mary Elliott Pottery, Geelong Rd. Craft Cottage, Anderson St. Barbara Peake's Studio, Sarabande Cr. Redwood

The Western District

Some famous Australians have been born and bred in this south-western part of Victoria. Many have been members of the land-owning families whose gracious homesteads are dotted about this beautiful pastoral area. The Western District supports one-third of Victoria's best sheep and cattle, and the region's merino wool is acknowledged to be the finest in the land.

Many of the Western District towns boast splendid pioneer buildings. Of special interest are **Hamilton**—recognised as the 'Wool Capital of the World'—and the attractive little towns of **Coleraine** and **Casterton**. Several of the district's historic homesteads are open for inspection, including 'Warrock' (near Casterton), which has 33 original farm buildings still in operation. Of particular interest to nature lovers are the remaining colonies of the eastern barred bandicoot.

Warrnambool, situated on the south coast, is the commercial capital of the Western District and a gateway to the Great Ocean Road. The winter visits of southern right whales are a popular attraction.

The heart of the Western District is fairly flat grazing land. To the east, the volcanic lake area around **Camperdown** offers great fishing and water sports. To the south, a rugged coastline stretches from **Anglesea** to the tiny hamlet of **Nelson**, at the mouth of the Glenelg River. To the north, the high rocky ranges of the Grampians break through the gently rolling countryside. An excellent scenic route to Halls Gap is along the Mt Abrupt Road from **Dunkeld**.

The Grampians, near Dunkeld

Further information can be obtained from local tourist information centres, especially the Hamilton and District Tourist Information Centre, Lonsdale St, Hamilton; (055) 72 3746; and the Warrnambool Tourist Information Centre, 600 Raglan Pde, Warrnambool; (055) 64 7837. **See also:** Individual town entries in A–Z listing.

The Wimmera

Travelling through the Wimmera on a hot summer day is an unforgettable experience. The Wimmera is the granary of the State; the wheat fields stretch as far as the eye can see, an endless golden plain broken only occasionally by a gentle ripple in the terrain. In the south-east corner, however, are the Grampians, surrounded by a network of lakes, understandably popular with anglers and water-sports lovers.

The region takes its name from an Aboriginal word meaning 'throwing stick'. Evidence of occupation by the original inhabitants, the Wotjobaluk and Jardwa tribes, can still be seen: canoe trees are common and there are many rock-art sites in the Grampians area. The Ebenezer Mission Station at Antwerp, near Dimboola, founded by Moravian missionaries to Christianise the Aboriginal population, has been restored by the National Trust and local inhabitants.

Horsham, with its delightful private, public and Botanical gardens, intriguing Olde Horsham Village and an excellent regional art gallery, makes a good base from which to explore the whole region. If you are visiting in March, do not miss the annual Wimmera Machinery Field Days, held at the Victorian College of Agriculture and Horticulture, Dooen, and the Labour Day weekend annual fishing competition on the Wimmera River. Natimuk, 34 km west of Horsham, is the centre for visitors drawn to climb Mt Arapiles, a 356-metre sandstone monolith.

The agricultural life of the last century has been remembered at **Warracknabeal**, the largest wheat-receiving centre in the State, where an agricultural machinery museum houses huge steam-powered chaff-cutters, headers and tractors and depicts the history of the wheat industry. Near Dimboola, set along the banks of the Wimmera River, is one entrance to the Little Desert National Park. Little Desert is something of a misnomer because the park is not little, and it does not look like a desert. There is a proliferation of plant and animal life, particularly in spring when the scrub and heathlands come into bloom.

For further information, contact Wimmera Tourism, 20 O'Callaghan's Pde, Horsham; (053) 82 1832. **See also:** Individual town entries in A–Z listing.

Gallery, Geelong Rd. Torquing Art, Bristol Rd. Torquair Scenic Flights, Blackgate Rd. **In the area:** Southern Rose, 1 km S; rose gardens, tearooms and restaurant. Museum of early Australian horse-drawn carriages near Bellbrae, 6 km W. Pottery Studios in Moores Rd, Bellbrae. Rebenberg Winery (open weekends) and Downunda Weaving Studio at Mt Duneed, 11 km N. Experimental wind-power generator at Breamlea, 10 km NE. **Tourist information:** Shire Offices, Grossmans Rd; (052) 61 4202, and Mary Elliott Pottery, Geelong Rd; (052) 61 3310. **Accommodation:** 2 motels, 4 caravan/camping parks. **See also:** The Great Ocean Road.
MAP REF. 210 F11, 217 E10, 227 Q9

Traralgon Pop. 19 699

Situated on the Princes Hwy, 164 km SE of Melbourne, Traralgon is one of the Latrobe Valley's main cities, the others being Moe and Morwell. It is a residential area based on an industrial core. **Of interest:** Walking tours; heritage drive. Band rotunda and miniature railway at Victory Park. **In the area:** Tambo Cheese Factory, 3 km E of town; cheese and local craft sales, viewing cheese-making. Giant mountain ash trees and ferns at Tarra–Bulga National Park; picnics, walks, scenic drives and nature study. Tarra–Bulga Visitor Centre at Balook, Grand Ridge Road. Loy Yang power station, 5 km S. **Tourist information:** Lloyd St, Moe; (051) 27 6928. **Accommodation:** 2 hotels, 9 motels, 5 caravan/camping parks.
MAP REF. 225 K7

Walhalla Pop. 15

The tiny goldmining town of Walhalla is tucked away in dense mountain country in south-east Gippsland. The drive, 46 km N from Moe passes through some spectacular scenery. Walhalla is set in a narrow, steep valley, with sides so sheer that its cemetery has graves that have been dug lengthways into the hillside. **Of interest:** Historic buildings and relics of gold-boom days have been preserved. Long Tunnel Extended Goldmine, named after the most successful in the State; open at weekends and holidays, guided tours. Old Fire Station; hand-operated fire engine and fire memorabilia. Spett's Cottage (1871); furnished in the period. Museum, opposite Rotunda; craft shop adjacent. Post Office; crafts. Old bakery (1865), oldest surviving building in town; near rebuilt hotel. Museum, Spett's Cottage, Band Rotunda and Windsor House (1890), all classified by the National Trust. Walhalla Coach Company; drives along main road. **In the area:** Alpine Walking Track, and Baw Baw National Park, which edges western side of town. At Erica, 12 km W: timber industry display at Erica Hotel; Railway Museum in Henty St; Mountain Saddle Safaris. Thomson River, 4 km S; fishing, picnicking, canoe trail, white-water rafting. Moondarra State Park, 30 km S. Scenic road between Walhalla and Jamieson, 140 km N. **Tourist information:** Erica Hotel, Walhalla Rd, Erica; (051) 65 3252. **Accommodation:** Limited. **See also:** Gippsland Lakes.
MAP REF. 225 J5

Wangaratta Pop. 15 984

The Ovens Hwy to Bright and the Victorian Alps, through the Ovens Valley, branches off the Hume Fwy at Wangaratta, 66 km SW of Wodonga. The surrounding fertile area produces wool, wheat, tobacco, hops and table wine grapes. The city is well planned with good areas of parkland. **Of interest:** In cemetery, grave of Daniel 'Mad Dog' Morgan, the bushranger. His headless body was buried here, the head having been sent to Melbourne for examination. Kooringa Native Plants. Wangaratta Woollen Mills. Mrs Stell's House in Miniature, detailed replica, at Visitor Information Centre, cnr Tone Rd and Handley St. IBM plant, opened 1984, supplies all IBM personal computer requirements for Australia, New Zealand and South-east Asia. Annual Festival of Jazz in Nov. Country Music Festival, New Years Eve Concert and 2-day Rodeo—5 days in all. **In the area:** Airworld Aviation Museum, 7 km S; world's largest collection of flying antique civil aircraft, as well as antique bicycles, cars, motor cycles and trucks; restaurant, adventure playground. Glenrowan, 16 km SW; famed for its Kelly history. Ned was captured here after a bloody gunfight at the local hotel and was subsequently condemned and hanged in Melbourne. Visitor Information Centre in the town focuses on the history of the Kelly Gang. Eldorado, 20 km E; interesting old gold township with the largest gold dredge in the southern hemisphere, built in 1936; historical museum, general store with tourist information, pottery open

Tarra-Bulga National Park, near Traralgon

weekends. Nearby Reedy Creek; popular with gold-panners and gem-fossickers. Road 27 km s to Moyhu leads to beautiful King Valley and Paradise Falls; area includes tiny townships of Whitfield, 54 km s, Cheshunt and Carboor; network of minor roads allows exploration of unspoiled area. King Valley Scenic Drive beside the river to Whitfield and Powers Lookout. Many vineyards in area, including John Gehrig Winery; Brown Brothers Milawa Vineyards, 16 km SE, family winery since 1889; Baileys Bundarra Vineyards (1870), 7 km N of Glenrowan, tastings and vineyard antiques; Auldstones Winery; Booth Brothers, 4 km N of Baileys. Warby Range State Park, 12 km W; good vantage points, picnic spots, variety of bird and plant life. Newton's Prickle Berry Farm at Whitfield. Brookfield Pottery at Everton, 22 km SE. 'Carinya' Ladson Store at Tarrawingee, 11 km SE. Byrne House and Gallery at Byrne, 25 km s. Wombi Toys at Whorouly, 25 km SE. **Tourist information:** Cnr Tone Rd and Handley St; (057) 21 5711. **Accommodation:** 2 hotels, 1 hotel/motel, 11 motels, 3 caravan/camping parks. **See also:** Wine Regions.
MAP REF. 233 M6

Warburton   Pop. 2504

Warburton was established with the gold finds of the 1880s; however, by the turn of the century it had found its niche as a popular tourist town with fine guest houses. It is surrounded by the foothills of the Great Dividing Range and is only about an hour's drive from Melbourne. **Of interest:** Swingbridge Gallery and Crafts. **In the area:** The Acheron Way begins 2 km E of Warburton, giving access to views of Mt Donna Buang, Mt Victoria and Ben Cairn, on the scenic 37-km drive to St Fillans. Mt Donna Buang, 7 km NW; popular day-trip destination from Melbourne, sometimes snow-covered in winter. Upper Yarra Dam, 23 km NE; picnic facilities. To the south of the town along Warburton Hwy is an attractive area of vineyards: Yarra Burn, Lillydale and Oak Ridge Estate. Countryside around Warburton is ideal for bushwalking, riding and birdwatching. Tommy Finn's Trout Farm at Millgrove, 3 km W. Yellingbo State Fauna Reserve, 25 km SW. Yarra Junction Historical Museum, 10 km W. Department of Conservation and Natural Resources leaflet giving details of a walk from

Flagstaff Hill, Warrnambool

Powelltown, 27 km s, to East Warburton can be obtained from tourist information outlet; this is one branch of the Centenary Trail (the other branch leads from Warburton to Baw Baw National Park). Between Powelltown and Noojee; rainforest gully walk to Ada Tree, giant mountain ash. **Tourist information:** 4 Bell St, Yarra Glen; (03) 730 1609. **Accommodation:** 1 hotel, 3 motels, 1 caravan/camping park.
MAP REF. 211 O6, 214 H9, 224 G4

Warracknabeal   Pop. 2687

On the Henty Hwy, 350 km NW of Melbourne, Warracknabeal is in the centre of a rich wheat-growing area. The name is Aboriginal, meaning 'the place of the big red gums shading the water course'. **Of interest:** Historical Centre, 81 Scott St; many items and displays of area's history. Self-guide leaflets available for tour of historic buildings; some classified by the National Trust, including Warracknabeal Hotel (1872), with iron lacework, and original log lockup (1872) built when Warracknabeal acquired its first permanent policeman. Wheatlands Agricultural Machinery Museum; farm machinery used over the past century; picnic/barbecue facilities. Lions Park, on Yarriambiack Creek; picnic spots and fauna park. Vintage Machinery and Vehicle Rally during Wheatlands Easter Carnival. **In the area:** Sections of the dog fence, some 30 km N; vermin-proof

barrier erected in 1883 from the Murray near Swan Hill to the border. Lake Hindmarsh, 74 km N. Jeparit, 45 km W; Wimmera–Mallee Pioneer Museum. Lake Buloke, 56 km E; duck-shooting in season. **Tourist information:** 119 Scott St; (053) 98 1632. **Accommodation:** 4 hotels, 3 motels, 1 caravan/camping park. **See also:** The Wimmera.
MAP REF. 228 H6

Warragul   Pop. 8910

Most of Melbourne's milk comes from this prosperous dairy-farming area 103 km from Melbourne. **Of interest:** West Gippsland Arts Centre, Civic Place. Vintage Craft Park, Copelands Rd. **In the area:** Darnum Musical Village, 8 km E. Wildflower sanctuary at Labertouche, 16 km W. Nature reserves and picnic spots at Glen Cromie, Glen Nayook and Toorongo Falls. Mountain country near Neerim South, 19 km N. Gippsland cheeses at Neerim South (Gippsland Blue, Jindi Brie); at Yarragon, 13 km E (Gippsland Food and Wine); Trafalgar, 21 km E; and Traralgon, 60 km E (Tambo Cheese Factory). Gourmet Deli Trail (brochure available), for a further food trip. **Tourist information:** Lloyd St, Moe; (051) 27 6928. **Accommodation:** 1 hotel, 2 motels, 1 caravan/camping park.
MAP REF. 211 P10, 224 H6

Warrnambool   Pop. 25 500

A beautiful seaside city located 263 km SW of Melbourne, where the Princes Hwy meets the Great Ocean Road, Warrnambool combines history and thriving progress on the shores of Lady Bay. First-class sporting, cultural and entertainment facilities and beautifully developed and maintained parks and gardens have resulted in Warrnambool being awarded Victoria's prestigious Premier Town title a record 3 times. **Of interest:** Flagstaff Hill, Merri St, unique 19th-century Maritime Village; Entrance Gallery orientation centre introduces visitors to Maritime Village experience; includes Flagstaff Hill tapestry, with themes of Aboriginal history, sealing, whaling, exploration, immigration and settlement. Over 100 ships were wrecked on the coast near Warrnambool; famous earthenware Loch Ard Peacock, recovered from Loch Ard wreck in 1878, is on permanent display at Flagstaff Hill Maritime Museum. The Mahogany Ship Restaurant specialises in seafood and

overlooks Warrnambool's picturesque Lady Bay and the Museum. Annual visit of rare southern right whales; usually May–Oct. (viewing platform east of town at Logans Beach). The Kid's Country Treasure Map (available at Tourist Information Centre); informative way for whole family to enjoy Warnambool. Performing Arts Centre, Art Gallery, Timor St. Botanic Gardens, Botanic Rd (designed by Guilfoyle in 1879). Fletcher Jones Gardens, Raglan Pde. Lake Pertobe Adventure Playground, Pertobe Rd, a children's paradise. The Potter's Wheel, Liebig St. Time and Tide Museum, Stanley St; shells, musical instruments and memorabilia. Annual Wunta Fiesta in Feb., 3-day May Racing Carnival and Melbourne–Warrnambool Cycling Classic in Oct. Heritage Trail Walk and arrow tour of city start at Tourist Information Centre (self-guide leaflets available). Thunder Point Reserve, end of Macdonald St. Middle Island, off Pickering Point; colony of fairy penguins. Wollaston Bridge, over 100 years old and of unusual design, on northern outskirts of town. **In the area:** Historic Shipwreck Trail, highlighting wrecks along the coast from Moonlight Head (112 km E) to Port Fairy (29 km W), allows visitors to explore Victoria's 'Shipwreck Coast'. Tower Hill State Game Reserve, 14 km W, is one of Victoria's largest and most recently active volcanoes; nature walk starts at the National History Centre. Robert Ulmann Studio, 4 km E; paintings of Australian flora and fauna. Allansford Cheese World, 10 km E; dairy promotion store, cheese tasting and sales, viewing of cheese, butter and honey production. Ralph Illidge Sanctuary, 32 km E; wildlife, picnic area and nature walks. Timboon Farmhouse and Cheese and Berry World; at Timboon, 53 km E of Warrnambool. Port Campbell National Park, 54 km SE; 32-km stretch of scenic and historic coastline, incorporates a magnificent series of sheer cliffs, deep caverns, great archways, grottos, island gorges, blowholes and spectacular offshore rock stacks. World-famous Twelve Apostles; 77 km SE of Warrnambool. Helicopter and joy flights along the coast. **Tourist information:** 600 Raglan Pde; (055) 64 7837. **Accommodation:** 10 hotels, 23 motels, 8 caravan/camping parks. **See also:** The Great Ocean Road.
MAP REF. 226 I9

Wedderburn　　　Pop. 764

Once one of Victoria's richest goldmining towns in the 'Golden Triangle', Wedderburn is on the Calder Hwy, 74 km NW of Bendigo. Gold can still be found in and around the town—nuggets worth over $20 000 were discovered in a local backyard in the 1950s. **Of interest:** Government Battery on northern edge of town. Hard Hill area, former gold diggings and Christmas Reef Mine. Museum and General Store (1910); restored building furnished and stocked as it was at turn of century. Coach-building factory, and old bakery converted into a kiln for a group of potters, using local clay. **In the area:** Wychitella Forest Reserve, 16 km N; wildlife sanctuary. Mount Korong, 16 km SE; picnics and some rock scrambling, as well as bushwalking. **Tourist information:** Shire Offices, High St; (054) 94 3200. **Accommodation:** 1 hotel, 1 caravan/camping park.
MAP REF. 229 N8

Welshpool–Port Welshpool
Pop. 241

Welshpool is a small dairying town and Port Welshpool is a deep-sea port servicing fishing and oil industries. Barry Beach Marine Terminal, 8 km S of the South Gippsland Hwy, services the offshore oil rigs in Bass Strait. **In the area:** Excellent fishing and boating. Agnes Falls, 19 km NW, the State's highest. At Toora, 11 km W: panoramic views from Mt Fatigue, off South Gippsland Hwy; scenic drive; accommodation at historic Ambleside guest house or Gumnuts Weaving Gallery; Franklin River Reserve has picnic facilities and nature walk. At Port Welshpool; Maritime Museum. Tarra–Bulga National Park, 56 km N. **Accommodation:** 1 motel, 2 caravan/camping parks.
MAP REF. 225 J10

Winchelsea　　　Pop. 969

This township, in the centre of a farming area, is on the Barwon River, 37 km W of Geelong. It originated as a watering-place and shelter for travellers on the road to Colac from Geelong. **Of interest:** Barwon Bridge; graceful stone arches, opened 1867 to handle increasing westward traffic. Barwon Hotel (1842), houses a museum of Australiana. Barwon Park Homestead, National Trust property, 3 km N on Inverleigh Rd; open first Sun. of month. Alexandra's Antiques and Art Gallery, Main St. Lake Modewarre, 14 km E; good fishing and water sports. **Tourist information:** Shire Offices; (052) 67 2104. **Accommodation:** 1 motel, 1 caravan/camping park.
MAP REF. 210 D10, 217 A8, 227 P8

Wodonga　　　Pop. 39 975

Wodonga is the Victorian city in a twin-city complex astride the Murray in north-east Victoria. Albury–Wodonga is a fast-growing city being developed as a decentralised region by the Federal, Victorian and NSW State Governments and, with the attractions of the Murray and nearby Lake Hume, it makes a good base for a holiday. **Of interest:** Wodonga has a number of historic buildings still in use. The city has about 30 km of bicycle paths. The Linc Inn, Lincoln Hwy, offers teas. Miniature steam railway; runs on 3rd Sun. of month, Diamond Park, off Lincoln Causeway. Sumsion Gardens, Church St; beautiful lakeside park. Stud Cattle Complex at Showgrounds. In Melrose Dr, largest outdoor tennis centre in Australia. **In the area:** Hume Weir, 15 km E; picnic facilities, inspections of Hume Weir Trout Farm. Military Museum at Bandiana, 4 km SE. Wodonga is close to 4 areas of interest: Upper Murray, mountain valleys of north-east Victoria, Murray Valley, and the Riverina district. Short drive 36 km S leads to picturesque historic township of Yackandandah. Towns of Beechworth (47 km), Wangaratta (68 km), both south-east, and Rutherglen, 42 km W; well worth visiting. **Tourist information:** Information Centre, Lincoln Causeway; (060) 41 3875. **Accommodation:** Albury–Wodonga, 3 hotels, 55 motels, 13 caravan/camping parks. **See also:** The Mighty Murray.
MAP REF. 127 P13, 233 O4, 234 B2

Wonthaggi　　　Pop. 5751

Once the main supplier of black coal to the Victorian Railways, Wonthaggi, situated 8 km from Cape Paterson in south Gippsland, is South Gippsland's largest town, and has many original buildings. Wonthaggi began as a tent town in 1909 when the coal mines were opened up by the State Government following industrial unrest in the coalfields in NSW. The mines operated until 1968. **In the area:** State Coal Mine, 1.5 km S on Cape Paterson Rd; tours of re-opened Eastern Area Mine; Museum of mining activities, with experienced ex-coalminer as guide; picnic shelter and facilities. Scenic drives

to beaches at Inverloch, 13 km SE, and Tarwin Lower, 35 km SE. Self-drive tour of 25 km links places of interest in area. Cape Paterson, 8 km S, within Bunurong Marine Park; surfing, swimming and fishing. **Accommodation:** 2 hotels, 2 motels, 2 caravan/camping parks.
MAP REF. 211 N13, 224 F9

Wycheproof
Pop. 777

A railway line runs down the middle of the main street of this little township on the edge of the Mallee, 140 km from Bendigo. **Of interest:** Centenary Park, Broadway; picnic/barbecue facilities, children's playground, historic log cabin. Willandra Historical Museum, Broadway. 'Mt Wycheproof', a mere 43 m high and the smallest mountain in the world. Craft Shops. **In the area:** Peppercorn Drive, 5 km NW; country crafts, antique kitchenware. **Tourist information:** Shire Offices, 367 Broadway; (054) 93 7400. **Accommodation:** 2 hotels, 1 motel, 1 caravan/camping park.
MAP REF. 126 G13, 229 L5

Yackandandah
Pop. 601

About 27 km S of Wodonga, this exceptionally attractive township, with avenues of English trees and traditional verandahed buildings, has been classified by the National Trust. Yackandandah is in the heart of the north-east goldfields country (gold was discovered here in 1852), but today it is better known for its historic buildings. **Of interest:** Number of original buildings in High St, including Post Office, several banks and general stores; also Bank of Victoria (1865), now a historical museum. Self-guide walking tour brochure available. Art and craft from Yackandandah Workshop, cnr Kars and Hammond Sts, and Haldane Artist Studio in High St. Wildon Thyme, High St; local art and craft, tea-rooms and restaurant. Ray Riddington's Premier Store and Gallery, High St. Country Music Festival held March, Labour Day weekend. Yackandandah Trail and Coach Rides; horse or coach rides, 2 hr to full day. Yack Track Tours; 4WD tours for wine tasting, gold panning and bushwalking, booking essential. **In the area:** At Allans Flat, 10 km NE, Mr Red's Farm, with nursery and native fauna park, and Schmidt's Strawberry Winery. Lavender Patch Plant Farm, 4 km W on Beechworth Rd. Picturesque Indigo Valley, 6 km W; classified by National Trust. Road leads through rolling hills along valley floor to Barnawatha. Koendidda Historic Homestead, Pooleys Rd, near Barnawartha; b & b accommodation, dinner by arrangement. Creeks and old diggings in Yackandandah area still yield specimens of alluvial gold to amateur prospectors. At Dederang, 25 km SE, art, craft and plants. At Leneva, 16 km NE, Wombat Valley Tramways; small-gauge railway operates at Easter or by arrangement for groups. **Tourist information:** Finders Bric-a-Brac and Old Wares, Courthouse, William St; (060) 27 1222.

Accommodation: 2 hotels, 1 caravan/camping park.
MAP REF. 233 O6, 234 A3

Yarram
Pop. 2006

This old-established South Gippsland town, 225 km by road from Melbourne, has some interesting original buildings, and a pleasant golf course inhabited by relatively tame kangaroos. It is situated between the Strzelecki Ranges and Bass Strait. **Of interest:** Tarra Spinning Wheels, Alberton Rd; spinning wheels, boat wheels, beds, general wood turning. Seabank Fishing Contest in March, Labour Day Weekend. Tarra Festival at Easter. **In the area:** To the south, historic towns of Alberton (6 km), Tarraville (11 km) and Port Albert (14 km); Christ Church (1856) in Tarraville is the oldest church in Gippsland. The Ninety Mile Beach, very popular with surfers and anglers, begins just north of Port Albert. Woodside (29 km E) and Seaspray (68 km NE); beaches are patrolled during the summer season. Fishing beaches: Mann's (16 km E), or McLoughlin's (29 km E). To the north; Australian Omega Navigation Facility with 427-m-high steel tower. In the Strzelecki Ranges, 27 km NW, Tarra–Bulga National Park; hilly country, densely forested with mountain ash, myrtle and sassafras, spectacular fern glades, splendid river and mountain views, rosellas and lyrebirds, the occasional koala. Walking tracks in both parks, two caravan parks at Tarra Valley.

Yackandandah

Horseriding nearby. Eilean Donan Gardens and Riverbank Nursery, Tarra Valley; architectural charm and splendid gardens. At Hiawatha, short drive from Yarram (circuit 46 km); Minnie Ha Ha Falls, on Albert River, picnic facilities. Horses for hire at Hiawatha. Wron Wron Forest, on Hyland Hwy, 16 km N; wildflowers in spring. Tarra Valley Festival at Easter. **Tourist information:** Ooly Dooly Motors, Commercial Rd; (051) 82 5119. **Accommodation:** 2 hotels, 3 motels, 3 caravan/camping parks.
MAP REF. 225 K9

Yarragon   Pop. 708

This small highway town in the Latrobe Valley is situated 120 km E of Melbourne in an agricultural and dairying district. It is a convenient base for exploring the Upper Latrobe and Tanjil River valleys in the mountainous area to the north and for scenic drives along the beautiful Grand Ridge Road to the south. **Of interest:** Antiques, crafts, gallery, specialty shops, gourmet food and boutique wines. **In the area:** Mt Worth State Park, 10 km S. At Childers, 16 km SE: Sunny Creek Berry Farm and Windrush Cottage for teas. Thorpdale, 22 km SE, known for its potatoes; potato bread from bakery. Potato Festival held March, Labour Day weekend. Trafalgar Lookout, Narracan Falls and Henderson's Gully near Trafalgar, 8 km E. At Darnum, 7 km W, musical village housing hundreds of musical instruments. Grand Ridge Rd, spectacular scenic 140-km drive traversing top of Strzelecki Ranges. **Tourist information:** Gippsland Food and Wine, Princes Hwy; (056) 34 2451. **Accommodation:** 1 motel.
MAP REF. 211 Q10, 224 H7

Yarrawonga–Mulwala
Pop. 3603

A pleasant stretch of the Murray and the attractive Lake Mulwala have made these border towns an extremely popular holiday resort. The 6000-ha lake was created in 1939 during the building of the Yarrawonga Weir, which controls the irrigation waters in the Murray Valley. **Of interest:** Around the lake and along the river, sandy beaches and still waters provide an ideal environment for all kinds of water sports, picnicking and general relaxation. The towns have excellent sports facilities, including a 45-hole golf course. The islands and backwaters of the lake contain abundant birdlife. Cruises

Kinglake National Park, near Yea

can be taken on the lake. The Yarrawonga and Mulwala foreshore areas have green lawns and shady willows, and facilities include children's playgrounds, giant water-slides, kiosk, barbecues and boat-ramps. Past Links Communications Museum; in Tourist Centre, Irvine Pde, Yarrawonga. Old Yarra Mine Shaft houses a large collection of gems, minerals and fossils. Carinya Pottery and Hallworth House Gallery, Woods Rd. Tudor House Clock Museum, Lynch St. Daily cruises on the *Paradise Queen* and the *Lady Murray*. Ski club conducts exhibitions and lessons. Tunzafun Amusement Park, Melbourne St. Robb & Co.; horse-drawn coach rides. Linley Park Animal Farm and Gardens, Corowa Rd, Mulwala; native and exotic animals. Canoe and boat hire, horseriding. **In the area:** Byramine Homestead and Country Gardens, 16 km W. Opposite, Fyffe Field Winery. Matata Deer Farm at Cobram, 42 km W. Historical Museum at Katamatite, 35 km SW of Yarrawonga. Fishing in Murray River (no licence required). **Tourist information:** Irvine Pde, Yarrawonga; (057) 44 1989. **Accommodation:** 4 hotels, 2 hotel/motels, 16 motels, 10 caravan/camping parks. **See also:** The Mighty Murray.
MAP REF. 127 N13, 233 K3, 233 K4

Yea   Pop. 995
The town, 58 km N of Yarra Glen, stands beside the Yea River, a tributary of the Goulburn. Set in attractive pastoral and dairy-farming land, it is well situated for touring to Mansfield, Eildon and the mountains, and to the gorge country between Yea and Tallarook, as well as south-east to Marysville. There are some beautiful gorges and fern gullies close to the Yea–Tallarook road, and the area provides easy access to the mountain country south of Eildon Weir. **Of interest:** Yea Dairy Co., trading as Ballantyne's Cheeses; specialty cheesemakers. Helen's Cafe, Station St; skier's breakfasts. **In the area:** Kinglake National Park, 30 km SW; beautiful waterfalls, tall eucalypts, fern gullies, impressive views. Pick-your-own fruit at Berry King Farm, Two Hills Rd, Glenburn, 30 km S. Farm holidays at Glenwaters, Glenburn. Spectacular Wilhelmina Falls, 32 km S via Melba Hwy. Murrindindi Cascades 11 km away in Murrindindi Reserve; wildlife includes wombats, platypuses and lyrebirds. Grotto at Caveat, 27 km N of town. Mineral springs at Dropmore, 47 km N, off back road to Euroa. Ibis rookery at Kerrisdale, 17 km W. Several good campsites along Goulburn River. Flowerdale Winery, Whittlesea–Yea Rd, Flowerdale. **Tourist information:** Shire Offices; (057) 97 2209; Goulburn Tourism, 320 High St, Nagambie; (057) 94 2647. **Accommodation:** 2 motels, 1 caravan/camping park.
MAP REF. 211 N2, 232 H11

Victoria

Other Map Coverage

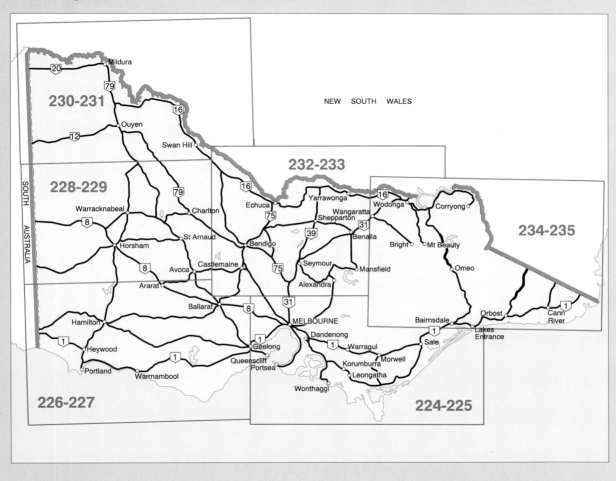

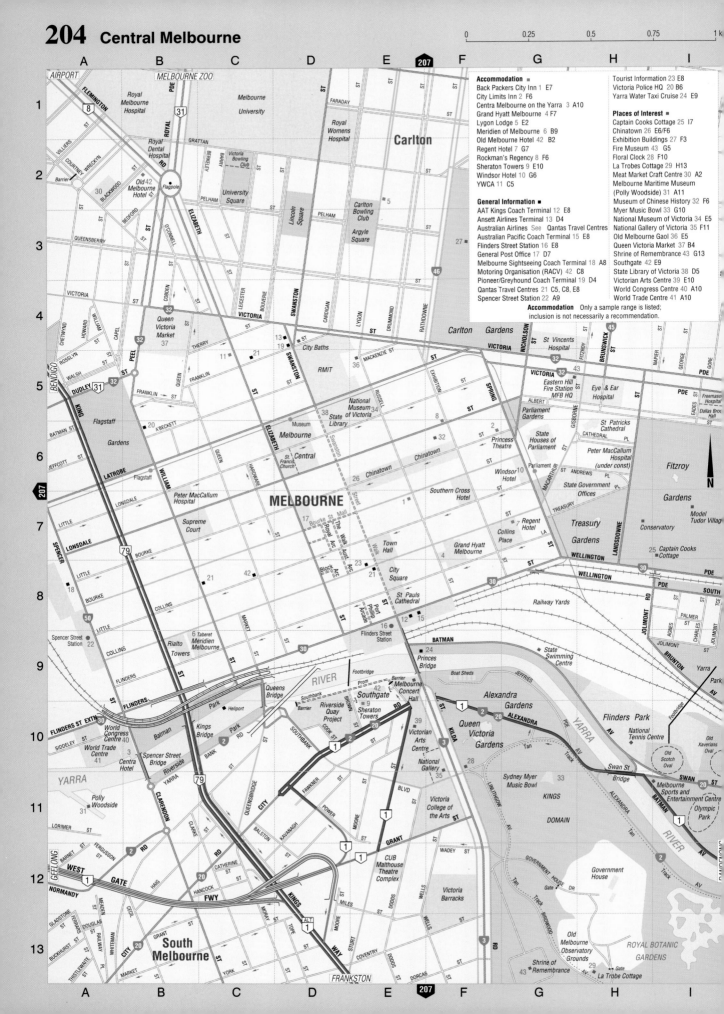

A B C D **210** E F G H

1

2

3

4

5

6 **210**

7

8

9

10

11

12

13

MELBOURNE AIRPORT

Greenvale Centre
Gellibrand Hill Park
Victoria Police
Domestic & International Terminals

TULLAMARINE FWY

ORGAN PIPES NATIONAL PARK

CALDER

Calder Park Thunderdome

Keilor Public Golf Course

Tullamarine Country Club

Keilor North

Tullamarine

MELTON HIGHWAY

Sydenham

Taylors Lakes

Keilor

Keilor Park

Keilor Downs

Keilor Park Recreation Reserve

Airport West

WESTERN
BALLARAT

Department of Defence

Department of Communications Radio 3RN 3LO

TAYLORS RD

Green Gully Reserve

Kealba

Brimbank Park

Keilor Cemetery

Keilor East

Keilor SEC Terminal Station

Nidd

Rockbank

FREEWAY

St Albans

Commonwealth of Australia Office of Defence Production

Avondale Heights

Ma

Commonwealth of Australia Department of Defence

WESTERN HIGHWAY

Albion
Selwyn Park

Braybrook

Medway Golf Course

Ordnance Factory

Deer Park

Ardeer

GLENGALA RD

Sunshine

Devonshire

Dobson Reserve

Skinner Reserve

RAAF Depot

Commonwealth of Australia Office of Defence Production

TILBURN RD FORREST

Sunshine Golf Course

WRIGHT ST

Sunshine Rd

Tottenham

Hansen Reserve

Derrimut Grasslands

Somerville

Brooklyn

Footscray Cemetery

BOUNDARY RD

Tarneit

Mt Derrimut

DOHERTYS

Crematorium and Lawn Cemetery

PRINCES FWY

WEST GATE FWY

DOCKLANDS

Spotswood

Truganina

FITZGERALD RD

Blackshaws

Newport Lakes Parkland

Newport

GEELONG

KOROROIT CREEK

Altona Lakes Public Golf Course

Newport Railway Workshops

Laverton Lake Recreation Reserve

Victorian Baseball and Softball Park

Altona

Cherry Lake

Altona Sports Park

Hogans Road Reserve

Laverton RAAF Base

AB Shaw Reserve

Grant Reserve

Hoppers Crossing

Laverton RAAF Base

Aircraft

Laverton

CENTRAL AV

Kooringal Golf Course

Werribee Plaza Shopping Centre

Mossfiel Reserve

QUEEN ST

Galvin Park

HIGHWAY

Department of Agriculture

Altona Meadows

SNEYDES RD

Wyndham Centre
Werribee Racecourse

Werribee

State Research Farm

Point Cook RAAF

Wyndham Vale

FREEWAY

PRINCES BYPASS

Zoological Park
State Equestrian Centre
Werribee Park

Point Cook Metropolitan Park

Point Cook

PRINCES

MALTBY

Melbourne Water Werribee Treatment Complex
Werribee Mansion

Point Cook RAAF Base

N

PORT PH

A B C D **210** E F G H

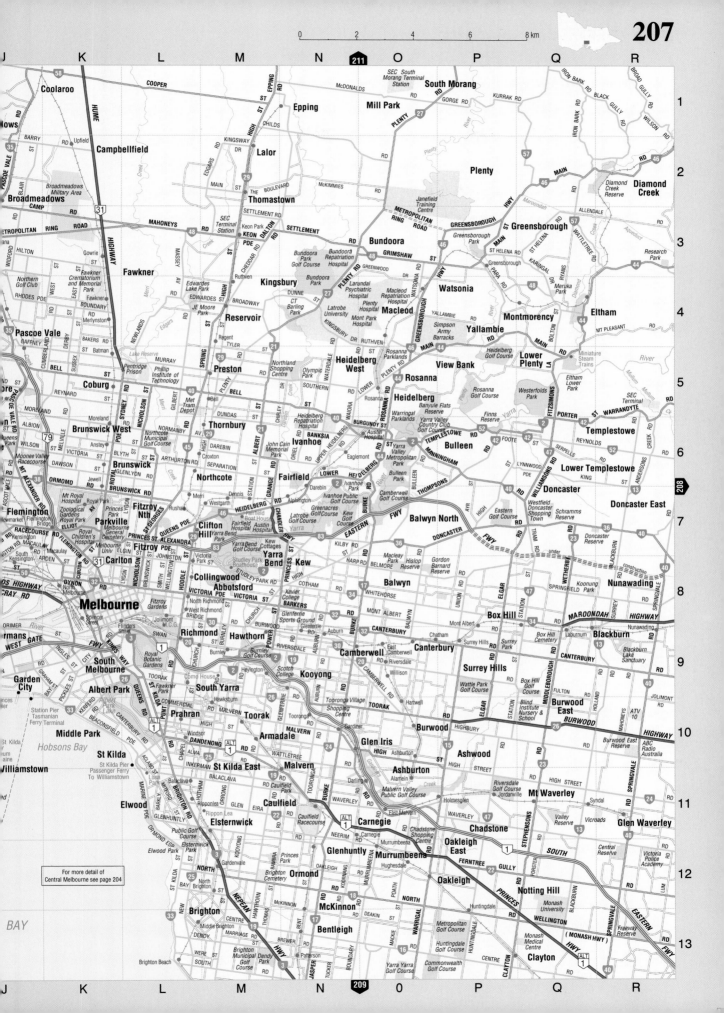

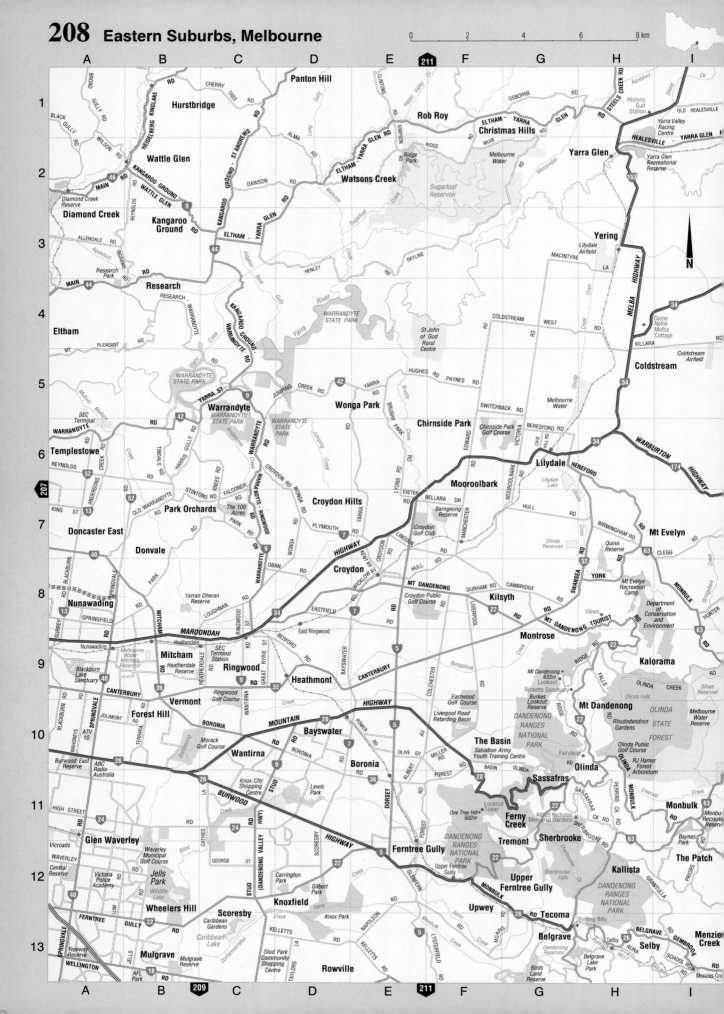

0 10 20 30 40 50 km

TO BENALLA

Seymour
Tallarook
Broadford
Kilmore
Wallan
Beveridge
Kalkallo
Mickleham
Craigieburn
Whittlesea
Yan Yean
Hurstbridge
Greensborough

MELBOURNE

Box Hill
Ringwood
Croydon
Glen Waverley
Brighton
Mentone
Mordialloc
Chelsea
Seaford
Frankston

Cranbourne
Pakenham
Officer
Beaconsfield
Berwick
Narre Warren
Lyndhurst

Mornington
Somerville
Moorooduc
Tyabb
Hastings
Bittern
Crib Point
Stony Point
Balnarring
Red Hill
Flinders
Somers

Cowes
Ventnor
Rhyll
Newhaven
San Remo
Bass
Kilcunda
Dalyston
Wonthaggi

Ruffy
Terip Terip
Merton
Bonnie Doon
Mansfield
Barjarg
Yarck
Molesworth
Alexandra
Eildon
Thornton
Acheron
Taggerty
Buxton
Marysville
Narbethong
Healesville
Yarra Glen
Coldstream
Seville
Woori Yallock
Wandin
Silvan
Olinda
Monbulk
Emerald
Cockatoo
Gembrook
Warburton
Yarra Junction
Launching Place
Millgrove
Big Pats Creek
Noojee
Neerim
Drouin
Warragul
Darnum
Yarragon
Trafalgar
Moe
Thorpdale
Narracan
Mirboo North
Leongatha
Korumburra
Poowong
Loch
Nyora
Lang Lang
Koo-wee-rup
Tooradin
Pearcedale
Cannons Creek
Warneet
Grantville
Corinella
Glen Forbes
Bena
Kongwak
Outtrim
Meeniyan
Dumbalk
Mirboo
Koonwarra

WESTERN PORT
FRENCH ISLAND
PHILLIP ISLAND

TO INVERLOCH
TO FOSTER
TO MORWELL

BELLARINE PENINSULA

Indented Head
Indented Head

St Leonards
South Red Bluff

DRYSDALE -
ST LEONARDS RD

EDWARDS POINT WILDLIFE RESERVE

Edwards Point

Swan Bay

Duck Island

PORT PHILLIP BAY

210

HISTORICAL HOMES: The Mornington Penins...
array of magnificently preserved historical hom...
Visit Coolart at Somers, a century-old mansio...
in landscaped gardens, or the simple 1844 drop sla...
McCrae Homestead. Sages Cottage at Baxter...
an excellent day tour destination, a serene ru...
set in large grounds with an animal sanctuary.

Queenscliff Golf Course

Swan Island

Queenscliff Steam Railway

Queenscliff
Black Lighthouse
Fort Queenscliff

The Rip

Searoad Passenger Ferry

Ferry

Mud Islands

DOLPHIN SWIMS: Join professional divers and swim with the friendly bottlenose dolphins that inhabit the bay. Tours depart Sorrento Pier on weekends from September to May.

Point Nepean
Nepean Bay
Observatory Point
Ticonderoga Bay
Fort Nepean
POINT NEPEAN NP
Cheviot Beach
COMMONWEALTH LAND
Weeroona Bay
Collins Bay
Portsea
POINT NEPEAN NP
Portsea Golf Course
Point King
London Bridge
Sorrento Golf Course

Mount Ma...
Balcombe Point

Mount F
Public F
Mt Mart
160m

Martha Point

Dromana Bay
Safety Beach

ARTHURS SEAT STATE PARK: Originally named after a similar mountain near Edinburgh, Scotland during the first exploration of Port Phillip Bay. Take a ride on the 72-seat chairlift for spectacular views of the Peninsula and Bay. Visit Arthurs Seat Fauna Park or enjoy a short walk to scenic Flinders Lookout.

Portsea Surf Beach

Sorrento

Capel Sound

MARINE DR
PENINSULA

Dromana

Eastern Lighthouse
McCrae
McCrae Homest

MORNINGTON RD

Arthurs Seat Chairlift
Arthurs Seat 309m
ARTHURS SEAT SP

BOUNDARY

Sorrento Back Beach
The Sisters
Collins Settlement Historic Site

Sorrento Downs Golf Course

Jubilee Point
Diamond Bay

Koonya Beach

Blairgowrie

Rosebud West

Rosebud

ARTHURS SEAT SP

Rosebud Golf Course

Sheepwash Ck

16

POINT NEPEAN NATIONAL PARK: This magnificent park extends from the tip of Port Nepean to Cape Schanck. An unusual transporter service operates, taking visitors to Cheviot Beach, Observatory Point and the historical Fort Nepean. Numerous walking tracks provide easy access to London Bridge, Cape Schanck Lighthouse and endless spectacular coastal scenery.

Spray Point

Koreen Point

White Cliffs

Rye

Tootgarook

Tootgarook Market

NEPEAN

Nepean

PURVES RD

MAIN CREEK RD

Rosebud Country Club

Rosebud Picnic Park

ARTHURS SEAT RD

71

SHANDS RD

MAIN RIDGE

The Divide

Observation Hill

DUNDAS ST
CANTEBURY JETTY RD
BROWNS RD
POINT NEPEAN NATIONAL PARK

TRUEMANS RD
BROWNS RD

FLINDERS RD

Drum Drum
Aloc Ck

Boneo Market

Boneo

MORNINGTON

School Hill 184m

BALDRYS RD

Musk

Rye Ocean Beach

SANDY RD

MORNINGTON PENINSULA

POINT NEPEAN NATIONAL PARK

Capri Beach

Boags Rocks
Gunnamatta Surf Beach

National Golf Course

Cape Schanck Golf Course

67 ROSEBUD

FLINDERS RD

MEAKINS RD

Stockyard Ck

Double Ck

Spring Rd

71

The Pinnac 77m

WINERIES: ❶
Balnarring Vineyard 9 L7
Coolart Valley Vineyard 17 J8
Craig Avon Vineyard 11 K7
Dromana Estate 6 I7
Elan Vineyard 5 L6
Hanns Creek Estate 12 K8
Karina Vineyard 7 I7
Kings Creek Vineyard 10 L7
Main Ridge Estate 16 I8
Merricks Estate 19 K9
Moorooduc Estate 2 K5
Paringa Estate 18 J9
Peninsula Estate 15 I8
Port Phillip Estate 13 J8
Red Hill Estate 21 I9
Stonier's Merricks 20 K9
Stumpy Gully Vineyard 3 L5
Tanglewood Downs 4 K6
T'Gallant 14 J8
The Briars Vineyard 1 J5
Tucks Ridge 22 J9
Willow Creek 8 K7

TOURIST INFORMATION:
Phillip Island (Phillip Island Rd, Newhaven)
Mornington (cnr Main & Elizabeth Sts)
Queenscliff (cnr Bellarine Hwy & Grubb Rd)

BASS STRAIT

N

Cape Schanck Lighthouse

Bushranger Bay

Cape Schanck

Picnic Point

The Arch

Simmons Bay

Cairns Bay

The Blowhole

Point

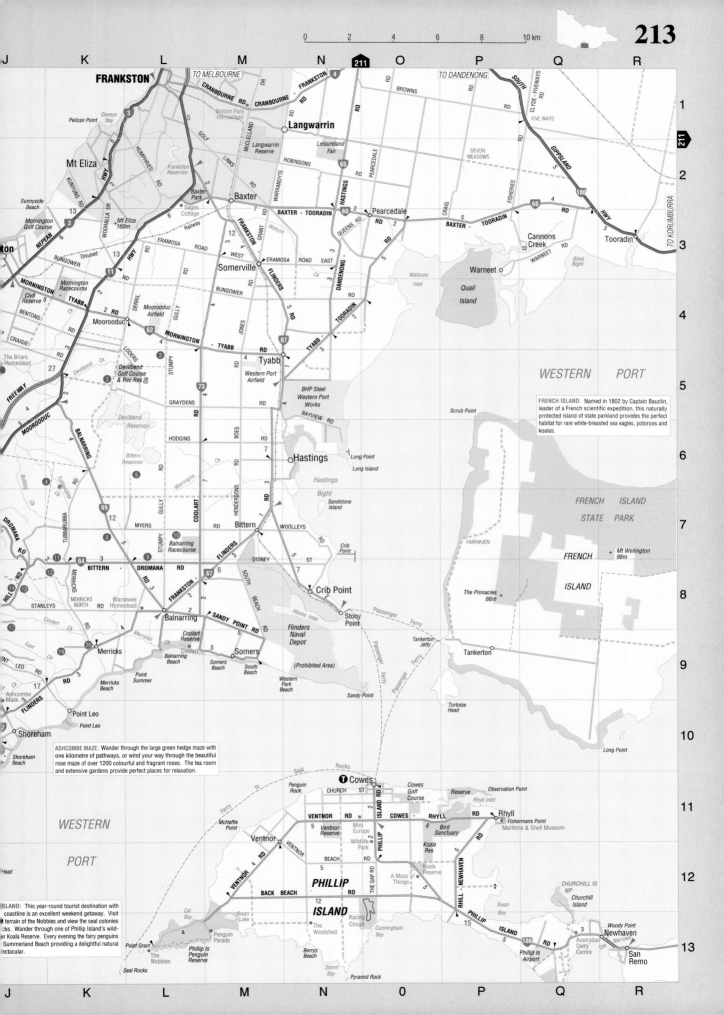

0 2 4 6 8 10 km

FRANKSTON

TO MELBOURNE

CRANBOURNE RD

CRANBOURNE - FRANKSTON

TO DANDENONG

211

BROWNS RD

Mt Eliza

Langwarrin

Pelican Point

Daveys Bay

Ballam Park Homestead

Leisureland Fair

DEVON MEADOWS

FIVE WAYS

Sunnyside Beach

Mornington Golf Course

Mt Eliza 160m

Sages Cottage

Baxter

Langwarrin Reserve

ROBINSONS RD

PEARCEDALE RD

BAXTER - TOORADIN RD

Pearcedale

CRAIG RD

BAXTER - TOORADIN

Cannons Creek

FISHERIES RD

WARNEET RD

Tooradin

TO KORUMBURRA

Mornington Racecourse

Disused Railway

Somerville

ERAMOSA ROAD WEST

ERAMOSA ROAD EAST

QUEENS RD

Blind Bight

TYABB RD

DERRIL RD

Mornooduc Airfield

BUNGOWER RD

FLINDERS RD

DANDENONG RD

TOORADIN RD

Warneet

Quail Island

WESTERN PORT

Mooroduc

The Briars Homestead

LODERS RD

STUMPY GULLY RD

JONES RD

MORNINGTON - TYABB RD

Tyabb

Watsons Inlet

Devilbend Golf Course & Rec Res

GRAYDENS RD

Western Port Airfield

TYABB RD

BHP Steel Western Port Works

Scrub Point

FRENCH ISLAND: Named in 1802 by Captain Bauclin, leader of a French scientific expedition, this naturally protected island of state parkland provides the perfect habitat for rare white-breasted sea eagles, potoroos and koalas.

Devilbend Reservoir

HODGINS RD

BOES RD

BAYVIEW RD

FREEWAY

MOOROODUC

Bittern Reservoir

COOLART RD

HENDERSONS RD

Hastings

Long Point

Long Island

Hastings Bight

Sandstone Island

FRENCH ISLAND STATE PARK

DROMANA RD

TUBBARUBBA RD

Warringine Ck

MYERS RD

STUMPY GULLY RD

Bittern

WOOLLEYS RD

FAIRHAVEN

Mt Wellington 98m

FRENCH ISLAND

Balnarring Racecourse

FLINDERS RD

DISNEY ST

Crib Point

The Pinnacles 66m

BITTERN - DROMANA RD

FRANKSTON -

SOUTH BEACH RD

Crib Point

Passenger Ferry

Tankerton Jetty

STANLEYS

Balnarring

SANDY POINT RD

Coolart Reserve

Somers

Stony Point

Flinders Naval Depot

Passenger Ferry

Tankerton

MERRICKS RD

Warrawee Homestead

Balnarring Beach

Coolart

Somers Beach

South Beach

(Prohibited Area)

Tortoise Head

HILL RD

STANLEYS

Merricks

Point Summer

Merricks Beach

Western Park Beach

Sandy Point

LEO RD

Ashcombe Maze

FLINDERS RD

Point Leo

Point Leo

Long Point

Ck

Shoreham

Shoreham Beach

ASHCOMBE MAZE: Wander through the large green hedge maze with one kilometre of pathways, or wind your way through the beautiful rose maze of over 1200 colourful and fragrant roses. The tea room and extensive gardens provide perfect places for relaxation.

Seal Rocks

Penguin Rock

Cowes

CHURCH ST

ISLAND RD

Cowes Golf Course

Observation Point

Rhyll Inlet

Rhyll

Fishermans Point

WESTERN

PORT

McHaffie Point

Ventnor

VENTNOR RD

VENTNOR RD

VENTNOR RD

VENTNOR BEACH RD

Ventnor Reserve

Mini Europe Wildlife Park

THE GAP RD

PHILLIP

COWES - RHYLL

RHYLL RD

Bird Sanctuary

Koala Res

A Maze 'n' Things

Koala Reserve

Maritime & Shell Museum

RHILL RD

NEWHAVEN RD

PHILLIP ISLAND RD

CHURCHILL IS NP

Churchill Island

PHILLIP

ISLAND

BACK BEACH RD

Cat Bay

Swan Lake

The Woolshed

Racing Circuit

Cunningham Bay

Swan Bay

PHILLIP ISLAND RD

Australian Dairy Centre

Woody Point

Newhaven

ISLAND: This year-round tourist destination with coastline is an excellent weekend getaway. Visit terrain of the Nobbies and view the seal colonies cks. Wander through one of Phillip Island's wild-r Koala Reserve. Every evening the fairy penguins Summerland Beach providing a delightful natural ectacular.

Point Grant

Penguin Parade

Berrys Beach

Storm Bay

Pyramid Rock

The Nobbies

Phillip Is Penguin Reserve

Phillip Is Airport

186

San Remo

The Narrows

0 2 4 6 8 10 km

WINERIES: ①
Bianchet Winery B8 1
Brahams Creek Winery I9 2
Chum Creek Winery D6 3
Coldstream Hills D8 4
De Bortoli Winery and
  Restaurant C5 5
Domaine Chandon Australia C7 6
Fergusson Winery and
  Restaurant
Kellybrook Winery and
  Restaurant A8 20
Lillydale Vineyards D10 8
Lirralirra Estate A8 9
Long Gully Estate D6 10
Monbulk Winery C11 11
Mount Delancy C10 12
Oakridge Estate D10 13
St Huberts Vineyard C8 14
Shantell Vineyard D5 15
Warramate Vineyard D8 16
Yarra Burn Vineyard and
  Restaurant G9/10 17
Yarra Edge Winery A8 21
Yarra Ridge Vineyard B7 18
Yering Station Vineyards B7 19

KINGLAKE NATIONAL PARK: Home to numerous lyrebirds and wombats, the Kinglake National Park areas were established to protect the remaining wet eucalypt forests on the Great Dividing Range. Tranquil walks through fern gullies and forested spurs take you to the Wombelano and Mason's Falls.

TOOLANGI-BLACK RANGES: Toolangi (once) home of C.J. Dennis, author of 'The Sentimental Bloke' is a mountainous berry producing area nestled in the Black Ranges State Forest. Picturesque roadways provide easy access to the spectacular Wilhelmina Falls and Murrindindi Cascades. There are excellent riding tours avaliable in the area, taking you along rugged mountain tracks and tranquil river paths. Trout and Blackfish can be caught in the Murrindindi River.

GULF STATION: Now owned by the National Trust, Gulf Station at Yarra Glen is one of Victoria's oldest pastoral properties dating back to the 1850s. Visitors can step back in time, explore the original timber buildings, cottage gardens and participate in farm activities.

HEALESVILLE SANCTUARY: Home to over 200 of Australia's unique birds, animals and reptiles, including some endangered species. Healesville Sanctuary, open every day of the year, is recognised as Australia's top wildlife park. Spend the day venturing among friendly kangaroos, emus and wombats in naturally designed enclosures.

SILVAN RESERVOIR: Located on the edge of beautiful Olinda State Forest, Stonyford picnic ground at the magnificent Silvan Reservoir provides excellent BBQ facilities for the perfect break on a day trip to the area. Visit the Tulip Farm or simply stop along the Monbulk Road for breathtaking views of the region.

PUFFING BILLY: This superbly restored vintage steam train ambles its way from the ferny stands of Belgrave through the cool rainforest to Emerald Lake.

TOURIST INFORMATION:
Healesville (278 Maroondah Hwy
Marysville (18 Murchison St)

TO YEA

TO ALEXANDRA

GREAT DIVIDING RANGE

KINGLAKE NATIONAL PARK

Kinglake

Healesville

Yarra Glen

Christmas Hills

Lilydale

Coldstream

Wandin North

Seville

Wandin Yallock

Woori Yallock

Yarra Junction

Warburton

Millgrove

Launching Place

Don Valley

Gladysdale

Three Bridges

Powelltown

Silvan

Olinda

Monbulk

Emerald

Cockatoo

Avonsleigh

Clematis

Menzies Creek

Belgrave

Upwey

Upper Ferntree Gully

Gembrook

Yellingbo

Marysville

Buxton

Narbethong

Steels Creek

Dixons Creek

Toolangi

Mittons Bridge

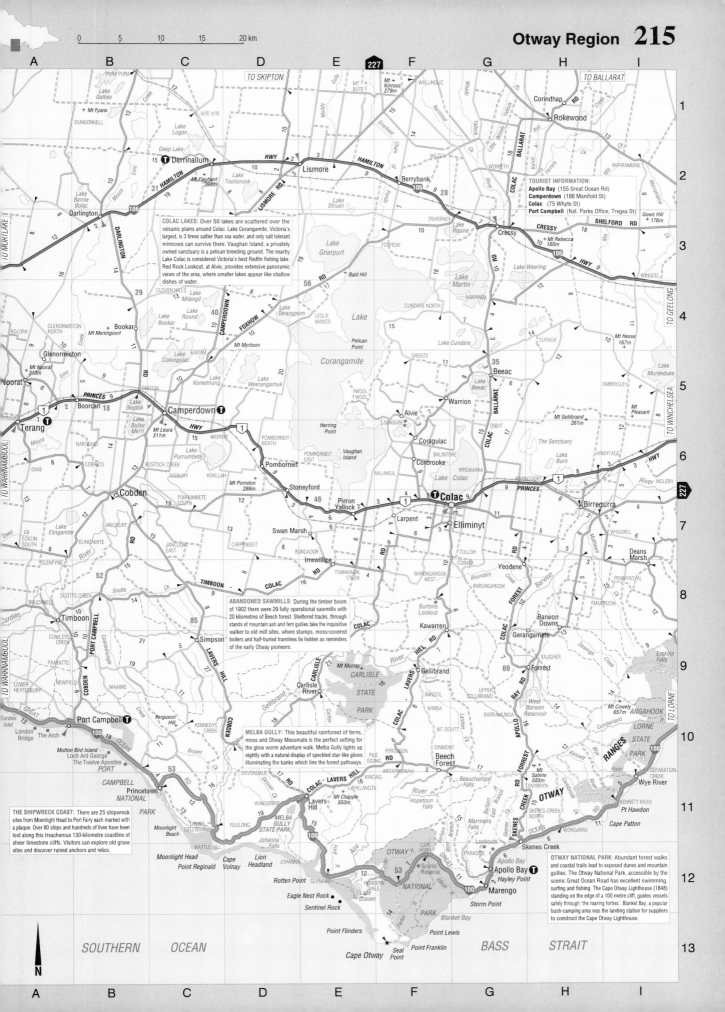

0   5   10   15   20 km

A   B   C   D   E   F   G   H   I

227

TO SKIPTON   TO BALLARAT

1

Corindhap   RD
Rokewood

2

TOURIST INFORMATION:
Apollo Bay (155 Great Ocean Rd)
Camperdown (188 Manifold St)
Colac (75 Whyte St)
Port Campbell (Nat. Parks Office, Tregea St)

Derrinallum   HAMILTON   HWY
Lismore   HAMILTON
Berrybank   106   28

Cressy   CRESSY   SHELFORD   RD
106   HWY

COLAC LAKES: Over 50 lakes are scattered over the volcanic plains around Colac. Lake Corangamite, Victoria's largest, is 3 times saltier than sea water, and only salt tolerant minnows can survive there. Vaughan Island, a privately owned sanctuary is a pelican breeding ground. The nearby Lake Colac is considered Victoria's best Redfin fishing lake. Red Rock Lookout, at Alvie, provides extensive panoramic views of the area, where smaller lakes appear like shallow dishes of water.

Mt Rebecca
160m
3

Lake
Martin

Mt Hesse
167m
4

Beeac   35

Corangamite

Warrion   5

Darlington
106   HAMILTON

Deep Lake   15
Lake Tooliorook
Mt Elephant
394m
Lake Struan

Lake Gnarpurt

Lake
Weering
12

Mt Pleasant

Lake
Murdeduke

OMBERSLEY

Glenormiston
NORTH   Bookar
Mt Meningoort

CLOVEN HILLS
Lake Milangil

Lake Terangpom

Lake Cundare
EURACK

Mt Gellibrand
261m

Noorat
Mt Noorat
313m

Lake
Round
Lake Bookar
Mt Myrtoon   40

LESLIE
MANOR

Alvie   Coragulac
Cororooke

Lake
Burn

TARMYTAGE   HWY

Camperdown   PRINCES   HWY
Terang   1   Boorcan   18
Mt Leura
311m

Pomborneit

Herring
Point

Pomborneit
NORTH

Vaughan
Island

Colac   Colac   PRINCES   1   Birregurra

227

6

Cobden

Mt Porndon
289m   46
Stoneyford

Pirron
Yallock
Larpent   Elliminyt

Deans
Marsh
7

ABANDONED SAWMILLS: During the timber boom of 1902 there were 29 fully operational sawmills with 20 kilometres of Beech forest. Sheltered tracks, through stands of mountain ash and fern gullies take the inquisitive walker to old mill sites, where stumps, moss-covered boilers and half-buried tramlines lie hidden as reminders of the early Otway pioneers.

Swan Marsh

Irrewillipe   TIMBOON -   COLAC

Yeodene

Barwon
Downs
8

Timboon   85
Simpson

Kawarren
Gerangamete   69
Forrest   9

Port Campbell   100   18

MELBA GULLY: This beautiful rainforest of ferns, moss and Otway Messmate is the perfect setting for the glow worm adventure walk. Melba Gully lights up nightly with a natural display of speckled star-like glows illuminating the banks which line the forest pathways.

Beech
Forest
10

London
Bridge   The Arch   53
Mutton Bird Island
Loch Ard George
The Twelve Apostles   PORT

Wye River   10

Princetown   CAMPBELL
NATIONAL   PARK

Lavers
Hill   Cape Patton   11

THE SHIPWRECK COAST: There are 25 shipwreck sites from Moonlight Head to Port Fairy each marked with a plaque. Over 80 ships and hundreds of lives have been lost along this treacherous 130-kilometre coastline of sheer limestone cliffs. Visitors can explore old grave sites and discover ruined anchors and relics.

Skenes Creek

Moonlight Head
Point Reginald   Cape Volnay   Lion
Headland

Apollo Bay   12
Marengo

OTWAY NATIONAL PARK: Abundant forest walks and coastal trails lead to exposed dunes and mountain gullies. The Otway National Park, accessible by the scenic Great Ocean Road has excellent swimming, surfing and fishing. The Cape Otway Lighthouse (1848) standing on the edge of a 100 metre cliff, guides vessels safely through 'the roaring forties'. Blanket Bay, a popular bush-camping area was the landing station for suppliers to construct the Cape Otway Lighthouse.

Rotten Point
Eagle Nest Rock
Sentinel Rock

Point Flinders   Point Lewis

N

SOUTHERN   OCEAN   *BASS   STRAIT*
13

Cape Otway   Seal
Point   Point Franklin

A   B   C   D   E   F   G   H   I

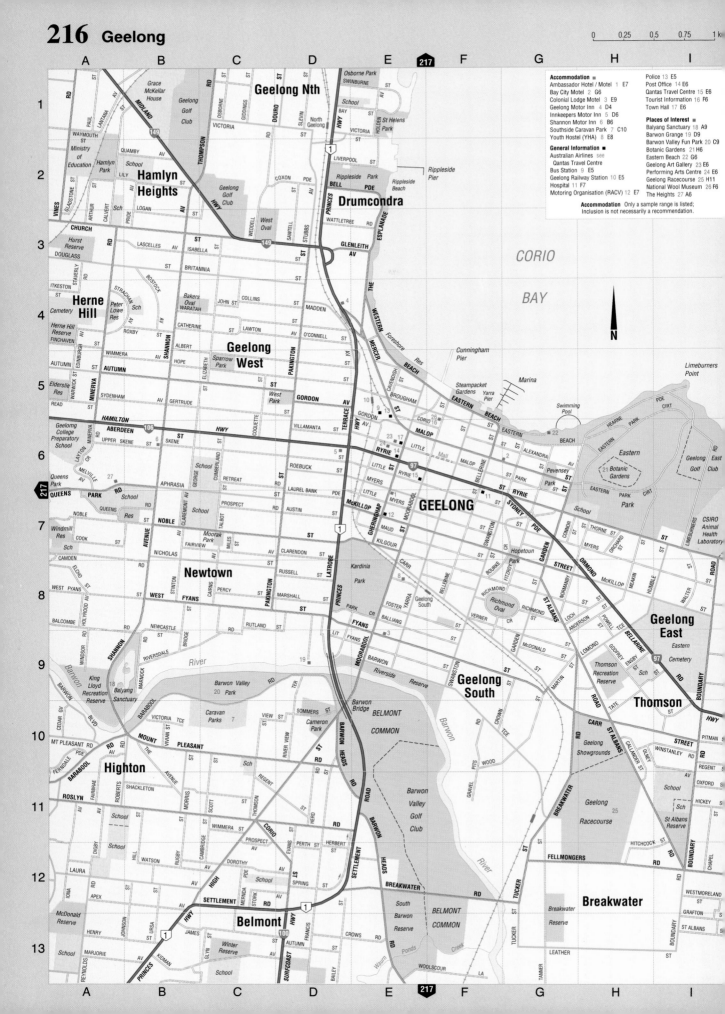

Geelong Nth

Hamlyn Heights

Drumcondra

Herne Hill

Geelong West

CORIO BAY

Newtown

GEELONG

Highton

Geelong South

Geelong East

Thomson

Belmont

Breakwater

Accommodation ■
Ambassador Hotel / Motel 1 E7
Bay City Motel 2 G6
Colonial Lodge Motel 3 E9
Geelong Motor Inn 4 D4
Innkeepers Motor Inn 5 D6
Shannon Motor Inn 6 B6
Southside Caravan Park 7 C10
Youth Hostel (YHA) 8 E8

General Information ■
Australian Airlines see
   Qantas Travel Centre
Bus Station 9 E5
Geelong Railway Station 10 E5
Hospital 11 F7
Motoring Organisation (RACV) 12 E7

Police 13 E5
Post Office 14 E6
Qantas Travel Centre 15 E6
Tourist Information 16 F6
Town Hall 17 E6

Places of Interest ■
Balyang Sanctuary 18 A9
Barwon Grange 19 D9
Barwon Valley Fun Park 20 C9
Botanic Gardens 21 H6
Eastern Beach 22 G6
Geelong Art Gallery 23 E6
Performing Arts Centre 24 E6
Geelong Racecourse 25 H11
National Wool Museum 26 F6
The Heights 27 A6

Accommodation Only a sample range is listed;
Inclusion is not necessarily a recommendation.

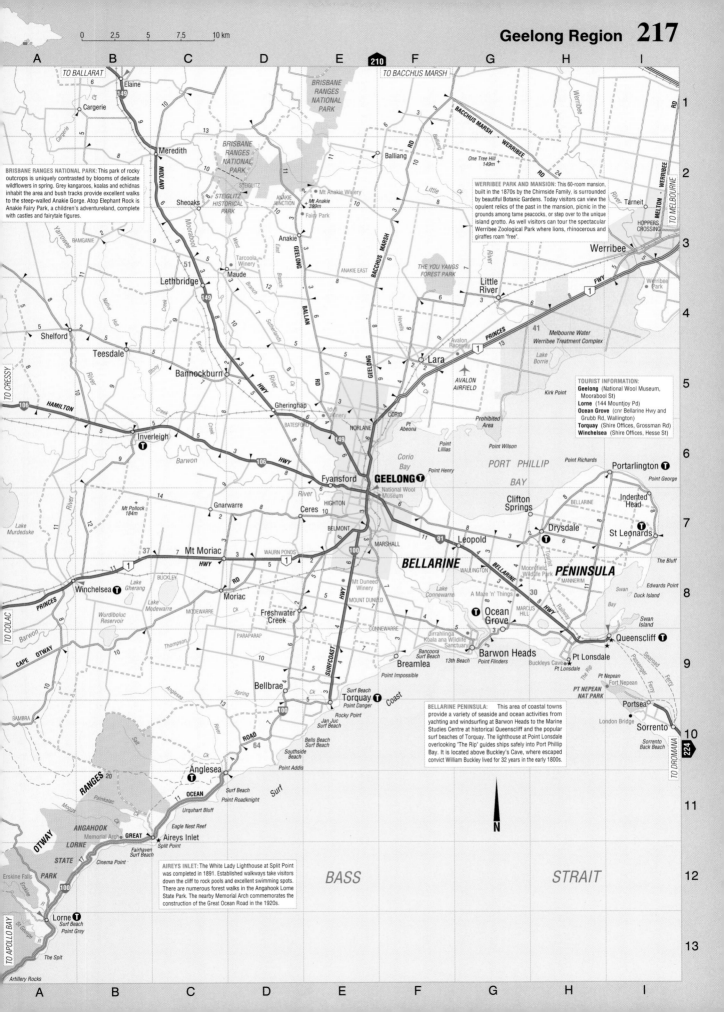

0   2.5   5   7.5   10 km

A   B   C   D   E   F   G   H   I

TO BALLARAT
Elaine
Cargerie
Meredith
Sheoaks
Lethbridge
Maude
Shelford
Teesdale
Bannockburn
Gheringhap
Inverleigh
Fyansford
Gnarwarre
Ceres
Mt Moriac
Winchelsea
Moriac
Freshwater Creek
Bellbrae
Torquay
Anglesea
Aireys Inlet
Lorne

BRISBANE RANGES NATIONAL PARK: This park of rocky outcrops is uniquely contrasted by blooms of delicate wildflowers in spring. Grey kangaroos, koalas and echidnas inhabit the area and bush tracks provide excellent walks to the steep-walled Anakie Gorge. Atop Elephant Rock is Anakie Fairy Park, a children's adventureland, complete with castles and fairytale figures.

BRISBANE RANGES NATIONAL PARK
STEIGLITZ HISTORICAL PARK
Anakie
Anakie Junction
Mt Anakie Winery
Mt Anakie 399m
Fairy Park
Anakie East

TO BACCHUS MARSH
Balliang
Little River
Werribee
Tarneit
HOPPERS CROSSING
TO MELBOURNE
Lara
Avalon Raceway
AVALON AIRFIELD
THE YOU YANGS FOREST PARK
One Tree Hill 149m
Lake Borrie
Melbourne Water Werribee Treatment Complex
Kirk Point
Prohibited Area

WERRIBEE PARK AND MANSION: This 60-room mansion, built in the 1870s by the Chirnside Family, is surrounded by beautiful Botanic Gardens. Today visitors can view the opulent relics of the past in the mansion, picnic in the grounds among tame peacocks, or step over to the unique island grotto. As well visitors can tour the spectacular Werribee Zoological Park where lions, rhinocerous and giraffes roam "free".

TOURIST INFORMATION:
Geelong (National Wool Museum, Moorabool St)
Lorne (144 Mountjoy Pd)
Ocean Grove (cnr Bellarine Hwy and Grubb Rd, Wallington)
Torquay (Shire Offices, Grossman Rd)
Winchelsea (Shire Offices, Hesse St)

GEELONG
National Wool Museum
NORLANE
CORIO
Pt Abeona
Point Lillias
Point Wilson
Point Henry
Corio Bay
PORT PHILLIP BAY
Point Richards
Point George
Portarlington
Indented Head
St Leonards
Clifton Springs
Drysdale
BELLARINE
Leopold
Moorfield Wildlife Park
Lake Connewarre
A Maze 'n' Things
BELLARINE PENINSULA
MANNERIM
The Bluff
Edwards Point
Duck Island
Swan Bay
Swan Island
Ocean Grove
Queenscliff
Barwon Heads
Pt Lonsdale
Buckleys Cave
Point Flinders
13th Beach
Jirrahlinga Koala ana Wildlife Sanctuary
Bancoora Surf Beach
Breamlea
Point Impossible
Pt Nepean
Fort Nepean
PT NEPEAN NAT PARK
Portsea
London Bridge
Sorrento
Sorrento Back Beach
TO DROMANA

HIGHTON
BELMONT
MARSHALL
Mt Duneed Winery
MOUNT DUNEED
WALLINGTON
MARCUS HILL
CONNEWARRE
PARAPARAP
Point Danger
Rocky Point
Jan Juc Surf Beach
Bells Beach Surf Beach
Southside Beach
Point Addis
Surf Beach
Point Roadknight
Urquhart Bluff
Eagle Nest Reef
Split Point
Fairhaven Surf Beach
Cinema Point

BELLARINE PENINSULA: This area of coastal towns provide a variety of seaside and ocean activities from yachting and windsurfing at Barwon Heads to the Marine Studies Centre at historical Queenscliff and the popular surf beaches of Torquay. The lighthouse at Point Lonsdale overlooking 'The Rip' guides ships safely into Port Phillip Bay. It is located above Buckley's Cave, where escaped convict William Buckley lived for 32 years in the early 1800s.

AIREYS INLET: The White Lady Lighthouse at Split Point was completed in 1891. Established walkways take visitors down the cliff to rock pools and excellent swimming spots. There are numerous forest walks in the Angahook Lorne State Park. The nearby Memorial Arch commemorates the construction of the Great Ocean Road in the 1920s.

OTWAY RANGES
ANGAHOOK LORNE STATE PARK
Memorial Arch
Erskine Falls
Artillery Rocks
The Spit
Point Grey
Surf Beach
TO APOLLO BAY
TO CRESSY
TO COLAC

BASS **STRAIT**

N

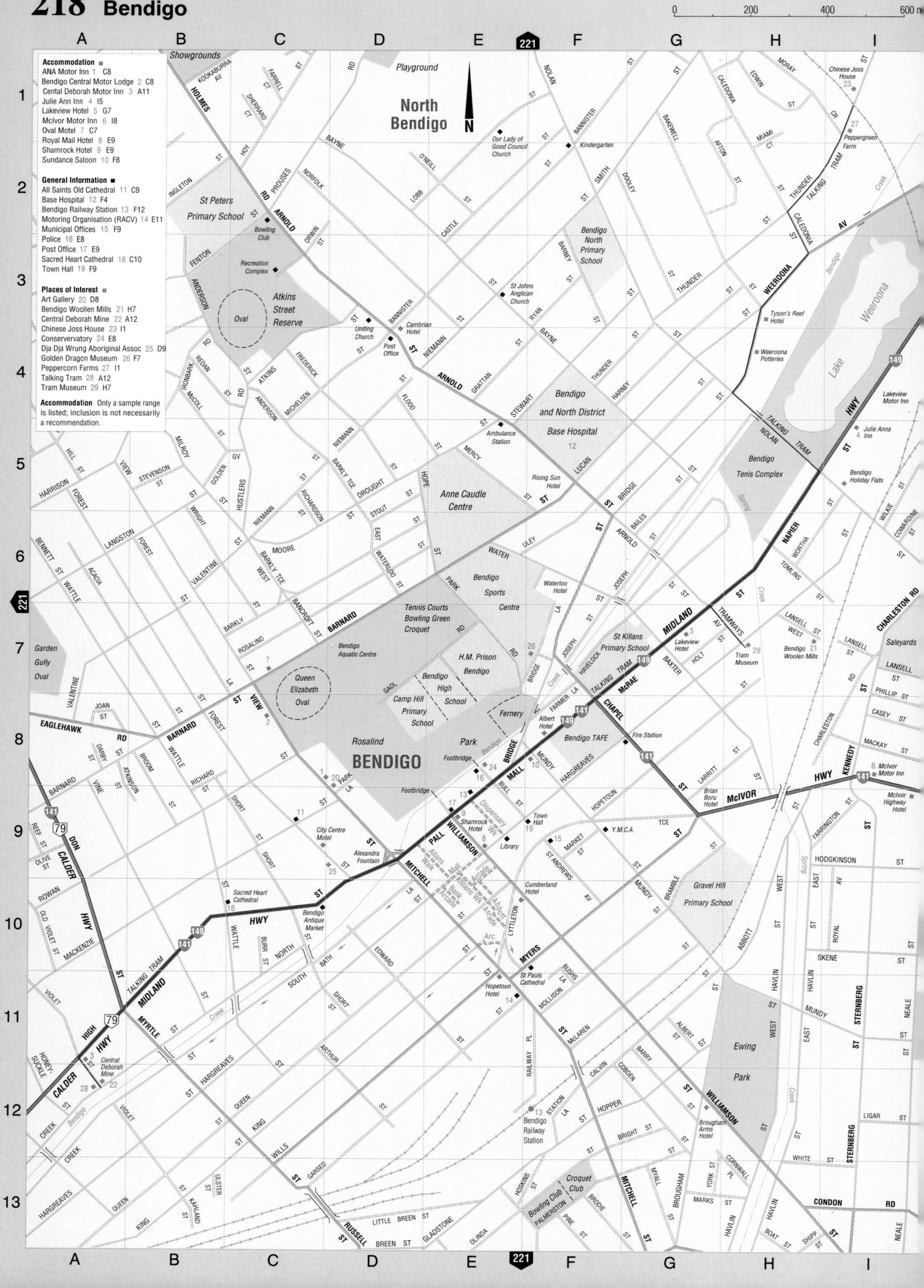

0   200   400   600 m

Accommodation ■
ANA Motor Inn 1 C8
Bendigo Central Motor Lodge 2 C8
Cental Deborah Motor Inn 3 A11
Julie Ann Inn 4 I5
Lakeview Hotel 5 G7
McIvor Motor Inn 6 I8
Oval Motel 7 C7
Royal Mail Hotel 8 E9
Shamrock Hotel 9 E9
Sundance Saloon 10 F8

General Information ■
All Saints Old Cathedral 11 C9
Base Hospital 12 F4
Bendigo Railway Station 13 F12
Motoring Organisation (RACV) 14 E11
Municipal Offices 15 F9
Police 16 E8
Post Office 17 E9
Sacred Heart Cathedral 18 C10
Town Hall 19 F9

Places of Interest ■
Art Gallery 20 D8
Bendigo Woollen Mills 21 H7
Central Deborah Mine 22 A12
Chinese Joss House 23 I1
Conservervatory 24 E8
Dja Dja Wrung Aboriginal Assoc 25 D9
Golden Dragon Museum 26 F7
Peppercorn Farms 27 I1
Talking Tram 28 A12
Tram Museum 29 H7

Accommodation Only a sample range
is listed; inclusion is not necessarily
a recommendation.

North
Bendigo
N

BENDIGO

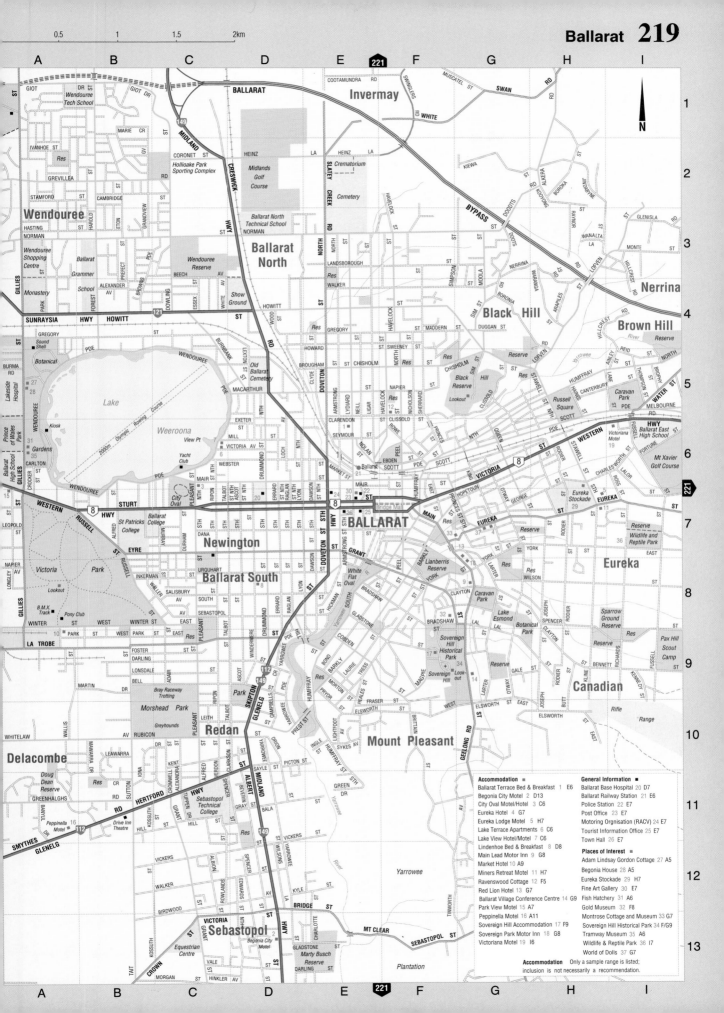

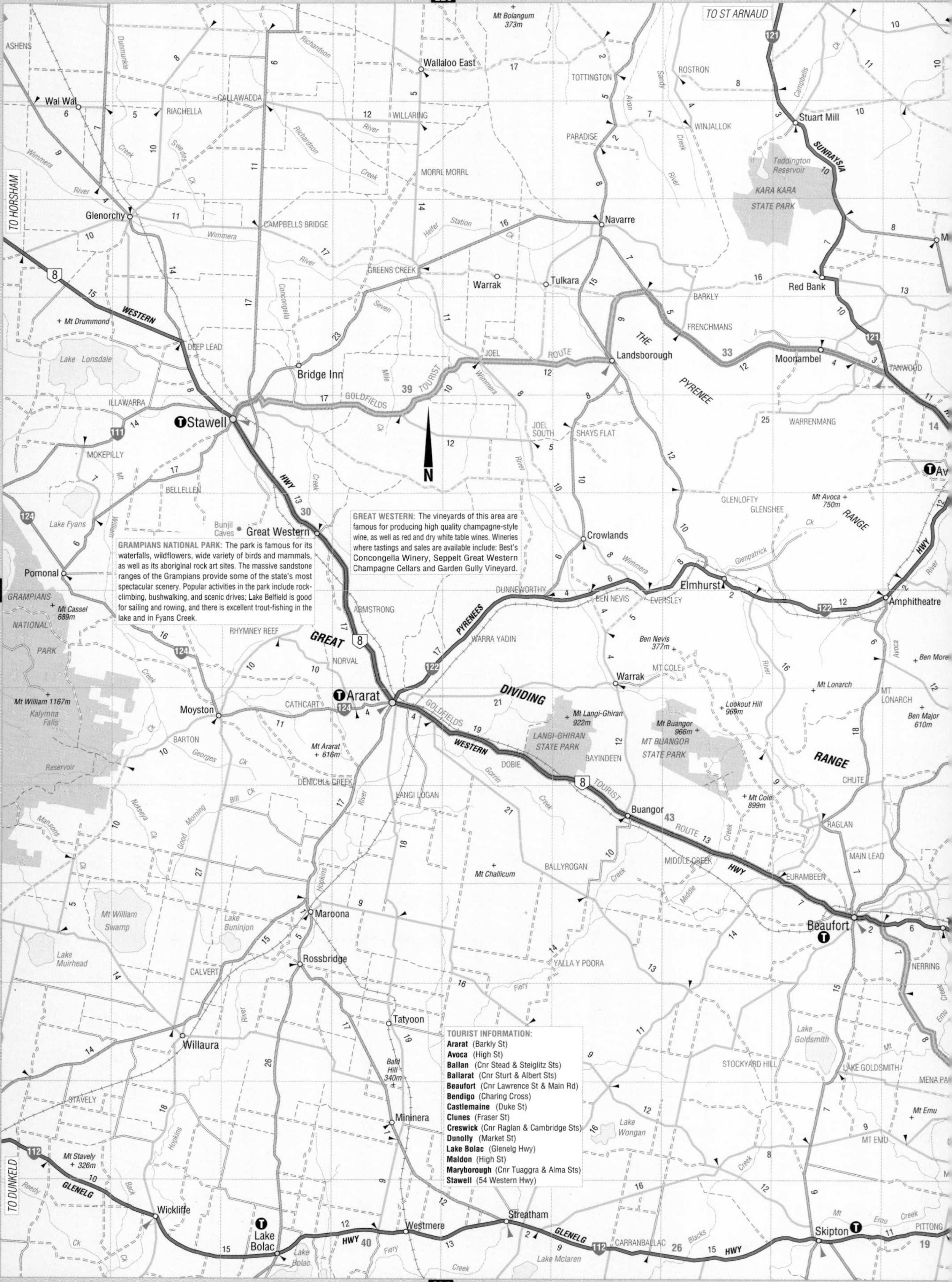

A
B
C
D
E
F
G
H
I
229
227
228
TO ST ARNAUD
TO HORSHAM
TO DUNKELD
Mt Bolangum 373m
ASHENS
Wallaloo East
TOTTINGTON
ROSTRON
Wal Wal
CALLAWADDA
RIACHELLA
WILLARING
PARADISE
WINJALLOK
Stuart Mill
Teddington Reservoir
KARA KARA STATE PARK
SUNRAYSIA
MORRL MORRL
Glenorchy
CAMPBELLS BRIDGE
Navarre
GREENS CREEK
Warrak
Tulkara
Red Bank
BARKLY
FRENCHMANS
Mt Drummond
WESTERN
DEEP LEAD
Lake Lonsdale
Bridge Inn
JOEL
Landsborough
THE PYRENEE
Moonambel
TANWOOD
GOLDFIELDS 39 TOURIST ROUTE
ILLAWARRA
Stawell
JOEL SOUTH
SHAYS FLAT
WARRENMANG
MOKEPILLY
BELLELLEN
GLENLOFTY
GLENSHEE
Mt Avoca 750m
Lake Fyans
Bunjil Caves
Great Western
Crowlands
GREAT WESTERN: The vineyards of this area are famous for producing high quality champagne-style wine, as well as red and dry white table wines. Wineries where tastings and sales are available include: Best's Concongella Winery, Seppelt Great Western Champagne Cellars and Garden Gully Vineyard.
GRAMPIANS NATIONAL PARK: The park is famous for its waterfalls, wildflowers, wide variety of birds and mammals, as well as its aboriginal rock art sites. The massive sandstone ranges of the Grampians provide some of the state's most spectacular scenery. Popular activities in the park include rock-climbing, bushwalking, and scenic drives; Lake Belfield is good for sailing and rowing, and there is excellent trout-fishing in the lake and in Fyans Creek.
Pomonal
GRAMPIANS NATIONAL PARK
Mt Cassel 689m
DUNNEWORTHY
BEN NEVIS
EVERSLEY
Elmhurst
Amphitheatre
ARMSTRONG
RHYMNEY REEF
GREAT DIVIDING RANGE
PYRENEES
WARRA YADIN
Ben Nevis 377m
NORVAL
MT COLE
Warrak
Mt Lonarch
MT LONARCH
Ben More
Mt William 1167m
Kalymna Falls
Moyston
CATHCART
Ararat
Mt Langi-Ghiran 922m
LANGI-GHIRAN STATE PARK
Lookout Hill 969m
Mt Buangor 966m
MT BUANGOR STATE PARK
Ben Major 610m
BARTON
Mt Ararat 616m
BAYINDEEN
DOBIE
CHUTE
Reservoir
DENICULL CREEK
LANGI LOGAN
Buangor
Mt Cole 899m
RAGLAN
43 ROUTE 13
MIDDLE CREEK
MAIN LEAD
BALLYROGAN
Mt Challicum
EURAMBEEN
Mt William Swamp
Maroona
Lake Buninjon
Beaufort
Lake Muirhead
Rossbridge
CALVERT
YALLA Y POORA
NERRING
Tatyoon
Willaura
Bald Hill 340m
STOCKYARD HILL
Lake Goldsmith
LAKE GOLDSMITH
MENA PA
STAVELY
Mininera
Lake Wongan
Mt Emu
MT EMU
Mt Stavely 326m
GLENELG HWY
Wickliffe
Lake Bolac
Westmere
Streatham
CARRANBALLAC
Lake Mclaren
Skipton
PITTONG
TOURIST INFORMATION:
Ararat (Barkly St)
Avoca (High St)
Ballan (Cnr Stead & Steiglitz Sts)
Ballarat (Cnr Sturt & Albert Sts)
Beaufort (Cnr Lawrence St & Main Rd)
Bendigo (Charing Cross)
Castlemaine (Duke St)
Clunes (Fraser St)
Creswick (Cnr Raglan & Cambridge Sts)
Dunolly (Market St)
Lake Bolac (Glenelg Hwy)
Maldon (High St)
Maryborough (Cnr Tuaggra & Alma Sts)
Stawell (54 Western Hwy)

GOLDFIELDS REGION: The cities and towns of this region came to a peak of style and affluence in the 1880s, an affluence built on the first gold discoveries in the 1850s. The towns display all the frivolity and grandeur of Victorian architecture.

MALDON: The National Trust has declared Maldon the 'first notable town' in Victoria; interesting collections of 19th-century buildings, and collection of European trees.

GARDENS: There are many fine historic and public gardens scattered throughout the region. Public gardens of particular note include the Botanic Gardens of Castlemaine, Daylesford and Malmsbury, and the Queen Mary Gardens at St Arnaud. Many of the cities and towns of the region have spectacular seasonal displays; Ballarat is famous for its begonias; Bendigo has special plantings for its famous Easter Fair and for the Spring racing season. One of the most famous private gardens, open to the public, is Buda Historic Home and garden at Castlemaine.

BENDIGO'S TALKING TRAM: Visitors can take a tram ride through the historic centre of Bendigo and enjoy a potted history provided by a recorded commentary.

SPA TOWNS: Daylesford and nearby Hepburn Springs are popular holiday centres, set in attractive hill country. They are both 'spa' towns, with 65 documented mineral springs, many with hand pumps.

MT BUNINYONG: An extinct volcanic crater that rises 750 metres above sea level. A sealed road leads up to the lookout which offers stunning 360° views.

SOVEREIGN HILL: This re-created gold-mining township is one of Victoria's major tourist attractions and should not be missed.

BENDIGO, BALLARAT, Castlemaine, Maryborough, Maldon, Dunolly, Daylesford, Creswick, Clunes, Eaglehawk, Epsom, Harcourt, Malmsbury, Trentham, Blackwood, Bacchus Marsh

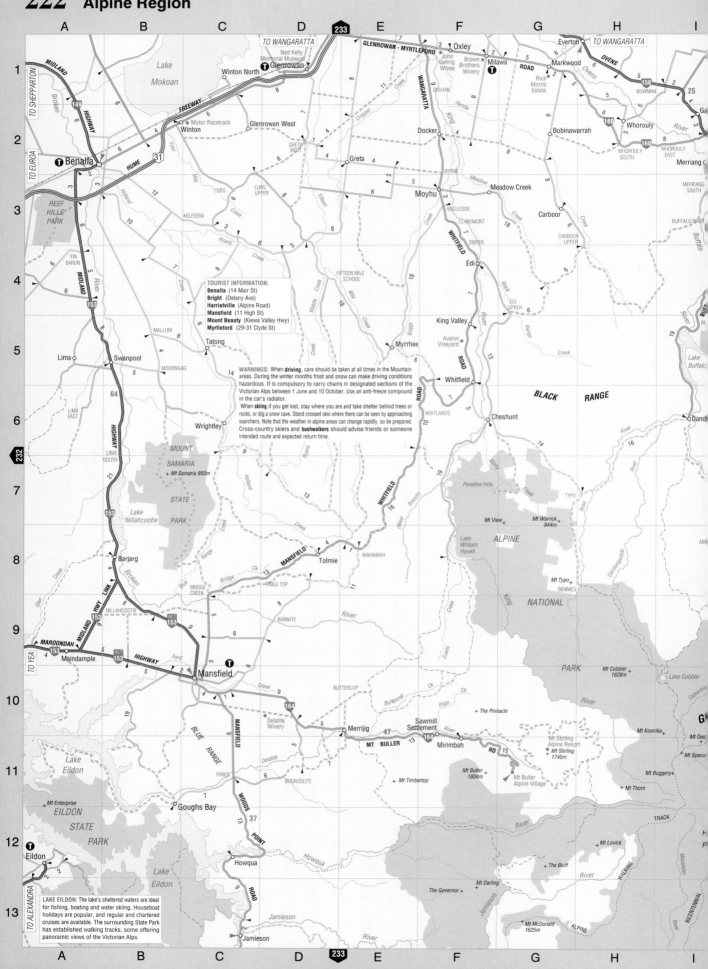

TOURIST INFORMATION:
Benalla (14 Mair St)
Bright (Delany Ave)
Harrietville (Alpine Road)
Mansfield (11 High St)
Mount Beauty (Kiewa Valley Hwy)
Myrtleford (29-31 Clyde St)

WARNINGS: When **driving**, care should be taken at all times in the Mountain areas. During the winter months frost and snow can make driving conditions hazardous. It is compulsory to carry chains in designated sections of the Victorian Alps between 1 June and 10 October. Use an anti-freeze compound in the car's radiator.
When **skiing**, if you get lost, stay where you are and take shelter behind trees or rocks, or dig a snow cave. Stand crossed skis where there can be seen by approaching searchers. Note that the weather in alpine areas can change rapidly, so be prepared. Cross-country skiers and **bushwalkers** should advise friends or someone intended route and expected return time.

LAKE EILDON: The lake's sheltered waters are ideal for fishing, boating and water skiing. Houseboat holidays are popular, and regular and chartered cruises are available. The surrounding State Park has established walking tracks, some offering panoramic views of the Victorian Alps.

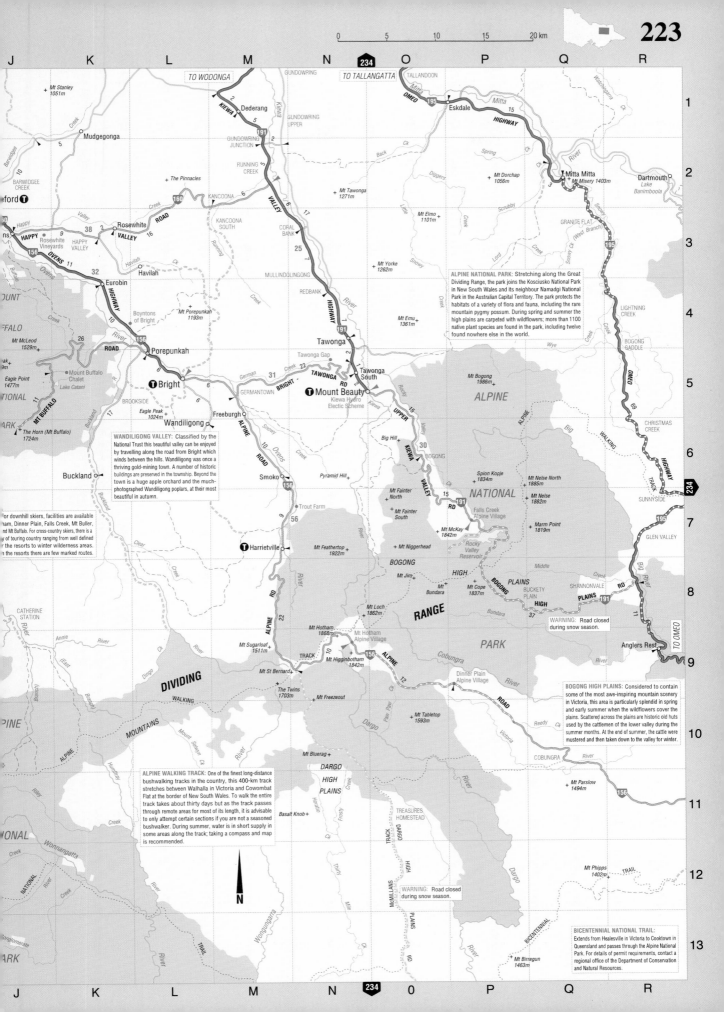

ALPINE NATIONAL PARK: Stretching along the Great Dividing Range, the park joins the Kosciusko National Park in New South Wales and its neighbour Namadgi National Park in the Australian Capital Territory. The park protects the habitats of a variety of flora and fauna, including the rare mountain pygmy possum. During spring and summer the high plains are carpeted with wildflowers; more than 1100 native plant species are found in the park, including twelve found nowhere else in the world.

WANDILIGONG VALLEY: Classified by the National Trust this beautiful valley can be enjoyed by travelling along the road from Bright which winds between the hills. Wandiligong was once a thriving gold-mining town. A number of historic buildings are preserved in the township. Beyond the town is a huge apple orchard and the much-photographed Wandiligong poplars, at their most beautiful in autumn.

For downhill skiers, facilities are available ...ham, Dinner Plain, Falls Creek, Mt Buller, ... Mt Buffalo. For cross-country skiers, there is a ...y of touring country ranging from well defined ... the resorts to winter wilderness areas. ...n the resorts there are few marked routes.

ALPINE WALKING TRACK: One of the finest long-distance bushwalking tracks in the country, this 400-km track stretches between Walhalla in Victoria and Cowombat Flat at the border of New South Wales. To walk the entire track takes about thirty days but as the track passes through remote areas for most of its length, it is advisable to only attempt certain sections if you are not a seasoned bushwalker. During summer, water is in short supply in some areas along the track; taking a compass and map is recommended.

BOGONG HIGH PLAINS: Considered to contain some of the most awe-inspiring mountain scenery in Victoria, this area is particularly splendid in spring and early summer when the wildflowers cover the plains. Scattered across the plains are historic old huts used by the cattlemen of the lower valley during the summer months. At the end of summer, the cattle were mustered and then taken down to the valley for winter.

BICENTENNIAL NATIONAL TRAIL: Extends from Healesville in Victoria to Cooktown in Queensland and passes through the Alpine National Park. For details of permit requirements, contact a regional office of the Department of Conservation and Natural Resources.

WARNING: Road closed during snow season.

WARNING: Road closed during snow season.

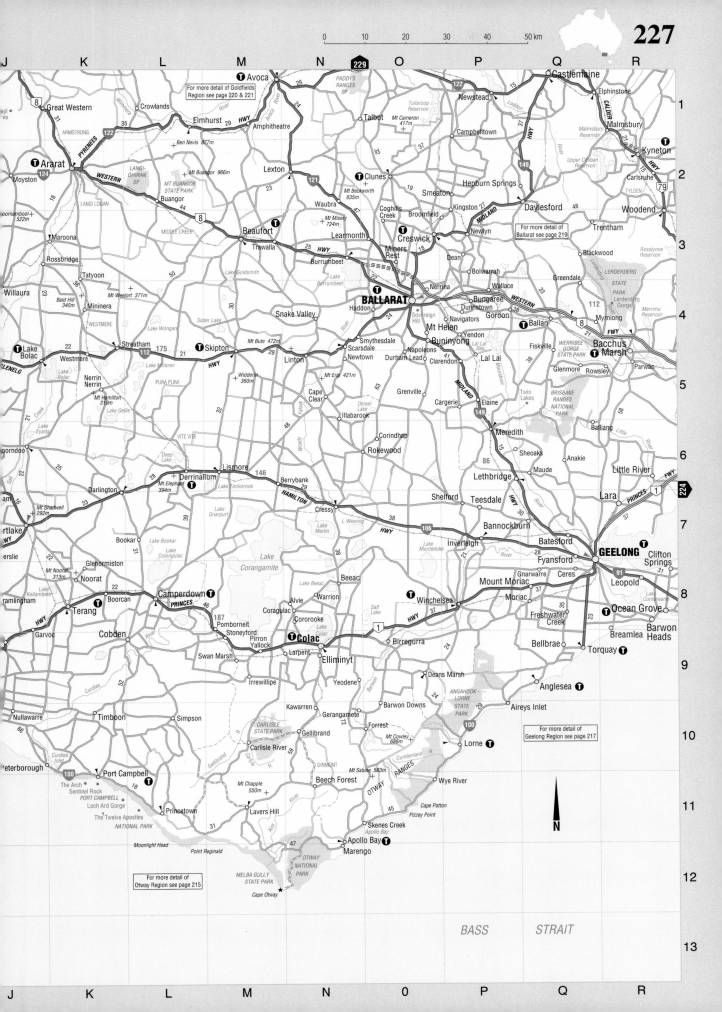

230

A B C D E F G H I

1

Tempy
Speed
Patchewollock
Turriff
SUNRAYSIA
22
27

Lake
Agnes

Mt Observatory
+ 93m

WYPERFELD

2

SCORPION
SPRINGS
CP

BIG DESERT

NATIONAL

35
Lasce

BIG DESERT

3

WILDERNESS PARK

PARK

LAKE
ALBACUTYA
PARK

T Hopetoun
25

Lake
Coorong

Lake
Albacutya

45

Mt Shaugh
184m +

4

MT SHAUGH
CONSERVATION
PARK

WIMMERA

Ross Lake

T Rainbow
Kenmare
41
HWY
Beulah

5

SOUTH AUSTRALIA
VICTORIA

Lake
Hindmarsh

32
Ellam

107
GALAQUIL

Jeparit T
45
HENTY
143
35

6

Yanac
Netherby
Lorquon
42
45
37
31
45
HWY
Warracknabe

287

SANDSMERE

KATYIL

138
BORUNG
42

Bordertown
Diapur
T Nhill

7

8
Wolseley
43
WESTERN
40
HWY
8
Kiata
Gerang
Gerung
39

Miram
Serviceton
Kaniva T
158

Dimboola
19
57

8

LITTLE DESERT NATIONAL PARK

48

Wimmera R

KALKEE

24

BANGHAM

45

25
17

Pimpinio
Jung
WIM

9

Frances
Lake
Cadnite

Minimay
34
Goroke T

Gymbowen
Mitre
Lake
Wyn Wyn
Mitre
Lake

Natimuk T
27

Murtoa T
31
14

Horsham T

BINNUM

31

MT ARAPILES-
TOOAN
STATE
PARK
18
32

Mt Arapiles
370m +
HWY

Haven
Taylors
Lake

10

Kybybolite
32
35

Lake
Morea

99
130
40

Noradjuha
40

Pine
Lake
41
WESTERN

Flat Rock
Caves
124

11

Hynam
Naracoorte
Apsley
21
WIMMERA
Clear Lake

64

Mt Talbot 320m +

DIFFICULT RANGE
Mt Difficult
810m +
Dadswells
Bridge

40
32
14

Lake
Wallace

Wombelano
North
Lake

Toolondo
Reservoir

HENTY

Wartook
Reservoir
61

Naracoorte
Caves
30

Edenhope T
32
Douglas

White
Lake

Lake
Kanagulk

THE BLACK RANGE

Mackenzie
Falls

12

Bool
Lagoon

Wrattonbully
34

River
21

BLACK RANGE
STATE PARK
107

Aboriginal
Paintings

GRAMPINS

13

GLENROY
Comaum
Coonawarra

Poolaijelo
29
Balmoral

DERGHOLM
STATE
PARK

Glenelg River
Chetwynd River

ENGLEFIELD
VASEY

Rocklands
Reservoir

VICTORIA RANGE

NATIONAL
Cave of Fishes
Cave of Hands
Lake
Bellfield

PARK

226

A B C D E F G H

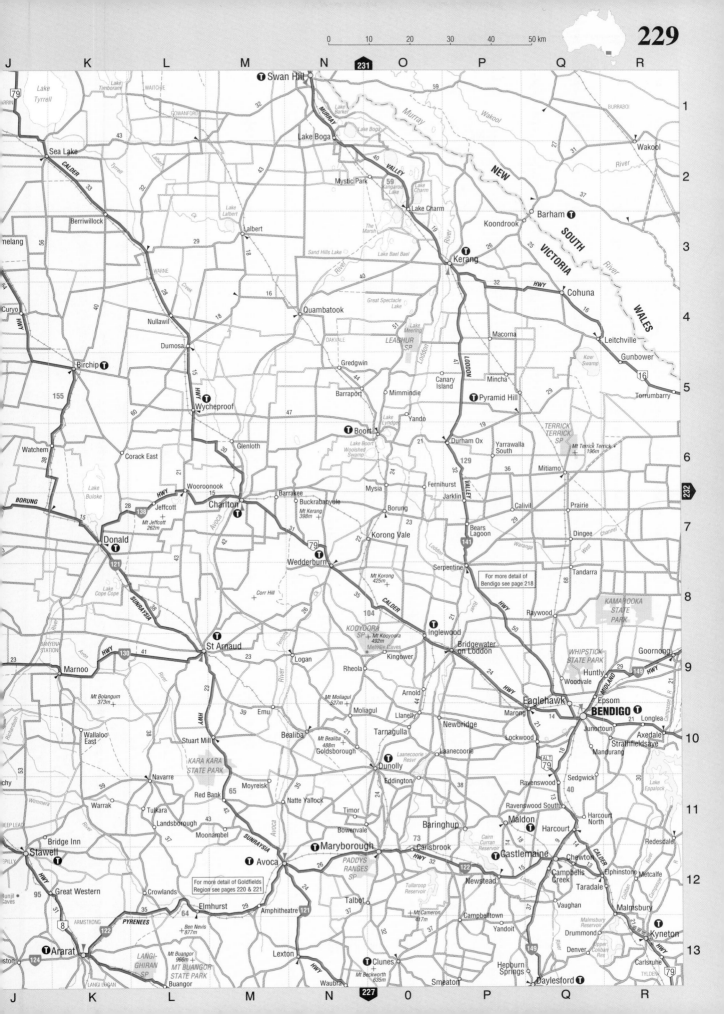

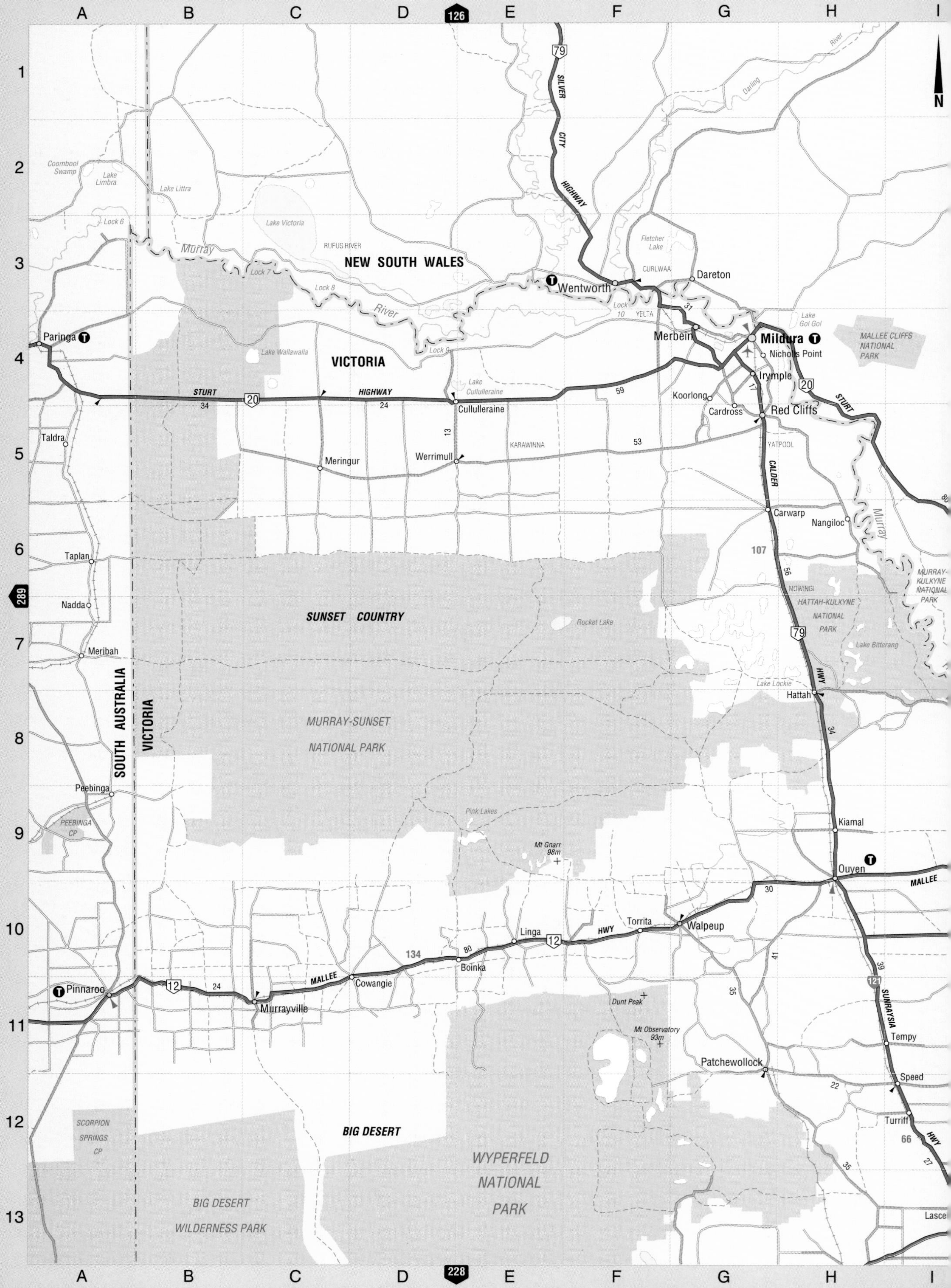

A B C D **126** E F G H I

1

2

Coombool Swamp

Lake Limbra

Lake Littra

Lock 6

Lake Victoria

RUFUS RIVER

NEW SOUTH WALES

3

Murray

Lock 7

Lock 8

River

Fletcher Lake

CURLWAA

Wentworth

Dareton

79

SILVER

CITY

HIGHWAY

4

Paringa

Lake Wallawalla

VICTORIA

Lock 9

Lake Cullulleraine

Lock 10

YELTA

31

Merbein

Lake Gol Gol

Mildura

Nichols Point

MALLEE CLIFFS
NATIONAL
PARK

Irymple

STURT

HIGHWAY

20

34

24

Cullulleraine

59

Koorlong

Cardross

Red Cliffs

20

STURT

5

Taldra

13

Meringur

Werrimull

KARAWINNA

53

YATPOOL

CALDER

Murray

6

Taplan

Carwarp

Nangiloc

107

56

NOWINGI

289

7

Meribah

SUNSET COUNTRY

Rocket Lake

HATTAH-KULKYNE
NATIONAL
PARK

79

Lake Bitterang

MURRAY-
KULKYNE
NATIONAL
PARK

Lake Lockie

Hattah

HWY

34

8

SOUTH AUSTRALIA

VICTORIA

MURRAY-SUNSET

NATIONAL PARK

9

Peebinga

PEEBINGA
CP

Pink Lakes

Mt Gnarr
98m

Kiamal

Ouyen

MALLEE

10

Linga

80

Boinka

HWY

Torrita

Walpeup

30

41

39

121

SURAYSIA

134

12

11

Pinnaroo

12

24

MALLEE

Cowangie

Murrayville

Dunt Peak

Mt Observatory
93m

35

Patchewollock

Tempy

22

Speed

12

SCORPION
SPRINGS
CP

BIG DESERT

WYPERFELD

66

Turriff

35

27

13

BIG DESERT

WILDERNESS PARK

NATIONAL

PARK

Lasce

A B C D **228** E F G H

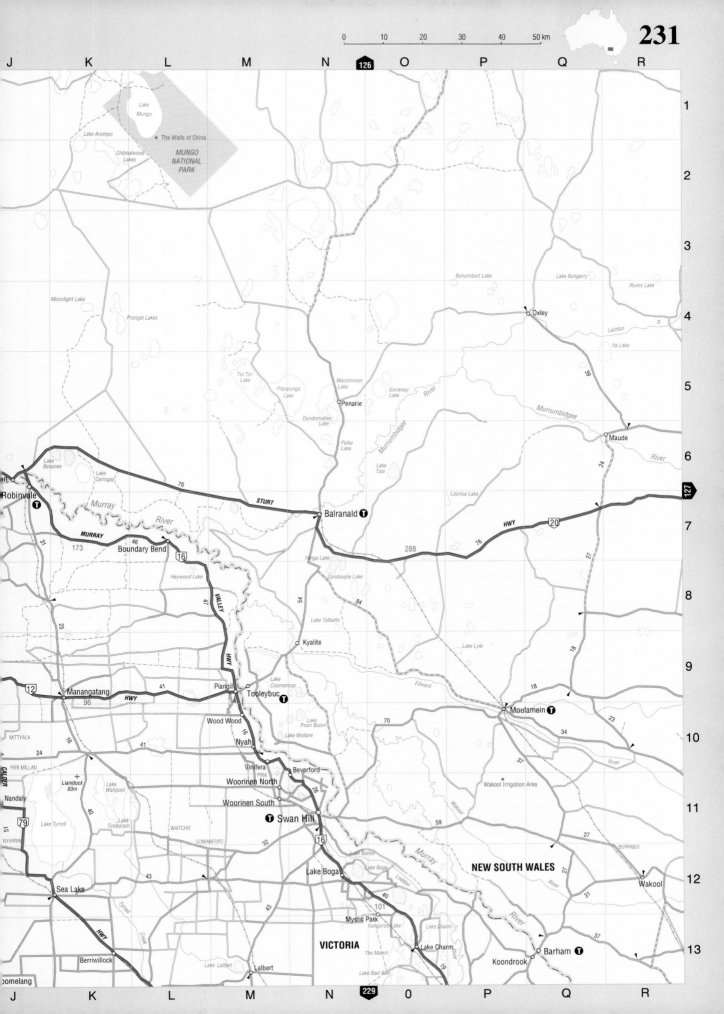

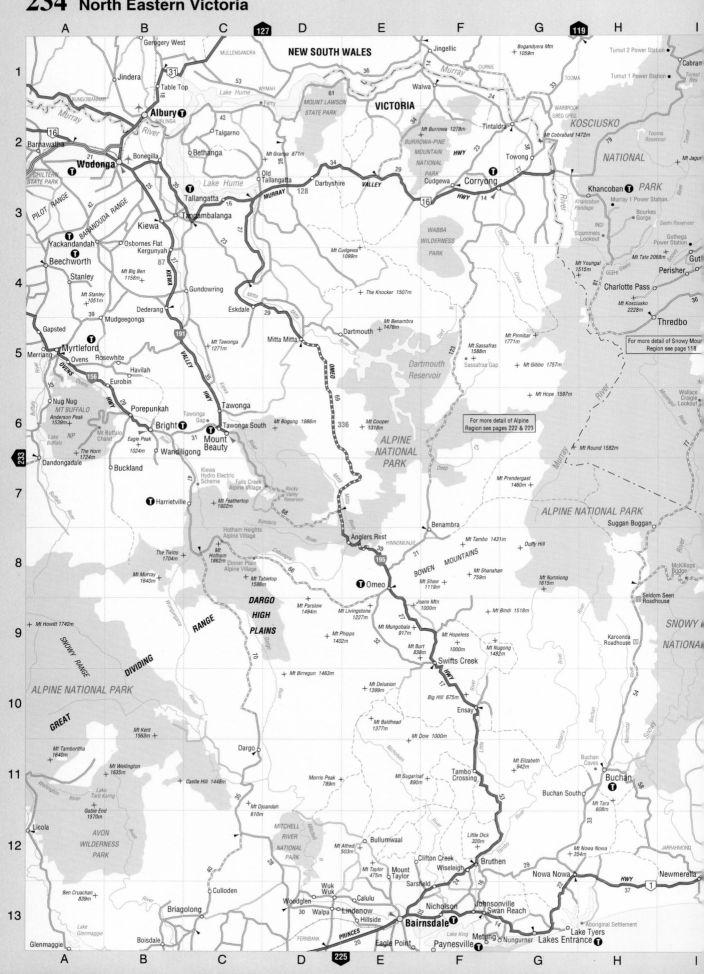

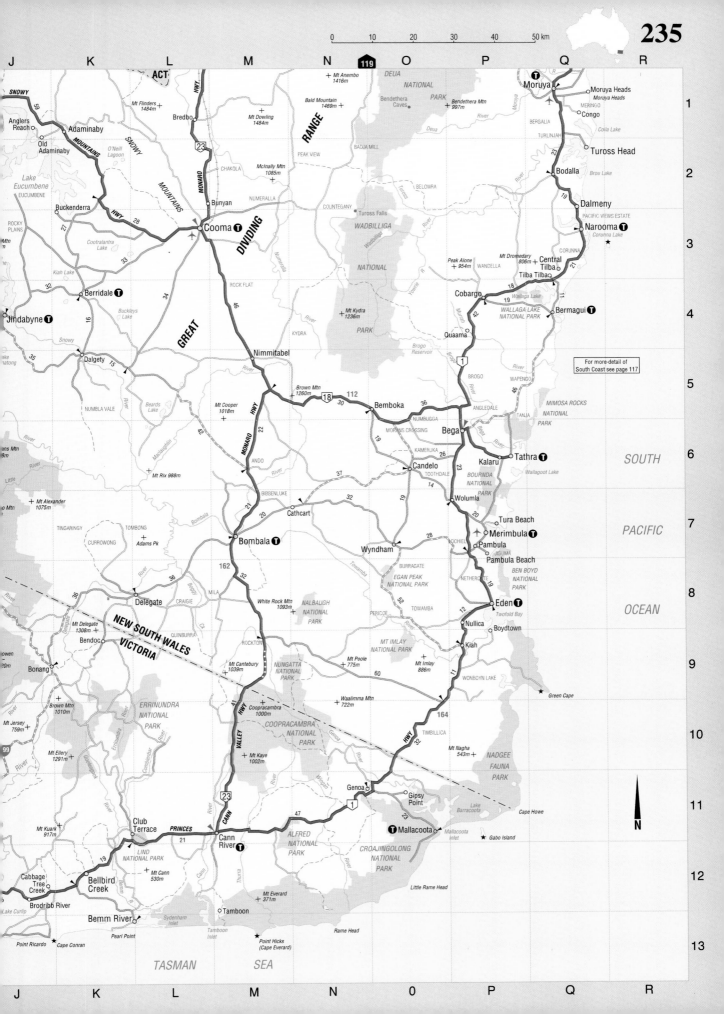

South Australia

The Adelaide biennial Arts Festival, the Barossa Valley Vintage, *Schutzenfest*, Australian Formula One Grand Prix, the Greek Glendi Festival, the Cornish Kernewek Lowender—from the number and variety of festivities held every year, it seems clear that South Australians enjoy making the most of life. For the visitor, these festivals provide an excellent chance to discover a community at its liveliest.

This energetic spirit also seems to indicate that South Australians have triumphed over what might seem to be rather depressing statistics: it is the driest state in the driest continent, two-thirds is near-desert and eighty-three per cent receives an annual rainfall of less than 250 millimetres. But these facts are easily forgotten when you visit the lush green Barossa Valley or explore the beauty of the Flinders Ranges.

As a result of innovative social changes in the 1960s, today South Australia's conservative image has virtually disappeared. It seems apt that its initial settlement began as the result of one man's ideas of how to create a model colony. Edward Gibbon Wakefield believed that the difficulties of other Australian colonies were caused by the ease with which anyone could obtain land. He claimed that if land were sold at two pounds an acre, only men of capital could buy; those who could not would provide a supply of labour, and the finance generated would encourage investment and the development of resources. In 1834 he tested his ideas in the Gulf St Vincent area. Lieutenant-Colonel Light was dispatched as Surveyor-General to select a site.

Today, although South Australia's economy remains traditionally agrarian, secondary industry provides nine out of ten jobs. Olympic Dam is one of the world's biggest copper-mines and probably the biggest uranium-mine. The Leigh Creek coalfields meet most of the state's power needs.

South Australia also boasts most of the world's opals. Coober Pedy, the main opal-mining town, produces ninety per cent of Australia's opals.

The gulf lands of South Australia enjoy a Mediterranean climate. The further north you go, the hotter and more inhospitable the temperatures become. Adelaide, with its average annual rainfall of 585 millimetres, enjoys a midsummer average maximum temperature of about 28.3°C and a midwinter average maximum of 15°C. Seventy-two per cent of the population lives here, making South Australia the most urbanised of all the states. Adelaide inherited its orderly and pleasant layout from its first Surveyor-General, Colonel Light, and many of its attractive original stone buildings have survived. The Mount Lofty Ranges make a picturesque backdrop. With the Stuart Highway now completely sealed, it is possible to drive from Port Augusta to central Australia on an all-weather road. Certain precautions should be taken before negotiating other roads in the north and west desert regions. (**See:** Outback Motoring.) If you feel intrepid, the opal towns of Coober Pedy and Andamooka are fascinating. Temperatures climb to over 50°C in Coober Pedy during summer (much of the town is built underground), so choose a cool period for your trip.

The spectacular Flinders Ranges have passable roads, although some are unsealed. Wilpena Pound and Arkaroola are the main resort bases. The Heysen Trail (commemorating South Australian painter Sir Hans Heysen) is a well-defined hiking trail that reaches from Cape Jervis almost to Quorn, with extensions into the Flinders Ranges.

Both the Yorke and Eyre Peninsulas have attractive, unspoiled coastlines. Port Lincoln, on the Eyre Peninsula, is a popular base for big-game fishing and on the Yorke Peninsula the three little towns of Wallaroo, Moonta and Kadina, collectively known as Little Cornwall, with their history of copper mining, are well worth a visit.

South of Adelaide is Victor Harbor, the south coast's largest resort. A little further on is the Coorong National Park, near the mouth of the Murray at Lake Alexandrina. Here the river completes its 2600-kilometre course. A trip along the Riverland section of the Murray reveals historic river towns, bountiful citrus orchards and extensive vegetable crops, all maintained by irrigation from the Murray. The lakes and lagoons at the river's mouth abound with birdlife and offer excellent fishing and seasonal duck-shooting. On the southern Victorian border is Mount Gambier, the commercial centre of the south-east, which has Australia's largest pine forest and the beautiful Blue Lake.

The fame of South Australia's wine regions now extends well beyond Australian shores. McLaren Vale on the Fleurieu Peninsula produces excellent wines, and the Riverland region is responsible for much of the national vintage. The Clare Valley, Adelaide Hills and Coonawarra wine regions all have distinct specialities determined by soil and climate. In the famed Barossa Valley region, there are more than forty wineries. The valley was originally settled by German Lutherans who planted orchards, olive groves and vineyards and built charming towns and wineries very much in their native European style. To explore this area, particularly during the Vintage Festival every odd-numbered year, is to discover a region and lifestyle unique in Australia.

Scott's Cove view to Cape Torrens, Kangaroo Island

Adelaide

An Elegant City

Adelaide is a gracious, well-planned city set on a narrow coastal plain between the rolling hills of the Mount Lofty Ranges and the blue waters of Gulf St Vincent. Surrounded by parkland, Adelaide combines the vitality of a large modern city (population nearly one million) with an easy-going Australian lifestyle.

Thanks to Colonel Light's excellent planning and foresight, Adelaide is well endowed with greenery. The city centre is completely surrounded by parklands, known as the Green Belt, with children's playgrounds and sports fields, barbecues, and tables and chairs under shady trees. At **Rymill Park** there is a children's boating lake with canoes and dinghies for hire. Flanagan's Riverfront Restaurant is set in parkland overlooking the waters of **Torrens Lake** near the Weir, north of North Terrace. At **Veale Gardens** to the

south of the city there are fountains, rockeries and formal rose gardens. Further east along South Terrace is the **Adelaide-Himeji Garden**, a blend of traditional Japanese lake, mountain and dry gardens. The gate is modelled on that of a temple, and a water bowl is provided for visitors to purify themselves by washing their hands and mouths. The beautiful, formal **Botanic Gardens** have sixteen hectares of Australian and imported plants and man-made lakes where children can feed ducks and swans; guided tours are available. While there, try not to miss the Palm House, an extensive glasshouse brought out from Germany in 1871. In the north-east corner of the gardens is the **Bicentennial Conservatory**, said to be the largest conservatory in the southern hemisphere, housing exotic tropical plants from all over the world. Two serpentine

viewing paths on upper and lower levels have wheelchair access.

Near the tree-lined boulevard of **North Terrace** on the edge of the city centre there are some fine colonial buildings: Holy Trinity Church is the oldest church in South Australia; the foundation stone was laid by Governor Hindmarsh in 1838, and the clock was made by Vulliamy, clockmaker to King William IV. Near this western end of North Terrace is the **Adelaide Gaol**, last used in 1988 and now open for inspection each Sunday. Also on North Terrace are the grand **Newmarket Hotel**, built in 1884, and the **Lion Centre**, home to the Mercury Cinema, the Jam Factory craft workshops and outlet and the biennial Fringe Festival.

The historic Adelaide Railway building, also in North Terrace, has been restored

Adelaide skyline

Hotels

Adelaide Hilton International
233 Victoria Sq., Adelaide
(08) 217 0711
Hindley Parkroyal
65 Hindley St, Adelaide
(08) 231 5552
Hyatt Regency
North Tce, Adelaide
(08) 231 1234
Terrace Intercontinental Adelaide
150 North Tce, Adelaide
(08) 217 7552

Family and Budget

Adelaide Paringa Motel
15 Hindley St, Adelaide
(08) 231 1000

Austral Hotel
205 Rundle St, Adelaide
(08) 223 4660
YMCA
76 Flinders St, Adelaide
(08) 223 1611

Motel Groups: Bookings

Flag 13 2400
Best Western (008) 22 2166
Travelodge (008) 22 2446

This list is for information only;
inclusion is not necessarily a
recommendation.

magnificently for the **Adelaide Casino**. The casino is part of the Adelaide Plaza Complex, which includes the **Adelaide Convention Centre**, **Exhibition Hall** and the luxurious **Hyatt Regency Hotel**.

Further along is the **Old Parliament House**, which today houses Australia's only museum of political history and has an excellent audiovisual display and delightful restaurant. On the corner of King William Road is the present **Parliament House**. Nearby is **Government House**, the oldest building in Adelaide, in a beautiful garden setting.

The **State Library**, on the corner of Kintore Avenue, holds many major collections. In the Mortlock Wing volumes on South Australia share space with Donald Bradman's trophies in a beautifully restored Victorian building. Behind the Library is the **Migration Museum**, the first museum to tell the stories of Australia's migrants. Close by, in the former armoury, is the **Police Museum**. Back on North Terrace, the **South Australian Museum** and the **Art Gallery of South Australia** rub shoulders. The museum holds the world's largest collection of Aboriginal artefacts and features this in a range of exhibits. The museum shops offer a wide range of books, posters and souvenirs for locals and visitors. The collections of the Art Gallery give one of the best overviews of Australian art available. It also houses important collections of sculptures, paintings and decorative arts from around the world.

The **University of Adelaide** is also on North Terrace. Walk through the landscaped grounds to see the blend of classic and contemporary architecture, and visit the **Museum of Classical Archaeology** in the grounds to view some 500 objects, many dating back to the third millennium BC. **Elder Hall**, with its spectacular pipe organ, is a fine concert venue.

At the eastern end of North Terrace is **Ayers House**, headquarters for the National Trust of South Australia. Sir Henry Ayers bought the property in 1855; the house was extended and became one of the major venues for social functions during Ayers' seven terms as Premier of the state. A charming nineteenth-century residence with slate roof and shuttered bay windows, Ayers House has an elegant formal restaurant and a more relaxed bistro extending into the courtyard, enabling visitors to enjoy the historic surroundings whilst dining. The Aboriginal Cultural Institute **Tandanya** is on the corner of Grenfell Street and East Terrace.

Back in the heart of the city on King William Street, is another important reminder of Adelaide's heritage, **Edmund Wright House**. Built in 1878, the building with its elaborate Renaissance facade is used for civil weddings. Other historic buildings in the city include the Town Hall in King William Street, with formal portico entrance and graceful tower, the General Post Office, and the Treasury Buildings on the corner of Victoria Square.

In North Adelaide there are fine old colonial buildings, from delightful stone cottages to stately homes and grand old hotels with lacework balconies and verandahs. **St Peter's Cathedral** in King William Road is one of Australia's finest cathedrals and is a fitting backdrop to the beautiful **Pennington Gardens**. There is a particularly fine view from **Light's Vision** on Montefiore Hill. A bronze statue of Colonel Light overlooks the city with its broad streets and spacious parks.

The **River Torrens** flows through many of Adelaide's parks. The banks are landscaped, lined with gums and willows, and perfect for a lazy picnic lunch. A fleet of *Popeye* motor launches cruises the river, providing a delightfully different way of travelling to the **Adelaide Zoological Gardens**. The zoo has an enormous collection of animals and reptiles and is noted for its variety of Australian birdlife. There is a walk-through aviary sheltering many types of unusual land and water birds, and a nocturnal house designed to display those animals and birds that are most active at night. The zoo grounds are in a perfect setting with magnificent trees (including exotic species), rock beds and rose gardens.

Also situated on the curving banks of the Torrens is the famous **Festival Centre**, hub of Adelaide's biennial festival, held in even-numbered years. This streamlined, modern building contains a 2000-seat lyric theatre, drama and experimental theatres and an imposing amphitheatre for outdoor entertainment. The building has been acclaimed by international critics as one of the finest performing venues in the world. The Southern Plaza incorporates a spectacular environmental sculpture by West German artist O. H. Hajek. There are also some fine contemporary tapestries and paintings hung inside the building. Guided tours are conducted, and restaurant and bar facilities are available. The Centre has walkways linking it to King William Road, Parliament House, Adelaide Railway Station and the Casino. Nearby is an attractive old band rotunda in **Elder Park**.

Adelaide has a bustling shopping complex centred around **Rundle Mall**. The paved mall has trees and a fountain, modern sculpture, colourful fruit- and flower-stalls and seats where you can sit and watch the passing parade. Buskers and outdoor cafes give the area a European atmosphere. Surrounding arcades and streets have everything from major department stores to tiny specialist boutiques. King William Street is lined with bank and insurance buildings, and in Hindley Street there are clusters of restaurants and continental food shops. A

Festival Centre

bonus for shoppers is the free Bee-line bus service which operates in the inner-city area.

Make a trip to **Melbourne Street** in North Adelaide for some of the city's most exclusive shops; **Unley Road** for exclusive boutiques and **Magill Road** for antiques and second-hand treasures; the **Parade** at Norwood combines all of the above with great delis, coffee shops, home design stores and bookshops. **King William Road** at Hyde Park has a number of stylish specialty shops and boutiques. The **Jam Factory and Craft Centre**, close to the city at 169 Payneham Road, St Peters, features high-quality contemporary South Australian crafts.

A real shopping experience is a visit to the **Central Market** behind the Hilton Hotel, with its stalls packed high with fresh produce (open Tuesday, Thursday, Friday and Saturday). Nearby arcades sell clothing, wine and spirits. In recent years, the east end of the city around **Rundle Street** has experienced a rebirth, with busy coffee houses, pubs, restaurants and a host of absorbing craft shops and boutiques. The **East End Market** has become the street's focus on

weekends, selling everything from fresh fish, meat and vegetables to clothing and jewellery. In Norwood, the **Orange Lane Markets** (Saturday and Sunday) feature second-hand goods, homemade produce, local crafts and stalls. The **Brickworks Market** at Thebarton (Friday, Saturday and public holiday Mondays) sells produce and bric-a-brac, and is part of a six-hectare complex featuring an amusement park and international restaurants. Other markets featuring fresh foodstuffs and a variety of other goods are the **Junction Market** in Prospect Road, Kilburn (Saturday, Sunday and public holiday Mondays), and the **Reynella Markets** at 255 Old South Road, Reynella (Friday, Saturday, Sunday and public holiday Mondays).

Adelaide is renowned for its restaurants. The city is credited as being the birthplace of modern Australian cuisine. Some of the best restaurants are tiny and crowded with fast service and super cheap prices. Others are set in historic buildings, serving international class cuisine in gracious surroundings. **Hindley Street** offers a wide range of cosmopolitan eating. **Gouger Street**, near the Central Market, is known as $10 street—

if you can't get a good meal for less than $10, you're in the wrong street—it is particularly famous for its seafood cafes and South Australian seafood is something special.

Adelaide also has some fine old pubs. Some are friendly 'locals', others incorporate restaurants, wine bars and dancefloors. The **Old Lion Hotel** in North Adelaide is a handsome 1880s bluestone building with a first-class restaurant, a sheltered courtyard and popular disco. It is typical of the new boutique-style hotel where beer is brewed on the premises; there are a number of these hotels within the inner-city area.

Not to be missed in Adelaide are the marvellous beaches, stretching right along the coastline with wide sandy shores and clear blue waters. Most are only a short drive from the city centre and perhaps the most famous is **Glenelg**. The best way to see it is by taking the famous **Bay Tram** from Victoria Square to the top of Jetty Road in Glenelg. Spoil yourself by dining at the **Ramada Grand Hotel**, or stroll down Jetty Road to the shopping centre. The **Magic Mountain Waterslide and Amusement Centre** provides entertainment. Restaurants abound, and Greek food here is a specialty. Grand old homes and guesthouses along the foreshore are a reminder of Glenelg's days as a seaside resort for the wealthy. The first settlers came ashore here in 1836 and proclaimed the colony of South Australia under a gum tree. The **Old Gum Tree** remains, with a commemorative plaque. HMS *Buffalo* played a significant part in South Australia's early settlement and a replica of the vessel at Glenelg is an appropriate setting for a maritime museum and restaurant.

Other beaches include **Brighton, West Beach, Henley, Grange** and **Semaphore**. At Semaphore, **Fort Glanville** is the oldest fortress in South Australia. A restaurant in the restored Customs House (1850) overlooks the esplanade and the ocean. The Semaphore to Fort Glanville Tourist Railway runs south along the seafront for more than 2 kms, from the Semaphore Jetty to Fort Glanville and the nearby caravan park, and operates daily during school holidays and on all public holidays and Sundays during the summer months. South, near Hallett Cove, is the **Hallett Cove Conservation Park**, established to preserve the remnants of glacial features that probably occurred 270 million years ago. Many beaches have sailboards and catamarans for hire, while the jetties are used for promenading, swimming and fishing.

Adelaide's suburbs have much to offer the visitor. A short drive west towards the suburb of **Grange** is **Sturt's Cottage** (built in 1840), home of Captain Charles Sturt, the famous pioneer and explorer. Managed by the Charles Sturt Memorial Museum Trust, its period furniture and many of Sturt's belongings recall the early days of South Australia.

In **Wayville**, just south-west of the city, is **The Investigator, Science and Technology Centre** with hands-on 'gizmos' and fun for all the family; located in the International Pavilion, Wayville Showgrounds (enter from Rose Tce). Also at the showgrounds in early September, the **Royal Adelaide Show** brings the country to the city.

Port Adelaide has many imposing buildings, a reminder of the port's heyday in the 1880s. The police station and court-house, town hall, shipping and transport building and Ferguson's bond store are noteworthy. The historic **Port Dock Station Railway Museum** in

Australian Formula One Grand Prix

Lipson Street contains a large collection of locomotives and rollingstock, platform displays, a theatrette and an operating HO-gauge model railway; visitors can ride miniature steam trains. The nearby **Maritime Museum**, complete with lighthouses and ships, is also in Lipson St. A few blocks away is the **South Australian Historical Aviation Museum** in Mundy St. Cruises and fishing trips are available from Port Adelaide and Outer Harbour.

At **St Kilda**, further north, there is an **Electric Transport Museum** where you can take trips on restored trams. A guided walk along the 1.7km boardwalk of the **Mangrove Walking Trail** is an experience not to be missed.

Near the suburb of **Rostrevor**, east of the city, the **Morialta Conservation Park** has a ruggedly beautiful gorge and many walking-tracks. **Brownhill Creek Recreation Park** has giant pine and gum trees in a quiet valley setting. There are barbecue facilities and pretty picnic spots. **Belair National Park** has picnic grounds, bushland, a children's playground and the former summer residence of the Governor. **Cleland Conservation Park** shows kangaroos, koalas, wombats and other native fauna in their natural surroundings.

Tour around Adelaide's attractions at your leisure in the city's only road-registered tram replica complete with on-board commentary. Board or alight the **Explorer Tram** as many times as you wish at any of the stopping points; the tram returns to any given point approximately every 2¼ hours.

The longest guided busway system in the world, **The O-Bahn**, runs north-east from the city centre. It travels beside the River Torrens in its own landscaped park from Adelaide to a major shopping centre at **Tea Tree Plaza**, and has a station at **Paradise**, a suburb named by early settlers. Walking-paths follow the busway track to Tea Tree Plaza, with views over reservoirs, foothills and the city.

Cowell Jade, at **Unley**, sells jewellery and carvings made from South Australian jade. The **South Australian Society of Model and Experimental Engineers** headquarters, in the nearby suburb of **Millswood**, has field days (open to visitors) twice a month. For magnificent views of Adelaide, take a trip to **Windy Point Lookout** or to the summit of **Mount Lofty**. At night, the lights of the city look particularly impressive. Adelaide is, until at least 1996, the **Formula One Grand Prix** city of Australia. This exciting race is through city streets, open parklands and the racecourse in November; the course is regarded by many as the best street circuit in the world. As well, Adelaide offers sports enthusiasts horse-racing at **Victoria Park, Morphettville** and **Cheltenham**; greyhound-racing at **Angle Park**; tennis, squash, swimming and golf. The **Adelaide Aquatic Centre** in **North Adelaide** features pools, waterslides, fountains, river rapids and waterfalls. The **Municipal Golf Course** in North Adelaide commands splendid views of the city. The **Adelaide Oval**, on King William Road, is a venue for interstate and international cricket matches, while the **Memorial Drive Tennis Courts** have played host to international players since 1929. Memorial Drive also is used for outdoor concerts and performances by visiting entertainers. The Ice Arena at 23 East Terrace in the suburb of Thebarton has skating and the world's first indoor artificial ski-slope.

For further information on Adelaide and South Australia, contact South Australian Tourism Commission Travel Centre, 1 King William St, Adelaide; (08) 212 1505, fax (08) 303 2249.

Tours from Adelaide

One of Adelaide's greatest assets is its close proximity to a number of fascinating regions. Vineyards and wineries, rolling hills and quaint villages, seaside resorts and beautiful wildlife reserves are all within an easy drive of South Australia's capital.

The Barossa Valley, 50 km from Adelaide via the Sturt Highway

A must for visitors to Adelaide is the Barossa Valley, Australia's premier wine-producing region. In this area to the north-east of Adelaide there are more than forty wineries and a multitude of historic buildings and galleries, with restaurants and cafes serving top-class cuisine. In August the Barossa Classic Gourmet Weekend offers visitors the opportunity to sample and enjoy fine wines and gourmet food. The Barossa Music Festival is held in October. Visit Gawler, Lyndoch, Tanunda, Nuriootpa and Angaston, detouring at will to the smaller villages and visiting the tasting facilities at the wineries; make sure the driver is happy to forgo this pleasure! Alternatively, extend your visit and stay overnight at the many and varied accommodation outlets in the area. (See also: Festival Fun; Vineyards and Wineries; individual entries in A–Z listing.)

The Clare Valley, 135 km from Adelaide via the Sturt Highway and Highway 32 (Highway 83 optional north of Tarlee)

The Clare Valley produces superb wines and the region is known nationally for its riesling. Driving north through Kapunda, Australia's first mining-town, you will pass some of the state's richest pastoral country, noted for its stud sheep. The wine towns begin at Auburn and continue to Watervale and Sevenhill to Clare. The area is noted for its prize-winning red and white table wines. Sevenhill Cellars winery was started by two Jesuit priests in 1848 and still operates today. Slightly further afield, there are some fine colonial buildings, such as the magnificent Martindale Hall at Mintaro (open daily), which was used in the film *Picnic at Hanging Rock*. The area also has many charming parks and picturesque picnic spots. (See also: Vineyards and Wineries; individual entries in A–Z listing.)

The Wine Coast, 42 km from Adelaide via the South Road

Another trip for wine-lovers is to the vineyards of the Fleurieu Peninsula. There are over fifty wineries in the area, often in picturesque bush settings. Most are well signposted and have wine tastings and cellar-door sales. Hardy's, D'Arenberg, Seaview and Coriole are some of the names to recognise. Stop for lunch in McLaren Vale at The Barn, a gallery-restaurant complex in a historic old coach-station, or enjoy a light snack at Pipkins. Your return trip could include a visit to the nearby beaches Moana, Port Noarlunga and Christies Beach. (**See also:** Vineyards and Wineries; The Fleurieu Peninsula; individual entries in A–Z listing.)

Seppeltsfield, Barossa Valley

The Adelaide Hills and Hahndorf, 25 km from Adelaide via the South Eastern Freeway

The Adelaide Hills are only half an hour's drive from the city. Stop on the way at Cleland Wildlife Park in the Cleland Conservation Park, to see native birds and animals in a natural bush setting. The Gorge Wildlife Park at Cudlee Creek is open every day. The hills themselves are a blend of gently rolling mountains, market gardens and orchards with farm buildings nestled in valleys off winding roads. Go off the main highway to visit Stirling (the nearby Mount Lofty Botanic Gardens offer magnificent views of Piccadilly Valley) and Aldgate, then Bridgewater with its historic waterwheel (1860), now part of the restored mill which houses the wine-making and maturation plant for Petaluma's premium sparkling wines; wine tasting and tours available. Mount Lofty (725 m) offers panoramic views of Adelaide.

Hahndorf is probably the best-known and most interesting town in the area. Settled by Silesian and Prussian refugees in 1838, its main street is lined with magnificent old elms and chestnut trees. Most of the buildings have been carefully restored and the town has a leisurely, old-world feel about it. The Hahndorf Academy and Art Gallery has a permanent exhibition of paintings by Sir Hans Heysen, who lived in the town for many years and depicted the area's beauty so well. A German folk-museum is next door, and both are open daily. The bakeries here sell delicious *apfelstrudel*, cheesecake and Black Forest cake, and small shops offer interesting local handicrafts and home-made preserves. Other attractions include a model train village, a clock museum and a strawberry farm. The heritage of the town is celebrated with several festivals including *Schutzenfest*, where each January visitors are treated to German-style food and beverages, music and entertainment; **Founders Day**, also in January, with its colonial heritage theme; and **Blumenfest**, the festival of flowers held in November. Settlers Hill Pioneer Village at Hochstens, Hahndorf, is a recreation of a turn-of-the-century town. Two of South Australia's oldest townships, Nairne and Mount Barker, lie to the east and southeast of Hahndorf.

In the little town of Oakbank, the Great Eastern Steeplechase, Australia's biggest picnic race meeting, is held with

Horse-drawn carriage, Hahndorf

great fanfare every Easter. North of Oakbank are Apple World at Forest Range and an archive and historical museum at Lobethal. Spennithorne Herb and Flower Farm is open for pick-your-own herbs, near Lobethal. At Woodside, Melba's Chocolates offer daily tours and tastings. From Hahndorf you can take the back road through winding hills and farmland to the old gold-mining town of Echunga, and return to Adelaide via the sleepy township of Mylor, where Warrawong Sanctuary, a leader in the preservation of rare and endangered animals, offers guided tours. Stop at the Belair National Park on your return trip to Adelaide. There are some beautiful walks, fireplaces for picnics and a wildlife park.

Stay in one of the many home-style accommodation houses dotted throughout the Adelaide Hills and experience inexpensive, quality bed-and-breakfast accommodation or rent a self-contained, historic cottage. Aboriginal rock art and environmental tours through the Hills are available. For further information, contact the Adelaide Hills Tourist Information Centre, 64 Main St, Hahndorf; (08) 388 1185. (**See also:** Vineyards and Wineries; Festival Fun; individual entries in A–Z listing.)

The Fleurieu Peninsula, 112 km from Adelaide to its furthest point via the South Road

The Fleurieu Peninsula extends south of Adelaide and has much to offer. Down the length of the west coast there are idyllic sandy beaches, such as Maslin (Australia's first official nudist beach), Sellicks and Christies Beach, right to the tip at wild but

beautiful Cape Jervis. Some beaches have sheltered coves, some have excellent surf, still others are ideal for fishing. Inland there are historic buildings, particularly at Willunga, where public buildings vie with small cottages for the visitor's attention. The almond orchards around here are a marvellous sight, especially when they bloom in late winter. There are a number of conservation parks, ideal for keen walkers as well as those looking for a quiet picnic spot. There is a pleasant scenic drive around Myponga Conservation Park. Only 84 km from Adelaide is Victor Harbor, one of the state's most popular seaside resorts. The sandy beach is perfect for swimming. Across the causeway is rugged Granite Island and The Bluff (Rosetta Head) has a whaling museum and a licensed restaurant. Further around is Port Elliot on splendid Horseshoe Bay. Further east is Goolwa, the historic river port at the mouth of the Murray River; here one of the focal points is the Signal Point Visitor Centre. A ferry will take you across to Hindmarsh Island for panoramic views of the area. Driving back to Adelaide, do not miss Strathalbyn on the banks of the Angas. Milang, 20 km to the south-east, is on the shores of Lake Alexandrina. Take your camera—the birdlife is fascinating. (**See also:** The Fleurieu Peninsula; individual entries in A–Z listing.)

National Motor Museum, Birdwood, 46 km from Adelaide via the North-East Road

The National Motor Museum (open daily) houses the most important motor vehicle collection in Australia. Veteran vintage and classic cars and motorcycles number over 300 and the grounds are a perfect venue for a picnic. At Gumeracha, on Torrens Gorge Ring Route en route from Adelaide, is the Toy Factory, where those not scared of heights can climb the largest wooden rocking horse in the world. Drive back to Adelaide through Mount Torrens to the small town of Lobethal, which was founded in the 1840s. The Archives and Historical Museum houses a most remarkable exhibit: the old Lobethal College, complete with shingled roof, which was built in 1845; open Sunday afternoons. Fairyland Village at Lobethal has fourteen chalets, each depicting a fairytale or a nursery rhyme. There is an enjoyable scenic route through Basket Range and Norton Summit back to Adelaide.

Festival Fun

Because good food and wine go hand in hand with festivities, it seems appropriate that South Australia is both the nation's wine capital and the Festival State. During the year, a wide variety of festivals is held throughout South Australia from the cultural extravaganza of the Adelaide Festival to the country-town carnivals. In November the city is galvanised by the roar of the **Australian Formula One Grand Prix**, which will be held in Adelaide until at least 1996.

For three weeks in March of each even-numbered year, Adelaide becomes the cultural centre of Australia as it hosts the **Adelaide Arts Festival**. During this time the city is like a giant magnet, drawing to it throngs of people from interstate and overseas. Hotels are often booked months ahead; restaurants, taxi services and retailers do a roaring trade.

Since it started in 1960, the Adelaide Festival has grown from a modest 51 performances to over 300, with as many as 30 competing for attention in one day, including many concerts, carnivals and street-theatre occasions for free. The cosmopolitan atmosphere and the world-renowned guest artists

have ranked this festival as an outstanding international event.

Although the Festival emphasises performances in theatre, dance, musical recitals, opera and ballet, it is not confined solely to the performing arts. There are exhibitions, lectures, a writers' week, an artists' week to celebrate the visual arts, poetry readings, and plenty of outdoor activities to coincide with this three-week-long cultural feast.

The focal point is the Adelaide Festival Centre, which stands on 1.5 hectares on the banks of the River Torrens, just 2 minutes' walk from the commercial heart of the city. The Festival Centre is the permanent home of the South Australia Theatre Company, which presents at least 10 major productions annually.

When the Festival is not on, Adelaide visitors and residents still use the parks and gardens surrounding the centre, and the two restaurants and terrace-style cafe, which are open 6 days a week.

Each odd-numbered year, in May, the Festival Centre organises a youth festival, 'Come Out', which focuses its attention on the arts for children and young people.

The **Barossa Valley Vintage Festival**, in Australia's premier wine-producing district, just one hour's drive from Adelaide, is also held in odd-numbered years. The mellow autumn weather and picturesque towns of the Barossa Valley draw large crowds to this event, which is traditionally a thanksgiving celebration for a successful harvest. The seven-day festival, held the week after Easter, is strictly *gemütlichkeit*—happy and friendly. There is music and dancing, good food, wine tasting, a vintage fair, float processions and a *weingarten*—a big feast featuring German folk songs. The grand finale takes the form of a spectacular fair held in the oval of Tanunda Park, where dancers in colourful national costumes dance around an 18-metre-high maypole, while food and wine are served in the marquees surrounding the oval. The **Barossa Classic Gourmet Weekend** in August combines the pleasures of wine, food and good music over two days.

During the long weekend in May the Clare Valley wineries host the **Gourmet Weekend**, which includes tastings and a progressive luncheon on the Sunday around the wineries.

A theatrical performance, Adelaide Arts Festival

McLaren Vale is the venue for the **One Continuous Picnic** festival, held in October, when wineries and restaurants offer opportunities to sample the vintages of the Wine Coast. It is part of the **McLaren Vale Bushing Festival**, a time of fun and festivity, with craft exhibitions, parades, picnic days and formal balls to celebrate the new vintage.

The **Riverland Wine Festival** is held in November each odd-numbered year. The region's wineries combine with local restaurants to provide good food and wine, jazz music and other entertainment.

South Australia is a State of many cultures, which accounts for the many ethnic festivals held throughout the year. The largest of these is the *Schutzenfest* held at Hahndorf, a historic German-settled town in the lovely Adelaide Hills. Traditionally a shooting festival to raise funds for the Hahndorf Academy, it has grown into the biggest German-style beer festival held outside Germany. Located just 35 kilometres from Adelaide, the tranquil countryside is transformed into a bustling carnival with 'oompah' music, imported German beer, German folk dancers in colourful national costume, and restaurants serving platters of *sauerbraten* and *apfelstrudel*. The hot, thirsty month of January is ideal for drinking steins of ice-cold beer while listening to brass bands and waiting for a variety of *würst* (cold sausage meats) to be served at your table.

In March, the Greek community organises the **Glendi Festival** to coincide with the Greek National Day. In odd-numbered years in May, the colourful **Kernewek Lowender** (Cornish family festival) is held, centred around Kadina, Moonta and Wallaroo on the scenic Yorke Peninsula. Quaint old miners' cottages, abandoned mining installations and numerous museums remind visitors of the heyday of copper mining. There is music and Cornish dancing, a pasty-making competition and a hilarious wheelbarrow race.

In October in even-numbered years, the Italian community launches a festival in the city and in country areas to promote its culture and lifestyle. The festival brings cultural groups of a region together in a shared celebration of their heritage.

During the June long weekend Barmera becomes the country music capital of the state, when visitors from all over Australia attend the **Country Music Festival. Citrus Week** promotes the Riverland citrus industry, with various events being held in all the towns in the region.

South Australia boasts many other festivals, among them the **Tunarama Festival** at the major fishing port and resort of Port Lincoln, held every Australia Day long weekend. Australia's only festival dedicated to a fish, it includes a street procession, sports, competitions, displays, a fireworks spectacular and the famous tuna-tossing event; there is fun for the whole family in a gala atmosphere on the beautiful Tasman Terrace foreshore. In April the people of Laura, a small town in the lower Flinders Ranges, organise a **Folk Fair** that attracts thousands of visitors.

Each Easter Monday, the **Great Eastern Steeplechase** is raced at Oakbank racecourse. This event is billed as the largest picnic meeting in the southern hemisphere and is a carnival that leads up to the running of the Adelaide Cup in May at Morphettville racecourse.

One event looked forward to by children and adults is the Christmas Pageant in the city streets of Adelaide. Floats depicting nursery rhymes and fairytale characters thrill all those who line the streets to welcome Father Christmas to South Australia.

Information on all the SA festivals can be obtained from the South Australian Tourism Commission Travel Centre, 1 King William St, Adelaide; (08) 212 1505. **See also:** Individual town entries in A–Z listing.

Aboriginal corroboree dance, Adelaide Arts Festival

South Australia from A to Z

Aldinga Pop. 3541

This small town 45 km S of Adelaide is 4 km from the west coast of the Fleurieu Peninsula. **Of interest:** St Ann's Church of England (1866) and Uniting Church (1863). **In the area:** Aldinga Beach, 4 km SW; good swimming, surfing, diving and fishing, and bush trails through Aldinga Scrub Conservation Park (leaflets available). Maslin, Australia's first nude bathing beach, 6 km N. McLaren Vale, 12 km NE, centre of wine-growing region with over 50 wineries. **Tourist information:** Aldinga Bay Holiday Village, Esplanade, Aldinga Beach; (085) 56 5019. **Accommodation:** Limited. **See also:** The Fleurieu Peninsula.

MAP REF. 283 K10, 284 B7, 287 B3, 289 K9

Andamooka Pop. 471

Andamooka is a lonely outback opal field around 600 km N of Adelaide, to the west of the saltpan Lake Torrens. It is off the beaten track, conditions are harsh, weather is severe and water precious. There are rough shacks along the dirt road, with many people living in dugouts to protect themselves from the extreme heat. Visitors who have obtained a precious-stone prospecting permit from the Mines Department in Adelaide can stake out a claim and try their luck. Looking for opals on mullock dumps left by miners requires permission from the owners of a claim. There are tours of the area and showrooms with opals for sale. The road to Andamooka is fair, but quickly affected by rain. **Of interest:** Duke's Bottle Home, made entirely of empty beer bottles. Annual Family Fun Day and White Dam Walk, Easter; Opal Festival Oct. **In the area:** Roxby Downs, 30 km W, service town for nearby Olympic Dam mining operations for copper, gold, silver and uranium; tours of mining operations available. At Woomera, 120 km S, Heritage Centre and Missile Park with displays of rockets and aircraft. **Tourist information:** Opal Creek Showroom, Main St; (086) 72 7193. **Accommodation:** 1 hotel/motel, 1 motel, 1 caravan/camping park.

MAP REF. 290 G4

Angaston Pop. 1819

Angaston is in the highest part of the Barossa Valley: within 79 km of the coast, it is 361 m above sea level. The town is named after prominent 1830s Barossa Valley settler, George Fife Angas. **Of interest:** Angas Park Fruit Co., Murray St, produces dried fruit and nuts; open daily. Angaston Galleria, Murray St, and Bethany Arts and Crafts, Washington St, for home-made goods, local and Australian art and craft. A Clothes Revival, Murray St, for clothes of yesteryear and collectables. **In the area:** Collingrove Homestead (1850), 7 km SE; National Trust owned property, once belonging to Angas pioneering family, viewing, accommodation and meals (closed Fri. in winter). Springton Gallery, Herbig Tree and Robert Hamilton & Son Winery at Springton, 27 km SE. Wineries: Saltram Wine Estates and Yalumba Winery, 2 km W and S of Angaston respectively, and Henschke's Wines near Keyneton (check opening times), 10 km SE: all open for tastings and sales. Magnificent view of Barossa Valley from Mengler's Hill Lookout, 8 km SW. **Tourist information:** Angaston Galleria, 18 Murray St; (085) 64 2648. **Accommodation:** 2 hotels, 1 motel. **See also:** Vineyards and Wineries.

MAP REF. 283 O4, 286 I4, 287 D1, 289 M7

Ardrossan Pop. 1008

Ardrossan, 148 km NW of Adelaide, is the largest port on the east coast of the Yorke Peninsula. An important outlet for wheat and barley, it is an attractive town with excellent crabbing and fishing from the jetty. **Of interest**: Ardrossan and District Historical Museum, Fifth St. The stump jump plough was invented here in the late 1800s; restored plough on display on cliffs at end of First St in East Tce. **In the area:** Salt and dolomite mines. BHP Lookout, 2 km S. For keen divers, *Zanoni* wreck off coast, 20 km SE; permission required to dive. Clinton Conservation Park, 40 km N. Coastal walks, wildlife tours, campfires, as package, 4 km W. **Tourist information:** Ardrossan Independent Store, First St; (088)37 3209. **Accommodation:** 2 hotel/motels, 2 caravan/camping parks.

MAP REF. 282 H4, 289 J6

Arkaroola Pop. 10

Founded in 1968, Arkaroola is a remote village settlement in the northern Flinders Ranges, about 660 km N of Adelaide. This privately owned property of 61 000 ha has been opened as a flora and fauna sanctuary. The rugged outback country is crossed by incredible quartzite ridges, deep gorges and rich mineral deposits, and is a haven for birdlife and rare marsupials. **Of interest:** Mineral and Fossil Museum, Outdoor Pastoral Museum, Astronomical Observatory (check viewing times), pioneer cottage. **In the area:** Marked walking-trails; self-guiding pamphlets from Information Centre. Old Cornish-style smelters (1861) and scenic waterholes, 12 km NW at Bolla Bollana. About 18 km further west, old log cabin (1856) at Yankaninna Homestead. Famous Mt Painter, 10 km N; further 20 km N, breathtaking views from

The Yorke Peninsula

Settled primarily as agricultural country, Yorke Peninsula was put on the map by the discovery of rich copper-ore deposits in 1861 and the influx of thousands of miners, including so many from Cornwall that the **Wallaroo–Moonta–Kadina** area became known as Little Cornwall.

The drive down the highway on the east coast is mainly within sight of the sea.

Many of the east-coast towns have excellent fishing from long jetties once used for loading grain ships. Also beach, surf and rock fishing are excellent, as is crabbing.

The west coast of Yorke Peninsula is lined with safe swimming beaches and spectacular coastal scenery. **Port Victoria**, the last of the windjammer ports, was once the main port of call for sailing ships transporting grain. Further north, Moonta's old stone buildings give it a sense of history and the Moonta mines tell of its mining heyday.

The southern tip of the Peninsula includes **Innes National Park** with its desolate countryside and impressive coastal scenery. Visit the site of a once-flourishing township, **Inneston**. **Pondalowie Bay** is a must for surfers. Rocky cliff tops and windswept headlands offer spectacular views across Investigator Strait.

For further information, contact the Yorke Peninsula Tourist Information Centre, Victoria Sq., Kadina; (088) 21 2093. **See also:** Individual entries in A–Z listing.

The Eyre Peninsula

The Eyre Peninsula is a vast region stretching from Whyalla in the east to the Western Australian border in the west, and, in a north–south direction, from the Gawler Ranges to Port Lincoln. Spencer Gulf borders the eastern edge of the Peninsula, along which are located a number of small coastal towns featuring sheltered waters, safe swimming, white sandy beaches and excellent fishing from either shore or boat. The charm of the peaceful resort towns of **Cowell**, **Arno Bay** and **Port Neill** has a natural appeal. Cowell has the added appeal of being one of the world's major sources of jade.

Whyalla is the second largest city in South Australia and acts as an important gateway to Eyre Peninsula. Located near the top of Spencer Gulf, this bustling, industrially based city also offers a wide range of attractions for the visitor.

The southern Eyre Peninsula encompasses the tourist resort towns of **Tumby Bay**, famous for fishing and beautiful offshore islands; **Coffin Bay**, with magnificent sheltered waters; and the jewel in the crown, the city of **Port Lincoln**, nestled on blue Boston Bay.

In stark contrast to the sheltered waters of Spencer Gulf, the west coast is exposed to the full force of the Southern Ocean and offers some of the most spectacular coastal scenery to be found anywhere in Australia. This rugged coast is

Point Labatt, on the western side of Eyre Peninsula

punctuated by a number of bays and inlets and, not surprisingly, resort towns have flourished where shelter can be found from precipitous cliffs and pounding surf. **Elliston**, **Venus Bay**, **Streaky Bay**, **Smoky Bay** and **Ceduna** all offer the visitor a diverse range of coastal scenery, good fishing and water-related activities.

Ceduna provides a vital service and accommodation facility for east–west traffic across Australia, and acts as a gateway information centre for visitors approaching the region from the west.

The hinterland of the Eyre Peninsula encompasses the picturesque Koppio Hills in the south, the vast grain-growing tracts of the central region and the

timeless beauty of the Gawler Ranges in the far north.

The Nullarbor, the western corridor into the region, is a vast treeless plain, bordered in the south by towering limestone cliffs that drop sheer to the pounding Southern Ocean. Here schools of southern right whales can be seen along the coastline between June and October on their annual breeding migration. Sightings of these beautiful creatures occur regularly and are on the increase.

For further information on the area, contact the Whyalla Tourist Centre, Lincoln Hwy, Whyalla; (086) 45 7900. **See also:** Individual entries in A–Z listing.

Freeling Heights overlooking Yudnamutana Gorge and Siller's Lookout over Lake Frome (a salt lake). The radioactive Paralana Hot Springs, 27 km N, originate deep within the earth's crust, along a great earth fracture. Gammon Ranges National Park, 20 km SW, has extensive wilderness areas; recommended for experienced bushwalkers only. Balcanoona Homestead, Big Moro Gorge (with rock pools) and Chambers Gorge (with Aboriginal rock carvings) 20 km S of Arkaroola. Ridgetop Tour, a spectacular 4WD trip across Australia's most rugged mountains. Scenic flights and guided tours available. **Tourist information:** Visitors Information Centre, (086) 48 4848. **Accommodation:** 4 motels, 1 caravan/camping park. **See also:** The Flinders Ranges; National Parks.
MAP REF. 285 G2, 291 M4, 484 D12

Balaklava Pop. 1439

Balaklava has a picturesque setting on the banks of the River Wakefield, 91 km N of Adelaide. The town was named after a famous battle in the Crimean War. **Of interest:** National Trust Museum, May Tce, has relics of district's early days; open Sun. Country Crafters, George St; local craft. Courthouse Gallery and Shop, Edith Tce; community art gallery. Urlwin Park Agricultural Museum, Short Tce. Lions Club Walking Trail, along Wakefield River and through town; brochure available at Council offices. Agricultural Show in Sept. Balaklava Racing Club; 4 meetings in autumn. Festival of Gardens and Galleries in Oct. **In the area:** Devils Gardens, 7 km NE on Auburn Rd, and The Rocks Reserve, 10 km E, both with picnic facilities. Beach-side town of Port Wakefield, 26 km W at head of Gulf St Vincent. **Tourist information:** Council Offices; (088) 62 1811. **Accommodation:** 2 hotels, 1 caravan/camping park.
MAP REF. 283 K1, 289 K5

Barmera Pop. 1859

The sloping shores of Lake Bonney make a delightful setting for the Riverland town of Barmera, 214 km NE of Adelaide. Lake Bonney is ideal for swimming, water-skiing, sailing, boating and fishing. The irrigated land is given over mainly to vineyards, but there are also apricot and peach orchards and citrus groves. Soldier settlement after World War I marked the beginning of today's community-oriented town. **Of interest:**

Donald Campbell Obelisk, Queen Elizabeth Dr; commemorates Campbell's attempt on world water speed record in 1964. Bonneyview Wines, Sturt Hwy; tastings, sales, gallery, restaurant and picnic facilities; open daily. SA Country Music Festival in June. **In the area:** At North Lake, 10 km NW, Napper's Old Accommodation House (1850), built on the overland stock route from NSW; ruins preserved by National Trust. At Overland Corner, 19 km NW on Morgan Rd (1859), now also National Trust museum; self-guided historical walking trail. Rocky's Country Hall of Fame for country music fans, 5 km NE on Renmark Bypass; open daily. At Cobdogla, 5 km W, Irrigation Museum has world's only working Humphrey Pump, as well as steam rides, historic displays and picnic areas; check operating days. Cobdogla Coloured Wool; spinning demonstrations, lamb-feeding, coloured fleeces. Moorook Loch Luna Game Reserve, 16 km SW, includes Wachtels Lagoon with birdlife and walking trail around foreshore, wetlands cruise available; nearby, Yatco Lagoon abounds with birdlife. At Monash, 8 km NE, Wein Valley Estate, tastings and sales, Mon.–Sat. **Tourist information:** Barmera Travel Centre, Barwell Ave; (085) 88 2289. **Accommodation:** 2 motels, 1 hotel/motel, 3 caravan/camping parks. **See also:** Festival Fun.
MAP REF. 289 Q6

Beachport Pop. 443

The site of the south-east's first whaling station, in the 1830s, Beachport is a quiet little town 51 km S of Robe. Rivoli Bay nearby provides safe swimming beaches as well as shelter for lobster boats. **Of interest:** Old Wool and Grain Store, Railway Tce; National Trust Museum with whaling, shipping and local history exhibits. Military Museum, Beach Rd; open daily. Artifacts museum, McCourt St; Aboriginal heritage. Jubilee Lagoon Park in town centre; barbecues, tennis, playgrounds, and skateboard track. **In the area:** Lake George, 4 km N, is a haven for waterbirds and popular for windsurfing and fishing. Beachport Conservation Park, between Lake George and the Southern Ocean, has Aboriginal shell middens; also walking trails (self-guiding leaflets available). Bowman Scenic Drive off McArthur Pl. offers spectacular views of the Southern Ocean. Swimming in Pool of Siloam, on Scenic

Drive; lake with high salt content and reputed therapeutic benefits. Woakwine Cutting, 10 km N on Robe Rd; extraordinary drainage project, with observation platform and machinery exhibit. Canunda National Park, 20 km S, 40-km stretch of spectacular windswept sand dunes and virgin bushland, with fascinating flora and fauna. Seaspray walk along cliff top; self-guiding leaflet from ranger at Southend. **Tourist information:** District Council, McCourt St; (087) 35 8029. **Accommodation:** 1 hotel, 1 motel, 2 caravan/camping parks.
MAP REF. 287 F11

Berri Pop. 3733

The commercial centre of the Riverland region, Berri is 227 km NE of Adelaide. Originally a wood-refuelling stop for the paddle-steamers and barges which plied the Murray, the town was first proclaimed in 1911. This is fruit- and vine-growing country, dotted with peaceful picnic and fishing areas. **Of interest:** Water Tower Lookout (17 m), Fiedler St; panoramic views of river and town. River crossings on Riverland's only twin ferries crossing Murray River; vehicular, 24-hr free service. Nearby, sculpture and cave memorial to Jimmy James, Aboriginal tracker. Houseboats, canoes for hire. Easter Festival and rodeo held annually. **In the area:** Large range of dried fruit and confectionery from Berri Fruit Tree Kiosk, 3 km W on Sturt Hwy. Berri Estates winery and distillery, largest wine-making facility in Australia, 13 km W on Sturt Hwy, near town of Glossop; tastings and sales Mon.–Sat. Berrivale Orchards, 4 km N on Sturt Hwy; tastings and sales of Berri fruit juices; also educational audiovisual on Riverland's history and various stages in processing of fruit; open Mon.–Fri., Sat. morning. Wilabalangaloo flora and fauna reserve, 5 km N, off Sturt Hwy; walking trails, spectacular scenery, museum and paddlewheeler; check opening times. On the Sturt Hwy, opposite access to Wilabalangaloo reserve, the Big Orange, the largest orange in the world; open daily. Rollerama roller skating centre adjacent. On Morgan Rd, art and craft exhibits at the Parlour Australiana Gallery, also accessed from the Big Orange. Martin's Bend, 2 km E; popular for water-skiing and picnicking. Township of Monash, 12 km NW on Morgan Rd. Wine tastings and sales (Mon.–Sat.) at Wein Valley Estate,

off Morgan Rd. Katarapko Game Reserve, 10 km sw, features Kia Kia Nature Trail for bushwalkers. **Tourist information:** 24 Vaughan Tce; (085) 82 1655. **Accommodation:** 1 hotel/motel, 3 motels, 1 caravan/camping park.
MAP REF. 126 A8, 289 Q6

Blinman   Pop. 30

Blinman, 478 km N of Adelaide near the northern boundary of the Flinders Ranges National Park, was a thriving copper-mining centre from 1860 to 1890. The countryside is magnificent, particularly when the wild hops bloom. **Of interest:** Several historic buildings, including hotel (1869), post office (1862) and police station (1874), all in main street. **In the area:** Great Wall of China, impressive ironstone-capped ridge, 10 km s on Wilpena Rd. Further south, beautiful Aroona Valley, with ruins of old Aroona Homestead; nearby Mt Hayward and Brachina Gorge. 'Almost ghost' town of Beltana, 60 km N, declared a historic reserve. Midway between Blinman and Parachilna is Angorichina, located 15 km w in scenic Parachilna Gorge; nearby, the Blinman Pools, fed by a permanent spring. Scenic drive east through Eregunda Valley to Chambers Gorge with rock pools and Aboriginal carvings; then north, spectacular Big Moro Gorge on Arkaroola Rd. **Accommodation:** 1 hotel/motel, 1 caravan/ camping park.
MAP REF. 285 E6, 291 K6

Bordertown   Pop. 2235

Bordertown is a quiet town on the Dukes Hwy, 274 km SE of Adelaide. Growth was stimulated after 1852 when it became an important supply centre for the goldfields of western Victoria. Today the area is noted for wool, cereals, meat and vegetable production. **Of interest:** Robert J.L. Hawke, former Australian Prime Minister, was born here and his childhood home, in Farquhar St, has been renovated and includes memorabilia; open Mon.–Fri. Town parks offer picnic facilities. Bordertown Wildlife Park, Dukes Hwy; native birds and animals, including pure white kangaroos. **In the area:** Historic Clayton Farm, 3 km s; vintage farm machinery and thatched buildings; open Sun.–Fri. Clayton Farm Vintage Field Day held Oct. long weekend. At Mundalla, 10 km sw: Mundalla Hotel (1884), now National Trust Museum, and Wirrega Council Chambers.

At Padthaway, 42 km sw, 1882 homestead houses Padthaway Estate winery; accommodation and meals available. Picnic areas among magnificent red gums and stringybarks at Padthaway Conservation Park. Bangham Conservation Park, 30 km SE, near Frances. **Tourist information:** Council Chambers, 43 Woolshed St; (087) 52 1044. **Accommodation:** 2 hotels, 3 motels, 1 caravan/ camping park.
MAP REF. 228 A7, 287 I7, 289 R13

Burra   Pop. 1191

Nestled in Bald Hills Range, 154 km N of Adelaide, Burra is a former copper-mining centre. The district of Burra Burra (the name is Hindi for 'great great') is now famous for stud merino sheep, and Burra serves as the market town for the surrounding farmland. *Breaker Morant* was filmed here. Copper was discovered in 1845 and copper to the value of almost $10 million was extracted before the mine closed in 1877. **Of interest:** A passport system (details from Tourist Information Office) gives visitors access to walk or drive around 11 km of heritage buildings, museums, mine shafts and lookout points. Daily 2-hr bus tours of town and its mining history from Tourist Information Office; bookings essential. Burra Creek miners' dugouts, alongside Blyth St, where more than 1500 people lived during the boom period; 2 dugouts preserved. Burra cemetery, off Spring St. Burra Mine Open Air Museum, off Market St, includes ore dressing tower, powder magazine; spectacular views of open-cut mine and town. Nearby

Brachina Gorge, near Blinman

Enginehouse Museum, built in 1858 and reconstructed in 1986; alongside archaeological excavation of 30-m entry tunnel to Morphett's Shaft. Market Square Museum, across from Tourist Information Office. Malowen Lowarth Museum, Kingston St, in original miner's cottage. Underground cellars of old Unicorn Brewery, Bridge Tce. Also in Bridge Tce, Paxton Square Cottages (1850), 33 two-, three- and four-roomed cottages built for Cornish miners, now restored as accommodation for visitors. In Burra North: police lockup and stables (1849), Tregony St; Redruth Gaol (1857), off Tregony St; and Bon Accord Mine buildings (1846), Railway Tce, now a museum complex. Picturesque spots alongside creek for swimming, canoeing and picnicking. **In the area:** Chatswood Farm Gallery, 14 km s at Hanson. Wineries in the Clare Valley, about 30 km sw. Picturesque Burra Gorge, 27 km E. Scenic 90 km drive, Dares Hill Drive, begins 30 km N on Broken Hill Rd. **Tourist information:** 2 Market Sq.; (088) 92 2154. **Accommodation:** 4 hotels, 1 motel, 1 caravan/ camping park.
MAP REF. 289 M4

Ceduna   Pop. 2753

Near the junction of the Flinders and Eyre Hwys, 786 km NW of Ceduna is the last major town you go through before crossing the Nullarbor from east to west. It is the ideal place to check your car and stock up with food and water before the long drive. The port at Thevenard, 3 km E, handles bulk grain, gypsum and salt. The fishing-fleet is noted for its large

National Parks

Nowhere else in Australia can wildlife be seen in such close proximity and in such profusion as in the parks of South Australia. To protect its valuable native animals and plants and to conserve the natural features of the landscape, this State has set aside 17 per cent of its total area as national, conservation and recreation parks, and regional and game reserves.

In addition to 14 national parks, the SA National Parks and Wildlife Service also manages 200 conservation parks, 14 recreation parks, 9 game reserves and 4 regional reserves. The main criteria for each category, as stated in the National Parks and Wildlife Act of 1972, were as follows:

- **National parks** Areas with wildlife or natural features of national significance.
- **Conservation park**s Areas for the preservation and conservation of native flora and fauna representative of South Australia's natural heritage, although historical features may also be included in these parks.
- **Recreation parks** Areas for outdoor recreation in a natural setting.
- **Game reserves** Areas suitable for the management and conservation of native game species, usually duck and quail. Hunting of some species during restricted open seasons.
- **Regional reserves** A new category established in 1988 which protects, at present, 4 large areas within South Australia considered to contain important wildlife and natural features, but where natural resources, such as minerals, may be needed in the future.

The range of climatic zones in South Australia enables visitors to enjoy the attractions of these parks throughout the year; coastal parks are cool in summer and autumn, while mountain areas are ideal to visit in winter and spring.

The Flinders Ranges, which extend for 430 kilometres, contain the **Flinders Ranges National Park**, which, with its total area of 94 908 hectares, is one of the major national parks in Australia. The Wilpena section, located in the south of the park, comprises the famed Wilpena Pound and the Wilpena Pound Range, covering an area of 10 000 hectares. The Pound is one of the most extraordinary geological formations in Australia. Developed in the Cambrian period, it is a vast oval rock bowl, ringed with sheer cliffs and jagged rocks and with a flat floor covered with trees and grass. A homestead dating back to 1889 still stands. At Arkaroo Rock,

Coffin Bay National Park

native rock paintings indicate that this was a significant area in Aboriginal mythology.

Twenty-five kilometres north of Wilpena is the Oraparinna section of the park. The 68 500 hectares of this section were a sheep station last century, at one time maintaining more than 20 000 sheep. Further north, near the **Gammon Ranges National Park**, Arkaroola offers both motel accommodation and a serviced camping ground. The park, an arid, isolated region of rugged ranges and deep gorges, offers visitors the opportunity to experience an extensive wilderness area. The mountains sparkle with exposed formations of quartz, fluorspar, hematites and ochres, making the region a gem-hunter's paradise. The Gammon Ranges (camping is permitted) are a sanctuary for many native birds and animals, including the western grey kangaroo, the big red kangaroo, the grey euro or hill kangaroo and the yellow-footed rock wallaby.

Further north, in the state's arid lands, over 8 million hectares have been set aside to protect the unique desert environment. These desert parks include the **Lake Eyre National Park, Witjira National Park, Innamincka Regional Reserve** and the **Simpson Desert Conservation Park**. Lake Eyre, the central

feature of the park of the same name, is one of the world's greatest salinas or salt lakes, found 16 metres below sea level. Contrarily, it is both the hub of a huge internal drainage system while being located in the driest part of the Australian continent. Vegetation is sparse but after heavy rains when the area floods, the ground is covered with colourful wildflowers and the animal and bird populations, attracted by the plant rejuvenation, rise accordingly. Care needs to be taken when visiting; only 4WD vehicles can access the park and campers must be fully self-sufficient.

Witjira National Park, located 120 km north of Oodnadatta, is an area of vast desert landscapes; gibber plains, sand dunes, salt pans and mound springs, upwellings of the Great Artesian Basin. Visitors may explore this extremely arid environment from the park's oasis, Dalhousie Springs.

The **Innamincka Regional Reserve** covers much of the flood-out country of the Cooper and Strzelecki Creeks from the Queensland border. These arid wetlands, which comprise a series of semi-permanent overflow lakes, hold many surprises for birdwatchers.

The **Simpson Desert Conservation**

Park, for the more adventurous park visitor, consists of spectacular red sand dunes which in places can run parallel for hundreds of kilometres, salt lakes, floodout plains, hummock grasslands, gibber desert, gidgee woodland, tablelands and mesas.

Visitors who wish to enjoy the attractions of the parks and reserves in this vast desert area must obtain a Desert Parks Pass (included in the **Desert Parks South Australia Handbook** and maps kit), from the SA National Parks and Wildlife Service (SA NPWS), PO Box 102, Hawker, SA 5434; telephone (086) 48 4244. The pass is valid from the date of purchase; it allows twelve months bush camping in Lake Eyre National Park, Witjira National Park, Innamincka Regional Reserve and the Simpson Desert Conservation Park and Regional Reserve, and also Flinders Ranges and Gammon Ranges National Parks. Maps and information on each park and reserve are included along with a vehicle identification sticker and three renewal forms.

One of the finest national parks in South Australia is **The Coorong**, 185 kilometres from Adelaide, south of the mouth of the mighty Murray River. The Coorong a corruption of the Aboriginal word *karangh*, meaning 'narrow neck' is a series of saltwater lagoons fed by the Murray and separated from the sea by the Younghusband Peninsula.

In the park are six island bird sanctuaries, prohibited to the public, but which can be viewed through binoculars. These islands house rookeries of pelicans, crested terns and silver gulls. The ocean beach of the Coorong is a favourite haunt of fishermen, but you can take the pleasant drive along the coast road beside the waterway, stopping to camp or picnic. There are more than 160 species of birds in the tea-tree and wattle thickets along this road. At dusk, big grey kangaroos and red-necked wallabies come out to feed on the grassed open areas.

On the southern flat plains of South Australia, near Naracoorte, is Bool Lagoon Game Reserve. The lagoon's natural cycle of flooding and drying out is perfect for breeding of waterbirds. In spring, when the water is deepest, thousands of black swans crowd the lagoon, creating a wildlife spectacle. In summer and autumn, when the water is shallow, waterfowl and waders flock to feed on the rich plant life. Bool Lagoon is also the largest permanent ibis rookery in Australia. Dense thickets of paperbark and banks of reeds in its central reaches provide safe places for breeding. A boardwalk network provides access to wildlife without disturbing the natural environment.

A conservation park in the south-east

Cape Du Couedic lighthouse, Flinders Chase Nat. Park

of the State, preserves the **Naracoorte Caves**. These limestone caves enclose a wonderland of stalagmites, stalactites, shawls, straws and other calcite formations. Four caves, including Blanche Cave, the first to be discovered, in 1845, are open for inspection by guided or adventure tours. A museum is set up within Victoria Fossil Cave, where a tour shows visitors skeletons of such extinct animals as giant browsing kangaroos, a hippopotamus-sized wombat, the marsupial lion and the Tasmanian tiger.

Flinders Chase National Park, situated at the western end of Kangaroo Island, is in wild and rugged country that has mild summers. It is popular with bushwalkers, who enjoy hiking through trackless forests of gum and mallee scrub.

Seal Bay Conservation Park, also on Kangaroo Island, allows visitors the unique opportunity to view breeding colonies of Australia sea lions. The adjoining **Cape Gantheaume Conservation Park** is a wilderness area attracting experienced bushwalkers.

A twelve-month Kangaroo Island Pass, available from the NPWS office at Kingscote (PO Box 39, Kingscote 5223; telephone (0848) 22 381) gives access to all parks on the island where an entrance fee is charged.

On the Yorke Peninsula is **Innes National Park**, where birdwatching is a favourite pastime; there is good fishing at the beaches; and walking trails lead to the coastal beach and to the historic site of Inneston. This small settlement, now in ruins, once housed miners who dug for gypsum, used for plaster and chalk; for many years nearly every schoolchild in Australia was taught with the aid of blackboard chalk mined here and shipped from Stenhouse Bay.

The Eyre Peninsula, bordered to the north by the Eyre Highway, contains several parks. At **Coffin Bay National Park** and **Lincoln National Park** the main

feature is the coastal scenery. As well, the opportunities for bush camping, birdwatching and bushwalking in delightful natural surroundings attract visitors.

Coffin Bay is only 50 kilometres west of Port Lincoln. The park takes in all of the Coffin Bay Peninsula, the western coast of which faces the Great Australian Bight while the southern side has the calming influence of sandy beaches and several offshore islands.

A 25 kilometre drive south of Port Lincoln finds **Lincoln National Park**, which occupies much of the Jussieu Peninsula, surrounded by small islands. At its northern tip, on Stamford Hill, the Flinders Monument commemorates a visit by Matthew Flinders in 1802. Beach fishing is popular, but rip tides and sharks prevent swimming.

The salt lakes of **Lake Gilles Conservation Park**, also on Eyre Peninsula, are birdwatching country.

A unique and successful experiment of familiarising people with native fauna is evidenced at the Cleland Wildlife Park in the centre of the larger **Cleland Conservation Park**, located on the slopes of Mount Lofty overlooking Adelaide. Here visitors are able to walk freely among the animals, which are housed in conditions similar to their native habitat.

Located within Adelaide's southern suburbs is **Belair National Park**, the most popular park in the State. The park's bushland setting, together with its resident birds and animals and many recreational facilities, attract family groups.

Camping and entrance fees are charged at many of South Australia's national parks.

For further information on camping restrictions, entry permits and fees, and general advice on visiting national parks, contact SA NPWS Information Centre, 55 Grenfell St, Adelaide 5000 (GPO Box 1782, Adelaide 5001); (08) 207 2000.

whiting hauls. Snapper, salmon, tommy ruff and crab are other catches. Ceduna is set on Murat Bay and the sand coves, sheltered bays and offshore islands of this bay make it an ideal base for a beach holiday. There was a whaling station on St Peter Island in the 1850s. According to map references in Swift's *Gulliver's Travels*, the tiny people of Lilliput might well have lived on one of the islands visible from Thevenard: St Peter Is. and St Francis Is. The beaches are ideal for swimming, fishing, water-skiing, windsurfing and boating. **Of interest:** Old Schoolhouse National Trust Museum, Park Tce; pioneering items, artefacts from atomic testing at Maralinga and historic medical room; open Mon.–Sat. Gaanywea camel day rides and safaris, from Nullarbor Roadhouse, May–Oct. **In the area:** Oestmann's Fish Factory at Thevenard Boat Haven; open daily. At Denial Bay, 13 km W: McKenzie Ruins, site of original settlement; also oyster farm. Denial Bay and Davenport Creek, west, and Decres Bay, Laura Bay and Smoky Bay, all south-east, for picnicking and safe fishing (boat charter available at Ceduna); all within day-tripping distance from town. Amazing sand dunes and excellent surf at Cactus Beach, near Penong, 54 km W. At Penong, 75 km W; restored woolshed, museum, local crafts; 10–4 daily. Southern right whales can be seen June–Oct. along coast west of Ceduna. Overseas Telecommunications Earth Station, 37 km N, links Australia with countries in Asia, Africa and Europe; open for inspection weekdays, tours available. Spectacular coastline includes prominent headland at Point Brown, 56 km S. **Tourist information:** Kendall Airlines, 58 Poynton St; (086) 25 2780. **Accommodation:** 1 hotel/motel, 4 motels, 5 caravan/camping parks. **See also:** The Eyre Peninsula.
MAP REF. 297 N10

Clare   Pop. 2575

Set in rich agricultural and pastoral country, this charming town was first settled in 1842; it was named after County Clare in Ireland. The area is renowned for its prize-winning table wines. Wheat, barley, fruit, honey, stud sheep and wool are other important regional industries. The first vines were planted by a group of Jesuit priests at Sevenhill in 1848. The priests are still producing table and sacramental wines from the Sevenhill Cellars. The Clare Valley wineries host a Gourmet Weekend on the May long weekend. Horseracing adds to carnival atmosphere of Clare Valley Easter Festival. **Of interest:** National Trust museum housed in old police station (1850), cnr Victoria Rd and West Tce; open Sat., Sun. and holidays. Inchiquin Lake, White Hut Rd. Lookouts at Billy Goat Hill, from Wright St, and Neagles Rock, Neagles Rock Rd. Maynard Memorial Park, Pioneer Ave; walking tracks and picnic facilities. Plaque commemorates arrival of Burke and Wills in 1862. Historic town walk self-guiding leaflets available. Clare Fine Art, Main North Rd; work of prominent Australian craftspersons, paintings. **In the area:** Stately Wolta Wolta Homestead, West Tce, on western edge of town, built by pioneer pastoralist John Hope in 1846 and still owned by Hope family; open for inspection Sun. 10–1. Over 20 wineries (some open for inspection, most for cellar-door sales; check opening times): around Clare—Jim Barry Wines, Tim Knappstein Wines, Leasingham Wines, Wendouree Cellars, Tim Adams' Wines, Duncan Estate Winery; around Sevenhill (7 km S)—Sevenhill Cellars (established 1851, with monastery buildings, including St Aloysius Church (1864), Paulett Wines, Pike's Polish Hill River Estate, The Wilson's Vineyard; around Penwortham (10 km S)—Skillogalee Wines, Waninga Wines, Penwortham Cellars, Mitchell's Winery; around Mintaro (15 km SE)—Mintaro Cellars; around Watervale (12 km S)—Crabtree Watervale Wines, Eaglehawk Estate (also wine museum), Rosenberg Cellars, Mount Horrocks Winery; around Auburn (26 km S)—Taylors Wines, Grosset Wines. Also at Mintaro, fascinating Heritage town, 15 km SE: historic Martindale Hall (featured in the film *Picnic at Hanging Rock*); accommodation, dining, and tours afternoons daily; slate quarry, operational since 1856 (not open for tours). Also at Auburn, town of historical and cultural interest, many historical buildings maintained by National Trust; self-guided walking tour leaflets available. Birthplace of poet C.J. Dennis in 1876, Stonehurst accommodation house. Scenic drive to Blyth, 13 km W; native flora and fauna in Padnaindi Reserve; Medika Gallery, originally a Lutheran church (1886), specialising in Australian bird and flower paintings, open daily. Scenic drive 12 km S to Spring Gully Conservation Park; stand of rare red stringybarks. Bungaree Station Homestead (1841), 12 km N, historic merino sheep station; tours and accommodation; knitting yarns, original patterns and hand-knitted Bungaree jumpers available from Station Store. Geralka Rural Farm, 25 km N of Clare. **Tourist information:** Main North Rd; (088) 42 2131. **Accommodation:** 2 hotels, 1 hotel/motel, 2 motels, 2 caravan/camping parks. **See also:** Festival Fun.
MAP REF. 289 L4

Cleve   Pop. 738

An inland town on Eyre Peninsula, settled in 1853 by Europeans, Cleve is surrounded by rich farming country. **Of interest:** Cleve Fauna Park, Fourth St. Old Council Chambers Museum, Third St. Eyre Peninsula Field Days (agricultural shows) held around Aug. every even year. **In the area:** Scenic drive along escarpment of Cleve–Cowell Hills. Cowell, 43 km E, and Arno Bay, 26 km SE, both have good swimming beaches and fishing jetties. Hincks (35 km W) and Bascombe Well (90 km W) Conservation Parks. **Tourist information:** Whyalla Tourist Centre, Lincoln Hwy, Whyalla, (086) 45 7900. **Accommodation:** 1 hotel/motel.
MAP REF. 288 F4

Coffin Bay   Pop. 343

A picturesque holiday town and fishing village in a sheltered bay, 51 km NW of Port Lincoln; sailing, water-skiing and swimming are popular here. The coastal scenery in this area is magnificent and fishing is excellent. Oysters cultivated in Coffin Bay are amongst the best in Australia. The bay's unusual name was bestowed by Matthew Flinders in 1802 to honour his friend Sir Isaac Coffin. **Of interest:** Oyster Farm, The Esplanade; also renowned for its lobster. Oyster Walk, a delightful 2½ km foreshore walkway between caravan park and Crinolin Point. **In the area:** Coffin Bay National Park and Kellidie Bay Conservation Park surround township; wildflowers in spring. Camping in national park areas; permit required. Farm Beach and nearby 'Anzac Cove', location for film *Gallipoli*. Yangie Trail drive, 10 km S, through bush to Point Avoid and Yangie Lookout for coastal views and surf beaches. Old stone buildings in Wangary, 29 km N. Further 50 km N, scenic stretch of Flinders Hwy between Mount Hope and Sheringa. Blacksmith's museum at

Alternative Accommodation

The South Australian Host Farms Association is a group of farming families who welcome guests to their homes. There are over 50 properties, varying from outback stations to sheep and wool farms, horse studs and dairy farms, vineyards and orchards.

The range of host farm accommodation includes self-contained cottages, shearers' quarters and accommodation in the homestead as a member of the family; many host farms offer bed and breakfast or welcome guests to dine with the family. Guests can also observe, or become involved in, seasonal activities on the property.

Bed and Breakfast Town and Country is an association of hosts willing to share their establishments with visitors. The accommodation ranges from modest to luxury in a wide variety of settings, including historic self-contained cottages, homestay and small guest houses.

Houseboats. With a meandering section of the Murray River flowing through the south-east section of the State, beautiful scenery, temperate weather and good shore facilities, houseboating is a viable and enjoyable holiday alternative.

From Murray Bridge to Renmark and Paringa, with several towns in between, houseboats ranging from 'monsters' sleeping 10 to 12 to those sleeping 4 to 6 can be hired. Some are equipped with dinghys, sundecks, air-conditioning, microwaves, colour TV and videos, while others have the bare essentials for comfort such as refrigerators, barbecues and heating. Booking is recommended for December and January.

For further information, contact the nearest South Australian Tourism Commission Travel Centre.

Koppio, 45 km NW. **Tourist information:** Beachcomber Agencies, The Esplanade; (086) 85 4057. **Accommodation:** 1 motel, 1 caravan/camping park. **See also:** The Eyre Peninsula.
MAP REF. 288 C7

Coober Pedy   Pop. 2491
In the heart of South Australia's outback, 848 km N of Adelaide on the Stuart Hwy, is the opal-mining town of Coober Pedy. This is the last stop for petrol between Cadney Park (155 km N) and Glendambo (253 km S) on the Stuart Hwy. The name 'Coober Pedy' is Aboriginal for 'white fellows in a hole'—most of the population live in dugouts (at a constant 24°C underground) as protection from the severe summer temperatures, often reaching 45°C, and the cold winter nights. There is also a complete lack of timber for building. The countryside is desolate and harsh, and the town has reticulated water provided from a bore 23 km N, and treated by reverse esmosis. Opals were discovered here in 1911 and today there are hundreds of mines. Anyone can try their luck after obtaining a precious stones prospecting permit from the Mines Department in Coober Pedy: takes 2–3 days. Trespassers on claims can be fined a minimum of $1,000. **Of interest:** Guided tours of working mines and tours and demonstrations of opals being cut and polished. Jewellery and polished stones available for purchase. Big Winch Lookout and Old Timers Mine, a mine museum and interpretive centre with self-guided walks, on eastern edge of town. Umoona underground mine, Hutchison St; museum and motel. Underground churches, Hutchison St, including St Peter and St Pauls, and the Catacomb Church, east of town. Desert Cave, Hutchison St; underground pictorial mining display, premier building and 4-star motel, underground shopping gallery. Underground Pottery, west of town, features locally made pottery. Coober Pedy races, held Oct. long weekend. **In the area:** Opal fields are pocked with diggings; beware of unprotected mine shafts. Avoid entering any field area unless escorted by someone who knows the area. The Breakaways, 30 km N, colourful 40 sq. km reserve containing unique landscape, ancient seabed. **Tourist information:** Council Offices, Hutchison St; (086) 72 5298. **Accommodation:** 1 hotel/motel, 9 motels, 2 caravan/camping parks. **See also:** The Outback.
MAP REF. 295 R11

Coonalpyn   Pop. 266
This tiny town on the Dukes Hwy, 180 km SE of Adelaide, makes a good base to explore the Mt Boothby (30 km SW) and Carcuma (20 km NE) Conservation Parks, see grey kangaroos, echidnas, emus and mallee fowl in their natural environment. **Of interest:** Melaleuca Crafts, Dukes Hwy; locally made pottery and clothing. **Tourist information:** Bakery and Craft Shop, Dukes Hwy; (085) 71 1200. **Accommodation:** 1 hotel, 1 caravan/camping park.
MAP REF. 287 F5, 289 O11

Coonawarra   Pop. 40
The history of Coonawarra goes back to 1890, when John Riddoch subdivided 2000 acres of his own vast landholding for the development of orchards and vineyards. Although the vines flourished and excellent wines were made, demand was not high until a resurgence of interest in the 1950s and 1960s, when the region became recognised as an important wine-growing area. The rich terra rossa soil and dedicated viticulturalists and winemakers now combine to produce award-winning white and red table wines. **Of interest:** Chardonnay Lodge, Penola Rd, has a motel, restaurant, art gallery and wine information centre. **In the area:** Wineries: Bowen Estate, Brands Laira, Hollick Wines, Hungerford Hill, James Haselgrove, Katnook Estate, Ladbroke Grove Wines, Leconfield Coonawarra, Mildara Wines, Penowarra Wines, Redman Winery, Rouge Homme, St Mary's Vineyard, The Ridge Wines, Wynns Coonawarra Estate, Zema Estate. **Tourist information:** Tourist Information Centre, Arthur St, Penola; (087) 37 2855. **Accommodation:** 1 motel. **See also:** Vineyards and Wineries.
MAP REF. 226 A2, 228 A13, 287 I11

Cowell   Pop. 695
A small, pleasant township 108 km S of Whyalla, Cowell is on the almost landlocked Franklin Harbour. One of the world's major jade deposits is in the district, and Cowell is the processing centre for Australia's only commercial jade-mining operation. The sandy beach is

safe for swimming and the fishing is excellent. Oyster farming is a new local industry and in season, fresh oysters can be purchased from various outlets. **Of interest:** Old post office and attached residence, (1888), Main St; now Franklin Harbour National Trust Historical Museum. Open-air Agricultural Museum, Lincoln Hwy. Jade Workshop, Lincoln Hwy, for viewing the grading of the stone; opposite, at the Cowell Jade Motel, displays of jewellery and sales (open daily). Lionel Deer's Camels, Kimba Rd. Smithy's Shell House, Warnes St. **In the area:** Franklin Harbour Conservation Park, south of Cowell, has good fishing spots. Swimming and fishing locations abound, including Port Gibbon, 15 km S, and Point Price Sandhills, 5 km further on. Arno Bay, 48 km S, is a popular holiday resort with sandy beaches and a jetty for fishing. Entrance Island, accessible only by boat. **Tourist information:** Council Offices, Main St; (086) 29 2019. **Accommodation:** 2 hotels, 1 motel, 2 caravan/camping parks. **See also:** The Eyre Peninsula. MAP REF. 288 G4

Crystal Brook   Pop. 1282

Originally part of a vast sheep station, this town, 25 km SE of Port Pirie, is now a thriving centre for the sheep, dairy and beef industries of the region. **Of interest:** National Trust Museum, Brandis St; local history collection in first two-storey building in town, which was original butcher's shop and bakery. Underground bakehouse to view. Crystal Crafts, Bowman St: local craft. Picnicking and swimming in creekside parks. Agricultural Show annually in Aug. **In the area:** Bowman Park, 5 km E, surrounds ruins of Bowman family property, Crystal Brook Run (1847); excellent Native Fauna Zone, including reptile collection, regular feeding of animals and demonstrations of snake venom extraction (open afternoons daily). Heysen Walking Trail runs through Bowman Park. Guided walking tours through southern Flinders Ranges available. Gladstone, 21 km NE, set in rich rural country in Rocky River Valley: railway yards contain one of world's few junction points of 3 different gauges—narrow, standard and broad —interlaid in one siding; tours of Gladstone gaol (1881); Trend Drinks Factory, home of 'Old Style Ginger Beer' (tours available). Laura, 32 km N; boyhood town of C.J. Dennis, author of *The Songs*

of a Sentimental Bloke, also Folk Fair (held in April) and cottage craft industry and art galleries; many historic buildings, (self-guided walking tour leaflet available). Picturesque Beetaloo Valley and Reservoir, W of Laura. Near Wirrabara, 50 km N, scenic walks through pine forests. Salt lakes around Snowtown, 50 km S; Lochiel–Ninnes Road lookout for superb view of inland lakes and countryside. Yacka, 40 km SE; sheepdog trials in Aug. **Tourist information**: District Council Offices, Bowman St; (086) 36 2150. **Accommodation:** Crystal Brook, 2 hotels, 1 caravan/camping park. Gladstone, 1 caravan/camping park. Laura, 1 caravan/camping park. MAP REF. 289 K2

Edithburgh   Pop. 453

Located on the cliff top at the southern tip of Yorke Peninsula, Edithburgh overlooks Gulf St Vincent and Troubridge Shoals, a chain of tiny islands. **Of interest:** Edithburgh Museum, Edith St; historical maritime collection. Native Flora Park (17½ ha), Ansley Tce. Town jetty, end of Edith St, built in 1873. Rockpool at cliffbase is excellent for swimming. Offshore skindiving is popular and nearby Sultana Bay is good for boating, fishing, swimming and sailboarding. State Sailboarding Championships held in Oct. **In the area:** Coobowie, 5 km N, popular coastal resort with caravan park and fuchsia nursery. Tours to Troubridge Island Conservation Park; ½ hour by boat. Scenic drive along coast passes wreck of *Clan Ranald*. **Tourist information:** Edithburgh Caravan Park, O'Halloran Pde; (088) 52 6056. **Accommodation:** 1 hotel, 2 motels, 1 caravan/camping park. MAP REF. 282 G9, 288 I9

Elliston   Pop. 242

Nestled in a small range of hills on the shore of Waterloo Bay, Elliston is a pleasant coastal town and the centre for a cereal-growing, mixed-farming and fishing community. Widely known for its rugged and scenic coastline, excellent fishing and safe swimming beaches, Elliston is a popular holiday destination. **Of interest:** Town hall mural, Main St; an art history of town and district. **In the area:** Clifftop walk at Waterloo Bay; fossilised weevil cocoons (shaped like a Dutch clog), believed to be over 100 000 years old, can be found. Talia Caves, 40 km N. Good surfing just north of town near Anxious Bay. Lock's Well and

Sheringa Beach to south, for surf fishing. Scenic drives north and south of town offer outstanding views of magnificent coastline; spectacular views also from Cummings Monument Lookout, just off hwy near Kiana, 52 km S. Day trip to summit of Mt Wedge and return via Bramfield. Flinders Island, 35 km offshore; limited accommodation. **Tourist information:** Rally's Roadhouse, Beach Tce; (086) 87 9170. **Accommodation:** 1 hotel/motel, 2 caravan parks. **See also:** The Eyre Peninsula. MAP REF. 288 B4

Gawler   Pop. 13 835

Settled in 1839, Gawler, 40 km NE of Adelaide, is the centre for a thriving agricultural district and also the gateway to the Barossa Valley. **Of interest:** Historical buildings, including Gawler Mill, telegraph station (now a folk museum) and old post office, west of Murray St. Old Eagle Foundry, King St; local iron lace made there. Walking tour of Church Hill district, a State Heritage Area. Brochures detailing self-guided walking, driving and cycling tours from Tourist Office. Para Para (1862), Penrith Ave; historic residence open Sat. and Sun. during renovation. Anglican Church, interesting pipe organ, bellringing Thurs. or by arrangement. Dead Man's Pass Reserve, end Murray St; picnic facilities and walking trails. **In the area:** Willaston post office, 2 km N; restored to original. Astronomical Society of SA's observatory at Stockport, 30 km N; public viewing nights; enquire at Tourist Office. Scholz Park Museum at Riverton, 54 km N. Wellington Hotel at Waterloo, 76 km N, near Manoora, once Cobb & Co. staging point. **Tourist information:** 61 Murray St; (085) 22 6814. **Accommodation:** 1 hotel, 1 motel, 2 caravan parks. MAP REF. 283 M5, 287 C1, 289 L7

Goolwa   Pop. 3018

Goolwa is a rapidly growing holiday town 12 km from the mouth of the Murray near Lake Alexandrina. Once a key port in the golden days of the riverboats, the area has a strong tradition of shipbuilding, trade and fishing; today, the lakes area is ideal for boating, fishing and aquatic sports and popular with birdwatchers and photographers. Southern right whales visit the bay July–Sept. **Of interest:** Many historic buildings, including distinctive railway superintendent's house (1852), known as 'the

Kangaroo Island

Only 120 kilometres south-west of Adelaide, Kangaroo Island, the third largest Australian island, shows nature at its wildest and purest form in a magical combination of sun and sea, native flora and fauna. A walk through bush or along coastal cliffs may provide glimpses of koalas, echidnas or, of course, kangaroos; there are also many species of birds and wildflowers.

To reach the island, visitors may fly from Adelaide (Air Kangaroo Island and Lloyds Aviation) or go by ferry. The vehicular ferry *Island Seaway* journeys from Port Adelaide to Kingscote. The *Philanderer III* and The *Navigator* both operate from Cape Jervis to Penneshaw.

There is no public transport on the island, but land and sea tours are available and hire vehicles include cars, mopeds and bicycles. Taxis and a private bus service operate to Kingscote and the airport. Kangaroo Island's waters—freshwater, surf, rocks and ocean—offer excellent fishing; big-game-fishing charters are available and fishing equipment can be hired.

At the three main towns, **Kingscote**, **American River** and **Penneshaw**, there is a range of accommodation from hotels and motels, through self-contained flats and cottages to camping and cabins.

American River, a small resort nestled in a protected pine-fringed bay, is ideal for fishing (charter boats available), scuba

Sea Lion, Seal Bay

diving and canoeing. **Pelican Lagoon** is a sanctuary for birds and fish. Penneshaw overlooks the passage separating the island from the mainland. Fairy penguins promenade on the rocks here at night.

The coastline of the island varies from the several kilometres of safe swimming beach at **Emu Bay** on the north to the rugged cliffs and roaring surf of the south. However, in the south, **D'Estrees Bay**'s wide deserted beach is ideal for fishing, shell collecting and exploring—there is an old whaling station at Point Tinline. **Cape Gantheaume** and **Seal Bay Conservation Parks** are located on this exposed

southern coast. Seal Bay is the home of a permanent colony of sea lions, with fur seals and leopard seals frequent residents. Also on the south coast are fascinating limestone formations in the caves at **Kelly Hill Conservation Park**. At **Cape Borda**, on the north-west tip of the island, is one of the most picturesque of Australia's old lighthouses; there are guided tours daily, arranged through the National Parks and Wildlife Service at Kingscote. Other attractive spots along the northern coast include the rugged rocks at **Harveys Return**; **Western River Cove** with its idyllic white beach; a superb protected bay at **Snelling Beach**; and **Stokes Bay**, where a secret tunnel leads to the beach. On the west coast, which is dominated by the soaring eucalypt forests of the **Flinders Chase National Park**, are two of the island's natural wonders: **Admirals Arch**, a huge arch where on sunny afternoons stalactites can be seen in silhouette, and the **Remarkable Rocks**, huge, unusually shaped granite boulders.

For further information, contact the Kangaroo Island Tourist Information Centre, National Parks and Wildlife Service, 37 Dauncey St, Kingscote, (0848) 2 2381. Island camping passes can be purchased from National Parks and Wildlife Service. **See also:** Entry for Kingscote in A–Z listing.

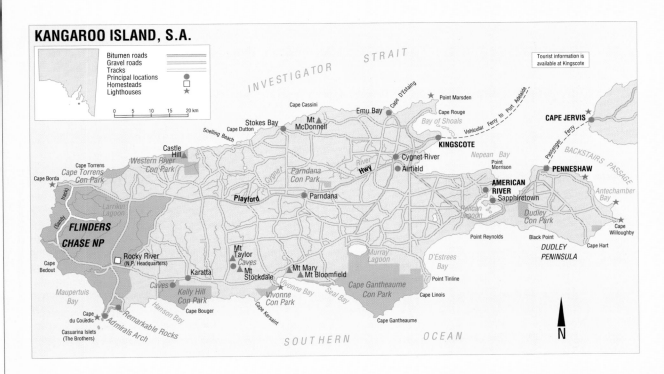

round-roofed house', and RSL Club, in former stables of Goolwa Railway (1853), both in B.F. Laurie Lane, off Cadell St. First railway carriage used in South Australia, horse-drawn and between Goolwa and Port Elliott in the 1850s, displayed in Cadell St. Steam train rides between Goolwa and Victor Harbor; enquire at Tourist Office. National Trust Museum, Porter St; housed in former blacksmith's shop dating from 1870s. Next door, in original but rebuilt cottage, Goolwa Print Room. Both Goolwa hotels, the Goolwa in Cadell St and the Corio in Railway Pl, date from 1850s. Signal Point Visitor Centre, The Wharf, has a computerised display of the river and district before European settlement, and the impact of development. Wooden Boat Festival in Feb. every odd-numbered year. Folk Festival Oct. **In the area:** Excellent fishing. Bird sanctuary east of Goolwa; swans, pelicans and other waterfowl; also bird hide. Nearby, the Barrages, desalination points that prevent salt water from reaching the Murray. MV *Aroona* and PS *Mundoo* cruise to mouth of the Murray, the Barrages, Lake Alexandrina and the Lower Murray. Hindmarsh Island, via ferry, for different view of Murray mouth. Malleebrae Woolshed, 2 km N; wool displays, shearing videos, art and craft (open by appointment). Scenic flights available; airport 5 km N. Currency Creek, 8 km N: Canoe Tree, Tonkin's Currency Creek Winery (with restaurant and fauna park) and creekside park and walking trail. Tooperang Trout Farm, 20 km NW. **Tourist information:** Old Library Bldg, cnr Cadell St and Goolwa Tce; (085) 55 1144. **Accommodation:** 4 motels, 2 caravan/camping parks. **See also:** The Fleurieu Peninsula.
MAP REF. 283 M12, 284 G12, 287 C4, 289 L10

Hawker   Pop. 345
This outback town in the centre of the northern Flinders Ranges is 400 km N of Adelaide. Once a railway town, it is now the centre of a unique area that attracts visitors from both Australia and overseas, who marvel at the colouring and grandeur of the many ranges that make up the Flinders. **Of interest:** Museum at Hawker Motors, cnr Wilpena and Cradock Rds. Historic buildings: old railway station complex (1885), Hawker Hotel (1882), post office (1882). Self-guided Historic Walk brochure

available. Horseracing carnival May, art exhibition Sept.–Oct. Henley-on-Arkaba fun-day Oct. **In the area:** Moralana Scenic Drive, 42 km N, joins roads to Wilpena and Leigh Creek. Further north, Arkaroo Rock, with paintings by Adnajamathana tribe; nearby Rawnsley Bluff, majestic southern rampart of Wilpena Pound. Scenic flights and 4WD tours available. Merna Mora Station, 46 km N; station holidays available. Rock paintings at Yourambulla Caves, 11 km S. Historic Kanyaka ruins, south off main road to Quorn. Walking trail and scenic lookout at Jarvis Hill, 5 km SW. Scenic drive west through Yappala, past Middle and Buckaringa Gorges to Gordon (check road conditions before departure). From Hawker, ruins at Wilson, Hookina, Wonoka and Willow Waters (check directions before departure). **Tourist information:** Hawker Motors, cnr Wilpena and Cradock Rds; (086) 48 4014. **Accommodation:** 1 hotel/motel, 1 motel, 2 caravan/camping parks. **See also:** The Flinders Ranges; National Parks.
MAP REF. 285 D9, 291 K9

Innamincka   Pop. 14
This tiny settlement, 1027 km NE of Adelaide, is built around a hotel and trading post on the Strzelecki Track, and is on the banks of Cooper Creek in wet periods. Motorists intending to travel along the Track should read the section on Outback Motoring before attempting the journey. There are no supplies or petrol between Lyndhurst and Innamincka. **Of interest:** Ruins of Australian Inland Mission hostel. Cullymurra Waterhole on Cooper Creek; picturesque spot, excellent fishing and Aboriginal carvings. **In the area:** Graves of explorers Burke and Wills near Innamincka; famous 'Dig Tree' 40 km over border in Qld. Coongie Lakes, 103 km NW (road conditions can vary considerably; 4WD recommended); freshwater lakes are a haven for wildlife. **Accommodation:** 1 hotel/motel. **See also:** The Outback.
MAP REF. 293 Q7, 484 G6

Jamestown   Pop. 1359
Jamestown is an attractive, well-planned country town 205 km N of Adelaide. The surrounding country produces stud sheep and cattle, cereals, dairy produce and timber. The importance of agriculture in the area means Jamestown's Agricultural Show in Oct. is regarded as one of the best in the State. **Of interest:** Railway

Station Museum; open Sun. afternoons. Parks ideal for picnicking along banks of Belalie Ck. Annual Christmas pageant. **In the area:** Scenic drive through Bundaleer Forest Reserve, 9 km S, up towards New Campbell Hill for panoramic view of plains stretching towards Mt Remarkable and The Bluff. Around Spalding, 34 km S, series of open waterways with picnic areas and trout fishing opportunities; Geralka Rural Farm, 49 km S, a working commercial farm with tourist facilities. At Gladstone, 29 km SW: railway yards for train enthusiasts; tours of gaol (1881); and tours of Trend Drinks Factory, home of 'Old Style Ginger Beer'. Appila Springs, scenic picnic spot 8 km from Appila, 24 km NW. **Accommodation:** 3 hotel/motels, 1 caravan/camping park.
MAP REF. 289 L2

Kadina   Pop. 3536
The largest town on the Yorke Peninsula, Kadina is the chief commercial centre of the region. The town's history is related to the boom copper-mining era during the 1800s and early 1900s, when thousands of Cornish miners flocked to the area; the community is still proud of its ancestry. A Cornish festival, the 'Kernewek Lowender', is held in conjunction with the towns of Wallaroo and Moonta in May every odd-numbered year. Bowling Carnival annually at Easter. **Of interest:** Historic hotels, including the Wombat, Taylor St, and Royal Exchange, Digby St, with iron lace balconies and shady verandahs. National Trust Kadina Museum complex includes Matta House, (1863) home of manager of Matta Matta Copper Mine; agricultural machinery, printing museum, blacksmith's shop and old Matta mine. Banking and Currency Museum, unique private museum, Graves St; open daily except Thurs. (closed June). Wallaroo Mines site; open for signposted self-guided walking tour. Brochures detailing self-guided walking tours of town available from Tourist Office. **In the area:** Towns of Moonta (18 km SW) and Wallaroo (10 km W), both of interest. Creative Activities network; expert tutoring in arts and crafts. Yorke Peninsula Field Days (agricultural shows) held at Paskeville (19 km SE) in Sept. every even year. **Tourist information:** Victoria Sq.; (088) 21 2093. **Accommodation:** 2 hotels, 2 motels, 1 caravan/camping park. **See also:** Festival Fun; The Yorke Peninsula.
MAP REF. 288 I5

The Flinders Ranges

Maralana Scenic Drive, south of Wilpena Pound

The Flinders Ranges are part of a mountain chain which extend for 430 kilometres from its southern end (between Crystal Brook and Peterborough) to a point about 160 kilometres east of Marree. The most spectacular peaks and valleys are in two areas: the first north-east of Port Augusta and the second north of Hawker. The Flinders, while similar in scale to many of Australia's mountain ranges, are totally different in both colouration and atmosphere. There is something unique in the contrast of the dry, stony land and richly lined rock faces—the characteristics of a desert range—with the rich vegetation of the river red gums, casuarinas, native pines and wattles that clothe the valleys and cling to hillsides and rock crevices. In spring, after rain, the display of wildflowers is breathtaking, carpeting the whole region with masses of reds, pinks, yellows, purples and white. The wildflowers, together with the natural beauty of the rock shapes, pools, caves and twisted trees that abound in the Flinders Ranges, make them a favourite haunt of photographers and artists. Many paintings by Sir Hans Heysen embody the shape and spirit of the ranges.

The Flinders is served by reasonably good roads. A pleasant trip, which will take in the best of the scenery, is the drive north-east from Port Augusta over Pichi Richi Pass to **Hawker** and from there on the loop road to **Parachilna**, circling the Wilpena Pound area.

But it is better to stay and explore, preferably on foot or by 4WD. There are kilometres of signposted tracks in the ranges, but as it is still only too easy to lose your way, it is important to be equipped with a good map and to follow a planned route. Drivers should avoid using the secondary roads after rain; they can be treacherous when wet.

The best-known feature of the Flinders is **Wilpena Pound**, an elevated basin covering about 50 square kilometres and encircled by sheer cliffs, which are set in a foundation of purple shale and rise through red stone to white-topped peaks. The only entrance is a narrow gorge, through which a creek sometimes flows. The external cliffs rise to over 1000 metres, but inside is a gentle slope to the floor of the plain. The highest point in the Pound is **St Mary's Peak**, at 1188 metres, which dominates the northern wall and provides a magnificent view over the mountains. Within the Pound are low, rounded hills and folded ridges, grasslands and pine-clad slopes that run down to the gums along Wilpena Creek. It is a wonderland of birdlife—rosellas, galahs, red-capped robins, budgerigars and wedgetailed eagles are common here. Bushland possums and rare yellow-footed wallabies also can be seen.

There is a well-organised resort at **Wilpena**, catering for levels of accommodation from camping to modern motel. Near the Pound in this central section of the ranges are **Warren Gorge**, **Buckaringa Gorge**, **Brachina Gorge**, **Yourambulla Cave** with its Aboriginal drawings, the **Hills of Arkaba**, considered the most

beautiful spur in this region, **Bunyeroo** and **Aroona Valleys** and the **Flinders Ranges National Park**.

Some features in the northern section of the Flinders—**Willow Springs Lookout**, the **Great Wall of China**, a long rocky escarpment, and **Mount Chambers** and **Chambers Gorge**, which can be reached by vehicle or on foot—are spectacular.

Another region of the Flinders, **Arkaroola** in the far north of the ranges, also invites exploration. The 61 000-hectare privately run **Arkaroola–Mt Painter Sanctuary** is situated in rugged outback country featuring quartzite razorback ridges over elongated valleys, once the sea bed of a great continental shelf that has left a legacy of rippled rock with embedded marine fossils. There is a profusion of wildlife: emus, ducks, parrots, cockatoos and galahs, possums, marsupial mice and yellow-footed rock wallabies all abound here.

From the heavily timbered slopes in the southern ranges, through picturesque gorges and rolling plains to the arid ranges of the north, the Flinders offers a variety of experiences. In addition to its unique flora and fauna, its rugged beauty and panoramic vistas, the region contains an important Aboriginal heritage and traces of early pioneering days.

For further information on the area, contact Flinders Ranges and Outback of South Australia Regional Tourism, PO Box 666, Adelaide 5001; (08) 303 2346. **See also:** National Parks; and individual entries in A–Z listing. **Note** detailed map of Flinders Ranges on page 285.

Kapunda
Pop. 1979

Situated 80 km N of Adelaide on the edge of the Barossa Valley, Kapunda is a market town for the surrounding farm country. Copper was discovered here in 1842 and Kapunda became Australia's first mining town. At one stage the population rose to 5000 and there were 16 hotels in the town. A million pounds' worth ($2m) of copper was dug out before the mines closed in 1878. Celtic Festival, annually, weekend before Easter, and Antique and Craft Fair Nov. **Of interest:** Many historic buildings; Heritage Trail and Historic Mine Walking Trail (maps available from Tourist Information Office). 'Map Kernow' (Son of Cornwall), 8-m-tall bronze statue at southern entrance to town, end of Main St. Historical Museum (1870s), Hill St. High School's main building, off Clare Rd; formerly residence of famous cattle king Sir Sidney Kidman. **In the area:** Scenic drive 26 km NE through rich sheep, wheat and dairy country to Eudunda; walks and scenic lookouts in area. Scholz Park Museum and Heritage-listed railway station at Riverton, 14 km N. At Marrabel, 25 km N, South Australia's biggest rodeo, held every Oct. Historic local stone buildings at Tarlee, 16 km w. **Tourist information:** 5 Hill St, (085) 66 2902. **Accommodation:** 1 hotel, 1 caravan/camping park.
MAP REF. 283 N3, 289 M6

Keith
Pop. 1176

Keith is a farming town on the Dukes Hwy, 241 km SE of Adelaide. In the centre of the former Ninety Mile Desert, now called Coonalpyn Downs, the area has been transformed from infertile scrubby pasture to productive farming by the use of plant nutrition and modern farming methods. **Of interest:** The main road is named Heritage St in recognition of the town's past. Pride of place is the former Congregational Church (1910) with its 11 locally made leadlight windows depicting the town's life and pioneering history. The Old Mouse, National Trust Buildings and Penny Farthing Coffee and Crafts add to the streetscape. Old Settlers Cottage (1894), Emu Flat Rd. **In the area:** Mount Rescue Conservation Park, 16 km N, vast expanse of sandplain with heath, pink gums and native wildlife. Ngarkat Conservation Park, 25 km NE. Mt Monster Conservation Park, 10 km s, with panoramic views and diverse wildlife. **Accommodation:** 1 hotel/

motel, 1 motel, 1 caravan/camping park.
MAP REF. 287 G6, 289 P12

Kimba
Pop. 682

A small township on the Eyre Hwy, Kimba is at the edge of SA's outback. This is sheep and wheat-growing country. **Of interest:** Historical museum, Eyre Hwy, featuring Pioneer House (1908), school and blacksmith's shop. The Big Galah, Eyre Hwy. Locally mined and crafted jade, including rare black jade, at adjacent Gem Shop. Sturt pea garden on Hwy. **In the area:** Walking trail from the edge of town, 3 km through bushland to White's Knob lookout. Gawler Ranges, north-west, a vast wilderness area; check road conditions. Lake Gilles Conservation Park, 20 km NE; Caralue Bluff, 20 km w; rock climbing and diverse flora and fauna. Pinkawillinie Conservation Park, 45 km w. **Tourist information:** Kimba Halfway Across Australia Gem Shop, Eyre Hwy; (086) 27 2112. **Accommodation:** 1 hotel/motel, 1 caravan/camping park.
MAP REF. 288 F2

Kingscote
Pop. 1443

Kingscote is the largest town and principal port of Kangaroo Island, 120 km sw of Adelaide. Kingscote was the first officially settled part of SA, in 1836. A vehicular ferry arrives here from Port Adelaide and there is an airfield nearby (travelling time, about 7 hrs or 30 min. respectively). **Of interest:** Cairn on foreshore marks State's first post office. Hope Cottage, National Trust Folk Museum, Centenary Ave. Town's cemetery is oldest in State. Rock pool and Brownlow Beach for swimming. Fishing from jetty for tommy ruffs, trevally, garfish and snook. Chriso's Wagon Rides, from The Esplanade; Clydesdale-drawn wagon rides in summer. **In the area:** Jumbuk Shearing demonstrations, Birchmore Rd, 17 km s. Eucalyptus oil distillery, Wilsons Rd, 20 km s off South Coast Rd. The small resort town of American River, a fishing village, about 50 km E, and, on the north-east coast of Dudley Peninsula, the village of Penneshaw, where the vehicular ferry arrives from Cape Jervis, about an hour away. Folk Museum in former Old Penneshaw School. Dudley, Cape Hart and Pelican Lagoon Conservation Parks on peninsula. Antechamber Bay, about 20 km SE of Penneshaw, for swimming, fishing

and bushwalking. On western end of island, Flinders Chase National Park, one of SA's most important parks and sanctuary for some of Australia's rarest wildlife. Cape Borda Lighthouse. Remarkable Rocks and Admiral's Arch, south-west. Guided tours available for Seal Bay, Kelly Hill Caves, and Cape Willoughby Lighthouse. **Tourist information:** National Parks and Wildlife Service, 37 Dauncey St; (0848) 22 381. **Accommodation:** 2 hotels, 4 motels, 2 caravan/camping parks. **See also:** Kangaroo Island.
MAP REF. 288 I11

Kingston S.E.
Pop. 1425

At the southern end of the Coorong National Park in Lacepede Bay, Kingston S.E. is a farming town and seaside resort. It was first named Maria Creek after a ship wrecked in the bay. The multitude of shallow lakes and lagoons in the area are a haven for birdlife and a delight for naturalists and photographers. **Of interest:** Unusual analemmatic sundial, adjacent to Apex Park, in East Tce. Post office (1867), Hanson St, one of seven selected nationally for a special Commonwealth Stamp Issue in 1982. National Trust Pioneer Museum (1872), Cooke St. Cape Jaffa Lighthouse (1860s; dismantled and re-erected in 1970s), Marine Pde. Maria Memorial, a granite cairn, commemorates massacre of 27 shipwrecked Europeans by Aborigines in 1840. Giant 'Larry Lobster' at entrance to town, Princes Hwy. **In the area:** Mt Scott Conservation Park, 20 km E. Jip Jip Conservation Park, 50 km NE. **Tourist information:** The Big Lobster, Princes Hwy; (087) 67 2555. **Accommodation:** 3 motels, 1 caravan/camping park. **See also:** The Coorong.
MAP REF. 287 F9

Lameroo
Pop. 567

A quiet little settlement 212 km E of Adelaide on the Mallee Hwy. **Of interest:** 18-hole golf course, Mallee Hwy. **In the area:** Baan Hill Reserve, 20 km sw, a natural soakage area surrounded by sandhills and scrub; picnic facilities. Ngarkat Conservation Park, 25 km s. Byrne Homestead (1898), built of pug and pine, 3 km along old Yappara road. Billiat Conservation Park, 37 km N. **Tourist information:** Council Offices; (085) 76 3002. **Accommodation:** 1 hotel/motel.
MAP REF. 287 H4, 289 Q10

Leigh Creek
Pop. 1378

Leigh Creek, in the Flinders Ranges, is the second-largest town N of Port Augusta. The economy is based on the large open-cut coalfield. The open-cut eventually consumed the original Leigh Creek township, and in 1982 residents moved to the new township about 13 km S. An extensive development and tree-planting scheme has transformed the new site into an attractive oasis. **In the area:** Visitors' viewing area for coal workings, 3 km from turnoff to coalfields, on Hawker to Marree Hwy; free tours of coalfields on Sat. (Mar.–Oct.) and school holidays. Aroona Dam, 4 km W, in steep-sided valley with richly coloured walls; scenic picnic area near gorge. Rugged Gammon Ranges National Park, 64 km E; wilderness area, recommended for experienced bushwalkers only. Lakes Eyre, Frome and Torrens, all dry salt pans, which occasionally fill with water. Lyndhust and Marree, 38 km and 119 km N, respective endpoints of Strzelecki and Birdsville Tracks. At Lyndhurst, unique gallery of sculptures by noted talc-stone artist 'Talc Alf'; open to visitors. **Tourist information:** Hawker Motors, cnr Wilpena and Cradock Rds, Hawker; (086) 48 4014. **Accommodation:** 1 motel, 1 caravan/camping park.
MAP REF. 285 D3, 291 K5, 484 C13

Loxton
Pop. 3322

Known as the Garden City of the Riverland region, Loxton is 251 km NE of Adelaide. The surrounding irrigated land supports thriving citrus, wine, dried-fruit, wool and wheat industries. The area was first named Loxtons Hut, after a boundary rider from the Bookpurnong Station built a primitive pine and pug hut here. Like all towns in the region, Loxton has a strong sense of community and civic pride. There are many landscaped parks and gardens, a modern shopping centre and extensive sporting facilities. The largest war-service settlement scheme in SA was carried out here. **Of interest:** Loxton District Historical Village on riverfront with 28 re-created buildings, including bank, bakery, sheds and railway station, as well as machinery and implements from pioneer days of late 1880s to mid-1900s; open daily except Christmas Day. Nearby, pepper tree planted by Loxton over 110 years ago. River cruises available. Art galleries and craft shops selling local paintings and

Sand dunes, Coorong National Park, near Kingston S.E.

handcrafts. Fisherama held in Jan., Mardi Gras in Feb. and Historical Village Fair, Easter in odd-numbered years. **In the area:** Sample excellent wines at Penfolds Winery, Bookpurnong Road (to Berri) in Loxton North; tastings and sales Mon.–Sat. Nearby, Medea Cottage Fruit Train for herbs and unusual perennials; open daily. Kia Kia Nature Trail, for bushwalkers, in Katarapko Game Reserve, 10 km NW; canoes for hire. Picnics at Habels Bend, 3 km NW, on sandy shores of river. Lock 4 and Moore's Woodlot (60 000 trees watered and fertilised by factory waste), 14 km N. Unique wood sculpture display, SE on Paruna Rd; open daily. **Tourist information:** East Tce; (085) 84 7919. **Accommodation:** 1 hotel/motel, 1 caravan/camping park.
MAP REF. 126 A8, 289 Q6

Lyndoch
Pop. 956

At the southern end of the Barossa Valley and a 40-minute drive from Adelaide, Lyndoch is one of the oldest towns in SA. Early industry was farm-oriented, and four flour mills were known to operate in the area. The nearby Para River was used to operate a water mill in 1853. Vineyards were established early, but the first winery was not set up until 1896. Some 8 wineries in the area are family-owned, and range from very small to one of the largest in the Barossa. **Of interest:** SA Museum of Mechanical Music, Barossa

Valley Hwy; open daily. **In the area:** Wineries: Wards Gateway Cellar, Chateau Yaldara Winery, Charles Cimicky Wines, Burge Family Winemakers, Grant Burge Wines, Orlando Wines, Kies Estate Cellars, Kellermeister Wines, Barossa Settlers. Barossa Reservoir and Whispering Wall, NW of Williamstown, 8 km S. Kersbrook, 22 km S; historic buildings and trout farm. **Tourist information:** Barossa Valley Visitors Centre, 68 Murray St, Tanunda; (008) 81 2662 or (085) 63 0600. **Accommodation:** 1 motel, 1 caravan/camping park.
MAP REF. 283 N5, 286 C8, 287 C1, 289 M7

McLaren Vale
Pop. 1469

Centre of the Wine Coast or Southern Vales winegrowing region, in which about 50 wineries flourish, McLaren Vale is 24 km S of Adelaide. Winemaking really began in 1876 when Thomas Hardy bought Tintara Vineyards; Hardy's Tintara today is the largest winery in the area. **Of interest:** Annual Wine Bushing Festival in late Oct. celebrates release of new vintage, and includes wine tastings and vineyard tours. Historic buildings include Hotel McLaren, Willunga Rd, Congregational Church and Salopian Inn, Willunga Rd. Almond Train, Main Rd; selection of almond products from local production housed in restored railway carriage. **In the area:** Many historic buildings have now been put to use as

tea-rooms, restaurants, wineries and galleries. The wineries are often in bushland settings; most are open for inspection, tastings and cellar-door sales; information and maps at information centres. **Tourist information:** The Cottage, Main Rd; (08) 323 8537. **Accommodation:** 2 motels, 1 caravan/camping park. **See also:** Festival Fun; Vineyards and Wineries.
MAP REF. 283 L10, 284 C6, 287 B3, 289 L9

Maitland   Pop. 1066

Maitland, a modern, well-planned town in the centre of the Yorke Peninsula, is the supply centre for the surrounding rich farmland. Wheat, barley, wool and beef cattle are the main primary industries here. Parks surround the town centre. **Of interest:** Self-guided nature and history trail; information from local District Council, Elizabeth St. St John's Anglican Church (1876), cnr Alice and Caroline Sts; stained-glass windows depicting Biblical stories in Australian settings. Lions Bicycle Adventure Park, off Elizabeth St. Maitland National Trust Museum, in former school, cnr Gardiner and Kilkerran Tces. The Artist's Window, Robert St; local art and craft. **In the area:** Paradean Gardens and teas, 10 km SE; check opening times. **Tourist information:** Yorke Peninsula Tourist Information Centre, Victoria Sq., Kadina; (088) 21 2093. **Accommodation:** 2 hotels.
MAP REF. 282 F3, 288 I6

Mannum   Pop. 2025

Mannum, 82 km E of Adelaide, is one of the oldest towns on the Murray, with a lively past. Picturesque terraced banks overlook the river. Wool, beef and cereals are produced in the region and the town is the starting point for the Adelaide water-supply pipeline. The first paddle-steamer on the Murray, the *Mary Ann*, left Mannum in 1853 and the first steam car was built here in 1894 by David Shearer. **Of interest:** Recreation Reserve, on banks of Murray; picnic spots, barbecue facilities and lookout tower. Also PS *River Murray Princess*. 'Leonaville' (1883), River Lane, built by town's first private developer, Gottlieb Schuetze. At Arnold Park, Randell St, PS *Marion*, built 1898, now National Trust Museum. Twin ferries to eastern side of river and scenic upriver drive alongside river. Mannum River Festival in spring.

Lookout off Purnong Rd to east offers sweeping views of area. **In the area:** Award-winning Choni Leather, 10 km NW on Palmer Rd. Scenic drive along Purnong Rd runs parallel to bird sanctuary for 15 km. Excellent scenic drive from Wongulla to Cambrai, begins 20 km N. Mannum Waterfalls Reserve, 10 km S, for picnics, swimming and scenic walks. Boats and houseboats for hire and river cruises available at weekends during summer. Pleasure cruises, weekends in summer. Water sports at Walker Flat. **Tourist information:** PS *Marion* Museum, Arnold Park, Randell St; (085) 69 1303. **Accommodation:** 1 motel, 2 caravan/camping parks.
MAP REF. 283 P7, 287 E2, 289 N8

Marree   Pop. 85

Marree is a tiny outback town 645 km N of Adelaide at the junction of the infamous Birdsville Track and the rugged road to Oodnadatta, which leads to the Kingoony–Alice Springs road. There are remnants of the old date palms planted by the Afghan traders who drove their camel trains into the outback with supplies in the 1800s. Desolate saltbush country surrounds the town, which is now a small service centre for the vast properties of the north-east of the state, for far northbound travellers. **In the area:** The Frome, 6 km N, a sandy watercourse which floods after heavy rains, surging across the Birdsville Track, often leaving travellers stranded for weeks. Lake Eyre, 90 km N, accessible via Marree and Muloorina Station. Mungeranie Roadhouse, 204 km N of Marree on the Birdsville Track, has fuel, food, accommodation, emergency repairs and a camping area. Oodnadatta Track, southern section (check track conditions with Marree police before departing; read section on Outback Motoring; fuel available only at Marree and William Creek, 210 km NW). Ruins of railway sidings from original Ghan line to Alice Springs at Curdimurka Siding and Bore, about 90 km W; annual Outback Ball held here in Sept. Bubbler Mound Springs and Blanchecup Mound Springs, 6 km S of the Oodnadatta Track, near Coward Springs, 136 km W; at Coward Springs: extensive pond formed by warm water bubbling to the surface; old date palms, remnants of an old plantation. **Accommodation:** 1 hotel. **See also:** The Outback.
MAP REF. 291 J1, 484 B11

Melrose   Pop. 205

Melrose is the oldest town in the Flinders Ranges, a quiet settlement at the foot of Mt Remarkable, 268 km N of Adelaide. **Of interest:** Historical buildings: old police station and court house (1862), Stuart St, now a National Trust Museum; ruins of Jacka's Brewery (former flour mill, 1877), Lambert St; North Star Hotel (1881), Nott St; Mt Remarkable Hotel (1857), Stuart St. Melrose Inn, Nott St; now National Trust property but privately owned. Heritage Walk available. Serendipity Gallery, Stuart St. Pleasant walks and picnic spots along creek. Panoramic views from War Memorial and Lookout Hill, Joe's Rd. Further on, Cathedral Rock. **In the area:** Walking trail (allow 5 hrs return) from town to top of Mt Remarkable (956 m); superb views. Mt Remarkable National Park, 2 km W. Booleroo Steam and Traction Preservation Society's Museum, Booleroo Centre, 15 km E; open by appointment. Near Murray Town, 14 km S: scenic lookouts at Box Hill, Magnus Hill and Baroota Nob; scenic drive west through Germein Gorge. Murraytown sheep property, 3 km SW; visitors welcome. **Tourist information:** Council Offices, Stuart St; (086) 66 2014. **Accommodation:** 1 hotel, 1 caravan/camping park.
MAP REF. 289 K1, 291 J12

Meningie   Pop. 818

Meningie is set on the edge of the freshwater Lake Albert and at the northern tip of the vast saltpans of the Coorong National Park, 159 km from Adelaide. It is a farming area, and over 40 professional fishermen are employed on the lakes and the Coorong; fishing is a significant industry in the town. The area abounds with birdlife such as ibises, pelicans, cormorants, ducks and swans. Sailing, boating, water-skiing and swimming are popular. **In the area:** Camp Coorong, 12 km S; aboriginal museum and cultural centre. The Coorong, stretching south and west, with its inland water, islands, ocean beach and wildlife. Scenic drive west following Lake Albert, adjacent to Lake Alexandrina, the largest permanent freshwater lake in Australia (50 000 ha). The channel between Lakes Alexandrina and Albert is crossed by a free ferry service at Narrung, 39 km NW. Poltalloch Homestead (1876) at Narrung. **Tourist information:** Melaleuca Centre, 76 Princes Hwy; (085) 75 1259. **Accommodation:** 1 hotel,

2 motels, 1 caravan/ camping park. **See also:** The Coorong.
MAP REF. 283 P13, 287 E5, 289 N11

Millicent   Pop. 5118
A thriving commercial and industrial town, Millicent is 50 km from Mt Gambier in the middle of a huge tract of land reclaimed in the 1870s. Today rural and fishing industries contribute to the area's prosperity, with extensive pine forests supporting two paper mills and a sawmill. **Of interest:** On northern edge of town, gum trees surround a fine swimming lake and picnic area. Award-winning National Trust Museum and Admella Gallery, Mt Gambier Rd; housed in original primary school (1873) with several theme rooms, plus farming equipment, 19 horse-drawn carriages and T-Class locomotive. Shell Garden, Williams Rd; unusual display surrounded by fuchsias, ferns and begonias. Radiata Festival Week held in March. **In the area:** Tantanoola, 21 km SE, home of famous Tantanoola Tiger, shot by Tom Donovan in 1890s. The 'tiger' (in reality a Syrian wolf), stuffed and now displayed in a glass cage in the Tantanoola Tiger Hotel. Underground caves within Tantanoola Caves Conservation Park featuring fascinating limestone formations; open daily, wheelchair access. Also at Caves, Trevor Peters' 4-acre garden and restored National Trust cottage; open daily. Scenic drive to Mount Burr, 10 km NE through magnificent pine forests. National Trust Woolshed (1863) at Glencoe, 29 km SE; tours available. Massive sand dune system within Canunda National Park; accessed at Southend, 27 km W, leaflet for self-guided walk available. **Tourist information:** Admella Gallery, 1 Mt Gambier Rd; (087) 33 3205. **Accommodation:** 1 hotel/motel, 2 motels, 2 caravan/camping parks.
MAP REF. 287 G12

Minlaton   Pop. 796
Minlaton is a prosperous town serving the nearby coastal resorts of Yorke Peninsula. The town, 209 km W of Adelaide, was originally called Gum Flat because of the giant eucalypts in the area. Pioneer aviator Harry Butler, pilot of the *Red Devil*, a 1916 Bristol monoplane, was born here. The plane is displayed at the Harry Butler Museum in Main St. **Of interest:** Fauna park, Main St; adjacent to Harry Butler Memorial. National Trust Museum, Main St. Jolly's Vintage Tractor and Engine Collection, Main St, open daily. **In the area:** Ostrich farm at Curramulka, 15 km NE. Gum Flat Homestead Gallery, 1 km E; pioneer homestead with local artists' work. At Port Vincent, 25 km E: swimming, yachting and waterskiing; annual yacht race in Jan.; Grainstore Galleries and Doll Museum. Short drive, 16 km NW, to Port Rickaby and Bluff Beach, a unique bay with abundant birdlife. Farm holidays and horsedrawn wagon holidays at Brentwood, 14 km SW. **Tourist information:** Council Offices, Main St; (088) 53 2102. **Accommodation:** 1 hotel/motel, 1 caravan/camping park.
MAP REF. 282 F7, 288 I7

Mintaro   Pop. 80
The township nestles among rolling hills and rich pastoral land, 15 km E of Clare. Classified as a Heritage Town, Mintaro is a timepiece of early colonial architecture. Many of the buildings display the fine slate for which the district is world-renowned; the quarry opened in 1854. **Of interest:** Early colonial buildings, inc. 18 Heritage listings, and 2 historic cemeteries. **In the area:** Magnificent classic architecture of Martindale Hall (1880), 3 km SE; location for film *Picnic at Hanging Rock*; tours, 10–4 daily; overnight accommodation and dining available. Self-contained accommodation at a number of historic cottages. **Accommodation:** 1 hotel
MAP REF. 289 L4

Moonta   Pop. 2723
The towns of Moonta, Kadina and Wallaroo form the corners of the area known as the 'Copper Triangle' or 'Little Cornwall'.

The Marree Hotel

Moonta is a popular seaside resort 163 km NW of Adelaide, with pleasant beaches and good fishing at Moonta Bay. A rich copper-ore deposit was discovered here in 1861 and soon thousands of miners, including many from Cornwall, flocked to the area. The mines were abandoned in the 1920s with the slump in copper prices and rising labour costs. The Poona mine now operates at Moonta, bringing life back to the mines area. **Of interest:** The town has many stone buildings, a charming city square (Queen Square) and a picturesque town hall, opposite the Square in George St. All Saints Church (1873), cnr Blanche and Milne Tces. Galleries include the Pug 'n' Dabble, Robert St. The 'Kernewek Lowender', a Cornish festival, is held, in conjunction with Kadina and Wallaroo, in May every odd-numbered year. **In the area:** Moonta Mines State Heritage Area, Arthurton Rd, about 2 km SE; booklet available. Highlights include Moonta Mines National Trust Museum (old primary school); typical Cornish miner's cottage (1870) furnished in period style; and pump house, various shafts and tailings heaps and mines offices. On weekends, public and school holidays, Moonta Mines Railway takes visitors from old railway station, Blanche Tce, through mines area. **Tourist information:** Town Hall, George St; (088) 25 2622. **Accommodation:** 2 hotels, 1 motel, 2 caravan/camping parks. **See also:** Festival Fun; The Yorke Peninsula. MAP REF. 282 F1, 288 I5

Morgan   Pop. 446

Once one of the busiest river ports in SA, Morgan is a quiet little township 164 km NE of Adelaide. **Of interest:** Self-guided Heritage Trail leaflets cover all historical sites, including the impressive wharves (1877), standing 12.2 m high, constructed for the riverboat industry. Customs house and courthouse near railway station, reminders of town's thriving past. Picnic/barbecue facilities, with children's play area, near customs house. Port of Morgan Historic Museum in old railway buildings on riverfront, off High St. PS *Mayflower* (1884), still operating; enquiries to Museum's caretaker. Nor-West Bend private museum, Renmark Rd; open by appointment. Houseboats for hire. **In the area:** Fossicking for fossils near township. Morgan Conservation Park, across river. White Dam Conservation Park, 9 km NW. **Tourist information:** Morgan Roadhouse, Fourth St; (085) 40 2205, and Council Offices Fourth St; (085) 40 2013. **Accommodation:** 1 hotel, 1 hotel/motel, 1 motel, 1 caravan/camping park. MAP REF. 283 R1, 289 O5

Mount Gambier   Pop. 21 153

Lieutenant James Grant, in 1800, sighted and named Mount Gambier, an extinct volcano. Mount Gambier township is built on its slopes in the centre of the largest pine plantations in Australia. Surrounded by rich farming and dairy country, the town is 460 km from Adelaide on the Princes Hwy. The Hentys built the first dwelling in the area in 1841 and by 1850 a weekly postal service to Adelaide was operating. The local white Mount Gambier stone used in most of the buildings, together with many fine parks and gardens, make it an attractive city. **Of interest:** Historic buildings include town hall (1862) and post office (1865), in Bay Rd, and many old hotels; Heritage Walk leaflet from Tourist Information Centre. Open caves at Cave Gardens, Bay Rd, adjacent to town hall, and Umpherston Cave, Jubilee Hwy East. Engelbrecht Cave, Jubilee Hwy, water-filled cave or sinkhole. Old Court house Law and Heritage Centre, Bay Rd, National Trust museum; open daily. Lewis' Museum, Pick Ave; open daily. Lady Nelson Tourist and Interpretive Centre, Jubilee Hwy East; full-scale replica of *Lady Nelson* forms part of Centre's structure. Dimjalla Park, Jubilee Hwy East; fun park, barbecue areas. Riddoch Art Gallery, Commercial St East; housed within complex of 19th century buildings. Yoey's Cheese and Gourmet Shop, Commercial St West; local and imported cheeses. Blue Lake Festival, held 10 days in Nov. **In the area:** Mount Gambier's four crater lakes, particularly Blue Lake (197 m at its deepest), which changes from dull grey to brilliant blue each Nov. and then reverts at end of summer; scenic 5 km drive offers several lookouts. Pumping Station, providing town's water supply; inspections daily. Tours of CSR Softwoods; inspection of treatment process, including pines being felled, trimmed and cut ready for loading; contact Tourist Centre for details. Haig's Vineyard, 4 km S. Mount Schank, 12 km S; views of surrounding district. Animal and Reptile Park, 10 km N, off Penola Rd, animal nursery, native gardens, train carriage. Tarpeena Fairy Tale Park, 22 km N on Penola Rd. Glencoe Woolshed (1863), National Trust building, 23 km NW; open Sun. afternoons or by appointment. Chant's Place flora and fauna park at Kongorong, 25 km SW. Glenelg River cruises from Victorian town of Nelson, 36 km SE; tours of spectacular Princess Margaret Rose Caves. **Tourist information:** Jubilee Hwy East; (087) 24 1730. Accommodation: 3 hotels, 1 hotel/motel, 18 motels, 6 caravan/camping parks. MAP REF. 226 A5, 287 I13

Murray Bridge   Pop. 12 725

Murray Bridge is SA's largest river town. Only 80 km from Adelaide, a modern freeway links the two cities. First settled in the 1850s, the town overlooks a broad sweep of the Murray and still retains some of the feeling of the time when it was a centre for the bustling riverboat traders. Water sports, river cruises and excellent accommodation make Murray Bridge a perfect holiday spot. **Of interest:** Captain's Cottage Museum, Thomas St. Butterfly House, Jervois Rd. Puzzle Park, also in Jervois Rd, a funpark for adults as well as children. Rock Rose Farm, Doyle Rd; herb garden and small animals. Cottage Box chocolate factory, Wharf Rd; open daily. Sturt Reserve, on banks of the river; fishing and swimming, and excellent picnic and playground facilities. Big River Challenge Festival each Nov. incorporates speedboat racing, water-skiing events and land-based sporting challenges. **In the area:** Charter and regular cruises on MV *Barrangul* and MV *Zane Grey*; houseboats for hire. Cruises lasting 2, 3 or 5 days on PS *Proud Mary* and PS *River Queen*. Avoca Dell, 5 km upstream, for boating, water-skiing and mini-golf; picnic facilities. Thiele Reserve, east of river, popular for water-skiing. Other riverside reserves include Hume, Long Island, Swanport and White Sands. Mypolonga, 14 km N, centre of beautiful citrus and stone-fruit orchards and rich dairying country. Earthworks Pottery, 9 km NE, on Karoonda Rd. Willow Glen Wines, 10 km S on Jervois Rd. Monarto Zoological Park, 10 km W off old Princes Hwy; open range zoo with many endangered species; open Sun. Riverglen Marina, 11 km S; houseboats and mooring. Several lookouts, including White Hill, west on Princes Hwy, and east at new Swanport Bridge. **Tourist information:** Community Information and Tourist Centre, South Tce; (085) 32 6660. **Accommodation:** 2 hotels, 4

The Coorong

The Coorong National Park curves along the southern coast of South Australia for 145 kilometres, extending from Lake Alexandrina in the north almost to the small township of Kingston S.E. in the south. A unique area, it has an eerie desolation, a silence broken only by the sounds of any of the 400 species of native birds wheeling low over the scrub and dunes and the thunder of the Southern Ocean.

The Coorong proper is a shallow lagoon, a complex of low-lying saltpans and claypans. Never more than 3 kilometres wide, the lagoon is divided from the sea by the towering white sandhills of Younghusband Peninsula, known locally as the Hummocks.

One of the last natural bird sanctuaries in Australia, the Coorong is home for giant pelicans, shags, ibises, swans and terns. During the summer, access is gained by turning off at **Salt Creek**, leaving the Princes Highway, and following the old road along the shore. The coastal scenery is magnificent. Explore the unspoiled stretches of beach where the rolling surf washes up gnarled driftwood and beautiful shells. Year-round access is from a point further south known as the '42 mile'; the final 1.5 kilometres is suitable for 4WD or walking.

For those who wish to explore in comfort, **Meningie** in the north and the fishing port of **Kingston S.E.** have a range of accommodation and can be used as touring bases. Camping is permitted in the Coorong National Park; however, in the Younghusband Peninsula section it is allowed in designated areas only. Permits must be obtained from the NPWS (see below).

The area is rich in history as well as being a naturalists' haven; pick up the Coorong Tourist Brochure for details. An interpretive programme is available during Easter and summer school holidays. Fishing, boating and walking are popular.

For further information, contact the National Parks and Wildlife Service Office, Salt Creek; (085) 75 7014. **See also:** Entries for Kingston S.E. and Meningie in A–Z listing.

The Fleurieu Peninsula

Starting 22 kilometres south of Adelaide, the Fleurieu Peninsula region stretches from O'-Halloran Hill for about 90 km to Cape Jervis on the west coast, and east around the vast fresh waters of Lake Alexandrina, where the Murray River meets the sea.

The ocean scenery varies from magnificent cliff faces and roaring surf to wide, sandy beaches and sheltered bays and coves. Maslin Beach is renowned as Australia's first nude bathing beach. Cape Jervis, at the tip of the Peninsula, commands a spectacular view across Backstairs Passage.

McLaren Vale is the centre of the Wine Coast or Southern Vales wine-producing district. With over 50 wineries, many in historic buildings and with attached restaurants, this is certainly an area in which to linger.

Victor Harbor is one of South Australia's most popular beach resorts. Either walk or take the old horse tram along the causeway to Granite Island to see the colony of fairy penguins. On the way to **Goolwa**, spend time in **Port Elliot** to take in its history and perhaps take a ride to Goolwa on the Cockle Train, a steam train restored from the original line opened in 1854; for operating times enquire at Tourist Information Centre.

There is superb fishing at Goolwa, once a busy port but now the starting point for leisurely paddle-steamer cruises up the Murray, and cruises to Hindmarsh Island and the Barrages.

For further information on the area, contact the Victor Harbor Tourist Information Centre, Torrens St, Victor Harbor; (085) 52 4255. **See also:** Individual entries in A–Z listing. **Note** detailed map of Southern Vales on page 284.

Yankalilla Bay on the Fleurieu Peninsula

Struan House, Naracoorte

motels, 5 caravan/camping parks.
MAP REF. 283 P9, 287 D3, 289 N9

Naracoorte   Pop. 4711

Situated 390 km SE of Adelaide, Naracoorte was first settled in the 1840s. The area is world-renowned for its limestone caves. Beef cattle, sheep and wheat are the local primary industries. **Of interest:** Sheep's Back Wool Museum, housed in former flour mill (1860), MacDonnell St; incorporates National Trust Museum, Art Gallery and Tourist Information Centre. Naracoorte Museum, Jenkins Tce, houses 100 collections, including coins, candles, gemstones and antiques. Regional Art Gallery, Smith St. Mini Jumbuk Factory, Smith St; woollen products. Restored locomotive on display in Pioneer Park. Jubilee Park and Swimming Lake, off Park Tce; 28 ha shaded by gums and surrounded by lawns. For anglers, trout and redfin abound in local streams and creeks. **In the area:** Tiny Train Park, 3 km S; trains, mini-golf. Naracoorte Caves, 12 km SE, in Conservation Park; Victoria Fossil Cave is of world significance, containing unique fossilised specimens of Ice Age animals, while Blanche Cave and Alexandra Cave have spectacular stalagmites and stalactites; guided tours daily, and beginners' and advanced adventure tours (bookings required). Bool Lagoon Game Reserve 17 km S, sanctuary for ibises and a wide variety of waterbirds; guided boardwalks and bird hide. Coonawarra wine region, 40 km S, and Padthaway and Keppoch wine districts, about same distance north-west. St Aubins host farm, 40

km N; Wongary host farm, 25 km S. **Tourist information:** MacDonnell St; (087) 62 1518. **Accommodation:** 2 hotels, 1 hotel/motel, 4 motels, 2 caravan/camping parks. **See also:** National Parks.
MAP REF. 228 A11, 287 H9

Nuriootpa   Pop. 3321

The Para River runs through the town of Nuriootpa, its course marked by fine parks and picnic spots, including Coulthard Reserve off Penrice Rd. The town is the commercial centre of the Barossa Valley. **Of interest:** Coulthard House, pioneer settler's home, now Barossa Information Centre. St Petri Church, First St. The Pheasant Farm, award-winning restaurant, Samuel St. **In the area:** Wineries, including Elderton, Kaesler, Penfolds, Stockwell Wines and Wolf Blass; sales and tastings, and vineyard tours. Also Tarac Distillers. Day tours of Barossa Valley available. **Tourist information:** Barossa Valley Visitors Centre, 68 Murray St, Tanunda; (008) 81 2662 or (085) 63 0600. **Accommodation:** 1 hotel, 1 motel, 1 caravan/camping park. **See also:** Vineyards and Wineries.
MAP REF. 283 N4, 286 G3, 289 M6

Old Noarlunga   Pop. 2000

A small village in the Southern Vales winegrowing region, Old Noarlunga is situated 32 km S of Adelaide on the Fleurieu Peninsula. **Of interest:** The Horseshoe Mill (1844); Church of St Philip and St James (1850), Church Hill Rd; Uniting Church, Malpas St; old Jolly Miller Hotel (1850), now Noarlunga Hotel, Patapinda

Rd; and Market Square, where first public market was held in 1841. **In the area:** Port Noarlunga and Christies Beach, 10 km NW, and Moana and Maslin Beaches, 3 km and 6 km S, all offer good swimming and fishing. About 8 km north of Port Noarlunga, Hallett Cove has tracks left by glaciers hundreds of millions of years ago. Lakeside Leisure Park at Hackham, 4 km N. At McLaren Vale, 5 km S, some 50 vineyards and wineries. At Myponga, 27 km S, Myponga Reservoir, for barbecues or picnics; several historic buildings. **Tourist information:** Noarlunga Hotel, Patapinda Rd; (08) 386 2061. **Accommodation:** 1 hotel, 1 motel, 1 caravan/camping park.
MAP REF. 283 K9

Oodnadatta   Pop. 180

A tiny but famous outback town 1050 km NW of Adelaide, Oodnadatta is an old railway town with a well-preserved sandstone station (1890), now a museum. It is thought the name Oodnadatta originated from an Aboriginal term meaning 'yellow blossom of the mulga'. Petrol and supplies available. **In the area:** Witjira National Park, gateway to Simpson Desert, 120 km N; free hot thermal ponds in Dalhousie Mound Springs. Camping and accommodation at Mt Dare Homestead, within park, or at Springs. The Oodnadatta Track runs from Marree to Oodnadatta and continues to join Stuart Hwy at Marla, 200 km W. Painted Desert, 100 km SW; scenic drive. **Tourist information:** Pink Roadhouse, Ikatura Tce; (086) 70 7822. **Accommodation:** 1 hotel, 1 caravan/camping park.
MAP REF. 292 B7

Paringa   Pop. 588

Paringa, 4 km from Renmark, is the eastern gateway to the Riverland region. **Of interest:** Paringa Suspension Bridge (1927). Bert Dix Memorial Park, adjacent to Paringa Bridge. Houseboat marina, Lock 5 Rd; houseboats for hire. Billy Boiling Championships and Bush Picnic held in Aug. **In the area:** Headings Cliff lookout tower, 12 km N on Murtho Rd; fine views of surrounding irrigated farmland and river cliffs. Murtho Forest Park; picnic and camping facilities. E & WS Lock 5 and Weir, Lock 5 Rd. Also on Lock 5 Rd, Margaret Dowling National Trust Park, area of natural bushland. The Black Stump, root system of river red gum estimated to be 500–600 years old; found on Murtho Rd.

Dunlop Big Tyre (14 m high, 26 m wide) spans Sturt Hwy at Yamba, 12 km SE; also fruit fly depot. Scenic drive, 36 km E into Victoria, to see delicate blossoms at Lindsay Point Almond Park in early spring. **Tourist information:** Council Offices, Murtho Rd; (085) 85 5102. **Accommodation:** 1 hotel/motel, 1 caravan/camping park.
126 A7, 230 A4, 289 R5

Penola   Pop. 1147

Penola, 52 km N of Mount Gambier, is the oldest town in the south-east of SA, and contains fine examples of slab and hewn-timber cottages, erected in the 1850s and maintained and restored. Many famous names are associated with Penola. Poets Adam Lindsay Gordon, John Shaw Neilson and Will Ogilvie all spent time here. The first school in Australia catering for all children regardless of income or social class was established here in 1866 by Mother Mary McKillop, who has recently been beatified. The stone classroom in which she taught is on the corner of Portland St and Petticoat Lane. **Of interest:** John Riddoch Interpretive Centre, Arthur St, housed in former Mechanics Institute; audiovisual, poetry recitals. In Petticoat Lane, heritage buildings and arts and crafts. Self-guided Heritage walk; details from Tourist Information Centre. **In the area:** Yallum Park Homestead (1880), 8 km W, historic two-storeyed Victorian homestead built by John Riddoch, founder of Coonawarra wine industry. Penola Conservation Park, 10 km W; picnic areas and signposted interpretive walk. The Coonawarra vineyards, 10 km N, produce magnificent table wines from 15 wineries; most open for tastings and cellar-door sales. **Tourist information:** Arthur St; (087) 37 2855. **Accommodation:** 2 hotels, 1 hotel/motel, 1 caravan/camping park.
MAP REF. 226 A3, 287 I11

Peterborough   Pop. 2138

Peterborough is a railway town 250 km N of Adelaide, surrounded by grain-growing and pastoral country. It is the principal town on the important Port Pirie to Broken Hill railway line. **Of interest:** The Steamtown Peterborough Railway Preservation Society runs limited historic narrow-gauge steam train journeys from town to Orroroo or Eurelia on holiday weekends during winter. Rann's Museum, Queen St; exhibits of historic

railway equipment and farm implements. The RoundHouse Exchange, housing unique railway turntable and other railway equipment; tours available. The Gold Battery, end Tripney Ave, an ore-crushing machine; open by appointment. Saint Cecilia, Callary St, a gracious home (with some splendid stained glass) built originally as a bishop's residence; accommodation, dining and murder mystery nights. Art gallery, Main St, adjacent to Tourist Information Centre. Victoria Park, Grove St; picnic facilities and children's playground. **In the area:** Terowie, 24 km SE; old railway town with many historic buildings. At Orroroo, 37 km NW: historic buildings and Yesteryear Costume Gallery with display of fashion from 1850; nearby, scenic walk among Aboriginal carvings along Pekina Ck; panoramic views from Black Rock Peak, east. At Magnetic Hill, 8 km W of Black Rock, a vehicle with the engine turned off rolls uphill! **Tourist information:** Main St; (086) 51 2708. **Accommodation:** 3 hotels, 1 hotel/motel, 1 motel, 1 caravan/camping park.
MAP REF. 289 L1, 291 L13

Pinnaroo   Pop. 645

This little township on the Mallee Hwy is 6 km from the Victorian border. **Of interest:** Australia's largest cereal collection (1300 varieties), Pinnaroo Institute, Railway Tce Sth. Historical Museum in railway station, Railway Tce Sth. Working printing museum, South Tce; animal park and aviary with parrots and other native birds. Farm-machinery museum at showgrounds, Homburg Tce. **In the area:** Walking Trail in Karte Conservation Park, 30 km NW, on Karte Rd. Gum Family Collection, 25 km N at Kombali; stationary engine museum. Peebinga Conservation Park, 42 km N, on Loxton Rd. Scorpion Springs Conservation Park, 28 km S; walking trail at Pine Hut Soak. Ngarkat Conservation Park, 48 km S. Pertendi Walking Trail, 49 km S. **Tourist information:** Council Offices; (085) 77 8002. **Accommodation:** 2 hotels, 1 motel, 1 caravan/camping park.
MAP REF. 126 A11, 230 A11, 287 I3, 289 R9

Port Augusta   Pop. 14 595

Port Augusta, a thriving industrial city at the head of Spencer Gulf and in the shadow of the Flinders Ranges, is the most northerly port in SA. It is 317 km from Adelaide and is a vital supply centre for

the outback areas of the State and the large sheep stations of the district. Port Augusta is an important link on the Indian-Pacific railway and the famous *Ghan* train to Alice Springs, which departs from Adelaide. The city has played an intrinsic role in SA's development since the State Electricity Trust built a series of major power stations here. Fuelled by coal from the huge open-cut mines at Leigh Creek, the stations generate more than one-third of the state's electricity. **Of interest:** Wadlata Outback Centre, Flinders Tce, for introduction to the sights and sounds of the outback. Homestead Park Pioneer Museum, Elsie St has a large photographic collection, pleasant picnic areas, blacksmith's shop, old steam train and crane, as well as rebuilt 130-year-old pine-log Yudnappinna Homestead. Royal Flying Doctor Service Base, Vincent St; open weekdays. School of the Air, southern end of Commercial Rd; tours available during term time. Curdnatta Art and Pottery Gallery in town's first railway station, Commercial Rd. Self-guided Heritage Walks (2 hr) include town hall (1887), Commercial Rd, courthouse (1884) cnr Jervios St and Beauchamp's Lane, with cells built of Kapunda marble, and St Augustine's Church (1882), Church St, with magnificent stained glass. McLellan Lookout, Whiting Pde, site of Matthew Flinders landing in 1802; panoramic views, picnic facilities in adjacent park. Red Cliffs lookout, end of McSporran Cres.; excellent view of Gulf and Flinders Ranges; adjacent area is site for Australian Arid Lands Botanic Gardens. Australian National Railway Workshops, Carlton Pde; guided tours on Tues. **In the area:** Conducted tours of Northern power station, 4 km E, weekdays. Scenic drive 23 km NE to splendid Pichi Richi Pass, where Railways Preservation Society runs old steam engines during school holidays, to the historic town of Quorn, 39 km NE, and to Warren and Buckaringa Gorges, 21 km and 37 km further north, respectively. Winninowie Conservation Park, 30 km SE. Hancocks Lookout, 38 km SE towards Wilmington, offers views of surrounding country, Port Augusta and Whyalla; turnoff road dangerous when wet. Mt Remarkable National Park, 63 km SE, has rugged mountain terrain, magnificent gorges and abundant wildlife. Historic Melrose, 65 km SE, is the oldest town in Flinders Ranges. **Tourist information:** Wadlata Outback Centre, Flinders Tce;

(086) 41 0793. **Accommodation:** 6 hotels, 9 motels, 3 caravan/camping parks. MAP REF. 285 A12, 290 I11

Port Broughton   Pop. 681

A small port on the extreme north-west coast of the Yorke Peninsula, Port Broughton is 169 km from Adelaide. On a protected inlet of the sea, the town is a major port for fishing boats and is renowned for its deep-sea prawns. **Of interest:** Safe swimming beach along foreshore. Charter boats and dinghies. Historical Museum, Bay St (previously old council chambers) and Cottage Museum, Kadina Rd, contain much of town's history. Historic walking trail. Shandelé porcelain dolls made and displayed, Harvey St. **In the area:** Fisherman's Bay, 10 km N; popular fishing, boating and holiday spot. Heritage copper-mining towns of Moonta, Wallaroo and Kadina, 47 km S. Clare Valley and surrounding wine districts 100 km E. **Tourist information:** Yorke Peninsula Tourist Information Centre, Victoria Sq., Kadina; (088) 21 2093. **Accommodation:** 1 hotel, 1 hotel/motel, 2 caravan/camping parks. MAP REF. 289 J3

Port Elliot   Pop. 1203

Only 5 km NE of Victor Harbor, Port Elliot is a charming, historical coastal town with the main focus these days on scenic Horseshoe Bay, the town's beach. The town was established in 1854, the same year Australia's first public iron railway operated between Goolwa and Port Elliot. **Of interest:** Along The Strand: National Trust historical display within Port Elliot railway station (1911), council chamber (1879), police station (1853) and St Jude's Church (1854); guided walks available, (085) 54 2024. Spectacular views from Freeman's Knob, end of The Strand. Port Elliot Art Pottery, Main Rd. **In the area:** Middleton Winery, 11 km NE via Middleton. **Tourist information:** Old Library Bldg, cnr Cadell St and Goolwa Tce, Goolwa; (085) 55 1144. **Accommodation:** 2 hotels, 1 motel, 1 caravan/camping park. MAP REF. 283 L12, 284 E12, 287 C4, 289 L10

Port Lincoln   Pop. 11 345

Port Lincoln is attractively sited on the clear waters of Boston Bay, which is three times the size of Sydney Harbour.

The port, 250 km due west of Adelaide across St Vincent and Spencer Gulfs, was discovered by Matthew Flinders in 1802 and settled in 1839. It was originally chosen as the State's capital. With its sheltered waters, Mediterranean climate, scenic coastal roads and attractive farming hinterland, Port Lincoln is becoming an increasingly popular tourist resort. It is the base for Australia's largest tuna fleet and is also an important export centre for wheat, wool, fat lambs and live sheep, frozen fish, lobster, prawns and abalone. The coastline is deeply indented, offering magnificent scenery: sheltered coves, steep cliff faces and impressive surf beaches. The Tunarama Festival, held every Australia Day weekend, celebrates the opening of the tuna season. **Of interest:** Boston Bay; swimming, water-skiing, yachting and excellent fishing. Mill Cottage Museum (1867) and Settler's Cottage Museum; both in picturesque Flinders Park. Old Mill lookout, Dorset Place; views of town and bay. Lincoln Hotel (1840), Tasman Tce, oldest hotel on Eyre Peninsula. Axel Stenross Maritime Museum, north end of town; First Landing site nearby. Rose–Wal Memorial Shell Museum in grounds of Eyre Peninsula Old Folks Home. Arteyrea Gallery, Washington St; community art centre. Barbed Wire and Fencing Equipment Museum; open by appointment only, (086) 82 1162. M.B. Kotz Collection of Stationary Engines, Baltimore St. Lincoln Cove, off St Andrews Tce, with marina and holiday charter boats. *Dangerous Reef Explorer* ferries visitors to reef, home for large sea lion colony, and a commercial tuna farm. Apex Wheelhouse, original wheelhouse from tuna boat *Boston Bay,* adjacent to Kirton Point Caravan Park, Hindmarsh St. **In the area:** Skippered boat charter available for game fishing, diving, day fishing and island cruises. Yacht charters available. Regular launch cruises of Boston Bay and Boston Island. Several pleasant parks close to town and vast natural reserves abounding in wildlife, no more than a day's outing away. Winter Hill Lookout, 5 km NW on Flinders Hwy. Greenpatch Farm, 15 km NW; native animals, bird-feeding, open Wed.–Sun. At Koppio, 38 km NW: Koppio Smith Museum; Kurrabi Lodge, local crafts; Tod Reservoir; museum with heritage display and picnic area. Coffin Bay, 49 km NW; lookout, Coffin Bay Oyster Farm for fresh oysters and other seafood, also

Oyster Trail, boat hire, and nearby Coffin Bay National Park. Boston Bay Wines, 6 km N on Lincoln Hwy; cellar-door sales on weekends or by appointment, (086) 84 3600. Tiny Tots Gnome Village, Lincoln Hwy. Karlinda Collection, adjacent to post office at North Shields, 16 km N; shells, marine life and Deepwater Trawl Fish Exhibit. At Poonindie, 20 km N, an intriguing church (1850) with two chimneys. Award-winning Quandong Farm, 45 km N; orchids, quandong seedlings and trees. Tumby Bay, 48 km N, a small beach resort. Lincoln National Park, 20 km S, offers wildlife and cliff-top walk to view impressive coastal scenery, permit required. Southernmost tip of Eyre Peninsula, known as Whalers Way, offers stunning coastal scenery; permit required, available from tourism outlets. On road to Whalers Way: Constantia Designer Craftsmen, world class furniture factory and showroom (guided tours available); historic Mikkira sheep station, open winter. Offshore islands for boating enthusiasts: Boston and Thistle Islands offer accommodation for 'getaway' holidays; Thistle and Wedge Islands (both privately owned), popular with bluewater sailors and fishermen. **Tourist information:** Eyre Travel, Civic Centre, Tasman Tce; (086) 82 4577. **Accommodation:** 5 hotels, 7 motels, 2 caravan/camping parks. **See also:** Festival Fun; The Eyre Peninsula. MAP REF. 288 D7

Port MacDonnell   Pop. 677

Port MacDonnell was once a thriving port. Today it is a quiet, well-planned fishing town, 28 km S of Mount Gambier. The rock-lobster fishing fleet here is the largest in SA. **Of interest:** Old Customs House (1860) with National Trust classification. Maritime Museum, Meylin St; salvaged artefacts from shipwrecks, plus photographic history of town. **In the area:** 'Dingley Dell' (1862, but restored), home of poet Adam Lindsay Gordon, now a museum, 2 km W. Cape Northumberland Lighthouse, on dramatically beautiful coastline west of town. Devonshire teas at Ye Olde Post Office Tea Rooms at Allendale East, 6 km N. For keen walkers, track to summit of Mt Schank, 10 km N; crater of extinct volcano, with picnic facilities. Mt Schank Fish Farm, for fresh fish, yabbies. Heading east, surf fishing at Orwell Rocks. Sinkholes for experienced cave divers at Ewens Ponds and Picaninnie

The Outback

Motorists contemplating travel in the outback should prepare their vehicles well and familiarise themselves with expected conditions before setting out.

The outback of South Australia covers almost 60 million hectares and is one of the most remote areas of the world; conditions are harsh, the climate extreme and distances are daunting.

The countryside is usually dry, barren and dusty, but freak rains and heavy floods can transform the land. Dry creek beds and water holes fill, wildflowers bloom and birdlife flocks to the area. The enormous salt **Lake Eyre** has been filled rarely since Europeans first saw the desert.

The main road to the Northern Territory, the Stuart Highway, is a sealed all-weather road. From **Port Augusta** to **Alice Springs** the road covers a distance of 1243 kilometres. Turn off the highway to visit **Woomera**, the new mining town of **Roxby Downs**, the opal-mining town of **Andamooka**, and **Tarcoola**.

Petrol, food and supplies are available at Port Augusta, **Pimba**, **Glendambo**, **Coober Pedy**, **Cadney Park Roadhouse**, **Marla**, and **Kulgera** just over the Northern Territory border.

The notorious Birdsville Track starts at **Marree**, once a supply outpost for Afghan camel traders, and follows the route originally used to drove cattle from south-west Queensland to the railhead at Marree. The track skirts the fringes of the Simpson Desert, with its giant sand dunes, and the desolate Sturt's Stony Desert. Artesian bores line the route, pouring out 64 million litres of salty boiling water every day. The road is fair; however, sometimes it is washed out by torrential rains and travellers can be left stranded for weeks. Sandstorms are another problem. Petrol and supplies are available at Marree and **Mungeranie**, and at **Birdsville** over the Queensland border.

The Strzelecki Track begins at **Lyndhurst**; a harsh, dusty road, it stretches 494 kilometres to the almost deserted outpost of **Innamincka**, with no stops for petrol or supplies.

Only experienced and well-equipped outback motorists should consider driving along the Birdsville and Strzelecki Tracks.

For further information on the area, contact Flinders Ranges and Outback of South Australia Regional Tourism, PO Box 666, Adelaide 5001, (08) 303 2346. **See also:** Individual entries in A–Z listing.

Remote outback scene

Ponds Conservation Parks, 7 km and 20 km E. **Tourist information:** Council Offices, Meylin St; (087) 38 2207. **Accommodation:** 1 hotel, 1 motel, 2 caravan/camping parks.
MAP REF. 287 H13

Port Pirie   Pop. 14 110

Huge grain silos and smelters' chimneys dominate the skyline of Port Pirie, 227 km N of Adelaide on Spencer Gulf. Situated on the tidal Port Pirie River, the city is a major industrial and commercial centre. The first settlers came in 1845; wheat farms and market gardens were established around the sheep industry in the region. Broken Hill Associated Smelters began smelting lead in 1889 and today the largest lead smelters in the world treat thousands of tonnes of concentrates annually from the silver, lead and zinc deposits at Broken Hill, NSW. Wheat and barley from the mid-north of the State are exported and there is a thriving fishing industry. Port Pirie is also a vital link in the road and rail routes to Alice Springs, Darwin, Port Augusta and Perth. Wheat farms, rolling hills and the ocean are all close by. Swimming, water-skiing, fishing and yachting are popular summer sports on the river. **Of interest:** Regional Art Gallery at Tourism and Arts Centre, Mary Elie St; local and touring exhibitions. National Trust Museum Buildings, Ellen St, include old Victorian pavilion-style railway station; open daily. Historic residence 'Carn Brae',

Florence St, antique exhibits and a collection of over 2500 dolls; open daily. The waterfront; loading and discharging of Australian and overseas vessels. Tours of Pasminco Metals BHAS smelting works; details from Tourism Centre. Northern Festival Centre in Memorial Park, Gertrude St, cultural heart of the State's north and venue for local and national performances. Port Pirie Festival of Country Music held in Oct. Blessing of the Fleet and associated festivals, early Sept.; reminder of role of Italians at turn of century in establishing fishing industry. **In the area:** Weeroona Island, 13 km N. Port Germein, beach resort 24 km N; wooden jetty said to be longest in southern hemisphere. Southern reaches of beautiful Flinders Ranges are within 50 km; further east, ruggedly beautiful Telowie Gorge, lined with giant red river gums. **Tourist information:** Tourism and Arts Centre, Mary Elie St; (086) 33 0439. **Accommodation:** 2 hotels, 1 hotel/motel, 4 motels, 3 caravan/camping parks.
MAP REF. 289 J2

Port Victoria   Pop. 313

A tiny township on the west coast of the Yorke Peninsula, Port Victoria was once the main port for sailing ships carrying grain from the area; the last windjammer sailed from here in 1949. **Of interest:** Port Victoria Geology trail; booklet available. Swimming and jetty fishing, from original 1888 jetty, end of Main St.

National Trust Maritime Museum on jetty; check opening times. Wardang Island, Aboriginal reserve, 10 km off coast, can be visited with permission from Point Pearce Community Council. **In the area:** Conservation Islands are breeding grounds for several bird species. New underwater Heritage Trail in waters around Wardang Island, for scuba divers visits to 8 wrecks; self-guiding leaflet available. **Tourist information:** Yorke Peninsula Tourist Information Centre, Victoria Sq., Kadina; (088) 21 2093. **Accommodation:** 1 hotel/motel, 2 caravan parks. **See also:** The Yorke Peninsula.
MAP REF. 282 E4, 288 I7

Quorn   Pop. 1056

Nestled in a valley in the Flinders Ranges, 331 km N of Adelaide, Quorn was established as a railway town in 1878. Part of the Great Northern Railway, the line was built by Chinese and British workmen. Closed in 1957, part of the line through Pichi Richi has been restored; a steam locomotive operates Mar.–Nov., taking passengers on the 33-km round trip. **Of interest:** Many historic buildings; Historic Walk leaflet available. Quorn Mill (1878), Railway Tce; once a flour mill, now art gallery, museum, motel and restaurant. Quornucopia Galley, Railway Tce. Nairana Craft Centre, First St. **In the area:** Colourful rocky outcrops of Dutchman's Stern, 6 km N. Junction Gallery, 16 km N on Yarrah Vale Rd. Warren Gorge, 22 km N,

Steam locomotive, Quorn

popular with climbing enthusiasts; Buckaringa Gorge, 32 km N, scenic picnic areas. Kanyaka Homestead 42 km N, ruins of sheep station that supported 70 families from the 1850s to the 1870s. Kanyaka Death Rock, also 42 km N, overlooking a permanent waterhole, once an Aboriginal ceremonial ground. Scenic drive 50 km S to Devil's Peak, Pichi Richi Pass, Mt Brown, Mt Brown Conservation Park and picturesque Waukarie Falls, 16 km away; walking trails. Towns of Bruce and Hammond, 22 km and 38 km SE; 1870s architecture. Hammond has unusual museum in original bank building. **Tourist information:** 3 Seventh St; (086) 48 6491 or (086) 48 6031. **Accommodation:** 2 hotels, 2 hotel/motels, 1 motel, 1 caravan/camping park.
MAP REF. 285 B12, 291 J11

Renmark Pop. 4256

Renmark is at the heart of the oldest irrigation area in Australia, 260 km NE of Adelaide on the Sturt Hwy. In 1887 the Chaffey brothers from Canada were granted 250 000 acres to test their irrigation scheme. Today lush orchards and vineyards thrive with the water piped from the Murray. There are canneries, wineries and fruit-juice factories. Wheat, sheep and dairy cattle are other local industries. The first community-run hotel in the British Commonwealth, the Renmark Hotel, is an impressive three-storeyed building overlooking a sweeping bend of the river. **Of interest:** National Trust Museum 'Olivewood', cnr Renmark Ave (Sturt Hwy) and 21st St; former Chaffey homestead. Old hand-operated wine-press, on display in Renmark Ave, and one of the Chaffeys' original wood-burning irrigation pumps, on display outside Renmark Irrigation Trust Office, Murray St, original Chaffey Bros. office. *PS Industry*, built in 1911, now floating museum moored adjacent to Tourist Centre, Murray Ave. Rivergrowers Ark packing shed, Renmark Ave, near 19th St; sales of local products; group tours available. Zenith Art Gallery, Murtho St; Ozone Art Gallery, Murray Ave. Houseboats for hire. **In the area:** Renmano Winery, 5 km SW on Sturt Hwy; tastings and sales Mon.–Sat. Unique collection of fauna, particularly reptiles, at Bredl's Wonder World of Wildlife, 7 km SW on Sturt Hwy; open daily. Ruston's Roses, 3000 varieties, 7 km SW off Sturt Hwy; open Oct.–end May. Angove's winery and distillery,

Bookmark Ave, 5 km SW; tastings and sales Mon.–Fri. Danggali Conservation Park, 60 km N, vast area of mallee scrub with bluebush and black oak woodland and abundance of bird and animal life; permit required. **Tourist information:** Tourist and Heritage Centre, Murray Ave; (085) 86 6704. **Accommodation:** 1 hotel/ motel, 4 motels, 3 caravan/camping parks. **See also:** Festival Fun.
MAP REF. 126 A7, 289 R5

Robe Pop. 730

A small, historic town on Guichen Bay, 336 km S of Adelaide, Robe is a fishing port and holiday centre. The rugged, windswept coast has many beautiful and secluded beaches, including 17 km of Long Beach, north of town. Lagoons and salt lakes are all round the area and wildlife abounds. Fairy penguins appear on the beach in the evening in summer. In addition there are interesting historic sites; many of the town's original buildings remain and have been restored. In the 1850s it was a major wool port. From 1857, 16 500 Chinese disembarked at Robe and travelled overland to the goldfields to avoid the Victorian Poll Tax. **Of interest:** National Trust buildings and small art and craft galleries; especially Smillie and Victoria Sts. Robe Historic Interpretation Centre in Library building, Victoria St, has displays and tourist information; leaflets on self-guided Heritage walks and drives available. Old Customs House Museum, (1863), Royal Circus. Karatta House, off Christine Dr, summer residence of Governor Sir James Fergusson in 1860s. Caledonian Inn (1858), Victoria St; accommodation and meals. Authorised landing strip for light aircraft. **In the area:** Lakeside (1884), Main Rd, 2km SE; historic home with accommodation, also caravan park. Waterskiing on adjacent Lake Fellmongery. Narraburra Woolshed, 14 km SE; sheep and wool activities. Beacon Hill, 2 km S, provides panoramic town and area views. Little Dip Conservation Park, 13 km S; complex moving sand dune system, salt lakes and freshwater lakes, where wildlife abounds. The Obelisk at Cape Dombey, 3 km W; northern vantage point for views of area. Crayfish fleet anchors in Lake Butler (Robe's harbour); fresh crays and fish are available Oct.–end Apr. **Tourist information:** Robe Library, Victoria St; (087) 68 2465. **Accommodation:** 2 hotels, 6 motels, 3 caravan/camping parks.
MAP REF. 287 F10

Roxby Downs Pop. 1999

A modern, newly established township built to accommodate the employees of the Olympic Dam Mining Project, Roxby Downs is 85 km N of Pimba, which is just off the Stuart Hwy, 555 km N of Adelaide. A road from Roxby Downs joins the Oodnadatta Track just south of Lake Eyre South, 125 km N of Roxby. **In the area:** Olympic Dam Mining Complex, 15 km N; tours of mining operations available. Heritage Centre and Missile Park, 90 km S at Woomera. **Tourist information:** Council Offices, Richardson Place; (086) 71 0010. **Accommodation:** 1 motel, 1 caravan/camping park.
MAP REF. 290 F4

Stansbury Pop. 513

Situated on the lower east coast of Yorke Peninsula, Stansbury was originally known as Oyster Bay because it was once one of the best oyster beds in South Australian waters. In days gone by, ketches shipped grain across the gulf from Stansbury to Port Adelaide. A popular holiday resort, the town has scenic views of Gulf St Vincent. The bay is ideal for water sports, including diving and waterskiing. **Of interest:** Museum, North Tce; in first Stansbury School (1878) and residence. Jetty fishing. **In the area:** Lake Sundown, 15 km NW, one of many salt lakes in area; photographer's delight at sunset. **Tourist information:** Yorke Peninsula Tourist Information Centre, Victoria Sq., Kadina; (088) 21 2093. **Accommodation:** 1 hotel, 2 motels, 2 caravan parks.
MAP REF. 282 G8, 288 I8

Strathalbyn Pop. 2623

An inland town with a Scottish heritage, on the Angas River, Strathalbyn is 58 km S of Adelaide and a designated heritage township. Picturesque Soldiers Memorial Gardens follow the river through town, offering shaded picnic grounds. **Of interest:** National Trust Museum, Rankine St; housed in old police station and courthouse. St Andrew's Church (1848), Alfred Pl. Old Provincial Gas Company (1868), South Tce; now Gasworks Gallery. Antique and craft shops. Collectors, Hobbies and Antique Fair annually, Aug. **In the area:** Lakeside resort of Milang, 20 km SE; museum. Langhorne Creek, 15 km E; winegrowing district. Pottery at Paris Creek, near Meadows, 15 km NW; iris gardens open Oct.–Mar. **Tourist information:**

Old Railway Station, South Tce; (085) 36 3212. Accommodation: 3 hotels, 1 caravan park.
MAP REF. 283 N10, 284 I7, 287 C3, 289 M9

Streaky Bay   Pop. 957

Streaky Bay, 727 km NW of Adelaide, is a holiday resort, fishing port and agricultural centre for the cereal-growing hinterland. The explorer Matthew Flinders named the bay because of the streaking effect caused by seaweed in its waters. The town is almost surrounded by small bays and coves, pleasant sandy beaches and spectacular towering cliffs. Crayfish and many species of fish abound in Streaky Bay waters and fishing from boat or the jetty is good. **Of interest:** Static Engine Museum, Alfred Tce. Old School House Museum, Montgomery Tce. Hospital Cottage (1864), the first building in Streaky Bay. **In the area:** Magnificent coastal scenery and rugged cliffs. Point Labatt Conservation Park, 55 km S, has only permanent colony of sea lions on Australian mainland. Murphy's Haystacks, 40 km SE off Flinders Hwy, a sculptural group of ancient pink granite rocks. Port Kenny, 62 km S on Venus Bay; excellent fishing. Further 12 km S, fishing village of Venus Bay; nearby, breathtaking views from Needle Eye Lookout. Spectacular limestone caves at Talia, 88 km S. **Tourist information:** Council Offices, Alfred Tce; (086) 26 1001. **Accommodation:** 1 hotel/motel, 1 motel, 1 caravan/camping park. **See also:** The Eyre Peninsula.
MAP REF. 297 P12

Swan Reach   Pop. 230

Swan Reach is a quiet little township on the Murray River, about 100 km E of Gawler. Picturesque river scenery and good fishing are making it an increasingly popular holiday resort. **In the area:** Sandleton Museum; 23 historic buildings depicting life of early settlers. Houseboats for hire. Punyelroo, 7 km S; fishing, boating and water-skiing. Swan Reach, 11 km W, and Ridley Conservation Parks, 5 km S. Junction of Rivers Marne and Murray, 15 km S; picnic facilities. Water sports at Walker Flat, 26 km S. Yookamurra Sanctuary, 21 km NW; conservation project, including eradication of feral animals and restocking with native animals. Guided walks for pre-European atmosphere;

overnight accommodation; booking essential, (08) 388 5380. **Accommodation:** 1 hotel, 1 caravan/camping park.
MAP REF. 283 R5, 287 E1, 289 N7

Tailem Bend   Pop. 1502

A railway-workshop town at the junction of the Dukes and Princes Hwys, 107 km SE of Adelaide, Tailem Bend has excellent views across the Murray as the river bends sharply towards Wellington. **Of interest:** Picnic/barbecue facilities, children's playground. Gumi Racing Festival held each Feb. **In the area:** Scenic drive via vehicular ferry across river to Jervois; cheese factory here (tours by appointment); then 11 km S to Wellington, where river meets lake. At Wellington, restored courthouse complex (1864); includes cells, stables, post and telegraph office, courtyard and kiosk. Historic buildings, SE on Dukes Hwy: old woolshed on left, approaching Cooke Plains; Braeside Homestead on left, after town. Old Tailem Town Pioneer Village, 5 km N of Tailem Bend; open daily. **Tourist information:** 15 Railway Tce; (085) 72 3537. **Accommodation:** 2 hotels, 1 motel, 2 caravan/camping parks.
MAP REF. 283 Q10, 287 E3, 289 N9

Tanunda   Pop. 3087

The town of Tanunda is the heart of the Barossa Valley. It was the focal point for early German settlement, growing out of the village of Langmeil, established in 1843, part of which can be seen in the western areas of town. The National Trust has classified Goat Square, site of the old market square, surrounded by century-old cottages. **Of interest:** Fine Lutheran churches. Historical museum, Murray St; former 1865 post and telegraph office houses collections specialising in German heritage. Old Siegersdorf Winery, Barossa Valley Way; Kev Rohlach Collection, from local heritage to technology. Barossa Kiddypark, Magnolia St; funpark with rides. **In the area:** Local wineries include St Hallett Wines, Rockford Wines, Charles Melton Wines, Bethany Wines, High Wycombe Wines, Basedow Wines, Old Barn Wines (also has local crafts), Veritas Winery, Hardy's Siegersdorf, Chateau Dorrien, Peter Lehmann Wines and Krondorf Wines. Story Book Cottage and Whacky Wood, Oak St, for children. Norm's Coolie Sheep Dogs, south off Barossa Valley

Way; 3 performances weekly. The Keg Factory, St Hallett Rd; makers of kegs, barrel furniture and wine racks. Bethany, 4 km S, first German settlement in the Barossa; pretty village with creekside picnic area, pioneer cemetery, attractive streetscapes and two wineries. At Kersbrook, 40 km S; ballooning. **Tourist information:** Barossa Valley Visitors Centre, 68 Murray Street; (008) 81 2662 or (085) 63 0600. **Accommodation:** 1 hotel, 1 hotel/motel, 2 motels, 1 caravan/camping park. **See also:** Festival Fun; Vineyards and Wineries.
MAP REF. 283 N4, 286 F5, 287 D1, 289 M7

Tintinara   Pop. 316

A quiet little town 206 km SE of Adelaide in the Coonalpyn Downs. **Of interest:** Post office (1865), Becker Tce. **In the area:** Historic Tintinara Homestead, 9 km W; historic buildings. Mt Boothby Conservation Park, 20 km W. Access to Mt Rescue Conservation Park, 15 km E; sandplains with heath, native fauna, Aboriginal campsites and burial grounds. **Tourist information:** Heart of the Park Tourist and Craft Shop, Becker Tce; (087) 57 2220. **Accommodation:** 1 hotel, 1 motel, 1 caravan/camping park.
MAP REF. 287 G5, 289 P11

Tumby Bay   Pop. 1147

Tumby Bay is a pretty coastal resort 49 km N of Port Lincoln on the east coast of the Eyre Peninsula. The town is noted for its long crescent beach and white sand. Lawns and picnic/barbecue facilities along the foreshore. **Of interest:** C. L. Alexander National Trust Museum, housed in old wooden schoolroom; open Fri. and Sat. afternoons. Police station (1871). Two jetties, one more than 100 years old. **In the area:** Rock and surf fishing. Island Lookout for panoramic views. Rugged but beautiful scenery at Poonta and Cowley's Beaches; catches include snapper, whiting and bream. Koppio, about 40 km W, through attractive fertile countryside, with National Trust classified Smithy Museum. Tod Reservoir Museum in Koppio hills. At Port Neill, 42 km N, grassed foreshore for picnics and safe swimming beach. Vic and Jill Fauser's Museum (open daily) and 1 km N, Port Neill Lookout for spectacular views. At Wanilla, wildflowers in spring. At Thuruna, excellent fishing. Lipson Cove, where visitors can walk

Murphy's Haystacks, near Streaky Bay

across to Lipson Island at low tide. Fishing, sea lions, dolphins and birdlife at Sir Joseph Banks Group of islands; charter tours available. Trinity Haven Scenic Drive. **Tourist information:** Hales Minimart, 1 Bratten Way; (086) 88 2584. **Accommodation:** Tumby Bay, 2 hotels, 1 motel, 1 caravan/camping park; Port Neill, 1 hotel, 2 caravan/camping parks. **See also:** The Eyre Peninsula.
MAP REF. 288 E6

Victor Harbor   Pop. 5930
A popular coastal resort town and unofficial capital of the Fleurieu Peninsula, Victor Harbor is 84 km S of Adelaide. Established in the early days of whaling and sealing in the 1830s, 'Victor' overlooks historic Encounter Bay, protected by Granite Island. Whale-watching and golfing. **Of interest:** Historical buildings: Adare (1860s), The Drive, Mount Breckan (1879), Renown Ave, Newland Memorial Congregational Church (1869), Victoria St, and St Augustine's Church of England (1869), Burke St. Telegraph Station Art Gallery, Coral St; housed in former telegraph station (1866). **In the area:** Granite Island, joined to mainland by 1 km causeway; walk or take horse-drawn tram across. Chairlift (operates SA school holidays and weekends) offers magnificent views of land and sea. Penguin rookeries and seals to be seen also. Greenhills Adventure Park, 3.5 km N on banks of Hindmarsh River. Native animals and birds at Urimbirra Wildlife Park, 5 km N. Opposite, Nangawooka Flora Reserve with over 1000 named trees and plants. At Mt Compass, 24 km N; pottery, strawberry and blueberry farms, begonia farm, nursery and Tooperang Trout Farm. The

Steam Ranger, a railway service, operates between Victor Harbor and Goolwa, via Port Elliot. North, both Hindmarsh and Inman Rivers provide good fishing and peaceful picnic spots. Spring Mount Conservation Park, 14 km NW. Glacier Rock at Inman Valley, 19 km NW, shows effect of glacial erosion. Hindmarsh Valley Falls, 15 km NE; pleasant walks and spectacular waterfalls. The Bluff, or Rosetta Head, 5 km S, worth 100-m climb for views. Waitpinga Beach, 17 km SW. Deep Creek Conservation Park, 50 km SW, has Heysen Trail for walking, and spectacular flora and fauna; park is well-known for its rugged cliffs and orchids and ferns in its gullies. Talisker Conservation Park (adjacent to Deep Creek Conservation Park) is site of historic silver–lead mine; old mine buildings and diggings. At tip of Fleurieu Peninsula is Cape Jervis, 70 km SW, with splendid views. **Tourist information:** Torrens St; (085) 52 4255. **Accommodation:** 3 hotels, 8 motels, 3 caravan/camping parks. **See also:** The Fleurieu Peninsula.
MAP REF. 283 L12, 284 D13, 287 C4, 289 L10

Waikerie   Pop. 1748
Waikerie, the citrus centre of Australia, is surrounded by an oasis of irrigated vegetables, orchards and vineyards in mallee-scrub country in the Riverland. Situated 170 km NE of Adelaide, the town has beautiful views of the river gums and magnificent sandstone cliffs along the Murray. The name means 'anything that flies' and the river and lagoons teem with birdlife; the mallee scrub is a haven for parrots and other native birds. **Of interest:** Co-op Fruit-packing House, Sturt Hwy, largest in Australia. Lions Park, on

riverfront; picnic/barbecue facilities, children's playground. Harts Lagoon, Ramco Rd; bird wetlands. Houseboats for hire. **In the area:** Orange Tree kiosk, Sturt Hwy, 2 km E; fruit products and river-viewing platform. Internationally acclaimed as a glider's paradise, joy rides and courses available from Gliding Club, off Sturt Hwy, 4 km E. Terrigal Fauna Park, Baldock Rd, 4 km E. On northern side of river near Lock 2, close to Taylorville, spectacular fossil deposit area, one of few in Australia where crystallised gypsum fossils are found in abundance. Devlin's ghost sighted, 11 km E. Holder Bend Reserve and Maize Island Conservation Park, 6 km NE. At Blanchetown, 42 km W, first of Murray's 6 SA locks; lookout at Blanchetown Bridge; floating restaurant. Brookfield Conservation Park, 11 km W, home of southern hairy-nosed wombat. **Tourist information:** Waikerie Travel Centre, 20 McCoy St; (085) 41 2295. **Accommodation:** 1 motel, 1 hotel/motel, 1 caravan/camping park.
MAP REF. 289 P5

Wallaroo   Pop. 2465
Situated 154 km NW of Adelaide, Wallaroo is a key shipping port for the Yorke Peninsula, exporting barley and wheat. Processing of rock phosphate is another major industry here. The safe beaches and good fishing in this historical area make it a popular tourist resort. In 1859 vast copper-ore deposits were discovered. A smelter was built, thousands of Cornish miners arrived and Wallaroo and surrounding areas boomed until the 1920s, when copper prices dropped and the industry gradually died out. The nearby towns of Moonta and Kadina

form part of the trio known as 'Little Cornwall', and the area still has many reminders of its colourful past. The 'Kernewek Lowender', a Cornish festival, is held in conjunction with Moonta and Kadina in May every odd-numbered year. **Of interest:** Cemetery, Moonta Rd, holds grave of Caroline Carleton, author of 'Song of Australia'. Number of charming old Cornish-style cottages in district. National Trust Wallaroo Heritage and Nautical Museum, in town's first post office (1865) in Jetty Rd; collection of maritime exhibits. Wallaroo Historical Walks brochure available at museum or town hall, Irwine St; guided tours on Sun. Historic buildings include old railway station, Owen Tce, customs house (1862) and Hughes chimney stack (1865), Jetty Rd, which contains over 300 000 bricks and is more than 7 m square at its base. **In the area:** Wallaroo Mines site in Kadina, 10 km E; open for signposted self-guided walking tour. Towns of Moonta and Kadina. Bird Island, 10 km S, for crabbing. **Tourist information:** Yorke Peninsula Tourist Information Centre, Victoria Sq, Kadina; (088) 21 2093. **Accommodation:** 3 hotels, 1 motel, 3 caravan/camping parks. **See also:** Festival Fun; The Yorke Peninsula.
MAP REF. 288 I4

Whyalla
Pop. 25 526

In 90 years Whyalla, northern gateway to the Eyre Peninsula, has grown from a small settlement known as Hummock Hill to the largest provincial city in the State and an important industrial centre based on steel. It is famous for its heavy industry, particularly the enormous BHP iron and steel works and ore mining at Iron Knob and Iron Monarch in the Middleback Ranges. A shipyard operated from 1939 to 1978, and the largest ship ever built in Australia was launched from here in 1972. Whyalla is a modern, well-planned city with a good shopping centre, safe beaches, fishing, boating and excellent recreational facilities. The area enjoys a sunny, Mediterranean-type climate. **Of interest:** Whyalla Maritime Museum, Lincoln Hwy; features now landlocked 650 tonne corvette *Whyalla*; and Tanderra Building, housing collection of models, including what is believed to be largest OO gauge model railway in Australia. Mount Laura Homestead Museum (National Trust), Ekblom St; check opening times. Whyalla Art Gallery, Darling Tce; open daily. Foreshore redevelopment includes

attractive beach, jetty, and landscaped area very popular for picnics, and marina. Hummock Hill lookout from Queen Elizabeth Dr; spectacular views. Flinders Lookout, Farrel St; Ada Ryan Gardens, Cudmore Tce; mini-zoo and picnic facilities under shady trees. Guided tours of BHP steel works; bookings at Tourist Centre (for safety reasons, visitors must wear closed footwear). Wildlife and reptile sanctuary, south-east on Lincoln Hwy, near airport, offers Nocturnal Walk Guided Tour; bookings essential. Whyalla Tourist Drive; brochure from Tourist Centre. Whyalla Show held in Aug. **In the area:** Port Bonython, 20 km E, and Point Lowly, 34 km E; Point Lowly Lighthouse (1882), oldest building in area (not open for inspection); and scenic coastal drive through Fitzgerald Bay to Point Douglas. Whyalla Conservation Park, 10 km N off Lincoln Hwy, near Port Bonython turnoff. At Iron Knob, 50 km N: iron ore quarries (tours available); BHP Mining Museum and Iron Knob Mineral and Shell Display. Lake Gilles Conservation Park, 72 km W; varied birdlife, kangaroos, western pigmy possums and reptiles. **Tourist information:** Lincoln Hwy; (086) 45 7900. **Accommodation:** 5 hotels, 1 hotel/motel, 5 motels, 2 caravan/camping parks. **See also:** The Eyre Peninsula.
MAP REF. 288 I1, 290 H13

Willunga
Pop. 1164

An historic township first surveyed in 1839, Willunga the Aboriginal word *willaunga* means 'the place of green trees', is just south of the famous Southern Vales winegrowing regions and is Australia's major almond-growing centre. **Of interest:** Historic pug cottages and fine examples of colonial architecture. National Trust police station and courthouse (1855), Main St. Church of England, St Andrews Tce, has Elizabethan bronze bell. Bush Inn (1889) and Vanessa's Restaurant, both Main Rd. Delabole Quarry (1842); operated for 60 years, now a National Trust site. Almond Blossom Festival held annually in late July. **In the area:** Cowshed Gallery at Yundi, 9 km E. Mt Magnificent Conservation Park, 12 km E; western grey kangaroos in bushland, scenic walks and picnic areas. Strawberry farm, 4 km N. Kyeema Conservation Park, 14 km NE. **Tourist information:** The Cottage, Main Rd, McLaren Vale; (08) 323 8537. **Accommodation:** 1 hotel.
MAP REF. 283 L10, 284 C7, 287 B3, 289 L9

Wilmington
Pop. 250

A tiny settlement formerly known as Beautiful Valley, Wilmington is 290 km N of Adelaide in the Flinders Ranges. **Of interest:** Police station (1880), now a private residence, and old coaching stables (1880) at rear of Wilmington Hotel, both Main St. Beautiful Valley Aussie Relics Museum, Melrose Rd; open all week. **In the area:** Many scenic drives. Hancock's Lookout, 7 km W, at top of Horrocks Pass off road to Port Augusta, for views of Spencer Gulf. Mount Remarkable National Park, 13 km S, with crystal-clear mountain pools, dense vegetation and abundant wildlife; Mambray Creek and spectacular Alligator Gorge in park. Historic Melrose, 21 km S, oldest town in the Flinders. Booleroo Steam and Traction Preservation Society's Museum (open by appointment), Booleroo Centre, 48 km SE. Hammond, 26 km NE; historic railway town. At Carrieton, 56 km NE: historic buildings; Aboriginal carvings, 5 km along Belton Rd; scenic drive to deserted Johnberg. **Tourist information:** General Store, Main St; (086) 67 5155. **Accommodation:** 1 hotel, 2 caravan/camping parks.
MAP REF. 285 B13, 291 J12

Wilpena
Pop. 20

Wilpena, 429 km N of Adelaide, is the small settlement outside Wilpena Pound. The Pound, part of the Flinders Ranges National Park, is a vast natural amphitheatre surrounded by colossal peaks that change colour as the light falls on them through the day. The only entrance is through a narrow gorge and across Sliding Rock. In 1900 a wheat farmer built a homestead within the Pound, but a flood destroyed the log road and the farm was abandoned. **In the area:** Bushwalking and mountain climbing in surrounding countryside. Numerous walking trails into Wilpena Pound, including one to St Mary's Peak, the highest point (1188 m). Aboriginal rock carvings and paintings at Arkaroo Rock on slopes of Rawnsley Bluff, south, and at Sacred Canyon, south-east. Rawnsley Park Station, 20 km S on Hawker Rd; demonstrations of sheep-drafting and shearing Sept.–Oct. Appealinna Homestead (1851), 16 km N off Blinman Rd; ruins of house built of flat rock from creek bed. Scenic drives— most of area within confines of Flinders Ranges National Park (headquarters at Oraparinna Station)—to Stokes Hill

Vineyards and Wineries

South Australia provides about 65 per cent of the wines and 83 per cent of the brandy made in Australia. In the equable dry climate of the southern and eastern regions of the State, kilometres of vineyards stretch over valleys, plains and hillsides. The State has eight distinct grape-growing regions: the Barossa Valley, the Wine Coast or Southern Vales region of the Fleurieu Peninsula, the Clare Valley, Murraylands, Riverland, the Adelaide Hills, the Coonawarra area, and Boston Bay on Eyre Peninsula.

The **Barossa Valley**, Australia's most famous wine-producing area, is located about 55 kilometres north-east of Adelaide. It is a warm and intimate place of charming old towns, with vineyards spreading across undulating hills in well-tended, precise rows. Visitors can view the valley from a hot-air balloon and afterwards enjoy a champagne breakfast.

The Barossa Valley was named in 1837 by Colonel Light in memory of Barrosa in Spain, where he had fought a decisive battle in 1811. The recorded spelling 'Barossa' was an error that was never rectified. The district was settled in 1839 by English and German settlers. Today the Barossa has a distinctive culture and atmosphere that derives from this German concentration in the mid-nineteenth century and is evidenced in the vineyards, the stone buildings, the restaurants, the bakeries and the Lutheran churches that dot the valley.

The Barossa produces brandy, dry and sweet table wines, and fortified styles of wine. Some of the most famous wineries of the Barossa are Yalumba, Orlando,

Penfolds and Seppelts. Some of these wineries are still run by members of the same families that established them over one hundred years ago. Others have been taken over by big international companies, but the distinctive qualities of the wine remain. There are many medium-size wineries making excellent wines, such as Wolf Blass, Basedows and Krondorf, and many boutique wineries specialising in producing a small number of quality wines, including Barossa Settlers, Henschke, Grant Burge and Elderton.

The **Wine Coast** or **Southern Vales** region, particularly suitable for red wines, is on the Fleurieu Peninsula, just south of Adelaide. Nestled in the gentle folds of the Mount Lofty Ranges with a westerly view to the sea lies McLaren Vale, the centre of this winegrowing area. There are over fifty wineries in the region, among them Chapel Hill, Hardy's Reynella, James Haselgrove, Seaview and Wirra Wirra, and they range from very large to very small. In most of the wineries, the person at the cellar door is the person who makes the wine, so meet your maker at McLaren Vale!

The vineyards of the **Clare Valley** are about 130 kilometres north of Adelaide and produce fine table wines, riesling, chablis and some terrific reds. Two of the better known of the twenty-odd wineries in this district are Eaglehawk Estate and Leasingham Wines.

The **Murraylands** region extends from Middleton Estate Wines at Middleton, north-east to Willowglen Wines near Murray Bridge. Another wine region that includes a stretch of the Murray River near

the Victorian border is **Riverland**. Famous for a wide range of products from top-quality table wines to ouzo and brandy, the region is represented by such wineries as Kingston Estate at Kingston on Murray eastwards to Angove's near Renmark.

There are vineyards scattered throughout the **Adelaide Hills**. Wineries to the north (south-east of the Barossa Valley) include Hamiltons, Craneford and Grand Cru Estate; this area is noted especially for its riesling. Closer to Adelaide are Petaluma and Stonyfell Wineries.

Many vineyards at **Coonawarra** in the far south-east produce red wines from a small area of unique rich, volcanic soil; examples are Ladbroke Grove, Mildara and Rouge Homme. Further vineyards have been established in the south-east at Keppoch and Padthaway.

Boston Bay, perched on the southern tip of the spectacular Eyre Peninsula, is one of Australia's newest wine regions. Its reputation as the 'home of the great white shark' is fast changing to 'home of great white wines', with national award recognition for the region's first major vintage.

Most of the South Australian wineries are open for inspection, tastings and cellar-door sales.

For further information about hours of inspection and winery tours, contact the South Australian Tourism Commission Travel Centre, 1 King William Street, Adelaide; (08) 212 1505. **See also:** Individual entries in A–Z listing. **Note** detailed maps of Southern Vales and Barossa Valley on pages 284 and 286 respectively.

Vineyards in the Clare Valley

Lookout, 2 km NE; Bunyeroo and Brachina Gorges, Aroona Valley, 5 km NW; Moralana Scenic Drive, 25 km S. Organised tours, 4WD tours and scenic flights available. **Tourist information:** Wilpena Pound Motel; (086) 48 0004. Accommodation: 1 motel, 2 caravan/camping parks. **See also:** The Flinders Ranges.
MAP REF. 285 D8, 291 K8

Woomera   Pop. 1600

Established in 1947 as a site for launching British experimental rockets, Woomera was, until 1982, a prohibited area to visitors. The town, 490 km NW of Adelaide, is still administered by the Defence Department. **Of interest:** Missile Park and Heritage Centre; displays of rockets, aircraft and weapons. Breen Park picnic area. **In the area:** Roxby Downs, 78 km N, service centre for Olympic Dam mining operations; tours of mining operations available. Andamooka opal field, 107 km E; tours available. Accommodation: 1 hotel, 1 caravan/camping park.
MAP REF. 290 F7

Wudinna   Pop. 573

Wudinna is a small settlement on the Eyre Hwy, 571 km NW of Adelaide. The township has become an important service point for central Eyre Peninsula. **Of interest:** Gawler Ranges Gallery, Eyre Hwy; all goods locally made. **In the area:** Wudinna is the gateway to the

timeless Gawler Ranges; Wilderness Safaris available. Mt Wudinna, 10 km NE, second largest granite outcrop in Australia; summit (261 m) offers panoramic views of countryside; recreation area at base. Turtle Rock, nearby ancient granite rock looking surprisingly like its namesake. Signposted tourist drives to all major rock formations. Prolific wildlife and wildflowers in spring throughout area. At Minnipa, 37 km NW: Grain Research Centre; Yarwondutta Rock; recreation areas at Minnipa Hill and Tcharkulda Hill. **Tourist information:** Gawler Ranges Gallery, Eyre Hwy; (086) 80 2333. **Accommodation:** 1 hotel/motel, 1 motel, 1 caravan park.
MAP REF. 288 C1, 290 B13

Yankalilla   Pop. 408

A small, quiet settlement just inland from the west coast of the Fleurieu Peninsula, 35 km west of Victor Harbor. **Of interest:** In Main St: Uniting Church (1878); Bungala House, gifts and pottery; leatherwork, woodwork and gumnut creations at craft shops in the area; Yankalilla Hotel, country-style counter meals; historical museum; tearooms. **In the area:** Tiny seaside town of Normanville, 4 km W. Bay Tree Farm, Cape Jarvis Rd, Second Valley, 14 km W; herbs, flowers, afternoon teas. Steep hillsides and gullies of Myponga Conservation Park, 14 km NE; home of western grey kangaroo. Glacier Rock, 22 km E; 500

m-yr-old Cambrian Kanmantoo quartzite. Myponga, 14 km NE; begonia farm and Myponga Reservoir for barbecues or picnics. **Tourist information:** Council Offices, Main St; (085) 58 2048. **Accommodation:** Yankalilla, 1 hotel. Normanville, 1 motel, 2 caravan/camping parks.
MAP REF. 283 J11, 287 B4, 289 K10

Yorketown   Pop. 738

Principal town at the southern end of the Yorke Peninsula, Yorketown's shopping centre services the surrounding cereal-growing district. Yorketown is surrounded by extensive inland salt lakes (some are pink), which are still worked. **In the area:** Toy Factory, 5 km NE; locally crafted wooden toys. Rugged coastal scenery and desolate country at tip of Peninsula, including Innes National Park, 77 km SW. Inneston, historic mining town within park, managed as historic site by NPWS. Surfing at Daly Head, 50 km W. Corny Point, at north-western tip of Peninsula, 55 km NW, has lighthouse and lookout; camping and fishing. **Tourist information:** Yorke Peninsula Tourist Information Centre, Victoria Sq., Kadina; (088) 21 2093. **Accommodation:** 1 hotel, 1 hotel/motel, 1 caravan/camping park. **See also:** Yorke Peninsula.
MAP REF. 282 F8, 288 I8

Wudinna, gateway to the Gawler Ranges

South Australia

Location Map

Other Map Coverage
Central Adelaide 276
Adelaide Approach & Bypass Routes 277
Adelaide & Southern Suburbs 278
Northern Suburbs, Adelaide 280
Adelaide Region 282
Southern Vales Region 284

Flinders Ranges Region 285
Barossa Valley Region 286

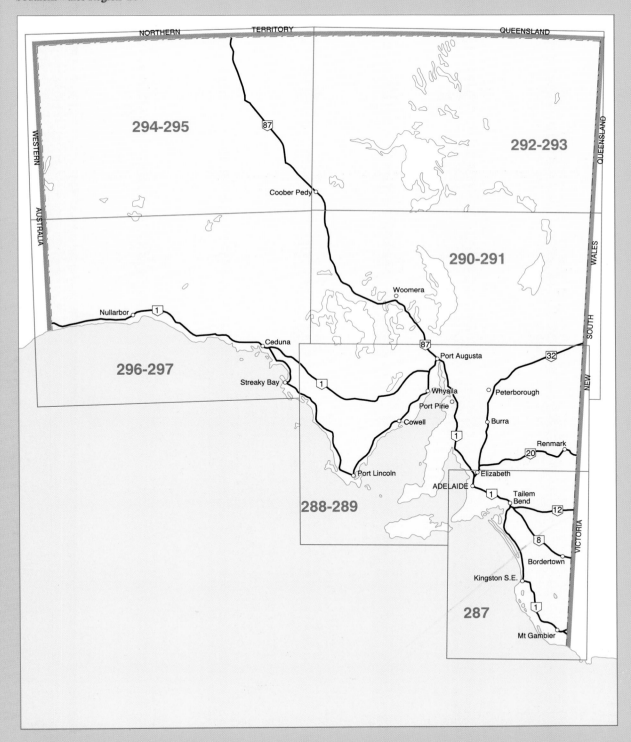

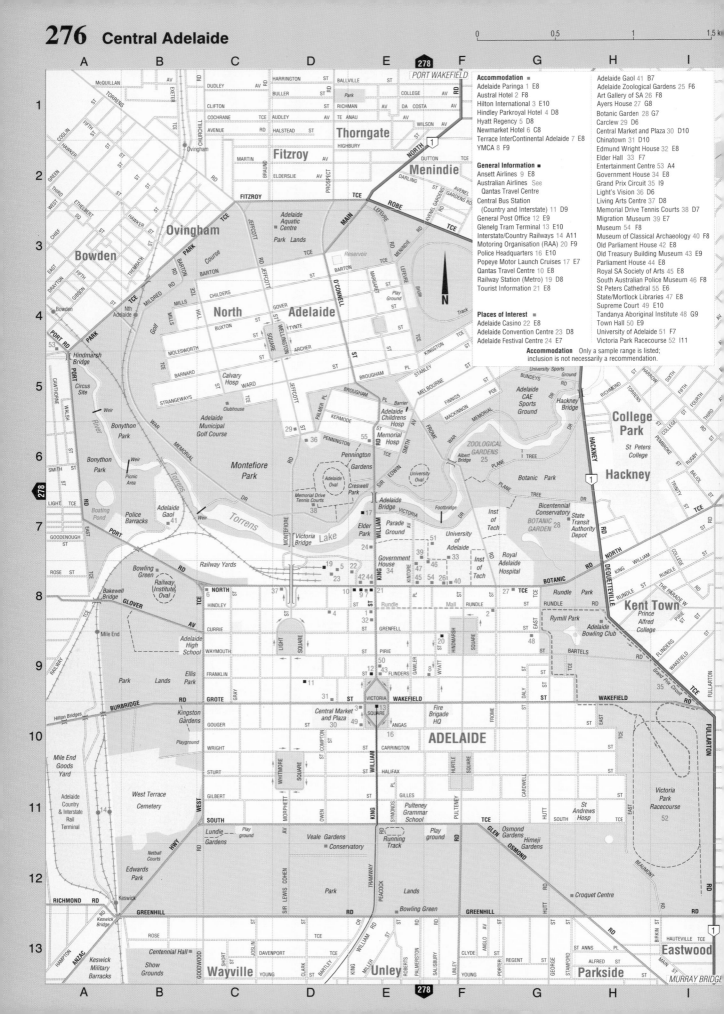

276 Central Adelaide

Accommodation
Adelaide Paringa 1 E8
Austral Hotel 2 F8
Hilton International 3 E10
Hindley Parkroyal Hotel 4 D8
Hyatt Regency 5 D8
Newmarket Hotel 6 C8
Terrace InterContinental Adelaide 7 E8
YMCA 8 F9

General Information
Ansett Airlines 9 E8
Australian Airlines   See
  Qantas Travel Centre
Central Bus Station
  (Country and Interstate) 11 D9
General Post Office 12 E9
Glenelg Tram Terminal 13 E10
Interstate/Country Railways 14 A11
Motoring Organisation (RAA) 20 F9
Police Headquarters 16 E10
Popeye Motor Launch Cruises 17 E7
Qantas Travel Centre 10 E8
Railway Station (Metro) 19 D8
Tourist Information 21 E8

Places of Interest
Adelaide Casino 22 E8
Adelaide Convention Centre 23 D8
Adelaide Festival Centre 24 E7

Adelaide Gaol 41 B7
Adelaide Zoological Gardens 25 F6
Art Gallery of SA 26 F8
Ayers House 27 G8
Botanic Garden 28 G7
Carclew 29 D6
Central Market and Plaza 30 D10
Chinatown 31 D10
Edmund Wright House 32 E8
Elder Hall 33 F7
Entertainment Centre 53 A4
Government House 34 E8
Grand Prix Circuit 35 I9
Light's Vision 36 D6
Living Arts Centre 37 D8
Memorial Drive Tennis Courts 38 D7
Migration Museum 39 E7
Museum 54 F8
Museum of Classical Archaeology 40 F8
Old Parliament House 42 E8
Old Treasury Building Museum 43 E9
Parliament House 44 E8
Royal SA Society of Arts 45 E8
South Australian Police Museum 46 F8
St Peters Cathedral 55 E6
State/Mortlock Libraries 47 E8
Supreme Court 49 E10
Tandanya Aboriginal Institute 48 G9
Town Hall 50 E9
University of Adelaide 51 F7
Victoria Park Racecourse 52 I11

Accommodation   Only a sample range is listed;
inclusion is not necessarily a recommendation.

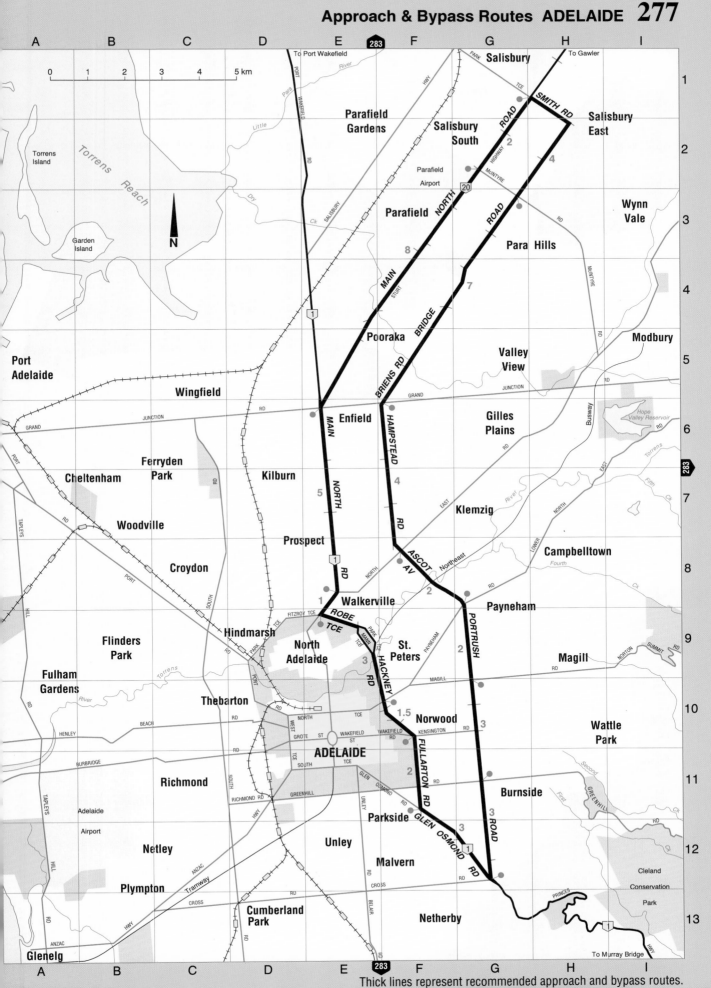

Thick lines represent recommended approach and bypass routes.

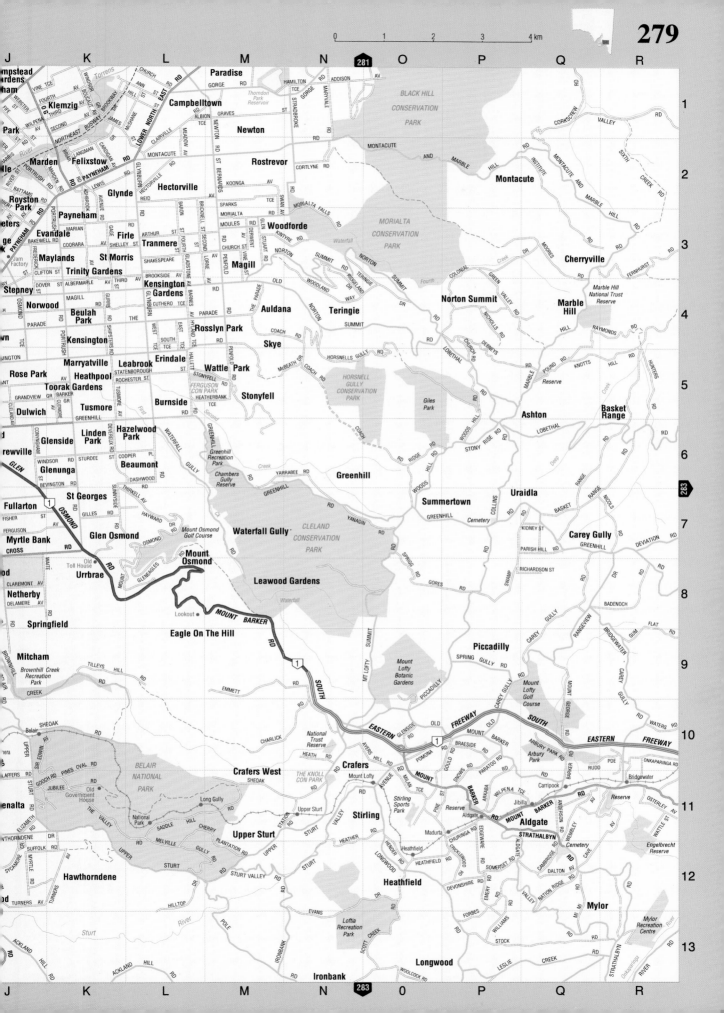

A   B   C   D   E   283   F   G   H   I

1

Salt Crystallization Pans

BROOKS WHITE RD COLEMAN
GREYHOUND RD CASSON
PLAIN RD SYMES

PORT WAKEFIELD
PRINCES HWY

RD MILL

ST KILDA RD
RD ROBINSON

MIDDLE VALE DR SHORT ST

2

Australian Electric Transport Museum

Waterloo Corner

Speed Kartway

UNDO RD

SUMMER

BURTON RD

St Kilda

3

Barker Inlet

Salt Crystallization Pans

Bolivar Sewage Treatment Works

HODGSON

4

Light Passage

Bolivar

5

Outer Harbor

Torrens Reach

JONES RD

Little Para

WHITES RD
DANIEL

6

VICTORIA RD

Outer Harbor
North Haven Golf Course

Outer Harbor

North Haven

Mutton Cove

Lipson Reach

7

DR

LADY GOWRIE

OSBORNE RD
RD
Midlunga
GEDVILLE RD

Osborne

Torrens Island

GULF

8

ST VINCENT

Largs Bay

MILITARY
STRATHFIELD TCE
RD
Draper

Taperoo

Port Adelaide River

Power Station

Garden Island

North Arm

Salt Crystallization Pans

9

MILITARY RD
RAILWAY TCE
FLETCHER
JETTY

VICTORIA
ST

Largs North

Largs Bay

RD
MEAD
WILLS

Hindmarsh Reach

MINNIPA RD
MOONTA RD

Port Adelaide

Drain

Gillman

MAGAZINE

Dry Creek

Dry Creek

10

ESPLANADE

HARGRAVE
Peterhead

Peterhead

Semaphore

Birkenhead

RD

ELDER ST

GRAND
EASTERN ST

OCEAN STEAMERS

FRANCIS ST

KAPARA
North Arm Road

CORMACK

WINGFIELD RD
SOUTH
FRANCIS

RAFFERTY
TCE

CORMACK

Wingfield

PLYMOUTH

ROSBERG RD

CHURCHILL RD

CAVAN

WALDAF

Semaphore South

MILITARY RD
HART ST
SWAN
BOWER ST

Glanville

SEMAPHORE
CAUSEWAY
RD

Exeter

ST VINCENT ST
COMMERCIAL RD

Port Waterfront Markets

S.A. Maritime Museum

BEDFORD ST

GRAY TCE

MAY

PDE

JUNCTION

HANSON
NTH

RD

Ottoway

INDAMA ST
WIRRIGA

NAMEENA ST
BIRRALEE

GRAND

CROMWELL

BRUNSWICK

11

Fort Glanville

SANSOM RD
FAIRFORD
TCE

Ethelton

Commercial Road

RD

PORT RD

GRAND

ADDISON

Athol Park

GLENROY ST
GLENLOY ST
ELY

DUDLEY

GATESHEAD ST

Angle Park

DAYS RD

TAMINGA ST

Tube Mills

Kilburn

CHURCHILL RD

Semaphore Park

RECREATION PDE

MILITARY

BARTLEY

CORDGAN
WEST

Delfin Island

WEBB
OLD PORT RD
FREDERICK

OSBURG RD

DOBURG RD

TORRENS ST

Rosewater

GEORGE ST PARK

Pennington

BURLEIGH AV
WILSON ST
NINTH AV

CARDIGAN
COWAN

Mansfield Park

TRAFFORD
LIBERTY

Greyhound Racing Club

Regency Golf Course

Regency Park

CAMIRA ST
SOUTH

JERSEY
LIVINGSTONE

12

Riverside Golf Course

LOCHSIDE DR

POPLAR ST

TAPLEYS HILL RD

PORT RD

Queenstown

Alberton

Cheltenham

Cheltenham Racecourse

RIDLEY ST

Woodville

REGENCY TCE

GODDALN
REGENCY

Ferryden Park

REGENCY RD

Croydon Park

Dudley Park

REGENCY

13

West Lakes
LAKES

Football Park

TURNER DR
BREBNER DR

West Lakes Shore

West Lakes

Royal Park

POPLAR ST

GORDON ST
PORT RD

Hendon

Albert Park

WEST LAKES BLVD
MAY ST
FINDON RD

CHELTENHAM ST

Woodville

Woodville Park
WOODVILLE RD

BELMORE

Kilkenny

ARDOMA RD
DAVID
NTH

PYM

RD
BEATRICE

Devon Park

Tennyson

A   B   C   D   E   278   F   G   H

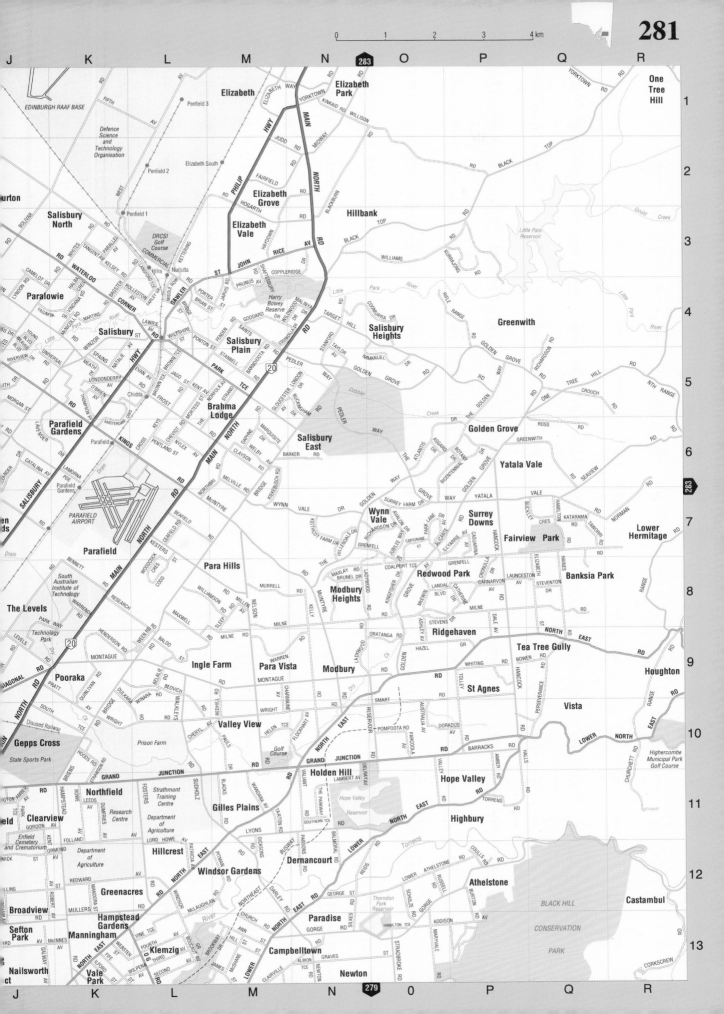

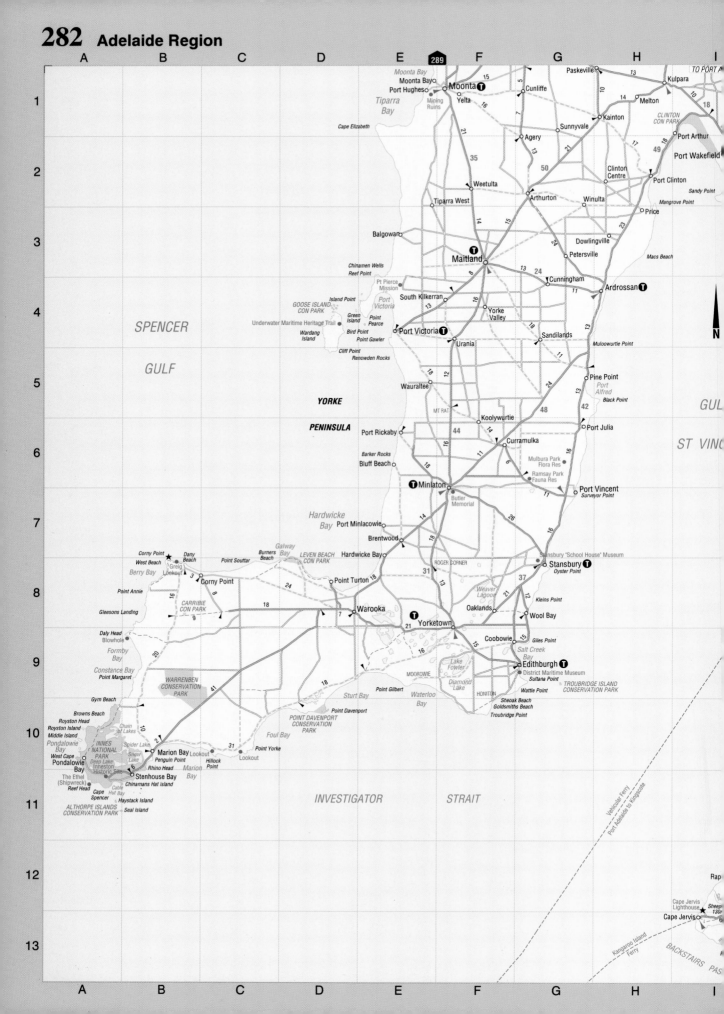

282 Adelaide Region

289

Moonta Bay
Moonta Bay
Port Hughes
Mining Ruins
Moonta
Yelta
Cunliffe
Paskeville
Kulpara
TO PORT A
13
15
16
5
10
14
Melton
Clinton Con Park
18
Tiparra Bay
Cape Elizabeth
21
Agery
Sunnyvale
Kainton
17
49
Port Arthur
Port Wakefield
35
50
Clinton Centre
18
Weetulta
Arthurton
Winulta
Port Clinton
Sandy Point
Tiparra West
Price
Mangrove Point
14
15
23
Balgowan
Dowlingville
24
Petersville
Macs Beach
Chinamen Wells
Reef Point
Maitland
8
13
24
Cunningham
11
Ardrossan
Pt Pierce
Mission
South Kilkerran
16
Yorke Valley
13
Island Point
Port Victoria
Green Island
Point Pearce
13
SPENCER
GOOSE ISLAND
CON PARK
Underwater Maritime Heritage Trail
Wardang Island
Bird Point
Point Gawler
Port Victoria
Urania
18
Sandilands
Muloowurtie Point
GULF
Cliff Point
Renowden Rocks
11
18
12
Pine Point
Port Alfred
Black Point
Wauraltee
MT RAT
Koolywurtie
13
42
YORKE
24
48
PENINSULA
Port Rickaby
44
14
Port Julia
Barker Rocks
Bluff Beach
16
Curramulka
Mulbura Park
Flora Res
16
Port Vincent
Surveyor Point
18
11
Ramsay Park
Fauna Res
6
Minlaton
Butler Memorial
11
Hardwicke
Bay
14
Port Minlacowie
Brentwood
18
26
16
Hardwicke Bay
ROGER CORNER
Corny Point
Dany Beach
Stansbury "School House" Museum
West Beach
Berry Bay
Greig Lookout
Point Souttar
Burners Beach
Galway Bay
LEVEN BEACH
CON PARK
Point Turton
18
31
Stansbury
Oyster Point
3
Corny Point
13
Point Annie
8
24
37
Gleesons Landing
CARRIBIE
CON PARK
18
7
Warooka
Weaver Lagoon
21
12
Kleins Point
9
Oaklands
Wool Bay
Daly Head
Blowhole
21
Yorketown
Giles Point
Formby
Bay
20
16
Coobowie
15
Salt Creek
Bay
Constance Bay
Point Margaret
WARRENBEN
CONSERVATION
PARK
41
18
MOOROWIE
Edithburgh
District Maritime Museum
Sultana Point
Gym Beach
Point Gilbert
Lake Fowler
Diamond Lake
TROUBRIDGE ISLAND
CONSERVATION PARK
Browns Beach
Royston Head
Royston Island
Middle Island
Chain
of Lakes
Point Davenport
Sturt Bay
Waterloo
Bay
HONITON
Sheoak Beach
Goldsmiths Beach
Troubridge Point
Pondalowie
Bay
West Cape
INNES
NATIONAL
PARK
Spider Lake
Snow Lake
10
Marion Bay
Lookout
POINT DAVENPORT
CONSERVATION
PARK
Wattle Point
Pondalowie
Bay
Deep Lake
Inneston
Historic Site
2
Penguin Point
Rhino Head
Hillock Point
31
Lookout
Foul Bay
Point Yorke
The Ethel
(Shipwreck)
Reef Head
Cape
Spencer
Stenhouse Bay
Chinamans Hat Island
Cable
Hut Bay
Marion
Bay
Haystack Island
Seal Island
INVESTIGATOR
STRAIT
ALTHORPE ISLANDS
CONSERVATION PARK

GUL
ST VIN

N

Vehicular Ferry
Port Adelaide to Kingscote

Rap

Cape Jervis
Lighthouse
Sheep
130r
Cape Jervis
Kangaroo Island
Ferry
BACKSTAIRS PAS

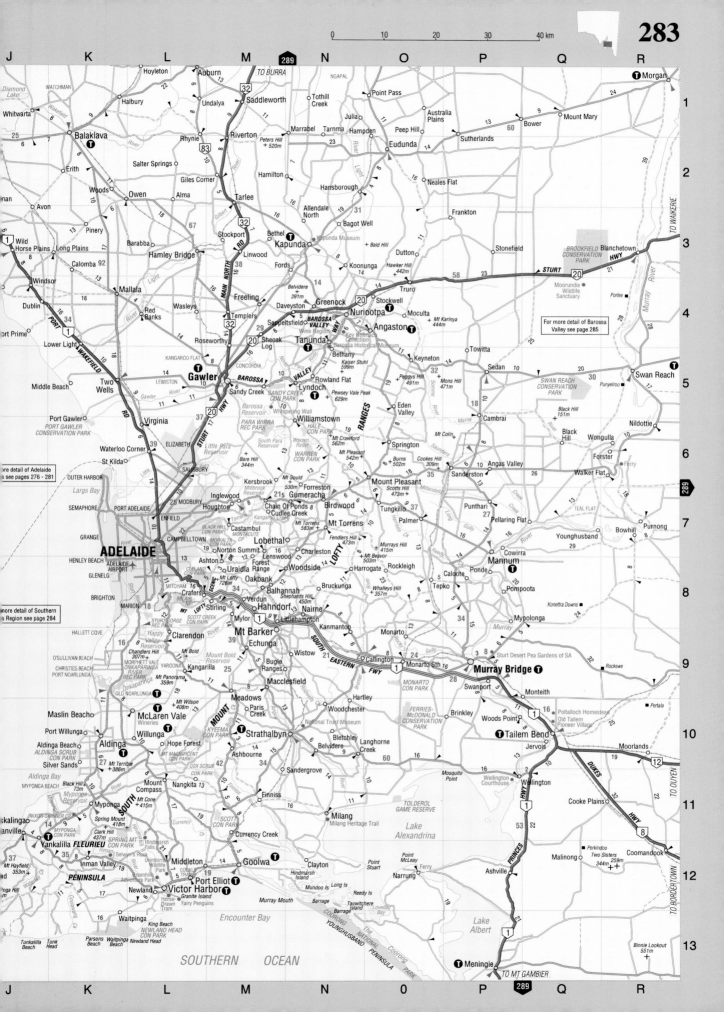

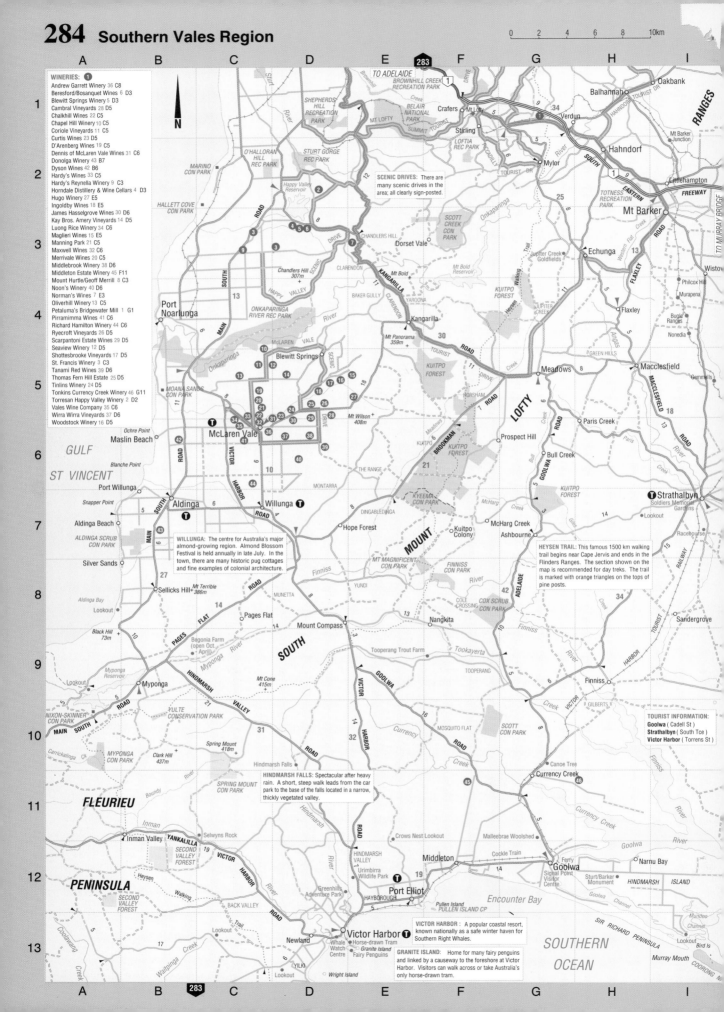

WINERIES: ❶

Andrew Garrett Winery 36 C8
Beresford/Bosanquet Wines 6 D3
Blewitt Springs Winery 5 D3
Cambrai Vineyards 28 D5
Chalkhill Wines 22 C5
Chapel Hill Winery 10 C5
Coriole Vineyards 11 C5
Curtis Wines 23 D5
D'Arenberg Wines 19 C5
Dennis of McLaren Vale Wines 31 C6
Donolga Winery 43 B7
Dyson Wines 42 B6
Hardy's Wines 33 C5
Hardy's Reynella Winery 9 C3
Horndale Distillery & Wine Cellars 4 D3
Hugo 27 E5
Ingoldby Wines 18 E5
James Hasselgrove Wines 30 D6
Kay Bros. Amery Vineyards 14 D5
Luong Rice Winery 34 C6
Maglieri Wines 15 E5
Manning Park 21 C5
Maxwell Wines 32 C6
Merrivale Wines 20 C5
Middlebrook Winery 38 D6
Middleton Estate Winery 45 F11
Mount Hurtle/Geoff Merrill 8 C3
Noon's Winery 40 D6
Norman's Wines 7 E3
Oliverhill Winery 13 C5
Petaluma's Bridgewater Mill 1 G1
Pirramimma Wines 41 C6
Richard Hamilton Winery 44 C6
Ryecroft Vineyards 26 D5
Scarpantoni Estate Wines 29 D5
Seaview Winery 12 D5
Shottesbrooke Vineyards 17 D5
St. Francis Winery 3 C3
Tanami Red Wines 39 D6
Thomas Fern Hill Estate 25 D5
Tinlins Winery 24 D5
Tonkins Currency Creek Winery 46 G11
Torresan Happy Valley Winery 2 D2
Vales Wine Company 35 C6
Wirra Wirra Vineyards 37 D6
Woodstock Winery 16 D5

SCENIC DRIVES: There are many scenic drives in the area; all clearly sign-posted.

WILLUNGA: The centre for Australia's major almond-growing region. Almond Blossom Festival is held annually in late July. In the town, there are many historic pug cottages and fine examples of colonial architecture.

HEYSEN TRAIL: This famous 1500 km walking trail begins near Cape Jervis and ends in the Flinders Ranges. The section shown on the map is recommended for day treks. The trail is marked with orange triangles on the tops of pine posts.

TOURIST INFORMATION:
Goolwa (Cadell St)
Strathalbyn (South Tce)
Victor Harbor (Torrens St)

HINDMARSH FALLS: Spectacular after heavy rain. A short, steep walk leads from the car park to the base of the falls located in a narrow, thickly vegetated valley.

VICTOR HARBOR: A popular coastal resort, known nationally as a safe winter haven for Southern Right Whales.

GRANITE ISLAND: Home for many fairy penguins and linked by a causeway to the foreshore at Victor Harbor. Visitors can walk across or take Australia's only horse-drawn tram.

Scale: 0 10 20 30 40 50 km

A B C D E 291 F G H I

THE FLINDERS RANGES: An ancient range of rugged mountains with spectacularly steep ridges of rock and tree-lined gorges. Sheer ruggedness, wild scenery, plentiful wildlife, unique flora and vestiges of long Aboriginal and short European occupation - all combine to make this region one of the greatest natural attractions in the country. Autumn, winter and spring are the best seasons to visit.

PARALANA HOT SPRINGS: The springs originate deep within the earth's crust and are the last vestige of volcanic action in Australia with near boiling water flowing from the ground.

RIDGE TOP TOUR: Described as one of the most spectacular tours in Australia, this 4WD circuit of the ranges, from Arkaroola, offers breathtaking views of the ancient landscape.

GAMMON RANGES NATIONAL PARK: The granite peaks of the Gammon Ranges rear up between the great salt lakes of Lake Frome and Lake Torrens. The Park is renowned for its untamed wilderness; it is drier, wilder and lonelier than the Flinders Ranges National Park. To see the best of the Park, it is necessary to bushwalk, as roads do not penetrate far into the Park.

WARNING: Bushwalking over the rugged terrain in this region is often very demanding. Bushwalkers should ensure that ample water is carried, about 1 litre per person per hour in hot conditions, food, map and matches or a lighter. A wide-brimmed hat, protective clothing and sturdy footwear are also essential. Someone should be informed of details of route and expected return time. A booklet 'Bushwalking in the Flinders Ranges' is available at the Flinders Ranges National Park Headquarters.

Driving in this region, particularly the northern section requires caution. While most major roads are sealed, many are not. Dust, corrugations and water are the main hazards. It is imperative that motorists obtain full information before proceeding on their journey. If you are off the main roads, check you have informed someone of your route, destination and arrival time; ensure you have adequate essential supplies. **Always** remain with your vehicle if it breaks down.

FLINDERS RANGES NATIONAL PARK: Incorporates most of the central Flinders Ranges. The Park offers a wide range of outdoor recreational activities, rugged mountain scenery, peaceful tree-lined gorges, abundant wildlife and a seasonal wealth of wildflowers.

TOURIST INFORMATION:
Hawker (cnr Wilpena and Cradock Rds)
Port Augusta (Wadlata Outback Centre, Flinders Terrace)
Quorn (3 Seventh Street)
Wilmington (General Store, Main St)

KANYAKA RUINS: This once gracious homestead dates back to the 1850s, when it supported around 70 families. Drought and poor seasons forced the owners off the land. Today restoration and interpretive signposting provides visitors with an interesting insight into the past.

TO MARREE
TO WOOMERA
TO WHYALLA
TO PORT PIRIE
TO BROKEN HILL
TO PETERBOROUGH

Wilpoorinna
South Hill 207m
Witchelina
FARINA
Tent Hill 247m
Mt Livingston 616m
Paralana Hot Springs

Mt Lyndhurst 286m
Avondale
Mount Lyndhurst
Mt Thomas 689m
Mt Pitt 855m
Mt Painter 790m
Umberatana
Arkaroola
Arkaroola Airstrip

Ochre Cliffs
Lyndhurst
Mt Ogilvie
Mt Bourne
Mt Clive
Mandarin Caps 655m
Yankaninna
GAMMON
Benbonyathe Hill
Wooltana

Mt Parry 369m
Mt Telford 350m
Mt Rose 756m
Owieandana
Mt McKinley 1051m
Weetootla Gorge
Balcanoona
RANGES

Myrtle Springs
Coalfield
Mt Coffin 835m
Patsy Springs
Mt Jeffery 727m
Mt Serle 933m
Mt Serle
Italowie Gorge
NATIONAL

Copley
Leigh Creek
Leigh Creek
Angepena
Hawker Hill
Balcaroona Creek
PARK
Wertaloona

Moolooloo North
Maynards Well
Big Moro Gorge

Mt Deception 685m
Mt Hack 1083m
Mt Uro
Nantawarrina
Wearing Gorge
FROME

Sliding Rock Creek
Sliding Rock Mine (Ruins)
Chambers Gorge
LAKE FROME

Beltana Roadhouse
Beltana
Puttapa
Old Warraweena (Ruins)
Mulga View
Mt Chambers 433m
REGIONAL

Mt Stuart
Narrina
RESERVE

Patawarta Hill 1009m
Mt Lyall 390m
Mt Frome 394m

Glass's Gorge
Angorichina
Eregunda Valley

Parachilna
Parachilna Gorge
Blinman
Wirrealpa
Frome Downs

Motpena
Angorichina Tourist Village
Great Wall of China

Mt Falkland
153
Commodore
Balcoracana

FLINDERS
Aroona (ruin)
Oraparinna
Martins Well
Erudina

Brachina Gorge
Mt Caernarvon 920m

RANGES
Mt Rupert 655m
Bunyeroo Valley
Willow Springs

NATIONAL
Merna Mora
St Marys Peak
Park Headquarters
Stokes Hill Lookout

Lookout
Wilpena
Moralana
Wilpena Pound
Sacred Canyon
Curnamona

Mern Merna
Lake Torrens
Walking
Rawnsley Park

South Gap
Mt Aleck 1128m
Heysen Trail
Willippa

Beda Hill 200m
Burnett Hill 442m
Wonoka Historic Site (ruin)
Arkaba
Warcowie
Wilyerpa Hill 880m

Wallerberdina
Arkaba
Wonoka
Bibliando

Mt Orkola 503m
Yappala
Mt Plantagenet 949m
Willow Waters (Ruins)
Glenorchy

Hawker
Yourambulla Caves
Baratta

Buckaringa Gorge
Middle Gorge
Kanyaka Ruins
Milang
Mt Victor 464m
Mt Victor
Plumbago
Koonamore

Mt Arden 839m
Warren Gorge
WILSON
Cradock
Yednalue
Melton
Four Brothers

THE DUTCHMANS STERN CP
66
47
Belton
Marchant Hill 799m
Spotswood Hill
Weekeroo Hill 568m

Quorn
105
Price Hill 756m
Wirra Downs
Waukaringa

Port Augusta
Devils Peak
Pichi Richi Railway
Bruce
Carrieton
Minburra
Tattawuppa Hill 611m

Stirling North
Mt Brown 965m
Hammond
Johnberg
Wabricoola
Yunta

Tassie Hill 268m
Horrocks Pass
Ivy Glen
Yalpara
Meadow Downs
BARRIER HWY

Wilmington
94
Willowie
Eurelia
YALPARA CP
Oulnina Hill 710m
Oulnina Park

ARMY TRAINING RESERVE
Blanche Harbor
WINNINOWIE CON PARK
Hancocks Lookout
MOUNT REMARKABLE NP
Morchard
Orroroo
BLACK ROCK CP
Dare Hill 452m
Panaramatee

Pekina Hill 732m
Orroroo Aboriginal Rock Carvings
Paratoo

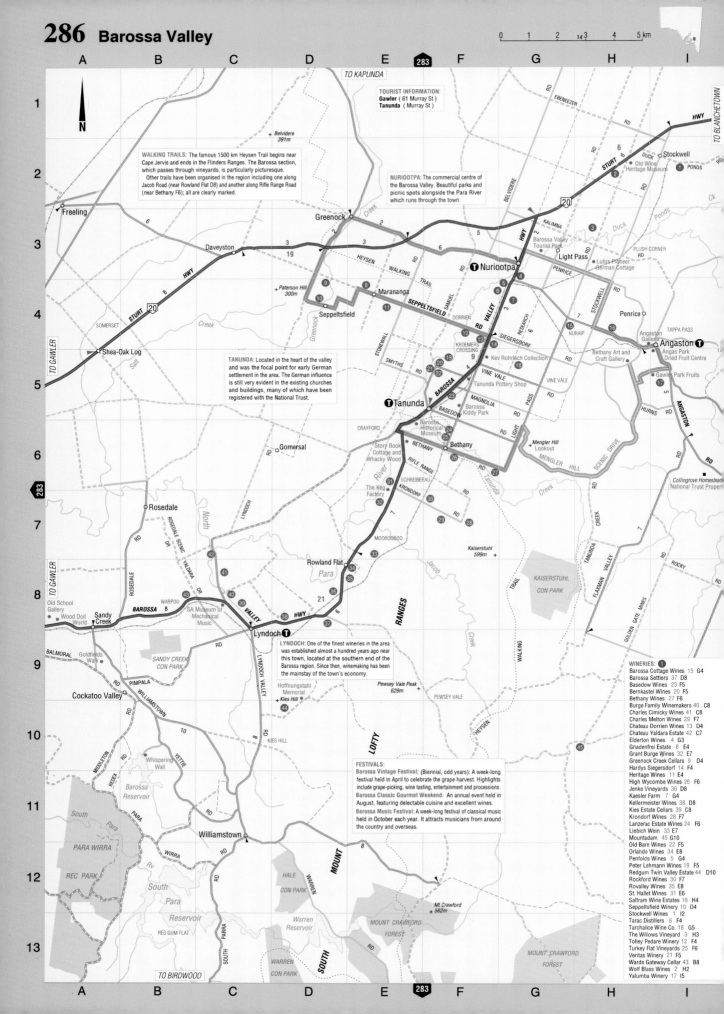

TO KAPUNDA

WALKING TRAILS: The famous 1500 km Heysen Trail begins near Cape Jervis and ends in the Flinders Ranges. The Barossa section, which passes through vineyards, is particularly picturesque. Other trails have been organised in the region including one along Jacob Road (near Rowland Flat D8) and another along Rifle Range Road (near Bethany F6); all are clearly marked.

NURIOOTPA: The commercial centre of the Barossa Valley. Beautiful parks and picnic spots alongside the Para River which runs through the town.

TANUNDA: Located in the heart of the valley and was the focal point for early German settlement in the area. The German influence is still very evident in the existing churches and buildings, many of which have been registered with the National Trust.

LYNDOCH: One of the finest wineries in the area was established almost a hundred years ago near this town, located at the southern end of the Barossa region. Since then, winemaking has been the mainstay of the town's economy.

FESTIVALS:
Barossa Vintage Festival: (Biennial, odd years): A week-long festival held in April to celebrate the grape harvest. Highlights include grape-picking, wine tasting, entertainment and processions.
Barossa Classic Gourmet Weekend: An annual event held in August, featuring delectable cuisine and excellent wines.
Barossa Music Festival: A week-long festival of classical music held in October each year. It attracts musicians from around the country and overseas.

WINERIES: ①
Barossa Cottage Wines 15 G4
Barossa Settlers 37 D8
Basedow Wines 23 F5
Bernkastel Wines 20 F5
Bethany Wines 27 F6
Burge Family Winemakers 40 C8
Charles Cimicky Wines 41 C8
Charles Melton Wines 29 F7
Chateau Dorrien Wines 13 D4
Chateau Yaldara Estate 42 C7
Elderton Wines 4 G3
Gnadenfrei Estate 8 E4
Grant Burge Wines 32 E7
Greenock Creek Cellars 9 D4
Hardys Siegersdorf 14 F4
Heritage Wines 11 E4
High Wycombe Wines 26 F5
Jenke Vineyards 36 D8
Kaesler Farm 7 G4
Kellermeister Wines 38 D8
Kies Estate Cellars 39 C8
Krondorf Wines 28 F7
Lanzerac Estate Wines 24 F6
Liebich Wein 33 E7
Mountadam 45 G10
Old Barn Wines 22 F5
Orlando Wines 34 E8
Penfolds Wines 5 G4
Peter Lehmann Wines 19 F5
Redgum Twin Valley Estate 44 D10
Rockford Wines 30 F7
Rovalley Wines 35 E8
St. Hallet Wines 31 E6
Saltram Wine Estates 16 H4
Seppeltsfield Winery 10 D4
Stockwell Wines 1 I2
Tarac Distillers 6 F4
Tarchalice Wine Co. 18 G5
The Willows Vineyard 3 H3
Tolley Pedare Winery 12 F4
Turkey Flat Vineyards 25 F6
Veritas Winery 21 F5
Wards Gateway Cellar 43 B8
Wolf Blass Wines 2 H2
Yalumba Winery 17 I5

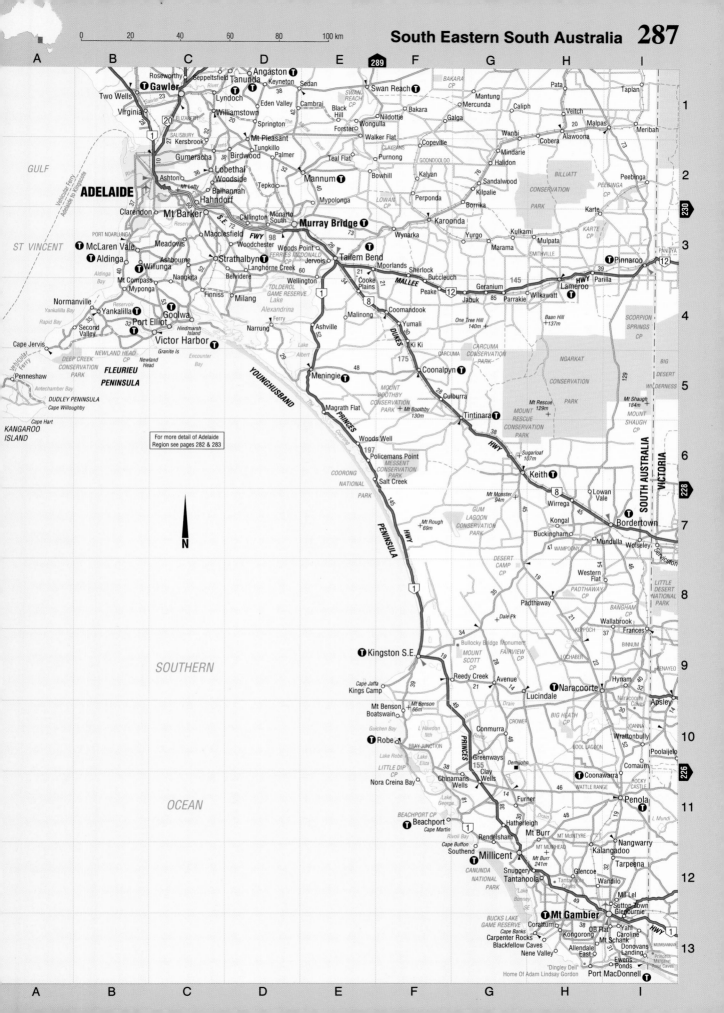

0 20 40 60 80 100 km

J K L M N O P Q R

SOUTH AUSTRALIA / NEW SOUTH WALES

DANGGALI CONSERVATION PARK

Melrose
Booleroo Centre
Murray Town
Wirrabara
Appila
Stone Hut
Hornsdale
Tarcowie
Yatina
Peterborough
Nantabibbie
Oodla Wirra
Doughboy Hill
Wright Hill +517m
Alderman Reservoir

Nelshaby
Napperby
Laura
Caltowie
Jamestown
Whyte Yarcowie
Terowie
PANDAPPA CONSERVATION PARK
Boiekevie Hill 539m
Ironback Hill 378m
Faraway Hill 216m

Crystal Brook
Narridie
Georgetown
Gladstone
Huddleston
Spalding
Booborowie
Hallett
Mt Bryan 932m
Curoona

Redhill
Koolunga
Collinsfield
Lake View
Brinkworth
Condowie
Hart
Andrews
Leighton
Hilltown
Mount Bryan
Mt Cone 793m
Burra
Redbanks
Stein Hill 612m

Snowtown
Blyth
Bumbunga
Kybunga
Clare
Sevenhill
Mintaro
Penwortham
Farrell Flat
Black Springs
Emu Downs
Worlds End
Florieton

Balaklava
Bowmans
Erith
Salter Springs
Auburn
Saddleworth
Manoora
Waterloo
Marrabel
Hampden
Morgan
Cadell
Weston Flat
POOGINOOK CONSERVATION PARK

Port Wakefield
Port Clinton
Owen
Riverton
Tarlee
Eudunda
Neales Flat
Frankton
Bower
Sutherlands
Mount Mary
Qualco
Ramco
Taylorville
Waikerie
Overland Corner
Renmark
Paringa

Avon
Pinery
Hamley Bridge
Kapunda
Dutton
Truro
Stonefield
Blanchetown
New Well
Notts Well
Lowbank
Kingston
Moorook
Monash
Glossop
Lyrup
Beri

Windsor
Dublin
Mallala
Wasleys
Freeling
Greenock
Nuriootpa
Angaston
Keyneton
Sedan
New Residence
Myrla
Loveday
Winkie
Loxton

Two Wells
Virginia
Gawler
Roseworthy
Seppeltsfield
Tanunda
Lyndoch
Williamstown
Eden Valley
Cambrai
Swan Reach
Bakara
Galga
Wunkar
Pyap
Taplan

Elizabeth
Kersbrook
Gumeracha
Birdwood
Palmer
Black Hill
Nildottie
Wongulla
Walker Flat
Copeville
Mantung
Mercunda
Caliph
Pata
Paruna
Meribah

ADELAIDE
Ashton
Woodside
Balhannah
Lobethal
Mt Pleasant
Tungkillo
Springton
Forster
Purnong
Bowhill
Kalyan
Wanbi
Cobera
Alawoona
Veitch

Clarendon
Mt Barker
Hahndorf
Callington
Monarto South
Mannum
Mypolonga
Perponda
Halidon
Sandalwood
Mindarie
BILLIATT CONSERVATION PARK
Peebinga

Macclesfield
Woodchester
Murray Bridge
Wynarka
Karoonda
Kilpalie
Borrika
Karte
PEEBINGA CP

McLaren Vale
Meadows
Strathalbyn
Langhorne Creek
Woods Point
Jervois
Tailem Bend
Moorlands
Sherlock
Buccleuch
Marama
Kulkami
Mulpata
Pinnaroo

Willunga
Aldinga
Ashbourne
Belvidere
Wellington
Peake
Geranium
Jabuk
Parrakie
Wilkawatt
Lameroo
Parilla

Myponga
Nangkita
Finniss
Milang
Cooke Plains
Coomandook
Yumali
One Tree Hill
Baan Hill
SCORPION SPRINGS CP

Normanville
Yankalilla
Goolwa
Narrung
Ashville
Ki Ki
CARCUMA CONSERVATION PARK
NGARKAT CONSERVATION PARK

Second Valley
Port Elliot
Victor Harbor
Lake Alexandrina
Lake Albert
Meningie
Coonalpyn
Colburra

Cape Jervis
FLEURIEU PENINSULA
DEEP CREEK CONSERVATION PARK
Magrath Flat
MOUNT BOOTHBY CONSERVATION PARK
Tintinara
MOUNT RESCUE CONSERVATION PARK
Mt Shaugh 184m
MOUNT SHAUGH CP

COORONG NATIONAL PARK
Policemans Point
Woods Well
Salt Creek
MESSENT CONSERVATION PARK
Keith

YOUNGHUSBAND PENINSULA
GUM LAGOON CONSERVATION PARK
Mt Monster 94m
Lowan Vale
Wirrega
Kongal
Bordertown
Buckingham
Mundulla
Wolseley
Serviceton

SOUTH AUSTRALIA / VICTORIA

SOUTHERN OCEAN

For more detail of Adelaide Region see pages 282 & 283

GULF ST VINCENT

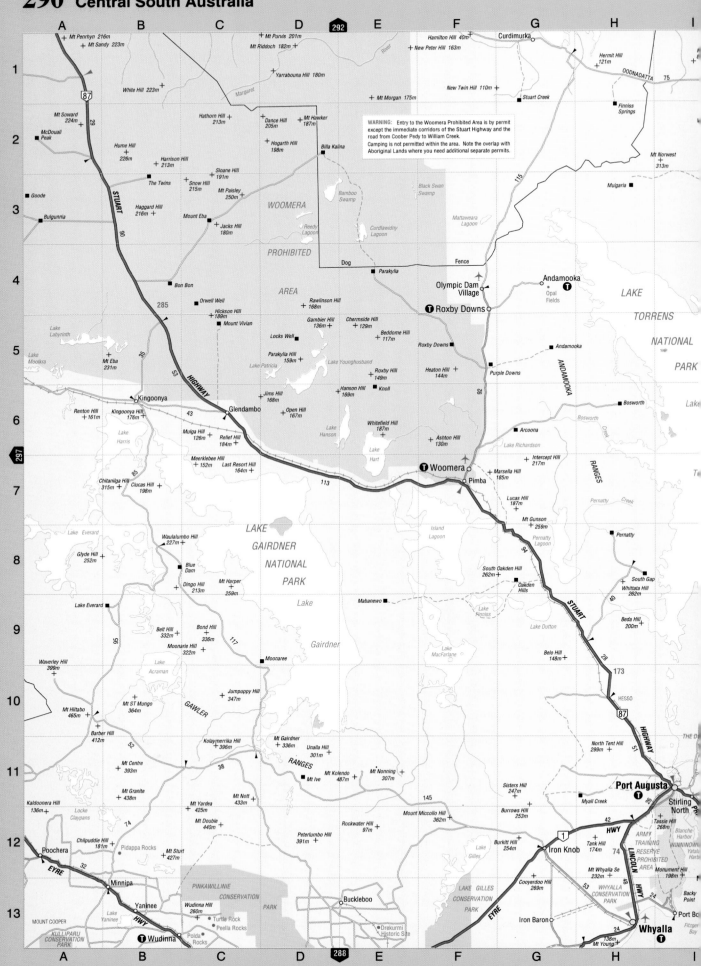

WARNING: Entry to the Woomera Prohibited Area is by permit except the immediate corridors of the Stuart Highway and the road from Coober Pedy to William Creek.
Camping is not permitted within the area. Note the overlap with Aboriginal Lands where you need additional separate permits.

STRZELECKI
REGIONAL RESERVE

WARNING: In outback Australia, long distances separate some towns. Travellers should familiarise themselves with prevailing conditions before departure, and take care to ensure their vehicle is roadworthy and that they carry adequate supplies of petrol, water and food.

In northern Australia, rainfall during the 'wet' season (Oct-March) can make some roads impassable. Full information on road conditions should be obtained before departure.

If visitors intend diverting off public roads within Aboriginal Land areas, a permit is required from the relevant Aboriginal authority.

Lake Callabonna

Winnathee

Hawker Gate House

Prospect Hill 218m

Mt Gardiner 374m

Mt Babbage 369m

Moolawatana

Smithville House

Mount Freeling

Mt Livingston 616m

Mount Fitton

Tent Hill 247m

Mt Neil 571m

Farina

Wilpoorinna

Paralana Hot Springs

Turleys Gate

Starvation Lake

Packsaddle

Mt Lyndhurst 286m

Mount Lyndhurst

Mt Pitt 855m

Mt Painter 790m

Arkaroola

Mandarin Caps 655m

Pine View

Lyndhurst

Avondale

Mt Coffin 835m

Mt Serle 933m

Mt Mckinlay 1051m

GAMMON RANGES NATIONAL PARK

Wooltana

Weetootla Gorge

LAKE FROME REGIONAL RESERVE

Copley

Leigh Creek

Leigh Creek

Mt Jeffery 727m

Balcanoona

Boughams Gate

Teilta

Maynards Well

Mt Deception 685m

NORTH FLINDERS RANGES

Lake Frome

Lake Culberta

Beltana

Beltana

Sliding Rock

Mt Hack 1083m

Old Warraween A (Ruins)

Lake Karpi

Lake Carnanto

Patawarta Hill 1009m

Narrina

Wearing Gorge

Chambers Gorge

Mt Chambers 433m

Lake Moko

Parachilna

Blinman

Wirrealpa

Lake Millyera

Lake Tarkarooloo

Dog Fence

124

Motpena

Commodore

For more detail of Flinders Ranges see page 285

Frome Downs

Lake Namba

Lake Yentaawena

Eurinilla

Morphetts

FLINDERS RANGES NATIONAL PARK

Oraparinna

Reaphook Hill 388m

Mt Caernarvon 920m

Benagerie

SOUTH AUSTRALIA

NEW SOUTH WALES

Mt Rupert 655m

Lookout

Wilpena

Moraiana

Wilpena Pound

Wilpena

Martins Well

Wilpena

Erudina

Mulyungarie

Mooleulooloo

MUNDI MUNDI PLAIN

Burnett Hill 442m

Mt Aleck 1128m

Rawnsley Park

Curnamona

Wonoka Historic Site (ruin)

Arkaroola

Willippa

Wilyerpa Hill 880m

Bibliando

Killawarra

Old Telechie

Umberumberka Reservoir

Ghost Town

Mt Plantagenet 949m

Baratta

Hawker

Yourambulla Peak Caves

FLINDERS

Sessions Creek

Mt Victor 464m

Bimbowrie

Wompinie

Cockburn

Hut Hill 618m

Cradock

Plumbago

Outalpa Hill 496m

Outalpa

HIGHWAY 32

Mingary

Aroona

Tepco

SOUTH

Belton

Marchant Hill 799m

Spotswood Hill

Weekeroo Hill 568m

Weekeroo

Wiawera

Olary

Ballara

Price Hill 756m

Wirra Downs

Waukaringa

223

Carrieton

Johnberg

Meadow Downs

Mannahill

Maldorky Hill 428m

Mutooroo

Burta

Hammond

Ivy Glen

Eurelia

Yalpara

Tattawuppa Hill 611m

Wadnaminga

Browns Hill 152m

Willowie

Morchard

Orroroo

BARRIER

Yunta

Oulnina Hill 710m

Oulnina

BENDA RANGE

Booleroo

Pekina Hill 732m

Pekina

Dawson

Nackara Hill 661m

Nackara

Paratoo

Dare Hill 452m

Oulnina Park

Melrose

Booleroo Centre

Nantabibbie

Oodla Wirra

Tarcowie

Yatina

Murray Town

Wirrabara

Hornsdale

Mannanarie

Peterborough

Doughboy Hill 602m

Wright Hill 517m

Alderman Reservoir

DANGGALI CONSERVATION PARK

Appila

Mt Lock 743m

Gumbowie

Belalie

Stone Hut

Boiekevie Hill 539m

Ironback Hill 378m

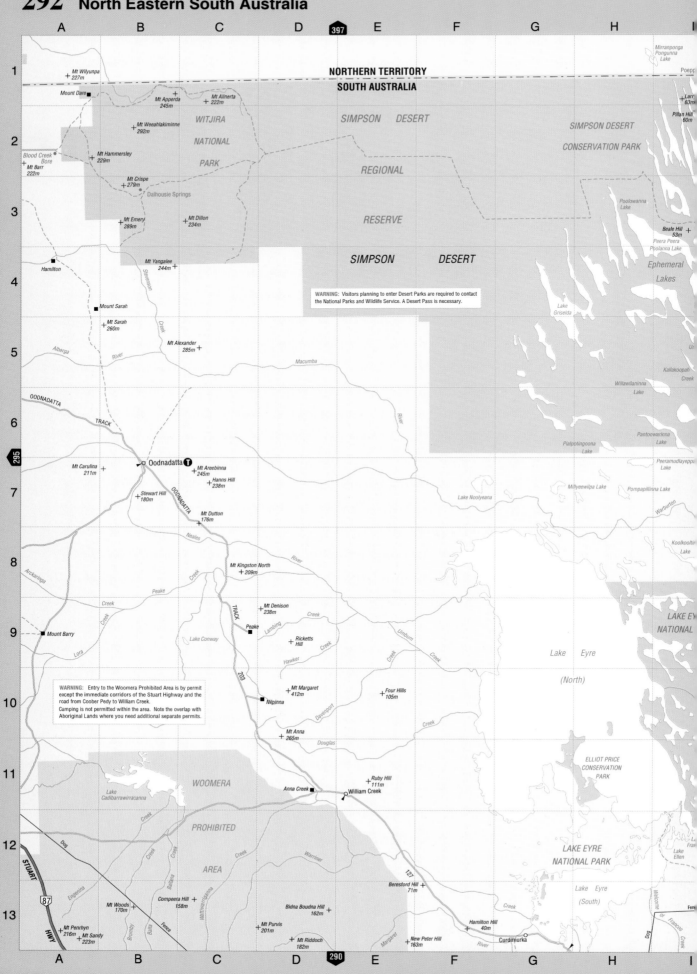

NORTHERN TERRITORY

SOUTH AUSTRALIA

WITJIRA NATIONAL PARK

SIMPSON DESERT

SIMPSON DESERT CONSERVATION PARK

REGIONAL

RESERVE

SIMPSON DESERT

Ephemeral Lakes

WARNING: Visitors planning to enter Desert Parks are required to contact the National Parks and Wildlife Service. A Desert Pass is necessary.

Mirranponga Pongunna Lake

+ Mt Wilyunpa 227m

■ Mount Dare

+ Mt Apperda 245m

+ Mt Alinerta 222m

+ Mt Weeahlakiminne 292m

+ Mt Hammersley 229m

Blood Creek Bore

+ Mt Barr 222m

+ Mt Crispe 279m

Dalhousie Springs

+ Mt Emery 289m

+ Mt Dillon 234m

■ Hamilton

+ Mt Yangalee 244m

Stevenson Creek

■ Mount Sarah

+ Mt Sarah 260m

+ Mt Alexander 285m

Alberga River

Macumba

OODNADATTA TRACK

+ Mt Carulina 211m

○ Oodnadatta Ⓣ

+ Mt Areebinna 245m

+ Hanns Hill 238m

+ Stewart Hill 180m

OODNADATTA TRACK

+ Mt Dutton 176m

Neales

+ Mt Kingston North 209m

River

Arckaringa

Creek

Peake

Creek

Lora

■ Mount Barry

Creek

TRACK

+ Mt Denison 238m

Lambing Creek

■ Peake

+ Ricketts Hill

Lake Conway

Hawker Creek

Umbum Creek

203

+ Mt Margaret 412m

■ Nilpinna

+ Four Hills 105m

Davenport Creek

Creek

Lake Eyre (North)

Lake Eyre National Park

WARNING: Entry to the Woomera Prohibited Area is by permit except the immediate corridors of the Stuart Highway and the road from Coober Pedy to William Creek.
Camping is not permitted within the area. Note the overlap with Aboriginal Lands where you need additional separate permits.

+ Mt Anna 265m

Douglas

WOOMERA

+ Ruby Hill 111m

ELLIOT PRICE CONSERVATION PARK

Lake Cadibarrawirracanna

Creek

■ Anna Creek

⊙ William Creek

PROHIBITED

AREA

Dog Creek

Baltana Creek

Engenina

Matthwartingenna

Creek

Warriner

Creek

127

Beresford Hill 71m

LAKE EYRE NATIONAL PARK

Lake Ellen

STUART HWY

87

+ Mt Woods 170m

Bramley

Baltana Fence

Compeera Hill 158m

Bidna Boudna Hill 162m

Margaret

Hamilton Hill 40m

Lake Eyre (South)

Welcome Creek

+ Mt Penrhyn 216m

+ Mt Sandy 223m

+ Mt Purvis 201m

+ Mt Riddoch 182m

+ New Peter Hill 163m

River

⊙ Curdimurka

Lake Griselda

Poolowanna Lake

Beale Hill 53m

Peera Peera Poolanna Lake

Kallakoopah Creek

Wiltawilaninna Lake

Pialpotingoona Lake

Pantoowarinna Lake

Peeramudlayeppa Lake

Millyeewilpa Lake

Pompapillinna Lake

Lake Noolyeana

Warburton

Koolkooltinna Lake

Larr

Pillan Hill 60m

397

390

295

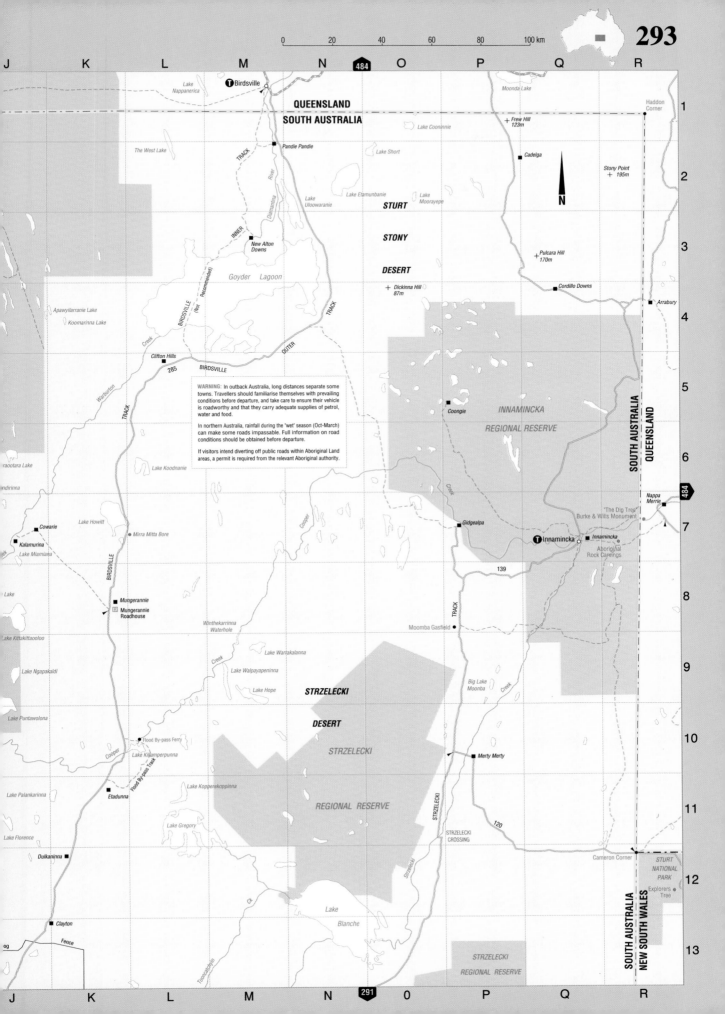

0   20   40   60   80   100 km

484

J   K   L   M   N   **484**   O   P   Q   R

Lake Nappanerica

T Birdsville

QUEENSLAND
SOUTH AUSTRALIA — 1

Moonda Lake

Haddon Corner

Pandie Pandie

The West Lake

Lake Cooninnie

Lake Short

+ Frew Hill
123m

■ Cadelga

Stony Point
+ 195m

2

Lake Etamunbanie

Lake Uloowaranie

Lake Moorayepe
Lake

STURT

New Alton Downs

+ Pulcara Hill
170m

3

STONY

Goyder   Lagoon

DESERT

+ Dickinna Hill
87m

■ Cordillo Downs

■ Arrabury   4

Apawyilarranie Lake

Koomarinna Lake

Clifton Hills

285

BIRDSVILLE (Not Recommended)

BIRDSVILLE

INNER

OUTER   TRACK

■ Coongie

INNAMINCKA

REGIONAL RESERVE

SOUTH AUSTRALIA   QUEENSLAND   5

Warburton   Creek

Lake Koodnanie

WARNING: In outback Australia, long distances separate some towns. Travellers should familiarise themselves with prevailing conditions before departure, and take care to ensure their vehicle is roadworthy and that they carry adequate supplies of petrol, water and food.

In northern Australia, rainfall during the 'wet' season (Oct-March) can make some roads impassable. Full information on road conditions should be obtained before departure.

If visitors intend diverting off public roads within Aboriginal Land areas, a permit is required from the relevant Aboriginal authority.

6

raootara Lake

ndirinna

Lake Howitt

Cooper   Creek

Nappa Merrie

484

"The Dig Tree"
Burke & Wills Monument

7

● Mirra Mitta Bore

■ Gidgealpa

T Innamincka   ○ Innamincka

Aboriginal Rock Carvings

Cowarie

Kalamurina

Lake Miamiana

TRACK

BIRDSVILLE

139

Lake

■ Mungerannie

Mungerannie Roadhouse

Winthekarrinna Waterhole

TRACK

Moomba Gasfield ●

8

ake Kittakittaooloo

Lake Warrakalanna

Lake Walpayapeninna

9

Lake Ngapakaldi

STRZELECKI

Lake Hope

Big Lake Moomba   Creek

Lake Puntawolona

DESERT

10

Flood By-pass Ferry

Lake Killamperpunna

STRZELECKI

■ Merty Merty

Flood Bypass Track

Lake Kopperekoppinna

Lake Palankarinna

Etadunna   ●

REGIONAL   RESERVE

STRZELECKI

120   11

Lake Florence

Lake Gregory

STRZELECKI CROSSING

Cameron Corner

Dulkaninna ■

Strzelecki   Ck

STURT NATIONAL PARK   12

Explorers Tree ●

Clayton ■

Fence

Lake Blanche

SOUTH AUSTRALIA
NEW SOUTH WALES

13

Toomaatchyin

**STRZELECKI
REGIONAL RESERVE**

J   K   L   M   N   **291**   O   P   Q   R

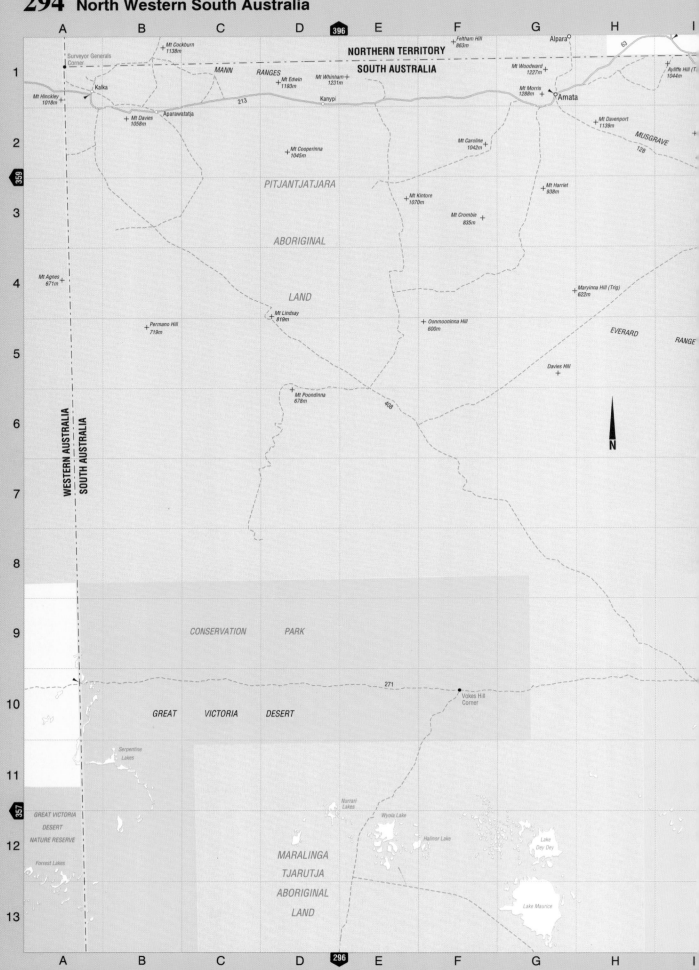

294 North Western South Australia

A B C D **396** E F G H I

1 Surveyor Generals Corner
Mt Cockburn 1138m
Mt Hinckley 1018m
Kalka
MANN RANGES
Mt Edwin 1193m
Mt Whinham 1231m
Kanypi
213
Feltham Hill 863m
NORTHERN TERRITORY
SOUTH AUSTRALIA
Alpara
Mt Woodward 1227m
Mt Morris 1288m
Amata
Ayliffe Hill (T 1044m
63

Mt Davies 1058m
Aparawatatja
Mt Davenport 1139m
MUSGRAVE
128

2 Mt Cooperinna 1045m
Mt Caroline 1042m
PITJANTJATJARA
Mt Kintore 1070m
Mt Harriet 938m

3 ABORIGINAL
Mt Crombie 835m

4 Mt Agnes 671m
LAND
Mt Lindsay 819m
Oonmooninna Hill 600m
Maryinna Hill (Trig) 622m
EVERARD

5 Permano Hill 719m
Davies Hill
RANGE

6 Mt Poondinna 678m
408
N

7

8

9 CONSERVATION PARK

10 271
Vokes Hill Corner
GREAT VICTORIA DESERT

11 Serpentine Lakes

12 GREAT VICTORIA DESERT NATURE RESERVE
Forrest Lakes
Nurrari Lakes
Wyola Lake
Halinor Lake
Lake Dey Dey
MARALINGA TJARUTJA

13 ABORIGINAL LAND
Lake Maurice

A B C D **396** E F G H

WESTERN AUSTRALIA
SOUTH AUSTRALIA

359
357

J K L M N O P Q R

396 397

0 20 40 60 80 100 km

NORTHERN TERRITORY
SOUTH AUSTRALIA

Victory Downs
Mount
24 Cavenagh
Victory Downs

Mt Cecil
551m

Mt Darling
544m
Mt Parlue
478m
Mt Mead
376m
Mt Hearne
306m

1

Sentinel Hill
910m

Mt Warrabillinna
1125m

PITJANTJATJARA

Tieyon

Eringa

Mt Barr
222m

2

ABORIGINAL

Mt Howe
519m

LAND   Echo Hill
604m

Marryat
Creek

Mt Britton
334m

a Hill (Trig)
regon

3

Hamilton
Creek

Marble Hill
523m

Lambin A (Ruin)

143

Chandler
Mt Chandler
551m

44

Alberga
River

Todmorden

4

Mimili

Mt Illbillee
917m

STUART

HIGHWAY

OODNADATTA

TRACK

5

EVERARD   RANGE

Mintabie

Marla

Welbourn Hill

87

6

292

Ammaroodinna Hill
359m

CENTRAL

83

Neales
River

MARALINGA

Wintinna

Arckaringa

7

TJARUTJA

AUSTRALIA

Cadney Park
Roadhouse

Mount Willoughby

Mt Arckaringa
243m

Arckaringa

8

ABORIGINAL

LAND

RAILWAY

Evelyn
Creek

Evelyn Downs

Poothoura
Creek

Lora

Mount Barry

9

MU JUNCTION

Pootnoura

Algebuīlcullia
Creek

153

10

TALLARINGA

Wooroing
Creek

265

CONSERVATION

Dog   Fence

Giddi-giddinna
Creek

Oolgelima

Ck

11

WOOMERA

PARK

Manguri

STUART

Coober Pedy

Long Creek

PROHIBITED

WARNING: Entry to the Woomera Prohibited Area is by permit
except the immediate corridors of the Stuart Highway and the
road from Coober Pedy to William Creek.
Camping is not permitted within the area. Note the overlap with
Aboriginal Lands where you need additional separate permits.

Mabel   Creek

HIGHWAY

12

AREA

87

Wilkinson
Lakes

Dog

Fence

Lake
Phillipson

Wirrida

Mt Penrhyn
216m

13

J K L M N O P Q R

297

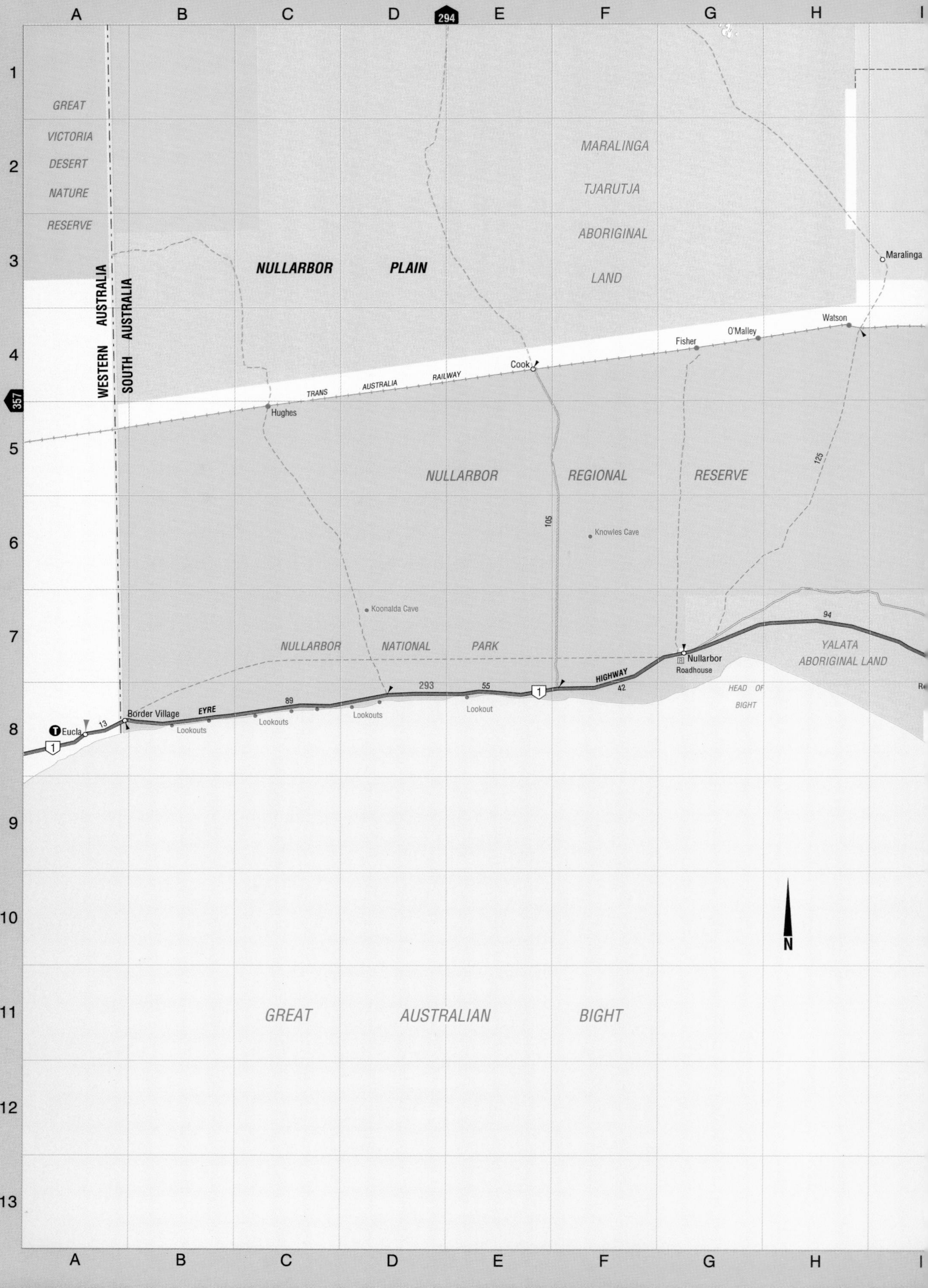

A B C **294** D E F G H I

1

GREAT

VICTORIA

2 *DESERT*

NATURE *MARALINGA*

RESERVE *TJARUTJA*

3 *ABORIGINAL*

NULLARBOR **PLAIN** *LAND* Maralinga

Watson

Fisher O'Malley

357 Cook

TRANS AUSTRALIA RAILWAY

Hughes

5 *NULLARBOR* *REGIONAL* *RESERVE* 125

105

6 Knowles Cave

Koonalda Cave

7 *NULLARBOR* *NATIONAL* *PARK* 94 *YALATA*

Nullarbor *ABORIGINAL LAND*

Roadhouse

Border Village **EYRE** 293 55 **HIGHWAY** 42 *HEAD OF*

8 Eucla 13 89 Lookout *BIGHT*

Lookouts Lookouts Lookouts

9

10 **N**

11 *GREAT* *AUSTRALIAN* *BIGHT*

12

13

A B C D E F G H

0   20   40   60   80   100 km

J   K   L   M   N   O   P   Q   R

MARALINGA

TJARUTJA

ABORIGINAL

LAND

Wilkinson Lakes

WARNING: Entry to the Woomera Prohibited Area is by permit
except the immediate corridors of the Stuart Highway and the
road from Coober Pedy to William Creek.
Camping is not permitted within the area. Note the overlap with
Aboriginal Lands where you need additional separate permits.

WOOMERA

PROHIBITED

AREA

Ingomar

Mc Douall Peak

Muckanippie

Mulgathing

Bulgunnia

Carnes

West Point Hill
230m

Lake Anthony

Half Moon
Lake

Mt Christie
233m

Warrior

Gibraltar Rocks   Gibraltar
Rocks

PARTRIDGE RANGE

TRANS

Barton

AUSTRALIA

Mungala

Mount
Christie

Wynbring

RAILWAY

Malbooma

Tarcoola

Wilgena Hill
253m

Lake
Moolkra

Lake
Labyrinth

Ifould Lake

Mt Finke
361m

Bulpara Hill
237m

Renton Hill
161m

143

YELLABINNA   REGIONAL

RESERVE

Dog

290

Lake Everard

Colona

55

Roadhouse

Nundroo

202   EYRE

Tallala Hill
84m

39

Bookabie

Bookabie Hill
149m

Dog   Fence

Bookabie School
Ruin

Cundilippy

35

Cooper Hill
126m

Penong

1

73

HIGHWAY

Woolshed Hill
134m

YUMBARRA

CONSERVATION   PARK

Koonibba Hill
169m

Coppudurba Hill
147m

OTC Satellite
Communication Station

Nuckulla Hill
264m

PUREBA

CONSERVATION PARK

Yarlbrinda Hill
348m

Waverley Hill
399m

FOWLERS BAY

Point Fowler

Lake MacDonnell

Hyde Pt

Ceduna

Thevenard

St Peter Island

Smoky Bay

Eyre Island

NUYTS
ARCHIPELAGO
CONSERVATION
PARK

ISLES OF
ST FRANCIS
CP

EYRE

FLINDERS

Smoky Bay

ACRAMAN
CREEK
CP

Point De Mole

Point Brown

Nurka Hill
130m

Oak Hill
111m

92

Carawa

173

109

Haslam

Streaky
Bay

Cape Bauer

Olive Islands

Corvisart Bay

Point Westall

Monument

Searcy Bay

Streaky Bay

CALPATANNA
WATERHOLE
CP

Calca

Mt Hall
208m

Cape Radstock

VENUS BAY
CP

Murphys Haystacks

HIGHWAY

Mt Cooper
672m

KULLIPARU
CONSERVATION
PARK

Port Kenny

Mt Damper
152m

Wallala Hill
166m

Pimbaacla Hill
121m

Wirrulla

HIGHWAY

YANTANABIE

Kaldoonera Hill
136m

49

Cungena

Locke
Claypans

Chandada

62

Poochera

33

Minnipa

Mt Hiltabo
465m

Barber Hill
412m

67

Dog

Fence

288

295

Western Australia

The Golden West

Even a casual glance at a map of Australia will quickly reveal that a motor touring holiday in Western Australia requires a great deal of thought and advance planning. For one thing, just getting there from the eastern states involves travelling huge distances, so fly/drive or Moto-Rail facilities are well worth investigation; and, given that it is almost one-third the size of the whole of Australia, unless you have unlimited time and energy, touring by road is only going to get you to certain sections. The south-west region is relatively easily and pleasantly covered by car, but to travel the unique north and north-east requires more time and careful planning.

The vast distances to be covered are such that it is worth considering some touring by air when planning your itinerary and budget. Ansett WA operates tours, varying in length, to all the spectacular remote regions. There is a network of almost 100 heritage trails across the state, each designed by the local community. Once you have settled your method of travel, you will find an amazing state waiting to be explored. Despite the fact that the Dutch had mapped the western coastline of Australia as early as the sixteenth century, it was not until 1826 that a British party from Sydney landed at King George Sound (Albany) and then only for fear of possible French colonisation. Three years later Perth, the first non-convict settlement in the country, was founded by Captain James Stirling. Due mainly to the ruggedness and sheer size of the land, the West remained pretty much as it had always been until 1892. In that year gold was discovered at Coolgardie and the first economic boom for the region began. Today, of course, it is an immensely rich mineral state, its thriving economy still growing.

The beautiful city of Perth has the best climate of any Australian capital: midwinter average maximum temperature of 18°C, a year-round average of 23°C and an average of almost eight hours of sunshine a day. The climate in the north of the state is tropical, and as you travel south it becomes subtropical and then temperate.

It is easy to assume from the map that Perth is a coastal city, though actually it is nineteen kilometres inland, up the broad and beautiful Swan River, home of the black swan. A city of over one million people, Perth is large enough to offer excitement and variety, yet compact enough to be seen quite easily. King's Park, 404 hectares of natural bushland, is only a short drive from the city centre, and nearby ocean beaches provide year-round swimming and surfing.

Once you start touring, the Swan Valley is a must, whether or not you are interested in wine. Up in the Darling Range the valley is fertile and beautiful. The vineyards flourish on the rich loam that is perfect for grape-growing, and at the end of a day's drive you can sample some notable results of these conditions.

Nearby Rottnest Island is low, small, sandy and only twenty kilometres off the coast from Fremantle. Regular air and ferry services from Perth will take you to this popular holiday island, where even the surrounding sea has been declared a sanctuary. Conditions for skin-diving could not be better.

Although Victoria has claimed the title of Australia's 'Garden State', the southern corner of the state is still the 'garden of Western Australia', ablaze every spring with wildflowers. Hardwood forests of massive karri and jarrah trees soar above the hundreds of different species of wildflowers that bloom from September to November. Great surfing beaches and coastal panoramas add to the attractions of the south-west region, with such popular locations as Margaret River, Busselton and Yallingup.

North-east of this well-vegetated corner, and 596 kilometres from Perth, is the one-time gold-boom area around Kalgoorlie–Boulder, surrounded by ghost towns such as Coolgardie and Broad Arrow. South of Kalgoorlie–Boulder the modern town of Kambalda owes its prosperity to nickel. Further east you reach the Nullarbor Plain; further north are the Great Victoria and Gibson Deserts.

Along the Brand Highway, 424 kilometres north of Perth, is Geraldton, situated between Western Australia's agricultural heartland and the beautiful coastline. Here you can sample freshly caught crays, and a little farther north you can see a range of flora and fauna in the Kalbarri National Park and explore the spectacular coastal gorges and cliffs.

The Pilbara region has some of the country's most spectacular gorges in Karijini (Hamersley Range) National Park. This is where Western Australia's second economic boom began, with the exploitation of the dramatic Hamersley Range, which is literally a mountain of iron. The Range stretches for 320 kilometres, yet from the air seems dwarfed by endless stretches of red sand. At the State's very top is the Kimberley Region, with the spectacular King Leopold Range in the west and Bungle Bungle National Park in the east. The region's economy is based on diamond mining, as well as the more traditional cattle industry, supported by the Ord River irrigation scheme. A visit to this remote, dramatic region with its gorges and rivers is a unique experience—in keeping with many areas of Australia's largest State.

Purnululu (Bungle Bungle) National Park

Perth

A Friendly City

The city itself appears to sit on the edge of a lake; in fact it is the wide expanse of the Swan River. Within easy reach of the city lie clean surf beaches, rolling hills, tranquil forests and well-kept parklands. Blessed with a Mediterranean-type climate and a river setting, Perth is a city made for an outdoor lifestyle. The **Swan River** winds through Perth and its suburbs, widening to the size of a lake at Perth and Melville Waters; and the Canning River provides another attractive waterway through the southern suburbs.

The city centre, 19 kilometres upstream from the port of Fremantle, is on the Swan River and is ringed by a series of gardens, parks and reserves, including the magnificent 404-hectare **Kings Park**. The green slopes of Mount Eliza in Kings Park contrast dramatically with Perth's impressive skyline, and the serene blue hills of the Darling Range can be seen in the distance.

Perth was founded by Captain James Stirling in 1829, but the progress of the isolated Swan River Settlement, made up entirely of free settlers, was slow at first and it was not until the first shipment of convicts arrived in 1850 that the colony found its feet. The convicts were soon set to work building roads, bridges and several fine public buildings, and in 1856 Perth was proclaimed a city. Gold discoveries in the state in the 1880s gave Perth another boost and the recent diamond finds in the Kimberley and the reopening of gold-mines in the Kalgoorlie–Boulder region have stimulated new growth.

Perth's citizens live mainly in pleasant suburbs that stretch north and south of the city, bounded by the Indian Ocean on the west and the Darling Range on the east. There are quite large Greek and Italian communities and smaller groups from the Netherlands, Germany, Poland and Yugoslavia, although most of the population these days is Australian-born.

Perth's city centre is compact, making it easy to find your way around. Also you can travel by bus or train within the city's **Free Transit Zone** (FTZ) without paying a fare, day or night, seven days a week. A free bus service, the City Clipper, circles the city every ten minutes during the day; other **Clipper** services connect the city with East and West Perth, and Northbridge.

Most of Perth's shops and arcades are in the blocks bounded by St Georges Terrace and William, Wellington and Barrack Streets, centring around **Hay Street Mall**, **Raine Square Shopping Plaza**, and **Murray Street Mall** and **Forrest Chase**. Perth's shopping area and business district is linked by pedestrian malls, overpasses and underground walkways enabling access unhampered by motor vehicles. Perth's unique **London Court**, an Elizabethan-style arcade, runs from Hay Street Mall to St Georges Terrace. At the Hay Street entrance, four knights on horseback 'joust' above a replica of Big Ben every fifteen minutes, while St George and the Dragon do battle above the clock over the St Georges Terrace entrance. Perth's decorative **Town Hall** on the corner of Hay and Barrack Streets was built by convicts between 1869 and 1879.

Stately **St Georges Terrace**, Perth's financial and professional heart, is worth strolling down for its wealth of historic buildings, cheek by jowl with towering

City view from Kings Park

London Court arcade

Hotels

Burswood Resort Hotel
Great Eastern Hwy, Victoria Park
(09) 362 7777
Hilton International (Parmelia)
Mill St, Perth
(09) 322 3622
Hyatt Regency
99 Adelaide Tce, Perth
(09) 225 1234
Sheraton
207 Adelaide Tce, Perth
(09) 325 0501

Family and Budget
All Seasons Freeway
55 Mill Point Rd, South Perth
(09) 367 7811

**Jewell House Private Hotel
(YMCA)**
180 Goderich St, Perth
(09) 325 8488

Motel Groups: Bookings
Flag 13 2400
Best Western (008) 22 2166
Hospitality Inns (008) 99 8228
Quality Pacific (008) 09 0600
Travelodge (008) 22 2446

This list is for information only; inclusion
is not necessarily a recommendation.

modern glass giants. Start at the western end, where you will see the mellow brickwork of **Barracks Arch** (all that remains of the Tudor-style Pensioner Barracks built in 1863) in front of Parliament House. When Parliament is not sitting, there are guided tours Monday to Friday.

Continuing along St Georges Terrace you reach the charming Cloisters, a former boys' school dating back to 1858, which has been integrated into the modern complex behind, and nearby is an ecclesiastical-looking building, another former boys' school and now the headquarters of the National Trust. The Palace Hotel, a grand old Victorian iron-lace balconied hotel, has been modified as a banking chamber and forms an impressive exterior facade for Perth's larges\t building, the R & I Bank Tower. Further along the terrace is an ornate Victorian church—Trinity Church Chapel—and the arched entrance to London Court. The handsome **Treasury Building** on the corner of Barrack Street overlooks **Stirling Gardens**, part of the **Supreme Court Gardens** and a popular picnic spot for shoppers and city workers. **St George's Cathedral** and the **Deanery** are another two interesting old buildings at this end of St Georges Terrace. Tucked behind the imposing modern **Council House** on the opposite side is one of Perth's oldest buildings, the **Old Court-house**, built in 1836, and the turrets of the Gothic-style **Government House** in its lush private gardens.

Further along is the modern **Perth Concert Hall**, which seats 1900 and is used for everything from hard rock to opera. Inside, a restaurant, a tavern and a cocktail bar cater for music-lovers.

Just north of the city centre in Northbridge is the attractive **Perth Cultural Centre** complex. Here the **Art Gallery of Western Australia** displays nationally and internationally renowned artworks. Nearby is the **Alexander Library**, and the original Perth Gaol, built in 1856 and within the modern complex of the **Western Australian Museum**. A blue whale skeleton, Aboriginal artefacts and veteran and vintage cars are among the exhibits.

A visit to the Cultural Centre could be combined with a meal at one of the many reasonably priced restaurants in this area, as **Northbridge** is also the centre of Perth's nightlife. Numerous hotels, nightclubs and piano bars offer live entertainment and dancing until dawn.

At the City West shopping complex in **West Perth** are the **Omni Theatre** and the **Scitech Discovery Centre**; the specially constructed theatre presents visitors with real adventure experiences, and the centre has a hands-on science and technology display.

Kings Park, just west of the city centre, is one of Perth's major attractions. Within this huge natural bushland reserve there are landscaped gardens and walkways, lakes, children's playgrounds, lookouts and the **Botanic Gardens** on Mount Eliza Bluff, where a blaze of Western Australian wildflowers is to be seen in spring. You can drive by car through the park or hire a bicycle, stopping at the many scenic lookouts over the city and river; or you can wander on foot along the many walking trails right to the top of Mount Eliza.

Other city parks include Hyde Park, with its waterbirds, ornamental lake and English trees, and the beautiful Queens Gardens, with a replica of London's Peter Pan statue. Just outside the city centre is Lake Monger, a favourite picnic spot which is also the home of black swans, ducks and other varieties of birds. Matilda Bay offers grassed areas and ample shade, with stunning views of the Swan River and Perth city skyline. The **Swan River Estuary Marine Park** includes three areas at Alfred Cove, Pelican Point and Milyu, about halfway between the Narrows and Canning Bridges.

A pleasant way to visit **Perth's Zoo**,

with its magnificent garden environment and nocturnal house, is to catch a ferry from the Barrack Street Jetty. The trip can be combined with a visit to the **Old Mill**, on the South Perth foreshore. This picturesque whitewashed windmill, built in 1838, now houses an interesting collection of early colonial relics.

Further north along the coast at **Sorrento** is **Hillarys Boat Harbour**. A day can easily be spent here, enjoying the atmosphere and variety of Sorrento Quay or experiencing the thrill of Underwater World, where you are transported through a submerged acrylic tunnel on moving walkways to see the enormous variety of underwater life. From September to November, charter boats offer visits to view whales basking between Perth and Rottnest Island. **Carnac Island**, a nature reserve fifteen kilometres off the coast near Perth, has a colony of sea-lions and its main beach is accessible in daylight hours by private boat.

Swimming and surfing are part of the joy of Perth and several beautiful Indian Ocean beaches—including Cottesloe, Swanbourne (a nude bathing beach), Port, City, Scarborough and Trigg Island—are within easy reach of the city, and the sheltered Swan River beaches dotted along Perth's riverside suburbs are even closer.

There are many other places of interest around Perth, including the historic port of **Fremantle**, which underwent a complete facelift in preparation for the America's Cup challenge. In Fremantle you can relive the past by strolling along the streets of terraced houses, or visiting

the city's magnificent historic buildings and the many galleries, museums and craft workshops. Cottesloe Civic Centre, in Broome Street, **Cottesloe**, is one of Perth's showplaces and the magnificent grounds of this beautiful Spanish-style mansion are open during office hours. The **University of Western Australia**, with its Mediterranean-style buildings and landscaped gardens in the riverside suburb of **Crawley**, is also worth seeing. The university's new **Fortune Theatre** has been built as a replica of Shakespeare's Fortune Theatre in Elizabethan London. Adventure World in the suburb of **Bibra Lake** includes rides, a wildlife park, animal circus and Australia's largest swimming pool among its attractions.

Perth's sporting facilities are excellent, with two racecourses, **Ascot** and Belmont Park; night pacing at Gloucester Park (the famous WACA cricket ground is near here); greyhound racing at Cannington and speedcar and motorcycle racing at the Claremont Showgrounds. Major athletics meetings, rugby and soccer matches are held at Perry Lakes Stadium (built for the 1962 British Empire and Commonwealth Games), and Australian Rules football finals at Subiaco Oval. Hockey is played at the Commonwealth Hockey Stadium, the first Astroturf stadium in Australia. The Superdrome hosts many international sporting events.

By night, Perth offers a wide range of entertainment: the modern Perth Entertainment Centre (home of the Perth Wildcats basketball team), in Wellington Street, seats 8000. At the Burswood Casino, across the river at Rivervale, you can try your luck at the tables, or enjoy the five-star splendour of the hotel. Another resort complex is Raddison Observation City Resort Hotel on the coast at Scarborough. Perth offers an excellent range of accommodation to suit all requirements—from the many five-star hotels to convenient self-contained family accommodation and dozens of quality hotels and motels.

During February and March, the Festival of Perth combines the visual arts, theatre, music and film.

For further information on Perth and Western Australia, contact the Western Australian Tourist Centre, Albert Facey House, cnr Forrest Place and Wellington St, Perth; (09) 483 1111 or (008) 99 3333.

Kings Park

Tours from Perth

With the sparkling Indian Ocean surf beaches beckoning from the west, the peaceful Darling Range on the east and the Swan River meandering through Perth from Fremantle to the Swan Valley vineyards, there are many enjoyable trips within easy reach of Perth.

A delightful way to visit the vineyards is by river. Cruisers operate wine-tasting tours; the *Lady Houghton* and the *Miss Sandalford* leave Barrack Street Jetty. Refreshments are served on board, and lunch is served at Mulberry Farm. At Houghtons Winery, you can tour the vineyard and sample a variety of wines.

Other cruises will take you to the historic riverside home Tranby. From, Wednesday to Saturday nights, in season, you can have dinner aboard a vessel that leaves the Barrack Street Jetty in the early evening and returns at midnight.

There is a daily ferry service from the Barrack Street Jetty to Rottnest Island–Perth's popular hideaway, once the site of the infamous Rottnest Native Prison. (**See**: Rottnest Island.)

Travel to Adventure World on Transperth Route 600; buses depart Perth central bus station daily. Adventure World is open most weekends, and daily in peak season and school holidays. If you have any enquiries regarding tours, information is available from the Western Australian Tourist Centre, Albert Facey House, cnr Forrest Place and Wellington St, Perth; (09) 483 1111 or (008) 99 3333.

Fremantle, 19 km from Perth via the Stirling or Canning Highways

A visit to this fascinating old port can make an interesting round trip by car if you return via the opposite side of the river. Fremantle is also easily accessible by bus, train and boat. **See** Fremantle entry in A–Z listing.

Historic Guildford in the Swan Valley, 18 km from Perth via Guildford Road or the Great Eastern Highway

This tour takes you near the vineyards of the Swan Valley, noted for their high-quality wines, to Guildford, one of the earliest settlements in the state. Many reminders of the colony's early days remain, including Woodbridge, a gracious, towered, two-storey mansion overlooking the river, beautifully restored and furnished by the National Trust. The Mechanics Hall in Meadow Street houses a folk museum, and a rail museum in the nearby suburb of Bassendean is also of interest. The Vines Resort, 15 km north of Guildford, has a world-class golf course and sporting and fitness facilities for guests. Whiteman Park, 7 km north of Guildford, has train and tram rides, a picnic area and the Trade Village, where tradesmen ply traditional crafts.

Walyunga National Park, 35 km from Perth via Guildford Road and the Great Northern Highway

The Avon River flows swiftly through a narrow gorge of the Darling Range in this beautiful bushland park.

John Forrest National Park, 28 km from Perth on the Great Eastern Highway

This huge bushland park in the Darling Range is popular with tourists. Walking trails, streams, waterfalls and a safe swimming pool for children are among its attractions. At weekends enjoy a Devonshire tea at the old Mahogany Inn, built in 1837 and now the oldest licensed inn in Western Australia.

Mundaring Weir, 42 km from Perth via the Great Eastern Highway

This water catchment area which provides water for the goldfields, over 500 km away, is surrounded by picnic areas. A visit to the O'Connor Museum will help you to understand the construction and operation of this complex water scheme. Kalamunda History Village is nearby.

Serpentine Dam, 54 km from Perth via the South Western Highway

The picnic grounds here overlook the Serpentine Dam, which is set among peaceful hills and beautiful landscaped gardens of wildflowers.

Pioneer World, Armadale, 29 km from Perth via the Albany Highway

Pioneer World is a reconstruction of the days of the gold rush when every town boasted a blacksmith and a coach-house. Nearby is Araluen Botanic Park, a refreshing oasis of beautiful gardens and waterfalls. Close to Armadale, Tumbulgum Farm features a farm show, an Aboriginal culture show and Mundijong's Showcase WA, offering a superb range of WA-made products for purchase. At nearby Gosnells, the Cohuna Wildlife Park has an abundance of Australian fauna, including a koala sanctuary.

Pinjarra, 84 km from Perth on the South Western Highway

This picturesque old town on the Murray River, only 19 km east of Mandurah, is becoming a popular base for exploring the area. Several historic buildings in the town include the National Trust's Old Blythewood, a former coaching-house built in the 1830s. Later used as a family homestead, it is now open to the public daily (closed Friday). A novel way of seeing the surrounding country is on board a steam train that occasionally runs from Pinjarra to Dwellingup, a quiet little timber-town in the foothills of the Darling Range. **See also:** Entry in A–Z listing.

Rottnest Island

Commodore Willem de Vlamingh referred to Rottnest Island as a 'terrestrial paradise' when he landed there in 1696, and holidaymakers still flock to the island to enjoy its peace, beauty and unique holiday atmosphere. A low, sandy island, just 20 kilometres north-west of Fremantle, Rottnest is a public reserve. Only 11 kilometres long and about 5 kilometres wide, the island has an attractive coastline, with many small private bays and coves, sparkling white beaches and turquoise waters. Vlamingh named it Rottnest, or Rat's Nest, for the island's quaint marsupial resident, the quokka, which he believed to be a type of rat.

Quokka

The Rottnest Hotel, completed in 1864, was originally the summer residence of the governors of Western Australia. Now commonly known as the **Quokka Arms**, it is a good place to stay, or just to enjoy a relaxing drink in the beer garden. **Rottnest Lodge Resort** has modern convention facilities in an informal setting. Other accommodation includes chalets, cabins, hostels and a camping area.

There is no lack of things to do on Rottnest. Cars are not permitted (which contributes to the wonderful sense of peace), but you can hire a bicycle and explore the island. You may even catch a glimpse of peacocks and pheasants, which were introduced at the turn of the century. Special coach tours of the island are conducted during the summer months (from the end of September to the end of April). A tramway operates, daily except Christmas day, on a 7-kilometre route from the historic settlement area to the Oliver Hill Battery. There are tennis courts, a 9-hole golf course and bowling facilities. You can hire a boat, dinghy or canoe, play mini-golf or go trampolining; or you can just laze on the beach in the sunshine.

The *Underwater Explorer*, a glass-bottomed pleasure cruiser, leaves regularly from Main Jetty, giving glimpses of shipwrecks, reefs and a startling array of fish. Ferries operate daily services to Rottnest from Barrack Street Jetty in Perth and also from Fremantle and Hillarys Boat Harbour. There are daily flights from Perth. As all wildlife on Rottnest is protected, no pets and no guns of any description, including spear guns, are allowed on the island.

For further information, contact the Rottnest Island Authority; (09) 372 9729 or the Information Kiosk, Main Jetty.

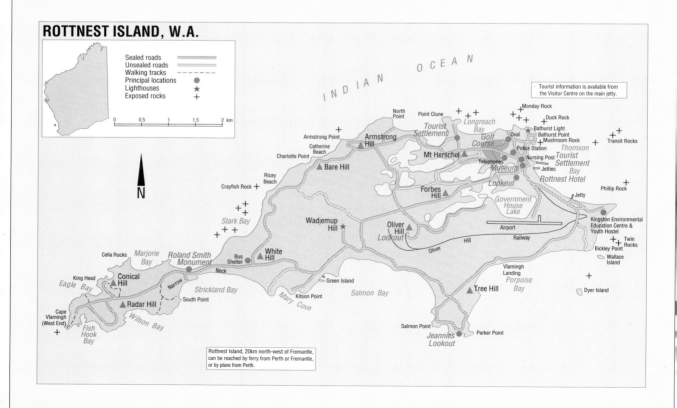

ROTTNEST ISLAND, W.A.

Sealed roads
Unsealed roads
Walking tracks
Principal locations   ●
Lighthouses   ★
Exposed rocks   +

0   0.5   1   1.5   2 km

N

INDIAN OCEAN

Tourist information is available from the Visitor Centre on the main jetty.

North Point
Point Clune
Monday Rock
Duck Rock
Armstrong Point
Armstrong Hill
Tourist Settlement
Longreach Bay
Golf Course
Oval
Bathurst Light
Bathurst Point
Mushroom Rock
Transit Rocks
Catherine Beach
Mt Herschel
Police Station
Thomson
Charlotte Point
Telephones
Nursing Post
Tourist Settlement
Ricey Beach
Bare Hill
Museum
Jetties
Bay
Crayfish Rock
Forbes Hill
Lookout
Rottnest Hotel
Phillip Rock
Government House Lake
Jetty
Stark Bay
Wadjemup Hill
Oliver Hill Lookout
Airport
Railway
Kingston Environmental Education Centre & Youth Hostel
Celia Rocks
Marjorie Bay
Roland Smith Monument
Bus Shelter
White Hill
Oliver   Hill
Twin Rocks
Bickley Point
Wallace Island
King Head
Conical Hill
Neck
Green Island
Vlamingh Landing
Porpoise Bay
Eagle Bay
Narrow
Strickland Bay
Kitson Point
Salmon Bay
Tree Hill
Dyer Island
Radar Hill
South Point
Mary Cove
Cape Vlamingh (West End)
Wilson Bay
Salmon Point
Jeannies Lookout
Parker Point
Fish Hook Bay

Rottnest Island, 20km north-west of Fremantle, can be reached by ferry from Perth or Fremantle, or by plane from Perth.

Western Australia from A to Z

Albany   Pop. 18 826

Albany is WA's oldest town and one of its most picturesque. On the edge of King George Sound and the magnificent Princess Royal Harbour, and known as the 'heart of the Great Southern', the town overlooks both the coast and the inland towards the spectacular Stirling and Porongurup Ranges. Situated 406 km S of Perth, Albany has a surprisingly English feel about it. The town dates back to 1826, when a military post was established to give the English a foothold in the West. Whaling was important in the 1840s and in the 1850s Albany became a coaling station for steamers bound from England. As WA's most important holiday centre, it offers visitors a wealth of history with its impressive stone colonial buildings and a rich variety of coastal, rural and mountain scenery. Its harbours, weirs and estuaries provide excellent fishing. **Of interest:** Colonial Buildings Historic Walk; self-guide brochure from Tourist Information Centre. Old Post Office–Intercolonial Communications Museum, opposite cnr Stirling Tce and Spencer St. Some Victorian shopfronts in Stirling Tce, at base of York St. Historical and environmental exhibits in Albany Residency Museum (1850s), Residency Rd, originally home of Resident Magistrates; open daily. Old Gaol and Museum (1851), Residency Rd; actually two gaols in one. Vancouver Arts Centre, Vancouver St; House of Gems, Frenchman Bay Rd, Old Farm (1836), Middleton Rd, Strawberry Hill; site of Government Farm for Albany, begun in 1872. Patrick Taylor Cottage (1832), Duke St; faithfully restored, extensive collection of period costume and household goods. Extravaganza Gallery, next to Esplanade Hotel, Middleton Beach; vintage and veteran cars, arts and crafts. Two restored forts: Princess Royal Fortress (commissioned 1893), Forts Rd, and Princess Royal Fort, Albany's first federal fortress, on Mt Adelaide; open for inspection. Also Mt Adelaide Forts Heritage Trails, starting point cnr Apex Dr and Forts Rd; self-guide leaflets available. The Amity, Princess Royal Dr, full-scale replica of brig that brought Major Lockyer and party of convicts to establish settlement of Albany in 1826. On Princess Royal Dr, Amity Crafts; local art and craft. Anzac Light Horse Memorial statue, near top of Mt Clarence, off Marine Dr. Spectacular view from here and from John Barnesby Memorial Lookout at Mt Melville. 'Genevieve 500', international classic car race, and Skywest Albany Ocean Yacht Race held in Nov. **In the area:** Jolly Barnyard family farm, 3 km N; deer farm, 6 km N. 'Locomotion' tourist railway, 15 km E; train rides, historic trams, art and craft, tearooms, holiday accommodation. Jimmy Newhill's Harbour (20 km S), Frenchman Bay (25 km S), Emu Point (8 km NE), and Oyster Harbour (15 km NE) have good beaches for swimming and fishing. Cheyne's Beach Whaling Station (25 km N), which ceased operation in 1978, now houses Albany Whaleworld; in its heyday, the Station's chasers took up to 850 whales per season. To the south are The Gap and Natural Bridge (18 km), the Blow Holes and The Gorge (19 km), with a sheer drop to the sea. To the east, Nanarup (20 km) and Little Beach (40 km) have sheltered waters. Towards Denmark, west of Albany, are Cosy Corner (20 km), and West Cape Howe National Park (30 km), one of the south coast's most popular parks; walking trails, fishing, swimming, hanggliding and one of the best lookouts on coast. Torbay Head in park is southernmost point in WA. Care should be taken when exploring the coast; king waves can be dangerous and have been known to rush in unexpectedly, causing loss of life. To the north, Porongurup National Park (37 km), with its huge granite peaks, and Stirling Range National Park (80 km), offer mountain climbing, memorable bushwalks and breathtaking scenery. Many brilliantly coloured wildflowers in spring, some unique to area. At Camp Quaranup, site of old quarantine station, south on Geake Point; historical walk. Torndirrup National Park, 17 km S, for fine coastal views. Willowie Game Park, 30 km E. Two Peoples Bay Nature Reserve, 40 km E. **Tourist information:** Cnr Peels Pl and York St; (098) 41 1088. **Accommodation:** 5 hotels, 9 motels, 10 caravan/camping parks. **See also:** The Great Southern.
MAP REF. 351 N12, 354 G13

Augusta   Pop. 838

Set on the slopes of the Hardy Inlet, the town of Augusta overlooks the mouth of the Blackwood River, the waters of Flinders Bay and rolling, heavily wooded countryside. Augusta is one of the oldest settlements in WA and a popular holiday resort. Jarrah, karri and pine forests supply the district's 100-year-old timber industry. **Of interest:** Historical Museum and Lumen Christi Catholic Church, both in Blackwood Ave. Crafters Croft, Ellis St; art and craft. Dragon Boat racing March. Augusta Spring Flower Show Sept.–Oct. **In the area:** Jewel Cave, 8 km N, world famous for its magnificent and colourful limestone formations. Moondyne Cave, 8 km N; guided adventure tours. Miniature railway, 18 km N of Bussell Hwy. Alexandra Bridge, 10 km N; charming picnic spot with towering jarrah trees and beautiful wildflowers. Lake Cave and Mammoth Cave, both 30 km N. Cape Leeuwin, 8 km SW, most south-westerly point of Australia, where

The Goldfields

The land that boasted the first goldmining boom in Western Australia is almost as forbidding as that of the far north-west. This is the vast region to the east of Perth that contains the famous towns of Kalgoorlie–Boulder, Coolgardie, Norseman, Kambalda, Leonora, Gwalia and Laverton. Although some towns, like Gwalia, are colourful but nearly deserted reminders of the great rush days, all are once again active goldmining areas, with Kalgoorlie–Boulder the main centre.

The western gold rush began in 1892 with strikes around **Coolgardie**. The town sprang up from nowhere and enjoyed a boisterous but short life. With great optimism diggers flocked to the area. In 1900 there were 15 000 people, today Coolgardie has a population of 1063. The grand old courthouse, built at the height of the boom, is used as a museum and has a record of life on the fields as it once was.

In 1893 Irishman Paddy Hannan made a bigger strike of gold at **Kalgoorlie**. The area became known as the Golden Mile, reputedly the richest square mile in the world. Kalgoorlie and its twin town Boulder boasted a population of 30 000 in 1902.

The modern **Kalgoorlie–Boulder** is a prosperous goldmining centre, producing 70 per cent of the gold mined in Australia. At Hannans North Historical Mining Complex visitors can don a hard hat and cap lamp and go below the surface, where guides explain the hardships endured by the miners in their search for gold. To the south is **Kambalda**, a new boom town, founded on rich nickel deposits.

Most of the towns north of Kalgoorlie are alive again as a result of the current goldmining operations. Deep underground mines are being replaced by massive open-cuts, which create their own adjacent table-top mountains of overburden. The little town of **Menzies**, is a shadow of its former self. The renovated, stately old Gwalia Hotel just outside **Leonora** is one of the few buildings left in what was once one of the State's most prosperous goldmining centres.

Kanowna once boasted a population of 12 000. Now all that remains is old and new mine workings, and historic markers describing what used to be. Siberia, Broad Arrow, Niagara and Bulong are the exotic names of some of the towns that flourished and died in a few short years. Nevertheless, mining is once again active in most of these areas.

See also: Individual town entries in A–Z listing.

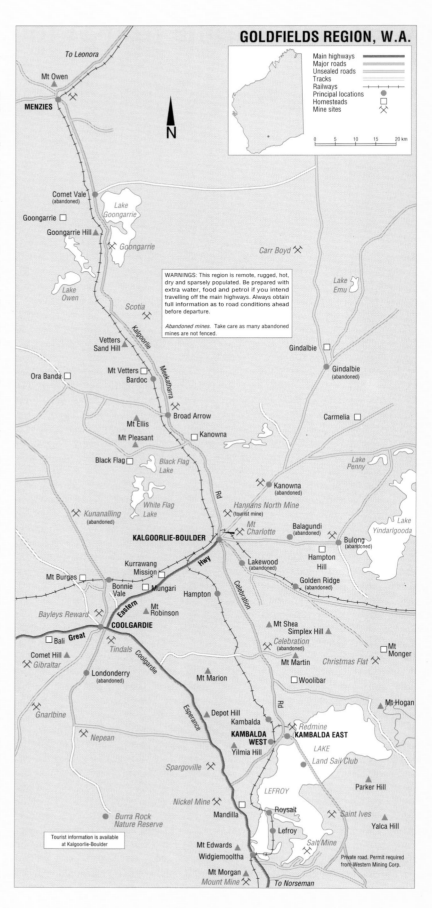

GOLDFIELDS REGION, W.A.

Main highways
Major roads
Unsealed roads
Tracks
Railways
Principal locations
Homesteads
Mine sites

0   5   10   15   20 km

WARNINGS: This region is remote, rugged, hot, dry and sparsely populated. Be prepared with extra water, food and petrol if you intend travelling off the main highways. Always obtain full information as to road conditions ahead before departure.

Abandoned mines. Take care as many abandoned mines are not fenced.

Tourist information is available at Kalgoorlie-Boulder

Private road. Permit required from Western Mining Corp.

Indian and Southern Oceans meet; lighthouse and water wheel, both built in 1895. Hillview Lookout, 6 km W. Picturesque coastline near Augusta offers fine swimming and surfing. Good fishing in both river and ocean. Marron (freshwater lobster) can be caught in season. Marron Fishing Licences required and obtainable from Post Office, Blackwood Ave. **Tourist information:** Leeuwin Souvenirs, Blackwood Ave; (097) 58 1695; Augusta–Margaret River Tourist Bureau, cnr Tunbridge Rd and Bussell Hwy, Margaret River; (097) 57 2147. **Accommodation:** 1 hotel/motel, 1 motel, 4 caravan/camping parks.
MAP REF. 349 D12, 354 D11

Australind   Pop. 4407

The popular holiday resort of Australind is located 11 km N of Bunbury on the Leschenault Estuary. Fishing, crabbing, swimming and boating on the estuary and the Collie River are the main attractions. **Of interest:** Henton Cottage (1841), Paris Rd; displays of local art and craft. Restored Church of St Nicholas (1842), Paris Rd; said to be smallest church in WA. Gem and Rock Museum, Old Coast Rd. **In the area:** To north, pleasant beach towns of Binningup (26 km) and Myalup (30 km). Kemerton Industrial Park (SCM Chemicals), 15 km N; guided tours. **Tourist information:** Harvey Tourist and Interpretative Centre, South West Hwy, Harvey; (097) 29 1122. **Accommodation:** 3 caravan/camping parks.
MAP REF. 346 C13, 354 D10

Balladonia Roadhouse

Pop. 10
Balladonia is on the Eyre Hwy, 191 km E of Norseman. At this point, the road crosses gently undulating dryland forest surrounding the Fraser Range. Claypans typical of the region and old stone fences built by pioneer farmers in the 1800s can be seen. In July 1979, debris from the US Skylab fell to earth near the town. **In the area:** Balladonia Station Homestead, (1882), off north side of highway, behind old telegraph station, 28 km E of Balladonia Hotel complex; gallery of paintings depicting history of Balladonia and Eyre Hwy. Newmans Rocks, 50 km W on Eyre Hwy; signposted. **Tourist information:** Roadhouse; (090) 39 3453. **Accommodation:** 1 hotel/motel, 1 caravan/camping park (with limited

facilities). **See also:** Crossing the Nullarbor.
MAP REF. 357 K9

Beverley   Pop. 818

On the Avon River, 130 km E of Perth, is the town of Beverley. **Of interest:** Delightful picnic spots beside Avon River. Aeronautical Museum, Vincent St, showing development of aviation in WA, includes a biplane built in 1929 by local aircraft designer Selby Ford; 9–4 daily. Dead Finish, Hunt Rd; one of the oldest buildings in town. Constructed in 1872 in the then centre of Beverley, it was first used as a hotel, but with the coming of the railway in 1886 the town centre moved nearer the station, leaving Dead Finish out of the mainstream. Barry Ferguson's Garage, Hunt Rd, display of old hand-operated machinery; open normal trading hours. Colonial Collectables, off Vincent St; memorabilia, antiques and tearooms. Cross-country Regatta, held by gliding club Jan. Agricultural Show in Aug. The Avon Ascent, self-guide drive tour of the Avon Valley; leaflet available. **In the area:** Restored St Paul's Church (consecrated 1862), opposite original town site, 5 km NW. Magnificent view from top of nearby Seaton Ross Hill. Farm Fresh Yabby Company 8 km SE; yabby farming, check opening times. Yenyening Lakes, 36 km SE; popular recreation area for water-skiing, motorboating, yachting, swimming. County Peak (362 m), 35 km SE; popular hiking and picnic area; spectacular views from summit. Restored church, St John's in the Wilderness (consecrated 1895), 27 km SW. Avondale Discovery Farm, 6 km W; 10–4 daily. **Tourist information:** Aeronautical Museum, Vincent St; (096) 46 1555. **Accommodation:** 2 hotels, 1 caravan/camping park.
MAP REF. 346 I5, 354 F7, 356 B9

Boyup Brook   Pop. 584

A small township near the junction of Boyup Creek and the Blackwood River, Boyup Brook is a market centre for the district's sheep, dairy-farming and timber industries. Shaded pools, charming cottages and farms are scenic features. Blackboys and huge granite boulders line the river valley. **Of interest:** Old Railway Museum, Railway Pde; pioneering memorabilia. Sandy Chambers Art Studio, Gibbs St; artworks, aviaries and camels. Flax Mill, on Blackwood River, off Barron St. Haddleton

Flora Reserve, Arthur River Rd. Pioneer Garden, Kojonup Rd; picnic/barbecue facilities. Carnaby Collection of beetles and butterflies at tourist centre. Bicentennial Walk Trail; details from tourist centre. Country Music Awards held in Feb. Autumn Art Affair in May. Blackwood River Marathon Relay in Oct.; running, canoeing, horseriding, swimming and cycling, to Bridgetown. Upper Blackwood Agricultural Show in Nov. **In the area:** Glacial rock formations at Glacier Hill, 18 km S. Scotts Brook Winery, 18 km SE; open by appt. Vintage engines and old timber-mill at Wilga, 22 km N. Harvey Dickson Country Music Centre, 5 km NE. School and teacher's house (1900), at Dinninup, 21 km NE. Blackwood Crest Winery at Kulikup, 40 km NE. Locally produced woollen goods at Stormboy Jumpers, 20 km W on Jayes Rd; apply tourist centre for appt. Visits to local farms (wheat, sheep, pig, goat, deer, angora) can be arranged through tourist centre. Boyup Brook Flora Drive; details from tourist centre. **Tourist information:** Cnr Bridge and Able Sts; (097) 65 1444. **Accommodation:** 1 hotel, 1 caravan/camping park. **See also:** The Great Southern.
MAP REF. 350 E2, 354 F10, 356 A12

Bremer Bay   Pop. 250

Bremer Bay, a popular holiday destination 181 km NE of Albany, was named in 1849 by Surveyor-General John Septimus Roe in honour of the captain of HMS *Tamar*, Sir Gordon Bremer. The township was built around the Old Telegraph Station at the mouth of Wellstead Estuary (named after John Wellstead, who first settled in the area in the 1850s). **Of interest:** Fishing, boating, scuba diving, water-skiing. Tavern, in Franton Way, and rammed-earth church, in John St, overlooking estuary. **In the area:** Fitzgerald River National Park, 17 km E. Military museum at Jerramungup, 60 km N. **Tourist information:** Roadhouse, Gnombup Tce; (098) 37 4093. **Accommodation:** 1 hotel, 1 caravan/camping park. **See also:** The Great Southern.
MAP REF. 356 E13

Bridgetown   Pop. 2017

Bridgetown is a quiet spot set in undulating country in the south-west corner of WA. Here the Blackwood River, well stocked with marron and trout, curves through some of the prettiest country in the State. Bridgetown was first settled in

1857 and the first apple trees were planted soon after. **Of interest:** Bridgetown Pottery, Brierley Jigsaw Gallery (in Tourist Centre) and Gentle Era craft shop, all in Hampton St. Geegelup Pottery, Mount St. Orchard Studio, Hampton St. Elizabeth Endisch Studio, Steere St. Bridgedale (1862), on South West Hwy, near bridge and overlooking river; constructed of local clay and timber by John Blechynden, first settler in area, and restored by National Trust; check opening times. St Paul's Church (1911), Hampton St; paintings by local artist. Memorial Park, Hampton St; peaceful picnic location. Kalara Park Stud, Doust St; visits by appt. Bowling Carnival in March. Wildflower season and apple blossom time begin Oct. Apple-orchard packing sheds worth a visit. Also in Oct., annual art exhibition and flower show, golf tournament, and two other major sporting events: the Blackwood Classic, a 3-day power-boat event over a 250 km course, and the Blackwood Marathon Relay, which attracts international and local competitors for running, canoeing, swimming, horseriding and cycling over a 58.3 km course. Agricultural Show and Blues Music Festival in Nov. **In the area:** Sutton's Lookout, off Phillip St, and Hester's Hill, 5 km N, offer fine views. Greenbushes Historical Park, 18 km N; historical displays on tin-mining industry. Donnelly Whippole Well, 15 km S. Bridgetown Jarrah Park, 20 km SW, for picnics and bushwalking. Geegelup Heritage Trail (52 km), retracing early history of agriculture, mining and timber industries; details from Tourist Centre. Scenic drives through rolling green hills, orchards and valleys and into karri and jarrah timber country for which the south-west is famed. **Tourist information:** Hampton St; (097) 61 1740. **Accommodation:** 2 hotels, 1 hotel/motel, 1 caravan/camping park. **See also:** The South-west.
MAP REF. 350 C3, 354 E11, 356 A12

Brookton   Pop. 576

An attractive town 137 km SE of Perth, near the Avon River in the heart of fertile farming country, Brookton was founded in 1884 when the Great Southern Railway line was opened. **Of interest:** In Robinson Rd, Old Police Station Museum, St Mark's Anglican Church (1895) and Old Railway Station, which houses Tourist Centre and art and craft shop. Lions Picnic Park, off Corrigin Rd, at eastern entrance to town. Old Time Motor Show held March every even-numbered year. **In the area:** Nine Acre Rock on Brookton–Kweda Rd, 12 km E, one of the largest natural granite outcrops in the area, and unusual home of pioneer Jack Hansen. Reserve and picnic ground at Boyagin Rock, 18 km SW. Yenyening Lakes nature reserve, 35 km NE; picnic/barbecue facilities. Brookton Pioneer Heritage Trail; details from tourist centre. **Tourist information:** Old Railway Station, Robinson Rd; (096) 42 1316. **Accommodation:** 2 hotels, 1 caravan/camping park.
MAP REF. 346 I7, 354 F8, 356 B9

Broome   Pop. 8906

Broome is situated on the coast at the southern tip of the Kimberley region. It is bounded by wide beaches and turquoise water and enjoys a warm climate with plenty of sunshine. Closer to Bali than to Perth, and with an international airport, the town is lively and cosmopolitan. The discovery of pearling grounds off the coast in the 1880s led to the foundation of Broome township in 1883. By 1910 Broome was the world's leading pearling centre. However, the industry began to suffer when world markets collapsed in 1914. Today with increasing tourism, Broome is again rapidly expanding into the most populous town in the Kimberley. **Of interest:** Many fascinating old buildings; self-guide Broome Heritage Trail (2 km) introduces buildings and places of historic interest. Chinatown, a reminder of Broome's early multicultural mix. Historical Society Museum, in Old Customs House, Saville St. Library, Haas St. Captain Gregory's House, Carnarvon St; not open to public. Kimberley Kreations Gallery in Matso's Store, Hamersley St; specialises in Kimberley art. Bedford Park, Hamersley St, contains relics of Broome's history. Courthouse (former Cable House), Hamersley St; gardens and markets open Sat. Broome Crocodile Park, Cable Beach Rd. Shell House, Guy St; one of largest shell collections in Australia. Sun Pictures, Carnarvon St; opened 1916 and believed to be oldest operating picture garden in world. On Port Dr, Chinese Cemetery and Japanese Cemetery (graves of many early Japanese pearl divers). Pioneer Cemetery in Apex Park. Each Aug.–Sept., Shinju Matsuri, or Festival of the Pearl, recalls Broome's heyday. Kimberley Tourism and Trade Expo held May; entertainment, food stalls and displays. Fringe Arts Festival held May–June. Broome Race Round and Cup Day June–July. Sailfish Premiere in July. Mango Festival in Nov. **In the area:** Beaches are ideal swimming spots and prized by collectors for their beautiful shells. Cable Beach (3 km from town centre), which stretches for 22 km, was named after the underwater cable that links Broome to Java. At Gantheaume Point, when the tide is out, giant dinosaur tracks, believed to be 130 million years old, can be seen. A natural phenomenon, visible at most full moons during the dry season (April–Oct.), is the Staircase to the Moon, caused by the moonlight reflecting off the exposed mudflats at extreme low tides; best seen from southern end of Dampier Tce (dates and times from tourist centre). Hovercraft Spirit of Broome visits local beaches. Broome area has good fishing all year round. Cable Beach Club, Auski and Roebuck Bay resorts. Broome Bird Observatory at Roebuck Bay, 18 km E. Safaris, cruises, scenic flights and short tours. Charter boats offer 6- to 10-day Kimberley expeditions with excursions to such attractions as coral reefs, Roley Shoals, Prince Regent River and waterfalls at Kings Cascades. Willie Creek Pearl Farm, 35 km N; tours include pearl farm and history of pearling industry. Day tours north to Lombardina Mission (190 km) and Cape Leveque (320 km). **Tourist information:** Cnr Bagot St and Great Northern Hwy; (091) 92 2222. **Accommodation:** 6 hotels, 1 hotel/motel, 5 caravan/camping parks. **See also:** The Kimberley.
MAP REF. 360 H8

Bunbury   Pop. 24 003

Bunbury, 'Harbour City', is the second largest urban area in WA and serves as the major port and commercial centre for the south-west region. Situated 180 km S of Perth on the Leschenault Estuary, at the junction of the Preston and Collie Rivers, it is one of the State's most popular tourist resorts, with a warm temperate climate, beautiful beaches along the coast, and the foothills of the Darling Range in the distance. Bunbury, originally called Port Leschenault, was first settled in 1838, and the whalers who anchored in Koombana Bay provided a market for the pioneer farmers. Today the port is the main outlet for the thriving timber industry, mineral sands and the produce of the fertile hinterland. **Of interest:** Visitors can drive along the breakwater, which extends into Koombana Bay, to view the modern harbour facilities. King Cottage (1880), Forrest Ave; fascinating historical museum, open weekends. Shell Museum, Mangles St; collection of shells from around the world, Aboriginal artefacts and minerals. Tree-lined pathways lead to Boulter's Lookout, Haig Cres; a vantage point for views of the city and suburbs, surrounding hills and farmland. Bunbury Lighthouse, Ocean Dr; notable landmark, painted in bold black and white checks with lookout at base. Marlston Hill Lookout, Apex Dr; Art Gallery, Wittenoom St. Centenary Gardens, cnr Wittenoom and Prinsep Sts, in city centre; peaceful picnic spot with kiosk. Grassed foreshore of estuary picnic/barbecue facilities, children's playground and boat ramp. Excellent beaches, and a surf club at Ocean Beach. Koombana Bay is ideal for water-skiing and yachting; dolphins inhabit the bay. Good fishing for bream, flounder, tailor and whiting in the bay, also deep-sea fishing. Succulent blue manna crabs can be caught in season in the estuary. There is a great variety of birdlife in the bush near the waters of the inlet. Big Swamp Bird Park, Prince Phillip Dr. Historic old wooden jetty in outer harbour; popular for fishing and crab-

bing. Miniature railway in Forrest Park, Blair St. Bunbury Show and Peters Aqua Spectacular, both held in March. Discover Bunbury—The Good Life, in Nov. **In the area:** Gelorup Museum, 12 km S. Wirrawee Adventure Playground, at Stratham, 17 km S. St Mark's, Picton, 5 km SE, oldest church in WA, erected in 1842. Although restored, church still retains some of its original timber structure. Boyanup Transport Museum, 20 km SE. At Australind, 11 km N, Church of St Nicholas (1860), thought to be smallest church in WA. Spring Hill Homestead (1855), 26 km N, off Old Coast Road; not open to public. Pleasant scenic drive off Old Coast Road with good crabbing and picnicking spots. Bunbury Heritage Trails; details from tourist centre. **Tourist information:** Old Railway Station, Carmody St; (097) 21 7922. **Accommodation:** 6 hotels, 10 motels, 3 caravan/camping parks. **See also:** The Southwest.
MAP REF. 346 C13, 354 D10

Busselton
Pop. 8936

First settled in the 1830s, Busselton is one of the oldest established areas in WA. Nowadays it is a pleasant seaside town at the centre of a large rural district. Situated 228 km S of Perth, on the sweeping shores of Geographe Bay and the picturesque Vasse River, the town is a very

popular holiday resort. Inland there are jarrah forests that supply the local timber industry, and agricultural land carrying dairy and beef cattle and vineyards. Fishing is also important, with crayfish and salmon in season. **Of interest:** Prospect Villa (1855), Pries Ave; two-storey colonial building (now motel) with antiques. Opposite, first steam locomotive used in WA. St Mary's (1844), Peel Tce; oldest stone church in State. Villa Carlotta (1897), Adelaide St; boarding school for 50 years, now guest house. Oceanarium and Nautical Lady Entertainment Centre, both near jetty on beachfront. Old Courthouse Arts Centre, Queen St. Old Butter Factory Museum, Peel Tce; on riverbank, has exhibits that include old butter- and cheese-making equipment. Wonnerup House (1859), Layman Rd, National Trust Museum; fine example of colonial Australian architecture and furnished in period style. Old school and teacher's house, Layman Rd; restored buildings of local undressed timber. Busselton Jetty, (2 km long), on beachfront near Queen St; longest timber jetty in Australia. Partially destroyed by Cyclone Alby in 1978, but still very popular with fishermen. Vasse River Parkland, Peel Tce; barbecue/picnic facilities. Archery Park and Minigolf, Bussell Hwy. The bay has good sheltered beaches for swimming and the western coast is ideal for surfing.

Camel riding on Cable Beach, Broome

Coastline near Carnarvon

Festival of Busselton held Jan. Down South Dive Classic in Nov. **In the area:** Several protea nurseries near Busselton open to visitors. Bunyip Craft Centre, 7 km E. Orchid farm at Vasse, 9 km W. Wildwood Pottery, 16 km W. Quindalup Fauna Park, 20 km W; birds, fish, tropical butterflies and native mammals. Bannamah Wildlife Park, 26 km W. Country Life Farm, 26 km W; hayrides and boat rides, children's farm. Yallingup, 32 km SW, for surfing enthusiasts; also sheltered rock pool. Yallingup Caves open daily. Over 20 wineries in Woodlands–Metricup district, 30 km SW, and around town of Margaret River, 47 km SW. Many scenic drives in area; to west, Eagle Bay (30 km), Sugar Loaf Rock, (35 km) and Cape Naturaliste (39 km), all offer excellent views of rugged coast. Wildflower, scenic and 4WD tours available. Farm holidays at Kerriley Park, 24 km SW. Augusta–Busselton Heritage Trail; details from tourist centre. **Tourist information**: Civic Centre, Southern Drive; (097) 52 1091. **Accommodation:** 4 hotels, 8 motels, 12 caravan/camping parks. **See also:** The South-west.
MAP REF. 349 F3, 354 D10

Caiguna   Pop. 10
This is the first stop for petrol and food after the long drive from Balladonia, 181 km W. This section of Eyre Highway is one of the longest straight stretches of sealed road in the world. **In the area:** Afghan Rocks, 14 km E; natural freshwater dams, used as resting place by camel drivers in 1890s. **Tourist information:** Roadhouse; (090) 39 3459. **Accommodation:** 1 motel, 1 caravan/ camping park. **See also:** Crossing the Nullarbor.
MAP REF. 357 M9

Carnamah   Pop. 367
Carnamah is a small, typically Australian country town, 290 km N of Perth. Wheat- and sheep-farming are the local industries. **Of interest:** Historical Society Museum, McPherson St; old farm machinery reflecting agricultural heritage. **In the area:** MacPherson Homestead (1880), 1 km E. Several old goldmining and ghost towns 40–50 km E; area rich in minerals and popular with gemstone enthusiasts. Yarra Yarra Lakes, 2 km W, where waters range in colour from red to green to blue; lakes attract many varieties of migratory birds and are surrounded by wildflowers in season. Perenjori, 58 km NE. Tathra National Park, 50 km SW; variety of wildflowers in spring. Lake Indoon, 61 km SW, for water-skiing. **Tourist information:** Carnamah Hotel, McPherson St; (099) 51 1023. **Accommodation:** 1 hotel/motel, 1 caravan/camping park.
MAP REF. 354 E3

Carnarvon   Pop. 6901
Carnarvon, at the mouth of the Gascoyne River, 904 km N of Perth, is the commercial centre of the highly productive Gascoyne region. The district was sighted as long ago as 1616 by Dirk Hartog. Another explorer, Willem de Vlamingh, landed at Shark Bay in 1697. The first pioneers arrived in 1876 and by the 1880s there were a number of settlers in the region. Today most of the land is used for pastoral activities, with sheep and beef cattle. The Gascoyne River often flows beneath its bed, and its resources have been tapped for irrigation. The Overseas Telecommunications Commission (OTC) earth station (no longer operating) and Radio Australia base are both located at nearby Browns Range. The USA National Aeronautics and Space Administration (NASA) operated here between 1964 and 1974. Carnarvon has warm winters and takes on a tropical appearance when the bougainvilleas and hibiscus bloom. The main street, built in the 1880s, is a gracious 40 m wide, to enable camel trains to turn. **Of interest:** Museum, Correia Arcade. Jubilee Hall (1887), Francis St. Pioneer Park, Olivia Tce. Rotary Park, North West Coastal Hwy. Fishing for snapper or groper, or game fishing for marlin or sailfish; charter boats available. Yachting Regatta held March. Mirari Tropical Festival in May. Dry River Regatta held between July and Sept. **In the area:** On Babbage Island, 5 km off Carnarvon; museum at lighthouse keeper's cottage. Prawning factory; tours organised by tourist centre during season, usually mid-April to late Oct. One Mile Jetty, almost 1500 m long. Pelican Point, good spot for picnics and swimming. OTC earth station with its mammoth 157-m diameter reflector (known as the 'Big Dish') at Browns Range, 8 km E; open to visitors; scenic views of area from platform of disc. Six km along highway from centre of Carnarvon, is turnoff at South River Rd to Munro's Banana Plantation (5 km from turnoff). In season, fresh-picked bananas, melons and other fruit and vegetables for sale. At Department of Agriculture Research Station, 3 km from South River Rd turnoff, inspections of experimental farmings; bookings through tourist information. Miaboolya Beach, 22 km N, has good fishing, crabbing and swimming. The hot water from Bibbawarra artesian bore, 16 km N, surfaces at 70°C; picnic area. There are blowholes 70 km N where the water is dramatically forced some 20 m into the air. About 1 km S of the blowholes is a superb sheltered beach; search for

oysters on the rocks, but beware of king waves and tides. Excellent fishing at Cape Cuvier, 30 km N of blowholes. Drive 55 km E inland from Carnarvon, along Gascoyne Rd, leads to Rocky Pool, deep freshwater billabong ideal for swimming and picnics. **Tourist information:** Robinson St; (099) 41 1146. **Accommodation:** 5 hotel/motels, 7 caravan/camping parks.
MAP REF. 355 B8

Cocklebiddy   Pop. 11
The ruins of an Aboriginal mission station can be seen at this tiny settlement on the Eyre Hwy, between Madura and Caiguna, about 280 km from the SA border. **In the area:** Cocklebiddy Cave, for experienced speleologists only (directions available at Roadhouse). Bird observatory and Post Office Historical Society Museum at Eyre on coast, 47 km S (4WD only). **Tourist information:** Roadhouse; (090) 39 3462. **Accommodation:** 1 motel, 1 caravan/camping park (limited facilities). **See also:** Crossing the Nullarbor.
MAP REF. 357 N8

Collie   Pop. 7684
Collie, the centre of WA's only coal-producing region, plays an integral part in the State's development. The town is set in dense jarrah forest, 202 km S of Perth, near the winding Collie River, and has an abundance of attractive parks and gardens. The drive into Collie from the South West Hwy, climbing the Darling Scarp, offers some of the finest views in WA. **Of interest:** Tourist coal mine, Throssell St; guided tours daily. Historical museum, Throssell St, in old Roads Board buildings; traces history of area and of coal industry. Opposite, steam locomotive museum with some fine restored trains. Also in Throssell St, old police station (1926) and post office (1898). Old courthouse cnr Wittenoon and Pendleton Sts. Impressive All Saints' Anglican Church, Venn St, built in Norman style. Art gallery at Tourist Bureau, Throssell St; collection of local art. Soldiers Park, Steer St, on banks of Collie River; shady trees and lawns, ideal for picnics. Minninup Pool off Mungalup Rd, also popular spot, surrounded by bushland and, in season, beautiful wildflowers. **In the area:** Harris Dam, 10 km N. Wellington Dam, 27 km W, in heart of Collie River Irrigation Scheme; major

tourist attraction with fishing, pleasant bushwalking tracks and recreation areas with grassy picnic spots. Delicious marron, or freshwater crayfish, abounds in dam Dec.–April. (Inland Fishing Licence required; available from post office or Tourist Bureau). Scenic drive to Collie River, 5 km W, takes visitors through some magnificent scenery. Muja open-cut mines and Muja power station, 15 km E. ('*Muja*', Aboriginal word used to describe bright yellow Christmas tree that grows in area.) **Tourist information:** Throssell St; (097) 34 2051. **Accommodation:** 5 hotels, 1 hotel/motel, 3 motels, 1 caravan/camping park.
MAP REF. 346 E13, 354 E10, 356 A11

Coolgardie   Pop. 1063
The old goldmining town of Coolgardie is one of the best-known 'ghost towns' in Australia. Alluvial gold was discovered here in 1892 and Coolgardie grew from nothing to a boom town of 15 000 people, 23 hotels, 6 banks and 2 stock exchanges in just 10 years. The main street was wide enough for camel trains to turn, splendid public buildings were erected and ambitious plans were made for the future. Sadly, the gold soon petered out. By 1985 there were only 700 people in the town; however, at the beginning of the 1990s, with an increase in tourism, there is a wave of confidence emerging and the population is increasing. **Of interest:** Historic buildings in Bayley St include: Goldfields Exhibition building (1898), most comprehensive prospecting museum in WA; Post Office (1898); Old Gaol; Denver City Hotel (1898), with handsome verandahs; Ben Prior's Open-air Museum, with wagons, horse- and camel-driven vehicles; Railway Lodge, wonderfully preserved building entering into 'ghost town' atmosphere. Railway station (1896), Woodward St; transport exhibition and display of famous Varischetti mine rescue. Warden Finnerty's house (1895), McKenzie St; striking example of early Australian architecture and furnishings. St Anthony's Convent, Lindsay St; now boarding-school for Aboriginal Self Help Group Concerned Parents Society (CAPS). Goal Tree, Hunt St. Lions Bicentennial Lookout, near southern end of Hunt St. Lindsay's Pit Mine Lookout, Ford St. Coolgardie Day and Camel Races, both held in Sept. **In the area:** Camel farm, 4 km W. Kurrawang Emu Farm, 20 km E. Cemetery, 1 km W, evokes harsh early days of gold

rush. Eastern Goldfields Heritage Trail; details from tourist centre. **Tourist information:** Bayley St; (090) 26 6090. **Accommodation:** 1 hotel, 3 motels, 2 caravan/camping parks. **See also:** The Goldfields.
MAP REF. 356 G7

Coral Bay   Pop. 726
The Ningaloo Coral Reef system approaches the shore at Coral Bay, 150 km S of Exmouth. Unspoilt expanses of white beaches offer good swimming, snorkelling, boating and fishing. **In the area:** Ningaloo Marine Park, just off beach. Views of reef from glass-bottomed boats. Diving equipment for hire. Numerous shipwreck sites at Pt Cloates, 8 km N, and ruins of Norwegian Bay whaling station (1915). **Tourist information:** Bayview Restaurant and Shop; (099) 42 5966. **Accommodation:** 1 motel, 2 caravan/camping parks.
MAP REF. 355 C5

Corrigin   Pop. 725
Rich farming country surrounds Corrigin, 230 km SE of Perth. **Of interest:** In Kunjin St, folk museum with historical exhibits, including photographs; also miniature railway and steam train. Turkish mountain gun from Gallipoli, RSL monument; Gayfer St. Art and craft shop, Walton St. Agricultural Show in Sept. Creative Arts Exhibition in Nov. **In the area:** Dog Cemetery, 5 km W. Observation tower, 3 km W, affords good views; on Wildflower Scenic Drive, Trott Dr (well signposted). Gorge Rock, 20 km SE; picnics. **Tourist information:** Shire Offices, Lynch St; (090) 63 2203. **Accommodation:** 1 hotel, 1 motel, 1 caravan/camping park.
MAP REF. 347 N7, 354 G8, 356 C9

Cossack   Pop. 1 & 1 dog
Cossack, once called Tien Tsin, has had a chequered history. It was the first port in the north-west, and has been a thriving pearling centre, the focus of a gold rush and the location for a factory producing turtle products. Today it is a ghost town. **Of interest:** Historic buildings: in Pearl St, courthouse (now museum), bond store, post and telegraph office; in Perseverance St, police quarters. Cemetery, off Perseverance St; headstones reflect town's colourful past. Located at mouth of Harding River, Cossack is ideal area for picnics, fishing, crabbing or

swimming. Boats for hire. Cossack Fair and Regatta in June. **In the area:** To north-west, Wickham (8 km), a modern company town, and Point Samson (18 km), a popular seaside resort. **Tourist information:** Roebourne Tourist Bureau, Queen St, Roebourne; (091) 82 1060. **Accommodation:** Backpackers hotel. **See also:** The Pilbara.
MAP REF. 358 A2

Cranbrook   Pop. 306

In the 1800s sandalwood was exported from Cranbrook to China, where it was used as incense. Today this attractive town, near the foothills of the Stirling Range, 320 km SE of Perth, is a sheep- and wheat-farming centre. **Of interest:** Annual Wildflower Display, Sept.–Oct. **In the area:** Gateway to the Stirling Arch, Salt River Rd; picnic area, native garden and tourist information. Stirling Range National Park, 15 km SE. Lake Poorarrecup, 55 km SW; popular spot in summer. Sukey Hill Lookout, 5 km E, off Saltriver Rd. High-quality table wines produced at Frankland district vineyards, 50 km W. Frankland Heritage Trail; details from tourist centre. **Tourist information:** Shire Offices, Gathorne St; (098) 26 1008. **Accommodation:** 1 hotel, 1 caravan/camping park.
MAP REF. 351 L6, 354 G11, 356 B13

Cue   Pop. 394

Cue, 640 km NE of Perth on the Great Northern Hwy, grew up as a boom town, an important centre for the Murchison goldfields. Today its well-kept stone buildings are a silent testimony to those frenzied days. **Of interest:** Buildings in Austin Street (classified by National Trust) include: bandstand built over a well, water from which was said to have started a typhoid epidemic, and impressive government offices. Masonic Lodge (1899), Dowley St, built largely of corrugated iron. **In the area:** Ghost town left from mining boom; Tuckanarra, 40 km N. Day Dawn, 5 km W, where town was established on site of gold reef; town disappeared when reef died out in 1930s. Ghost town of Big Bell, 30 km W, another crumbling reminder of gold boom; current open-pit mine opened in 1989 (access restricted). Walga Rock, monolith 50 km W, one of largest in Australia; largest gallery of Aboriginal rock paintings in WA. Wilgie Mia Red Ochre Mine, 64 km NW; gemstone fossicking. Cue Heritage Trail;

details from tourist centre. **Tourist information:** Dorsett's Guesthouse, Austin St; (099) 63 1291. **Accommodation:** 1 hotel, 1 caravan/camping park.
MAP REF. 355 I12, 356 C1, 358 B13

Dampier   Pop. 1810

A model town with all modern conveniences, Dampier lies on King Bay, facing the unique islands of the Dampier Archipelago. Hamersley Iron Pty Ltd established the town as a port outlet for ore mined from two of the world's richest iron-ore deposits, Tom Price and Paraburdoo. The town's deepwater port with its export facilities sees over 400 million tonnes of ore loaded each year. Salt is harvested from ponds near the port. **Of interest:** Jurat Park, Haig Close; picnic/barbecue facilities and children's playground. Tours of the Hamersley Iron port facility, Mon.–Fri.; bookings (091) 44 4600. Boating, sailing, fishing, diving, windsurfing and swimming. Game fishing; charter boats for hire. In the first weekend of Aug., Dampier and Karratha hold their FeNaCLNG festival (Fe: iron; NaCl: salt; LNG: liquefied natural gas). A major feature of the festival is the Dampier Classic, a game-fishing competition for which almost 100 fish are caught, tagged and released. **In the area:** North West Shelf Gas Project on Burrup Peninsula 8 km NW; Visitors Centre open weekdays, except public holidays. Nearby Hearsons Cove, popular tidal swimming beach and picnic area. Aboriginal rock carvings on Burrup Peninsula; details from tourist centre. Pilbara Railway Historical Society Museum, 10 km W, home of 'Pendennis Castle' steam locomotive; open Sun. **Tourist information:** King Bay Holiday Village, The Esplanade; (091) 83 1440. **Accommodation:** 2 motels, 1 caravan/ camping park. **See also:** The Hamersley Range; The Pilbara.
MAP REF. 355 G1

Denham–Shark Bay
Pop. 943

Two peninsulas form the geographical feature of Shark Bay, 833 km from Perth. Denham is the most westerly town in Australia and the main centre of the Shark Bay region. Dirk Hartog, the Dutch navigator, landed on an island at the entrance to Shark Bay in 1616. Pearling developed as the main industry and the population was a mixture of Malays, Chinese and Europeans. Until recently

Shark Bay was known only for its excellent fishing, but today its most spectacular tourist attraction is the wild dolphins of Monkey Mia, who after years of love and understanding come of their own accord to be fed. **In the area:** Francois Peron National Park, 7 km N. Eagle Bluff, 20 km S, habitat of sea eagle and good fishing spot. Catamaran MV Explorer offers a variety of cruises. Safaris and coach tours also available. Nanga Station, 50 km S; this half-million-acre sheep station also has motel units, restaurant, tourist facilities, sailboards and dinghies for hire on beach, and charter fishing. Zuytdorp Cliffs, 160 km W and extending south to Kalbarri, offer striking scenery; 4WD only. Shell Beach, 40 km S; 110-km stretch of unique Australian coastline comprising countless tiny shells. Hamelin Pool, 100 km SE; historic displays in Flint Cliff Telegraph Station and Post Office Museum (1894), and stromatolites ('living rocks' communities) in nature reserve. **Tourist information:** Shark Bay Visitor and Travel Centre, 83 Knight Tce, Denham; (099) 48 1253. **Accommodation:** 1 hotel/motel, 1 motel, 4 caravan/camping parks.
MAP REF. 355 B10

Denmark   Pop. 1586

The attractive coastal town of Denmark, 54 km W of Albany, is at the foot of Mt Shadforth, overlooking the tranquil Denmark River. The town is known for its good fishing, sandy white beaches and scenic drives through farming country and karri forests. The dense hardwood forests supply timber for the mills in the area. **Of interest:** Historical Museum, Mitchell St. Denmark Gallery, Strickland St. Cottage Industries Shop, Mitchell St. Alpaca stud and tourist farm, Scotsdale Rd. Jassi Skincraft, Glenrowan Rd off Mt Shadforth Scenic Drive; local handcrafts, wines and sheepskin products. Esplanade Parkland, along the riverbank, with shaded picnic areas, recreation and sports facilities. Winery and Craft Centre in Old Butter Factory, North St. Mt Shadforth Lookout, top of Isley Dr, for magnificent views of countryside. Winter Festival held in Aug. Art and Craft Market Days in Dec. and Jan. and on Easter Sat. **In the area:** Knoll Drive, 3 km E. Wynella Museum, 15 km W. William Bay, 18 km W; sheltered swimming beach. Greens Pool–William Bay National Park, 23 km W. Parry's Beach, 25 km W, for fishing, with salmon in season, and Ocean Beach,

8 km s, for surfing. Picturesque town of Albany, 54 km E; rich history and beautiful beaches. A pleasant drive through the Valley of the Giants, 45 km w, reveals the massive karri and tingle trees. Boating, fishing, bushwalking and scenic drives in area of Nornalup, 50 km w, and Walpole, 66 km w, adjacent to Walpole–Nornalup National Park. Some dozen wineries in Denmark–Mount Barker–Albany region, 15 km E. Farm holidays at Rannock West, 32 km w, cattle and sheep property. Scotsdale Rd–McLeod Rd Tourist Drive (details from tourist centre), provides excellent views of coast and attractions along way. Denmark Timber, Mokare and Wilson Inlet Heritage Trail; details from tourist centre. **Tourist information:** Strickland St; (098) 48 1265. **Accommodation:** 2 hotels, 2 motels, 5 caravan/camping parks. **See also:** The Great Southern.
MAP REF. 351 K12, 354 G12

Derby
Pop. 3022
Derby operates as an administrative centre for a hinterland rich in pastoral and mineral wealth. The town is located on King Sound, 220 km NE of Broome, and is an ideal base for expeditions into the outback regions of the Kimberley. Roads have been greatly improved in recent years, including the Gibb River road, spanning the 645 km from Derby to the junction of the Great Northern Hwy between Wyndham and Kununurra. However, as rain usually closes the road between Nov. and March, it is always advisable to check local conditions before setting out. **Of interest:** In Loch St: Botanic Gardens; Old Derby Gaol; museum, including photographic display, at Wharfinger House. In Clarendon St: Raintree Craft Shop; Art Gallery; Royal Flying Doctor Service. In Stanley St: Ngunga Craft Shop. Country Music Festival held July. Boab Festival, also held July, features rodeo, mardi gras and Derby's famous mud football. **In the area:** Prison Tree, 7 km s, boab (or baobab) tree reputedly used as prison in early days. Close by, Myall's Bore, an enormous cattle trough, 120 m long. Mowanjum Corporation, 10 km s. Fitzroy River empties into King Sound, 48 km s. Tours available to spectacular Windjana Gorge and remarkable Tunnel Creek, with its colonies of flying foxes, 145 km and 184 km E respectively; also Pigeon's Cave, hideout of Aboriginal outlaw. King Leopold Ranges, 200 km E. Mitchell Plateau,

580 km NE, via Gibb River Rd and Kalumburu Rd; includes spectacular Mitchell Falls, King Edward River and Surveyor's Pool; in this remote region, visitors must be entirely self-sufficient. Motor yacht charter to Buccaneer Archipelago and Walcott Inlet available. Charter flights over Kimberley coast and Cockatoo and Koolan Islands. Pigeon Heritage Trail, from Derby to Windjana Gorge and Tunnel Creek National Park, following adventures of Pigeon, Aboriginal outlaw active in 1890s; details from tourist centre. **Tourist information:** 1 Clarendon St; (091) 91 1426. **Accommodation:** 3 hotels, 1 caravan/camping park. **See also:** The Kimberley.
MAP REF. 352 B9, 361 J7

Dongara–Port Denison
Pop. 1677
These quiet towns are on the coast 359 km N of Perth. Dongara has beaches, reef-enclosed bays and an abundance of delicious rock lobster. There is good fishing in the waters around Port Denison, which also has swimming and golf. **Of interest:** Fisherman's Lookout, near Leander Point, Port Denison, gives panoramic views of harbour. Historic buildings include Anglican rectory and church, and old police station in Waldeck St; Royal Steam Flour Mill (1894)), the 'Old Mill', on Brand Hwy; and Russ Cottage (1870), St Dominicks Rd. Restaurant, store, blacksmith's shop and accommodation in historic cottage; all on Brand Hwy. Dongara's main street,

Moreton Tce, shaded by huge 85-year-old Moreton Bay fig trees. Dongara Cemetery, Dodd St; headstones date back to 1874. Heritage Trail from Old Mill to Russ Cottage; details from tourist centre. Blessing of the Fleet held Nov. **In the area:** At Western Flora Caravan Park, 60 km s of Dongara; wildflowers in river and bushland setting. Eneabba, 81 km s of Dongara; mineral sand mining, with large concentrations of rutile. Holiday towns of Leeman (38 km) and Green Head (50 km) sw of Eneabba. Historic hamlet of Greenough, 40 km N; deer and emu park in Georgina Rd. **Tourist information:** Old Police Station Building, 5 Waldeck St; (099) 27 1404. **Accommodation:** 2 hotels, 1 motel, 4 caravan/camping parks.
MAP REF. 354 C3

Donnybrook
Pop. 1570
The township of Donnybrook, the home of the Granny Smith apple, is at the heart of the oldest apple-growing area in WA, 210 km s of Perth. Gold was discovered here in 1897, but it was mined for only 4 years. Donnybrook stone has been used in construction State-wide. Apple Festival is held Easter in odd-numbered years. **Of interest:** On South West Hwy, Anchor and Hope Inn (1865), once staging post for mail coaches. Rotary Lookout, Trigg St. Arboretum, junction Irishtown Rd and South West Hwy. Trigwell Place, near river at southern end of town; picnic/barbecue facilities and children's playground. **In the area:** Glen Mervyn

Dolphins at Monkey Mia, near Denham

Western Wildflowers

The sandplains, swamps, flats, scrub and woodlands of south-western Australia light up with colour in spring as the 'wildflower State' puts on its brilliant display. The plains can become carpeted, almost overnight, with the gold of everlastings or feather flowers or the red and pinks of boronia and leschenaultia. The banksia bushes throw up their red and yellow cylinders along the coast and in the woodlands, grevilleas spill their flowers down to the ground and orchids proliferate. Flowering gums become a mass of red and the felty kangaroo paws invade the plains. Lilies, banksias, parrot bush, flame peas, feather flowers and native foxgloves—all are displayed in a magnificent abundance.

There are over 8000 named species and 2000 unnamed species of wildflowers in Western Australia, giving the State one of the richest floras known to man. Around 75 per cent of them are unique to the region, although they may have family connections with other plants of northern or eastern Australia. Isolation by the barrier of plain and desert that separates the west from the eastern States has caused plants on both sides to pursue their own evolution; some families of plants are unique to the west.

On even a short trip to Perth, visitors can see a wide variety of Western Australian wildflowers. At **King's Park** close to the city, wildflower species abound and give a brilliant display in the August to October period. Visitors in any part of the south-west at that time will see wildflowers all around them. Often, however, it is in the State's national parks that the full beauty of massed wildflower displays is best seen. Only 25 kilometres east of Perth on the Great Eastern Highway is the **John Forrest National Park**, on the edge of the Darling Range escarpment. On these undulating hills and valleys the undergrowth of the jarrah forest is rich in flowering plants—red and green kangaroo paw, swamp river myrtle, blue leschenaultia and pink calytrix are the most common. Fifty kilometres north of Perth is the **Yanchep National Park**, a place of coastal limestone and sandy plains, covered with wildflowers. There are many places farther north that are worth visiting, if only for the unique quality of their scenery. One such is the **Kalbarri National Park**, 670 kilometres north of Perth, at the mouth of the Murchison River. The park contains magnificent flowering trees and shrubs of banksia, grevillea and melaleuca, while the ground beneath is

Sturt Desert Peas, Pilbara region

covered with many species, such as leschenaultia, twine rushes and sedges. Prolific displays of wildflowers also can be found throughout the wheat belt, forests and sandplains of the south-west.

The **Dryandra State Forest**, a few kilometres from Narrogin in the south-west, has magnificent woodlands of wandoo and powderbark, with brown mallet and bush thickets. An important sanctuary for mallee fowl and numbat, this forest contains a number of species of dryandra.

Another interesting area of Western Australia is the **Stirling Range National Park**, 400 kilometres south of Perth and near the Porongurup Range. The Stirlings are very jagged peaks that rise above flat farmlands. The scenery is magnificent and wildflowers abound, many unique to the region. There are banksias here, as well as dryandra, cone bushes, cats paws, and a number of mountain bells, which have red or pink flower heads. The bare granite domes and the boulders of the Porongurup Range tower over slopes of flowering trees such as *Banksia grandis* and creepers such as the clematis.

There are many coastal parks around Albany. The **Torndirrup National Park** is an area of coastal hills and cliffs and such scenic features as the Gap, the Blowhole and the Natural Bridge. In the stunted,

windswept coastal vegetation there are many wildflowers, including the endemic giant-coned *Banksia praemorsa* and the Western Australian Christmas tree with its brilliant orange flowers.

Twenty-five kilometres east of Albany is the peaceful and beautiful **Two Peoples Bay** flora and fauna reserve, which has thickets of mallee, banksia and peppermint, together with many flowering shrubs and plants. Along the coast west of Albany is the **Walpole–Nornalup National Park**, where dense karri forest mingles with red tingle, jarrah, marri, casuarina and banksia, and many wildflowers including the tree kangaroo paw, the babe-in-cradle orchid and the potato orchid.

Although most wildflowers occur in the south-west of the State, northern areas also have displays peculiar to climatic changes and times of rainfall. While enjoying Western Australia's brilliant flora, visitors should remember that wildflowers are protected under the State's *Native Flower Protection Act*.

For further information on national parks and wildflower display areas, contact the Western Australian Tourist Centre or the Department of Conservation and Land Management, 50 Hayman Rd, Como WA 6152; (09) 334 0333.

Dam, 30 km NE; picnic/barbecue facilities. At Balingup, 20 km S: Old Cheese Factory, now art and craft centre; Tinderbox, for herbs and herbal remedies; Bailiwick woodwork; and, 2 km from town, Golden Valley Tree Park. Scenic drives; details from tourist centre. **Tourist information:** 'Old' Railway Station, South West Hwy; (097) 31 1720. **Accommodation:** 2 hotels, 1 motel, 1 caravan/camping park. **See also:** The South-west.
MAP REF. 354 E10

Dumbleyung Pop. 292
Dumbleyung lies in the central south of WA, 217 km E of Bunbury and 224 km N of Albany. **Of interest:** Dumbleyung Craft and Tourist Shop, Absolon St. **In the area:** Lake Dumbleyung, 10 km W, where Donald Campbell established a new world water-speed record in 1964; area ideal for swimming, boating, bird-watching and picnicking. Wheatbelt Wildflower Drive, beginning at Kukerin, 39 km E; includes Tarin Rock Nature Reserve. Kukerin Tracmach Vintage Fair held Sept.–Oct. Historic Schools Heritage Trails, 4 scenic drives; details from tourist centre. **Tourist information:** Shire Offices, Harvey St; (098) 63 4012. **Accommodation:** 1 hotel, 1 caravan/camping park.
MAP REF. 347 M13, 354 G10, 356 C11

Dunsborough Pop. 656
Dunsborough is a quiet town on Geographe Bay, west of Busselton, popular because of its fine beaches. **Of interest:** Greenacres, shell museum, off Naturaliste Tce. Bush Cottage Markets, Commonage Rd. Hutchings Museum, Newbury Rd. Moonshine Brewery and Rivendell Gardens, both in Wildwood Rd. **In the area:** Bannamah Wildlife Park, 2 km W. Yallingup Caves and surfing beach, 8 km W. Wineries 6 km SW. Shearing Shed, Wildwood Rd, 15 km SW; shearing demonstrations, wool craft; check opening times. Gunyulgup Galleries, 4 km S of Yallingup. Cape Naturaliste Lighthouse, 13 km N; open daily except Wed. Also several walking tracks in area. Torpedo Rock, 10 km W; Sugarloaf Rock, 12 km N; Canal Rocks, 15 km SW. Good beaches at Meelup, 5 km N; Eagle Bay, 8 km N; and Bunker Bay, 12 km N. Scuba diving, snorkelling, canoeing; 4WD day tours, wildflower tours, winery and craft tours, and day trips to Pemberton; details from tourist centre.

Tourist information: Naturaliste Tce; (097) 55 3517. **Accommodation:** 1 hotel, 1 motel, 2 caravan/camping parks.
MAP REF. 349 C2, 354 D10

Dwellingup Pop. 383
This quiet little town is 24 km SE of Pinjarra and 109 km from Perth. The road into Dwellingup offers panoramic views of the Indian Ocean and Peel Inlet. The impressive jarrah forests nearby supply the local timber mill and bauxite is mined in the area. Centre for new Conservation and Land Management tourist venture. **Of interest:** Real country-style meals in friendly Dwellingup Community Hotel, Marrinup St. Hotham Valley Tourist Railway runs old-style steam train between Pinjarra and Dwellingup, and into jarrah forest; check running times. **Tourist information:** Murray Tourist Centre, George St, Pinjarra; (09) 531 1438. **Accommodation:** 1 hotel.
MAP REF. 346 E9, 354 E9

Esperance Pop. 7066
Wide sandy beaches, scenic coastline and the offshore islands of the Recherche Archipelago are all attractions of Esperance, on the south coast of WA. The town, 720 km from Perth via Wagin, is both the port and service centre for the highly productive agricultural and pastoral hinterland. The first permanent settlers came in 1863. The town boomed during the 1890s as port for the goldfields, but it was not until the 1950s, when scientists realised that the heath plains could be transformed into fertile pasture and farming country, that the town's development began in earnest. **Of interest:** Municipal Museum, James St; collection of machinery, furniture and farm equipment from yesteryear, also display of Skylab, which fell to earth over Esperance in 1979. Public Library, Windich St; collection of books on history of Esperance. Art and craft centre on the Esplanade. Fishing and seal watching from Tanker Jetty. Esperance Diving Academy, Esplanade. Boat charters for deep-sea fishing available, also motorcycle tours and horseriding. **In the area:** Rotary Lookout, or Wireless Hill, 2 km W, offers excellent panoramas of bay, township and farmlands. Wind Farm, SECWA research programme, at Salmon Beach, 5 km W; landscape of windmills. Pink Lake, 5 km W; dense saltwater lake that really is pink. Twilight Bay, 12 km W, on tourist loop, for swimming and

fishing, and nearby Picnic Cove, with sheltered swimming beach. Views of bay and islands from Observatory Point and Lookout, 17 km W. Dalyup River Wines, 42 km W; open 10–4 weekends. The Recherche Archipelago, or Bay of Isles, off Esperance, consists of 105 small unspoiled islands, a haven for native fauna. Two-hr launch cruises around Gull, Button, Charlie and other islands; landing not permitted. Regular cruises during Jan. to Woody Island, SE of Esperance (50 min. by boat); developed as a tourist attraction, overnight camping facilities. Parrot Farm, 15 km E, on Fisheries Rd. Cape Le Grand National Park, 56 km E, with spectacular coastline and many attractive beaches; scenic walks and beautiful wildflowers for which the region is famous. Magnificent view from Frenchmans Peak, in park. Cape Arid National Park, 120 km E, popular with fishermen, campers and 4WD. **Tourist information:** Museum Village, Dempster St; (090) 71 2330. **Accommodation:** 3 hotels, 6 motels, 6 caravan/camping parks. **See also:** Crossing the Nullarbor; National Parks.
MAP REF. 356 H12

Eucla Pop. 30
Eucla is just 12 km from the WA/SA border, on the Eyre Hwy. **In the area:** A cross on an escarpment overlooking the ocean and the sand-covered ruins of the old telegraph station and former town site, 5 km S, is dedicated to all Eyre Hwy travellers and is illuminated at night. The highway westward from Eucla descends to the coastal plain via Eucla Pass. Midway down the Pass (about 200 m) a track to the left leads to the old town site and ruins amongst the sand dunes. Nine-hole golf course, 7 km N. Weebubby Cave, 12 km N; experienced cavers only. **Tourist information:** Roadhouse; (090) 39 3468. **Accommodation:** 1 motel, 1 caravan/camping park. **See also:** Crossing the Nullarbor.
MAP REF. 296 A8, 357 R8

Exmouth Pop. 3128
Exmouth is one of the newest towns in Australia and was founded in 1967 as a support town for the US Naval Communications station. The station, an RAN facility run by a civilian contractor, is the main source of employment for people living in Exmouth. The town has many modern sporting and community facilities. Excellent year-round fishing and

The Kimberley

Until relatively recently the Kimberley region in the far north of Western Australia was a place only for hardened pioneers and prospectors. Now, with the National Highway completed, it is on Australia's travel map and it can offer both excitement and adventure. In addition, the 40-tonne, 18-metre ketch-rigged motor yacht *Opal Shell* cruises along the Kimberley coast out of Derby.

There are two seasons throughout the Kimberley. The northern towns generally have higher maximum temperatures and the southern coastline towns experience a higher humidity and average minimum temperature. The long dry period in winter brings delightful weather, while the green season brings higher temperatures, with monsoonal rains usually falling between December and March.

The gateway to the Kimberley is the old pearling town of Broome. In the boisterous days of the early 1900s the pearling fleet numbered some 400 luggers with 3000 crewmen. Today Broome is rapidly expanding into one of Western Australia's most popular tourist destinations. There are many points of interest, including a set of dinosaur tracks believed to have been embedded in limestone 130 million years ago, and Buccaneer Rock, reputed to be the place where Dampier was wrecked in the *Roebuck* in 1699.

Further north-east is **Derby**, on King Sound near the mouth of the Fitzroy River, a centre for the beef-cattle industry of the Fitzroy Valley and the King Leopold Ranges. Just 7 kilometres south of the town is a centuries-old boab tree. Shaped like an inverted wineglass and 14 metres in diameter, it is hollow and is reputed to have been used as a cell for prisoners.

Derby is an ideal base for excursions to Windjana Gorge and Tunnel Creek in the Napier Range, and Geikie Gorge near the town of **Fitzroy Crossing**. These are among the most colourful and spectacular of all the river gorges of northern Australia.

The old gold settlement of **Halls Creek**, 16 kilometres from the site of the present town, was the scene of the first gold rush in Western Australia in 1885. Scores of diggers perished of hunger and thirst and very little gold was found. Nearby is the meteorite crater at Wolfe Creek, the second largest in the world, with an average depth of 50 metres. The meteorite is believed to have struck the earth about one million years ago. Also near Halls Creek is the China Wall, a natural white stone wall above a placid creek.

The most northerly town and safe port harbour in Western Australia is **Wyndham**, the terminus of the Great Northern Highway and now also the port for the Ord River irrigation area as well as for the east Kimberley cattle stations. A 100-kilometre route from Wyndham to **Kununurra** winds through spectacular ancient gorge country. Kununurra is the base for nearby attractions such as Lake Argyle, Hidden Valley National Park and the Bungle Bungle National Park. South of Lake Argyle is the Argyle diamond mine, the world's largest. Kununurra is then linked to **Darwin** by the National Highway, which is often used by travellers making a round trip of Australia.

See also: Individual town entries in A–Z listing. **Note** detailed map of Kimberley Region on page 352.

The Ord River

The introduction of the Ord River Scheme was a far-sighted move to develop the tropical north of Western Australia. During the rainy season, the rivers of the Kimberley become raging torrents and at times the waters of the Ord River empty more than 50 million litres a second into Cambridge Gulf. With the end of the monsoon rain, the rich seasonal pastures die and the land becomes dry again. The Ord River Dam was built to harness this tremendous wealth of water for agriculture.

The Kimberley Research Station was established in 1945 to investigate the likelihood of producing crops on the black alluvial soil of the plains. The land was found to be suitable for a variety of tropical crops. By 1963 the Diversion Dam at Kununurra was built to divert water from the river into supply channels. **Lake Argyle**, 72 kilometres south of the Carr Boyd Range, is the main storage reservoir. It is the largest man-made lake in Australia, and holds nine times the volume of water of Sydney Harbour, its normal capacity being 5674 million cubic metres. This vast expanse of water is dotted with islands that were once peaks rising above the surrounding valleys. The water of the Ord is now capable of irrigating 72 000 hectares of land. A third of the projected irrigation area will be along the Keep River Plain in the Northern Territory.

The area is becoming increasingly attractive to tourists. Surrounding Lake Argyle are rugged red slopes, a haven for native animals such as the bungarra lizard, the brush-tailed wallaby and the grey kangaroo. Looking out over the lake is a tourist village, with a modern hotel/motel, caravan and camping facilities and areas of shaded lawns. There are lake cruises and, for the more energetic, fishing trips, bushwalks or tennis.

The Durack homestead, **Argyle Downs**, is also to be found here; once the residence of the Durack family, the homestead was moved to its present site to prevent it being covered by the waters of the lake. A fascinating memorial to the early settlers of the district, it re-creates life as it once was in the Kimberley.

The town of **Kununurra**—the name means 'big water'—has been established as the residential and administrative centre of the Ord River Scheme.

See also: Individual town entries in A–Z listing; The Kimberley.

its beaches has made Exmouth a main tourist destination. The town is situated on the north-eastern side of North West Cape, which juts out north from the mainland. The Cape is the nearest point in Australia to the continental shelf, so there is an abundance of fish and other marine life in the surrounding waters. Turtle-nesting November–Jan. Coral spawning March. Whale sharks March–May, and humpback whales and manta rays Aug.–Oct. **Of interest:** Exmouth House of Dolls, Craft St. Ocean Exhibits Museum, Pellew St. **In the area:** Beaches for swimming, snorkelling, fishing. Shothole Canyon Rd provides easy access into one of many spectacular gorges in Cape Range National Park; park's Milyering Visitor Centre, 52 km SW. Yardie Creek Gorge in the park has deep blue waters, multi-coloured rock, and abundant wildlife. Charles Knife Canyon Rd has picnic spots, scenic lookouts and walking trail. Prawn fishery, 23 km S; inspections during season early May–late Oct. Learmonth RAAF base, 34 km S. Charter fishing available at Bundegi Beach jetty, 14 km N. Panoramic views from Vlaming Head Lighthouse, 19 km N; guided tours. Wreck of SS *Mildura* nearby. Ningaloo Marine Park, 14 km W of Cape, largest coral reef in WA; 500 species of fish and 220 species of reef-building corals. Daily coral-viewing trips from both Exmouth and Coral Bay. Safari tours of Cape. Lightfoot Heritage Trail; details from tourist centre. **Tourist information:** Thew St; (099) 49 1176. **Accommodation:** 2 motels, 4 caravan/camping parks. MAP REF. 355 C3

Fitzroy Crossing   Pop. 1119

In the Kimberley, where the road north crosses the Fitzroy River, is the settlement of Fitzroy Crossing, 260 km inland from Derby. Once a sleepy little hamlet, the last few years have seen unprecedented growth of the town as a result of Aboriginal settlement, mining by BHP at Cadjebut, 50 km E, and an increase in the number of visitors to the nearby Geikie Gorge National Park. **In the area:** Picturesque waterholes, which support abundance of fish and other wildlife. Magnificent Geikie Gorge, 20 km NE; sharks, sawfish and stingrays, which have adapted themselves to fresh water, abound, as do barramundi and freshwater crocodiles. Regular boat trips available May–Oct. Fitzroy River Lodge tourist complex on Great Northern Hwy. **Tourist information:** Fitzroy River Lodge; (091) 91 5141. **Accommodation:** 1 hotel, 1 motel, 3 caravan/camping parks. **See also:** National Parks. MAP REF. 352 H11, 361 M9

Fremantle   Pop. 27 000

The largest port in the State and western gateway to Australia, Fremantle is a bustling city 19 km S of Perth. It is a city of contrasts, with galleries and museums, beautiful sandy white beaches and many historic buildings as a reminder of the city's heritage. Captain Charles Fremantle arrived in May 1829 to take possession of 'the whole of the west coast of New Holland', and was followed one month later by Captain James Stirling, who arrived with a small group to found the first colony in Australia made up entirely of European free settlers. The engineer C. Y. O'Connor, who began the Goldfields Water Scheme, was also responsible for building the artificial harbour that turned Fremantle into an important port. The city was the first stop for many migrants arriving in Australia and as a result has a large European population. With its old-world charm and colourful cosmopolitan culture, Fremantle is one of the most fascinating port cities in the world. **Of interest:** Many coffee shops and restaurants in South Terrace–Cappucino Strip. Maritime Museum, Cliff St, built in 1860s and a fine example of colonial Gothic architecture. Fremantle Museum and Arts Centre, Finnerty St; during summer, courtyard used for musical performances. Boat museum on Victoria Quay, not far from Maritime Museum. Energy Museum, Parry St. Film and Television Institute, Adelaide St. Round House (1830), end of High St, oldest building in WA; 12-sided structure, constructed as gaol. Joan Campbell's Pottery Workshop, near The Round House, in converted boatshed. Magnificent Samson House (1900), cnr Ellen and Ord Sts; guided tours. Shell Museum, Beach St. Spare Parts Puppet Theatre, Short St; permanent puppet display and regular performances. Endeavour Replica, Mews Rd. Fremantle Gaol (1851–59), forbidding building of local stone; no longer in use as prison and open to visitors. Fremantle Prison Museum, with displays recording penal system in WA, adjacent to prison. Warders' Quarters, Henderson St; Georgian terrace. Old Customs House (1853), Cliff St, also in Georgian style. St John's Church and Square (1882). Gracious Town Hall in Kings Square, cnr William and Adelaide Sts; opened in 1887. Quaint old building at 5 Mouat St; originally housed German Consulate and shipping offices. Port Authority Building, Cliff St; Fremantle's tallest building, with panoramic views from roof viewing area. Impressive Fremantle Markets, Henderson St; range of food, including delicious seafoods, handcrafts, antiques, clothing and souvenirs Fri–Sun. Adjacent to Marine Tce and the Esplanade, modern Challenger Harbour marina facilities developed for first Australian defence of the America's Cup, yachting's most prestigious trophy. Fremantle's large fishing fleet, which works Australia's most valuable fishing grounds (mainly lobster), and its considerable Italian community, give the city a Mediterranean flavour. There are pavement cafes and excellent restaurants. Sail & Anchor Hotel on South Tce, Australia's first pub brewery, serves specialty beers. Fremantle Crocodile Park at Fishing Boat Harbour, off Mews Rd; both saltwater and smaller freshwater species. Fremantle Festival held Nov. **In the area:** Swimming at Port, Leighton and South Beaches. Ferries to Rottnest Island, 20 km W, leave from wharf daily; charter boats to Rottnest also available. Daily tram tours; details from tourist centre. **Tourist information:** Town Hall Shop, King Sq., High St; (09) 430 2346. **Accommodation:** 10 hotels, 2 hotel/motels, 1 motel, 3 caravan parks. MAP REF. 342 B11, 346 C5, 348, 354 D7

Gascoyne Junction   Pop. 34

Located 178 km E of Carnarvon, at the junction of the Gascoyne and Lyons Rivers, the town is the administration centre for the Shire of Upper Gascoyne. The old-fashioned pub is a good rest stop before enjoying the many scenic attractions of the Kennedy Ranges National Park, 60 km N. **Tourist information:** Carnarvon District Tourist Bureau, Robinson St, Carnarvon; (099) 41 1146. **Accommodation:** 1 hotel. MAP REF. 355 E8

Geraldton   Pop. 24 361

The key port and administration centre for the Midwest region, Geraldton is 424 km N of Perth on Champion Bay. A year-round sunny climate, combined with a

mild winter, makes it one of the State's most popular holiday resorts. The city itself is flourishing, with a modern shopping centre, interesting museums and excellent accommodation. The beaches are sandy and white and the fishing is good. Rich agricultural land surrounds Geraldton and the district is noted for its beautiful spring wildflowers and picturesque countryside. The Houtman Abrolhos Islands, which were first sighted and named in the sixteenth century, lie 64 km off the coast and are used mainly as a base for rock-lobster fishermen. **Of interest:** St Francis Xavier Cathedral, Cathedral Ave, designed by Mons. John C. Hawes, architect responsible for some fine buildings in and around Geraldton. Sir John Forrest Memorial, Marine Tce. Geraldton Museum (includes Maritime Display building and Old Railway building), Marine Tce; collection of earthenware pots and wine vessels, bronze cannon, coins and other relics from shipwrecks off coast. Queens Park Theatre (1922), Cathedral Ave, surrounded by gardens. Art Gallery, cnr Durlacher St and Chapman Rd. Old Gaol Craft Centre, Bill Sewell Complex, Chapman Rd. Tourist Lookout and Wishing Well on Waverley Heights, Brede St, for panoramic views. Point Moore Lighthouse (1878), Willcock Dr. Fishing is popular and many varieties can be caught; town's breakwater is good location. At Fisherman's Wharf, during season (mid-Nov.–end June), watch huge hauls of lobster being unloaded. Geraldton–Midwest Sunshine Festival held in spring. **In the area:** Good fishing at Sunset Beach, 6 km N; fishing and surfing at Drummond Cove, 10 km N; and mouth of Greenough River, 10 km S. Greenough River is also a favourite place for picnics, with safe swimming for children. Greenough hamlet, 24 km S; National-Trust-restored-village preserved to look as it did in 1880s; guided tours. Ellendale Bluffs and Pool, 45 km SE; permanent waterhole at base of steep rock face. Chapman Valley, 35 km NE; farming district with brilliant wildflower displays in spring. From Mill's Park Lookout, on Waggrakine Cutting, 15 km NE; views over Moresby Range and coastal plain towards Geraldton. Kalbarri National Park, 170 km N. The sheer coastal rock faces and deep gorges of the Murchison River, at Kalbarri, 164 km N, are stunningly beautiful. Farm holidays available near Badgingarra, 250 km S, halfway between Geraldton and Perth. Geraldton Heritage Trail; details from tourist centre. **Tourist information:** Bill Sewell Community Recreation Complex, cnr Bayley St and Chapman Rd; (099) 21 3999. **Accommodation:** 5 hotels, 5 motels, 5 caravan/camping parks.
MAP REF. 354 C2

Gingin   Pop. 473

Situated 83 km N of Perth and 30 km from the coast, Gingin is mainly a centre for sheep- wheat- and cattle-farming. As an interesting day trip from Perth, it offers alternative return trips touring coastal centres or inland via the scenic Chittering Valley. The town is built around a loop of Gingin Brook, which rises from springs not far from town and flows strongly all year round. **Of interest:** Gingin has the charm and appeal of an English village and offers some fine examples of traditional Australian architecture, including St Luke's Anglican Church (1860s), Granville (1871), Uniting Church (1868) and Dewar's House (1886), all in Weld St; and Philbey's Cottage (1906), Brockman St. **In the area:** Horseriding, horse-drawn vehicle rides, demonstrations of sheep-shearing and sheepdog work all available; details from tourist information. At Bullsbrook, 30 km S: the Maze, Bullsbrook Antiques and Cottage Crafts. At Bindoon, 24 km E: Neroni Wines, Chittering Valley Estate and Kay Road Art and Craft Gallery. At Lower Chittering, 30 km SE: Golden Grove Citrus Orchard, Sewell Leisure Park, 44 km NE; golf, rides, flora and fauna, picnic/barbecue facilities. **Tourist information:** Shire Offices, 7 Brockman St; (09) 575 2211. **Accommodation:** 1 hotel, 1 caravan/camping park.
MAP REF. 354 E6

Guilderton   Pop. 385

Guilderton is at the mouth of the Moore River, 94 km from Perth, and is a popular day trip and holiday destination. There is excellent fishing in both the river and the sea, and safe swimming for children. Many Dutch relics have been found here, possibly from the wreck of the Gilt Dragon in 1656. **In the area:** Seabird, 20 km N, small but growing fishing village offering 'away from it all' tranquillity with safe beach and ample recreational options. Ledge Point, 28 km N, centre built around fishing industry, providing activities for all age groups; sporting facilities, safe swimming and boating, and picnic facilities complement relaxed lifestyle and friendly atmosphere of this holiday spot. World famous Ledge Point to Lancelin windsurfing classic held in Jan. **Tourist information:** Shire Offices, 7 Brockman St, Gingin; (09) 575 2211. **Accommodation:** 1 caravan/camping park.
MAP REF. 354 D6

Halls Creek   Pop. 1305

In the heart of the Kimberley, 2832 km from Perth, at the edge of the Great Sandy Desert, is Halls Creek, site of WA's first gold discovery in 1885. In the years 1885–1887, 10 000 men came to the Kimberley fields in search of gold, then gradually drifted away, leaving 2000 on the diggings. Today in the area, mineral exploration is still being carried out and the pastoral industry is being supported by steady beef prices. **Of interest:** Arts Centre, Great Northern Hwy; Aboriginal art and artefacts and jewellery made from Halls Creek gold. Russian Jack Memorial, Thomas St, honours European early settlers. **In the area:** China Wall, natural quartz formation, 6 km N; picnic spot above creek. Prospecting at Old Halls Creek, 16 km E; mud-brick ruins of original settlement. Caroline Pool, off Duncan Rd, near old town site; picnic spot with swimming Oct.–May. Ruby Queen Mine, and Sawpit Gorge for fishing, swimming and picnicking, both 40 km SE. Town also offers a relaxing staging point for travellers who wish to visit such wonders as the Wolfe Creek Meteorite Crater, 148 km S (almost 1 km wide, 49 m deep and second largest meteorite crater in world), and Purnululu (Bungle Bungle) National Park, 165 km SE. Aerial tours and 4WD safaris available. **Tourist information:** Great Northern Hwy; (091) 68 6262. **Accommodation:** 1 hotel, 1 motel, 1 caravan/camping park. **See also:** The Kimberley.
MAP REF. 353 N11, 361 P9

Harvey   Pop. 2597

The thriving town of Harvey is set in some of the finest agricultural country in Australia, 139 km S of Perth. Bordered by the Darling Range and the Indian Ocean, the fertile coastal plains make perfect dairying country. The town's irrigation storage dams, with their recreation areas, have become a popular tourist attraction. **Of interest:** J. Knowles' House and Store (1890), Harvey St, first business in Harvey; now museum.

Wave Rock, near Hyden

Next door, Harvey Historical Society Museum, housed in old Harvey railway station (1914). L'Arancio Cafe, site of town's famous 'Big Orange' Tourist Complex; train rides, wildlife park, restaurant and craft shop. Harvey Tourist and Interpretative Centre, South West Hwy; industry displays, including dairy industry in Moo Shoppe, and crafts. Harvey Internment Camp Memorial Shrine, South Coast Hwy, built by prisoners of war in 1940s; check opening times. Harvey Show held in Oct. **In the area:** Harvey Weir, 3 km E, off Weir Rd. Jardup, restored home of Clarke family, early settlers in district, 9 km E on road to Stirling Dam; art gallery, open Sun. Scenic drive (7 km) around NW side of dam leads to Harvey Falls and Trout Ladder; popular fishing spot. Myalup and Binningup beaches, 25 km W, off Old Coast Rd, are wide and sandy, ideal for swimming, fishing and boating. Emu Tech Farm, Old Coast Rd, Myalup; restaurant and picnic area. Logue Brook Dam, 10 km N; popular venue for bushwalkers, swimmers, water-skiers and trout fishermen. Timbermill Workshop at Yarloop, 15 km N; working exhibit, closed Tues. Yarloop Heritage Trail; details from tourist centre. Yalgorup National Park, 35 km NW. Kemberton Industrial Park (SCM Chemicals), 18 km S; guided tours. **Tourist information:** South West Hwy; (097) 29 1122. **Accommodation:** 1 hotel, 1 motel, 2 caravan/ camping parks. **See also:** The Southwest.
MAP REF. 346 D11, 354 E9

Hopetoun
Pop. 206
Hopetoun is a peaceful holiday resort overlooking the Southern Ocean. The town is 59 km S of Ravensthorpe and offers some rugged but beautiful coastal scenery and wildflowers all year round. The town was once called Mary Anne Harbour and has a colourful history. **Of interest:** The beaches with their white sand, the sheltered bays and the excellent fishing are the main attractions. Chatterbox Craft, Veal St; local art and crafts. **In the area:** Dunn's Swamp, 5 km N, for picnics, bushwalking and birdwatching. Fitzgerald River National Park, 10 km W, features the Barrens, a series of rugged mountains, undulating sandplains and steep narrow gorges; Hamersley Inlet, within the park, is a scenic picnic and camping spot. Take care fishing from rocks—king waves can roll in unexpectedly. **Tourist information:** Hardware and Tackle Store, Veal St; (098) 38 3088. **Accommodation:** 1 hotel, 1 motel, 1 caravan/camping park.
MAP REF. 356 F12

Hyden
Pop. 150
Hyden is in the Shire of Kondinin, 351 km from Perth, in the semi-arid eastern wheat-growing area of WA. **In the area:** Fascinating rock formations, the most famous of which is Wave Rock, 4 km E of Hyden; 2700 million-yr-old granite outcrop rising 15 m, like a giant wave about to break. Wildlife park, coffee shop and caravan park with chalets at Wave Rock. Pioneer Town, collection of Australiana, at base of rock. Lace collection (from 1600) at Wave Rock Wildflower Shop. Other rock formations within walking distance of Wave Rock; Hippo's Yawn, The Falls and The Breakers. Aboriginal rock paintings at Mulka's Cave, 18 km N of Wave Rock; nearby is The Humps, another unusual granite formation. Signposted 72 km scenic tour introduces natural attractions of region. **Tourist information:** Wave Rock Wildflower Shop, Wave Rock Rd, 4 km E of town; (098) 80 5182. **Accommodation:** 1 hotel/motel, 1 caravan/ camping park.
MAP REF. 354 I8, 356 D9

Jurien
Pop. 603
On the shores of an attractive, sheltered bay between Perth and Geraldton, Jurien is a lobster-fishing centre. The town is also a growing holiday centre because of its magnificent safe swimming beaches, excellent climate and reputation as a fisherman's paradise. Jurien boat harbour, a 17½ ha inland marina, offers excellent facilities for the boating enthusiast. **Of interest:** Tours of rock-lobster processing factory during fishing season. Badgingarra Shears (shearing competition) held Aug. Blessing of the Fleet in Nov. Slalom Carnival (windsurfing in Cervantes) held in Dec. **In the area:** Cockleshell Gully, 31 km N, has great diversity of flora and fauna. Stockyard Gully National Park, 50 km N (4WD only); walk through Stockyard Gully Tunnel (300 m long), along winding underground creek; flashlight necessary. Spectacular sand dunes along coast. Nambung National Park, boundary 55 km S; check road conditions before leaving Jurien if taking coastal track; main, signposted route further inland recommended. The Pinnacles, further 17 km within park, thousands of spectacular calcified spires, around 30 000 years old, scattered over some 400 ha of multi-coloured sand; guided tours by coach daily. Waddi Farms, Koonah Rd, Badgingarra, 60 km SE; displays of wildflowers, emu farm, native gardens, shop and restaurant; complex sited off Brand Hwy. **Tourist information:** Shire Offices, Bashford St; (096) 52 1020. **Accommodation:** 1 hotel/motel, 1 caravan/camping park.
MAP REF. 354 C4

Kalbarri
Pop. 1521
This popular holiday resort is ideally located, between Geraldton and Carnarvon,

National Parks

The national parks of Western Australia are tourist attractions in themselves: their spectacular displays of wildflowers create a paradise for photographers and a colourful wonderland for bushwalkers and campers.

Western Australia has more than 8000 named species and 2000 unnamed species of wildflowers, growing undisturbed in their natural surroundings. One quarter of these species cannot be found anywhere else in the world and they lure admirers from interstate and overseas. The best months to see them are from August to October. This is also the best time for camping trips and bushwalking.

Within a 100 kilometre radius of Perth there are 10 National Parks well worth a visit. **Yanchep National Park**, about 50 kilometres north on a belt of coastal limestone, has forests of massive tuart trees. Islands on Loch Ness within the park are waterfowl sanctuaries. Yanchep is also famed for its underground limestone caves and displays of spring wildflowers.

Some 80 kilometres north-east of Perth is the **Avon Valley National Park;** its most popular attractions are upland forests and river valleys, as well as the beautiful wildflowers that abound in season. The highest point in the park is Bald Hill, which gives panoramic views of the Avon River. After winter rains, a tributary of the Avon, Emu Spring Brook, spills 30 metres in a spectacular waterfall.

A cluster of national parks to the east of Perth includes **John Forrest National Park**, which was Western Australia's first proclaimed national park. With the Darling Escarpment within its boundaries, the park features granite outcrops, dams and waterfalls, creeks and rock pools.

Other nearby national parks are **Kalamunda, Greenmount, Gooseberry Hill** and **Lesmurdie Falls**. All are within 20–25 kilometres from Perth. Lookouts at various vantage points offer panoramic views over the suburbs and cities of Perth. The Bibbulmun Track, once an Aboriginal walking trail, begins its 500-kilometre route in Kalamanda National Park.

Proclaimed as the State's first flora and fauna reserve in 1894, **Serpentine National Park** is about 60 kilometres south from Perth and a firm favourite of day picnickers to the falls area within the park. Jarrah and marri forests, and wildflowers in spring are some of the park's attractions.

Stirling Range National Park, 450 kilometres south-east of Perth, is one of Australia's outstanding reserves. Surrounded by a flat, sandy plain, the Stirling Range rises abruptly to over 1000 metres, its jagged peaks veiled in swirling mists. The cool, humid environment created by these low clouds contribute to the survival of more than 1000 species of flowering plants, some of which, like the mountain bells, are found nowhere else in the world.

Brilliant displays of wildflowers are also a feature of the nearby **Porongurup National Park**, where the granite domes of the Porongurup Ranges are clothed in a luxuriant forest of karri trees. The South Western Highway bisects the **Shannon National Park,** 358 kilometres south of Perth. A base from which to explore the park is located at the former timber-milling townsite of Shannon. The remainder of the park consists of towering karri and jarrah forests, surrounding the Shannon River, which empties into the sea at Broke Inlet to the south.

Spectacular coastal scenery is the main attraction of the **Torndirrup National Park** on the Flinders Peninsula, 460 kilometres south of Perth. Also on the south coast are outstanding parks, including **Cape Le Grand National Park,** with its wide beaches and magnificent bays, protected by imposing granite headlands, located 40 kilometres east of Esperance.

Two other parks are near Esperance, both to the west of the township. **Stokes National Park** hugs the coastline around Stokes Inlet and features long sandy beaches and rocky headlands backed by sand dunes and low hills. Stokes Inlet and its associated lakes support a rich variety of wildlife. Inland from Stokes about 100 kilometres, lies Peak Charles National Park. A walk to the ridge of this ancient granite peak allows sweeping views of its companion, Peak Eleanora, and over the

Millstream–Chichester National Park

Purnululu (Bungle Bungle) National Park

dry sandplain heaths and salt-lake systems of the surrounding country.

One of the loveliest sections of the south coast of Western Australia is **Fitzgerald River National Park**, through which the rugged Barren Range (named by Matthew Flinders) stretches from west to east. The park's 330 000 hectares comprise gently undulating sandplains, river valleys, precipitous cliff edges, narrow gorges, and beaches for swimming and rock fishing. The park contains many rare species of flora and fauna, including unique species of flowering plants; one, the exotic royal hakea, resembles a flame shooting from the earth.

Along the lower south-west coast is **Walpole–Nornalup National Park,** 18 166 hectares of wilderness in which creeks gurgle under tall eucalypts, rivers meander between forested hills and inlets rich in fish create a haven for anglers and boating enthusiasts. A network of roads and walking tracks, through forests of karri and tingle, attracts bushwalkers and birdwatchers to enjoy the variety of animal and bird life.

About 100 kilometres east is **West Cape Howe National Park**, the spectacular coastline of which includes the gabbro cliffs of West Cape Howe and the granite of Torbay Heads, fronting the cold waters of the Southern Ocean. Extensive coastal heath, swamps, lakes and karri forest cover the inland, and the park is popular with anglers, bushwalkers, rock climbers and hang-gliding enthusiasts.

Unusual rock formations are to be found at Nambung National Park, 230 kilometres north of Perth on the coast. Here a moonscape of coloured quartz is studded with fantastic limestone pillars ranging in size from stony 'twigs' to columns more than 2 metres tall. This is the unique Pinnacle Desert, a favourite subject for photographers.

Keeping to the coast but travelling further north, the visitor will discover the wild beauty of ancient landscapes, unsurpassed at **Kalbarri National Park**. Its 186 050 hectares encompass the lower reaches of the Murchison River, which winds its way through spectacular gorges to the Indian Ocean. Sea cliffs in layers of multi-coloured sandstone loom over the crashing white foam at Red Bluff.

In the Pilbara, 1400 kilometres north of Perth, is **Karijini (Hamersley Range) National Park**, part of a massive block of weathered rock over 450 kilometres long. Within this huge, spectacular park are many well-known gorges, including Dales Gorge, its strata in horizontal stripes of blue, mauve, red and brown dating back almost 2000 million years. Further north, still in the Pilbara, **Millstream–Chichester National Park** contains almost 20 000 hectares of clay table-lands and sediment-capped basalt ranges. At Millstream, on the Fortescue River, natural freshwater springs have created an oasis in arid country. In contrast, there are the Chichester Ranges: rolling hills, hummocks of spinifex, white-barked snappy gums on the uplands, and pale coolibahs along the usually dry watercourses.

In the far north of Western Australia are the national parks of the Kimberley region—mountain ranges formed millions of years ago. The largest of these parks, **Geikie Gorge**, has an area of 3136 hectares and is 20 kilometres north-east of Fitzroy Crossing. The multi-coloured cliffs are reflected in the placid waters of the Fitzroy River, which flows through the gorge. The area is too rugged for extensive walking, but organised boat trips go up the river through the gorge, enabling visitors to view one of Australia's most beautiful waterways.

Other nearby national parks are Windjana Gorge and Tunnel Creek, both northwest of Geikie Gorge. Tunnel Creek, a permanent watercourse, flows underground for 750 metres. The tunnel is high and wide. It is possible to walk through; some deep wading may be necessary. South of Lake Argyle is **Purnululu (Bungle Bungle) National Park**, with its tiger-striped, beehive-shaped domes.

Hidden Valley National Park, only 2.5 kilometres east of Kununurra, has features typical of the Kimberley: banded sandstone outcrops similar to those of the Bungle Bungle massif, boab trees, red soil dotted with eucalpyts, and black kites circling overhead. Aboriginal rock paintings are also a feature of the park.

For further information on Western Australia's national parks, contact the Department of Conservation and Land Management, 50 Hayman Rd (GPO Box 104), Como, WA 6152; (09) 334 0333.

661 km N of Perth. The town's picturesque setting on the estuary of the Murchison River, its year-round sunny climate and the spectacular gorges of the river running through the Kalbarri National Park attract a growing number of tourists each year. Kalbarri is also renowned for its excellent fishing and the brilliance and beauty of more than 500 species of wildflowers. **Of interest:** Kalflora, off Ajana Rd, with wide range of Kalbarri wildflowers. In Grey St: Doll and Marine Museum, Fantasy Land and Gemstone Mine. Echoes Restaurant, Porter St, overlooking river; fully licensed and serves fresh seafood. Kalbarri Entertainment Centre, Porter St; bicycles for hire. **In the area:** Kalbarri National Park, large area of magnificent virgin bushland surrounding town; picnic/barbecue facilities, camping not permitted. Horseriding at Kalbarri Big River Ranch, 3 km E, within park. Also within park, 11 km E, spectacular Murchison River gorges with abundance of wildlife and native flora; canoe safaris and abseiling adventure tours available. Coach tours of park and joy flights over gorges available. Red Bluff, 4 km S of town, ideal for swimming, fishing and rock climbing. Rainbow Jungle and Tropical Bird Park, 4 km S. Cairn at Wittecarra Creek, 4 km S, marks what is believed to be site of first permanent landing of Europeans in Australia: two Dutchmen sent ashore for their part in *Batavia* mutiny in 1629. Meanarra Lookout, 7 km SE. Z Bend and The Loop lookouts, 30 km NE. Coastal gorges, with precipitous red cliffs dropping to the Indian Ocean below, are a majestic sight throughout the area; coach tours and joy flights available. **Tourist information:** Allen Community Centre, Grey St; (099) 37 1104. **Accommodation:** 1 hotel/motel, 2 motels, 4 caravan/camping parks. MAP REF. 355 C13

Kalgoorlie–Boulder

Pop. 25 016

At the heart of WA's largest goldmining area is the city of Kalgoorlie–Boulder, centred on the famous Golden Mile, reputed to be the richest square mile in the world. Over 1300 tonnes of gold have been mined from this small area. Paddy Hannan discovered gold in 1893 and the rush began. By 1902 the population was 30 000 and there were 93 hotels operating. Men made fortunes overnight and the impressive stone buildings and

magnificent wide streets recall the town's fabulous boom past. Rather than walk daily to the Great Boulder Mine, the miners set up their tents on the Golden Mile, which soon grew into the town of Boulder. Kalgoorlie is 597 km E of Perth. One of the greatest difficulties facing the miners in this semi-desert area was lack of water. Determination and the brilliant scheme initiated by the engineer C. Y. O'Connor saved the day. A pipeline was established, carrying water an incredible 563 km from a reservoir near Perth. The water began flowing in 1903. Goldmining continues, with renewed vigour now that the price of gold has risen. The Kalgoorlie–Boulder region is also an important pastoral district, with high-quality wool being produced. **Of interest:** Some fine examples of early Australian architecture to be seen. Buildings worthy of note in Hannan St include: Exchange and Palace Hotels, Australia Hotel, Government Buildings and Kalgoorlie Post Office. Distinctive Kalgoorlie Town Hall, (1908) has impressive staircase and display of paintings by local artists. Museum of the Goldfields in former British Arms Hotel (1899), Hannan St, with fascinating display recalling heyday of gold-rush boom. Goldfields Aboriginal Art Gallery next to museum. Close to museum is Paddy Hannan's Tree, Outridge Tce, marking spot where gold was first found in Kalgoorlie. Also in Hannan St, bronze statue of Paddy Hannan. School of Mines Museum, Egan St; world-class display, including most of minerals found in WA. Hannans North Historical Mining Complex, Broad Arrow Rd; underground and surface tours, and gold-pouring demonstrations. Super Pit Lookout, off Eastern Bypass Rd; open daily. Boulder Town Hall (1908), Burt St, with regular art exhibits. Goldfields War Museum, Burt St. Eastern Goldfields Historical Museum, Burt St, in Boulder railway station. Picturesque Cornwall Hotel (1898), Chesapeake St. Royal Flying Doctor Base, Killarney St, serves one of largest areas in Australia, tours weekdays. Hammond Park, Lyall St; wildlife sanctuary with small lake and scale model of Bavarian castle. Mt Charlotte Reservoir and Lookout, off Sutherland St; storage for Kalgoorlie's vital fresh-water supply. The Loop Line, tourist railway line around the Golden Mile. **In the area:** Kurrawang Emu Farm, 18 km W; tours, Aboriginal artefacts; closed Sun. Kal-

goorlie–Boulder is an ideal base from which to visit old goldmining towns, some now ghost towns, in the district. Coolgardie (37 km SW), Broad Arrow (38 km N), Ora Banda (54 km N), Kookynie (200 km N) and Leonora–Gwalia (235 km N) are all within a day's drive and are all active again. WA's only two-up school, 7 km N of Kalgoorlie, on eastern side of road to Menzies. Eastern Goldfields Heritage Trail; details from tourist centre. **Tourist information:** 250 Hannan St, Kalgoorlie; (090) 21 1966. **Accommodation:** Kalgoorlie; 13 hotels, 9 motels, 4 caravan/camping parks. Boulder, 8 hotels, 2 motels, 2 caravan/camping parks. **See also:** Crossing the Nullarbor; The Goldfields. MAP REF. 356 H6

Kambalda
Pop. 4259

Kambalda's goldmining history lasted from 1897 to 1906, during which time 30 000 ounces of gold were produced. When the gold petered out, so did the town. In 1966, however, rich nickel deposits were discovered and the town has since boomed. Today Kambalda, 634 km E of Perth, consists of two well-planned centres (Kambalda East and Kambalda West), several km apart, and is noted for its environmental protection policy. **Of interest:** Several pleasant picnic areas in centre of town. Red Hill Lookout, off Gordon Adams Rd; excellent views of area, including vast Lake Lefroy. **In the area:** Land yachting on salt bed of lake. Defiance Open Cut Gold Mine Lookout, 20 km S; obtain entry permit from town's Western Mining office. Eastern Goldfields Heritage Trail; details from tourist centre. **Tourist information:** Irish Mulga Dr, Kambalda West; (090) 27 1446. **Accommodation:** 1 hotel, 1 caravan/camping park. **See also:** The Goldfields. MAP REF. 356 H7

Karratha
Pop. 11 325

Karratha was established on Nickel Bay in 1968 as a result of the continuing development of the Hamersley Iron Project, when there was a lack of suitable land for expansion at Dampier and a need for a regional centre was emerging. The town's growth gained even greater momentum with the development by Woodside Petroleum of the immense offshore gas reserve on the North West Shelf and Karratha now has the best service facilities in the north-west. Karratha's

The South-West

The south-west corner of Western Australia is a lush green land. Its gently rolling hills are crossed by rivers winding through deep-sided valleys. The soils are fertile and the farms prosperous. Along the coast there are beautiful bays, and inland, majestic towering karri and jarrah forests. The countryside is dotted with picturesque orchards and in any season the vibrant colours of many wildflowers can be seen; Western Australia is one of the richest areas of flora in the world. The Mediterranean climate ensures warm, dry summers and mild, wet winters.

Pinjarra, 84 kilometres south of Perth, is one of the State's oldest districts.

Near **Harvey** there is fine agricultural land and the undulating farms stretch to the foothills of the Darling Range. To the north-west is **Yalgorup National Park** (one of only three sites in Western Australia with stromatolites), where the lakes attract a wide variety of birdlife. The Old Coast Road, which edges down the coast to Bunbury, is a perfect choice if you want to go off the beaten track.

The coast of the south-west is fascinating: an unusual mixture of craggy outcrops and promontories, sheltered bays with calm waters and beaches pounded by rolling surf. From **Cape Leeuwin** it is possible to see the sun rising over one ocean and setting over another. The length of the coast, together with the many rivers and estuaries, makes the south-west an angler's paradise. The Murray, Harvey and Brunswick rivers and their tributaries are only some of the streams annually stocked with trout.

The main port for the south-west, **Bunbury** rests on Geographe Bay looking out over the Indian Ocean. It is a perfect holiday town, flanked by golden beaches and peaceful rural farmland. One of the oldest towns in the State, **Busselton**, sited on the Vasse River, has a wealth of pioneer houses, many restored and open to the public.

Leeuwin–Naturaliste National Park combines a scenic coast with magnificent wildflowers and the tall timbers of karri and jarrah forests.

Yallingup is known for its excellent surf and spectacular limestone caves. Dripping water has created strange shapes in the limestone, with magic colours reflected in the glittering underground water.

Bridgetown, **Donnybrook** and **Greenbushes** are small townships tucked away in green, hilly country and pretty apple orchards. Goldmining flourished briefly here at the turn of the century. **Manjimup** and Pemberton are world famous for the source of their timber, the karri and jarrah trees. Here some of the world's tallest trees reach straight up, often 80 and 90 metres, to the sky. The Pemberton, Scott, Warren and Brockman National Parks are nearby, introduced to protect the unique environment.

See also: Individual town entries in A–Z listing. **Note** detailed map of Margaret River Region on page 349.

The Great Southern

The Great Southern, also known as the Rainbow Coast, is bounded by a rugged coastline and the roaring Southern Ocean. During the winter months spectacular rainbows regularly occur. The coast gives way to an amazingly beautiful hinterland with rivers winding through forests, ancient mountain ranges and gentle valleys.

The district has an important historical heritage. **Albany** was the first town in Western Australia, established two and a half years before the Swan River colony. Major Edmund Lockyer landed here in 1826 to claim the western half of the continent as British territory.

Albany is the unofficial capital of the area, and retains a charming English atmosphere from the colonial days. The town looks out over the magnificent blue waters of Princess Royal Harbour in King George Sound. Albany has a number of fine old homesteads, museums and galleries. There are numerous scenic drives around the coast, to the Gap, the Natural Bridge and the Blowholes. There are also stretches of golden sand and secluded bays. The fishing is superb. **Denmark**, a holiday resort, lies on the banks of the tranquil Denmark River, and the little village of **Nornalup** nestles near the Frankland River. Near Nornalup is the awe-inspiring Valley of the Giants, with tingle and karri trees towering over the tangled undergrowth and vivid splashes of wildflowers.

The Great Southern has a new industry—viticulture. The vineyards around **Mt Barker** have already produced award-winning wines. Mt Barker itself is the gateway to the Stirling and Porongurup mountain ranges, both within the confines of national parks. The Porongurup Range has granite peaks dominating giant hardwood trees and a maze of wildflowers and creepers. There are many easy climbs, rewarded by panoramic views: Castle Rock, Howard's Peak and Devil's Slide are three of the most popular.

The high jagged peaks of the Stirling Range (the highest is Bluff Knoll at 1037 metres) tower over virgin bushland. From a distance, with the changing light, the vegetation varies from heathery shades to blues and reds. The peaks can sometimes be seen shrouded in mist, and on occasions even tipped with snow.

There are more than 100 species of birds in the park and a great deal of native wildlife. Look also for the beautiful wild orchids, Stirling banksia and mountain bells.

The inland area of the Great Southern is dotted with small towns including Tambellup with its colonial buildings, and the thriving towns of **Katanning**, **Kojonup**, **Gnowangerup** and **Jerramungup**, are all surrounded by peaceful rural farmland.

See also: Individual town entries in A–Z listing. **Note** detailed map of Albany Region on page 350.

Lake Argyle, south of Kununurra

near to perfect warm winter temperatures make it just the place for visitors to escape the southern cold and soak up the sun in a clean, modern town. **Of interest:** Largest shopping centre outside Perth. Swimming, boating, golf, bowls. Views from TV Hill Lookout, Millstream Rd. Scenic flights, day tours and safari tours of Pilbara outback available. Jaburara Heritage Trail (3½ km) includes sites of Aboriginal rock carvings; details from tourist centre. Also Chichester Range Camel Trail. **Tourist information:** Lot 4548, Karratha; (091) 44 4600. **Accommodation:** 2 motels, 3 caravan/camping parks. **See also:** The Hamersley Range; The Pilbara.
MAP REF. 355 G1

Katanning   Pop. 4139
A thriving township 186 km N of Albany, Katanning's well-planned streets have some impressive Victorian buildings. The countryside is given over to grain-growing and pastoral activities, and is noted for its fine merino sheep. **Of interest:** Old Mill Museum (1889), cnr Clive St and Austral Tce; outstanding display of vintage roller flour-milling process. Majestic Kobeelya mansion (1902), Brownie St; country retreat now owned by Baptist Church; open for inspection by appt. All Ages Playground, Clive St; miniature steam railway with 600 m of track. Old Winery, Andrews Rd; newly restored. Dore St; largest country-based sheep-selling facility in WA; regular sales on Thurs. throughout year, also ram

sale in Aug. Meatworks on Wagin Rd; guided tours by appt; apply tourist centre. Katanning Triathlon held Feb. Arts Exhibition Sept.–Oct. Katanning Caboodle in Dec. Katanning Show held in Oct. **In the area:** Lakes surrounding town offer swimming, boating and water-skiing. Stirling Range National Park, 80 km S. At Gnowangerup, 60 km SE, work of local wood carver John Davis; subjects include native birds. Katanning–Piesse Heritage Trail; details from tourist centre. **Tourist information:** Flour Mill, cnr Austral Tce and Clive St; (098) 21 2634. **Accommodation:** 3 hotels, 2 motels, 2 caravan/camping parks. **See also:** The Great Southern.
MAP REF. 351 L1, 354 G10, 356 B11

Kojonup   Pop. 1023
Situated on the Albany Hwy, 154 km N of Albany, Kojonup takes its name from the Aboriginal word *kodja*, meaning 'stone axe'. In 1837, when surveying the road from Albany to the newly established Swan River settlement, Alfred Hillman was guided to the Kojonup Spring by local Aborigines. Later a military outpost was set up on the site, and this marked the beginning of the town. **Of interest:** Kojonup Spring and picnic area. Military Barracks Museum (1845), Barracks Pl. Elverd's Cottage (1850s), Soldier Rd; display of tools and implements of early years. Sundial in Hillman Park, on Albany Hwy. Walsh's Cattle Complex, Broomehill Rd. **In the area:** Wide variety of flora (including more

than 60 species of orchids) and fauna (especially birds). Yeedabirrup Rock, 10 km E, one of many granite monoliths in area. Also in area; locally made jarrah furniture, hand-turned blackboy articles and woollen jumpers. Farmstay and farm tour at 'Kalpara'; details from tourist office. **Tourist information:** Benn Pde; (098) 31 1686. **Accommodation:** 1 hotel, 1 hotel/motel, 1 motel, 1 caravan/ camping park. **See also:** The Great Southern.
MAP REF. 351 J2, 354 F10, 356 B12

Kondinin   Pop. 312
The small settlement of Kondinin is 278 km E of Perth. There are sheep stud-farms nearby. Kondinin Craft Shop, Gordon St; local craft. **In the area:** Kondinin Lake, 8 km W, popular with water-skiing and yachting enthusiasts after a rainy winter. **Tourist information:** Kondinin Craft Shop, Gordon St; (098) 89 1130. **Accommodation:** 1 hotel, 1 motel, 1 caravan/ camping park.
MAP REF. 347 P8, 354 H8, 356 C9

Kulin   Pop. 321
A centre for the sheep and grain-growing farms of the district, Kulin lies 283 km SE of Perth. **Of interest:** The *Eucalyptus macrocarpa* are a spectacular feature of the local flora. **In the area:** Several species of native orchids in the bush. Jilakin Rock and Lake, 18 km E. Buckley's Breakaway (pit caused by granite decomposing to kaolin), 58 km E, has unusual coloured rock formations. Dragon Rocks Nature Reserve, 75 km E. **Tourist information:** Shire Offices, Johnston St; (098) 80 1204. **Accommodation:** 1 hotel/motel, 1 caravan/camping park.
MAP REF. 347 O9, 354 H8, 356 C10

Kununurra   Pop. 4061
Kununurra is situated along Lake Kununurra on the Ord River, and holds the magnificent Hidden Valley National Park within its boundaries. The town supports several industries, including agriculture and mining. It is the major centre for the Argyle Diamond Mine (the largest diamond mine in the world) and the Ord River Irrigation area. **Of interest:** Ord River Festival, held Aug.; includes float parade, rodeo, mardi gras, art and craft exhibitions and famous Ord Tiki Race and water-ski display. **In the area:** Three-hr minibus tours of local attractions; details at Tourist Bureau.

Hidden Valley National Park, 2 km E. Warringarri Aboriginal Arts, 2 km N. Kelly's Knob Lookout, 2 km N; good vantage-point for viewing surrounding irrigated land. Melon Farm, Ivanhoe Rd, 8 km N and Banana Farm, River Farm Rd, 9 km N; tasting and sales, every day May–Oct. Top Rockz Gallery, 10 km N. Ivanhoe Crossing, 13 km N, popular fishing spot. Kimberley Research Station, 16 km N. Middle Springs, 30 km N, and Black Rock Falls, 32 km N, are wet-season attractions. Pump Station, 6 km W. Cruises on Lake Kununurra from Pump Station and upstream past the Everglades and rugged gorges teeming with birdlife. Fishing is good, with barramundi a prized catch. Kununurra is a major starting point for flights over and ground tours of the remarkably coloured and shaped Bungle Bungles, the Mitchell Plateau, Kalumburu and the wilderness of the lower Ord River. El Questro Station 100 km W; rugged scenery, hot springs, Aboriginal rock art, fishing, boating, camping, accommodation. At Lake Argyle, 72 km S in Carr Boyd Range; tourist village with hotel, caravan park and camping area. The lake, created by the Ord River Dam, contains 9 times the volume of water in Sydney Harbour, transforming mountain peaks into rugged islands; it is one of the largest man-made lakes in the southern hemisphere. Durack Homestead, 70 km S, reconstructed homestead of Durack family, now pioneer museum and memorial to settlers of district. Sleeping Buddha/Elephant Rock, 10 km S. Pandanus Wildlife Park, Nimberlee Art Gallery and Zebra Rock Gallery, all 16 km S. Visits to Argyle Diamond Mine available; also charter flights and bush camping holidays. **Tourist information:** Coolibah Dr; (091) 68 1177. **Accommodation:** Kununurra, 2 hotels, 2 motels, 5 caravan/camping parks. Lake Argyle, 1 hotel/motel, 1 caravan/camping park. **See also:** The Kimberley; The Ord River.
MAP REF. 361 R5, 392 B13, 394 B2

Kwinana Pop. 13 517
Kwinana, 20 km S of the port of Fremantle, is a symbol of WA's rapidly developing industrial strength. Containing the BP Oil Refinery and Alcoa's Alumina Works, it is one of the nation's major industrial centres. Construction of the Kwinana complex, built on Cockburn Sound, one of the world's finest natural harbours, was begun in 1951. **Of interest:** Escorted group tours of local industries. Hull of the wrecked SS *Kwinana*, at Kwinana Beach, filled with cement and used as a diving platform for swimmers. **In the area:** Seaside resort city of Rockingham, 10 km S; cruises to offshore islands, Cape Peron (7 km W) and Penguin Island (10 km SW). **Tourist information:** Rockingham and Districts Tourist Centre, 43 Kent St, Rockingham; (09) 592 3464. **Accommodation:** 1 motel.
MAP REF. 346 C6, 353 Q2, 354 D8

Lake Grace Pop. 596
A pleasant country town with first-class service facilities, situated 252 km N of Albany in the peaceful rural countryside of the central south wheat belt, Lake Grace derives its name from the shallow lake just west of the settlement. **Of interest:** Wildlife sanctuary, South Rd. Restored Inland Mission hospital, Stubbs St, last in WA. Old railway buildings under restoration. **In the area:** Lookout, 5 km W. Roe Heritage Trail; details from tourist centre. **Tourist information:** Lake Grace Newsagency; (098) 65 1029. **Accommodation:** 1 hotel, 3 motels, 1 caravan/camping park.
MAP REF. 347 Q11, 354 H9, 356 D10

Lake King Pop. 29
A crossroads centre with a tavern and store, Lake King is a stopping place for visitors travelling across arid country and through Frank Hann National Park to Norseman. **Of interest:** Interdenominational community church. **In the area:** Frank Hann National Park, 35 km E, with cross-section of heath flora of inland sandplain east of wheat belt; park is traversed by Lake King–Norseman Rd, a formed gravel all-weather road. (No visitor facilities or supplies available between Lake King and Norseman.) Wildflowers in season. Hollands Track, early goldfields access route. Lakes in area include Lake King, 5 km W, and Lake Pallarup, 15 km S. Mt Madden cairn and lookout, 25 km SE; picnic area. Pioneer well at Pallarup, 18 km S. **Tourist information:** Morgane St, Ravensthorpe; (098) 38 1163. **Accommodation:** 1 hotel/motel, 1 caravan park.
MAP REF. 356 E10

Lancelin Pop. 531
This quiet little fishing town on the shores of Lancelin Bay is 127 km N of Perth. A natural breakwater extends from Edward Island to Lancelin Island, providing a safe harbour and a perfect breeding ground for fish. There are rock lobsters to be caught on the offshore reefs outside the bay. Lancelin is fast becoming known as the sailboard mecca of WA and affords a colourful spectacle each Dec. with large numbers of international and interstate windsurfers taking part in the annual Ledge Pt ocean race. Long stretches of white sandy beach provide an ideal swimming area for children. **Of interest:** Large off-road area for dune buggies. WA dune-buggy championships held Easter. **In the area:** Track (4WD only) leads 55 km N to Nambung National Park; check road conditions before setting out. **Tourist information:** The Centre Store, Gingin Rd; (096) 55 1054. **Accommodation:** 1 hotel, 1 hotel/motel, 2 caravan/camping parks.
MAP REF. 354 D6

Laverton Pop. 1197
Laverton, situated 360 km NE of Kalgoorlie, is a modern satellite town sustained by the nickel mine at Windarra, 28 km W, and goldmining operations. With an annual rainfall of around 200 mm, summers are hot and dry; April–Oct. is recommended time to travel. From Laverton to Ayers Rock (1200 km), all roads are unsealed, and the following points should be noted:
- Permit required to divert from the Laverton–Yulara Road. Obtained from Aboriginal Planning Authority in Perth or Alice Springs.
- Water is scarce.
- Supplies are available at Laverton. Fuel and accommodation at Warburton and Giles.
- Check on road conditions at the Laverton Police Station or at Shire Offices: roads can be hazardous when wet.
Tourist information: Shire Offices, MacPherson Pl; (090) 31 1202. **Accommodation:** 1 hotel, 1 caravan/camping park. **See also:** The Goldfields.
MAP REF. 356 I3

Leonora Pop. 1194
A busy mining centre 240 km N of Kalgoorlie, Leonora has a typical Australian country-town appearance, with its wide streets and verandahed shopfronts. The town is the centrepoint of and railhead for the north-eastern goldfields, with mining of gold, copper and nickel at Laverton, 120 km NE and Leinster, 134 km NW. **In**

the area: Small goldmining town of Menzies, 110 km S. Most of the country is flat mulga scrub, but after good rains there are brilliant wildflowers Aug. and early Sept. Leonora has 3 major gold producers on its doorstep, including the famous Sons of Gwalia. The township of Gwalia, 2 km S, has an impressive museum that captures the miners' lifestyle; walk the 1 km Heritage Trail. Malcolm, 20 km NE, good picnic spot, and Malcolm Dam. Old mine workings and ghost town of Kookynie, 92 km SE; the Grand Hotel still offers a warm welcome. **Tourist information:** Shire Offices; (090) 37 6044. **Accommodation:** 2 hotels, 1 motel, 1 caravan/camping park. **See also:** The Goldfields.
MAP REF. 356 G3

Madura   Pop. 15

The Hampton Tablelands form a backdrop to Madura, 195 km from the WA/SA border, on the Eyre Hwy. The settlement dates back to 1876 when horses for the Indian Army were bred here. **In the area:** Old roadhouse ruins, 4WD only, 5 km W; directions from Roadhouse. **Tourist information:** Roadhouse; (090) 39 3464. **Accommodation:** 1 motel, 1 caravan/camping park. **See also:** Crossing the Nullarbor.
MAP REF. 357 O8

Mandurah   Pop. 23 343

The popular holiday resort of Mandurah is on the coast 72 km S of Perth. The Murray, Serpentine and Harvey Rivers meet here, forming the vast inland waterway of Peel Inlet and the Harvey Estuary. The river waters and the Indian Ocean offer excellent conditions for yachting, boating, swimming, water-skiing and fishing, and the town becomes a mecca for tourists in holiday periods. **Of interest:** Hall's Cottage, Leighton Rd; small whitewashed cottage, built in 1845 by two of the colony's earliest settlers. Christ Church (1870), cnr Pinjarra Rd and Sholl St, has hand-carved furniture. Mandurah Farm World, Fremantle Rd; group bookings only. Kerryelle's Collectors Museum, Gordon Rd. Boats for hire and cruises on inlet and river. Watch for dolphins, which can sometimes be seen in estuary. Waters also attract abundance of birdlife. Mandurah Estuary Bridge is a particularly good fishing spot. King Carnival Amusement Park in Hall Park. Beaches at Halls Head, just over old traffic bridge; also Peel Pottery. **In the area:**

Pleasant picnic areas near numerous storage dams in nearby Darling Range. Boating and swimming at Waroona and Logue Brook Dams. Bavarian Castle Fun Park, Old Coast Rd, 2 km S. Threlfall Galleries, 10 km S. Dawes Channel, 10 km S; channel being dug between inland waterways and ocean; popular for fishing and boating. Cape Bouvard Studios, Henry Rd, Melros, 15 km S. Lakes Clifton and Preston, 20 km S, two long, narrow lakes running parallel to coast; Cape Bouvard Wines, Mt John Rd, 22 km S (weekends only). Hamel Forestry Department Nursery, 42 km SE; open for inspection. Durago Gallery, Amarillo Dr, Karnup, 14 km N. Peel Estate Winery, Fletcher Rd, Baldivis, 20 km N. Western Rosella Bird Park, 5 km E. Houseboats for hire. **Tourist information:** 5 Pinjarra Rd; (09) 535 1155. **Accommodation:** 2 hotels, 5 motels, 11 caravan/camping parks.
MAP REF. 346 C8, 354 D8

Manjimup   Pop. 4353

Fertile agricultural country and magnificent karri forests surround Manjimup, 307 km S of Perth. This is the commercial centre of the south-west corner of WA and one of the State's most diversified horticultural regions, contributing to the town's more recent growth. The first settlers arrived here in 1856 and Manjimup's history has been closely tied to the timber industry since then. **Of interest:** Manjimup Regional Timber Park, Rose St; attractions include: Visitors Centre, blacksmith's shop, Timber Museum with excellent display on development of timber industry in WA, Age of Steam Museum, art and craft gallery, historical hamlet fire tower lookout, picnic/barbecue facilities. WA Chip and Pulp (Paper Wood Co.) mill, Eastbourne Rd; guided tours. Yallambee Gem Museum, Chopping St. **In the area:** Piano Gully Wines, 10 km S; tastings 10–4 daily. Diamond Wood-chip Mill, 12 km S; guided tours. Diamond Tree Fire Tower, 9 km S, in use 1941–74; may not be climbed, but surrounded by picnic area. Warren National Park, 40 km S; ideal for bushwalkers, peaceful picnic location. Constable Wines, Graphite Rd, 8 km W. One Tree Bridge, 21 km W. Pleasant walk along river edge, near bridge, to Four Aces: four magnificent karri trees, standing in line, believed to be 300–400 years old. Abundant bird and other wildlife at Donnelly River Holiday

Village 28 km W; also horseriding. King Jarrah, 4 km E; 47-m-high tree estimated to be 600 years old. Fonty's Pool, 10 km SW; popular swimming pool and picnic area with spacious lawns and gardens. The 19-km round trip to Dingup, northeast of Manjimup, goes through farmland and forest. Dingup Church (1896) and historic Dingup House (1870). Southern Wildflowers farm at Quininup, 33 km SE. Timber tours depart from Timber Park in Manjimup. King Jarrah Heritage Trail; details from tourist centre. Also abseiling, rockclimbing, bushcraft, horse-drawn picnic excursions, safari tours; details from tourist office. **Tourist information:** Cnr Rose and Edward Sts; (097) 71 1831. **Accommodation:** 4 motels, 3 caravan/camping parks. **See also:** The South-west.
MAP REF. 350 D6, 354 E11, 356 A13

Marble Bar   Pop. 383

Widely known as the 'hottest town in Australia' because of its consistently high temperatures, Marble Bar lies 203 km SE of Port Hedland. The town takes its name from the unique bar of red jasper that crosses the Coongan River, 6 km from town. Alluvial gold was discovered at Marble Bar in 1891, and in 1931 at Comet Mine. Today the major industries are primarily mining of tin, copper and gold, and pastoral activities. Marble Bar is a very typical WA outback town. **Of interest:** Government buildings, cnr Francis and Contest Sts, built of locally quarried stone in 1895, and still used by police and mining registrar. Marble Bar State Battery, Newman–Tabba Rd; not open to public. **In the area:** Jasper deposit at Marble Bar Pool, from which town takes its name, 4 km W; and nearby Chinaman's Pool, ideal picnic spot. The scenery in the area is beautiful, especially in winter and after rainfall, when the spinifex is transformed into a multitude of flowering plants. Rugged ranges, rolling plains, steep gorges, deep rock pools and many natural scenic spots abound. Town of Nullagine, 111 km S, in mineralrich area, dotted with old goldmines. Scenic gorges, picnic spot and swimming at Coppin's Gap, 68 km NE, and Kitty's Gap, further 6 km. Annual Marble Bar Cup and Ball held in June–July, over long weekend. **Tourist information:** BP Garage; (091) 76 1041. **Accommodation:** 1 hotel/motel, 1 motel, 1 caravan/camping park. **See also:** The Pilbara.
MAP REF. 358 E2

Margaret River
Pop. 1725

Margaret River is a pretty township nestled on the side of the Margaret River near the coast 280 km from Perth. The town is noted for its world-class wines, magnificent coastal scenery, surfing beaches, wineries and spectacular cave formations in the district. **Of interest:** Rotary Park, Bussell Hwy; heritage walk trails start from park (details from tourist centre). Old Settlement Craft Village. Greek Chapel, Wallcliffe Rd. Margaret River Gallery and Margaret River Pottery, both on Bussell Hwy. Melting Pot Glass Studio, Boodjidup Rd. Eagles Heritage, Boodjidup Rd; large collection of birds of prey. Inn and restaurant, Farrelly St; formerly 1885 homestead. **In the area:** Among over 20 wineries of Cowaramup (10 km N), Willyabrup (20 km N) and Margaret River areas is Leeuwin Estate Winery, 8 km S; tasting-room, function room with Australian paintings, picnic/barbecue facilities. Bellview Shell Museum, and timber mill, both at Witchcliffe, 6 km S. Marron Farm, 11 km S. Vardos Clydesdale Museum and Village, 20 km S. Boranup Gallery, Caves Rd, Boranup, 20 km S. Berry Farm, 13 km SE. Mammoth Cave, 21 km SW, with fossil remains of prehistoric animals; 4 km on is Lake Cave. At Cowaramup, 10 km N, Cowaramup Pottery, Antique-a-Brac, Quinda Crafts and Silverthread Silversmith. Gunyulgup Gallery, Caves Rd, Yallingup, 45 km N. Ellensbrook Homestead (1853–5), National Trust property, 15 km NW. Prevelly, 8 km W; Gracetown, 15 km NW; Coastal areas of Redgate, 10 km S; and Hamelin Bay, 34 km S. Augusta–Busselton, Margaret River and Hamelin Bay Heritage Trails; details from tourist centre. **Tourist information:** Cnr Tunbridge Rd and Bussell Hwy; (097) 57 2911. **Accommodation:** 1 hotel, 4 motels, 4 caravan/camping parks.
MAP REF. 349 C7, 354 D11

Meekatharra
Pop. 1414

Meekatharra lies 768 km NE of Perth on the Great Northern Hwy. Gold, copper and other minerals are mined, and there are huge sheep and cattle stations in the area. Meekatharra was once important as the railhead for cattle which had travelled overland from the Northern Territory or the East Kimberley. **Of interest:** Royal Flying Doctor Service base, Main St. School of the Air, High St; open to the public during school term.

Boranup Beach, south of Margaret River

Old Courthouse, Darlot St. **In the area:** Old goldmining towns, relics of mining equipment and mine shafts can be seen. Since the upturn in gold prices several mines, such as Peak Hill and Nannine have reopened. State Battery relics, Main St. Peace Gorge (The Granites), 5 km W. Mt Gould, 15 km W. Mt Yagahong, 40 km SE. Bilyuin Pool, 88 km NW. **Tourist information:** Shire Offices, Main St; (099) 81 1101. **Accommodation:** Meekatharra, 2 hotels, 2 motels, 1 caravan/camping park. Sandstone (to SE), 1 hotel, 1 caravan park.
MAP REF. 358 C12

Merredin
Pop. 3068

A main junction on the important Kalgoorlie–Perth railway line, Merredin is situated 259 km E from Perth. During the late 1800s, Merredin grew up as a shanty town as miners stopped on their way to the goldfields. The town has excellent parks and recreation facilities. **Of interest:** Wildlife Park, Cummings St. Harling Memorial Library, Barrack St, and Old Railway Station Museum, Gt Eastern Hwy. CBH wheat storage and transfer depot, Gamenya Ave, built in 1966 with additions in 1978; largest horizontal storage in southern hemisphere, with a capacity of 220 000 tonnes. **In the area:** Pumping Station No. 4, 3 km W; designed by C. Y. O'Connor in 1902 and fine example of early industrial architecture, station closed 1960 to make way for

electrically driven stations. Hunts Dam, 5 km N, for picnics and bushwalking. Lake Chandler, 45 km N. Mangowine Homestead, 56 km N at Nungarin; National Trust property. Museum at Koorda, 140 km NW; several wildlife reserves in vicinity. Totadjin Dam Reserve, 16 km SW; Totadjin Rock has wave formation similar to that at Wave Rock. Bruce Rock, 50 km SE, with museum, craft centre and Australia's smallest bank. Folk Museum at Kellerberrin, 55 km W. Durakoppin Wildlife Sanctuary, 27 km N of Kellerberrin, and Gardner Flora Reserve, 35 km SW. Merredin Peak Heritage Trail; details from tourist centre. **Tourist information:** Barrack St; (090) 41 1668. **Accommodation:** 2 hotels, 4 motels, 2 caravan/camping parks. **See also:** Crossing the Nullarbor.
MAP REF. 347 P1, 354 H6, 356 C8

Mingenew
Pop. 357

The little township of Mingenew is in the wheat district of the mid-west, 378 km N of Perth. **Of interest:** Mingenew Museum, Victoria St, in small, original Roads Board office; pioneer relics. Mingenew Hill Lookout and Pioneer Memorial, off Mingenew–Mullewa Rd, for views. Mingenew Rural Expo and Wildflower Display, both in Sept. **In the area:** Picnic spots at Depot Hill, 15 km W. Superb beaches and excellent fishing at Dongara, 53 km W. WA's first coal shafts can be seen in Irwin Gorge at

Coalseam Park, 32 km NE; rock-hunting in riverbed, wildflowers in spring. **Tourist information:** Post Office building; (099) 28 1060. **Accommodation:** 1 hotel, 1 caravan/camping park.
MAP REF. 354 D2

Morawa
Pop. 624

Renowned for its plentiful grain harvests, Morawa is situated in the mid-west, 394 km N of Perth. Spring is the perfect time to visit, when the wildflowers are in brilliant bloom. **Of interest:** Historical Museum, Prater St. St David's Anglican Church, Prater St. Holy Cross Catholic Church, Davis St. Jo's Taxidermy, Winfield St; open daily. **In the area:** Koolanooka Springs reserve and Koolanooka Hills mine site, 24 km E; ideal for picnics. Bilya Rock Reserve, 4 km W. **Tourist information:** Shire Offices; (099) 71 1004. **Accommodation:** 1 hotel/motel, 1 caravan/camping park.
MAP REF. 354 E3

Mount Barker
Pop. 1520

Mount Barker is a quiet, friendly town in the Great Southern district of WA. It is 360 km from Perth, with the Stirling Ranges to the north, and the Porongurups to the east. Mt Barker was discovered by Europeans in 1829, and the first settlers arrived in the 1830s. Vineyards in the area, though relatively new, have produced some top-quality wines. **Of interest:** Old police station and gaol (1868), Albany Hwy; now museum. **In the area:** Lookout on summit of Mt Barker, easily pinpointed by its 168-m-high television tower, provides splendid panoramic views of area and well worth the 5-km drive. Privately owned St Werburgh's Chapel (1872), 12 km W; small mud-walled chapel overlooking Hay River Valley. Historic town of Kendenup, 16 km N; WA's first gold discovery made here. Narrikup Country Store and Kalangadoo Krafts, 16 km S; large collection of art and craft. Porongurup National Park, 24 km E; granite peaks and brilliant seasonal wildflowers. Farm holidays at Warrawing sheep farm, 42 km E. Stirling Range National Park, 80 km NE; tall peaks, picturesque plains, native flora and fauna. Lake Poorrarecup, 50 km NW. Area also noted for orchids and brown and red boronia, which bloom Sept.–Nov. Mt Barker Heritage Trail; details from tourist centre. Ten wineries in the area; details from tourist centre. **Tourist information:** 57 Lowood Rd; (098) 51 1163. **Accommodation:** 1 hotel, 2 motels, 1 caravan/camping park, self-contained chalets, 1 lodge. **See also:** The Great Southern.
MAP REF. 351 M9, 354 G12, 356 C13

Mount Magnet
Pop. 1076

The former goldmining town of Mount Magnet, 562 km from Perth on the Great Northern Hwy, is now a popular stopping-place for motorists driving north to Port Hedland. The surrounding land is used for pastoral farming. Spectacular wildflowers in spring. **In the area:** The Granites, 7 km N, picnic spot with some Aboriginal rock art. Fossick for gemstones, but take care as there are dangerous old mine shafts. Ghost town, Lennonville, 11 km N. **Tourist information:** Hepburn St; (099) 63 4172. **Accommodation:** 2 hotels, 1 motel, 1 caravan park.
MAP REF. 354 G1, 355 I13, 356 B2

Mullewa
Pop. 739

Gateway to the Murchison goldfields, Mullewa is 99 km from Geraldton. **Of interest:** Kembla Zoo, Stock Rd. Our Lady of Mount Carmel Church and Monsignor John C. Hawes Priesthouse Museum, both in Maitland Rd. Water Supply Reserve, Lovers Lane; native plants. Annual Wildflower Show held Aug.–Sept. Agricultural Show in Sept. **In the area:** Waterfalls after heavy rain; 5 km N, near airport. Wildflowers at Tallering Peak and Gorge, 58 km N. The Woolly Baa Baa, Tallering Station, 40 km NE; gallery, sheepskin and wool products, accommodation, camping; open April holidays–mid-Oct. Butterabby grave site, 18 km S. St Mary's Agricultural School and Pallotine Mission, both near Tardun, 40 km SE. Bindoo Hill Glacier Bed, 40 km SW; scenic drive includes Coalseam National Park. Tenindewa Pioneer Well, 18 km W. Mons. Hawes Heritage Trail; details from tourist centre. **Tourist information:** Shire Offices; (099) 61 1007, or Jose St. **Accommodation:** 1 hotel, 1 hotel/motel, 1 caravan park.
MAP REF. 354 D1

Mundaring
Pop. 1542

Mundaring is situated on the Great Eastern Hwy, 34 km E of Perth. The picturesque Mundaring Weir, 8 km S of the town, set in wooded hilly country, is the source of water for the eastern goldfields. The original dam was opened in 1903, and the pumping station was used until 1955. The attractive bush setting makes the weir a popular picnic spot in summer. **Of interest:** Sculpture Park, Jacoby St; sculptures by WA artists. **In the area:** The C. Y. O'Connor Museum, 8 km S; collection of models of Eastern Goldfields water supply. Old Mahogany Inn (1837), 7 km W, served as military outpost to offer protection to travellers from hostile Aborigines. Lake Leschenaultia, 10 km NW; camping, swimming, canoeing, walking, picnic/barbecue facilities, also miniature scenic railway; open daily. John Forrest National Park, on high point of Darling Range, 26 km E; picnic spot and natural pool at Rocky Pool. **Tourist information:** Shire Offices, 7000 Great Eastern Hwy; (09) 295 1400. **Accommodation:** 1 hotel, 1 hotel/motel.
MAP REF. 346 E4, 354 E7

Mundrabilla
Pop. 11

A tiny settlement on the Eyre Hwy where travellers can break the journey across the continent. There is a bird and animal sanctuary behind the motel. **Tourist information:** Roadhouse; (090) 39 3465. **Accommodation:** 1 motel, 1 caravan/camping park.
MAP REF. 357 Q8

Nannup
Pop. 472

Nannup is a quiet, friendly town in the Blackwood Valley, 290 km S of Perth. The surrounding countryside is lush, gently rolling pasture alongside jarrah and pine forests. **Of interest:** Old police station (1922), Brockman St. Arboretum, Brockman St. Art and craft centre, Warren Rd. Bunnings Timber Mill, Warren Rd; largest jarrah sawmill in State; open for inspection. Robz Art Gallery, and Needful Things, both Warren Rd; local art and craft. Crafty Creations, Warren Rd; local art and craft, especially jarrah goods. Gemstone Museum, Warren Rd. **In the area:** Walking trails; self-guide leaflets available. Scenic drives around area's jarrah forest and pine plantations. Canoeing on Blackwood River. Barrabup Pool, 10 km W. Tathra Wines, 14 km NE. Nannup Heritage Trail; details from tourist centre. **Tourist information:** 4 Brockman St; (097) 56 1211. **Accommodation:** 1 hotel/motel, 2 caravan/camping parks.
MAP REF. 350 A4, 354 D11

Narrogin Pop. 4638

Narrogin is important as the centre of prosperous agricultural country and as a major railway junction. Sheep, pigs and cereal farms are the main primary industries. The town is 189 km SE of Perth on the Great Southern Hwy, and its name is derived from an Aboriginal word meaning 'waterhole'. The annual Three Day Horse Competition, held in Sept., attracts entrants from Australia and overseas. **Of interest:** Old Butter Factory, at exit to Wagin; memorabilia, craft workshops, gardens. Courthouse Museum (1894), Egerton St; originally school and later district courthouse. Foxes Lair, Williams Rd; 5 ha of natural bushland. Lions Lookout, Kipling St; panoramic views of Narrogin. Restoration Group Museum, Federal St; fully restored cars, stationary engines and other machinery. Centenary Park, picnic/barbecue facilities; also pathway marked with 100 commemorative tiles designed by local artists. Spring Festival end Oct. **In the area:** Unusual rock formations, 11 km E, at Yilliminning and Birdwhistle Rocks. Facey homestead, 40 km NE; mini-zoo and local crafts; open daily. Dryandra Forest, 30 km NW; numbats and mallee fowl. South Central Wheatbelt Heritage Trail; details from tourist centre. **Tourist information:** 23 Egerton St; (098) 81 2064. **Accommodation:** 2 hotels, 2 motels, 1 caravan/camping park.
MAP REF. 347 J10, 354 F9, 356 B10

New Norcia Pop. 73

Spanish Benedictine monks established a mission at New Norcia in 1846 to help the Australian Aborigines. Today St. Gertrude's (1908) is a boarding residence for 200-odd girls who attend New Norcia Catholic College. The handsome Spanish-inspired buildings come as a surprise, surrounded by dusty Australian paddocks and distant bushland. The settlement is in the secluded Moore Valley, and wheat, wool and other farm products are grown. **Of interest:** Museum and art gallery, Great Northern Hwy; priceless collection, including gifts sent by Queen Isabella of Spain, fine paintings and Roman, Egyptian and Spanish artefacts; gallery's shop also sells locally made products and souvenirs. Heritage Trail (2 km) includes inspection of oldest operating flour mill in WA (built 1879); also abbey church, cemetery, 19th-century blacksmith's forge and historic olive press; details from tourist centre.

Benedictine Community tour incl. monastery, guesthouse, chapels, garden. **Tourist information:** Museum and art gallery, Great Northern Hwy; (096) 54 8056. **Accommodation:** 1 hotel, 1 guest house.
MAP REF. 354 E6

Newman Pop. 5627

This town was built by Mt Newman Mining Co. to house employees involved in the extraction of iron ore. Mt Newman ships its ore from Port Hedland, and the two towns are connected by a 426-km railroad. In 1981 responsibility for the town was handed over to the local shire. With the sealing of the National Hwy and improved tourist facilities in the town, Newman has become a popular stopover. **Of interest:** Tours of Mt Whaleback mine, Newman Dr, largest open-cut mine in world. Mining and pastoral museum, behind tourist centre. Radio Hill Lookout, off Newman Dr. Walking trail and climb from museum to Lookout. **In the area:** Ophthalmia Dam, 15 km N; swimming and barbecues. Good views from Mt Newman, 20 km N. Aboriginal rock carvings, rock pools and waterholes at Wanna Munna, 70 km W, and Punda (4WD only), 75 km NW. Kalgans Pool, 51 km NW; popular day trip, conventional vehicles with care. Eagle Rock Falls and pool, 69 km NW; permanent pools, picnic spots; falls may require 4WD. **Tourist information:** Cnr Fortescue Ave and

Sand goanna

Newman Dr; (091) 75 2888. **Accommodation:** 1 motel, 3 caravan/camping parks. **See also:** The Hamersley Range; The Pilbara.
MAP REF. 358 E6

Norseman Pop. 1398

Norseman, 200 km S of Kalgoorlie, is the last large town on the Eyre Hwy for travellers heading east towards SA. Gold put Norseman on the map back in the early 1890s, and the richest quartz reef in Australia is still being mined today. The town is steeped in goldmining history, with the colossal tailings dumps a reminder of the area's wealth. The area is popular with amateur prospectors and gemstone collectors; gemstone fossicking permits are available from Norseman Tourist Bureau. There is a quarantine checkpoint for westbound travellers at Norseman, so visitors should make sure they are not carrying fruit, vegetables, honey, used fruit and produce containers, plants or seeds. **Of interest:** Historical Collection of mining tools and household items; Battery Rd. Post Office (1896), cnr Prinsep and Ra Sts. Heritage Trail (33 km), following original Cobb & Co. route, includes descent into a 'decline'; details from tourist centre. Statue in Roberts St commemorating horse called Norseman who allegedly pawed at the ground and unearthed a nugget of gold, thus starting a gold rush in area. Mine tours of massive open-cut mine conducted weekdays. Norseman Tourist Reception Centre, Roberts St, has complete visitor facilities, day parking and barbecues. **In the area:** Dundas Rocks, 22 km S, are 550 million years old; excellent picnic area and old Dundas town site nearby. Easy drive up Beacon Hill (otherwise known as Mararoa or Lookout Hill), 2 km E, yields good views of surrounding salt lakes (spectacular when seen at sunrise and sunset), old mines and Jimberlana Dyke, reputedly one of oldest geological areas in world. Mt Jimberlana, 7 km E; walking trail to summit for good views. Peak Charles, 50 km S, then 40 km off hwy; magnificent views, but only for energetic climbers. Gemstone leases on Eyre Hwy and off Kalgoorlie Hwy; details from tourist centre. Frank Hahn National Park, 50 km E of Lake King township, traversed by Lake King–Norseman Rd. Twice-daily bus tours of town, the 'decline', Beacon Hill and part of Heritage Trail. **Tourist information:** 68 Roberts St; (090) 39 1071.

Accommodation: 2 hotels, 2 motels, 1 caravan/ camping park. **See also:** Crossing the Nullarbor; The Goldfields. MAP REF. 356 H9

Northam   Pop. 6560

The regional centre of the fertile Avon Valley at the junction of the Avon and Mortlock Rivers, Northam is an attractive rural town. On the Great Eastern Hwy, 100 km E of Perth, it is an important supply point for the farms of the eastern wheat belt. Northam is also a major railway centre and the main depot for the Goldfields Water Scheme, which takes water as far east as Kalgoorlie. WA's largest military training camp is on the outskirts of town. **Of interest:** Old Police Station (1866), Courthouse (1896), Town Hall (1897); all in Wellington St, and Flour Mill (1871), Newcastle St. Old Railway Station Museum, Fitzgerald St. Avon Valley Arts Society art and craft shop, Wellington St. Weir across Avon River, near Peel Tce bridge, forms lake that attracts both black and white swans and many other species of native birdlife. Byfield House, Gordon St; elegant, late-Victorian home built by James Byfield, now restored to its original grandeur and operating as bed and breakfast accommodation. Shamrock Hotel (1886), Fitzgerald St; fully renovated. Morby Cottage, Old York Rd, built in 1836 by one of Northam's first families, the Morrells, stands as tribute to district's early settlers. Sir James Mitchell House (1905), Duke St; classified by National Trust. Annual scenic cycling tour of wheat belt begins at Northam in May. **In the area:** Restored Buckland Homestead (1874), 8 km N; stately home set in landscaped gardens; contains collection of antique furniture, silver and paintings. At Dowerin, 58 km NE: museum, craft centre and Hagbooms Lake. Muresk Agricultural College, former early farming property, 10 km S. Blue Gum Camel Farm, located near Spencer Brook Rd, at Clackline, 19 km SW; camel- and trail-riding in picturesque bushland surroundings. Also in area: hot-air ballooning, horseriding, gliding, canoeing. In spring, wildflowers abound near Wubin, 190 km N. Northam–Katrine Heritage Trail and Farming Heritage Trail; details from tourist centre. **Tourist information:** Fitzgerald St; (096) 22 2100. **Accommodation:** 4 hotels, 1 motel, 1 caravan/camping park. MAP REF. 346 H2, 354 F7, 356 A8

Northampton   Pop. 786

Northampton nestles amidst gentle hills in the valley of Nokarena Brook, 48 km N of Geraldton. Inland there is picturesque country with vivid wildflowers in spring. The drive west leads to the coast, with beaches for swimming and fishing. **Of interest:** Chiverton House Folk Museum, Hampton Rd. Gwalla church site and cemetery, Gwalla St. St Mary's Convent and Church, Main St, designed by Mons. Hawes. Miners' cottages (1860s), Brook St. **In the area:** Alma Schoolhouse and disused Ghurka lead mine, 12 km N. At Horrocks Beach, 20 km W, pleasant bays, sandy beaches and good fishing. Near coast at Port Gregory, 47 km NW, labour-hiring depot for convicts, dating from 1800s; this squat building with slits for windows was probably erected as protection from hostile Aborigines. Hutt Lagoon, near Port Gregory, turns pink in light of midday sun. **Tourist information:** Nagle Centre, Main St; (099) 34 1488. **Accommodation:** 2 motels, 1 caravan/camping park. MAP REF. 354 C1

Northcliffe   Pop. 190

Magnificent virgin karri forests surround the little township of Northcliffe, 32 km S of Pemberton, in the extreme south-west corner of the State. Unique flora and fauna is to be found in this area. **Of interest:** In Wheatley Coast Rd: Pioneer Museum, with historical relics and photographs; and at Tourist Centre, rock and mineral collection, Aboriginal Interpretation Room and photographic folio of native flora and birds. Earthworm Farm, North St; 10–4 daily. Northcliffe Art and Craft, Wheatley Coast Rd; local art and craft. South West Timber Trekking Company, off Wheatley Coast Rd; horseriding on forest tracks. Forest Park, off Wheatley Coast Rd; Hollow Butt Karri, Twin Karri walking trails and picnic areas. Warren River; fishing. **In the area:** Mt Chudalup, 20 km S; giant granite outcrop with walking trail to summit for panoramic views. Sandy beaches of Windy Harbour and Salmon Beach, 29 km S; ideal for fishing and swimming. Cliffs at Point D'Entrecasteaux, 27 km S; popular with climbers. D'Entrecasteaux (5 km S), Warren (20 km NW) and Shannon (30 km E) National Parks, with Bibbulmun Track linking all three. Boorara Tree (once used as fire lookout) and Lane–Poole Falls, 24 km SE. **Tourist information:** Adjacent to Pioneer

Museum, Wheatley Coast Rd, in town centre; (097) 76 7203. **Accommodation:** 1 hotel, 1 caravan/camping park. MAP REF. 350 C9, 354 E12, 356 A13

Onslow   Pop. 881

Onslow, on the NW coast of the State, is important as the base for the oilfields off the coast at Barrow Island. The town was originally located at the mouth of the Ashburton River, but was moved to its site on Beadon Bay after constant cyclones. The remains of the old town site can still be seen. Onslow was a bustling pearling centre and in the 1890s gold was discovered. US submarines refuelled here during World War II, and the town was bombed by the Japanese. In 1952 it was the mainland base for Britain's nuclear experiments at Monte Bello Islands. **In the area:** Excellent fishing. Native fauna includes emus, red kangaroos, sand goannas, bustards and a wide variety of birdlife. In spring, after rain, the wildflowers bloom, including the Sturt desert pea and Ashburton pea. **Tourist information:** Shire Offices; (091) 84 6001. **Accommodation:** 1 hotel, 2 caravan/camping parks. MAP REF. 355 E2

Pemberton   Pop. 934

The town of Pemberton, 335 km S of Perth, is nestled in a quiet valley, surrounded by towering karri forests. This lush forest area has some of the tallest hardwood trees in the world, and, in spring, brilliant flowering bush plants. **Of interest:** Pemberton is known as a centre for high-quality woodcraft, and there are a number of craft outlets: Pemberton Arts and Craft, Broadway Ave; Wooddawn Woodcrafts, Ellis St; Warren River Arts and Craft, Jamieson St; Woodcraftsman's Studio, Jamieson St; Fine Woodcraft, Dickinson St. In Brockman St: Museum, with collection of historic photographs and authentic forestry equipment, includes tourist centre. Trout and Marron Hatchery supplies fish for WA rivers and dams; daily tours. Fishing in local rivers; Inland Fishing Licence required for trout and marron. Wineries with cellar-door sales and/or tastings include Warren Vineyard, Dickinson St; Gloucester Ridge, Burma Rd; Mountford Wines, Bamess Rd. Pemberton Sawmill, Brockman St; guided tours Mon.–Fri. **In the area:** Gloucester Tree, signposted off Brockman St, tallest fire lookout in world; over 60 m high with 150 rungs

spiralling upwards; open for climbing during daylight hours. Further south are picturesque Lane Poole Falls and at Northcliffe, pioneer museum. The Cascades, 8 km S; popular for picnics, bushwalking and fishing. King Trout Farm, 9 km S. Brockman Sawpit, 13 km S; restored to show how timber was sawn in 1860s. Moon's Crossing, 18 km S, for picnics; 4WD in winter. Marron and dairy farm, 1 km N. Big Brook Dam and Arboretum, 7 km NW. Donnelly River Wines, 35 km NW. Piano Gully Vineyard, 24 km NE, off South West Hwy. Eagle Springs marron farm, 18 km W. Sandy beaches line the rugged coast at Windy Harbour, where fishing is good. Warren (9 km S), Brockman (13 km S) and Beedelup (18 km W) National Parks all close by. Some of best accessible virgin karri forest in Warren National Park, where tallest of karri trees (89 m) can be found. Swamp Willow Farm on Hawke Rd near park, 12 km S; local wood craft. Tramcars based on 1907 Fremantle trams operate daily through tall-timber country between Pemberton and Northcliffe; details from tourist centre. Also available: Forest Industry tours into logging and regrowth areas; Mon.–Fri.; scenic bus tours, daily; 4WD adventure tours, 2 hrs– overnight; horseriding, incl. pub crawl; details from tourist centre. **Tourist information:** Brockman St; (097) 76 1133. **Accommodation:** 1 hotel/motel, 2 motels, 1 caravan/camping park. **See also:** The South-west.
MAP REF. 350 C7, 354 E12, 356 A13

Karri forest near Pemberton

Perenjori   Pop. 250
On the Northam–Mullewa Hwy (known as the 'Wildflower Way'), 352 km NE of Perth, Perenjori lies on the fringes of the Murchison goldfields and the great sheep stations of the west. **Of interest:** Historical Museum behind tourist centre, Fowler St. Arts and Crafts Centre, Russell St. **In the area:** Fossickers will find many gemstones in this mineral-rich region. The wildflower season lasts from July to Sep. and there are many scenic drives. The salt lakes attract a variety of waterbirds. Old goldmining and ghost towns include Rothsay, 67 km E (working mine not open for inspection); Warriedar, 107 km E; and Nows Nest, 176 km E. Care should be taken, as unfenced pits make the area dangerous. Mongers Lake Lookout, 35 km E. Camel Soak, picnic spot; 47 km E. Aboriginal Stones at Damperwah Soak, 40 km NE. Perenjori–

Rothsay Heritage Trail (180 km), recalls district's early goldmining days; details from tourist centre. **Tourist information:** Fowler Street; (099)73 1105. **Accommodation:** 1 hotel, 1 caravan/camping park.
MAP REF. 354 E3

Pingelly   Pop. 763
On the Great Southern Hwy, 154 km SE of Perth, Pingelly is part of the central southern farming district. The cutting of sandalwood was once a local industry, but today the land is given over to sheep and wheat growing. **Of interest:** Community Craft Centre, Parade St. Courthouse Museum, Parade St. Apex Lookout, Stone St, for fine views of town and country. **In the area:** Historic St Patrick's Church (1873) at Mourambine, 10 km E. Tuttanning Flora and Fauna Reserve, 21 km E. Yealering Lake and picnic ground, 58 km E. Dryandra Reserve, 40 km SW, with unique examples of flora; fauna includes the numbat, WA's fauna emblem. Timber also produced in reserve, which has been called an ecological oasis. Boyagin Rock

Picnic Ground and Reserve, 26 km NW. Moorumbine Heritage Trail; details from tourist centre. **Tourist information:** Shire Offices, 17 Queen St; (098) 87 1066. **Accommodation:** 2 hotels, 1 motel, 1 caravan/camping park.
MAP REF. 347 J8, 354 F8, 356 B10

Pinjarra   Pop. 1779
Pinjarra is a pleasant drive 84 km S of Perth, along the shaded South Western Hwy or the scenic Old Coast Road. The town has a picturesque setting on the banks of the Murray River in one of the earliest established districts in WA. The Alcoa Refinery, 4 km NE of town on South West Hwy, is the largest alumina refinery in Australia. Pinjarra is becoming increasingly popular with tourists as a base from which to explore the area. Bus tours are available from the Tour Reception Centre at the Pinjarra Refinery. **Of interest:** St John's Church (1845), Heritage Rose Garden, Henry St., Liveringa (1880), Edenvale (1888), George St; homes of early settlers. Old School (1896) and Teacher's House, Henry St. **In the area:** Marrinup Falls,

Crossing the Nullarbor

The trip from Adelaide to Perth along the Eyre Highway is one of Australia's great touring experiences. It is far from monotonous, with breathtaking views of the Great Australian Bight only a few hundred metres from the road in many places. There is nothing quite like a long straight road stretching as far as the eye can see ahead and in the rear-vision mirror.

If you are planning a return journey, it is well worth considering driving one way and putting the car on the train for the return. As there is a limited amount of space for cars, train bookings need to be made well in advance, even at off-peak times. (**See:** Planning Ahead.)

The Eyre Highway is bitumen for its entire length. The highway is extremely well signposted, with indications of the distance to the next town with petrol and other services.

If the journey is undertaken at a sensible pace, it can be surprisingly relaxing, especially during the quieter times of year. The standard of accommodation is good and reasonably priced, with a friendly atmosphere in the bars and dining rooms of the large motel/roadhouses that are strategically situated along the highway. Many friendships have been made during the trip across the Eyre Highway as the same carloads of travellers meet at stopping-places each night.

Although the highway is bitumen, there are certain hazards. The road can have breakaways on the shoulders in places, requiring caution when drivers are overtaking. And it can be difficult to overtake the big semitrailers as they thunder along the highway, particularly when they 'tailgate' to save fuel. Overtaking also can be hazardous in damp conditions when the spray from the vehicle in front completely cuts visibility ahead. On the other hand, the semitrailer drivers are usually courteous and signal when it is safe to overtake. Kangaroos also can be a problem, especially at dusk or after rain.

The setting sun can make driving somewhat unpleasant for drivers travelling in a westerly direction. Also, do not forget the time changes that you will encounter on the way! (**See also:** Time Zones.)

Above all, it is most important to have a safe, reliable car. The settlements along the highway are mainly motels with garage and roadhouse. You could have a long wait for mechanical or medical help.

Eyre Highway

The trip begins properly at **Port Augusta**, 330 kilometres north-east of Adelaide, at the head of Spencer Gulf. Port Augusta is a provincial city that services a vast area of semi-arid grazing and wheat-growing country to the north and west. As you head out of the city on the Eyre Highway, you see the red peaks of the Flinders Ranges soaring above the sombre bluebush plains; these are the last hills of any size for 2500 kilometres. Through the little towns of **Kimba** and **Kyancutta** the scenery can vary from mallee scrub to wide paddocks of wheat. This area was once called Heartbreak Plains, a reminder of the time when farmers walked off their land in despair, leaving behind them the crumbling stone homesteads that today dot the plains.

The highway meets the sea at **Ceduna**, a small town of white stone buildings and limestone streets set against a background of blue-green sea. The waters of the Great Australian Bight here are shallow and unpredictable, but they yield Australia's best catches of its most commercially prized fish, whiting. On the outskirts of Ceduna is a warning sign about the last reliable water. This marks the end of cultivated country and the beginning of the deserted, almost treeless land that creeps towards the Nullarbor Plain. The highway stays close to the coast and there is always a little scrub and other vegetation on the plains, or on the sand dunes that lie between the highway and the ocean.

Further north the Nullarbor Plain covers an area greater than the State of Victoria. The name 'Nullarbor' is a corruption from the Latin words meaning 'no trees' and the name is apt. Geologists believe that the completely flat plain was once the bed of a prehistoric sea, which was raised to dry land by a great upheaval of the earth.

West of Ceduna the traveller will find **Penong**, a town of 100 windmills, and the

breathtaking coastal beauty around Point Sinclair and Cactus Beach. Then on to **Nundroo** and south to the abandoned settlement of **Fowlers Bay**, once an exploration depot for Edward John Eyre and now a charming ghost town best known for its fishing. At the **Yalata Roadhouse**, run by the Yalata Aboriginal Community, there are genuine artefacts for sale at reasonable prices. Between **Nullarbor** and **Border Village** are five of the most spectacular coastal lookouts anywhere on the Australian coastline, where giant ocean swells pound the towering limestone cliffs that make up this part of the Great Australian Bight. From June to October an added bonus is the chance of spotting the majestic southern right whale on its annual migration along the southern part of the continent. Fuel, refreshments and accommodation are all available at Penong, Nundroo, Nullarbor and Border Village.

The stone ruins of an Aboriginal mission remain at **Cocklebiddy**. The road continues until it reaches the first real town in more than 1200 kilometres, **Norseman**, an ideal stopping-place.

From here you turn north to **Kalgoorlie** or south to **Esperance** on the coast. At **Kalgoorlie–Boulder** you will see one of the longest-established and most prosperous goldmining centres in Western Australia. After a working life of more than 90 years, the mines around Kalgoorlie still produce more than 70 per cent of Australia's gold. Set in vast dryland eucalypt forest, the town is picturesque in frontier style.

Esperance, on the other hand, offers coastal scenery including long, empty beaches. Nearby, wildflowers spread across the countryside in spring.

The undulating forest and wildflower scrub continues for a further 250 kilometres until the road reaches the wheat- and wool-growing lands around the towns of **Southern Cross** and **Merredin**. The farmland becomes increasingly rich as it rises into the Darling Range, the beautiful, wooded mountain country that overlooks Perth. At the end of this long journey Perth glitters like a jewel on the Indian Ocean— a place of civilisation and style, of beaches, waterways and greenery.

For further information on the Eyre Highway, see South Australian entries for **Ceduna, Kimba, Penong** and **Wudinna** and Western Australian entries for **Balladonia, Caiguna, Cocklebiddy, Eucla, Mundrabilla** and **Madura**. **See also:** Individual town entries in A–Z listing.

3-km walk from Scarp Rd. Alcoa Scarp Lookout, 14 km E. Athlone Angora Stud and Goat Farm, 16 km E. Scarp Pool, 20 km SE, popular for picnics and swimming. Fairbridge Village, 5 km N. Whittakers Mill, for bushwalking, camping and barbecues, and Dandalup Studio (art and craft), both at North Dandalup, 10 km N. Old Blythewood (1840s), 4 km S, has served as post office, coach stop and family home. Lake Navarino Forest Resort and Waroona Dam, 33 km S; watersports, fishing, walking, horseriding, tours. Hotham Valley Tourist Railway runs old-style steam train between Pinjarra and Dwellingup (Sun., May–Oct.). Farm holidays available at Nanga Dell Farm near Waroona, 24 km S. Yalgorup National Park on coast, 48 km SW of Waroona. Pinjarra Heritage Trail; details from tourist centre. **Tourist information:** Murray Tourist Centre (in Edenvale stately home), George St; (09) 531 1438. **Accommodation:** 1 hotel, 1 motel, 1 caravan/camping park. **See also:** The South-west.
MAP REF. 346 D9, 354 E8

Point Samson
Pop. 180

Point Samson was named in honour of Michael Samson, who accompanied the district's first settler, Walter Padbury, on his 1863 journey. The town was established in 1910 as the major port for the Roebourne district, replacing Cossack, where the harbour had silted up following a cyclone. The port was very active for many years, but today Point Samson supports a small fishing industry and its extremely attractive setting has made it a popular beach resort. **Of interest:** Point Samson's sandy beach is protected by a coral reef, making it perfect for swimming, fishing and skindiving. The tidal rivers contain an immense variety of marine life, from barramundi to mud crabs. Offshore waters have some of the best game fishing along the entire coast. Swimming and picnicking at Honeymoon Cove on Johns Creek Rd; boat ramp and jetty at nearby John's Harbour. Trawlers Tavern for local seafood. **In the area:** Fishing boat harbour at Sam's Creek, 1 km N. Samson Reef can be explored at low tide. Emma Withnell Heritage Trail; details from tourist centre. **Tourist information:** Point Samson Fisheries, Point Samson Rd; (091) 87 1414. **Accommodation:** 1 caravan park.
MAP REF. 355 H1, 358 A1

Port Hedland
Pop. 11 344

Port Hedland's remarkable growth has been due to the iron-ore boom, which started in the early 1960s. The town was named after Captain Peter Hedland, who discovered the harbour in 1829. Today Port Hedland handles the largest tonnage of any Australian port. Iron ore from some of the world's biggest mines is loaded on to the world's biggest ore carriers. Gathering of salt is another major industry, with about 2 million tonnes exported per annum. The Spinifex Spree, held Aug., is ten days of sport, social and cultural activities. Aboriginal population represent several language groups. International airport, also serves north-west region of the State. **Of interest:** Stairway to the Moon, viewed from Cooke point on certain dates, April–Oct.; details from tourist centre. Observation Tower at tourist centre, Wedge St. Lions Park, Hunt St, has pioneer relics. Royal Flying Doctor Base, Richardson St. Visitors are welcome at wharf, where ore is loaded on to giant ships. BHP mine tours can be booked through tourist centre. Don Rhodes Mining Museum, Wilson St. At Two Mile Ridge, opposite the fire brigade in Wilson St, are some Aboriginal carvings in limestone ridge (no public access). Old St Matthew's Church (1917), Edgar St; art gallery and exhibition centre, historic building. Olympic pool in McGregor St, next to Civic Centre. The 2-km-long trains operated by BHP Iron Ore arrive 6 times daily. Heritage trails include Port Hedland cemetery; graves of early gold prospectors and Japanese pearl divers. **In the area:** Swim, picnic and fish at Pretty Pool, next to Cooke Point caravan park. Giant cone-shaped mounds of salt, piled high awaiting export, 8 km S at Cargill Salt. Tour of bauxite mine and alumina refinery, 8 km E; Wed. and Sun. Stone carvings at Woodstock, 300 km SE. Port Hedland Heritage Trail; details from tourist centre. Whale-watching July–Oct. Good fishing; charter boats for hire. Birdlife is abundant in district: watch for bustards, eagles, cockatoos, galahs, ibises, pelicans and parrots. **Tourist information:** 13 Wedge St; (091) 73 1650. **Accommodation:** 6 hotel/motels, 3 caravan/camping parks. **See also:** The Pilbara.
MAP REF. 358 C1, 360 B13

Ravensthorpe
Pop. 392

Ravensthorpe, situated 533 km SE of Perth, is the centre of the old Phillips River goldfield. Copper mining was also important here, reaching a peak in the late 1960s. Many old mine shafts can be seen around the district. Wheat and sheep are the local industries. **Of interest:** Historical Society Museum, Morgan St. Several historic buildings: Anglican Church, Dunn St; old mine manager's house, Carlisle St; Dance Cottage (museum), Palace Hotel and newly restored Commercial Hotel (now Community Centre), all in Morgan St. **In the area:** Ravensthorpe Range, 3 km N, and Mt Desmond, 10 km SE, for panoramic views. WA Time Meridian at first rest bay west of town. Fitzgerald River National Park, 46 km S; now Biosphere Reserve for UNESCO. Old copper smelter, 2 km E. Annual wildflower display in Sept. features over 600 species from Fitzgerald River National Park. Rock-hunting; check locally to avoid trespass. Catlin Creek Heritage Trail and short scenic drives, leaflets available; details from tourist centre. **Tourist information:** Community Centre, Morgan St; (098) 38 1277. **Accommodation:** 1 hotel/motel, 1 motel, 1 caravan/camping park.
MAP REF. 356 F11

Rockingham
Pop. 36 675

At the southern end of Cockburn Sound, 45 km S of Perth, Rockingham is a coastal city and seaside resort. Begun in 1872 as a port, the harbour fell into disuse with the opening of the Fremantle inner harbour in 1897. Today its magnificent golden beaches and protected waters are Rockingham's main attraction. **Of interest:** Museum, Kent St. Lookout at Point Peron, Peron Rd. WA Waterski Park, St Albans Rd. Sunday markets, Flinders Lake. Cockburn Yacht Regatta held Jan. **In the area:** Nearby Penguin Island, with a colony of fairy penguins. Garden Island, home to HMAS *Stirling*, naval base; normally closed to public, but accessed by bus tour from Perth weekly; causeway link to mainland not open to public. Kwinana Industrial Complex, 10 km N. Scenic drive 48 km inland to Serpentine Dam, WA's major water conservation area. Brilliant wildflowers, gardens and bushland surround dam and Serpentine Falls are close by. Shoalwater Bay Islands Marine Park, 6 km NW, extends from just south of Garden Island to Becher Point in Warnbro; cruises, including dolphin cruises, available. Marapana Deer Park, 16 km S. Baldivis Estate Winery, 15 km SE. Peel Estate Winery, 17 km

SE. Old Rockingham Heritage Trail and Rockingham–Jarrahdale Heritage Trail; details from tourist centre. **Tourist information:** 43 Kent St; (09) 592 3464. **Accommodation:** 2 hotels, 1 motel, 3 caravan/camping parks.
MAP REF. 346 C6, 354 D8

Roebourne   Pop. 1213

Named after John Septimus Roe, the State's first surveyor-general, Roebourne was established in 1864 and is the oldest town on the north-west coast. It was developed as the capital of the North-West and at one time was the administrative centre for the whole area north of the Murchison River. The town was the centre for the early mining and pastoral industries in the Pilbara; it was connected to the port of Cossack, and later to Point Samson, by tramway for the transport of passengers and goods. Although now overshadowed by the iron-ore and other industries, Roebourne has retained its own special character. **Of interest:** Old stone buildings (some classified by National Trust) include police station, Queen St; Post Office (1887), Shell St; hospital (1887) and courthouse in Hampton St; Holy Trinity Church (1894), Withnell St; Union Bank (1889, now Shire library) and Victoria Hotel, last of town's five original pubs, in Roe St. Old Roebourne Gaol (1886), Queen St, with art and craft centre Aboriginal art gallery; open daily. Good views from top of Mt Welcome, Fisher Dr. Wirraway Art Gallery, Hampton St. Royal Show, July. Roebourne Cup annually July–Aug., at racecourse on main hwy. **In the area:** Emma Withnell Heritage Trail, 52 km round trip, taking in towns of Wickham (15 km) and Cossack (17 km, restored buildings, archaeological project, art gallery) and terminating at Point Samson. Fishing at Cleaverville; 25 km N. **Tourist information:** Old Goal, Queen St; (091) 82 1060. **Accommodation:** 1 hotel/ motel, 1 caravan/camping park. **See also:** The Pilbara.
MAP REF. 355 H1, 358 A2

Southern Cross   Pop. 982

A small but flourishing town on the Great Eastern Hwy, 368 km E of Perth, Southern Cross is a unique town, being the centre of a prosperous agricultural and pastoral area and a significant gold-producing area. **Of interest:** First courthouse in eastern goldfields (1893), Antares St; now history museum, open daily. Other historic buildings include

Post Office (1891), Antares St, and Railway Tavern (1890s), Spica St. Newly restored Palace Hotel. The town and its wide streets, originally designed to allow camel trains to turn around, are named after stars and constellations. Goldmining activities around Southern Cross, Marvel Loch (35 km S) and Bullfinch (36 km N). **In the area:** Wildflowers bloom on sandplains in spring. Koolyanobbing, 56 km N; built for miners extracting iron ore and now ghost town since closure in 1983. Several interesting rock formations; areas around ideal for picnicking. Hunt's Soak, 7 km N, also has picnic area. Old State Battery, 34 km S. **Tourist information:** Shire Offices, Antares St; (090) 49 1001. **Accommodation:** 2 hotels, 1 motel, 1 caravan/camping park. **See also:** Crossing the Nullarbor.
MAP REF. 356 E7

Three Springs Roadhouse
Pop. 473

Sir John Forrest named Three Springs, which is 170 km SE of Geraldton. WA's finest talc, exported for use in the ceramics industry, is mined here from an open-cut mine 13 km E. Of interest: At town entrance, information bay and path through living display of wildflowers. Heritage Walk, including wildflowers; details from tourist centre. **In the area:** Yarra Yarra Lake system, 5 km W, attracts many migratory birds. Emu Farm, 14 km W on Eneabba Rd; open daily. Wildflower farm adjacent. Eneabba, major mineral sands mining centre, 56 km W. Blue Waters, near Arrino, 18 km N; picnic area amid river gums. Pink Lakes, 6 km E, Cockatoo Canyon, 6 km W, and old copper-mine ruins, 7 km NW. Wildflower Drives (best between Aug. and Nov.); details from tourist centre. **Tourist information:** Thomas Street; (099) 54 1041. **Accommodation:** 1 hotel/motel.
MAP REF. 395 K10

Tom Price   Pop. 3634

The huge iron ore deposit now known as Mt Tom Price was discovered in 1962, after which the Hamersley Iron Project was established. The construction of a mine, two towns (Tom Price and Dampier) and a railway between the mine followed, all of which was achieved in a remarkably short period of time. **Of interest:** Nameless Festival held in Aug. **In the area:** Proximity of Tom Price to spectacular Karijini (Hamersley Range)

National Park, 38 km N, and chance to tour open-cut mining operation make town a popular stopping-place. Views of remarkable scenery around Tom Price from Mt Nameless lookout, 6 km W, via walking trail. Aboriginal carvings, 4WD tours to site, 10 km S; details from tourist centre. **Tourist information:** Central Rd; (091) 89 2375. **Accommodation:** 1 hotel, 1 motel, 1 caravan/camping park. **See also:** The Hamersley Range; The Pilbara.
MAP REF. 355 I4, 358 B5

Toodyay   Pop. 604

The historic town of Toodyay, nestled in the Avon Valley, has many charming old buildings recalling its pioneering past. Situated 85 km NE of Perth, Toodyay is surrounded by picturesque farming country and, to the west, virgin bushland. **Of interest:** Classified by the National Trust as a historic town, Toodyay has many buildings of historic significance in or near Stirling Tce. Connor's flour mill, built in the 1870s, is an imposing structure, now housing the local tourist centre, displays and a fascinating steam engine, still in working order. Old Newcastle Gaol Museum (1865), Clinton St, and police stables (1870), opposite, were built by convicts with random rubble stone. **In the area:** Hoddywell Archery Park, 8 km S. On Perth road, 4 km SW Coorinja Winery, begun in 1870. White Gum Company, 9 km SW, just off road to Perth, flower farm; native and exotic flowers under cultivation. Trout farm, 12 km SW; fishing and sales. Blink Bonney Cottage, 14 km SW; crafts and tearoom. Emu farm, 15 km SW; 10–4 daily. Avon Valley National Park, 25 km SW; spectacular scenery and seasonal wildflowers. Northam, 27 km SE, and, nearby, Avon River Weir; sanctuary for swans. Grassy riverbank is a delightful picnic spot. **Tourist information:** Connor's Mill, Stirling Tce; (09) 574 2435. **Accommodation:** 2 hotels, 2 caravan/camping parks.
MAP REF. 346 G2, 354 E7, 356 A8

Wagin   Pop. 1293

The prosperous rural countryside surrounding Wagin supports grain crops and pastures for livestock, especially sheep. Wagin's development has been tied to its important location as a railway-junction town, 177 km E of Bunbury. The annual 2-day 'Woolorama' in March is attended by sheep farmers from all over Australia

The Hamersley Range

Stretching more than 300 kilometres through the heart of the mineral-rich Pilbara, the Hamersley Range forms a wild and magnificent panorama. The mountains slope gently up from the south to the flat-topped outcrops and Western Australia's highest peak, **Mt Meharry**. In the north they rise majestically from golden spinifex plains.

Although today the main activity in the area is centred on mining towns like **Tom Price**, **Paraburdoo** and **Newman**, visitors will find many other areas of interest.

Spectacular gorges have been carved by the waters of the Fortescue and other rivers. Precipitous walls of rock are layered in colours from reddish brown to green and blue to pink in the changing light. The gorges are up to 100 metres deep, with water flow at their base sometimes only one metre wide. Others have

wide, crystal-clear pools reflecting the colour of the sky. Lush green vegetation thrives and the gorges are cool oases in the harsh climate.

Tom Price is a good base from which to explore the beauty of the Hamersley Ranges. The **Wittenoom Gorge** is a popular spot because it is so easily accessible (camping is not permitted). At Yampire Gorge there is a well once used by Afghani camel-drivers in the 1800s. The breathtaking **Dales Gorge**, approached through Yampire Gorge, is 45 kilometres long. Here are found crystal-clear pools and the splendid Fortescue Falls. The small but intriguing **Rio Tinto Gorge,** and **Hamersley Gorge** with its folded bands of coloured rock, are also quite beautiful.

One particularly enchanting oasis in the Hamersley Range area is the tropical paradise of **Millstream–Chichester National Park**, on the Fortescue River, inland from Roebourne. Thousands of birds flock to this delightful spot, where ferns, lilies,

palms and rushes grow in abundance. There are two long, deep, natural pools. The springs produce over 36 million litres of water a day from an underground basin, which is piped to Roebourne, Dampier, Karratha, Wickham and Cape Lambert. In contrast to the **Karijini (Hamersley Range) National Park**, the scenery in the Millstream–Chichester National Park varies from magnificent views over the coastal plain to the deep permanent river pools of tropical Millstream. This attractive spot offers excellent swimming conditions and pleasant camping areas.

The Hamersley Range is rugged, exciting country, and is enticing and often beautiful. Keep in mind, however, that you are travelling in remote areas. Old roads are being improved and new ones constructed in an effort to open up one of the oldest areas in the world.

See also: Individual town entries in A–Z listing.

The Pilbara

In the far north-west of their State, the Western Australians are moving mountains with giant earth-movers that chew their way through the red iron ore. The discovery of vast mineral wealth has created a major economic breakthrough for the State. The arid Pilbara region, one of the most heavily mineralised areas in the world, also contains some of the oldest rock formations in the world—perhaps 2000 million years old. The iron ore boom has created employment opportunities in this desolate land of sand spinifex, mulga scrub and massive red mountains, and model towns have sprung up. Gardens, swimming pools, golf courses and communal activities help compensate for the isolation and harsh climate. The largest towns of the Pilbara are company towns, residential and administrative centres for the iron ore mines, or ports for the export of ore. **Dampier**, on King Bay, is a modern iron ore company town, with a major salt industry nearby. Offshore is the Woodside North West

Shelf Gas Project. The project is the largest single resource development ever undertaken in Australia and includes a 1500-kilometre pipeline for the domestic market. Another side to the town can be found within the attractions of the Dampier Archipelago, comprising 42 islands of which 25 are incorporated into reserves for flora and fauna. The area is a natural playground with fishing, diving, swimming, boating, camping and bushwalking allowed around and on several of these outcrops.

Roebourne, the oldest town in the north-west, has been a centre for the pastoral, copper and pearling industries. The old pearling port of **Cossack** is a short drive away. Inland on the Fortescue River, lush ferns, palms and lilies grow near the deep pools at **Millstream**, the source of water for many Pilbara towns. The **Millstream–Chichester National Park** is also well worth a visit. To the south, the fishing village of Onslow and its offshore islands is the perfect holiday retreat.

Karratha is a modern town and regional centre, as is **Wickham**. Wickham's port at Cape Lambert has the longest and tallest jetty in Australia, standing

3 kilometres long and 18.5 metres above water. At **Port Hedland**, streamlined port facilities cope with more tonnage than any other port in the country. Ore mined inland at **Tom Price**, **Newman**, **Paraburdoo** and other centres is railed on giant trains to the ports for export.

The fishing here is good, with many world records being set. Swimming can be dangerous: sharks, sea snakes and poisonous fish frequent the waters. **Tom Price** affords easy access to the magnificent gorges in the **Karijini (Hamersley Range) National Park**, with their many-coloured walls, deep cool waters and lush green growth. And, of course, there is **Marble Bar**, living up to its reputation as the hottest place in Australia and keeping alive the tradition of 'the great Australian outback'.

Despite great improvements to the main roads—many are sealed—they are still liable to deterioration, and can have long stretches of rough and dangerous surface. It is wise to check on local conditions before setting out.

See also: Individual town entries in A–Z listing; Outback Motoring.

and attracts crowds of over 25 000. **Of interest:** Wagin Historical Village, Ballagin Rd; collection of early pioneer artefacts, set in 16 authentic old buildings. Town has some fine Victorian buildings and shopfronts in Tudhoe and Tudor Sts. Giant Ram (7 m high), Arthur Rd, and adjacent park with ponds and waterfalls. Great Southern Gamebirds, Ware St; many varieties of native birds. **In the area:** Corralyn Emu Farm, 4 km N. Granite Mt Latham, 6 km W, affords scenic views and opportunities for bushwalkers. Puntapin, another rock formation, 6 km SE, used as a water-catchment area. Wildflowers abound in spring. Lakes Norring, 13 km SE, for picnics, swimming, sailing and water-skiing; and Dumbleyung, 30 km E, for sightseeing. Rockleigh Farm, 18 km SW, for farm holidays. Wagin Heritage Trail; details from tourist centre. **Tourist information:** Shire Offices, Arthur Rd; (098) 61 1177; Wagin Historical Village, Ballagin Rd. **Accommodation:** 3 hotels, 1 motel, 1 caravan/camping park. **See also:** The Great Southern.
MAP REF. 347 K13, 354 G10, 356 B11

Walpole
Pop. 290

Walpole is literally where the forest meets the sea. Surrounded by the Walpole–Nornalup National Park where a variety of trees grow, including karri, jarrah, and the tingle species, which is unique to the area. The area is known for its wildflowers in season as well as its wildlife. **Of interest:** Pioneer Cottage, Pioneer Park; opened in 1987 to commemorate district pioneers, cottage follows basic design of early pioneer homes, but is not intended as a replica. Bibbulmun Track (530 km), leading S from Kalamunda, 30 km E of Perth, ends at Walpole. **In the area:** Knoll Drive, 3 km E. For bushwalkers, Nuyts Wilderness area, 7 km W, and other walking trails, while anglers have choice of ocean, river and inlet. Valley of the Giants, 16 km E; Fernhook Falls, 32 km NW; Mt Frankland, 29 km N; Circular Pool, on Frankland River, 11 km NE; and Peaceful Bay, 28 km SE. Tingle trees on Hilltop Rd, near Circular Pool. Coalmine Beach Heritage Trail; details from tourist centre. **Tourist information:** Pioneer Cottage, Pioneer Park; (098) 40 1111. **Accommodation:** 1 hotel/motel, 1 motel, 2 caravan/camping parks.
MAP REF. 354 F12

Original town site, Wyndham

Wanneroo
Pop. 6745

Just a short drive from Perth, the district around Wanneroo stretches along 50 km of constantly changing coastline. **Of interest:** Botanic Golf, Burns Beach Rd. Dizzy Lamb Park, cnr Karoborup Rd and Wanneroo Rd. Hillarys Boat Harbour, Sorrento Quay and Underwater World, all at junction of Whitfords Ave, Hepburn Ave and West Coast Dr. Mindarie Keys Resort, Ocean Falls Bvd. Gumnut Factory and Wanneroo Weekend Markets, both in Prindiville Dr, Wangara. Conti Estate Wine Cellars and Restaurant, and Magic Wildflowers, both in Wanneroo Rd. International competitors are attracted to regular meetings at Wanneroo Motor Racing Circuit. **In the area:** Kristen Leigh Creations, Dellamarta Rd, Wangara; Australian wildflowers made into jewellery. Lakes Joondalup, 1 km W, Jandabup, 4 km E, and Gnangara, 7 km SE, are close by. Vineyards in area open for inspection and cellar-door sales: Faranda Wines, 2 km S; Conti Estate Wines, 4 km S; and Hartridge Wines, 10 km NW. Wildflower Cottage, 10 km N. Yanchep National Park, 27 km NW; Gloucester Lodge Museum in park. **Tourist information:** Joondalup Railway Station; (09) 300 0155 or WA Coach Service 3–6 Dellamarta Rd, Wangara; (09) 309 1680. **Accommodation:** 3 caravan/camping parks.
MAP REF. 346 C3, 354 D7

Wickepin
Pop. 245

Wickepin dates back to the 1890s, when the first settlers came to the district. The town is 214 km SE of Perth in farming country. **Of interest:** Good examples of Edwardian architecture in Wogolin Rd. **In the area:** The town has become well known following the publication of Albert Facey's autobiography *A Fortunate Life*; the house he built still stands 15 km S of Wickepin. Toolibin Lake reserve, 20 km S, attracts wide variety of waterfowl. Tiny town of Yealering and Yealering Lake, 30 km N. Sewell's Rock Nature Reserve, 14 km E of Yealering, ideal for picnics and nature walks. Albert Facey Heritage Trail; details from tourist centre. **Tourist information:** Wickepin Newsagency and Milkbar, 56 Wogolin Rd; (098) 88 1070. **Accommodation:** 1 hotel, 1 caravan/camping park.
MAP REF. 347 L9, 354 G9, 356 B10

Wickham
Pop. 1973

Construction of Wickham, 40 km N of Karratha, was begun in 1970 by the Cliff's Robe River Iron Associates. Today the town is still company-owned and -operated, now by Robe River Iron Associates. Wickham is the sister town to Pannawonica, and it is here that iron ore mined out of Pannawonica is processed before being exported from nearby Cape Lambert. **Of interest:** Tours of processing plant and port operations commence at Robe River Visitors Centre, Wickham Dr, Mon.–Fri. Boat Beach off Walcott Dr. Lookout at Tank Hill for views of town. Annual Cossack to Wickham Fun Run held July–Aug. **In the area:** Wharf at Cape Lambert, 10 km NW, is tallest and longest open-ocean

wharf in Australia. Point Samson, 9 km W, popular beach resort with game fishing. Restored town of Cossack, 8 km SE, once pearling port. Roebourne, 10 km S, oldest town in north-west; old gaol and government buildings. **Tourist information:** Roebourne Tourist Bureau, Queen St, Roebourne; (091) 82 1060. **Accommodation:** Limited budget accommodation. **See also:** The Hamersley Range; The Pilbara.
MAP REF. 355 H1, 358 A2

Williams   Pop. 371

This historical town enjoys a picturesque setting on the banks of the Williams River, 161 km SE of Perth. **In the area:** Dryandra State Forest, 25 km N. **Accommodation:** 1 hotel, 1 motel, 1 caravan/camping park.
MAP REF. 346 I11, 354 F9, 356 B10

Wittenoom   Pop. 50

Wittenoom is situated at the mouth of Wittenoom Gorge on the northern face of the magnificent Karijini (Hamersley Range) National Park. The town lies 289 km from Roebourne, 300 km from Port Hedland, 240 km from Newman and 130 km from Tom Price. Wittenoom was established in 1947 as a service centre for the workers of the blue asbestos mining industry, but world demand had declined by 1966 and mining ceased. **In the area:** Karijini (Hamersley Range) National Park, surrounding and south of town; renowned for its spectacular gorges. Mt Meharray (1245 m), WA's highest peak, is just inside eastern boundary of park. Wittenoom Gorge extends southward; 12-km scenic drive. Yampire Gorge, 52 km SE, used as watering-spot by camel drivers; turnoff 24 km E gives access to other gorges. Dales Gorge, 60 km SE; permanent waterfalls, Fortescue Falls and Fern Pool. Kalamina Gorge and pool, 35 km W of Dales Gorge; the most accessible gorge in the National Park. Joffre, Hancock, Weano and Red Gorges, joining below Oxer Lookout, begin 97 km W of Wittenoom; 30–45 m deep at junction; Weano Gorge, section 1 m wide and 30 m deep, the most accessible of this group. Oxer Lookout has breathtaking view. Hamersley Gorge, 53 km W; permanent pools for swimming, coloured folds in rock. Warning: Although the asbestos mine at Wittenoom was closed in 1966, there is still a significant health risk from microscopic asbestos fibres created by the milling process; these fibres are present in tailing dumps near the Wittenoom mine site and in landfill used in and around the town site. While the risk from airborne asbestos fibres to short-term visitors in the town is considered to be significantly low, **warning is given that inhaling asbestos fibres may cause cancer.** Any activity that disturbs asbestos tailings and generates airborne fibres should be avoided. Visitors travelling through Wittenoom are advised to take the following precautions:

- Keep to main roads in the town and gorge areas.
- When driving in windy or dusty conditions, keep car windows closed.
- Avoid parking on or adjacent to asbestos tailings.
- Prevent children playing in asbestos tailings in the town or at mine site.
- Camp only in designated camping areas. Camping is not allowed in the Wittenoom Gorge.

Tourist information: Wittenoom Souvenir and Tourist Shop, Sixth Ave; (091) 89 7096. **Accommodation:** 1 hotel, 1 caravan/camping park.
MAP REF. 355 I3, 358 C4

Wyndham   Pop. 860

Wyndham is the most northerly town and safe port harbour in WA. The town consists of two main areas: the original town site of Wyndham port, situated on Cambridge Gulf, and Wyndham East (or 'Three Mile', as it is known), on the Great Northern Hwy, the residential and shopping area. In October 1985 the meatworks, representing Wyndham's main industry, closed. Today Wyndham is a service town for the pastoral industry, mining exploration, tourism and nearby Aboriginal communities. Port now handles live cattle shipment to Indonesia. **Of interest:** Historic buildings in main street (Great Northern Hwy) include Port Post Office (now tourist information centre), Durack's Store, courthouse and Anthon's Landing. Warriu Park Aboriginal Monument; in town centre. Port display next to Marine and Harbours Offices, near wharf. Crocodile-spotting from the wharf. Crocodile Farm, Priority Rd, Wyndham Port; daily feeding. Annual Top of the West Festival held Aug. **In the area:** Afghan cemetery, 1 km E. Abundant birdlife at Marlgu Billabong, 11 km E. The Grotto, rock-edged waterhole, at base of volcanic hole estimated to be 100 m deep, 36 km E (2 km off road), is a cool, shaded oasis with safe year-round swimming. Huge boab tree, 1500–2000 yrs old, in Three Mile Caravan Park. The 100-km sealed road to Kununurra passes through splendid gorge country. To south-east, Aboriginal rock paintings (18 km), and prison tree estimated to be 2000–4000 years old (22 km). Five Rivers Lookout, 2 km N, atop Bastion Range, offers spectacular views of Kimberley landscape, mountain ranges, Cambridge Gulf, Wyndham port and rivers. Alligator Airways resort on Drysdale River, 80 km NW. El Questro Station, 100 km SW; this vast cattle station offers accommodation and touring options; details from the tourist office. **Tourist information:** Old Post Office building, O'Donnell St, Wyndham Port; (091) 61 1054. **Accommodation:** 1 hotel, 1 hotel/motel, 1 caravan/camping park. **See also:** The Kimberley.
MAP REF. 353 O1, 361 Q4, 392 A12, 394 A2

Yalgoo   Pop. 80

Yalgoo lies 216 km E of Geraldton along an excellent road in real Australian outback country. Alluvial gold was discovered in the 1890s. Small traces of gold are still found in the district, which encourages fossicking by locals and visitors. **Of interest:** Courthouse Museum, Gibbons St. Restored Dominican Convent Chapel, Henty St. **In the area:** Joker's Tunnel, 10 km S on Paynes Find Rd, carved through solid rock by early prospectors and named after Joker mining syndicate. Golden Grove zinc mine, 300 employees, 50 km S; open for inspection, check details at tourist information. Area harbours abundant native wildlife and there are prolific wildflowers in season (July–Sept.). Station holidays at Yuin Station, Yalgoo, Thundelara Station, 80 km SE, and Barnong Station, 54 km SW. **Tourist information:** Shire Offices; (099) 62 8042. **Accommodation:** 1 motel, 2 caravan parks.
MAP REF. 354 F1, 356 A2

Yallingup   Pop. 150

Yallingup is known for its excellent surf, with the Australian Surf Championships held in the area. Its caves were a well-known attraction before the turn of the century. **Of interest:** Caves House Hotel, off Caves Rd, built by government as holiday hotel in 1903. Early visitors arrived from Busselton via horse and buggy along dirt road, a journey of 2½

hours. Hotel was rebuilt in 1938 after a fire, using locally milled timber; now has award-winning accommodation and restaurant. **In the area:** Yallingup Caves, 2 km E; open daily. Gunyulgup Gallery, 2 km S. At Rivendell Gardens, 10 km SE, Devonshire teas and pick-your-own strawberries in season. Canal Rocks and Smith's Beach, with good fishing, surfing and swimming, as well as spectacular scenery, 5 km SW. Only a short drive to top-class wineries of Metricup district (20 km S) and Margaret River area (40 km S). Wineries near to Yallingup include: Hunts Foxhaven Estate (3 km S), open by appointment; Wildwood (5 km S); Cape Clairault Wines (10 km S); Happ's Vineyard and Pottery (8 km SE); and Moonshine Brewery and Abbey Vale Vineyards (11 km SE). Goanna Galley and Bush Cottage Market, 8 km SE; local art and craft. Shearing Shed, Wildwood Rd, 10 km SE; shearing demonstrations and woolshop; check opening times. **Tourist information:** Civic Centre, Southern Dr, Busselton; (097) 52 1091. **Accommodation:** 1 hotel/motel, 1 motel, 3 caravan/camping parks. **See also:** The South-west.
MAP REF. 354 C10

Yanchep   Pop. 1577

Within easy driving distance from Perth is the resort of Yanchep, 51 km to the north. **In the area:** Yanchep National Park , 15 km E, covering 2799 ha of natural bushland. In park, Gloucester Lodge Museum; startling limestone formations in Crystal Cave (open to public) and launch cruises on freshwater Loch McNess (Sun.). Marina at Two Rocks, 6 km NW. Wild Kingdom wildlife park and zoo, 3 km NE, halfway between Yanchep and Two Rocks. Wreck of *Alkimos,* south of Yanchep, is said to be guarded by a ghost. Gnangara Lake, 30 km SE; picturesque location with picnic facilities. **Tourist information:** Information Office, Yanchep National Park; (09) 561 1004 and 935 Wanneroo Rd, Wanneroo; (09) 405 4678. **Accommodation:** 1 hotel/motel.
MAP REF. 346 C2, 354 D7

York   Pop. 1562

Founded in 1830, York is the oldest inland town in WA, set on the banks of the Avon River in the fertile Avon Valley. The town has a wealth of historic buildings, carefully preserved. Many festivals and events held annually, including the York Jazz Festival Sept–Oct. **Of interest:** Post Office, courthouse and police station, all in Avon Tce, were built of local stone in 1895. Restored two-storey mud-brick building, Settlers' House (1850), also in Avon Tce, offers old-world accommodation. Castle Hotel, fine example of early coaching inn and York's first licensed hotel, and Romanesque-style Town Hall (1911), with impressive dimensions, both in Avon Tce. Old railway station (1886), Railway Rd, now houses railway museum. Old hospital (now offers group accommodation), Brook St, has its original shingle roof. Residency Museum (1843), Brook St; colonial furniture and early photographs. York's fine churches include Holy Trinity (consecrated 1858), Suburban Rd; St Patrick's (1886), South St; and Uniting Church (1888), Grey St. All in Avon Tce: Art Gallery, York Pottery and Loder Antiques. Also in Avon Tce: Motor Museum, Australia's best collection of veteran, classic and racing cars (and some bicycles and motorcycles); and Balladong Farm, offering visitors the chance to handfeed many friendly animals. De Ladera Alpaca Farm, North Rd; alpacas and other animals, picnic/barbecue facilities. Suspension Bridge across river in Low St, erected originally in 1906. Follow signs from Castle Hotel to Pioneer Drive and then to Mt Brown; lookout. Facilities also at Avon Park, Low St, and Railway Park, Railway Rd. **In the area:** Near Quairading, 64 km E, Toapin Weir and Mt Stirling, offering panoramic views. Self-guide leaflet outlines the Quairading District Heritage Trail. York, York to Goldfields, Guildford to York and Farming Heritage Trails; details from tourist centre. **Tourist information:** 105 Avon Tce; (096) 41 1301. **Accommodation:** 3 hotels, 2 motels, 1 caravan/camping park.
MAP REF. 346 H4, 354 F7, 356 A8

Old hospital, now a hostel, York

Western Australia

Location Map

Other Map Coverage

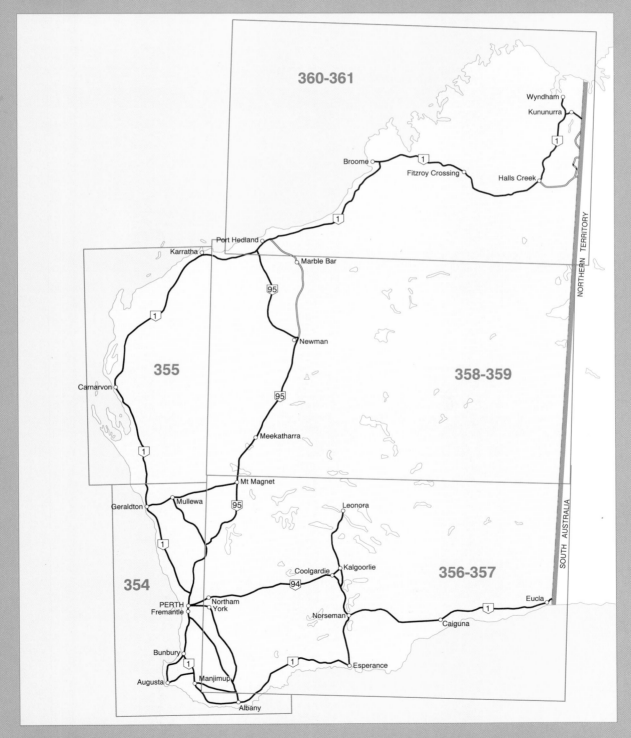

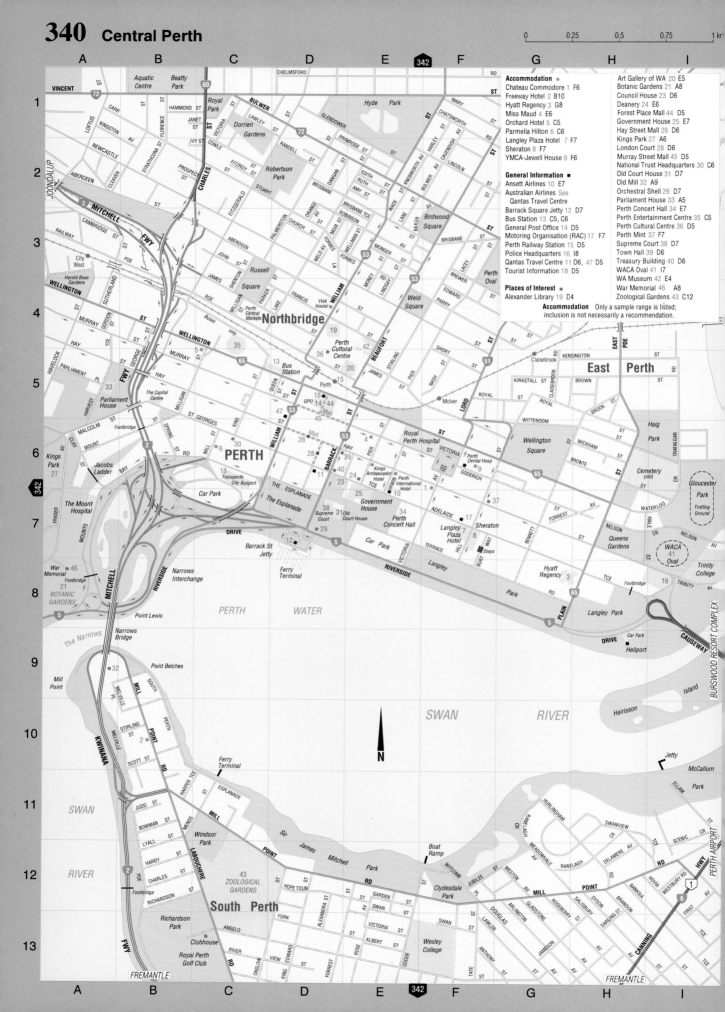

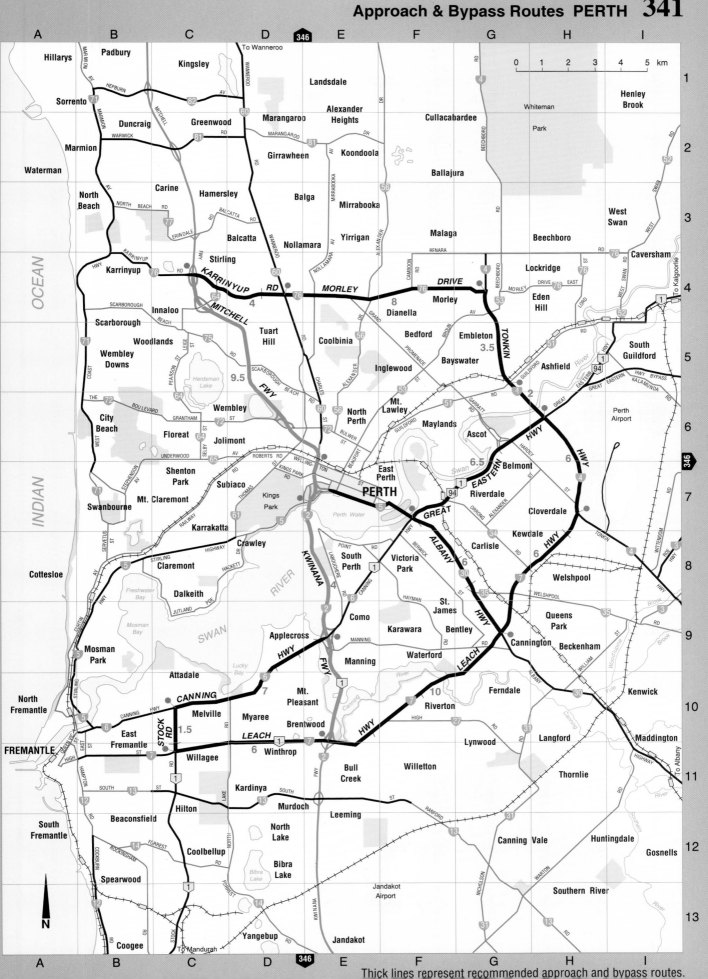

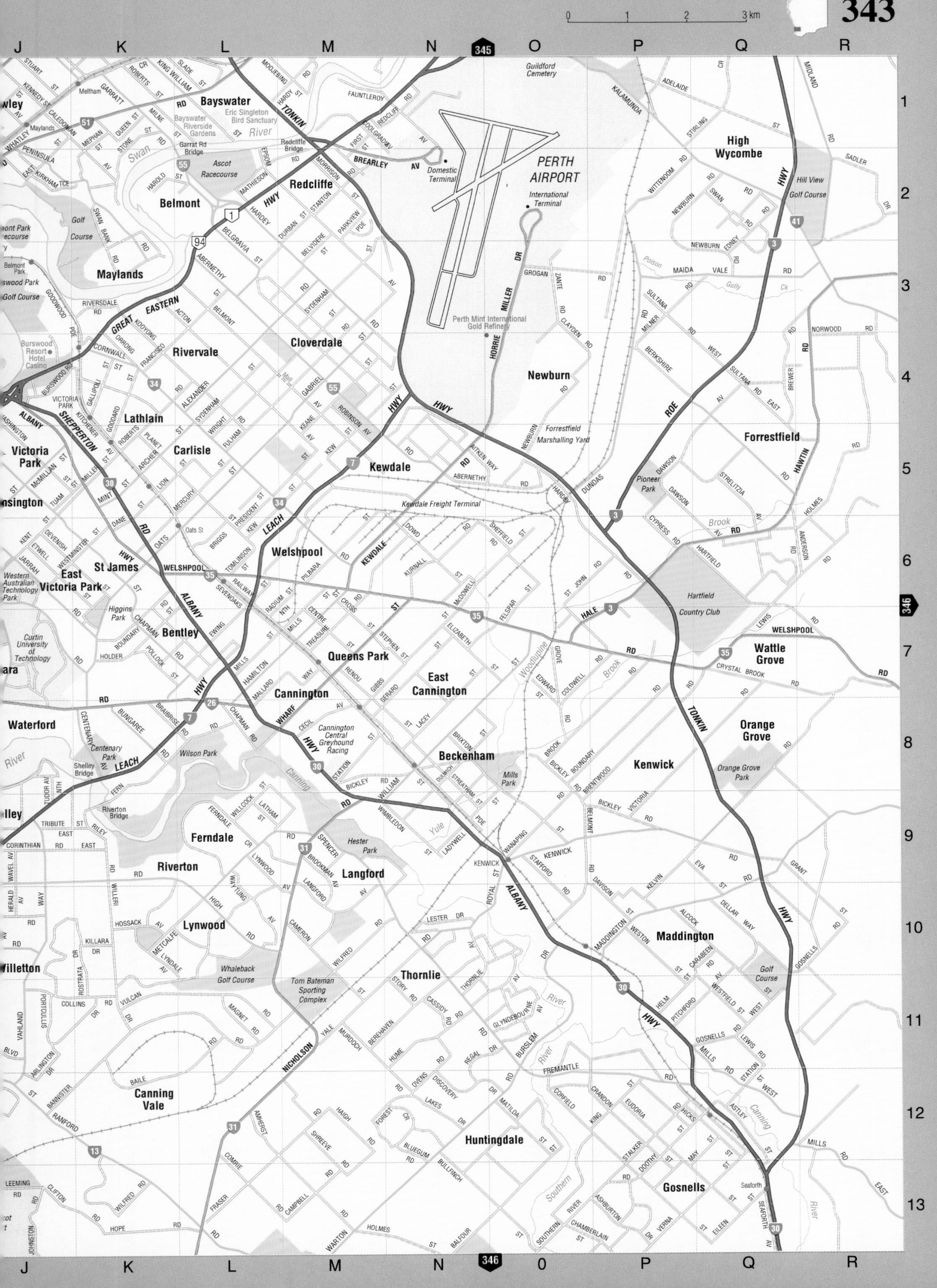

0 1 2 3 km

J K L M N O P Q R

PERTH AIRPORT

Domestic Terminal
International Terminal

Guildford Cemetery

Bayswater
Eric Singleton Bird Sanctuary
Bayswater Riverside Gardens
Redcliffe Bridge
Garrat Rd Bridge

Ascot Racecourse

Belmont
Redcliffe
Maylands

High Wycombe
Hill View Golf Course

Belmont Park
Swan River
Golf Course

Burswood Resort Hotel Casino

GREAT EASTERN HWY

Rivervale
Cloverdale
Newburn

Perth Mint International Gold Refinery

Forrestfield Marshalling Yard

Victoria Park
Lathlain
Carlisle

Kewdale

ROE HWY

Forrestfield

East Victoria Park
St James

Kewdale Freight Terminal

Welshpool
Kewdale

Pioneer Park

Hartfield Country Club

Welshpool

Curtin University of Technology
Western Australian Technology Park

Bentley

Queens Park

East Cannington

Hale

Wattle Grove

Cannington

Beckenham

Mills Park

Kenwick

Orange Grove
Orange Grove Park

Waterford

Cannington Central Greyhound Racing

Centenary Park
Shelley Bridge
Wilson Park

LEACH

Riverton Bridge

Ferndale

Riverton

Hester Park

Langford

Kenwick

ALBANY HWY

Maddington
Golf Course

Lynwood

Willetton

Whaleback Golf Course

Tom Bateman Sporting Complex

Thornlie

TONKIN HWY

Canning Vale

Huntingdale

Gosnells

J K L M N O P Q R

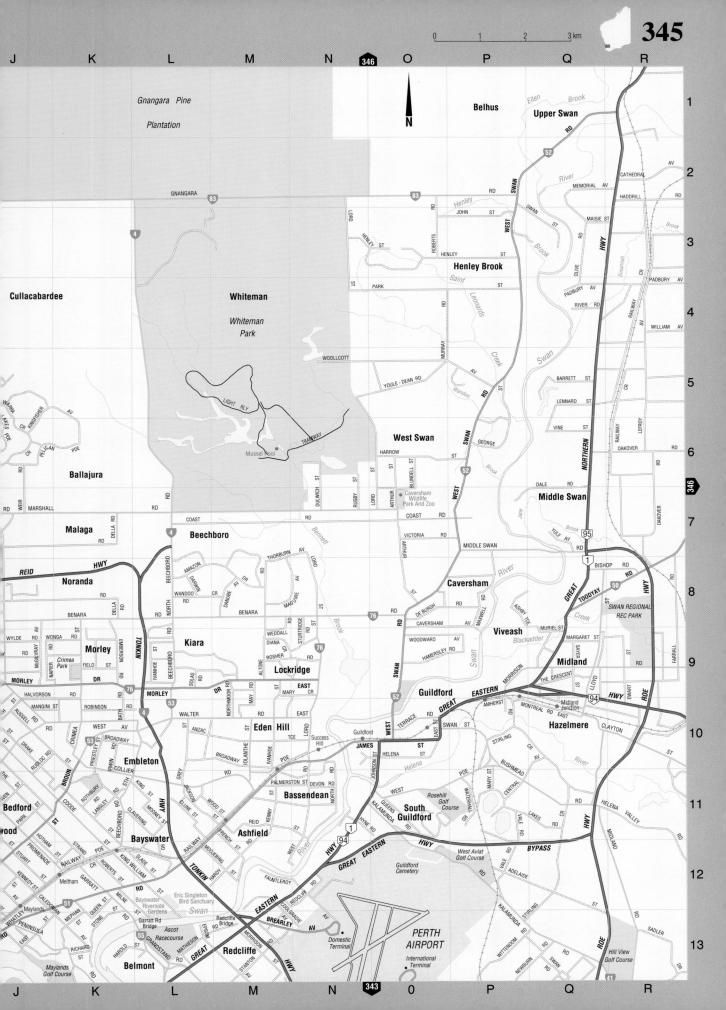

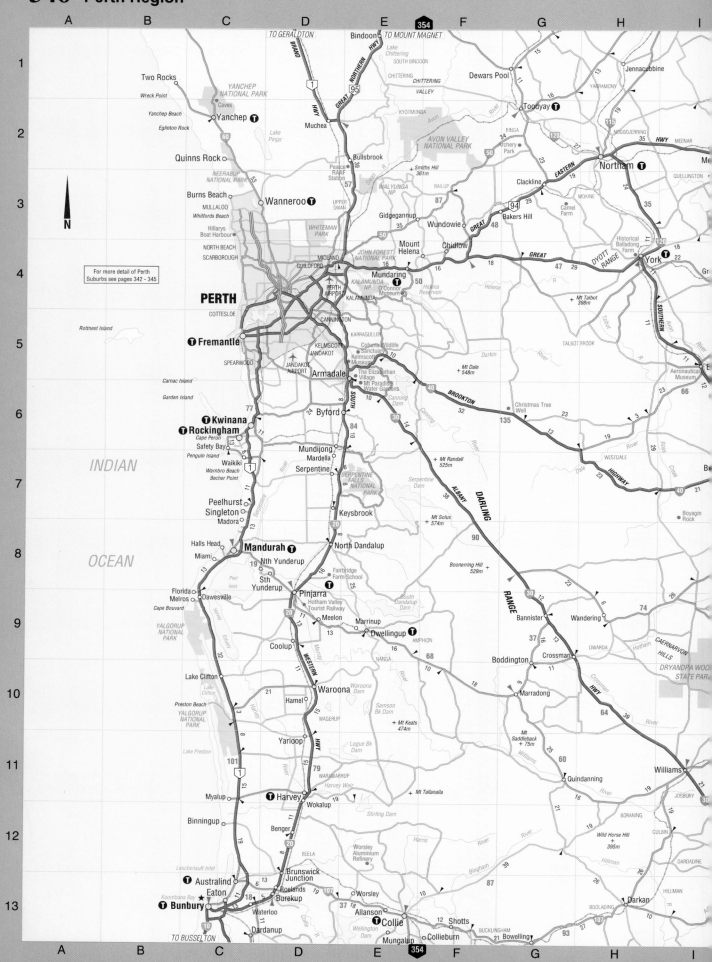

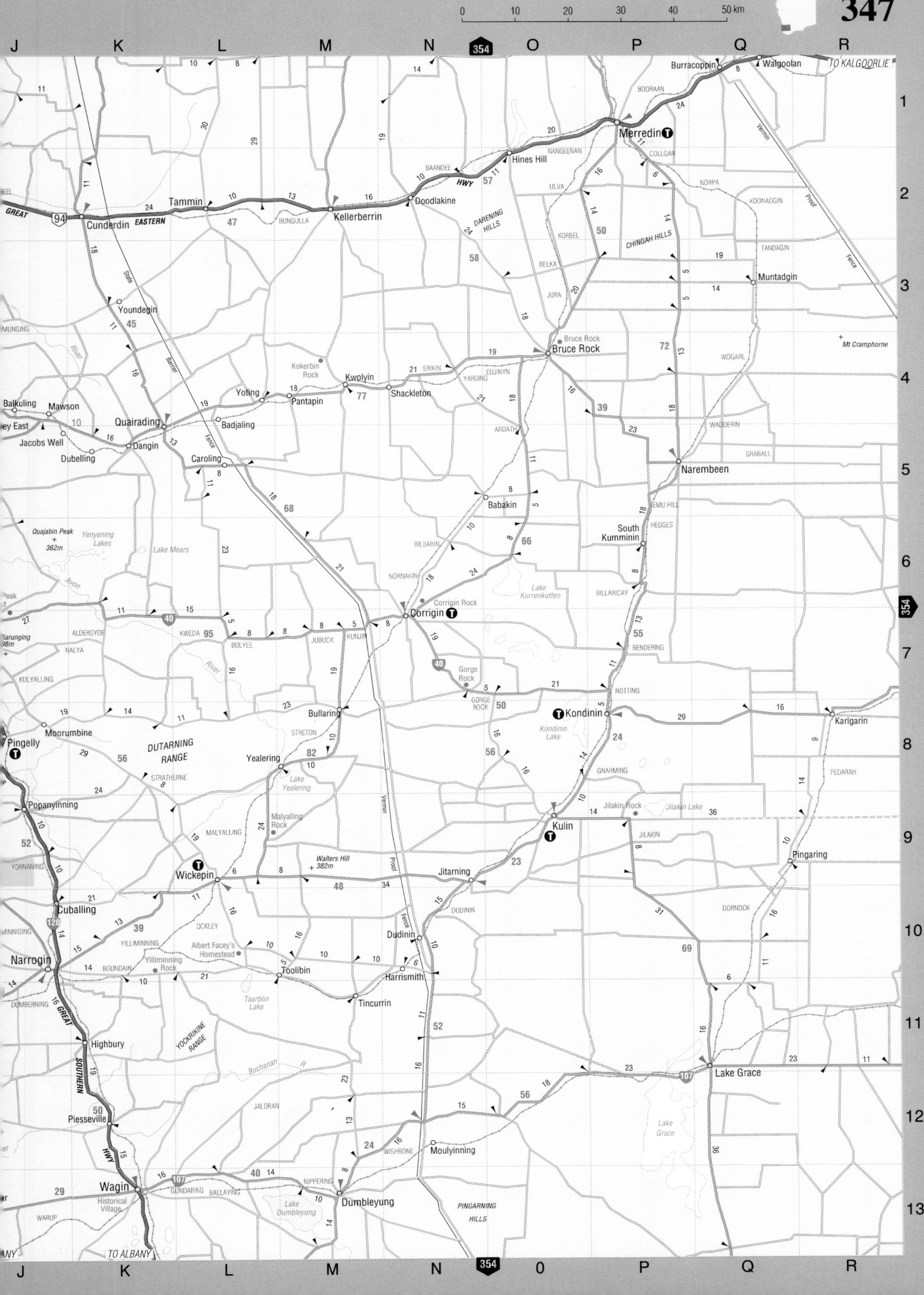

0 10 20 30 40 50 km

TO KALGOORLIE

Burracoppin Walgoolan
Merredin
Hines Hill
Tammin Doodlakine
Cunderdin Kellerberrin
GREAT EASTERN HWY
Bungulla
Youndegin
Muntadgin
CHINGAH HILLS
Mt Cramphorne
Balkuling Mawson
Quairading Yoting Pantapin Kwolyin Shackleton Bruce Rock
Jacobs Well Badjaling
Dubelling Dangin
Caroling
Narembeen
Quajabin Peak + 362m
Yenyening Lakes
Lake Mears
Babakin
South Kumminin
HEDGES
Lake Kurrenkutten
Bilbarin
Nornakin
Corrigin Rock
KWEDA Corrigin BENDERING
BULYEE JUBUCK KUNJIN
Gorge Rock
GORGE ROCK
Pingelly Moorumbine
Bullaring NOTTING Kondinin Karlgarin
STRETON
DUTARNING RANGE Yealering Kondinin Lake
Lake Yealering PEDARAH
Popanyinning
MALYALLING Jilakin Rock Jilakin Lake
Malyalling Rock JILAKIN
YOGNANING Kulin Pingaring
Wickepin Walters Hill + 382m Jitarning
Cuballing DUDININ DORNOCK
OCKLEY
YILLIMINNING Dudinin
Narrogin Albert Facey's Homestead Toolibin Harrismith
Yilliminning Rock Lake Grace
BOUNDAIN Taarblin Lake Tincurrin
Highbury YOCKRIKINE RANGE
Buchanan R
JALORAN
Piesseville WISHBONE Moulyinning Lake Grace
Wagin NIPPERING Dumbleyung
Historical Villages GUNDARING BALLAYING Lake Dumbleyung PINGARNING HILLS
WARUP
TO ALBANY

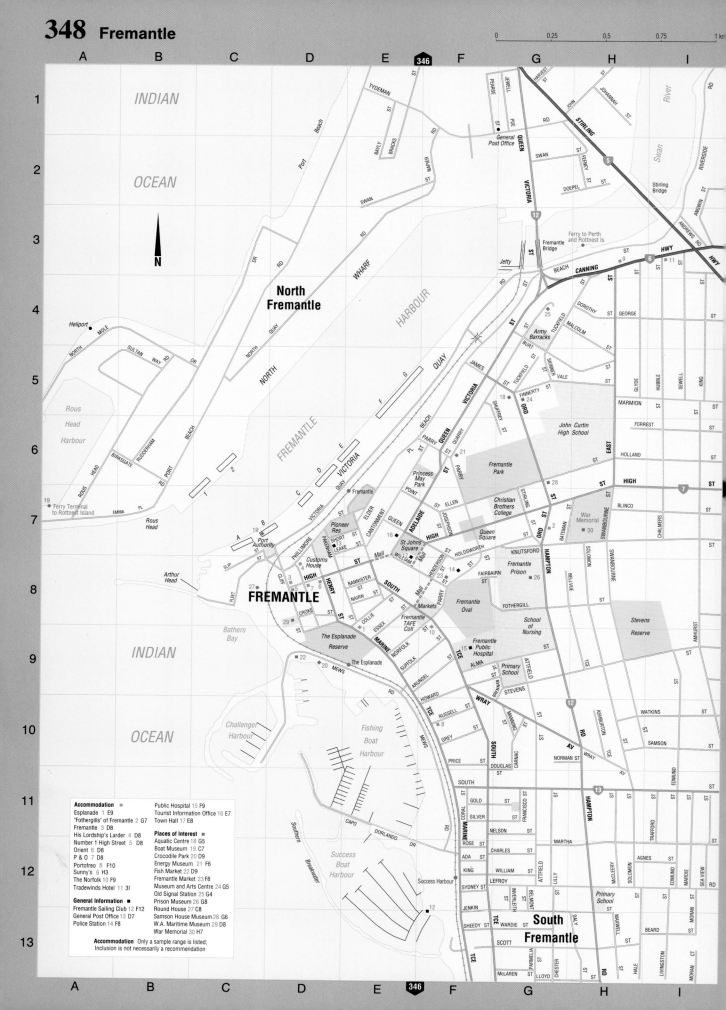

348 Fremantle

Accommodation ■
Esplanade 1 E9
"Fothergills' of Fremantle 2 G7
Fremantle 3 D8
His Lordship's Larder 4 D8
Number 1 High Street 5 D8
Orient 6 D8
P & O 7 D8
Portofreo 8 F10
Sunny's 9 H3
The Norfolk 10 F9
Tradewinds Hotel 11 3I

General Information ■
Fremantle Sailing Club 12 F12
General Post Office 13 D7
Police Station 14 F8

Public Hospital 15 F9
Tourist Information Office 16 E7
Town Hall 17 E8

Places of Interest ■
Aquatic Centre 18 G5
Boat Museum 19 C7
Crocodile Park 20 D9
Energy Museum 21 F6
Fish Market 22 D9
Fremantle Market 23 F8
Museum and Arts Centre 24 G5
Old Signal Station 25 G4
Prison Museum 26 G8
Round House 27 C8
Samson House Museum 28 G6
W.A. Maritime Museum 29 D8
War Memorial 30 H7

Accommodation Only a sample range is listed;
Inclusion is not necessarily a recommendation

0   5   10   15   20km

A   B   C   D   E   F   G   H   I

354
TO BUNBURY

WINERIES: 1
Amberley Estate C3 7
Ashbrook Estate C5 23
Brookland Valley Vineyard C5 15
Cape Clairault Wines C4 8
Cape Mentelle C7 26
Chateau Xanadu C7 27
Cullens Willyabrup Wines C5 21
Eagle Bay Estate C2 1
Evans and Tate C5 16
Fermoy Estate C5 10
Freycinet Estate C8 30
Gralyn C5 20
Green Valley Vineyard C9 33
Happ's Vineyard C3 3
Hay Shed Hill Winery C5 26
Hunts Foxhaven Estate B3 2
Leeuwin Estate C8 32
Lenton Brae C5 12
Moonshine Brewery C3 6
Moss Brothers C4 13
Mosswood C5 11
Pierro C5 18
Redgate C8 31
Ribbon Vale Estate C5 19
Rivendell Vineyard C3 5
Rosa Brook Estate C5 19
Sandalford Wines C5 17
The Berry Farm E8 29
Treeton Estate D5 27
Vasse Felix C5 22
Wildwood C3 4
Willespie C5 24
Woodlands C5 14
Woody Nook C5 9
Wrights C5 25

Cape Naturaliste

Bunker Bay
Rocky Point
Sugarloaf Rock
MEELUP
Eagle Bay
Eagle Bay
Point Piquet
Gannet Rock
Sail Rock
Castle Point
Castle Rock
Hutchings Antique Museum
Bird Rock
Bannamah Wildlife Park
Greenacres Shell Museum
Dunsborough
Dunsborough Beach
Dunn Bay

GEOGRAPHE BAY

Peppermint Grove Beach

TUART FOREST NATIONAL PARK

Capel

BUSSELL
25

FISHING: The length of the coast, together with the many rivers and estuaries make the region an angler's paradise. Many of the rivers and streams are stocked annually with trout.

WONNERUP
Wonnerup Beach
Old Railway Jetty
Nautical Lady Entertainment Centre
St Mary's Church
Busselton
Oceanarium
Old Butter Factory Museum
Ballarat Engine

LUDLOW
Wonnerup Estuary
Wonnerup House
LUDLOW FOREST
RUABON
TUTUNUP

TUART FOREST NATIONAL PARK: The park is home to a variety of animals, including the Western Ringtail Possum, an endangered species. The park also protects the state's largest remaining area of Tuart Forest. Tuart, a species of hardwood, only grows on coastal limestone, and hence is unique to the limestone coast of south-western Western Australia.

Yallingup
Yallingup Cave
Gunyulgup Galleries
Canal Rocks
Cape Clairault

CAVES RD

Toby Inlet
Molloy Ditch
The Broadwater
VASSE

MARYBROOK
Carbunup River
BUSSELL HWY
NORTH JINDONG
JINDONG
KALOORUP
YELVERTON
METRICUP

BUSSELTON: One of the oldest established areas in Western Australia, Busselton, today, is a pleasant seaside town at the centre of a large rural district. The festival of Busselton, held in January, draws large crowds.

Four Mile Hill
YOONGARILLUP
The Whistle Stop Station
WALSALL
ACTON PARK
BOALLIA
CHAPMAN HILL
Chapman Hill

VASSE
HIGHWAY
TO NANNUP

WHICHER RANGE

LEEUWIN-NATURALISTE NATIONAL PARK

INDIAN OCEAN

Cowaramup Point
Gracetown

Cowaramup

TREETON

THE RAPIDS CONSERVATION PARK

AUGUSTA-BUSSELTON HERITAGE TRAIL: This trail, which runs from Augusta to Vasse, basically retraces the original track, which, in the 1830s, linked these two towns.

OSMINGTON

BRAMLEY
KILCARNUP
Cape Mentelle
Rotary Park
Margaret River
Eagles Heritage
Prevelly

MOWEN
Mt Yates
ROSA GLEN
Bellview Shell Museum
Margaret River Marron Farm
Pioneer Settlers Memorial
The Berry Farm

TOURIST INFORMATION:
Busselton (Civic Centre Complex, Southern Drive)
Dunsborough (Naturaliste Tce)
Margaret River (Cnr Tunbridge Rd and Bussell Hwy)
Augusta (Blackwood Ave)

Witchcliffe
Mammoth Cave
BOBS HOLLOW
Lake Cave
Cape Freycinet

Boranup Galleries

LEEUWIN-NATURALISTE NATIONAL PARK

FOREST GROVE
Warner Glen Bridge
Canoe Hire
WARNER GLEN
ALEXANDRA BRIDGE

BLACKWOOD CONSERVATION PARK
Sues Bridge

HIGHWAY BROCKMAN

CAVES RD
Boranup Hill
BORANUP
Boranup Beach
North Point
Boranup Lookout
Boranup Maze

LEEUWIN-NATURALISTE NATIONAL PARK: This narrow strip of protected coastline combines a scenic coast with magnificent wildflowers and the tall timbers of Karri and Jarrah Forests.

BROCKMAN HIGHWAY

STEWART RD

Karridale
East Hill
Hamelin Bay
Hamelin Island
Foul Bay
Cape Hamelin

KUDARDUP

Molloy Island River Cruises
SCOTT NATIONAL PARK

CAVES: There are over 350 caves in this region, lying along the Leeuwin-Naturaliste ridge; only some of the caves are open to the public. They include Mammoth Cave, Jewel Cave, Lake Cave and Yallingup Cave - all of which have guided tours daily in summer. Moondyne Cave is an "adventure cave" open to the public; tour guide provided.

CAVES RD
Moondyne Cave
Jewel Cave
Hillview Lookout & Golf Course

BUSSELL HWY

LEEUWIN-NATURALISTE NATIONAL PARK

Green Hill
Augusta
Historical Museum
The Landing Place
Flinders Bay

SURFING: The sheltered bays and excellent beaches that dot the coastline of the Yallingup-Margaret River region offer ideal surfing conditions.

CAPE LEEUWIN: From the cape it is possible to see the sun rising over one ocean and setting over another.

Old Waterwheel
Whale Rescue Memorial
Matthew Flinders Memorial
Seal Island

Cape Leeuwin

SOUTHERN OCEAN

D'ENTRECASTEAUX NATIONAL PARK
Gingilup Swamps
Lake Quitjup

N

354

TO BUNBURY

Capel River

NEWLANDS

Kirup

Grimwade

Wilga

Balgarup River

Mullalyup

SOUTH

Balingup

The Old Cheese Factory

WESTERN

Gregory Tree

Dinninup

Kulikup

Muradup

Jarrahwood

TO BUSSELTON

104

Blackwood River

Greenbushes

28

Boyup Brook

Country Music Centre

Whinston Hills

41

BRIDGETOWN: A quiet spot set in undulating country in the south-west corner of the state. Here the Blackwood River, well stocked with marron and trout, curves through some of the prettiest country in the state. Bridgetown was first settled in 1857 and the first apple trees were planted soon after.

Bridgetown

Blackwood River

Mayanup

71

River

NATIONAL PARKS IN WESTERN AUSTRALIA:
The following guidelines will help ensure that your visits to the state's national parks are both safe and enjoyable:
   a) Remember that open fires are hazardous, only use the barbeques provided or portable stoves.
   b) When driving in the park, always stick to approved tracks which are clearly marked.
   c) Domestic animals and firearms are not permitted in parks as all native plants and wildlife are protected.

Nannup

23

46

23

VASSE

37

HWY

42

Henry Hill+

Tweed River

Tone River

Boywerup Rock

51

TO AUGUSTA

10

92

76

MANJIMUP: This is the commercial centre of the south-west corner of WA, and the state's largest apple-growing area. Dairying, beef, sheep and vegetable farming are other pastoral activities. The wood chip mill represents a flourishing industry contributing to the town's more recent growth.

27

37

47

River

103

The Four Aces

One Tree Bridge

Palgarup

10

Pioneer Cairn

Pioneer Cemetery

Yerriminup River

Perup River

28

River

Deanmill

Manjimup

Wilgarup River

6

36

354

River

5

Jardee

Fontys Pool

15

10

Nyamup

102

Quabicup Hill+

59

Unicup Lake

Kutunilup Lake

PEMBERTON: The town of Pemberton is nestled in a quiet valley, surrounded by towering Karri forests. This lush forest area has some of the tallest hardwood trees in the world, and, in spring, brilliant flowering bush plants.

Diamond Tree Tower

Bunnings Diamond Mill

100 Year Old Forest

Big Brook Dam

BEEDELUP NP

Beedelup Falls

River

MUIRS

94

94

HWY

Tone

Lake Jasper

Donnelly

16

Gloucester Tree

Pemberton

Cascades

35

103

Lake Muir

Byenup Lagoon

102

Rocky Gully

+ Benjerup Hill

River

WARREN NATIONAL PARK

King Trout Farm

BROCKMAN NP

Brockman Saw Plt

Marianne North Tree

Moons Crossing

Tordit Gurrup Lagoon

Yeagarup Lake

Big Brook Arboretum

31

PEMBERTON

SOUTH

SHANNON

1

WESTERN

Mt Rae+

Warren River

TRAMWAY

27

10

Northcliffe

Muirillup Rock

SHANNON NATIONAL PARK

Chitelup Hill

+ Callcup Hill

D'ENTRECASTEAUX

Meerup

River

Boorara Tree (or Firetower)

Lane Poole Falls

Mt Johnson 285m+

+ Granite Peak 402m

MOUNT FRANKLAND

Lymburner Falls

Warren Beach

NATIONAL PARK

Creek

Doggerup

27

River

Shannon River

Gardner River

Lake Maringup

BEADMORE RIDGE

Mt Mitchell +

NATIONAL PARK

+ Mt Frankland 411m

ALBANY REGION: Also known as the Rainbow Coast, this area is bounded by a dramatically rugged coastline and the roaring Southern Ocean. During the winter months spectacular rainbows regularly occur. The coast gives way to an amazingly beautiful hinterland with rivers winding through forests, ancient mountain ranges and gentle valleys.

Point D'Entrecasteaux

Flat Is

Ledge Is

Sandy Is

Farnhook Falls

68

Deep River

Gladstone Falls

Broke Inlet

Circular Pool

Mt Romance Em

BUSHWALKING: Most of the national parks in the region have established walking trails. It is advisable to:
   Always carry drinking water.
   Be prepared for sudden changes in weather.
   Wear long pants, long sleeved shirt and sturdy shoes as the bush can be very prickly.

Walpole

VALLEY OF THE GIANTS

66

1

Nornalup

WALPOLE-NORNALUP NATIONAL PARK

Tingle Tree

SOUTH

COAST

Irwin Inlet

Cliffy Head

Chatham Is

Mandalay Beach

Long Point

Mt Hopkins+

Nornalup Inlet

Saddle Is

Rocky Head

Rame Head

Foul Bay

Point Nuyts

Casuarina Isles

Goose Is

Point Irwin

SOUTHERN   OCEAN

WALPOLE: Walpole is literally where the forest mee... Surrounded by the Walpole - Nornalup National P... a variety of trees, including Karri, Jarrah and the Ting... unique to the area, all grow. The area is known for its ... in season as well as its wildlife.

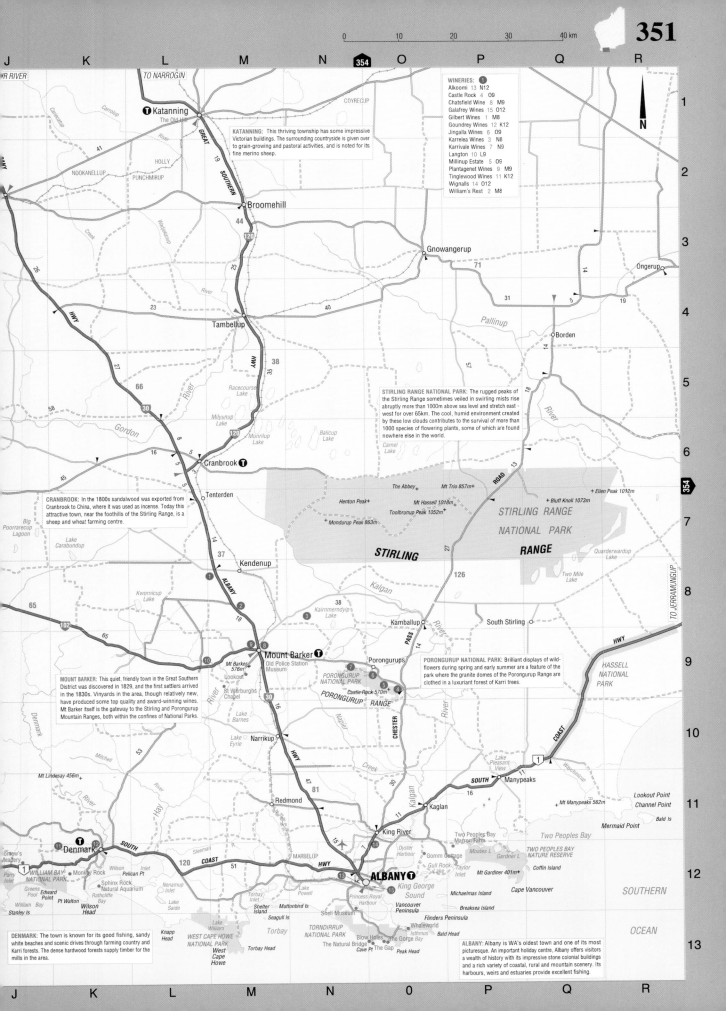

WINERIES:
Alkoomi 13 N12
Castle Rock 4 O9
Chatsfield Wine 8 M9
Galafrey Wines 15 O12
Gilbert Wines 1 M8
Goundrey Wines 12 K12
Jingalla Wines 6 O9
Karrelea Wines 3 N8
Karrivale Wines 7 N9
Langton 10 L9
Millinup Estate 5 O9
Plantagenet Wines 9 M9
Tinglewood Wines 11 K12
Wignalls 14 O12
William's Rest 2 M8

KATANNING: This thriving township has some impressive Victorian buildings. The surrounding countryside is given over to grain-growing and pastoral activities, and is noted for its fine merino sheep.

STIRLING RANGE NATIONAL PARK: The rugged peaks of the Stirling Range sometimes veiled in swirling mists rise abruptly more than 1000m above sea level and stretch east - west for over 65km. The cool, humid environment created by these low clouds contributes to the survival of more than 1000 species of flowering plants, some of which are found nowhere else in the world.

CRANBROOK: In the 1800s sandalwood was exported from Cranbrook to China, where it was used as incense. Today this attractive town, near the foothills of the Stirling Range, is a sheep and wheat farming centre.

PORONGURUP NATIONAL PARK: Brilliant displays of wildflowers during spring and early summer are a feature of the park where the granite domes of the Porongurup Range are clothed in a luxuriant forest of Karri trees.

MOUNT BARKER: This quiet, friendly town in the Great Southern District was discovered in 1829, and the first settlers arrived in the 1830s. Vinyards in the area, though relatively new, have produced some top quality and award-winning wines. Mt Barker itself is the gateway to the Stirling and Porongup Mountain Ranges, both within the confines of National Parks.

DENMARK: The town is known for its good fishing, sandy white beaches and scenic drives through farming country and Karri forests. The dense hardwood forests supply timber for the mills in the area.

ALBANY: Albany is WA's oldest town and one of its most picturesque. An important holiday centre, Albany offers visitors a wealth of history with its impressive stone colonial buildings and a rich variety of coastal, rural and mountain scenery. Its harbours, weirs and estuaries provide excellent fishing.

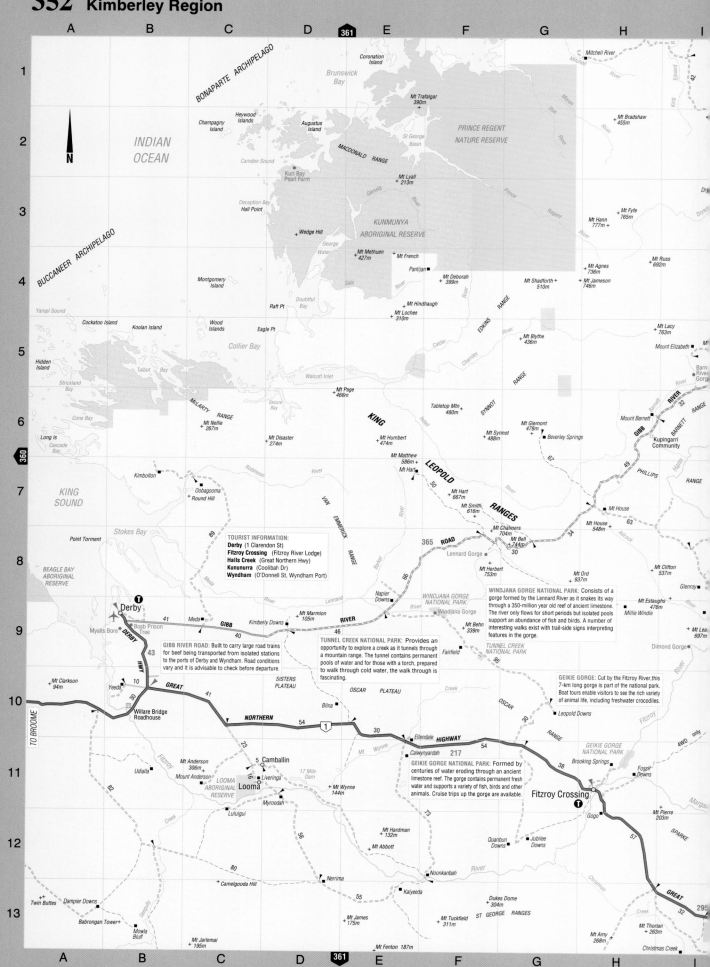

TOURIST INFORMATION:
Derby (1 Clarendon St)
Fitzroy Crossing (Fitzroy River Lodge)
Halls Creek (Great Northern Hwy)
Kununurra (Coolibah Dr)
Wyndham (O'Donnell St, Wyndham Port)

GIBB RIVER ROAD: Built to carry large road trains for beef being transported from isolated stations to the ports of Derby and Wyndham. Road conditions vary and it is advisable to check before departure.

TUNNEL CREEK NATIONAL PARK: Provides an opportunity to explore a creek as it tunnels through a mountain range. The tunnel contains permanent pools of water and for those with a torch, prepared to walk through cold water, the walk through is fascinating.

WINDJANA GORGE NATIONAL PARK: Consists of a gorge formed by the Lennard River as it snakes its way through a 350-million year old reef of ancient limestone. The river only flows for short periods but isolated pools support an abundance of fish and birds. A number of interesting walks exist with trail-side signs interpreting features in the gorge.

GEIKIE GORGE: Cut by the Fitzroy River, this 7-km long gorge is part of the national park. Boat tours enable visitors to see the rich variety of animal life, including freshwater crocodiles.

GEIKIE GORGE NATIONAL PARK: Formed by centuries of water eroding through an ancient limestone reef. The gorge contains permanent fresh water and supports a variety of fish, birds and other animals. Cruise trips up the gorge are available.

20 40 60 80 km

J K L M N 361 O P Q R

1

DRYSDALE RIVER
NATIONAL PARK

Forrest

River

River

OOMBULGURRI
ABORIGINAL RESERVE

Kneebone

Banjo

Drysdale

Creek

MIRIMA (HIDDEN VALLEY) NATIONAL PARK:
A rugged area of ancient sandstone hills and valleys
and of special significance to the Aboriginal people.
The park has several pleasant walking trails along the
valley and ridges which offer spectacular views of both
the park and Kununurra.

DNER **PLATEAU**

Carson

Durack

Creek

2

MAITLAND RANGE

BOAB: A symbol of the region, the
boab, sometimes called the 'bottle tree',
produces furry brown nuts on which
local artists carve scenes or animals.

Wyndham

14

56

42

4wd
only

Home Valley

Mt Cockburn North
486m

COCKBURN
RANGE

69

MIRIMA
(HIDDEN VALLEY)
NATIONAL PARK

Kununurra

45

VICTORIA

Lake
Kununurra

Ord

KEEP
RIVER
NATIONAL
PARK

River

Kerr

River

Ellenbrae

Creek

165

34

41

1

101

Mt Hensman
384m

HWY

34

52

20

Newry

3

Russ

River

283

Ellenbrae

El Questro

Dunham
Pilot Dam

61

Mt Brooking
379m

Durack
Homestead

TO KATHERINE

4

Pimple Peak

Chapman

Blackfellow

Creek

DURACK

River

Durack

BLUFF

FACE

RANGE

Pentecost Downs

Salmond

Pentecost

River

56

HIGHWAY

1

Dunham River

CARR BOYD RANGE

Lake
Argyle

Rosewood

The Twins
318m

38

RD

DUNCAN

5

ARGYLE DIAMOND MINE: The world's largest
diamond mine. The pink diamonds from the mine
along with other precious gems can be purchased
at various outlets in Kununurra.

151

Glenhill

Pompeys Pillar
Iron Deposits

Mt Quirk
323m

Mt Mary

Waterloo

6

: In outback Australia, long distance separate some
avellers should familiarise themselves with prevailing
before departure, and take care to ensure their vehicle
rthy and that they carry adequate supplies of petrol,
food.

Argyle Diamond
Mine

29

Bow

Ck

Lissadell

Spring Creek

80

258

394

n Australia, rainfall during the "wet" season (Oct-March)
some roads impassable. Full information on road
should be obtained before departure.

DURACK RANGE

River

Wilson

Bow River

34

Castlereagh Hill

Texas Downs

Mt Jarrad
530m

32

OSMOND RANGE

Osmond

Mt John
526m

Creek

Mt Elder

36

Mistake Creek

7

intend diverting off public roads within Aboriginal Land
ermit is required from the relevant Aboriginal authority.

Mt Lush
778m

Turkey Creek

55

Mable Downs

VIOLET HILL
ABORIGINAL LAND

Mt Remarkable
748m

NORTHERN

Mt Panton
340m

8

Bedford Downs

72

Chamberlain

4WD
only

Mt King
950m

26

Ord

River

4WD
only

Mt Ranford

Mt Buchanan
417m

PURNULULU
(BUNGLE BUNGLE)
NATIONAL PARK

RANGE

Ord

Mt Napier
487m

WESTERN AUSTRALIA

NORTHERN TERRITORY

Tableland

Mt Wells
983m

74

163

Little

HWY

Trane

Fitzroy

NARRIE RANGE

Mt Warton
437m

Tullewa Hill

71

52

GREAT

River

DIXON

Panton

River

PURNULULU (BUNGLE BUNGLE) NATIONAL PARK:
Considered one of Australia's greatest national wonders.
The ecology of the park is very delicately balanced as the striped
rock formations have a skin of beach lichen and orange
silica which if broken, exposes the soft sandstone underneath
to erosion. The southern end of the park contains the
spectacular beehive formations and awe-inspiring gorges.
Vehicle access is limited to 4WD only.

Kirkimbie

90

9

gorge

LEOPOLD RANGES

Lansdowne

Mt Laptz

Mt Laptz
245m

4WD
only

Gold

Little

Alice Downs

Springvale

14

Panton

River

RANGE

Mt Coghlan
622m

Nicholson

River

Marella
Gorge

Nicholson

BUCHANAN HWY

10

t Frederick

Leopold

Mt Winifred

Mt Cummings

O'Donnell

Mt Amhurst
719m

22

Moola Bulla

Mt Barrett
692m

Saunders Creek

Sophie Downs

Chinas Wall

Elvire

River

Flora Valley

59

RD

80

DUNCAN

11

Mt Ball
554m

MUELLER RANGE

Mount Amhurst

Glidden

Halls Creek

16

29

Koongie Park

Mt Flora
458m

Flora Valley

173

30

Turner

Stun

Mt Wittenoom
428m

12

Mt Huxley
537m

Mt Fairbairn
338m

Phillip

Margaret

River

Lamboo

34

40

River

Canning

55

Stock

Route

Heritage

Trail

DENISON PLAINS

47

13

Margaret River

11

Louisa Downs

1

Mt Ramsay
421m

Ruby Plains

Wolfe

Mary

Creek

Gordon
Downs

GARDNER RANGE

Mt Dockrell
542m

98 HIGHWAY

CANNING STOCK ROUTE: Once the longest
and loneliest stock route, the 1500-km track
enabled the beef cattle from the Kimberley region
to be driven to the southern goldfields. Today
it is well-known as a 4WD route.

Bohemia Downs

J K L M N 361 O P Q R

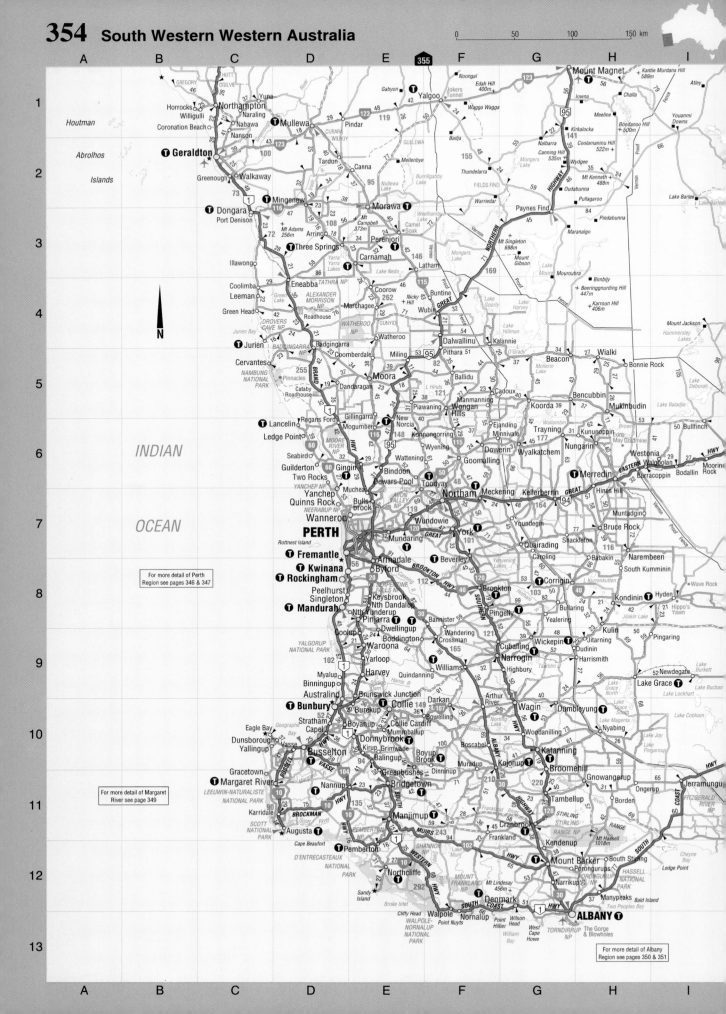

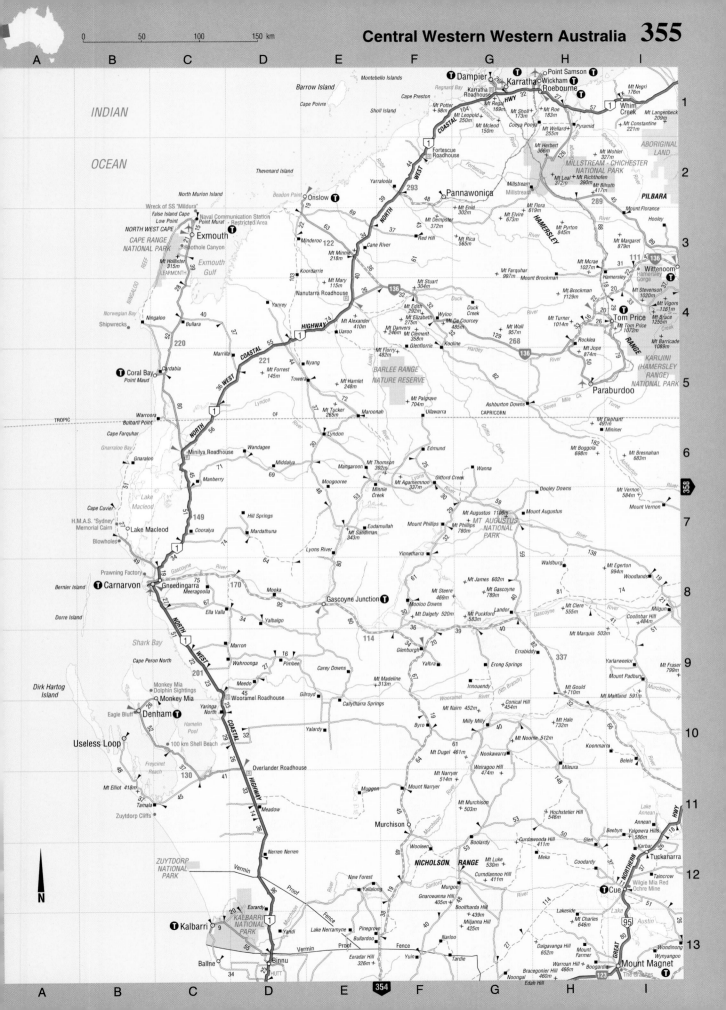

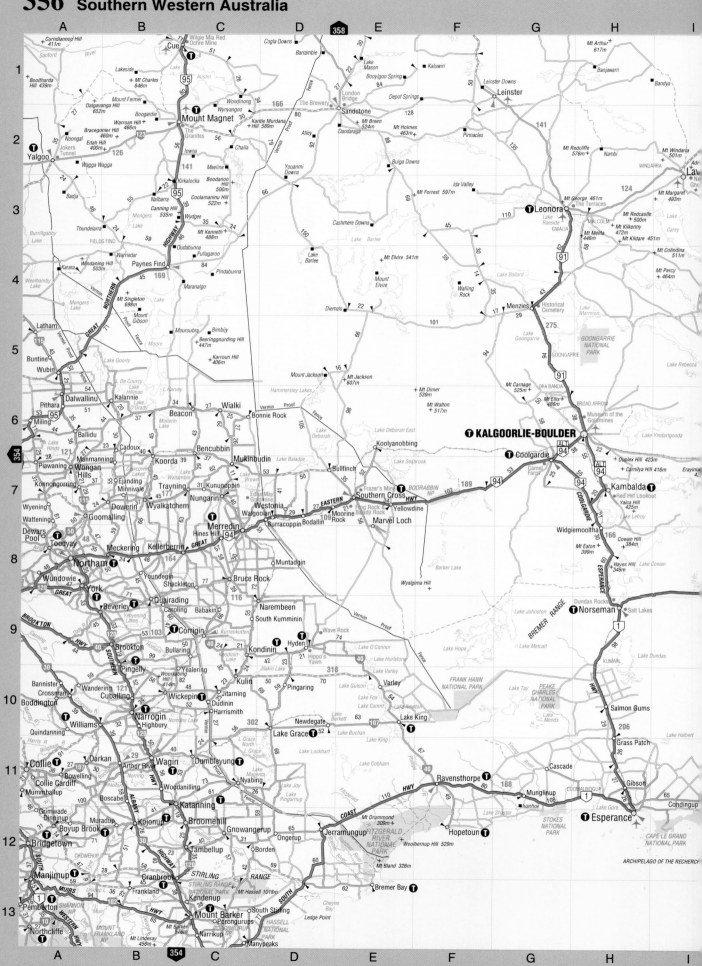

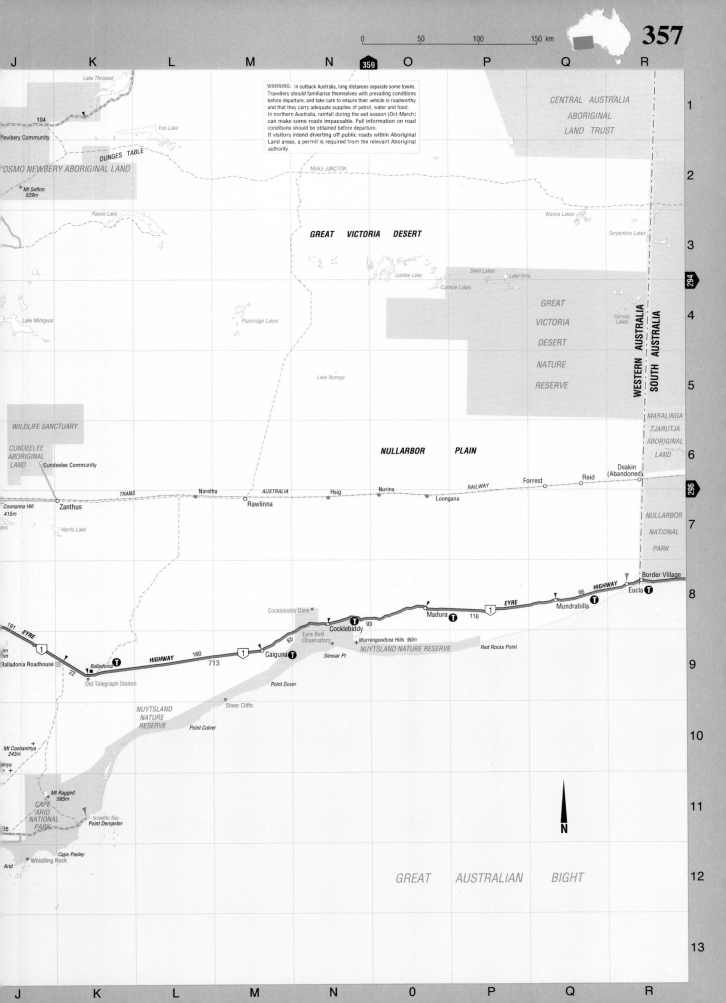

50   100   150 km

WARNING: In outback Australia, long distances separate some towns. Travellers should familiarise themselves with prevailing conditions before departure, and take care to ensure their vehicle is roadworthy and that they carry adequate supplies of petrol, water and food.
In northern Australia, rainfall during the wet season (Oct-March) can make some roads impassable. Full information on road conditions should be obtained before departure.
If visitors intend diverting off public roads within Aboriginal Land areas, a permit is required from the relevant Aboriginal authority.

Lake Throssel

104

Yeo Lake

CENTRAL AUSTRALIA
ABORIGINAL
LAND TRUST

ewbery Community

DUNGES TABLE

OSMO NEWBERY ABORIGINAL LAND

NEALE JUNCTION

Mt Sefton
529m

Wanna Lakes

Serpentine Lakes

Rason Lake

GREAT   VICTORIA   DESERT

Lake Minigwal

Plumridge Lakes

Jubilee Lake

Shell Lakes   Lake Ilma

Carlisle Lakes

GREAT

VICTORIA

DESERT

NATURE

RESERVE

Forrest
Lakes

294

Lake Nyanga

WESTERN AUSTRALIA

SOUTH AUSTRALIA

WILDLIFE SANCTUARY

MARALINGA
TJARUTJA
ABORIGINAL
LAND

CUNDEELEE
ABORIGINAL
LAND

NULLARBOR   PLAIN

Cundeelee Community

Deakin
(Abandoned)

Forrest   Reid

Coonanna Hill
415m

TRANS   AUSTRALIA   RAILWAY

Naretha   Haig   Nurina   Loongana

296

Zanthus   Rawlinna

NULLARBOR

Harris Lake

NATIONAL

PARK

Border Village

191   EYRE   66   HIGHWAY   Eucla
Cocklebiddy Cave   Madura   116   Mundrabilla
1   65   Cocklebiddy   93
Eyre Bird   EYRE
Observatory   1
Balladonia Roadhouse   Balladonia   HIGHWAY   160   1   Caiguna   Slessar Pt
22   Old Telegraph Station   713   Wurrengoodyea Hills 90m
NUYTSLAND NATURE RESERVE   Red Rocks Point

Mt Coobaninya
243m

Point Dover

NUYTSLAND
NATURE
RESERVE

Sheer Cliffs

Point Culver

Mt Ragged
585m

CAPE
ARID
NATIONAL
PARK

Israelite Bay
Point Dempster

N

Cape Pasley
Whistling Rock

Arid

GREAT   AUSTRALIAN   BIGHT

1
2
3
4
5
6
7
8
9
10
11
12
13

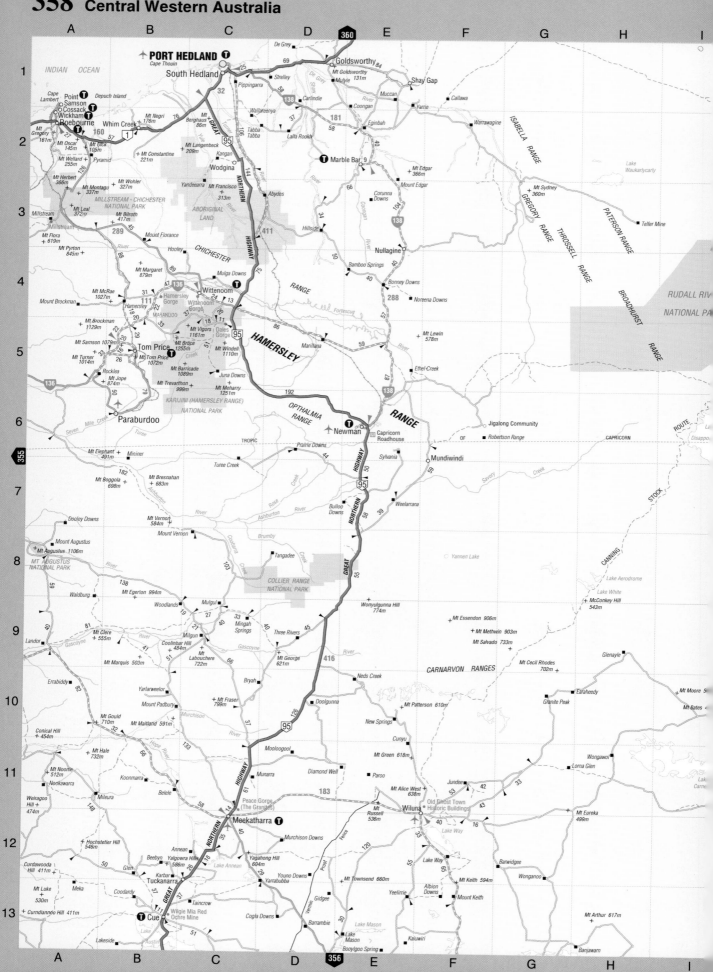

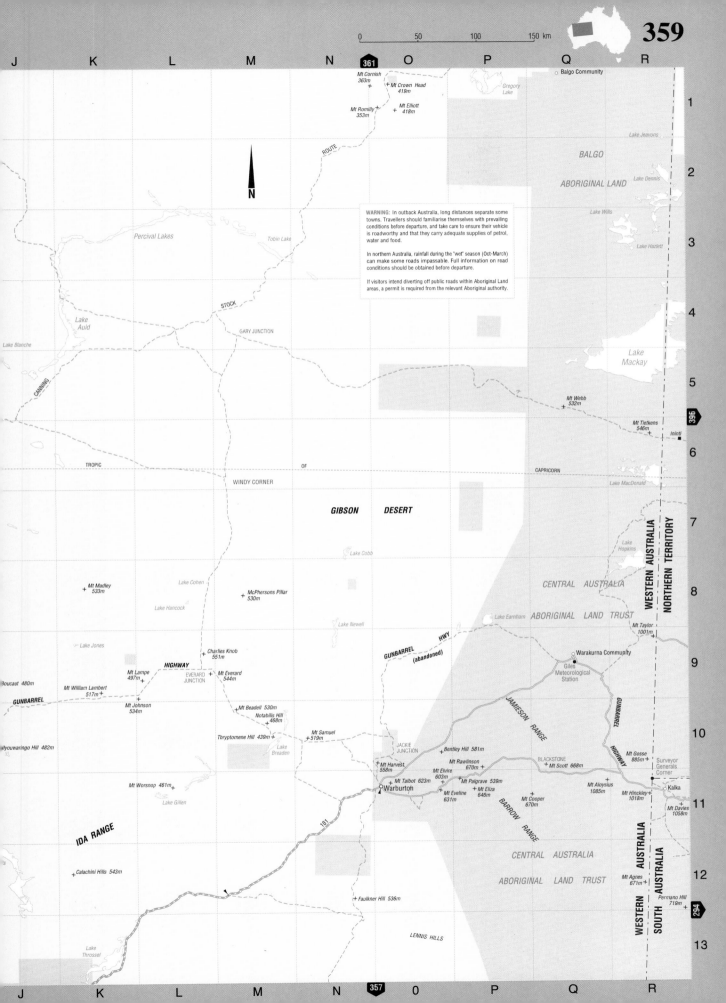

0 50 100 150 km

361

1

○ Balgo Community

Mt Cornish
363m
+ Mt Crown Head
419m

Mt Elliott
818m

Mt Romilly
353m

Lake Jeavons

BALGO

2

ABORIGINAL LAND

Lake Dennis

ROUTE

Percival Lakes

Tobin Lake

Lake Wills

Lake Hazlett

3

WARNING: In outback Australia, long distances separate some towns. Travellers should familiarise themselves with prevailing conditions before departure, and take care to ensure their vehicle is roadworthy and that they carry adequate supplies of petrol, water and food.

In northern Australia, rainfall during the 'wet' season (Oct-March) can make some roads impassable. Full information on road conditions should be obtained before departure.

If visitors intend diverting off public roads within Aboriginal Land areas, a permit is required from the relevant Aboriginal authority.

STOCK

Lake
Auld

Lake Blanche

GARY JUNCTION

4

Lake
Mackay

5

CANNING

Mt Webb
532m

396

Mt Tietkens
546m
+ Ininti

TROPIC

OF

CAPRICORN

Lake MacDonald

6

WINDY CORNER

GIBSON DESERT

7

Lake Hopkins

Lake Cobb

Mt Madley
533m

Lake Cohen

McPhersons Pillar
530m

CENTRAL AUSTRALIA

8

Lake Hancock

Lake Newell

Lake Earnham

ABORIGINAL LAND TRUST

Mt Taylor
1001m

Lake Jones

Charlies Knob
551m

HWY

GUNBARREL

Warakurna Community

Boucaut 480m

HIGHWAY

Mt Lampe
497m
EVERARD
JUNCTION

Mt Everard
544m

(abandoned)

Giles
Meteorological
Station

9

Mt William Lambert
517m

GUNBARREL

Mt Johnson
534m

Mt Beadell 530m

Notabilis Hill
468m

JAMIESON RANGE

GUNBARREL

10

llyouwaringo Hill 482m

Thryptomene Hill 439m

Mt Samuel
+ 519m

JACKIE
JUNCTION

Bentley Hill 581m

Mt Rawlinson
670m

BLACKSTONE

Mt Scott 668m

Mt Gosse
885m

HIGHWAY

Surveyor
Generals
Corner

Mt Worsnop 461m

Mt Harvest
558m

Mt Elvire
603m

Mt Talbot 623m

Mt Palgrave 539m

Mt Aloysius
1085m

Mt Hinckley
1018m

Kalka

11

Lake Gillen

Warburton

Mt Eveline
631m

Mt Eliza
646m

Mt Cooper
670m

Mt Davies
1058m

IDA RANGE

BARROW RANGE

CENTRAL AUSTRALIA

Mt Agnes
671m

12

Calachini Hills 543m

ABORIGINAL LAND TRUST

181

Faulkner Hill 536m

Permano Hill
719m

294

WESTERN AUSTRALIA

SOUTH AUSTRALIA

LENNIS HILLS

13

Lake
Throssel

357

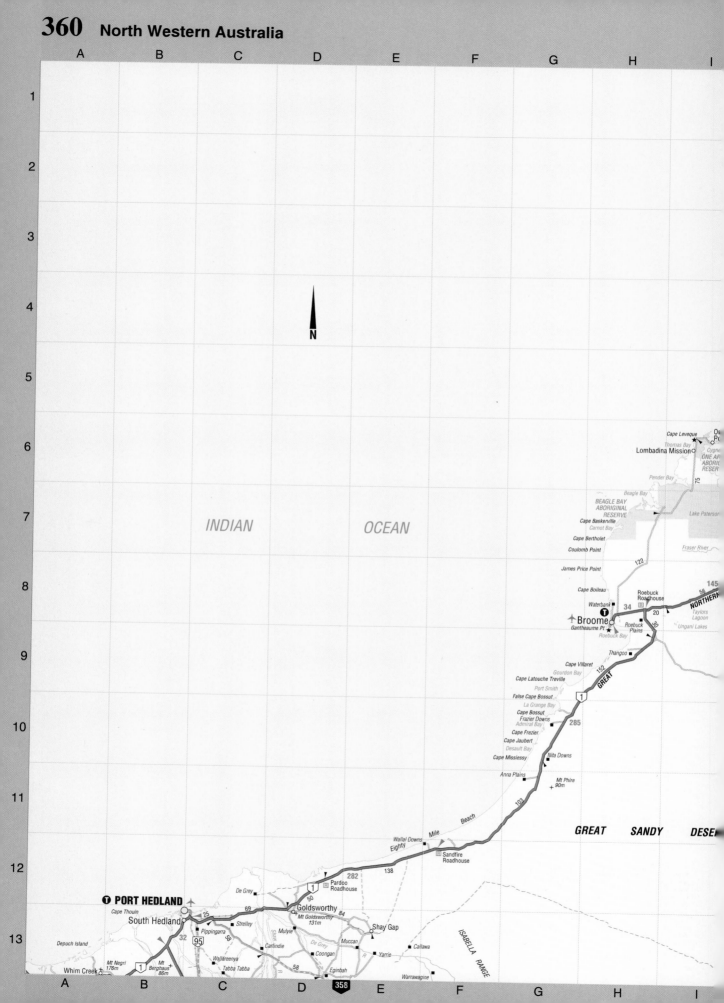

A B C D E F G H I

1
2
3
4

N

5
6

INDIAN   OCEAN

Cape Leveque ★   O
                                    Po
        Thomas Bay ○   Cygne
Lombadina Mission ○   ONE A
                                    ABORIC
                                    RESER
            Pender Bay

            Beagle Bay
        BEAGLE BAY
        ABORIGINAL
        RESERVE   Lake Paterson
Cape Baskerville   75
Carnot Bay

Cape Bertholet   Fraser River

Coulomb Point

James Price Point   122

Cape Boileau   145
                                    56
Cape Boileau
        Roebuck   NORTHERN
        Roadhouse
Waterbank   34   20
        ✈ Broome ○ T   Roebuck   30   Taylors
Gantheaume Pt ★   Plains   Lagoon
        Roebuck Bay   Ungani Lakes
                        Thangoo

Cape Villaret
        Gourdon Bay   152
Cape Latouche Treville   GREAT
        Port Smith
False Cape Bossut   1
        La Grange Bay
Cape Bossut
Frazier Downs
        Admiral Bay   285
Cape Frezier
Cape Jaubert
        Desault Bay
Cape Missiessy   Nita Downs

        Anna Plains   Mt Phire
                                    + 90m

7
8
9
10
11

GREAT   SANDY   DESE
        103
        Mile
        Beach
Wallal Downs
        Eighty   Sandfire
                        Roadhouse

12

        138   GREAT   SANDY   DESE

        282
        1   Pardoo
        50   Roadhouse
De Grey   Goldsworthy   84
        69   Mt Goldsworthy
                        131m
T PORT HEDLAND ✈   Shay Gap
Cape Thouin   25
South Hedland   Strelley   ISABELLA
        32   Pippingarra   RANGE
Depuch Island   95   Mulyie   Muccan
                        Callawa
        Cartindie   Coongan
        Walláreenya   Yarrie
Whim Creek   Mt Negri   Tabba Tabba   Eginbah
        176m   1   Mt   58
        Berghaus   Coongan   Warrawagine
        86m   Eginbah

13

A B C D 358 E F G H

J K L M N O P Q R

0 50 100 150 km

TIMOR SEA

Cape Londonderry
Cape Talbot
Cape Bougainville
Cape Rulhieres ★
Cape Bernier

JOSEPH BONAPARTE GULF

Vansittart Bay
Napier Broome Bay
Cone Mtn 178m
Admiralty Gulf

Kalumburu Mission
20

Mt Connor 312m
Carson River
Mt Leeming 244m
Mt Casuarina 221m

KALUMBURU ABORIGINAL LAND

OOMBULGURRI ABORIGINAL LAND

MITCHELL PLATEAU
Theda
Mt Nicholls 143m

Bigge Island

62
21
313
42

DRYSDALE RIVER NATIONAL PARK

Mt Anderson 485m

Mitchell River
Doongan
Mt Mongona 366m
Mt Fraser 366m

Cambridge Gulf

Mt Connection 183m

York Sound

Mt Trafalgar 390m
34

GARDNER PLATEAU

Drysdale River

Brunswick Bay

PRINCE REGENT NATURE RESERVE

Mt Lyall 213m

Wyndham ⊤
14
56
165
Home Valley
69
⊤
Kununurra

KEEP RIVER NP

HIDDEN VALLEY NP

Champagny Island

KUNMUNYA ABORIGINAL LAND

Mt Hann 777m
Mt Methuen 427m

Mt Russ 692m
66
Mt Cockburn North 671m
34
41
45
36
1
34
27

Deception Bay
Hall Point

Mt Deborah 399m
Mt Shadforth 510m
El Questro
Mt Hensman 384m

Cockatoo Island
Koolan Island
Koolan

Mt Lochee 310m
Mt Lacy 763m
Mount Elizabeth 35
Gibb River
27
Dunham Pilot Dam
Dunham River
151
56

Lake Argyle Tourist Village
Lake Argyle

Collier Bay
Calder

Mt Blythe 436m
Old Beverley Springs
Mt Quirk 323m
Rosewood

Mt Nellie 267m
Secure Bay

Mt Page 466m

KIMBERLEY REGION

Mt Synnot 488m
Mt Glemont 478m
81
Mount Barnett
1
29
Lissadell
Spring Creek
80

Mt Disaster 274m

Kimbolton
Oobagooma

Mt Humbert 474m
67
34
Mt Lush 778m
Texas Downs
Mt John 526m
Mistake Creek

Mt Hart 667m
50
63
32

DURACK RANGE

CARR BOYD RANGE

HIGHWAY

Robinson

Mt Smith 616m
Mt Chalmers 704m
30
Mt House 548m
Mt Clifton 537m
Glenroy
72
Mt Jarrad 530m

Turkey Creek
55

VIOLET HILL ABORIGINAL LAND

Bedford Downs

Mt Buchanan 417m

KING LEOPOLD
365
69
Napier Downs

Mt Herbert 753m
Mt Ord 937m
22
Mt Brennan 532m
Mt Warton 437m
Tableland

Mt Wells 983m
Mt King 950m
26
163
Mt Napier 487m

DUNCAN

Meda
40
Kimberly Downs
46

Mt Broome 931m
Mt Estaughs 476m
Mornington

RANGES

WINDJANA GORGE NATIONAL PARK

Mt Behn 339m
98

Mt Leake 697m
Lansdowne
Mt Laptz 245m
74
52
Springvale
14
Alice Downs

PURNULULU (BUNGLE BUNGLE) NATIONAL PARK

90

41
43

Mt Percy 201m

GEIKIE GORGE NATIONAL PARK

HIGHWAY

Mt Coghlan 622m
Nicholson
80

10
41
Willare Bridge Roadhouse
Blina
30
Ellendale
30
Leopold Downs
38
Fossil Downs
Mt Amhurst 719m
Mt Barrett 692m
22
Saunders Creek
Wittenoom 428m

30
54
Camballin
217
54
⊤ Fitzroy Crossing
Mt Elma 317m
Moola Bulla
Halls Creek ⊤
55
BUCHANAN HWY
80

Mount Anderson
21
Mt Wynne 144m
Mt Pierre 203m
Mt Ball 554m
Mt Flora 458m
Flora Valley

Looma
Myroodah
Mt Hardman 132m
Quanbun
Mount Amhurst
57
Mt Huxley 537m
Mt Fairbairn 338m
NORTHERN
34
16
29
40
55

DENISON PLAINS
Wallamunga

Luluigui
80
Noonkanbah
Jubilee Downs
Mt Ramsay 421m
1
47
Ruby Plains
Sturt

Dukes Dome 304m
Margaret River
Louisa Downs
Gordon Downs

56
55
Mt James 175m
Mt Tuckfield 311m
Mt Amy 268m
Mt Thorlan 263m
295
111 **GREAT**
19
11
Mt Dockrell 500m
47

Mt Jarlemai 195m
Mt Fenton 187m
Cherrabun
Mt Piper 337m
Christmas Creek
Bohemia Downs
Louisa Downs
90
Mt Junction 626m

WOLFE CREEK CRATER NP

Mt Josephine 419m
Carranya
Sturt Creek
Mt Frederick 530m

Lake Jones
Lake Betty
Lake Mclernon
Billiluna Community

Tilley Claypan

Lake Lanagan

TANAMI
TRACK

AUSTRALIA TERRITORY

WESTERN NORTHERN

ROUTE

Balgo Community

Mt Cornish 363m
Mt Crown Head 419m
Gregory Lake

Mt Romilly 353m
Mt Elliott 418m

BALGO ABORIGINAL LAND

Lake Jeavons

CANNING STOCK

For more detail of Kimberley Region see pages 352 & 353

WARNING: In outback Australia, long distances separate some towns. Travellers should familiarise themselves with prevailing conditions before departure, and take care to ensure their vehicle is roadworthy and that they carry adequate supplies of petrol, water and food.
In northern Australia, rainfall during the wet season (Oct-March) can make some roads impassable. Full information on road conditions should be obtained before departure.
If visitors intend diverting off public roads within Aboriginal Land areas, a permit is required from the relevant Aboriginal authority.
Beware of man-eating crocodiles in rivers and estuaries.

392

394

1
2
3
4
5
6
7
8
9
10
11
12
13

J K L M N O P Q R

Northern Territory

Outback Australia

There are only three main highways that take motorists into the Northern Territory: the Barkly Highway from Mount Isa in Queensland, the Stuart Highway from South Australia and the Victoria Highway from the extreme north-east of Western Australia. Given the enormous distances involved, you may well decide to fly, either to Darwin or to Alice Springs, and then hire a car. Alternatively, airlines, coach companies and tour operators offer day and extended coach tours, coach camping tours, adventure and safari trek tours which allow you to discover this unique, relatively uninhabited and exciting Territory in experienced hands.

Six times the size of Great Britain, with a population similar to that of Newcastle in New South Wales, and boasting the famous 'red centre' and the world's largest monolith, the Northern Territory abounds with staggering statistics.

The first, unsuccessful, attempt to settle this huge, forbidding region was in fact not on the mainland at all, but on Melville Island, in 1825, and it was not until 1869 that a town called Palmerston was established on the coast, the town which was later to become Darwin. Originally the Territory was part of New South Wales, when that state's western boundary extended to the 129th east meridian. Later it was annexed to South Australia and it did not come under Commonwealth control until 1911. In July 1978 the Territory attained self-government.

In terms of monetary value, the Territory's main industry is mining. Gold, bauxite, manganese ore, copper, silver, iron ore and uranium all contribute to this industry. The tourist industry ranks second in importance, but beef cattle farming is by no means unimportant, even though sixteen hectares or more are often required to support one animal. Poor soil, huge distances from markets and winter droughts all combine to render commercial crop-growing virtually impossible.

The 'dry season', between the months of May and October, is the best time to visit the Northern Territory; and 'dry' *means* dry -— during the 'wet season' Darwin has an average annual rainfall of 1500 millimetres, while only 25 millimetres falls in the 'dry season'. July is the Territory's coolest month. Temperatures in Darwin range then between 20° and 30°C. In 'the Alice' (as Alice Springs is affectionately known) the average maximum in August is 22.5° C, cooling at night to a low of around zero.

The Northern Territory's two main centres are more than 1500 kilometres apart. Darwin, at the 'Top End', has a population of about 70 000. It suffered extensively from Cyclone Tracy in 1974 and has since been virtually rebuilt. It is renowned for its relaxed lifestyle and beautiful beaches. Darwin makes a perfect jumping-off spot for exploring the Top End region.

If, however, you are 'going it alone' by car, you should research your trip thoroughly before setting out; read the section on Outback Motoring and bear in mind that the dry season is definitely the most pleasant weather for touring. Always be sure to make full enquiries as to conditions before leaving sealed roads. Both the Stuart and Barkly Highways are now all-weather roads, sealed for their entire length. Even so, any driving at night should be undertaken with care.

East of Darwin is the spectacular Kakadu National Park. Further east is Arnhem Land, which can be explored by extended coach tour or adventure tour. Many Aboriginal reserves require entry permission from an Aboriginal Land Council. These reserves belong to the Aborigines; much of the land is sacred to them and should be respected by visitors.

South of Darwin is Katherine with its spectacular gorge, on the southern fringe of Arnhem Land. Freshwater crocodiles are common in the Katherine River, so its dramatic beauty is best viewed from either bank. From Katherine, the Stuart Highway continues south through the Tanami Desert to Alice Springs. The only town of any size along the way is Tennant Creek. South of this desert outpost are the Devil's Marbles, a random pile of granite boulders, some of which are almost perfect spheres. An Aboriginal legend says that they are eggs laid by the mythical Rainbow Serpent.

Many people outside Australia think of Alice Springs as one of the most important towns in Australia. Certainly, it has been immortalised on film and in snapshots countless times. No other town, or even tiny settlement, is nearer to the geographic centre of the country. In 1872 Alice Springs was simply a repeater station for the Overland Telegraph Service. Today it is not only the centre for the outback cattle industry but also a lively tourist centre with a population of over 20 000.

Uluru (Ayers Rock), 450 kilometres to the south-west in Uluru National Park, is the world's biggest monolith: one enormous rock, nine kilometres in circumference and rising 348 metres above the plain on which it stands. The Aborigines made it a part of their sacred rituals, and guides will explain the mythology of the cave paintings at its base.

The magnificent Kata Tjuta (The Olgas) and, closer to the Alice, the prehistoric palms at Palm Valley, the dramatic Kings Canyon, Standley Chasm and Ormiston Gorge, all add their own fascination to the many wonders of the Northern Territory.

Sunset over the Olgas

Darwin

A Relaxed City

The first coastal town established in the Northern Territory was Palmerston, in 1864. Located at the mouth of the Adelaide River, it was quickly abandoned after a disastrous wet season in 1865.

Another expedition, led by Surveyor-General George Goyder, established a base at Adam Bay about fifty kilometres east of present-day Darwin. After surveying the area, he recommended that Port Darwin, which had been discovered in 1839 and named after Charles Darwin, would be the best place for a settlement. The town was officially called Palmerston, but the locals referred to it as Port Darwin to distinguish it from the original settlement. The name was officially changed to Darwin in 1911 when the Federal Government took control of the Territory.

In its early days, Darwin's development was hampered by its isolation. During World War II, however, the Stuart Highway was completed, linking Darwin with the railhead at Alice Springs, but after recovering from bomb damage in the war, growth was still slow.

The new Darwin's prosperity is based largely on the mineral wealth of the Northern Territory. It is the exploitation of this resource that has finally led to Darwin's development into the modern city it is today, despite the major setback when Cyclone Tracy struck in 1974.

A new Darwin grew out of the ruins of the cyclone, as befits the city's role as the capital of a self-governing territory. Until recently, Darwin had been largely maintained by the Commonwealth Government because of its strategic location, as much as for its function as a route centre and supply base for a grazing and mining area by no means yet fully developed.

Life for the early citizens was hard and changed very little until World War II. Graziers and agriculturalists could only hope to cope with the violent climatic changes. Development of modern techniques saw the population grow to 45 000 by 1974, when Cyclone Tracy struck. Now the figure has pushed past 70 000, which says something for either the hardiness of its people or the desirability of the city as a place to live, or perhaps a bit of both. With Broome, in Western Australia, Darwin is one of Australia's most multicultural settlements, embracing people of forty-seven racial and cultural backgrounds. Chinese people have always formed a major part of the city's population and, in more recent years, Timorese and South-east Asian refugees have been arriving in Darwin and many have stayed. Quite large contingents of armed-forces personnel are also stationed at bases around Darwin.

Temperatures in the city area itself average around 28°C; there is very little or no rain during the 'dry'. In the 'wet', maximum temperatures average close to 34°C with high relative humidity, which

Tropical palms line the entrance to Government House

can be uncomfortable for people from more equable climes. But always Darwin is good for sailing, swimming, water-skiing or soaking up the sun.

City sightseeing is conveniently done from air-conditioned motor coaches that make regular tours. The main features to see are the splendidly tropical 34-hectare **Botanical Gardens**, the few surviving historic buildings, churches, memorials, the **Reserve Bank**, the **Supreme Court**, Darwin's busy **harbour** area and the **Beaufort Darwin Centre** (including a world-class hotel and the **Performing Arts Centre**) on the Esplanade overlooking the harbour. A lookout on the Esplanade commemorates the fiftieth anniversary of the bombing of Darwin in 1942. Day and half-day cruises around the harbour are available.

The city's business district is much like any other similar-sized city, but the relaxed and tropical atmosphere has a distinct character of its own. Modern air-conditioned shopping centres now serve Darwin's suburbs, which are in two main sections, divided by the airport.

Christchurch Cathedral was completed and consecrated in March 1977. It incorporates the porch from its predecessor, which was destroyed by Cyclone Tracy. During the war it was a garrison church and came under fire from Japanese bombers. The new cathedral, built at a cost of $800 000, features a stained-glass window in memory of the trawler-men lost at sea during the cyclone. The altar, weighing 2.5 tonnes, has been hewn from a solid jarrah log believed to be more than 400 years old. Not far from the cathedral is the 'Tree of Knowledge', an ancient, spreading banyan tree. There are several other interesting places of worship in Darwin, particularly the **Chinese Temple**. Visitors are welcome to inspect the interior.

One of Darwin's most historic hotels, the **Old Victoria** in the Smith Street Mall, has been restored into a modern shopping complex, at the same time retaining its colonial character with 'punkahs' to cool the Balcony Bar.

For those with cultural interests, the city boasts a theatre group which welcomes visitors' participation in its workshops held in **Brown's Mart**, another building that survived Tracy. The **Beaufort Centre** includes a 1000-seat theatre for the performing arts. Cinemas are located in Mitchell Street, at Parap and at Nightcliff.

Several art galleries, including some

Sunset over Mindil Beach

Hotels
Beaufort
The Esplanade, Darwin
(089) 82 9911
Diamond Beach Hotel Casino
Gilruth Ave, Mindil Beach
(089) 46 2666
Melia
32 Mitchell St, Darwin
(089) 82 0000

Family and Budget
Darwin
10 Herbert St, Darwin
(089) 81 9211
Poinciana Inn
84 Mitchell St, Darwin
(089) 81 8111

Top End
Cnr Daly and Mitchell Sts, Darwin
(089) 81 6511
YWCA
119 Mitchell St, Darwin
(089) 81 8644

Motel Groups: Bookings
Best Western (008) 22 2166
Travelodge (008) 22 2446

This list is for information only: inclusion is not necessarily a recommendation.

which feature the art and craft of the Aboriginal people, can be seen in the city area. The elegant colonial architecture of **Government House** (near the southern end of the Esplanade) and **Old Admiralty House** (on the Esplanade), now an art gallery and garden cafe, is a reminder of the city's past. The **Museum of Arts and Sciences** at Bullocky Point houses important collections of Aboriginal, Balinese and New Guinean artefacts, as well as works by Australia's most famous painters.

At the end of the Esplanade, at Doctors Gully off Mitchell Street, **Aquascene** provides the opportunity at feeding times to hand-feed the ocean fish, which come in to the jetty. For feeding times, call 81 7837. At the entrance to the Wharf Precinct is a marine complex housing the **Australian Pearling Exhibition** which features static, audio visual and live displays on pearl farming. The award-winning **Indo Pacific Marine** coral reef ecosystem exhibit is also part of the complex. At Temira Crescent on the outskirts of the city centre, is the **Myilly Point** Heritage Precinct, headquarters for the National Trust. The Trust building houses an information centre and gift shop.

The **East Point Military Museum** at **Fannie Bay** displays artillery, war planes and other militaria close to the gun turrets that were constructed during World War II. Fannie Bay is also the site where Ross and Keith Smith landed their Vickers Vimy aircraft in 1919, completing the first flight from the UK to Australia. One of the most beautiful spots in the world to build a prison, Fannie Bay has some fine beaches. The **Fannie Bay Gaol Museum** features various displays including one on Cyclone Tracy. Darwin boasts of its beautiful sunsets and the nearby **East Point Reserve** is a popular viewing place.

Darwin's best-known annual event is probably the Beer Can Regatta, held each September. The competing boats and other floating craft are constructed out of beer cans, a commodity of which there never seems to be a shortage in this city!

Darwin's restaurants offer an excellent choice of cuisine, from the fare of simple steak houses to French, Italian and Indonesian menus. There are also some wine bars which offer varied menus and pleasant settings for lunch and dinner.

To the north of the city area, Darwin's suburbs have been virtually rebuilt since 1974. The tropical climate has encouraged a lush regrowth and the gardens are a feast of beautiful bougainvilleas, hibiscus and alamanders. The rebuilt houses have been designed to better withstand any future cyclonic onslaught.

Sporting interests are well served. There is a golf course, a speedway track, a race-course at Fannie Bay, and the usual facilities for tennis, squash, bowls and football (Aussie Rules and Rugby). An **Olympic Pool** is located on Ross Smith Avenue. Sea wasps are common in the waters off Darwin, so swimming in the sea for much of the year is not recommended.

Darwin is the natural jumping-off point for touring the Top End. The good hotels and motels are as well-found as their counterparts in other Australian capitals. The pressure on these services is often great and a range of alternative, less luxurious, accommodation has developed which can still be very comfortable. Many of the numerous caravan parks in Darwin are occupied by permanent residents, so it is worth booking ahead.

The **Diamond Beach Casino** in Darwin is a few metres from the shores of **Mindil Beach**. As well as gambling facilities, this thirty-million-dollar complex offers luxury accommodation, restaurants and discos, sporting and convention facilities. The **Mindil Beach Sunset Market** operates on the foreshore from May to September; watch the setting sun while browsing through the food, art and craft stalls.

For further information on Darwin, contact the Darwin Region Tourism Association, 31 Smith St Mall (PO Box 4292, Darwin 0801); (089) 81 4300.

Fogg Dam offers an opportunity to view wildlife

Tours from Darwin

The eight million hectares of the Arnhem Land Aboriginal Land, one of Australia's most fascinating wilderness areas, lie to the east of Darwin. It is a land that changes from broken mountains to vast plains, irrigated by constantly flowing rivers. An entry permit is required, which tourist agencies arrange through local government authorities. In the 'dry', many tours of places of interest in and around the city are available, by bus or hire car. Safaris by air and four-wheel-drive take sporting enthusiasts to less accessible areas for sightseeing, shooting and fishing.

The best month for the bush is July when, on a clear night, the stars seem to get in your eyes and you would not swap your cutlet of barramundi, grilled in the traditional manner on a shovel over an open fire, for the finest dish in the world. Almost any time from April to September is suitable for getting back to nature. When you do, it is hard to conceive that Darwin, serving all this vastness, has an airport that can take not only jumbo jets but also the supersonic Concorde.

Fogg Dam, 70 km from Darwin via the Arnhem Highway

A sunrise or sunset tour of this area offers an excellent opportunity to view animals and birds on the move between their feeding-grounds and where they sleep.

Not only is Fogg Dam a likely spot to see a crocodile, but you will also see many wallabies. The nearby swamps are the haunt of the elegant jabiru stork. Other birds in abundance are the pelican, egret, galah, cockatoo and kitehawk. The tour route then goes on to the Marakai Plains where many species of birds can be seen. Millions of dollars were lost in this area when the rice irrigation scheme at Humpty Doo failed. Stop at Reptile World at Humpty Doo, which has the largest range of snakes in Australia (250 species), as well as many lizards.

Kakadu National Park, 250 km from Darwin via the Arnhem Highway

Recently placed on the World Heritage List, Kakadu is rich in natural and cultural heritage. Apart from abundant wildlife, the scenery here is dramatic and there are many fine examples of ancient Aboriginal art at sites throughout the park. The drive is fascinating, and can be topped off by a cruise on the South Alligator River. You would be unlucky not to see crocodiles, as well as wallabies, and the birdlife is prolific; however, sightings of buffalo are becoming rare. The Arnhem Highway is sealed all the way to Jabiru, and you could

Tourist boat on the Adelaide River

do the trip in your own car or a hired car.

Approximately 100 kilometres south of Jabiru are the Jim Jim Falls, accessed only by four-wheel-drive. There are many good camping spots on Jim Jim Creek and other billabongs. The deep and clear stretches of water on Nourlangie Creek, west of the Kakadu Highway, afford excellent opportunities for fishing. The safari guides have local knowledge and can show you far more than if you explore on your own. **See also**: Aboriginal Art; The Top End.

Howard Springs, 35 km from Darwin via the Stuart Highway

There is safe swimming here in a spring-fed pool surrounded by monsoon forest. Avid birdwatchers can spot fifty or more species in a few hours; varieties of reptiles abound. Picnic areas and a kiosk are provided. On the way you could visit Nostalgia (one of Darwin's oldest homes) and the Territory Oils Art Centre.

Territory Wildlife Park at Berry Springs, 50 km from Darwin via the Stuart Highway

A tourist development of international standard, located in more than 400 ha of bushland at Berry Springs, the Territory Wildlife Park is designed to display only animals native and feral to the Northern Territory. The exhibits are all connected by a 4 km link road and include open-moated enclosures with kangaroos, wallabies, dingoes, bustards, buffalo and banteng; a naturally occurring lagoon where native birds can be viewed from a hide; an aquarium which features an acrylic walk-through tunnel for underwater viewing of large freshwater fish; a series of aviaries which display birds in natural habitats; a walk-through rainforest aviary; and the second largest nocturnal house in the world, artificially moonlit, where visitors can see about fifty species of mammals, birds and reptiles. The park is a project of the Conservation Commission of the NT. Adjacent to the Territory Wildlife Park is the Berry Springs Nature Park which features a spring-fed swimming area. The park is an ideal location for a picnic.

Crocodile Farm, 40 km from Darwin via the Stuart Highway

Australia's first and largest commercial crocodile farm with over 7000 inmates, ranging in length from a few centimetres to four metres. There are feeding displays and tours daily. Be adventurous and try some farm-raised crocodile delicacies.

Ferry trips to the Cox Peninsula and Harbour Cruises

Daily trips depart from the wharf in Darwin Harbour to Mandorah on the Cox Peninsula, ideal for a relaxed day on the beach, swimming or fishing. Cruises on the harbour provide a delightful way to view the city shores; sunset cruises are also popular. There is also a wide range of fishing tours available around various locations in Darwin Harbour..

Cruises on the Adelaide River, 64 km from Darwin via the Arnhem Highway

The *Adelaide River Queen* offers 2.5 hour cruises for crocodile-viewing.

Air tours

Several tours by air from Darwin are available, including day or weekend trips to Jim Jim Falls and fishing and shooting trips. A three-day air tour into Western Australia, including a jungle cruise at Lake Kununurra, the Hidden Valley, the Carr Boyd Ranges, Lake Argyle and the Ord River, makes a most enjoyable trip, if you can spare the time.

Crocodile farm, near Darwin

Northern Territory from A to Z

Adelaide River   Pop. 356
A small settlement set in pleasant country, 112 km s of Darwin on the Stuart Hwy, Adelaide River is the starting-point for visits to Rum Jungle, an old uranium-mining area (30 km NW), Litchfield Park with its clear pools and spectacular waterfalls (30 km N), the Daly River district (110 km SW), and the Batchelor and Tipperary experimental farming areas (40 km N and 90 km SW). **Of interest:** War memorial and Australian War Graves. **In the area:** Majestic Orchids, part of Hydro Majestic, 48 ha horticultural and recreational development, 7 km SW of Berry Springs Nature Park and near Litchfield Park entrance; 16 ha orchid-growing area. Freshwater Lake Bennett, 35 km N, recreation resort for picnicking, camping, swimming, sailing, canoeing, fishing and bushwalking. 4WD tours available. **Accommodation:** 1 hotel/motel, 1 caravan/camping park.
MAP REF. 388 E8, 392 F7

Aileron   Pop. 50
On the Stuart Hwy, 139 km N of Alice Springs. **Of interest:** Rest-stop; Aboriginal art; native wildlife; Sunday roast lunch. **Accommodation:** 1 hotel/motel.
MAP REF. 397 J6

Alice Springs   Pop. 20 448
Alice Springs is at the heart of the Red Centre, almost 1500 km from the nearest capital city. It is the gateway to the NT's biggest single tourist attraction, Uluru (Ayers Rock). A modern and well-maintained town in the heart of the MacDonnell Ranges, some 350 000 visitors a year pass through between May and Sept. In this period, cloudless skies and warm days usher in refreshingly cool nights. The rest of the year is very hot and dust storms are common. Rains, usually brief, can come at any time of year. While there is plenty to see in the town itself, many natural wonders lie within a day's journey. 'The Alice', as it is affectionately called, offers a variety of restaurants, together with an international casino, sports grounds, a swimming pool and an 18-hole golf course. There is a wide variety of

View over Alice Springs

The Red Centre

An ideal way to see the multitude of tourist attractions in the Red Centre is to base yourself in Alice Springs and to take advantage of the many and varied coach tours which operate from there.

Of course, what you should not miss is **Uluru (Ayers Rock)**. About 450 kilometres south-west of the Alice, the world's greatest monolith rises majestically 348 metres above a wide, sandy floodplain which is covered in spinifex and desert oak. The rock is 9 kilometres in circumference and with the movement of the sun during the day, it changes colour through shades of fiery red, delicate mauve, blues, pinks and browns. When rain falls, it veils the rock in a torrent of silver.

Ayers Rock Resort at Yulara is about a 20-minute drive north of Uluru. The resort offers a range of accommodation: the top-class Sails in the Desert Hotel, the Outback Pioneer Hotel and Lodge, the Four Seasons Desert Gardens four-star resort, Spinifex Lodge, Emu Walk self-contained service apartments, and well-equipped camping grounds.

An excellent way to familiarise yourself with the region is to spend an hour or so at the Yulara Visitors Centre. Displays depict the geology, history, flora and fauna of the region and there is a spectacular collection of photographs. Audiovisual shows are held regularly.

Yulara is a self-contained township; it has accommodation for the resort's staff (about 500), a supermarket, and other shops and services.

Yulara, with its prize-winning design, does not intrude into the landscape but blends into the ochre colours of the desert around. If you can, allow for a stay of at least three days. This will give you time to see a sunrise and a sunset, to explore Uluru and visit Kata Tjuta (The Olgas).

According to Aboriginal legends, Uluru and Kata Tjuta were created and given their distinctive forms during the Tjukurpa or creation period. At the base of Uluru, there are cave paintings and carvings made thousands of years ago by members of the Loritja and Pitjanjatjara tribes. It is not difficult to appreciate that this is a sacred place of ancient times.

Do not attempt the 1.6-kilometre climb of Uluru unless you are fit and well, and have a good head for heights. As the climb follows a religious track, the Anungu (the traditional owners) would prefer visitors took other discovery walks within the park.

Taking the 9-kilometre circuit walk around the base of Uluru, you will see the Mutitjulu (Sound Shell), a cavity as smooth as if formed by the sea, and the Taputji (Kangaroo Tail), a 160-metre strip of stone. Tours include the Mala Walk, the Edible Desert Walk (Aboriginal bush tucker) and the Liru Walk, conducted by Aboriginal guides.

Some 50 kilometres to the west are **Kata Tjuta (The Olgas)**, a cluster of rounded, massive rocks which are equally mysterious. They too are dramatic and vividly coloured, lacking only the majesty of Uluru's great bulk. The tallest dome of Kata Tjuta, Mount Olga, is 546 metres above the oasis-like 'Valley of the Winds' that runs through the rock system. Ernest Giles, who first saw Mount Olga and named it after the Queen of Spain, described the rocks as 'minarets, giant cupolas and monstrous domes ... huge memorials of the ancient times to the earth'.

Curtin Springs cattle station and roadside inn is on the Lasseter Highway, 82 kilometres east of Yulara. Accommodation is available; also tours from Yulara to Mount Conner.

Ross River Homestead, 88 kilometres east of Alice Springs, is a delightful place to base yourself for exploration of the East MacDonnells. This ranch-style homestead resort features a range of outback experiences in comfortable surroundings. The historic pub bar has an interesting display of antiques. **Trephina Gorge, John Hayes Rockhole, N'Dhala Gorge** and **Corroboree Rock** are in the area.

The **Arltunga Historical Reserve**, 110 kilometres south-east of Alice Springs, has been set aside to preserve memorabilia of the gold-mining era in the region. Little evidence remains of the shanty town that grew up after 1887 when alluvial gold was found here. You can explore the stone ruins, scattered workings, gravestones and go down a mine. The Visitors Centre displays historical exhibits, and there is a gaol and a restored police station. Camping is available in a private camping ground next to the reserve and there is good fossicking in the area.

If you take advantage of the organised Ross River tour from Alice Springs, you will be able to visit these attractions, and also hear much of the folklore relating to the Eastern Aranda Aborigines, sample billy tea and damper, and learn how to throw a boomerang or crack a whip.

A turning off the Stuart Highway about 140 kilometres south-west of Alice Springs leads to the **Henbury meteorite craters** and, a further 200 kilometres west, the spectacular beauty of **Kings Canyon** within Watarrka National Park. The **Kings Canyon Frontier Lodge** and **Kings Creek Campground** are good accommodation bases from which to see these attractions.

The Henbury craters are believed to have been formed several thousand years ago when a falling meteor broke into pieces and hit the earth. The largest of the twelve craters is 180 metres wide and 15 metres deep. The smallest is six metres wide and only a few centimetres deep.

Kings Canyon, 323 kilometres southwest of Alice Springs, is one of the most interesting and scenic areas of the Centre. The climb to the rim of the canyon is fairly arduous, but well worth the effort. Even more spectacular views can be obtained by crossing the tree-trunk bridge—a nerve-racking experience, as there is no handrail—to the north wall. The Lost City and the Garden of Eden are superb sights here.

An interesting day-tour from Alice Springs is the beautiful **Standley Chasm**. About 50 kilometres west of Alice Springs, this colourful cleft in the West MacDonnells is only five metres wide. At midday when the sunlight reaches the floor of the chasm, turning the walls a blazing red, it is a memorable sight. **Simpsons Gap National Park**, 18 kilometres west of Alice Springs, can be visited at the same time and has walking access.

Further west, about 133 kilometres from Alice Springs, are **Glen Helen** and **Ormiston Gorges**. Located on the Finke River, their colours were captured by Aboriginal artist Albert Namatjira and today lend themselves to photography, as does the sunrise on Mount Sonder, which can be seen to the west. Glen Helen Lodge is an accommodation base for the West MacDonnells or a day tour is available at Alice Springs.

A day tour from Alice Springs will take you to **Palm Valley** and the **Finke River Gorge,** 155 kilometres south-west. The Finke River is one of the oldest watercourses in the world and to walk along its bed is an unforgettable experience.

Palm Valley, with its rock pools, cycad palms and *Livistona* palms unique to the area, is yet another of the incredible sights of the Centre. The valley's plant life has such a 'prehistoric' appearance, to enter the area is like taking a trip back in time.

These two attractions can also be visited by taking a two-day tour from Alice Springs, staying overnight at Glen Helen. Also worth a visit is the restored **Hermannsburg Mission**, 125 kilometres west of Alice Springs, on the way to Palm Valley.

Much nearer 'home', the Alice Springs **Telegraph Station Historical Reserve** is only three kilometres north of town. The site of the original settlement in the Alice Springs area, the station and all the original stone buildings have been restored by the Conservation Commission of the Northern Territory. These buildings house furnishings and artifacts from early this century and a historic interpretative display; there are guided tours half-hourly. The Reserve occupies 570 hectares and offers opportunities for bushwalking, picnicking and wildlife observation. A small waterhole, the original water source for the settlement, from which Alice Springs obtained its name, is adjacent to the old station buildings.

The telegraph station was originally built to link Port Augusta to Darwin, thence by submarine cable to Java. The line was completed in 1872 and was used from then until 1932, when operations were transferred to the site at the corner of Parsons Street and Railway Terrace in Alice Springs.

For further information about the attractions of the Red Centre, contact the tourist information centre, Centrepoint Building, cnr Gregory Tce and Hartley St, Alice Springs; (089) 52 5800. **Note** detailed map of Red Centre on page 390.

Uluru (Ayers Rock) with wildflowers

shops and a number of art galleries, including some that specialise in Aboriginal art. The Todd River, which runs through the town, is dry except after flash floods; for the annual Henley-on-Todd Regatta in Oct. the boats are carried or fitted with wheels. The few areas of land that can be irrigated support small dairy and fruit-growing enterprises, but the main produce of the area is beef cattle from huge runs. The site of the town was discovered by William Whitfield Mills in 1871, when he was surveying a route for the Overland Telegraph Line. He named the Todd River after the South Australian Superintendent of Telegraphs, Sir Charles Todd, and a nearby waterhole Alice Springs after his boss's wife. The first settlement was at the repeater station, built for transmitting messages across the continent. All of the thick-walled stone buildings have been restored and can be viewed. About ten years before Mills, John McDouall Stuart recorded in his diary that he passed about 50 km W of the site. Stuart also discovered and named Central Mt Sturt (since renamed Central Mt Stuart) in 1860, after Captain Sturt, who had commanded an earlier expedition in which he (Stuart) had taken part, but the South Australian Government renamed it in Stuart's honour after he had completed his successful expedition to the northern coast of Australia. John Ross, a pastoralist seeking new grazing lands, also helped look for a route for the telegraph line. The repeater station was for many years the only reason for the existence of a handful of people in this remote area, but in 1888 the South Australian Government became eager to open up the country and sent surveys north seeking suitable sites for railheads. The township of Stuart, 3.2 km from the telegraph station, was gazetted in the same year; but the railway remained unbuilt and Stuart stagnated. Regular supply was maintained by the expensive and slow camel train from Port Augusta. Even the discovery of gold at Arltunga, 96 km E of the settlement, did little to develop Stuart. The Federal Government took control of the NT from SA in 1911. From that time the township began to develop steadily, if still slowly. The Australian Inland Mission stationed Sister Jane Finlayson there in 1916. She was supposed to stay only one year, but the

growing needs of the area led to the establishment of Adelaide House nursing hostel in 1926. The railway was finally completed in 1929 and the first train reached Stuart in Aug. that year. The service became known as 'The Ghan', after the Afghan camel drivers it had replaced. The white population increased from 40 in 1926 to 200 in 1931 as the supply of materials became more reliable and less expensive. As the township grew there came the need for better identification: there was too much confusion between Stuart and the telegraph station Alice Springs, only 3 km apart, so the name Stuart was dropped in favour of Alice Springs. Now it is the jumping-off point for tourists who visit the Red Centre. **Of interest:** Royal Flying Doctor Service base, Stuart Tce; tours daily. School of the Air, Head St; open to visitors weekday mornings. Araluen Arts Centre, Larapinta Dr; focal point for performing and visual arts, and art galleries. Strehlow Research Centre; collection of artefacts of the Arunta people. Panorama 'Guth', Hartley St; 360° landscape painting of Central Australia. Aboriginal Art and Culture Centre, Todd St. Flynn Memorial Church, Todd Mall; built in memory of founder of RFDS. Old Stuart Gaol, Parsons St. Lasseter's Casino, Barrett Dr. Technology, Transport and Communications Museum, Memorial Dr. Olive Pink Flora Reserve, cnr Barrett Dr and Causeway; Australia's only arid-zone botanic garden. Country Music Festival held in April; annual Bangtail Muster street parade and sports carnival, and Lions Camel Cup in May; Shell Oil Finke Desert Race and Gemtree World Paddymelon Bowls Championship in June; Show Day in July; and Harts Range race meeting, Old Timers Fete and Alice Springs Rodeo in Aug.; and Corkwood Festival (Central Australian art, craft, music and dance) in Nov. **In the area:** Views from top of Anzac Hill at N end of town. Old telegraph station, 3 km N, off Stuart Hwy; historic reserve with original buildings and equipment. Old Timers' Museum, 5 km S; exhibits of 1890s pioneering era. Pitchi Richi Sanctuary, 3 km SW; features clay sculptures by William Ricketts, and open-air pioneer museum. Frontier Camel Farm, 7 km SE, off Ross Hwy; reptile house, camel rides and museum with displays highlighting importance of camels and their Afghan masters in early development

of central Australia. Nearby, Mecca Date Gardens, Australia's first commercial date farm. The Old Ghan still runs on 23.5 km of private line between MacDonnell Siding and Ewaninga (trip includes meal at siding stop); train is feature of Ghan Preservation Society rail museum at MacDonnell Siding, 10 km S. Chateau Hornsby, NT's only commercial winery, 11 km E: Emily Gap, Jessie Gap and Ruby Gap Nature Parks (13, 18 and 141 km); Corroboree Rock Conservation Park (48 km); Trephina Gorge and N'Dhala Gorge Nature Parks (80 and 98 km); Ross River Homestead (88 km); and Arltunga Historical Reserve (110 km). To west: Simpsons Gap and Ormiston Gorge and Pound National Parks (18 and 132 km); Standley Chasm (50 km); Ellery Creek Big Hole, Serpentine Gorge, Glen Helen Gorge and Redbank Gorge Nature Parks (93, 104, 133 and 170 km); Hermannsburg Mission (125 km); and Gosse Bluff meteor crater (210 km). To north: Ryan Well and Central Mt Stuart Historical Reserves (126 and 216 km); Barrow Creek Telegraph Station (284 km); Wycliffe Well and Bonney Well (392 and 422 km); and Devils Marbles (420 km). To north-east: Gemtree; fossicking for garnet or zircon (140 km)To south: Ewaninga Rock Carvings Conservation Reserve (39 km); and Chambers Pillar Historical Reserve (149 km). To south-west: Henbury Meteorites Conservation Park (147 km); Palm Valley in Finke Gorge National Park (155 km); Kings Canyon in Watarrka National Park (323 km); and Uluru National Park (450 km). Great variety of tours of varying duration covering scenic attractions, Aboriginal culture and specialist interests, many 'off beaten track'. Experience these by bus or coach, limousine, 4WD safari, Harley Davidson motorcycle, camel, horse, aircraft, helicopter or balloon. **Tourist information:** Centrepoint Building, cnr Gregory Tce and Hartley St; (089) 52 5800. **Accommodation:** 2 hotels, 16 motels, 6 caravan/ camping parks. **See also:** Aboriginal Art; The Red Centre. MAP REF. 391 K3, 397 J9

Barkly Homestead Pop. 20

On the junction of the Barkly Hwy, 185 km from the junction of the Stuart and Barkly Hwys. **Accommodation:** 1 motel, 1 caravan/ camping park. MAP REF. 395 N11, 397 N1

The Top End

With improved roads and the vast increase in tourism in Australia, Darwin has become a major tourist destination. There is accommodation to suit either luxury or family means. Darwin itself is a winter haven, with its excellent beaches, abundance of fish and warm weather, but its real attraction is as a base for exploring the wild and fascinating country at the 'Top End'. Here you might see wide billabongs covered with lilies, clouds of geese wheeling above the trees, crocodiles sunning themselves on waterside rocks, plunging waterfalls, rows of pillar-like ant hills, spectacular cliff and rock features, caves and cliffs carrying the Aboriginal cave paintings of the past.

The Northern Territory Government has created a number of reserves to preserve the features of the region and to make them accessible to travellers. The most spectacular of these, in an area fast becoming one of the top natural tourist attractions in Australia, is **Kakadu National Park** in the dense and wild country along the East Alligator River, bordering Arnhem Land.

Kakadu has World Heritage status; it is considered to be of outstanding worth for both its natural features and its cultural significance. Situated 250 kilometres from Darwin, it encompasses an area of 1 307 300 ha (approx. 20 000 square kilometres). The park is leased to the Australian Nature Conservation Agency (ANCA) to manage for all visitors to enjoy.

Kakadu contains a wealth of archaeological and rock-art sites that provide insights into Aboriginal culture. The park's traditional owners are willing to share their knowledge and understanding of their land, so visitors will appreciate the importance of Kakadu and share responsibility for its protection.

Kakadu is unique in that it encompasses an entire river catchment, the black-soil floodplains and paperbark lagoons of the South Alligator River system, and within it are found all the major habitat types of the Top End. The park is rich in vegetation, ranging from pockets of rainforest through dwarf shrubland to open forest and swamps. The abundant wildlife includes several animals unique to the area, such as the banded pigeon, the rock possum and a species of rock wallaby. There are emus, a rich variety of pigeons

Jim Jim Falls, Kakadu National Park

and parrots, many marsupials, freshwater and saltwater crocodiles, waterbirds and rivers teeming with fish. Features within the park include Yellow Waters, a spectacular wetlands area with prolific birdlife, particularly in the dry season, and Nourlangie Rock, where there is Aboriginal rock art. A spectacular point in the park is the Jim Jim Falls, 215 metres high and with a sheer drop of 152 metres of water pouring (in the wet season) over a rugged and colourful escarpment.

North of the Jim Jim Falls is the East Alligator River, a well-known fishing ground where barramundi can be caught and where the river reaches wind through spectacularly beautiful country. Visits to some isolated locations within the park are subject to a permit system and limited visitor numbers because of the sensitive nature of those areas.

As crocodiles are present in park, swimming is not recommended and those who fish from the banks of rivers or from boats should take care.

Accommodation in the park consists of hotels, caravan parks, a youth hostel and private camping-grounds. Facilities are available for disabled persons. Fuel, food and provisions may be obtained at Jabiru township and at Border Store.

Visitors over sixteen years of age pay a park use fee (valid for fourteen days).

Two small parks close to Darwin are **Berry Springs**, 65 kilometres south, and **Howard Springs**, 35 kilometres southeast. Berry Springs is noted for its warm water, a continual 20° C for pleasant and safe swimming, and its birdlife. More than 120 species of birds have been recorded, the most colourful ones including rainbow lorikeets, the northern rosella, red-winged parrots, rainbow birds and blue-faced honeyeaters. At Howard Springs, the pool

is surrounded by rainforest, including pandanus palms, milkwood, red ash, white cedar, wild nutmeg and camphorwood trees. Again, the park abounds in birds and other wildlife.

Along the Stuart Highway, known as 'the track', 354 kilometres south-east of Darwin are the town of **Katherine** and the spectacular **Nitmiluk (Katherine Gorge) National Park**. Here the clear river flows between the brilliantly coloured walls of the gorge, towering 60 metres high. A boat tour through the gorge is guaranteed to be a highlight of any holiday.

A further 110 kilometres south-east of Katherine is the **Mataranka Pool Reserve**, near the Mataranka Homestead, where thermal springs are surrounded by lush tropical forest and the water is permanently at body temperature. Four-wheel-drive wildlife safaris can be arranged in Darwin and they are an ideal way to see the country and to experience something of life in the Top End.

There are major roads to all these Top End attractions. However, if you are contemplating an unguided tour of the region, it is vital that you recognise that should you stray into some unknown areas you may get into difficulties. **See also:** Outback Motoring.

For further information on Kakadu contact Park Manager, Kakadu National Park, PO Box 71, Jabiru NT 0886; (089) 79 9101. *Visitor Guides* to the park are available from the ANCA: GPO Box 636, Canberra ACT 2601; and GPO Box 1260, Darwin NT 0800; or from Park Headquarters. For further information on the Top End contact the Darwin Region Tourism Association, 31 Smith St Mall (PO Box 4292, Darwin 0801); (089) 81 4300. **Note** detailed map of Kakadu National Park on page 387.

National Parks

There are nearly 90 parks, reserves and protected areas in the Northern Territory. The major ones are grouped in two sections, separated by 1500 kilometres of road. One group is at the Top End, close to Darwin, and the other at the southern end, around Alice Springs in central Australia.

Best-known of all the parks in the Centre is **Uluru** (Ayers Rock–Mount Olga) National Park, which contains the monolith Uluru (Ayers Rock) and Kata Tjuta (The Olgas) rising abruptly from the surrounding plains. The area is of vital cultural and religious significance to the Anangu (the traditional owners), whose ancestors have lived in the area for at least 10 000 years.

An easy way to explore Uluru's attractions is either by undertaking the Circuit Walk or joining a guided coach party tour around the nine-kilometre rock base to see significant traditional sites, such as the Mutitjulu Cave containing elaborate Aboriginal paintings, and Kantju Gorge.

The climb to the 348-metre-high summit is strictly for those with a good head for heights. It should not be attempted by anyone who is unfit or unwell, or in hot weather; injuries are common.

Further west, the great domes of Kata Tjuta are separated by deep clefts, many of which hold sweet water and support abundant wildlife. The name Kata Tjuta means 'many heads'. There are several walks—Lookout, Valley of the Winds, Olga Gorge—which take from one to two hours to complete. Please keep to these marked tracks and consult a ranger before attempting any unmarked walks.

The town of Alice Springs lies in the MacDonnell Ranges, the land of the Aranda people and a paradise for photographers and artists. Cutting through the ranges are spectacular gorges offering some of the finest scenery in Australia—crimson and ochre rock walls bordering deep blue pools and slopes covered with spring wildflowers.

Within the **West MacDonnells National Park** are several scenic highlights. The best-known is Ormiston Gorge and Pound, where fish bury themselves in the mud as a string of waterholes shrink to puddles, then wait for the rains to fill them again. The deepest part of Ormiston Creek is a magnificent permanent pool the Aranda believed to be inhabited by a great water-snake. At the far end of the gorge, the walls are curtained by a variety of ferns and plants, including the lovely Sturt's desert rose and the relic *Macrozamia*.

Finke Gorge National Park, a scenic wilderness straddling the Finke River, includes the picturesque Palm Valley. This valley is a refuge for cycad palms and the ancient *Livistona mariae*, estimated to be about 5000 years old. The park is particularly rugged and visitors who do not join tours are advised to use 4WD.

Closer to Alice Springs is **Simpsons Gap,** only 8 kilometres west, that is best seen on foot. There are several walking tracks, as well as guided ranger tours, through rocky gaps, along steep sided ridges overlooking huge gums and timbered creek flats.

Between Finke and Uluru lies **Watarrka National Park**, its main attraction being the beautiful Kings Canyon. Waterholes, rock formations, and abundant

Yellow Waters wetlands area, Kakadu National Park

The East MacDonnells near Alice Springs

wildlife provide excellent photographic and bushwalking opportunities.

The East MacDonnells contain five parks and reserves including **Trephina Gorge Nature Park** and **Arltunga Historic Reserve**, rich in Aboriginal history and culture. The **Corroboree Rock Conservation Reserve** protects the sacred grounds of the Aranda.

The **Ewaninga Rock Carvings Conservation Reserve** contains a small group of rock outcrops on which prehistoric Aboriginal carvings trace a maze of wavy lines, circles and animal tracks. The rock engravings in **N'Dhala Gorge National Park** are so ancient that their meaning is unknown to the present-day Aboriginal people of central Australia.

South-west of Alice Springs, just off the Stuart Highway, are the twelve **Henbury Meteorite Craters**, which were formed several thousand years ago. This is a haunt of the ferocious-looking, but harmless, bearded dragon lizard.

At the Top End of the Territory are several impressive national parks, including the scenic Kakadu. Located 348 kilometres south of Darwin is **Nitmiluk (Katherine Gorge) National Park**. This fascinating river canyon, with its abundant wildlife and Aboriginal rock paint-

ings, is best seen from a tour boat. When the Katherine River flows peacefully in the dry season (May-October), anglers will boast with delight of the good catches of barramundi and other species of fish that are found in the gorge's deep pools.

Litchfield Park, 100 kilometres south of Darwin, features four spectacular waterfalls that flow throughout the year. The Lost City with its fascinating sandstone formation and Sandy Creek Falls are on 4WD tracks. Swimming, photography, wildlife observation and bushwalking, ranging from a 20-minute stroll to an extended wilderness walk, are all popular activities.

One of the newest parks in the Territory, **Gregory National Park**, features tropical and semi-arid plant life, together with spectacular range and gorge scenery. Significant Aboriginal sites and evidence of early European settlement and pastoral history are also features. Boat tours are available at Timber Creek on Victoria River. Vehicle access within the park is by 4WD only.

In **Gurig National Park**, on the Cobourg Peninsula, a wilderness lodge, Seven Spirit Bay, overlooks Coral Bay and is reached from Darwin by air. The complex offers a true wilderness

experience. Fishing, sailing, a trip to historic ruins at Victoria, and exploration of the area's natural environment are the park's other attractions.

Note: In national parks and reserves and other areas, it is wise to heed local advice on the dangers of swimming because of the possibility of lurking crocodiles. The saltwater crocodile (found mainly in river estuaries) is highly dangerous. The freshwater or Johnstone's crocodile (found in billabongs and rivers) is generally regarded as harmless though it has been known to attack humans in circumstances where it has felt threatened.

For more information about the Territory's parks and reserves, contact the Conservation Commission of the Northern Territory, PO Box 496, Palmerston NT 0831; telephone (089) 89 4411. For Kakadu and Uluru, contact the Australian Nature Conservation Agency (ANCA), GPO Box 636, Canberra ACT 2601, telephone (06) 250 0200; or PO Box 1260, Darwin NT 0801, telephone (089) 81 5299. **See also:** The Top End. **Note** detailed map of Kakadu National Park on page 387.

Barrow Creek
Pop. 30

On the Stuart Hwy, 283 km N of Alice Springs. Originally a water stop for cattle-droving. **Of interest:** Old Telegraph Station (1872). **Accommodation:** 1 hotel.
MAP REF. 397 J4

Batchelor
Pop. 635

In the heart of the Coomalie area. Former town for Rum Jungle Uranium Mine, now a major education centre for the training of Aboriginal teachers at Batchelor College. **Of interest:** Mini replica of Karlstein Castle of Bohemia. Swimming at Rum Jungle Lake. Parachuting and gliding. **In the area:** Batchelor is gateway to Litchfield Park, 40 km W, with its spectacular waterfalls (Wangi, Sandy Creek, Florence and Tolmer) and pockets of scenic rainforest. Fishing for barramundi on Daly River, 70 km SW (4WD). **Tourist information:** Rum Jungle Motor Inn, Rum Jungle Rd; (089) 76 0123. **Accommodation:** 1 motel, 1 caravan/camping park.
MAP REF. 388 D7, 392 E6

Borroloola
Pop. 594

Small settlement on the McArthur River. Once one of the north's larger and more colourful frontier towns, it is now very popular with fishing enthusiasts. Local Aboriginal basket-weaving. **Of interest:** Museum in old police station (1886), off Robinson Rd. Borroloola Fishing Classic, held every Easter. **In the area:** Cape Crawford, 110 km SW; gateway to the Gulf area. **Tourist information:** McArthur River Caravan Park, Robinson Rd; (089) 75 8734. **Accommodation:** 1 hotel, 1 caravan/camping park; cabins.
MAP REF. 393 N13, 395 O3

Daly Waters
Pop. 298

Situated 4 km N of the junction of the Stuart and Carpentaria Hwys. **Of interest:** Historic pub (1893), Stuart St. **In the area:** Tree (1 km N), reputedly marked with the letter S by explorer John McDouall Stuart. **Tourist information:** Daly Waters Pub, Stuart St; (089) 75 9927. **Accommodation:** 1 hotel, 1 motel, 1 caravan/ camping park.
MAP REF. 395 J3

Dunmarra
Pop. 30

At the junction of the Stuart and Buchanan Hwys, 363 km N of Tennant Creek. **Accommodation:** 1 motel, 1 caravan/ camping park.
MAP REF. 395 J4

Elliott
Pop. 423

On the Stuart Hwy, 254 km N of Tennant Creek. **In the area:** Lake Woods, 13 km W, NT's largest lake; water is curious milky white. **Accommodation:** 1 hotel, 1 motel, 2 caravan/camping parks.
MAP REF. 395 J6

Glen Helen
Pop. 42

On Namatjira Drive, 136 km W of Alice Springs, Glen Helen is an excellent base for exploring the superb scenery of Ormiston Gorge, 12 km NE, the 'jewel of the MacDonnell Ranges'. At Glen Helen Gorge, 300 m E, you can walk along the bed of the Finke River between towering, rugged red cliffs. Helicopter flights available to surrounding areas, including Mt. Sonder. Glen Helen Lodge has won many awards for its food and accommodation standards and its hospitality, including Yapalpa Restaurant. **In the area:** Finke River Gorge, 37 km SE amazing rock formations: the 'amphitheatre', 'sphinx' and 'battleship'. Red cabbage palms (*Livistona mariae*) in nearby Palm Valley, found nowhere else in the world. Hermannsburg, 25 km SW; restored Aboriginal mission, birthplace of artist Albert Namatjira. Redbank Gorge, 24 km W. **Tourist information:** Glen Helen Lodge, Namatjira Dr; (089) 56 7489. **Accommodation:** Glen Helen Lodge.
MAP REF. 390 E3, 396 H9

Jabiru
Pop. 1731

A mining town within the Kakadu National Park, 247 km from Darwin on the Arnhem Hwy, Jabiru has a range of services enhanced to cater for special environmental requirements necessary to limit the effect of the town on the surrounding World Heritage National Park. **Of interest:** Gagudju Crocodile Hotel, Flinders St, hotel built in shape of 250-m-long crocodile; design was approved by the Gagudju people, to whom the crocodile is a totem. Kakadu Frontier Lodge and Caravan Park, Civic Dr, laid out in traditional Aboriginal circular motif. Jabiru Olympic Swimming Pool, Civic Dr, largest in NT; also 9-hole golf course. **In the area:** Inspection of Ranger Uranium Mine, 6 km E; daily tours May–Oct. (information from Kakadu Air Services at Jabiru Air Terminal).

Scenic flights over the unique Kakadu territory with its virtually inaccessible sandstone formations standing some 400 m above vast floodplains, seasonal waterfalls, wetland wilderness and remote beaches. Daily tours to Arnhem Land. Boat, gorge and waterfall, and safari tours available. **Tourist information:** 6 Tasman Plaza; (089) 79 2548. **Accommodation:** 1 hotel, 1 caravan/ camping park. **See also:** The Top End.
MAP REF. 387 H5, 389 Q4, 392 I5

Katherine
Pop. 7064

In times of drought—sometimes for years on end—you can travel northern Australia for 2000 km and more before you see the sheen of flowing water in a permanent river. Perhaps it is the instant impact of the incredible contrast between unending arid plain and Katherine Gorge that heightens its dramatic beauty. The town of Katherine is 337 km S of Darwin, by a stretch of bitumen that reaches from horizon to horizon in an almost ruler-straight line. Nowadays Katherine's economic mainstays are the Mt Todd goldmine, tourism and the Tindal RAAF airbase, 27 km SE, but still this neat township is the centre of scientific agricultural experiments designed to improve the efficiency of the traditional beef cattle industry on which it was founded. Indeed it is sited in some of the NT's most promising agricultural and grazing country. The township is located on the southern side of the Katherine River and has good facilities, including several churches, parks, sporting clubs, a bowling ground, a golf course and showground. **Of interest:** Katherine Museum, Gorge Rd. Railway Station Museum, Railway Tce. School of the Air, Giles St. O'Keefe House, Riverbank Dr; one of oldest homes in town. **In the area:** The Katherine River was named after a beautiful daughter of one of the sponsors of John McDouall Stuart, who discovered it in 1862. The gorge, named Nitmiluk by the Aboriginal people, towers above the sparkling, slow-moving water in the dry season. The ancient rock walls are dotted with caves. Aboriginal paintings, from miniatures to huge murals, decorate both faces above the floodline. The scene changes in the wet, when the water-level often rises 18 m as the river boils through. The caves are swamped and a bigger flood than average may wash away another piece of an irreplaceable art form that was developed thousands of years ago. The rock is grey, black and ochre, the vegetation bright green. Fifty-eight species of reptiles and amphibians have been identified in the area, including a burrowing frog, the freshwater crocodile, a tortoise with a neck so long it looks like a snake when its body is submerged, three kinds of frogs that climb trees, a lizard without legs, pythons that often grow to 2 m, and many poisonous snakes. In the higher reaches of the gorge kangaroos and wallabies in mobs of hundreds at a time crowd in to drink. You may catch a barramundi—if you don't hook a tortoise or crocodile. The only way to see the gorge properly is by flat-bottomed boat. You can hire a canoe yourself and camp in the gorge overnight, or take a guided tour; cruises run daily. There are three easily-reached pools in the gorge. No motorboats are allowed in the gorge May – October. The weather is always hot, but there is little humidity for the nine not-quite-so-hot months of the year. You will need a top covering over cotton clothes in the early morning and at night from about mid-April to mid-July. Historic Springvale Homestead, 8 km W, is the oldest remaining homestead in the NT, having been built by Alfred Giles in 1879. An Aboriginal Corroboree is performed here three times a week. Manyal-

laluk (formerly Eva Valley Station), 100 km SE of Katherine, offers visitors the experience of Aboriginal culture combined with the magnificent scenery of a wilderness park. Edith Falls, for picnics, swimming and camping, 62 km NE. Mataranka Homestead, 115 km S, has a thermal pool believed to have therapeutic powers. The tourist resort here has excellent facilities. There is rock art in the Land of the Lightning Brothers, 140 km SW, and at Muniyung, 170 km SE. Tours available include guided tours of Cutta Cutta Caves, 26 km S, heli tours and scenic flights, 4WD safaris, barramundi fishing tours and horse trail rides. Boat tours on Victoria River at Timber Creek, 285 km W, in Gregory National Park; also fishing and bushwalking. **Tourist information:** Cnr Stuart Hwy and Lindsay St; (089) 72 2650. **Accommodation:** 2 hotel/motels, 7 motels, 8 caravan/camping parks. **See also:** Aboriginal Art; The Top End.
MAP REF. 392 H10

Kulgera
Pop. 25
About 20 km from the SA border on the Stuart Hwy. **Of interest:** Town's name is Aboriginal for 'place of weeping eye', named for 45 m-high rocks where water continuously trickles down the sides. Museum and animal centre. **Tourist information:** Kulgera Hotel, Stuart Hwy;

(089) 56 0973. **Accommodation:** 1 hotel, 1 caravan park.
MAP REF. 396 I13

Larrimah
Pop. 20
On the Stuart Hwy, 90 km N of Daly Waters. **Of interest:** Museum; Crocodiles and buffalo at Green Park, Stuart Hwy. **Tourist information:** Green Park Tourist Complex, Stuart Hwy; (089) 75 9937. **Accommodation:** 1 hotel, 2 caravan/camping parks.
MAP REF. 392 I12, 394 I2

Mataranka
Pop. 180
This settlement, 110 km SE of Katherine, has a well-developed tourist resort with a thermal spring pool nearby. **Of interest:** Stockyard Museum and Territory Manor Wildlife Park, both on Stuart Hwy. **In the area:** Camping, horse-trail riding, scenic flights, 4WD safaris and barramundi fishing. Elsey National Park, 5 km E; swimming, fishing, camping, canoeing, pleasant walks and Mataranka thermal pool. Elsey Cemetery, 25 km S, graves of outback pioneers immortalised by Mrs Aeneas Gunn (who lived at Elsey Station Homestead 1902-3) in *We of the Never Never*. Replica of Elsey Homestead, museum. **Accommodation:** 1 hotel, 2 motels, 2 caravan/camping parks. **See also:** The Top End.
MAP REF. 392 I11, 394 I1

The spectacular Katherine Gorge

Aboriginal Art

Art is an essential element in Aboriginal culture, often using symbols to communicate ideas which cannot be expressed in any other way. Traditional art serves this purpose throughout the Australian continent, but the actual form of expression varies considerably from region to region.

Much of the artwork at Uluru (Ayers Rock), for example, is symbolic and may appear to the uninitiated eye to be quite abstract. Aboriginal artists in Central Australia also traditionally used the ground as their 'canvas'; large sand paintings are made with coloured earths, feathers and other natural objects to represent the travels of the 'Dreaming' ancestors, the ancient beings that created the landforms on the vast plains. These sand paintings are intricate patterns made up of varying combinations of circles, lines, dots and tracks.

The designs found in the traditional art of the Top End, particularly at the spectacular art sites in Kakadu National Park, are quite different in style: here the visitor can see examples of 'X-ray' art, so named because great attention is given to internal detail. This style has been practised in other civilisations, but is believed to have reached its highest level of expression in Western Arnhem Land.

Some of the galleries where Aboriginal art can be seen are:

Alice Springs

The **Alice Springs Aboriginal Art and Culture Centre** located at 86–88 Todd Street features works by Central Australian and Western Desert artists and craftspeople. Stock includes paintings on canvas and bark, watercolours, carvings, weavings, weapons, didjeridus, seed necklaces and ornaments, silk fashion batiks, books and cassettes. Worldwide mail-order and delivery services available.

The origin of the Ewaninga Rock Carvings (39 kilometres south of Alice Springs) is lost in time. More correctly known as petroglyphs, the carvings are considered to be the work of an ancient culture, since present-day Aborigines do not understand their meaning. The rock carvings form a part of the Ewaninga Rock Carvings Conservation Reserve.

Uluru Region

The **Maruku Arts and Crafts** complex, next to the Ranger Station, at entrance to Uluru National Park, specialises in works of more than 800 artists and craftsmen from the tribal groups in the area—Pitjantjatjara, Yankunytjatjara, Matuntjara and Luritja.

Anangu cave art sites around Uluru and Kata Tjuta (the Olgas), 50 kilometres west of Uluru, are extremely vulnerable.

Protection of this art is given a high priority by the Anangu, the traditional owners, and measures are being taken to ensure it is not damaged. Unlike some other cave art in Australia, the pigments used in the paintings are water-based and are very susceptible to damage from moisture, such as sweat from human hands.

Darwin

The **Museum of Arts and Sciences** at Bullocky Point houses a fine permanent collection of Aboriginal art. Each September it also brings together the finest traditional and contemporary Aboriginal art from around Australia for the National Aboriginal Art Award, which coincides with the Danggalaba Festival of Aboriginal Art and Life. The award gives visitors the opportunity to see and purchase some of the best bark and sand paintings, carvings, fabric prints and contemporary art offered in Australia.

Raintree Gallery at 18 Knuckey Street has a wide range of northern Australian Aboriginal paintings and artefacts for both collectors and gift buyers. The stock includes canvas and bark paintings, carvings, weapons, weavings, fashion garments, books, musical instruments and cassettes. A gift shop is open at least six days a week, just off the Smith Street Mall. Worldwide packing and mailing facilities are available.

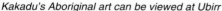

Kakadu's Aboriginal art can be viewed at Ubirr

Kakadu National Park

The rock art in Kakadu National Park is among the finest in the world, and represents a close personal and spiritual relationship between man and the environment. The richness of Kakadu's Aboriginal art can be viewed at **Nourlangie Rock** and **Ubirr**, both of which are accessible by road. There are four main periods of art and much can be learned about the early history of the Aborigines—some of the occupation sites have been carbon-dated at 23 000 years, and others go back even earlier.

The main subject of the *pre-estuarine* period (which ended with the rise of the sea-level 7000 to 9000 years ago) was man the hunter, with stone axes, simple spears and boomerangs. The *estuarine* period is marked by the introduction of paintings representing the estuarine species of animals, especially the barramundi fish. This was also the era when 'X-ray' art emerged, with its depiction of the internal organs and skeletons of animals. Between 2000 and 4000 years ago freshwater systems began to replace estuarine conditions. This is reflected in the art with the depiction of freshwater species such as the long-necked tortoise and the magpie goose. The *contact* period began when Aboriginal people were subject to intense contact with outsiders. The Europeans' activities and their material possessions, particularly rifles and steel axes, are most graphically portrayed in the main gallery at Ubirr.

Katherine

The township of Katherine has developed historically as the regional centre for a diverse group of Aboriginal communities. The artefacts available at **Mimi Arts and Crafts Gallery** in Lindsay Street reflect this diversity in art, from the desert communities of the west to the coastal communities in the east, and include contemporary music, weavings, canvas and bark paintings. Aboriginal-designed fabrics are also available from the Pearce Street shop.

Tennant Creek

Anyinginyi Art and Crafts, 139 Patterson Street, specialises in the art work of the four groups that share this part of the country: the Warlpiri (renowned for their sand paintings), and the Warumungu, Kaititja and Alyawarre, whose paintings and carvings depict aspects of life from the Tanami and Barkly regions.

Arnhem Land

A group of ancient rock paintings, ranging from simple stick figures and handprints to more intricate and heavily symbolic paintings, was discovered in 1988 in caves deep in escarpment country in an area known as **Umorrduk,** near Mount Borradaile, 225 kilometres east of Darwin. Tours are available from Darwin, travelling through Kakadu National Park and Arnhem Land, to visit these 20 000-year-old rock-art sites in Gummulkbin tribal lands.

A more comprehensive listing of outlets that specialise in Aboriginal arts and crafts is available from the Darwin Regional Tourism Association, 33 Smith St. Mall; (089) 814300.

Aboriginal-operated Tours

For over 60 000 years the Aboriginal people have developed a unique understanding of the relationship between the physical and spiritual world. Today many Aborigines work professionally to share their knowledge with visitors.

There is a wide range of Aboriginal operated tours available throughout the Northern Territory, each offering an insight into the Aboriginal culture of that area.

The Northern Territory Tourism Commission has produced an excellent brochure *Come Share our Culture* which includes specific details of the tours available. To obtain a copy, contact the Darwin Regional Tourism Association, 33 Smith St Mall, Darwin; (089) 814300.

Aboriginal corroboree

Aboriginal Lands

Since the declaration of the *Aboriginal Land Rights (Northern Territory) Act* 1976, visitors **must** obtain a permit to enter Aboriginal Land.

It should be noted that as a general rule, Land Councils have been asked by traditional owners not to issue entry permits for unaccompanied tourist travel. This does not affect visitors travelling on organised tours on to Aboriginal Land where tour bookings include the necessary permit.

When making an application for entry to any Aboriginal Land, applicants must state the reason for entry, dates and duration of intended stay, names of persons travelling, and itinerary and routes to be used while on these lands. Permits can be issued only after consultation and approval of the relevant Aboriginal communities. Processing permit applications can take four to six weeks. It is the right of traditional owners of Aboriginal Land to refuse entry permits. Applications and any enquiries must be directed, in writing, to the relevant Land Council listed below.

All public roads that cross Aboriginal Lands are exempt from the permit provisions; the exemption covers the immediate road corridor only. If there is a likelihood of a need for fuel stops, travellers should seek transit permits from the relevant Land Councils. For those roads that are not designated as public roads, travellers should seek advice from the Land Councils before departure. Some towns within Aboriginal Land are also exempt from the provisions.

By agreement with the Tiwi Land Council, Australian Kakadu Tours runs the Putjamirra tourist camp (with tent accommodation) on Melville Island. Entry permission for visitors is arranged by the tour operator.

Bathurst Island artists and craftspeople have found expanding markets for their paintings, carvings, screen prints, batik, pots and other artefacts. The annual Northern Territory Barra Classic fishing tournament is held on Bathurst Island in September.

The relevant land councils to whom applications for permits and any inquiries must be directed, are:

Alice Springs and Tennant Creek Regions:
Central Land Council
33 Stuart Hwy
PO Box 3321
Alice Springs NT 0871
(089) 51 6320

Darwin, Nhulunbuy and Katherine Regions:
Northern Land Council
PO Box 42921
Casuarina NT 0811
(089) 20 5100

Melville and Bathurst Islands:
Tiwi Land Council
PO Box 38545
Winnellie NT 0821
(089) 47 1838

Gulf of Carpentaria

Gove

The Gove Peninsula, named after W.H.J. Gove, an Australian airman killed in the area during World War II, is situated at the far north-east point of Arnhem Land.

The whole of the peninsula is set aside as Aboriginal Land and the main centres are **Yirrkala** and **Nhulunbuy**. Gove Resort, and Hideaway Safari Lodge near Nhulunbuy's airport, offer visitors long white beaches and good fishing.

Nine kilometres west of Nhulunbuy, near Dundas Point, is **Melville Bay**, which the explorer Matthew Flinders described as the best natural harbour on the Gulf of Carpentaria. Accommodation is limited.

The **Yirrkala Mission**, near Mount Dundas, provides a residential base for many of the Aborigines in the area. Its name became familiar during the struggle by its people to win title to their land. The *Aboriginal Land Rights (Northern Territory) Act* was finally assented to on 16 December 1976. It represents to the people of Yirrkala the culmination of years of struggle to win recognition for their claims to land on which their people have lived for many thousands of years. The Yirrkala area is noted for Aboriginal carvings of birds and fish.

The easiest way to visit Nhulunbuy is by air (either commercial or charter). If you plan to explore by 4WD and without a tour guide, a permit is required from the Northern Land Council.

For further information contact the Darwin Regional Tourism Association, 33 Smith St Mall, Darwin; (089) 81 4300.

Noonamah Pop. 8
On the Stuart Hwy, 38 km S of Darwin.
Accommodation: 1 hotel/motel.
MAP REF. 388 D4, 392 F5

Pine Creek Pop. 437
On the Stuart Hwy, 92 km NW of Katherine, Pine Creek experienced a brief gold-rush in the 1870s; today the town is experiencing a resurgence following the reopening of goldmining operations. **Of interest:** Numerous historic buildings, including restored railway station and track, and open-air goldmining museum in National Trust reserve. **In the area:** Gold fossicking (licence required). Gold-mine tours; scenic drive; hunting safaris. Douglas Hot Springs Nature Park, 64 km N, off Stuart Hwy (52 km W) and Butterfly Gorge Nature Park, 14 km S of Springs (4WD); bushwalking. **Accommodation:** 1 hotel/motel, 1 caravan/camping park.
MAP REF. 387 A13, 389 J13, 392 G8

Renner Springs Pop. 19
On the Stuart Hwy, 161 km N of Tennant Creek. **Accommodation:** 1 hotel/motel.
MAP REF. 395 J8

Ross River Pop. 30
Settlement 85 km E of Alice Springs. **Of interest:** Overnight horse and camel safaris; horse, camel and wagon rides at Ross River Homestead ranch-style outback resort; also whipcracking, boomerang-throwing, and billy tea and damper. **In the area:** Trephina Gorge, 17 km NW. N'Dhala Gorge, 11 km SW; Aboriginal rock engravings and ancient fossil deposits. Arltunga Historical Reserve, 25 km E. **Tourist information:** Ross River Homestead, Ross Hwy; (089) 56 9711. **Accommodation:** Ross River Homestead; backpackers' bunkhouse, 30 cabins, 1 camping/caravan park.
MAP REF. 391 O3, 397 K8

Tennant Creek Pop. 3480
According to legend, Tennant Creek was founded when a beer wagon carrying building supplies destined for the nearby Overland Telegraph Station broke down at the site of the present town. The township is 507 km N of Alice Springs, on the Stuart Hwy. Gold and copper deposits account for its development today, and the town has grown into a thriving regional centre

Trephina Gorge near Ross River

for the Barkly Tablelands. **Of interest:** Civic Centre, Peko Rd; impressive art, gem and mineral collection. Travellers Rest Area, Purkiss Reserve, Ambrose St; picnic area with full facilities and adjacent swimming pool. **In the area:** Gold Stamp Battery and Museum, 1 km E; one of very few batteries still operational. The Dot Mine, 5 km W; 1930s goldmine, day and night tours. Telegraph Station, 10 km N; tours. Nobles Nob, 16 km E, once richest open-cut goldmine of its size in world. Three Ways Roadhouse, junction of Stuart and Barkly Hwys, 25 km N; nearby, John Flynn Historical Reserve. Attack Creek Historical Reserve, 73 km N, site of encounter between John McDouall Stuart and local Aborigines. Mary Ann Dam, 4 km NE; popular for swimming, canoeing, windsurfing, cycling and bushwalking. The Devil's Marbles, 103 km S; huge 'balancing rocks'. Less well-known but equally impressive, though smaller, the Devils Pebbles, 16 km NW. **Tourist information:** New Coach Transit Centre, Paterson St; (089) 62 3388. **Accommodation:** 1 hotel/motel, 3 motels, 1 youth hostel, 2 caravan/camping parks. **See also:** Aboriginal Art.
MAP REF. 395 K11

Ti Tree Pop. 50
On the Stuart Hwy, 194 km N of Alice Springs. **Of interest:** Aboriginal art at Aakki Gallery. **Accommodation:** 1 motel, 1 caravan/camping park.
MAP REF. 397 J6

Timber Creek Pop. 100
Located 290 km SW of Katherine on the Victoria Hwy. **Of interest:** Boat tours, cruises, scenic flights. **In the area:** Gregory National Park, 15 km W; Keep River National Park, 175 km W; rugged scenery, Aboriginal rock art, wildlife.

Tourist information: Timber Creek Hotel, (089) 75 0722. **Accommodation:** 2 hotels/motels, 2 caravan/camping parks. **See also:** National Parks.
MAP REF. 392 E12, 394 E2

Victoria River Pop. 6
Located where the Victoria Hwy crosses the Victoria River, between Timber Creek and the junction with Delamere Road. **Tourist information:** Victoria River Wayside Inn, Victoria Hwy; (089) 75 0744. **Accommodation:** 1 hotel/motel, 1 caravan/camping park.
MAP REF. 392 F12, 394 F2

Victory Downs Pop. 15
Situated on the border with SA, just off the Stuart Hwy, 316 km from Alice Springs.
MAP REF. 295 M1, 396 I13

Wauchope Pop. 7
On the Stuart Hwy, 115 km S of Tennant Creek. **In the area:** Devil's Marbles, 8 km N, Wycliffe Well, 18 km S; well-known for large selection of international beers. Old Wolfram mines, 10 km E (4WD only). **Tourist information:** Wauchope Well Hotel, Stuart Hwy; (089) 64 1963. **Accommodation:** 1 hotel, 1 caravan/camping park.
MAP REF. 395 K13, 397 K2

Yulara Pop. 2169
Situated on outskirts of Uluru National Park, this township is the location for the world-class Ayers Rock Resort, offering full visitor facilities and comfortable air-conditioned accommodation in all price brackets. **Of interest:** Visitors Centre provides displays and information on national park. Tours include Edible Desert Experience, and Uluru Experience Night Star Talk, which offers nocturnal sky viewing and narration of Aboriginal and European legends relating to the night sky. **In the area:** Uluru (Ayers Rock), 20 km SE; Australia's famous sandstone monolith. Kata Tjuta (The Olgas), 50 km W. Tours can be booked at Visitors Centre or reception in accommodation areas. **Tourist information:** Visitors Centre; (089) 56 2240. **Accommodation:** 3 hotels, backpackers' units, apartments, caravan/camping ground. **See also:** The Red Centre.
MAP REF. 396 F12

Touring the Territory

Many people will not want to embark on a tour of the Northern Territory's outback areas alone. Fortunately, an enormous variety of accompanied tours leave from all capital cities, enabling even the least intrepid visitor to see Australia's magnificent centre. These tours range from quite basic holidays under canvas, travelling by coach or 4WD between overnight stops, to air-conditioned coaches (for those who prefer a few 'home comforts'), choosing a route served by motel, hotel or tourist camp accommodation.

The main tourist season operates from approximately April to September, but intending visitors are now exhorted to 'See Alice while she's hot' and excellent reductions on travel and accommodation costs during the 'off season' months between October and March are being offered. This is the 'hot season', and if you do not like intense heat, it may be a better idea to save up until you can afford the higher in-season prices.

On a camping tour, it is usual for campers to help put up the tents, prepare, serve and wash up after meals, and generally clean up, but all this lends itself to making the holiday a truly 'different' experience. It does also mean, however, that adaptability is an advantage, since you cannot choose the people who accompany you.

Another way to tackle the outback is to join a convoy expedition, where you drive your own vehicle, but are guided by experts. Motoring organisations arrange such tours, but departure times are limited and you will not be permitted to join the tour if your vehicle is not in an acceptable condition.

If you do decide to travel alone on roads that are off the beaten track, it is wise to take a few precautions for your own security. It is not advisable to pick up hitch-hikers or to camp, other than in a lockable caravan, outside organised sites. **See also:** Outback Motoring.

The 'Ghan' train is another way of avoiding the long, boring stretches of road. To travel one way by train and return by air is a time-saving way of seeing the Centre. There is a great variety of organised tours operating from Alice Springs which will convey you to the main tourist attractions of the region. This is an excellent way of seeing the Centre. Coach operators also combine a one-way rail trip (approximately 22 hours) with a return coach journey.

Overnight stop, Devil's Marbles

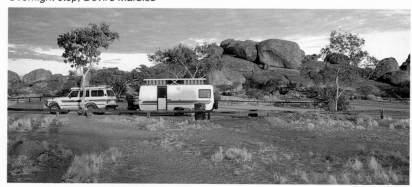

Sportsman's Territory

Even though the Northern Territory has an area of 135 million hectares—six times the size of Great Britain and one-sixth of the Australian continent—there are few places where you can legally shoot game. Even fishing is restricted in some areas.

Every kind of firearm must be registered. The possession of high-powered rifles and pistols is tightly controlled. Visitors with a high-powered weapon properly licensed in their home state or country may be allowed it in the Territory if a valid certificate or licence is produced at a police station. The police must be satisfied that the weapon is safe, that the applicant is over twenty-one years and that there is a 'substantial reason' for carrying the weapon. The term 'substantial reason' does not include sporting purposes. Visitors carrying firearms must report to police within two days of entering the Territory. The booklet *Before You Shoot,* available at any NT police station, outlines licensing requirements for shooters and firearms in the Territory.

Firearms are prohibited in the Territory's main sanctuaries and protected areas. Sanctuaries now in existence include: Cobourg Peninsula, Tanami Desert, Woolwonga Aboriginal Land, Daly River Aboriginal Land, Murgenella River and the Arnhem Land Aboriginal Land. All Aboriginal Lands are protected areas. It is an offence to take firearms or traps into any protected area. Penalties range from fines of up to $400 to imprisonment for up to twelve months. Maps showing existing sanctuaries and protected areas can be seen at police stations. Firearms and shooting are prohibited in NT parks, except for the hunting reserves — Howard Swamp, Lambell's Lagoon, Harrison Dam and Marrakai (all in the Top End). Further information about these reserves, and the necessary permits that must be obtained prior to arrival, is available from the Northern Territory Conservation Commission, Gaymark Building, Palmerston; (089) 89 4411.

Property owners rarely give permission for strangers to shoot on their land. Trigger-happy tourists are known to have caused serious stock losses in the Territory and those who shoot on private property without permission from the owner are liable to find themselves under fire. Some fish are protected in some areas, but fishing is otherwise unrestricted both inland and in the sea. Visitors who want to mount a hunting, shooting and fishing expedition in the Territory could well save themselves heavy fines and confiscation of guns and gear by booking into an organised safari through a hometown travel agency.

Northern Territory

Location Map

Other Map Coverage
Central Darwin 384
Darwin & Northern Suburbs 385
North Eastern Suburbs, Darwin 386
Kakadu Region 387
Darwin Region 388
Alice Springs Region 390

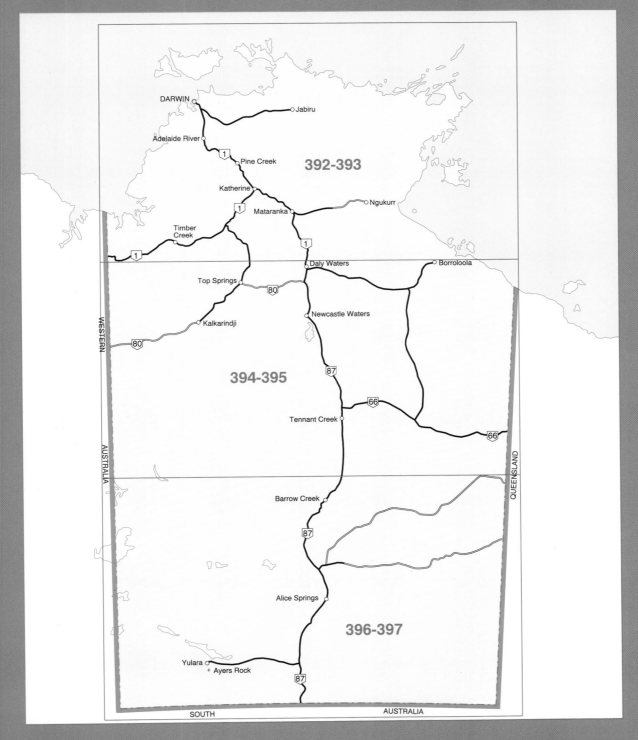

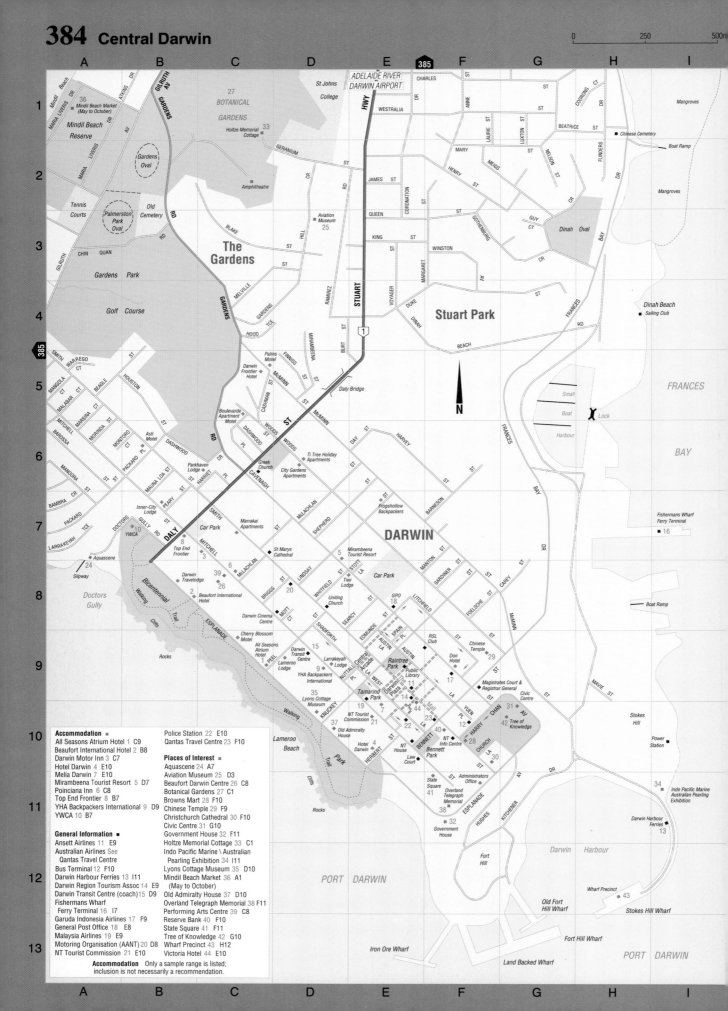

0   250   500m

Accommodation ■
All Seasons Atrium Hotel 1   C9
Beaufort International Hotel 2   B8
Darwin Motor Inn 3   C7
Hotel Darwin 4   E10
Melia Darwin 7   E10
Mirambeena Tourist Resort 5   D7
Poinciana Inn 6   C8
Top End Frontier 8   B7
YHA Backpackers International 9   D9
YWCA 10   B7

General Information ■
Ansett Airlines 11   E9
Australian Airlines See
  Qantas Travel Centre
Bus Terminal 12   F10
Darwin Harbour Ferries 13   I11
Darwin Region Tourism Assoc 14   E9
Darwin Transit Centre (coach) 15   D9
Fishermans Wharf
  Ferry Terminal 16   I7
Garuda Indonesia Airlines 17   F9
General Post Office 18   E8
Malaysia Airlines 19   E9
Motoring Organisation (AANT) 20   D8
NT Tourist Commission 21   E10

Police Station 22   E10
Qantas Travel Centre 23   F10

Places of Interest ■
Aquascene 24   A7
Aviation Museum 25   D3
Beaufort Darwin Centre 26   C8
Botanical Gardens 27   C1
Browns Mart 28   F10
Chinese Temple 29   F9
Christchurch Cathedral 30   F10
Civic Centre 31   G10
Government House 32   F11
Holtze Memorial Cottage 33   C1
Indo Pacific Marine \ Australian
  Pearling Exhibition 34   I11
Lyons Cottage Museum 35   D10
Mindil Beach Market 36   A1
  (May to October)
Old Admiralty House 37   D10
Overland Telegraph Memorial 38   F11
Performing Arts Centre 39   C8
Reserve Bank 40   F10
State Square 41   F11
Tree of Knowledge 42   G10
Wharf Precinct 43   H12
Victoria Hotel 44   E10

Accommodation   Only a sample range is listed;
  inclusion is not necessarily a recommendation.

0 0.25 0.5 0.75 1km

A B C D E F G H I

1 2 3 4 5 6 7 8 9 10 11 12 13

East Point

East Point

Rocks

Dudley Point

Artillery War Museum

East Point Reserve

Mangroves

Boat Ramp

Creek

DARWIN AIRPORT

TOTEM DE LATOUR RD

Ludmilla

FITZER TUDAWALI ST

BAGOT ABORIGINAL RESERVE

NADPUR

BENWERRIN

CAMARA ST

RAAF Base

BUKATILLA
CARRYONG
CALOOLA
CAREELA
COLLENDINA CURRINGA
DAMALA DAMALA BELLARA
COORADIL

NARROWS

The Narrows

WILMOT Dwyer Park

BILLEROY
AMAROO RD GANDARRA CIR

Waratah Sports Club

KURRINGAL CT

BAYVIEW

GEORGE ST

PHILLIP

HINKLER

Ross Smith Memorial Fannie Bay Gaol Museum

ROSS

DICK WARD DR

Fannie Bay Racecourse

Richardson Park

SMITH

PLAYFORD

GILBERT
LUDMILLA TCE
WELLS
BRENAN
PORTER

FLEMING ST

Trailer Boat Club
Boat Ramp
Sailing Club

Vesteys Beach

Olympic Pool
Waterslide

FANNIE BAY

Ski-ing and Yachting Area

Boat Ramp

Fannie Bay

POINT RD

EAST

ELIZABETH

CHRISTIE

BROWN
HOLTZE

DONIGRAVE
GILES
LAMPE ST

KELLAWAY
GREGORY

MACDONALD

URQUHART ST
PARAP PL GORDON ST

Parap

HUDSON

FYSH

HWY

BISHOP

BRENNAN DR

Water Ski Club

Boat Ramp

CONACHER Museum and Art Gallery

Bullocky Point
Rocks

Darwin High School

Darwin Bowling Club

SEALE

DRYSDALE

SOMERVILLE

RAILWAY

BISHOP ST
JOLLY ST

Winnellie

TIGER

WOOLNER

STUART

ILIFFE ST

QUARRY
CR
VERBURG
Primary School

GRAHAM

Mangroves

Sacred Heart College

St Johns College

Botanical Gardens

GILRUTH AV

The Gardens

Mindil Beach

MARARA LIVERIS DR
MINDIL BEACH
RESERVE
MARA LIVERIS

Diamond Beach Hotel Casino

Myilly Point

GERANIUM ST

Amphitheatre

Gardens Oval NTFL

Tennis Courts

GARDENS

STUART HWY

WESTRALIA

EDEN ST
CHARLES ST
ANNE ST
MARY ST
HENRY ST
NELSON ST

ASHLEY

BEATRICE

MEIGS

Stuart Park

Boat Ramp

Dinah Oval

Mangroves

Sadgroves Creek

CHIN QUAN Gardens Park

Golf Course

Indo Pacific Museum

Cullen Beach

KAHLIN TCE
SMITH
MITCHELL
MALABAS
HOUSTON
KIRKLAND SQ
SCHULTZE
BAROSSA
PACKARD
WOODS ST

BLAKE ST
MELVILLE
GARDENS
HOOD TCE

RAMIREZ

STUART ST

McAINSH

CORONATION
MARGARET
WINSTON AV
GOTHENBURG

QUEEN
KING
VOYAGER
DUKE

DINAH
BEACH
BAY
DR

Dinah Beach

Small Boat Harbour

Lock

Mangroves

Emery Point
Elliott Point

ALLEN
WHITTLE CR
NIMMO PL
STEELE
HERRING
TEMIRA
MARELLA
MAMOORA

Larrakeyah

Military Area

ALLEN AV
STEVENS
NURSES WALK

LARRAKEYAH TCE

Slipway Aquascene

Patrol Boat Harbour

Doctors Gully

Bicentennial

ESPLANADE

DALY ST

MITCHELL
CAVENAGH
SMITH
WOODS
SHEPHERD
HARVEY ST
McMINN
BARNESON

Daly Bridge

DARWIN

DAV

FRANCES ST

Stokes Hill

Old Power Station

FRANCES BAY

PEEL
LINDSAY
WHITFIELD
EDMUNDS
SHADFORTH LA
WEST LA
KNUCKEY
HERBERT
HARRY CHAN
LITCHFIELD ST
AUSTIN
CAREY

Lyons Cottage

Old Admiralty House

Lameroo Beach

Overland Telegraph Memorial

Government House

BENNETT
ESPLANADE

Chinese Temple

MAVIE

HUGHES
WITCHENER

Darwin Harbour

Fort Hill

PORT DARWIN

Iron Ore Wharf

Stokes Hill Wharf
Fort Hill Wharf
Land Backed Wharf

For more detail of Central Darwin see page 384

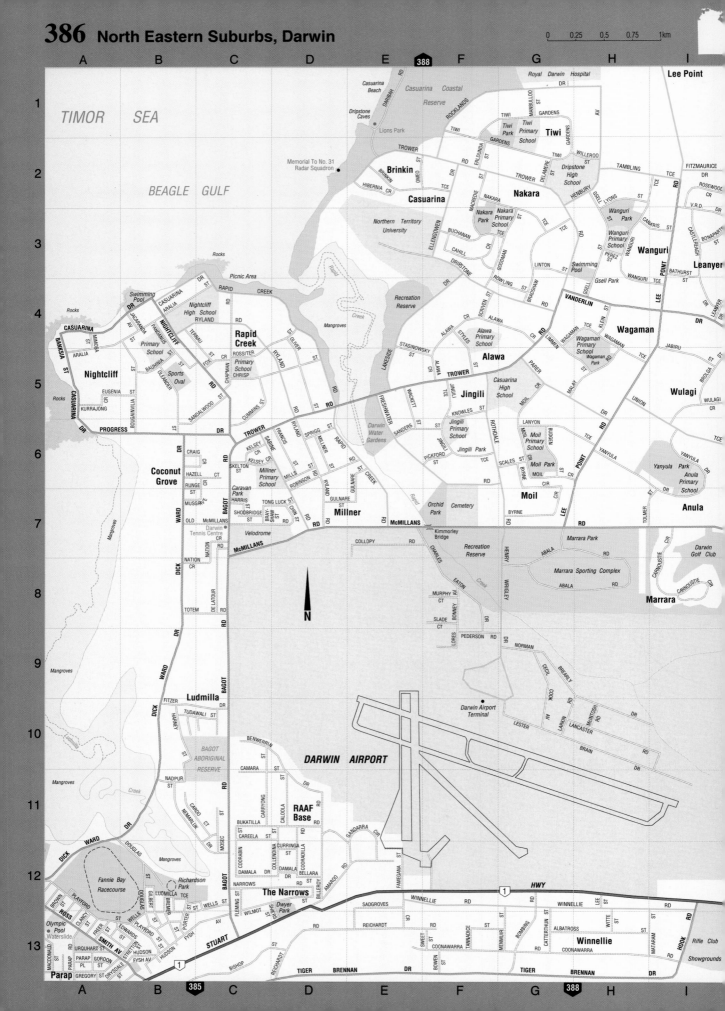

0   10   20   30   40   50 km

N

Van Diemen
Gulf

Finke Bay

KAKADU

ARNHEM

LAND

LAND

ARNHEM

PLATEAU

ABORIGINAL

LAND

TRUST

NATIONAL

PARK

Point Stuart
(Gurnaynjarr)

POINT STUART
COASTAL RESERVE

CARMOR
PLAIN

Swim
Creek
Plains

POINT STUART
RAINFOREST
RESERVE

Melaleuca

Cashew
Plantation

West Alligator Head

Pococks Beach

Field Island
(Gardangarl)

Barron Island
(Djidbordu)

Point Farewell
(Gularri)

Midnight Point
(Mandola)

Cunningham Channel

CAIRNCURRY PLAIN

CULALY PLAIN

Mt Hooper
(Mayambanjdju)

Munmarlary
(Manmularri)

CSIRO
Kapalga
Field Research
Station

BOGGY PLAIN (NANJBAGU)

Four Mile Hole
Camping area

Two Mile Hole
Camping area

Park Entrance
Station

Kakadu
Holiday
Village

Gungarre
Monsoon
Rainforest Walk

Boat
ramp

Mamukala Wetlands
Walk

Chirracarwoo Lagoon

Nourlangie
Billabongs

Red Lilly
Billabong

Yellow Waters
Walk

Leichhardt Billabong

Yellow Waters

Gagudju Vista Lodge

Cooinda

Boat ramp
Camping area
Boat ramp

Mardugal
Billabong Walk
Camping area

Boat ramp

Alligator
Billabong

Gnarl-ah-rogie Hill

Jim Jim Billabong

Spring Peak

Kunkamoula
Billabong
(Gunkumulu)

Camping area
Black Jungle Spring
(Giyamungkurr)

Mundogie Hill

Dird Djahdjam
Hill

Mt Basedow

Magela Plain
(MARNANJ)

Oenpelli Hill
(Injalak)

Cannon Hill
(Ngamarr-kanangka)

Ubirr (Obiri Rock)

Ubirr Art Site Walk
Meri (Mel)
Camping area

Border Store

Boat ramp

East Alligator
Ranger Station

Djaburluku (Jabiluka)
Camping area

Djawumba Hill

JABILUKA
MINERAL
LEASE

Gadjuduba
Camping area

MUDGINBERRI

RANGER
MINERAL
LEASE

Jabiru East

Park
Headquarters

HWY

Jabiru

Gagudju
Crocodile
Hotel

Ranger Uranium
Mine

Mt Brockman

Malabanjbandju
Camping area

Lligadjarr
Wetlands Walk

Burdulba (Baroalba)
Camping area

Muirella Park
Camping area
Boat ramp

Nourlangie
Rock

Nourlangie
Art Site Walk

Camping area

Mt Cahill
152m

Mirrai
Lookout

Baboalba Springs
(Gubara)

KOONGARRA
MINERAL LEASE

Koongarra

Sandy
Billabong

Table Top

Deaf Adder
Gorge

Mamurdi Hill

Turkey Dreaming
(Imagirrk)

Oenpelli
(Gunbalanya)

Mary River
Roadhouse

Moline Goldmine

Pine Creek

TO KATHERINE

TO DARWIN

TO ADELAIDE RIVER

TO STUART

Mount Harris Mine
(abandoned)

Mt George
274m

Long
Billabong
Camping area

Maguk
(Barramundie Gorge)
Camping area

Maguk
Plunge
Pool
Walk

Jim Jim Falls
Plunge Pool Walk

Camping area

Jim Jim Falls
(Barrkmalam)

Twin Falls
(Gungkurdul)

Goodparla

Old Goodparla

Bukbukluk
Lookout

Ikoymarrwa
Lookout

Waterfall
Creek
Falls

Gunlom
(Waterfall Creek)
Camping area

Gunlom
Lookout
Walk

Kambolgie
Camping area

CONSERVATION
ZONE

Gimbat

Coronation Hill
(Guratba)

Mt Evelyn

Big Sunday
(Nilyanjurrung)
338m

Frances Creek
(ruins)

Esmeralda

Union Hill

Cullen Hill

McCarthy Hill

Aston Hill

Ranford Hill

Coronet Hill

Walter Spring

Eva Spring
Wells Springs

Bloomfield
Springs

Ngartluk
Billabongs

Birdie Creek

Cooper Creek

BOATING: Boat tours available; details provided at Park Headquarters. Boat ramps provided throughout the Park.
When boating:
Take safety equipment including life jackets, safety light and oars.
Do not overload boat.
Carry extra fuel in tidal areas as making way against tidal flow can double fuel consumption.
Beware of mudbanks, snags and shifting sandbanks.
If stranded, stay with your boat until help arrives; remember, crocodiles inhabit the waters.
When planning a long trip, advise ranger of your destination, estimated return time and number of people on board.

CAMPING: Camping grounds are provided throughout the Park. Permits are required for camping outside designated camping grounds and can be obtained at Park Headquarters.

FISHING: Fishing is permitted using lures. Northern Territory bag limits apply. Cast nets, traps, live bait, spear guns and crab pots are not permitted. East of the Kakadu Highway, fishing is permitted only in specific areas.

ART SITES: Kakadu contains a wealth of archaeological and rock art sites which provide insights into Aboriginal culture and the environmental changes witnessed through generations.
The various styles of rock art that can be seen include the stick-like mimi figures (believed to be the oldest), x-ray style paintings which show the internal structure of animals and contact art which began with the arrival of non-Aboriginal people. The principle sites are at Ubirr and Nourlangie Rock.
Do not touch the paintings.
Keep to walking tracks and behind fences.

WALKING TRACKS: Numerous marked tracks of various lengths and degrees of difficulty have been constructed enabling visitors to view both the natural wonders of the Park and the richness of Aboriginal art.
Rangers conduct guided walks in the dry season; details are available at Park Headquarters.
Wear comfortable shoes and a hat.
Walk in the cooler hours of the day.
Carry a litre of water for every hour you intend to walk.
Keep to the marked tracks.
Do not walk alone.
If you get lost, do not wander, sit in the shade and wait for help.
Obtain a camping permit if bushwalking for more than one day.

WARNINGS: Freshwater and saltwater (estuarine) crocodiles are present in the Park. Both species can be dangerous, particularly the saltwater crocodile which may be found in both saltwater and freshwater.
Do not swim or paddle in natural waterways.
Do not allow children to play near the water's edge.

WARNINGS: In outback Australia, long distances separate some towns. Travellers should familiarise themselves with prevailing conditions before departure, and take care to ensure their vehicle is roadworthy, and that they carry adequate supplies of petrol, water and food.
In northern Australia, rainfall during the 'wet' season (October to March) can make some roads impassable. Full information on road conditions should be obtained before departure.
If visitors intend diverting off public roads within Aboriginal Land areas, a permit is required from the relevant Aboriginal authority.

PROTECTING THE PARK:
Drive carefully and keep to roads and carparks.
Pets are prohibited.
Fires to be lit only in fireplaces provided.
Use litter bins for rubbish.
All animals and plants in the Park are protected.
Avoid damage to rock paintings and other sacred sites.

FURTHER INFORMATION: Park Headquarters, P.O. Box 71, Jabiru NT 0886; (089)79 9101. The Park Headquarters, open daily, has displays providing interesting information about the Park; brochures and leaflets are available.

For more detail of Darwin Suburbs see pages 385 & 386

BEAGLE GULF

Shoal Bay

CAPE HOTHAM FORESTRY RESERVE
CAPE HOTHAM CONSERVATION RESERVE
Chambers Bay

Lee Point
Hope Inlet
CASUARINA
NIGHTCLIFF
SANDERSON
DARWIN AIRPORT
WINNELLIE
BERRIMAH
PALMERSTON

MARY RIVER CONSERVATION RESERVE

Charles Point
Radio Australia Transmitter Station
Point Margaret
Tapa Bay
Magnetic Anthills
Mandorah
14
COX PENINSULA
Mica Beach
Kings Table
Flagstaff Hill
DARWIN
Port Darwin
East Arm
West Arm
Middle Arm

Koolpinyah
Woolner
Lake Finniss
Lake Finniss Farm
Adelaide

SHADY CAMP RESERVE

IDA BAY
DELISSAVILLE WAGAIT LARRAKIA ABORIGINAL LAND TRUST
Belyuen
13
COX
11
Turnbull Bay
Bynoe Harbour
Observation Hill
21
PENINSULA

Peak Hill
Haycock Hill
Haycock Reach
Crocodile Farm
Humpty Doo
Noonamah
12

ARNHEM
25
Gows Reptile Park
Humpty Doo (Wariuk)
Magnetic Anthills
FOGG DAM CONSERVATION RESERVE
Fogg Dam
Bird Sanctuary
Beatrice Hill
Beatrice Hill Experimental Farm
MIDDLEPOINT
Tommy Policeman Lagoon
Coastal Research Station
18

Opium Creek Station
Helens Creek
Point S. Aba
WILDMAN RESERVE

MARRAKAI CONSERVATION RESERVE
55

STUART
11
HIGHWAY
12

TERRITORY WILDLIFE PARK
Berry Springs
Southport Ruins Historic Town
19
Tidy Hill
Magnetic Anthills
Tumbling Waters
Arthurs Hill
Lagoon Hill
ROAD
RANGE
14
24

Charlotte
Annie
Finniss
River

Acacia Store
12
Mantons Hill
Mt Daly
Roaming Buffaloes
LEANING TREE LAGOON NATURE PARK
Dennys Hill

DELISSAVILLE WAGAIT LARRAKIA ABORIGINAL LAND TRUST
ROAD
MARRAKAI
Corroboree Park Tavern
36
HIGHWAY
21
Old Mount Bundy Outstation
Mt Goyder 105m

Finniss River
11
Sweets Lookout
Mt Bennett
Mt Finniss
FINNISS
19

Darwin River Dam
Manton Reservoir
MANTON DAM PARK
8
Giants Reef
9
Johnny's Zoo Homestead

Buffalo Rise 43m
Luckie Hill
Mt Gunn
MARY RIVER CROSSING RESERVE
Annaburroo
Bark Hut Inn
McKinlay

DELISSAVILLE WAGAIT LARRAKIA
392
Two Sisters Hills 84m
ABORIGINAL LAND TRUST
Woolaning
Pethericks Rain Forest
Florence Falls
Ladelle Downs Outstation
Wangi
7
16
Burton Ck

DELISSAVILLE WAGAIT LARRAKIA ABORIGINAL LAND TRUST
River
Rum Jungle
Mt Charles
10
13
Meneling
Batchelor
84
11
Heaton Hill
Predictor Hill
Cameron Downs
Banyan
Banyan
17

Wild Horse Hill
Johns Hill
Bobs Hill
Lost Hill
Mount Ringwood
RINGWOOD RANGE
Mt Ringwood 195m
Mt Dougla 250r
Julie Peak

Welltree
Keri
Wangi Falls
TABLE TOP RANGE
Tolmer Falls
The Lost City
Blyth (aband)
LITCHFIELD PARK
Prospect Hill
43

Sargents
Stapleton
18
12
Adelaide River War Cemetery
Adelaide River
HIGHWAY
1
West
Robin Falls
Mt Tymn
15
DURAT
18
Mt Paqualin 195m
51
Mt Ellison 205m
Ban Ban Springs
STUART
12

Litchfield
Mt Litchfield 203m
Neds Knob
24
21

Mt Foelsche 113m

112
14
ROAD
Mt Smith
27
Mt Shoobridge
5
6
27
The Banyans
Mt Wells 263m

ROAD
29
Mt Thomas
Mt Pleasant 255m
Hayes Creek
Douglas
1
33
Emerald Springs
HIGHWAY

MALAK MALAK ABORIGINAL LAND TRUST
Elizabeth Downs
Marion Hill
RIVER
22
Mt Hayward 178m
DALY
Mt Green
27
Daly River
DALY RIVER NATURE PARK
17
Hermit Hill 95m
Quartz Knob
Mt Boulder 244m

Station
Tipperary
30
Kumbyechants
Ceres Downs
Douglas
18
DOUGLAS HOT SPRINGS NATURE PARK
BUTTERFLY GORGE NATURE PARK
24

ROCK CANDY RANGE
Daly
Wilton Wai Ck
Douglas Daly Experimental Station
Douglas River
Mt Muriel
Mt Briggs
Dollqo
Middle
Gypsy Ck
Stray Creek

0   10   20   30   40 km

392

J   K   L   M   N   O   P   Q   R

Finke Bay

CARMOR PLAIN

CULALY PLAIN

CAIRNCURRY PLAIN

+ Turkey Dreaming (Imakirrk)

1

Mt Hooper +
86m

Wildman

Alligator

+ Oenpelli Hill (Injalak)
Oenpelli •
Gunbalanya

Cannon Hill +
(Ngamarr-kanangka)

Ubirr •
Rock Paintings

12

2

+ Balkanini Hill

West

Alligator

+ Nardaba
Munmarlary (Manmularri)

MAGELA PLAIN

Cahills Crossing
Border Store

Alligator

N

4WD track

Four Mile Hole

33

BOGGY PLAIN

For more detail of Kakadu
National Park see page 387

Jowmbu Hill
Djawumba Hill +
Djarrdjarr +

○ Ja Ja

Mayaamarleprard
Waterhole

Magela

3

Bunga Ck

Cattle Ck

River

River

8

HIGHWAY

20

9

Njimbardi •

28

MUDGINBERRI

+ 16

Two Mile Hole

River

55

Kakadu Holiday Village

Chirracarwoo Lagoon

215

Park
Headquarters

11

Jabiru East

Jabiru ⊤

Ranger
Uranium Mine

4

Alligator

37

ARNHEM

Fox Ck

Flying Ck

21

21

58

Nourlangie
Billabongs

+ Djalandjal Hill

+ Mt Brockman
289m

ARNHEM

5

Wildman

KAKADU

Alligator Billabong

7

12

KOONGARRA

Nourlangie Rock
Cave Paintings

LAND

Alligator

Yellow Waters ○

Cooinda ○

10

11

+ Mt Cahill
152m

6

Namarrgon

Gnarl-ah-rogie Hill +

West

9

Jim Jim Waterfall

+ Table Knob

392

+ Spring Peak

+ Mt Basedow
230m +

+ Table Top 490m

ABORIGINAL

6

JIM JIM

HIGHWAY

NATIONAL

Jim

Deaf

Adder   Creek

7

ROAD

101

Kunkamoula Billabong

+ Mundogie Hill

+ Dird Djahdjam Hill

+ Mt Partridge

4WD track

Nourlangie Creek

LAND

Craig Creek

COINWONG   GORGE

+ Bokawh

Konbolu Hill +

Bamurmundie

Jim

TRUST

8

Long Billabong

KAKADU

55

PARK

Koongin Creek

Jim Jim Falls •

156

Mary River

+ Mt Masson

Goodparla ●

14

9

+ Mt George 274m

27

South

Creek

13

Twin Falls •

Old Goodparla (Aband) ▪

Alligator

10

Halfway Peak
217m +

Mary River ●

27

Waterfall Creek
Falls

+ Mt Callanan

18

Fisher

River

+ Mt Evelyn
366m

Creek

+ Mt Saunders
304m

Mt Daniels
142m

HIGHWAY

27

● Gimbat

Alligator

11

River

Coronation Hill (Guratba) +

Katherine

KAKADU

13

21

48

Mary River
Roadhouse

Big Sunday
338m +

River

12

28

Cullen

+ Mt Gardiner

+ Coronet Hill

+ Ngartluk Hill

Pine Creek ⊤

13

+ Cullen Hill

+ McCarthy Hill

Creek

WARNING: In outback Australia, long distances separate some
towns. Travellers should familiarise themselves with prevailing
conditions before departure, and take care to ensure their vehicle
is roadworthy and that they carry adequate supplies of petrol,
water and food.

+ Aston Hill

Ranford Hill +

In northern Australia, rainfall during the "wet" season (Oct-March)
can make some roads impassable. Full information on road
conditions should be obtained before departure.

▪ Bonrook

River

Two Sisters

If visitors intend diverting off public roads within Aboriginal Land
areas, a permit is required from the relevant Aboriginal authority.

Wandie

Fergusson

Birdie

Beware of man-eating crocodiles in rivers and estuaries.

A B C D **396** E F G H I

1

Ulambaura ■

10

Haasts Bluff ■
Haasts Bluff

18

Derwent Creek

Dashwood

Glen Helen ■

+ Mt Chapple
1166m

Milton Park ■

20

Amburla ■

TANAMI

2

Haasts Bluff ○

The Tre

Arumbera Ck

45

TROPIC OF CAPRICORN

Creek

Mt Zeil
+ 1510m

Mt Razorback
1231m
+

Redbank Gorge ■

Redbank

Creek

Ormiston Creek

15

Mt Hay
+ 1252m

Hamilton Downs ■

Ha
C
Youth

Sta
Ch

3

HAASTS BLUFF

ABORIGINAL LAND TRUST

17

20

Davenport Ck

REDBANK GORGE
NATURE PARK
+ Mt Sonder
1380m

Ormiston Gorge ●

WEST MACDONNELL

NATIONAL PARK

+ Mt Giles

Ellery

Ck

STANDLEY CHASM: This impressive chasm
in the West Macdonnells is only five metres
wide. It is a memorable sight at midday when
the sunlight reaches the floor of the chasm,
transforming the colour of the walls to a
blazing red.

○ Glen Helen
Glen Helen Lodge
GLEN HELEN GORGE
NATURE PARK
Glen Helen
Gorge

HEAVITREE

NAMATJIRA
18

Ochre Pits ●

Serpentine Gorge ●

Ellery Creek
Big Hole ●

RANGE

42

Iwupata

DRIVE

4

ABORIGINAL LAND TRUST

50

HERMANNSBURG

Gosse
Bluff ●

TNORALA
(GOSSE BLUFF)
CONSERVATION
RESERVE

47

Creek

Gilbert Creek

Finke

21

MACDONNELL

86 11

RANGES

78

DRIVE

River

WATERHOUSE

5

KRICHAUFF RANGE

19

Ipolera ●

Areyonga ●

LARAPINTA

Creek

Finke River

Hermannsburg ●

Mt Hermannsburg +

Namatjira
Monument

Ellery

PALM VALLEY: With its rock pools, cycad palms
and *Livistona* palms unique to the area, Palm
Valley is yet another of the incredible sights of the
Centre. The valley's plant life has such a "prehistoric"
appearance, to enter the area seems like taking a
trip back in time.

Palm ●
Valley

6

396

Walker Creek

Illara Creek

JAMES RANGES

Mc Minn

FINKE
GORGE
NATIONAL
PARK

4wd

Boggy Hole ●
Police Camp Ruins

Wallace Rockhole ●
Aboriginal Community
Camping ground & tours

JAMES RANGES

Hugh

Tidenvale

7

KINGS CANYON: One of the most interesting and
scenic areas of the Centre. Spectacular views can
be obtained by crossing the tree-trunk bridge to
the north wall. The Lost City and the Garden of
Eden are of particular note.

WATARRKA
NATIONAL
PARK

Creek

ILLAMURTA SPRINGS
CONSERVATION
RESERVE

4wd track

4wd track

Finke

Creek

Maloney Creek

Virginia Camel Farm ●

Orange

STUART

8

TO KINGS CANYON

Petermann Creek

PETERMANN HILLS

Temple Downs ■

4wd

HENBURY METEORITE CRATERS: Believed to have been formed
several thousand years ago when a falling meteor broke into
pieces and hit the earth. The largest of the twelve craters is 180
metres wide and 15 metres deep. The smallest is 6 metres wide
and only a few centimetres deep. This area is a haunt of the
ferocious-looking, but harmless, bearded dragon lizard.

29

200

CHANDLERS

9

LEVI RANGE

Creek

Palmer

51

Wallara Ranch
Roadhouse

37

River

11

HENBURY
METEORITE CRATERS
CONSERVATION
RESERVE

Henbury ●
Meteorite
Craters

Henbury ●

87

10

SEYMOUR RANGE

INSET: ULURU NATIONAL PARK

To Connellan Airport

LASSETER HIGHWAY

Yulara ○
Ayers Rock Resort

To Erldunda

Palmer Valley ■

River

11

KATITI ABORIGINAL LAND TRUST

To Docker River

KATA TJUTA
(THE OLGAS)

Sunset
Viewing
Area

Car Park

Car
Park

Olga Gorge
Walk

Valley of the Winds
Walk

Park Entrance Station

68

12

KATA TJUTA

ULURU NATIONAL PARK

DRIVE

Sunset Viewing
Area (Coaches)

Sunset Viewing
Area (Cars)

**ULURU
(AYERS ROCK)**

Cairn
863m

Ranger Station

0   2   4   6   8   10 km

MT SUNDAY RANGE

ERLDUNDA RANGE

13

TO ULURU

LASSETER

Imanpa ○

51

Mt Ebenezer
Roadhouse

Karinga Ck

HIGHWAY

55

4

To ULURU (Ayers Rock)
Erldunda to Ayers Rock - 260km
See inset for more detail.

Erldunda ●

TO COOBER PEDY

A B C D **396** E F G H

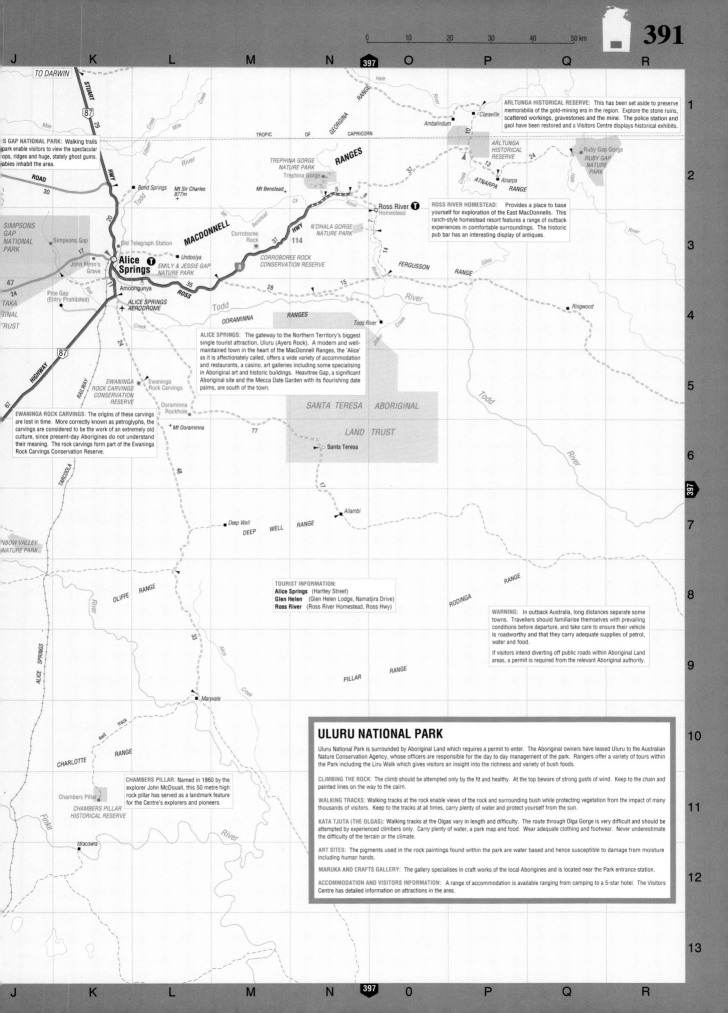

Scale: 0 10 20 30 40 50 km

Grid columns: J K L M N O P Q R
Grid rows: 1 2 3 4 5 6 7 8 9 10 11 12 13

TO DARWIN

STUART HWY 87 29

...S GAP NATIONAL PARK: Walking trails ...park enable visitors to view the spectacular ...ops, ridges and huge, stately ghost gums. ...abies inhabit the area.

ROAD 30

Bond Springs

Mt Sir Charles 877m +

Fifteen Mile Creek

Todd River

ARLTUNGA HISTORICAL RESERVE: This has been set aside to preserve memorabilia of the gold-mining era in the region. Explore the stone ruins, scattered workings, gravestones and the mine. The police station and gaol have been restored and a Visitors Centre displays historical exhibits.

Ambalindum

Claraville

Hale Creek

TROPIC OF CAPRICORN

GEORGINA RANGES

ARLTUNGA HISTORICAL RESERVE

10

24

Ruby Gap Gorge
RUBY GAP NATURE PARK

13

Atnarpa

ATNARPA RANGE

Hale River

River

TREPHINA GORGE NATURE PARK

Trephina Gorge

Mt Benstead +

Ck 5

37

8

Ross River

Ross River Homestead

ROSS RIVER HOMESTEAD: Provides a place to base yourself for exploration of the East MacDonnells. This ranch-style homestead resort features a range of outback experiences in comfortable surroundings. The historic pub bar has an interesting display of antiques.

SIMPSONS GAP NATIONAL PARK

Simpsons Gap

17

MACDONNELL RANGES

Corroboree Rock

N'DHALA GORGE NATURE PARK

14

FERGUSSON RANGE

Giles River

River

20

Old Telegraph Station

Alice Springs

John Flynn's Grave

47

2A

TAKA ...GINAL ...RUST

Pine Gap (Entry Prohibited)

11

Amoongunya

Undoolya

EMILY & JESSIE GAP NATURE PARK

35

ROSS

HWY 114

8

CORROBOREE ROCK CONSERVATION RESERVE

28

15

Todd River

River

Ringwood

ALICE SPRINGS AERODROME

24

OORAMINNA

RANGES

Todd River

Jinker Creek

ALICE SPRINGS: The gateway to the Northern Territory's biggest single tourist attraction, Uluru (Ayers Rock). A modern and well-maintained town in the heart of the MacDonnell Ranges, the 'Alice' as it is affectionately called, offers a wide variety of accommodation and restaurants, a casino, art galleries including some specialising in Aboriginal art and historic buildings. Heavitree Gap, a significant Aboriginal site and the Mecca Date Garden with its flourishing date palms, are south of the town.

HIGHWAY 87

67

RAILWAY

EWANINGA ROCK CARVINGS CONSERVATION RESERVE

Ewaninga Rock Carvings

24

Ooraminna Rockhole

+ Mt Ooraminna

77

SANTA TERESA ABORIGINAL

LAND TRUST

Santa Teresa

Todd River

EWANINGA ROCK CARVINGS: The origins of these carvings are lost in time. More correctly known as petroglyphs, the carvings are considered to be the work of an extremely old culture, since present-day Aborigines do not understand their meaning. The rock carvings form part of the Ewaninga Rock Carvings Conservation Reserve.

TARDOOLA

48

17

Allambi

Deep Well

DEEP WELL RANGE

...NBOW VALLEY ...NATURE PARK

OLIFFE RANGE

River

RANGE

RODINGA RANGE

TOURIST INFORMATION:
Alice Springs (Hartley Street)
Glen Helen (Glen Helen Lodge, Namatjira Drive)
Ross River (Ross River Homestead, Ross Hwy)

WARNING: In outback Australia, long distances separate some towns. Travellers should familiarise themselves with prevailing conditions before departure, and take care to ensure their vehicle is roadworthy and that they carry adequate supplies of petrol, water and food.

If visitors intend diverting off public roads within Aboriginal Land areas, a permit is required from the relevant Aboriginal authority.

ALICE SPRINGS

33

Alice Creek

PILLAR RANGE

Maryvale

4wd track

CHARLOTTE RANGE

CHAMBERS PILLAR: Named in 1860 by the explorer John McDouall, this 50 metre high rock pillar has served as a landmark feature for the Centre's explorers and pioneers.

Chambers Pillar

CHAMBERS PILLAR HISTORICAL RESERVE

Finke River

Idracowra

ULURU NATIONAL PARK

Uluru National Park is surrounded by Aboriginal Land which requires a permit to enter. The Aboriginal owners have leased Uluru to the Australian Nature Conservation Agency, whose officers are responsible for the day to day management of the park. Rangers offer a variety of tours within the Park including the Liru Walk which gives visitors an insight into the richness and variety of bush foods.

CLIMBING THE ROCK: The climb should be attempted only by the fit and healthy. At the top beware of strong gusts of wind. Keep to the chain and painted lines on the way to the cairn.

WALKING TRACKS: Walking tracks at the rock enable views of the rock and surrounding bush while protecting vegetation from the impact of many thousands of visitors. Keep to the tracks at all times, carry plenty of water and protect yourself from the sun.

KATA TJUTA (THE OLGAS): Walking tracks at the Olgas vary in length and difficulty. The route through Olga Gorge is very difficult and should be attempted by experienced climbers only. Carry plenty of water, a park map and food. Wear adequate clothing and footwear. Never underestimate the difficulty of the terrain or the climate.

ART SITES: The pigments used in the rock paintings found within the park are water based and hence susceptible to damage from moisture including human hands.

MARUKA AND CRAFTS GALLERY: The gallery specialises in craft works of the local Aborigines and is located near the Park entrance station.

ACCOMMODATION AND VISITORS INFORMATION: A range of accommodation is available ranging from camping to a 5-star hotel. The Visitors Centre has detailed information on attractions in the area.

397

A B C D E F G H I

1

2

TIMOR

Cape Van Diemen
Point Jahleel
MELVILLE
ISLAND
Vashon Head
Danger Pt
Minjilang
CROKER
ISLAND
Cape Croker
McCluer
Grant Island

SEA

Deception Point
Pularumpi
Milikapiti
BATHURST
ISLAND
TIWI
ABORIGINAL LAND
TRUST
Cape Keith
COBOURG
PENINSULA
GURIG NATIONAL PARK
Cape Cockburn
Murgenella St

3

Paru
Nguiu
Pickertaramoor
Conder Point
Cape Gambier
Greenhill
Island
Endyalgout
Island
Morsel
Island
Van Diemen
Gulf
Mt Permain
220m
Oenpelli
Gunbalanya

4

Beagle
Gulf
Cape Hotham
Clarence Strait
CAPE HOTHAM
FORESTRY RES
CAPE HOTHAM
CONSERVATION RES
Gunn Point
Point Stuart
Field Island
Cooper
East

5

For more detail of Darwin
Region see pages 388 & 389

DARWIN
Radio Australia
Transmitter Station
Mandorah
Belyuen
Howard
Springs
Koolpinyah
Woolner
MARY RIVER
CONSERVATION
RESERVE
Swim Creek
Plains
ARNHEM
Melaleuca
Munmarlary (Manmularri)
Ja Ja
Jabiru
Cahills Cr
Border St
Ubirr
Rock Paintings

6

Noonamah
Berry
Springs
Humpty
Doo
Humpty Doo (Warluk)
Acacia Store
Fogg
Dam
MARRAKAI
CONSERVATION
RESERVE
Point Stuart
Helens Creek
HIGHWAY
Kakadu Holiday Village
219
Mt Brockman
289m
Nourlangie Rock
KAKADU
Mt Cahill
152m
Yellow Waters
Cooinda
NATIONAL

Finniss
River
Darwin
River Dam
DELISSAVILLE
WAGAIT LARRAKIA
ABORIGINAL
LAND TRUST
Rum Jungle
Batchelor
Banyan
Wangi
Falls
War Cemetery
Tortilla Flats
Mount Ringwood
Mt Douglas
250m
Mt Masson
Mary River
Station
Goodparla
Jim Jim Falls
Twin Falls
PARK

7

Point Blaze
Fog Bay
North Peron
Island
Wangi
Welltree
Keri
LITCHFIELD
Adelaide River
Ban Ban
Spring
STUART
112
Mt George
274m
Gimbat
Mt Evelyn
366m

8

South Peron
Island
Reynolds
Anson Bay
Cape Ford
Litchfield
Robin
Falls
PARK
Elizabeth Downs
MALAK MALAK
ABORIGINAL
LAND TRUST
Daly
Douglas
Douglas Daly
Experimental Station
DOUGLAS
HOT SPRINGS
NATURE
PARK
Hot Springs
Setay Valley
Hayes Creek
Butterfly
Gorge
Esmeralda Farm
1
Pine Creek
The Banyans
KAKADU
River

Cape Dombey
Tipperary
Daly River
Middle
Creek
Ooloo
Umbrawarra
Gorge
Bonrook
Mt Lambell 317m
Birdie

9

Joseph
Bonaparte
Gulf
Moyle
DALY RIVER
PORT KEATS
ABORIGINAL
Wadeye
Community
LAND TRUST
River
Bonalbo
Jindare
Claravale Station
Morrisons
Mariliyum
90
Edith Falls
19
NITMILUK
Katherine
Gorge
O'Sullivans
House
Mt Felix 332m
Eva Valley
BESWICK
ABORIGINAL
LAND
TRUST

10

Pearce Point
Treachery Bay
Swamp Point
MACADAM RANGE
FISH RIVER
FORESTRY
RESERVE
WINGATE MOUNTAINS
Fish
Dorisvale
Claravale
Florina
Ferguson
iKintore Caves
HIGHWAY
42
Mt Shepherd
232m
29
Katherine
Tindal
RAAF
Base
Manbulloo
Cutta
Cutta
Caves
112
Maranboy
Barunga

11

Cambridge
Gulf
Turtle Point
Fitzmaurice
Wombungi
76
125
King
O'Brien
Ck
1
58
52
Dry River
Mataranka
We Of The Never Never
Graves
ELS

12

Wyndham
Mt Connection 183m
Legune
NORTHERN
TERRITORY
WESTERN
AUSTRALIA
YAMBARRAN RANGE
Bradshaw
Angalarri
Mt Thymanan 304m
Innesvale
Willeroo
GREGORY
NATIONAL
PARK
24
28
38
DELAMERE
Gorrie
Larrimah

361
56
Kununurra
HIDDEN
VALLEY NP
36
1
Mt Cockburn
North
671m
VICTORIA
45
KEEP
RIVER
NP
PINKERTON
RANGE
Bulla
Auvergne
Victoria
Kneebone
Bulla
58
Timber Creek
Timber
Creek
Police Station
& Store
63
131
VICTORIA
Coolibah
Fitzroy
Victoria
River
Crossing
Old Delamere
Delamere
23
96
ROAD
Western Creek
STU

13

HIGHWAY
Newry
27
80
Jasper Gorge
GREGORY
NATIONAL
PARK
Gregory
ROAD
44
Gilnockie
Sunday Creek

NOTE: The following towns Borroloo
Timber Creek, while located on Ab
Land, are open towns.
No entry permit is required.

394

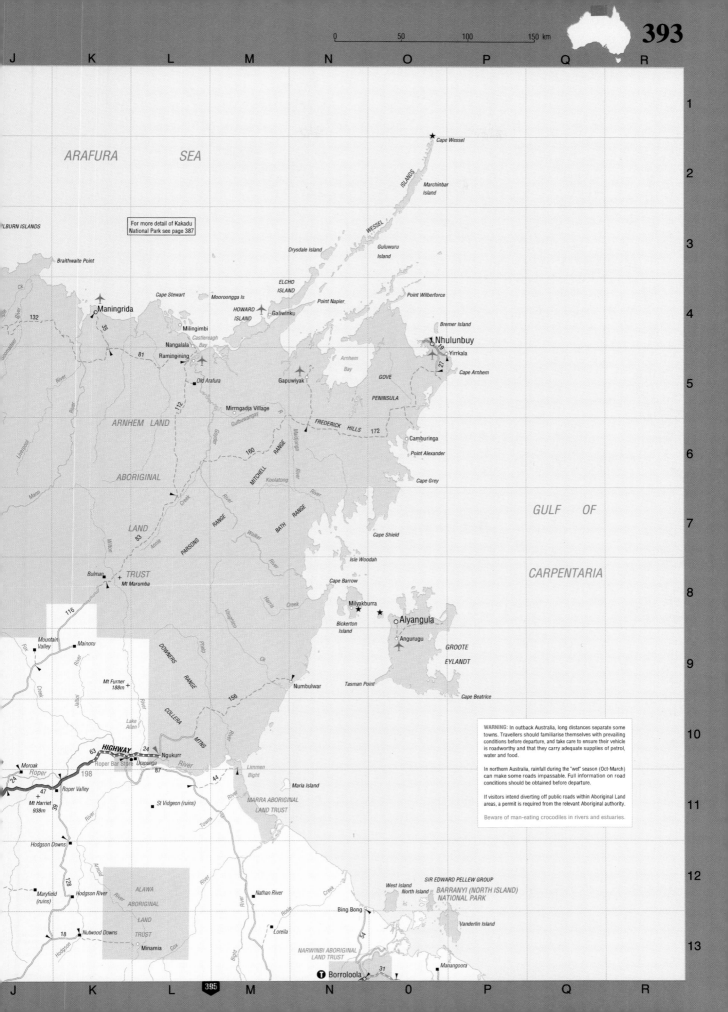

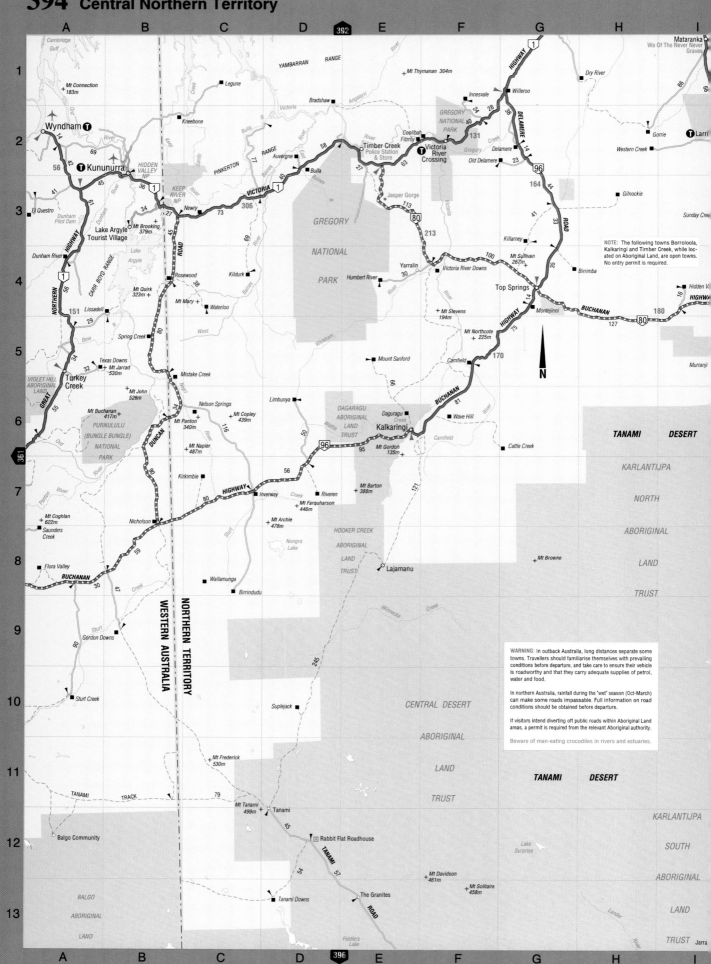

NOTE: The following towns Borroloola, Kalkaringi and Timber Creek, are located on Aboriginal Land, are open towns. No entry permit is required.

WARNING: In outback Australia, long distances separate some towns. Travellers should familiarise themselves with prevailing conditions before departure, and take care to ensure their vehicle is roadworthy and that they carry adequate supplies of petrol, water and food.

In northern Australia, rainfall during the "wet" season (Oct–March) can make some roads impassable. Full information on road conditions should be obtained before departure.

If visitors intend diverting off public roads within Aboriginal Land areas, a permit is required from the relevant Aboriginal authority.

Beware of man-eating crocodiles in rivers and estuaries.

Scale: 0 50 100 150 km

393

GULF OF

CARPENTARIA

J K L M N O P Q R

St Vidgeon (ruins)

MARRA ABORIGINAL LAND TRUST

Hodgson Downs

West Island
North Island
SIR EDWARD PELLEW GROUP
BARRANYI (NORTH ISLAND) NATIONAL PARK

Maryfield (ruins)
128
Hodgson River
Nathan River
Rose
Lorella
Bing Bong
SW Is
Centre Is
Vanderlin Island
Manangoora

ALAWA ABORIGINAL LAND TRUST

18
Nutwood Downs
Minamia

88
Borroloola
31
NARWINBI ABORIGINAL LAND TRUST
24
Greenbank

Waters
CARPENTARIA
Bauhinia Downs
35
Billengarrah
Tawallah
18
43
65
26
Seven Emu

139
Cooee Hill
Tanumbirini
273
33
Broadmere
63
113
95
Spring Creek
36
Pungalina

Shenandoah
21
O T Downs
37
44
HIGHWAY
Cape Crawford Roadhouse
Robinson River

1
43
58
Balbirini
37
Mallapunyah
Foelsche
Robinson River
Calvert

Newcastle
115
Kiana
Calvert Hills
Wollogorang
Westmoreland

Beetaloo
43
TABLELANDS
Wallhallow
CHINA WALL
Walford
DOOMADGEE ABORIGINAL LAND

Newcastle Waters
Elliott
STUART
Cresswell Downs
WAANYI/GARAWA

72
229
Eva Downs
Anthony Lagoon
Benmara
ABORIGINAL

Renner Springs
Tarrabool Lake
377
TABLELANDS HWY
CONNELLS LAGOON CONSERVATION RESERVE
LAND TRUST
Mt Oscar 115m

Mt Willieray 369m
Helen Springs
39
95
Springvale

Muckaty
100
Brunette Downs
100
Mittiebah

HIGHWAY
Corella Lake
LAWN HILL NATIONAL PARK

87
Banka Banka
50
Brunchilly
70
Lake Sylvester
76
65
Gallipoli

Churchills Head Rock
136
45
Rockhampton Downs
46
Alexandria
21

Stuart Memorial
WARUMUNGU ABORIGINAL LAND
77
Buchanan
Cigarette Creek
98

Phillip Creek
29
John Flynn Memorial
98
187
Alroy Downs
O'Shanassy
91

Warrego
25
18
Three Ways Roadhouse
66
BARKLY
54
TABLELAND
Camooweal
66

24
Devils Pebbles
31
Tennant Creek
89
Barkly Homestead
Avon Downs Police Station
30
13
Microwave Repeater Station

87
114
122
HIGHWAY
141
66
Soudan
30
26
71
66

McLaren Creek
261
Avon Downs
56
CAMOOWEAL CAVES NP

52
Kurundi
69
21
Barrys Caves
21
Six Mile Waterhole
Austral Downs

DEVILS MARBLES CON RES
Mt Cairns 597m
Epenarra
Big Ranken Waterhole
22 Mile Waterhole

Devils Marbles
27
Wauchope
Bullock Waterhole
Mt Michael 243m

Wycliffe Well Roadhouse
17
Singleton
Wycliffe Well
49
WARRABRI ABORIGINAL LAND

Numagalong (aband)
Hatches Creek

J K L M N O P Q R

397

NORTHERN TERRITORY
QUEENSLAND

BARKLY

GULF OF CARPENTARIA

A B C D E F G H I

1
TANAMI
TRACK
79
Mt Tanami 499m
45
Balgo Community
CENTRAL DESERT
ABORIGINAL
LAND
TRUST
Lake Surprise
TANAMI DESERT

2
NORTHERN TERRITORY
WESTERN AUSTRALIA
Rabbit Flat Roadhouse
TANAMI
34
57
Tanami Downs
The Granites
Lander River

3
BALGO
ABORIGINAL
LAND
YININGARRA
ABORIGINAL
LAND
TRUST
Lake Lucus
Lake White
Fiddlers Lake

4
Lake Willis
LAKE MACKAY
ABORIGINAL
LAND
TRUST
MALA
ABORIGINAL
LAND
TRUST
ROAD
189
Mt Patricia 577m
PAWA
ABORIGINAL
LAND
TRUST
Mount Barkly
Old Mo
85

5
Mt Farewell 603m
Mt Singleton 808m
Mount Doreen
Mt Hardy 840m
31
28
38
YUENDUMU
ABORIGINAL
LAND
TRUST
Mt Campbell 628m
Mount Denison
Yuelamu
Coniston
Mt Stafford 1049m
Mt Leichhardt 1139m
Anningie

6
Lake Mackay
Mt Nicker 632m
Vaughan Springs
77
Yuendumu
26
Mt Gardiner 999m
Coniston (ruins)
178
YALPIRAKINU
ABORIGINAL
LAND
TRUST
TANAMI
61
Napperby

7
359
YUNKANJINI
ABORIGINAL
LAND
TRUST
Mt Cockburn 846m
Nyirripi
Newhaven
Lake Bennett
118
Central Mount Wedge
Mount Wedge
29
Lake Lewis
Mt Hammond 750m
Mt H 721m
288
64 ROAD

8
TROPIC
Lake Macdonald
Ininti
Kintore
Mt Leisler 901m
Pinpirnga
Tinki
OF
Ualki
Ilipila
HAASTS BLUFF
CAPRICORN
273
Warren Creek Bore
Mt Liebig
Mt Liebig 1524m
Derwent
Papunya
Ulambaura
Haasts Bluff
Haasts Bluff
51
31
44
Glen Helen
Mt Zeil 1510m
Mt Sonder 1380m
Narwietooma
23
Mt Chapple 1166m
Milton Park
39
Mt Hay 1252m
Hamilton
You
NAMATJIRA
47

9
Mt Forbes 762m
ABORIGINAL
LAND
TRUST
29
29
MACDONNELL
RANGES
LARAPINTA
T 46
Glen Helen
Gosse Bluff
47
Ipolera
19
Areyonga
91
24
Hermannsbu
Palm Valley
FINKE GORGE NP
Wallace
Aboriginal

10
Mt Murray
Lake Neale
WATARRKA
NP
Ulpanyali
Lila
Kings Canyon
35
Wunmera
Kings Creek
63
Mt Lewis 100m
Tempe Downs
47
Wallara Ranch
52
Henb
Meteo
Cra
47

11
CENTRAL
AUSTRALIA
Lake Hopkins
Mt Harris 1067m
Mt Taylor 1001m
Warakurna Community
Giles Meteorological Station
PETERMANN
203
233
PETERMANN
ABORIGINAL
LAND
TRUST
RANGES
50
Wallara
Wallera Range
Angas Downs
18
52
242
Mount Ebenezer
HWY
Erldur
56

12
Mt Gosse 885m
Stevensons Pk 1319m
Butlers Dome 1111m
The Olgas
Mt Olga 1069m
Yulara
18
39
LASSETER
ULURU NATIONAL PARK
93
Curtin Springs
41
Mygdora Lake
Ayers Rock
68
Mt Conner 863m
Mt Conner (ruins)

13
Mt Elliott 573m
Mt Scott 668m
Mt Aloysius 1085m
ABORIGINAL
LAND
Surveyor Generals Corner
Kalka
Mt Cockburn 1138m
MANN
Aparawatatja
RANGES
NORTHERN TERRITORY
SOUTH AUSTRALIA
Mt Morris 1288m
Amata
Mt Davenport 1139m
Alpara
Mulga Park
141
Mt Cuthbert 1036m
Victory Downs
Victory
Cave
2

A B C D E F G H I
294 394 295

0 50 100 150 km

J K L M N O P Q R

1

395

Barkly Homestead

BARKLY

141

66

Soudan

261

Barrys Caves

Ranken Ck

Lorne Ck

Avon Downs Police Station

30

26

30 13 Camooweal

Microwave Repeater Station

71

HWY

66

Crater Of Caves

CAMOOWEAL CAVES NP

87

WARUMUNGU ABORIGINAL LAND

Gosse River

122

21

Avon Downs

Six Mile Waterhole

56

2

RLANTIJPA SOUTH ORIGINAL AND TRUST

McLaren Creek

27

52 Kurundi 69

21

Epenarra

DEVILS MARBLES CON RES

Devils Marbles

Mt Cairns 597m

Big Ranken Waterhole

22 Mile Waterhole

Austral Downs

70

Numagalong (Aband)

Wauchope

17 19

Singleton

Wycliffe Well

21

Hatches Creek

49

Mt Michael 243m

Bullock Waterhole

56

3

Wycliffe Well Roadhouse

Highway

23

Ali-Curung

Murray Downs

23

Elkedra River

Elkedra

95

Annitowa

147

HIGHWAY

21

Lake Nash

Georgina Ck

Georgina Downs

Stokes

SANDOVER

Georgina

Georgina River

4

WARRABRI ABORIGINAL LAND TRUST

110

41

Mt Nelson 554m

Mt Stirling 575m

Tara

Barrow Creek

80

24

37

Ooratippra

10

15

Argadargada

OORATIPPRA ABORIGINAL LAND

Woodroffe

Urandangi

5

UART

44 90

Wilora

Mt Tops 705m

ALYAWARRA ABORIGINAL LAND TRUST

HIGHWAY

Ammaroo

579

157

River River Sandover River

Oratippra

Mt Hogarth 338m

93

6

Tree Store & Police Station

ree 50 25

Woola Downs

Mt Octy 696m

Mt Skinner 677m

135

ANGARAPA ABORIGINAL LAND TRUST

Sandover

Utopia

Derry Downs

45

43

Arapunya

Arthur

Lucy Creek

TARLTON DOWNS ABORIGINAL LAND

HIGHWAY

101

Manners Creek

Tobermorey

DONOHUE

122

432

7

Maggie

Ewart 803m

Mt Byrne 711m

Chianina

Mount Skinner

24

Atartinga

Waite River

Delmore Downs

Creek

Alcoota

29

Bundey

MacDonald Downs

14

Delny

Mount Swan

16

33

Mt Swan 633m

Dneiper

Huckitta

Mt Sainthill 549m

Baikal

Old Jinka Homestead

Creek

95

48

Tarlton Downs

PLENTY

43

Marqua

NORTHERN TERRITORY

QUEENSLAND

HWY

Mt Idamea 184m

8

85

27

Bushy Park

40

Mt Riddock 1102m

Mt Campbell 1051m

SANDOVER

Red Cliff 658m

82

Mueller

26

34

PLENTY

Harts Range Police Station

55

Mount Riddock

Mt Palmer

30

485

75

HIGHWAY

18

Jervois

41

Mt Brassey 1138m

Quartz Hill

58

River

Atula

Mt Reinecke 283m

Mt Winnecke 258m

Mt Woods 265m

Mt Wooldridge 288m

Western Channel

Hay

TOOMBA RANGE

Mt Whelan 189m

8

68

19

29

72

Yambah

The Garden

52

Claraville

RANGES

Mt Ruby 852m

Indiana

TROPIC

OF

CAPRICORN

9

Bond Springs

Mt Sir Charles 877m

MACDONNELL

ARLTUNGA HISTORICAL RES

Atnarpa

RUBY GAP NATURE PARK

Carter Knoll

Illogwa River

55

SIMPSONS GAP NP

impsons Gap

62

Alice Springs

107

Ross River

Ross River Historic Homestead

89

Amoonguna

Todd River

Ringwood

9

24

17

wupataka

Ewaninga Rock Carvings

SANTA TERESA ABORIGINAL LAND TRUST

88

Todd River

Limbla

62

Numery

Hale River

10

101

85

Mt Ooraminna 649m

199

Ooraminna Rockhole

Santa Teresa

17

Allambi

Todd River Downs

WARNING: In outback Australia, long distances separate some towns. Travellers should familiarise themselves with prevailing conditions before departure, and take care to ensure their vehicle is roadworthy and that they carry adequate supplies of petrol, water and food.

Deep Well

ugh ange Creek

75

217

In northern Australia, rainfall during the 'wet' season (Oct-March) can make some roads impassable. Full information on road conditions should be obtained before departure.

11

RAILWAY

53

Chambers Pillar

Idracowra

Horseshoe Bend

For more detail of The Red Centre see pages 390 & 391

If visitors intend diverting off public roads within Aboriginal Land areas, a permit is required from the relevant Aboriginal authority.

River

11

Andado

Old Andado

95

16

SIMPSON

DESERT

SIMPSON

DESERT

NATIONAL

434

12

Umbeara

Finke

34 36

31

Mt Peebles 262m

New Crown

Finke River

PARK

12

51

22

147

60

Mt Cecil 551m

Mt Parlue 478m

Mt Mead 376m

Mt Grundy 397m

NORTHERN TERRITORY

SOUTH AUSTRALIA

Mt Wilyunpa 227m

Mount Dare

WITJIRA NATIONAL PARK

Mt Alinerta 222m

SIMPSON

CONSERVATION

DESERT

PARK

Poeppel Corner

13

t Howe

Tieyon

J K L M N O P Q R

295 292

Queensland Sunshine State

To visitors from other states, as well as to many Queenslanders, the Sunshine State is holiday country, evoking dreams of long, golden days, tropical islands set in jewel-blue seas and the chance to get 'a really good tan'. The first settlers in the tropical north, however, were there for grimly practical reasons.

In 1821, Sir Thomas Brisbane, Governor of New South Wales, sent John Oxley, his Surveyor-General, to explore the almost unknown country north of the Liverpool Plains. Oxley's task was to find a suitable site for a penal settlement and he decided on Moreton Bay. In 1824, troops and convicts arrived at Redcliffe, but a lack of fresh water and the hostility of the Aborigines persuaded them to move south and they settled at the present site of Brisbane. By 1859, the settlement was well established and the free settlers were urging separation from New South Wales; and so, on 10 December, the state of Queensland was proclaimed.

Having gained legislative independence, the population of just 23 000 then set about achieving economic independence. Fortunately, the new state was well endowed with excellent farming land, and wool and beef production were soon established on the western plains and tablelands. It was not long before sugar production, worked by 'kanaka' labour from the Pacific Islands, became much more important, and it has remained so.

As well as being blessed with fertile land which produces grain, sugar, dairy produce, wool, mutton, beef, cotton, peanuts and timber, Queensland is immensely rich in minerals, and the vast Mount Isa mining complex in the west produces copper, lead and zinc in enormous quantities.

Over the years, Queensland has been developing another, very different, form of industry—tourism. Its attraction as a holiday destination is very much due to its climate.

In the west, the climate is very similar to that of the arid Red Centre, with fierce daytime heat, but on the coast the temperature rarely exceeds 38°C and for seven months or so of the year the weather is extremely pleasant. If you are unused to high humidity, however, the period from December to April can be uncomfortably damp.

Four geographic and climatic regions run north to south, neatly dividing the state. In the west is the Great Artesian Basin: flat and hot. Parched and bare during drought, it becomes grassy after rain, thanks to a complex system of boreholes which distribute water through channels and allow grazing. The tablelands to the east are undulating and sparsely timbered, broken up by slow, meandering rivers. The backbone of Queensland is the Great Dividing Range—most spectacular in its extreme north and south, where it comes closest to the coast. Although the coastal region is the area most popular with visitors, Queensland's hinterland is lushly beautiful and its national parks, with many species of bird, animal and plant life unique to the state, total more than a million hectares. The state's highway and road system is good in the south-east and close to the larger northern towns, but elsewhere roads tend to be narrow and poorly graded and conditions deteriorate during drought or heavy rain.

The two main towns of the tropical northern region are Townsville and Cairns. The more northerly Cairns is fast becoming a fashionable holiday centre and makes an excellent base for deep-sea fishing and for exploring the region, with its lush sugar-lands, mountainous jungle country and the wilds of the Cape York

Peninsula. The Atherton Tableland is a rich volcanic area west of Cairns, with superb lakes, waterfalls and fern valleys. Stretching along this coastline are Queensland's famed islands: Lizard, north of Cooktown to Green Island, Dunk, Hinchinbrook, Magnetic, the beautiful Whitsundays, Great Keppel, Heron, Fraser and Lady Musgrave. If you are planning an island holiday, make sure your choice fits in with your idea of a tropical paradise. Many islands are extensively developed for tourism; others are quiet and offer simple accommodation. Beyond, and protecting them from the South Pacific, is the outer Great Barrier Reef, the world's largest and most famous coral formation.

South of the Reef is the Sunshine Coast. This scenic coastal region, with its leisurely pace and its wide variety of natural attractions and sporting facilities, offers an alternative to the more commercialised Gold Coast. Bribie Island, the weird and wonderful shapes of the Glass House Mountains and the beautiful Lakes District are nearby.

Brisbane, Australia's third city, is a far-spread capital, built on both sides of the Brisbane River. An easygoing, friendly city, its parks and gardens lush with subtropical plants, Brisbane has a year-round average of seven and a half hours of sunshine a day. The Gold Coast, seventy-five kilometres to its south, is the heart of holiday country. Luxuriously developed, it offers a wide range of accommodation, glittering nightlife, seemingly endless golden beaches and incessant sun. Inland is rich and rolling wheat and dairy farming country, its peaceful setting a far cry from the tropical north or the mining areas of Mount Isa—which goes to prove, once more, that the Sunshine State is a very diverse place indeed.

Eastern edge of Cape Tribulation National Park

Brisbane

A Subtropical City

The best place from which to see and understand the layout of Brisbane is from the lookout on **Mount Coot-tha**, eight kilometres south-west of the city centre and easily distinguished by its television towers. Brisbane sprawls over the series of small hills below, with the Brisbane River wandering lazily through the suburbs and city and out into **Moreton Bay**, thirty-two kilometres downstream. Surprisingly little use is made of the river for public transport, and most riverside houses back on to rather than face it.

Moreton and Stradbroke Islands look like a protective mountain range against the Pacific Ocean, far to the east. On a good day you can see the rugged mountains behind the Gold Coast to the south, and northward the strange **Glass House Mountains** just south of the Sunshine Coast.

The **City Hall**, Brisbane's best-known building, is now lost among the cluster of high-rise office buildings that dominate the skyline.

Brisbane, although it has developed into an international tourist destination following its hosting of the Commonwealth Games in 1982 and World Expo in 1988, still does not bustle like the larger southern capitals, and the suburban architecture, except for the newer, western areas, is predominantly the traditional galvanised-iron-roofed timber houses on stumps that residents think sensible and visitors find quaint. What is occasionally lacking in paint is more than made up for by colourful subtropical trees and shrubbery.

The city started inauspiciously as a convict settlement as far removed from Britain, and even from Sydney, as possible. In 1799 Matthew Flinders sailed into Moreton Bay on the sloop *Norfolk*. In 1823 John Oxley, then Surveyor-General, on board the cutter *Mermaid* sailed up the river that flowed into the bay and called it the Brisbane, after the Governor of New South Wales, Sir Thomas Brisbane.

The first troops and convicts arrived in 1824 on the brig Amity. The original settlement at Redcliffe was soon abandoned, mainly because of a lack of fresh water, and barracks were built on the present site of the city centre, previously investigated by Oxley. The penal settlement was closed in 1839 and the region was opened for free settlement in 1842.

Today Brisbane is a busy city with a modern and extensive public transport system, a wide selection of restaurants, entertainment and night-life, parks and gardens which thrive in the subtropical climate, and a population of over one million.

Among many interesting early buildings is the **Observatory** or **Old Windmill** on Wickham Terrace, overlooking the city. Built in 1828, the mill proved unworkable, so convicts were pressed into service to crush the grain on a treadmill. In 1934 a picture of the mill was the first television image transmitted in Australia, sent to Ipswich, thirty-three kilometres away.

The restored **Commissariat Stores**, at North Quay below the old **State Library** building, were built by convicts in 1829. The nearby **Treasury Building** at the top of Queen Street, an impressive Italian Renaissance structure built of local grey sandstone, was commenced in 1888. (It is to have a new lease of life as Brisbane's first casino, opening in 1995.) **Newstead House**, a charming building overlooking the river at Breakfast Creek, was built in 1846 by Patrick Leslie, the first settler on the Darling Downs. He sold it to his brother-in-law Captain John Wickham, RN, resident of the Moreton Bay Colony, and it was the centre of official and social life in Brisbane until the first **Government House** was built in 1862. It is Brisbane's oldest home and has been restored by a Trust to illustrate a bygone past. Government House, a classic colonial building with additions made between 1882 and 1895, was also the original University. It is now part of the **Queensland University of Technology** complex at the bottom of George

City skyline

Hotels

Chancellor on the Park
Cnr Leichhardt St and Wickham Tce,
Spring Hill
(07) 831 4055
The Beaufort Heritage
Cnr Edward and Margaret Sts, Brisbane
(07) 221 1999
Brisbane Hilton
190 Elizabeth St, Brisbane
(07) 231 3131
Sheraton Brisbane Hotel and Towers
249 Turbot St, Brisbane
(07) 835 3535

Family and Budget

Kingsford Hall Private Hotel
114 Kingsford Smith Dr, Hamilton
(07) 862 1317

Queensland Countrywomen's Association Club
89–95 Gregory Tce, Spring Hill
(07) 831 8188
Story Bridge Motor Inn
321 Main St, Kangaroo Point
(07) 393 1433
Wickham Terrace Motel
491 Wickham Tce, Spring Hill
(07) 839 9611

Motel Groups: Bookings

Flag 13 2400
Best Western (008) 22 2166
Travelodge (008) 22 2446

This list is for information only; inclusion is not necessarily a recommendation.

Street and is the home of the National Trust of Queensland. Nearby **Parliament House** was designed by Charles Tiffin in a 'tropical Renaissance' style and was opened in 1868. The **Parliament House Annexe** (irreverently called the 'Taj Mahal') is a modern tower block behind Parliament House overlooking the river. The exclusive **Queensland Club** is diagonally opposite Parliament House and was built during the 1880s.

The **General Post Office** in Queen Street was built between 1871 and 1879 on the site of the female convict barracks. The small church behind the Post Office in Elizabeth Street beside **St Stephen's Catholic Cathedral** is the third oldest building in Brisbane, having been dedicated in 1850. The **Customs House** at Petrie Bight at the bottom of Queen Street was built in 1884. The **Deanery**, built in 1849, behind **St John's Anglican Cathedral** in Ann Street, became a temporary residence for the first Governor of Queensland, Sir George Bowen. The proclamation announcing Queensland as a separate colony was read from its balcony in 1859. It became the residence of the Dean of Brisbane in 1910. Further south along Ann Street is **All Saints' Church**, which dates from 1861.

Earlystreet Historical Village is a particularly fine collection of Queensland buildings and architecture at 75 McIlwraith Avenue, Norman Park, east of the city centre. Among the buildings are reconstructions of the ballroom and billiard-room of 'Auchenflower House', and 'Stromness', one of the first houses at Kangaroo Point. The village is open daily and afternoon teas are served on Sundays.

To the north of the city, another building open to the public is 'Miegunyah', a traditional Queensland house with verandahs and ironwork at Jordan Terrace, Bowen Hills. It is the home of the Queensland Women's Historical Society.

There are very few terrace houses in Brisbane, but a row at the **Normanby Junction** has been lovingly restored and incorporates two restaurants. A similar development has occurred on **Coronation Drive**. Brisbane's more impressive houses, including the famous old 'Queenslanders', are scattered throughout the inner-city suburbs. Many small cottages in the **Spring Hill**, **Paddington** and **Red Hill** areas are being restored. The **Regatta Hotel** on the river at Coronation Drive is worth a visit, and the famous **Breakfast Creek Hotel** has a popular beer garden serving excellent steaks.

The main city department stores are located in Queen Street, which, between Edward and George Streets, is now a mall. A modern plaza containing specialist shops is at the corner of George, Ann and Adelaide Streets. At the top of the Mall is the **Myer Centre**, a vast complex housing specialised shops, restaurants, food halls and 'Tops', an amusement and entertainment area. Two of the city's most popular markets are the kilometre-long stretch of Sunday craft markets at the **Riverside Centre** in Eagle St, and the **South Bank Markets**, held on Friday nights, Saturdays and Sundays.

For the sports enthusiast, Brisbane's famous '**Gabba**' ground at Woolloongabba hosts cricket matches and greyhound racing. There are four horseracing venues at Albion Park, Doomben, Eagle Farm and Bundamba. The **ANZ Stadium** at Nathan and the Chandler aquatic centre, indoor sports hall and velodrome were all built for the 1982 Commonwealth Games. The ANZ Stadium is now the home of the rugby league premiers, the Brisbane Broncos.

The **City Square** facing the **City Hall** is a popular spot for 'watching the world go by'. The **Anzac Memorial and Eternal Flame** is opposite **Central Railway Station** with its towering backdrop, the **Sheraton Brisbane Hotel and Towers**.

Across Victoria Bridge lies **South Bank Parklands**, 16 hectares of redeveloped and landscaped parklands with walking and bicycle paths, a man-made beach, a series of artificial canals where the South Ships cruise and several restaurants. The Gondwana Rainforest Sanctuary, the Butterfly and Insect House and Our World Environment Display are special features attracting visitors to Brisbane's newest open space.

For the art-lover, the **Queensland Art Gallery**, within the **Queensland Cultural Centre**, is on the southside riverbank. This impressive gallery includes significant Australian, British and European collections. The Cultural Centre also houses an auditorium, a three-theatre performing arts complex, the **State Library of Queensland** and the **Queensland Museum**. The **Civic Art Museum** in the City Hall, the **Museum of Contemporary Art** at South Brisbane and the **University of Queensland Art Museum** at St Lucia are excellent. Private galleries include the Philip Bacon Gallery at New Farm, the Ray Hughes Gallery at Red Hill, the Victor Mace Gallery at Bowen Hills, Para Galleries at South Brisbane, which specialises in Queensland artists, and the New Central Galleries, the Town Gallery, the Don McInnes Galleries, Barry's Gallery and two Aboriginal galleries in the city proper. The Potter's Gallery in Fortitude Valley has pottery by local artists for sale.

Mt Coot-tha

Only eight kilometres from Brisbane's city centre, Mt Coot-tha offers city dwellers an attractive 'breathing space'. Here the Brisbane City Council has plans for an ambitious development scheme which will make the best recreational use of the area.

Brisbane's newest Botanic Gardens are in the foothills of Mt Coot-tha. The tropical display house, in the form of a futuristic-looking dome, has a superb display of tropical plants and is open daily. The arid-zone garden and cactus house are nearby. The gardens also include a lagoon and pond, a demonstration garden, ornamental trees and shrubs, areas of Australian and tropical rainforest, and a large collection of Australian native plants.

Situated in the Botanic Gardens is the Sir Thomas Brisbane Planetarium. The largest planetarium in Australia, it accommodates 144 people and was named after the 'founder of organised science in Australia'. When Sir Thomas was Governor of New South Wales, in 1821 he set up an astronomical observatory at Parramatta. His observations resulted in the publication of *The Brisbane Catalog of Stars*.

Various programmes are shown at the Planetarium's Star Theatre. A representation of the night sky is projected on to the interior of the dome and the movements of sun, moon and stars are described as they occur. Special effects can also be obtained by additional projectors to demonstrate more unusual phenomena in the sky.

Programmes are shown in the afternoon and evening, Wednesday to Sunday, with an additional afternoon show at weekends. Children under six are not admitted.

The planetarium complex also contains an observatory which can be used by members of the public, by prior arrangement, to view the day or night sky.

Outside again, there are many picnic areas at Mt Coot-tha, including a particularly attractive spot at the J.C. Slaughter Falls. The Mount Coot-tha Restaurant (BYO) on Sir Samuel Griffith Drive is open daily for lunches and morning and afternoon teas. The view from this vantage-point is superb, across the city and Moreton Bay, and sometimes as far as the Lamington Plateau in the south and the Glass House Mountains in the north.

Perhaps the best view of all from Mt Coot-tha is at night when the lights of the city of Brisbane are spread out before you — a breathtaking sight. Even if you have only one evening in Brisbane, it is worth making the short trip to the lookout to take in this memorable scene.

Botanic Gardens

The **Leichhardt Street** area of Spring Hill has developed as a centre for arts and crafts enthusiasts.

Brisbane's annual Warana Festival, a feast of art, craft and cultural activities, occurs in September. Also held annually are the Royal National Exhibition (in August) at Bowen Hills and the Spring Hill Fair (usually on the second weekend in September) in the streets of Spring Hill. The Biennial International Festival of Music begins in late May in odd-numbered years. The Brisbane International Film Festival is held in Aug.–Sept.

Queensland University is built mainly from Helidon freestone on a superb site on the river at St Lucia. A second university, **Griffith**, is in beautiful bush country in the southern suburb of Nathan. **Government House** at Bardon was built in 1865 for Johann Heussler, who brought German farm-workers to the state, and it became the official residence in 1920.

The old **Queensland Museum** is an ornate building on the corner of Bowen Bridge Road and Gregory Terrace. The main **Post Office** in Queen Street has a museum of telegraphic material. The **Queensland Maritime Museum** in Stanley Street, South Brisbane, incorporates the old South Brisbane dry dock. Nearby are the newly developed **Riverside Esplanade** walking and bicycle paths leading to Kangaroo Point, with access to picnic areas.

The old **Botanic Gardens** next to Parliament House are magnificent. In contrast, New Farm Park, which is close to the city via the Valley, has 12 000 rose bushes that are at their best between September and November, jacaranda trees that blossom in October and November, and poinciana trees in November and December. The **Mount Coot-tha Botanic Gardens**, five kilometres from the city, feature a Tropical Display Dome and the superb Sir Thomas Brisbane Planetarium. The nearby **J.C. Slaughter Falls Park** is popular for picnics, barbecues and bushwalks.

Self-guide leaflets outlining **Heritage Trails** within the city and suburbs, and a booklet listing a wide choice of attractions and eating-places are available from the **Brisbane Visitors and Convention Bureau** on the ground floor of the City Hall in King George Square, or the Queen St Mall Information Booth.

Brisbane is famous for its seafood, and several good restaurants allow you

Story Bridge

the opportunity to come to grips with the awesome Queensland mudcrab, Moreton Bay bugs, tiger prawns and delicious reef fish and barramundi. Popular venues are Pier Nine Oyster Bar and Restaurant at Eagle Street Pier; Michael's Riverside Restaurant at the Riverside Centre in Eagle Street; Rumpoles in Turbot Street; Muddie's in Edward Street; the Milano Italian Restaurant in the Queen Street Mall; Oxley's Wharf Restaurant on the river at **Milton**; and the exotic Cat's Tango in St Lucia. Chinatown in **Fortitude Valley** offers oriental shopping and dining.

Because of its vast size (the Brisbane City Council controls an area of 1220 square kilometres), the city's public transport network is extensive. Council buses take most of the load, while modern electric air-conditioned trains run to many areas. An excellent pocket map is produced by the Metropolitan Transit Authority. Small ferries operate from the city to Kangaroo Point, East Brisbane and New Farm Park. Golden Mile operates river and bay cruises from North Quay, including popular cruises to **Lone Pine Koala Sanctuary**. The City Ferry Cruise, operated by the Brisbane City Council, leaves the Edward Street ferry terminal (near the Botanic Gardens), travelling downstream to Breakfast Creek and upstream to Queensland University. The magnificent paddle-wheeler *Kookaburra Queen* cruises the river daily and is a good place to dine.

There are plenty of hotels and motels offering accommodation in and near Brisbane, together with a number of caravan parks within easy reach of the central city area. And, of course, the tourist mecca of the Gold Coast is only a relatively short distance away.

Several of Brisbane's attractions lie just outside the main city area. Views from the surrounding hills are good, particularly from Bartley's Hill lookout at **Hamilton**. There is also the Historical Observation Tower at the Boardwalk in **Newstead**, a 33-m tower affording outstanding city views. The *Southern Cross*, Sir Charles Kingsford Smith's Fokker tri-motor aircraft, is on display at Brisbane airport in Airport Drive. Just across the river is **Fort Lytton**, a garrison built in 1880 and opened to visitors in 1989. Brisbane's famous Lone Pine Koala Sanctuary, with its photogenic koalas and other fauna, is eleven km away at **Fig Tree Pocket**. Samford Alpine Adventureland at **Samford**, twenty-one km from the city, offers grass-skiing, a 700-m bobsled, and swimming and picnic areas. Amazons Aquatic Adventureland at Jindalee, twelve km from the city, has family waterslide entertainment and picnic areas. **Bunya Wildlife Sanctuary Park**, fourteen km north at Cash's Crossing, has a wildlife sanctuary, World Koala Research Station and picnic and barbecue facilities. Brisbane Forest Park at **The Gap**, twelve km from the city, provides 'bushranger' and wildlife tours in its 25 000 ha of bushland. Tours of the Golden Circle tropical fruit cannery at Northgate are available.

The **Australian Woolshed**, fourteen km north-west of the city, offers a true taste of Australia and features trained rams, sheep-shearing demonstrations and tame koalas and kangaroos.

For further information on Brisbane, contact the Brisbane Visitors and Convention Bureau, City Hall, King George Square; (07) 221 8411 or (0055) 31756.

Tours from Brisbane

There is a variety of things to see and do around Brisbane. Most tours can be done in one day, but some will be better enjoyed if you plan an overnight stop.

The Brisbane forest parks concept is being developed as breathing space for the city, and many new national parks have been declared in the surrounding area, so as well as visiting the famous beaches, take advantage of these parks—they are well worth a visit.

Redcliffe, 34 km from Brisbane via Gympie Road

Drive to Redcliffe via Petrie and a detour to the North Pine Dam. The Redcliffe Peninsula is almost completely surrounded by the waters of Moreton Bay. The sandy beaches are safe for swimming and the fishing is good. High on the volcanic red cliffs there are spectacular views far across Moreton Bay to Moreton and Stradbroke Islands, famous for their natural surroundings and mountainous sand dunes. The Redcliffe jetty is a favourite spot for local anglers. **See also:** Entry in A–Z listing.

Bribie Island, 47 km from Brisbane via Bruce Hwy

See: Other Islands

Wynnum–Manly and Redland Bay, 35 km from Brisbane via Routes 23, 30 and 44

You will not have to drive very far to enjoy the bayside suburbs of Wynnum and Manly, south-east of Brisbane on the shores of Moreton Bay. Manly has five marinas and is the headquarters of the Royal Queensland Yacht Squadron. There is a golf course at Wynnum, and other sporting facilities. Continue on to Redland Bay, a peaceful tourist resort. The area is famed for its market gardens and the Strawberry Festival (on the first Saturday of each September). Wayside stalls sell fruit and flowers at weekends. Boats can be hired all along this coast, so that you can do your own exploring, or go fishing, or you can visit the islands of Moreton Bay. **See also:** Entry in A–Z listing.

The Gold Coast, 70 km from Brisbane via the Pacific and Gold Coast Highways

See: City of the Gold Coast.

Gold Coast Hinterland, about 100 km from Brisbane via the Pacific Highway and Nerang

If possibly you are bored by the Gold Coast, simply drive west. The nearby McPherson Ranges have some of Australia's finest scenery: rainforest, deep ravines, waterfalls, and a spectacular view of the coast.

Tamborine Mountain, 70 km from Brisbane via the Pacific Highway

Tamborine Mountain, some 30 km from Oxenford, is a retreat from the bustle of Brisbane. Here walking tracks lead through the rainforest, where palms, staghorns, elkhorns, ferns and orchids grow in profusion, to waterfalls and lookouts. Picnic and barbecue facilities are located in the area and in the nearby Joalah, Knoll and Palm Grove National Parks. **See also:** National Parks.

O'Reilly's Guest House, Lamington National Park, 112 km from Brisbane via the Mt Lindesay or Pacific Highways and Canungra

Lamington National Park is one of the wildest and finest in Queensland. On a plateau at the top is O'Reilly's Guest House, and it is worth making this a full weekend's trip, though an advance booking should be made. A maze of walking tracks and an elevated treetop walkway allow you to see the area's many attractions. But if walking is not for you, you can just sit in the sun, breathe in the refreshing mountain air and admire the superb scenery or feed the birds. The subtropical rainforest here has an abundance of wildlife, which has been protected for many years. Information on the area is available at the tourist information centre in Canungra or from the ranger at O'Reilly's. **See also:** National Parks.

Binna Burra, Lamington National Park, 108 km from Brisbane via the Mt Lindesay or Pacific Highways and Canungra

If you chose to walk from O'Reilly's to Binna Burra Lodge it would be a distance of some 22 km. It is a much longer trip by road. Binna Burra Lodge is a good centre from which to enjoy the great variety of walks in the area, but a sensible pair of shoes is a must. Bring a sweater, too—it can get cold even in summer. If you plan to spend a weekend 'wilderness camping' in the mountains, a permit is necessary and can be obtained from the Chief Ranger at Binna Burra. Information is available in Canungra about the many walks and places of interest on the way. Those who prefer more comforts can plan to stay overnight at the Binna Burra Lodge, but book accommodation in advance. **See also:** National Parks.

Toowoomba, 127 km from Brisbane via the Warrego Highway

A comfortable distance from Brisbane for a day trip, this drive takes you past some pretty, small towns and old farmhouses. Stop at Marburg on the way to admire the old timber pub with its latticed verandah. Toowoomba's most popular tourist attraction is its parks and gardens, with a touch of England in the magnificent oaks, elms, plane trees and poplars. The gardens are best seen during September when the city has its Carnival of Flowers. The carnival is usually held over the last week of September, and includes a procession, dancing and entertainment in the streets. The Blue Arrow Drive around the city, laid out by the city council, is a must for the visitors. You could return to Brisbane via the New England and Cunningham Highways. **See also:** Entry in A–Z listing.

The Jondaryan Woolshed Historical Museum and Park, 176 km from Brisbane via the Warrego Highway

The Jondaryan Woolshed was built in 1859, with space for eighty-eight blade shearers to handle some 200 000 sheep a season. Now an ideal outing for all the family, it has been developed as a working memorial to the early pastoral pioneers. As well as the Woolshed, see the blacksmith's shop, the one-roomed schoolhouse, and the dairy. There is also a fascinating collection of old agricultural machinery. Open every day except Good Friday and Christmas Day; conducted tours operate on the hour.

The Bunya Mountains, 250 km from Brisbane via the Warrego and Brisbane Valley Highways

This three-hour drive is often spectacular, but hairpin bends make the journey unsuitable for cars towing caravans or trailers. Because there is so much to see along the way, it would be wise to stay overnight either camping or at a hotel. On the way, Savages Crossing is a good place for a picnic, and the Bellevue Homestead at Coominya is worth a detour. A major National Trust project, the homestead has been moved from its original site and rebuilding and restoration is continuing. Further on, stop to see the Koomba Falls and King House at Maidenwell. There are many more places to visit on the way to the mountains and all are fully signposted. Most of the area is set aside as the Bunya Mountains National Park; there are two major camping sites in the park. Bushwalkers will enjoy the excellent graded tracks. If you have time, and do not want to camp, continue on to Kingaroy, the peanut-growing area, where there is plenty of accommodation. **See also:** National Parks.

Mt Glorious, 40 km from Brisbane via Waterworks Road

One of the more interesting short drives from Brisbane through mountainous country due west of the city is to Mt Glorious, via Mt Nebo, and then back via Samford. From Mt Glorious it is possible to extend this drive to take in the delights of Lake Wivenhoe, only 15 km further on. Spectacular views of the mountainous Brisbane Forest Park. Stop at McPhee's and Jolly's Lookouts before arriving at the pretty town of Mount Nebo. Hear bellbirds and whipbirds in the Manorina National Park. In the Maiala National Park at Mt Glorious there are many well-documented short and long walks through the lush rainforest. At the information centre for the Brisbane Forest Park (60 Mt Nebo Rd, The Gap; (07) 300 4855), you can view exhibits of Queensland's native freshwater fish at the Walkabout Creek aquatic study centre, and then dine in the restaurant upstairs.

The Sunshine Coast, 100 km from Brisbane to its nearest point via the Bruce Highway
See: Sunshine Coast.

Beerwah and Buderim past the Glass House Mountains, 100 km from Brisbane via the Bruce Highway and the Glass House Mountains Tourist Road

Travelling past the Glass House Mountains, you will see the ten spectacular trachyte peaks named by Captain Cook as he sailed up the coast in 1770. The sun shining on the rock-faces reminded him of glasshouses in his native Yorkshire. Further north from Beerwah is the Queensland Reptile and Fauna Park, reputed to be one of the best such parks in Australia. Here venomous snakes, including taipans, and lizards of

Gold Coast hinterland

all sizes, can be seen. A recent addition is the two-hectare Crocodile Environment Park, where guided tours allow visitors to view crocodiles and alligators in their natural surroundings. Continue on through Landsborough to Buderim. Visit the art galleries and the Pioneer Cottage, one of Buderim's earliest houses, which retains much of its original furnishings from last century. **See also:** Entries in A–Z listing.

The Big Pineapple and Sunshine Plantation, 115 kilometres from Brisbane via the Bruce Highway

Seven kilometres south of Nambour, the Sunshine Plantation is the largest and most popular tourist attraction on the Sunshine Coast. On the pleasant drive up the Bruce Highway, you will pass colourful roadside stalls offering tropical fruit at prices that amaze the southern visitor.

The Big Pineapple itself is a 16-m-high replica of a pineapple, with a top-floor observation deck which looks out on the plantation of tropical fruit below. Two floors of audiovisual displays tell the story of the pineapple and there is a Polynesian-style restaurant and tropical market. Ride on a sugarcane train through more than 40 ha of pineapples, mangoes, avocados, sugarcane, and nuts and spices. An attractive animal farm is fun for children. The 'Nutmobile' will take you to the Magic Macadamia, a giant nut. Here the complete process, from cracking the nut to the final product, is revealed. Admission to the Big Pineapple and the industry display is free.

Miva Station, 202 km from Brisbane, and Susan River Homestead, 284 km from Brisbane, both via the Bruce Highway

At Miva Station via Gympie you can camp in your own tent, although an extra charge will secure one already erected on site. Trail riding and hay rides are popular, or you can go canoeing or fishing. If you are very quiet you may see a lungfish or platypus in the creek. The area is a bird and animal sanctuary. At the Susan River property, 15 km past Maryborough on the Hervey Bay road, if you stay at the homestead, full board is provided. Here you can join in the mustering, swim in the pool, or simply feed the emus and wallabies. For further information about Station and Farm Holidays, contact the Queensland Government Travel Centre; (07) 221 6111.

City of the Gold Coast

The Gold Coast, Australia's premier holiday destination, boasts 42 kilometres of golden, unpolluted beaches stretching from Southport in the north to Coolangatta in the south, with a lush subtropical backdrop in the Gold Coast hinterland—the 'green behind the gold'.

Situated only one hour's drive south of Brisbane, this international resort city offers a multitude of man-made and natural attractions, and, of course, superb surfing beaches—Main Beach, Southport, Surfers Paradise, Broadbeach, Mermaid Beach, Miami, Burleigh Heads, Tallebudgera, Palm Beach, Currumbin, Tugun, Kirra and Coolangatta.

With almost 300 days of sunshine each year—an average winter maximum of 22°C and average summer maximum of 28°C—it is no wonder the region is the country's holiday playground, attracting three million visitors annually.

Accommodation caters for all budgets, ranging from international five-star-plus hotels and resorts to hotels, motels, apartments, guest houses, caravan parks, camping grounds and backpackers' hostels. It is estimated there are more than 15 000 rooms with more than 50 000 beds available on the Gold Coast.

Nightlife, entertainment, sporting facilities, shopping and restaurants guarantee to satisfy all tastes. In fact, the Gold Coast is said to have the largest number of restaurants per square kilometre in Australia to tantalise all tastebuds.

Surfers Paradise with its towering skyline, beachfront esplanade, glitz and glamour is the hub of the Gold Coast, while the Gold Coast hinterland is a subtropical hideaway with 7 national parks complete with massive trees, spectacular views, cascading waterfalls and bush walks only thirty minutes from the hustle and bustle of the city.

Moving west from the coastline into the hinterland, the terrain climbs steadily to 1000 metres to breathtaking scenery in the Numinbah Valley and at Springbrook. Highlights here include the 190-metre-high Purlingbrook Falls, Winburra Lookout and the Hinze Dam.

In the Numinbah Valley on the southern Queensland border is the Natural Arch, a spectacular waterfall that plummets through a stone archway into a rock pool below. This is an excellent spot for picnics, barbecues and bush walks.

Mount Tamborine rainforests and Lamington National Park provide the backdrop to Beaudesert Shire. The more adventurous are easily tempted into tackling the rugged ranges and gorges of Lamington National Park, the largest preserved natural subtropical rainforest in Australia, with 160 kilometres of graded walking tracks.

The 'old-time' flavour of the hinterland has been preserved in the design of the area's buildings, some of which date back to the early 1900s.

At the southern end of the Gold Coast the bustling twin towns of Coolangatta–Tweed Heads sit on opposite headlands at the mouth of the Tweed River. Both towns are thriving holiday centres with a range of top accommodation, shopping resorts, restaurants, entertainment and tourist facilities.

At **Coomera:** Warner Bros Movie World, based on the world-famous Hollywood movie set, is a theme park and part of a fully operational studio. The only one of its kind in the southern hemisphere, it (along with the Australiana-theme park Dreamworld and Australia's largest water park Wet 'n' Wild) is only 23 kilometres north of Surfers Paradise. Nearby is the exclusive Sanctuary Cove residential resort, which incorporates the Hyatt Hotel, two golf courses and a marina. The links-style Hope Island Golf Club is one of the Gold Coast's newest international golf

Marina Mirage resort, Southport

Beach at Surfers Paradise

courses. Just south is Cable Ski World at Coombabah.

At **Southport:** Sea World, on The Spit at Main Beach, is the largest marine park in the southern hemisphere. Its world-class attractions include performing dolphins, false killer whales, a monorail, a skyway, water-ski ballet, helicopter rides, an Endeavour replica and an Old Fort. It adjoins the Sea World Nara Resort. The Gold Coast's fourth major theme park, Motor World is scheduled to open in late 1994. Also on The Spit overlooking the Broadwater is Fisherman's Wharf, a complex of specialty shops, outdoor cafes and restaurants. The Gold Coast's major cruise boats operate from its jetties. Also along the Broadwater is Mariner's Cove with marina, shopping and restaurants and Marina Mirage, an upmarket shopping and boating complex opposite the Sheraton Mirage Hotel. Visitors can enjoy a variety of water sports on the Broadwater, including jet skiing, sailing, windsurfing, parasailing, hovercraft rides and bungee jumping.

At **Surfers Paradise:** Attractions include Ripleys Believe It or Not Museum, Hoyts cinema complex, resort shopping, restaurants, many international hotels including the Gold Coast's newest five-star hotel, the Marriott Surfers Paradise Resort, numerous nightclubs and the sport of 'people watching'. Near Surfers at Bundall, the Gold Coast Arts Centre has an art gallery, cinema and a performing arts complex. Five kilometres inland from Surfers is Royal Pines Resort. The complex includes a 5-star hotel, convention facilities, a 27-hole golf course and a marina.

At **Broadbeach:** Pacific Fair Shopping Resort on the Nerang River, which recently had a $168 million facelift. Conrad Jupiters, Australia's largest casino, is linked by monorail to the Oasis Shopping Resort and the Pan Pacific Hotel. Cascade Park and Gardens on the Nerang River has man-made waterfalls and still-water pools, ideal for picnicking. One way to view the area is by an open-cockpit flight in a Tiger Moth plane.

At **Mermaid Beach:** A huge cinema complex close to family restaurants, a variety of specialty restaurants.

At **Miami:** The Miami Hotel features live music and dancing, food and beer.

At **Burleigh Heads:** Burleigh Knoll Environmental Park, Burleigh Heads National Park and Fleay's Fauna Centre are all worth a visit.

Inland at **Mudgeeraba** are the Gold Coast War Museum, Skirmish, Movie Militaria and the Boomerang Farm.

At **Tallebudgera:** Tally Valley art and craft markets, the Camp Eden Health Resort and the Playroom rock venue.

At **Currumbin:** Feed the thousands of lorikeets that flock to the Currumbin Sanctuary daily. The Chocolate Expo Factory is opposite. Visit Olson's Bird Gardens, Mount Cougal National Park and the Currumbin Rock Pool.

At **Coolangatta:** Foyster Mall links the main street with the beachfront. The Land of Legend, a fairytale and fable exhibition, delights children. Captain Cook Memorial and Lighthouse at Point Danger.

At **Tweed Heads:** Across the border from Coolangatta, try your luck on the pokies at Twin Towers Services Club and Seagulls Rugby League Club.

For further information on the Gold Coast, contact the Gold Coast Tourism Bureau, 5th Floor, 105 Upton St, Bundall; (075) 74 0999. There are information centres at Cavill Mall, Surfers Paradise, (075) 38 4419, and Beach House, Marine Pde, Coolangatta, (075) 36 7765. **See also:** Entries in A–Z listing. **Note** detailed map of the Gold Coast on page 469.

Queensland from A to Z

Airlie Beach
Pop. 2524

Since 1987 Airlie Beach has been part of the town of Whitsunday. Centre of the thriving Whitsunday coast, Airlie Beach offers many restaurants and eating-places, several major resorts with all facilities, top-grade holiday accommodation and a large range of activities and services for visitors. Twenty km from the Bruce Hwy at Proserpine, Airlie overlooks the Whitsunday Passage and islands, and has its own beach and marina. At Airlie and Shute Harbour, passengers can secure transport to the outer reef and reef-fringed islands. **Of interest:** Annual Fun Race held Sept. **In the area:** Neighbouring Shute Harbour and islands of Whitsunday Passage. Conway National Park, renowned for its natural beauty and habitat of the rock wallaby and many species of butterfly. **Tourist information:** Cnr Mandalay St and Shute Harbour Rd; (079) 46 6673. **Accommodation:** 1 hotel, 8 motels, 4 caravan/camping parks, 3 resorts.
MAP REF. 476 I2

Allora
Pop. 950

North of Warwick on the Toowoomba road, Allora is in a prime agricultural area. **Of interest:** Historical museum, Drayton St. Talgai Homestead (c. 1860); accommodation and meals. **In the area:** Goomburra State Forest and Valley, 35 km E. Main Range National Park, 50 km E; camping and picnic areas and extensive walking tracks through dense rainforest. **Tourist information:** 49 Albion St (New England Hwy); (076) 61 3686. **Accommodation:** 1 caravan/camping park.
MAP REF. 466 E12, 475 L7

Aramac
Pop. 326

This small pastoral township is 67 km N of Barcaldine. Originally called Marathon , it was renamed by explorer William Landsborough as an acronym of Sir Robert Ramsay Mackenzie, Colonial Secretary in 1866 and Premier of Qld from 1867–8. **Of interest:** Tramway Museum housing old engines and rolling stock. **In the area:** The Lake, 68 km NE; popular for swimming, fishing and bird-watching. **Tourist information:** Shire Offices; (076) 51 3311. **Accommodation:** 1 hotel, 1 caravan park.
MAP REF. 476 B8, 483 P8

Atherton
Pop. 5206

Atherton is the agricultural hub of the Atherton Tableland, where plantations of maize, peanuts, macadamia nuts and tropical fruits dot the rural and rainforest landscape. This farming town is 100 km SW of Cairns on the Kennedy Hwy and is surrounded by a patchwork of dense rainforest that abounds in varied birdlife and tropical vegetation. **Of interest:** Old Post Office Museum, Herberton Rd. Maize Festival held Sept. and Tablelands Band Festival Nov. Other festivals on Tableland include Tobacco Festival at Dimbulah (May), Tin Festival at Herberton (Sept.) and Torimba Forest Festival at Ravenshoe (Oct.). Fascinating Facets in the Crystal Caves, a man-made underground attraction comprising tunnels and chambers and displaying minerals, gemstones and agate; Main St. **In the area:** Atherton Tableland, one of oldest land masses in Australia, provides picturesque alternative to coast route; rainforest-fringed volcanic crater lakes, spectacular waterfalls and fertile farmlands. At Tolga, 5 km N: Woodworks and a peanut factory. Mareeba, 32 km N, tobacco- and rice-growing area; rodeo held July. Lake Tinaroo, 15 km NE; swimming, fishing, water-skiing, houseboats and sailing. Cruises on crater lakes, Lakes Eacham and Barrine, set in national parks 25 km E through historic Yungaburra; steeped in Aboriginal legend, lakes are well known for their crystal-clear waters and picturesque beauty. The Curtain Fig Tree, 2.5 km S of Yungaburra; spectacular aerial roots in curtain formation. Mt Hypipamee National Park, 26 km S; sheer-sided explosion crater

Airlie Beach

124 m deep. At Malanda, 25 km SE: Malanda Falls Environmental Park with signposted rainforest walk at edge of town. McHugh Road Lookout, 20 km S of Malanda; offers panoramic views. At Herberton, 19 km SW: Foster's Winery and Historical Village with over 30 restored buildings. **Tourist information:** 42 Mabel St; (070) 91 3608. **Accommodation:** 5 motels, 4 caravan/camping parks. **See also:** Atherton Tableland; The Far North.
MAP REF. 473 C13, 479 K7

Ayr   Pop. 8637
This busy sugar town on the north side of the Burdekin delta is surrounded by intensively irrigated sugarcane fields which are the most productive in Australia. Visitors are welcome at the Inkerman Sugar Mills during the crushing season (June–Dec.). Townsville, 82 km N, is the outlet for the bulk sugar. **Of interest:** Ayr Nature Display, Wilmington St; fine collection of butterflies and beetles. Burdekin Cultural Complex, comprising 530-seat theatre, library and activities centre. Beautiful Cooktown orchid blooms March–Aug. **In the area:** Home Hill, Ayr's sister town, on opposite side of the Burdekin River. Alva Beach, 18 km N; beach walks, birdwatching, swimming and fishing. Mt Kelly Orchids, 16 km SW; orchid displays and sales, Devonshire teas; by appt. **Tourist information:** Community Information Centre, Queen St; (077) 83 2888. **Accommodation:** 6 hotels, 6 motels, 4 caravan parks.
MAP REF. 479 O13

Babinda   Pop. 1268
A swimming-hole and picnic area known as The Boulders is a feature of interest 10 km W of this small sugar town, which is 57 km S of Cairns in the Bellenden Ker National Park. Qld's two highest mountains, Mt Bartle Frere (1611 m) and Mt Bellenden Ker (1591 m), and the Josephine Falls, are in the park. **Of interest:** Deeral Cooperative; makes footwear and Aboriginal artefacts. **In the area:** Deeral, 14 km N of Babinda, is the departure point for cruises through the rainforest and saltwater-crocodile haunts of the Mulgrave and Russell Rivers. **Accommodation:** Limited.
MAP REF. 479 L8

Barcaldine   Pop. 1530
A pastoral and rail town, Barcaldine is 108 km E of Longreach. All the streets are named after trees, and citrus fruits thrive on local bore water. **Of interest:** Beta Farm Slab Hut, cnr Pine and Bauhinia Sts; restoration of early settler's hut. Folk Museum, cnr Gidyes and Beech Sts. 'Tree of knowledge', ghost gum in main street, meeting-place for 1891 shearers' strike, which resulted in formation of Australian Labor Party. Australian Workers' Heritage Centre, Ash St; opened May 1991 on centenary of shearers' strike. **In the area:** Marraroo Gallery, 1 km W; unique Qld colonial and Aboriginal contemporary works. Lake Sanderson, 25 km E, reputedly largest man-made lake in western Qld; native wildlife. North Delta Station, 32 km E; outback station at work, accommodation. Red Mountain scenic drive, 55 km E, on Richmond Hills Station; visits by appt. Botanical Walk, 9 km S, through variety of bushland. **Tourist information:** Oak St; (076) 51 1724. **Accommodation:** 6 hotels, 4 motels, 2 caravan/camping parks.
MAP REF. 476 B9, 483 P9

Bargara   Pop. 2703
This popular surf beach, 13 km E of Bundaberg, is patrolled by one of Qld's top surf clubs. Nearby beaches include Nielson Park and Kelly's. **Of interest:** Professional and amateur competitions at 18-hole golf course. **In the area:** Mon Repos Environmental Park, 3 km N, largest and most accessible mainland turtle rookery in Australia; giant sea turtles come ashore to lay their eggs Nov.–Feb.

Millaa Millaa Falls, near Atherton

In 1912 Bert Hinkler, then an engineering apprentice, flew to a height of some 9 m in home-made glider off Mon Repos beach, marking start of his distinguished aviation career. **Tourist information:** Real Estate House, 20 Bauer St; (071) 59 2966. **Accommodation:** 1 hotel/motel, 5 motels, 3 caravan/camping parks, 2 resorts.
MAP REF. 477 P12

Beaudesert   Pop. 4028
Beaudesert is a major market town on the Mount Lindesay Hwy, 66 km SW of Brisbane, near the NSW border. A road west leads to the Cunningham Hwy, and the road east leads to the Gold Coast via Tamborine. The district is noted for dairying, agriculture and beef cattle. **Of interest:** Historical Museum, Jane St. Popular Beaudesert race meetings. Australian Rodeo Championships held Nov.–Jan. **In the area:** Woollahra Farmworld, Gleneagle, 5 km N. Dartington Park, 12 km S, and Bigriggen Park, 30 km SW; recreation areas, picnic/barbecue facilities. Lamington National Park, 40 km S. Mt Barney National Park, 55 km SW. Kooralbyn Valley Resort, 30 km SE. **Tourist information:** Historical Museum, Jane St; (075) 41 1284. **Accommodation:** 3 hotels, 3 motels, 1 caravan park.
MAP REF. 467 L12, 475 N7

Beenleigh   Pop. 16 388
Midway between Brisbane and the Gold Coast, Beenleigh is now almost a satellite town of Brisbane. The Beenleigh Distillery on the Albert River has been producing rum from local sugar since 1884. Rocky Point Sugar Mill, 20 km E, is Australia's only privately owned mill. **In the area:** Coomera, 20 km S; several family attractions include Movie World theme park, Dreamworld family fun park and Wet 'n' Wild Water Park. **Accommodation:** 2 motels, 3 caravan/camping parks.
MAP REF. 465 P13, 467 N10, 475 N6

Biggenden   Pop. 686
Set in the shadow of Mt Walsh National Park and The Bluff, 100 km SE of Bundaberg, this agricultural centre holds a Rose Festival in Sept. every second year. **In the area:** Magnetite mine, 5 km S; inspection tours. Coalstoun Lakes National Park, 3 km N; protects two volcanic crater lakes. Mt Woowoonga, 20 km N; forestry reserve, bushwalking,

Aerial view of Birdsville

picnic/barbecue facilities. Chowey Bridge (1905), 20 km NW; concrete arch railway bridge (1 of 2 surviving in Aust.), picnic facilities nearby. Mt Walsh National Park, 8 km S; wilderness park popular with experienced bushwalkers. **Tourist information:** Cnr Mulgrave and Bourgong Sts, Bundaberg; (071) 52 2333. **Accommodation:** 1 hotel, 1 hotel/motel, 1 caravan/camping park. MAP REF. 475 L1

Biloela
Pop. 6200

This modern, thriving town in the fertile Callide Valley is situated at the crossroads of the Burnett and Dawson Hwys, 142 km SW of Rockhampton. The name is Aboriginal for 'white cockatoo'. Underground water provides irrigation for lucerne, cotton and sunflower crops. **Of interest:** Greycliffe Homestead, Gladstone Rd; open by appt. Advance Australia Fair, Dawson Hwy; rural-oriented theme park, combines hi-tech of farming life with charms of rural living. **In the area:** Boating and swimming at Callide Dam, 5 km E. Callide open-cut coal mine and power station; viewing platform 15 km E. Cotton Ginnery, 2 km N; tours March–July, video offseason. Lyle Semgreen Gems at Jambin, 32 km N; open by appointment. At Banana, 47 km W: Bindiggin; displays of dolls, bottles and rocks. Mt Scoria, 14 km S; solidified volcano core. **Tourist information:** Callide St; (079) 92 2405. **Accommodation:** 2 hotels, 5 motels, 4 caravan/camping parks. **See also:** Capricorn Region. MAP REF. 477 L11

Birdsville
Pop. 102

The well known Birdsville Track starts here on its long path into and across SA. The first settlers arrived in Birdsville, nearly 2000 km by road west of Brisbane, in the 1870s and at the turn of the century it was a thriving settlement, with 3 hotels, 3 stores, several offices and a doctor. When the toll on cattle crossing the border near the town was abolished after Federation in 1901, prosperity declined and the population diminished. **Of interest:** Museum, McDonald St; Australiana, domestic artefacts and range of working farm equipment. Ruins of Royal Hotel, Adelaide St; reminder of Birdsville's boom days. Birdsville Pub, also Adelaide St; comes into its own on first weekend in Sept. when Birdsville Races are held. Population then swells to about 3000 and has been known to consume about 50 000 cans of beer over period of race meeting! Hotel is an important overnight stop for tourists travelling down the Track, west across the Simpson Desert (4WD country), north to Mount Isa or east to Brisbane. **(Travel in this area can be hazardous, especially in wet season (approx. Oct.–March). Supplies of food and water should always be carried, as well as petrol, oil and spare parts. Check noticeboard at police station, which details local conditions, before setting out. See also: Outback Motoring.)** The famous 'Flynn of the Inland' founded the first Australian Inland Mission at Birdsville and there is still a well-equipped medical outpost, run by Frontier Services, in the town. Birdsville's water comes from a 1219-m-deep artesian bore, one of the hottest in Qld. The water comes from the ground almost at boiling point and four cooling ponds bring it to a safe temperature. Electricity is supplied by two diesel-run generators. **In the area:** Big Red, 40 km W; biggest sand dune in the Western Desert. **Accommodation:** 1 hotel/motel, 1 caravan/camping park. **See also:** The Channel Country. MAP REF. 293 M1, 484 D2

Blackall
Pop. 1578

Centre of some of the most productive sheep and cattle country in central Qld, Blackall has many studs in its vicinity. In bygone days the cattle rustler Captain Starlight roamed the district. In 1892 the legendary Jackie Howe set the almost unbelievable record of shearing 321 sheep with blade shears in less than 8 hours, at Alice Downs Station, 25 km N. Blackall sank the first artesian bore in Qld in 1885; it still pumps up 6.82 million litres of hot water daily. **Of interest:** Jackie Howe statue, junction Short and Shamrock Sts. Millions-of-years-old petrified tree stump. **In the area:** Steam-driven Blackall Wool Scour (1906), 4 km N, on Clematis St; under restoration. Idalia National Park, 100 km SW; habitat of rare yellow-footed rock wallaby. Farm holidays at Avington Outback Holiday Station. **Tourist information:** Short St; (076) 57 4637. **Accommodation:** 5 hotels, 2 motels, 1 caravan/camping park. MAP REF. 476 C11, 483 P11

Blackwater
Pop. 6760

This major mining town is 190 km W of Rockhampton on the Capricorn Hwy. The name comes from the discolouration of the local waterholes caused by ti-trees. Coal mined in the area is railed to Gladstone for use at the power station before export. The town's population is made up of workers of many nationalities and it displays what is claimed to be the most varied collection of national flags this side of the United Nations. Cattle is the traditional industry. **Of interest:** Inspection tours of Utah mine; bookings necessary. **In the area:** Expedition

Sunshine Coast

A chain of sun drenched beaches bathed by the cobalt-blue Pacific stretches from Rainbow Beach southward to Bribie Island to form Queensland's Sunshine Coast. This scenic coastal region, with its average winter temperature of 25°C, its leisurely pace, and its wide variety of natural attractions and sporting facilities, offers an alternative to the more commercialised Gold Coast.

While huge waves thunder on to white sand beaches to provide year-round surfing, the calmer waters of protected beaches ensure safe swimming, boating and water-skiing. Rivers and streams alive with fish lure the angler, and forest-fringed lakes become perfect picnic spots for the family.

The Sunshine Coast is blessed with many wonders of nature. The coloured sands of Teewah in **Cooloola National Park**, between Tewantin and Rainbow Beach, rise in multi-coloured cliffs to over 200 metres. Geologists say that these sandcliffs are over 40 000 years old and claim the main colouring is either the result of oxidisation or the dye of vegetation decay. However, an Aboriginal legend relates that the colours come from a rainbow killed by a boomerang when it came to the rescue of a young woman.

Another marvel of nature is the **Glass House Mountains**, formed by giant cores of long-extinct volcanoes.

The **Noosa** area, at the northern end of the region, has facilities for fishing, boating and golf. Poised on the edge of Laguna Bay is the resort town of **Noosa Heads**, with its 430-hectare national park. This coastal park contains a network of walking tracks that wind through rainforests, giving spectacular ocean views of such unusual rock formations as Hell's Gates, Paradise Caves, Lion's Rock, Devil's Kitchen and Witches' Cauldron. The park also houses an animal sanctuary and there are coastal lakes inhabited by elegant black swans, pelicans, ducks and cranes.

The southernmost town of the Sunshine Coast is **Caloundra**, 'the beautiful place', where Aborigines once came down from the hills to feast on seafood.

The hinterland of the Sunshine Coast is like a huge cultivated garden, covered with pineapples, sugarcane, ginger and citrus, dotted with dairy farms and enclosing within its folds cascading waterfalls, lush rainforests and bubbling streams. Looming majestically behind this garden of plenty is the **Blackall Range**, a world apart with art and craft galleries, Devonshire tea places, comfortable pubs and a feeling of 'olde England'. The scenic drive through the townships of Mapleton, Flaxton, Montville and Maleny is one of the best in south-east Queensland. The **Kondalilla National Park** and **Mapleton Falls National Park** are a must for nature lovers. Kondalilla, an Aboriginal word meaning 'rushing waters', is apt, as the park has an 80-metre waterfall that drops into a valley of rainforest. The Mapleton Hotel offers authentic country-pub hospitality with panoramic views from the traditional Queensland verandah. Visit the miniature English village with its castles, churches, thatched cottages and inns. A number of art and craft cottages surround Montville's Village Green. Take in the view from the picture window at the De'Lisle Gallery while being surrounded by works of art from the Sunshine Coast's best artists. Mary Cairncross Park, at the southern end of the range, gives breathtaking views of the coast and the Glass House Mountains. **Nambour** is conveniently located, just off the Bruce Highway, for trips to the mountains of the Blackall Range or to the beach.

The Sunshine Coast has accommodation to suit all tastes and budgets, from beachfront caravan parks through to luxury 5-star international motels. And if you enjoy dining out, there are dozens of fine restaurants where you can indulge your tastebuds.

For more information on the Sunshine Coast, contact Tourism Sunshine Coast Ltd, 126 Alexandra Pde, Alexandra Headland; (008) 07 2041. **See also:** Individual town entries in A–Z listing. **Note** detailed map of Sunshine Coast on page 470.

Glass House Mountains

Lake Moogerah, near Boonah

Range (732 m), discovered by Ludwig Leichhardt. Blackdown Tableland National Park, 50 km SE; picnic/barbecue facilities at Horseshoe Lookout and Mimosa Creek camping area. **Tourist information:** Clermont St, Emerald; (079) 82 4142. **Accommodation:** 3 motels, 2 caravan/camping parks. **See also:** The Capricorn Region.
MAP REF. 476 I9

Boonah   Pop. 2100
Eighty-six km SW of Brisbane between Warwick and Ipswich, Boonah is the main town in the Fassifern district, a highly productive agricultural and pastoral area. Its location was noted as a 'beautiful vale' by the colonial administrator and explorer Captain Logan in 1827, and by explorer Allan Cunningham in 1828. **Of interest:** Fassifern German Festival held Sept. **In the area:** Templin Historical Village, 5 km N; Sun.–Thurs. 9.30–3.30. Fassifern Valley National Park, 12 km W. Lake Moogerah, 20 km SW, for water sports. The Scenic Rim, ring of mountains bordering shire; popular for scenic drives, bushwalking, trail-riding, rock-climbing, skydiving and water sports. Picnic spots and recreation facilities for day trippers; camping and accommodation for those with more time. Coochin Coochin, historic homestead, 14 km S; not open to public. **Tourist information:** Shire Offices, High St; (074) 63 1599. **Accommodation:** 2 hotels, 1 motel, 1 caravan/camping park.
MAP REF. 467 J12, 475 M7

Boulia   Pop. 281
Situated on the Burke River, 365 km W of Winton, 305 km S of Mt Isa and 200 km E of the NT border, Boulia is the capital of the Channel Country. **Of interest:** Stone Cottage Museum (1880s), Pituri St; town's oldest house, now displays historic relics of region, also Aboriginal artefacts. The Red Stump in main street warns travellers of dangers of Simpson Desert. Artificial 'Min Min' light, Herbert St. Koree Yuppiree Tree, near Boulia State School, thought to be last known corroboree tree of Pitta Pitta tribe. Varied birdlife to be seen around river. Boulia rodeo held Aug. **In the area:** Mysterious Min Min light, first reportedly sighted near ruins of Min Min Hotel (130 km E), has been seen within 24 km of town. Wills Creek, to north, another reminder in area of ill-fated explorers Burke and Wills. **Travel by road in wet season not possible. See**: Outback Motoring. **Tourist information:** Shire Offices, Herbert St; (077) 46 3188. **Accommodation:** 1 hotel/motel, 1 caravan park. **See also:** The Channel Country.
MAP REF. 482 F8

Bowen   Pop. 8312
A relaxed town exactly halfway between Mackay and Townsville, Bowen was named after Qld's first Governor. The town was established in 1861 on the protected shores of Port Denison and was the first settlement in North Qld. It boasts an excellent climate with an average of 8 hours' sunshine daily. Bowen is famous for its tomatoes and, particularly, for its tropical mangoes, in season (Nov.–Jan.). **Of interest:** Signposted Golden Arrow tourist route starting at Salt Works, Don St. Historical murals in Powell, Herbert and George Sts. Historical Museum, Gordon St. Annual Art, Craft and Orchid Expo in Aug. Coral Coast Festival in Oct. **In the area:** Excellent small bays 7 km; fishing, snorkelling and safe swimming. At Delta, 7 km N, coffee plantation. Collinsville coal mines and power station, 92 km SW. Day trips to resort on Stone Island. Boat racing and charter fishing and diving. **Tourist information:** Courthouse, Herbert St. **Accommodation:** 3 hotels, 5 motels, 7 caravan/camping parks.
MAP REF. 476 H1

Buderim   Pop. 7499
Buderim is a delightful town just inland from the Sunshine Coast, high on the fertile red soil of Buderim Mountain, between the Bruce Hwy and Mooloolaba on the coast. It is a popular residential and retirement area. **Of interest:** Blue Marble and Fine Art Images galleries, Burnett St. Pioneer timber cottage (1876), Ballinger Rd; one of Buderim's earliest houses, faithfully restored and retaining many of its original furnishings. Buderim Festive Markets, in Old Ginger Factory, Burnett St. Buderim Forest Park, Quorn Close; waterfalls and walking tracks. **In the area:** Self-guide Forest Glen–Tenawha Tourist Drive, includes Super Bee honey factory, Forest Glen Deer Sanctuary and Moonshine Valley Winery with tastings and sales of wines made from locally grown tropical fruits and Italian restaurant. **Tourist information:** Cnr Aerodrome Rd and Sixth Ave, Maroochydore; (074) 79 1566. **Accommodation:** 2 motels, 2 caravan/camping parks.
MAP REF. 467 N1, 470 G9, 475 N4

Bundaberg   Pop. 38 074
Bundaberg, 368 km N of Brisbane, is the southernmost access point to the Great Barrier Reef and an important provincial city in the centre of the fertile Burnett River plains. The district is known for its sugar (the area's main crop), timber, beef production and, in more recent years, tomatoes, avocados and small crops. Bundaberg is a city of parks and botanical gardens; its wide streets lined with

poincianas provide a brilliant display in spring. Several famous Australians have called Bundy home: aviator Bert Hinkler, in 1928 the first man to fly solo from England to Australia; singer Gladys Moncrieff; cricketer Don Tallon; and rugby league star Mal Meninga. Sugar has been grown in the area since 1866. Raw sugar is exported from an extensive storage and bulk terminal facility at Port Bundaberg, 16 km NE. Industry sidelines include the distilling of the famous Bundaberg Rum, refined sugar production, and the manufacture and export of advanced Austoft cane-harvester equipment. **Of interest:** Alexandra Park and Zoo, Quay St, on Burnett River; children's playground and cacti garden. Bundaberg Rum Distillery, Avenue St, East Bundaberg; guided tours to see Famous Aussie Spirit being made. The Potters Centre, Bourbong St; local pottery, watercolours and handcrafts. Boyd's Antiquatorium, Bourbong St; boasts best Edison Gramophone collection in Australia. Schmeider's Cooperage and Craft Centre, Alexandra St, East Bundaberg; demonstrates ancient art of barrel-making. Hinkler House Memorial Museum, Mt Perry Rd, Nth Bundaberg; repository of aviation history within Botanical Gardens. Also Botanical Gardens Railway; steam train rides around lakes; and Bundaberg Historical Museum. Unique winery for tropical-fruit wine and Sunny Soft Drinks, Mt Perry Rd, Nth Bundaberg. Banio's Horseriding Centre, Patterson's Rd, North Bundaberg; 300 acres of picturesque riverside country. **In the area:** Unexplained mystery, 25 km N: 35

strange craters said to be 25 million years old. Pennyroyal Herb Farm, 6 km S; snacks at Culinary Corner. The Paradise Park, 6 km S; bird and animal sanctuary and nursery. Dreamtime Reptile Reserve, 8 km S on Childers Rd; educational tours. Avocado Grove, 10 km S; subtropical gardens. Currajong Gardens and Nursery, 61 km SW, near Gin Gin. Bauers Gerbera Nursery nearby. Hummock Lookout, 7 km E; views over city, 'patchwork quilt' of canefields and coast. Surfing beaches at Bargara–Nielson Park and Kelly's Beach (15 km E), Moore Park (21 km N) and Elliott Heads (18 km SE). Turtles can be seen at Mon Repos Environmental Park, 14 km E, Nov.–Feb. Tours to view migrating humpback whales, mid-Aug.–mid-Oct. Fishing at Burnett Heads, 18 km E, at river mouth. House of Rare Bits, The Esplanade, Burnett Heads; locally made handicrafts and Devonshire teas. Poseidon Seashells, Rickets Rd, Burnett Heads; coral, seashells, local shellcraft. Cruises to Lady Musgrave Island, uninhabited coral cay, on either MV *Lady Musgrave* (departs Burnett Heads) or by seaplane with Bundaberg Seaplane Tours. Flights to Lady Elliot Island resort. **Tourist information:** Cnr Mulgrave and Bourbong Sts; (071) 52 2333. **Accommodation:** Many hotels, 33 motels, 8 caravan/camping parks (most with cabins).
MAP REF. 477 P12

Burketown
Pop. 200

The centre of rich beef country, Burketown is 230 km W of Normanton. The Gulf is accessible by boat from Burketown, which sits on the Albert River and on the east–west dividing line between the wetlands to the north and the beginning of the Gulf Savannah grass plains to the south. **Of interest:** 100-year-old bore, which issues boiling water. Burketown Pub (1860s), original customs house; oldest building in the Gulf. Burketown to Normanton telegraph-line, post office and cemetery offer insights into town's historic past. **In the area:** Original Gulf meatworks just north of town. Nicholson River wetlands, 17 km W, breeding grounds for crocodiles and variety of fish and birdlife. Escott Lodge, 17 km W, operating cattle station and tourist resort with camping and accommodation. **Tourist information:** Burke Shire Council; (077) 45 5100 or Old Post Office and Museum; (077) 45 5177. **Accommodation:** 1 hotel/motel, 1 caravan/camping park. **See also:** Gulf Savannah.
MAP REF. 481 E9

Burrum Heads
Pop. 770

This pleasant holiday resort on Hervey Bay, 45 km N of Maryborough off Bruce Hwy, offers excellent fishing. **In the area:** Burrum River National Park, near town, and Woodgate National Park, 5 km N by boat. **Tourist information:** Phillips Travel, 45 Burrum St; (071) 29 5211. **Accommodation:** 1 hotel/motel, 2 caravan/camping parks.
MAP REF. 477 P13

Caboolture
Pop. 12 716

A major dairying centre just off the Bruce Hwy, 46 km N of Brisbane, Caboolture is

Horseshoe Bay, near Bowen

noted for its butter, yoghurt and cheese. The area is also rich in Aboriginal history and relics. The district was opened up in the 1860s for grazing, sugar and cotton. **Of interest:** Caboolture Historical Village, faithfully restored. **In the area:** Distinctive landmark of Glass House Mountains, 22 km N. Popular fishing resorts of Donnybrook and Toorbul (20 and 22 km NE), and Beachmere on Deception Bay (13 km SE). Bribie Island, 23 km E, family day tripping destination; picnic areas, fishing and safe swimming. Abbey Museum, on road to Bribie Island, traces growth of Western civilisation. **Tourist information:** Shire Offices, Hasking St; (074) 95 3122. **Accommodation:** 3 motels, 2 caravan/camping parks. MAP REF. 467 M4, 475 N5

Cairns   Pop. 64 463

A modern, colourful city and capital of the tropical Far North. The cosmopolitan esplanade traces the bay foreshore and parks and gardens abound with colour and tropical trees and plants. Cairns' location is superb: the Great Barrier Reef to the east, the mountain rainforests and plains of the Atherton Tableland to the west, and palm-fringed beaches to the north and south. Cairns has gained world-wide prominence as one of the great black marlin fishing locations and is now further enhanced by easy access to the Great Barrier Reef for snorkelling enthusiasts, scuba divers and those who

simply wish to see the coral from glass-bottomed boats. **Of interest:** Cairns Red Explorer bus from Lake St; links 9 stops and attractions in and around city. Cairns Museum, cnr Lake and Shields Sts. Big-game fishing boats moor at Marlin Marina, end of Spence St. Trinity Wharf and The Pier shopping and entertainment complex. Freshwater Connection historical complex, which is also departure point for 100-year-old Kuranda Scenic Railway, through Barron Gorge to rainforest village of Kuranda, 34 km NW. Wetland areas, including the Esplanade, provide opportunities for birdwatching. Flecker Botanic Gardens, Collins St; exotic trees and shrubs, 200 varieties of palms, area devoted to plants used by Aborigines. Walking track links gardens to Centenary Lakes Parkland. Jack Barnes Bicentennial Mangrove Boardwalk, Airport St; two educational walks through mangroves, with viewing platforms. Rusty's Bazaar, Grafton and Sheridan Sts; Sat. & Sun. markets with local handicrafts, home-made produce, plants and new and secondhand goods. Royal Flying Doctor Service Visitor Centre, Junction St, Edge Hill. Doll and Bear Museum, Mayers St, Manunda. Fun in the Sun Festival held Oct. **In the area:** Bulk sugar terminal, Cook St, Portsmith; guided tours during crushing season. Marlin Coast, extending from Machans Beach (10 km N) to Ellis Beach, 26 km of spectacular coastline. Vic Hislop

Rafting on Barron River, near Cairns

Shark Show, 8 km N. Popular seaside spot of Holloways Beach, 11 km N. Wild World and Outback Opal Mine, 22 km N. Hartley's Creek Crocodile Farm, 40 km N. Reef and islands can be explored by private charters, daily cruises and air (seaplane and helicopter). Longer cruises to resort islands and reef on catamaran *Coral Princess*. Access to nearby Green, Fitzroy and Frankland Islands on cruise vessels. Cairns also offers easy access to wilderness areas of Cape York, Daintree and Atherton Tableland. Sugarworld Gardens, 8 km S at Edmonton. Delightful rural settings of Barron and Freshwater Valleys, north and south of Cairns; attractions include Crystal Cascades, Barron Gorge hydro-electric power station and Copperlode Dam (Lake Morris); bushwalking, hiking, whitewater rafting and camping. Off-road safaris (4WD) to Cape York and Gulf Savannah. At Injinoo, Cape York: Panjinka Wilderness Lodge; fishing, sailing, walking, wildlife; 4WD. Information from Dept of Environment & Heritage, (070) 52 3096; or Far North Qld Coach and Off Road Association, (070) 31 4565. **Tourist information:** Cnr Grafton and Hartley Sts; (070) 51 3588. **Accommodation:** 50 hotels, numerous motels from 5-star, international-standard hotels to family and budget; 9 caravan/camping parks. **See also:** The Far North; Cape York. MAP REF. 472, 473 G9, 479 L6

Caloundra   Pop. 22 094

This popular holiday spot on the Sunshine Coast is 96 km N of Brisbane via a turnoff from the Bruce Hwy. The main beaches are Kings, Shelly, Moffat, Dicky, Golden and Bulcock. The main shipping channel to Brisbane is just offshore. Pumicestone Passage (a State marine park) to the south, between Bribie Island and the mainland, has sheltered waters for fishing, boating, water-skiing and sailboarding. **Of interest:** Queensland Air Museum, at aerodrome, Pathfinder Dr. Teddy Bear World, Bowman Rd; museum, water-slide, mini-golf. **In the area:** Old Lighthouse, Golden Beach, 4 km S. Wreck of SS *Dicky* (1893), Dicky Beach, 4 km N. At Currimundi, 4 km N: Indoor skydiving centre, Nicklin Way; also Lake and Seaside Environment Park. Opals Down Under and House of Herbs, Bruce Hwy, 9 km N. Suncoast Crayfish Farm, off Glenview Rd, 9 km N. Aussie World and Ettamogah Pub, Bruce Hwy, 10 km N; pure *Australasian Post*.

Pt Cartwright Lookout, 12 km N. Glass House Mts, 29 km SW. **Tourist information:** Caloundra Rd; (074) 91 0202. **Accommodation:** 2 hotels, 11 motels, 12 caravan/camping parks. **See also:** Sunshine Coast.
MAP REF. 467 N2, 470 I13, 475 N4

Camooweal   Pop. 234
On the Barkly Hwy, 188 km NW of Mount Isa, Camooweal is the last Qld town reached before crossing the NT border, 13 km W. **Of interest:** Shire Hall (1922–3) and Freckleton's Store, both classified by National Trust. Ellen Finlay Park; picnic/barbecue areas. Cemetery; headstones tell local history. **In the area:** Camooweal Caves, within national park, 25 km S; challenge to experienced potholers. **Tourist information:** Inland Qld Tourism and Development Board, Marian St, Mount Isa; (077) 43 7966. **Accommodation:** 1 hotel, 1 motel, 1 caravan park.
MAP REF. 395 Q12, 397 Q1, 482 B1

Cannonvale   Pop. 2402
Cannonvale is the first of the three seaside resorts along the Shute Harbour road from the Proserpine turnoff, and is a suburb of the town of Whitsunday. Located 3 km from Airlie Beach, Cannonvale is fast becoming a vital centre for service and manufacturing businesses in the region. **Of interest:** Wildlife Park, Shute Harbour Rd. **In the area:** Airlie Beach and Shute Harbour, neighbouring resorts to south. Conway National Park, 10 km S. Tours to Whitsunday Islands. **Tourist information:** Cnr Mandalay St and Shute Harbour Rd, Airlie Beach; (079) 46 6673. **Accommodation:** 1 motel, 3 caravan/camping parks, 1 resort.
MAP REF. 476 I2

Cardwell   Pop. 1294
From Cardwell, 58 km S of Ingham, a beautiful view is obtained of Rockingham Bay and many islands, including the well known Hinchinbrook, all of which may be visited by boat from Cardwell. Departure point for 4-day walk on Hinchinbrook Is. Local fishing and snorkelling is generally excellent. **Of interest:** Museum, Victoria St. National Parks Display Centre, Victoria St; information about local national parks and Great Barrier Reef Marine Park. **In the area:** Scenic drives in Cardwell Forest, with spectacular coastal scenery, and Kirrama

Gold panning statue, Charters Towers

Range, 9–10 km N, on Kennedy Rd. Murray Falls in State Forest Park, 20 km NW; camping and picnic area. Houseboats and yachts for hire. Cruises available. **Tourist information:** Hinchinbrook Travel, 13 Victoria St; (070) 66 8539. **Accommodation:** 1 hotel, 6 motels, 5 caravan/camping parks.
MAP REF. 479 L10

Charleville   Pop. 3513
Charleville marks the terminus of the Westlander rail service and is at the centre of a rich pastoral district carrying some 800 000 sheep and 100 000 cattle. The town has an interesting history. Charleville's river, the Warrego, was explored by Edmund Bourke in 1847, and in 1862, William Landsborough camped nearby when searching for Burke and Wills. By the 1890s, Charleville was a frontier town with its own brewery, 10 pubs and 500 registered bullock teams. Cobb & Co. had a coach-building factory here in 1893. The last coach on Australian roads ran to Surat in 1923. A monument 19 km N of the town marks the spot where Ross and Keith Smith landed with engine trouble on the first flight from London to Sydney in 1919. Amy Johnson also landed here, in 1920. Qantas started flights from Charleville in 1922. Charleville is the heart of the Mulga Country; the mulga provide welcome shade and in drought are cut down and used as sheep

fodder. **Of interest:** Historical Museum in restored Qld National Bank building (1880), Albert St; amazing 5-m-long 'vortex gun' used in unsuccessful rainmaking experiments in 1902. Skywatch at Meteorological Bureau at airport; powerful telescopes, guided presentation evenings. 'Weary Willie' swagman statue in main street. National Parks and Wildlife Service Research Centre, Park St. Cobb & Co. coach can be hired for town tours. Booga Woongaroo Festival held Oct. **In the area:** Tree blazed by Landsborough in 1862, 16 km S; guide required. **Tourist information:** Town Hall Building, Wills St; (076) 57 3057. **Accommodation:** 4 hotels, 3 motels, 2 caravan/camping parks.
MAP REF. 474 A3, 485 Q3

Charters Towers   Pop. 9016
This peaceful and historic city once had a gold rush population of some 30 000. Between 1872 and 1916, Charters Towers produced ore worth 25 million pounds ($50m). On 25 December 1871 a young Aboriginal boy named Jupiter made the first strike while looking for horses that had bolted during a thunderstorm. He brought some quartz back to his employer, Hugh Mosman, who rode to Ravenswood to register his claim, and the gold rush was on. The Government rewarded Mosman and he adopted and educated Jupiter. Charters Towers is 135 km inland from Townsville in hot, dry country on the road and rail line to Mount Isa. Cattle-raising is the main industry in the Dalrymple Shire, together with citrus and grapes and another gold boom— there are 3 large goldmines open in the area. **Of interest:** Much classic early Australian architecture with verandahs and lacework still remains, particularly facades in Mosman and Gill Sts. Historic homes: Ay-Ot-Lookout(1890s), Hodgkinson St, and Pffither House (1890s), Paul St. Zara Clark Museum, Mosman St; local history, open Sat.–Sun. Tourist centre in restored Stock Exchange, Mosman St. Buckland's Hill lookout, Fraser St. **In the area:** Mount Leyshon goldmine, 24 km S. Old Venus gold treatment battery, 5 km E; 2 guided tours daily. Ravenswood, 88 km E; small mining town. Burdekin Falls Dam, 150 km SE; camping. **Tourist information:** Mosman St; (077) 87 2374. **Accommodation:** 5 hotels, 6 motels, 3 caravan/camping parks. **See also:** The Far North.
MAP REF. 476 D1, 483 R1

Gladstone Region

Gladstone, only 6 hours' drive north of Brisbane, offers the closest major southern access to the Great Barrier Reef. Reef trips depart daily from Gladstone's marina and regularly from Town of 1770.

With its gracious palm-studded city centre, Gladstone faces the harbour and offers accommodation ranging from international hotels to caravan parks, as well as restaurants serving the region's famous mud crabs. Gladstone, the outlet for Central Queensland's mineral and agricultural wealth, is a world-class port and one of Australia's busiest.

The hinterland west of Gladstone features national parks, rainforests and an historical village, and is ideal for trail-riding, camping, walking and fishing.

South of the city, nestled in the delta of the picturesque Boyne River, **Boyne Island** is linked by a bridge to its twin beachside community, **Tannum Sands**. In an easy blend of scenery and industry, a major smelter on the island produces a quarter of Australia's aluminium output.

Further south, the **Agnes Water–Town of 1770** area is renowned for its unspoiled parkland with natural springs, palm groves, pockets of wilderness, and rare birds, animals and plants. The secluded white beaches with their crystal-clear waters are virtually unaltered since Captain Cook landed here in 1770.

Heron Island, a world-famous coral cay resort, is on the Barrier Reef just off Gladstone. **Wilson Island**, another beautiful coral cay, offers camping holidays in comfortable seclusion. Locally based helicopters, as well as a host of vessels moored in the Gladstone marina, enable visitors to explore this tropical paradise. A large charter-boat fleet departs regularly for fishing and diving trips or to take campers to the reef islands.

For further information contact Gladstone Area Promotion and Development Ltd, 56 Goondoon St, Gladstone; (079) 72 4000. **See also:** Individual town entries in A–Z listing.

Heron Island, offshore from Gladstone

Childers
Pop. 1473

Childers is a picturesque sugar town, 53 km s of Bundaberg. Much of it was destroyed by fire in 1902; Today it is a National Trust Town. **Of interest:** Historic Childers, self-guide town walk taking in many historic buildings: Old Butcher's Shop (1896), North St; Grand Hotel and Federal Hotel, Churchill St; Royal Hotel, Randall St; Gaydon's Building (1894), Churchill St, now Pharmaceutical Museum, art gallery and tourist centre; and Historic Complex, Taylor St, includes school, cottage and locomotive. **In the area:** Cane Cutters' Cottage, Apple Tree Creek, 5 km N; crafts and Devonshire teas. Isis Central Sugar Mill, Cordalba, 10 km N; tours July–Nov. Woodgate National Park, 45 km E; accommodation. **Tourist information:** Pharmaceutical Museum, Churchill St; (071) 26 1994. **Accommodation:** 4 hotels, 4 motels, 2 caravan/camping parks. MAP REF. 475 M1, 477 P13

Chillagoe
Pop. 502

Chillagoe, once a thriving town where copper, silver, lead, gold and wolfram were mined, is now a small outback town where the recent development of tourism, international-standard marble mines and the Red Dome gold mine have returned the town to some of its former glory. **Of interest:** Local museum gives glimpse of history of town, with relics of old mining days on display. **In the area:** Rugged limestone outcrops in Chillagoe Mungana National Park, 8 km s, contain many magnificent caves; guided tours. **Tourist information:** Far North Qld Promotion Bureau, cnr Grafton & Hartley Sts, Cairns; (070) 51 3588. **Accommodation:** 1 hotel, 1 motel, 1 caravan/ camping park. MAP REF. 478 I7

Chinchilla
Pop. 3152

Chinchilla is a prosperous town in the western Darling Downs, 354 km w of Brisbane on the Warrego Hwy. Ludwig Leichhardt named the area in 1847 from Jinchilla, the local Aboriginal name for cypress pines. Grain-growing is the traditional industry, as well as cattle, sheep, pigs, timber and, more recently, grapes and watermelons. **Of interest:** Chinchilla Historical Museum, Villiers St; working steam engines and 1880s slab cottage. Newan's Collection of Petrified Wood, Boyd St. Fishing on Charley's

Display at the Historical Museum, Chinchilla

Creek and Condamine River. Polocrosse Carnival held 3rd weekend in July. **In the area:** Barakula State Forest, 40 km N, Qld's largest commercial forest. Petrified wood, fossils and gemstones fossicking near Eddington, 20 km SW. Cactoblastis Hall at Boonarga, 8 km E. **Tourist information:** Chinchilla Historical Museum, Villiers St; (076) 62 7014. **Accommodation:** 1 hotel/motel, 3 motels, 1 caravan/camping park. MAP REF. 474 I4

Clermont
Pop. 2727

Centre of a fertile region which breeds cattle and sheep and grows wheat, sorghum, safflower and sunflower as well as hardwood timber, Clermont is 350 km sw of Mackay, just off the Gregory Hwy. Nearby is the Blair Athol open-cut mine, the largest seam of steaming coal in the world. About 170 houses were built in 1982 in Clermont for coal workers. The town, which takes its name from Clermont in France, was established over 120 years ago (the first inland settlement in the tropics) after the discovery of gold. At first the settlement was at Copperfield, but was moved to the present site when gold was discovered. Many remnants of the gold rushes can still be seen. **In the area:** Picnics and bush walks at Theresa Creek Dam, 5 km SW. Copperfield Store, 5 km SW; original shop from copper-mining era, now a museum. Copperfield Chimney, 8 km SW; last remaining chimneys from copper-mining days. Clermont and District Historical Museum, 4 km NW on Charters Towers Rd.

Tourist information: Shire Offices, Daintree St; (079) 83 1133. **Accommodation:** 4 hotel/motels, 2 motels, 1 caravan park. MAP REF. 476 G7

Cleveland
Pop. 9270

Centre of the Redland Shire, 35 km SE of Brisbane, Cleveland was nearly the capital for the new colony of Qld; however, when Governor Gipps and his official party arrived for an inspection, the tide was out and the trudge over the mudflats created a less than favourable impression. **Of interest:** Ye Olde Court House (1853); built by Francis Bigge for timber-getters, later first police station and courthouse, now restaurant. Cleveland Lighthouse (1847), Cleveland Point; guided timber-carrying vessels. Close by, The Old Lighthouse (1864), wooden structure, restored and relocated, held Australian record for length of tenancy by one attendant: 50 years by James Froy. Grand View Hotel (1849), restored; built by Francis Bigge in anticipation of influx of holidaymakers when Cleveland was named the capital of Qld, it became known as Bigge's Folly. Main bar exhibits murals depicting historic events of the day. Bayside Markets, Bloomfield St; held Sun. Cleveland is departure point for barges and water taxis to Nth Stradbroke and other Moreton Bay islands. **In the area:** Ormiston House (1862), overlooking bay at Ormiston, 5 km N; open Sun., March–Nov. Its builder, Captain Louis Hope, pioneered Qld's sugar industry at this location. Whepstead Manor

Lakefield National Park, near Cooktown

(1874), at Wellington Point, 7 km N; an historic old Queenslander with beautifully landscaped grounds, now restaurant and function centre. **Tourist information:** Shire Offices, Bloomfield St; (07) 286 8586. **Accommodation:** 2 motels. MAP REF. 467 N8

Clifton   Pop. 805

Located between Toowoomba and Warwick, Clifton is the centre of a rich grain-growing and dairying area. **Of interest:** Historic buildings, including Club Hotel (1889), King St, and Church of St James and St Johns (1890s), cnr Tooth St and Mears Pl. **In the area:** Tours of local peanut factory, 5 km E. Arthur Hoey Davis (Steele Rudd), author of *On Our Selection*, grew up at East Greenmount, 10 km N. Sister Kenny, remembered for her method of treating poliomyelitis, is buried at Nobby, 8 km N. Also at Nobby, Rudd's Pub (1893); museum in part of dining room. **Tourist information:** Shire Offices, King St; (076) 97 3299. **Accommodation:** Limited. MAP REF. 466 E11, 475 L7

Cloncurry   Pop. 2309

An important mining town, 124 km E of Mount Isa, Cloncurry has an interesting history. In 1861, John McKinlay of Adelaide, leading an expedition to search for Burke and Wills, reported distinctive traces of copper in the area. Six years later, pioneer pastoralist Ernest Henry discovered the first copper lodes. A rail link to Townsville was built in 1908. During World War I, Cloncurry was the centre of a copper boom and in 1916 it was the largest source of copper in Australia, with four smelters operating. After copper prices slumped following the war, a pastoral industry took its place. In 1920 a new Qantas air service linked Cloncurry to Winton and in 1928 the town became the base for the famous Royal Flying Doctor Service. In 1974 a rare type of exceptionally pure 22-carat gold, resembling crystallised straw, was discovered. It is now used for jewellery-making. The Cloncurry Shire is mainly cattle country, and Cloncurry is a main railhead for transporting stock. **Of interest:** John Flynn Place, Daintree St; incorporates Fred McKay Art Gallery and RFDS Museum, cultural centre, outdoor theatre and Cloncurry Gardens. Cloncurry–Mary Kathleen Memorial Park, McIlwraith St; 4 buildings from abandoned town of Mary Kathleen, re-erected and used to display items of historic interest. Royal Flying Doctor Service Historical Museum, cnr King and Gregory Sts. Cloister of Plaques (RFDS memorial), Uhr St. Courthouse (1884), Shaeffe St. Afghan Cemetery, Henry St. Chinese Cemetery, Flinders Hwy. Old Qantas hangar at aerodrome. Saleyards in Sir Hudson Fyshe Dr. Agricultural Show held June; Merry Muster Rodeo Aug. **In the area:** Rotary Lookout, near Normanton Rd turnoff. Ruins of Great Australia Copper Mine, 2 km S. Alluvial gold workings at Soldiers Cap, 48 km SW. Kuridala ghost town, 88 km SE; amethyst fossicking a further 8 km and signposted. Walkabout Creek Hotel at McKinlay, 105 km SE, location for film *Crocodile Dundee*. Burke and Wills cairn on Corella River, 50 km W. Ruins of old gold-mining town of Mount Cuthbert, 10 km from Kajabbi (77 km NW). **Tourist information:** Cloncurry–Mary Kathleen Memorial Park, McIlwraith St; (077) 42 1361. **Accommodation:** 2 hotels, 2 motels, 1 caravan park. **See also:** Gulf Savannah. MAP REF. 482 G3

Cooktown   Pop. 1342

Captain James Cook beached the *Endeavour* here in 1770 to repair damage after running aground on a coral reef. Gold was discovered at the Palmer River in 1872 and by 1877 Cooktown was a booming, brawling gold rush port with 37 busy pubs and a transient population of some 18 000 people a year (including 6000 Chinese). Cooktown now has only three hotels left and the town's main industry is tourism. Located 240 km north of Cairns, it is the departure point to tour Cape York Peninsula. The surrounding district has good agricultural potential and the town is also supported by prawning, fishing and tin mining. **Of interest:** Cooktown Cemetery, with graves of tutor, early immigrant and heroine Mrs Mary Watson, and the nearby Chinese Shrine to the many who died on the goldfields. Grassy Hill offers views across the reef, township and hinterland. James Cook Historical Museum (est. 1945) with collection tracing Cooktown's 2 centuries of history, incl. an anchor from the *Endeavour*. Cooktown Sea Museum, featuring maritime history of area; also shell collection. Discovery Festival, featuring re-enactment of Cook's landing, held June long weekend. **In the area:** Bicentennial National Trail (5000 km) for walkers and horseriders runs from Cooktown to Healesville in Vic. Lakefield National Park, 58 km NW; rivers, lagoons and swamps provide habitat for great variety of wildlife and are crucial area for crocodile conservation. Lizard Island, 90 km NW, with resort, national park and beautiful secluded beaches. Quinkan Aboriginal Art Galleries near Laura, 145 km W; guided tours of hundreds of cave paintings, best seen May–Nov. **Tourist information:** Cooktown Sea Museum, cnr Helen and Walker Sts; (070) 69 5680. **Accommodation:** 3 hotels, 6 motels, 3 caravan/camping parks. **See also:** Atherton Tableland. MAP REF. 479 K3

Coolangatta
Pop. part of Gold Coast
Coolangatta is the most southerly of Qld's coastal towns, with its twin town of Tweed Heads across the border in NSW. Twin Towns Services Club and Seagulls Rugby League Club feature international shows, poker machines and dining. At Point Danger is the Captain Cook Memorial and Lighthouse. **In the area:** Coolangatta Airport at Bilinga services the Gold Coast for domestic flights, charters, joy flights and tandem sky diving. For those who prefer to keep their feet on the ground, the Tom Beaston Outlook (Razorback Lookout) behind Tweed Heads provides splendid views. **Tourist information:** Beach House, Marine Pde; (075) 36 7765. **Accommodation:** 2 hotels, 2 motels, many holiday units. **See also:** City of the Gold Coast.
MAP REF. 469 I10, 475 O7

Crows Nest   Pop. 1154
This small town, 45 km N of Toowoomba, acquired its name from Jim Crow, an Aboriginal from the Kabi-Kabi tribe who once made his home in a hollow tree near what is now the police station. A life-size memorial in Centenary Park commemorates this. **Of interest:** Salts Antiques, Thallon St; open weekends. John French VC Memorial Library, William St. Carbethon Folk Museum and Pioneer Village, Thallon St. **In the area:** Authentic split-timber and shingle pioneer's hut north on Crows Nest–Cooyar Rd. Crows Nest Falls

National Park, 6 km N (look for sign to Valley of Diamonds); walking tracks to falls and gorge, picnic facilities and camping (above falls). Ravensbourne National Park, 25 km S. Farm holidays at Listening Ridge and Blue Haze host farms. **Tourist information:** 541 Ruthven St, Toowoomba; (076) 32 1988. **Accommodation:** 1 caravan/camping park.
MAP REF. 466 F5, 475 L5

Croydon   Pop. 220
This Gulf town is 561 km from Cairns. Restoration work within the Croydon Historic Precinct, the remains of the much larger town of the 1800s, is transforming the surviving town into a showpiece. **Of interest:** Old gaol, butcher shop, general store and hospital. Gaslights still stand on footpaths, and old courthouse and mining warden's office still have their original furnishings. Outdoor Museum, featuring a display of early mining machinery from age of steam. Guided walking tours of town. Terminus of Normanton to Croydon railway. **Tourist information:** Shire Offices; (077) 45 6125. **Accommodation:** 1 hotel, 1 roadhouse, 1 caravan/camping park. **See also:** Gulf Savannah.
MAP REF. 478 E9

Cunnamulla   Pop. 1683
A western sheep town renowned for its friendliness and hospitality, Cunnamulla is on the Warrego River, 122 km N of the NSW border. It is the biggest wool-loading station on the Qld railway network,

with some 2 million sheep in the area, plus beef cattle and Angora goats. Explorers Sir Thomas Mitchell and Edmund Kennedy were the first white visitors in 1846 and 1847, and by 1879 it had become a town with regular Cobb & Co. services. **Of interest:** In 1880 a daring but disorganised villain, Joseph Wells, held up the local bank and tried to escape with the loot, but could not find his horse. Irate locals bailed him up in a tree, demanding justice and their money back. The tree, in Stockyard St, is still a landmark. Historical Society display in Bicentennial Museum, John St; history of wool-growing district. Yupunga Tree in Centennial Park, Jane St; picnic/barbecue facilities. Cunnamulla–Eulo Opal Festival held in Aug. **In the area:** Wildflowers in spring. Varied birdlife, including black swans, brolgas, pelicans and eagles. Visits to shearing sheds in season. Farm holidays at Carpet Springs, 80 km W. Yowah opal fields, 190 km W via Eulo on Paroo River. **Tourist information:** Cordale Enterprises, Jane St; (076) 55 1416. **Accommodation:** 4 hotels, 3 hotel/motels, 1 motel, 1 caravan/camping park.
MAP REF. 485 P7

Currumbin
Pop. part of Gold Coast
Situated at the mouth of the Currumbin Creek, this part of the Gold Coast has many attractions for visitors. **Of interest:** Currumbin Sanctuary, 20 ha reserve, owned by National Trust of Qld;

Beach at Coolangatta

The Great Barrier Reef

The Great Barrier Reef is a living phenomenon. Its coloured coral branches sit upon banks of limestone polyps that have been built up slowly over thousands of years from the seabed. The banks of coral are separated by channels of water, shading from the delicate green of the shallows to the deepest blue. The reef area is over 1200 kilometres long, stretching from near the coast of western Papua New Guinea to Breaksea Spit, east of Gladstone on the central Queensland coast. It is only between 15 and 20 kilometres wide in the north, but south of Cairns the reef area can extend up to 325 kilometres out to sea. The Great Barrier Reef was proclaimed a marine park in 1979 and a management programme was undertaken to balance the interests of scientists, tourists and fishing enthusiasts, and to preserve the reef for future generations. With over 700 islands scattered through the tropical sea, and the banks of reefs darkening the water, this sun-drenched, tropical paradise attracts thousands of visitors each year to its resorts.

The coral presents an incredibly beautiful picture. Visitors can see it from semi-submersible vessels, which allow occupants to go underwater without getting wet, or from glass-bottomed boats; or, even better, they can swim around using snorkels or diving gear. The colours of

purple, pink, yellow, white and red are intermixed and made more startling by the spectacular shapes of the coral. There are more than 340 varieties of identified coral, the most common being the staghorns, brain corals, mushroom corals, organ pipes and blue corals. Spread among these are waving fields of soft coral, colourful anemones, sea urchins and sea slugs. Shellfish of all kinds, ranging from great clams to tiny cowries, cling to the reef while shoals of brightly coloured tropical fish—among them red emperors, coral trout, sweetlip, angel-fish, parrot-fish and demoiselles—glide and dart through the coral gardens. Multitudes of seabirds nest on the islands of the reef through spring and summer.

Three island resorts, Green Island, Heron Island and Lady Elliot Island, are coral cays—actually part of the reef—and at low tide it is possible to walk on the coral ledges that surround them. Other resort islands are continental islands, having once been part of the mainland, and are generally more wooded and mountainous.

The Barrier Reef is Australia's most beautiful tourist attraction, and the best way to see it is by boat. If you do not have your own yacht, and the holiday budget will not stretch to chartering one, there are many excellent cruises available through

the reef and its islands. Charter boats, scuba diving and fishing trips are also available.

The resort islands off the reef and the Queensland coast offer different styles of living to suit various tastes in holidays and entertainment. Their common denominator is their beautiful setting and a consistency of climate, broken only by the sudden and short-lived downfalls of the monsoonal period from December to February.

Southern Reef Islands
The Southern Reef extends offshore from Bundaberg to Rockhampton. One of the uninhabited islands, North West Island, is the largest coral cay in the Great Barrier Reef. It is the major breeding site for two species of bird—the white-capped noddy and the wedgetailed shearwater—and is also a major nesting site for the green turtle. A catamaran service to the island operates from Yeppoon.

Great Keppel Island, 48 kilometres north-east of Rockhampton, offers 30 kilometres of white, sandy beaches and unspoiled tropical island scenery. Great Keppel Island is for everyone, from families and couples to young singles.

Resort pool, Great Keppel Island

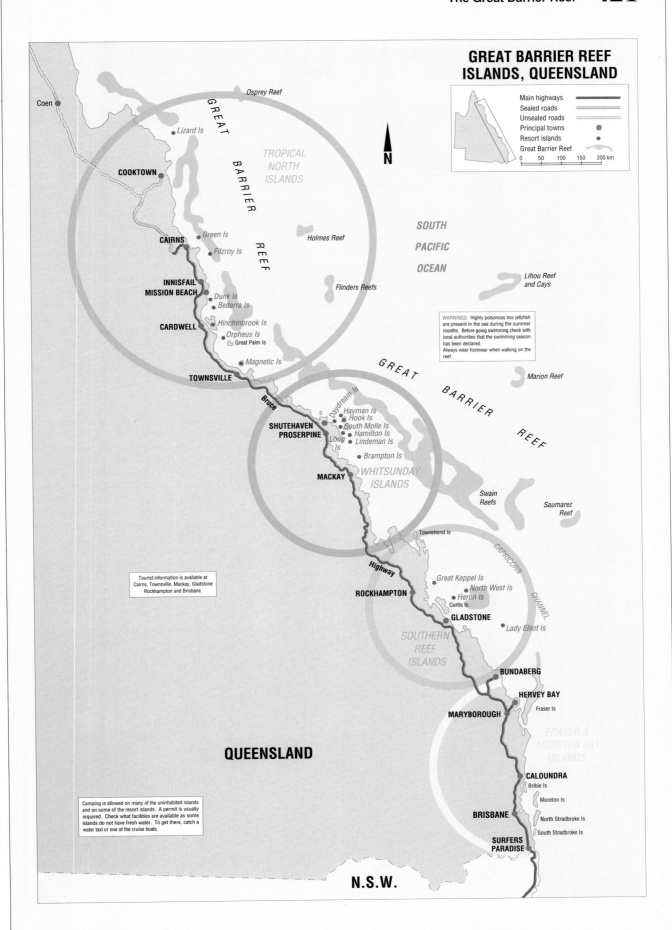

GREAT BARRIER REEF ISLANDS, QUEENSLAND

Main highways		
Sealed roads		
Unsealed roads		
Principal towns	●	
Resort islands	●	
Great Barrier Reef		

0   50   100   150   200 km

Coen

Osprey Reef

GREAT

Lizard Is

COOKTOWN

BARRIER

TROPICAL
NORTH
ISLANDS

N

Green Is

CAIRNS

Fitzroy Is

REEF

Holmes Reef

SOUTH
PACIFIC
OCEAN

INNISFAIL
MISSION BEACH

Dunk Is
Bedarra Is

Flinders Reefs

Lihou Reef
and Cays

CARDWELL

Hinchinbrook Is
Orpheus Is
Great Palm Is

WARNINGS: Highly poisonous box jellyfish
are present in the sea during the summer
months. Before going swimming check with
local authorities that the swimming season
has been declared.
Always wear footwear when walking on the
reef.

Magnetic Is

GREAT

TOWNSVILLE

Marion Reef

Bruce

BARRIER

Daydream Is

Hayman Is
Hook Is

REEF

SHUTEHAVEN
PROSERPINE

South Molle Is
Hamilton Is

Long
Is

Lindeman Is

Brampton Is

MACKAY

WHITSUNDAY
ISLANDS

Swain
Reefs

Saumarez
Reef

Townshend Is

CAPRICORN

Highway

Great Keppel Is

CHANNEL

Tourist information is available at
Cairns, Townsville, Mackay, Gladstone
Rockhampton and Brisbane.

North West Is

ROCKHAMPTON

Heron Is
Curtis Is

GLADSTONE

Lady Elliot Is

SOUTHERN
REEF
ISLANDS

BUNDABERG

HERVEY BAY

Fraser Is

MARYBOROUGH

FRASER &
MORETON BAY
ISLANDS

QUEENSLAND

CALOUNDRA

Bribie Is

Moreton Is

Camping is allowed on many of the uninhabited islands
and on some of the resort islands. A permit is usually
required. Check what facilities are available as some
islands do not have fresh water. To get there, catch a
water taxi or one of the cruise boats.

BRISBANE

North Stradbroke Is

South Stradbroke Is

SURFERS
PARADISE

N.S.W.

The resort accommodates around 500 people and offers many well-organised activities: tennis, water-skiing, island safari trips, skindiving, parasailing and coral viewing. During school holidays the Keppel Kids' Klub organises games and activities. **Getting there:** Light plane from Rockhampton, or a launch from Rosslyn Bay near Yeppoon.

Heron Island is a very small, genuine coral island, 72 kilometres offshore from Gladstone. Heron is only about 1 kilometre across, with a continuous white sand beach and coral reef. It is a true coral cay with part of the reef emerging at low tide. The island has dense palms, pandanus, pisonia, tournefortia and she-oaks, and is world famous for its birdlife, including sea eagles, noddy terns, muttonbirds and of course herons. Over 1150 types of fish have been recorded in the lagoon. The island and reefs are a national park and wildlife sanctuary, and there is a Marine Biological Research Station. It is a mecca for divers, and scuba gear may be hired. Turtles come ashore to lay their eggs from October to March, and hatching can be seen from late December to May. The resort overlooks the island's boat harbour and accommodates around 280 people. **Getting there:** Catamaran or helicopter from Gladstone (daily services).

Lady Musgrave Island, 2 hours by catamaran north-north-east of Bundaberg, is a superb coral cay with a navigable lagoon 13 kilometres in circumference. An underwater observatory is available for day trippers to view the coral and prolific sealife at close quarters. The island hosts a myriad of birdlife in its gigantic pisonia trees. Turtles nest on the beaches from November through February. The island is uninhabited, but permits are available from the Marine Parks Authorities for camping; numbers are limited to 50 at any one time. **Getting there:** Plane from Brisbane, or by catamaran aboard MV *Lady Musgrave* from Bundaberg, or MV *1770* from Town of 1770.

Lady Elliot Island, 80 kilometres northeast of Bundaberg at the southern end of the Great Barrier Reef, is a small, sand-covered coral cay. Lady Elliot is extremely popular with snorkellers and divers. Surrounded by 40 metres of deep water and yet right on the reef, the island has 10 major dive areas. As it is a coral cay, divers and snorkellers can simply walk into the water and be among the spectacular reefs in a few moments. The island is surrounded by beautiful coral gardens built by hundreds of different varieties of coral. The aquamarine depths are rich with marine life. Sighting exotic fish, giant velvety clams, green turtles, starfish and huge manta rays is normal during an underwater venture. On land, the island is becoming known as one of the most significant bird rookeries off the Australian coast, with up to 56 species of birds nesting on the island. In the summer months it is possible to see green turtles laying their eggs. The resort is low-key, with simple but comfortable accommodation for a small number of people. **Getting there:** Light plane from Bundaberg.

Whitsunday Islands

The magnificent Whitsunday Islands in the Whitsunday Passage include Lindeman, South Molle, Daydream, Hayman, Hook, Hamilton and Long Island. These are only the resort islands; there are over 73 uninhabited islands. Hamilton and Hayman Islands have marinas and excellent service facilities. All islands have anchorage and their own individual attractions and sporting activities.

Brampton Island is a mountainous island of 8 square kilometres in the Cumberland Group, 32 kilometres from Mackay and south of the major group of the Whitsundays. It is a national park and wildlife sanctuary with lush forests, palm trees and fine white beaches. The island is surrounded by coral reefs, particularly in the passage between Brampton and Carlisle Islands. The resort's world-class facilities include an aquatics centre and a golf course. The island has a beautiful resort beach overlooking neighbouring Carlisle Island. Daily activities vary from cruises to the Great Barrier Reef, to water sports, palm-frond weaving, archery, snorkelling and bushwalking. **Getting there:** Light plane or launch from Mackay.

Lindeman Island, 67 kilometres north of Mackay, is another beautiful national park island. It is some 20 square kilometres in area and 73 islands in the Whitsunday Group can be seen from the peak of Mt Oldfield. The island, noted for its birds and butterflies, is covered by extensive walking tracks and has seven secluded sandy beaches. The island's Club Med resort has all the benefits and services associated with that group. The island will appeal to young professionals, sporty types, nature lovers and young families. The island's golf course is one of the most

Underwater Observatory, Hook Island

picturesque in Australia. **Getting there:** From Proserpine, light plane; from Hamilton Island, light plane or water taxi; from Shute Harbour, light plane or launch; from Mackay, light plane or launch.

Hamilton Island is 16 kilometres from Shute Harbour. The island's grazing land was transformed in the early 1980s into one of the most complex island resorts in Australia. Extensive facilities have made Hamilton almost a town on its own, with a school, banks and post office. Its 200-berth marina hosts the nation's most famous yachts, particularly during Hamilton Race Week in May each year. The resort has the largest hotel of any type in Australia, accommodates over 2000 people and features a wide range of activities and entertainment, including facilities for windsurfing, sailing, scuba diving, parasailing, fishing, tennis and squash. There are also hot spas, a gymnasium, a fauna park and a waterside village. The catamaran *Southern Spirit* offers 7-night cruises around the Whitsundays. **Getting there:** Plane from Melbourne, Sydney, Brisbane, Cairns, Proserpine, Shute Harbour and Mackay, or launch from Shute Harbour.

Long Island is a mountainous, bushy island in the Whitsunday Group, 9 kilometres from Shute Harbour and 43 kilometres from Proserpine. Excellent walking tracks climb through the rainforest to give postcard views of the other islands. Scrub turkeys are friendly and common. Island oysters are yours for the opening. The island is part of the Conway National Park system, one of the most beautiful waterways in the world. Long Island has 3 resorts. The Island Resort is a fun-filled location with an exciting range of activities in a beautiful setting. Palm Bay Hideaway Resort, the nature-lover's favourite, is 2 kilometres down the island's coast and offers peaceful, relaxed family and group accommodation, as well as catering to the single visitor. Paradise Bay is ideal for the keen fisherman or families who want to get away from it all. **Getting there:** Launch or helicopter from Shute Harbour or Hamilton Island.

South Molle Island is situated in the heart of the Whitsunday Passage, 8 kilometres from Shute Harbour. The island is only 4 kilometres by 2.4 kilometres in area, lightly timbered, with numerous inlets, quiet bays, coral gardens and reefs. Walking tracks take hikers to the island's peaks for uninterrupted views of the Whitsunday Passage. The well-known resort

View from South Molle Island

accommodates around 500 people and offers a wide range of entertainment and activities, including a golf course and gymnasium, as well as a reef pontoon with a fish observation chamber and a platform for swimmers, snorkellers and scuba divers. **Getting there:** Launch, helicopter or seaplane from Shute Harbour.

Daydream Island 5 kilometres from Shute Harbour, is a small island (1.2 kilometres by half a kilometre) of volcanic rock and coral. Foliage is dense and tropical, while the beaches end in spectacular coral gardens offshore. The luxurious resort, totally rebuilt in 1990, has a beautifully appointed 303-room hotel at the northern end of the island. Trips to the outer reef and other islands are available. **Getting there:** Launch or helicopter from Shute Harbour or Hamilton Island.

Hook Island is renowned for its breathtaking Underwater Observatory, a must for the visitor, where coral and other reef marine life can be seen in their natural habitat. Accommodation is in 12 bunk-style units, and there is a walking track with great views. The island is 90 minutes by launch from Shute Harbour and most cruises visit Hook Island. It is a perfect retreat from the hustle and bustle of city life. **Getting there:** Launch from Shute Harbour.

Hayman Island is the most northerly of the Whitsunday Group and the closest to the outer reef. There are some 80

varieties of bird in the island's tropical bushland. Hayman is a luxury resort offering culinary delights, enjoyment and relaxation to its pampered guests; its hotel is a member of the leading Hotels of the World group. Fishing, sightseeing trips, scenic flights or diving adventures can be arranged. **Getting there:** Launch from Abel Point Marina, Airlie Beach or plane from Airlie Beach, Townsville, Mackay or Cairns, but accommodation bookings must be made first with the island.

Tropical North Islands
This group of islands is located off the north coast of Queensland between Townsville and Cooktown. Generally speaking, the Reef in this section is closer to the mainland than it is further south. The resort islands include Magnetic, Orpheus, Hinchinbrook, Bedarra, Dunk, Fitzroy, Green and Lizard.

Magnetic Island is only a 29-minute catamaran ride across Cleveland Bay from Townsville. The island is a seaside 'suburb' of Townsville, with some 2500 permanent residents. Over 2709 hectares of this 5184-hectare mountainous island is a national park and bird sanctuary, with good walking tracks. Trees are mostly pines, with she-oaks, pandanus, poincianas and banyans giving variety. Hotels and accommodation places range from economy to resort. Buses and taxis operate on the island. **Of interest:** The Koala Park Oasis at Horseshoe Bay, Shark World at Nelly Bay, horseriding, snorkelling, beautiful beaches and excellent fishing. **Getting there:** Vehicular ferry, catamaran or water taxi from Townsville.

Orpheus Island, a small, volcanic island surrounded by coral reefs, is 80 kilometres north of Townsville and 16 kilometres off Lucinda Point. The island is a densely wooded national park, and some 50 varieties of birds have been seen. Turtles regularly nest on the beaches and it is the base for a giant-clam farm. There is a 5-star exclusive resort on the island. **Getting there:** Plane from Townsville or Cairns.

Hinchinbrook Island is the largest island national park in the world; all of its 642 square kilometres are totally protected, and even insecticides are banned. There are rugged mountain ranges with thick tropical vegetation and waterfalls, which contrast with long sandy beaches and secluded coves on the eastern side. A marine research station has been set up at Cape Ferguson to study the ecology of mangroves. Permits to camp on the island may be obtained from the National Parks and Wildlife Service in Townsville or Cardwell. A small, pleasant resort at Cape Richards accommodating a maximum of 30 people offers natural, unsophisticated holidays. **Getting there:** Resort's launch collects visitors from Cardwell.

Bedarra Island is a very small, heavily wooded island, 6 kilometres from the mouth of the Hull River near Tully. The island is an oasis of untouched tropical beauty. There are 2 resorts: Bedarra Bay, which accommodates 32 people, and the exclusive Bedarra Hideaway, which has 16 individual units. No day visitors are permitted on the island. **Getting there:** Plane from Townsville or Cairns to Dunk Island and launch from Dunk Island.

Dunk Island, a national park 5 kilometres off the coast near Tully, is one of the most popular of the resort islands. The island's resort is owned by Australian Airlines and can accommodate 200 guests in various degrees of luxury. There are extensive walking tracks through the island's superb

rainforest. More than 90 varieties of birds have been identified. Butterflies and wild orchids complete the tropical picture. The writer E.J. Banfield (Beachcomber) lived on the island from 1897 to 1913, and the film *Age of Consent* was made here. **Getting there:** Plane from Townsville or Cairns, or launch from Clump Point near Mission Beach.

Fitzroy Island, 30 kilometres from Cairns, covers 324 hectares. The island offers magnificent native flora and fauna, secluded sandy beaches and giant clams being bred to restock the Reef. Visitors to the lighthouse are rewarded with breathtaking 360-degree panoramas. The island, once a well-kept secret of divers and boat and fish enthusiasts, now has accommodation ranging from villa-style to bunkhouse, with communal amenities. **Getting there:** Catamaran from Cairns.

Green Island, 27 kilometres from Cairns, is a coral cay surrounded by beautiful patches of reef and crested with thick tropical vegetation. The resort is currently undergoing reconstruction due for completion late 1994, but is better known as the daily host to visitors from Cairns, who can see the reef through glass-bottomed

boats and at the underwater observatory. There is a theatrette showing colour films of the reef and a display of coral and other marine and animal life. **Getting there:** Catamaran from Cairns.

Lizard Island, 95 kilometres north-east of Cooktown, caters for a small number of guests in a resort built in homestead style, facing a beautiful lagoon. The reefs around this national park are magnificent, with excellent fishing, including the famous black marlin. Big-game fishing enthusiasts descend on Lizard Island during the marlin season (September to November). The first 'tourist' was Captain James Cook in August 1770. He landed and climbed Cook's Look (359 metres) to spy out a safe passage through the reefs to the open sea. The island takes its name from the large but harmless monitor lizards he found. **Getting there:** Plane from Cairns.

For further information on the islands of the Great Barrier Reef, contact the Queensland Tourist and Travel Corporation, 36th Floor, Riverside Centre, 123 Eagle Street, Brisbane; (07) 833 5400; or any Queensland Government Travel Centre.

Arthur Bay, Magnetic Island

Other Islands

Fraser Island If you like sand, sea, sailing, fishing and plenty of peace and quiet, Fraser Island would be your ideal holiday place. One hundred and twenty-three kilometres long, Fraser is the largest sand island in the world and the largest island on Australia's east coast. It acts as a breakwater, protecting the coast from Bundaberg to well south of Maryborough, and forms the eastern shores of Hervey Bay, a magnificent stretch of sheltered water ideal for sailing, and which attracts hundreds of fishermen each year for the annual tailor season.

Fraser's remote and abundant sand dunes are particularly attractive to those with 4WD or beach buggies, but the island is large enough to accommodate them in certain areas without upsetting the peace and quiet. Apart from its long stretches of beautiful beach, Fraser Island has a unique area of freshwater lakes and tangled rainforests. There are over 40 lakes on the island, all of them above sea level, and the dense forests surrounding them attract a wide range of bird and animal life.

An odd feature of the island is its ever-moving creeks, which may run parallel to the ocean for several kilometres, then spill through a dune, carving a new course through the sand to the sea.

The island is accessible by air service from Brisbane, Maroochydore, Maryborough, Hervey Bay or Toowoomba, or by barge from Inskip Point (Rainbow Beach) and Hervey Bay. Visitors to the island are required to have permits.

Kingfisher Bay Resort Village is at North White Cliffs, on the western side of the island opposite Mary River Heads.

There are 5 areas of accommodation on the ocean side of Fraser Island: at Orchid Beach, Happy Valley, Eurong, Dilli Village and Cathedral Beach Camping Park. Korawinga Lodge at Eurong has time-share units.

The Orchid Beach island village is at the northern end of the island, overlooking the 32-kilometre sweep of Marloo Bay and the main surf beach—a rarity on Queensland islands, as those further north are sheltered from the surf by the Barrier Reef. All these holiday centres offer family accommodation.

Moreton Bay Islands

Bribie Island is a largely undeveloped island, 69 kilometres north of Brisbane, reached via a turnoff on the Bruce Highway and a 1-kilometre bridge across Pumicestone Passage. Bribie is about 31 kilometres long, the northern tip being opposite Caloundra on the Sunshine Coast. Matthew Flinders landed on the southern tip in 1799. Apart from the townships of **Bongaree** on the mainland side and **Woorim** on the surf side, little has changed since those days. Bribie is a wildlife sanctuary, with excellent fishing, boating and crabbing. **Accommodation:** 4 motels, 6 caravan/camping parks.

Moreton Island, predominantly a national park, is a remarkable wilderness island only 35 kilometres east of Brisbane. Apart from rocky headlands, the island is mostly huge sandhills, native scrub, banksias and freshwater lakes, which attract over 125 species of birds. A lighthouse at the northern tip was built in 1857 and still guides shipping into Brisbane. There are no roads on the island, but the occasional 4WD vehicle uses the tracks and the magnificent 40-kilometre-long beach. Mt Tempest (280 m) is probably the highest permanent sandhill in the world. The pleasant tourist resort of **Tangalooma** is on the leeward side and its latest attraction are the wild dolphins which come to be fed each night as soon as the tide is high enough. There are several campsites in the park. Transport is by launch or air from Brisbane.

North Stradbroke Island or 'Straddie', as it is affectionately called, is a large and unspoiled island directly east of Brisbane across Moreton Bay. It is a popular spot for fishermen, surfers and weekenders. The small settlements of **Dunwich** and **Amity Point** are on the leeward side, and **Point Lookout** is on the north-east corner. Dunwich started as a quarantine station for the port of Brisbane in 1828, and from a typhoid plague in 1850 there are some historic local gravestones. Point Lookout has the only hotel on the island, some impressive rocky headlands, and great fishing and surfing. The 500-hectare **Blue Lake National Park** offers walks through coastal woodland, and a variety of wildlife. Vehicular ferries sail regularly from Redland Bay and Cleveland to Dunwich. **Accommodation:** 2 resorts, 1 motel, 9 caravan/ camping parks.

South Stradbroke Island was separated from North Stradbroke Island by a cyclone in 1896, and the channel between them is called Jumpinpin. South Stradbroke stretches down to Southport on the Gold Coast, the protected Broadwater being a well-used boating playground. The island is almost uninhabited. Day cruises operate from Southport. **Accommodation:** 1 resort.

For further information, contact the Queensland Tourist and Travel Corporation, 36th Floor, Riverside Centre, 123 Eagle Street, Brisbane; (07) 833 5400; or any Queensland Government Travel Centre.

Maheno wreck, a well known landmark on Fraser Island

Railway station, Emerald

free-ranging animals in open areas, twice-daily wild lorikeet feeding, walk-through rainforest aviary with pools and waterfalls, rides through sanctuary on miniature railway. Opposite, Chocolate Expo Factory; convention centre. **In the area:** The Land of Legend, 3 km S; thousands of dolls displayed in fairytale settings. Olson's Bird Gardens, Currumbin Valley, 9 km W; large landscaped aviaries amid subtropical setting. Mt Cougal National Park, 22 km SW, at end of Currumbin Creek Rd; rainforest area for bushwalking and picnicking. **Tourist information:** Beach House, Marine Pde, Coolangatta; (075) 36 7765. **Accommodation:** 1 hotel, 8 motels, 2 caravan/camping parks. **See also:** City of the Gold Coast.
MAP REF. 469 G10

Daintree   Pop. 200
This quaint, unspoilt township lies in the heart of the Daintree River catchment basin surrounded entirely by the McDowall Ranges, 115 km N of Cairns. The area has an abundance of native plant life, birds and exotic tropical butterflies, and Australia's prehistoric reptile, the estuarine crocodile, can be seen lurking in the mangrove-lined creek and tributaries of the Daintree River. **Of interest:** Daintree Timber Museum. Local art and craft shops, restaurants and a truly old-time local store. River cruises operate. **In the area:** Daintree Coffee Plantation, 5 km W. Daintree Butterfly Farm, 2 km S. Wonga-Belle Orchid Garden, 17 km S; 3.5 ha of lush landscaped gardens.

Daintree Rainforest Environmental Centre, 11 km N via ferry; boardwalk through rainforest. Cape Tribulation, 35 km N, where rainforest meets reef; bushwalking, crystal-clear creeks and forests festooned with creepers and vines, palm trees, orchids, butterflies and cassowaries. Bloomfield Falls, 85 km N, via Cape Tribulation. **Tourist information:** Macrossan St, Port Douglas; (070) 99 5599. (Also at Marina Mirage, Wharf St, Port Douglas.) **Accommodation:** 1 Eco-Tourist Lodge, 1 caravan/camping park.
MAP REF. 473 B1, 479 K5

Dalby   Pop. 9385
Dalby is a pleasant, well planned country town at the crossroads of the Warrego, Bunya and Moonie Hwys, 84 km NW of Toowoomba on the Darling Downs. It is the centre of Australia's richest grain-growing area, and cattle, pigs and sheep further add to the wealth of the district. **Of interest:** Dalby Pioneer Park Museum, Black St; early buildings, household and agricultural items, craft shop. Obelisk in Edward St marks spot where explorer Henry Dennis camped in 1841. Cactoblastis Memorial Cairn in Myall Creek picnic area pays homage to the voracious Argentinian caterpillar, which eradicated the dreaded prickly pear cactus in 1920s. Dalby Cultural and Administration Centre, Drayton St; theatre, cinema, art gallery and restaurant. Harvest Festival held Oct. **In the area:** Lake Broadwater, 29 km SW; boating and water-skiing when full. In Lake Broadwater Environmental Park; 3-km walk,

picnic/barbecue facilities, birdwatch tower, camping. Jimbour House, 29 km N; grounds open daily. Bunya Mountains National Park, 60 km NE. **Tourist information:** Thomas Jack Park, cnr Drayton and Condamine Sts; (076) 62 1066. **Accommodation:** 2 hotels, 5 motels, 2 caravan/camping parks. **See also:** Darling Downs.
MAP REF. 466 A4, 475 K5

Dirranbandi   Pop. 460
A small pastoral township and railhead on the Balonne River, Dirranbandi is south-west of St George, close to the NSW border. **Tourist information:** Balonne Shire Council, Victoria St, St George; (076) 25 3222. **Accommodation:** 1 motel.
MAP REF. 122 C2, 474 E8

Eidsvold   Pop. 587
The Eidsvold goldfield was extremely productive for 12 years from 1888 and remains an attractive haunt for fossickers. The district is recognised as the State's best producer of quality beef cattle. **Of interest:** Historical Museum, including Knockbreak Homestead (1850s), George Schafer and Eric Schultz Collection of rocks and minerals, Noel Duncan Bottle Collection, and local history section, especially goldmining. **In the area:** Waruma Dam, 48 km N via Burnett Hwy; swimming, sailing and water-skiing. **Tourist information:** Historical Museum, Mt Rose St; (071) 65 1277. **Accommodation:** 1 hotel/motel, 1 motel, 1 caravan/camping park.
MAP REF. 475 J1, 477 M13

Emerald   Pop. 6557
An attractive town, 263 km W of Rockhampton at the junction of the Capricorn and Gregory Hwys, Emerald is the hub of the Central Highlands. As well as the cattle industry, grain, oilseeds, soybeans and cotton are important. **Of interest:** Shady Moreton Bay fig trees line Clermont and Egerton Sts. Railway station (1901), Clermont St; classified by National Trust. Pioneer Cottage complex, Harris St. Pastoral College, Capricorn Hwy. **In the area:** Gregory coalfields, 60 km NE. Fairbairn Dam, 19 km S, for picnics and water sports. **Tourist information:** Clermont St, Biloela; (079) 82 4142. **Accommodation:** 3 hotels, 6 motels, 6 caravan/camping parks. **See also:** The Capricorn Region.
MAP REF. 476 H9

Emu Park
Pop. 1919

On the way to this pleasant seaside resort, 45 km NE of Rockhampton, is St Christopher's Chapel, built by the US Army in 1942. Emu Park has excellent picnic spots and a safe beach. **Of interest:** Historical Museum, Hill St. On headland overlooking Keppel Bay, unusual and graceful 'singing ship' memorial to Captain Cook, who discovered the bay on voyage up east coast in May 1770. Memorial represents a billowing sail, mast and rigging. Hidden organ pipes create musical sounds with sea breezes. **In the area:** Koorana Crocodile Farm, Emu Park–Rockhampton Rd, 20 km W; boardwalk viewing on guided tours. **Tourist information:** Historical Museum, Hill St; (079) 39 6080. **Accommodation:** 2 motels, 1 caravan/camping park.
MAP REF. 477 M8

Eromanga
Pop. 90

A centre for extensive oil exploration, 103 km W of Quilpie, the refinery at Eromanga produces around 1.5 million barrels of oil a year. Named from an Aboriginal word meaning 'hot, windy plain', Eromanga is reputedly the furthest town from the sea in Australia. **Of interest:** Royal Hotel, once Cobb & Co. staging post, with some original 19th-century buildings. **Tourist information:** Quilpie Shire Council, Brolga St, Quilpie; (076) 56 1133. **Accommodation:** 1 hotel, 1 caravan/camping park.
MAP REF. 485 K4

Esk
Pop. 882

Esk, in the Upper Brisbane Valley, is the largest town in the Esk Shire and known for its lakes and dams. **Of interest:** Numerous shops selling antiques and local craft. Arts and Crafts Show in Nov. **In the area:** Somerset Dam and Lake Wivenhoe, source of Brisbane's main water supply, and Atkinson Dam—all popular swimming, fishing and boating spots. Lake Wivenhoe, 70 km NW of Brisbane, picnic/barbecue facilities and restaurant; also State's main centre for championship rowing. At Coominya, 22 km SE of Esk: historic Bellevue Homestead; also camel races held in Sept. Further north in shire, some of finest grazing country in Brisbane Valley; this is deer country, where progeny of small herd of deer presented to Qld by Queen Victoria in 1873 still roam. **Tourist information:** Shire Offices, 2 Redbank St; (074) 24

1200. **Accommodation:** 3 hotels, 6 motels, 1 caravan/camping park.
MAP REF. 466 I5, 475 M5

Eulo
Pop. 42

Once the main centre for opal mining in the area, Eulo lies near the Paroo River, 64 km W of Cunnamulla. **Of interest:** Eulo Queen Hotel; owes its name to Isobel Robinson (nee Richardson), who ran hotel and virtually reigned over opal fields at turn of century. Paroo Lizard Race Track, venue for World Lizard Racing Championships, held Aug.–Sept., next to hotel. Destructo Cockroach Monument commemorates death of racing cockroach. Eulo Date Farm, west of town; enquire at caravan park for inspection. **In the area:** Currawinya National Park, 100 km SW; birdwatching and fishing. **Tourist information:** Paroo Shire Hall, James St; (076) 55 2121. **Accommodation:** 1 hotel, 1 caravan/camping park.
MAP REF. 485 O7

Gatton
Pop. 5098

First settled in the 1840s, this thriving agricultural town in the Lockyer Valley is midway between Ipswich and Toowoomba, and 96 km W of Brisbane on the Warrego Hwy. Sawmilling, dairy cattle, small-crop farming and raising of beef cattle, pigs and calves, are the main activities of the area, which also includes the towns of Grantham, Helidon and

Lake Wivenhoe, near Esk

Withcott. **In the area:** Qld Agricultural College, now part of Queensland Univ., 5 km E; opened 1897. Helidon, 14 km W, noted for its spa water; also for Helidon freestone, used in many Brisbane buildings. Grantham, 7 km SW, renowned for its fresh fruit and vegetables; many roadside stalls offer locally grown produce. **Tourist information:** Gatton Tourist Information Centre and Lakeside Diner, Apex Lake Dr; (074) 62 3430. **Accommodation:** 3 hotels, 1 hotel/motel, 1 motel, 3 caravan/camping parks. **See also:** Darling Downs.
MAP REF. 466 H8, 475 L9

Gayndah
Pop. 1750

Gayndah claims to be Qld's oldest town, having been founded in 1848. It is on the Burnett River and the Burnett Hwy, just over 100 km W of Maryborough. An Orange Festival is held every odd-numbered year, June long weekend. **Of interest:** Original school (1863), still in use. Several homesteads in district built in 1850s. Capper St; location for film *The Mango Tree*. Historical Museum, Simon St; includes Ban Ban Springs homestead. **In the area:** Ban Ban Springs, 26 km S; natural spring and popular picnic area. Claude Warton Weir Recreation Area, 3 km W; fishing and picnics. **Tourist information:** Cnr Mulgrave and Bourbong Sts, Bundaberg; (071) 52 2333. **Accommodation:** 1 motel, 1 caravan/camping park.
MAP REF. 475 K1

Georgetown
Pop. 310

A township on the Gulf Developmental Road to Croydon and Normanton. Once one of many small goldmining towns on the Etheridge Goldfield. The area is now noted for its gemstones, especially agate and onyx. Georgetown is also a transshipping centre for beef road-trains. **In the area:** Gemfields at Agate Creek, 95 km SW, and O'Briens Creek, 129 km NE. Tallaroo hot springs, 55 km E. Undara Volcanic National Park, 129 km E. **Tourist information:** Etheridge Shire Council; (070) 62 1233. **Accommodation:** 1 hotel, 1 motel, 2 caravan/camping parks. **See also:** Gulf Savannah.
MAP REF. 478 H10

Gin Gin
Pop. 907

Some of Qld's oldest cattle properties are in the area of this pastoral town on the Bruce Hwy, 52 km W of Bundaberg. The district is known as Wild Scotsman

Country, after James McPherson, Qld's only authentic bushranger. **Of interest:** The Residence, Mulgrave St; former police sergeant's home housing district's pioneering memorabilia. **In the area:** Mystery Craters, 17 km NE; curious formation of 35 craters, estimated to be about 25 million years old. Yellow Windmills Nursery and Goat Farm, 21 km N. Lake Monduran, 24 km N, held back by Fred Haigh Dam, Qld's second largest; boating and picnic facilities. Currajong Gardens, 9 km S; indoor and outdoor plants incl. exotic and rare cacti. Moonara Craft Spinning, 25 km W; demonstrations, from fibre to product, daily. **Tourist information:** Cnr Mulgrave and Bourbong Sts, Bundaberg; (071) 52 2333. **Accommodation:** 2 motels, 1 caravan/camping park.
MAP REF. 477 O12

Gladstone   Pop. 23 462

Matthew Flinders discovered Port Curtis, Gladstone's impressive deepwater harbour, in 1802, but it was not until the 1960s that its potential began to be utilised. As an outlet for Central Qld's mineral and agricultural wealth, Gladstone, 550 km N of Brisbane, is now one of Australia's most prosperous seaboard cities. Its harbour is one of Australia's busiest, handling more shipping tonnage per annum than Sydney. One reason for this growth is the opening up of the almost inexhaustible coal supplies in the hinterland. Another is that the world's largest single alumina plant is at Parsons Point, operated by the multinational-backed Queensland Alumina Limited.

Millions of tonnes of bauxite from Weipa on the Gulf of Carpentaria are processed annually into millions of tonnes of alumina, the halfway stage of aluminium. Comalco has built an aluminium smelter at Boyne Island. A large power station has been built in Gladstone to supply power to the alumina refinery and smelter, as well as feeding into the State's electricity grid. Chemical processing is a new regional industry. Gladstone's most important tourist feature is its proximity to the southern section of the Great Barrier Reef. The city is renowned for its mud crabs and prawns, and has won the State Tidy Towns Competition 6 times. **Of interest:** Self-guide Gladstone Visitor Circuit, by car or foot. Historic Kullaroo House (1911) and Grand Hotel (1897), Goondoon St. Gladstone Regional Art Gallery and Museum, cnr Goondoon and Bramston Sts. Potter's Place, art gallery and craft shop, Dawson Hwy. Tondoon Botanic Gardens, end Glenlyon St. Picnic/barbecue facilities at Barney Point Beach and Friend Park, Barney St. Also at Reg Tanna Park, Glenlyon St, with Railway Dam. Waterfall at bottom of Auckland Hill, end Auckland St; floodlit at night. Views of harbour and islands from Auckland Hill Lookout. Radar Hill Lookout, Goondoon St. Round Hill Lookout, West Gladstone. Auckland Inlet, anchorage alongside James Cook Park; finishing-line for annual Brisbane to Gladstone yacht race, highlight of 10-day Harbour Festival held Easter. **In the area:** Tours of Gladstone Power Station, north of town. Curtis Island, Gladstone Harbour; family

recreation area. Quoin Island Resort, 20 min. by ferry; fishing, swimming, live entertainment, day trippers welcome. Ferry harbour cruise; includes lunch on Quoin Is. Lake Awoonga, 30 km S; picnic and camping areas, water-based recreation, walking trail and varied wildlife. Port Curtis Historical Village, 26 km SW at Calliope River. **Tourist information:** 56 Goondoon St; (079) 72 4000. **Accommodation:** 21 motels, 7 hotel/motels, 7 caravan/camping parks. **See also:** Gladstone Region.
MAP REF. 477 N10

Goondiwindi   Pop. 4331

This attractive modern country town at the junction of the five highways is on the picturesque Macintyre River, which was discovered by explorer Allan Cunningham in 1827 and forms the State border. The Aboriginal word *goonawinna* means 'resting place of the birds'. The district's thriving economy is based on cotton, wheat, beef and wool and a growing manufacturing sector. The Spring Festival in Oct. coincides with the blooming of jacarandas and silky oaks. **Of interest:** Botanic Gardens of Western Woodlands (25 ha); access from Barwon Hwy, 1 km NW. Statue of famous racehorse Gunsynd, the 'Goondiwindi Grey', in Apex Park, McLean St. Customs House Museum, opposite that Park. Historic Victoria Hotel, Marshall St. Univ. of Qld Pastoral Veterinary Centre, Leichhardt Hwy (N). Tours of Bulk Grains depot and cotton gin by arrangement. **In the area:** Boobera Lagoon, 20 km SW into NSW; wildlife sanctuary. **Tourist information:** McLean St; (076) 71 2653. **Accommodation:** 2 hotels, 2 hotel/motels, 7 motels, 3 caravan/camping parks. **See also:** Darling Downs.
MAP REF. 122 H2, 474 I8

Gordonvale   Pop. 2658

This town is 24 km S of Cairns. **In the area:** Gillies Hwy, with 295 bends, leads west to Atherton. Goldsborough Valley State Forest, walking, swimming, canoeing, picnicking; 6 km W (15 km off Gillies Hwy). Bellenden Ker National Park, 10 km S; spectacular views from summit of Walsh's Pyramid. The Mulgrave Rambler, 15 km steam train ride along cane railway system through canefields and rainforest; includes visit to spectacular orchid nursery (charter only). Hambledon Sugar Mill at Edmonton, 16 km N. **Tourist information:** Cnr Grafton

Boyne River, Gladstone

Rainbow Beach, near Gympie

& Hartley Sts, Cairns; (070) 51 3588.
Accommodation: 4 hotels, 1 caravan/
camping park.
MAP REF. 473 G11, 479 L7

Gympie   Pop. 10 791

The city of Gympie started with the
'Great Australian Gold Rush', 1867 version, led by James Nash. The field proved
extremely rich, and some 4 million
ounces had been found by the time the
gold petered out in the 1920s. By then
dairying and agriculture were well established and Gympie continued to prosper.
On the Mary River and 182 km N of
Brisbane by the Bruce Hwy, Gympie is
the major provincial city servicing the
Cooloola region. It is an attractive city,
with jacarandas, flowering silky oaks,
cassias, poincianas and flame trees very
much in evidence. **Of interest:** Woodworks Museum, Frazer Rd. Gympie
Gold Rush Festival held mid-Oct. **In the
area:** Goldmining Museum at Mon-
kland, 5 km S; nearby, cottage of Andrew
Fisher, first Queenslander to become
Prime Minister (1908). Part of the Bicentennial National Trail runs through Kilkivan, 51 km NW. Goomeri, 26 km
further W; known as 'clock town' because of unique memorial clock in town
centre. Borumba Dam, for picnics and
water sports, 51 km SW via Imbil and
Imbil Forest Drive. Rock pools and
views at Mothar Mountain. Peaceful
fishing resort of Tin Can Bay and small
resort of Rainbow Beach with its coloured sands, 77 km E through vast pine
forests. Ferry to Fraser Island operates
from Inskip Point north of Rainbow

Beach. Cooloola National Park, 50 km E.
Mary Valley Scenic Way runs south between Gympie and Maleny via Kenilworth. **Tourist information:** Bruce
Hwy, Lake Alford; (074) 82 5444. **Accommodation:** 14 hotels, 7 motels, 4
caravan/camping parks.
MAP REF. 475 M3

Hervey Bay   Pop. 22 205

Hervey (pronounced Harvey) Bay is the
large area of water between Maryborough and Bundaberg that is protected by
Fraser Island. The name is also that of a
thriving city that comprises the pleasant
strip of seaside resorts along its southern
shore, some 34 km NE of Maryborough,
including Gatakers Bay, Pialba, Scarness, Torquay, Urangan, Burrum Heads,
Toogoom, Howard and Torbanlea. An
ideal climate makes the area popular with
residents of nearby Maryborough and
Bundaberg, and during the winter
months there is a regular influx of visitors
from the south. Hervey Bay is actively
promoted as 'Australia's family aquatic
playground'. As there is no surf, swimming is safe even for children. Fishing is
the main recreation and boats may be
hired and fresh yabbies caught for bait.
Of interest: Hervey Bay Historical Society Museum, Zephyr St, Scarness, recalls pioneer days. In Pialba: Village
Pottery, Old Maryborough Rd (open for
tour of manufacturing process); Polyme-
tric Products, Old Maryborough Rd,
(model village and ships, woodwork);
Wide Bay Gallery, Main St (paintings).
Golf'n'Games, Cypress St Torquay; 18-
hole mini-golf, 120-m water slide. Cairn

at Dayman Point, Urangan, commemorates landing by Matthew Flinders in
1799 and the 2-Force commandoes who
trained there on the *Krait* in World War
II. Pier 1 km long at Urangan, used by
fishermen. Sun. markets at Urangan and
Nikenbar. Yachting regatta held at Scarness every Easter. Other attractions include Neptune's Aquarium (performing
seals and sharks), Nature World Wildlife
Park (lorikeets, koalas, other marsupials,
reptiles and crocodiles) and Vic Hislop's
Shark Show. Day trips to Fraser Island.
Humpback whales visit Hervey Bay
early Aug.–mid-Oct. on their annual migration; viewing cruises available.
Humpback Whale Festival held Aug.
Monthly craft market, cnr Deaman Camp
and Torquay Rds. **In the area:** Hervey
Bay Marine Park. Quiet seaside resorts at
Toogoom and Burrum Heads, 15 km N.
Historic Brooklyn House at Howard, 25
km NW. Go-kart track, 2 km W. Susan
River Homestead, 15 km W, for farm
holidays. **Tourist information:** Polyme-
tric Products, Old Maryborough Rd, Pialba; (071) 28 2603. **Accommodation:** 4
hotel/motels, 18 motels, 20 caravan
parks.
MAP REF. 475 N1, 477 Q13

Home Hill   Pop. 3197

Sister town to Ayr, Home Hill is on the
south side of the Burdekin River, 84 km
S of Townsville. The towns are joined by
a high-level bridge as the river is liable
to flood. **Of interest:** Tours of Inkerman
Sugar Mill during crushing season (June-
Dec.). Ashworth's Rock Shop and Museum; also art and craft. **In the area:**

The Far North

Sitting in a tropical garden through dusk and into lush evening, dining superbly on king prawns, Queensland mud crabs and a chilled bottle of white wine, you will find it hard to believe you are at 'the end of the line'—**Port Douglas**, the most northerly of the easily accessible coastal towns of Queensland.

This is part of the continuing joy of travelling in the north—a region larger than most European countries and considered by many to be the most diversely beautiful and exciting part of Australia.

This Port Douglas scene typifies the beauty of coastal Queensland; the restaurant looks down from a jungle-covered hill that looms over the small town and the 7 kilometres of ocean beach. By day the dense tropical forest is revealed in showers of coloured flowers against the intense green of the jungle. The lavish rainforest and the rush of sparkling mountain streams are lasting impressions for the traveller in the north.

Cairns, 1766 kilometres from Brisbane, is the stepping-stone to a variety of sightseeing excursions. A major city for tourism, Cairns is often known as the 'capital of Far North Queensland'. Nestling beside Trinity Bay, this scenic city is an ideal base for visiting the surrounding tourist attractions. From Cairns, you can relax on a launch cruise that takes you to see the wonders of the Great Barrier Reef or to explore uninhabited islands. Aerial tours from Cairns take you over the Great Plateau, with its lush tablelands and spectacular waterfalls.

Four-wheel drive tours of the region with an Aboriginal guide are available. Visitors are educated on the local Aboriginal sites, Dreamtime legends and native flora. Details available at Port Douglas Dive Centre. Near Mission Beach, members of the Giramay Aboriginal Tribe share with visitors the beauty of the Murray Falls area as well as their knowledge of the environment.

The pleasant climate in winter and early spring is one of the main attractions of this city. Visitors can enjoy snorkelling or other water sports, while fishermen flock to Cairns from September to December to catch the big black marlin. Cairns itself is a picturesque city. Delicate ferns, tropical shrubs and fragrant flowers thrive in the Botanical Gardens, where a walking track joins the Centenary Lakes Parkland, created in 1976 to mark the city's hundredth anniversary. Two lakes, one saltwater and the other freshwater, provide a haven for wildlife among native trees and shrubs. You can also see orchids growing to perfection in orchid nurseries, which form the basis of one of Cairns' important export industries.

There are dozens of places around Cairns, all within easy driving distance on good roads, that will claim the traveller's attention. Port Douglas is only one of them. The 60-kilometre journey from Cairns passes through a magnificent stretch of coastal scenery as the Cook Highway winds past white coral beaches, through archways of tropical forest, and past the islands that dot the azure northern waters. Port Douglas, despite its increasing popularity with tourists, still retains some of its fishing-village atmosphere. The motels and holiday units are all set back from the beachfront. Just out of town is the Sheraton Mirage Resort, with 300 rooms but only 3 storeys high.

Just north of Port Douglas (and remember to stop at the cemetery that contains the graves of many pioneer settlers who were lured north by the Palmer River gold rush) is the sugar town of **Mossman**, where the crushing plant can be inspected from July to October. During these months cane farmers once created raging fires to prepare the cane for harvesting; however nowadays cane is more often harvested green. These days the fabled strong man of the north, the cane cutter, is seldom seen, having exchanged his machete for a seat on an ingenious machine that cuts

Bally Hooley Steam Express; Mossman

Turtle Bay, near Cairns

the cane and throws it, in a shower of short sticks, into the hopper that trails behind. Sugar-growing is a major industry of the north, and the waving fields of cane wind through the mountains for hundreds of kilometres down the lush coastal plain.

Near Mossman is one of those perfect places that seem so plentiful in the north, the Mossman River Gorge. A short walk under the dense green canopy of the rainforest leads to the boulder-strewn river, which rushes in a series of cascades through the jungle-sided gorge. It is a place to picnic, to swim or simply to bask in the rays of the North Queensland sun.

There are many such places, particularly on the edge of the Atherton Tableland, where the mountains have thrown up fascinating geological oddities and where waterfalls spill. For example, near **Atherton** township there are two volcanic lakes, Barrine and Eacham, where walking tracks through the rainforest give beautiful water views and a chance to see the abundant wildlife—parrots, waterfowl, turtles, platypuses, goannas and many marsupials.

South-west of **Malanda** is Mt Hypipamee National Park, where visitors can walk beneath huge rainforest trees, past staghorn ferns and orchids, along Dinner Creek to the falls and up to the crater, a funnel of sheer granite walls that fall away into dark and forbidding water.

Ten kilometres away from the Malanda Falls, where water cascades over a fern-swathed precipice into a delightful swimming pool, is the huge Curtain Fig Tree, which has resulted from a strangling fig taking over its host tree, climbing higher and higher and throwing down showers of roots to support its massive structure. There are dozens of other waterfalls in this area. Near **Millaa Millaa** is Falls Circuit, where the Millaa Millaa Falls, Zillie Falls and Elinjaa Falls are sited amid a magnificent panorama of rainforest mountains and plains.

There are four main highways linking the tablelands with the coast. They are all magnificent scenic routes, although the roads are narrow and winding in some parts. Undoubtedly, however, the most novel and popular way of getting up to the tableland is by the scenic railway to **Kuranda**, built to serve the Herberton tin mine in the 1890s, and now regarded as one of the most difficult feats of engineering in Queensland. The track climbs 300 metres in 20 kilometres to traverse the Barron Gorge, and part of it runs over a viaduct along the edge of a 200-metre precipice. The lovely old carriages have rear platforms with decorative iron railings where travellers can stand and take in the superb uninterrupted view. The Kuranda railway station, festooned in tropical plants, ferns and orchids, is a

much-photographed stopover before the descent to Cairns.

The Atherton and Evelyn Tablelands are areas of volcanic land at altitudes between 600 and 1000 metres, mild in climate and supporting dairying, maize and tobacco-farming. Gradually the tablelands change to dry, rough country, where tin, copper, lead and zinc was once mined. Beyond the main tableland settlement of Atherton is the fascinating mining town of **Herberton**, with its Historical Village and old houses proclaiming its boom days of the late nineteenth century.

Southward from Cairns the plain is flanked by the Walter Hill Range on the seaward side and the Bellenden Ker Range, with its superb rainforest. A turn off the highway beyond the town of Innisfail leads into the tropical holiday resort area, where many small towns nestle in the encroaching forest and peep through palms across the sand to the Barrier Reef islands. Further south is the Hinchinbrook Channel, opposite the large continental island of Hinchinbrook.

For further information on the Far North, contact the Far North Qld Promotion Bureau Ltd, cnr Grafton & Hartley Sts, Cairns; (070) 51 3588. **See also:** Individual town entries in A–Z listing. **Note** detailed map of Cairns Region on page 473.

Groper Creek, 16 km W, is noted for its fishing and giant mud crabs; camping, caravan and picnic areas. **Tourist information:** Community Information Centre, Queen St, Ayr; (077) 83 2888. **Accommodation:** 2 hotels, 1 motel, 2 caravan/camping parks.
MAP REF. 479 O13

Hughenden   Pop. 1592
The explorer William Landsborough camped at this spot on the Flinders River in 1862, while unsuccessfully searching for the missing Burke and Wills expedition. A year later a cattle station was established, and Hughenden came into existence. The town is on the Townsville–Mount Isa rail line and the Flinders Hwy, 250 km W of Charters Towers. It is a major centre for wool and cattle produced in the Flinders Shire. **Of interest:** Landsborough Tree, Stansfield St E; William Landsborough camped here St Patrick's Day 1862. Dinosaur Display Centre, Gray St; 14-m replica of Muttaburrasaurus, most complete dinosaur fossil found in Australia. Dinosaur Festival held July in even-numbered years. **In the area:** At Prairie, 40 km E, both on Flinders Hwy: mini-museum at Prairie historical relics at Cobb & Co. Yards. Porcupine Gorge National Park, 62 km N; 'mini-Grand Canyon'. Gemstone fossicking at Cheviot Hills, 200 km N. **Tourist information:** Ilfracombe Shire Offices, Devon St; (076) 58 2233. **Accommodation:** 1 hotel, 2 hotel/motels, 2 motels, 2 caravan/camping parks.
MAP REF. 483 N3

Ilfracombe   Pop. 350
This town, 28 km E of Longreach on the Landsborough Hwy, was developed in 1891 as a transport nucleus for Wellshot Station, the largest sheep station in the world (in terms of stock numbers) at that time; the head station was in itself the size of a town. The first Qld motorised mail service departed from Ilfracombe in 1910. **Of interest:** Folk Museum. **Tourist information:** Outback Qld Tourist Authority, Council Offices, Coronation Dr, Blackall; (076) 57 4255. **Accommodation:** 1 hotel, 1 caravan/camping park.
MAP REF. 476 A9, 483 N9

Ingham   Pop. 5075
A major sugar and sightseeing town near the waterways of the Hinchinbrook Channel, Ingham is on the Bruce Hwy,

111 km N of Townsville. The town has a strong Italian and Spanish Basque cultural background. **Of interest:** Macknade Mill, oldest sugar mill still operating on original site. Victoria Sugar Mill, largest in southern hemisphere; guided tours in crushing season, June–Nov. **In the area:** Wallaman Falls National Park, 51 km W; noted for spectacular scenery, excellent camping, swimming and picnic spots, and 300-m-high Wallaman Falls. Jourama Falls National Park, 25 km S. Herbert River Gorge National Park, 100 km NW. Mt Fox, extinct volcano, 65 km SW. Cemetery, 5 km E; interesting Italian mausoleums. Forrest Beach, 20 km E, 16 km of sandy beaches overlooking Palm Group of islands; stinger net swimming enclosures installed in summer. Lucinda, 22 km NE on banks of Herbert River, base for fishing holidays; Taylor's Beach, 24 km NE, popular family seaside spot. Hinchinbrook and Orpheus resort islands offshore. **Tourist information:** Bruce Hwy; (077) 76 1381. **Accommodation:** 8 hotels, 2 motels, 2 caravan/camping parks.
MAP REF. 479 M10

Inglewood   Pop. 1007
An early hostelry called Brown's Inn grew into the town of Inglewood, in the south-western corner of the Darling Downs, 108 km W of Warwick. Beef cattle and sheep are raised, and lucerne, grain and fodder crops are irrigated from Coolmunda Dam, 20 km E, which attracts boating enthusiasts as well as many pelicans and swans. **Accommodation:** 2 motels, 3 caravan/camping parks.
MAP REF. 123 J1, 475 J8

Injune   Pop. 394
This small cattle and timber town, 89 km N of Roma, is the southern gateway to the Carnarvon National Park. Explorer Ludwig Leichhardt called the region 'ruined Castle Valley'. **In the area:** Carnarvon National Park, 154 km N; spectacular sandstone scenery with gorges and escarpments, and major Aboriginal art sites: Art Gallery and Cathedral Cave. Carnarvon Gorge Oasis Lodge adjacent to park. **Tourist information:** BP Central, Bowen St, Roma; (076) 22 3399. **Accommodation:** 1 hotel, 1 motel.
MAP REF. 474 F2

Innisfail   Pop. 8520
Innisfail is a prosperous, colourful town on the banks of the North and South

Johnstone Rivers, 92 km S of Cairns. Sugar has been grown here since the early 1880s and its contribution to the area is celebrated with 9-day gala Sugar Festival held end August. The famous Opera Festival is held in Dec. Besides sugar, bananas and other tropical fruit are grown, beef cattle are raised, and the town has a prawn and reef fishing fleet. **Of interest:** Local history museum, Edith St. Chinese Joss House, Owen St. Cane Cutter Monument, Fitzgerald Esplanade. Several lovely parks with riverside picnic facilities. **In the area:** Flying Fish Point and Ella Bay, 5 km N, for swimming and camping. Palm-fringed shoreline of Bramston Beach, 23 km N. Johnstone River Crocodile Farm, 8 km NE. Mt Bartle Frere (1611 m), 25 km NW, Qld's highest peak, with track to summit. Johnstone River Gorge, accessed from Palmerston Hwy, 18 km W; walking tracks lead to several waterfalls. Tea plantation at Nerada, 28 km W. Palmerston National Park, 30 km W, from where road leads to Atherton Tableland. Australian Sugar Museum at Mourilyan, 7 km S. Etty Bay, 15 km S, with fine beach and picnic area; also natural history museum. Innisfail is excellent base for exploration of quieter lagoons and islands (including Dunk) of Great Barrier Reef. **Tourist information:** Johnstone Shire Regional Information Centre, Australian Sugar Museum, Bruce Hwy, Mourilyan; (070) 63 2306. **Accommodation:** 2 hotels, 7 motels, 4 caravan/camping parks.
MAP REF. 479 L8

Ipswich   Pop. 65 346
In 1827 a convict settlement was established on the Bremer River to work the limestone deposits in the nearby hills. The limestone was ferried down river to Brisbane in whaleboats. In 1828 explorer Allan Cunningham used Limestone Hills, as the settlement was known, as the starting point for his exploration of the Darling Downs to the west. In 1842 it was renamed Ipswich after the city in Suffolk, England, and the enormous coal deposits in the area speeded development. The railway from Brisbane arrived in 1876, displacing the busy river trade and Cobb & Co. services. Ipswich is 40 km SW of Brisbane on the way to both Toowoomba and Warwick. Coal mining, earthenware works, sawmills, abattoirs and foundries make it a major industrial centre. **Of interest:** Many historic buildings, including Claremont (1858),

Atherton Tableland

Few people visiting the peaceful and productive Atherton Tableland realise just what a wild and remote place it was only a hundred years ago. The area was unknown to Europeans until a colourful and aptly named prospector, James Venture Mulligan, led several expeditions south-west from **Cooktown** between 1874 and 1876, having previously discovered the spectacular Palmer River goldfields in 1873. The northern Aboriginal tribes bitterly resented the miners' intrusion on their land, and during the 1860s and 1870s there were a great many skirmishes between new settlers and natives, and several massacres.

In 1874 Mulligan, leading a party from Cooktown, named the Hodgkinson and St George Rivers and Mt Mulligan, north of the tobacco town of **Dimbulah**. He returned in 1875 and found a beautiful river flowing north, which he presumed was the Mitchell before it swung west to the Gulf of Carpentaria. He had in fact discovered the Barron River, which eventually flows east to the Pacific coast. Mulligan travelled up the Barron and camped at Granite Creek, where **Mareeba** now stands. He travelled over rich basaltic plains, now the tobacco fields on the Kuranda road, until stopped by dense, impenetrable jungle near what is now **Tolga**. He marvelled at huge cedar and kauri trees, but skirted the jungle westwards and camped 3 kilometres from the site of **Atherton**. In the ranges nearby he discovered the Wild River and traces of tin. However, as the nearest ports were Cooktown and Cardwell, some 500 kilometres away, Mulligan considered the area too isolated for tin mining.

Convinced that there was gold in the Hodgkinson River valley, Mulligan set off again and found extensive strikes as he prospected the valley. The Hodgkinson gold rush started as soon as he reported his find, most of the diggers coming from Cooktown and the Palmer River. The towns of **Kingsborough** and **Thornborough** quickly sprang up in 1876 between Mt Mulligan and Mareeba. In two years the population was some 10 000, but the field was not as golden as the Palmer.

This caused an unusual situation, the interior being opened up before a direct route to the coast had been discovered and a port founded. During 1876 several difficult tracks were cut down the steep, densely jungled coastal ranges towards Port Douglas and Trinity Bay. Rivalry developed between the two anchorages, with Trinity Bay eventually being dominant and becoming **Cairns**. Some epic hauls up the range were recorded. A double team of bullocks, yoked four abreast, took ten tonnes of mining machinery from Port Douglas to Kingsborough; in 1881, 80 bullocks hauled up the complete battery for the Great Northern tin mine at **Herberton**. An impressive monument at the foot of the Cairns–Kuranda road, the Kennedy Highway, commemorates the trailblazers who opened tracks from the Tableland to the coast and the outlet for the Hodgkinson gold.

The railway line from Cairns to **Kuranda**, on the edge of the Tableland, is only 34 kilometres long but took 4 years to build, cost 20 workers their lives, and has 15 tunnels. It was completed in 1888, and the prosperity of the Atherton Tableland, and Cairns, was assured.

In April 1877, John Atherton settled at the junction of Emerald Creek and the Barron River, and formed Emerald End station. When he found alluvial tin in the headwaters of the creek, he reputedly yelled 'Tin-hurroo' to his mate: hence the name of the area, **Tinaroo**. Atherton was interested in cattle, not tin, but he led others to major tin lodes on the Wild River, discovered by Mulligan four years earlier. Mining commenced and the town of Herberton came into existence. The Tate River field was also an important find, and tin proved to be more influential in the development of the area than the short-term excitement of gold.

In 1880, Atherton built a wide-verandahed shanty at Granite Creek, a popular camping ground halfway between Port Douglas and Herberton, used by men flocking to the new field. This became Mareeba. Eventually the railway linked Herberton and Ravenshoe with Cairns. Today, Herberton is an interesting historic town that holds an annual Tin Festival in September. The local museum, called the Tin Pannikin, is in a classic old (unlicensed) pub, and is a tourist 'must'.

Ravenshoe (pronounced Ravens-ho, not Raven-shoe) is on the Palmerston Highway, 93 kilometres west of Innisfail, and is 30 kilometres south of Atherton on the Kennedy Highway. It is noted for its gemstones and the fine cabinet timbers grown and milled in the area. The Torimba Forest Festival shows off the district's products every October.

Mount Garnet, 47 kilometres west of Ravenshoe, is an old copper-mining town where tourists can pan the tailings to find alluvial tin.

The rich dairy country around **Malanda**, 14 kilometres south-east of Atherton, supplies milk for what is known as the longest milk run in the world: to Weipa, Mount Isa, Darwin, and into Western Australia. The Malanda Show is held every July.

Millaa Millaa, 24 kilometres south of Malanda, has a cheese factory, and the Millaa Millaa, Zillie and Elinjaa waterfalls are nearby. McHugh Lookout gives an excellent view of the southern Tableland.

Tinaburra is a popular tourist settlement on Tinaroo Dam. Nearby on the Malanda–Yungaburra road is the amazing and much-photographed Curtain Fig Tree.

For more information on the Atherton Tableland, contact the Far North Qld Promotion Bureau Ltd, Cnr Grafton & Hartley Sts, Cairns; (070) 51 3588. **See also:** Individual town entries in A–Z listing. **Note** detailed map of Cairns Region on page 473

Elinjaa Falls, near Millaa Millaa

Gooloowar (1864), Ginn Cottage and grammar school. **In the area:** Northeast: College's Crossing (7 km), Mt Crosby (12 km) and Lake Manchester (22 km), popular swimming and picnic spots. Redbank Railway, 10 km E. Restored historic homestead Wolston House at Wacol, 16 km E. Swanbank Power Station, 12 km SE; trains run by Qld Pioneer Steam Railway Co-op, first weekend April–Dec. St Brigid's Church, Rosewood, 20 km SW; largest wooden church in South Pacific. **Tourist information:** Council Offices, South St; (07) 280 9811. **Accommodation:** 4 hotel/motels, 7 motels, 7 caravan/camping parks. MAP REF. 467 K9, 475 M6

Isisford   Pop. 150

Established in 1877 by travelling hawkers William and James Whitman, Isisford is 117 km S of Longreach. First called Wittown, the name of the town was changed in 1880 to recall the ford in the nearby Barcoo River and the proximity of Isis Downs Station homestead. **Of interest:** Bicentennial Museum, Centenary Dr. **In the area:** Huge, semicircular prefabricated shearing shed, erected in 1913, at Isis Downs Station, 20 km E; largest in Australia. Visits by arrangement; (076) 58 8203. Oma Waterhole, 10 km W; popular spot for fishing and water sports. **Tourist information:** Shire Offices; (076) 58 8277. **Accommodation:** 2 hotels, 1 caravan/camping park. MAP REF. 476 A11, 483 N11

Julia Creek   Pop. 572

A small cattle and rail township on the Flinders Hwy, Julia Creek is 134 km E of Cloncurry. A sealed road runs north to Normanton in the Gulf Savannah. The town is an important cattle-trucking centre. **Of interest:** McIntyre Museum, Burke St. Julia Creek Rodeo held May. **Tourist information:** Shire Offices, Julia St; (077) 46 7166. **Accommodation:** 2 hotels, 1 motel, 1 caravan/camping park. **See also:** Gulf Savannah MAP REF. 482 I3

Jundah   Population 100

Jundah (an Aboriginal word for 'women'), 219 km SW of Longreach, was gazetted as a town in 1880. For about 20 years the area was important for opal mining, but lack of water eventually caused the mines to close. **Of interest:** Barcoo Historical Museum. **In the area:** Jundah Opal Fields, 27 km NW. **Tourist information:** Barcoo Shire Council, Dickson St, Jundah; (076) 58 6133. **Accommodation:** 1 hotel, 1 caravan/camping park. MAP REF. 483 L12

Karumba   Pop. 708

Karumba, 69 km N of Normanton, is situated at the mouth of the Norman River and is the centre of the prawning industry in the Gulf of Carpentaria. A barramundi fishing industry also operates out of the town. **Of interest:** Slipway once used by Empire Flying Boats Service, which ran from Sydney to England.

Old cemetery on road to Karumba Point. Boat hire and accommodation at Karumba Pt. **In the area:** Town is surrounded by flat wetlands extending 30 km inland, habitat of saltwater crocodiles and many species of birds, including brolgas and cranes. Karumba is easiest point of access to the Gulf; charter vessels available for fishing and exploration of the Gulf and Norman River; also *The Ferryman* cruises on the Norman River. **Tourist information:** Carpentaria Shire Council, Normanton; (077) 45 1166. **Accommodation:** 1 hotel/motel, 2 caravan/camping parks. **See also:** Gulf Savannah. MAP REF. 478 B8, 481 H8

Kenilworth   Pop. 257

West of the Blackall Range, through the Obi Obi Valley, is Kenilworth, famous for its Kenilworth Country Foods handcrafted cheeses. This enterprise began as the Kraft cheese factory closed and 6 employees mortgaged their homes to start the venture. **Of interest:** Kev Franzi's Movie Museum and Photo Workshop, on Eumundi Rd; 2-hr shows. **In the area:** Little Yabba Creek, 8 km S; picnic spot with bellbirds. Lake Borumba, 32 km NW; sailing and water-skiing. Imbil Forest Drive from Lake Borumba, 39 km N, through forests and farmlands to Gympie. **Tourist information:** Cnr Sixth Ave and Aerodrome Rd, Maroochydore; (074) 79 1566. **Accommodation:** 1 hotel, 1 motel, camping facilities. MAP REF. 475 M4

Killarney   Pop. 827

This attractive small town is on the Condamine River, 34 km E of Warwick, and very close to the NSW border. **In the area:** Noteworthy mountain scenery. Dagg's and Brown's waterfalls, 1–2 km S. Cherrabah Homestead Resort, 7 km S; horseriding, golf, sailing and bushwalking. Queen Mary Falls National Park, 7 km E. **Tourist information:** 49 Albion St (New England Hwy), Warwick; (076) 61 3122. **Accommodation:** 1 caravan/camping park, 1 resort. MAP REF. 123 M1, 475 L8

Kingaroy   Pop. 6672

This prosperous agricultural town is famous for its peanuts and for its best-known citizen, Sir Johannes (Joh) Bjelke-Petersen, former Premier of Qld. Peanuts, maize, wheat, soy and navy

Peanut silos behind original Council Chambers, Kingaroy

beans are grown, and specialised agricultural equipment is manufactured. Kingaroy is 233 km NW of Brisbane and its giant peanut silos are a distinctive landmark. Kingaroy claims the title 'Peanut Capital of Australia', and also 'Baked Bean Capital of Australia', with 75% of Australia's navy beans grown in the district. **Of interest:** In Haly St: Kingaroy Bicentennial Heritage Museum; at Tourist Information Centre, videos on peanut and navy bean industries; at Garden of Rocks, landscaping with semi-precious stones and petrified wood. **In the area:** Mt Wooroolin scenic lookout, 3 km W. Bunya Mountains National Park, 56 km S. **Tourist information:** Haly St (opp. silos); (071) 62 3199. **Accommodation:** 5 hotels, 6 motels, 2 caravan/camping parks.
MAP REF. 475 L3

Kuranda
Pop. 616

This 'village in the rainforest' at the top of the Macalister Range is best known to tourists who have taken the 34-km trip from Cairns on the 100-year-old scenic railway. **Of interest:** Railway station with platforms adorned by lush ferns and orchids. Wildlife Noctarium; rainforest animals normally only active at night. Butterfly Sanctuary, said to be world's largest, with over 2000 butterflies in aviary; also static museum display. Tjapukai Aboriginal Dance Theatre; 2 performances daily. Also Rainforestation; Pamagirri Aboriginal dancers. Local markets held Wed.–Fri. and Sun. **In the area:** Guided tours of river and rainforest. Kuranda Rainforestation offers army-duck rides in rainforest, while Paradise in the Rainforest offers scenic rides on 'tractor train'. Barron Falls, spectacular after heavy rain. **Tourist information:** Cnr Grafton & Hartley Sts, Cairns; (070) 51 3588. **Accommodation:** 2 hotels, 3 motels, 1 caravan/camping park. **See also:** Atherton Tableland; The Far North.
MAP REF. 479 L6

Kynuna
Pop. 18

On the Landsborough Hwy, 161 km NW of Winton, Kynuna was established in the 1860s and was a staging point for Cobb & Co. coaches. **Of interest:** Kynuna's only hotel is the famous Blue Heeler. 'Surf' Carnival held Sept. **In the area:** Combo Waterhole, scene of the events described in 'Waltzing Matilda', 24 km

SE on western side of old Winton–Kynuna road. **Tourist information:** Blue Heeler Hotel, Landsborough Hwy; (077) 46 8650. **Accommodation:** 1 hotel/motel, 2 caravan/camping parks.
MAP REF. 482 I5

Laidley
Pop. 2315

Laidley, 75 km from Brisbane, is between Ipswich and Gatton, in the Lockyer Valley. It is the principal town for the Laidley Shire, a rural area of the Greater Brisbane Region regarded as 'Queensland's country garden'. **Of interest:** Historic home, Das Neumann Haus (1893); tourist centre, arts and craft, art gallery. Country Market, last Sat. in month, William St. Festival Week and Fire in the Valley Duathon held Sept. **In the area:** Laidley Pioneer Village, 1 km S; original buildings from old township. Adjacent, Narda Lagoon, flora and fauna sanctuary. Derby Cottage Farmstay, 23 km S. Lake Dyer, 1 km W, with picnic/barbecue facilities; Lake Clarendon, 17 km NW. Scenic Drives; leaflets available. **Tourist information:** Cnr William and Patrick Sts; (074) 65 1805. **Accommodation:** Limited.
MAP REF. 466 H9, 475 M6

Landsborough
Pop. 1150

Just off the Bruce Hwy, Landsborough is 9 km S of the Caloundra turn-off. **Of interest:** In Maleny St: Historical Museum, De Maine Pottery. Bottle, gemstone and shell museum on Glass House Mountains Dr. **In the area:** Queensland Reptile and Fauna Park, 4 km S. Big Kart Track, 5 km N. **Tourist information:**

Scenic railway, Kuranda

Landsborough Museum, Maleny St; (074) 941 755. **Accommodation:** 1 motel, 1 caravan/camping park.
MAP REF. 467 M2, 470 E13

Logan City
Pop. 132 000

Captain Patrick Logan, one of the founders and first Commandant of the Moreton Bay Penal Settlement, first discovered the area now known as Logan City. On 21 August 1862 he reported the sighting of a 'very considerable river which empties itself into the Moreton Bay ... I have named it the Darling'. This river later became the Logan River, an acknowledgment by Governor Darling of Logan's 'zeal and efficient service'. The region was named after Logan when it was first declared a shire in 1978, and it became a city in 1981. Midway between Brisbane and the Gold Coast, Logan is Qld's fastest growing city. Using its close proximity to both Brisbane and the Gold Coast (a little more than half an hour from each), it has a strong and vigorous economic base influenced by its location. **Of interest:** Mayes Cottage (1871), Mawarra St; National Trust Building, once home of early pioneers. Daisy Hill Forest Park (430 ha), Daisy Hill Rd; picnics, bushwalking and horseriding. Kingston Butter Factory Community Art Centre, Milky Way, off Kingston Rd. Logan Hyperdome, off Pacific Hwy; largest shopping complex in Australia. **Tourist information:** 4195 Pacific Hwy, Loganholme; (07) 801 3400. **Accommodation:** 4 motels, 11 caravan/camping parks.
MAP REF. 467 M9

Longreach
Pop. 3607

Longreach has a relatively small human population, but if you count the 800 000 sheep and 20 000 beef cattle in the area, it becomes the most important and prosperous town in the Central West. On the Thomson River, it is a friendly, modern town of broad streets, some 700 km by road or rail west of Rockhampton. It was here, in 1870, that Harry Redford, better known as Captain Starlight, with four mates rounded up 1000 head of cattle and drove them 2400 km into SA over wild unmapped country that only 10 years before had been the downfall of Burke and Wills. There Starlight sold the cattle. Unfortunately, since they did not belong to him, he was arrested in Adelaide and brought back to Qld to be put on trial at Roma. Despite the evidence, the jury found him not guilty, probably because of the pioneer philosophy that if you are daring enough to carry out that sort of deed, you deserve to get away with it! The events were the basis for Rolf Boldrewood's novel *Robbery Under Arms*. Although Qantas (**Q**ueensland **A**nd **N**orthern **T**erritory **A**ir **S**ervices) actually started in Winton, it soon moved its base to Longreach and then began regular operations. The same hangar used then became Australia's first aircraft factory and the first of 6 DH-50 biplanes was assembled there in 1926. The world's first Flying Surgeon Service started from Longreach in 1959. **Of interest:** Several historical buildings: Uniting Church (1892), Galah St, built for Grazier's Association; courthouse (1892), Eagle St; post office (1902), cnr Duck and Galah Sts. Stockman's Hall of Fame and Outback Heritage Centre, Capricorn Hwy; exhibition hall, theatre with audiovisuals, library and resource centre. School of Distance Education, Capricorn Hwy; tours during term. Preview Centre for proposed Qantas Founders' Museum in Qantas Park, Eagle St. Longreach Pastoral College, Capricorn Hwy. Jackson's Weapon Museum, Cassowary St. Pamela's Doll Display and Syd's Outback Collection Corner, Quail St. Cruises on Thomson River; *Yellowbelly Express* and Billabong Boat Cruises. **In the area:** Folk Museum at Ilfracombe, 27 km E. Outback station accommodation at Lorraine, Oakley and Toobrack Stations. **Tourist information:** Qantas Park; (076) 58 3555. **Accommodation:** 5 hotels, 5 motels, 2 caravan/camping parks. MAP REF. 483 N11

Main street, Mackay

Lucinda–Dungeness
Pop. 784

Lucinda, the port for Ingham's sugar has the world's longest offshore sugar-loading jetty. The conveyor belt, (5.76 km long), loads 2000 tonnes of sugar an hour. Charter boats leave the Dungeness harbour for fishing, cruising and trips to the islands, including popular Hinchinbrook. **In the area:** Unique Italian cemetery, 3 km N; mausoleums and architecture. Wallaman Falls, 80 km S; 300-m-high single fall, highest in Qld. **Tourist information:** Lucinda Point Hotel, Halifax Rd; (077) 77 8103. **Accommodation:** 1 hotel/motel, 1 caravan/camping park. MAP REF. 479 M10

Mackay
Pop. 40 250

Mackay is often called the sugar capital of Australia, producing one-third of the nation's sugar crop. Five mills operate in the area, and the bulk-sugar loading terminal is the world's largest. Sugar was first grown in 1866, a mill was built and in the same year Mackay became a town. It became a major port in 1939 when an ingenious breakwater was built, making it one of Australia's largest artificial harbours. The nearby Hay Point coal-loading terminals handle the massive output from the Central Qld coalfields. Gazetted in 1918, Mackay is now an attractive and progressive tropical city. Besides sugar and coal, the town's economy depends on beef cattle, dairying, timber, grain, seafood, and the growing of tropical fruit. Tourism is a growth industry, with cruises to Brampton, Lindeman, Hamilton, the Great Barrier Reef and the Whitsunday Islands. **Of interest:** Self-guiding Heritage Walk of historic buildings, including Commonwealth and National Banks, town hall, courthouse, police station and customs house. Queens Park and Orchid House, Goldsmith St. Mackay Entertainment Centre, Gordon St. Tourism Mackay, Nebo Rd; building is replica of old Richmond sugar mill. Mt Bassett Weather Station and lookout; Mt Pleasant Reservoir and lookout; both just north of town. Numerous beaches: Harbour, Town, Blacks, Bacasia, Illawong, Lamberts and Shoal Point. Illawawong Fauna Park at Illawong Beach. Festival of the Arts held July; Sugartime Festival Sept. **In the area:** Furleigh sugar mill, 15 km N. Cape Hillsborough National Park, 40 km N. Eungella National Park, 84 km NW. Polstone Sugar Cane Farm 15 km W. Greenmount historic homestead, 20 km W, near Walkeston. Kinchant Dam, 20 km W of Walkerston. At Mirani, Juipera Walkabout, contact museum. Orchidways, on Homebush Rd, 25 km S of Mackay; orchid farm. At Homebush, craft and art gallery. Hay Point coal-loading terminal lookout, 30 km S. Cape Palmerston National Park, 80 km S; 4WD access only. Cruises to Great Barrier Reef and Whitsunday Islands. **Tourist information:** The Mill, Nebo Rd; (079) 52 2677. **Accommodation:** 19 hotels, 29 motels, 10 caravan/camping parks. MAP REF. 477 J4

Maleny
Pop. 789

A steep road climbs west to Maleny, 50 km SW of Maroochydore on the Blackall Range. This is excellent dairy country. From Mary Cairncross Park, an area of thick rainforest, there is a fine view of the Glass House Mountains to the south. These ten spectacular trachyte peaks were named by Captain Cook as he sailed up the coast in 1770, for the sun shining on the rockfaces reminded him of glasshouses in his native Yorkshire. **Of interest:** Art and craft galleries. Fig Tree Cottage for pottery and opals. **In the area:** Scenic drive from Maleny through Montville and Flaxton to Mapleton, one of best in south-east Qld. Most of Sunshine Coast can be seen: views across to Moreton Island, and closer, pineapple

and sugarcane fields. Montville, 17 km NE, has many excellent potteries and art and craft galleries. Various museums, antique shops, fruit stalls, Devonshire tea places and tourist attractions along the way. Flaxton, 3 km further N; miniature English village and clock museum. Kondalilla and Mapleton Falls National Parks, 7 km W of Montville. **Tourist information:** Montville Tourist Information Centre, Main St, Montville; (071) 42 9214. **Accommodation:** 1 hotel, 3 motels, 1 caravan/camping park. **See also:** Sunshine Coast.
MAP REF. 467 L2, 470 B11

Mareeba   Pop. 6795

This town is at the centre of the main tobacco-growing region of Australia. Farms in the Mareeba–Dimbulah area are irrigated from Lake Tinaroo. Mining and cattle are also important industries. **Of interest:** In Mason St: Bicentennial Lakes, park with plantings to encourage wildlife; picnic facilities, children's playground. Mareeba Rodeo held in July. **In the area:** Pinevale Ranch, 10 km E; day horseriding. Aerodrome 11 km S. Mareeba Coffee Estates, 7 km W. Granite Gorge, 12 km W. Dirt and sealed road via Dimbulah crosses Great Dividing Range to Chillagoe (145 km W), old mining town with fine limestone caves. **Tourist information:** Shire Offices; (070) 92 1222. **Accommodation:** 4 hotels, 2 motels, 4 caravan/camping parks. **See also:** Atherton Tableland; Cape York.
MAP REF. 473 C10, 479 K7

Maroochydore   Pop. 28 509

A well-established and popular beach resort, Maroochydore is the business centre of the Sunshine Coast, 112 km N of Brisbane. **Of interest:** Famous surfing beaches and Maroochy River, with its pelicans and swans, offers safe swimming. Cotton Tree, at river mouth, popular camping area. **In the area:** Yacht Harbour, beach and Pilot Station at Mooloolaba, 5 km S. Fairytale Castle and Ski n Skurf water-skiing park at Bli Bli, 10 km N. Nostalgia Town, 11 km N via Bli Bli; emphasises humour in history. Mooloolah River National Park, 10 km S (access difficult). Maroochy Airport has daily flights to and from Sydney. River cruises up Maroochy River to Dunethin Rock through sugarcane fields. **Tourist information:** Cnr Sixth Ave and Aerodrome Rd; (074) 79

1566. **Accommodation:** 2 hotels, 11 motels, 4 caravan/ camping parks.
MAP REF. 467 N1, 470 H9, 475 N4

Maryborough   Pop. 20 790

Maryborough is an attractive provincial city, 3 hours drive north of Brisbane and situated on the banks of the Mary River. The Mary River was discovered in 1842 and in 1847 a wool store was established near the original town site. A village and port soon grew to handle wool being grown inland. It was officially proclaimed a port in 1859, and a municipality in 1861. The city itself is well planned. Maryborough is promoted as the Heritage City, and visitors are encouraged to take the Heritage Walk and drive through the suburbs to see the excellent architecture of a bygone era. The climate is dry subtropical with warm moist summers and mild winters, and several seaside resorts are nearby. **Of interest:** Some fine examples of early Qld colonial architecture, including Baddow House, Queen St, furnished in period style. St Paul's bell tower (1887) has one of the last sets of pealing bells in Qld. Fruit Salad Cottage Heritage Museum, Banana St. Brennan & Geherty's Store, Lennox St; property of National Trust. Pioneer gravesites and original township site in Alice St, Baddow, and historic time gun outside city hall; signposted walk. Several parks: Queen's Park, unusual domed fernery and waterfall; Elizabeth Park, rose gardens; Anzac Park; and Ululah Lagoon, near the golf links, scenic waterbird sanctuary where

black swans, wild geese, ducks and waterhens may be hand-fed. Heritage City Market, every Thurs. Mary River cruises. **In the area:** Hervey Bay, Rainbow Beach, Tin Can Bay, Burrum Heads and Woodgate seaside resorts; all offer fishing. Also at Hervey Bay; tours to see humpback whale migration. Fraser Island, just off coast; World-Heritage-listed sand island. Teddington Weir, 15 km S. Tuan Forest, 24 km SE. Pioneer museum at Brooweena, 49 km W on Biggenden Rd. Houseboats for hire. Farm holidays available. **Tourist information:** 30 Ferry St; (071) 21 4111. **Accommodation:** 5 hotel/motels, 8 motels, 6 caravan/camping parks.
MAP REF. 475 M1

Mary Kathleen   Pop. Nil

Well known to many Australians because of the controversial issue of uranium mining, Mary Kathleen was once a small mining town on the Barkly Hwy between Mount Isa and Cloncurry. The area has now been returned to its natural state, leaving no trace of the former inhabitants. In late 1982 the mine was shut down and by the end of 1983 the houses were sold and removed to new areas. Four buildings have been re-erected in the Mary Kathleen Memorial Park at Cloncurry. **In the area:** Mount Frosty, off Mt Isa Rd; popular swimming-hole and fossicking area for minerals and gemstones. **Note: Not recommended for children; hole is some 9 m deep with no shallow areas.**
MAP REF. 482 F3

Cadman Cottage, Montville, near Maleny

Cape York

The Cape York Peninsula is a vast triangular area as large as Victoria, with **Cairns** in the lower east corner, **Normanton** in the lower west, and **Thursday Island** as a dot at the northern tip. It is virtually uninhabited except for several Aboriginal communities, isolated cattle stations, and a string of small settlements along the telegraph line to **Bamaga** at the northern tip. Areas in the north of the peninsula are being considered as a site for the world's first commercial spaceport.

The first European exploration of Cape York was in the 1840s and the 1860s, by the Jardine brothers, John Bradford, Robert Jack, and the ill-fated Edmund Kennedy and his famous Aboriginal guide Jacky Jacky. Little has changed since then. Vegetation varies from gums and anthills in the south to swamps and jungle in the north. Many areas of the Cape are national parks and a sanctuary for much of Australia's unique wildlife, including crocodiles, orchids and insect-eating pitcher plants. Further information and permits may be obtained from Dept of Environment & Heritage, McLeod St,

Cairns; (070) 52 3096.

There are two distinct seasons: the wet and the dry. During the wet virtually all road transport stops and the only movement is by regular flights with Flight West into Bamaga. Some 50 kilometres on a dirt track brings the comfortable Pajinka Wilderness Lodge, managed by the Injinoo Aboriginal Community, for those who don't want to rough it. **There are almost no sealed roads or bridges in the area**.

All Aboriginal communities are self-sufficient and may be visited, but **it is essential that a permit be obtained in writing beforehand**. The main settlements are **Lockhart River** and **Portland Roads** on the east coast; Bamaga at the tip; and **Edward River**, Weipa South, and **Aurukun** on the Gulf. The Ang-Gnarra Aboriginal Corporations at Laura offer a guide and ranger service to visitors. Details available at the caravan park.

For the motorist with an adventurous spirit, the Cape is the ideal place to go exploring. A reliable and well-equipped 4WD vehicle, preferably equipped with a winch, is essential for this area. It is possible to drive north from Cairns or Mareeba to Bamaga through Laura and Coen. The Royal Automobile Club of Queensland provides an excellent map and information sheet and it is essential

reading before an expedition north is planned. **Conditions on the track are unpredictable and the RACQ or police at Cairns should be contacted before heading north**. August to October are the recommended travel months. It should be realised that there are limited facilities and fuel north of Coen. You can drive for days without seeing another car. The Laura, Kennedy, Stewart, Archer, Wenlock, Dulhunty and Jardine Rivers must be forded. During good dry conditions it is possible to take a conventional car, with care, north to Coen and west to Weipa.

Weipa, on the Gulf of Carpentaria, has the world's largest deposits of bauxite, the raw material for aluminium. Comalco offers conducted tours of the bauxite mining operation. Once mined the bauxite is shipped to the huge alumina plant at Gladstone on the central Queensland coast. The first European to see the red bauxite cliffs was the Dutch explorer Captain Willem Jansz in 1606. Direct access to Weipa is by regular Ansett flights from Cairns.

For further information on Cape York, contact the Far North Qld Promotion Bureau Ltd, cnr Grafton & Hartley Sts, Cairns; (070) 51 3588. **See also:** Individual town entries in A–Z listing.

Thursday Island

An unusual place with a magnificent winter climate, Thursday Island is Queensland's most northerly administration centre. Situated 35 kilometres north-west off the tip of Cape York Peninsula in the Torres Strait, it is a colourful outpost. Its population of around 2900 is made up of islanders, a minority of Europeans, and Malays, Polynesians, Chinese and Japanese. At Rosie's Shop, at the corner of Douglas and Blackall Streets, a range of Torres Strait Islander and Aboriginal artefacts are available for purchase. The Harbours and Marine Department's Torres Strait Pilot Service operates from its excellent harbour, once the base for 150 pearling luggers. Ferry

and day cruises depart from the harbour and operate between Bamaga, Horn Island, Punsand Bay and Pajinka Lodge Cape York.

Fishing boats, Thursday Island

For further information on Thursday Island, contact the Far North Qld Promotion Bureau Ltd, cnr Grafton & Hartley Sts, Cairns; (070) 51 3588.

Miles
Pop. 1260

Ludwig Leichhardt passed through the Miles district (340 km w of Brisbane) on three separate expeditions. He named the place Dogwood Creek, after the shrub that grows on the banks of the creek. In 1878 the western railway line reached 'Dogwood Crossing', and Cobb & Co. continued the journey to Roma. The town was renamed Miles after a local member of parliament. The area has always been good sheep country, but today the emphasis is on cattle, mainly Herefords, and wheat; tall silos dominate the surrounding plains. After the spring rains, the wildflowers are magnificent. Also gorges, walks, wildlife and fishing. **Of interest:** Historical village, Warrego Hwy; 'pioneer settlement' with all types of early buildings and war museum, displays of vehicles and implements. **In the area:** Possum Park, 21 km N; historical display, caravans and camping, and ex-airforce ammunition store, underground bunkers converted for accommodation. Myall Park Botanical Gardens at Glenmorgan, 100 km SW. **Tourist information:** Miles and District Historical Village, Warrego Hwy; (076) 27 1492. **Accommodation:** 3 hotels, 3 motels, 2 caravan/camping parks.
MAP REF. 474 I4

Millaa Millaa
Pop. 325

Located 75 km inland from Innisfail, Millaa Millaa is renowned for the many spectacular waterfalls in the area. The town's main industry is dairying. **Of interest:** Eacham Historical Society Museum, and Old Millaa Millaa Cheese Factory. **In the area:** Millaa Millaa Falls, Zillie Falls and Elinjaa Falls, all seen from 15 km gravel road that leaves and rejoins Palmerston Hwy east of town. Lookout to west of town offers excellent panoramic views of district. **Accommodation:** 1 hotel, 1 caravan/camping park. **See also:** Atherton Tableland; The Far North.
MAP REF. 479 L8

Millmerran
Pop. 1159

This town on the Condamine River produces eggs, cotton, grain, vegetables, cattle and wool. **Of interest:** Ned's Corner: camp oven meals, Australiana, yarns and poetry, bullock team; by appt only. Historical Society Museum, Charlotte St. Bottle and Brick Museum, Mary St. **Tourist information:** 541 Ruthven St,

Hotel and bottle tree, Mitchell

Toowoomba; (076) 32 1988. **Accommodation:** 1 hotel, 1 motel, 1 caravan/camping park.
MAP REF. 466 A10, 475 K6

Miriam Vale
Pop. 447

Situated on the Bruce Hwy, 150 km N of Bundaberg, this small township is renowned for its mud crab sandwiches. Watch for the Giant Crab. The twin towns of Town of 1770 and Agnes Water lie 25 km E. Captain Cook, while on his voyage of discovery in Australian waters, made his second landing here. The estuary and beaches provide an ideal spot to get away from it all and the fishing is excellent. **Tourist information:** Gladstone Area Promotion and Development Ltd, 56 Goondoon St, Gladstone; (079) 72 4000. **Accommodation:** 1 hotel, 1 motel, 1 caravan/camping park.
MAP REF. 477 N11

Mission Beach
Pop. 814

This quiet tropical 8-km-long beach is backed by coconut palms and heavy rainforest, close to Tully. Day trips to Dunk and the surrounding Family Group of islands (excluding Bedarra) can be taken from the jetty at Clump Point. At the southern end of the beach, a cairn at Tam O'Shanter Point commemorates the ill-fated 1848 Cape York expedition of Edmund Kennedy. **In the area:** Giramay Walkabouts; aboriginal cultural experience and full-day adventure trek. Art and craft galleries. Horseriding, boat and jet-ski hire, game fishing, water taxis.

Riverboat cruises on *River Rat* through mangroves and rainforest include fishing, mud-crabbing and crocodile spotting. Many walks along beach, or into rainforest where you can meet the cassowary. Whitewater rafting on Tully River, 10 km inland; superb scenery and swimming in the top reaches. Tully Railway Station; tropical plants. Tully Sugar Mill; tours weekdays in crushing season. **Tourist information:** Cassowary Dr, Wongaling; (070) 68 8559. **Accommodation:** 1 hotel, 6 motels, 5 caravan/camping parks.
MAP REF. 479 M9

Mitchell
Pop. 1101

This typical western country town, on the banks of the Maranoa River, lies on the Warrego Hwy between Roma and Charleville and was named after Sir Thomas Mitchell, explorer and Surveyor-General of NSW, who visited the region in 1845. **Of interest:** Old Courthouse, Cambridge St; new display and local crafts. **In the area:** Neil Turner Weir, 3.5 km NW. Unsealed tourist road leads north into Great Dividing Range and former stronghold of local turn-of-century bushrangers, the Kenniff brothers. Region behind Carnarvon National Park, 256 km N, is little known; sufficient petrol and supplies must be carried for return trip. Rutland and Arcoona Stations offer accommodation. **Tourist information:** Booringa Shire Council; (076) 23 1133. **Accommodation:** 5 hotels, 2 motels, 2 caravan/camping parks.
MAP REF. 474 D3

Aerial view of Mount Isa

Monto
Pop. 1339

Monto, on the Burnett Hwy, 250 km inland from Bundaberg, is the centre of a rich dairying, beef cattle and agricultural district. The Monto Dairy Festival is held on the June long weekend every even-numbered year. **In the area:** Cania Gorge National Park, 25 km N; spectacular sandstone formations. **Tourist information:** Cnr Mulgrave and Bourbong Sts, Bundaberg; (071) 52 2333. **Accommodation:** 2 motels, 1 caravan/camping park.
MAP REF. 477 M12

Mooloolaba – Alexandra Headland
Pop. part of Maroochydore

Because of its excellent clean, sandy beach and variety of restaurants and nightlife, Mooloolaba is equally in demand for family and young people's holidays. The Mooloolaba Esplanade, offering beachside resort shopping, rises to the bluff at Alexandra Headland. Alexandra Headland beach is a popular board-riding location. Few visitors forget the panoramic sweeping views up the beach to the Maroochy River and Mudjimba Island, with Mt Coolum creating an impressive backdrop. One of the safest anchorages on the eastern coast is at Mooloolaba Harbour. It is the finishing point for the annual Sydney-to-Mooloolaba Yacht Race and the starting point for the Mooloolaba-to-Gladstone Race. **Of interest:** Wharf complex, The Spit, Mooloolaba; dozens of specialty shops. Underwater World oceanarium,

cnr River Esplanade and Parkyn Pde; 80-m transparent tunnel for viewing 3 separate marine environments, also freshwater section and seal pool. Harbour is also base for Sunshine Coast's main prawning and fishing fleet, for yachting and game-fishing trips to near offshore reefs, and for pilot vessels that guide ships into Port of Brisbane. Para-flying off Mooloolaba Beach. **Tourist information:** Cnr Aerodrome Rd and Sixth Ave, Maroochydore; (074) 79 1566. **Accommodation:** 2 hotels, 10 motels, 3 caravan/camping parks.
MAP REF. 470 I9

Moranbah
Pop. 6525

Just off the Peak Downs Hwy, 200 km SW of Mackay, this town services the huge open-cut coal mines of Goonyella/Riverside and Peak Downs, managed by BHP Australia Coal Ltd. Coking coal is railed to the Hay Point export terminal just south of Mackay. **Of interest:** Inspections of Goonyella/Riverside Mine and Peak Downs Mine. **Tourist information:** Shire Offices, Goonyella Rd; (079) 41 7254. **Accommodation:** 2 hotel/motels, 1 motel, 2 caravan/camping parks.
MAP REF. 476 H6

Mossman
Pop. 1771

Mossman, the sugar town of the north, situated 78 km N of Cairns on the Cook Hwy, is surrounded by towering green mountains and fields of green sugarcane. **Of interest:** Mt Demi (1159 m) towers over town. Tours of Mossman Central Mill during cane-crushing season (June–

Dec.). Bally Hooley Steam Express, genuine steam train, transports tourists from Port Douglas (20 km SE) through canefields and on to tour of mill. Bavarian Festival held June. **In the area:** Popular beaches Cooya, Newell and Wonga; latter two provide public facilities. Mossman Gorge, 9 km S; short walk through rainforest to picturesque cascades. Silky Oaks Wilderness Lodge, backing on to Daintree National Park, 10 km W. Karnak Playhouse Theatre, 12 km N. High Falls Farm at Miallo, 15 km N. Wonga Belle Orchid Garden, 20 km N. Exotic jungle river cruises on Daintree River, 25 km N. Cape Tribulation National Park, 64 km N; largest tract of tropical rainforest in Australia. **Tourist information:** Cnr Grafton & Hartley Sts, Cairns; (070) 51 3588. **Accommodation:** 2 hotels, 2 motels, 1 caravan/camping park. **See also:** The Far North.
MAP REF. 473 B3, 479 K6

Mount Isa
Pop. 23 667

In 1923, John Campbell Miles discovered a rich silver-lead deposit on the western edge of the Cloncurry field. Today the progressive city of Mount Isa is the most important industrial, commercial and administrative centre in northwest Qld. 'The Isa' is a company town, with Mount Isa Mines operating one of the largest silver-lead mines in the world. Copper and zinc are also mined and processed. Ore trains run 900 km E to Townsville for shipment. 'The Isa' is an oasis of civilisation with excellent amenities and facilities in the otherwise hot and monotonous spinifex and cattle country surrounding it. The famous Rotary Rodeo, held Aug. attracts rough-riders from all over Qld and almost doubles the population of Mount Isa for the period of the festivities. **Of interest:** Surface and underground mine tours; advance bookings essential. Silver smelter stack, Australia's tallest free-standing structure (265 m). In Church St: John Middlin Mining Display and Visitors Centre; Frank Aston Underground Museum, opp K Mart. National Trust Tent House, Fourth Ave. Kalkadoon Tribal Centre and Cultural Keeping Place, Marian St. Riversleigh Fossil Display, Civic Centre, West St. Mt Isa Potters Gallery, Alma St. Flying Doctor Service base, Barkly Hwy. School of Distance Education, Kalkadoon High School. City Lookout, Hilary St. Donaldson Memorial Lookout and Walking Track. Country

Music Festival held April; Agricultural Show in June; Art Society Exhibition Aug. **In the area:** Man-made Lake Moondarra, 15 km N; swimming, water sports, picnic/barbecue facilities. Lake Julius, 100 km N, offers Aboriginal cave paintings, fishing, water-skiing, nature trails and abandoned goldmine. Air charter companies provide flights to excellent barramundi fishing grounds near Birri Fishing Lodge at Birri Beach on Mornington Island and Sweers Island, in Gulf of Carpentaria. Mount Frosty, old limestone mine and swimming-hole; popular area for fossickers. Lake Corella, 90 km E; Burke and Wills memorial cairn. Camooweal, 188 km W on Barkly Hwy, last Qld town before crossing NT border. Gunpowder Resort, 140 km NW, where activities range from bull-catching to water-skiing. Tours of Riversleigh Fossil Site, 200 km NW, and Lawn Hill National Park, 500 km NW. Copper City Tours; full day bush tours. **Tourist information:** Marian St; (077) 43 7966. **Accommodation:** 4 hotels, 13 motels, 8 caravan parks.
MAP REF. 482 E3

Mount Morgan   Pop. 2782
Found only 32 km SW of Rockhampton, the crater of the Mount Morgan open-cut gold, silver and copper mine is one of the world's largest man-made holes, measuring some 800 m across and 274 m deep. In the golden heyday of the mine, the town had 15 000 people. Mine tours available daily. **Of interest:** Museum, East St. Courthouse and other historic buildings have National Trust classifications. **In the area:** The Big Dam for swimming, boating and picnics. **Tourist information:** Mount Morgan Railway Station, Burnett Hwy; (079) 38 2122. **Accommodation:** 3 hotels, 1 hotel/motel, 2 caravan/camping parks. **See also:** The Capricorn Region.
MAP REF. 477 L9

Mourilyan   Pop. 446
Located 7 km S of Innisfail, Mourilyan is the bulk-sugar outlet for sugar produced in the Innisfail area. **Of interest:** Australian Sugar Museum, Bruce Hwy. **In the area:** On Old Bruce Hwy, south-west: tours of South Johnstone Sugar Mill (8 km) in season, July–Oct.; National-Trust-classified Paronella Park (15 km), ruins of Spanish castle set in rainforest; suspension bridge, waterfall and picnic and camping areas. Natural History Museum, 7 km E near Etty Bay; butterflies, shells, insects. Etty Bay, 8 km E; quiet tropical beach with caravan/camping park. **Tourist information:** Australian Sugar Museum, Bruce Hwy; (070) 63 2306. **Accommodation:** 1 hotel.
MAP REF. 479 L8

Mundubbera   Pop. 1118
Centre of an important citrus-growing area, Mundubbera is on the Burnett Hwy, 410 km NW of Brisbane. **Of interest:** 'Enormous Ellendale' or 'Big Mandarin' Information Centre features displays on citrus-growing industry. **In the area:** Golden Mile Orchard, 13 km W; open weekdays for inspection. Rare Neoceratodus, or lungfish, is found in Burnett River nearby (exhibit on display at Information Centre). Jones Weir, Auburn River National Park, 40 km SW. Gurgeena and Binjour Plateaux; peanut-, maize- and bean-growing areas to northeast. **Tourist information:** 'Enormous Ellendale' Information Centre; (071) 65 4549. **Accommodation:** 2 motels, 1 caravan/camping park.
MAP REF. 475 K1

Murgon   Pop. 2210
Murgon, known as the beef capital of the Burnett, is one of the most attractive inland towns in southern Qld. Settlement dates back to 1843 and the name comes from an Aboriginal word meaning 'lily pond'. Beef, dairying and mixed crops are the main industries. The town is 101 km inland from Gympie and 46 km N of Kingaroy. **Of interest:** Vic Rewald's Lapidary Display, Nutt St; semi-precious polished gemstones collection. Queensland Dairy Museum, Gayndah Rd; adjacent, relocated Trinity Homestead, one of district's original buildings. Murgon Cheese Factory, Macalister St. Goschnick's Farm Machinery Museum, Bunya Hwy. **In the area:** Cherbourg Emu Farm at Cherbourg Aboriginal Community, 5 km SW; walk-through enclosures, educational displays and sales of emu products and Aboriginal artefacts. Bjelke-Petersen Dam, 15 km SE; popular water sports and recreation area. Jack Smith's Scrub Environment Park, 15 km NE; nature walk, scenic views. Adjacent, Boat Mountain Environment Park.

Australian Sugar Museum, Mourilyan

National Parks

The diverse landscapes of Queensland's national parks lure visitors by the million each year. They are drawn not only to the endless stretches of sandy beaches and magnificent Great Barrier Reef cays and islands off the coast, but also to the cooler mountainous regions of the southern ranges, the inland plains and sem-arid areas and the wilderness of Cape York.

Many parks and reserves are accessible by conventional vehicle, some by 4WD only; their major attraction is the climate—beautiful one day, glorious the next! Certainly, daytime temperatures in the north and west can reach a searing 40°C or more, and the monsoonal period (November to March) brings the occasional cyclone and rainfall that can be measured in metres, but other than these extremes, the climate makes for pleasant day visits and extended bushwalking, camping and other recreation-based activities.

Today Cape York Peninsula is like a magnet to tourists, even though the only aim of thousands of visitors may be simply to stand at its tip. The peninsula's vast and monotonous country is interspersed with surprising pockets of forest, broad vegetation-fringed rivers and occasional waterfalls, all the home of a wide variety of wildlife. **Jardine River/Heathlands, Rokeby** and **Iron Range National Parks** are destinations for keen and experienced wilderness explorers. However, a growing number of visitors divert to **Lakefield**, the State's second largest national park, encompassing 537 000 hectares. Its fringing rainforest, paperbark woodland, open grassy plains, swamps and coastal mudflats leading to mangroves along Princess Charlotte Bay, offer a variety of attractions for the most demanding visitor. Basic campsites are located along many watercourses.

Within a several-hundred-kilometre radius of Cairns are scores of national parks catering for all tastes. **Chillagoe–Mungana Caves National Parks**, three hours' drive from Cairns, are dominated by weird limestone outcrops, castle-like pinnacles that house a wonderland of colourful caves. Guided tours are conducted daily. Once Queensland's leading mineral producing area, it is popular with fossickers.

About 50 kilometres from Cairns is the **Atherton Tableland**, on which lie several national parks. Here visitors can follow walking tracks through rainforest at **Mt Hypipamee**, or visit the 65-metre-wide **Millstream Falls**, or the crater lakes of **Eacham** and **Barrine**.

A north Queensland visit would not be complete without a train trip to Kuranda via **Barron Gorge National Park**, or a visit to the **Bellenden Ker**, **Lumholz**, **Cape Tribulation** and **Daintree National Parks**. This undeveloped mountainous country, with its scenic waterfalls and lush rainforest, should not be missed.

One of the most breathtakingly beautiful scenic reserves in Australia is **Carnarvon National Park**, 720 kilometres by road north-west of Brisbane. The Carnarvon Gorge section of this 251 000-hectare park, a dramatic, twisting chasm of soft sandstone gouged from vertical white cliffs, is a popular destination for campers. Graded tracks lead through forests of eucalypt, she-oaks, tall cabbage palms and relic macrozamia palms. Two major Aboriginal art sites, the Art Gallery and Cathedral Cave, contain rock paintings of great significance. Visitor numbers to the gorge are limited year-round.

Some 300 kilometres east of Carnarvon National Park and north-west of Monto is **Cania Gorge National Park**, featuring prominent sandstone cliffs up to 70 metres high, cave formations, dry rainforest on sheltered slopes and open eucalypt forest. Though not as extensive as Carnarvon Gorge, this park protects a valuable scenic resource and provides an important wildlife habitat. **Auburn River National Park**, south-west of Mundubbera, protects an area of open eucalypt forest and dry scrub. The Auburn River flows through this 389-hectare park over a jumbled mass of pink granitic boulders. Over time, water erosion has sculptured the river's rock pools and cataracts. Vegetation along the river banks includes stunted figs, and bottle trees are common.

Cape Tribulation National Park

Daintree National Park

Rainforest species occur in some areas and small lizards can be seen sunbaking on rocks near the water.

Queensland's coastal islands range from large, steep continental types to coral cays, many of them lying between the mainland and the outer Great Barrier Reef. Several national park islands have been developed for tourism; these include Hinchinbrook, the world's largest national park island, 39 900 hectares of wilderness and quiet beaches. More than 90 per cent of the 100 islands in the Whitsunday–Cumberland Group (including **Conway National Park**) are national parks and 6 of these islands have resorts. Sail-yourself yachts are a novel way to visit some of the more isolated spots.

Eungella National Park, 83 kilometres west of Mackay, is the Aboriginal 'Land of the Clouds'. It is one of Queensland's wildest and most majestic parks, and the cool freshness under the canopy of rain-forest makes it a perfect destination for a day trip. Many visitors, however, choose to camp by the Broken River, where the normally shy platypus can be seen swimming casually in the creek waters.

Cape Hillsborough National Park, 50 kilometres north of Mackay, is often referred to as 'the island you can drive to', because it combines the beauty of an island with the accessibility of the mainland. A wide variety of wildlife includes kangaroos, wallabies, possums, echidnas and 100 species of birds.

Launches and charter vessels from Gladstone will take visitors to Heron, North West and Tryon Islands, all rich in coral and marine life and a paradise for snorkellers and scuba divers. The Capricorn–Bunker islands are outstanding rookeries of the loggerhead and green turtles and the summer nesting-grounds for thousands of wedgetailed shearwaters and white-capped noddies.

Eurimbula National Park is south-east of Gladstone, near the twin com-munities of Agnes Water–Town of 1770. Over 200 years ago Captain Cook and his crew chose this picturesque stretch of coast, with its broad sandy beaches be-tween small rocky headlands, for their first landing in what is now Queensland. Bo-tanically this is a key coastal area, pres-erving a complex array of vegetation, including some plants common in south-ern areas and others found in northern forests.

Lady Musgrave Island is a charming coral cay reached from Bundaberg and Town of 1770. Around the cay's edge, exposed to wind and salt spray, grows a vegetation fringe of casuarina and pan-danus, which protects the shady pisonia forest on the inner part of the island. The sheltered lagoon is used by many yach-ties, and by day trippers for snorkelling and reef-viewing in glass-bottomed boats.

Situated only 3 kilometres east of Bundaberg and covering 40 hectares is the Baldwin Wetlands, containing the **Baldwin Swamp Environmental Park**. Walking tracks and a boardwalk allow observation of the park's wildlife. **Mon Repos Environmental Park**, 14 kilometres east of Bundaberg, is eastern Australia's largest mainland turtle rookery. The turtle season extends from November to March. Visitors to the information centre get some basic knowledge of sea turtles and acceptable human interaction with them. This ensures that a visit to the rookery is an enlightening and enjoyable experience.

Woodgate National Park, south of Bundaberg, is at the mouth of the Burrum River near Woodgate township. This coastal park of 5490 hectares provides an essential habitat for wildlife; plant communities in the park include mangroves lining the Gregory and Burrum Rivers, wallum heathland, eucalypt and angophora forests, ti-tree swamps and small pockets of palm forest. Roads within the park are gravel or sand, and 4WD vehicles are recommended, although at times conventional vehicle access is possible.

Off Hervey Bay is the world's largest sand island, Fraser Island. The northern third of the island is **Great Sandy National Park**. This and two parks further south, **Moreton Island** and **Cooloola National Parks**, require 4WD vehicles for access; the latter offers excellent boating opportunities, particularly on the Noosa River.

Noosa National Park, 160 kilometres north of Brisbane, offers the visitor a wide variety of coastal scenery. Walking tracks lead to lookouts from which can be seen such unusual rock formations as Hell's Gates, Boiling Pot and Fairy Pool.

Further south towards Brisbane lie the **Glass House Mountains**, eroded volcanic plugs that rise suddenly from the landscape. First sighted by Captain Cook in 1770, four of these—**Mts Coonoorwin**, **Beerwah**, **Tibrogargan** and **Ngungun** are national parks.

Bunya Mountains National Park, 250 kilometres north-west of Brisbane, was established to preserve the last remaining community of bunya pine forest. It was here that Aborigines used to gather about every third year to feast on bunya nuts.

The crescent of national parks, or Scenic Rim, around Brisbane, includes (among many) **Mount Mistake**, **Main Range**, **Mount Barney**, **Lamington** and **Springbrook National Parks**. These offer Brisbane residents and visitors panoramic views, extensive walking tracks, picnic facilities and a range of recreational opportunities. Lamington attracts visitors by the thousands to its cool rainforest, rich in elkhorn and staghorn ferns and over 700 species of orchid.

Nine small national park areas at **Tamborine Mountain** also attract many day visitors to their rainforests, waterfalls and lookouts.

Girraween National Park, 'Place of Flowers', lies south of Stanthorpe and close to the New South Wales border, and offers visitors the best floral displays in the State. This is a photographer's paradise, while the park's massive granite outcrops provide a challenge for the rock climber.

For more information about Queensland's national parks, including the requirement for camping and driving permits, contact the Department of Environment Naturally Queensland Centre, 160 Ann St, Brisbane (PO Box 155, Brisbane Albert St 4002); (07) 227 8185. **See also:** Individual town entries in A–Z listing.

Lawn Hill National Park, close to the NT border

Tourist information: 118b Lamb St; (071) 68 1984. **Accommodation:** 1 hotel/motel, 1 motel, 2 caravan parks. MAP REF. 475 L3

Muttaburra   Pop. 195

Muttaburra, 114 km N of Longreach, was developed as a town in the late 1870s, the name being derived from an Aboriginal word meaning 'meeting of the waters'. **In the area:** Formerly part of an inland sea, the area has many fossil remains. The name 'Muttaburrasaurus' was given to a previously unknown dinosaur, the fossilised bones of which were discovered here. Full-sized replica of dinosaur in Edkins St. Fishing, water-skiing and agate fossicking. **Tourist information:** Muttaburra Motors and Cafe, Edkins St; (076) 58 7140. **Accommodation:** 1 hotel, 1 caravan/camping park. MAP REF. 476 A7, 483 N7

Nambour   Pop. 10 355

Nambour is a busy provincial town, 106 km N of Brisbane, just off the Bruce Hwy. The district was settled in the 1860s, mainly by disappointed miners from the Gympie goldfields, and sugar has been the main crop since the 1890s. Small locomotives pulling trucks of sugarcane regularly trundle across the main street to Moreton Central Mill during the crushing season. Pineapples and tropical fruit are grown extensively. Nambour is the Aboriginal name for the red-flowering ti-tree that grows locally. **In the area:** Spectacular Glass House Mountains to south, and scenic Blackall Ranges to west. Major tourist attractions, the Sunshine Plantation, home of the Big Pineapple, and CSR Macadamia Nut Factory, 7 km S. Moonshine Valley Winery, Forest Glen deer sanctuary and Super Bee honey factory, 10 km further S on Forest Glen–Tanawha Tourist Drive. Beach resorts of Maroochydore and Mooloolaba, 20 km E at mouth of Maroochy and Mooloolah Rivers. **Tourist information:** Sunshine Plantation, Bruce Hwy, Woombye; (071) 42 1333. **Accommodation:** 3 hotels, 5 motels, 2 caravan/camping parks. **See also:** Sunshine Coast. MAP REF. 467 M1, 470 E8, 475 N4

Nanango   Pop. 2571

Gold was mined here from 1850 to 1900, but the area, 24 km SE of Kingaroy, now relies on beef cattle, beans and grain. The

Noosa

1400-megawatt Tarong Power Station and Meandu Coal Mine, 18 km SW, also are of economic importance to the area. **Of interest:** Astronomical Observatory, Faulkners Rd; day and night viewings. **In the area:** Yarraman and Benarkin Forest Drives, including Coomba Falls. Bunya Mountains National Park, 84 km W. Berlin's Gem and Historical Museum, 17 km SW; open daily. **Tourist information:** Shire Offices, Drayton St; (071) 63 1307. **Accommodation:** 3 hotels, 3 motels, 4 caravan/camping parks. MAP REF. 475 L4

Nebo   Pop. 160

Nebo is situated 100 km SW of Mackay on the Peak Downs Hwy. Beef cattle and grain-farming are the major industries. **Of interest:** Nebo Museum, Reynolds St. Annual rodeo in July. **Tourist information:** Shire Offices, Reynolds St; (079) 50 5133. **Accommodation:** 1 hotel, 1 motel, 1 caravan/camping park. MAP REF. 476 I5

Nerang   Pop. 10 174

This small township in the Gold Coast hinterland is 10 km from Southport. **In the area:** At Carrara, 5 km S, weekend Hinterland Country Market. Hinze Dam on Advancetown Lake, 8 km S; swimming and sailing, picnic/barbecue facilities. Spectacular scenery in Numinbah Valley area. Natural Arch National Park, 38 km S; popular picnic spot with walking tracks through rainforest, and lookout nearby. Glow-worms in cave under arch. Towards Spring-

brook, 42 km S: Wunburra Lookout on Springbrook Plateau; Best of All View, off Repeater Station Rd; Purlingbrook Falls in Springbrook National Park. **Tourist information:** Albert Shire Council, Nerang–Southport Rd; (075) 78 0211. **Accommodation:** 2 hotels, 3 motels, 1 caravan/camping park. MAP REF. 467 N12, 469 C5, 475 N7

Noosa   Pop. 17 776

Noosa Heads is the most northerly of the Sunshine Coast resorts and is renowned for its natural scenery. A combination of the Noosa National Park, a protected main beach facing north, the Noosa River and lakes system, and Qld sunshine, has resulted in a fashionable resort with a relaxed atmosphere, temperate weather and safe year-round swimming. Wildlife abounds in the area. There are excellent restaurants and accommodation, but without Gold-Coast-style high-rise development. Tewantin, 6 km up the river, was first settled in the 1870s as a base for timber-cutters. The area formerly known as Noosaville, on the river between the two centres, is a relaxed family-style resort. **Of interest:** Noosa Regional Gallery Pelican St, Tewantin. Selina Antiques, Sunshine Beach Rd, Noosa Junction. Walking and surfing in Noosa National Park, between Noosa Heads and Sunshine Beach and walking distance from Hastings St; rocky headlands, sandy coves and patches of rainforest. Views of river and lakes from Laguna Lookout. At Tewantin: Big Shell, Coloured Sands Art Gallery and House of Bottles. **In the area:** Camel rides on Noosa's north shore beach; horseriding through the bush. All 20–40 km N: Teewah coloured sand-hills, stranded freighter *Cherry Venture*, Noosa River Everglades and Cooloola National Park; may be accessed by 4WD vehicles, and boat tours depart from Noosaville. Noosa Lakes system, navigable for 50 km into Cooloola National Park, is ideal for boating, sailing and windsurfing. Houseboat holidays are popular. Boreen Point, quiet holiday and sailing centre on Lake Cootharaba, 21 km N of Tewantin. Sat. markets at Eumundi, 16 km SW. **Tourist information:** Hastings St, Noosa Heads; (074) 47 4988, or Sunshine Beach Rd, Noosa Junction; (074) 47 3755. **Accommodation:** 21 hotels/motels, 4 caravan/camping parks. **See also:** Sunshine Coast. MAP REF. 470 H1, 475 N3

Darling Downs

The 72 500 square kilometres of black volcanic soil on the Darling Downs produce 90 per cent of the State's wheat, 50 per cent of its maize, 90 per cent of its oilseeds, two-thirds of its fruit and one-third of its tobacco, as well as oats, sorghum, millet, cotton, soybeans and navy beans. It is a major sheep, cattle and dairying area and the home of several famous bloodstock studs.

Allan Cunningham was the first white man to ride across these fertile plains in 1827. The Darling Downs is rural Australia at its best, with a touch of England in the magnificent oaks, elms, plane trees and poplars of **Toowoomba's** parks, and the colourful rose gardens of **Warwick** in the south. The climate is cooler and more bracing than in the rest of the State.

Driving across the Downs with its neat strips of grainfields, lush pastures, patches of forest and national parks, and well-established homesteads, gives the visitor an impression of beauty and quiet prosperity.

The Warrego Highway leads northwest from Toowoomba to the wheatfields and silos of **Dalby**, the hub of the Downs. Gowrie Mountain is a popular lookout. At **Jimbour**, 27 kilometres north-west of Dalby, stands the stately two-storey Jimbour House. On an elevated site with panoramic views of the Jimbour Plains, this historic home in landscaped gardens was constructed between 1874 and 1876, mainly from local materials, including cedar from the Bunya Mountains. Part of an earlier (1870) bluestone building still stands at the rear of the house.

The New England Highway, the main Sydney to Brisbane route, turns into the Cunningham Highway at Warwick, and descends from the Downs towards the coast through Cunninghams Gap, discovered in 1827. Main Range National Park has lovely rainforest, palms and native wildlife. An alternative inland route between Brisbane and Melbourne is the Newell Highway, which runs west from Warwick to **Goondiwindi** and then south through **Moree** and **Narrabri**. A less-used but scenic route is the Heifer Creek Way through the Lockyer Valley from near **Greenmount East** to **Gatton**.

For further information on the Darling Downs, contact the Southern Downs Tourist Association, 49 Albion St (New England Hwy), Warwick; (076) 61 3122. **See also:** Individual town entries in A–Z listing.

Scene near Cunninghams Gap

Normanton
Pop. 1189

Normanton, 151 km from Croydon, is the central town of the Gulf Savannah and is situated on a high gravel ridge on the edge of the savannah grasslands that extend to the west and the wetlands that extend to the north. The town is also the terminus of the historic Normanton to Croydon railway, and the Normanton railway station is the home of the *Gulflander*. **Of interest:** Penitentiary, Haig St. Restored Bank of NSW building, Little Brown St. Town well, Landsborough St; no longer in use. **In the area:** Fishing and camping at Walkers Creek, 32 km NW, and Norman River at Glenore, 23 km S. Lakes on outskirts of Normanton abound with jabirus, brolgas, herons and other birds. At Shady Lagoons, 18 km E; bush camping, birdwatching, wildlife. Dorunda Station, 170 km NE; working cattle station, offering accommodation, and barramundi and saratoga fishing in lake and rivers. Karumba, 69 km NW; prawn-fishing centre for Gulf region. **Tourist information:** Shire Offices; (077) 45 1166. **Accommodation:** 3 hotel/motels, 1 motel, 1 caravan/camping park. **See also:** Cape York; Gulf Savannah.
MAP REF. 478 C8, 481 H9

Oakey
Pop. 3425

On the Warrego Hwy, 29 km from Toowoomba, this town is the base for Australian Army Aviation. **Of interest:** Horse-drawn vehicles and memorabilia, and bronze statue of racehorse Bernborough at Tourist Centre, Campbell St. Oakey Historical Museum, Warrego Hwy. Flypast, Museum of Australian Army Flying, at army base; large collection of original and replica aircraft (most in flying condition) and aviation memorabilia. **In the area:** Acland Coal Mine Museum, 18 km N. Jondaryan Woolshed (1859), on Warrego Hwy, 22 km NW, with space for 88 blade shearers; shearing demonstrations, billy tea and damper, sales of goods at wool store. Australian Heritage Festival held at Woolshed in Aug. Horse-drawn caravan holidays. **Tourist information:** Bernborough Crafts and Tourist Centre, 68 Campbell St; (076) 91 1595. **Accommodation:** 4 hotels, 2 motels.
MAP REF. 466 D6, 475 K5

Palm Cove
Pop. 2800

Part of the Marlin Coast, serene Palm Cove, 27 km N of Cairns, offers visitors

Railway station, Normanton

an inviting selection of world-class accommodation with an equally splendid range of boutiques, art galleries and souvenir shops—all set on a tropical beach. Dive and tour bookings to the Barrier Reef are available, as are pick-up services for a host of day tours to the Atherton Tableland and surrounding areas. There is also convenient access to Mossman and Port Douglas. **In the area:** Wild World, Australian Wildlife Showpark, 5 km S; exotic range of flora and fauna. Outback Opal Mine at Clifton Beach, 7 km S; simulated mine with displays of Australia's most famous stone. Bungy tower in rainforest, McGregor Rd Smithfield; 14 km S. **Tourist information:** Cnr Hartley and Grafton Sts, Cairns; (070) 51 3588. **Accommodation:** 12 motels, 3 resorts, 2 caravan/camping parks.
MAP REF. 473 F7

Pittsworth
Pop. 2110

Pittsworth is a typical Darling Downs town, situated 40 km SW of Toowoomba on the road to Millmerran. It is the centre of a rich grain and dairying district. Cotton is grown with the help of irrigation. **Of interest:** Some buildings, especially in Hume St, listed by National Trust. Folk Museum, Pioneer Way; pioneer cottage, blacksmith's shop and early school. Great Australian Team Truck Pull held in Dec. **Tourist information:** Sunkist Cafe, Yandilla St; (076) 93 1246. **Accommodation:** 1 hotel/motel, 1 motel, 1 caravan/camping park.
MAP REF. 466 C9, 475 K6

Pomona
Pop. 885

This small farming centre is in the northern hinterland of the Sunshine Coast, 33 km S of Gympie. Mt Cooroora (439 m) dominates the town and in July each year tests the skill of mountain runners from world-wide, with the 'King of the Mountain' race and festival. **Of interest:** Majestic Theatre; cinema museum and annual film festival. **In the area:** Lake Cootharaba, 18 km NE; large, shallow saltwater lake on Noosa River where Mrs Eliza Fraser spent time with Aborigines after wreck of *Stirling Castle* on Fraser Island in 1836. **Tourist information:** Hastings St, Noosa Heads; (074) 47 4988. **Accommodation:** 1 hotel.
MAP REF. 470 B1

Port Douglas
Pop. 3660

Just 65 km N of Cairns, along one of the most scenic coastal drives in Australia, Port Douglas offers the contrast of cosmopolitanism in a tropical, tree-covered mountain setting. Once a small, sleepy village, Port Douglas has become an international tourist destination, particularly since the opening of the Sheraton Mirage Hotel, a resort complex with a golf course and marina, just out of town. The township, hidden off the main highway, is surrounded by lush vegetation and pristine rainforests. This setting, along with its proximity to the Great Barrier Reef, makes it an ideal holiday destination. **Of interest:** Ben Cropp's Shipwreck Museum, end of Macrossan St, in Anzac Park. Sun. market in park. Rainforest Habitat, Port Douglas Rd;

Old goldmining equipment, Ravenswood

flora and fauna in natural surroundings. Regatta in Sept. Tours from town include: horse trail-riding, rainforest hiking, Native Guide rainforest tours, 4WD safaris, coach tours, reef tours to Outer Barrier Reef and Low Isles, tours on famous steam train Balley Hooley, the *Lady Douglas* paddlewheel cruise, and tours to Wetherby cattle station. **In the area:** Flagstaff Hill, end Murphy St; commands breathtaking views of Four Mile Beach and Low Isles. Sugar town of Mossman and picturesque Mossman Gorge, 15 km N; Daintree River rainforest cruises begin further 40 km N. **Tourist information:** 23 Macrossan St and Shop 18, Marina Mirage, Wharf St; (070) 99 5599. **Accommodation:** 3 resorts, 47 motels, 4 caravan/camping parks. **See also:** The Far North. MAP REF. 473 C4, 479 K6

Proserpine   Pop. 3034
A sugar town, Proserpine is close to Airlie Beach, Shute Harbour and the islands of the Whitsunday Passage. **Of interest:** Bulk sugar mill, Hinschen St; tours during crushing season. **In the area:** Conway National Park, 10 km SE; spectacular views across islands of Whitsunday Passage. Lake Proserpine at Peter Faust Dam, 20 km W; boats for hire, waterskiing, fishing, swimming, picnic/barbecue facilities. **Tourist information:**

Beach Plaza, The Esplanade, Airlie Beach; (079) 46 6673. **Accommodation:** 4 motels, 2 caravan/camping parks. MAP REF. 476 I2

Quilpie   Pop. 624
Quilpie, 217 km W of Charleville, was established as a centre for the large sheep and cattle properties in the area, but is better known as an opal town. It takes its name from the Aboriginal word *quilpeta*, meaning 'stone curlew'. **Of interest:** Opal sales in town and opal workings outside town. Altar, font and lectern of St Finbarr's Catholic Church, Buln Buln St, made from opal-bearing rock. Mardi Gras and horseracing Sept., week before Birdsville Races. **In the area:** Lake Houdrahan, 6 km N on river road to Adavale; water sports and popular recreation area. Duck Creek Opal Mine at Cheepie, 75 km E. **Tourist information:** Shire Offices; (076) 56 1133. **Accommodation:** 1 hotel, 1 motel, 1 caravan/camping park. **See also:** The Channel Country. MAP REF. 485 M4

Ravenswood   Pop. 120
Ravenswood, friendly and 'not quite a ghost town', is 88 km E of Charters Towers via Mingela. One hundred years ago it was the classic gold-rush town. Visitors will find interesting old workings and perhaps a little gold along with

the nostalgia. **Of interest:** Several restored old buildings in town, including courthouse, shops and present ambulance centre. **In the area:** Burdekin Dam, 70 km SE; popular recreational area. **Tourist information:** Railway Hotel, Barton St; (077) 70 2144. **Accommodation:** 2 hotels, 1 motel/camping park, free camping in showgrounds. MAP REF. 476 E1

Redcliffe   Pop. 39 073
Redcliffe was actually the first European settlement in Qld. Matthew Flinders landed here in 1799 while exploring Moreton Bay and the spot was simply named for what he found: red cliffs. In 1824, John Oxley and Commandant Miller arrived with the first convicts and troops to set up the new Moreton Bay penal colony, which was abandoned the following year in favour of Brisbane. The Aborigines, one of the reasons for the move, called the place Humpybong, meaning 'dead houses', and the name is still used for the Redcliffe Peninsula, which comprises the towns of Woody Point, Margate, Clontarf, Scarborough and Redcliffe. The City of Redcliffe was proclaimed in 1959 and is a fast-growing separate-but-satellite area of Brisbane, 35 km S via the 2.6-km-long bridge known as the Houghton Hwy, which in 1979 replaced the old Hornibrook Hwy. Fishing and boating are popular pastimes. **Of interest:** Historical museum and self-guiding Heritage Walk. **In the area:** Redcliffe is departure point for vehicular ferry to Moreton Island, where sand dunes are reputed to be highest in world. Popular Tangalooma resort on western side of island. **Tourist information:** Jetty Building, Redcliffe Pde; (07) 284 5595. **Accommodation:** 6 hotels, 3 motels, 11 caravan/camping parks. **See also:** Tours from Brisbane. MAP REF. 467 N6, 475 N5

Redland Bay   Pop. 2576
Some 30 km SE of Brisbane on the shores of Moreton Bay, the famous red soil of this area grows excellent vegetables and strawberries, mainly for the Brisbane market. It is a popular Sunday afternoon drive from the city. Nearby Cleveland is the main centre of the Redland area, and beaches at Wellington Point, Victoria Point and Redland Bay offer safe swimming and boating. **Of interest:** Strawberry Festival held Sept. **In the area:** Roseworld, 2 km S; exhibition gardens

The Capricorn Region

This rich and varied slice of Queensland stretches inland from Rockhampton and the Capricorn Coast out to Jericho, and straddles the Tropic of Capricorn. The area includes the Capricorn Coast, Rockhampton City and surrounds, the Central Highlands and the Rural Hinterlands, and is drained by the Fitzroy, Mackenzie, Comet, Nogoa and Dawson Rivers. The district was first opened up by gold- and copper-mining around **Emerald** in the 1860s, and the discovery of sapphires around **Anakie**. The original owners of the land have left their heritage in superb and mysterious rock paintings on the silent stone walls of the Carnarvon Ranges to the south. Cattle have been the economic mainstay since European settlement, but vast tracts of brigalow scrub were cleared after World War II to grow wheat, maize, sorghum and safflower. These days coal has become king, with mainly American companies gouging out enormous deposits for local and Japanese markets. On a smaller scale, professional and amateur fossickers are still finding gems, and with a great deal of enjoyment.

For a pleasurable tour of the region, drive west from **Rockhampton**, the commercial and manufacturing capital, along the Capricorn Highway. Detour to Blackdown Tableland National Park where there are waterfalls, rock pools and camping areas; the turnoff is between **Blackwater** and **Dingo**. (You will need a permit from the Queensland National Parks office in Rockhampton to enter the park.) At Emerald turn south to Springsure, then east to **Biloela** on the Dawson Highway. Continue north on the Burnett Highway via **Mount Morgan** back to Rockhampton.

Mount Hay Gemstone Tourist Park, 41 kilometres from Rockhampton, allows visitors to fossick for thunder-eggs and rhyolite, which may be cut and polished at the factory in the park. Utah's Blackwater coalmine produces 4 million tonnes of coking coal and almost 3 million tonnes of steaming coal annually. Tours can be arranged.

Emerald is the main town in the Central Highlands region, with the central-western railway continuing much further west to Longreach and the Channel Country. Clermont and the Blair Athol coalfields are 106 kilometres to the north-west. The

gemfields of Anakie, **Rubyvale**, **Sapphire**, **The Willows** and **Tomahawk Creek** are west of Emerald, and are popular with tourists seeking a different holiday. (A fossicker's licence is necessary.)

Springsure, 66 kilometres south of Emerald, is one of Queensland's oldest towns, having been surveyed in 1854. It produces beef and grain. Nearby is the Old Rainworth Fort at **Burnside**, a fascinating piece of Australiana, where early farm equipment, wool presses and the like are on display. It was built in 1853 from local stone.

Rolleston, 70 kilometres to the southeast, is the turnoff to the magnificent Carnarvon National Park, 103 kilometres further south. The park is some 28 000 hectares of rugged mountains, forests, caves and deep gorges, some of which are Australia's earliest art galleries, with countless Aboriginal paintings and engravings, which in places extend in a colourful frieze for more than 50 metres.

The Callide open-cut mine is situated near **Biloela**, the principal town in the Callide Valley. The nearby Callide Power Station supplies the Rockhampton, Moura and Blackwater districts as well as Biloela.

What are known as the 'Snowy Mounts' are actually huge piles of salt in the Fitzroy River delta between **Bajool** and **Port Alma**. Underground salty water is pumped to the surface into pools called crystallisers, and the salt is 'harvested' during October–November after solar evaporation.

For further information on the Capricorn Region, contact the Capricorn Information Centre, The Spire, Gladstone Rd, Rockhampton; (079) 27 2055. **See also:** Individual town entries in A–Z listing.

Botanic Gardens, Rockhampton

showing most varieties of roses. Venman Environmental Park, Mt Cotton, 12 km sw; fauna sanctuary with walking tracks and picnic/barbecue area. King Country Nursery at Thornlands, 10 km N; rainforest setting with picnic facilities. At Cleveland, 15 km N: Bayside Markets on Sun. Cleveland is departure point for boats to Stradbroke Island, while Redland Bay is departure point for Russell, Lamb, Macleay and Karragarra Islands. Off Victoria Point, 6 km N: Coochiemudlo Island, quiet but popular. Islands are all excellent places to picnic, swim and explore; full range of facilities and services. **Tourist information:** Cnr Waterloo and Russell Sts, Cleveland; (07) 821 0057. **Accommodation:** 4 motels, 5 caravan/camping parks. **See also:** Tours from Brisbane.
MAP REF. 467 O9, 475 N6

Richmond   Pop. 631

This small town on the Flinders Hwy, 500 km from Townsville, serves the surrounding sheep and cattle properties. **Of interest:** Restored Cobb & Co. coach, Goldring St. Richmond Rodeo held May. **In the area:** The area is rich in fossils. **Tourist information:** Shire Offices, Goldring St; (077) 41 3277. **Accommodation:** 1 hotel, 1 hotel/motel, 2 motels, 1 caravan park.
MAP REF. 483 L3

Rockhampton   Pop. 55 768

Rockhampton is called the beef capital of Australia, with some 2.5 million cattle in the region. Gold was discovered at Canoona, 60 km NW of Rockhampton, in 1858; however, cattle became the major industry, with Herefords the main breed, since successfully cross-bred with more exotic breeds to produce disease-resistant herds. Rockhampton straddles the Tropic of Capricorn. It is a prosperous city on the Fitzroy River and has considerable architectural charm. Many of the original stone buildings and churches remain, set off by flowering bauhinia and brilliant bougainvilleas. The Capricana Springtime Festival is held Sept.; Camp Draft and Rough Riding Championships are an annual feature. The city has several well-established secondary industries, including two of Australia's largest meat processing and exporting factories. **Of interest:** Quay St, alongside river, classified by National Trust; buildings include ANZ Bank (1864) and Customs House (1901). Botanic Gardens on Athelstane

Cotton fields, St George

Range, accessed via Spencer St; fine tropical display, also Japanese-style garden, koala park and walk-in aviary. Cliff Kershaw Gardens, Bruce Hwy; feature Braille Trail. Fitzroy River Barrage, Savage St, provides 63 700 million litres of water and separates tidal salt water from upstream fresh water. The Capricorn Spire (14 m) at Curtis Park, Gladstone Rd, marks exact line of Tropic of Capricorn. **In the area:** Dreamtime Cultural Centre, Bruce Hwy, North Rockhampton; largest Aboriginal cultural centre in Australia. Old Glenmore historic homestead, 5 km N, has displays and historic buildings. Rockhampton Heritage Village, Gangalook, 20 km N; heritage buildings, hall of clocks, pioneering tools, steam engine. St Christopher's Chapel, Emu Park Rd, 20 km N; built by American servicemen. Limestone caves, Olsen's Capricorn Caverns and Cammoo caves systems, 32 km N; conducted tours. Pleasant drive to top of Mt Archer. Yeppoon and Emu Park beaches, 25–30 km NE. Mt Morgan Mine and Museum, 38 km SW. Thunder-eggs fossicking at Mt Hay Gemstone Tourist Park, 41 km W on Capricorn Hwy. Great Keppel Island Resort, 13 km off Capricorn Coast. Underwater Observatory off Middle Island. **Tourist information:** The Spire, Gladstone Rd; (079) 27 2055. **Accommodation:** 18 hotels, 8 hotel/motels, 31 motels, 8 caravan/camping parks. **See also:** The Capricorn Region.
MAP REF. 477 L9

Roma   Pop. 5669

Roma is on the Warrego Hwy, 261 km W of Dalby, with the Carnarvon Hwy going south to St George, and north to Injune and the Carnarvon Gorges. It was named

after the wife of Sir George Bowen, Qld's first Governor. In 1859 it became the first gazetted settlement after the separation from NSW. The Mt Abundance cattle station was established in 1857 and sheep and cattle have been the area's economic mainstay ever since. The famous trial of Harry Redford, alias Captain Starlight, was held in Roma in 1872. In 1863 the SS *Bassett* brought vine cuttings to Roma and Qld's first wine-making enterprise got under way. Australia's first natural gas strike was made at Hospital Hill in 1900, and the gas from this source was used, briefly, to light the town. Further deposits were found periodically, and 'oil' (actually gas and condensate) caused excitement in the area in the early 1960s. Roma now supplies Brisbane with gas via a 450-km pipeline. **Of interest:** Oil rig, named 'Big Rig' by locals; erected as landmark at eastern entrance to town on Warrego Hwy. Romavilla Winery, Injune Rd; tastings and sales. Campbell Park; picnics and walks. Cultural Centre, cnr Bungil and Injune Rds; mural by local artists. Largest inland cattle market in Australia, on Warrego Hwy. **In the area:** Meadowbank Museum, 15 km W on Warrego Hwy. Carnarvon National Park, 251 km NW; Aboriginal cave paintings, varied scenery, guided tours, walks, accommodation. **Tourist information:** BP Central, Bowen St; (076) 22 3399. **Accommodation:** 10 hotels, 8 motels, 4 caravan/camping parks.
MAP REF. 474 F4

St George   Pop. 2512

Situated at a major road junction, St George is in the centre of a rich cotton-growing district. It is on the Balonne

River, 118 km N of Mungindi by the Carnarvon Hwy, and 292 km sw of Dalby by the Moonie Hwy. As St George has a rainfall of only 500 mm a year, an extensive irrigation programme is carried out by means of a dam and three weirs. Cotton-growing and harvesting is completely mechanised; planting is from Oct. to Nov., and harvesting from April to June. The cotton ginnery may be inspected by appointment during the harvesting months. Wheat, barley, oats and sunflowers are also irrigated, and sheep and cattle are raised. **Of interest:** Balonne Creative Arts Group, Klinge Lane; local craft. Riversands Winery, Lower Alfred St; open daily. **In the area:** Rosehill Aviaries, 64 km w; one of Australia's largest private collections of Australian parrots. Fishing for Murray cod, yellowbelly and freshwater jew on Balonne River. **Tourist information:** Shire Offices, Victoria St; (076) 25 3222; or Merino Motor Inn; (076) 25 3333. **Accommodation:** 2 hotels, 2 hotel/motels, 2 motels, 3 caravan/camping parks.
MAP REF. 474 F7

Sarina   Pop. 3094
In the sugar belt, Sarina lies 37 km s of Mackay on the Bruce Hwy. The area has many fine beaches, including Sarina, Armstrongs, Campwin, Grasstree, Halftide and Salonika. Sarina produces molasses and ethyl alcohol as byproducts of the sugar industry. **Of interest:** Plane Creek Central Sugar Mill. CSR Distillery, Bruce Hwy; tours available. Flea market, Broad St, last Thurs. in month.

Shute Harbour

Agricultural Show in Aug. Beach Aqua Carnival Sept. **In the area:** To north: Tours of Campwin Beach Prawn Farm (8.5 km) and The Big Prawn, Grasstree Beach (13 km). Viewing gallery at Hay Point and Dalrymple Bay coal terminal complex, 12 km N. **Tourist information:** Broad St; (079) 43 1501. **Accommodation:** 4 hotels, 3 motels, 3 caravan/camping parks.
MAP REF. 477 J4

Shute Harbour   Pop. 200
Shute Harbour (or as it is known to older residents, Shute Haven) is a suburb of the town of Whitsunday. It is also the second largest marine passenger terminal in Australia, second only to Sydney's Circular Quay. Shute Harbour's first marina is a 400-berth project. The jetty at Shute Harbour, 36 km NE of Proserpine, is the best place to start exploring the 80 or so tropical islands that bask in the beautiful Whitsunday waters. Hayman, Daydream, South Molle and Lindeman Islands are the best known. Every morning big and small launches, yachts and glass-bottomed boats take tourists on board for a memorable, picturesque day out. Booking offices, souvenir and food outlets are on the main jetty, with fuel available nearby. Try boom-net riding on one of the 3-island tours available daily. You can even fly by seaplane to Hardy's Lagoon on the outer Barrier Reef for a few hours' snorkelling amongst the coral. An extensive fleet of sail and power vessels of varying sizes and classes is available for charter. Ex-America's Cup challenger

Gretel takes visitors on day trips through the Whitsunday Islands. There are also day trips to the pontoon at Hardy Reef for swimming, snorkelling and scuba diving. The brigantine *Romance* offers 5-night cruises off the islands and the Reef. **Of interest:** Spectacular views from Lions Lookout. Heritage Doll Museum, Shute Harbour Rd, adjacent to Whitsunday Airport. **In the area:** Airlie Beach (5 km N), Conway National Park (15 km s), the Great Barrier Reef (30 min. by air, 90 min. by boat) and Whitsunday Islands. **Tourist information:** Beach Plaza, The Esplanade, Airlie Beach; (079) 46 6673. **Accommodation:** 2 motels.
MAP REF. 476 I2

Southport
Pop. part of Gold Coast
At the northern end of the Gold Coast strip, Southport is packed with attractions to suit the holidaymaker. It also serves as the commercial and administrative centre for the Gold Coast. **Of interest:** Sea World at The Spit is a marine park where a full day can happily be spent and dolphins, sea lions and false killer whales delight visitors. Other attractions include a replica of the *Endeavour*, the Johnson Water Ski Show and a monorail. The Gold Coast's fourth major theme park, Motor World is scheduled to open late 1994. Also on The Spit are Marina Mirage, Mariner's Cove and Fisherman's Wharf (tourist complexes with speciality shops, restaurants, outdoor cafes and weekend entertainment), and the Southport Yacht Club. **In the area:** Attractions of the Gold Coast and its hinterland. **Tourist information:** Cavill Mall, Surfers Paradise; (075) 38 4419. **Accommodation:** Low and high-rise hotels and motels, self-contained apartments, caravan/camping parks. **See also:** City of the Gold Coast.
MAP REF. 469 E5

Stanthorpe   Pop. 4187
The main town in the Granite Belt, 225 km sw of Brisbane and in the mountain ranges along the border between Qld and NSW, Stanthorpe came into being after the discovery of tin at Quartpot Creek in 1872. Silver and lead were discovered in 1880, but the minerals boom did not last. The area has produced excellent wool for more than a century, but is best known for large-scale growing of apples, pears, plums, peaches and grapes. Stanthorpe is

915 m above sea level and is often the coolest part of the State. Spring is particularly beautiful with fruit trees and wattles in bloom. There are 90 varieties of wild orchids found in the area. **Of interest:** Museum, High St. Art Gallery and Library Complex, Weeroona Park, Marsh St. Apple and Grape Harvest Festival held March (even-numbered years); Brass Monkey Month July; Spring Wine Festival Oct. **In the area:** Granite Belt wineries: Mt Magnus at Pozieres (14 km NW); Heritage at Cottonvale (12 km NW); Old Caves, just north of Stanthorpe; Granite Cellars Stone Ridge, Felsberg, Mountview and Kominos, near Glen Alpin (10 km S); Rumbalara at Fletcher (14 km S); Golden Grove, Winewood, Bungawarna and Robinson's Family Winery, near Ballandean (19 km S); Bald Mountain at Wallangarra (30 km S). Sunworld Park at Eukey, 13 km SE; displays of sun- and wind-powered instruments. Storm King Dam, 26 km SE; popular for canoeing and water-skiing. Mt Marlay for excellent views. Sundown National Park; wilderness area with camping on Severn River in south-west of park. Girraween National Park, 32 km S; camping, bushwalking, rock climbing and spectacular wildflower displays. **Tourist information:** 61 Marsh St; (076) 81 2057. **Accommodation:** 5 hotels, 6 motels, 3 caravan/camping parks. MAP REF. 123 L2, 475 L8

Strathpine   Pop. 10 108
Immediately behind Brisbane and to the north is the Pine Rivers Shire, a peaceful rural district that includes the closest forested areas and national parks to Brisbane. Taking advantage of this rural setting so close to the city are a number of art and craft industries. Brisbane's oldest and largest country market is held on Sun. at Albany Creek, 6 km S of Strathpine. Locally produced artworks, food and produce are sold while buskers entertain and craft demonstrations are given. **In the area:** Alma Park Zoo at Kallangur, 11 km N; Australian native animals, grizzly bears, camels and many other animals and birds. Friendship Farm for children features baby animals. Bunya Park Wildlife Sanctuary at Eatons Hill, 8 km SW; Australian native animals in typical bush setting. Samford Grass Ski, 15 km SW. Australian Woolshed at Ferny Hills, 16 km SW; shearing, spinning, trained rams, working sheepdogs, woolshed dancing and traditional

Girraween National Park, near Stanthorpe

Australian food. Bush dances with bush band. Number of national parks, and Brisbane Forest Park just minutes from Brisbane. **Tourist information:** Shire Offices, 220 Gympie Rd; (07) 205 0555. **Accommodation:** Limited. MAP REF. 462 C3

Tambo   Pop. 351
Tambo, 101 km SE of Blackall on the Matilda Hwy, was established in the mid-1860s. From a point where the town now stands, explorer Thomas Mitchell first saw the Barcoo River. **Of interest:** Old Post Office Museum, Arthur St. **In the area:** Salvator Rosa section of Carnarvon National Park, 120 km E; area named by Major Mitchell, who was reminded of landscapes painted by 17th-century artist. Access to park via Dawson Development Rd and Cungelella Station; 4WD recommended. Permission to camp in park must be obtained from Qld NPWS. **Tourist information:** Tambo News and Gear, Arthur St (Matilda Hwy); (076) 54 6288. **Accommodation:** 1 hotel, 1 hotel/motel, 1 motel, 1 caravan/camping park. MAP REF. 476 D12, 483 R12

Taroom   Pop. 705
Taroom is almost 300 km due W of Maryborough, on the Dawson River and Leichhardt Hwy. Cattle-raising is the main industry. **Of interest:** Coolibah tree in main street, marked 'L.L.' by Ludwig Leichhardt on his 1844 trip from Jimbour

House near Dalby to Port Essington (Darwin). Museum, Kelman St; old telephone exchange equipment, farm machinery, local history. Two-day Agricultural Show in May. Leichhardt Festival Sept. **In the area:** Rare Livistona palms near hwy 15 km N. Reedy Creek Homestead, 115 km NW; outback holidays on working cattle station. Isla Gorge National Park, 55 km N. Robinson Gorge, 108 km NW. **Tourist information:** Shire Offices, Yaldwyn St; (076) 27 3211. **Accommodation:** 1 hotel, 1 hotel/motel, 1 motel, 1 caravan/camping park. MAP REF. 474 H1

Texas   Pop. 816
Quite the opposite in size to its US namesake, Texas lies on the Dumaresque River and the Qld–NSW border, 55 km SE of Inglewood. **Of interest:** Historical Museum in old police station (1893). Agricultural show held July. **In the area:** Glenlyon Dam, 51 km SE; good fishing. **Tourist information:** 40 High St. **Accommodation:** 1 motel, 1 caravan/camping park. MAP REF. 123 J13, 475 J9

Theodore   Pop. 502
Grain and cotton are the main crops around this town on the Leichhardt Hwy, 220 km N of Miles. It was named after Edward Theodore, a Premier of Qld. **Of interest:** Theodore Hotel, The Boulevard; only cooperative hotel in Qld. Dawson Folk Museum, Second Ave. Fishing on Glebe Weir. **In the area:** Isla Gorge National Park, 35 km S. Cracow, 52 km SE, where gold was produced from famous Golden Plateau mine 1932–76. **Tourist information:** Callide St, Biloela; (079) 92 2405. **Accommodation:** 1 hotel, 1 caravan/camping park. MAP REF. 477 K12

Thuringowa   Pop. 36 000
Thuringowa is a growing city surrounding the city of Townsville. It depends not only on its established grazing and sugar industries but on such diversification as tropical fruit plantations, including mango and pineapple, extensive mixed vegetable farming, the Qld Nickel Refinery at Yabulu and, increasingly, tourism. Some of north Qld's best beaches, stretching along more than 120 km of coastline, provide visitors with surfing and fishing. **In the area:** Australian farm display at Alligator Creek, 18 km SE; also

The Channel Country

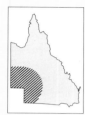

The remote Channel Country is an endless horizon of sweeping plains in Queensland's far-west and south-west corner. It seldom rains in the Channel Country itself, but after the northern monsoons the Georgina, Hamilton and Diamantina Rivers and Cooper Creek completely take over the country as they flood through hundreds of channels in their valiant efforts to reach Lake Eyre. There is scarcely any gradient. After the 'wet without rain', the enormous quantities of water carried by these rivers usually vanish into waterholes, saltpans and desert sands; lush grass, wildflowers and bird and animal life miraculously appear, and cattle are moved in for fattening.

The region is sparsely populated, except for large pastoral holdings and scattered settlements linked by very essential beef-roads. The Diamantina Development Road runs south from Mount Isa through Dajarra and Boulia to Bedourie, then swings east across the many channels of the Diamantina River and Cooper Creek through Windorah to the railhead at Quilpie, then on to Charleville, a journey of some 1335 kilometres.

Boulia, proclaimed the capital of the Channel Country, was first settled by Europeans in 1877. It is 305 kilometres south of Mount Isa and 365 kilometres west of Winton. A friendly, relaxed town on the Burke River, its name comes from an Aboriginal word meaning 'clear water'. Burke and Wills filled their water-bags here. The first mail service was by horse from Cloncurry, and a telegraph station was established in 1884.

Bedourie, 198 kilometres further south, is the administrative centre for the Diamantina Shire, and has a store, school, police station and Flying Doctor medical clinic. It has ample artesian water, without the usual pungent smell, and swimming is popular. The hotel serves petrol as well as beer.

South of Bedourie the Diamantina Road swings east for the partly sealed drive to **Windorah**, on Cooper Creek. The name means 'place of large fish'. During drought the area is a dustbowl, during the monsoonal period a lake. There is a good pub in town and sheep-raising is the only industry.

A good but narrow sealed road leads 237 kilometres east to **Quilpie**, the eastern gateway to the Channel Country. Cattle, sheep and wool are railed to the coast from here. The name derives from the Aboriginal word for the stone curlew, and all but one of the streets have birds' names. Opals have been found here since 1880. Although it is on the Bulloo River, the town's water supply is obtained from a near-boiling artesian bore.

The Kennedy Developmental Road from Winton to Boulia is sealed for most of its 256 kilometres. A welcome stop is the bush pub at Middleton. Visitors are sure to be told about the Min Min light, a totally unexplained phenomenon that often appears at night near the old Min Min pub, some 130 kilometres from Boulia. One theory says it is an earthbound UFO that chases cars and then disappears.

Betoota has one building (a pub) that basks in the centre of a very large, virtually featureless gibber plain. It is the only stop on the lonely 394-kilometre drive from Windorah to Birdsville, and Betoota can be truly welcome. The pub is open every day and sells fuel.

Birdsville, the most isolated settlement in Queensland, is 11 kilometres from the South Australian border, with the Simpson Desert to the west. It is at the top end of the Birdsville Track to Marree in South Australia.

Thargomindah is a small settlement on the eastern fringe of the Channel Country, 187 kilometres from Cunnamulla. Around the turn of the century Cobb & Co. was operating regularly to Cunnamulla, Hungerford, Charleville, Noccundra and Eromanga.

Noccundra, 142 kilometres even further west, has a permanent population of 3, but they can put you up at the pub and sell you petrol and car parts. Waterholes on the nearby Wilson River are the places for yellow-belly and catfish, brolgas, pelicans, emus and red kangaroos.

Visitors should realise that summer in the Channel Country can become unbearably hot. The best time to go is between April and October, and particularly for the wildflowers, which usually bloom in late August or early September.

For further information on the Channel Country, contact the Outback Qld Tourism Authority, Library Building, Shamrock St, Blackall; (076) 57 4255. **See also:** Individual town entries in A–Z listing.

Channel country

wildlife park at Billabong Sanctuary. Haughton River Company's Invicta Sugar Mill at Giru, 27 km SE. Tropical Agriculture Research Station at Lansdowne Station, Woodstock, 33 km S. Internationally recognised Australian Institute of Marine Science at Turtle Bay on Cape Bowling Green, 97 km SE. **Tourist information:** Bruce Hwy, Townsville; (077) 78 3555. **Accommodation:** 3 hotels, 2 hotel/motels, 1 motel, 5 caravan/camping parks.
MAP REF. 479 N12

Tin Can Bay – Rainbow Beach

Pop. 1355

Half an hour's drive north-east of Gympie takes travellers to Tin Can Bay and Rainbow Beach. These two hamlets are popular fishing, prawning and crabbing areas; the quiet waters of Tin Can Bay are ideal for boating and fishing, while Rainbow Beach has good surfing. **Of interest:** In Aug., Amamoor Creek State Forest Park in Mary Valley becomes 'home among the gum trees' when annual Country Music Muster is held. **In the area:** Road south from Rainbow Beach (4WD) leads to coloured sands and beaches of Cooloola National Park. North, at Inskip Point, ferry to Fraser Island. Fully equipped boats for hire at Carlo Point for cruising, fishing, swimming. **Tourist information:** 8 Rainbow Beach Rd, Rainbow Beach; (074) 86 3227. **Accommodation:** 1 hotel, 4 motels, 4 caravan/camping parks.
MAP REF. 475 N2

Toowoomba

Pop. 75 990

The garden city of Toowoomba has a distinctive charm and graciousness in its wide, tree-lined streets, colonial architecture and many fine parks and gardens. It is at its best in Sept. for the Carnival of Flowers. Toowoomba is 127 km W of Brisbane, on the rim of the Great Dividing Range. It began in 1849 as a village near an important staging post for teamsters and travellers, and was known as 'The Swamp'. Aborigines pronounced this as T'wamp-bah, or Toowoomba. Today it is the commercial centre for the fertile Darling Downs, with butter and cheese factories, sawmills, flour mills, tanneries, engineering and railway workshops, a modern iron foundry, clothing and shoe factories. It has an active cultural and artistic life. **Of interest:** Self-guide Russell St Heritage Walk. Cobb & Co. Museum, Lindsay St; traces history of horse-drawn vehicles. St Patrick's Cathedral (1880s), James St. St Luke's Anglican Church (1897), cnr Harries and Ruthven St. Parks include: Lake Annand, McKenzie St, for birdlovers; Laurel Bank, scented gardens; Botanic Gardens and adjacent Queens Park, Lindsay St; and Waterbird Habitat, McKenzie St. Ascot House (1870s), Newmarket St; teas, lunches. Royal Bull's Head Inn (1847), Brisbane St; fully restored by National Trust. Toowoomba Art Gallery, Linton Gallery and Gould Gallery, Ruthven St; Downs Gallery, Margaret St. Willow Springs Adventure Park, Spring St. **In the area:** Several self-guide scenic drives: many picnic spots on 48-km circuit to Spring Bluff and Murphy's Creek; railway station at Spring Bluff, although closed, has superb gardens; 100-km circuit to Heifer Creek, known as Valley of the Sun, provides some spectacular scenery; 255-km circuit takes in Bernborough Centre, Jondaryan Woolshed, Cecil Plains Cotton Ginnery, Millmerran Museum and Pittsworth Folk Museum. Picnic Point, 5 km E; mountain views and Carnival Falls. Balyarta Fragrant Gardens, Highfields Orchid Park, Danish Flower Art; all at Highfields, 15 km N. Talopea Gallery, Black Forest Hill Cuckoo Clock Centre; at Cabarlah, 20 km N. Acland Coal Mine Museum, near Oakey, 25 km NW. **Tourist information:** 541 Ruthven St; (076) 32 1988. **Accommodation:** 28 motels, 4 caravan/camping parks. **See also:** Tours from Brisbane; Darling Downs.
MAP REF. 466 F8, 475 L6

Townsville

Pop. 75 990

In 1864 a sea captain named Robert Towns commissioned James Melton Black to build a wharf and establish a settlement on Cleveland Bay to service the new cattle industry inland. Townsville was gazetted in 1865 and declared a city in 1903. Today Australia's largest tropical city, Townsville has an international airport and its rapid expansion is evidenced by the Sheraton Breakwater Island Casino-Hotel, The Breakwater Entertainment Centre and the Great Barrier Reef Wonderland, as well as the Victoria Bridge Complex and the Lakes Project. There are, however, many

Tin Can Bay

handsome historic buildings, particularly in the waterfront park area around Cleveland Bay. The city's busy port handles minerals from Mount Isa and Cloncurry; beef and wool from the western plains; sugar and timber from the rich coastal region; and its own manufacturing and processing industries. Townsville is the administrative, commercial, education and manufacturing capital of northern Qld. Among its impressive new public buildings is the James Cook University, which offers Australia's first tourism degree. Adjacent is the Institute of Education. A 20-min. catamaran trip across the bay takes you to Magnetic Island National Park and resort, or you may walk the length of the Strand with its tropical parks, waterfall and overhanging bougainvillea gardens. At the end of the Strand is the Rockpool development, which allows year-round swimming. Flinders Mall in the heart of the city has the Cotters Market every Sun. morning. Townsville is becoming a renowned centre for research into marine life and is the headquarters for the Great Barrier Reef Marine Park Authority. An annual attraction is the 10-day Festival of Townsville, Sept.–Oct. **Of interest:** Sheraton Breakwater Casino, Western Breakwater, end Flinders St. Great Barrier Reef Wonderland, Flinders St East; aquarium with touch-tank and walk-through transparent underwater viewing-tunnel, also Omnimax theatre. Billabong Sanctuary, entry from Muntalunga Dr; koala-feeding and crocodile shows. Museum of Tropical Queensland, Flinders St, adjacent to Wonderland. Perc Tucker Regional Art Gallery, Flinders Mall. Jezzine Military Museum, end The Strand. Copper refinery at Stuart; conducted tours. Queen's Gardens, cnr Paxton and Gregory Sts. Botanic Gardens, Kings Rd. Historic Flinders Street East. Castle Hill Lookout, off Burke St. Town Common Environment Park, Pallarenda Rd; coastline park. Maritime Museum, Palmer St, South Townsville. **In the area:** Four-day cruises to Cairns via resort islands and Reef on catamaran *Coral Princess*. Reef day trips and dive cruises. Day sailing around Magnetic Island. Daily connections to resort islands: Magnetic, Orpheus, Hinchinbrook, Dunk and Bedarra. Day outback tours, rainforest and whitewater rafting tours. Mt Spec, Crystal Creek National Park, Hidden Valley and Paluma, all 80–100 km NW. Mt Elliott National Park (25 km S), on Bruce Hwy,

Busy port of Townsville

and Pangola Park (32 km S) at Spring Creek, Giru; waterfalls, bush walks, swimming, picnic and camping facilities. Australian Institute of Marine Science at Cape Ferguson, 46 km S. **Tourist information:** Bruce Hwy; (077) 78 3555. **Accommodation:** 74 hotel/motels, 15 caravan/camping parks. **See also:** The Far North.
MAP REF. 471, 479 N12

Tully
Pop. 2715

Situated at the foot of Mt Tyson, Tully receives the highest annual rainfall in Australia, averaging around 4200 mm. Major industries are sugarcane, bananas, tropical fruit, cattle and timber. **Of interest:** Beautiful railway station, Booth Hwy; has profusion of tropical plants. **In the area:** Fishing, whitewater rafting, canoeing and reef and island cruising. Popular picnic spot on Tully River near Cardstone, 44 km W. Spectacular rainforests at Mission Beach and Clump Point (9 km NE), Bingil Bay (25 km NE), and Kareeya Gorge and Murray Falls (40 km S). **Tourist information:** Bruce Hwy; (070) 68 2288. **Accommodation:** 2 hotels, 1 motel, 1 caravan/camping park.
MAP REF. 479 L9

Warwick
Pop. 10393

An attractive city on the Darling Downs, Warwick is 162 km SW of Brisbane on the Cunningham Hwy, and 82 km S of Toowoomba on the New England Hwy. The area was first explored by Allan Cunningham in 1827; in 1840 the Leslie brothers arrived from the south and established a sheep station at Canning Downs, and other pastoralists followed. The NSW Government asked Patrick Leslie to select a site for a township, and in 1849 Warwick was surveyed and established. It was the first town, after Brisbane, in what became Qld. The railway line from Ipswich was opened in 1871, and Warwick became a city in 1936. In what seemed to be a minor incident in 1917, Prime Minister Billy Hughes was hit by an egg while addressing a crowd on the controversial conscription issue of the day. He asked a local policeman to arrest the man and the policeman refused. The result was the formation of the Commonwealth Police Force. Warwick is on the willow-shaded Condamine River, 453 m above sea level, and calls itself 'the Rose and Rodeo City'. The surrounding rich pastures support many famous horse and cattle studs, and produce some of Australia's finest wool and grain. Fruit, vegetables and timber grow well, and its dairy products and bacon are famous. **Of interest:** Pringle Cottage (1870), Dragon St; museum housing large photo collection, vehicles and machinery. Leslie Park in Palmerin St. Jubilee Gardens, cnr Alice and Helene Sts, for superb displays of

Whitsunday Passage

roses. Warwick Regional Art Gallery, Albion St. Antique and Collectables Fair in Jan. Rock Swap held Easter. Celebrated Warwick Rodeo in Oct. **In the area:** Leslie Dam, 15 km W, for water sports and picnics. Queen Mary Falls National Park, 45 km E via Killarney, and Carr's Lookout, a further 14 km. Main Range National Park, 50 km NE. Cherrabah Homestead Resort, 35 km E near Killarney. Richmond Homestead (c. 1898) and Talgai Homestead (c. 1860), both via Allora, 26 km N; accommodation and meals. Goomburra State Forest Park, east of Allora: Scenic Rim, Sylvester's Lookout, Mt Castle, the Hole in the Wall; picnic/barbecue facilities, camping. **Tourist information:** 49 Albion St (New England Hwy); (076) 61 3122. **Accommodation:** 13 hotels, 10 motels, 3 caravan/camping parks. **See also:** Darling Downs.
MAP REF. 123 M1, 466 F13, 475 L7

Weipa   Pop. 2510
Located on the west coast of Cape York, Weipa is home of the world's largest bauxite mine, operated by Comalco. This small mining town provides a comprehensive range of services and facilities for those travellers just wishing to visit or those calling in for urgently needed repairs or reprovisioning. **Of interest:** Guided tours of bauxite mine provide comprehensive coverage of whole mining process at Weipa. **In the area:** Tours of local areas such as Rocky Point, Trunding, Nanum and Evans Landing

also give insight into town's development and lifestyle. Number of fishing and camping areas near Weipa developed for well-equipped tourist. **Tourist information:** Cnr Grafton & Hartley Sts, Cairns; (070) 51 3588. **Accommodation:** Limited. **See also:** Cape York.
MAP REF. 480 B7

Whitsunday   Pop. 6093
Named by Captain Cook in 1770, Whitsunday Island (uninhabited) is the largest in the group. The mainland town of Whitsunday is one of Australia's fastest-growing tourist destinations. Whitsunday (including the suburbs of Airlie Beach, Cannonvale and Shute Harbour) depends on the tourism industry, and offers a large range of activities for 500 000 visitors each year. Stretching along 15 km of the coastline, Whitsunday town was gazetted in 1987. **Of interest:** Scenic and bush walks through areas behind town in Conway National Park. Whitsunday Festival of Sail held Aug.–Sept. Whitsunday Gamefishing Championships on June long weekend. Mardi Gras in Sept. Annual game-fishing tournament in Nov. **In the area:** Coral-viewing and tours of Great Barrier Reef and Whitsunday Islands. Extensive half- and full-day mainland tours, taking in Cedar Creek Falls, rainforests and other major attractions. **Tourist information:** Beach Plaza, The Esplanade, Airlie Beach; (079) 46 6673. **Accommodation:** 2 hotels, 20 motels, 7 caravan parks, 4 resorts.
MAP REF. 477 J2

Winton   Pop. 1156
Banjo Paterson wrote Australia's most famous song, 'Waltzing Matilda', on Dagworth Station near Winton in 1895. Combo Waterhole was then part of Dagworth, and the ballad had its first public airing in Winton. The town is 173 km NW of Longreach on the Matilda Hwy, and at the headwaters of the Diamantina River. A major sheep area, Winton is also a large trucking centre for the giant road trains bringing cattle from the Channel Country to the railhead. In 1920 the first office of a company called Qantas was registered in Winton. The town's water supply comes out of deep artesian bores at a temperature of 83°C. **Of interest:** Swagman statue near swimming-pool. Gift Gem Shop, Elderslie St; 'Opal Walk' set up in the shop. Qantilda Pioneer Place, Elderslie St, complex of 5 buildings; includes relocated Dagworth Station lounge room, Qantas Room, old telephone exchange, radio display, Aboriginal artefacts, steam locomotive, vintage vehicles and collection of 8000 bottles. Outback Festival held Sept. in odd-numbered years. **In the area:** Aboriginal paintings and bora ceremonial grounds at Skull Hole, 40 km S. Opalton, 115 km S; ghost town and gemfields. Lark Quarry Environmental Park, 110 km SW; preserves tracks of dinosaur 'stampede'. Combo Waterhole, 141 km NW via Matilda Hwy. Outback tours. Farm holidays at Lorraine Station, 60 km SE. **Tourist information:** Qantilda Pioneer Place,

Gulf Savannah

The Gulf Savannah is a vast, remote, thinly populated region stretching east to the Undara Volcanic National Park, north from **Mount Isa** and **Cloncurry** to the mangrove-covered shores of the Gulf of Carpentaria, and west to the Queensland–Northern Territory border. The unfortunate Burke and Wills were the first white visitors, although the waters of the Gulf itself were first charted by Dutch navigators almost 400 years ago. The country is flat and open and has more rivers than roads. April to October is the recommended time to see the Gulf country. During the monsoon period, generally November–March, rain may close the dirt roads and on rare occasions may flood the sealed roads from Cloncurry and **Julia Creek**. Motorists should realise that this is not 'Sunday-driving' country and should plan accordingly. The safest way to travel in the monsoon period is by air out of Cairns, Mount Isa or Karumba. The Gulf Savannah is, however, an ideal corner of Australia if you want to get away from it all, and the people are exceptionally friendly and helpful.

The wide expanses of the Gulf Savannah region divide themselves into separate areas. The **Eastern Savannah** is easily reached via the Great Top Road (Gulf Development Road), which winds up the eastern face of the Dividing Range, passing above Cairns. As an alternative route to Georgetown, or for travellers with limited time to explore the outback, the Undara Loop is a leisurely 3-day round trip from Cairns through the Lynd Junction, Einasleigh and Forsayth to Georgetown. **Georgetown**, 411 kilometres from Cairns, is the centre of the Etheridge Goldfield, where nuggets can still be found. Completing the loop back to Cairns takes the traveller to Tallaroo Hot Springs, Mt Surprise and Undara Volcanic National Park, where visitors can see the lava tubes, a geological phenomenon.

From Georgetown the traveller can head west 150 kilometres to Croydon, terminus of the railway from Normanton, a historic link established to service Croydon, a rich goldmining town of the last century.

Normanton is the central town of the whole Gulf Savannah, with a population of 1189, although in the gold days of 1891 it counted some 3000 people. The former goldmining town of **Croydon** is 151 kilometres to the east. The strangely isolated railway between the two towns is not connected to any other system. It is used once a week by the Gulflander, the famous tourist train, which leaves Normanton every Wednesday and Croydon every Thursday. Many of Croydon's buildings have been classified by the National Trust and the Australian Heritage Commission.

Karumba, 69 kilometres north of Normanton on the mouth of the Norman River, is the centre of the Gulf prawning industry and home to the barramundi fishing industry. Keen fishermen Australia-wide come to Karumba to try their skills in what is described as the best light-tackle gear fishing in Australia. Grunter, king salmon and blue salmon are plentiful, and northern Australia's top table and sporting fish, the barramundi, is to be found in estuaries, rivers and foreshore waters. Experts consider barramundi one of Australia's finest fish, and eaten fresh they are superb.

The **Western Savannah** has endless flat grassed plains stretching as far as the eye can see, while the wetlands around Karumba stretch across the top of the Western Savannah above Burketown and beyond to the border. Here rivers which are some 8 kilometres apart overflow their banks during the monsoons and form an unbroken sheet of water.

The town of **Burketown**, close to the Gulf, usually makes the headlines during round-Australia car trials or when it is flooded. It can be isolated for long periods

Lawn Hill National Park

during the wet. Explorers Leichhardt and Landsborough termed the surrounding area the 'Plains of Promise', and today, like most of the Gulf region, it is cattle country. Barramundi fishing and bird-watching attract adventurers; a well-equipped 4WD vehicle is advisable.

Lawn Hill National Park, 262 000 hectares of rare vegetation, incorporates the Riversleigh Fossil Field Section. The park is to the west of the **Gregory Downs Hotel**, a welcome watering-hole for the traveller. Here, 60-metre sheer sandstone walls form Lawn Hill Gorge with emerald green water at their base. The National Park Service has established 20 km of walking tracks to enable visitors to see safely this beautiful country.

When travelling on the sealed beef-road from Cloncurry to Normanton, motorists notice the Bang Bang Jump-up, a change in terrain height, 29 kilometres north of the Donors Hill Station turnoff.

Flight West operate regular flights from both Cairns and Mt Isa, and this is probably the best way to appreciate the vast beauty of the Gulf Savannah and its many sleepy, winding rivers.

Although towns in this area are fully serviced, motorists are advised to carry basic supplies of food and water in case of breakdown. Check local road conditions before departure from service points and, if possible, notify someone of your destination and expected time of arrival. ABC Radio also issues reliable road reports.

The Gulf Savannah is a new frontier in Australia that is opening up to those who are in search of interesting but authentic educational and adventure experiences. To assist visitors, an organisation of Savannah Guides has been formed. These guides are professional interpreters who have lived in the Gulf Savannah for many years and are able to offer a wide range of knowledge concerning the wilderness environment. There are guide stations at: Kowanyama Aboriginal Community; Hells Gate, 183 km west of Burketown; Undara Lava Lodge, Volcanic National Park, 144 kilometres east of Georgetown; and Adels Grove, Cape Crawford, NT (in Lawn Hill National Park), 109 km south-west of Borroloola NT.

For further information on the area, contact Savannah Guide Headquarters, 55 McLeod St, Cairns; (070) 51 4658 or (070) 31 1631. **See also:** Individual town entries in A–Z listing.

Elderslie St; (076) 57 1618. **Accommodation:** 4 hotels, 2 motels, 2 caravan/camping parks.
MAP REF. 483 L7

Wondai   Pop. 1156

This typical small country town in the South Burnett is 23 km S of Murgon and 31 km N of Kingaroy. The surrounding area produces peanuts and a variety of grains; other industries include dairying, beef and pork production, timber milling and dolomite mining. **Of interest:** Museum, Mackenzie St. **In the area:** Gem-fossicking areas surround district. Boondooma Dam, 50 km NW near Proston; recreation area and water sports. **Tourist information:** Shire Offices, Scott St; (071) 68 5155. **Accommodation:** 2 hotels, 1 hotel/motel, 1 motel, 1 caravan/camping park.
MAP REF. 475 L3

Yandina   Pop. 707

Yandina lies 10 km N of Nambour on the Bruce Hwy and is the home of the world-famous Ginger Factory and Gingertown, where visitors may enjoy ginger 'goodies'. The processing of the crop can be observed from the tower platform at the factory and the Ginger Bell paddlesteamer offers river cruises from the factory to a working ginger farm. **Of interest:** Carinya, historic homestead on Bruce Hwy on northern edge of town. The Queenslander; antiques and fascinating bric-a-brac. Wappa Dam, nearby; pleasant picnic spot. **In the area:** At Eumundi, 8 km N, Sat. morning country markets; goods range from locally grown fruit and vegetables to art and craft. Old and impressive Imperial Hotel, near markets. **Tourist information:** Cnr Aerodrome Rd and Sixth Ave, Maroochydore; (074) 79 1566. **Accommodation:** 1 hotel, 1 caravan/camping park.
MAP REF. 470 E6

Yeppoon   Pop. 7542

This popular coastal resort, 40 km NE of Rockhampton, lies on the shores of Keppel Bay. Yeppoon and the strip of beaches to its south—Cooee Bay, Rosslyn Bay, Causeway Lake, Emu Park and Keppel Sands—are known as the Capricorn Coast. Great Keppel Island Resort is 13 km offshore. **Of interest:** Yeppoon Pineapple Festival held Sept. **In the area:** Capricorn International Resort, 85 000-ha Japanese development, 8 km N. Cooberrie Park, 15 km N; noted flora and fauna reserve with picnic facilities. Byfield State Forest, 17 km further N; home of extremely rare Byfield fern, picnic facilities. Nearby at Waterpark Creek, Upper Stony and Red Rock. Catamaran service daily to Great Keppel Is., weekly to North West Island, largest coral cay on Great Barrier Reef. Coral Life Marineland, Kinka Beach, 13 km S; has unique living displays of coral and marine life. **Tourist information:** Ross Creek Roundabout; (079) 39 4888. **Accommodation:** 3 hotels, 1 hotel/motel, 8 motels, 3 caravan/camping parks.
MAP REF. 477 M8

Yungaburra   Pop. 807

On the edge of the Atherton Tableland, 13 km from Atherton and inland from Cairns, the town is known for its National Trust Historic Precinct listing. **Of interest:** Self-guide Historic Precinct Buildings walk. Rockhounds Shop, Cedar St; mineral display and gem-fossicking information. Artists Gallery, Mulgrave Rd. Produce and craft markets held 4th Sat. of each month, Mulgrave Rd. **In the area:** Curtain Fig Tree, 2.5 km SW; spectacular example of strangler fig. Lakes Eacham (5 km E) and Barrine (10 km E), volcanic crater lakes. **Tourist information:** Cnr Grafton & Hartley Sts, Cairns; (070) 51 3588. **Accommodation:** 1 hotel, 3 motels.
MAP REF. 473 E13

Rosslyn Harbour, Yeppoon

Queensland

Other Map Coverage
Central Brisbane 460
Brisbane Approach & Bypass Routes 461
Brisbane & Northern Suburbs 462
Southern Suburbs, Brisbane 464
Brisbane Region 466
Gold Coast Approach & Bypass Routes 468

Gold Coast Region 469
Sunshine Coast Region 470
Townsville 471
Cairns 472
Cairns Region 473

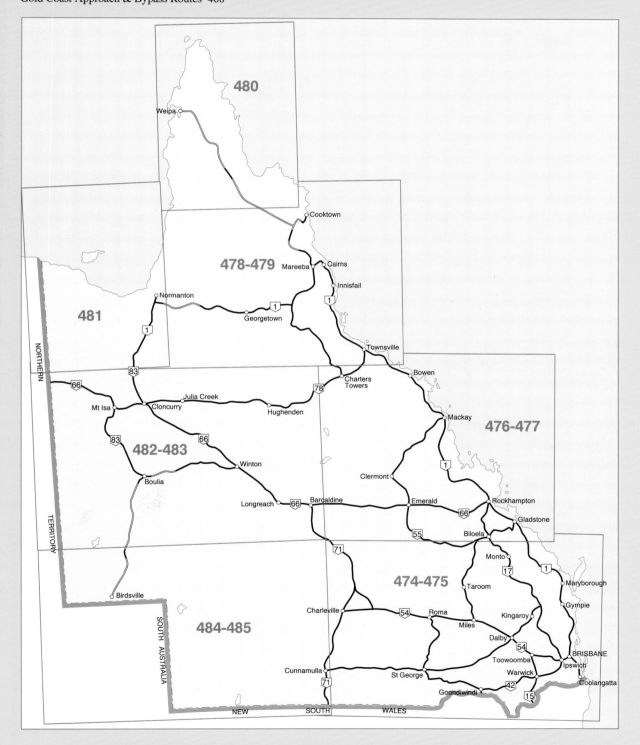

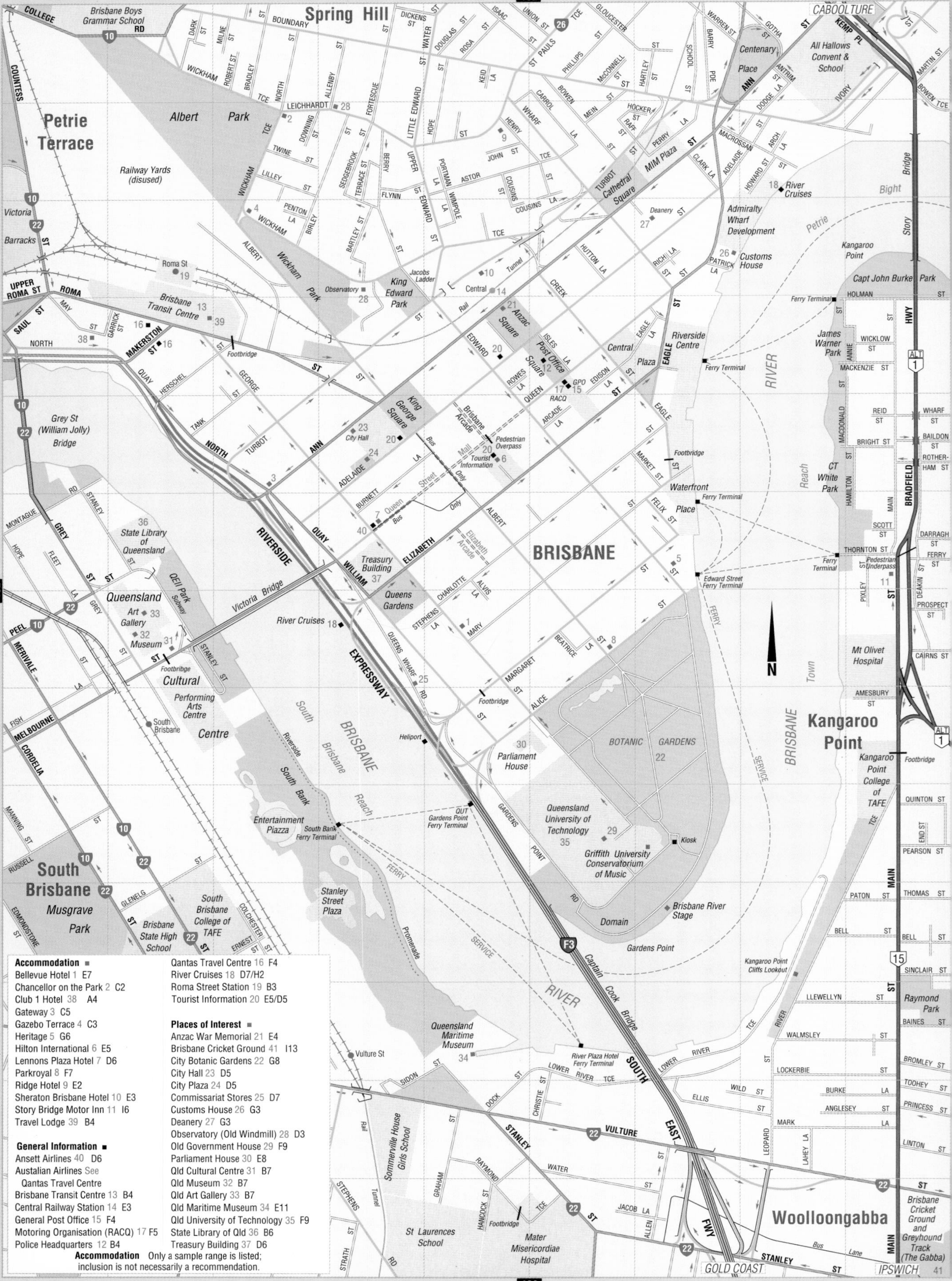

Spring Hill

Petrie Terrace

Albert Park

Railway Yards (disused)

Victoria Barracks

BRISBANE

Kangaroo Point

South Brisbane

Musgrave Park

Woolloongabba

Accommodation
Bellevue Hotel 1 E7
Chancellor on the Park 2 C2
Club 1 Hotel 38 A4
Gateway 3 C5
Gazebo Terrace 4 C3
Heritage 5 G6
Hilton International 6 E5
Lennons Plaza Hotel 7 D6
Parkroyal 8 F7
Ridge Hotel 9 E2
Sheraton Brisbane Hotel 10 E3
Story Bridge Motor Inn 11 I6
Travel Lodge 39 B4

General Information
Ansett Airlines 40 D6
Australian Airlines See
  Qantas Travel Centre
Brisbane Transit Centre 13 B4
Central Railway Station 14 E3
General Post Office 15 F4
Motoring Organisation (RACQ) 17 F5
Police Headquarters 12 B4

Qantas Travel Centre 16 F4
River Cruises 18 D7/H2
Roma Street Station 19 B3
Tourist Information 20 E5/D5

Places of Interest
Anzac War Memorial 21 E4
Brisbane Cricket Ground 41 I13
City Botanic Gardens 22 G8
City Hall 23 D5
City Plaza 24 D5
Commissariat Stores 25 D7
Customs House 26 G3
Deanery 27 G3
Observatory (Old Windmill) 28 D3
Old Government House 29 F9
Parliament House 30 E8
Qld Cultural Centre 31 B7
Qld Museum 32 B7
Qld Art Gallery 33 B7
Qld Maritime Museum 34 E11
Qld University of Technology 35 F9
State Library of Qld 36 B6
Treasury Building 37 D6

Accommodation Only a sample range is listed; inclusion is not necessarily a recommendation.

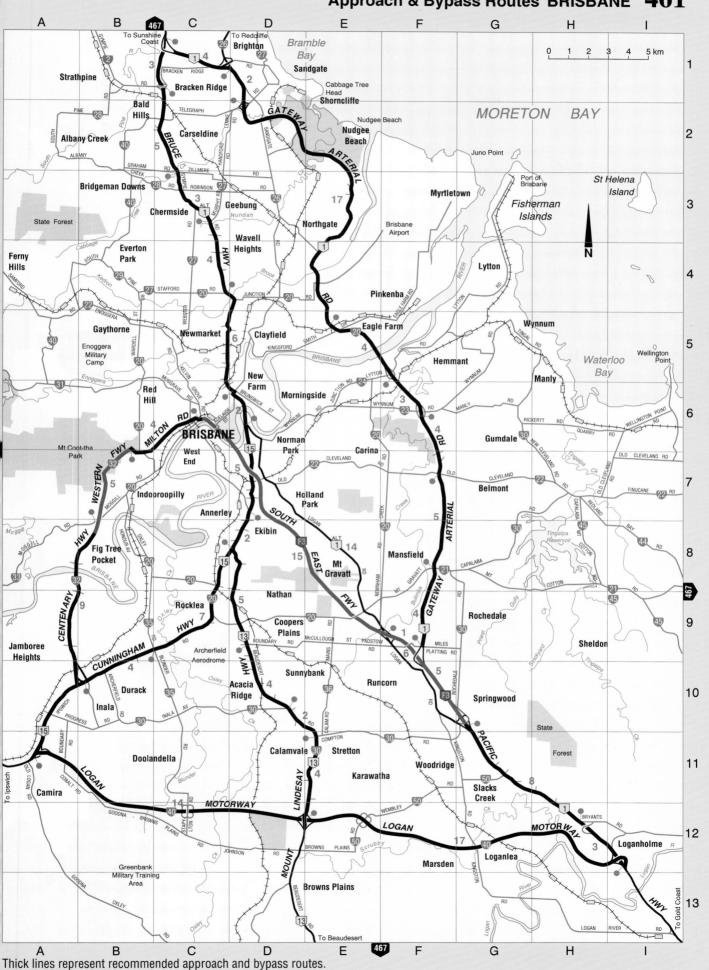

Thick lines represent recommended approach and bypass routes.

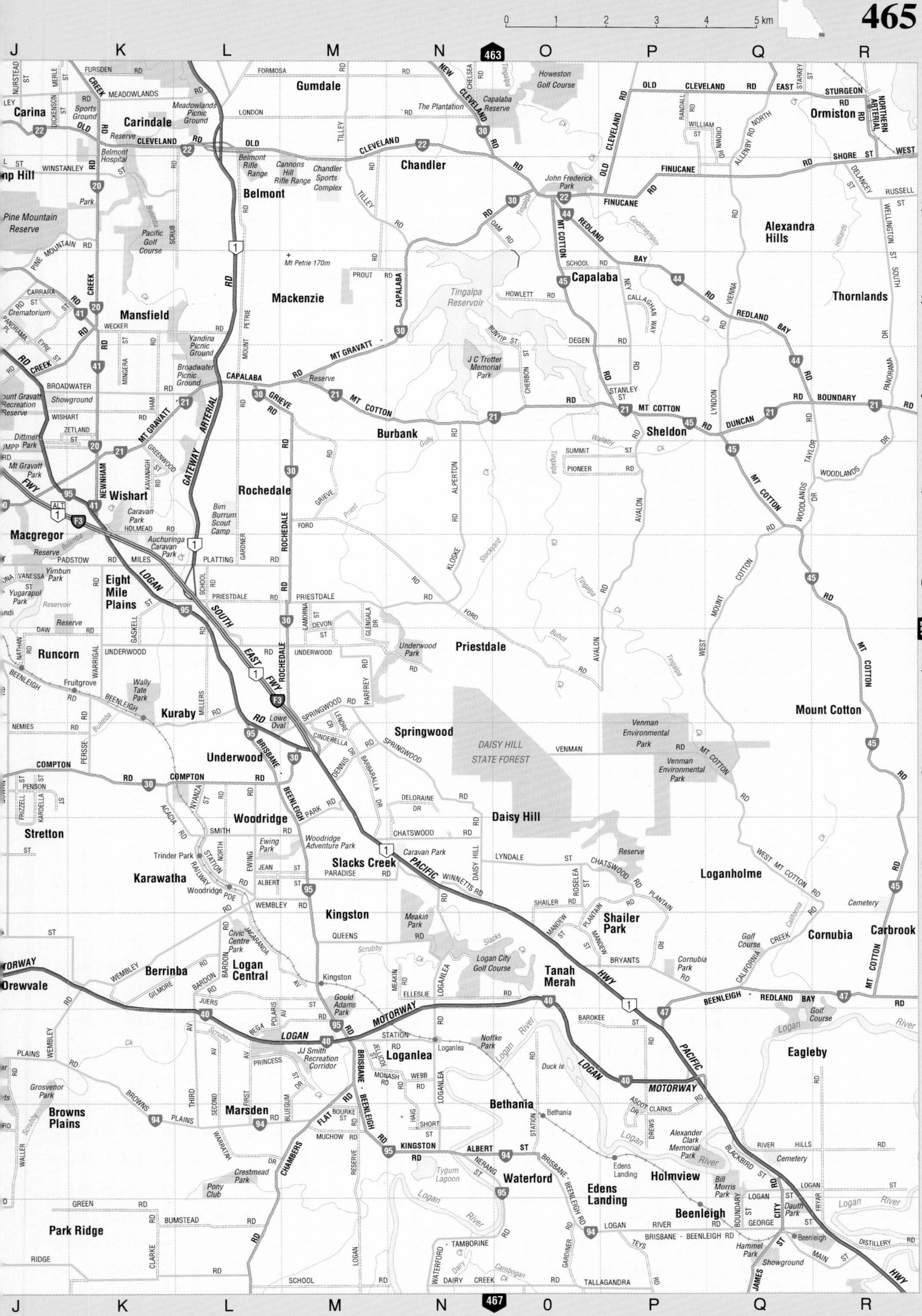

0 1 2 3 4 5 km
463
467
J K L M N O P Q R
1 2 3 4 5 6 7 8 9 10 11 12 13
Carina
Carindale
Gumdale
Chandler
Belmont
Ormiston
Alexandra Hills
Thornlands
Capalaba
Mackenzie
Mansfield
Burbank
Sheldon
Wishart
Rochedale
Macgregor
Eight Mile Plains
Runcorn
Priestdale
Kuraby
Springwood
Mount Cotton
Underwood
Daisy Hill
Woodridge
Stretton
Karawatha
Slacks Creek
Loganholme
Kingston
Shailer Park
Cornubia
Carbrook
Berrinba
Logan Central
Tanah Merah
Drewvale
Eagleby
Loganlea
Browns Plains
Marsden
Bethania
Waterford
Edens Landing
Holmview
Beenleigh
Park Ridge
Howeston Golf Course
Capalaba Reserve
The Plantation
Belmont Hospital
Belmont Rifle Range
Cannons Hill Rifle Range
Chandler Sports Complex
John Frederick Park
Pine Mountain Reserve
Pacific Golf Course
Mt Petrie 170m
Tingalpa Reservoir
Crematorium
Yandina Picnic Ground
Broadwater Picnic Ground
J C Trotter Memorial Park
Showground
Mt Gravatt Park
Caravan Park
Bim Burrum Scout Camp
Auchuringa Caravan Park
Yimbun Park
Yugarapul Park
Underwood Park
Wally Tate Park
Lowe Oval
DAISY HILL STATE FOREST
Venman Environmental Park
Ewing Park
Woodridge Adventure Park
Trinder Park
Meakin Park
Logan City Golf Course
Cornubia Park
Civic Centre Park
Gould Adams Park
JJ Smith Recreation Corridor
Noffke Park
Duck Is
Grosvenor Park
Alexander Clark Memorial Park
Bill Morris Park
Dauth Park
Crestmead Park
Pony Club
Tygum Lagoon
Hammel Park
Showground
Cemetery
Golf Course
GATEWAY ARTERIAL
LOGAN MOTORWAY
PACIFIC HWY
SOUTH EAST FWY
MT GRAVATT - CAPALABA RD
OLD CLEVELAND RD
MT COTTON RD
REDLAND BAY RD
BEENLEIGH - REDLAND BAY RD
BRISBANE - BEENLEIGH RD
Logan River

TO KINGAROY
TO KINGAROY
475
Cooranga North
Haly Mountain 956m
Mt Kiangarow 1146m
BUNYA MOUNTAINS NATIONAL PARK
ALICE CREEK
Ellesmere
Brooklands
Tarong
Meandu Creek
Tarong Power Station
BRISBANE
RANGE
South Nanango
Rocky Hill
17
Mt Monsildale 726m
Avoca Vale
Mt Spencer 445m
Linville

Bell
Mt Mowbullan 1106m
Wengenville
Pimpimbudgee
Maidenwell
Yarraman
Upper Yarraman
D'AGUILAR
COOYAR
RANGE
Neumgna
17
Blackbutt
Benarkin
BALFOUR
Moore
48
19
HWY

Jimbour
22
WARMGA
KOONDAI-I
UPPER KOONDAI-I
WOODLAWN
YAMSION
RANGEMORE
COOYAR CREEK UPPER
35
Cooyar
Kooralgin
Googa Googa
BLACKBUTT
Colinton
Nurinda
12

Kaimkillenbun
21
Squaretop
MALLING
Malling
WOODLEIGHTON
NUTGROVE
GREAT
6
Wutul
Woolshed Mtn 485m
BIARRA
Harlin
Yimbun
14
Toog

Moola
Maclagan
NARKO
THORNVILLE
DIVIDING
25
NEW
Mt Shem 631m
Mt Japheth 664m
ANDURAMBA
Sugarloaf 544m
RANGE
Ivory Ck
32

Quinalow
Peranga
EVERGREEN
MOUNT DARRY
DOCTORS CREEK
Cookes Hill 737m
ENGLAND
46
Mt Tin Tin 390m
Bluff Mtn 520m
THE BLUFF
Mt Deongwar 548m
Ottaba
BRISBANE

Dalby
54
BLAXLAND
IRVINGDALE
Kulpi
5
Haden
HWY
JONES GULLY
Virginia
Barnes Hill
Queen Mab Mtn 527m
Pinelands
733m
Kipper
Gallanani
Esk

KOMMAMURRA
AUCHMAH
Brymaroo
PLAIN VIEW
CAIRNS
MULDU
NEUVE
Crows Nest
Bald Hill No2 763m
CROWS NEST FALLS NATIONAL PARK
Cressbrook Dam
Mt Hallen

WARREGO
27
Bowenville
13
11
Acland
Coal Mine Museum
GREENWOOD
Goombungee
NARA
DOUGLAS
PECHEY
12
7
RANGE
Lake Perseverance
49
33
Buaraba
Mt Hallen 388m

21
Jondaryan
Woolshed
54
28
DEVON PARK
SABINE
BODDUA
Hampton
Ravensbourne
PERSEVERANCE
RAVENSBOURNE NATIONAL PARK
Buaraba Creek
Coo

Oakey
15
HWY
KELVINHAUGH
MUNIGAMEEN
Meringandan
32
13
Cabarlah
Mt Perseverance 807m
Mt Cross 625m
Murphys Creek
Yellow Gully 410m
Mount Taram

Norwin
MYWYBILLA
5
14
MOUNT IRVING
TANGKAM
YARGULLEN
Aubigny
Kingsthorpe
Highfields
GOWRIE
CAWDOR
19
Ballard
Byars Hill

BONGEEN
NORILLEE
Mount Tyson
11
Biddeston
8
29
WELLCAMP
16
POSTMANS RIDGE
LOCKYER
Lake Clarendon

LINTHORPE
IRONGATE
ROSSVALE
BEAUARABA
ATHOL
BUNKERS HILL
WESTBROOK
Withcott
19
Helidon
54
Gatton
WARREGO
13
Glenore Grove

Springside
WALLINGFORD
Southbrook
17
44
Bunkers Hill 633m
SHEPPERD
WYREEMA
VALE VIEW
21
TOOWOOMBA
35
CARPENDALE
LILYDALE
Tenthill
8
Winwill
Forest Hills
Plainland
Hat

YARRANLEA
Pittsworth
19
25
UMBIRAM
42
NEW
PRESTON
HODGSON VALE
STOCKYARD
FLAGSTONE CREEK
Ma Ma Creek
Ropeley
Woodlands
Blenheim
Laidley

Pampas
Brookstead
6
SUGARLOAF RAMSAY
Mt Campbell 719m
GREAT
Mount Whitestone
Upper Tenthill
Mt Bines 451m
Cal

Yandilla
Mt Perkins 673m
16
Greenmount
Emu Creek
BUDGEE
Mount Sibley
Mount Sylvia
Mount Berryman
INGOLSBY
Hidden Vale

Millmerran
TUMMAVILLE
SPRING LESLIES BRIDGE
Felton East
51
Mt Kent 602m
Nobby
WEST HALDON
Hirstglen
DIVIDING
Mt Cooper 712m
Mt Haldon 906m
JUNCTION VIEW
EAST HALDON
Mt Zahel 871m
Thornton
Mt Lowe 938m
Rosevale

FELTON SOUTH
BACK PLAINS
14
NEVILTON
12
PILTON
8
ENGLAND
Mt Phillips 910m
Mt Mistake 1092m
MISTAKE
MOUNTAINS
LITTLE

ELLANGOWAN
RYEFORD
Clifton
39
KINGS CREEK
SPRING CREEK UPPER
GREAT
Grass Tree Knob 805m
Kangaroo Mtn 770m

ROCKY CREEK
MOUNT EMLYN
Leyburn
11
VICTORIA HILL
ELPHINSTONE
SPRING CREEK
DIVIDING
RANGE
Mt Castle 1137m
MOUNT MISTAKE NATIONAL PARK
FRA

TALGAI
Allora
13
KITAL
BERAT
MAIN RANGE NATIONAL PARK
Mt Cordeaux 1135m
Mt Edwards
Lake Moogerah
Mou

Pratten
THANES CREEK
BONY MOUNTAIN
MT MARSHALL
Dalrymple
21
CUNNINGHAM
57
Mt Mitchell 1167m
18
Clintonvale
Freestone
Spicers Peak 1219m
Mt Grenville
Moo

Karara
CUNNINGHAM
42
GREYMARE
CUNNINGHAM
WILLOWVALE
UPPER FREESTONE
15
Mt Huntley 1265m
Mt Asplenium 1280m
CROI

TO GOONDIWINDI
475
Warwick
15
TO STANTHORPE
Leslie Dam

0 10 20 30 40 50 km

J K L M 475 N O P Q R

1

For more detail of Sunshine Coast see page 470

Sommer Mtn 789m
Mt Cabinet 732m +
Mt Denmark 732m +
CONONDALE NP
Bolloumba
Obi Obi
MAPLETON FALLS NP
KONDALILLA NP
Dulong
Flaxton
Nambour
Bli Bli
NINDERRY
TO NOOSA HEADS
Didillibah
Mt Langley 868m +
Mt Ramsden 792m +
CONONDALE RANGE
Donovans Knobs 662m
Witta
Hunchy
Woombye
Buderim
Maroochydore
Point Cartwright
Montville
Palmwoods
Mons
Forest Glen
Movie Museum
North West Mtn +599m
Mount Kilcoy
Mt Marysmokes 657m+
Mt McLean 465m
Reesville
Maleny
Wootha
Eudlo
Diamond Valley
Mooloolah
SUNSHINE COAST
MOOLOOLAH RIVER NP
Currimundi Environmental Park

2

Mt Kilcoy 351m
Stanmore
Booroobin
Bellthorpe
Crohamhurst
Bald Knob
Bald Knob 465m
Long Range Weather Forecasting Observatory
DULARCHA NP
Mt Mellum 404m+
Landsborough
Old Reptiles Fauna Park
Caloundra
Peachester
Coochin Ck
Beerwah
11
21

Kilcoy
KALANGARA
25
HWY
WINYA
Mt Beerwah 556m +
Mt Coonowrin 375m
Mt Ngungun 236m
Mt Tibrogargan 282m
Glass House Mountains
PUMICESTONE NATIONAL PARK

3

Glenfern
Neurum
Durundur
Woodford
Mt Beerburrum 276m
Beerburrum
36
North West Channel

Villeneuve
Mt Archer 460m
D'Aguilar
Mt Tunbubudla 294m
Donnybrook
Toorbul
White Patch
Bribie Island

4

Mt Delaney 373m
Delaneys Ck
Bracalba
Elimbah
Wamuran
Caboolture Historical Village
Mt Mee 495m
Campbells Pocket
Rocksberg
Caboolture
Morayfield
Moodlu
BANKSIA BEACH
Bellara
Woorim
North Point
Cape Moreton
MORETON ISLAND NATIONAL PARK

Lake Somerset
Mount Mee
40
23
Mt Byron + 617m
Mt Pleasant 524m
Mount Pleasant
Burpengary
Bongaree
Beachmere
Deception Bay
Skirmish Point
Bulwer
Cowan Cowan Point

5

Somerset Dam
Crossdale
Mt Sim Jue + 611m
Upper Laceys Creek
Dayboro
Narangba
FRESHWATER CREEK NP
Deception Bay
Rothwell Memorial
MORETON
Pearl Channel
Tangalooma
Mt Tempest 280m
SOUTH
Moreton Island

D'AGUILAR RANGE
Bryden
Dundas
Brisbane Forest Park
Mt D'Aguilar 742m +
Mt Samson 742m
Mt Samson
Mt Lawson 473m
Closeburn
Dakabin
Kallangur
Redcliffe
Scarborough
Margate
Moreton Island Tourist Resort

6

For more detail of Brisbane Suburbs see pages 462-465

Hydro Power Station
Mt Glorious
Upper Cedar Creek
Yugar
Highvale
Samford
Lawnton
Strathpine
CASHS CROSSING
SANDGATE
Bramble Bay
BAY

CABBAGE TREE RANGE
CHERMSIDE
BRISBANE
AIRPORT
NEWMARKET
FORT LYTTON NP
ST HELENA ISLAND NP
Fisherman Islands
St Helena Island
Mud Island
PACIFIC

7

Fernvale
Wanora
Borallon
Mt Crosby
INDOOROOPILLY
BRISBANE
MORNINGSIDE
WYNNUM
WELLINGTON POINT
Amity Point
KOORINGAL

8

Marburg
Walloon
Rosewood
IPSWICH
CAPALABA
Cleveland
Old Court House
Peel Island
Dunwich
Rocky Point
Capt. Cook Memorial
Point Lookout
WILD FLOWER RESERVE
Mt Hardgrave 219m
Blue Lake Beach

SOUTHERN IPSWICH BYPASS
Ebenezer
Loamside
Ripley
Purga
SUNNYBANK
LOGAN
Victoria Point
Redland Bay
Gemstone Display
Lamb Island
Macleay Island
BLUE LAKE NATIONAL PARK
North Stradbroke Island
OCEAN

9

Peak Crossing
Mt Goolman + 454m
Mt Blaine + 457m
GREENBANK MILITARY TRAINING AREA
LOGAN CITY
BETHANIA JUNCTION
Loganholme
Eagleby
Alberton
Russell Island
Native Companion Lagoon
Ibis Lagoon

10

Flinders
Mt Elliot 436m
Harrisville
Limestone Ridge
Mt Welcome 332m
Maclean Bridge
Waterford
BEENLEIGH
Yatala
Rum Distillery
Steiglitz
Woongoolba
Cabbage Tree Point
Fish Habitat Reserve

11

Roadvale
MUNBILLA
Kagaru
Cedar Grove
Jimboomba
Wolfdene
Dog Monument
Ormeau
Norwell
Jacobs Well
South Stradbroke Island
Santa Barbara
Sanctuary Cove
Couran

12

Boonah
Milford
Sugarloaf + 408m
Veresdale
Woodhill
Gleneagle
Mt Dunsinane 322m
Boyland
Tamborine Village
Nth Tamborine
Eagle Heights
Mt Tamborine
Maudsland
Oxenford
Movie World
Upper Coomera
Dreamworld
Boyankil
Currigee
Sea World
Fishermans Wharf
MAIN BEACH
Southport
Surfers Paradise
GOLD

13

For more detail of Gold Coast see page 469

Bromelton
Beaudesert
Boys Town
Josephville
Mt Mahomet 445m
Laravale
Kerry
Tabooba
Canungra
Witheren
Gilston
Advancetown
Mudgeeraba
Wongarra
Nerang
Mt Nathan 938m
Bond University
BROADBEACH
GOLD COAST
BURLEIGH HEADS
BURLEIGH HEADS NP

Beechmont
Tallebudgera
TO TWEED HEADS

J K L M 475 N O P Q R

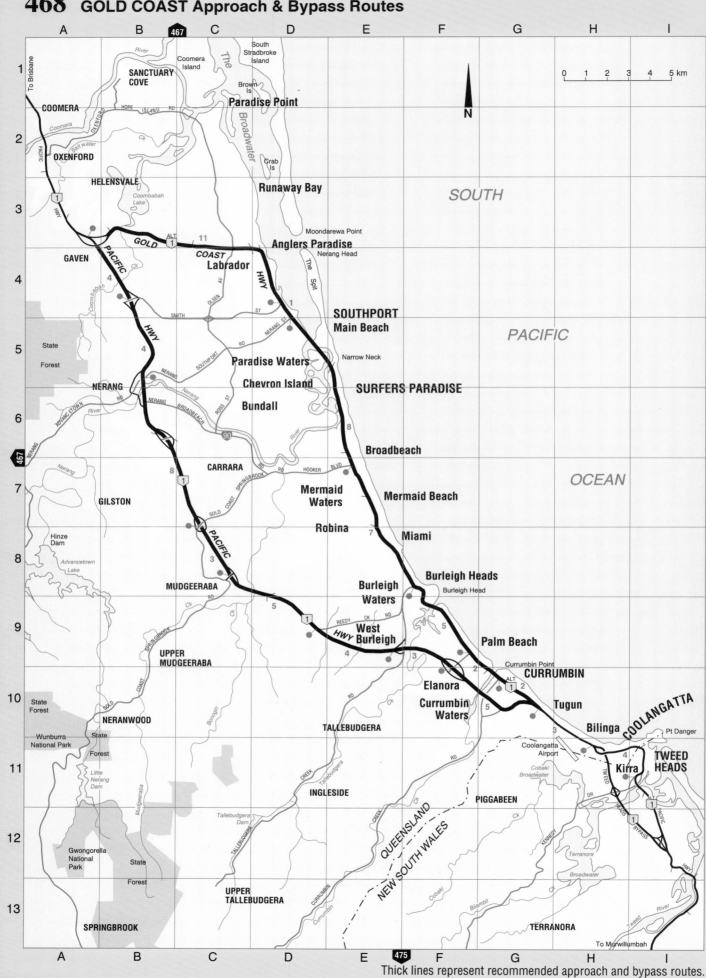

Thick lines represent recommended approach and bypass routes.

0 2 4 6 8 10 km

DREAMWORLD: A family oriented entertainment complex set amid landscaped gardens & natural bushland. It features various exciting rides, a computerised animated koala theatre, a water playground, specialty shops and a restaurant.

SANCTUARY COVE: Exclusive residential resort with waterfront shopping village, marina, golf courses, tennis complex & Hyatt Regency Hotel.

WARNER BROS MOVIE WORLD: Based on the world-famous Hollywood movie set, it is a theme park as part of a fully operational movie studio.

SOUTH STRADBROKE ISLAND: Cruises leave from Southport for this uninhabited island.

WET 'N' WILD WATER PARK: An amazing variety of waterslides and pools set in a landscaped barbeque and picnic area.

NERANG: A pleasant town on the Nerang River. Further inland, the Nerang River valley has attractive picnic spots and swimming holes.

TOURIST INFORMATION:
Coolangatta (Marine Parade)
Surfers Paradise (Cavill Mall)

ADVANCETOWN LAKE: Sailing (no power boats), picnic and barbeque facilities, scenic drives and the Hinze Dam.

WAR MUSEUM: Indoor & outdoor displays of army memorabilia, military equipment & adventure games.

CURRUMBIN SANCTUARY: Australian fauna, including waterbirds, koalas and kangaroos. Visitors can feed the brightly coloured lorikeets twice daily.

PURLINGBROOK FALLS: One of the most spectacular falls in the hinterland. Resorts such as Binna Burra and O'Reillys are in the nearby Lamington National Park.

OLSON'S BIRD GARDENS: Exotic pheasants, colourful parrots and tiny finches are displayed in huge walk - through landscaped aviaries.

THE SETTLEMENT: Historical village created with genuine pioneer buildings faithfully restored and furnished.

TO BRISBANE

SOUTH STRADBROKE ISLAND

SOUTH PACIFIC OCEAN

Coomera
Oxenford
Helensvale
Nerang
Southport
Surfers Paradise
Broadbeach
Mermaid Beach
Miami
Burleigh Heads
Palm Beach
Currumbin
Elanora
Tugun
Bilinga
Coolangatta
Tweed Heads
Mudgeeraba
Advancetown
Springbrook

N

TO MURWILLUMBAH

0 2 4 6 8 10 km

A **B** **C** **D** **E** 475 **F** **G** **H** **I**

TO GYMPIE

Pomona

Mt Cooroora

YUROL STATE FOREST

BRUCE

Black Mtn

BLACK MOUNTAIN

Cooroy

Mt Cooroy

RANGE

HIGHWAY

RD

Mt Eerwah

Eumundi

Eumundi Brewery
Eumundi Markets

Mt Tinbeerwah

Lake MacDonald

TINBEERWAH

TEWANTIN STATE FOREST

TEWANTIN

Noosaville

NOOSA

NOOSA-TEWANTIN: A highly developed tourist infrastructure of restaurants, boutiques, apartment-style accommodation & resorts have not impacted on the area's great natural beauty. Drive up Viewland Drive to Laguna Lookout for a spectacular view of the area.

Lake Cooroibah

Laguna Bay

NOOSA RIVER

NOOSA NATIONAL PARK: This 430 hectare coastal park contains a network of walking tracks that wind through rainforest, giving spectacular views of the ocean and several unusual rock formations.

North Head

Dolphin Point

Noosa Heads

Alexandria Bay
Roaring Caves
Devils Kitchen
Cooks Monument

Laguna Lookout

Coral

NOOSA AIRPORT

EUMUNDI

DOONAN

Lake Weyba

LAKE WEYBA

Marcus Beach

Sea

NOOSA NATIONAL PARK

Peregian Beach

DAVID LOW WAY

Thunder Egg Farm

NORTH

STATE FOREST

MAROOCHY

TOURIST INFORMATION:
Alexandra Headland (Alexandra Pde)
Caloundra (Caloundra Rd)
Maroochydore (Cnr Aerodrome Rd & Sixth Ave)
Noosa Heads (Hastings St)
Woombye (Sunshine Plantation, Bruce Hwy)

KENILWORTH

BLACKALL

STATE FOREST

BELLI PARK

Belli

Gheerulla

North Arm

Mt Bottle & Glass

Cedar

Cooloolabin Dam

COOLOOLABIN

KIAMBA

Rocky

Wappa Dam

Ginger Factory

Yandina

Mt Combe

Kiamba Falls

STATE FOREST

Poona Dam

Mt Ninderry

YANDINA: The home of the world-famous ginger factory and Gingertown, where visitors may partake of ginger "goodies". The processing of the crop can be observed from the tower platform at the factory and the Ginger Bell Paddlesteamer offers river cruises from the factory to a working ginger farm.

YANDINA

MAROOCHY RIVER

MAROOCHY RIVER

Mt Peregian (Emu Mtn)

ENVIRONMENTAL PARK

SOUTH

COOLUM

Coolum Beach

Point Perry

Point Arkwright

Yaroomba

PACIFIC

Mt Coolum 208m
MOUNT COOLUM NP

Marcoola Beach

SUNSHINE MOTORWAY

DAVID LOW WAY

Connors Knob

MAPLETON FALLS NATIONAL PARK

KIDAMAN CREEK

OBI OBI

Mapleton

NAMBOUR

MAPLETON RD

Dulong

Nambour

Flaxton Gardens

Model English Village

KURREELPA

NAMBOUR: The centre of the sugar industry on the Sunshine Coast. The sugar mill is open for public tours (July - Nov.) and cane trains can be seen during harvest time rattling through the town carrying their loads to the mill.

HIGHWAY

Bli Bli

Bli Bli Castle
Nostalgia Town

DIDILLIBAH

MUDJIMBA

Mudjimba Island

MAROOCHY AIRPORT

MAROOCHY RIVER

Twin Waters Resort

Channel Island
Goat Island
Pincushion Island

Endeavour Replica

Maroochydore

HINTERLAND: The inland towns including Mapleton, Flaxton, Montville, Maleny and Palmwoods are renowned for their galleries, antique shops, craft shops, inns, guest-houses and tea shops. The surrounding area is particularly scenic and ideal for bushwalking and picnicking. Note that the road linking Palmwoods and Montville is steep and winding.

Witta

KENILWORTH

MALENY

Flaxton

KONDALILLA NP

Kondalilla Falls

OBI OBI GORGE NP

HUNCHY

Petrie

Macadamia Nut Factory

Woombye

Big Pineapple

Moonshine Valley Winery

MONS

Deer Sanctuary

MAROOCHYDORE

SUNSHINE MOTORWAY

Buderim

ALEXANDRA HEADLAND

Mooloolaba

Underwater World

BUDDINA

STATE FOREST

Montville

Montville Art Galleries

RANGE

ROAD

Baroon Pocket Dam

THE BIG PINEAPPLE: This 16 m high fibreglass replica of a pineapple is one of the best-known landmarks on the Sunshine Coast and is situated on an 112-hectare subtropical plantation. Other attractions include train rides, Nutmobile rides to the Macadamia Nut Factory, boat tours, restaurants and a tropical fruit market.

Forest Glen

MONTVILLE RD

WOOMBYE

Paynter

BUDERIM: Fertile red soil and a warm climate combine to establish the prize-winning gardens evident through-out this delightful village. Nearby Buderim Forest Park and Foote Sanctuary have bushwalking tracks through the rainforest.

Super Bee Honey Factory
TANAWAH

MOOLOOLAH RIVER NATIONAL PARK

MOTORWAY

WARANA

Maleny

Howells Knob Lookout

REESVILLE

MALENY

MONTVILLE ROAD

MOOLOOLAH

Eudlo

Mooloolah River

Mt Sippy 180m+

RANGE

Ettamogah Village

PALM VIEW

Suncoast Crayfish Farm

SUNSHINE MOTORWAY

BOKARINA

WURTULLA

Currimundi Environmental Park

CURRIMUNDI

Mary Cairncross Park

Landsborough

Bald Knob 465m

MALENY

DIAMOND VALLEY

Mooloolah

WOOTHA

MARY CAIRNCROSS PARK: Considered the best vantage point in the Blackall Range for spectacular views that extend back to the coast. The park also features walking tracks through the rainforest.

BALD KNOB

STATE FOREST

DULARCHA NP

Ewen Maddock Dam

Mooloolah River

CALOUNDRA RD

Racecourse

NICKLIN WAY

Golf Course

Moffat Head

Caloundra

Queensland Air Museum

CALOUNDRA AIRPORT

Caloundra Airport

CONNONDALE

BOOROOBIN

Stanley

Long Range Weather Forecasting Observatory

CROHAMHURST

RANGE

BELLTHORPE STATE FOREST

GLASS HOUSE MOUNTAINS: A group of 13 volcanic peaks that dominate the landscape ten km south of Landsborough. Formed by giant cores of long-extinct volcanoes they were first sighted by Captain Cook in 1770. Four of them - Mounts Coonoowrin, Beerwah, Tibrogargan and Ngungun - are national parks.

Historical Museum

GLASSHOUSE MOUNTAINS STATE FOREST

Landsborough

BRUCE

Peachester

TO BRISBANE

467

CALOUNDRA: A popular holiday destination, renowned for its relaxed lifestyle and beaches. Pumicestone Passage is a haven for all types of water sports, famous for its fishing, and harbours Bulcock Beach and Golden Beach, two of the safest beaches on the Sunshine Coast.

KINGS BEACH
Deepwater Point

Bribie Island

Pumicestone Passage

OCEAN

N

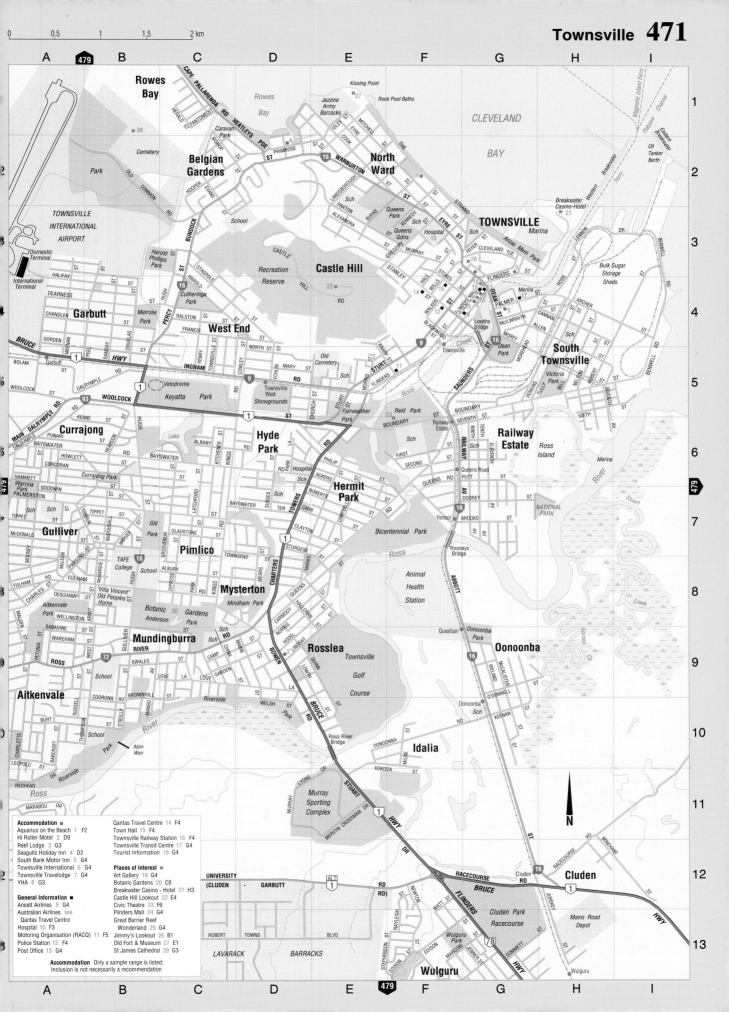

Accommodation ■
Aquarius on the Beach 1 F2
Hi Roller Motel 2 D9
Reef Lodge 3 G3
Seagulls Holiday Inn 4 D2
South Bank Motor Inn 5 G4
Townsville International 6 G4
Townsville Travelodge 7 G4
YHA 8 G3

General Information ■
Ansett Airlines 9 G4
Australian Airlines see
 Qantas Travel Centre
Hospital 10 F3
Motoring Organisation (RACQ) 11 F5
Police Station 12 F4
Post Office 13 G4

Qantas Travel Centre 14 F4
Town Hall 15 F4
Townsville Railway Station 16 F4
Townsville Transit Centre 17 G4
Tourist Information 18 G4

Places of Interest ■
Art Gallery 19 G4
Botanic Gardens 20 C8
Breakwater Casino - Hotel 21 H3
Castle Hill Lookout 22 E4
Civic Theatre 23 F6
Flinders Mall 24 G4
Great Barrier Reef
 Wonderland 25 G4
Jimmy's Lookout 26 B1
Old Fort & Museum 27 E1
St James Cathedral 28 G3

Accommodation Only a sample range is listed;
Inclusion is not necessarily a recommendation

A B C D E F G H I

Accommodation ■
All Seasons Sunshine Tower 1 G8
City Caravan Park 2 F8
Hilton Hotel 3 I9
Holiday Inn 4 H8
Pacific Coast Guest House 5 H10
Pacific International 6 I9
Radisson Plaza 7 I9
Tuna Towers 8 H8
Youth Hostels 9 H9,H10

General Information ■
Ansett Airlines 10 H9
Australian Airlines See
  Qantas Travel Centre
Bus Station 11 I10
Cairns and Far North
  Environment Centre 12 E7
Cairns Railway Station 13 H10
Hospital 14 G8
Motoring Organisation (RACQ) 15 I9
Police 16 I9
Post Office 17 I9
Qantas Travel Centre 18 I9
Tourist Information 19 H9

Places of Interest ■
Flecker Botanic Gardens 20 D6
Hides of Cairns Hotel 21 H9
Museum 22 H9
Marlin Jetty 23 I9
Royal Flying Doctor Service 24 C6
The Pier 25 I9

Accommodation Only a sample range
is listed; inclusion is not necessarily a
recommendation.

0   0,5   1   1,5   2

Barron River Bridge
Barron River
Mangroves
Northern Treatment Works
GREENBANK RD
CAPTAIN COOK
Stratford
Aeroglen
KAMERUNGA RD
Savina Park
Mount Whitfield
Lumley Hill
Mt Whitfield Environmental Park

CAIRNS INTERNATIONAL AIRPORT
N

PORT OF CAIRNS
CAIRNS HARBOUR

Whitfield
Gloucester St
Aeroglen
AEROGLEN DR
AIRPORT AV

Edge Hill
Flecker Botanic Gardens
Centenary Lakes
Edge Hill Primary School
Stan Williams Park
Behan Soccer
Cemetery

Cairns North
SHERIDAN ST
ESPLANADE

CAIRNS
Stafford Point
Marlin Marina
The Pier 25
Boat Ramp

Manoora
Manunda
Parramatta Park
Trinity Bay High School
College of Technical & Further Education
Griffiths Park
Primary School

Parramatta Park Showground
B.M.X. Track
Barlow Park

Westcourt
Koppen Park
Sports Ground
Bungalow
HMAS Cairns Naval Patrol Boat Base

Mooroobool
Earlville
BRUCE HWY
MULGRAVE RD
Portsmith

Cannon Park Racecourse
Admiralty Island
TRINITY INLET
Mangroves

A B C D E F G H I

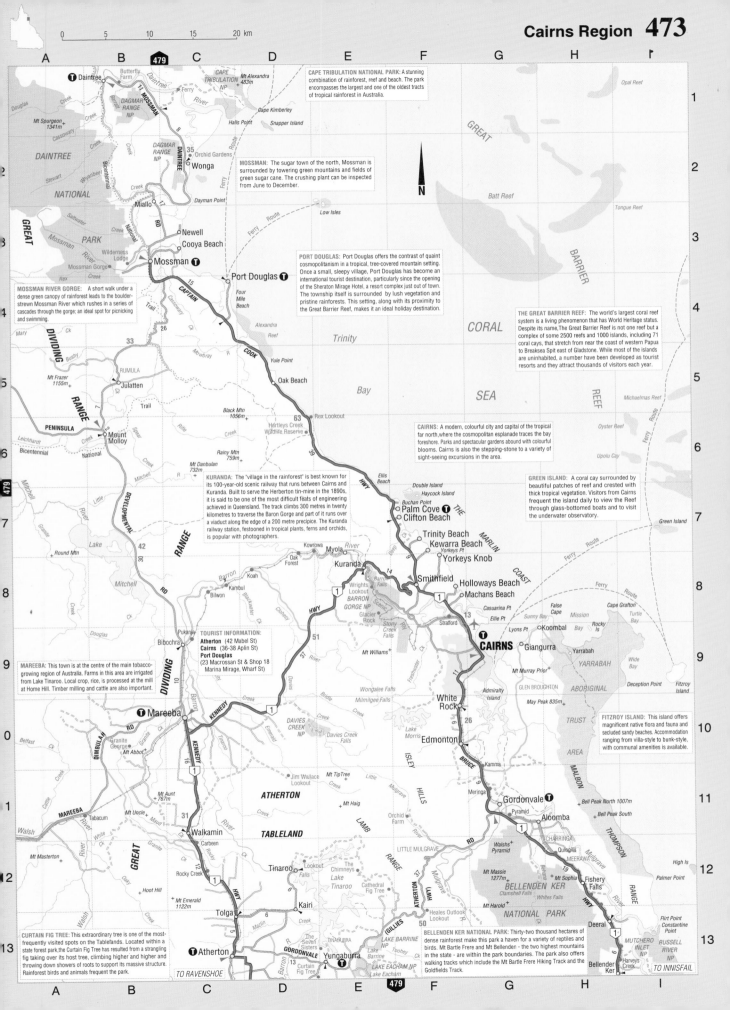

0   5   10   15   20 km

479

CAPE TRIBULATION NATIONAL PARK: A stunning combination of rainforest, reef and beach. The park encompasses the largest and one of the oldest tracts of tropical rainforest in Australia.

MOSSMAN: The sugar town of the north, Mossman is surrounded by towering green mountains and fields of green sugar cane. The crushing plant can be inspected from June to December.

PORT DOUGLAS: Port Douglas offers the contrast of quaint cosmopolitanism in a tropical, tree-covered mountain setting. Once a small, sleepy village, Port Douglas has become an international tourist destination, particularly since the opening of the Sheraton Mirage Hotel, a resort complex just out of town. The township itself is surrounded by lush vegetation and pristine rainforests. This setting, along with its proximity to the Great Barrier Reef, makes it an ideal holiday destination.

THE GREAT BARRIER REEF: The world's largest coral reef system is a living phenomenon that has World Heritage status. Despite its name, The Great Barrier Reef is not one reef but a complex of some 2500 reefs and 1000 islands, including 71 coral cays, that stretch from near the coast of western Papua to Breaksea Spit east of Gladstone. While most of the islands are uninhabited, a number have been developed as tourist resorts and they attract thousands of visitors each year.

MOSSMAN RIVER GORGE: A short walk under a dense green canopy of rainforest leads to the boulder-strewn Mossman River which rushes in a series of cascades through the gorge; an ideal spot for picnicking and swimming.

CAIRNS: A modern, colourful city and capital of the tropical far north, where the cosmopolitan esplanade traces the bay foreshore. Parks and spectacular gardens abound with colourful blooms. Cairns is also the stepping-stone to a variety of sight-seeing excursions in the area.

KURANDA: The "village in the rainforest" is best known for its 100-year-old scenic railway that runs between Cairns and Kuranda. Built to serve the Herberton tin-mine in the 1890s, it is said to be one of the most difficult feats of engineering achieved in Queensland. The track climbs 300 metres in twenty kilometres to traverse the Baron Gorge and part of it runs over a viaduct along the edge of a 200 metre precipice. The Kuranda railway station, festooned in tropical plants, ferns and orchids, is popular with photographers.

GREEN ISLAND: A coral cay surrounded by beautiful patches of reef and crested with thick tropical vegetation. Visitors from Cairns frequent the island daily to view the Reef through glass-bottomed boats and to visit the underwater observatory.

TOURIST INFORMATION:
Atherton (42 Mabel St)
Cairns (36-38 Aplin St)
Port Douglas
(23 Macrossan St & Shop 18
Marina Mirage, Wharf St)

MAREEBA: This town is at the centre of the main tobacco-growing region of Australia. Farms in this area are irrigated from Lake Tinaroo. Local crop, rice, is processed at the mill at Home Hill. Timber milling and cattle are also important.

FITZROY ISLAND: This island offers magnificent native flora and fauna and secluded sandy beaches. Accommodation ranging from villa-style to bunk-style, with communal amenities is available.

CURTAIN FIG TREE: This extraordinary tree is one of the most-frequently visited spots on the Tablelands. Located within a state forest park, the Curtain Fig Tree has resulted from a strangling fig taking over its host tree, climbing higher and higher and throwing down showers of roots to support its massive structure. Rainforest birds and animals frequent the park.

BELLENDEN KER NATIONAL PARK: Thirty-two thousand hectares of dense rainforest make this park a haven for a variety of reptiles and birds. Mt Bartle Frere and Mt Bellenden - the two highest mountains in the state - are within the park boundaries. The park also offers walking tracks which include the Mt Bartle Frere Hiking Track and the Goldfields Track.

TO RAVENSHOE   **479**   TO INNISFAIL

476

477

A B C D E F G H I

1
Landsborough
103
Murphy Tableland
Mt Ogilby 700m
Carnarvon
Expedition National Park
Mt Round 460m
Precipice NP
Cracow
Aubur
Mt Weldon 660m
Broadmere
Lonesome NP
Lynd Range
River
87

2
87 Augathella
Chesterton Range
Mt Boyd 614m
Mt Hotspur 696m
101
Mt Hutton 914m
Injune
Durham Downs
53
Great
68
Taroom
278
59
112
84
90 Hwy
Developmental Road
Wandoan
Guluguba
Leichhardt

3
Charleville 89 54
Warrego
Morven 44
Mungallala 176
Mitchell Hwy
18
36
Roma
82
Mt Combabula 354m
81
66
Dividing
Range
Royal Flying Doctor Base & Visitors Centre
71
Amby
Muckadilla
Mineral Hot Springs
87
Wallumbilla
54 44 Yuleba
Jackson 140 Dulacca
Drillham 55
Miles
45
Chinc

4
99 Hwy
79
Bonus Downs
35
45
55
33
114
58
125
39
Range
Condamine
37

5
71
Wyandra
43
Boatman Bore
202 Creek
Albany Downs
210
Surat
194
Carnarvon Hwy
64
Coalbah
Glenmorgan
Meandarra
83
The Gums
Bushy Park
46

6
Clifton
Thrushton NP
Begonia
River
Lake Kajarabie
116 Carnarvon
Bindle
114
Flinton
Westmar
68
Moonie
Southwood NP
74
Moo
92

7
485
Mitchell
Balonne Hwy
45
Boolba
109
St George
St George Irrigation Area
77
77
55
44
Moonie
182
55
39
BE

8
Charlotte Plains
Bollon
77
River
25
Nindigully
65
16 193 Commoron
Talwood 22 Toobeah
62
Goond
Noorama Sports Centre
Dirranbandi
44
118
Daymar
76
39
37
49
Boggabilla
20
Thallon
65
153
39
Bru

9
Queensland
New South Wales
Jobs Gate
Culgoa
Hebel
19
99
Gundabloui
Mungindi
26 River 41 42
18
18
Mastermans
30
42
90

10
Enngonia
Beulah
38
Goodooga
47
55
Angledool Lake
Opal Mines
107
50
57
74 38 142
OTC Satellite Tracking Station
Moree
29 Pallamallawa W
Gwydir Hwy
Hwy
42
27
21
Lightning Ridge
Collarenebri
68
Gravesend
50

11
71
Bullaroon
94
Narran
106
21
Cumborah
74
75
Rowena
89
53
97
36
Bingar
Terewah Or Narran Lake
70

12
Bourke
97 Brewarrina
64
Barwon
70
Mt Bendemeer 149m
Castlereagh River
Walgett
92
Burren Junction
50 Wee Waa
32
44 Nandewar Range
Narrabri
Grattai Mtn 1310m
103
Mount Kaputar NP
Barra
Oxleys Tableland
Mitchell 76
Mulga
Bogan
41
50
363
Namoi
Pilliga
57
CSIRO Observatory
Deriah Mtn 855m
Mt Byar 853m
Upp Hor
Upper

13
Ben Lomond
Byrock
62 32
56
Carinda
115
Wingadee
85
Gwabegar
Salt Caves
Boggabri
42
Upper N
Wilga Downs
Dijou Mountain 317m
Coronga Pk 415m
34
Colossal
32
25
Newell Hwy

125

122

A B C D E F G H I

0 20 40 60 80 100 km

N

J K L M N O P Q R

1
Childers Buxton Toogoom
Howard Torbanlea
Dallarnil Hervey Bay FRASER ISLAND
GREAT SANDY NATIONAL PARK
Biggenden Maryborough Eurong
35 Eidsvold 45 Mtn
Mundubbera Binjour Brooweena
Gayndah Coalstoun Lakes Mungar Owanyilla Maaroom Tuan

2
Tiaro
Gundiah Bauple
Tin Can Bay Rainbow Beach Double Island Point
Miva Neerdie
Tansey Woolooga Gunalda
COOLOOLA NATIONAL PARK
COOLOOLA COAST

3
Murgon Goomeri Kilkivan Gympie Cooran
Wondai Widgee Mtn 688m Lake Cootharaba
Proston Cloyna
Kingaroy Gallangowan Borumba Resvr Cooroy Tewantin Noosa Heads
Memerambi Imbil Emundi Peregian Beach
Kenilworth Coolum Beach
Dangore Mtn 599m Bli Bli SUNSHINE COAST

4
Taabinga Nanango Nambour Witta Maroochydore
Kumbia Brooklands Yarraman Linville Beerwah Buderim
CONONDALE NATIONAL PARK Caloundra
Bell Maidenwell Blackbutt Moore Harlin Glass House Mountains
Haly Mtn 956m D'AGUILAR Kilcoy
Kalmkillenbun Maclagan Cooyar Woodford Wamuran
Moola Toogoolawah Elimbah Bongaree
Dalby Kulpi Crows Nest Caboolture MORETON ISLAND NP
Brymaroo Haden Esk Burpengary Deception Bay
Bowenville Goombungee Hampton Samford Redcliffe MORETON ISLAND

5
SOUTH
Jondaryan Cabarlah Coominya STRATHPINE
Oakey Murphys Creek Gatton Lowood Samford BRISBANE Point Lookout
Kingsthorpe Grantham Fernvale Dunwich
TOOWOOMBA Laidley Rosewood Victoria Point NORTH STRADBROKE ISLAND
Springside Greenmount IPSWICH Redland Bay
Pittsworth Southbrook Peak Crossing Beenleigh
Felton East Thornton Jimboomba Tamborine Village SOUTH STRADBROKE ISLAND
Millmerran Pampas Nobby MT MISTAKE NP Roadvale Beaudesert Oxenford
Clifton Rosevale Kalbar Nerang Southport GOLD COAST
Leyburn Allora Aratula Boonah Mudgeeraba SURFERS PARADISE

7
PACIFIC
Pratten Clintonvale Mt Alford Burleigh Heads
Warwick Tannymorel Maroon Coolangatta
Karara MT BARNEY NP Hillview Springbrook Tweed Heads
Killarney Rathdowney Murwillumbah
Legume Woodenbong LAMINGTON NP Bogangar
Dalveen Mulli Mulli Tyalgum Uki Pottsville Beach
Pozieres Urbenville MT WARNING NP Burringbar
Amiens Applethorpe Mullumbimby Ocean Shores
Stanthorpe Haystack Mtn 878m Kyogle Nimbin Brunswick Heads
Glen Aplin RICHMOND RANGE Bangalow Byron Bay
QUEENSLAND Bonalbo Clunes Newrybar

9
OCEAN
Texas Ballandean Mummulgum Lismore Lennox Head
Wallangarra Tabulam Casino Alstonville Ballina
Tenterfield Drake Mallanganee Coraki Wardell
NEW SOUTH WALES Coraki Broadwater
Woodburn BROADWATER NP Evans Head

10
Baryulgil BUNDJALUNG NP
Torrington Mt Bajimba 1446m Mt Marsh 501m Chatsworth Iluka
Deepwater GIBRALTAR RANGE NP Laurence Road Maclean Yamba
Emmaville Copmanhurst Lawrence Tyndale Brooms Head
GWYDIR Carrs Creek Junction Ulmarra

11
Inverell Red Range Grafton YURAYGIR NP
Glen Innes Coutts Crossing Minnie Water
Gilgai Glencoe Wooli
Tingha Ben Lomond The Black Mtn 591m Red Rock
Bundarra Llangothlin GUY FAWKES NP Glenreagh Arrawarra
Guyra Mt Hyland 1439m Woolgoolga
Emerald Beach Moonee Beach

12
Coramba
Dorrigo Coffs Harbour
Armidale Ebor Bellingen Sawtell
NEW ENGLAND NP Urunga
Hillgrove Bowraville Valla Beach Nambucca Heads
Macksville Scotts Head

13
Stuarts Point South West Rocks

J K L M N O P Q R

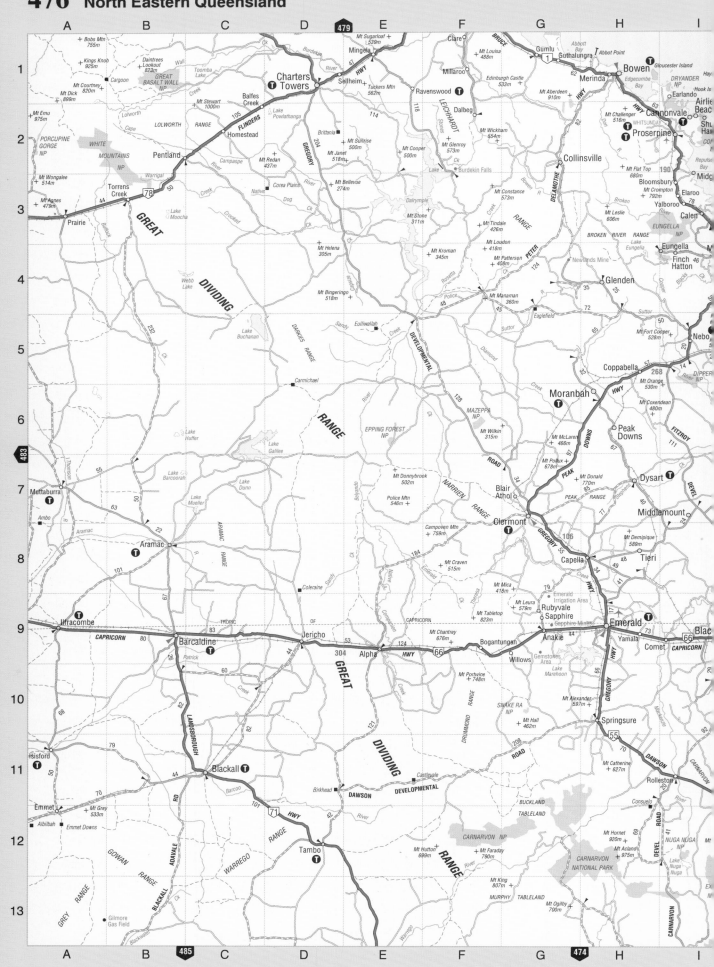

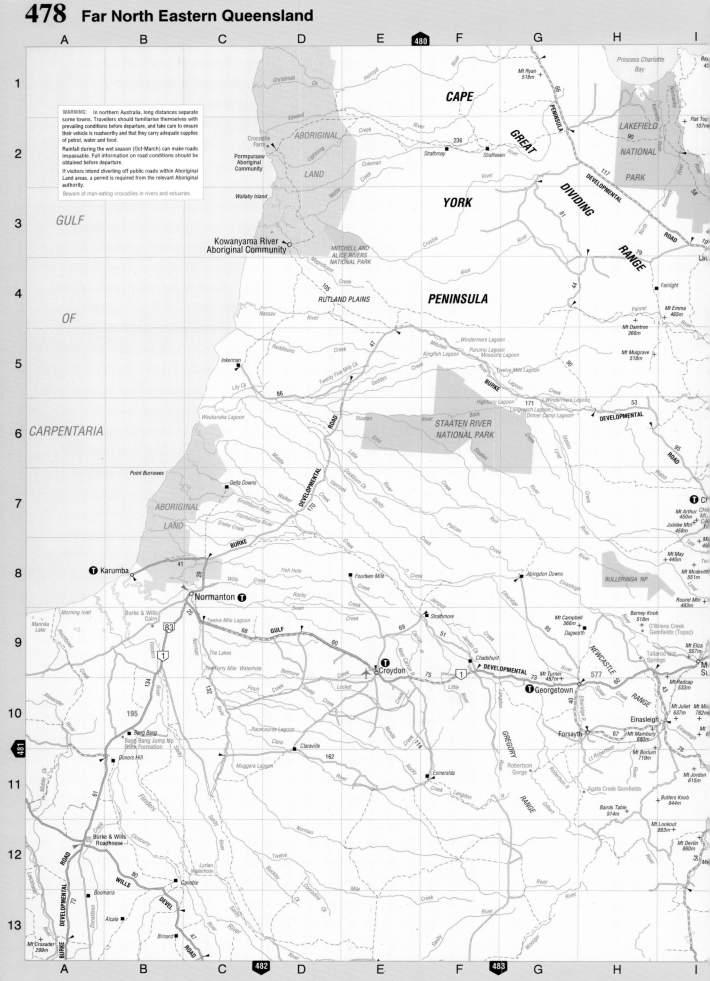

CAPE
GREAT
YORK
DIVIDING
RANGE
PENINSULA

GULF
OF
CARPENTARIA

ABORIGINAL
LAND

Princess Charlotte
Bay

LAKEFIELD
NATIONAL
PARK

Mt Ryan
518m

Strathmay   Strathaven

Crocodile
Farm

Pormpuraaw
Aboriginal
Community

Wallaby Island

Kowanyama River
Aboriginal Community

MITCHELL AND
ALICE RIVERS
NATIONAL PARK

RUTLAND PLAINS

Inkerman

Flat Top
107m

Fairlight

Mt Emma
465m

Mt Daintree
366m

Mt Mulgrave
518m

Windermere Lagoon
Purumu Lagoon Mosquito Lagoon
Twelve Mile Lagoon

BURKE

Highbury Lagoon
Longreach Lagoon Windermere Lagoon
Dinner Camp Lagoon

DEVELOPMENTAL

STAATEN RIVER
NATIONAL PARK

Point Burrowes

Delta Downs

ABORIGINAL
LAND

Smithburn River
Fitzmaurice River
Snake Creek

BURKE

DEVELOPMENTAL
ROAD

Karumba

Normanton

Burke & Wills
Cairn

Morning Inlet

Manrika
Lake

Pinchbowl

Fish Hole

Fourteen Mile

Rocky

Swan

Twelve Mile Lagoon

GULF

The Lakes

The Forty Mile Waterhole

Belmore

Croydon

Strathmore

Abingdon Downs

Mt Arthur
450m
Jubilee Mtn
458m

Mt May
445m

Mt Mcdevitt
551m

Round Mtn
493m

BULLERINGA NP

Barney Knob
518m
O'Briens Creek
Gemfields (Topaz)

Mt Campbell
366m
Dagworth

Chadshunt

DEVELOPMENTAL

Georgetown

Mt Turner
457m

577

NEWCASTLE
RANGE

Mt Eliza
557m

Tallaroo Hot
Springs

Mt Redcap
533m

Bang Bang

Bang Bang Jump Up
Rock Formation

Donors Hill

Racecourse Lagoon

Clara

Claraville

Muggera Lagoon

Esmeralda

GREGORY

RANGE

Robertson
Gorge

Agate Creek Gemfields

Bairds Table
914m

Mt Lookout
883m

Einasleigh

Forsayth

Mt Juliet
637m

Mt Mambury
680m

Mt Borlum
719m

Mt Jordon
615m

Butlers Knob
844m

Burke & Wills
Roadhouse

Boomarra

Alcala

Canobie

WILLS

DEVEL

ROAD

BURKE

DEVELOPMENTAL
ROAD

Lyrian
Waterhole

Brinard

Mt Crusader
299m

Mt Devlin
860m

236
66
117
81
44
90
53
171
95
79
19
95
105
47
86
170
41
29
25
68
60
134
195
132
69
51
75
73
40
67
76
162
114
61
72
80
47
54
58
90
43
75

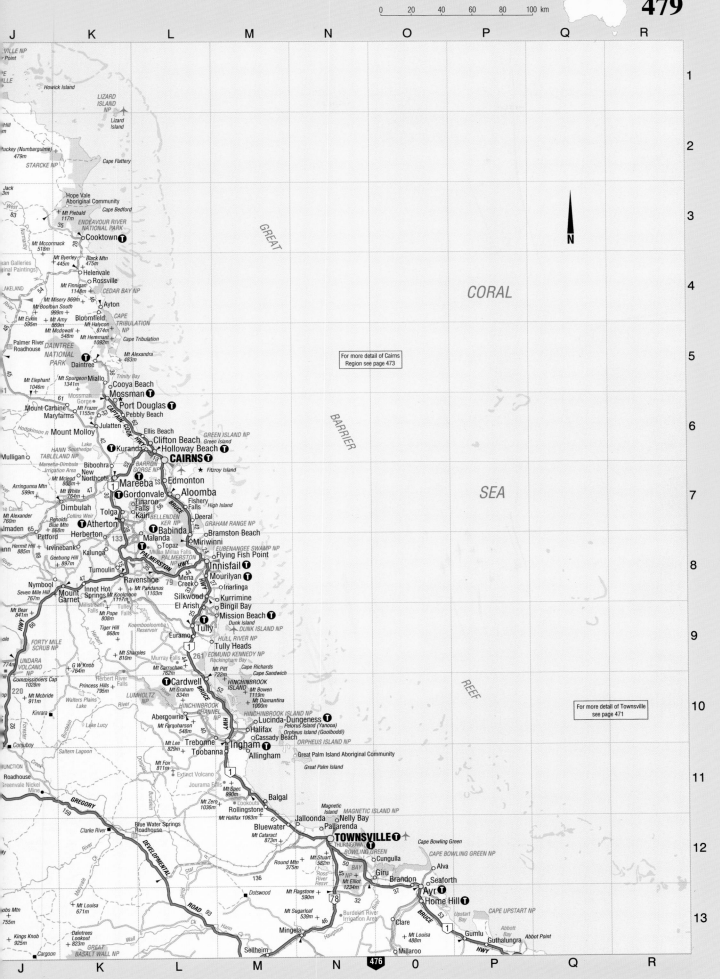

0 20 40 60 80 100 km

CORAL

SEA

GREAT

BARRIER

REEF

Howick Island

LIZARD ISLAND NP

Lizard Island

Cape Flattery

STARCKE NP

Jack 3m

Hope Vale Aboriginal Community

Cape Bedford

ENDEAVOUR RIVER NATIONAL PARK

Mt Piebald 117m

Cooktown

Mt Mccormack 518m

Mt Byerley 445m

Black Mtn 475m

Helenvale

Rossville

Mt Finnigan 1148m

CEDAR BAY NP

Mt Misery 869m

Ayton

Mt Boolbun South 999m

Bloomfield

Mt Amy 869m

CAPE TRIBULATION NP

Mt Eykn 595m

Mt Halycon 874m

Mt Mcdowall 548m

Mt Hemmant 1092m

Cape Tribulation

Palmer River Roadhouse

DAINTREE NATIONAL PARK

Mt Alexandra 483m

Daintree

Mt Elephant 1046m

Mt Spurgeon 1341m

Miallo

Cooya Beach

Trinity Bay

Mossman Gorge

Mossman

Mount Carbine

Mt Frazer 1155m

Port Douglas

Maryfarms

Julatten

Pebbly Beach

Ellis Beach

GREEN ISLAND NP

Mount Molloy

Green Island

Clifton Beach

Kuranda

Holloway Beach

HANN Southedge TABLELAND NP

Biboohra

BARRON GORGE NP

CAIRNS

Mareeba-Dimbula Irrigation Area

New Northcote

Fitzroy Island

Mareeba

Edmonton

Arringunna Mtn 599m

Mt Mcleod 808m

Gordonvale

Aloomba

Mt White 764m

Tinaroo Falls

Fishery Falls

High Island

Dimbulah

Tolga

Kairi

BELLENDEN KER NP

Deeral

GRAHAM RANGE NP

Atherton

Collins Weir

Reholds Blue Mtn 868m

Herberton

Babinda

Bramston Beach

Petford

Malanda

Miriwinni

Kalunga

Topaz

Millaa Millaa Falls

EUBENANGEE SWAMP NP

Irvinebank

PALMERSTON

Flying Fish Point

Geebung Hill 897m

Tumoulin

Innisfail

Mt Pandanus 1103m

Mena Creek

Mourilyan

Nymbool

Ravenshoe

Mt Koolmoon 1117m

Inarlinga

Seven Mile Hill 767m

Innot Hot Springs

Silkwood

Mount Garnet

Kurrimine

El Arish

Mt Bear 841m

Millstream Falls

Mt Pope 808m

Tully Falls

Bingil Bay

Mission Beach

Tiger Hill 868m

Dunk Island

DUNK ISLAND NP

FORTY MILE SCRUB NP

Koombooloomba Reservoir

Tully

UNDARA VOLCANO NP

Euramo

HULL RIVER NP

Commissioners Cap 1028m

G W Knob 764m

Tully Heads

Mt Sharples 810m

Murray Falls

EDMUND KENNEDY NP

Reckingham Bay

Mt Mcbride 911m

Herbert River Falls

Mt Carruchan 762m

Cape Richards

Cape Sandwich

Princess Hills 795m

Mt Pitt 722m

Kinrara

Cardwell

HINCHINBROOK ISLAND

Mt Graham 834m

Mt Bowen 1119m

LUMHOLTZ NP

Walters Plains Lake

Mt Diamantina 1000m

Lake Lucy

HINCHINBROOK CHANNEL NP

Saltern Lagoon

Abergowrie

HINCHINBROOK ISLAND NP

Conjuboy

Mt Farquharson 548m

Lucinda-Dungeness

Pelorus Island (Yanooa)

Halifax

Orpheus Island (Goolboddi)

Cassady Beach

ORPHEUS ISLAND NP

Mt Lee 829m

Trebonne

Ingham

Toobanna

Great Palm Island Aboriginal Community

Allingham

Mt Fox 811m

Great Palm Island

Extinct Volcano

Greenvale Nickel Mine

Roadhouse

Jourama Falls

GREGORY

Balgal

Mt Spec 990m

Clarke River

Mt Zero 1036m

Magnetic Island

MAGNETIC ISLAND NP

Rollingstone

Nelly Bay

Blue Water Springs Roadhouse

Mt Halifax 1063m

Jalloonda

Bluewater

Pallarenda

DEVELOPMENTAL

Mt Cataract 873m

TOWNSVILLE

THURINGOWA

Cape Bowling Green

CAPE BOWLING GREEN NP

Round Mtn 375m

Mt Stuart 582m

BOWLING GREEN BAY NP

Cungulla

Mt Louisa 671m

Ross River Resvr

Giru

Alva

Dotswood

Mt Elliot 1234m

Brandon

Seaforth

Mt Flagstone 590m

Ayr

Home Hill

Mt Sugarloaf 539m

Burdekin River Irrigation Area

Clare

CAPE UPSTART NP

Kings Knob 925m

Mingela

Haughton

Gumlu

Abbot Point

Cargoon

GREAT BASALT WALL NP

Sellheim

Millaroo

Guthalungra

Abbot Bay

Upstart Bay

For more detail of Cairns Region see page 473

For more detail of Townsville see page 471

0 20 40 60 80 100 km

N

TORRES STRAIT

BADU ISLAND
Mulgrave Hill 209m
Mt Augustus 399m
MOA ISLAND
High Island

Thursday Island
Horn Island
Cape York Wilderness Lodge
PRINCE OF WALES ISLAND
Endeavour Strait
Cape York
Bamaga
Newcastle Bay
Parslow Pt

GULF OF

Vrilya Point
Vehicle Ferry
JARDINE RIVER NATIONAL PARK
RICHARDSON RANGE
Left Hill 108m
Orford Bay
Puddingpan Hill 123m
Cridland Hill 112m
Helby Hill 150m
CAPTAIN BILLY LANDING

CARPENTARIA

ABORIGINAL LAND
376
216
Messum Hill 87m
Shelburne Bay

CORAL

Mapoon Aboriginal Community
Port Musgrave Bay
Ducie River
Palm Creek
Bertiehaugh
Conical Hill 86m
Briscoe Hill 147m
Cape Grenville
Temple Bay
Glennie 299m
GREAT DIVIDING
Huxley Hill 283m
Kennedy Hill 518m
Moreton Telegraph Station
Barret Hill 366m
Weymouth Bay

Duifken Point
Albatross Bay
Weipa
Mission R
PENINSULA
Batavia Downs
40
65
EMBLEY RANGE
48
Mt Dobson 495m
Bowden 345m
Mt Tozer 545m
IRON RANGE NP
Portland Roads
Cape Weymouth
Lockhart River Aboriginal Community

SEA

GREAT

Pera Head
Lagoon Creek
247
70
GEIKE RANGE
DEVELOPMENTAL
Iguana Mtn 244m
RANGE
Cape Direction
Direction Hill 146m
Mt Carter 671m
Jacks Khob 411m

Ward River
Coconut Ck
Mèrkunga Creek
ARCHER BEND NATIONAL PARK
Archer River
Bald Hill 441m
Geai Creek
Archer River Roadhouse
112
ROKEBY NATIONAL PARK
Birthday Mtn 438m
Table Mtn 458m
Night Island
Cape Sidmouth
Whale Hill 306m
Round Mtn 321m
MCILWRAITH RANGE

BARRIER

Aurukun Aboriginal Community
Coen River

Double Hill 411m
Claremont Isles

REEF

ABORIGINAL LAND
Kendall River
CAPE
Mt Croll 488m
Mt White 449m
Coen
Silver Plains
53
Port Stewart
Pipon Island
FLINDERS GROUP NP
Flinders Group Is
Cape Melville
St Pauls Hill 418m
CAPE MELVILLE NP

Christmas Ck
Holroyd River
YORK
ROAD
41
Kintore 405m
66
Mt Ryan 518m
Princess Charlotte Bay
Bathurst Bay
Bay Hill 432m
Barrow Point
CAPE MELVILLE NP
Howick Island

Edward River
Crocodile Farm
Pormpuraaw Aboriginal Community
Coleman River
236
Strathmay
Strathaven
90
LAKEFIELD NATIONAL PARK
Kennedy River
Flat Top Hill 107m
Saddle Hill 508m
LIZARD ISLAND NP
Lizard Island

Wallaby Island
Lightning
Matte River
Crosbie River
PENINSULA
GREAT DIVIDING RANGE
North River
58
83
Mt Jack 213m
Mt Piebald 117m
Mt Stuckey (Numbargulme) 479m
STARCKE NP
Cape Flattery

Kowanyama Aboriginal Community
MITCHELL AND ALICE RIVERS NATIONAL PARK
Hope Vale Aboriginal Community
Cape Bedford
ENDEAVOUR RIVER NATIONAL PARK

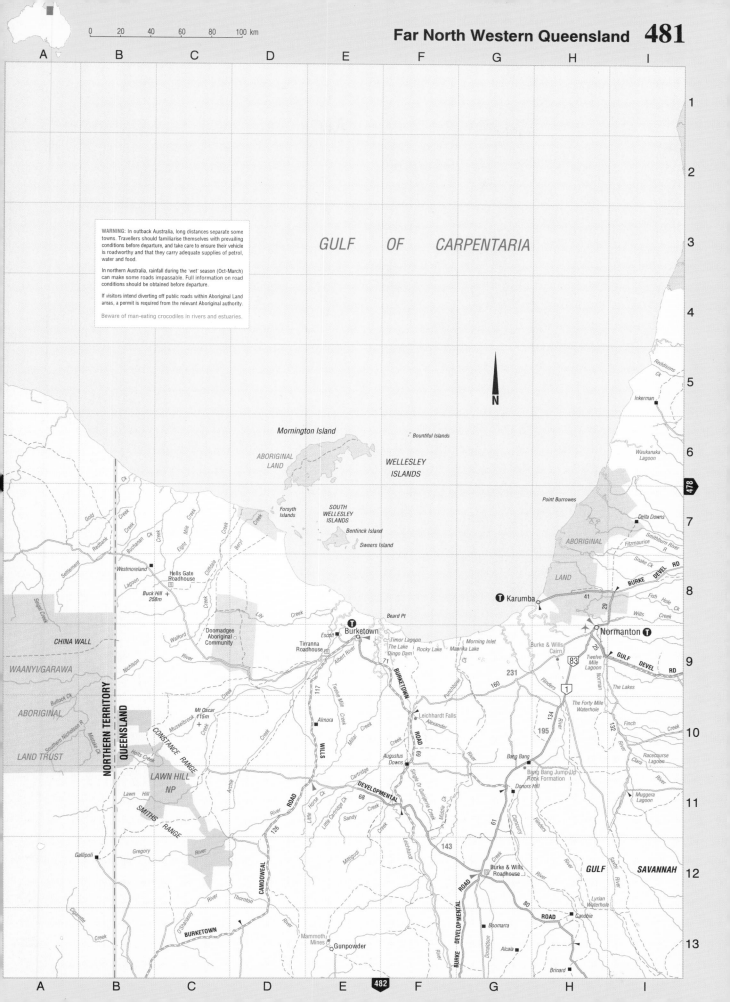

0 20 40 60 80 100 km

A B C D E F G H I

GULF   OF   CARPENTARIA

WARNING: In outback Australia, long distances separate some towns. Travellers should familiarise themselves with prevailing conditions before departure, and take care to ensure their vehicle is roadworthy and that they carry adequate supplies of petrol, water and food.

In northern Australia, rainfall during the 'wet' season (Oct-March) can make some roads impassable. Full information on road conditions should be obtained before departure.

If visitors intend diverting off public roads within Aboriginal Land areas, a permit is required from the relevant Aboriginal authority.

Beware of man-eating crocodiles in rivers and estuaries.

N

Mornington Island

Bountiful Islands

ABORIGINAL
LAND

*WELLESLEY
ISLANDS*

Forsyth
Islands

SOUTH
WELLESLEY
ISLANDS

Bentinck Island

Sweers Island

Point Burrowes

Reddisons Ck

Inkerman

Waukanaka
Lagoon

478

Delta Downs

Smithburn River

ABORIGINAL

Fitzmaurice

Snake Ck

LAND

BURKE DEVEL RD

Fish Hole Ck

Wills Creek

Gold

Redbank

Settlement

Creek

Buchanan Ck

Eight Mile Creek

Creek

Berryl

Cliffdale

Creek

Creek

Lily

Creek

Creek

Westmoreland

Lagoon

Hells Gate
Roadhouse

Buck Hill
258m

Doomadgee
Aboriginal
Community

Walford

River

Nicholson

Beard Pt

Escott

Burketown

Tirranna
Roadhouse

Albert River

Timor Lagoon
The Lake
Dingo Dam

Rocky Lake

Morning Inlet

Maanka Lake

Karumba

41

29

25

Normanton

Burke & Wills
Cairn

GULF

DEVEL

RD

83

Twelve
Mile Lagoon

231

160

Flinders

1

The Lakes

The Forty Mile
Waterhole

132

Finch

Creek

CHINA WALL

WAANYI/GARAWA

Bullock Ck

ABORIGINAL

Southern Nicholson R

LAND TRUST

Mistake Ck

NORTHERN TERRITORY

QUEENSLAND

CONSTANCE RANGE

Hells Creek

Mt Oscar
115m

Musselbrook

Creek

Creek

Arctic

Creek

117

Twelve Mile

Creek

Millar

Almora

Creek

Augustus
Downs

Alexander

Leichhardt Falls

BURKETOWN

ROAD

69

Single Or Quinterie Creek

Punchbowl

Ck

195

134

River

Racecourse
Lagoon

Clara

River

LAWN HILL
NP

Lawn

Hill

SMITHS

RANGE

Gregory

River

River

ROAD

126

CAMOOWEAL

Little Horse Ck

Little Cartridge Ck

Sandy

68

Cartridge

Creek

Leichhardt

Creek

DEVELOPMENTAL

ROAD

61

143

Middle Ck

Creek

Cloncurry

Flinders

Bang Bang

Bang Bang Jump-Up
Rock Formation

Donors Hill

Muggera
Lagoon

Gallipoli

O'Shanassy

River

Thornton

River

BURKETOWN

Mammoth
Mines

Gunpowder

River

Donaldson

BURKE DEVELOPMENTAL ROAD

80

Burke & Wills
Roadhouse

River

Sandy River

GULF SAVANNAH

Lyrian
Waterhole

ROAD

Boomarra

Alcala

Canobie

Brinard

Cigarette

Creek

482

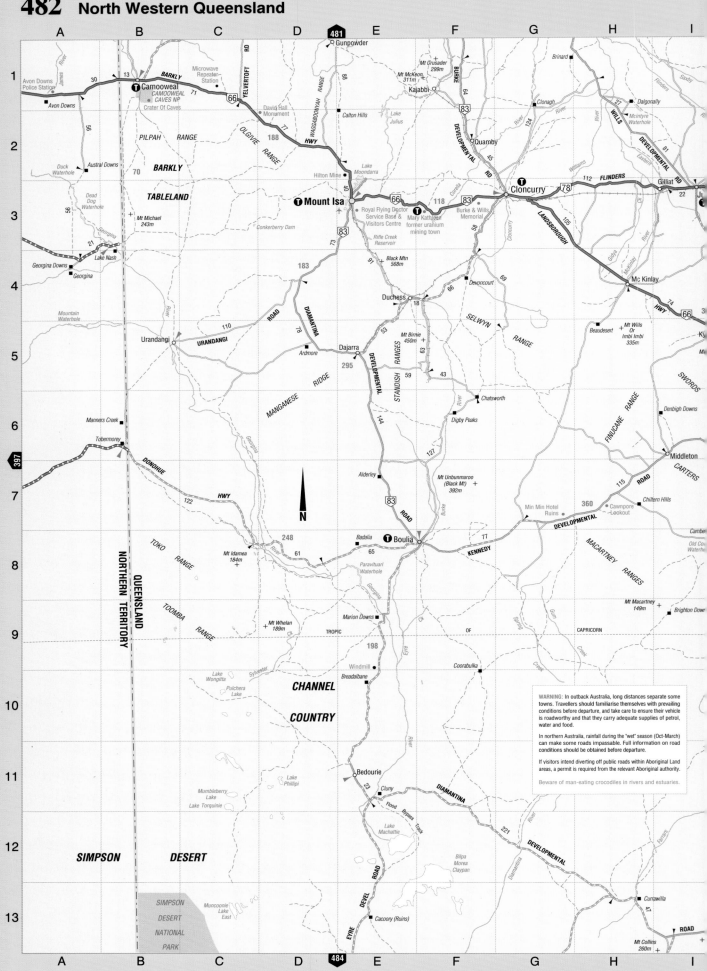

0 20 40 60 80 100 km
J K L M N O P Q R
478
479
1 2 3 4 5 6 7 8 9 10 11 12 13
476
485
Charters Towers
Sellheim
Balfes Creek
Homestead
Pentland
Torrens Creek
Prairie
Hughenden
Richmond
Maxwelton
Nonda
Nelia
Stamford
Corfield
Winton
Opal Fields
1st Flying Surgeon Service 1958
Muttaburra
Aramac
Morella
Longreach
Ilfracombe
Barcaldine
Jericho
Alpha
Blackall
Tambo
Isisford
Emmet
Yaraka
Stonehenge
Jundah
Windorah
Opalton
Mt Louisa 671m
Bobs Mtn 755m
Kings Knob 925m
Daintrees Lookout 823m
Mt Courtney 820m
Cargoon
GREAT BASALT WALL NP
Mt Stewart 1000m
Mt Emu 975m
Mt Dick 899m
PORCUPINE GORGE NP
WHITE MOUNTAINS NP
Mt Desolation 579m
Mt Wongalee 514m
Mt Agnes 479m
Mt Walker 479m
Arrara
Alderley
Compton Downs
Burleigh
Elmore
Clutha
Coleraine
Essex Downs
Albion Downs
Microwave Station
Barenya
Bonnie Downs
Dagworth
Mt Booka Booka 251m
Mt Boorooma 263m
Lorraine Station
Clyde
BLADENSBURG NP
Mt Williams 263m
Cork
Mt Davy 294m
LARK QUARRY ENVIRONMENTAL PARK
Velson Pk
Evesham
Darra
Elmore
Ambo
Dalkeith
Bimerah
Berrimpa
Budgerygar
Albilbah
Emmet Downs
Mt Grey 533m
IDALIA NATIONAL PARK
Gilmore Gas Field
Birkhead
Coleraine
Carmichael
Corea Plains
Mt Redan 437m
Mt Sunrise 500m
Mt Janet 518m
Mt Bellevue 274m
Brittania
Mt Helena 305m
Mt Bingeringo 518m
Lake Powlathanga
Lake Moocha
Webb Lake
Lake Buchanan
Lake Huffer
Lake Galilee
Lake Barcoorah
Lake Dunn
Lake Mueller
GREAT DIVIDING RANGE
GRAMPIAN HILLS
LOLWORTH RANGE
DARKIES RANGE
ARAMAC RANGE
CORYS RANGE
TULLY RANGE
FORSYTH RANGE
MOUNTAINS
MACEDON RANGE
GOWAN RANGE
GREY RANGE
WARREGO RANGE
CHEVIOT RANGE
KENNEDY DEVELOPMENTAL ROAD
FLINDERS HWY
LANDSBOROUGH HWY
CAPRICORN HWY
THOMSON DEVELOPMENTAL ROAD
JUNDAH ROAD
WINTON
ADAVALE BLACKALL ROAD
TROPIC OF CAPRICORN
Flinders River
Thomson River
Barcoo River
Cooper Creek
Aramac Creek
Campaspe River
Mayne River

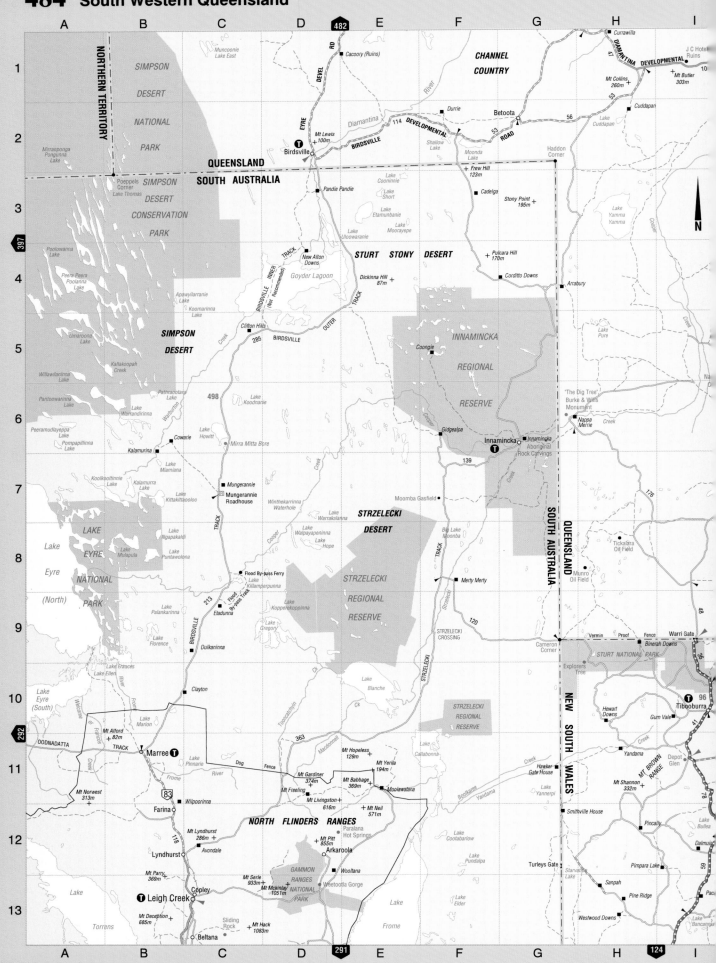

0 20 40 60 80 100 km

J K L M N O P Q R

483

1

Windorah

Gowan Range Road

Gilmore Gas Field

Landsborough

71

River

76

Jundah Quilpie Rd

Cheviot Range

50 57

Budgerygar

Grey Range

Adavale

Blackall

87

Augathella

2

38 Clifton

134

Diamantina

Adavale

Adavale

Charleville Road

179

84

71

Developmental

103

Blackwater Creek

Lake Dartmouth

Ambathala

3

Cornwall

Earlstoun

Bull Creek Opal Field

97

Boothulla

Charleville

54

Road

Royal Flying Doctor Base & Visitors Centre

Numerous Opal Fields

Oil Fields

Mt Bellalie 216m

Quilpie

Cheepie

210 Cooladdi

Hwy

79

4

Eromanga

36

Congie

Mt Prara 309m

99

Boatman Bore

5

McGregor Range

Oil Fields

234

Grey Range

76

Rd

Thargomindah

Toompine

Opal Mines

35

River

199

Wyandra

43

Norley Range

Quilpie

82

127

Bulloo

46

Coongoola

Clifton

6

474

Occundra

122

Lake Bullawarra

Repeater Station

Thargomindah

Blackgate Opal Field

130

Yowah Opal Field

198

68

Cunnamulla

54

Mitchell

Balonne

134

Hwy

7

Warrego

Charlotte Plains

Bulloo

Developmental

Road

Eulo

71

WARNING: In outback Australia, long distances separate some towns. Travellers should familiarise themselves with prevailing conditions before departure, and take care to ensure their vehicle is roadworthy and that they carry adequate supplies of petrol, water and food.

In northern Australia, rainfall during the "wet" season (Oct-March) can make some roads impassable. Full information on road conditions should be obtained before departure.

If visitors intend diverting off public roads within Aboriginal Land areas, a permit is required from the relevant Aboriginal authority.

Mud Springs

118

8

145

122

Lake Wyara

Kungie Lake

Mitchell

Noorama Sports Centre

9

Lake Numalla

Currawinya

NP

Adelaide Gate

Lake Callamulcha

Hungerford

Vermin Proof Fence

QUEENSLAND

Hamilton Gate

Waverley Gate

Parragundy Gate

Barringun

NEW SOUTH WALES

Jobs Gate

Berawinnia Downs

Sharoon

38

Teurika

Ourimbah

128

Maureen Joy

146

Enngonia

Beulah

10

Pindera Downs

Owen Downs

Barrajong

River

42 142

Clifton Downs

Colana

Koridina

Bullaroon

Whyjonta

86

85

417

Wanaaring

64

52

71

62

11

Barrona Downs

Fords Bridge

68

97

Bundarra

Murphys Lake

130

Brewarrina

Petita

The Range

85

Bogan

12

Gumpopla

Nantilla

Noonamah

163

Utah Lake

Bourke

Oxleys Tableland

Mt Bendemeer 149m

41

Allandy

Questa Park

Glendara

Tonga Lake

101

Mulga River

76

28

Quichra

Purnanga

Cawnalmurtee

Mt Mulyah 162m

Louth

Ben Lomond

Hwy

62 32

13

Oak Vale

Goodwood

Mandalay

Poloka Yantabangee Lake

Peery Lake

Polocara

Jinki Lake

Mt Wammiga 380m

Wilga Downs

Byrock

43

74

White Cliffs

Opal Mines

32

Thoolabool Range

Mt Deerina Range

Darling River

125

J K L M N O P Q R

Tasmania Heritage Island

Tasmania has certainly won many more hearts than it can claim square kilometres. It has only 68 000 of the latter, but it crams into them its rugged west, a central plateau broken by steep mountains and narrow river valleys, and an eastern coastal region offering a soft 'English' pastoral beauty. Its diverse charms have made it a popular tourist attraction for Australians from 'the mainland' for many years.

This dramatically beautiful island, however, has a far from beautiful early history. First sighted by Abel Tasman in 1624, it was later claimed by Captain Cook for the English and was first settled in 1803. For the next fifty years it was maintained primarily as a penal colony, although prosperous settlements developed around Hobart and New Norfolk. The convicts did the hard labour and lived in brutal conditions at Port Arthur. The only people treated more harshly than the convicts were the Aborigines, who resisted the takeover of their tribal lands. Political separation from New South Wales was granted in 1825 and transportation of convicts ceased in 1853. Today the ruins of Port Arthur have taken on a mellow charm and Tasmania is an infinitely more hospitable place.

Tasmania was first called Van Diemen's Land; these days it is known as the 'heritage island', 'treasure island' or the 'apple isle'. Its economy is basically agricultural with the major growth area being in quality specialised food products. The Tasmanian hydro-electric system has a greater output than that of the Snowy Mountains Scheme. Tasmania's high rainfall helps in this area. The climate offers mild summers and cool winters, with much of the mountain regions receiving heavy winter snowfall. Mid-December to late January is very popular with tourists; late spring or autumn are also pleasant. Even the winter months offer good touring.

When planning a trip to Tasmania note the heavy booking for the *Spirit of Tasmania* ferry service between Melbourne and Devonport from December to March. Either book well in advance or consider a fly/drive holiday, which can be a relaxing and economic alternative.

Tasmania's roads are well suited to relaxed meandering, many of them being winding and narrow. In a fortnight, however, you can happily complete what is virtually a round tour of the island.

Built on either side of the Derwent River, Hobart, the capital of Tasmania, is dominated by Mount Wellington. The Wrest Point Hotel-Casino, Australia's first casino, with its lavish entertainment and International Convention Centre, is now competing for first place as the city's best-known landmark, towering over Hobart's many colonial buildings. Port Arthur, Richmond with its beautiful bridge (the oldest in Australia) and the settlements of Bothwell and New Norfolk are within reach.

The Derwent Valley with its hopfields and apple orchards, lovely in blossom-time and in autumn, lies to the west. Further west is Lake Pedder; the flooding of this spectacular country was a source of great controversy when it was made part of the Tasmanian hydro-electric scheme. The surrounding country makes up the South West National Park, Tasmania's largest and one which has been given World Heritage status. The Lyell Highway then leads to the Cradle Mountain Lake St Clair National Park. Queenstown, surrounded by eerie white mountains, is the largest settlement in this wild, forested region. Nearby coastal Strahan was once a mining boom-town and is the starting-point of the Gordon River cruises. North of Queenstown, the town of Zeehan is currently enjoying a mining revival with the reopening of the Renison Bell Tin Mine.

The north coast is yet another contrasting area. Burnie is one of the larger towns and Stanley is a classified historic town situated beneath 'the Nut', an unusual peninsula. East of Burnie, the Bass Highway hugs the coast as far as Devonport, the terminal of the Bass Strait passenger/vehicle ferry *Spirit of Tasmania* and the centre of an apple-growing area. Inland is Launceston, Tasmania's second largest city. Situated on the River Tamar, Launceston has many old buildings. Only minutes from the city centre is the beautiful Cataract Gorge, and the nearby colonial villages of Evandale, Hagley, Westbury, Carrick, Perth, Longford and Hadspen are well worth a visit.

A mild climate, good surfing beaches and sheltered seaside resorts add to the attraction of the east-coast region. St Helens, 160 kilometres east of Launceston, is the principal resort town. Try not to miss Bicheno, a picturesque old port and one-time whaling-town. Further south, 'the Hazards', a red granite mountain range, tower up behind Coles Bay, at the entrance to the Freycinet National Park. Nearby Swansea offers top-class ocean and freshwater fishing.

An enriched sense of Tasmania's history can be gained from studying graveyard headstones: in St David's Park in the centre of Hobart; on Maria Island, the Isle of the Dead off Port Arthur, King Island and Sarah Island in Macquarie Harbour; at National Trust properties; and in towns like Stanley, Richmond, Ross, Evandale and Corinna.

Whether you complete a round trip or only explore parts of this island state, it is very likely that, by the time you come to leave, Tasmania will have won yet another heart.

Landscape near Mt Roland

Hobart

A Historic City

Hobart is an enchanting city built around a beautiful harbour and under the spell of nearby majestic Mount Wellington. A strong seafaring flavour and sense of the past give Hobart an almost European air. This feeling is heightened in winter when Mount Wellington is snow-capped and temperatures drop to a crisp 5°C. The rest of the year Hobart has plenty of days with sparkling blue skies, but temperatures rarely exceed 25°C.

Many of Hobart's beautiful early colonial sandstone buildings were erected by the unfortunate convicts who formed the majority of the first settlers in 1803.

Hobart's deepwater harbour on the broad estuary of the Derwent River soon became a thriving seaport and by 1842 Hobart was proclaimed a city. The harbour is still Hobart's lifeblood and the port is always busy with yachts. The suburbs nestle right up to the lower slopes of **Mount Wellington** and the city's population of 172 500 spreads both sides of the graceful **Tasman Bridge**, which made tragic world headlines in January 1975, when it was rammed by the bulk-carrier *Lake Illawarra*.

From the bridge you will see **Government House** and the **Royal Tasmanian Botanical Gardens** set in the Queen's Domain, a large parkland with sporting facilities and an adventure playground. Within the lovely old Botanical Gardens are a children's playground, a Japanese garden and a restaurant which serves lunch and teas.

In a matter of minutes from here you are in the heart of Hobart, which has been bypassed by the usual pressures of modern city life. Parking is no problem, but most of the city streets are one-way.

Hobart's waterfront retains much of its early character and it is not hard to imagine it in the early whaling days when Hobart Town was a lusty, brawling seaport known to sailors all round the world. Foreign ships tie up almost in the centre of town, battered whalers now replaced by Australian fishing-trawlers. Wander around to **Constitution Dock**, the haven

Hobart skyline viewed from Mt Nelson

for the yachts in the annual Sydney to Hobart Yacht Race; you can buy live seafood from the local fishermen.

Just around the corner, in Argyle Street, is the **Tasmanian Museum and Art Gallery**, which has a fine collection of early prints and paintings, Aboriginal artefacts and convict relics. From here it is only a short stroll to the **Theatre Royal**, which was built in 1837 and is the oldest theatre in Australia. It is worth going inside to glimpse its charming dolls'-house-scale Georgian interior. Dame Sybil Thorndike rated it as the finest theatre she had played in outside of London. Not far from the Theatre Royal are the **Criminal Courts** and **Penitentiary Chapel**, operated by the National Trust; guided tours are conducted daily.

Heading back towards the centre of the city, you will see Hobart's sandstone old **Town Hall**, built on the site of the original **Government House**, on the corner of Macquarie and Elizabeth Streets.

Australia's second oldest capital, Hobart has a wealth of beautiful Georgian buildings, mostly concentrated in **Macquarie and Davey Streets.** More than ninety of them have a National Trust classification and the **Anglesea Barracks**, in Davey Street, is the oldest military establishment in Australia still used by the army. The Cascade Brewery in **South Hobart**, over a century and a half old, offers conducted tours.

Several modern complexes blend in with the older buildings without destroying the overall scale and atmosphere. The largest landmark is the tower of Australia's first hotel-casino, **Wrest Point**, built on a promontory in the suburb of **Sandy Bay**, just out of town. Back towards the waterfront is the famous **Salamanca Place**, which displays the finest row of early merchant warehouses in Australia. Dating back to the whaling days of the 1830s, the whole area has been sympathetically restored and the warehouses are now used as art and craft galleries, restaurants and a puppet theatre. A colourful open-air craft market, where almost anything is sold for almost any price, is held here each Saturday. Children will particularly enjoy the nearby **Post Office Museum**, in Castray Esplanade, where they can see old telephones, letter-boxes and a small post office.

The steep **Kelly's Steps**, wedged between two old warehouses in Salamanca Place, lead to the heart of Hobart's unique **Battery Point**, a former mariners' village, which has retained its nineteenth-century character. Battery Point has many excellent restaurants offering a variety of cuisines, and several quaint cottage tearooms.

The area is also Hobart's mecca for antique-hunters. Just round the corner is the **Van Diemen Folk Museum**, with its interesting collection of colonial relics housed in Narryna, a gracious old town house, complete with a shady garden and an ornamental fountain. A short walk from here is the graceful old **St George's Anglican Church**, which was built between 1836 and 1847 and designed by two of Tasmania's most prominent colonial architects, John Lee Archer and James Blackburn. The **Tasmanian Maritime Museum** has a collection of old seafaring relics and documents.

Back towards the city, **St David's Park**, with its beautiful old trees, is an ideal place for a rest. One side of this park was Hobart Town's first burial ground and the pioneer gravestones, which date from 1804, make fascinating reading. Across the road, in Murray Street, is **Parliament House**, one of the oldest buildings in Hobart. Originally used as the Customs House, it was built by convicts between 1835 and 1841. Visitors may ask to see the tiny **Legislative Council Chamber**, which is exactly as it was when it was inaugurated. The ceiling has been painstakingly repainted in its original ornate pastel patterns and the benches have been refurbished in plush red velvet. The building was designed by John Lee Archer.

The **Allport Library and Museum of Fine Arts**, a library of rare books and a collection of antique furniture, china and silver, is also in Murray Street, within the **State Library**.

The main shopping area of Hobart is centred round the **Elizabeth Street Mall**, between Collins and Liverpool Streets. The **Cat and Fiddle Arcade and Square** is located between the Mall and Murray Street. Shoppers can relax in the modern square with its fountain and an animated mural which 'performs' on the hour. In the Mall, added to the hourly antics of the Cat and Fiddle Clock, there is entertainment provided by strolling buskers. Further along Elizabeth Street, in **Franklin Square**, you can play 'giant' chess.

Hobart offers a sophisticated nightlife with the Wrest Point Hotel-Casino, cabaret and revolving restaurant, and a range of licensed restaurants—from Japanese and Mexican to colonial-style. For a touch of 'olde-worlde' class you can sip cocktails in the drawing-room of **Lenna**, an Italianate former mansion (now a distinctive hotel-motel) in Battery Point, before dining in the lavishly decorated restaurant. Fresh seafood is a specialty of many of the city's restaurants. **Mures Fish Centre**, at Victoria Dock, offers a range from takeaway to the fisherman's basket (brimming with such delicacies as crayfish, mussels, squid and scallops). Hobart also has several interesting old pubs with a nautical flavour, such as the **Customs House Hotel** on the corner of Murray and Morrison Streets.

The suburbs of Hobart have much to offer the visitor. Nearby **Sandy Bay** is the site of both the **University of Tasmania** and a **Model Tudor Village**. Beyond this, just out of **Taroona**, is the convict-built **Shot Tower**, from the top of which you can get a superb view of the Derwent Estuary. Also part of the Shot Tower complex are a small museum and tearooms, both housed in an old (1855) building, as well as the original owner's

Hotels
Lenna of Hobart
20 Runnymede St, Battery Point
(002) 23 2911
Sheraton Hobart
1 Davey St, Hobart
(002) 35 4535
Wrest Point Hotel-Casino
410 Sandy Bay Rd, Sandy Bay
(002) 25 0112

Family and Budget
Hobart Pacific Motor Inn
Kirby Crt, West Hobart
(002) 34 6733
Hobart Tower Motel
300 Park St, New Town
(002) 28 0166
Taroona
178 Channel Hwy, Taroona
(002) 27 8748

Motel Groups: Bookings
Best Western (008) 22 2166
Innkeepers (008) 03 0111
Flag 13 2400

The above list is for information only; inclusion is not necessarily a recommendation.

Battery Point

A most delightful part of Hobart is the former maritime village **Battery Point**, perched between the city docks and Sandy Bay. Battery Point dates back to the early days of Hobart Town, when it became a lively mariners' village with fishermen's cottages, shops, churches, a village green and a riot of pubs with such evocative names as the Whalers' Return and the Neptune Inn. Miraculously, it has hardly changed since those days. To anyone strolling through its narrow, hilly streets—with enchanting glimpses of the harbour, yachts and mountains at every turn—it looks almost like a Cornish fishing-village.

Quaint **Arthurs Circus** is built around the former village green, now a children's playground. A profusion of old-fashioned flowers—sweet-william, honeysuckle, daisies and geraniums—grow in pocket-sized gardens.

Pubs such as the Knopwood's Retreat and the Shipwright's Arms add to the feeling that time has stood still. Knopwood Street and Kelly's Steps are reminders of two pioneer settlers: the Reverend Bobby Knopwood, Battery Point's first landowner, and the adventurer James Kelly, who owned a whaling-fleet and undertook a daring voyage around Van Diemen's Land.

Battery Point gets its name from a battery of guns set up on the promontory in front of a small guard-house in 1818. This soon became a signalling-station and is now the oldest building in Battery Point.

Today the Point has many inviting restaurants and tearooms, and several antique shops to explore, but it is still mainly a residential area. Most of the houses are tiny dormer-windowed fishermen's cottages, with a few grander houses such as Secheron, Stowell, Narryna and Lenna. An attractive leaflet with a detailed map, *Let's Talk About Battery Point*, is available from the Tasmanian Travel Centre, and the National Trust organises walking tours of the area, departing from the Wishing Well, Franklin Square, each Saturday morning.

Arthurs Circus

house, built in 1835. **North Hobart**, only a few minutes from the centre of the city, is the 'gourmet' food suburb, where a concentration of excellent restaurants and delicatessens have proliferated, to the delight of residents and visitors alike. Slightly further north, in the suburb of **New Town** is **Runnymede**, a National Trust homestead. Beautifully restored, it commands an attractive view over New Town Bay and **Risdon,** where Hobart's first settlement was pioneered. Further north, in the suburb of **Goodwood**, the **Derwent Entertainment Centre** stands beside the river and **Elwick Racecourse**. **Bellerive**, the ruins of an old fort at **Kangaroo Bluff**, was built to guard Hobart against a feared Russian invasion late last century. Some of Hobart's best beaches, including **Lauderdale**, **Cremorne** and **Seven Mile Beach**, are in this area. For surfers there is a wild ocean beach at **Clifton**, where the Australian surfing championships have been held.

There are dozens of scenic drives and lookouts around Hobart, with spectacular views from the pinnacle of **Mount Wellington** and from the old **Signal Station** on top of **Mount Nelson**. The **Waterworks Reserve** is an attractive picnic area only a few minutes' drive from town.

The hundreds of yachts moored near the prestigious **Royal Yacht Club** in Sandy Bay are evidence of one of Hobart's most popular sports. Other sports are well catered for with a public golf-course at **Rosny Park**, racing and trotting at **Glenorchy**, and public squash courts at **Sandy Bay**, **New Town** and **Bellerive**. The Southern Tasmanian Tennis Association Courts and an Olympic swimming-pool are in **Queen's Domain**. Tasmania's cricket headquarters is at Bellerive.

Hobart offers a complete range of accommodation, from the modern Sheraton Hobart Hotel and Wrest Point Hotel-Casino, with superb views from its 21-storey tower, to tiny Georgian cottage guest houses at Battery Point. Between these two extremes there are many modern hotels and motels and numerous guest houses, as well as caravan parks and holiday flats and cottages. 'Campercraft', small houseboats like floating caravans, can be hired throughout the state.

For further information, contact the Tasmanian Information Centre, 20 Davey St; (002) 30 8233.

Tours from Hobart

Hobart is within easy reach of a marvellous range of tourist attractions. To appreciate its superb natural setting, it is worth going on a scenic flight over the city and its surroundings, taking in the beautiful Derwent estuary, the patchwork fields of the Midlands, the Tasman Peninsula and the spectacular lakes and mountains of central and south-western Tasmania. Flight bookings can be made at the Tasmanian Information Centre, Hobart, which also can arrange half-day and full-day coach tours.

Mt Wellington, 22 km from Hobart via the Huon Road

The most popular short trip from Hobart is to the pinnacle of Mt Wellington, 1271 metres above the city, which commands panoramic views of the Derwent Valley to the north and the D'Entrecasteaux Channel to the south. A novel way to see the views is the half-day tour 'Mt Wellington Downhill': transport to the summit and a thrilling bike-ride back down.

Cadbury's Factory, Claremont, 14 km from Hobart on the Lyell Highway

A visit to this beautifully sited model factory, the biggest chocolate and cocoa factory in Australia, is another popular short trip. Privately-run coach tours leave daily and self-drive tours may be made Tuesday–Thursday. Information and bookings at Travel Centre. The factory is usually closed for two weeks in September and from the end of December to mid-January.

Richmond, 26 km from Hobart via the Eastern Outlet Road

Tasmania's oldest and most famous historic village, Richmond has the oldest bridge in Australia, and a wealth of mellow old colonial buildings, including Tasmania's oldest gaol and two historic churches. Prospect House, built in 1830, another historic building, is now a licensed restaurant and colonial accommodation property. **See also:** Entry in A–Z listing.

New Norfolk, 32 km from Hobart on the Lyell Highway

This historic town, in the centre of Tasmania's hop-growing country, is delightful in autumn when the leaves on the many English trees planted here last century turn to beautiful golden tones. Quaint old oast-houses are a feature of the landscape and the town's attractions include the historic Old Colony Inn, now a museum and tearooms set in charming grounds, and the famous Salmon

Richmond Bridge

Ponds, 11 km north-west at Plenty, the first successful trout hatchery in Australia. **See also:** Entry in A–Z listing.

Mt Field National Park and Russell Falls, 72 km from Hobart via the Lyell Highway and Gordon River Road

The road from New Norfolk to Mt Field passes through some of the loveliest parts of the Derwent Valley. A nature walk leads to the magnificent Russell Falls, cascades that drop 32 metres into a gorge of rainforest and tree ferns, from near the park entrance. This large scenic wildlife reserve shelters many native birds and animals, including the elusive Tasmanian devil. **See also:** National Parks.

Lake Pedder and Lake Gordon, 170 km from Hobart via the Lyell Highway and Gordon River Road

In clear weather, the road from Mt Field National Park to the township of Strathgordon is probably the most spectacular stretch of mountain highway in Australia. Unfortunately (from the visitor's point of view), there is very high rainfall in the area, which of course results in its unique natural topography. Motorists are advised to cancel trips on overcast days. Man-made Lakes Pedder and Gordon,

part of the Hydro-Electric Commission's giant Gordon River power development, are liberally stocked with trout. The underground power station at the Gordon Dam can be inspected on regular tours. You can hire boats and fishing tackle, and charter scenic cruises from Strathgordon, where a chalet is available for overnight accommodation. Enquiries should be directed to the Tasmanian Information Centre in Hobart. **See also:** National Parks; Dams for Power.

The Tasman Peninsula and Port Arthur, 151 km from Hobart via the Arthur Highway

There is so much to see on this fascinating trip that it would be well worth staying overnight at the narrow isthmus of Eaglehawk Neck or at Port Arthur. Once guarded by a line of tethered hounds to prevent convicts escaping, Eaglehawk Neck is now a base for game fishing charter boats. There are four unique coastal formations in the area: the spectacular Devil's Kitchen, the Blowhole, Tasman's Arch and the Tessellated Pavement. The old penal settlement of Port Arthur is Tasmania's number one tourist attraction. Other attractions in the area include Bush Hill, Remarkable Cave and Safety Cove, while a seaplane service

from Hobart provides flights around the peninsula. **See also:** Entries in A–Z listing; A Convict Past.

Huonville, 37 km from Hobart via Huon Road and the Huon Highway

You can make a scenic trip to Huonville, the centre of Tasmania's picturesque apple-growing district, via the shoulder of Mt Wellington on the Huon Highway, returning via the coastal town of Cygnet and along the Channel Highway, which commands spectacular vistas of the coastline and rugged Bruny Island. **See also:** Entry in A–Z listing.

Hastings Caves, 110 km from Hobart via the Huon Road and Huon Highway

These caves, 13 km from the small township of Hastings, are another popular attraction. There are regular guided tours of the only illuminated cave, Newdegate Cave, regarded as one of the most beautiful limestone caves in Australia. A natural thermal swimming-pool with an average temperature of 27°C is nearby. Motorists are warned that Dover is the last place to buy petrol *en route* to Recherche Bay. The Ida Bay Scenic Railway is another popular tourist attraction near Hastings. **See also:** Entry in A–Z listing.

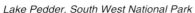

Lake Pedder, South West National Park

Tasmania from A to Z

Avoca Pop. 207

This small town with a mining background, on the Esk Main Road, also serves the small communities of Rossarden and Storys Creek, in the foothills of Ben Lomond, the highest mountain in north-east Tasmania. **Of interest:** Historic buildings include St Thomas's Church and parish hall, Falmough St. **In the area:** Bona Vista (1848), 1 km NW on Storys Creek Rd, once one of Tasmania's most attractive historic houses; private property, inspection possible by arrangement. **Tourist information:** Fingal Valley Neighbourhood House, Talbot St, Fingal; (003) 74 2344. **Accommodation:** Limited.
MAP REF. 527 O9

Beaconsfield Pop. 1088

The ruins of impressive brick buildings with Romanesque arches dominate this quiet town on the West Tamar Hwy, 46 km NW of Launceston. Formerly a thriving gold township (called Cabbage Tree Hill), the ruins are the remains of buildings erected at the pithead of the Tasmanian Gold Mine in 1904. When the mine closed 10 years later after water seepage, more than 6 million dollars' worth of ore had been won from the reef. In 1804 a party of officers established a settlement north of the town, called York Town. **Of interest:** Grubb Shaft Museum in one of old mine buildings; restored miner's cottage and original Flowery Gully School alongside museum. **In the area:** York Town monument, on Kelso–Greens Beach Rd. Batman Bridge, 7 km SE, near Sidmouth; A-frame reaches 100 m above River Tamar. Auld Kirk (1843) at Sidmouth, 9 km SE. **Tourist information:** Tamar Visitors Centre, Main Rd, Exeter; (003) 94 4454. **Accommodation:** 3 hotels.
MAP REF. 523 J5, 527 K5

Beauty Point Pop. 1137

This popular fishing and yachting centre on the West Tamar Hwy, 48 km NE of Launceston, is the oldest deepwater port in the area and was constructed to serve the Beaconsfield goldmine. Today cargo is loaded at Bell Bay on the eastern shore of the Tamar River. **Of interest:** Nearby Sandy Beach for safe swimming. **In the area:** Two northern resorts: Kelso, 15 km N, dates back to early York Town settlement; Greens Beach, 20 km N, at mouth of River Tamar. Marion's Vineyard at Deviot, 12 km S. **Tourist information:** Tamar Visitors Centre, Main Rd, Exeter; (003) 94 4454. **Accommodation:** 1 hotel, 1 motel, 1 caravan/camping park.
MAP REF. 523 K5, 527 K5

Bicheno Pop. 705

A fishing port and holiday resort on the east coast, 195 km from Hobart, Bicheno offers surf, rock, sea and estuary fishing. The town's mild climate, outstanding fishing, nearby fine sandy beaches and its picturesque setting make it one of

Old mine building, Beaconsfield

Tasmania's most popular holiday resorts. Licensed seafood restaurants and a range of accommodation add to its appeal. Originally a sealing and whaling town from about 1803, it later became a coal-mining port in 1854. Today crayfishing is the main local industry. **Of interest:** On Tasman Hwy: Sea Life Centre, with aquarium and seafood restaurant; and Bicheno Dive Centre, diving school and charters. Picturesque foreshore walkway, from Redbill Point north of town to Blowhole to south. Lookouts at top of town's twin hills. Fairy Penguin Rookery; access Gordon St. Grave of Aboriginal heroine Waubedebar in Lions Park, Burgess St. Adventure tours, including scuba diving, water-skiing and mountain-bike-riding. **In the area:** East Coast Bird Life and Animal Park, 7 km N; Tasmanian devils and other native fauna. Douglas Apsley National Park, 10 km NW. Freycinet National Park, 10 km S. Freycinet Vineyard, 18 km SE; tastings and sales. **Tourist information:** Bicheno Penguin Adventure Tours, Foster St; (003) 75 1333. **Accommodation:** 2 hotel/motels, 2 caravan/camping parks.
MAP REF. 527 Q10

Boat Harbour Pop. 109

The clear water and rocky points of this attractive resort make it an ideal spot for skindiving and spear fishing. Situated on the north-west coast, 31 km W of Burnie, it adjoins one of the richest agricultural areas in the State. **Of interest:** Shannondoah Cottage, Bass Hwy; local crafts, lunches, Devonshire teas. **In the area:** Boat Harbour Beach, 3 km N; safe swimming, marine life in pools at low tide, fishing, water-skiing and bushwalking. Rocky Cape National Park, 19 km NW. Good fishing and swimming at Sisters Beach, 5 km NW. Birdland Native

Gardens nearby within park. **Tourist information:** 48 Cattley St, Burnie; (004) 34 6111. **Accommodation:** 2 motels, 1 caravan/camping park.
MAP REF. 526 F4

Bothwell   Pop. 396

This peaceful old country town in the beautiful Clyde River valley, 74 km N of Hobart, has been proclaimed a historic village. It has 52 buildings either classified or recorded by the National Trust as worthy of preservation. Surveyed in 1824 and named by Lieut.-Governor Arthur after the Scottish town of the same name, it is now the centre of quality sheep and cattle country. It is possible that the first golf in Australia was played on the links at the nearby homestead of Ratho during the 1830s. This course still exists and is open to visitors with golf-club membership elsewhere. **Of interest:** Bothwell Grange (c. 1836), Alexander St; guest house, tearooms and art gallery. Lamont Weaving Studio, Patrick St; demonstrations, sales, tearoom. Peter Muere Woodturning, Queens St. St Luke's Church (1830), Dennistoun St. Georgian brick Slate Cottage (1836), High St; restored and furnished in style of day. **In the area:** Restored and operational Thorpe Water Mill, 2 km N on Interlaken Rd; tours by arrangement. Excellent fishing at Arthurs Lake, Penstock Lagoon, Great Lake and Lake Echo. Cottages. **Tourist information:** Council Offices, Alexander St; (002) 59 5503. **Accommodation:** 1 camping/caravan park. **See also:** Scenic Island State.
MAP REF. 525 K3, 527 L12

Branxholm   Pop. 262

This small, former tin-mining town on the Tasman Hwy, 90 km NE of Launceston, now serves the surrounding rich vegetable-growing and dairying district. **Of interest:** Pine plantations and Firth Memorial Grove, Mt Horror Rd, Mt Horror. Old tin-mine workings and lapidary. **Tourist information:** Rose's Travel, 11 Alfred St, Scottsdale; (003) 52 2186. **Accommodation:** 1 hotel, 1 caravan/ camping park.
MAP REF. 527 O5

Bridgewater   Pop. 8684

This town, only 19 km N of Hobart, is situated on the bank of the main northern crossing of the Derwent River. The causeway was built in the early 1830s by 200 convicts, who barrowed 2 million tonnes of stone and clay from the site. The original bridge was opened in 1849; the present one dates from 1946. **In the area:** At Granton, 1 km across bridge: Old Watch House (now petrol station), built by convicts in 1838 to guard causeway, has smallest cell used in Australia (50 cm square and 2 m high); and Black Snake Inn (1833), another convict-built building. **Tourist information:** Council Offices, Tivoli Rd, Gagebrook; (002) 03 33. **Accommodation:** Limited.
MAP REF. 520 H4, 525 L5

Bridport   Pop. 1165

Bridport is a popular holiday resort and fishing town on the north-east coast, 85 km from Launceston. **Of interest:** Fine beaches and excellent river, sea and lake fishing. **In the area:** Bowood (1839), historic homestead near town; not open to public. Views from Waterhouse Point and Ranson's Beach. Winegrowing at Piper's Brook, 18 km W. **Tourist information:** Rose's Travel, 11 Alfred St, Scottsdale; (003) 52 2168. **Accommoda-**

tion: 1 hotel, 1 hotel/motel, 1 caravan/ camping park.
MAP REF. 527 M4

Brighton   Pop. 1472

This town, near Hobart on the Midland Hwy, has always been an important military post. It was first established in 1826 and today the Brighton Army Camp is the main military base in Tasmania. The town was named after the English resort by Governor Macquarie in 1821. **Of interest:** Agricultural Show in Nov. **In the area:** Bonorong Park Wildlife Sanctuary, 2 km SE. Historic village of Pontville, 2 km N. **Tourist information:** Council Offices, Tivoli Rd, Gagebrook; (002) 63 0333. **Accommodation:** 1 hotel/motel. **See also:** Rural Landscapes.
MAP REF. 520 H3, 525 L5

Bruny Island   Pop. 520

Almost two islands, separated by a narrow isthmus, Bruny was named after the French Admiral Bruni D'Entrecasteaux, who surveyed the channel between the island and the mainland of Tasmania in 1792. Abel Tasman discovered the island in 1642 but did not land. Other European visitors in the 18th century included Furneaux (1773), James Cook (1777) and William Bligh (1788 and 1792). The first apple trees in Tasmania are said to have been planted here by a botanist with the Bligh expedition. Bruny Island ferry departs from Kettering, on the mainland, several times daily. **Of interest:** Fishing. Camel tours. On South Bruny: Bligh Museum, at Adventure Bay, exhibits island's recorded history. Lookouts at Adventure and Cloudy Bays. Lighthouse (1836) at Cape Bruny, second oldest in Australia. Walking tracks to Mt Mangana and Mt Bruny. Scenic reserve at Mavista Falls on Adventure Bay. On North Bruny: memorials to early navigators. Dennes Point beach on D'Entrecasteaux Channel, picnic/barbecue facilities. At Variety Bay, remains of convict-built church on private property near airstrip; conducted tours. **Tourist information:** Council Offices, Alonnah; (002) 93 1139. **Accommodation:** 1 hotel, 2 caravan/camping parks.
MAP REF. 525 L9

Buckland   Pop. 228

A stained glass window depicting the life of John the Baptist and dating back to the 14th century is in the church in this tiny

Colonial Accommodation

As a result of the popularity of this type of accommodation over the last few years, there are now over 150 properties, including host farms and colonial cottages, available for visitors.

    Host farms provide a wide variety of standard and type of service, and offer guests the opportunity to observe farm life or become involved in it.

    Colonial accommodation is provided in buildings or cottages established on their present sites before 1901. Although concessions are made to allow modern facilities to be incorporated, interiors are presented in colonial style by the use of genuine or reproduction furniture and other decoration.

For further information, contact the nearest Tasmanian Travel Centre.

township, 64 km NE of Hobart. History links the window with Battle Abbey, England, which stands on the site of the Battle of Hastings. The abbey was sacked by Oliver Cromwell in the 17th century, but the window was hidden before it could be destroyed. Two centuries later it was given to Rev. T.H. Fox, Buckland's first rector, by the Marquis of Salisbury. It is now set into the east wall of the Church of St John the Baptist, built 1846. Although the window has been damaged and restored several times in its long life, the original figure-work is intact. Also of interest is Ye Olde Buckland Inn, a 19th-century tavern and restaurant. **Tourist information:** Council Offices, cnr Vicary and Henry Sts, Triabunna; (002) 57 3113. **Accommodation:** 1 hotel.
MAP REF. 521 M2, 525 N4

Burnie
Pop. 20 505

The rapid expansion of Burnie, now Tasmania's 4th largest town, is based on one of the State's largest industrial enterprises, Associated Pulp and Paper Mills Ltd. Situated on Emu Bay, 148 km W of Launceston, Burnie has a busy deepwater port, which serves the west coast mining centres. Other important industries include plants for the manufacture of titanium oxide pigments, dried milk, chocolate products and cheese. **Of interest:** Lactos cheese factory, Old Surrey Rd; tastings and sales. Tours of Amcor, Marine Tce. Pioneer Village Museum, High St; reconstruction of Burnie's small tradesmen's shops at turn of century. Meals at restored Burnie Inn, town's oldest remaining building, re-erected in Burnie Park, Glen Osborne, historic building, Aileen Cres; offers b & b. Burnie's Athletic Carnival New Year's Day; cycling, foot racing and woodchopping. **In the area:** Local beauty spots include: on town's outskirts, Round Hill, for panoramic views; Fern Glade, 5 km W, for riverside walks and picnics; Emu Valley Rhododendron Gardens, 3 km S; Guide Falls at Ridgley, 17 km S; and 20 km S, Upper Natone Forest Reserve for picnics. Day tours to: Cradle Mountain, Gunns Plains, Leven Canyon and Fossil Cliffs, inland. Pieman River cruises. **Tourist information:** 48 Cattley St; (004) 34 6111. **Accommodation:** 4 hotels, 2 hotel/motels, 5 motels, 2 caravan/camping parks. **See also:** Scenic Island State.
MAP REF. 526 G4

The Hazards, Freycinet National Park, near Coles Bay

Campbell Town
Pop. 820

Campbell Town, on the Midlands Hwy, 66 km S of Launceston, is a national centre for selling stud sheep. The area's links with the wool industry go back to the early 1820s, when Saxon merinos were introduced to the Macquarie Valley, west of the town. Timber and stud beef are also important primary industries. The town and the Elizabeth River were named by Governor Macquarie for his wife, the former Elizabeth Campbell. **Of interest:** Wesleyan Chapel (1846), King St; owned by National Trust. National-Trust-classified buildings include: St Michael's Church (1857), King St; Balmoral Cottage (1840s), Bridge St; and St Luke's Church (1839), The Grange (1840), Campbell Town Inn (1840) and convict-built Red Bridge (1837), all in High St. Memorial to Harold Gatty, first round-the-world flight navigator, also in High St. **In the area:** Evansville Game Park, 30 km E. Trout fishing in local rivers and lakes, particularly Lake Leake, 30 km SE. **Tourist information:** 75 High St; (003) 81 1388. **Accommodation:** 2 hotels. **See also:** Scenic Island State.
MAP REF. 527 N10

Coles Bay
Pop. 120

This beautiful unspoiled bay, 39 km S of Bicheno on the Freycinet Peninsula, is a good base for visitors to the 70 000 ha Freycinet National Park. **Of interest:** Park's pleasant beaches, crystal-clear waters and colourful heathlands make it ideal for swimming, fishing and bushwalking. Abundant birdlife and variety of wildflowers, including 60 varieties of small ground orchid. Rock climbing on the Hazards and nearby cliffs. Opportunities for water-skiing, skindiving, canoeing and sailing. Charter boat trips to Schouten Island. Tours by arrangement. **Tourist information:** Park Ranger; (002) 57 0107. **Accommodation:** Coles Bay, 1 motel, 3 caravan/camping parks. Friendly Beaches, camping area. **See also:** National Parks.
MAP REF. 525 Q2, 527 Q11

Cygnet
Pop. 924

The centre of a fruit-growing district, 54 km from Hobart, the town was originally named Port de Cygne (meaning Swan Port) by the French Admiral Bruni D'Entrecasteaux because of the number of swans in the bay. **Of interest:** Good beaches and boat-launching facilities at Verona Sands, Randalls Bay and Egg and Bacon Bay. Port Cygnet Fishing Carnival held in March. **In the area:** Boating, fishing, bushwalks and gem fossicking. Deepings Woodturning, Nicholls Rivulet, 10 km W. Harts View and Winter Wood wineries, 10 km W; tastings and sales. At Gardners Bay, 6 km S: Talune Wildlife Park and Koala Gardens; picnic/barbecue facilities, cabin accommodation. Unique Lymington lace agate sometimes found at Drip Beach, Lymington, 12 km S. **Tourist information:**

National Parks

In 1863 legislation was introduced to preserve certain areas of Tasmania for their splendid scenic value. Today the Parks and Wildlife Service of Tasmania manages not only the State's 14 national parks but also many State reserves with their Aboriginal areas, caves, gorges, waterfalls, rivers, and historic sites that date back as far as 1803, when European settlers first landed on the island.

All parks are accessible year round, but some tourists believe the highland parks are best seen in summer and autumn, when the climate is more reliable, and when wildflowers bloom in profusion and flowering trees and shrubs are alive with birdlife.

The two areas to be declared the first national parks of Tasmania were Mount Field, just 80 kilometres north-west of Hobart, and Freycinet, on the central east coast. **Mount Field** is a popular tourist venue, offering such activities as climbing and bushwalking. It also provides the only developed skiing area in southern Tasmania. There are several delightful waterfalls within the park, the best-known being Russell Falls, which was discovered in 1856. Here the cascading water plunges in two stages into deep gorges shaded by tree ferns that filter sunlight and create a mosaic effect. There are two levels of forest, including the ancient pencil pine, 250-year-old gum trees, sassafras, giant tree ferns, the unique horizontal scrub and a variety of mosses, ferns, lichens and fungi. There is a wide range of walks from leisurely to strenuous, including the famed Lyrebird Walk, where you may see the black currawong, native to Tasmania, and hear the noisy yellow wattlebird or perhaps the endless repertoire of the lyrebird's mimicry.

Freycinet National Park offers the nature lover wide stretches of white sands, rocky headlands, granite peaks, quiet beaches and small caves, with windswept eucalypt forests on its slopes and excellent short or long walking tracks. Just north of the park is Moulting Lagoon, the breeding ground of the lovely black swan and a refuge for other waterfowl. Freycinet National Park also includes Schouten Island, separated from the Freycinet Peninsula by a 1 kilometre wide passage, and reached only by boat. Near the park is Coles Bay, a fishing and swimming resort with delightful coastal scenery.

A short distance north-west of Freycinet National Park is Tasmania's newest national park, **Douglas Apsley** (16 080 hectares). Proclaimed in 1990, this park contains the State's last large dry sclerophyll forest and can be traversed along a 3-day north–south walking track. Here forest-clad ridges contrast with patches of rainforest and river gorges. Waterfalls and spectacular coastal views add to the grandeur of the area. Facilities are basic.

Many of Tasmania's national parks are important wildlife reserves. One such park, the 13 899-hectare **Mount William National Park** in north-east Tasmania, is a sanctuary for an abundance of native animals, including the Forester kangaroo (Tasmania's only kangaroo), echidna, wombat, pademelon, Bennetts wallaby and Tasmanian devil. Spring brings a carpet of wildflowers to this park: the red and white heaths provide a background for the contrasting colours of the golden wattle and the guinea flower. At Lookout Point, thousands of rock orchids creep over and cover the granite rocks.

Fifty kilometres south-east of Launceston is **Ben Lomond National Park**, one of Tasmania's two main ski fields, with an alpine village, ski-tows, ski hire, a tavern with accommodation and a public shelter.

Steep, jagged mountains create a natural amphitheatre at the **Walls of Jerusalem National Park** (51 800 hectares) in the State's north central zone. Ancient forests of pencil pines ring tiny glacially formed lakes, making the park very popular with bushwalkers.

The central north coastal strip of **Asbestos Range National Park** is an important refuge for the rare ground parrot and the rufous wallaby. Its islands off Port Sorell provide an important breeding area for fairy penguins and the tidal and mud flats are ideal feeding grounds for a variety of migratory seabirds. On the

Dove Lake, Cradle Mountain Lake St Clair National Park

Wineglass Bay, Freycinet National Park

unspoiled beaches of this park, white sands come to life with thousands of soldier crabs.

Further west along the coast, **Rocky Cape National Park** (3064 hectares) encompasses rugged coastline with small sheltered beaches backed by heath-covered hills. It is known for its rock shelters once used by Aborigines.

Covering some of Tasmania's highest country is **Cradle Mountain Lake St Clair National Park**. There is a visitors centre near the entrance to the park at Cradle Mountain, and a nature walk into the nearby rainforest incorporates a suspended walkway. Cradle Mountain has a variety of fine bushwalks, including one of Australia's best-known walking routes, the 85 kilometre Overland Track. Here walkers can hike through forests of deciduous beech, Tasmanian 'myrtle', pandanus, King Billy pine and a wealth of wildflowers. At the other end of the park, the tranquil Lake St Clair, with a depth of over 200 metres, occupies a basin gouged out by two glaciers more than 20 000 years ago; cruises operate daily, and 6-day treks take in Mt Ossa (Tasmania's highest mountain) and the Pine Valley region. Lake St Clair was discovered by Europeans as early as 1826 and is now a popular spot for boating. There are several campsites. Cradle Mountain Wilderness Lodge lies on the northern boundary of the national park.

Although **Maria Island**, off the east coast, is not easily accessible it is well worth a visit. You can get there either by light aircraft or by passenger ferry from Triabunna or Louisville. On arrival, it seems as if you have stepped into another world, for on Maria Island no tourist vehicles are permitted. The island embraces magnificently coloured sandstone cliffs and is a refuge for over eighty species of birds. Forester kangaroos, emus and Cape Barren geese roam freely in this totally unspoiled landscape. Its intriguing history and historic buildings date back to the convict era of 1825 and provide a contrast to the now peaceful surroundings.

Tasmania's largest national park is **South West National Park**, which has 605 213 hectares of mainly remote wilderness country. Here there are dolerite- and quartzite-capped mountains, sharp ridges and steep valleys left by glaciers; the dense forests are made up of eucalypts, ancient Huon pines and shrubs and limbs of the Antarctic beech, all covered with mosses, ferns, lichens and the pink-flowered climbing heath. Mountain climbers will find a challenge in Federation Peak, Mount Anne and Precipitous Bluff, while anglers will be kept busy with trout fishing at Lakes Pedder and Gordon. A new bird hide at Melaleuca can be used in summer to observe the extremely rare orange-bellied parrot.

The 440 000-hectare **Franklin Gordon Wild Rivers National Park** forms the central portion of Tasmania's World Heritage Area. The Franklin attracts wilderness adventurers from around the world to test its challenging rapids. Along the slightly more placid Gordon River are stands of 2000-year-old Huon pine. Unusual buttongrass vegetation growing right to the edge of the water stains it to the colour of tea. The Lyell Highway, the road link between Hobart and the west coast, runs through the park. A number of excellent short walks lead off the highway to rainforests and spectacular lookouts.

A 2-hour drive from Hobart, through Geeveston to the south-east, brings visitors to the **Hartz Mountains National Park**. Most of the area is over 600 metres in altitude with Hartz Peak being 1255 metres high. There are basic facilities for the day visitor and no camping facilities, although camping is permitted. Bushwalking is popular, although all visitors are warned that the area is subject to sudden storms, even in summer.

At the southern end of Flinders Island in Bass Strait is **Strzelecki National Park** (4215 ha). Famed for its exhilarating views from Mt Strzelecki's granite summit, the park also boasts beaches and camping among she-oaks at Trousers Point.

In some of the many State reserves, limestone caves are a popular attraction. The cave interiors are dramatically lit to enhance the wonderland of limestone-derived calcite formations. The Hastings Caves, located 110 kilometres from Hobart, include a nearby thermal swimming pool with a year-round warm temperature. Set in a fern glade, the pool is surrounded by lawns and picnic areas. In the north central region, King Solomon and Marakoopa Caves are popular destinations.

For further information on Tasmania's national parks, contact the Parks and Wildlife Service, 134 Macquarie Street, Hobart (GPO Box 44A, Hobart 7001); (002) 33 6285.

Talure Wildlife Park, Gardners Bay; (002) 95 1775. **Accommodation:** 1 hotel, 1 caravan/camping park.
MAP REF. 520 F10, 525 L8

Deddington Pop. 50

In 1830 artist John Glover arrived from England and bought land on the site of this little town, 37 km SE of Launceston. He named his property Deddington after the village in the English Lake District where he had lived. **Of interest:** Deddington Chapel (1840), designed by Glover, classified by National Trust. John Glover's grave beside chapel. **Tourist information:** Council Offices, Smith St, Longford; (003) 91 1303. **Accommodation:** None.
MAP REF. 527 M8

Deloraine Pop. 2098

Scenic Deloraine, with Bass Strait to the north and the Great Western Tiers to the south, is an ideal base for exploring the many attractions of northern Tasmania. The surrounding rich countryside is used mainly for dairying and mixed farming. **Of interest:** Self-guide Heritage Walk. Deloraine Folk Museum, Emu Bay Rd; housed in Plough Inn, classified by National Trust, Gallery 9, West Barrack St. **In the area:** Tasmanian Smokehouse, 10 km W; sales of gourmet fish. Tasmanian Wildlife Park, 18 km W; specially designed noctarium for displaying nocturnal animals. Heidi Cheese Factory, Exton, 6 km E; tastings and sales. Scenic drives south to Liffey, Meander and Montana Falls; also to Central Highlands, through Golden Valley, to Great Lake, highest body of water in Australia. Excellent trout fishing on lake and in Mersey and Meander Rivers. A number of b & b. **Tourist information:** 29 Westchurch St; (003) 62 2046. **Accommodation:** 1 motel, 1 caravan/camping park. **See also:** Stately Homes.
MAP REF. 522 I11, 527 J7

Derby Pop. 200

Derby is a small tin mining town on the Tasman Hwy, 34 km from Scottsdale in the north-east. In its heyday, tin mining was a flourishing industry, but there has been a gradual swing to rural production, although tin is still worked. **Of interest:** Derby Tin Mine Museum, housed in old school (1890s), with tearooms; local history, gemstone and mineral displays, tin panning demonstrations. Reconstructed 'town' surrounding museum consists of 7 original buildings from area: miner's cottage, newspaper office, mining assay office, butcher's shop, general store, blacksmith's shop and two cells from old Derby gaol. In Main St: Wallaby's Woodcraft, woodturning; Taylor Made Crafts, in old bank, local crafts. **Tourist information:** Tin Mine Museum, Main St; (003) 54 2262. **Accommodation:** 1 hotel, 1 camping area.
MAP REF. 527 O5

Devonport Pop. 22 660

As the terminal for a vehicular ferry from Melbourne, Devonport has become a busy industrial and agricultural-export town, as well as a major tourist centre. Devonport has its own airport, and is ideally suited as a visitor base for seeing scenic northern Tasmania. **Of interest:** Self-guide leaflets from tourist centre. Showcase Gallery and Art Centre, Best St. Maritime Museum, Victoria Pde, The Bluff. Taswegia, printery museum, Formby Rd. Tiagarra, Tasmanian Aboriginal Culture and Art Centre at Mersey Bluff, parklands and beach resort promontory at river mouth; Tasmanian Aboriginal rock carvings outside display area. Home Hill, Middle Rd; tours of home of former Prime Minister Joseph Lyons and Dame Enid Lyons. **In the area:** Walking track (12 km) from The Bluff to Don River Railway and Museum, at Don, 6 km W. Forth, 13 km W, has spring of pure water claimed to have medicinal qualities. Braddon's Lookout, near Forth, with panoramic view of coastline. Tasmanian Aboretum (45 ha) at Eugenana, 10 km S; picnic area and

Lighthouse on the Bluff, near Devonport

walking tracks. **Tourist information:** 18 Rooke St; (004) 21 6226. **Accommodation:** 4 hotels, 2 hotel/motels, 2 motels, 3 caravan/camping parks. **See also:** Scenic Island State.
MAP REF. 522 E5, 526 I5

Dover Pop. 521

This attractive fishing port, south of Hobart, was once a convict station. The original Commandant's Office still stands, but the cells, which are underground just up from the wharf, can no longer be seen. Quaint old cottages and English trees give the town an old-world atmosphere. The 3 islands in the bay are called Faith, Hope and Charity. **Of interest:** Chartered fishing trips. Several old graves on Faith Island. Attractive scenery and unspoiled beaches make area ideal for bushwalking and swimming. Casey's Steam Museum, Main St; working steam engines. Several b & b. **In the area:** Southport, 21 km S, fishing port established in days of sealers and whalers; good fishing, swimming, surfing and bushwalking. Catamaran, 39 km S; most southerly town in Australia. Cockle Creek, further 2 km S, is start of extended South Coast Walking Track. **Tourist information:** Church St, Geeveston; (002) 97 1836. **Accommodation:** 1 hotel, 1 caravan/camping park.
MAP REF. 520 E12, 525 K9

Dunalley Pop. 306

This prosperous fishing village stands on the narrow isthmus connecting the Forestier Peninsula to the rest of Tasmania. The Denison Canal, spanned by a swing bridge, provides access to the east coast for small vessels. **Of interest:** Bangor Farm, off Arthur Hwy; conservation farm, home of Oyster Bay Aborigines and site of Abel Tasman's landing; tours of farm, middens, artefacts and nature reserves include lunch; bookings essential; (002) 53 5233. Tasman Memorial, Imlay St, marking first landing by Europeans on 2 December 1642, to north-east, near Cape Paul Lamanon. **Tourist information:** Council Offices, 12 Somerville St, Sorell; (002) 65 2201. **Accommodation:** 1 motel.
MAP REF. 521 M6, 525 O6

Eaglehawk Neck
Pop. 150

In convict days this narrow isthmus, which separates the Tasman from the

Forestier Peninsula, was guarded by a line of ferocious tethered dogs. Soldiers and constables also stood guard, to ensure that no convicts escaped from the notorious convict settlement at Port Arthur. The only prisoners to escape did so by swimming. The town today, in complete contrast, is a pleasant fishing resort. A charter tuna fishing fleet operates from Pirate's Bay. **Of interest:** Historic officers' quarters, next to Officers Mess, off Arthur Hwy; restored, open for inspection. **In the area:** Four unusual natural features in Tasman Arch State Reserve, off Arthur Hwy—Tasman's Arch, Devil's Kitchen, Blowhole and Tessellated Pavement—are within 4 km E of town. Coastal walking track leads from Devil's Kitchen to Waterfall Bay and on to Fortescue Bay. Good sailing in Eaglehawk Neck Bay. Dive centres near Blowhole and below Lookout; groups for diving and lessons. Port Arthur convict settlement, 21 km SW. **Tourist information:** Officers Mess, off Arthur Hwy; (002) 50 3635. **Accommodation:** 1 hotel, 1 motel. **See also:** A Convict Past; Tours from Hobart.
MAP REF. 521 N8, 525 O7

Evandale
Pop. 772

This little township, 19 km from Launceston, has been proclaimed an historic village. Founded in 1829, some of its buildings date from as early as 1809. Originally it was named Collins Hill, but was renamed in 1836 in honour of Tasmania's first Surveyor-General, G. W. Evans. It remains unspoiled by progress and retains many buildings of historical and architectural significance. **Of interest:** Self-guide Heritage Walk from Tourism and History Centre, High St. Also in High St: Solomon House (1836) offers Devonshire teas, accommodation; St Andrew's (1871) and Uniting (1839) churches; Blenheim (1840s), stained glass sales and inspection of workshop. Strickland's Gallery, Russell St; bronze castings and foundry inspection. Sunday market in Falls Park, Russell St. Village Fair and National Penny Farthing Championships held in Feb. Colonial cottages. **In the area:** Clarendon (1838), 8 km S near Nile; designed in grand manner and set in extensive formal gardens. Old inn at Nile also of historic interest. **Tourist information:** High St; (003) 91 8128. **Accommodation:** 2 motels. **See also:** Stately Homes.
MAP REF. 523 P12, 527 M8

Exeter
Pop. 394

Exeter serves a large fruit-growing area 24 km NW of Launceston. **In the area:** To north-east, former river resorts of Gravelly Beach and Paper Beach. Walking track (5 km return) leads from Paper Beach to Supply River. Near (400 m) mouth of Supply River, ruins of first water-driven flour mill in Tasmania, built 1825. Notley Fern Gorge, at Notley Hills, 11 km S; 10 ha rainforest reserve with picnic/barbecue areas. Brady's Lookout, rocky outcrop used by notorious bushranger Matthew Brady, in State Reserve, 5 km SE. Monument to John Batman's ship *Rebecca*, in which he crossed Bass Strait to Yarra River; ship was built at the once busy shipyards at Rosevears, 6 km SE. On Rosevears Dr, historic Rosevears Hotel, first licensed 1831; also Waterbird Haven, wetlands habitat with treetop hide. Tastings and sales at 10 wineries in West Tamar winegrowing area. **Tourist information:** Tamar Visitors Centre, Main Rd; (003) 94 4454. **Accommodation:** Limited.
MAP REF. 523 L7, 527 L6

Fingal
Pop. 428

Situated in the Esk Valley, 21 km inland from St Marys on the South Esk River, Fingal is the headquarters of the state's coal industry. The first payable gold in Tasmania was found in 1852 at The Nook, near Fingal. **Of interest:** Historic buildings include: St Joseph's Church, Grey St. Masonic Lodge, Brown St. In Talbot St: St Peter's Church; Holder Bros. General Store; and Fingal Hotel, with collection of over 280 different brands of Scotch whisky. Coal Shovelling Festival held Feb. or March; includes World Coal Shovelling Championships. **In the area:** Mathinna, 27 km N; extensive forestry development area with waterfalls nearby. White Gum Forest Reserve at Evercreech, further 3 km; 89 m white gum, picnic/barbecue areas, rainforest walking tracks. **Tourist information:** Fingal Valley Neighbourhood House, Talbot St; (003) 74 2344. **Accommodation:** 1 hotel. **See also:** Stately Homes.
MAP REF. 527 P8

Franklin
Pop. 462

This timber milling town, 45 km SW of Hobart, was the site of the first European settlement in the Huon district in 1804. It was named after Governor Sir John Franklin, who took up 259 ha on the banks of the Huon River. Timber milling has been an important local industry since the very early years. Orcharding and dairy farming are the other main industries. Country Cottage.

St Andrew's Church, Evandale

Scenic Island State

Wherever your holiday journey in Tasmania takes you, you will be sure to see magnificent scenery and to have many fascinating experiences along the way. Most travellers start their Tasmanian holiday in the north, where they have either taken their car off the ferry or have hired a car or mobile home for the journey south.

Probably the best way to see what Tasmania has to offer is to take the 'circle route', with as many diversions along the way as time permits to see and explore scenic or historic highlights. Such a tour of the island, which is small enough to allow you to see most of it in a short space of time, will take you through some of the most fascinating country that Australia has to offer. The incomparable wilderness of the west coast, the towering mountains of the central district, the gentle pastoral landscapes of the Midlands, the lavish orchard country around Launceston and the Huon Valley, the snug beaches, bays and villages of the east coast, are all relatively accessible on good roads.

You will soon find that not everything about Tasmania is small. The trees are taller here than on the mainland, nurtured by the temperate climate (Tasmania has the world's tallest hardwood trees, some exceeding 90 metres); mountains vault to the skies from wild forest land. The great inland lakes in the mountains feed savage rivers, some of which harness the State's great hydro-electric schemes. The hills and valleys are harshly carved by the weather and become gentle only in the rolling pastoral lands of the Midlands and the north.

In this romantic landscape, more reminiscent of Scotland than Australia, are set the remnants of a rich past of convict and colonial life—the prisons, churches, cottages and courthouses, the barracks, mansions and homesteads from the earliest days of European settlement.

From **Devonport**, the coast road west runs with the northern railway along the sea's edge, beneath the impressive cliffs that face Bass Strait. Along this road are the thriving towns of **Ulverstone**, **Burnie**,

Wynyard and **Stanley**, and the striking headlands of Table Cape, Rocky Cape and the Nut. They are worth a special trip, as is a detour down the side road from **Penguin** to the peaceful mountain farmland of Gunns Plains and the Gunns Plains caves. The road from **Forth** into the vast wilderness areas of the magnificent Cradle Mountain Lake St Clair National Park is also well worth a visit, but the turnoff to follow the circle route is at **Somerset**, from where you head south down the Murchison Highway through the rich farmlands towards the increasingly mountainous country of the west coast. An interesting diversion leads to **Corinna**, once a thriving town but now virtually abandoned, on the beautiful Pieman River, not far from its mouth. A launch trip from Corinna travels through deeply-cut river gorges west to the Indian Ocean.

Back on the main road, the mountain scenery is unique and quite spectacular. The towns here developed as a result of their mineral wealth. **Zeehan** now has only a small population, but at the turn of the century there were more than 10 000 inhabitants when tin mining was at its height. Many buildings of those days still stand. The larger town of **Queenstown** has grown up around the Mount Lyell copper mine, in a valley beneath bare, bleached hills, streaked and stained with the hues of minerals—chrome, purple, grey and pink. Nearby is **Strahan** on Macquarie Harbour, the only coastal town in the west. The harbour can be reached only by shallow-draught vessels through the notorious passage called Hell's Gates. Visitors can cruise through beautiful wilderness country along the Gordon River, past the ruins of the remote convict settlement on Sarah Island.

The road turns inland from these towns, avoiding the almost inaccessible southwest, and travels through the Franklin Gordon Wild Rivers National Park, across the Central Highlands past Lake St Clair and down the Derwent River valley through the town of **New Norfolk**, centre of the Tasmanian hop-growing industry. This valley, brilliantly coloured with foliage in autumn, is both of scenic and historical interest. It was settled by Europeans in 1808, the site having been chosen by Governor Macquarie.

A detour from the Hobart road leads to the lovely old town of Richmond, one of the many historic towns off the Midlands Highway that are not visited if the circle route is followed. (Some of the others are **Ross, Oatlands, Campbell Town,**

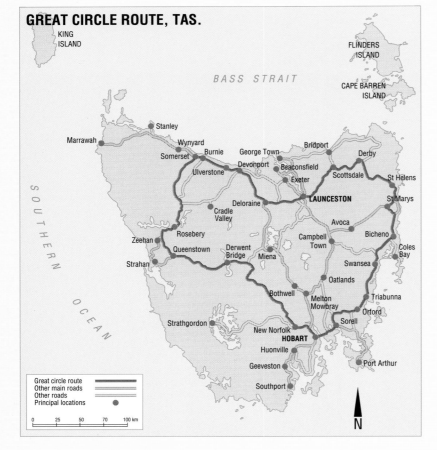

GREAT CIRCLE ROUTE, TAS.

KING ISLAND

FLINDERS ISLAND

CAPE BARREN ISLAND

BASS STRAIT

Marrawah

Stanley

Wynyard
Somerset Burnie George Town Bridport
Devonport Beaconsfield Derby
Ulverstone Exeter Scottsdale St Helens

Deloraine LAUNCESTON St Marys

Cradle Valley Avoca
Rosebery Bicheno
Zeehan Campbell Town
Queenstown Derwent Bridge Miena Coles Bay
Strahan Swansea

Oatlands

Bothwell Triabunna
Melton Mowbray Orford

Strathgordon Sorell

New Norfolk HOBART
Huonville

Geeveston Port Arthur

Southport

SOUTHERN OCEAN

Great circle route
Other main roads
Other roads
Principal locations

0   25   50   70   100 km

N

Bothwell and **Longford**, all set in the charming rolling countryside of the Midlands with their English trees framing or hiding the landowners' mansions.) Richmond is probably the best example, its old Georgian houses and cottages clustered together with its bridge, convict-built and the oldest freestone bridge still in use in Australia. The gaol pre-dates Port Arthur as a penal settlement; two churches, a courthouse, a schoolhouse, a rectory, the hotel granary, a general store and a flour mill were all built in the 1820s and 1830s.

Hobart, Australia's second oldest and most southerly city, is attractively sited on the Derwent River, with Mount Wellington looming above it. The port area at Salamanca Place, where the old bond stores and warehouses are sited, is a reminder of the days when the whaling fleet and the timber ships tied up at the wharf and sailors went out on the town. Battery Point with its barracks, workers' cottages and Arthur's Circus—its Georgian-style houses built around a circular green—is part of Hobart's beginnings.

There are many fine public buildings in the city, which help it to retain something of the feeling of its colonial days. There is modern-day fun in Hobart, too, since the Wrest Point Hotel–Casino developed as Hobart's best-known entertainment complex.

In complete contrast, the grim but beautiful penal settlement of **Port Arthur** is not far from Hobart, on the Tasman Peninsula. Here, within the forbidding

Scenery near Strahan

sandstone walls, visitors will feel something of the hopelessness and isolation of the thousands of convicts who passed through this settlement during its 47 years of existence.

South of Hobart is the scenic Huon Valley, particularly spectacular when the apple trees are in blossom. At the southern end of the route is Cockle Creek on Recherche Bay, where the South Coast walking track begins.

North on the circle route from Hobart the Tasman Highway traverses the east coast, a region enjoying a mild and equable climate throughout most of the year and with a number of attractive seaside resorts. Most are on sheltered inlets but within easy reach of surf beaches and

fishing grounds: towns like **Orford**, **Triabunna**, **Swansea**, **Bicheno**, **Scamander** and **St Helens**.

Off the Tasman Highway near Bicheno is the Freycinet National Park on the Freycinet Peninsula. There are many walking tracks through this park, which is dominated by the Hazards, a red-granite mountain range. Many varieties of the small ground orchid have been identified in the park and the birdlife is prolific.

The road cuts across the less developed farming country of the north and goes west to **Launceston**, the northern capital of Tasmania, 64 kilometres from the north coast at the junction of the North Esk, South Esk and Tamar Rivers. It is a smaller, more provincial city than Hobart, set in pleasant hilly countryside, and makes an excellent base from which to explore the rich coastal plain of the Tamar Valley and the mountain country to the north of the island's central plateau. Cataract Gorge, historic Franklin House and Entally House, and the hydro-electric station at Duck Reach, built in 1895, are all within easy reach of Launceston.

On to Devonport, where this description of the circle route began. Many of Tasmania's magnificent national parks are not far from the circle route highway, and a close scrutiny of the map will lead to many other interesting diversions.

For further information, contact the Tasmanian Information Centre, 20 Davey St; (002) 30 8233. **See also:** Individual town entries in A–Z listing; National Parks.

Dams for Power

Tasmania has the largest hydro-electric power system in Australia, producing nearly 10 per cent of the nation's electrical energy.

It is Tasmania's highland rivers that produce the volume of water necessary for these hydro-electric systems. The Derwent, Mersey, Forth, Gordon, King and Pieman Rivers have already been harnessed for power production.

Stage 1 of the Gordon River power development involved 4 major dams, the creation of Lakes Gordon and Pedder, and an underground power station. The lakes are stocked with trout and have already become tourist attractions.

Continuing development to harness and use this massive water power has included the construction of 4 other major

dams—Murchison, Mackintosh, Bastyan and Reece—and the creation of 4 new lakes. A spectacular rockfill has created Lake Pieman on the Lower Pieman River and will supply water for the third and biggest power station in the complex.

Driving between **Hobart** and **Queenstown**, you can see much of the Derwent power scheme, the most extensive of the hydro-electric developments, consisting of 10 power stations. The Derwent River rises in Lake St Clair, 738 metres above sea level, and all but the last 44 metres of its fall is utilised.

There are public viewing galleries at Tungatinah, Tarraleah, Liapootah and Trevallyn power stations, and overnight accommodation is available at Bronte Park and Tarraleah.

The power developments on the Mersey and Forth Rivers, although smaller than the Derwent scheme are far more spectacular, as the system lies within a very steep river valley. The scheme encompasses 7 power stations and rises at Lake Mackenzie, 1121 metres above sea level. A feature is the spectacular Lake Barrington, site for National and World Rowing Championships. Day trips may be arranged at any north-west-coast tourist centre.

For further information on HEC public viewing areas, roads open to the public, environmental issues, guided tours and accommodation, contact the Hydro-electric Commission, 4–16 Elizabeth St, Hobart 7000; (002) 30 5111.

Tourist information: Huon River Jet Boats, Esplanade, Huonville; (002) 64 1838. **Accommodation:** Limited. **See also:** Rural Landscapes.
MAP REF. 520 E9, 525 K7

Geeveston　　Pop. 826

This important timber town is the gateway to Tasmania's south-west World Heritage Area. **Of interest:** Esperance Forest and Heritage Centre, Church St; tourist complex incorporating Gateway to South-West (Huon Hwy), Hartz Gallery (wilderness art and craft) and 5 forest walks. **In the area:** Arve and Weld valleys west of town contain world's tallest (87 m) hardwood trees. Hartz Mountains National Park, 23 km SW, off Arve Rd. Tahune Forest Reserve, 27 km NW on Arve Rd; camping and recreation area. Cruises on Huon River. **Tourist information:** Church St; (002) 97 1836. **Accommodation:** Limited.
MAP REF. 520 D10, 525 K8

George Town　　Pop. 5026

Situated at the mouth of the River Tamar, George Town was first settled by Europeans in 1811, when it was named for King George III. Today it is a commercial centre, mainly as a result of the Comalco plant at Bell Bay and other industrial developments. **Of interest:** Self-guide walk. Monument on Esplanade commemorates unintentional landing in 1804, when Lieut.–Col. William Paterson and his crew in HMS *Buffalo* ran aground during storm. Devonshire teas and lunches at The Grove (c. 1838), cnr Elizabeth and Cimitiere Sts. **In the area:** Inspections of Comalco plant at Bell Bay, 6 km S. At Hillwood, 24 km S; pick-your-own strawberry farm. Ghost town of goldmining settlement at Lefroy, 10 km E; ruins, old diggings, cemetery. Pipers Brook winegrowing region, 33 km E; tastings and sales at several wineries. Low Head, 5 km N; surf beach and river beach; also Maritime Museum in Australia's oldest continuously used pilot station, opened 1803. Day and weekend cruises to Bass Strait islands on SS *Furneaux Explorer*. Several b & b. **Tourist information:** Main Rd; (003) 82 1700. **Accommodation:** 2 hotels, 1 hotel/motel, 1 motel. **See also:** Stately Homes.
MAP REF. 523 K4, 527 K5

Gladstone　　Pop. 200

The small township of Gladstone is one of the few communities in the far

Loading pulp wood, Huonville

north-east that still relies on tin mining. The district was once a thriving tin and goldmining area, with a colourful early history. Now many of these once-substantial townships are near-ghost towns or ghost towns. **In the area:** Geological formations in Gladstone–South Mt Cameron area. Boobyalla, old mining town, 20 km north-west. Moorina, 30 km SW; section of old cemetery contains graves of Chinese miners. Former tin mining town of Weldborough, 37 km SW, once headquarters for 900 Chinese miners. Mt William National Park, 25 km E; prolific flora and fauna and excellent beaches. Historic lighthouse at Eddystone Point, 35 km E. **Tourist information:** Rose's Travel, 11 Alfred St, Scottsdale; (003) 52 2186. **Accommodation:** 1 hotel.
MAP REF. 527 P4

Hadspen　　Pop. 1334

The township of Hadspen, which was first settled in the early 1820s, has many historic buildings some of which offer accommodation or meals. **Of interest:** Row of Georgian buildings, including Red Feather Inn (c. 1844), old coaching station. Hadspen Gaol (c. 1840). Church of the Good Shepherd; building commenced in 1858, funded by Thomas Reibey, who withdrew his support after a dispute with the bishop. Church was completed in 1961, almost 50 years after Reibey's death. Rutherglen Holiday Village. **In the area:** Entally House (1819), one of Tasmania's most famous historic

homes, 1 km W on banks of South Esk River; magnificent collection of Regency furniture and fine silverware. **Accommodation:** 1 hotel/motel, 1 caravan/camping park. **See also:** Stately Homes.
MAP REF. 523 N11, 527 L7

Hamilton　　Pop. 150

A classified historic town in a rural setting, Hamilton has retained many of its colonial buildings. **Of interest:** Glen Clyde House (c. 1840), Grace St; award-winning craft gallery and tearooms. Cottages and b & b. **In the area:** Meadowbank Lake, 10 km NW; popular venue for picnics, boating, water-skiing and trout fishing. **Tourist information:** Council Offices, Tarleton St; (002) 86 3202. **Accommodation:** 1 hotel.
MAP REF. 520 D1, 525 K4, 527 K13

Hastings　　Pop. 20

This small centre, about 100 km from Hobart on the Huon Hwy, attracts many tourists to its famous limestone caves, local gemstones and nearby scenic railway. **In the area:** Esperance Forest drive to Esperance River; begins off Hastings Rd. Hastings Caves, 13 km NW; regular guided tours of illuminated Newdegate Cave and swimming in thermal pool. Lune River, 2 km S, haven for gem collectors. Beyond river, 2 km further S, Ida Bay Scenic Railway; originally built to carry limestone, now carries passengers 7 km to Deep Hole and back; picnic facilities at both ends of track. **Tourist information:** Church St, Geeveston; (002) 97 1836. **Accommodation:** Limited. **See also:** Tours from Hobart.
MAP REF. 520 D13, 525 K9

Hawley Beach　　Pop. 1000

This popular seaside area near Port Sorrell is well known for its good fishing, excellent beaches and safe swimming. **Of interest:** Meals and accommodation at historic Hawley House (1878), Main Rd. **Tourist information:** 18 Rooke St, Devonport; (004) 21 6226. **Accommodation:** Limited.
MAP REF. 527 J5

Huonville　　Pop. 1524

Huonville is an important commercial centre serving the surrounding townships, and is the largest apple-producing

centre in the area. The valuable softwood now known as Huon pine was discovered in this district. **Of interest:** Daily river cruises, over rapids, to Glen Huon. Model Train World, Main Rd. Cottages and b & b. **In the area:** Apple Museum at Grove, 6 km NE. Scenic drives to western townships of Glen Huon, Judbury and Ranelagh, and east to Cygnet. Antique Motor Museum near Ranelagh, 5 km NW. Model Miniature Village at Glen Huon, 8 km W. At Port Huon, 10 km S: indoor sports centre, river cruises in estuary. **Tourist information:** Huon River Jet Boats, Esplanade; (002) 64 1838. **Accommodation:** 1 hotel. **See also:** Tours from Hobart.
MAP REF. 520 F8, 525 K7

Kettering Pop. 295

This township on the Channel Hwy serves a large fruit-growing district. The Bruny Island ferry leaves several times daily from the terminal at Kettering, with extra services provided during holidays. Oyster Cove Inn and marina, Ferry Rd. Variety of boats for hire; skippered cruises available. **In the area:** Bruny Island. Pleasant walks in Snug Falls Track area, near township of Snug, 8 km N. Also at Snug: Mother's Favourites; seafood. Good swimming and boating at Coningham Beach nearby. Monument to French explorer Admiral Bruni D'Entrecasteaux at Gordon, 21 km S. **Tourist information:** Talune Wildlife Park and Koala Gardens, Gardners Bay; (002) 95 1775. **Accommodation:** 1 hotel.
MAP REF. 520 H9, 525 L8

Kingston–Blackmans Bay
Pop. 12 907

Kingston Beach, 12 km S of Hobart, was discovered by Scottish botanist Robert Brown in 1804. **Of interest:** Display at Federal Government's Antarctic research headquarters, Channel Hwy. **In the area:** Scenic drives south through Blackmans Bay, Tinderbox and Howden; magnificent views of Droughty Point and Bruny Island from Piersons Point. Small blowhole at Blackmans Bay, at reserve on Talone Rd; spectacular in stormy weather. Walking tracks in Snug Falls area. **Tourist information:** Council Chambers, Channel Hwy; (002) 29 555. **Accommodation:** 2 hotel/motels.
MAP REF. 520 H7, 520 H8, 525 M7

Latrobe Pop. 2551

Situated on the Mersey River, 9 km SE of Devonport, Latrobe is in the area that was once the home of the 4 main Aboriginal groups together known as the North Tribe. After European settlement Latrobe became a busy town with its own shipyards. Today it is the site of one of the biggest cycling carnivals in Australia, the Latrobe Wheel Race, held at Christmas. **Of interest:** Many early buildings and shopfronts dating from 1840s, including some with National Trust classifications. Self-guide leaflet. Several renowned restaurants in Gilbert and Forth Sts. Court House Museum, Gilbert St; local history. Bell's Parade, picturesque reserve with picnic areas along riverbank. **In the area:** Historic homestead Frogmore, now host farm, 1 km SW. Several b & b.

Tourist information: Council Offices, Gilbert St; (004) 26 1041. **Accommodation:** 1 motel.
MAP REF. 522 E6, 526 I6

Launceston Pop. 66 747

Although it is Tasmania's second-largest city and a busy tourist centre, Launceston manages to retain a relaxed, friendly atmosphere. Nestling in hilly country where the Tamar, North Esk and South Esk rivers meet, Launceston is also at the junction of 3 main highways and has direct air links with Melbourne and Hobart. It is sometimes known as the Garden City because of its beautiful parks and gardens. **Of interest:** Yorktown Square, The Avenue, Quadrant Mall, Civic Square, and Prince's Square with its magnificent baroque fountain and fine surrounding buildings. Main shopping area around the Mall. Old Umbrella Shop, George St; unique 1860s shop preserved by National Trust. Penny Royal World, Paterson St, collection of buildings originally sited at Barton, near Cressy, and moved stone by stone to Launceston; complex includes accommodation, restaurants and tavern, museum, working water mill and corn mill, and graceful windmill. It is linked by restored tramway to Penny Royal Gunpowder Mill at old Cataract quarry site; boat trips on artificial lake. Parks include: 5 ha City Park with Monkey Island and conservatory; Design Centre of Tasmania nearby displays contemporary art and craft; Royal Park, formal civic park fronting on to South Esk River; and Zig

Kings Bridge, Launceston

Marakoopa Cave, near Mole Creek

Zag Reserve, leading to Cataract Gorge area. Queen Victoria Museum and Art Gallery, in Royal Park, with displays of Tasmania's mineral wealth, flora and fauna, Aboriginal and convict relics, early china and glassware, and colonial and modern art. *Lady Stelfox* departs from Ritchie's Mill Arts Centre, Bridge Rd, for cruises on lower reaches of Tamar. Guided tours of Boags Brewery, William St. Self-guide walking tours; leaflets from tourist centre. Garden Festival held Oct. **In the area:** One of Launceston's outstanding natural attractions, spectacular Cataract Gorge, 2 km w of city centre. Cataract Cliff Grounds Reserve, on north side of gorge; formal park with lawns, European trees, peacocks and licensed restaurant. Area linked to south side (swimming pool and kiosk) by scenic chairlift and suspension bridge; delightful walks on both sides of gorge. Landscaping around Trevallyn Dam, 6 km w, makes attractive picnic spot. Nearby, Australia's only hang-gliding simulator. Waverley Woollen Mills, 5 km E; tours include inspection of historic collection of plant machinery, creating industry for which Launceston earned national reputation. Launceston Federal Country Club Casino, 7 km SW. Punchbowl Reserve and Rhododendron Gardens, 5 km SW; native and European fauna in natural surroundings. Three historic houses: Franklin House, 6 km S; Entally House, 13 km SW at Hadspen; and Clarendon, near township of Nile, 28 km SE; all National Trust properties. Grindelwald Holiday Resort, near Legana, 12 km N; Swiss-style village on edge of Lake Louise, with shops, restaurant and chalet accommodation. St

Matthias' Church, 15 km N at Windermere. Tamar Valley wineries, 50 km N/NE, including St Matthias, Marions, Heemskerk, Rochecombe and Pipers Brook. Guided tours throughout northern Tasmania; details from tourist centre. Colonial cottages. **Tourist information:** Cnr St John and Paterson Sts; (003) 36 3133. **Accommodation:** 17 hotels, 26 holiday units, 12 motels, 1 caravan/ camping park. **See also:** Fisherman's Paradise; Scenic Island State; Stately Homes.
MAP REF. 523 N10, 527 L7

Lilydale   Pop. 333
At the foot of Mt Arthur, 27 km from Launceston, the township of Lilydale has many nearby bush tracks and picnic spots. **In the area:** Lilydale Falls Reserve, 3 km N; two oak trees grown from acorns from Windsor Great Park planted here on the coronation day of British King George IV, 12 May 1937. Scenic walks to top of Mt Arthur (1187 m). Hollybank Forest Reserve, 5 km S at Underwood; picnic/barbecue areas. At Lalla, 4 km w: Walker Rhododendron Gardens; Appleshed for local art and craft. Plant nursery, on northern slopes of Brown Mountain. Bridestowe Lavender Farm, near Nabowla, 26 km NE; sales of lavender products and tours in flowering season, Dec.–Jan. **Accommodation:** 1 hotel.
MAP REF. 527 M6

Longford   Pop. 2601
This quiet country town, 22 km S of Launceston, was first settled in 1813 when former settlers of Norfolk Island were given land grants in the area. Since

then it has had 3 name changes, having previously been known as Norfolk Plains and Latour. Now classified as a historic town, it serves a rich agricultural district. The municipality of Longford carries the largest head of stock in the State. **Of interest:** Self-guide leaflet on town and area. Many historic buildings, some convict-built. Christ Church (1839), Wellington St, noted for outstanding stained glass window; also pioneer gravestones. Targa Tasmania held March; motor racing and classic and veteran car displays. Country Club Hotel, Wellington St, with 'car in window'. **In the area:** Brickendon (1824), 2 km S; homestead built by William Archer and still owned by descendants. Longford Wildlife Park, 5 km N, conservation area for fallow deer and Australian fauna and flora; picnic/barbecue areas and man-made lake. At Perth, 5 km NE, historic buildings include Eskleigh, Jolly Farmer Inn, Old Crown Inn and Leather Bottell Inn. At Cressy, 10 km S: Connorville sheep station, established by Roderic O'Connor, whose descendants still produce superfine wool there. **Tourist information:** Council Offices, Smith St; (003) 91 1303. **Accommodation:** 1 hotel, 1 caravan/camping park. **See also:** Scenic Island State; Stately Homes.
MAP REF. 523 N13, 527 L8

Mole Creek   Pop. 249
This town, 74 km S of Devonport, serves an important farming and forestry district. The unique Tasmanian leatherwood honey from the blossom of the leatherwood tree, which grows only in the rainforests of the west coast of Tasmania, is produced here. Each summer, apiarists transport hives to the nearby leatherwood forests. **In the area:** Guided tours of fine limestone caves in State reserves: Marakoopa, 8 km w, and smaller, but still spectacular, King Solomon Cave, further 7 km w; glow-worm display at Marakoopa. **Tourist information:** 29 Westchurch St; (003) 62 2046. **Accommodation:** 1 hotel, 1 caravan/camping park.
MAP REF. 522 E12, 526 I7

New Norfolk   Pop. 5822
Mellow old buildings set among English trees and hop fields dotted with oast houses give this classified historic town a decidedly English look; the countryside has often been compared with that of Kent in England. On the Derwent River,

38 km NW of Hobart, the town owes its name to the fact that displaced settlers from the abandoned Norfolk Island settlement were granted land in this area. Although the New Norfolk district produces a majority of the hops used by Australian breweries, the chief industry today is paper manufacture. **Of interest:** Self-guide historic walk leaflet at Historical Centre in Council Chambers, Circle St; genealogical and other records also available. Scenic lookouts: Peppermint Hill, off Blair Rd; Pulpit Rock, off Rocks Rd. Old Colony Inn (c. 1835), Montague St; museum and tearooms. Oast House, Tynwald Park, Lyell Hwy; hops museum, art gallery and tearooms. St Matthew's Church (1823), reputedly oldest church still standing in Tasmania; craft centre in adjoining Close. Bush Inn (1815), Lyell Hwy; claims oldest licence in Commonwealth, although contested by Launceston Hotel. Jet boat rides on Derwent River rapids leave from Bush Inn. Hop Festival held March. **In the area:** Tours of Australian Newsprint Mills at Boyer, 5 km E. Famous Salmon Ponds at Plenty, 11 km NW; hatchery where first brown and rainbow trout in southern hemisphere were bred in 1864; also restaurant and museum. Mt Field National Park, with impressive Russell Falls, 40 km NW. **Tourist information:** Council Chambers, Circle St; (002) 61 2777. **Accommodation:** 3 hotels, 1 motel, 1 caravan/camping park. **See also:** Rural Landscapes; Scenic Island State; Stately Homes; Tours from Hobart.
MAP REF. 520 F4, 525 K6

Oatlands   Pop. 522
This classified historic town on the shores of Lake Dulverton, 84 km N of Hobart, attracts both lovers of history and anglers. It was named by Governor Macquarie in 1821 and surveyed in 1832. Many of the town's unique sandstone buildings were constructed in the 1830s and it is said that almost everyone lives in a historic house. **Of interest:** Convict-built courthouse (1829), Campbell St. Holyrood House (1840), High St; restaurant and historic gardens. St Peter's Church (c. 1838), William St. Callington Flour Mill (1836), Mill Lane. Lake Dulverton Wildlife Sanctuary, Esplanade. Several b & b. **In the area:** Trout fishing on Lake Sorell, 29 km NW, and adjoining Lake Crescent. **Tourist information:** Council Offices, 71 High St; (002) 54 0011. **Accommodation:** 1

hotel. **See also:** Rural Landscapes; Scenic Island State.
MAP REF. 525 M3, 527 M12

Orford   Pop. 502
Views from this popular holiday resort at the estuary of the Prosser River, on the Tasman Hwy, are dominated by Maria Island National Park, which is 20 km offshore. **Of interest:** Bushwalks, river and sea fishing, scuba diving and golf. **In the area:** The Thumbs Lookout, 2 km S; overlooks Maria Island. Beautiful 14th-century stained glass window in Church of St John the Baptist at Buckland, 18 km SW. Daily ferry service from Triabunna, 7 km NE, to Maria Island. **Tourist information:** Council Offices, cnr Vicary and Henry Sts, Triabunna; (002) 57 3113. **Accommodation:** 1 resort, 1 hotel/motel, 1 motel, 1 caravan/camping park. **See also:** Scenic Island State.
MAP REF. 521 N2, 525 O4

Penguin   Pop. 2876
The Dial Range rises over this quiet town, named after fairy penguins still found in rookeries nearby. **Of interest:** National-Trust-classified St Stephen's Church and Uniting Church, Main St. Hiscutt Park with working Dutch windmill; tulips in season. Tours of penguin rookeries, Dec.–early March. Old School Market, 2nd and 4th Suns in month. Town Fiesta held Nov. **In the area:** Magnificent view from summit of Mt Montgomery, 5 km S. Mason's Fuschia Fantasy, 6 km S on West Pine Rd; 750 varieties, viewing and sales p.m. and Sat.

Ferndean Wildlife Reserve, 6 km S; picnic spot with walking tracks. Pioneer Park at Riana (10 km). Pindari Deer Farm (15 km); deer-handling demonstrations. Beltana Ostrich Farm, South Riana (20 km); guided tours and viewing of chicks, Oct.–April. Scenic drive south-east to Ulverstone via coast road. **Tourist information:** Roelf Vos carpark; (004) 25 2839. **Accommodation:** 1 hotel, 1 caravan park. **See also:** Scenic Island State.
MAP REF. 522 A4, 526 H5

Poatina   Pop. 20
This modern plateau town, south-west of Launceston, was built to house the construction team working on the hydro-electric power station. **In the area:** Poatina underground power station, 5 km W; guided tours. **Tourist information:** Council Offices, Smith St, Longford; (003) 91 1303. **Accommodation:** None. **See also:** Dams for Power.
MAP REF. 527 K9

Pontville   Pop. 1125
Much of the freestone used in Tasmania's old buildings was quarried near this classified historic township. Pontville was founded in 1830 and many of its early buildings remain. On the Midland Hwy, 27 km N of Hobart, it is the seat of local government for the Brighton Municipality. **Of interest:** Historic buildings on or adjacent to Midland Hwy include: St Mark's Church (1841); 'The Sheiling' behind church (built in 1819 and restored in 1953); old post office; Crown Inn; and 'The Row', thought to

Callington Flour Mill, Oatlands

Rural Landscapes

Tasmania's homesick early settlers were amazingly successful in their attempts to tame their strange new antipodean home. They set about systematically clearing the more accessible lowlands of all traces of native bush, replacing it with neatly tilled fields fringed by hedgerows and the exotic trees familiar to them. Georgian farmhouses set in gardens with flower-beds and borders completed the picture.

Tasmania's main pastoral district is the beautiful Midlands area between **Brighton** and **Perth**, noted for stock raising and high-quality merino wool. This was one of the first farming areas established in Tasmania and its gently undulating plains are offset by mellow farmhouses, historic villages and a wealth of huge old English trees. The historic township of New Norfolk is the centre of Tasmania's long-established hop-growing district, which is a main supplier of hops for Australian beer. This enchanting countryside is enhanced by quaint old oast houses, or hop-drying kilns. Apples and dairy products are produced in the **Derwent Valley**, which is also an important beef-raising and wool-growing district.

The **Huon Valley**, south of Hobart, is the centre of Tasmania's famous apple-growing industry, which dates back to the early nineteenth century when Lady Franklin, wife of Governor Sir John Franklin, established a farm at **Franklin.**

Tasmania's richest and most highly productive farmland lies on the north-west coast, where the main industries are potato-growing and the raising of prime beef and dairy cattle.

See also: Individual town entries in A–Z listing.

Stately Homes

One of Tasmania's big attractions is its wealth of beautiful stately homes with a distinctly English air. You can dine in style in some, such as Prospect House in the historic township of **Richmond**, and stay in others.

Several of Tasmania's grand old mansions, such as Malahide and Killymoon, both on the Esk Highway near **Fingal**, are privately owned and cannot be inspected, but many of the State's finest homesteads are open daily to the public.

Superb Clarendon House, near **Nile**, and a short drive from Launceston, is probably Australia's grandest Georgian mansion. Completed in 1838 and owned by the National Trust, it has been meticulously restored and suitably furnished.

Three other stately homesteads within easy reach of **Launceston** are Franklin

House, just 6 kilometres south; Entally House at **Hadspen**; and Brickendon in **Longford**.

Franklin House is another elegant Georgian mansion owned by the National Trust.

Charming Entally House, the most historic of the Trust houses, was built in 1819. Set in superb grounds, Entally has a greenhouse, chapel and coach-house also open for inspection.

Two-storeyed, shuttered Brickendon, with its graceful metal front porch, looks French, but long stretches of hawthorn hedges and many old chestnuts, oaks, ash and junipers make it seem part of an English landscape.

The Grove in **George Town**, north of Launceston, is another privately owned historic house open to visitors. Built in the

1820s, it has been painstakingly restored by the present owners, who dress in period costume to serve lunch and teas.

Privately owned but operated by the Trust, the White House, in **Westbury**, near **Deloraine**, was built c. 1841 as a corner shop and residence. It stands on a corner of the town's Village Green and displays a fine collection of Staffordshire china.

Hobart has two historic homes open for inspection: the National Trust property Runnymede, in the suburb of **New Town**, and Narryna in **Battery Point**.

Graceful Runnymede, built c. 1836, has been restored and furnished by the Trust.

Narryna, a Georgian sandstone and brick townhouse with a walled courtyard, is set in an old-world garden shaded by elm trees. Also known as the Van Diemen's Land Memorial Folk Museum, it houses a significant collection of colonial artefacts.

The misleadingly named Old Colony Inn in **New Norfolk** serves lunches (with fresh trout as a specialty) and Devonshire teas. This beautiful old building set in delightful grounds has become one of Tasmania's most photographed tourist attractions. Despite its name, it was never used as an inn.

For further information, contact the National Trust of Australia (Tasmania), 413 Hobart Rd, Franklin Village 7249; (003) 44 6233. **See also:** Individual town entries in A–Z listing.

Prospect House, Richmond

have been built in 1824 as soldiers' quarters and now restored. **In the area:** Townships nearby with interesting historic buildings: Bagdad, 8 km N; Kempton, 15 km N, beyond Badgad; Tea Tree, 5 km E; and Broadmarsh, 10 km W. **Tourist information:** Council Offices, Tivoli Rd, Gagebrook; (002) 63 0333. **Accommodation:** Limited.
MAP REF: 520 H3, 525 L5

Port Sorell   Pop. 1494

Sheltered by hills, this well-established holiday resort at the estuary of the Rubicon River near Devonport has a mild climate. Named after Governor Sorell and established in 1822, it is the oldest township on the north-west coast. Unfortunately, many of its old buildings were destroyed by bushfires early this century, after it had been almost deserted for the thriving new port of Devonport. **Of interest:** Swimming, fishing, boating and bushwalking. Views from Watch House Hill, once site of old gaol and now bowling-green. Asbestos Range National Park across estuary. **In the area:** At neighbouring Shearwater, resort with 9-hole golf course. **Tourist information:** 18 Rooke St, Devonport; (004) 21 6226. **Accommodation:** 2 caravan/camping parks. **See also:** National Parks.
MAP REF. 522 G5, 527 J5

Queenstown   Pop. 3368

The discovery of gold and mineral resources in the Mt Lyell field last century led to the almost overnight emergence of the township of Queenstown. It is a town literally carved out of the mountains that tower starkly around it. Mining has been continuous in Queenstown since 1888, and the field has so far produced more than 670 000 tonnes of copper, 510 000 kg of silver and 20 000 kg of gold. The Mt Lyell Company, which employs most of the town's inhabitants, is engaged in a scheme to establish large-scale underground mining. The town has modern shops and facilities, but its wide streets, remaining historic buildings and unique setting give it an old mining-town flavour. In certain lights, multi-coloured boulders on the bare hillsides surrounding the town reflect the sun's rays and turn to amazing shades of pink and gold. **Of interest:** Guided tours of Mt Lyell Mine from Farmers Store, Driffield St, include viewing of mine workings and Mining Museum. Gallery Museum, cnr Sticht and Driffield Sts, depicts history

Antique shop, Richmond

of west coast in photographs and memorabilia. **In the area:** Spectacular views from Lyell Hwy as it climbs steeply out of town. Original (1833) Iron Blow goldmine, off Lyell Hwy, at Gormanston, 6 km SE. Ghost town of Linda, 9 km SE. Mt Jukes Rd lookout, 7 km SW; road leads to old mining settlement of Lynchford and Crotty Dam. Rafting on Franklin River. Mt Mullens and Franklin River scenic nature walk along old mining railway line between Queenstown and Zeehan. Lyell Tours; 4WD day or half-day tours to Bird River rainforest area. **Tourist information:** RACT, 18 Orr St; (004) 71 1974. **Accommodation:** 2 hotels, 2 hotel/motels, 3 motels, 1 caravan/camping park. **See also:** Scenic Island State; The West Coast; Dams for Power.
MAP REF. 524 E1, 526 F11

Railton   Pop. 996

This substantial country town south of Devonport owes its existence to the Goliath Portland Cement Company, representing one of Tasmania's major industries. Raw materials are taken from a huge quarry on the site and carried by an overhead conveyor to the crusher. **In the area:** Scenic drive through area known as Sunnyside to Stoodley Forest Reserve, 14 km S; picnic/barbecue areas and walking tracks. **Tourist information:** Kentish Museum, 93 Main St, Sheffield; (004) 91 1861. **Accommodation:** 1 hotel.
MAP REF. 522 F8, 526 I6

Richmond   Pop. 754

Charming Richmond, 26 km from Hobart, is one of the oldest and most important historic towns in Australia. The much-photographed Richmond Bridge is the oldest bridge in Australia (1823–25) and many of the town's buildings were constructed in the 1830s or even earlier. Some of these structures, including the bridge, were built by convicts under appallingly harsh conditions. Legend has it that the ghost of an overseer who was murdered by convicts still haunts the bridge. **Of interest:** Self-guide leaflet of town and area. Old Richmond Gaol (1825), Bathurst St, one of Australia's best preserved convict prisons; guided tours. St John's (1837), St John's Circle; oldest Catholic church in Australia still in use. St Luke's Church (1834–36), Torrens St; fine timber ceiling. General store and former post office (1832), Bridge St; oldest postal building in Australia. Also in Bridge St: galleries featuring local art and crafts, including Saddler's Court (c. 1848) and Peppercorn Gallery (c. 1850); restored Bridge Inn, one of town's oldest buildings, housing complex of shops; Old Hobart Town, model of Hobart in early 1800s; Toy Museum; and The Maze. Village Store (1836), one of oldest general stores still operating in Tasmania. Georgian mansion Prospect House (1830s) off Hobart Rd, haunted by ghost of Mrs Buscombe; meals and accommodation. **In the area:** Scenic drive north through Campania (7 km) and Colebrook (19 km). Colonial Cottages. **Tourist information:** Saddler's Court Gallery, 48 Bridge St; (002) 62 2132. **Accommodation:** 1 hotel, 1 caravan/ camping park. **See also:** Scenic Island State; Stately Homes; Tours from Hobart.
MAP REF. 521 J4, 525 M5

Ringarooma   Pop. 235

Farming and timber milling support this north-eastern town, which dates back to the 1860s. **In the area:** Views of Ringarooma and surrounding towns from Mathinna Hill. Pleasant drives on New River Rd and Alberton Rd. Old Tin Mining Rd to Branxholm, 16 km NE, gives glimpses of area as it was in days of early pioneers. **Tourist information:** Rose's Travel, 11 Alfred St, Scottsdale; (003) 52 2186. **Accommodation:** Limited.
MAP REF. 527 O6

Township of Ross

Rokeby
Pop. 3495

This old township on the eastern shore of the Derwent River was first settled in 1809. The first apples to be exported from Tasmania were grown here, as was the first wheat ever produced in Tasmania. Rokeby's rural character is now rapidly changing with the expansion of the Clarence Municipality. **Of interest:** Historic cemetery contains graves of many First Fleeters. Historic buildings include Rokeby Court, Rokeby House and St Matthew's Church (1843). Some chairs in church's chancel were carved from wood from ship in Nelson's fleet; organ, brought from England in 1825 and first installed in what is now St David's Cathedral, Hobart, is still in use. **In the area:** Historic buildings at Bellerive, 8 km NW. To south, excellent surfing at Clifton Beach; boating and swimming at South Arm. New Historic Centre at Rosny, 10 km NW. **Tourist information:** Council Offices, 38 Bligh St, Rosny Park; (002) 44 0600. **Accommodation:** Limited.
MAP REF. 519 O10, 521 J6, 525 M6

Rosebery
Pop. 1637

Gold was discovered at Rosebery in 1893 in what is now called Rosebery Creek. Huge deposits of lead and zinc were also discovered in the area. Goldmining has long since been abandoned and the town now owes its existence to the zinc mining company Pasminco-EZ. **In the area:** Montezuma Falls, highest waterfall in State, 5 km W; accessible by 4WD or walking track. **Accommodation:** 1 hotel, 1 caravan/camping park. **See also:** The West Coast.
MAP REF. 526 F9

Ross
Pop. 282

One of the oldest and most beautiful bridges in Australia spans the Macquarie River at this historic township. The bridge was designed by colonial architect John Lee Archer and built by convicts in 1836. The convict stonemason Daniel Herbert who worked on the bridge received a free pardon in recognition for his fine carvings. Ross was established in 1812 as a military post for the protection of travellers who once stopped there to change coaches. Today it is still an important stopping-place on the Midland Hwy between Launceston and Hobart. The district is famous for its superfine wool. **Of interest:** Self-guide leaflet on town and area. Ruins of woman's prison, off Bond St. Tasmanian Wool Centre, Church St; highlights area's links with wool industry. Avenue of English trees in Church St complements historic buildings: Scotch Thistle Inn and Coach House, former coaching stop, now licensed restaurant; and old Ross General Store and Tea Room, with range of Tasmanian crafts and Devonshire teas. In Bridge St: old barracks building, restored by local National Trust. Street leads to Ross Bridge (floodlit at night). Ross Rodeo held Nov. **In the area:** Some of the State's best trout-fishing lakes—Sorell, Crescent, Tooms and Leake—are within hour's drive of town. Cottages and b & b. **Tourist information:** 75 High St, Campbell Town; (003) 81 1388. **Accommodation:** 1 hotel, 1 caravan/camping park. **See also:** Scenic Island State.
MAP REF. 525 M1, 527 N10

St Helens
Pop. 1145

This popular resort on the shores of Georges Bay is renowned for its crayfish and flounder. The largest town on Tasmania's east coast, it has 3 freezing works in or near the settlement to handle the catch of the crayfishing and scallop fleet based in its harbour. **Of interest:** Bayside beaches, ideal for swimming; coastal beaches for surfing. Charter boats for deep-sea fishing. Excellent fishing for bream on Scamander River. Many local restaurants specialise in fish dishes. St Helens History Room, Cecilia St; guided tours of town and district. **In the area:** Bushwalks to view varied birdlife and abundant wildflowers. Scamander, 19 km S; swimming and fishing. Binalong Bay, 11 km NE; surf and rock fishing. Healey's Cheese Factory, at Pyengana, 28 km NW; sales of cheeses. Several coastal reserves in Bay of Fires district; camping areas, good beach fishing. **Tourist information:** St Helens Secretariat, 20 Cecilia St; (003) 76 1329. **Accommodation:** 1 hotel, 1 hotel/motel, 1 motel, 2 caravan/camping parks. **See also:** Scenic Island State.
MAP REF. 527 Q6

St Marys
Pop. 629

The position of this small township, at the junction of the Tasman Hwy and the Esk Main Rd, makes it a busy thoroughfare. At the headwaters of the South Esk River system, St Marys is about 10 km inland from the attractive east coast. **In the area:** Small coastal township of Falmouth, 14 km NE; early settlement of historical interest with several convict-built structures, also fine beaches, attractive rocky headlands and good fishing. Spectacular mountain and coast views to south through Elephant

The West Coast

The beautiful but inhospitable west coast, with its wild mountain ranges, lakes, rivers, eerie valleys and dense rainforests, is one of Tasmania's most fascinating regions. The majestic, untamed beauty of this coast is in complete contrast to the State's pretty pastures. The whole area has vast mineral wealth and a colourful mining history, reflected in its towns. The discovery of tin and copper in 1879 and 1883 started a rush to the west coast, booming at the turn of the century. Today **Queenstown**, the largest town, still depends almost entirely on the Mt Lyell copper mine, and the other main towns—Zeehan, Rosebery and Strahan—also owe their existence to mining.

It was not until 1932 that a rough road was pushed through the mountainous country between Queenstown and Hobart. Fortunately, modern road-making techniques have improved the situation and today west coast towns are linked by the Murchison, Zeehan and Waratah Highways, and the Lyell Highway (the original road to Hobart) has been brought up to modern standards. In fact, the flooding of Lake Bunbury has resulted in the re-routing of the highway, which now takes motorists around the lake itself, enhancing the spectacular entry to Queenstown. Driving round the west coast road circuit and seeing the superb mountain scenery and colourful towns of the area is an unforgettable experience. The only drawback is the area's exceptionally heavy rainfall, even in summer and autumn.

The little township of **Zeehan**, southwest of Rosebery, typifies the changing fortunes of mining towns. Following the rich silver-lead ore discoveries in 1882 its population swelled to 10 000 and the town boasted 26 hotels and the largest theatre in Australia, the Gaiety, where Dame Nellie Melba sang. Many of these fine buildings from the boom period can still be seen, including the Gaiety Theatre and the Grand Hotel. Zeehan's West Coast Pioneers Memorial Museum, housed in the former School of Mines, is a popular tourist attraction.

One of the most spectacular views on any highway in Australia can be seen as you drive into Queenstown. As the narrow road winds down the steep slopes of Mt Owen, you can see the amazingly bare hills—tinged with pale pinks, purples, golds and greys—that surround the town. At the turn of the century, the trees from these hills were cut down to provide fuel for the copper smelters, and heavy rains eroded their topsoil, revealing the strangely hued rocks beneath.

The first European settlement of the west coast was established in 1821, when the most unruly convicts from Hobart were dispatched to establish a penitentiary on **Sarah Island** in Macquarie Harbour and to work the valuable Huon pine forests around the Gordon and King Rivers. Sarah Island soon became a notorious prison and most of the unfortunate convicts who managed to escape died in the magnificent, but unyielding, surrounding bush. The horrors of that time are echoed in the name of the entrance to the harbour—Hell's Gates. Today the port of **Strahan** on Macquarie Harbour has thousands of visitors each year, all attracted to the spectacular Gordon River, one of Tasmania's largest and most remote wild rivers. Cruise boats make regular trips to Heritage Landing at the mouth of the river. On the return trip they stop along the way to allow visitors to see the old convict ruins on Sarah Island. Scenic flights depart from Strahan, to enable visitors to take in the beauty of more inaccessible areas. Another interesting trip from Strahan is to Ocean Beach, 6 kilometres from the town. This long, lonely stretch of beach, lashed by spectacular breakers, somehow typifies the magnificent wild west coast.

The magnificent scenic wilderness Melaleuca is reached only by plane or boat. Flights with Par Avion leave Cambridge Airport near Hobart daily. Boat Harbour in Tasmania's wild south-west is the departure point for the luxury launch *The Spirit of Huon* or the yacht *Golconda*. Fishing, hiking and sailing are offered in this incredibly rugged area of Tasmania; also sightings of the almost extinct orange-bellied parrot are becoming more frequent.

See also: Individual town entries in A–Z listing.

Landscape around Queenstown

Pass. **Tourist information:** St Helens Secretariat, 20 Cecilia St, St Helens; (003) 76 1329. **Accommodation:** 1 hotel.
MAP REF. 527 Q8

Savage River   Pop. 540

This township in the rugged west coast region serves the workers on the major Savage River iron-ore project, which has been financed by a consortium of American, Japanese and Australian interests. Ore deposits are formed into a slurry and pumped through an 85-km pipeline north to Port Latta on the coast, where they are pelletised and shipped to Japan. **Of interest:** Inspections of mine complex, Mine Rd. **In the area:** Former gold-rush township of Corinna, 28 km SW; good fishing, spectacular scenery and regular launch excursions on Arcadia II to Pieman Head. Old graves with Huon pine headstones are reminders of past. **Tourist information:** Council Offices, Smith St, Waratah; (004) 39 1231. **Accommodation:** 1 hotel.
MAP REF. 526 D7

Scamander   Pop. 407

This well-developed resort town, midway between St Marys and St Helens, offers excellent sea and river fishing, and has good swimming beaches. **Of interest:** Scenic walks and drives via forestry roads through plantations. Scamander River, noted for bream fishing; trout in upper reaches. **In the area:** Beaches and lagoons at Beaumaris, 5 km N. Trout Creek Reserve, 10 km W; fishing landing stage, picnic/barbecue facilities. **Tourist information:** St Helens Secretariat, 20 Cecilia St, St Helens; (003) 76 1329. **Accommodation:** 1 hotel/motel, 1 caravan/camping park. **See also:** Scenic Island State.
MAP REF. 527 Q7

Scottsdale   Pop. 2020

Scottsdale is the major town in Tasmania's north-east and serves some of the richest agricultural and forestry country on the island. A large food-processing factory specialises in the deep-freezing of vegetables grown in the district. **In the area:** Beach resort of Bridport, 23 km N. Bridestowe Lavender Farm near Nabowla, 13 km W; sales of lavender products and tours in flowering season, Dec.–Jan. Sideling Lookout, 16 km W. **Tourist information:** Rose's Travel, 11 Alfred St; (003) 52 2186.

Accommodation: 2 hotels, 1 motel, 1 caravan/camping park.
MAP REF. 527 N5

Sheffield   Pop. 992

This town, 30 km S of Devonport, stands at the foothills of the Great Western Tiers, in one of the most scenically attractive areas in the State. Sheffield is known as the Gateway to the Wilderness; Mt Roland is the area's outstanding natural feature. The town's economy is based on farming. **Of interest:** Community project: 28 murals on various buildings depict area's history. Kentish Museum, Main St; local history and hydro-electric exhibits. Steam Museum, cnr Main and Spring Sts. Red Water Creek and Heritage Society runs steam train weekends, daily in summer. Daffodil Festival held Sept. **In the area:** Lakes and dams of Mersey–Forth Power Development Scheme, 10 km W. Lake Barrington, created by scheme; major recreation area and international rowing venue. Devil's Gate Dam, 13 km W; spectacular scenery from viewing areas. Cradle Mountain Lake St Clair National Park, 61 km SW; bushwalking, spectacular rainforest and mountain scenery, flora and fauna. Numerous host farms and b & b. **Tourist information:** Kentish Museum, 93 Main St; (004) 91 1861. **Accommodation:** 1 hotel, 1 motel, 1 caravan/camping park. **See also:** National Parks.
MAP REF. 522 D9, 526 I6

Smithton   Pop. 3495

This substantial township is the administrative centre of Circular Head in the far north-west. It serves the most productive dairying and vegetable-growing area in the State, and also is the centre of one of Tasmania's most important forestry areas, with several large sawmills. Fishing is another important industry. **Of interest:** Fishing and boating on Duck River and at Duck Bay. Lookout tower on Tier Hill, at end of Massey St. **In the area:** Forestry Commission reserves throughout district for wide range of recreational activities. Rocky Cape National Park, 45 km E; walks, Aboriginal caves. Allendale Gardens at Edith Creek, 13 km S; rainforest walks and Devonshire teas. Graveyard at ghost town of Balfour, 40 km SW. Lacrum Dairy Farm at Mella, 6 km W; milking demonstrations, afternoon teas, cheese tastings and sales. Nearby Wombat Tarn has picnic/barbecue area, lookout, bushwalks,

children's playground. Possum Trot, at Redpa, 40 km SW; woodcraft, native gardens and rainforest bushwalks. Excellent surfing at Marrawah, 50 km SW. Seasonal scenic cruises on Arthur River, 70 km S. Cottage accommodation. **Tourist information:** Council Offices, Goldie St; (004) 52 1265. **Accommodation:** 1 hotel, 1 motel.
MAP REF. 526 D3

Somerset   Pop. 3257

At the junction of the Bass and Waratah Hwys, Somerset has become a satellite town for Burnie, 6 km E. **In the area:** Scenic drive from town, south through Elliott to small rural settlement of Yolla, which serves surrounding rich pastoral country. **Tourist information:** 48 Cattley St, Burnie; (004) 34 6111. **Accommodation:** 1 hotel, 1 hotel/motel, 1 motel, 1 caravan/camping park. **See also:** Scenic Island State.
MAP REF. 526 G4

Sorell   Pop. 3199

Named after Governor Sorell, this town is 27 km NE of Hobart. Founded in 1821, it played an important part in early colonial history by providing most of the grain for the State from 1816 to 1860. It also provided grain for NSW for more than 20 years. The area is still an important agricultural district, specialising in fat lambs. **Of interest:** Historic Blue Bell Inn and picnic/barbecue facilities in park, both in Somerville St. **In the area:** Saddleback Horseback Tours at Orielton, 6 km N; day or 2-night rides, bushman's meals; also Woodsdale Bush Lodge for horseriders and groups. Many Hobartians have holiday homes in extensive and popular beach area around Dodges Ferry and Carlton, 18 km S. **Tourist information:** Council Offices, 12 Somerville St; (002) 65 2201. **Accommodation:** 1 hotel.
MAP REF. 521 K5, 525 N6

Stanley   Pop. 576

This quaint little village, nestling under a huge rocky outcrop called the Nut, is steeped in history. It was the site for the headquarters of the Van Diemen's Land Company, set up in 1825 to cultivate land and breed high-quality sheep. Then its wharf handled whalers and sailing ships. Today these are replaced by modern crayfish and shark-fishing fleets, but little else has changed. The birthplace of

Australia's only Tasmanian prime minister, the Hon. J. A. Lyons, Stanley has been declared a historic town and for 5 of the last 6 years has won the Tasmanian Government award for the State's Premier Tourist Town. **Of interest:** Chairlift to top of the Nut (152 m). Historic buildings in wharf area: bluestone bond store, Wharf Rd; and former VDL Co. store, in Marine Park, designed by colonial architect John Lee Archer, who lived in township. Archer's own home, now Poet's Cottage, Alexander Tce, at base of the Nut; private residence, not open to public. Also in Alexander Tce, birthplace of J. A. Lyons, Lyons Cottage; open for inspection. Other historic buildings in Church St include: still licensed Union Hotel (1849), with its nest of cellars and narrow stairways; Commercial Hotel (1842), now private residence; and multi-award-winning Plough Inn (1843); authentic house museum, fine Tasmanian handcrafts, tourist information. Next door, Discovery Centre Folk Museum. Headstones in Burial Ground on Browns Rd, dating from 1828, include those on graves of John Lee Archer and explorer Henry Hellyer. Small colonies of fairy penguins near wharf and cemetery, and on Scenic Drive. Cottages. **In the area:** Highfield Historic Site (1835), headquarters of VDL Co., on Scenic Drive, 2 km N; homestead, chapel, schoolhouse, barn, stables, workers' cottages and remains of servants' quarters nearby; two arched gates are all that remain of former deer park. Popular picnic area and Big Tree (giant eucalypt) at Dip Falls, off hwy, 40 km SE, via Mawbanna. Pelletising plant of Savage River Mines at Port Latta, 20 km E, where ore is moved by conveyor to jetty for loading onto carriers. Self-guide leaflet *Things to See and Do* for Circular Head area. Many cottages and b & b. Circular Head Arts Festival held Sept., Agricultural Show Dec. **Tourist information:** 35 Church St; (004) 58 1226. **Accommodation:** 1 motel, 1 caravan/camping park. **See also:** Scenic Island State.
MAP REF. 526 E3

Strahan   Pop. 597

This pretty little port on Macquarie Harbour is the only town on Tasmania's forbidding west coast. Originally a Huon pine timber-milling town, its growth was boosted by the copper boom at the Mt Lyell mine. When the Strahan–Zeehan railway opened in 1892, it became a busy port. Today it handles freight to and from Queenstown and is used by crayfish, abalone and shark fishermen, but the use of the harbour is limited because of the formidable bar at Hell's Gates, the mouth of the harbour. Seaplane flights over Gordon River and Frenchmans Cap, landing at Sir John's Falls. **Of interest:** Excellent views of township and harbour from Water Tower Hill. On the Esplanade: self-guide leaflets and historical collection at Visitors Centre; NPWS World Heritage display at Customs House; colonial accommodation at stately Franklin Manor, built late last century. Mineral and gemstone museum, Innes St. Morrison's Mill, one of few remaining Huon pine sawmills. Cottages. **In the area:** Botanical Creek Peoples Park and Hogarth Falls on outskirts of town; picnic/barbecue areas. Surfing and trail rides at Ocean Beach, 6 km W; also mutton bird rookery. Picnic/barbecue areas and coastline views at Sand Dunes, 12 km N on Strahan–Zeehan Hwy. Cruises up Gordon River to Heritage Landing and infamous Sarah (or Settlement) Island, Tasmania's first and most brutal penal establishment. Cruises also across Macquarie Harbour to Hell's Gates. Strahan Wilderness 4WD tours following Old Abt Railway from Strahan towards Queenstown. **Tourist information:** Wharf, The Esplanade; (004) 71 7488. **Accommodation:** 2 hotels, 1 motel, 1 caravan/camping park. **See also:** Scenic Island State; The West Coast.
MAP REF. 524 D2, 526 E11

Swansea   Pop. 418

Swansea is a small town of historical interest on Great Oyster Bay, in the centre of Tasmania's east coast. It is the administrative centre of Glamorgan, the oldest rural municipality in Australia. The original council chambers (c. 1860) are still in use. **Of interest:** Self-guide leaflet on town and area. In Franklin St: Bark Mill and East Coast Pioneer Museum (c. 1885); restored working displays and tearooms. Morris' General Store (1838), Franklin St; run by Morris family for over 100 years. Community

The Nut, Stanley

A Convict Past

The ruins of the infamous Port Arthur settlement are the greatest single tourist attraction in Tasmania. The fact that they were a place of incarceration for more than 12 000 prisoners has been blurred by time but it is still possible, particularly in bleak weather, for the ruins to create something of the atmosphere of hopelessness and misery that existed there about 150 years ago.

Port Arthur is on the Tasman Peninsula, which extends from the Forestier Peninsula south-east of Hobart, screening Pitt Water and the Derwent estuary from the Tasman Sea. Both peninsulas are very beautiful, with sweeping pasture, timbered areas and a coastline of sheltered bays and towering cliffs. Many secondary roads, tracks and secluded beauty spots make it an ideal place for bushwalking. Accommodation includes a motor inn, self-contained villas and log cabins, guest house, colonial accommodation, a caravan park and youth hostel.

Eaglehawk Neck is on the isthmus between the two peninsulas. In the days of the penal colony, hounds were tethered in a tight line across the Neck to prevent escapes. The line was continually patrolled and guard posts were established in the nearby hills. No prisoner ever broke through this fearful barrier, although some did swim to freedom.

A major Port Arthur conservation project was completed in 1986. Among the buildings still standing are the church, penitentiary, guard tower, hospital and model prison. Buildings that have been restored include Exile Cottage, home of exiled Irish rebel William Smith O'Brien, the Commandant's House and the Junior Medical Officer's House. The restored former lunatic asylum is a museum and visitor centre. Guided tours of the whole site are conducted all year round, 9.30–3.30. The settlement was established by Governor Arthur in 1830 and, although transportation ceased in 1853, it was not abandoned until 1877. Many buildings were demolished by contractors and others were badly damaged by a bushfire in 1897. Today, nocturnal historical 'ghost tours' through the settlement are an unforgettable experience; they begin at 8 p.m. winter time and 9.30 p.m. during daylight saving. The site is open daily; an entrance fee allows visitors access to over 60 buildings, ruins and sites. Free guided tours are conducted and on audio tours Frank The Poet recounts his experiences as a Port Arthur convict.

In Port Arthur Bay stands the **Island of the Dead**, with its 1769 unnamed convict graves; 180 additional named graves mark the resting places of free settlers, prison staff and the military. The ferry *Bundeena* makes regular trips to this unique island cemetery.

For further information, contact Port Arthur Historic Site, 'Clougha', Port Arthur 7182; (002) 50 2363. **See also:** Individual town entries in A–Z listing.

Ruins at Port Arthur

Centre (c. 1860); museum with largest billiard table in Australia. Schouten House (c. 1841), Bridge St; once Swansea Inn, now restaurant and b & b. **In the area:** Views from Duncombes Lookout, 3 km S. Spikey Beach, 7 km S; picnic area with excellent rock fishing. Mayfield Beach, 14 km S; safe swimming and popular fishing area. Walking track from camping area to Three Arch Bridge. Cottages and b & b. **Tourist information:** Council Offices, Noyes St; (002) 57 8115. **Accommodation:** 1 hotel/motel, 1 motel, 2 caravan/camping parks. **See also:** Scenic Island State.
MAP REF. 525 P2, 527 P11

Triabunna   Pop. 831

When Maria Island was a penal settlement, Triabunna, 86 km NE of Hobart, was a garrison town and whaling base. Today it is a centre for the scallop and abalone industries, with an important export wood-chipping mill just south of the town. **Of interest:** On The Esplanade: Bicentennial Park with picnic/barbecue areas; National Trust-run Pioneer Park with machinery exhibits. Working Horse Museum, Vicary St. Daily ferry service to historic settlement of Darlington on Maria Island National Park. Charter fishing boats for hire. Local beaches for swimming, water-skiing and fishing. **Tourist information:** Council Offices, cnr Vicary and Henry Sts; (002) 57 3113. **Accommodation:** 1 hotel, 1 hotel/motel, 1 caravan/camping park. **See also:** National Parks; Scenic Island State.
MAP REF. 521 O1, 525 O4, 527 O13

Ulverstone   Pop. 9923

Situated 19 km W of Devonport, near the mouth of the Leven River, Ulverstone is a well-equipped tourist centre. **Of interest:** On Beach Rd: Riverside Anzac Park, with children's playground and picnic/barbecue areas; Fairway Park, with wildfowl reserve and giant water-slide. Weeda Copper, Eastland Dr; local copperware. **In the area:** Extensive beaches east and west of town provide safe swimming areas for children. Good beach, river and estuary fishing. Tours of hop fields. Scenic views at Preston Falls, 19 km S. Guided tours of Gunns Plains Caves, 24 km SW. Walking tracks to viewing platform at Leven Canyon, 41 km SW. Goat Island Sanctuary, 5 km W; walking access to island, low tide only. **Tourist information:** Roelf Vos carpark; (004) 25 2839. **Accommodation:**

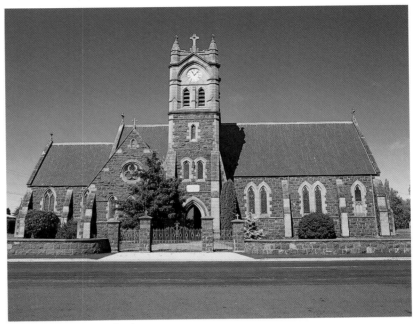
Holy Trinity Church, Westbury

2 hotels, 3 motels, 3 caravan/camping parks. **See also:** Scenic Island State.
MAP REF. 522 B5, 526 H5

Waratah   Pop. 360

This lonely little settlement, set in mountain heathland 100 km N of Queenstown, was the site of the first mining boom in Tasmania. In 1900 it had a population of 2000 and Mount Bischoff was the richest tin mine in the world. The deposits were discovered in 1871 by James 'Philosopher' Smith, a colourful local character, and the mine closed in 1935, with dividends totalling 200 pounds for every one pound of original investment. Today the town is experiencing a revival of mining activity at nearby Que River. **Of interest:** Self-drive tour of town. In Smith St: Waratah Museum and Gift Shop; adjacent, Philosopher Smith's Hut, replica of miner's hut with audio historical commentary; Atheneum Hall (c. 1887), with portrait of Smith. St James' Anglican Church (1880), first church in Tasmania to be lit by hydro power. **In the area:** River and lake fishing. Mining townships: Savage River, 38 km W, and fascinating former goldmining town Corinna, 66 km W. Cruises on Pieman River. **Tourist information:** Council Offices, Smith St; (004) 39 1231. **Accommodation:** 1 hotel, 1 caravan/camping park. **See also:** The West Coast.
MAP REF. 526 F7

Westbury   Pop. 1292

A village green, said to be unique in Australia, gives this town, 16 km E of Deloraine, a decidedly English air. Situated on the Bass Hwy, Westbury was first surveyed in 1823 and laid out on a bold scale in 1828, and has several fine old colonial buildings. **Of interest:** Self-guide leaflet on town and area. White House (c. 1841), Village Green, King St; house, bakehouse, coachhouse, courtyard, vintage cars, bicycles, wagons and dolls and toys in stable complex. On Bass Hwy: Hedge maze; Gemstone and Mineral Display; Pearn's Steam World, display of old tractors, farm machinery and motor vehicles. Maypole Festival, with Morris dancing on Village Green, held Nov. **In the area:** At Hagley, 5 km E: St Mary's Anglican Church, noted for fine east window, donated by Lady Dry, wife of Sir Richard Dry, first Tasmanian-born premier. At Carrick, 10 km E: fine examples of Georgian and Victorian buildings. Liffey Falls, 25 km S; picnic/barbecue area and walking tracks. Trout fishing at Brushy Lagoon, 15 km N. Colonial cottages. **Tourist information:** Old Bakehouse, 52 William St; (003) 93 1140. **Accommodation:** 1 hotel. **See also:** Stately Homes.
MAP REF. 523 K11, 527 K7

Wynyard   Pop. 4679

Situated within a short driving distance of many varied attractions, this small

The Bass Strait Islands

King Island and Flinders Island, Tasmania's two main Bass Strait islands, are ideal holiday spots for the adventurous. You can fish, swim, go bushwalking or skindive among the wrecks of the many ships that foundered off their shores last century. Each spring millions of muttonbirds make a spectacular sight as they fly in to nest in coastal rookeries.

King Island, at the western end of the strait, is a picturesque, rugged island with an unspoiled coastline of beautiful sandy beaches on the east and north coasts, contrasting with the forbidding cliffs of Seal Rocks and the lonely coast to the south. The lighthouse at Cape Wickham is the largest in Australia. There is a penguin colony on the breakwater at Grassy Harbour. Once famous for its seal population and now almost extinct sea lions, the island's main industries today are scheelite mining and farming. King Island dairy products have earned a reputation for their high quality. The unofficial capital is **Currie**, which has a kelp factory. Accommodation includes a hotel, 2 motels, numerous guest houses, several holiday flats and a caravan/camping park.

Flinders Island is renowned for its excellent fishing, its magnificent granite mountains and its gemstones, including the Killiecrankie 'diamonds', actually a kind of topaz. Strzelecki National Park, near the civic centre, **Whitemark**, provides challenging rock climbing. From Whitemark 4WD tours are available to hills and remote beaches. The island is also popular with scuba divers, naturalists and photographers. Accommodation on the island includes 2 hotels, 2 guest houses and several holiday flats. Flinders is one of more than 50 islands in the Furneaux Group that were once part of the land bridge linking Tasmania with the mainland.

In the 1830s the few surviving Tasmanian Aborigines were settled near **Emita** in an attempt to save them from extinction. All that remains of the settlement today is the graveyard and the chapel, Wybalenna, which has been restored by the National Trust.

Fishing is the main industry of the tiny community of **Lady Barron** to the south, a port village overlooking Franklin Sound and **Cape Barren Island**, the home of the protected Cape Barren goose.

For further information contact: King Island Shoppe, Edward St, King Island; (004) 62 1666; and Council Offices, Davey St, Flinders Island; (003) 59 2131.

Fisherman's Paradise

Fish are biting all year round in Tasmania, which is a fisherman's paradise by any standards. Tasmania is famous for three species of fish: trout in fresh water, bream in the estuaries, and tuna off the coast.

One area alone contains hundreds of lakes and lagoons stocked with trout of world-class size. This is the inaccessible 'Land of Three Thousand Lakes'. You are more likely, however, to choose from the huge range of developed areas brimming with trout in the central highlands region, such as Great Lake, Bronte Lagoon, Lake Sorell and Arthurs Lake. Brumby Creek, just 25 kilometres from **Launceston** between **Cressy** and **Poatina**, is rapidly gaining a reputation as one of the great trout waters of Australia.

As the trout season closes in May, game fish begin to move down the mild east coast and fishermen start hauling in the big ones: bluefin tuna often weighing in at over 45 kilograms. Then, as the bluefin leave in the midwinter months, schools of barracouta arrive in their thousands, and large Australian salmon schools return to the estuaries and along the shoreline.

In spring, one of the great sport fish of Tasmania, the tasty silver bream, arrives in the river estuaries. Many anglers regard this as one of the best fighting fish for its size.

Of course, in late spring and early summer the whole island is an angler's dream. January and February are peak inland trout-fishing months, and from February to March schools of Australian salmon swim close to the shoreline of Tasmania's many river estuaries, providing exciting fishing for the angler using a silver flash lure from the beach or rocks.

For further information on licence requirements, fees, bag limits, seasons and regulations, contact the Inland Fisheries Commission, 127 Davey St, Hobart 7000; (002) 23 6622. **See also:** Individual town entries in A–Z listing.

Trout fishing near Cressy

View of Wynyard from Table Cape Lookout

centre at the mouth of the Inglis River, west of Burnie, has become a well-developed tourist centre, offering a range of accommodation and sporting facilities. There are daily flights between the town's airport and Melbourne. The Waratah–Wynyard municipality is a prosperous dairying and mixed-farming district and the town has a large, modern dairy factory. **Of interest:** Excellent trout, fly and sea fishing. Tulip Festival held in Oct; Table Cape Tulip Farm open to visitors. **In the area:** Oldest marsupial fossil in Australia found at Fossil Bluff, 7 km N. Panoramic views from Table Cape Lookout, 5 km N. Mallavale Farm, Boat Harbour, 11 km NW; local crafts, teas. Excellent beach at Boat Harbour. Good swimming and fishing at Sisters Beach, further 5 km NW, within Rocky Cape National Park, 30 km NW. Also at Sisters Beach, adjoining National Park: Birdland Native Gardens; nature trail, aviaries, camellias, rhododendrons, displays, craft shop. Rhodo Garden at Lapoinya, 20 km SW; rhododendrons,

camellias, begonias, native birds and fauna; open daily. Scenic flights and walks. Cottages and farmstay. **Tourist information:** Council Offices, Saunders St; (004) 42 2221. **Accommodation:** 2 hotels, 1 hotel/motel, 1 motel, 2 caravan/camping parks. **See also:** Scenic Island State; National Parks.
MAP REF. 526 F4

Zeehan
Pop. 1132

Named after one of Abel Tasman's ships, this former mining town, situated 36 km NW of Queenstown, has had a chequered history and is now a National-Trust-classified historic town. Silver-lead deposits were discovered here in 1882. By 1901, Zeehan had 26 hotels and a population of 10 000, making it Tasmania's third largest town. Just 7 years later mining began to decline and Zeehan became almost a ghost town. In the boom period between 1893 and 1908, 8 million dollars' worth of ore had been recovered. Now the town is again on an

upward swing with the reopening of the Renison Bell tin mine. **Of interest:** Many 'boom' buildings in Main St: Gaiety Theatre, Grand Hotel, ANZ Bank, St Luke's Church, post office and courthouse (now art gallery). West Coast Pioneers Memorial Museum, Main St; mineral, historical, geological and biological collections. Beside museum, unique display of steam locomotives and rail carriages used on west coast. Scenic drive, 7.5 km round trip; includes Spray Tunnel, old train tunnel. **In the area:** Old mine workings at Dundas, 13 km E. Trial Harbour, 20 km W; popular fishing area. Unsealed roads to both areas often in poor condition; check before departure. Fishing and boating on Lake Pieman, 50 km NW. Trout fishing on Henty River, 25 km S. **Tourist information:** West Coast Pioneers Memorial Museum, Main St; (004) 71 6225. **Accommodation:** 1 hotel, 1 hotel/motel, 1 motel, 1 caravan/camping park. **See also:** Scenic Island State; The West Coast.
MAP REF. 526 E9

Tasmania

Other Map Coverage
Central Hobart 517
Hobart & Suburbs 518
Hobart Region 520
Launceston Region 522

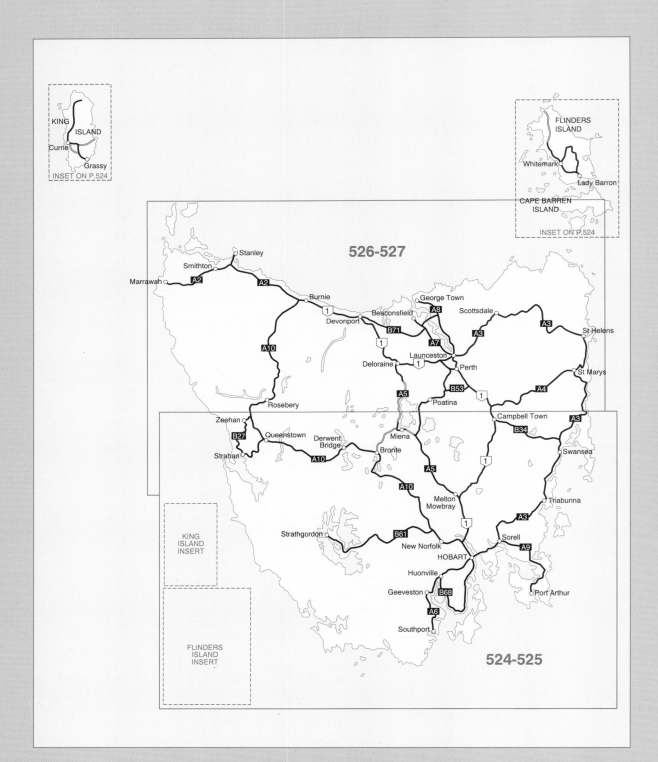

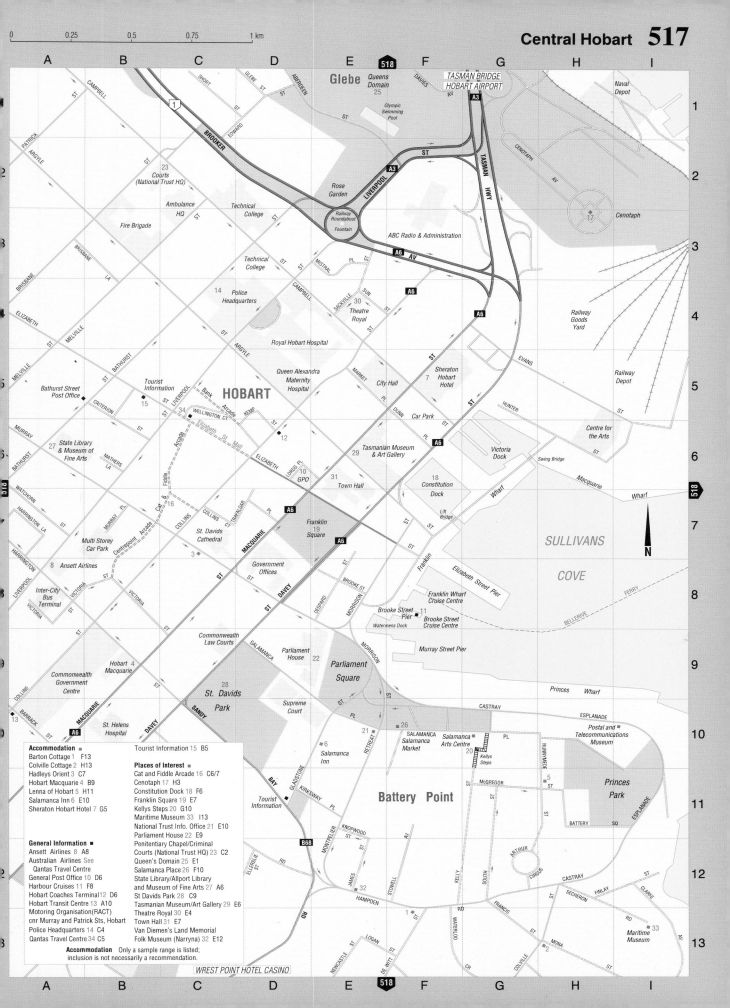

Glebe

Queens Domain 25

TASMAN BRIDGE
HOBART AIRPORT

Olympic Swimming Pool

Rose Garden

Railway Roundabout Fountain

ABC Radio & Administration

Courts (National Trust HQ) 23

Ambulance HQ

Technical College

Fire Brigade

Technical College

Police Headquarters 14

Theatre Royal 30

Royal Hobart Hospital

Queen Alexandra Maternity Hospital

City Hall

Sheraton Hobart Hotel 7

Railway Goods Yard

Railway Depot

Tourist Information 15

HOBART

Car Park

Centre for the Arts

Bathurst Street Post Office

State Library & Museum of Fine Arts 27

Tasmanian Museum & Art Gallery 29

Victoria Dock

Swing Bridge

Macquarie

Wharf

GPO 10

Town Hall 31

Constitution Dock 18

Wharf

SULLIVANS

Franklin Square 19

Lift Bridge

COVE

N

Multi Storey Car Park

St. Davids Cathedral

Ansett Airlines 8

Inter-City Bus Terminal

Government Offices

Elizabeth Street Pier

Franklin Wharf Cruise Centre

Brooke Street Pier 11
Brooke Street Cruise Centre

Watermens Dock

Murray Street Pier

Commonwealth Law Courts

Parliament House

Parliament Square 22

Princes Wharf

Commonwealth Government Centre

Hobart Macquarie 4

St. Davids Park 28

Supreme Court

CASTRAY

ESPLANADE

Postal and Telecommunications Museum

Hobart Transit Centre 13

St. Helens Hospital

Tourist Information

Salamanca Inn 6

Salamanca Market

Salamanca Arts Centre

Salamanca Place 26

Kellys Steps 20

Princes Park

Battery Point

McGregor

BATTERY

Maritime Museum 33

Tourist Information

Van Diemen's Land Memorial Folk Museum (Narryna) 32

WREST POINT HOTEL CASINO

A B C D E F G H I

520

Chigwell
BERRIEDALE ROAD
Berriedale
Elliss Point
Berriedale Bay
Derwent Haven
FORESHORE
BROOKER
MAIN
MARYS
HOPE
RD
Rosetta
Elwick Bay
B32
EAST
DERWENT
HWY
Bowen Bridge
DERWENT
RIVER
Risdon Cove
C324
HWY
PIPER
B32
EAST
RISDON
GARDEN
Risdon V

Montrose
MONTROSE
PITCAIRN
BRENT
ST
GROVE
RD
ELWICK
GOODWOOD
RD
B35
Elwick Racecourse
Derwent Entertainment Centre
HOWARD
ACTON CR
Prince Of Wales Bay
Goodwood
Risdon
RD
Porter Bay
East Risdon Nature Reserve
SUGARLOAF
Sugarloaf Hill
Risdon V

Glenorchy
CHAPEL
BAROSSA
TOLOSA
CLYDESDALE AV
LEONARD
ST
Derwent Park
DERWENT PARK
GORMANSTON
FLETCHER
BOWEN
LENNOX
ASHBOLT
RISDON
Lutana
Golf Course
RD
Royal Showgrounds
LAMPTON
AV
DERWENT
PARK
Cemetery
Recreation Reserve
Geilston Bay
GEILSTON
DERWENT
LINCOLN
KAROOLA
GOLF LINKS
Lindisfarne Recreation Reserve
Lindisfarne Point

West Moonah
ASHBOURNE GV
SPRINGFIELD AV
AMY ST
Moonah
BAYSWATER
ALBERT
BROOKER
New Town Bay
Selfs Point
Lime Kiln Point
B32
Natone Hill
Rose Bay
EAST DERWENT
Ros

Merton
DEVINES RD
Springfield
FLORENCE
HIGHFIELD
TOWER
NEW TOWN
RISDON
QUEENS
WALK
Runnymede
BELLEVUE
Cornelian Bay
B36
DOMAIN
HWY
Upper Domain
Lower Domain
Pavilion Point
Royal Botanical Gardens
Tasman Bridge
Government House
A3
TASMAN
HWY
Montagu Bay
Rosny

Lower Glenorchy Reservoir
Barrier
KALANG
AV
Lenah Valley
New Town CK RD
BRUSHY CK
POTTERY
Mt Stuart
Lookout
DOYLE
GILBIN
DARLING PDE
MT STUART
MELLIFONT
ARTHUR
NEWDEGATE
AUGUSTA
CLARE
STOKE
ARGYLE
LETITIA
BURNETT
CAMPBELL
FEDERAL
New Town
North Hobart
Glebe
BROOKER
Queens Domain
Upper Domain
Rose Garden
Naval Depot
Cenotaph
Macquarie Point
Rosny ESPL
Rosny Point
Ferry
RIVER

Knights Creek Reservoir
Barrier
Limekiln Gully Reservoir
Fossil Hill 340m
Brushy Hill 400m
Knocklofty
Knocklofty Park
West Hobart
WARWICK
PATRICK
MELVILLE
LIVERPOOL
COLLINS
LANSDOWNE CR
HILL
MURRAY
HARRINGTON
ELIZABETH
ST Mall
HOBART
Constitution Dock
Sullivans Cove
Salamanca Pl
Kellys Steps
Van Diemens Museum
Battery Point
Battery Pt Historic Area
Secheron Point

Mountain Park
PINNACLE
PINNACLE RD
Mt Wellington 1270m
Lookout
South Hobart
FOREST
MACQUARIE
ST
HAMPDEN
Cascades Brewery
CASCADE
MACQUARIE
DAVEY
Sandy Bay
KING
REGENT
GROSVENOR
NAPOLEON
For more detail of Central Hobart see page 517

Cascades
HUON
HWY
B64
Lower Reservoir
Upper Reservoir
WATERWORKS RD
Dynnyrne
YORK
A6
OUTLET
PROCTORS
University of Tasmania
SANDY
BAY
NELSON
WAIMEA
CHURCHILL
DERWENTWATER
Wrest Point
Wrest Point Hotel Casino
B68
Sandy Bay
Lower Sandy Bay
LIPSCOMBE

STRICKLAND
HUON HWY
O'Gradys Falls
Silver Falls
Ridgeway Park
Sandy Bay Rivulet
Ridgeway Reservoir
Vincents RD
OLINDA
Hobart Metriculation College
Recreation Reserve
NELSON
GV
Skyline Reserve
Skyline Reserve
Mount Nelson Signal Station Reserve
Mt Nelson
Lookout
Porter Hill
Pierces Reserve
Truganini Reserve
Tudor Court Model Village

Fern Tree
PINNACLE
HWY
Chimney Pot Hill
Chimney Pot Hill
RIDGEWAY
Ridgeway Park
SOUTHERN
PROCTORS
Cartwright
Badger Hill
The Lea Conservation Area
Rivulet
CHANNEL HWY

HUON
SUMMERLEAS
Browns River
SCOTTS
Ridgeway
Dixon
Taroona

A B C D E F G H I

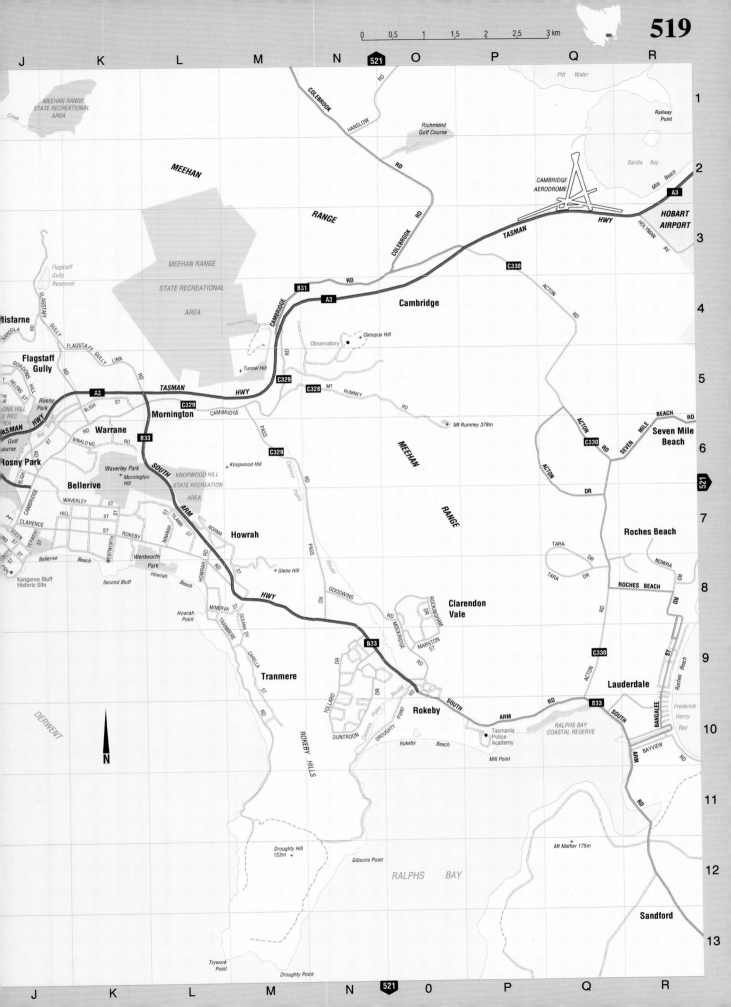

0   0,5   1   1,5   2   2,5   3 km

J   K   L   M   N   **521**   O   P   Q   R

1

Pitt   Water

Creek

MEEHAN RANGE
STATE RECREATIONAL
AREA

Railway
Point

Barilla   Bay

2

Mile   Beach

MEEHAN

CAMBRIDGE
AERODROME

A3

Richmond
Golf Course

HANSLOW

RD

RD

COLEBROOK

COLEBROOK

RANGE

TASMAN

HWY

HOBART
AIRPORT

HOLYMAN

AV

3

Flagstaff
Gully
Reservoir

MEEHAN RANGE

C330

Misfarne

STATE RECREATIONAL

ACTON

Flagstaff
Gully

FLAGSTAFF GULLY   LINK

AREA

B31

A3

RD

Cambridge

RD

4

GORDONS HILL

HELENS HILL

FLAGSTA FE GULLY

RD

RD

CAMBRIDGE

RD

Observatory

Canopus Hill

+ *Tunnel Hill*

RD

TASMAN   HWY

C329

C328

MT

A3

KAROOLA

RD

HWY

5

TASMAN

C329

RUMNEY

RD

Rosny
Park

ST

BLIGH

Mornington

CAMBRIDGE

PASS

+ *Mt Rumney 378m*

ACTON

RD

C330

Seven Mile
Beach

SEVEN

MILE

BEACH

RD

6

Warrane

BINALONG

RD

B33

SOUTH

C329

MEEHAN

ACTON

ST

Rosny Park

Rivulet

+ *Knopwood Hill*

ARM

KNOPWOOD HILL
STATE RECREATION

DR

521

BLIGH

Golf
Course

RD

Bellerive

WAVERLEY

Waverley Park
+ *Mornington*
Hill

AREA

RANGE

Roches Beach

7

CAMBRIDGE

HILL

ST

ST

ST

Howrah

Clarence

TARA

DR

NINABAH

ST

TULANBI

NORMA

Plains

CLARENCE

Bellerive   *Beach*

ROKEBY

WENTWORTH

ST

ST

ST

HOWRAH

ST

Glebe Hill

TARA

DR

ROCHES   BEACH

8

QUEEN

DERWENT

ST

ST

Wentworth
Park

RD

PASS

+ *Glebe Hill*

NOWRA

Kangaroo Bluff
Historic Site

Second Bluff

Howrah   Beach

HWY

GOODWINS

RD

RD

Howrah
Point

MINERVA

ST

RD

Rivulet

RD

RD

ROCKINGHAM

Clarendon
Vale

C330

Lauderdale

9

TRANMERE

OZEMA

DN

Plains

DR

MARSTON

ST

B33

ACTON

BANGALEE

ST

ST

CARELLA

Tranmere

TOLLARD

DR

DR

RD

MOCKRIDGE

B33

SOUTH

10

DERWENT

ST

DUNTROON

Clarence

DROUGHTY

POINT

Rokeby

SOUTH

ARM

Tasmania
Police
Academy

RALPHS BAY
COASTAL RESERVE

Frederick
Henry   Bay

BAYVIEW

RD

ARM

N

Rokeby   Beach

Mill Point

Ralphs Bay

11

Droughty Hill
153m +

Gibsons Point

Mt Mather 175m
+

RD

12

RALPHS   BAY

Sandford

13

Trywork
Point

Droughty Point

J   K   L   M   N   **521**   O   P   Q   R

A B C D 525 E F G H I

TO QUEENSTOWN
Hamilton
Glen Clyde House
Meadowbank Lake
A10
LYELL HWY
Mt Bethune 508m +
Mt Spode 521m +
Peckham Vale
Pelham
21
Taylors Tier 639m +
Kempton
Windsor Park
Quoin Mtn 900m +
Pleasant Mo
Fair Vie
Colebroc

MT FIELD NATIONAL PARK
Lake Webster
Mt Field East 1269m +
Fentonbury
10
Ellendale
Old MacDonalds Tourist Farm
Meadowbank Power Station
Meadowbank
Allanvale
Norton Mandeville
21 13
Clarendon
Elderslie Park
Huntingdon Tier 545m +
Elderslie
Dysart
MIDLAND HWY
1
11
Bagdad
28
HWY
Chauncy Vale

Lake Seal
Lake Nicholls
Russell Falls Trout Farm
Westerway
8
B61
Karanja 15
Glenora
Bushy Park
B61
Macquarie Plains
Gretna
Rosegarland
Derwent River
Jordan River
21
Mangalore Farm
Mangalore
12
Florentine Peak +
+ Mt Mawson
National Park
RD
GORDON RIVER
38
B62
Kinvarra
Plenty
Salmon Ponds
12
Mt Belmont 456m +
Black Hills
Mt Dromedary 989m +
Broadmarsh
Woodlands
Dromedary
Broadmarsh
Pontville
1
Brighton
Bonorong Park Wildlife Centre
Tea Tree

+ Mt Lord
Broad River
Glen River

Tyenna
11
Fitzgerald
Maydena
Uxbridge
Moogara
Feilton
Hayes
Magra
4
Toll House
Boyer
Australian Newsprint Mill
Jet Boat
B10
Granton
A10
Museum
32
21
Claremont
Berriedale
Cadbury's Chocolate Factory
Bridgewater
Old Beach
B32
Grasstree Hill 544m +
Grasstree Hill
Mt Direction 448m +
Risdon Cove Historic Site
Cove Hill 239m +
Motor Racing Circuit
Risdo

Mt Styx + 1080m
Styx River
Russell River
New Norfolk
Glenfern
Lachlan
Mt Lloyd
Leathercraft Workshops
Collins Cap
Malbina
Molesworth
Mt Faulkner 901m +
Glenlusk
Collinsvale
Glenorchy
GLENORCHY
MOONAH
LINDISFA
Risdo

SOUTH WEST NATIONAL PARK
SNOWY RANGE
Denison River
Little Denison River
Weld River
Plenty River
RANGE
WELLINGTON
WELLINGTON PROTECTED AREA
(PROPOSED)
+ Trestle Mtn
Collins Bonnet 1259m +
Mt Wellington 1270m
Lookout
12
MT STUART
HOBART
Battery Point
Wrest Point Casi
Sandy Bay
BELLE
HOW

525
+ Mt Weld 1338m
South Weld Forest Reserve
Lonnavale
Mountain River
Fern Tree
Ridgeway
B64
HWY
Neika
Leslie Vale
37 10
Longley
11
Sandfly
Grove
Apple Museum
A6
Crabtree
Lucaston Motor Museum
SOUTHERN
OUTLET
Kingston
Australia's Antarctic Headquarters
A6
Taroona
B68
Tudor Cou Model Villa
Shot Tower
Lookout
15
Kingston Beach
Opossum Ba
Blackmans Bay
South

Mt Picton + 1327m
Lake Picton
Huon River
Judbury
Ranelagh
Glen Huon
Apple Carver
HUON
6
Huonville
Boat Hire
B68
Woodstock
Upper Woodstock
Grey Mountain 831m +
Pelverata
Kaoota
Nierinna
Allens Rivulet
Margate
Electrona
Snug
HWY
12
Coningham
Howden
36
Cape Direc
Iron
Dennes Point
B66
Lowes Hill 212m +
NORTH
Barnes Ba

Lake Riveaux
Tahune Forest Reserve
Franklin
A6
Cradoc
Castle Forbes Bay
Port Huon
Egg Island
Glaziers Bay
CHANNEL
17
Woodturning & Tahune Wildlife Park
Cygnet
Nicholls River
Oyster Cove
Kettering
20
Woodbridge
Birchs Bay
Gardners Bay
5
Oyster Cove
Ferry
Roberts Hill 206m +
BRUNY

Waratah Lookout
HARTZ MOUNTAINS NATIONAL PARK
Hartz Peak 1255m +
Geeveston
Forest and Heritage Centre
44
HUON
Cairns Bay
Waterloo
Surges Bay
Glendevie
Petcheys Bay
Lymington
Wattle Grove
8
Garden Island Creek
15
15
Flowerpot
Fruit Farm
CHANNEL
Middleton
Simpsons Point
ISLAND
Church Hill 178m +
Memo
Early Na
Great Bay

SOUTH WEST NATIONAL PARK
Adamsons Peak 1226m +
Police Point
HWY
Hideaway Bay
9
Francistown
Surveyors Bay
Dover
Museum Point
Port Esperance
HWY
8
Raminea
Strathblane
Esperance River
Huon River
Gordon
Verona Sands
B68
15 48
CHANNEL
Simpsons Bay
Satellite Island
Alonnah
D'ENTRECASTEAUX
SOUTH BRUNY ISLAND
Adventure Bay
Lookout
B66

Hastings Cave
Thermal Springs
Hastings
3
A10
525
TO SOUTHPORT
Little Taylors Bay
Lunawanna
Partridge Island
Mt Mangana 571m +
Adventure Bay
Cookville
Fluted Cape
Captain Cook's Landing Pla
Bligh Museum

1 2 3 4 5 6 7 8 9 10 11 12 13

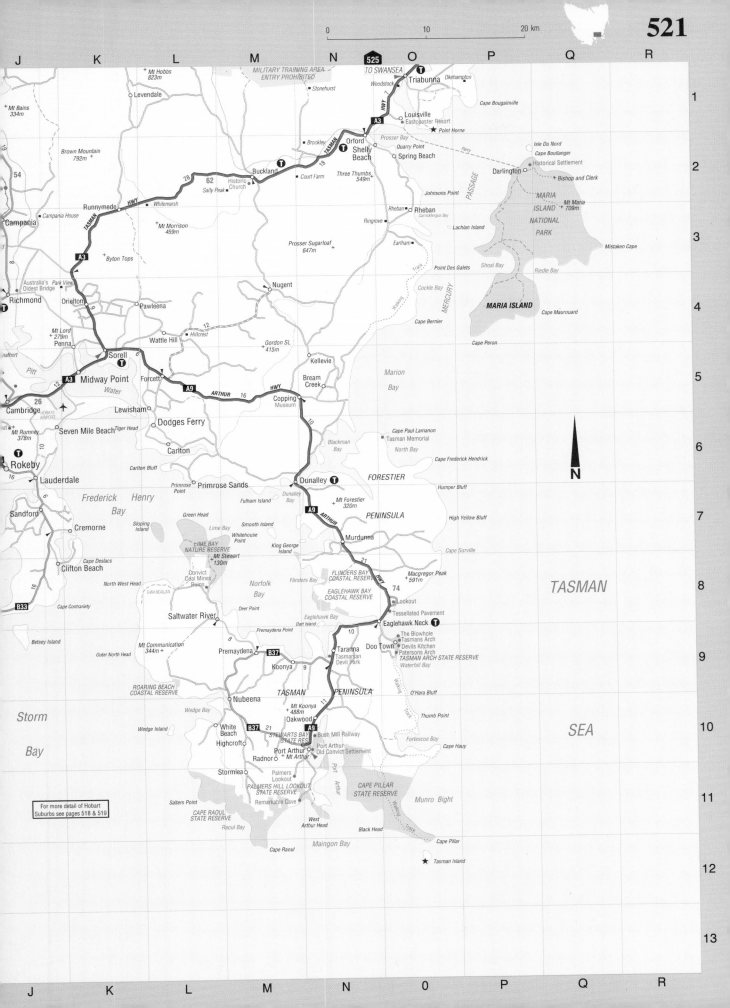

0   10   20 km

J   K   L   M   N   525   O   P   Q   R

TO SWANSEA

TO SWANSEA
Woodstock   Triabunna
Okehampton
1
Mt Bains 334m +   Levendale   Mt Hobbs 823m +   Stonehurst   HWY   Louisville Eastcoaster Resort   Cape Bougainville
A3
Brockley   Orford Shelly Beach   Prosser Bay   Point Horne
2
Brown Mountain 792m +   Buckland   Court Farm   Three Thumbs 549m +   Quarry Point   Spring Beach   Isle Du Nord   Cape Boullanger   Historical Settlement   Darlington   Bishop and Clerk
28   62   Historic Church   Sally Peak   TASMAN
Runnymede   Whitemarsh   MARIA ISLAND   Mt Maria 709m +
Campania   Campania House   Mt Morrison 469m +   Prosser Sugarloaf 647m +   Rheban   Carrickfergus Bay   Rheban   Lachlan Island   NATIONAL   Mistaken Cape
3
A3   Byton Tops   Ringrove   Earlham   PARK
Australia's Oldest Bridge   Park View   Nugent   Point Des Galets   Shoal Bay   Riedle Bay
Richmond   Orielton   Pawleena   Cape Bernier   MARIA ISLAND   Cape Maurouard
4
Mt Lord 279m +   Penna   Wattle Hill   Hillcrest   12   Gordon SL 415m   Cape Peron
Pitt   Sorell   6   Kellevie   Marion Bay
5
Midway Point   Forcett   ARTHUR   16   HWY   Copping Museum   MERCURY PASSAGE
A3   Water   Lewisham   Bream Creek
Cambridge   26   HOBART AIRPORT   Seven Mile Beach   Tiger Head   Dodges Ferry   10   Cape Paul Lamanon   Tasman Memorial
6
Mt Rumney 378m +   Carlton   Blackman Bay   North Bay   Cape Frederick Hendrick
Rokeby   Carlton Bluff   FORESTIER   Humper Bluff
Lauderdale   Primrose Point   Primrose Sands   Dunalley   High Yellow Bluff
7
Frederick Henry Bay   Fulham Island   Dunalley Bay   Mt Forestier 320m +   PENINSULA
Sandford   Green Head   Smooth Island   A9   ARTHUR
Cremorne   Sloping Island   Lime Bay   Whitehouse Point   Murdunna   Cape Surville
8
Cape Deslacs   LIME BAY NATURE RESERVE   Mt Stewart 130m +   King George Island   21   Macgregor Peak 591m +   TASMAN
Clifton Beach   Convict Coal Mines Ruins   74
B33   GWANDALAN   FLINDERS BAY COASTAL RESERVE
Cape Contrariety   North West Head   Norfolk Bay   Flinders Bay   EAGLEHAWK BAY COASTAL RESERVE
Betsey Island   Saltwater River   Deer Point   Eaglehawk Bay   Lookout   SEA
Outer North Head   Premaydena Point   Dart Island   Tessellated Pavement
9
Mt Communication 344m +   Premaydena   B37   8   10   Eaglehawk Neck   The Blowhole   Tasmans Arch
Koonya   9   Taranna   Doo Town   Devils Kitchen   Patersons Arch   TASMAN ARCH STATE RESERVE
ROARING BEACH COASTAL RESERVE   Tasmanian Devil Park   Waterfall Bay
Storm   Nubeena   TASMAN   PENINSULA   O'Hara Bluff
10
Bay   Wedge Bay   Mt Koonya 488m +   11   Thumb Point
Wedge Island   Oakwood   A9   Bush Mill Railway   Fortescue Bay   Cape Hauy
White Beach   B37   21   STEWARTS BAY STATE RES
Highcroft   Port Arthur   Port Arthur Old Convict Settlement
Radnor   Mt Arthur +
Stormlea   Palmers Lookout   Port Arthur   CAPE PILLAR STATE RESERVE   Munro Bight
11
Salters Point   PALMERS HILL LOOKOUT STATE RESERVE   Remarkable Cave
For more detail of Hobart Suburbs see pages 518 & 519   CAPE RAOUL STATE RESERVE   West Arthur Head   Black Head   Cape Pillar
Raoul Bay   Maingon Bay
12
Cape Raoul   Cape Pillar   Tasman Island
13

J   K   L   M   N   O   P   Q   R

A B C D E F G H I

1

2

SPIRIT OF TASMANIA: Ferries passengers and cars across Bass Strait between Melbourne and Devonport. This powerful sea voyager offers all the facilities of an ocean cruise-liner, accommodating passengers seeking luxury to the budget-conscious backpacker.

Spirit of Tasmania Ferry To Melbourne Victoria

N

3

BASS STRAIT

ASBESTOS RANGE NATIONAL PARK: Lying between Greens Beach and Port Sorell, this scenic northern coastal park has numerous isolated beaches, huge granite outcrops, sand dunes and grasslands covered in wildflowers. Mineral asbestos was mined last century at the northern point.

West Head

Badger Head

Pt Sorell

Port Sorell

ASBESTOS RANGE NATIONAL PARK

C721

Sulphur Creek

TO BURNIE

4 Penguin T B17 1 13

Hawley Beach
Shearwater
Port Sorell T
Bakers Beach

Rubicon Estate

C74

Ferndene

Ulverstone T Weeda Copper Craft Turners Beach Leith 12 24

Athlone
Northdown
B74 19 Wesley Vale

Squeaking Point

York Town *Browns*

5

Braeside Gawler B15 4 Forth B19 9 Don 6 Devonport T Searoad Terminal

Quoiba B71 11 Thirlstane 3 Moriarty 6

Branchs *Creek*

North Motton B17 Abbotsham B16 15 8

Spreyton 6 Latrobe T BASS 18 Harford C704 8 7 C740

FRANKFORD 65

Saxons

6

C124 Spalford Kindred 11 Melrose 10 3 Eugenana

1 Sassafras East

7 Gunns Plains Preston Central Castra 13 13 C132 Sprent 3 Paloona Paloona PS Lower Barrington B14 C150 31 Sassafras HWY *Robin Hood* C153 Franklin *Rubicon* 19 B71

Caves Warringa

8 C125 South Preston B15 10 Upper Castra Wilmot Lower 12 Lake Paloona Barrington 5 Nook B13 Railton T C160

Rosslyn *West Fran*

9 Nietta Wilmot Narrawa West Kentish Roland 8 Murals Theatrette Sheffield T B14 4 2 Stoodley Sunnyside Merseylea 10 Kimberley 50 22 BASS Parkham C711

Leven Canyon South Nietta 5 Forest Walk 10 C156 5 C160

10 Rainforest Walk *Charles Peak* 14 Erriba Rowing Staverton C140 C136 Claude Road 11 Paradise Beulah 8 C159 11 Weegena Moltema B13 1 C710 Reedy Marsh Weetah

Lower Beulah 9 Elizabeth Town Dunorlan

11 Moina C132 Wilmot Power Station Cethana Power Station 9 2 Gowrie Park Mt Roland 1234m C137

MOLE CREEK: Named after the creek which curiously "burrows" underground, this rural district is noted for its strong-flavoured, light amber leatherwood honey and its unusual breed of beef cattle 'Belted Galloways'. Mole Creek is near some limestone caves, notably King Solomons and Marakoopa, where the underground temperature is only 9°C year-round.

Wattle Bank HWY

Lemana Red Hills 10 Deloraine T

12 Daisy Dell Lorinna Liena King Solomons Cave B12 15 Mayberry Marakoopa Cave Mole Creek T Historic Farm Trowunna Wildlife Park *Mayfield* Chudleigh B12 24 Needles C168 C164 Montana C166

Lemana *Meander* LAKE HWY 6 C503 10 A5 Quamby Brook C5

13 CRADLE MOUNTAIN LAKE ST CLAIR NATIONAL PARK C139 Lemonthyme Power Station C171 *Mountleigh* C166 Caveside C169 C167

Dove *Iris* *Lake Cethana* *Forth* *Mersey* TO HOBART Go Va

A B C D 526 E F G H I

Grid columns: J K L M N O P Q R
Grid rows: 1–13

West Sandy Cape · *East Sandy Cape* · *Anderson Bay*

Bridport

Stony Head · *Noland Bay* · Lulworth · Weymouth · Bellingham

Five Mile Bluff · Beechford · *Turquoise Bluff + 167m* · Back Creek · Weymouth Farm · B82 · 28 · B84

Low Head ★ · Leura · C816 · Delamere Winery · Pipers Brook Winery · Heemskerk Winery · C827

Low Head · C807 · *Dam* · Lefroy · Pipers Brook · C818 · B82

George Town · Museum · Mt George 242m · B82 · EAST · C819 · C826 · *Bridestowe Lavender Farm*

Kelso · Bell Bay · A8 · C809 · Pipers River · Rochecombe Winery · Idlewilde · Retreat · *Fairbanks*

Clarence Point · Ilfraville · Bell Bay · B83 · Glen · Lebrina · Golconda · B81 · Vermont · Blumont · Nabowla

Beauty Point · Teddy Bear Park · B73 · TAMAR · The Glen · Tunnel · Wyena · Denison Gorge

Beaconsfield · Museum · Rowella · Kayena · Lower Turners Marsh · Bangor · Lilydale Falls · Lilydale North · C827 · Lisle

C715 · Sidmouth · C812 · Karoola · Lilydale · **TO SCOTTSDALE** · 527

Batman Bridge · Marion's Winery · Devoit · Hillwood · Mount Direction · Mt Direction +367m · C811 · Lalla Gardens · La Provence Winery

Flowery Gully · Robigana · Paper Beach · Leam · Turners Marsh · Underwood · Myrtle Bank · Myrtle Grove

C717 · Holwell · Stewarts Hill +419m · WEST · A7 · Gravelly Beach · Windermere · B83 · Targa · St Patricks River

Winkleigh · Loira · Exeter · Blackwall · Dilston · B81 · Patersonia · C404

Frankford · Lanena · Rosevears · St Matthias Winery · C824 · Nunamara · Mt Barrow 1413m

B71 · Glengarry · TAMAR RD · A7 · HWY · Rocherlea · TASMAN HWY · 70

Notley Hills · Notley Gorge · C731 · Legana · NEWNHAM · Mowbray

C714 · Black Sugarloaf 502m · FRANKFORD · Bridgenorth · C732 · 24 · Riverside North

Birralee · C732 · Rosevale · C734 · TREVALLYN · INVERMAY · WAVERLEY · A3

B72 · Glenburn · TAMAR RIVER · Penny Royal World · Cataract Gorge · **LAUNCESTON** · NEWSTEAD · Corra Linn · C401

Selbourne · C735 · SUMMERHILL · PROSPECT · KINGS MEADOWS · ST. LEONARDS · Illaro · C401

Glenvista · Country Club Casino · YOUNGTOWN · Franklin House · Relbia · White Hills

Westwood · C738 · Hadspen · Entally House · Longford Wildlife Park · C531 · Mt Arnon +314m · Breadalbane · C402

Violet Banks · BASS · Hagley · 44 · HWY · Carrick · Strathroy · B41 · LAUNCESTON AIRPORT · Western Junction

Westbury · B52 · Glenore · C511 · C513 · Pateena · MIDLAND · Perth · Evandale · Historic Town · C413

C501 · C506 · C507 · C505 · Whitemore · Oaks · West Lagoon · Newry · B52 · C416

Cluan · Bishopsbourne · Toiberry · C519 · Longford · East Lagoon · Woodstock · Rosebank · 34 · C419

B51 · C520 · C521 · Brickendon · Woolmers · Symmons Plains Raceway · Clarendon House · Deddington · Hampden

TO HOBART · 527

WINERIES: Pipers Brook is referred to as the centre of northern Tasmania's grape-growing area. Vineyards in the district are open to visitors for tours and tastings.

LILYDALE: Lilydale is Tasmania's "country garden" with an expansive Rhododendron Reserve and rows of ash trees originally planted for an unsuccessful tennis racquet and cricket bat manufacturing firm. Numerous pathways provide excellent bushwalking through forest parks and to the Lilydale Falls.

TAMAR RIVER: This magnificent broad river was the passageway of the first European settlement and exploration in northern Tasmania. Batman Bridge, one of the world's first cable-stayed truss bridges, is 30kms from Launceston and links the east and west banks.

TOURIST INFORMATION:
Bridport (11 Alfred St, Scottsdale)
Deloraine (29 Westchurch St)
Devonport (18 Rooke St)
Evandale (7 High St)
Exeter (Tamar Visitors Centre, Main Rd)
George Town (Main Rd)
Latrobe (Council Offices, Gilbert St)
Launceston (cnr St John and Paterson Sts)
Longford (Council Offices, Smith St)
Sheffield (93 Main St)
Ulverstone (Roelf Vos carpark)
Westbury (52 William St)

Grid columns: A B C D E F G H I
Grid rows: 1 2 3 4 5 6 7 8 9 10 11 12 13

SOUTHERN

OCEAN

526

Lake Margaret
A10
Mt Lyell Mine
Linda
HWY
Gormanston
Queenstown
B27
LYELL
B24
Ocean Beach
Strahan
Lynchford
King River PS
Regatta Point
36
Mt Owen 1146m
Mt Jukes 1168m
Point Hibbs
Cape Sorel ★
LYELL
A10
A10
LYELL
26
Bronte Park

Mt Gould 1491m
Mt Ida 1158m
Mt Olympus 1447m
Lake St Clair
Mt Hugel 1307m
Mt Rufus 1402m
Mt Gell 1439m
Derwent Bridge
BRONTE
Collingwood R
81
HWY
Mt Arrowsmith 981m
Lake King William
Mt King William I 1324m
Clark Dam
Butlers Gorge
Butlers Gorge PS
Tarraleah
A1

Sloop Point
Gorge Point
Birthday Bay
Modder
Hibbs Bay
Point Hibbs
Mt Darwin 1031m
Mt Sorell 1144m
PILLINGER
Sarah Island Convict Ruins
Frenchmans Cap 1443m
Mt Seal 878m
Mt King William III 1158m
FRANKLIN GORDON WILD RIVERS NATIONAL PARK
Part of World Heritage Area
Mt King William II 1372m
KING WILLIAM RANGE
PRINCE OF WALES RANGE
Liapootah PS
Wayatinah
Wayatinah

SOUTHERN

OCEAN

Spero Bay
Endeavour Bay
Wanderer
High Rocky Point
Hibbs R
Spero R
Spero
Mainwaring R
Mt Osmund 369m
Mt Discovery 680m
Mt Lee 734m
Lewis
Frederick Hill 518m
Mt Curly 1039m
Mt Humboldt 1079m
Mt Wright 1119m
Clear Hill 1198m
MOUNT NATIONAL
Gordon PS
Strathgordon
Lookout
Serpentine Dam
Mt Sprent 1058m
B61
Lake Gordon
ADAMSFIELD
Old Mine
Lookout
Mt Wedge 1146m
Mt Bowes 957m
Lookout Forest Walk
84

Low Rocky Point ★
Elliott Bay
Elliott Hill 209m
Hardwood Hill 412m
Nye Bay
Mt Gaffney 588m
Mulcahy Bay
Wreck Bay
Mt Hean 747m
SOUTH WEST NATIONAL PARK
Mt Giblin 878m
Lookout
Scotts Peak Dam
Edgar Dam
Mt Anne 1425m
Mt Orion 1119m
Mt Braddon 729m
FRANKLAND RANGE
ARTHUR RANGE
Part of World Heritage Area
Mt Norold 978m
Mt Rugby 771m
Bathurst Harbour
Mt Counsel 800m
Mike Hill
Point St Vincent
Port Davey
Stephens Bay
Mine
Mt Melaleuca
Melaleuca
Mt Melaleuca 595m
SOUTH WEST NATIONAL PARK
Island Bay
Window Pane Bay
South West Cape
Karama Bay
New Harbour
Louisa Bay
Cox Bight
Ile Du Golfe
De Witt Island
Flat Witch Island
MAATSUYKER GROUP
Maatsuyker Island ★

SOUTHERN

KING ISLAND

Cape Wickham
Cape Farewell
Phoques Bay
Lavinia Point
New Year I
Christmas I
Whistler Point
Egg Lagoon
Yambacoona
37
BASS STRAIT
Reekara
B25
Loorana
Dairy Factory
Sea Elephant Bay
Naracoopa
Parenna
Currie
Pegarah
Yarra Creek
Fitzmaurice Bay
29
Lymwood
Grassy
Bold Head
Pearshape
Seal Point
Surprise Point
Surprise Bay
Cataraqui Point
Seal Bay
Stokes Point

King Island   Flinders Island

Launceston
HOBART

FLINDERS ISLAND

Inner Sister Island
Stanley Point
Blyth Pt
Palana
Killiecrankie Bay
Killiecrankie
Cape Frankland
Leeka
29
FURNEAUX
Marshall Bay
Lughrata
Babel I
Prime Seal Island
Emita
Museum
B85
Memana
Arthur Bay
19
72
Whitemark
Long Point
Parry's Bay
Ranga
15
Sellars Lagoon
Cameron Inlet
GROUP
Trousers Pt
Loccota
Lady Barron
Great Dog I
Vansittart I
Puncheon Pt
Mt Chappell I
STRZELECKI NP
Anderson I
Badger I
Long I
FRANKLIN SOUND
Cape Barren Island
Mt Munro 716m
CAPE BARREN ISLAND
Cape Barren
BASS STRAIT
Preservation I
Sloping Pt
Clarke Island
Kent Bay
Forsyth I
Mt Kerford 499m
Passage I
BANKS STRAIT
Lookout Heads
Moriarty Point

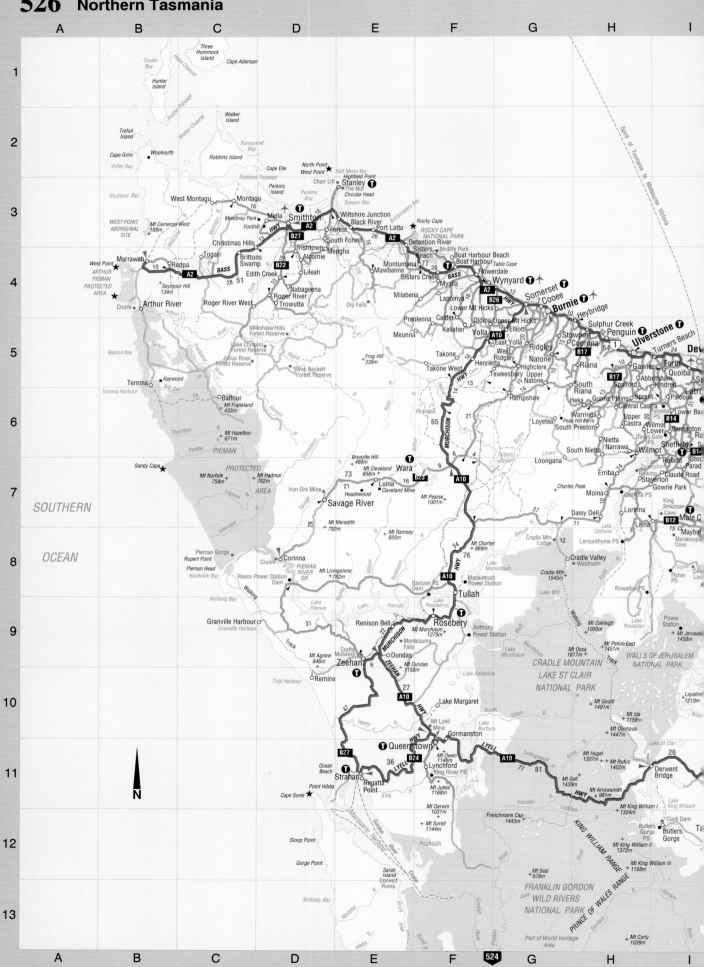

BASS STRAIT

Banks Strait

CAPE BARREN ISLAND

Kent Bay
Mt Kerford 499m
Preservation I
Sloping Pt
Forsyth I
Clarke Island
Passage I
Look Out Heads
Moriarty Point

Cape Portland
Swan Island
+ Vinegar Hill 52m
Cape Naturaliste
Poole
Great Mussel Roe Bay
Rushy Lagoon
Icena
Cape Portland
Mt William + 216m
MOUNT WILLIAM NATIONAL PARK

Tomahawk
Boobyalla
Waterhouse Island
Waterhouse Point
Ringarooma Bay
Croppies Point
Waterhouse
Anderson Bay
West Sandy Cape
East Sandy Cape
37

more detail of Launceston region see pages 522 & 523

Mt Cameron + 551m
Anson Park
Gladstone
B82
South Mt Cameron
Ansons Bay
Eddystone Pt — Eddystone Point
Bay Of Fires

Five Mile Bluff
Stony Head
Lulworth
Low Head
Beechford
Weymouth
Bellingham
Bridport
Back Creek
Pipers River
Vineyard
Pipers Brook
Lavender Farm
B84
North Scottsdale
Forester
Winnaleah
Herrick
Pioneer
Henderson Lagoon
The Gardens

George Town
Low Head
Lefroy
Bell Bay
B82
Retreat
Glen
Lebrina
Golconda
Lietinna
Scottsdale
Warrentina
Telita
Moorina
Derby
A3
Weldborough
99
Lotta
Goulds Country
Binalong Bay

Greens Beach
Kelso
Clarence Point
Beauty Point
Beaconsfield
Rowella
Sidmouth
Lower Turners Marsh
Bangor
Wyena
West Scottsdale
Springfield
A3
Legerwood
Cuckoo Hill 732m
Ringarooma
Pyengana
Goshen
Priory
Mt Pearson 373m
Goshen
St Helens Point
Akaroa
Stieglitz
Parnella
St Helens Island

SBESTOS RANGE NATIONAL PARK
Port Sorell
Sassafras East
Devonport
Exeter
Lanena
Windermere
Dilston
B81
Myrtle Bank
Targa
Nabowla
Lisle
Tonganah
Talawah
Trenah
Alberton
Mt Victoria 1208m
Mt Young + 903m
St Columba Falls
St Helens
Parkside
Beaumaris
Scamander

Frankford
B71
West Frankford
Holwell
Glengarry
Bridgenorth
Legana
Rocherlea
Waverly
St Patricks River
Patersonia
Nunamara
Tayene
Mt Barrow 1413m
Mt Saddleback 1277m
Upper Esk
Mathinna
Upper Scamander

Parkham
B72
Rosevale
Selbourne
Riverside
North
Hadspen
LAUNCESTON
Casino
Corra Linn
White Hills
Relbia
Burns Creek
Musselboro
Upper Blessington
ROSES TIER
Alpine Village
Legges Tor 1575m
Whisloca
Carr Villa
Mangana
Cornwall
Mt Nicholas 869m
St Marys
37
Falmouth

Elizabeth Town
Weetah
Exton
Westwood
Hagley
Carrick
Westbury
B52
Perth
Breadalbane
Western Junction
Blessington
English Town
BEN LOMOND NATIONAL PARK
Ormley
B43
Gray
Four Mile Creek

Deloraine
Osmaston
Glenore
Whitemore
Oaks
Toiberry
Longford
Bishopsbourne
Evandale
Hampden
Deddington
Storys Creek
Rossarden
B42
Fingal
A4
ROAD
St Marys
Chain Of Lagoons

A5
Golden Valley
Quamby Brook
Cluan
Bracknell
Liffey
Cressy
Kilrae
B53
Powranna
Nile
Clarendon
Rostrevor
Ormley
B42
Avoca
MAIN
74
Royal George
Seymour
Long Point
DOUGLAS APSLEY

Meander
Jackeys Marsh
Lifely Falls
Blackwood Creek
Richmond Hill
Epping Forest
Cleveland
Conara
Llewellyn Siding
Mt St John + 777m
A3
Birdlife Park
Waubs Harbour
Sealife Park

GREAT
66
Breona
Poatina PS
Lookout
The Glen
The Bend
Parknook
Rokeby
Woodford
Front Rocky Hill + 574m
Bicheno
Cape Lodi

WESTERN TIERS
A5
52
Cramps
B51
Pisa
Talenty
Campbell Town
B34
Meetus Falls
Ferndale
Greenlawn
Apslawn
Llandaff

Miena
14
Wilbursville
Mt Penny West + 1115m
St Patricks Plains
Shannon
Auburn
Goldsmith
Auburn
Ross
Front Rocky Hill
B34
Cranbrook
Mt Peter + 280m

33
Steppes
Waddamana
Ellinthrop
Mt Franklin 1102m
Snobs Point 971m
Mona Vale
Mt Hobgoblin 763m
Moulting Lagoon

Lake Echo PS
Dee Lagoon
Hermitage
Interlaken
Woodbury House
Tunbridge
Mount Morriston
Bark Mill
Swansea
Cape Tourville
The Hazards
Wineglass Bay
Cape Forestier

Glengowan
Sunny Banks
The Quoin
Rotherwood
Woodbury
Antill Ponds
Trefusis
The Gables
Hillcrest
Stonehouse
Mt Tooms 719m
Buxton Point
Great Oyster Bay
FREYCINET NATIONAL PARK
FREYCINET PENINSULA
Cape Degerando

Black Bobs
Dungrove Hill 690m
Forest Green
Cluny
Oatlands
York Plains
Nala
Pawtella
Lemont
Little Swanport
Pontypool
Little Swanport Hill 536m
Cape Baudin
Cape Sonnerat

Osterley
Hartfield
Cawood Hill 579m
Bothwell
Jericho
Lower Marshes
Andover
Stonehenge
Early Rise
Hermitage
Grindstone Bay
Isle des Phoques

A10
Ouse
Cluny PS
Montacute
Denholm
Tedworth
Stonor
Mt Seymour 739m
Crichton
Mt Seymour
Whiteford
RIVER TRAINING AREA ENTRY PROHIBITED
Ashgrove
Mt Murray
Grindstone Point

33
LYELL HWY
A10
Rathmore
Melton Mowbray
Stockman
Jericho
Tiberias
Tunnack
Baden
Mt Ponsonby 820m
Woodsdale
Rostrevor House
Triabunna
Cape Bougainville

Langloh
Hamilton
Hollow Tree
Windsor Park
Kempton
Colebrook
Rhyndaston
Eldon
Levendale
Louisville
Eastcoaster Resort

Lawrenny
Bonnie Vue
Woodstock
Stonehurst

10 20 30 40 50 km

525

Index of Place Names

To enable the ready location of the place names that appear in this gazetteer, each is followed by a map page number and grid reference, and/or the text page number on which that place name occurs. A page number set in bold type indicates the main text entry for that place name.

Sale Vic. 225 M6, 179, 190, **194**
Sale — Place name
Vic. — State
225 M6 — Sale appears on this map page
179, 190 — Sale is mentioned on these pages
194 — Main entry for Sale

The alphabetical order followed in the index is that of 'word-by-word', where all entries under one word are grouped together. Where a place name consists of more than one word, the order is governed by the first and then the second word. For example:
Green Bay
Green River
Greenbank
Greens Beach
Greenwood Forest
Greg Greg
Gregafell

Names beginning with Mc are indexed as Mac and those beginning with St, as Saint.

The following abbreviations and contractions are used in the index:
ACT — Australian Capital Territory
NSW — New South Wales
NT — Northern Territory
Qld — Queensland
SA — South Australia
St — Saint
Tas. — Tasmania
Vic. — Victoria
WA — Western Australia

Abbotsford NSW 98 I8
Abbotsford Vic. 207 M8, 149, 156
Abbotsham Tas. 522 C6, 526 H5
Abercorn Qld 477 M13
Aberdare State Forest NSW 112 B11, 112 C10, 113 D13
Aberdeen NSW 121 J3, 122 I13
Aberfeldy Vic. 225 J3
Abergowrie Qld 479 L10
Abermain NSW 112 C9, 113 H11
Abernethy NSW 112 C10, 121 K5
Acacia Ridge Qld 464 H7
Acheron Vic. 211 O2, 232 I12, 157, 199
Acland Qld 466 D5
Acraman Creek Con. Park SA 297 O11
Acton ACT 136 A3, 138 G9, 132
Adaminaby NSW 118 H5, 119 D8, 140 E9, 235 K1, **50**
Adavale Qld 485 N2
Adelaide SA 276, 278 I5, 283 K7, 287 B2, 289 K8, 237, **238–41**, 273
Adelaide River NT 388 E8, 392 F7, 364, 367, **369**
Adelong NSW 119 B6, 120 C13, **50**
Advancetown Qld 467 N13, 469 B6, 470 B6
Adventure Bay Tas. 520 H13, 525 M9, 494
Aeroglen Qld 472 C4
Agery SA 282 G2, 288 I5
Agnes Banks NSW 105 J6
Agnes Banks Nature Reserve NSW 105 J7
Agnes Water Qld 477 O11, **416**, 439, 443
Aileron NT 397 J6, **369**
Ainslie ACT 138 H8
Aireys Inlet Vic. 210 E12, 217 C11, 227 P9, 175
Airlie Beach Qld 476 I2, **408**, 415, 423, 451, 456
Airport West Vic. 206 I4
Aitkenvale Qld 471 A9
Akaroa Tas. 527 Q6
Alawa NT 386 F5
Alawoona SA 287 H1, 289 Q7
Albany WA 351 N12, 354 G13, **305**, 313, 314, 323
Albany Creek Qld 462 C6, 452
Albert NSW 120 A3, 125 R13, 127 R1
Albert Park SA 278 D1, 280 E13
Albert Park Vic. 207 K9, 148, 150
Alberton Qld 467 N10
Alberton SA 280 E12
Alberton Tas. 527 O6
Alberton Vic. 225 K9, 190, 201
Albion Qld 462 H9

Albury NSW 127 P13, 233 P4, 422 B2, **50–1**, 56, 71, 72
Alcomie Tas. 526 D4
Alderley Qld 462 F9
Aldgate SA 279 Q11, 243
Aldinga SA 283 K10, 284 B7, 287 B3, 289 K9, **246**
Aldinga Beach SA 283 K10, 284 A7, 246
Aldinga Scrub Con. Park SA 283 K10, 284 B7, 246
Alectown NSW 120 C5
Alexander Heights WA 344 H4
Alexander Morrison Nat. Park WA 354 D4
Alexandra Vic. 211 O2, 233 J11, **157**
Alexandra Bridge WA 349 E10, **305**, 333
Alexandra Headland Qld 470 H9, **440**
Alexandra Hills Qld 465 Q2
Alexandria NSW 99 M12, 103 O2
Alford SA 289 J4
Alfords Point NSW 102 F8
Alfred Cove WA 342 E9
Alfred National Park Vic. 119 E13, 235 M11
Alfred Town NSW 120 A12, 127 R10
Algester Qld 464 H8
Ali-Curung NT 397 K3
Alice Springs NT 391 K3, 397 J9, 363, 364, 369, 370–1, 372, 374, 378, 382
Allambie Heights NSW 99 O3, 101 N13
Allans Flat Vic. 201
Allansford Vic. 226 I9
Allanson WA 346 E13
Allawah NSW 103 K7
Allenby Gardens SA 278 F3
Allendale East SA 287 H13
Allendale North SA 283 N3, 289 M6
Allens Rivulet Tas. 520 G8
Allenvale Vic. 184
Alligator Creek Qld 452
Allingham Qld 479 M11
Allora Qld 466 E12, 475 L7, **408**, 456
Alma SA 283 L2, 289 L6
Almaden Qld 479 J7
Alonnah Tas. 520 G12, 525 L9
Aloomba Qld 473 G11, 479 L7
Alpara NT 294 G1, 396 F13
Alpha Qld 476 E9, 483 R10
Alpine National Park Vic. 119 A10, 222 F8, 223 J10, 223 P5, 225 K1, 233 N12, 233 Q9, 234 A10, 151, **168**, 186
Alstonville NSW 123 P3, 475 O9, 51
Althorpe Islands Con. Park SA 282 A11, 288 G10

Altona Vic. 206 F10, 210 I7
Altona Meadows Vic. 206 F12
Alva Qld 479 O12
Alvie Vic. 210 A10, 215 F5, 227 N8
Alyangula NT 393 O8
Amata SA 294 G1, 396 F13
Ambrose Qld 477 M10
Amby Qld 474 E4
American River SA 288 I11, 255, 258
Amiens Qld 123 L2, 475 L8
Amity Point Qld 467 P7, 425
Amoonguna NT 397 J9
Amphitheatre Vic. 220 I7, 227 M1, 229 M12
Anakie Qld 476 G9, 449
Anakie Vic. 210 F7, 217 D3, 227 Q6, 176
Anakie Gorge Vic. 158, **176**
Andamooka SA 290 G4, 237, **246**, 267, 274
Andover Tas. 525 M3, 527 N12
Andrews SA 289 L3
Anembo NSW 119 E7, 140 I7
Angahook–Lorne State Park Vic. 210 D12, 215 I10, 217 A11, 227 P9
Angas Valley SA 283 P6
Angaston SA 283 O4, 286 I4, 287 D1, 289 M7, 242, **246**
Angle Park SA 280 G11, 241
Anglers Reach NSW 118 G5, 119 C8, 140 D9, 235 J1
Anglers Rest Vic. 223 R9, 233 R10, 234 E8, 190
Anglesea Vic. 210 E11, 217 C11, 227 Q9, **157**, 175
Angourie NSW 94
Angurugu NT 393 O9
Angustown Vic. 192
Anna Bay NSW 112 H3, 121 M5
Annandale NSW 99 K10, 103 M1
Annangrove NSW 105 K7
Annerley Qld 464 H3, 467 M8
Ansons Bay Tas. 527 Q4
Anstead Qld 464 A6
Antechamber Bay SA 287 A5, 289 J11, 258
Antill Ponds Tas. 525 M2, 527 M11
Antwerp Vic. 197
Anula NT 386 I7
Anzac Village NSW 102 B5
Aparawatatja SA 294 B2, 396 C13
Apollo Bay Vic. 215 G12, 227 N11, **157**, 175
Appila SA 289 K1, 291 K13, 256
Appin NSW 105 J12, 116 G3, 119 I2, 121 J9
Applecross WA 342 G7
Applethorpe Qld 123 L2, 475 L8
Apslawn Tas. 525 P1, 527 L13

Blackall Qld 476 C11, 483 P11, **410**
Black Bobs Tas. 525 J3, 527 J12
Black Forest SA 278 G7
Black Hill SA 283 Q6, 287 E1, 289 N7
Black Hill Vic. 219 G4
Black Hill Conservation Park SA 283 M7
Black Hills Tas. 520 F3, 525 K5
Black Range State Park Vic. 137 G12, 226 G1
Black River Tas. 526 E3
Black Rock SA 265
Black Rock Vic. 209 A4
Black Rock Conservation Park SA 285 E13
Black Springs NSW 104 B8
Black Springs SA 289 M4
Blackburn Vic. 207 R9
Blackbutt Qld 466 G2, 475 L4
Blackdown Tableland Nat. Park Qld 477 J9
Blackfellow Caves SA 287 H13
Blackheath NSW 104 G6, 106 C5, 120 H7, 48, 75
Blackmans Bay Tas. 520 H8, 525 M7, **503**
Blacksmiths NSW 105 R2, 112 G10
Blacktown NSW 105 K8
Blackville NSW 120 H1, 122 H12
Blackwall Tas. 523 L7
Blackwater Qld 476 I9, 410, 449
Blackwood SA 279 J12
Blackwood Vic. 221 Q11, 158, 182
Blackwood Conservation Park WA 349 G9
Blackwood Creek Tas. 527 K9
Bladensburg National Park Qld 483 L7
Blair Athol Qld 476 G7, 417
Blair Athol SA 280 I12
Blairgowrie Vic. 210 I11, 212 D8, 224 B8, 154
Blakehurst NSW 103 J8, 105 L10
Blanchetown SA 283 R3, 289 O6, 271
Blandford NSW 121 J1, 123 J12
Blaxland NSW 104 I7, 107 P7
Blaxlands Ridge NSW 105 J5
Blayney NSW 120 F7, **57**
Blenheim Qld 466 H9
Blessington Tas. 527 N7
Bletchley SA 283 N10
Blewitt Springs SA 284 D5
Bli Bli Qld 467 N1, 470 G8, 475 N4
Blighty NSW 127 L12, 232 H1
Blinman SA 285 E6, 291 K6, **249**
Bloomfield Qld 479 K4
Bloomsbury Qld 476 I3
Blue Lake National Park Qld 467 P9
Blue Mountains NSW 106–7, 37, 44, **48**, 49, 58, 75
Blue Mountains National Park NSW 104 H6, 106 E12, 106 H3, 107 L12, 119 G1, 120 H8, 48, **58**, 75
Blue Water Springs Roadhouse Qld 479 K12
Bluewater Qld 479 M12
Bluff Qld 477 J9
Bluff Beach SA 282 E6, 261
Blumont Tas. 523 R5
Blyth SA 289 K4, 252
Boat Harbour Tas. 526 F4, **493–4**, 509, 515
Boat Harbour Beach Tas. 526 F4
Boatswain SA 287 F10
Bobbin Head NSW 100 H6, 52
Bobinawarrah Vic. 222 G1
Bodalla NSW 117 H1, 119 G8, 141 M10, 235 Q2
Bodalla State Forest NSW 141 L11
Bodallin WA 354 I6, 356 D7
Boddington WA 346 G10, 354 E9
Bogangar NSW 123 P1, 475 O8
Bogan Gate NSW 120 B6, 127 R4
Bogantungan Qld 476 F9
Boggabilla NSW 122 H2, 474 I8
Boggabri NSW 122 G8, 474 H13, **57**
Bogong National Park Vic. 178
Boinka Vic. 126 C10, 230 E10

Boisdale Vic. 225 M4, 234 B13
Bolivar SA 280 I4
Bollon Qld 474 D7
Bolwarra NSW 112 C7
Bolwarrah Vic. 210 E4, 221 O11, 227 P3, 232 B13
Bomaderry NSW 116 E12, 119 H4, 120 I11, **83**
Bombala NSW 117 A9, 119 E11, 235 M7, **57**
Bonalbo NSW 123 N2, 475 M8
Bonang Vic. 119 C12, 235 J9, 190
Bonbeach Vic. 209 E8
Bondi NSW 99 P11, 103 R1, 105 N10, 41
Bondi Junction NSW 99 P11, 103 R1
Bonegilla Vic. 127 P13, 233 P4, 234 B2
Boneo Vic. 212 F9
Bongaree Qld 467 N5, 475 N5, 425
Bongeen Qld 475 K6
Bonnells NSW 112 F12
Bonnells Bay NSW 105 Q2
Bonnet Bay NSW 102 H9
Bonnie Doon Vic. 211 Q1, 233 J10, 157, 174
Bonnie Rock WA 354 H5, 356 C6
Bonny Hills NSW 109 G9, 121 O1, 123 N11
Bonython ACT 139 C10
Booborowie SA 289 L3
Boobyalla Tas. 527 O3, 502
Bookabie SA 297 L9
Bookar Vic. 215 B4, 227 L7
Bool Lagoon SA 251, 264
Boolaroo NSW 76
Boolarra Vic. 224 I8
Boolba Qld 474 E7
Booleroo SA 291 J12
Booleroo Centre SA 289 K1, 291 J13, 260, 272
Booligal NSW 127 K6
Booloumba Qld 467 K1
Boonah Qld 467 J12, 475 M7, **412**
Boonanghi State Forest NSW 109 D3
Boondall Qld 462 H5
Boonoo Boonoo National Park NSW 123 M3
Boorabbin National Park WA 356 F7
Booragoon WA 342 G10
Booral NSW 121 L4
Boorcan Vic. 215 B5, 227 K8
Boorganna Nature Reserve NSW 109 B10
Boorhaman Vic. 233 L5
Booroobin Qld 467 L2
Booroorban NSW 127 K9
Boorowa NSW 119 C3, 120 D10
Boort Vic. 126 H13, 229 O6, **164**
Boothby SA 270
Booti Booti National Park NSW 121 N3
Booyal Qld 475 L1, 477 O13
Borallon Qld 467 K8
Borden WA 351 Q4, 354 H11, 356 C12
Border Ranges National Park NSW 123 O1, 475 N8, 76, 77, 81
Border Store NT 387 I3, 389 R2
Border Village NT 296 A8, 357 R8
Bordertown SA 228 A7, 287 I7, 289 R13, **249**
Boree Creek NSW 127 O10
Boreen Point Qld 445
Boronia Vic. 208 E10
Boronia Heights Qld 464 I13
Boronia Park NSW 99 J7
Bororen Qld 477 N11
Borrika SA 287 G2, 289 P8
Borroloola NT 393 N13, 395 O3, **376**
Borung Vic. 229 O7
Boscabel WA 351 J1, 354 F10, 356 B11
Boston Bay SA 273
Boston Island SA 266
Botany NSW 103 O5, 105 M10
Botany Bay NSW 103 N7
Botany Bay Nat. Park NSW 103 Q8, 105 M11
Bothwell Tas. 525 K3, 527 L12, 487, **494**, 501
Bouddi National Park NSW 105 O6, 108 G9, 108 H8, 69, 88

Boulder WA see Kalgoorlie–Boulder
Bouldercombe Qld 477 L9
Boulia Qld 482 F8, **412**, 453
Boulla Qld 453
Boundary Bend Vic. 126 G9, 231 L7
Bourke NSW 125 N6, 474 I11, 485 P12, **57**, **60**
Bournda National Park NSW 117 G8, 119 G10, 235 P6
Bowden SA 276 A3, 278 G3
Bowelling WA 346 G13, 354 F10, 356 A11
Bowen Qld 476 H1, **412**
Bowen Hills Qld 462 G10, 401, 403
Bowen Mountain NSW 104 I6
Bowenvale Vic. 229 N11, 186
Bowenville Qld 466 C5, 475 K5
Bower SA 283 P1, 289 N5
Bowhill SA 283 R7, 287 E2, 289 O8
Bowling Green Bay Nat. Park Qld 479 N12
Bowmans SA 283 J2, 289 K5
Bowning NSW 119 D4, 120 E11
Bowral NSW 116 C7, 119 H3, 120 I10, 45, **60**
Bowraville NSW 123 O8, 475 M13, 78
Box Hill Vic. 207 P8, 211 K7
Boyankil Qld 467 O11
Boyanup WA 354 D10, 309
Boydtown NSW 119 F11, 235 P9, 55, 66
Boyer Tas. 520 F4, 525 L5, 505
Boyland Qld 467 M12
Boyne Island Qld 477 N10
Boys Town Qld 467 L12
Boyup Brook WA 350 E2, 354 F10, 356 A12, **307**
Bracalba Qld 467 L4
Bracken Ridge Qld 462 F4
Bracknell Tas. 527 K8
Braddon ACT 136 E2, 138 H8
Brady Creek SA 289 M5
Braeside Vic. 209 E5
Brahma Lodge SA 281 M5
Braidwood NSW 119 F6, 120 G13, 141 L4, **60**, 79
Bramfield SA 288 B3, 254
Brampton Island Qld 477 J3, **422**
Bramston Beach Qld 479 L8
Branch Creek Qld 462 A6
Brandon Qld 479 O12
Branxholm Tas. 527 O5, **494**, 507
Branxholme Vic. 226 F6
Branxton NSW 113 F1, 121 K4
Braybrook Vic. 206 H7
Bray Park Qld 462 B2
Breadalbane NSW 119 E4, 120 F11
Breadalbane Tas. 523 O11, 527 M7
Breakfast Creek Qld 462 H10, 400, 403
Breakwater Vic. 216 H12
Bream Creek Tas. 521 N5, 525 O6
Breamlea Vic. 210 F10, 217 F9, 224 A7, 227 R8, 198
Bredbo NSW 119 D8, 140 G8, 235 L1
Bremer Bay WA 356 E13 , **307**
Brendale Qld 462 C4
Brentwood SA 282 E7, 288 I8, 261
Breona Tas. 527 J9
Brewarrina NSW 125 P5, 474 C11, 485 R12, **60**
Brewongle NSW 104 B4
Briagolong Vic. 225 M4, 234 C13, 185
Bribbaree NSW 119 A2, 120 B9
Bribie Island Qld 467 N4, 399, 404, 411, 414, **425**
Bridge Inn Vic. 220 C4, 229 J11
Bridgeman Downs Qld 462 E5
Bridgenorth Tas. 523 M9, 527 L6
Bridgetown WA 350 D3, 354 E11, 356 A12, **307–8**, 323
Bridgewater SA 243
Bridgewater Tas. 520 H4, 525 L5, **494**
Bridgewater Vic. 164, 180, 183

Mount Eliza Vic. 209 D13, 213 K2, 154
Mount Evelyn Vic. 208 I7
Mount Feathertop Vic. 168
Mount Field National Park Tas. 520 A2, 524 I5, **496**
Mount Forbes Qld 467 J10
Mount Frankland National Park WA 350 F10, 354 F12, 356 B13
Mount French National Park Qld 467 J12
Mount Gambier SA 226 A5, 287 I13, 237, **262**
Mount Garnet Qld 479 K8, 433
Mount Gravatt Qld 465 J4
Mount Grenville National Park Qld 466 I12
Mount Hallen Qld 466 I6
Mount Hawthorn WA 342 G1, 344 G12
Mount Helen Vic. 210 C5, 221 M13, 227 O4
Mount Helena WA 346 E4
Mount Hope SA 288 C5, 252
Mount Hotham Vic. 173
Mount Hunter NSW 104 I11
Mount Imlay National Park NSW 117 D12, 119 F12, 235 O9
Mount Isa Qld 482 E3, 399, **440–1**
Mount Kaputar National Park NSW 122 H7, 474 I12, **59**
Mount Keira NSW 114 A10
Mount Kilcoy Qld 467 J2
Mount Kosciusko NSW 140 A13, 62
Mount Kuring-gai NSW 100 G6
Mount Larcom Qld 477 M10
Mount Lawley WA 343 J1, 344 I12
Mount Lawson State Park Vic. 127 Q13, 233 R4, 234 D1
Mount Lewis NSW 98 E13, 102 H3
Mount Liebig NT 396 F8
Mount Lloyd Tas. 520 E5, 525 K6
Mount Lofty SA 237, 238, 241, 243, 251
Mount Macedon Vic. 210 H3, 224 A2, 232 D13, 177, 184
Mount Magnet WA 354 G1, 355 I13, 356 B2, **328**
Mount Magnificent Con. Park SA 283 L10, 284 E8
Mount Martha Vic. 212 I5, 155
Mount Mary SA 283 Q1, 289 N5
Mount Mee Qld 467 K4
Mount Mistake National Park Qld 466 H11, 475 L7, **444**
Mount Molloy Qld 473 B6, 479 K6
Mount Morgan Qld 477 L9, **441**
Mount Moriac Vic. 210 E9, 217 C8, 227 Q8
Mount Mulligan Qld 479 J6
Mount Napier State Park Vic. 226 G6
Mount Nebo Qld 405
Mount Nelson Tas. 518 G12
Mount Olga NT 396 E12, 370, 374
Mount Ommaney Qld 464 C6
Mount Osmond SA 279 L8
Mount Ousley NSW 114 C6
Mount Perry Qld 477 N13
Mount Pleasant NSW 114 A6
Mount Pleasant Qld 467 K5
Mount Pleasant SA 283 O6, 287 D2, 289 M7
Mount Pleasant Vic. 219 E10
Mount Pleasant WA 342 G8
Mount Pritchard NSW 102 A2
Mount Remarkable National Park SA 285 B13, 291 J12, 260, 272
Mount Rescue Conservation Park SA 287 G5, 289 P11, 258
Mount Richmond National Park Vic. 226 D8
Mount St. Thomas NSW 114 B13
Mount Samaria State Pk Vic. 222 B6, 233 K9
Mount Samson Qld 467 L6
Mount Schank SA 226 A6, 287 H13, 262
Mount Scott Conservation Park SA 287 G9
Mount Seymour Tas. 525 M3, 527 N13

Mount Shaugh Con. Park SA 126 A13, 228 A4, 287 I5, 289 R11
Mount Skillion State Forest NSW 109 E2
Mount Sonder NT 370
Mount Stirling Vic. 173
Mount Stuart Tas. 518 E7
Mount Surprise Qld 478 I9
Mount Sylvia Qld 466 G9
Mount Tamborine Qld 467 N12, 406
Mount Tarampa Qld 466 I7
Mount Taylor Vic. 119 A13, 225 P4, 234 E12
Mount Torrens SA 283 N7, 243
Mount Tyson Qld 466 C7
Mount Victoria NSW 104 F6, 106 B3, 120 H7, 75
Mount Warning National Park NSW 123 O1, 475 N8
Mount Waverley Vic. 207 Q11
Mount Wellington Tas. 487, 488, 490, 501
Mount White NSW 105 N5, 108 C9
Mount Whitestone Qld 466 G9
Mount William Nat. Park Tas. 527 Q4, **496**
Mount Wilson NSW 104 G5
Mount Worth State Pk Vic. 211 Q11, 224 H7
Mountain River Tas. 520 G7, 525 L6
Moura Qld 477 K11
Mourilyan Qld 479 L8, 432, **441**
Mowbray Tas. 523 O9
Mowbray Park NSW 104 H12
Moyhu Vic. 222 F3, 233 M7, 199
Moyreisk Vic. 220 I3, 229 M11
Moyston Vic. 220 B8, 227 J2, 229 J13
Muchea WA 346 D2, 354 E7
Muckadilla Qld 474 E4
Mudgee NSW 120 F4, 73, **80**
Mudgeeraba Qld 467 O13, 469 D8, 475 N7, 407
Mudgegonga Vic. 223 K1, 233 O7, 234 A5
Mudjimba Qld 440
Mukinbudin WA 354 H5, 356 C7
Mulambin Qld 477 M8
Mulbring NSW 112 D10
Mulgildie Qld 477 M12
Mulgoa NSW 104 I9, 119 H1, 120 I8
Mulgrave NSW 105 K7
Mulgrave Vic. 208 B13, 209 H2
Mullaley NSW 122 G10
Mullaloo WA 344 A1, 346 C3
Mullewa WA 354 D1, **328**, 331
Mulli Mulli NSW 475 M8
Mulliyup WA 350 B2
Mullumbimby NSW 123 P2, 475 N8, 61, **80**
Mulpata SA 287 H3, 289 Q9
Mulwala NSW 127 N13, 233 K3, **80**, 143, 193, **202**
Mumbil NSW 120 E4
Mummballup WA 354 E10, 356 A11
Mummulgum NSW 123 O3, 475 M9
Munbilla Qld 467 J11, 475 M7
Mundalla SA 249
Mundaring WA 346 E4, 354 E7, **328**
Mundaring Weir WA 328
Mundijong WA 346 D6
Mundingburra Qld 471 B9
Mundiwindi WA 358 F6
Mundoora SA 289 J3
Mundrabilla WA 357 Q8, **328**, 332
Mundubbera Qld 475 K1, **441**
Mundulla SA 287 H7, 289 Q13
Mungallala Qld 474 D3
Mungalup WA 346 E13
Mungar Qld 475 M1
Mungeranie SA 267
Mungerannie Roadhouse SA 293 K8, 484 C7
Mungindi NSW 122 E3, 474 F9
Munglinup WA 356 G11
Mungo National Park NSW 126 G5, 231 L2, 51, **59**, 92

Mungungo Qld 477 M12
Muntadgin WA 347 Q3, 354 H7, 356 D8
Munyaroo Conservation Park SA 288 H2
Muogamarra NSW 108 C11
Muogamarra Nature Reserve NSW 105 M6, 108 C11
Muradup WA 350 I2, 354 F10, 356 B12
Murarrie Qld 463 K11
Murchison Vic. 232 G7, 188, 194
Murchison WA 355 F11
Murdinga SA 288 D4
Murdoch WA 342 G12
Murdunna Tas. 521 N7, 525 O7
Murgenella River NT 382
Murgenella Settlement NT 392 I3
Murgon Qld 475 L3, **441**, **445**
Murphys Creek Qld 466 F7, 475 L6
Murrabit Vic. 181
Murramarang National Park NSW 141 O7
Murray Bridge SA 283 P9, 287 D3, 289 N9, 253, **262**, **264**
Murray River NSW 120 A7, 120 B10, 126 C7, 127 J12, 127 O13, 37, 50, 51, 53, 65, 68, 72, 79, 80, 86, 89
Murray River SA 283 P8, 283 R4, 289 N6, 289 P5, 243, 251, 263, 273
Murray River Vic. 230 B3, 230 H6, 231 K7, 231 O12, 232 C2, 232 F3, 233 J3, 233 N4, 234 A2, 167, 189, 192, **193**, 196, 202
Murray Town SA 289 K1, 291 J13, 260
Murray–Kulkyne Park Vic. 126 E8, 230 I6
Murray–Sunset National Park Vic. 126 B9, 230 C8, 289 R7, **168**
Murrayville Vic. 126 B11, 230 C11
Murrindindi Vic. 211 N3, 224 F1, 232 I12
Murringo NSW 94
Murrumba Qld 466 I5
Murrumbateman NSW 119 D4, 120 E12
Murrumbeena Vic. 207 O12
Murrumburrah NSW 119 B3, 120 C10, **72**
Murrurundi NSW 120 I1, 122 I12, **80**
Murtoa Vic. 228 I9, **188**
Murwillumbah NSW 123 P1, 475 N8, **80–1**
Musk Vic. 221 P9, 171
Musk Vale Vic. 210 E3, 221 O9
Musselboro Tas. 527 N7
Muswellbrook NSW 121 J3, 122 I13, **81**, 86
Mutchero Inlet National Park Qld 473 I13
Mutdapilly Qld 467 J10
Muttaburra Qld 476 A7, 483 N7, **445**
Myall Lakes National Park NSW 121 M4, 54, **59**, 61
Myalla Tas. 526 F4
Myalup WA 346 C11, 354 D9, 307, 319
Myamyn Vic. 226 E6
Myaree WA 342 F10
Myers Flat Vic. 163
Mylestom NSW 123 O8, 475 N12
Mylor SA 279 Q12, 283 M8, 284 G2, 243
Myola Qld 473 E7
Mypolonga SA 283 P8, 287 E2, 289 N8, 262
Myponga SA 283 K11, 284 B9, 287 B4, 289 K16, 264, 274
Myponga Conservation Park SA 283 K11, 284 A10, 243, 274
Myrla SA 289 P6
Myrniong Vic. 210 F5, 221 Q13, 227 Q4, 160
Myrrhee Vic. 222 E5
Myrtle Bank SA 279 J7
Myrtle Bank Tas. 523 Q7, 527 M6
Myrtleford Vic. 223 J2, 233 N7, 234 A5, **188**
Myrtletown Qld 463 L6
Mysia Vic. 229 O6
Mysterton Qld 471 C8
Mystic Park Vic. 126 H12, 229 O2, 231 O12, 196
Nabageena Tas. 526 D4

West Pymble NSW 98 I3, 100 G13
West Ridgley Tas. 526 G5
West Ryde NSW 98 G6
West Scottsdale Tas. 527 N5
West Swan WA 345 O6
West Wollongong NSW 114 C10
West Wyalong NSW 120 A8, 127 Q6, **92**
Westbourne Park SA 278 H7
Westbury Tas. 523 K11, 527 K7, 487, 506, **513**
Westcourt Qld 472 E11
Western Creek Tas. 527 J8
Western District Vic. 143, 152, 166, 170, 171, 182, **197**
Western Flat SA 287 H8
Western Junction Tas. 523 P12, 527 M7
Western River Con. Park SA 288 G11
Westerway Tas. 520 C2, 525 J5
Westlake Qld 464 C6
Westleigh NSW 100 E10
Westmar Qld 474 H7
Westmead NSW 98 B6
Westmeadows Vic. 207 J1
Westmere Vic. 220 D13, 227 K5
Weston ACT 138 D13, 139 B4
Weston Creek ACT 137 D4, 138 B13, 139 A4, 140 G3, 130
Weston Flat SA 289 O5
Westonia WA 354 I6, 356 D7
Westwood Qld 477 L9
Westwood Tas. 523 M11, 527 L7
Weymouth Tas. 523 O2, 527 L4
Whale Beach NSW 101 R3, 105 O7
Wharminda SA 288 E5
Wheatsheaf Vic. 221 P9
Wheeler Heights NSW 99 O1, 101 N10
Wheelers Hill Vic. 208 B12, 209 H1
Whim Creek WA 355 I1, 358 B2, 360 A13
Whipstick State Park Vic. 229 Q9, 232 C8
White Beach Tas. 521 L10, 525 N8
White Cliffs NSW 124 G8, 485 K13, **92–3**
White Dam Conservation Park SA 262
White Flat SA 288 D7
White Gum Valley WA 342 C11
White Hills Tas. 523 P11, 527 M7
White Mountains National Park Qld 476 A2, 483 O2
White Patch Qld 467 N4
White Rock Qld 473 F10
Whitefoord Tas. 525 M3, 527 N13
Whiteman WA 345 M4
Whiteman Park WA 346 D3
Whitemark Tas. 524 B11, 514
Whitemore Tas. 523 L13, 527 K8
Whitfield Vic. 222 F5, 233 M8, 186, 199
Whitsunday Qld 408, 415, 451, **456**
Whitsunday Islands Qld 477 J2, 415, 422, 436, 451, 456
Whitsunday Islands Nat. Park Qld 477 J2
Whitsunday Passage Qld 408, 422, 423, 448
Whittlesea Vic. 211 K4, 224 D2, 232 G13
Whitton NSW 127 N8, **93**
Whitwarta SA 283 J1, 289 K5
Whorouly Vic. 222 H1, 233 N7, 199
Whroo Vic. 192
Whyalla SA 288 I1, 290 H13, 247, **272**
Whyalla Con. Park SA 288 I1, 290 H13
Whyte Yarcowie SA 289 M2
Wialki WA 354 H5, 356 C6
Wickepin WA 347 L9, 354 G9, 356 B10, **336**
Wickham NSW 110 C6
Wickham WA 355 H1, 358 A2, 312, 334, 335, **336–7**
Wickliffe Vic. 220 B13, 227 J5
Widgiemooltha WA 356 H8
Wilberforce NSW 105 K6, 52
Wilbursville Tas. 525 K1, 527 K10
Wilby Vic. 127 N13, 233 K5
Wilcannia NSW 124 G11, 93

Wild Flower Reserve Qld 467 P8
Wild Horse Plains SA 283 J3, 289 K6
Wildman Reserve NT 388 I4
Wiley Park NSW 102 I4
Wilga WA 350 D1, 307
Wilkawatt SA 287 H4, 289 Q10
Willagee WA 342 E10
Willamulka SA 289 J4
Willandra National Park NSW 127 K4
Willare Bridge Roadhouse WA 352 B10, 361 J8
Willaura Vic. 220 B11, 227 J4
Willawarrin NSW 109 D1, 123 N9
Willawong Qld 464 G8
Willetton WA 343 J10
William Bay National Park WA 351 J12
William Creek SA 292 E11, 260
Williams WA 346 I11, 354 F9, 356 B10, **337**
Williamstown SA 283 N6, 286 C11, 287 C1, 289 M7
Williamstown Vic. 207 J10, 211 J7, 149, 150
Williamtown NSW 112 G6, 121 L5
Willigulli WA 354 C1
Willoughby NSW 99 N5
Willow Grove Vic. 211 R9, 224 I6
Willow Tree NSW 120 I1, 122 I11
Willowie SA 285 C13, 291 J12
Willowmavin Vic. 211 J2, 224 C1, 232 F12
Willunga SA 283 L10, 284 C7, 287 B3, 289 L9, 243, **272**
Willyabrup WA 327
Wilmington SA 285 B13, 291 J12, 265, **272**
Wilmot Tas. 522 B9, 526 H6
Wilmot Lower Tas. 522 C8, 526 H6
Wilora NT 397 J5
Wilpena SA 285 D8, 291 K8, 250, 257, **272**, **274**
Wilpena Pound SA 285 D8, 291 K8, **250**, 256, **257**, 272, 274
Wilson SA 256
Wilsons Prom. Marine Reserve Vic. 225 J13
Wilsons Prom. Marine Park Vic. 225 J11
Wilsons Prom. National Park Vic. 225 J11, 151, 153, **169**, 175, 184
Wilston Qld 462 F10
Wilton NSW 104 I13
Wiltshire Junction Tas. 526 E3
Wiluna WA 358 F11
Wimmera Vic. 228 D4, 164, 172, 174, 180, 188, 189, 192, **197**
Winburndale Nat. Res. NSW 104 C2, 120 G6
Winchelsea Vic. 210 D10, 217 A8, 227 P8, **200**
Windermere Tas. 523 M7, 527 L6, 504
Windjana Gorge National Park WA 352 F8, 361 L8
Windorah Qld 483 K13, 485 J1, 453
Windsor NSW 105 K6, 121 J7, 45, 49, 52, **93**
Windsor Qld 462 G10
Windsor SA 283 J4, 289 K6
Windsor Gardens SA 281 L12
Windy Harbour WA 330, 331
Wine Coast (Southern Vales) SA 284, **242**, 273
Wingala NSW 99 Q3, 101 O13
Wingen NSW 121 J2, 122 I12, 80, 86
Wingfield SA 280 M3
Wingham NSW 109 B13, 121 M2, 123 M12, **93**
Winkie SA 289 Q6
Winkleigh Tas. 523 K7, 527 K6
Winmalee NSW 104 I7, 107 O4
Winnaleah Tas. 527 O5
Winnellie NT 385 G6, 386 H13, 388 C2
Winninowie Con. Park SA 285 B13, 290 I12
Winslow Vic. 226 I8
Winston Hills NSW 98 B4
Winthrop WA 342 F10
Winton Qld 483 L7, **456**, **458**
Winton Vic. 222 B2, 233 L7
Winton North Vic. 222 C1

Winulta SA 282 G2, 289 J6
Winwill Qld 466 G8
Wirrabara SA 289 K1, 291 J13, 254
Wirrega SA 287 H7, 289 Q13
Wirrulla SA 297 Q11
Wiseleigh Vic. 119 A13, 225 P3, 234 F12
Wisemans Creek NSW 104 B5
Wisemans Ferry NSW 105 L4, 121 J6, 52, **93**
Wishart Qld 465 K5
Wistow SA 283 N9, 284 I3
Witchcliffe WA 349 C8, 327
Witches Falls National Park Qld 467 M12
Withcott Qld 466 F8
Witheren Qld 467 M13
Witjira National Park SA 292 C2, 397 M13, **250**, 251, 264
Witta Qld 467 L1, 470 A10, 475 M4
Wittenoom WA 355 I3, 358 C4, **337**
Wittenoom Gorge WA 358 C4, 335, 337
Wivenhoe Pocket Qld 467 J7
Woden ACT 138 E13, 139 C4
Woden Valley ACT 137 E4, 140 G3, 130
Wodgina WA 358 C2
Wodonga Vic. 127 P13, 233 O4, 234 B2, 163, 193, 194, **200**
Wokalup WA 346 D11
Woko National Park NSW 121 L1, 123 K12
Wokurna SA 289 J4
Wolfdene Qld 467 N10
Wolfe Creek Crater Nat. Park WA 361 P10
Wollemi Nat. Park NSW 104 H2, 120 H6, 81
Wollert Vic. 211 K5
Wollombi NSW 112 A13, 121 J5, 63
Wollomombi NSW 123 M8, 475 L13
Wollongong NSW 114, 116 H6, 119 I3, 121 J10, 54, **93–4**
Wollstonecraft NSW 99 L7
Wolseley SA 228 A7, 287 I7, 289 R13
Wolumla NSW 117 F8, 119 F11, 235 P7
Wombarra NSW 105 K13
Wombat NSW 119 B3, 120 C10
Wombat State Forest Vic. 158
Wombelano Vic. 228 E11
Wombeyan Caves NSW 120 G10, **84**
Wonboyn Lake NSW 66
Wondai Qld 475 L3, **458**
Wonga Qld 473 C2
Wonga Park Vic. 208 D5
Wongan Hills WA 354 F5, 356 A7
Wongarbon NSW 120 D3
Wonglepong Qld 467 M12
Wongulla SA 283 R6, 287 E1, 289 N7, 260
Wonthaggi Vic. 211 N13, 224 F9, 153, **200–201**
Wood Wood Vic. 126 G10, 231 M10
Woodanilling WA 354 G10, 356 B11
Woodbridge Tas. 520 G10, 525 L8
Woodburn NSW 123 P3, 475 N9, **94**
Woodbury Tas. 525 M2, 527 M11
Woodchester SA 283 N10, 287 D3, 289 M9
Woodenbong NSW 123 N1, 475 M8
Woodend Vic. 210 H3, 224 A1, 227 R3, 232 D12, 185
Woodford NSW 104 H7, 107 K8
Woodford Qld 467 L3, 475 M4
Woodforde SA 279 M3
Woodgate Qld 477 P13
Woodgate National Park Qld 413, 417, **444**
Woodglen Vic. 225 O4, 234 D13
Woodhill Qld 467 L11
Woodlands Qld 466 H8
Woodlands WA 344 D11
Woodridge Qld 465 L9
Woods SA 283 K2, 289 L6
Woods Point SA 283 P10, 287 E3, 289 N9
Woods Point Vic. 224 I2, 186
Woods Well SA 287 E6, 289 N12
Woodsdale Tas. 525 N4, 527 N13
Woodside SA 283 N8, 287 C2 , 289 M8, 243

Accident Action

Those vital first moments

Treating an unconscious person

1. CLEAR AIRWAY
Lie victim on side and tilt head back.

2. CLEAR MOUTH
Quickly clear mouth, using fingers if necessary. If breathing, leave on side.

3. TILT
IF NOT BREATHING, place victim on back. Tilt head back. Support the jaw, keeping fingers away from neck.

4. BLOW
Kneel beside victim's head. Place your widely open mouth over victim's slightly open mouth, sealing nostrils with your cheek. Blow until victim's chest rises.

5. LOOK, LISTEN
Watch chest fall. Listen for air escaping from mouth. Repeat steps 4 and 5, 15 times per minute.

6. RECOVERY POSITION
When breathing begins, place victim on side, head back, jaw supported, face pointing slightly towards ground.

NOTE: For an injured child, cover mouth and nose with your mouth. Blow until chest rises (20 times per minute).

7. IF UNCONSCIOUS
If victim is unconscious and trapped in the car, still tilt head back and support the jaw.

SEND SOMEONE FOR AN AMBULANCE.

DO NOT LEAVE AN UNCONSCIOUS PERSON.